The Spokan Indians

John Alan Ross

Published by Michael J. Ross
Spokane, Washington

The Spokan Indians

Sales: Additional copies of this book can be purchased from quality bookshops and online booksellers.

ISBN: 978-0-9832311-0-3

BISAC code: SOC021000

Library of Congress subject headings:
➤ Anthropology, culture, and society
➤ Anthropology--Fieldwork
➤ Anthropology--History
➤ Anthropology of Pacific North America
➤ Ethnography monograph
➤ Ethnohistory
➤ Indians of North America
➤ Spokane Indians

The image on the front cover is a modified version of a painting by Paul Kane, "Drying Salmon", originally published in his book *Wanderings of an Artist Among the Indians of North America, from Canada to Vancouver's Island and Oregon Through the Hudson's Bay Company's Territory and Back Again*. Reference details can be found in this book's bibliography. The image on the cover's spine was sketched, in pencil, by the author, from a pictograph of a Great Horned Owl (*snine?*) that was approximately 16 cm in length, from top to bottom. It contained red, black, and white pigments. The eyes were solid black, and the outline of the head and body were solid red. Such polychrome pictographs are rare. The author discovered it, just above Little Falls, during his fieldwork that culminated in *An Ethnoarchaeological Cultural Resource Survey of the Spokane Indian Reservation (1991-1993)*. The pictograph had been drawn on a huge white granite boulder, with an overhang that had protected the drawing from natural damage. Also, it was effectively hidden behind, and shaded by, a towering Ponderosa pine that was likely older than 250 years.

This ethnography is dedicated in fond memory to an extraordinarily kind and wonderful lady, Nancy Flett, my *sk'ʷúy*, who, for over thirty years, was always gracious in her hospitality, and a most knowledgeable and appreciative mentor of her people's past.

Nancy Flett (1906-1997)

Have not all races had their first unity from a mythology
that marries them to rock and hill?

William Butler Yeats, *The Trembling of the Veil*

Children of the Sun
we must honor our Mother
spirit of Spokan

Michael J. Ross

Contents

Figures

The following figures were sketched by the author: 13, 15-20, 23, 25, 26, 28, 29, 36-38.

Foreword

A foreword for a book is like a frame for a picture; both should draw the eye to the work's uniqueness. What best can draw the reader's eye to the uniqueness of John Ross's book is an understanding of the man, those who gave him the material for the book, and the conditions under which they collaborated. Indeed, the reader cannot appreciate the uniqueness of this work without knowing about Ross and the challenges he faced uncovering a culture that lay largely dormant in the minds of aging strangers, taught to distrust greatly the *suyápi* culture whence Ross came.

An ethnography is a written story about strangers. A great ethnography is one that captures and then reveals those strangers most truly. Ross writes a great ethnography. His story reflects the stories of the last ones who knew the old ways and no longer are here to tell about them. Those "old people" entrusted their stories to Ross, whom they accepted as a "legitimate listener," instead of their great-grandchildren claiming to be busy with things more important than old peoples' stories. The old people told Ross, "We are like ghosts." Their traditional culture was in its death throes; their way of life was no longer feasible, and worse, neglected or even disrespected by the young people. Ross writes for the old people who could not, and for their younger kin too busy to listen, hoping a "ghost" story can join the two together again. It is in this hoped-for union that the reader will recognize special magic, charm, and purpose of this work—crafted, lovingly, to keep alive a lost oral tradition.

Ross describes his occupation as "medical anthropologist." His chapter on medicine and health shows he is that; the other chapters show he is much more. To this day, his disciplined gait, posture, and demeanor reflect his early years at military school in the Northeast, followed by a stint in the U.S. Army. He worked three years as a medical technician in the military and out, including two years in Papua-New Guinea, before enrolling at the University of Montana, conducting fieldwork with the Flathead under Drs Carling Malouf and Verne Dusenberry. After taking a B.A. in anthropology there, he completed graduate studies in anthropology at Washington State University, with Dr. Deward E. Walker, Jr. and later with William Elmendorf. Ross was then hired to teach anthropology at Eastern Washington University in 1968, which he did passionately until retiring in 2000, climbing the ladder of assistant, associate, and full professor, and finally professor emeritus. His list of publications is thick; his list of enriched students is thicker. He was one of those rare college professors whom students remember vividly, because he was uncannily adept at bringing them from cocksure ignorance to thoughtful uncertainty.

Ross's home reflects well his personality. Over a dozen half-hull model ships line its basement walls, all intricately-crafted to scale and meticulously painted by Ross. He was also a carver of his two sons' toys, the owls for his yard and garden, a whimsical collection of black, wooden cetacean reliefs for his kitchen walls, and waterfowl decoys, among many others. He was also a painter; his letters often come branded with one of his impromptu pen-and-ink watercolors, often framed by recipients. He makes a palate of his garden as well, built around a pond and plants so natively alluring that hawks fish there. He is a scientist who is an artist, or vice versa. The fastidious passion and attention to detail in his art likewise shows through in his ethnography, a seamless amalgam of art and science.

Ross is a real physical specimen, an anomaly among academics of his time. Even at the gray-bearded, emeritus stage of his life, he looks as though he could play prop for the local rugby club (and still scrum down), if his uncauliflowered ears and relatively intact nose did not give him away. He is tall, angular, and stout, with legs molded by riding a bicycle over twenty miles to and from work every day for thirty some years, even—and knowing an inkling of his indomitable spirit—especially in the coldest days of winter. He does not suffer fools gladly, and if they were his students, he suffered real fools not at all, as some found out too late when asked to settle matters of perceived disrespect, as men, outside the classroom. (Luckily, none

1

took him up on the offer.) He was, and remains, a bear for hard work; he had to be, to climb the mountain this work cast in his path.

Ross started research for this work on the Spokane reservation in 1967. Before that, he had spent three years working with Colville Indians to the very near north. That background gave him a good foothold on Plateau culture and Interior Salish, places, people, and language. Ross also learned early on that he loved working with the old people—"elders" in more modern verbal garb. ("Old people," for *p'iᵂp'xᵂút* (*nt'č'miʔsc*), is used here.) Most of the time, and more of the time than Ross would have liked had traditional roles not failed, he did for the old people what their younger kin should have done. He filled the role of surrogate (great-)grandchild, whether it was taking the old people for punk wood, gathering roots or berries, or similar outings and errands.

Ross worked with many old people on the reservation over a forty-year span. Several were especially memorable: John Wynne, Nancy Flett, Paul Samuels, John B. Flett, Gib Eli, Norbert and Christine Abrahamson, Ann McCrea, Whitman Mathews, Sadie Boyd, Helen Sherwood, Nancy Lowley, Violet Seymor, Albert Peone, Lucy Peuse, Albert Sam, Alex Sherwood, and Ella McCarty. Women generally taught about plants and their uses; men generally taught about hunting and fishing. But there was overlap, and usually one who was a true culture-bearer contributed generally, with specific topics of expertise, such as medicine (Gib) or religion (Ella). Some were gifted story-tellers (Nancy); others had special skills in hunting or fishing (Sam, John, Paul) and making traditional tools, crafts, and implements (Sam, John). Those "culture-bearers," an unwieldy title from which they humbly would have shied, usually shared two characteristics: they were very bright, if not brilliant, and they never had been to an Indian boarding school. A lack of *suápi* schooling made for excellent teachers (*sxᵂm'em'eyéʔm* - "non-Indian teacher").

Wellpinit (latitude 47.888N, longitude 117.986W), lies at the heart of the Spokane reservation in northeastern Washington, about 45 miles (northwest) and 80 minutes from Ross's home in suburban Spokane. The drive to the reservation gave Ross time to consider his plan for the day, if he had not already, and the drive home to digest what he had learned that day. And to dream about the lost way of life he was recording: Not long ago, he recalls approaching the reservation one early low foggy morning, and he had a distinct feeling he could see ten to fifteen *spoqln* warriors returning from a successful horse-stealing venture. It is a pleasant drive, at least in summer, and ever inspiring as the Selkirk Mountains come into view. Ross wore out several pairs of boots hiking about the reservation, exploring its unbeaten paths and finding its sacred places. He knew the reservation as well as any *suyápi*, at least in the modern era, and as well as many *sqltmíxᵂ* (Indians). Ross realized that to understand *spoqín* culture he needed to know their land well, and he set about that task with a near-Prussian sense of discipline. Ross was not an arm-chair anthropologist.

One does not volunteer secrets to strangers. Ross's story reflects many secrets, showing he was no stranger, or a stranger with a very special status. He was trusted and given access to hidden places, throughout the land and in the old people's memories. He earned their trust the old fashioned way: he shared a lot of time with them, and he kept true to his word. *ʔesunéxwisti*. (What he thought, said, and did were consistent with one another, and held true.) He visited them when they were sick, and his wife Julie cooked traditional foods to take to them in hospital. He patched their roofs when they leaked. He did their laundry when they were too ill to do so. He was a man for others. *kᵂtispʔús* ("He was magnanimous").

In moribund native cultures, most of what remains of the old ways lies in old people's heads, a situation that both narrows and broadens the notion of fieldwork. Fieldwork happens whenever and wherever the old people are, ready, willing, and able to talk about the old ways. Sometimes fieldwork is in a pickup truck, driving for groceries; other times, at a hospital bedside, or sharing a cup of coffee. Ross was there, with the old people, when they needed help, comfort, or just somebody to listen. In those moments, at various times and places, they shared with him "things important to them," as they put it to him. Those "things important to them" are the guts and bones of Ross's book.

2

Ross takes friendship seriously. *Ex pede Herculem*, one example close to home suffices. When one of his friends was very sick and in hospital for a long time, Ross at least weekly sent him a care package of books, letters, articles clipped from newspapers and magazines, and a renewed promise that a visit by Ross was only a phone call away. The promise included Ross driving his truck hundreds of miles to the sick friend's side, with the makings for a sweat lodge, and that Ross treated the old people he loved with at least that much kindness and care. Ross was a sheltering tree for the old people. They knew it, and they took shelter there, with "things important to them."

That social context for research is critical to appreciating this work fully: it was done despite an often frigid climate. Worse yet, the old people were shamed by the misguided anger of their younger kith and kin, and held by their gracious hospitality to apologize for it to those they had invited into their home (their houses and reservation). The anthropologist, in turn, was caught having deftly to absorb or avoid the anger, and accept or politely deflect the apology, which can make research emotionally taxing, when gathering the information itself was often hard enough. It was made all the worse for Ross, because he often was taking the place, by default, of the old people's younger kin—prodigal (great-)grandchildren who rarely chose to come home and accept the baton of traditional knowledge and skills. Those sins by omission added resentment to already dark-clouded emotional weather.

When the resentment occasionally boiled over, younger kin would accuse Ross of "stealing our culture." (Truth be told, the accusers rarely had spent the time to learn the culture to which they now laid claim and charged Ross with theft.) The old people, however, freely gave of their cultural knowledge and language. They did not view it as a zero-sum game, where "if I give you some, I will have less." They could share their knowledge on Monday, and when they woke up on Tuesday, it still would be there. Whatever they knew of the old ways, they shared it with Ross, similar to the berries, salmon, or dried meat they shared with him, even when they had none to spare.

The old people did not understand the taunts of their younger kin. "How can I give away my culture and my language? It's not like giving away a blanket or a horse." For the younger kin, however, perhaps having learned *suyápi* lessons of materialism too well, whatever knowledge the old people gave any *suyápi* meant less for them. Those accusers should be glad now that Ross took what they would have denied him in the 1970s and 1980s, at AIM's apparent zenith. He has saved for them many pieces of their people's past that otherwise would have been lost forever. This book shows, marvelously, that Ross fought a river of anti-*suyápi* sentiment and out-swam its current.

The old people had seen the old ways and the new ways. Acculturation of their families toward *suyápi* ways was hard and sad for them to watch. Harder and sadder still was the young people's steadfast lack of interest in the old ways in the 1960s, 1970s, and 1980s. The old people would complain that their younger kin would rather watch TV than listen to traditional stories or learn cat's cradle, and that young men wanted to hunt deer with a scoped rifle through a pickup truck window parked at the side of the road. When one dear old woman's family put her in a rest home, the other old people were astonished. It just was not done in the old days. During their lives, horses gave way to cars, traditional games gave way to the casino, and traditional food gave way to a diet that wreaked havoc on the health of their families. When the old people were born, diabetes was unheard of among their people; during their lives, it became a cruel disabler and killer. Perhaps they enjoyed their long talks with Ross partly because it took them back to happier times.

The old people recognized that they were the tenuous bridge between the world of their *t'úpye?* (reciprocal kin term for great-grandparent vis-à-vis great-grandchild, and vice versa), lineally above and below them. They were the last with the skills and the knowledge of the old ways. The two worlds were so different that one *t'úpye?* could not fathom the world of the other *t'úpye?*. The old people, as the bridge between the two *t'úpye?*, had to fathom and reconcile both worlds; it was hard on them. They told Ross that they wanted to pass knowledge of the old ways on to future generations, perhaps to reassure themselves that something they treasured in their own time would not be lost. Pieces of their life experiences would be passed

3

on, just as keepsakes from their belongings would be passed on at their memorial feasts. The old people and Ross understood Ross's role as recorder for the last keepers of the old ways. If they were "ghosts," as they complained, Ross was their chosen "ghost writer."

The old people firmly believed that only the old (i.e., *sqltmix*ʷ) ways could fix many of the problems brought on by the new (i.e., *suyápi*) ways. Perhaps only the old ways could. They also instructed Ross that the new ways needed to be covered up for the old ways to work. For instance, for old medicine to work during a traditional healing, new things in the home, such as electric lamps, had to be turned off and covered up. The old people were convinced that sooner or later the young ones would realize that they needed the old ways to protect them from the harm brought by the new ways. They entrusted their knowledge of the old ways to Ross, not to preserve the old ways idly for preservation's sake, but to perpetuate them as intact as possible for that hoped-for epiphanic dawn in the minds of the young people.

John Wynne, at age 96, once told Ross that when Wynne was young, his family was one of the first to get electricity. Wynne bought a radio and brought it home to his parents. He played it for them for a while and they told him, lowering his voice, "You just brought the devil into our home." Wynne felt even more strongly about TV—which Wynne called the "real devil." For the old people, the *suyápi* had brought many devils into their home (their houses and the reservation): alcohol, drugs, diet, missionaries, boarding schools, materialism, uranium mining, casinos, and so on. While there might not be any way to get all of those devils out of their house, a record of what the house looked like before the devils were brought in offered a chance to rebuild a better home for their young people. That goal was foremost in their minds: save this knowledge of the old ways for the young people, so they can rebuild a better home for themselves some day.

At the same time, the old people bemoaned the young peoples' inability to make it in the natural world of their forefathers. The young people could no longer hunt, fish, or gather food, at least with the skill and desire of the old people. An elder once said, "You can't see a leaf fall until first you hear it leave the tree." Somewhat cryptically, he meant that one cannot survive in the woods until one knows Nature. The young people no longer knew the woods, nor wanted to, and that deeply troubled Abrahamson and his contemporaries. When one of his younger kin was trying to kill a coyote, he told Ross, "He's never going to get a coyote. He doesn't know the ritual. He hasn't been given permission."

Another of the old people told Ross candidly but joylessly, "You know more about the sweathouse than my grandson—its ritual and significance." Similar comments fell on Ross like mid-summer hail during his work with the old people. It is odd for strangers to give an outsider more inside information than they give younger members of their own group; it is odd for that outsider to hold that greater inside information; and it is odder still for the younger members to know how to respond to those older givers and the trusted outsider with more information. It causes confusion for all, and a host of other unsettling emotions, for the giver, the bearer, and those to whom it should have been given and by whom it should be borne.

Ross recalls that the old people had a special grace about accepting his presence in their homes and lives. "Their hospitality strained imagination," he would say. Every visit ended with Ross being handed something to take home—berries, salmon, dried meat, and the like, even when the givers themselves had none to spare. Ross tells a story to drive the point home. He picked up one of the old people, stranded hitchhiking in bad weather and passed by many *suyápi*. They came upon an accident involving cars that had passed the elderly hitchhiker by. The old person insisted on stopping to help the injured *suyápi*. Ross commented, "But they just passed you by." The old person responded, simply, "Yes, but they need help," as he got out of Ross's truck. Perhaps the same ethic drove the old people reflexively to overlook the young people's rejection of the traditional knowledge, and urged an often mystified Ross to save it for the young people: "Yes, but they will need help."

In forty years of working with the old people, Ross never was asked his religion or political party, or called on to interpret or defend *suyápi* culture. Occasionally, they would ask him things such as "Are we at war again?" But it rarely was more than rhetorical, or punctuation between more important talk about their

4

lives on or about the reservation. When they left the reservation, the clash of cultures seemed to confuse them, as when women would wear pants, but covered with a skirt. They were proud to be Indians, but often made to feel ashamed when off the reservation. Ross's favorite informer used the excuse of a bad bladder to stay at home and not have to leave the reservation. They were aware of life beyond the reservation, but the reservation was their life, and they gracefully accepted Ross's stepping into it.

Most old people were affectionate and kind to Ross, but without fanfare or physical demonstration. Nancy Flett once gave Ross a pair of beautifully-beaded buckskin gloves, and Ross complimented the fine stitching of the beads and intricate design. She hugged him spontaneously—once in decades—because he noticed the detail; he had gotten it. Some old people did not like *suyápi* but still recognized the value of Ross's work. One even told Ross point blank, "I don't like whites," but after a long pause followed with, "Well, I guess we're going to do some things together." Whether welcomed or sometimes only tolerated, Ross found ways to work with the old people. He was a wise scapegoat; he knew that he alone could not expiate all the crimes of his race; but that knowledge also did not stop him from trying.

Ross generally eschews attributing knowledge to certain old people, partly to avoid shaming them or their kin. Certain knowledge, when cast out of context before a *suyápi* audience, or a *sqltmix*ʷ audience largely acculturated to *suyápi* culture (including Roman Catholic or other Christian notions of morality, sexuality, and humanity), might bring shame. The old people themselves were not ashamed of that knowledge, or their sharing it; they were concerned that it might be misconstrued by those lacking the ken of its proper meaning and use. To respect them, Ross avoids specific attribution, and certainly not to cast any light on himself. He avoids seeking or taking credit, despite his masterful ferreting out the knowledge and presenting it so lucidly and exactingly.

For significant items—acts, objects, or concepts—Ross gives words in *npoqíniščn* (Spokane language), and occasionally in its mutually intelligible dialects, *nqlisélišcn* (Kalispel language or *nsélišcn* (Flathead). Ross does not simply catalogue those words for academic reference, although that would be a worthy end in itself. He does so to provide the best evidence of its existence. The native term substantiates something almost as well as holding it in the hand, and much better when the thing is found only in museums, in old black-and-white photographs, or in the minds of the old people. The word *sʔétw'l'* (greater sandhill crane, *Grus canadensis*) proves the point; that this bird is gone from *spoqIn* territory, but its name remains, like the grin of the Cheshire cat.

Some words present trickier puzzles, such as *mláqls* (raven - *Corvus corax*). Its etymology is lost except to a handful of linguists, as English werewolf (OE *werwulf* - 'man-wolf') is lost to most English speakers. *mláqls* once transparently meant 'excrement on his shirt' (*mnák* 'excrement' + = (*a*)*lqs* 'shirt, robe, clothes'), referring to something that happened to raven in the mythic period (when animals were people). Later sound changes obscured that meaning; still clear in neighboring and closely related *Coeur d'Alene* (*mnáčlqs* - 'raven'). In any case, words still allow a linguistic archeology dig, after the material culture is long gone. Ross lays many of the *npoqíniščn* diggings out on the table for further study.

The old people told Ross, "If we had a word for it, we had it." These days, young people may challenge *suyápi* anthropologists writing about their culture: "We never had gays;" "We never ate clay;" and so on. But when there are terms for berdache (and 'homosexual male' and 'lesbian') and geophagy (and the clay eaten), and more terms describing them, the argued ignorance is properly muted. Ross's work is remarkable in its linguistic and semantic detail; it will be important in keeping the record straight on traditional *spoqin* culture; indeed, the old people told Ross that the only way to understand the culture is through the language: "If you cannot speak my language, you'll see my face but not my soul."

Traditional culture fights against dilution and diminution—if not for out-and-out survival—on more than just the *suyápi* front (television, radio, Internet, and other media). It also battles a subtler, often powwow-enabled, pan-Indian front: dream-catchers, fancy dancers, totem poles, 'Indian' (turquoise) jewelry, 'Indian' tacos, and other foreign things from other tribes. Perhaps 'pan-Indian' can be justified as being better than 'no Indian,' but pan-Indian is not traditional *spoqín* culture, and not what the old people said they wanted for their younger kin. Sometimes little things are big things; the old people decried the introduced, foreign practice of frequently blowing (eagle leg bone) whistles during traditional dances. "That is not our way."

Finally, it seems some now question whether non-invasive ethnography can be done, or even whether ethnography should be done. One thinks of Cratylus's statement, purportedly challenging Heraclitus that "one cannot step twice into the same river." Is it true an ethnographer cannot step into the same culture twice (to do genuine ethnographic research), because his stepping into the culture itself changes the culture? Should one avoid a strongly 'authored' narrative in writing the ethnography? Can one ever escape the gravitational pull of one's ethno-centrifugal force in studying and then recording another culture? For those worried by such angels-dancing-on-the-head-of-a-pin queries, Ross's work will seem brazen and perhaps paint him as an *enfant terrible*. Yet he has bigger *sm̓ǐč* ('salmon') to catch and dry.

Ross spurns self-doubt about his role as an ethnographer and his right to step into, describe, and interpret *spoqín* culture. He boldly leapfrogs notions of reflexivity (how the ethnographer might affect the culture and vice versa), self-reflexivity (how the ethnographer's persona affects his own perception of the culture), and similar restrictive (and probably well-meaning) ideas. He models the Nike footwear credo; he "just do[es] it." And he does it very well, with a hands-on approach to describing the beloved strangers with whom he worked for about forty years. Ross must be forgiven for any transgressions, real or imagined. He is from a different era, when men were braver about pursuing their passions and stating their beliefs, and not easily cowed by slavish notions of political correctness. Yet it is primarily for these last stated reasons that the reader will find in this volume an uncommon, if nearly unheard-of event: the recovery of a near-lost tradition for those courageous enough to read and comprehend it.

Steve M. Egesdal
Honolulu, Hawaii
May 2006

Letter from a Tribal Member

This second foreword was kindly written and signed by George Hill—an internationally renowned Spokan artist and sculptor—to verify, as required by the Spokane Indian Tribal Council, the author's past and present relationships with the Spokan elders.

Let me introduce myself, I am George Hill, son of James Hill and Ina Brigman Hill, Grandson of George Hill, and Bessie Ferguson Hill and James Brigman, and Julia Flett Brigman. I am a member of the Spokane Nation. I have lived on the reservation all my life except for years in the U.S. Navy (Vietnam Veteran) and college in Santa Fe, New Mexico, where I majored in museum studies. I was the Director of the Spokane Tribal Culture program until recently when I resigned to pursue my passion as a fine arts sculpture. I am 56 years old.

I have known Professor Ross as a friend and professionally for 25 plus years. Before that I had heard our elders speak well of him.

John has been with our people, visiting and collecting knowledge since the 1960s. He was a friend and companion to tribal elders who still had a clear understanding of who we are as a people. The Elders welcomed John into their homes, passing knowledge on to him. I believe they did this knowing that the world was changing. Their grandchildren were being drawn into the hustle and bustle of today's world, forgetting their past.

These Elders knew that we would come back seeking this knowledge only to find it gone with them. By passing this knowledge on to John, they hoped to preserve it for future generations when they would come back seeking this knowledge.

Our tribal Elders would not have divulged this knowledge to John if they did not trust in his heart to do what was best. They entrusted John to ensure our people did not lose a part of their spirit. The Elders wanted this knowledge to survive and guide us.

By publishing this book, John is helping our people to know who they are. This book will give our young a base knowledge to incorporate their family/tribal histories into.

I fully support the publication of this book for the young and the future of our people.

George Hill
Spokane Indian Reservation
Wellpinit, Washington
2 August 2007

About the Author

John Alan Ross is an Emeritus Professor of Anthropology at Eastern Washington University, where he taught for thirty-two years. Prior to that, he and his wife lived among the Chimbu tribe in the Eastern Highlands of New Guinea for three years conducting medical research on kwashiorkor for the Australian Government Public Health Service. Since then his fieldwork has taken him to several countries overseas; but his primary focus has always been on the traditional culture of the American Plateau Indians. He lived and worked on the Colville and Flathead Reservations, and for forty years conducted fieldwork on the Spokane Indian Reservation, where his main interest was in the areas of religion, ethnomedicine, and syncretic medicine.

He has two sons, and currently lives with his wife in Spokane, Washington.

The above picture of Norbert and Christine Abrahamson, with the author, was taken in 1989 by Col. Dale Potter (Ret.). This elderly couple—97 and 93 respectively when they died—were very knowledgeable of the old ways. The author much enjoyed spending time with them. To the author's left is his old Datsun truck, filled with tules for the Museum of Anthropology, at Eastern Washington University. In his left hand is a gift of smoked salmon (*sq'ʷlesŧ*).

Acknowledgements

During my years of fieldwork with the Spokan (from 1968 to 2008), I received considerable assistance while trying to learn the past culture of the Spokan Indians. Therefore, I am extremely grateful to many on- and off-reservation Spokan, who graciously and patiently shared with me their memories of both wonderful and difficult times. While some Spokan requested anonymity, there are those who should be acknowledged for their kind assistance: Norbert and Christine Abrahamson, Glenn Galbraith, Nancy Lowley, Whitman Mathews, Ella McCarty (*c'np'x̌ʷtl'šéw'si*), Gibson Moses (*sx̌ʷlekʷ*), Albert Peone, Lucy Peuse, Charlie Quintasket (Lakes), Albert Sam, Paul Samuels, Violet Seymore, Alex and Margaret Sherwood, their son Robert, Louie and Jim Wynne, and John Wynne—all of whom truly epitomized the old ways of traditional hospitality. Tina and Arnold "Judge" Wynecoop, in particular, were quite supportive, including financial assistance for the editing process.

My principal mentor was Nancy Flett, my surrogate *yéye* and a most gracious lady who was always undaunted when traversing precipitous slopes on the reservation in search of native plants as well as historical and ethnographically significant sites. Her knowledge of indigenous flora was invaluable. After Nancy's death, her daughter Ann McCrea—one of a few remaining speakers of Spokan—kindly continued her mother's efforts to preserve their language, and was always willing to provide linguistic assistance and share her wisdom.

Of all the contributors and friends, I am indebted beyond words to Dr. Steve M. Egesdal, a tireless and dedicated linguist, polyglot, ethnographer, *translator* (*sx̌ʷnmicínm*), eclectic scholar, and accomplished athlete, who over the years conducted extensive and significant ethnographic and linguistic fieldwork with the Flathead, Kalispel, Okanogan, Spokan, and Thompson Indians. This remarkable scholar is a paragon of ceaseless enthusiasm, who never hesitated in providing considerable encouragement. He gave an inordinate amount of his personal time and effort in reading this manuscript and making many helpful suggestions, as well as identifying morphemes and providing correct interpretations of Spokan words. His deep emic knowledge of the "old Spokan" language, his remarkable ability to analyze its structural and functional elements, and his extensive field experience, demonstrated the value of further reconstruction of the ethnographic past—a synthesis of linguistics, ethnography, and archaeology. Several elders said, "When he speaks, it is like hearing and knowing the hearts of our old people again." One elder remarked, "He is one of the few *suyápi* to appreciate our present ways and beliefs, as he has of our past, a time he truly understands and respects."

I am indebted to my former professor Dr. Allan H. Smith, whom I relied upon for his extensive knowledge and detailed comparative ethnography of the Kalispel and Chewelah-Spokan Group. Smith's published and unpublished work—resplendent with drawings and photographs—is the most comprehensive ethnography of any Interior Plateau group, an invaluable contribution to the literature, and a testament to his diligence and skills as an ethnographer. I commend the staff and faculty of Lewis and Clark College Library for making available Smith's unpublished field notes pertaining to the Kalispel, the Kalispel-Spokan Group, and the Spokan Indians.

I am indebted to Dr. William W. Elmendorf (*silmíx̌ʷ*), a devoted scholar, gentleman, and teacher. He had developed a working facility with the Spokan language, which cleared paths to cultural knowledge otherwise closed to non-speaking outsiders. His keen ear for the language is reflected in his consistent and correct writing of it. He kindly made available to me—and many Plateau scholars—his extensive yet unpublished collection of Lakes and Spokan ethnographic and linguistic data (1935-36), which is used throughout this monograph. Even after his retirement, he discussed Spokan ethnography with me, often for many enjoyable hours.

My deepest thanks go to Dr. Nancy Turner, a dedicated professor of ethnobotany at Victoria University, who provided extensive editing of the chapter on medicine and health. I was quite fortunate for her gracious assistance because she is undoubtedly the most qualified expert in this field. She was remembered by many Spokan elders for her kindness in assisting the Spokane Tribe, and for her remarkable efforts in identifying the many edible, medicinal, and utilitarian plants used aboriginally. One elderly lady said, "As long as there are flowers, she will be with us."

Randy Bouchard and Dr. Dorothy Kennedy, two noted Plateau ethnographers and linguists who have pioneered outstanding studies in the Plateau and Northwest Coast, extended their much-appreciated assistance and hospitality to me. Special recognition is given to Dr. Katie Nielson for her reference research and assistance in the area of congenital defects.

Deane Osterman, an accomplished ethnobiologist working for the Kalispel Tribe, deserves great thanks for creating the Salish font needed for this manuscript, and for his invaluable help with identifying fish species and providing kinship charts. Kevin Lyons, an accomplished and oft-cited ethnoarchaeologist, also with the Kalispel Tribe, is commended for his moral support and invaluable assistance with primary and secondary ethnographic sources. Both Osterman and Lyons are highly qualified and dedicated in recovering and protecting the Kalispel people's history.

When writing what often seemed like an encyclopedia, there were some difficulties in locating citations of early historians. A gifted scholar and well-published ethnohistorian, Jack Nesbit deserves special acknowledgment for his invaluable time and assistance in locating certain references. He has an excellent reputation on the Spokane Indian Reservation as a devoted teacher of the ethnohistory of their elders. I am also grateful to his friend and colleague, Dr. Ian Maclaren, Professor of History and Classics at the University of Alberta. An expert on Canadian artist Paul Kane, he was able to clarify the identity of El-ko-ka-shin, a Spokan shaman and Bluejay. The research skills and efforts of ethnohistorian Dr. Larry Cebula are also much appreciated.

I am indebted to the distinguished Dr. Allan Scholz, an extremely talented and dedicated professor of biology, and former Director of the Upper Columbia United Tribes Fisheries Center at Eastern Washington University. Even while writing his own magnum opus on Columbia River fish, he spent considerable time reading this manuscript, gave constructive suggestions and corrections, and always gave freely of his knowledge concerning studies of Columbia River aquatic life. He has contributed his knowledge and time also to the Spokane Tribe and Tribal Fishery, as well as the Spokan students he has trained over the years, and whom he invariably acknowledges in his significant research and publications.

Dr. Charles Mutschler, archivist and head of Special Collections at Eastern Washington University, John F. Kennedy Memorial Library, is commended for his invaluable assistance and encouragement to me, and for his resourcefulness and dedication in preserving the Spokane Tribal History Collection for future scholars and the Spokane Indians. His most able and knowledgeable assistant, Elaine Zeiger-Breeding, was always helpful in recovering often obscure ethnographic documents concerning the Spokan. She should also be recognized for her personal time and efforts in saving and transcribing hundreds of nearly-lost Spokan language tapes. Garry Jeffries, Michael Lomax, Justin Otto, and Elizabeth Malia provided invaluable early reference assistance, and Sue Ratan's assistance with government records is much appreciated. Always a great joy and extremely helpful was Mahilani P. Gutina, whose knowledge dispelled the mystery of copying machines. My thanks to the staff of the Newberry Library in Chicago, the British Museum, and The Museum of Man in London, all of whom made available unpublished manuscripts relating to the Spokan. Nancy Compos, Dennis Fredrickson, Riva Dean, and Rayette Sterling—archivists at the Spokane Public Library—were always gracious, resourceful, and helpful, as was archivist David Kingma of Gonzaga University. The curators of the Allan H. Smith Kalispel Collection at Lewis and Clark College were most helpful. Doctoral candidate Marc Entze, in the History Department at WSU, is acknowledged for his kind assistance with the extensive McWhorter Collection. Archaeologist Madeline Perry, of the Bureau of Land Management, deserves credit for her ethnographic assistance. The Spokane Indian Tribal Council was always very supportive of my research, as was the Spokane Tribal Culture Committee. I am indebted for the kindness and resourceful efforts of Richard Bruce, Museum Assistant and Graphic Designer at the Northwest Museum Organization, as well as Jane Davey, a most competent and helpful archivist at the Museum of Arts and Culture.

Professor Charles Booth, Dr. Dan Sisson, Bob Banger, and Dr. Robert Boyd gave me much encouragement; the first three also provided constructive criticism of certain sections of the manuscript. I gratefully acknowledge the kind support of Bob May (*nqʷn'qʷn'él's*), who during the author's fieldwork assisted with ethnobotany and always provided fresh-baked bread. May's outstanding ethnobotonical collection shows his dedication to and love of the Spokan. Dana Komen of Eastern Washington University's Archaeological and Historical Services graciously shared her own Bluejay field inquiries with me, as well as securing numerous obscure secondary ethnographic references. Rebecca Stevens of Archaeological and Historical Services (AHS) kindly shared her unpublished ethnobiological research (MA Thesis) on mussels in the Interior Plateau. Stan Gough, Director of AHS at Eastern Washington University, was quite helpful in making available various Spokan lithic artifacts. Pam McKenney, a gifted artist and illustrator, diagramed the annual subsistence round. Much appreciated is the assistance of archaeologist Tim Smith (in researching secondary materials) and Dr. Ruthann Knudson. I am indebted to Keo Boreson's resourcefulness and kindness in sharing her extensive field knowledge of Plateau pictographs and petroglyphs.

My thanks go to all those Spokan elders who, from 1968 to 2008, contributed their experiences and knowledge while amassing the Spokane Tribal History Collection (STHC), under the careful guidance of Barry Carlson, Pauline Flett, and Ann McCrea. During the initial writing, I benefited from the efforts of several readers, such as long-time friend and Plateau ethnoarchaeologist Greg Cleveland, and George Hill, a Spokan Indian and talented artist and sculptor.

I also thank Ryan Cates for the graphics work he did on the owl pictograph used on the book's cover.

As a skilled woodworker with an eye for color and layout, my son Justin kindly provided helpful suggestions on the design of the book's cover. Not long after he was born, Justin was given the middle name of Kwistasket (*sxʷstasq't* - "Walks-in-heaven"), which had been the name of a famous Sinkaietk warrior.

I am most grateful to my son Michael for his meticulous work on every phase of this project: He performed the first full edit and reorganization of the manuscript; contributed an original haiku honoring the Spokan; created lists of Spokan terms (for use as word processor dictionaries); contributed a chart depicting caloric intake; prepared all the digital images (for inclusion as figures); performed part of the final full edit; managed the outsourced editing; developed a computer program to search for duplicate material; created the index for the back of the book; formatted the manuscript and the cover for printing; and published the book. Without his skills, efforts, and perseverance, this book would never have happened.

Last but not least, I wish to acknowledge my heart-felt gratitude to my wife, Julie, who, as an anthropologist and "field widow," never failed in her logistical and moral support during my many long absences while conducting fieldwork. She created two excellent cartographic diagrams, assisted in the design of the book's cover, and provided valuable encouragement, suggestions, and library research during the writing of this manuscript.

Introduction

Apart from Elmendorf's fieldwork, traditional Spokan culture has not been studied as extensively by anthropologists and historians as some other Interior Plateau groups. Fortunately, much of what is known of the Spokan pre-historical and early historical periods is based largely upon recorded observations, principally those of Work (1823, 1829, 1830), Cox (1831, 1832), Parker (1838, 1840, 1844), Hale (1846), Kane (1859), Gibbs (1855), Stevens (1855, 1860), Wilson (1866), Lord (1866, 1867), and DeSmet (1905), Lewis (1906), and Elliott (1918).

The first relatively comprehensive Spokan ethnography was by James Teit (1930), a Shetland Islander whose wife was a Spokan, and who viewed the Spokan as culturally and linguistically similar to the Flathead, Kalispel, and Pend d'Oreille—all of whom he collectively termed the Flathead Group. It was not until Verne Ray's (1933) extensive fieldwork with the Sanpoil and Nespelem that the annual subsistence cycles and fishing strategies in the Interior Plateau were properly recognized and documented, as well as the socioeconomic significance of ethnic interaction by these essentially riverine-oriented peoples. Later writings describing the Spokan and their dependence on and exploitation of resources, are by Elmendorf (1935-36), Hulbert and Hulbert (1936), Spier (1938), Ray (1936, 1939, 1942), Smith (1936-8), Swindell (1942), Walker (1967, 1968, 1973, 1977), Douglas (1972), Ruby and Brown (1982, 1986), and Bouchard and Kennedy (1984, 1985).

Extensive reconstructive ethnographic research with elderly Spokan concerning the transitional period (1804-1866) and late historical period (1904-1950) to early contemporary periods, was done by Elmendorf, who assiduously collected field data in 1935 and 1936 from mostly non-English speaking Spokan. Elmendorf developed a good working knowledge of the Spokan language, which allowed him access to the culture closed to other outsiders. His fine ear was matched by his fine hand in capturing the language in earlier Americanist orthography (Egesdal, pers. comm.). Consequently, his work is particularly significant because it linguistically delineates the extensive nomenclature of the gathering, hunting, and fishing technologies used by the Spokan, often prior to Euro-American contact. Elmendorf's later work with Spokan kinship (1961 and 1965) is also notable. With his extensive study and fluency of Interior Salish languages, Dr. Steve M. Egesdal has quietly, but significantly, been a most important resource to many Plateau scholars.

Anthropologists Teit, Ray, and Smith were also fortunate in having native-speaking informants—some of whom were born prior to tribalization (the unification of separate socio-political groups), i.e., the US federal government's reservation system.

The diaries of Elkanah and Mary Walker, Protestant missionaries to the Spokan (1838-1847), provide historically important observations regarding the dependence of the Spokan upon the Spokane River and its resources. Historians Ruby and Brown (1982) and Drury (1976) wrote several extensive and detailed accounts of the Spokan, largely synthesizing previous anthropological and historical writings, particularly those covering the early stages of the missionization and reservation periods. Ruby and Brown's 1983 book describing Plateau slavery, is also commendable and thorough.

Prodipto Roy's 1961 classic sociological study of Spokan assimilation is possibly the first account to view and critically appraise Spokan deculturation, the consequences of depopulation by warfare and epidemics, and the shift in Spokan culture from a subsistence orientation to agribusiness, due to Euro-American incursion.

Allan Smith's unpublished PhD dissertation (1941) established many of the socioeconomic paradigms that predate Anastasio's (1955) comprehensive ethnography, which explained the aboriginal intergroup relations, which helped regulate inter-ethnic utilization of resources both within the Plateau, and with other eastern Plateau groups (through the use of task groups). Walker's (1967) writing of mutual cross-utilization of economic resources in the Interior Plateau firmly established the importance and dependence of Interior

Plateau peoples upon fishing, as does Scholz's (1985) comprehensive description of fishing on the Middle and Upper Columbia.

The findings of Chalfant (1954 and 1974) and Anastasio (1955 and 1974), during the Indian Claims Commission hearings, addressed and helped to clarify intergroup ethnic relations, including task-force grouping during the aboriginal period. Chalfant (1974) and Chance (1981) provided significant ethnohistorical overviews of the Spokan and neighboring groups. Schalk (1977, 1981), Schalk and Cleveland (1983), and Thoms (1989) provided new insights into influences and changes regarding important food resources and their consequences upon southern Plateau peoples. These adjustments are probably similar to the Spokan's own shifting from seasonal subsistence to agriculture—a consequence of missionization and the demands of government agroindustrial programs.

One may wonder if this monograph was written mainly for the benefit of the descendants of my informants, who wanted those descendants to know more about the once-traditional Spokan culture, which they saw disappearing and is now essentially gone. It in fact was written primarily to assist anyone who wants to learn and appreciate how the Spokan Indians, as a highly mobile hunting-gathering and fishing people, successfully adapted for approximately 11,000 to 12,000 years in a natural environment—one which non-Indians have radically changed in a relatively brief period.

Throughout the many years and thousands of hours of living and working with the Spokan elders, I listened intently to whatever an elder wanted to tell me, whether during a brief session or one lasting all day. With few exceptions, the elder would speak only when no one else was present—sometimes prefacing it by saying he or she had not spoken or even thought of the subject for many years. These occasions gave these informants a chance to recall and explain what they remembered having seen or had been told of past beliefs and customs by their parents, grandparents, and even great-grandparents. These informants wanted me to record their words—their most valued bequest to their children and grandchildren, in hopes that the past Spokan cultural history may be read and kept by those heirs.

Over the years, I heard varying oral accounts of Spokan origins, of numerous practices and beliefs that remained with a few elders. Given the intertwining of what remains of a peoples' traditional culture—religion, mythology, economics, social and political organization, and medicine—a non-Indian observer may not understand how these people were able to flourish in an environment seasonally limited in key resources. One could not help but be impressed, even humbled, when older women, prior to digging roots, would acknowledge their physical needs, and, before any harvest, invariably first pray to various spiritual powers for a rich harvest. After any amount of harvest, these elders always gave thanks for their bounty. They saw the providence of nature as a complex combination of sacred beliefs and rituals acknowledging a special relationship with various powers and with an environment upon which they were totally dependent.

Unfortunately, as a result of Euro-American contact—in the form of change agents and introduced diseases—there was a radical shift within Spokan culture, as well as devastation to the natural ecosystem. After considerable loss of land, degradation of what remained, and reduced access, the Spokan and other Plateau peoples were unable to acquire critical and once-traditional food resources. The attitudes, laws, and federal policies of the whites institutionalized their belief that the lands and other resources of the Spokan could be taken and exploited at will.

Th early Euro-Americans, including many who were educated, used the terms "savage" and "primitive," which were not always intended as derogatory. During the Romantic Movement and the Enlightenment, Jean-Jacques Rousseau (1712-1778) wrote a treatise, *Discourse on Inequality*, which spoke of the natural goodness of man and the complimentary notion of the "Noble Savage" (Nature's Gentleman). That term was first used by John Dryden (1631-1700) in *The Conquest of Granada by the Spaniards* (1672), which claimed man is essentially good when in the "State of Nature." Rousseau felt society was unnatural and even corrupt, because it had destroyed man's "natural goodness" and was thus the source of inequality. Rousseau further believed that so-called primitive peoples lived in harmony with nature, free from civilization's corruption, and consequently these people were generous and morally courageous, and maintained a strict sense of fidelity.

Yet despite the Enlightenment ideology, during the Age of Exploration, many European countries engaged in colonialism and imperialism. They developed a notion of their technological, social, and moral superiority, which consequently caused the terms "primitive" and "savage" to slide into pejorative usage, and eventually helped rationalize acts of slavery, genocide, and ethnocide.

Understandably, many early explorers and entrepreneurs used the term "savage" or "sauvage" in conversation and when writing descriptions of indigenous people, but usually without any perceivable negative connotations. This is especially true of writers with field experience and, occasionally, those who *understand an Indian language* (*nsux^w n'et sqelix^w*), such as Franchère (1854), Cox (1831, 1832, 1957), Hale (1846), Kennedy (1823), Ross (1849, 1904), Wilson (1866), and Thompson (1916). This is apparent in their often insightful and objective ethnographic observations.

In writing this monograph, every attempt was made to report accurately only what was told to me by each elder, without making any conjectured interpretations or conclusions. As an ethnographer, and not a linguist, I have sometimes included the regional and/or generational variations of some Spokan words, which may have resulted from the speaker being non-Spokan or having parents from a different group or birthplace. The inclusion of Spokan words and phrases was partly to substantiate the historical truth of certain rituals, beliefs, and selected aspects of material culture that are now not recognized. These words were obtained from multiple sources, most of whom are/were not linguists. The diacritics were recorded as accurately as possible, but some of them may contain flaws. With apologies to his Indian informants, and to Steve Egesdal and Ann Macrae, the author assumes all responsibility for any errors in the diacritics of the Spokan words.

In each case where a Spokan word or phrase is known, the English version is italicized, and the Spokan version is listed immediately afterward, in parentheses, and formatted in a Salish font to indicate its correct pronunciation. For reference purposes: The special diacritics in the Salish font, *áčéíƛ̓óʕšú^{w}x̣ʔ*, are produced by typing the characters ACEIjLOPSUWX?, respectively (note the lowercase 'j' and the question mark).

14

Chapter I: Cultural, Linguistic, and Intergroup Affiliation

Southern Interior Culture Area

The intermontane semi-arid Plateau culture area is situated in the extensive low-elevation Columbia River basin, which is characterized by generally low local relief. It is bounded on the west by the Cascade Mountains, on the east by the Rocky Mountains, to the north by the Fraser River, and (less defined) to the south by the Blue Mountains. The most unique natural features of the Plateau are the numerous flood-scoured scabland channels characterized by basalt cliffs, steptoes, buttes, rock shelters, and thousands of small basins containing ponds, lakes, and extensive wetlands. "The varied recent geomorphic history of the region has created a mosaic of landform features and sub regions. Aeolian Uplands, all impose strong local-microclimatic organizations" (Quinn 1984:35).

Culturally, the Plateau was further divided by prehistoric and proto-historical (1740-1810) Amerindian adaptations, into two regions—the Northern Plateau and the Southern Plateau—presently delineated by the American and Canadian political boundary. The Northern Plateau peoples were more dependent upon fishing and hunting, whereas those of the Southern Plateau were principally oriented to plants, supplemented by hunting. Archaeological evidence establishes an early and successful continuous inhabitation from 11,500 BCE to roughly the 1800's (Ames *et al.* 1998:103-19). (See Appendix A for a traditional historical account.)

Apart from more recent comparative ethnographic and ethnohistorical work for the Indian Claims Commission by Chalfant (1954, 1974), Anastasio (1974), and Ray (1954, 1960), Teit's ethnographic fieldwork in the eastern Plateau (1904, 1908, 1909, 1930) represents the most comprehensive ethnographic cross-cultural Plateau studies. Teit worked extensively with various tribes whose members were still knowledgeable native-speakers, and who explained the traditional beliefs and rituals, and were, in some cases, adept at demonstrating subsistence strategies and skills. Verne Ray's ethnographies (1933, 1936, 1942) are invaluable for providing some understanding of the peoples of this region and generally within the eastern Plateau (1939).

Spinden (1908) argued that the Plateau was not a distinct culture area, due to environmental differences and certain attendant adaptations. Instead, he considered the Plateau a transitional area because of certain similarities with Northwest Coast Salish and the Interior Salish, and some similar culture elements of the Flathead and *Nez Perce* (*saptni*), "with their tipis and fierce war complex, seemed to be like Plains tribes" (Burns 1966:8). It is true that the Flathead and Nez Perce had incorporated numerous Plains features of socioeconomics, warfare, and kinship structure; but that does not satisfactorily flag them as a "borrowed culture." Characterization of the Plateau as an identifiable ethnic distribution is based primarily upon Teit's work (1930) with the Flathead Group, Spier's recognition of the individuality of Plateau culture (1930:224-325), and Ray's (1933, 1936) and Walker's (1967) descriptions of the eastern Plateau as a definite and unique culture area, based on linguistic groupings, subsistence orientation, and intergroup socioeconomic relationships.

Dinwoodie, in reviewing Ray's notion of "pacific ideal," concluded that "anthropologists interested in tracing the movements of peoples have been more impressed by the area's linguistic and cultural heterogeneity" (2000:919). Yet Hayden and Schulting, when studying the distribution of regional subsistence items, traditions, and technology, wrote:

> Because of the general homogeneity of the Plateau environment, the basic subsistence adaptations do not differ as dramatically as they do in interaction spheres with more heterogeneous environments. Nevertheless, there are some striking regional differences in subsistence technologies and their associated styles (1997:55).

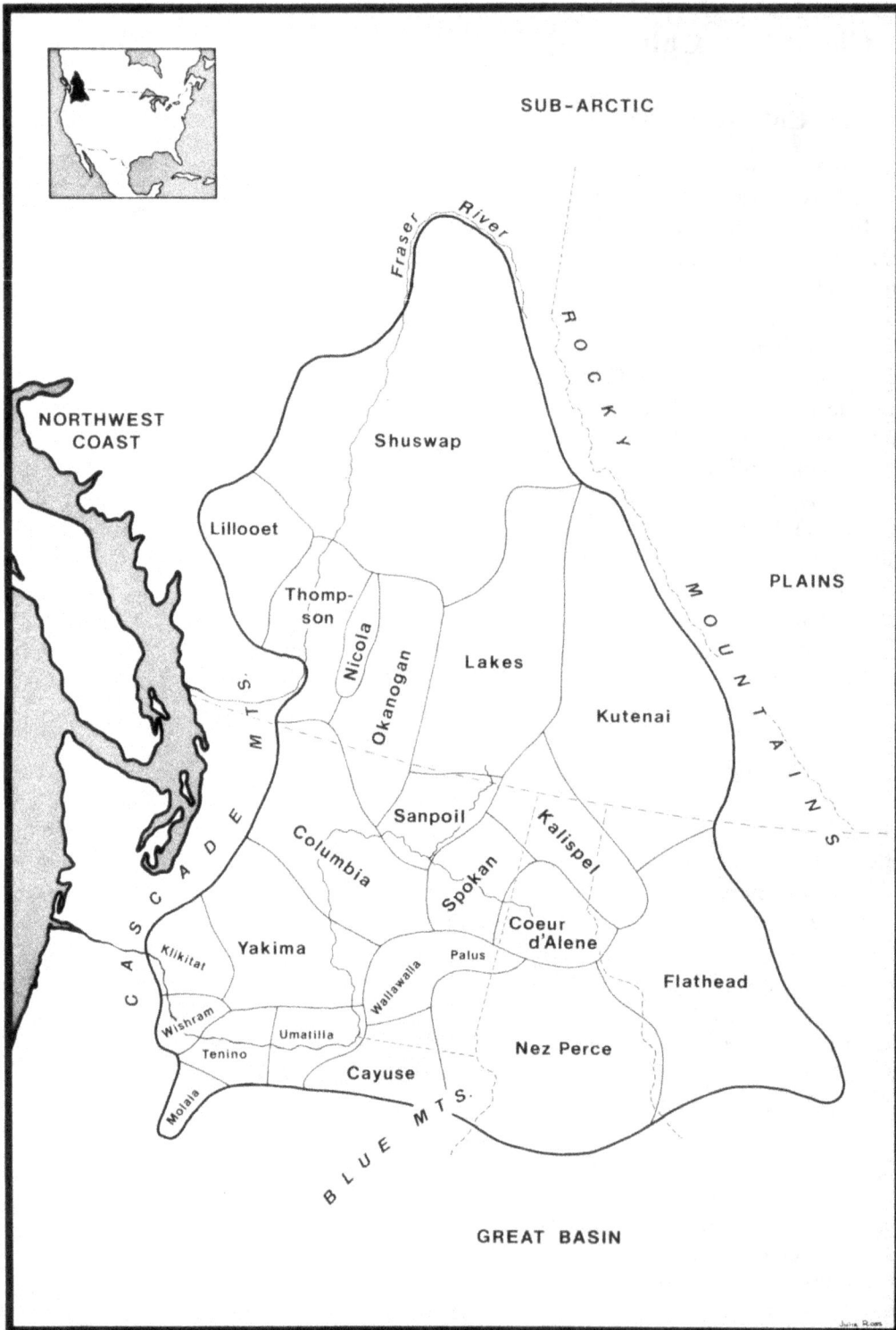

Figure 1. Plateau ethnic distribution (by Julie A. Ross, after Verne Ray)

16

Though Anastasio's extensive secondary research oversimplified certain behaviors and cross-culture differences, such as Ray's pacifism (1939:145), he satisfactorily demonstrated that the aboriginal Plateau was essentially a single social system:

[...] the norms of intergroup relations and the relevant ceremonies, ritual beliefs, and values form part of an intergroup culture. The component groups were bound together by their acceptance of this culture, which made it possible for them to perform a number of tasks jointly and which permitted the peaceful solution of disputes and other common problems. On this basis we would say that the area was a society, in the general sense of the term, and more specifically a political entity (Anastasio 1955:92).

Various early descriptions of the Spokan people, and Teit's comparative description of the mental and physical characteristics of the Flathead Group post-contact, describes the people as of "medium stature, well built, and good-looking. The ancient Flathead were noted for courtesy, affability, hospitality, liberality, kindness, honesty, truthfulness, and courage." Teit also notes other tribes' descriptions of the Spokan: They "are said to have partaken to a considerable degree the same temperament and physique as the Flathead." "The Sahaptain people considered the Spokan to be of a rather roving disposition, fond of trading, sports, and dancing, bold, and rather revengeful. Some tribes lower down the Columbia considered them as raiders and robbers. The Latah's Creek Spokan were more serious, reserved, and quieter than the others" (Teit 1930:325).

The major shared cultural features of the Plateau were a relatively simple political structure, with leadership by chiefs through inheritance, group consultation, and consensus. The need to maintain mutual cross-utilization of subsistence resources during a well-defined annual subsistence round was well established. Despite degrees of linguistic differences and cultural adaptation, groups within the Plateau culture area shared certain distinctive cultural features, which Walker succinctly summarized as:

- Location in a region of great environmental diversity.
- Adaptation to a riverine environment, with watercraft and elaborate fishing technology, which provided about half of the food base. Remaining food was secured from large game animals and relatively abundant tuberous roots. Most of the time there was a comfortable margin of survival in this culture area.
- Intensive interrelationships between local groups based on kinship, trade, and political ties. These interactions were facilitated by either common language, multilingualism, or a trade language.
- Band and composite band political organization, bilateral kinship, polygyny, primarily patrilocal residence, local communities rarely larger than 100 individuals, and winter residence in the major river valleys in semi-subterranean houses.
- Emphasis on democratic and peaceful relations among individuals and groups.
- Shaman-centered religions, with an emphasis on the individual vision quest for a tutelary spirit, annual observance of first fruits and first salmon ceremonies, and winter tutelary spirit dances. (1967:12)

Macro Band Distribution and Intergroup Relations

The following discussion of Spokan band distribution adheres essentially to a review of the aforementioned historical and anthropological literature of the southern Interior Plateau, but more specifically with the later findings of Teit (1928, 1930), Elmendorf (1935-6), Smith (1936-8, 1991), Ray et al. (1938), and Chalfant (1954, 1974), who conducted inquiries with Spokan-speaking elders. The Interior Salish-speaking Spokan (spo?qe?n'i) have traditionally been divided into the Lower Spokan (scqecióni), the Middle Spokan (sntu?t?úlixi or sntu?t?úli) of the Latah Creek area, and the Upper Spokan (snxumén?e) (Ray 1939; Teit 1930). Smith (1936-8) refers to the Middle Spokan as snxʷm'én'e?ey' ("salmon-trout people"), the Upper Spokan as sntutu?úli, and the Lower Spokan as sksstiɫeni. Collectively they all called themselves spokéni (Elmendorf 1935-6, 2:39). "The word Spokane conveyed nothing to the Indian except a place where one small

17

band lived. The Anglos gave the name to any of the bands living along the Spokane River" (Burns 1966:179). (See Appendix B.)

Macro band classification is primarily geographic, rather than linguistic, since the non-Indian terms (Lower, Middle, and Upper Spokan) refer to the relative aboriginal locations of the Spokan Group along the Spokane River. The Lower Spokan were members of the Central Interior Salish-speaking people, while the Middle and Upper Spokan belonged to the Interior Northern Salish (Ray 1936:106). "On the lowest [section of the] Spokane River population [cf. Ray's *snqelt*] was purely Colville, ... or of a closely related kinship speaking group" (Spokane Tribal History Collection [STHC]), as were those speakers of a Sanpoil and Colville dialect (STHC; Carlson 1972). Smith contended the Lower Spokan spoke an Okanogan language and dialect similar to the Northern and Southern Okanogan, Sanpoil, Colville, and Lakes—whereas the Middle and Upper Spokan spoke a dialect shared with the Kalispel, Flathead, and Pend d'Oreille (1953:94).

The approximate territorial lines of the Spokan bands are generally agreed upon. However, divisions customarily used to designate Plateau ethnic groups are often oversimplified. Consequently, attempts to establish precise pre-historical boundaries are quite difficult:

> The exactitude with which boundaries are drawn varies greatly [...] Where the village is the political unit boundaries are automatically exact so far as the settlements themselves are concerned, but intervening and tributary territory must be divided arbitrarily, or be used in common. In the typical organization of the Plateau, territorial segmentation is highly specific along river courses, but hunting territory is invariably used in common by a number of villages or small bands. An area may be frequented more or less exclusively by a larger band but this is a matter of convenience rather than principle and does not particularly affect the specificity of boundaries [...] The actual line of division [between villages] is seldom geographically intermediate, but is determined with regard to fishing grounds [...] It must be emphasized at this point that these distinctions and differences are largely formal and structural, not economically functional (Ray 1939:15-6).

People dependent upon a foraging economy of hunting, gathering, and fishing, were deliberate and careful when locating winter villages and other resource exploitation camps. Professor A. L. Kroeber, the acclaimed "Dean of American anthropologists," determined that the drainage systems correlated with the tribal distribution:

> In one respect drainage is often a good indicator of tribal boundaries. Except where streams are very large and the country is relatively uniform height, or political frontiers. This is expectable. The headwaters are usually the least habitable and valuable parts of a territory. Native settlement, being on the whole extremely light, concentrated in the valleys and along larger streams. The uplands frontiers were therefore unimportant, they tended to remain vague and general, and were not literally demarcated. Crests and watersheds, which are almost always easily observed, thus sufficed. The divide might be a high range or a spur between boundaries; the principle was the same (1939:216-7).

Teit also acknowledged the difficulties in establishing the aboriginal Spokan boundaries:

> The exact boundaries between the Spokane and the Columbia are rather vague. The Coeur d'Alene do not seem to know of any time when Columbia boundaries touched theirs. Some of them say that at one time parties of Columbia came close to their border on the southwest, and occasionally parties of the two tribes met; that at this time parties of Spokane seldom came south of Cheney or Sprague, but Ritzville, and sometimes Colfax. Spokane are said to have camped on Cow Creek and their parties often went right to the mouth. Colfax was considered to be in Palouse country, at least, in later days, but was to some extent within both Coeur d'Alene and Nez Perce spheres of influence. It seems not improbable that at one time the narrow strip of Palouse country above the mouth of the Palouse was neutral ground, the contiguous tribes of the Columbia, Spokan, Coeur d'Alene, and Nez Perce each making use to some extent of the part lying nearest to them. This neutral strip, and previous decimation of the Columbia population by disease, would make the expansion of the Yakima (*yiaqme?*) or Palouse in this direction very eastward (1963:330).

No groups in the interior Plateau recognized, nor were concerned with, exact aboriginal boundaries, particularly after the arrival of the horse. Yet it has become as issue in modern land litigation (Chalfant 1954, 1974). Exact ethnic boundaries would have proved dysfunctional in maintaining joint economic exploitation

18

of hunting and fishing resource areas. Major fishing stations, and even extensive *root fields* (q^wom), were traditionally mutually exploited by different groups; the principles of usufruct tended to dominate resource utilization—often based upon marriage ties, language, and traditional established use.

Canadian explorer John Warren Dease (1788-1863), Chief Trader of the Hudson's Bay Company (HBC), noted in 1827 how the Spokan were a population of 222 men (Lewis 1925, 2:107) divided into three distinct groups living along the Spokane River. Other descriptions of Spokan macro band designation and distribution are fairly consistent among early observers. George Gibbs, who served as geologist and interpreter during the government-sponsored Pacific Railroad Survey (1853-5), suggested that the so-called Spokan Group comprised eight groups, which is inconsistent with later ethnographic accounts. He probably included the Coeur d'Alene, Sanpoil and Nespelem, and the Okanogan. His groups were:

> [...] the *Spokehnish*, or *Spokanes*, lie south of the *Schwoyelpi*, and chiefly upon or near the Spokane river. The name applied by the whites to a number of small bands, is that given by the Coeur d'Alenes to the one living at the forks. They are also called *Sinkoman* by the Koottenaies. These bands are eight in number: The *Sin-slik-hoo-ish*, on the great plain above the crossings of the Coeur d'Alene [Spokane] river; the *Sintootoolish* [south Spokan], on the river above the forks; the *Sma-hoo-men-a-ish* [Upper Spokan], (Spokenis) at the forks; the *Skai-schil-t'nish*, at the old Chemakane [sic] mission [on Tschimakain Creek]; the *Schu-el-stish*; the *Sin-poil-schne*; and *Sin-speelish*, on the Columbia river; the last named band is nearly extinct. The *Sin-poil-schne* (*N'pochele*, or *San Puelles*) have already been included among the *Okinakanes*, though, as well as the *Sin-spee-lish* below them, they are claimed by the Spokanes. The three bands on the Columbia all speak a different language from the rest (Gibbs 1855, 1:414).

Though provocative, Gibbs's account cannot be dismissed out of hand, because fission and relocation of some groups may have ensued from the introduction of communicable disease into the Spokan, with the drastic reduction in population and ensuing millennium movements (Spier 1936; Du Bois 1938). Like Gibbs, Anson Dart, Superintendent of Indian Affairs for the Oregon Territory, also numbered eight bands (1851:216, 237-8), when referring to the Flathead Group, and citing the population as "two-thousand five hundred and twelve" (1851:216, 478-9). Cox also wrote that:

> Taking this place (Tschimakain) as the center of a circle whose radius shall not exceed sixty mile[s], it will include a population of near 2,000 souls, nine-tenths of whom rarely, if ever, leave the above specified ground for a length of time, unless it be for a few weeks in the spring. There are five or six bands, each of which has particular lands which they call theirs, and where they pass a portion of each year (Durham 1912, 1:78).

Cox had visited the region of the Spokan prior to Gibbs, and noted different locations of the three Spokan macro bands: "The Spokans have a small village at the entrance of their river, but their chief and permanent place of residence is about forty miles higher up, where we built our fort, and where the Pointed Heart River [Spokane River] joins the [Little] Spokan from the southeast" (Cox 1957 [1832]:261). Simms wrote, "The Spokanes have moved on both sides of the Spokane River, from its mouth to the Idaho line" (1875:361). Mooney (1896, pl. 88) evidently complied with Gibbs's 1877 mapping of Spokan territory, when he placed their northeastern boundary on the Columbia River, from the mouth of the Spokane River, down to approximately Grand Coulee; he placed their western territory boundary close to longitude 119° (i.e., east of the coulée), and their southern boundary at about Ritzville (Anon. 1958:n.p.).

Though different from Gibbs's aforementioned eight bands of Spokan, Cowley (1916) delineated six separate Spokan resident groups, as restated by Drury:

> The different bands of the Spokans were located mainly as follows: Enoch's band at the Falls, William Three Mountains' band west of Latah or Latah creek, Garry's band east of Hillyard, Paul's band on the Little Spokane, and Lot's band between Walker's prairie and the Columbia river. Batisté Peone's band, which was Catholic, occupied Peone prairie, where a Catholic mission had been established and under the care of Father Cataldo (1949:122).

Gibbs's statement that the Spokan had more than three bands was later recorded and expanded by historian J. Neilson Barry, identifying the Spokan collectively as Spo-kan, Sin-kp-mah-nah, or Spo-gan. He placed the Sin-too-too-lish near the present city of Spokane; Sin-slik-hoo-ish in the valley east of Spokane;

19

the Sma-hoo-men-a-ish at the junction of the Spokane and Little Spokane Rivers; the Skai-schil-tnish around the Tschimakain Mission; the Ske-cher-a-mouse, or Ske-chei-a-mouse, in the area of Chewelah; and the Schu-el-stish, or Schee-et-st-ish, at the banks of the Columbia River (1927:158).

More recent ethnographers (Ray 1933-36, Elmendorf 1935-6, and Smith 1936-8) maintain that the Spokan Group comprised three spatially unique macro bands (Ross 1995c). However, some contemporary Spokan state that Spokan ethnic affiliation has changed diachronically in oral history, and some groups became extinct through introduced Euro-American disease, while others became integrated. For example, the people at *Chewelah* (*sloúteᵂs* - "garter snake") were called *sloʔtéw'si* or *sƛtéʔusi* ("valley Indians") by both the Kalispel and the Spokan (Smith 1936-8:118). Their area of settlement within Colville Valley was known as *slʕ'ᵂtéw's*, and they spoke a mixture of Spokan and Kalispel (Elmendorf 1935-6, 1:79), which is actually a sub-dialect of Kalispel called *nlʕ'ᵂtéw'sišcn* (Egesdal, pers. comm.). As a result of intermarriage, their language was more similar to the Lower Spokan (Smith 1936-8:118). Elmendorf also stated how, despite certain notions of "tribal" endogamy, the Spokan and Kalispel intermarried (1935-6, 1:79). Teit, however, refers to the Chewelah as *šƛát'use* (1930:312). The designation *smtewsi* belonged to a small group of Spokan north of *Little Falls* (*scqesciłn* or *sxʷnítkʷ*) who, according to oral tradition, were completely decimated by an epidemic, before 1805.

On 18 June 1811, David Thompson became the first person to visit and acknowledge the Chewelah-Spokan Group (Elliott 1918, 1:11-6; Elmendorf 1935-36, 1:64), and again on 1 November 1811, during a trip to the Spokane River, via the *Colville Valley* (*sloʕᵂyew'si*) to Kettle Falls (Elliott 1918, 2:104-5). Kettle Falls was also called Colville Falls and Quiarpi Falls (Elliott 1917, 3:197 fn). The Chewelah-Spokan Group, established just prior to the reservation system, was further acknowledged by 1st Lt. M. C. Wilkinson (later Captain), during a tour in 1877 with Indian Agent Inspector E. C. Watkins (Wilkinson 1877:n.p.). As late as 1907, Indian Agent John M. Webster referred to this group "of Kalispels with a strong mixture of Spokane blood." Much of the contiguous riverine area occupied by the aboriginal Spokan was temporarily utilized not only by several ethnic groups, but also more distant groups because of the need for mutual exploitation of salmon. Intergroup relations were also facilitated by intermarriage, established trade, certain locally unavailable subsistence sources and prestige goods. Consequently, due to the vast fish resources of the Spokane River at that time, the Spokan spent most of the year on or near the river (Kennedy 1823)— particularly since "the Spokane subsistence base was one of the poorest in the Plateau as regards hunting" (Anastasio 1974, 4:26).

Jonathan Edwards (1847-1929), an early Protestant missionary, perhaps recognized different settlement patterns, and certainly revealed a calculating strategy for proselytizing Spokan Indians:

> There are five or six bands, each of which has certain lands which they claim as theirs, and where they pass a portion of each year. So far as I can learn they are somewhat regular in their removings. In this respect, let last year be a fair specimen. We shall have no great difficulty at almost any time, in knowing where to find a good collection. In April a large number gather on one plain to gather a root called popo [*p'úxʷp'uxʷ*] (1900:21).

Establishing aboriginal locations is made difficult by the seasonal mobility of cultural groupings, as well as inaccurate group name designations and multiple geonomic designations for natural features. For example, the Spokan did not refer to themselves as *Spokan Indian* (*spoqín*) in a collective sense, but rather used the ethnocentric terms *spoʔqeʔn'i*, *spqén* ("a round head"), and *spoqéne* ("echo") (Elmendorf 1935-6, 1:63, 4:11b; Ross 1995b:497), which are not derogatory, as translations may suggest. However, it is correct to follow Elmendorf's (1935-6) and Connolly's (pers. comm.) linguistic interpretation of the Spokan as being derived by early whites from the aboriginal geonomic designation and formation of Spokane Falls (see Appendix C). The Spokan adopted this designation, as did whites prior to the establishment of the reservation on 18 January 1881. Cowley was a Spokan-speaking missionary who, in 1874, served as Indian Sub-Agent to the Spokan. He claimed:

[...] Spokane is a white man's invention, a corruption of two or three Indian words. The name of the Indians who lived on the lower reach [Spokane River] was Spokaynish. There is an Indian word used by this tribe pronounced spo-kan-ee, with the accent on the final syllable. This word means sun, or sunlight, and has nothing to do with the name of the tribe (1916:2).

Cox mentions the term Spokane as the name of a chief known as *ilíx^wmspoqíni* or "the Son of the Sun" (1832:104), which may give credit to their collective designation as "Children of the Sun" (see Appendix D). Yet Meany (1923:284) feels the designation meant "chief of the sun people," and not the name of a particular chief, but rather his designated title. Though acknowledging the doubtful origin and existing ambiguity of the name Spokan, Mooney claimed that some signified the name as "Sun (people)" (1896:444), and, when speaking of the Spokan, Parker (1844) noted, "They denominate themselves the children of the sun, which in their language is Spokein" (Durham 1912, 1:67; Wynecoop 1969:75). Father Jean Pierre DeSmet wrote that they call themselves Children of the Sun, which in their language is "Spokan" (1847, 3:991-2). Swanton (1952:411) in 1842, was believed to have had minimal contact with the Spokan, whom Anastasio (1974, 4:159) also referred to the Spokan as "Children of the Sun."

There are other historical accounts (Hale 1846, 4:439; DeSmet 1847), and even more recent ones (Wynecoop 1969; Ruby and Brown 1981; Carlson and Flett 1989), suggesting that the ethnic designation for the Spokan should be translated as "Children of the Sun."

However, Edward Curtis (1868-1952) noted:

Etymologically the word seems to be related to *spúkani*, sun, but the force of the reference is not apparent. It may conceivably have originated among a tribe which; thus, described a related people living "toward the sun"; however, in the speech of the three tribes mentioned above [*špokénih, špokénik, šhpoknuh*], *spúkani* does not appear as the word for sun. In explanation of the term an informant said that when Garry was taken to Anglican Mission School at Red River (1825-29 and 1830-31) country to be educated, when asked what was his name; he replied, "*ɬúmhú-spúkani*" (Chief Sun); that by a misconception the white men took the last part of his name to be the name of his tribe. Intrinsically this is highly improbable and chronologically impossible; for the word "Spokanes" was used by the fur-trader Alexander Henry in 1811, and Garry went to school about 1825. No less impossible is the proposed derivation from a word meaning "wheat": it is hardly to be supposed that wheat was an article of such importance to the Spokan as to have given them a well-established cognomen as early as 1811 (1907-30, 7:56).

Historically, the name Spokan is mentioned for the first time by Thompson. Franchère kindly and understandably wrote, "Mr. Thompson kept a regular journal, and travelled, I thought more like a geographer than a fur-trader" (1854:121). Alexander Henry (1739-1824), a fur trader for the North West Company, conducted trade with Salishan and Shahaptian-speaking groups, including the Spokan, and contended, "The Spokanes are a tribe of the Flat Heads, speaking nearly the same language. They dwell along the Spokane River, seldom, if ever, go to the meadows [Plains] in search of buffalo, being content to live on the produce of their own lands" (Coues 1893, 2:711). The overland trail used by Thompson "became in later years in part the 'Mullan Road,' and in greater part the 'Colville Road,' which was used so heavily and so long in the commercial agricultural development of the Colville, Spokane, and Big Bend districts" (Elliott 1917, 8:261-262).

Etymologically, the name "Skeetshoo" (or "Schuihoo") was first applied to the Spokan Indians, then to the Spokane River (Elliott 1914, 4:262 fn and 276 fn), and eventually to the immediate area it drained. During 1804-06, Lewis and Clark wrote of the Indians and the falls, using the name "Skeetsomish" (Coues 1893, 3:990-2). On 8 June and 11 August 1811, Thompson also referred to the Spokane River and Coeur d'Alene Lake as "Skeetshoo" (Elliott 1911, 3:197; 1917, 3:182; 1925, 2:262 fn), as did Meany (1922, 13:212).

Parenthetically, the Euro-American policy of tribalization not only relocated many Amerindian peoples, but deprived groups of their aboriginal identity by replacing one group's designation with that assigned by other ethnic groups—sometimes a derogatory name, or the mispronunciation of the aboriginal term by non-Indians. Anthropologists are not always in agreement with what some Amerindian groups were called aboriginally. For example, the term *sntsuwe'stsene* is one designation for the Upper Spokan (Teit 1930:314), whereas Elmendorf (1965) prefers *sntu?c?lixi*. The Lower Spokan, according to Ray (1936:121), refer to themselves as *snkalt*, and were dialectically and culturally akin to the Sanpoil; but Elmendorf (1965) prefers the designation *scqescín*. However, Hale felt the Lower Spokan were a distinct tribe "not merely a component part of the Spokan" (Chalfant 1974:48). Yet (Ray 1936:12) feels that the name of the Middle Spokan, "Salmon Trout Fishers," is derived from the dialect name, which included the Middle and Upper Spokan collectively, and is fairly consistent with Elmendorf's usage (1965). Alexander Ross maintained the Sanpoil "were closely related to the Spokane Indians" (Twaites 1959, 3:276 fn); he was likely referring to the Lower Spokan. The Lower, Middle, and Upper Spokan collectively referred to themselves as *spoqíni* (Elmendorf, pers. comm.).

Yet Curtis contended, in his 1911 fieldwork, that the Spokan did not perceive themselves as a single entity:

> The Lower Spokan have a vague tradition that they once were enemies of the other two tribes. In ancient times there was war between the Middle Spokan and the Coeur d'Alênes, the last fight taking place about the beginning of the eighteenth century; but the Upper Spokan were frequently on friendly terms with both parties. In those days also ceased the old hostilities between the New Percé and the Upper and Middle Spokan (1911, 7:56).

John Work, an employee of the HBC, had a wife who "was of Spokane blood and a very intelligent woman" (Elliott 1914, 4:270 fn), and was of great assistance to her husband. He was a keen observer of indigenous cultures, and made important ethnographic reference to the Spokan in numerous reports—ones that recognized linguistic, cultural, and distribution differences between the Spokan and contiguous groups:

> The Spokan possess the lands of the river that bears their name from its discharge to above the falls near the Awl heart [Coeur d'Alene] country. They consist of three tribes, the Scaitseeuthinish who live at the lower falls, the Sinhomenish who remain above the Forks at the old Spokane Fort, and the Sintotoluh who dwell at the upper falls. This part of the country is less rugged than we have passed, towards the southward there are some pretty extensive plains and also tracts of high ground without wood. Chivereau [horses] are in some parts pretty numerous. Great numbers of salmon and trout ascend the river most seasons (Work 1829:20).

Curtis as well considered the Spokan to comprise separate groups, each of which "exercised exclusive control over fishing and camping grounds along the stream [Spokane River], although they shared the extensive prairie [*čłčewn*] south of the river for root-digging, and the hills north for gathering berries and hunting game" (1911, 7:74-5). He described the following location for the Spokan, stating each group was not a band, but rather a tribe:

> In eastern Washington, along the Spokane River below the Coeur d'Alenes (*sčicow'i*) [or *sč'sčícwi'*], were three small tribes known collectively as the Spokan, and distinguished as Upper, Middle, and Lower *špokán*, according to their respective positions on the river. The first-named held the country on both sides of the Spokane River from Post Falls, in Idaho, to the mouth of Latah Creek, a little below the Spokane Falls and the site of the present city of Spokane; and from Mount Carlton [Mount Spokane], on the north to a line about thirty miles south of the river. In their own language they were *sntu??uli*, the Muddy [Creek] People, *ntutuúli-mátg* being the name of Latah Creek. Their permanent winter camps were along this stream. Adjoining them on the west were *šinhoméné*, the Salmon-trout people, who claimed the country along the river a short distance below the mouth of Latah Creek to the present Tumtum [*st'cmt'sínen*], Washington. The *tskaisfsíhlni*, whose name is derived from the native appellation of the Little Falls of the Spokane about which their camps centered, held the territory from Tumtum to the mouth of the river [...] These were separate tribes, not bands of the same tribe. Each exercised exclusive control over its fishing and camping grounds along the stream, although they all shared the prairies south of the river for root-digging, and the hills on the north for gathering berries and hunting game (Curtis 1907-30, 7:54).

Through his extended residency, Curtis became interested in the dialectic variation between the Lower Spokan and what he called the other two tribes (Middle and Upper Spokan) of Spokan, correctly remarking how:

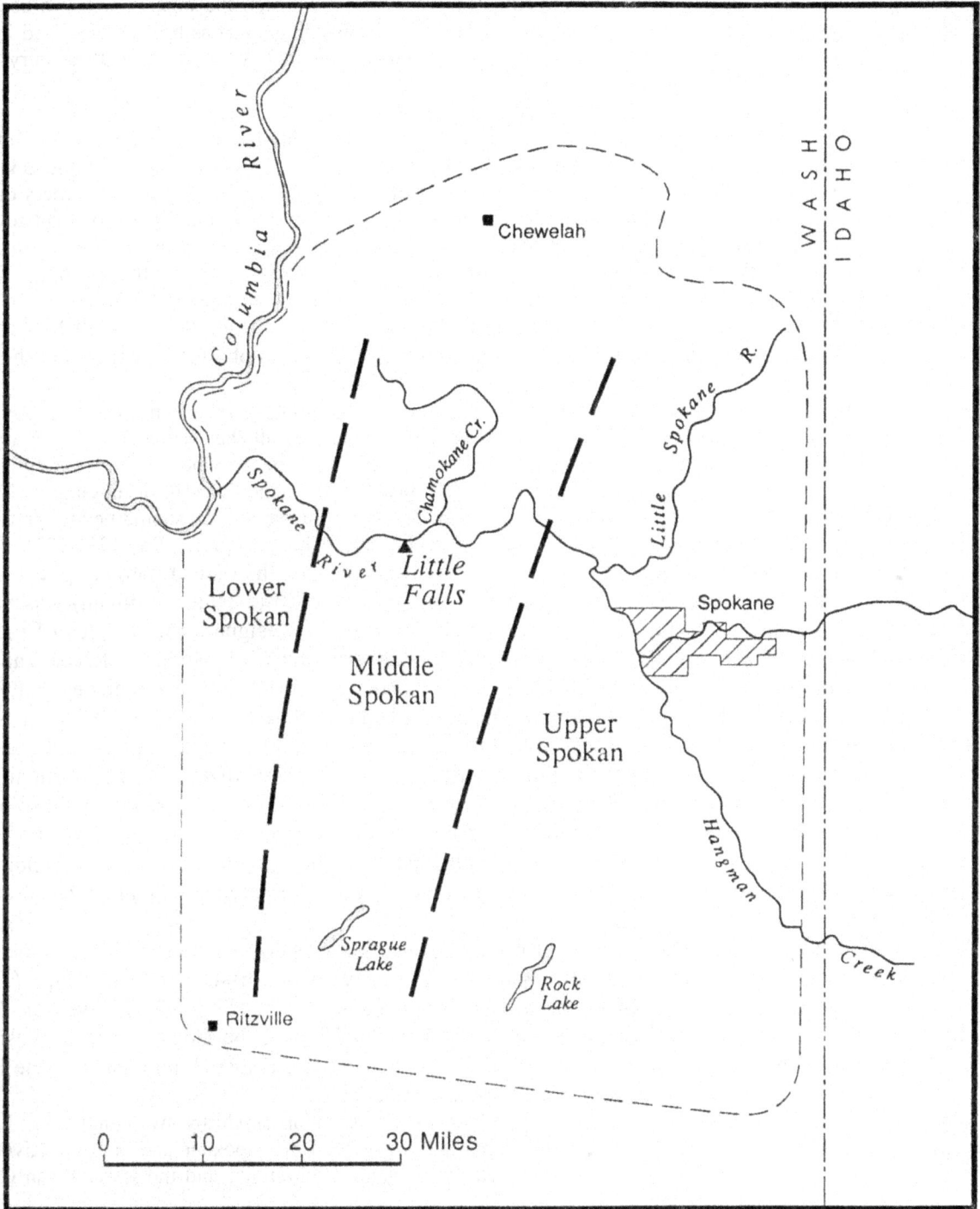

Figure 2. Spokan band distribution (by Julie A. Ross)

The language of the Lower Spokan was slightly different from that which the other two tribes used in common. The *sntu?t?úli* and the *snxʷmén?i* were closely allied in friendship as well as by language, and in the times of which we have our first definite information, shortly before the middle of the nineteenth century they were practically one (1911, 7:55).

James Teit, a later ethnographer of the Plateau, noted:

> The Spokan were in three main groups: (1) The Lower Spokan occupying the mouth and lower part of the Spokane River, including the present Spokane Indian Reservation. (2) The Upper Spokan, or Little Spokan, occupying the Little Spokane River and all the country east of the Lower Spokan to within the borders of the Coeur d'Alene and Kalispel. The plateau country south of the Spokane River, around Davenport and toward Palouse, was used as a summering and hunting ground by both these divisions, and it seems there was a distinct line between them. (3) The South or Middle Spokan occupied the whole Latah's Creek country, extending south along the borders of the Coeur d'Alêne. It seems that they did not go west of Cheney (1930:313-4).

The fieldwork of Verne Ray (1977:13) with certain Interior Salish aboriginal groups differs from the aforementioned descriptions by Teit (1930) and Curtis (1907-30) when he emphatically wrote that the Lower Spokan:

> [...] are not the same people as Teit designates by the term Lower Spokan, though the territory partially coincides. Teit assumed that peoples speaking the Spokan dialect extended all the way to the mouth of the Spokane River and that the local term Lower Spokan referred to all of the peoples below the Little Spokan Valley. But rather it designates a small group of peoples dialectically akin to the Sanpoil, occupying the lower most part of the Spokane River valley as indicated on the map. The name Lower Spokan should be interpreted as "peoples of the Lower Spokane Valley;" and not "lower Spokan-dialect speaking peoples." (Ray 1936:121)

Ray (1936:121-2) purported that the term "Spokan" was derived from the dialect name applicable to the Middle and Upper Spokan peoples, and in Teit's terminology, this group (the Middle Spokan) was included with the Lower Spokan. Ray further used the term "Middle Spokan" to designate the peoples of the Latah (Hangman) Creek Valley, and the term "Upper Spokan" for those of the Little Spokane River Valley and eastward. These are unfortunate confusions, as local usage in no way conformed to either designation. For example, Reverend Parker, when visiting a Middle Spokan village, confused them with the Upper Spokan, whom he considered a neighboring tribe (1840:288-91). The Middle Spokan were the peoples of the middle Spokane River country—the territories in each case extending for considerable distances both north and south of the river. Thus, "Upper" refers to their upriver location, not upper in the sense of north or those areas of somewhat higher elevation, as some contemporary Spokan have thought (P. Flett, pers. comm.). Teit's alternative terms of "Little Spokan" for the Little Spokane River Valley peoples, and "South Spokan" for those of the Latah Valley, are not objectionable, except they suggest a greater demarcation between these groups than existed.

A recent ethnohistory of the Spokan, based primarily upon Chalfant's concurrence with Ray's location of the three Spokan macro bands—presented before the Indian Claims Commission field hearings (1974)—corrected some errors and inconsistencies set forth by Curtis (1907-30) and Teit (1930). Based on this, the Spokan occupied the terraces of the Spokane River east to the territory of the Coeur d'Alene, west to the mouth and lower part of the Spokane River (Lugenbeel 1859), north to the Kalispel, and south to the Palouse (Grover 1855, 2:511-3; Teit 1930:309; Ray 1936). Chalfant concluded:

> The lower Spokan occupied the lower Spokane River Valley as far up as Curby, Washington, and also occupied the Tschimakain Creek vicinity. The middle Spokan lived on the Little Spokane and Spokane Rivers in the vicinity of the confluence, while the Upper occupied the Spokane city vicinity and the lower Latah Creek (1974:61).

In his 1865 annual report, Indian Agent Paige submitted the following description of the Spokan population and band distribution, and their reluctance to give up their land:

> This tribe is the largest in the district. They inhabit the country on the Spokane river, from its mouth to the boundary of Idaho, and number about one thousand. The tribe is divided into two bands called Upper and Lower Spokanes, under the rule, respectively, of the chiefs Gary and Lot [...] They are strongly averse to selling their

24

lands to the government; do not like the whites to settle in their country; are somewhat haughty in their deportment and refuse to accept presents from the department (1865:98-101).

However, the following year Paige amended his 1865 report, which now included the Middle Spokan, and reduced his population estimate to 750 (1866:73).

In summary, Elmendorf's extensive fieldwork provides the following linguistic designations and distribution of the three so-called Spokan macro bands—one that is most comparable to Teit's earlier findings, and has been adopted by most anthropologists:

Aboriginally the Spokan were comprised of three bands: Lower Spokan (*scqástsítni*) with a principal settlement at *scqástsítn* ('fishery', from *tsqá* 'fish running upstream') near Little Falls; Middle Spokan (*sntutuʔúli*) on Latah or Latah Creek (*ntuʔtʔúlm*, from *ntutu'úli* 'milky, cloudy, of water'); and Upper Spokan (*snxʷménʔí*) on the Little Spokane River and upriver from the junction with Latah Creek. The principal Middle Spokan village was a year round encampment (also known as *ntutu'úlm*) where Latah Creek joins the Spokane [River]. The Middle and Upper Spokan considered themselves as "all one people" [*tsqʼaistłmi*] in distinction to the Lower Spokan (Elmendorf 1935-6 and 1965).

Local historian William Stanley Lewis (1876-1941) maintained that, "Latah is an Indian word meaning 'place where we get food,' and was probably named from the locality being an excellent camas and course ground" (1955:32).

This formulation of Spokan divisions agrees essentially with that of Teit (1930), but differs from Ray (1936), who designated the "Lower Spokan" as an Okanogan-speaking group at the mouth of the Spokane River. "The Okanogan and Spokan groups were the closest relatives of each other" (Elmendorf 1965:71). The Lower Spokan settled mostly at *Indian Hill* (*čłčaƛxʷé*) and on *Long Prairie* (*lʔaičʔn*), and their language was similar to the Chewelah-Spokan Group (Smith 1936-8; Himmelberg 1997:2), with whom they shared resource areas and intermarried. Elmendorf noted, "There were probably at least two bands of the Chewelah [Chewelah-Spokan Group], as some people speak of their two winter camps" (1930:312).

Linguistic Groupings

The Spokan Indians of northeastern Washington spoke a Salishan language that was shared, in different dialects, with the contiguous Kalispel-Flathead dialect group (Smith 1965:67), being a *lingua franca* in the northeastern Plateau (Ross 1994:611). Smith (1965:74) believes Kalispel was probably more the *lingua franca* between the Chewelah-Spokan-Kalispel-Pend d'Oreille-Flathead (Elmendorf 1965:74). Burns wrote:

The Eastern [Lower] and Central [Middle] Spokanes, with the Kalispels, could comprehend each other's tongues; but the Coeur d'Alenes stood alone in their unique subgroup [... but] The Eastern [Upper] Spokanes were closely identified with the Coeur d'Alenes despite divergent dialects (1966:6).

Later, he is more correct when stating, "Both Central [Middle] and Eastern [Upper] tribes were dialectically akin to the Kalispel" (Burns 1966:179). Maximilian (1782-1867) wrote how the Flatheads "speak the same language as the Ponderas [Pend d'Oreille] and Spokein [Spokan] Indians" (1834, 24:227).

Elmendorf's research concluded that the "Spokan, Chewelah, Kalispel, Pend d'Oreille [*snčicuʔmšcn*], and Flathead are similarly mutually intelligible, with Spokane probably the most distinct dialect" (1965:65). Roehrig (1881:575) also studied similarities between Flathead, Kalispel, and Spokan. Cox, when referring to the Chewelah-Spokan Group, noted:

[...] a small tribe, consisting of not more than fifteen families, who occupied a few hunting lodges about midway between Spokan House and the Chaudiere Falls [Kettle Falls]. Their language is a dialect of that spoken by the natives of the above places, but approaching more nearly to the Spokan (Stewart and Stewart 1957:190-191).

25

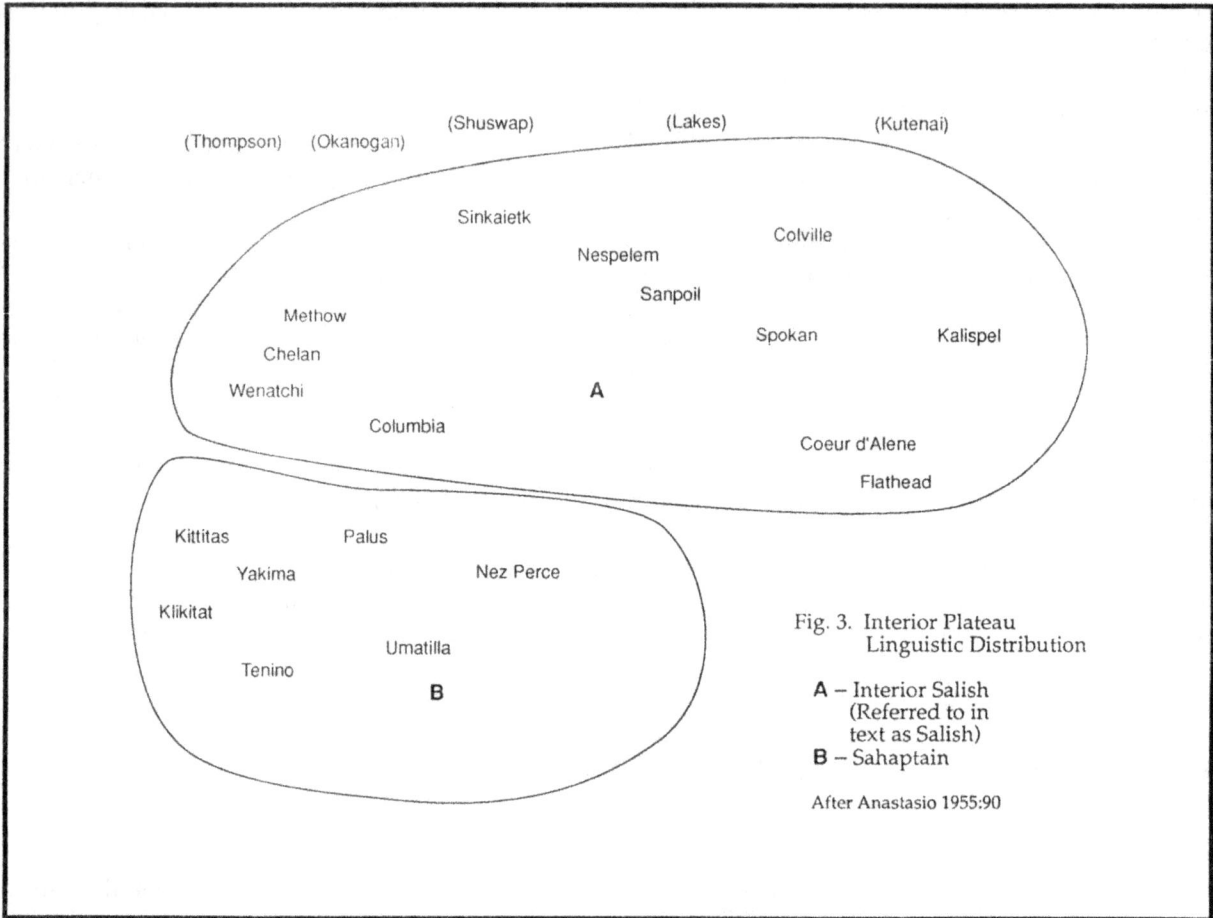

Figure 3. Interior plateau linguistic distribution

Simpson also considered the Spokan language as being a *lingua franca*:

> The Spokan Language is understood from the Lakes down to the Nez Percès or Louis's River and that of the Nez Percès Tribe down to the Cascades or lowest Portage but every thirty or forty Miles a different Language is spoken, having little affinity with each other (1847:95).

"According to Kalispel tradition, the Chewelah are a group of Kalispel who recently migrated to the region they now occupy because of a misunderstanding" (Ray 1936:121). The *Chewelah people* (*slo?téw'si* - "garter snake"), who intermarried with the Spokan and the Kalispel, were called *sk'ewíl'e?xʷ* by the Lakes. The town of Chewelah was called *sč'ewíl?e?* ("water snake").

Within the eastern Plateau there were two major language families: In the Southern Plateau was Sahaptian (Dalles, Klickitat, Nez Perce, Palouse, Umitilla *Walla Walla* (*walúle*), Wanapum, and Warm Springs); further north were the Salishan (Columbia, Coeur d'Alene, Kalispel, Okanogan-Colville, Thompson, and Sanpoil and Nespelem). Many of those located along the Columbia River spoke the Chinook Trade Jargon. Other dialects were Wasco-Wishram, Carrier, Chilcotin, and Kutenai.

Chinook Jargon was mentioned by the French-Canadian explorer and ethnographer Franchère: "The Chinook language is spoken by all nations from the mouth of the Columbia to the falls [Spokane Falls]. It is difficult to pronounce [...] being full of gutturals, like Gaelic" (1904, 6:336). More specifically, Gunter noted,

26

"The Chinook language is spoken to the north and south of the mouth of the Columbia and up the river as far as The Dalles" (1950:201). Chinook Jargon reflected primarily the need for common communication among all groups involved in riverine resource exploitation. In later years, the Spokan, who travelled extensively, became familiar with Chinook Jargon (Teit 1930:373). Although Chinook was a *lingua franca* along the Columbia River, Teit noted in the 1920s and early 1930s how:

> [...] sign language is still used considerably by elderly Coeur d'Alene in speaking with some Spokan and members of other tribes. Sign language was often used talking with strangers, when attempting to cross the Spokane River, they (whites) shouted to get the attention of the ferryman, and after a while, trading and hunting, and as gestures accompanying speech (1930:136).

Parker, when with the Spokan, recorded how "two women came to the river, and with uncommonly pleasant voices, together with the language of signs, the latter of which only I could understand [...] informed that the ferryman was gone upon a short hunt" (1840:288).

```
        Penutian stock          Mosan stock


  Chinookan         Sahaptian            Salishan
   family             family              family



 Tillamook        Bella          Coast         Interior
                  Coola          Salish           Salish



        4 Interior Salish dialects spoken by:

        1)   the Lower Spokan, Lakes, Colville, Sanpoil,
             Nespelem, and Southern Okanogan;

        2)   the Columbia, Chelan, Methow, and Wenatchi;

        3)   the Middle Spokan, Upper Spokan, Chewelah,
             Flathead, and Kalispel;

        4)   the Coeur d'Alene.
```

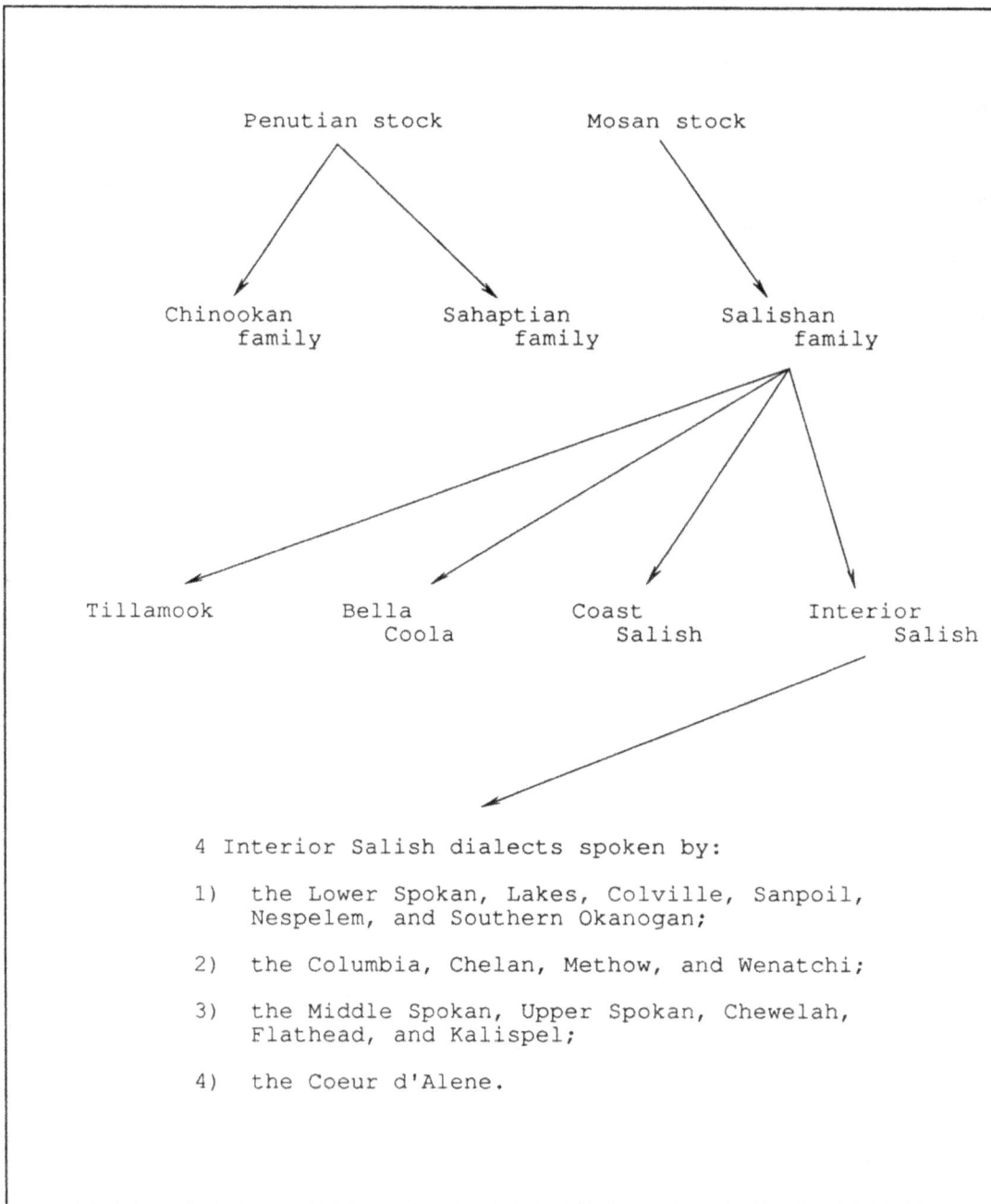

Figure 4. Interior Salish dialects

An early and invaluable description of Flathead sign language was collected by William Clark (1885:174). However, Elmendorf's fieldwork concluded that the "Blackfeet used sign language but the Spokans didn't—only a deaf mute talked with his hands." But, some Spokanes knew it: "according to Sam Boyd [the last Spokane Chief and Elmendorf's principal informant], Spokanes did use sign to a considerable extent" (1935-6, 1:68) (Durham 1912, 1:64).

Most people were polyglots, because of several factors: Many dialects were mutually intelligible; resource distribution—notably anadromous fish—lead to polyadic trade relationships; and intermarriage occurred among different dialectic and language groups.

The close proximity and resulting socioeconomic interrelationships between the Lower Spokan and the Sanpoil explain why "many were eventually allotted lands on the Spokane Indian Reservation. The Sanpoils were from the *snqelt* area. These peoples [...] were of great influence among the Spokanes. Many of the place-names are Colville in meaning, such as *čq'ew'sicn'* or *sk'ew'sikn'*" (STHC). Teit wrote that the *Sinpohellechach* were the Sanpoils at the mouth of the Sanpoil River, fifty-five miles west of the Spokane River, and were closely related to the Spokane Indians. More specifically, Teit also provided the linguistic designation of the Spokan groups:

- *Stsêkastsi'*, *Stkastsi'LEn*, *Stkastsi'LEnic* (the Lower Spokan). The name is derived from a place called *Stkasi'LEtsn*, near the mouth of the Spokane River. Some translate the name as "running fast," probably with reference to the river. Other, less-accepted translations of the name are "bad food," "bad eaters," or "poor feeders"—according to some, in reference to the people; according to others, derived from a place-name.
- *SntutuUli* or *Sntutu'U'* (the Middle Spokan). This name is translated "living together" by some, and "pounding" or "pounders" (meat or fish) by others. Most people think the term is derived from a place whose name was derived from the sound of pounding.
- *SnXo'mE'*, *SEnXomE'*, *SEnXomEnic'* (the Upper Spokan). This name is usually translated as "salmon-trout" or "salmon-trout people" (from *Xome'na* - "salmon-trout" or "steelhead," a fish once plentiful in tribe's area). Some think the term may originally have been the name of a locality in their country where the fish were abundant. Another translation of the name is "using red paint," but this is probably incorrect (1930:298).

There is no reason to dispute Elmendorf's linguistic designations for the Spokan: *Lower Spokan* (*scqesció ni* or *scqecíłni*), *Middle Spokan* (*snxmene?ey*), and *Upper Spokan* (*sntu?t?lix^wi* or *snxumén?e*). Elmendorf located a Spokan settlement (*snqált* or *snqelt*) of Inchelium, a group of Sanpoil he called the *sntpoéleci* or *san poʕwil'ši*, located immediately west of the confluence of the Spokane and Columbia Rivers, who spoke a dialect called *sx̣^wiy'e?łpi* (1935-6, 4:27). (For specific locations and designations of native Spokan villages, see Ray 1936, 2:99-152.)

Phonetically, the Spokan constituted a Spokan Group, albeit the Lower Spokan dialect was slightly different from the Middle and Upper Spokan (Curtis 1907-30 7:55; Elmendorf 1965; Ray 1936:107; Smith 1936-8; Spier 1936:8; Carlson 1972), due partly to spatial distribution along the Spokane River. However, Chalfant (1974) is probably correct in assuming that this divergence is also cultural, because the fishing terminology of the Lower Spokan for salmon varied from that of the Middle and Upper Spokan. For these reasons, the Reverend Samuel Parker (1838:283-4) also considered the Lower Spokan as culturally separate.

Aboriginal ethnic groups of the Columbia Basin maintained close and constant economic and social relationships with each other. For example, the Spokan had contact with the Chelan, Coeur d'Alene, Columbia, Colville, Methow, Nespelem, Sanpoil, Sinkaietk, Wenatchee, Flathead, Nez Perce, Kalispel, and Pend d'Oreille. The Kalispel, Flathead, and Pend d'Oreille spoke dialects most closely related to the Spokan, and linguistically compose what Teit designated as the Flathead Group (1930:295), and what Elmendorf designated as the Spokane-Kalispel-Flathead Group (1965:67). Despite some phonetic and cultural differences, they referred to themselves as *šee lictcén*, meaning Salish-speaking (Teit 1930:295-6). Elmendorf (1965:71) felt that the Spokan Group shared the greatest similarities with the Okanogan Group. Numerous names have been assigned to the Spokan by other aboriginal peoples—for example, *špokeí néms*, *špoqé én*, Yakima (*yi?áqm'e?*), Palouse, and Klickitat and *łê'cłuks* by the Wasco (Teit 1930:299); *spukán* by the Klamath and Modoc (Teit 1930:299); *Spokenish* by Gibbs (1855, 1:20); *Sinkoman* by the Kutenai (*gl'sé?*)

(Gibbs 1855, 1:20); *Spokin-nish* by Manypenny (Stevens 1855:428). Swanton referred to the Coeur d'Alene as "Skit-wish" or "Skitswish" (1952:411).

Within the Plateau, there existed dialectic polyglotism, and between major linguistic groupings there was some bilingualism, as with the Wasco-Wishram, Nez Perce-Palouse, and Cayuse-Nez Perce (French 1961; Walker 1973). This multilingualism reflected the needed continuous intergroup social and economic intercourse to facilitate trade and marriage: "Lexical resemblances indicate social and linguistical interaction among many with their immediate neighbors more than with their distant ones" (Rigsby 1996:144).

Consequently, the Spokan language was probably a *lingua franca* in the southeastern Plateau. The formulation of Spokan band divisions agrees essentially with that of Teit (1930), but differs from Ray (1936), who placed the Lower Spokan and Okanogan-speaking group at the mouth of the *Spokane River* (*čxʷiyy'ep*); i.e., all the Spokan at the mouth of the Spokane River spoke one language (Elmendorf, pers. comm.). Some missionaries spoke Chinook Jargon, e.g., Reverend Eells translated, recorded, and published a book of hymns in Chinook Jargon. Traditionally, many of those Spokan who inhabited contiguous areas with the Coeur d'Alene, along the Spokane River, are often referred to as the Spokane River Group. These linguistic abilities reinforced a commonly shared cultural core. Bilingualism and the concept of usufruct were probably responsible for later confusion by many non-Indians in delineating ethnic boundaries and the location of aboriginal groups.

When asked about the differences between some Indian languages and English, an elderly Spokan man replied, "All Indian languages are like the wind. You can feel and hear them, but not see them. Your language can be seen, but we can't feel or hear what you people really mean, only what you write, and that may not always be true."

Socioeconomic Intra-Areal Affiliations

Interior Plateau task-grouping interrelations facilitated the mutual exploitation of needed resources, trade, intermarriage, and maintained dyadic and polyadic task-grouping for warfare when venturing onto the Plains for bison-hunting, horse-stealing, and reciprocal trading, prior to 1809 (Thompson 1916:463, 548). Miller correctly stated, "That the Plateau people survived is a tribute to the task group system, with its totally integrated structure of economic cooperation" (2003:25). These groupings often required some Salish groups to coordinate with the Nez Perce for protection. "In these intertribal gatherings [...] councils were held to settle disputes, to preserve order, and to make important decisions" (Garth 1964, 20:45).

The Spokan traveled in relative safety through Nez Perce country and the areas of the Palouse territory, and even the Cayuse territory for hunting and trading. Most conflict among some groups was limited and sporadic, although conflict increased temporarily in eastern Washington with the introduction of the horse, in approximately 1730 (Haines 1938a:430). Yet the horse may have ultimately served to decrease conflict within the Interior Plateau because of the substantial cooperation required for hunting bison and trading for Plain's resources.

Sadly, political and ethnic factionalism was later introduced by Christian missionaries (Ross 1967), which had devastating effects upon many Plateau groups, and eventually wrought incalculable harm to peoples who once subscribed to universal animism for explaining their relationship to the natural and supernatural worlds. Because of the generally held premises of Franz Boas (1911) regarding the futility and validity of late-date ethnographic research with indigenous language loss, Chalfant's fieldwork was at a critical time (1951-1954) in collecting pertinent ethnography, along with that of Ray (1936 and 1939) and Elmendorf (1935-6) for locating aboriginal Spokan fishing stations:

> Major fishing stations were maintained during the salmon season along the Spokane river from its mouth to Spokane Falls at the city of Spokane, and on the lower part of the Little Spokane. Each division maintained major fishing sites in the vicinity of their villages. Thus, the range of the more permanent camp sites defined the portion of the river utilized by each group. The Lower Spokan had their main sites on the Spokane near its mouth, near

River Homes ten miles east of the mouth, at little Falls, and at Curby. The Little or Middle Spokane maintained their major villages and fishing stations at, and above and below, the confluence of the Little Spokane and Spokane. The Upper Spokan, whose major camps centered around the junction of Latah creek and Spokane river, utilized this confluence, the lower stretches of Latah creek and Spokane Falls for fishing [...] The Spokan also utilized major fishing stations quite distant from their home sites. many Spokan families annually travelled to the famed Kettle Falls on the Columbia to join in the intra-tribal salmon catches. A summer fishing camp was jointly occupied by the Upper Spokan and Coeur d'Alene at the outlet of Spokane river on Coeur d'Alene Lake in Idaho, where a weir was constructed and traps set to take salmon-trout, whitefish, speckled trout and suckers. Some Spokan, probably from the Lower division, joined with the Sanpoil and other tribal groups, including Coeur d'Alene, Yakima, Umitilla, Okanogan, and Colville, at the mouth of Sanpoil river on the Columbia where the Sanpoil maintained a large weir throughout the summer (Cox 1957 [1832]:85-6).

Canadian artist John Mix Stanley (1814-1872) created a lithograph (1862, 12 (1):134-135, Plate XXXVI) that illustrates Spokane Falls at the time.

Figure 5. "Falls of the Spokane"

Trade

All trading groups observed a well-developed protocol and strict division of labor. The women of various tribes basically controlled negotiations among themselves for all foodstuffs—whether hunted by men but later processed by women (such as dried deer meat or fish, including dried eel), and all materials the women made, such as tule mats, bags, and tanned deer hides, since "it was shameful and ridiculous for men to trade such things" (Elmendorf 1935-6, 2:66). More specifically, women were the sole purveyors when *trading food*

($n^?eymcín$), and men were the sole traders of horses, feathers, weapons, tools, drums, lithic products, or any other items they manufactured.

Intergroup trading assumed definite patterns of group socioeconomic interaction between Interior Salishan and Sahaptian groups during their seasonal movements, which required them to share subsistence areas within the Plateau. For example, Thompson (1916:466; Work 1971:41) wrote that the time for catching salmon along the Columbia River varied by as much as two months; similarly, roots matured at different times—given elevation, slope, exposure, and other natural conditions—thereby necessitating mutual utilization of food resource areas by various groups on a temporary basis. There were extensive root fields south and southwest of the Spokan, mutually harvested annually by numerous groups. The Spokane River provided a main communication route for trade goods, particularly items being exchanged from southwesterly tribes and coastal peoples:

> Probably the reason for the relative importance of this trail [Spokane River] may be found in the fact that an exceedingly important, parallel route led westward from the Colville to the Sinkaietk, and that the greater part of the goods which moved westward over the famous Pend Oreille river route continued their journey over this more northern route (Smith 1941:291).

The localization of certain natural resources was an important stimulus to the annual movements of groups, as well as a reason for conducting trading between groups. For example, Griswald cited how in 1877, "The Coeur d'Alene traded for bitterroot and salmon with the Spokane" (1970:45), and, "The Coeur d'Alene and Spokan Indians here carried on a brisk trade with the tribes of Montana, exchanging fish for buffalo robes" (Gaston 1927:165). Fresh or dried bison tongue was always considered a fine gift, and Work's group "Had 113 Buffalo Tongues salted in bags made of pannefliches" (Elliott 1914, 5:189). "The Coeur d'Alene [also] imported native tobacco from the Spokane because they did not grow the plant" (Griswald 1970:45). Bitterroot was traded to the Lakes from the Spokan (Elmendorf 1935-6, 1:30), probably for greenstone. Even prior to the horse, trade between the Spokan and Coeur d'Alene was conducted on a regular basis, and the Coeur d'Alene became quite dependent upon the Spokan, especially for salmon:

> The Coeur d'Alene had no salmon in their country, but salmon came close to the borders of their territory along the Spokane River. Some Coeur d'Alene bought what dried salmon they required from the Spokan; but large numbers of the tribe went to Spokane Falls and other parts of the Spokane River where they fished salmon for themselves with the Spokan tribe. As the two tribes were usually friendly, this opportunity was generally available (Teit 1930:197).

This lack of local resources was likely a factor in the development of long-established trading partners, whereby a man assumed the prerogatives, privileges, and trust of his father's trading partner's son. DeSmet claimed, "The Coeur d'Alene have still the reputation of being the best and most industrious Indians in the Rocky Mountain" (O'Hara 1909, 3:251-2).

Teit also acknowledged the dependence of the Coeur d'Alene upon the Spokan for certain berry, *root* (*sóx^{w}ep*), and nut crops.

> Thus soapberries (*Shepherdia*) and hazelnuts, which did not grow in the country of the Coeur d'Alêne, were obtained from the Spokan, who, in turn got them from the Colville Indians, in whose country they were plentiful. Bitterroot also did not grow in the Coeur d'Alêne country, which was procured from the Spokan, in whose country it grew abundantly. After the introduction of horses, many Coeur d'Alêne made trips to the district around Cheney and Sprague, in Spokan territory, to get it. The Spokan never raised any objections, as they had an abundance [...] The Spokan also allowed them to come to their territory and put up supplies of salmon [...] Some of the Coeur d'Alêne, however, preferred to buy dried salmon from the Spokan [...] It seems that in older times the Coeur d'Alêne did nearly all their trading with the Spokan, and comparatively little with other tribes. After they began to go out on the plains a trade sprang up in special articles with several of the Plains tribes. All parties going to the plains to hunt buffalo carried small quantities of western products to trade, for the Plains tribes were very fond of some of these, and were willingly to pay rather high prices. Thus salmon oil put up in sealed salmon skin, salmon pemmican mixed with it and put up in salmon skins, cakes of camas and other roots, cakes of certain kinds of berries, Indian hemp. And Indian-hemp twine were transported across the mountains (1930:112-4).

32

The general area of Little Falls was recognized as a major trading site for the Coeur d'Alene, Colville, Nez Perce, Sanpoil, Nespelem, and Palouse tribes who congregated primarily to fish, but also to exchange goods:

The *stsqaistsíłn* [Little Falls] bartered a good deal among themselves and with other tribes. They traded horses with each other and with the Nez Perce obtained from the Blackfeet during periods of peace [...] In getting hides from the Blackfeet, each party would travel part way to meet each other (Elmendorf 1935-6, 2:66-7).

Trade between the Spokan and the Coeur d'Alene was summarized by Chance and Hudson:

The Coeur d'Alene obtained most of the items they wanted from the Spokan who had a reputation throughout the Columbia plateau as traders and intermediaries of exchange. The Coeur d'Alene trade for soapberries, hazelnuts, bitterroot, dried salmon, dentalia, abalone and some other shells, flat circular beads, copper and iron, and slaves with the Spokan (1981:53).

An impetus for trade between eastern Plateau groups and western Plains tribes was the scarcity of bison in the Pacific Northwest, and the later acquisition of horses by eastern Salish and Sahaptian Indians. Horses permitted the Spokan and other groups to make a long annual "journey to the buffalo hunting grounds and here if they were lucky they killed and feasted to repletion, dried great quantities of meat and with meat and robes packed on their ponies" before returning home (Kingston 1932, 3:171).

Teit (1930:114) listed other highly desired Plateau products sought by western Plains groups, particularly horn and wood bows and arrows, various types of skins (particularly buckskin clothing), and dried salmon. They also traded products originally from coastal peoples, including greenstone pipes, finished or unfinished shells for necklaces, and western-bred horses, which were larger than horses from the Plains. Bancroft (1832-1918) noted that for "the Spokans the chief riches are their horses, which they obtain in barter from the Nez Percés" (1875, 1:273 fn). Warren Ferris (1810-1873), a trapper for the AFC, also wrote that horses were the principal wealth of the Flatheads (1940:146). Their effect upon trading was also acknowledged by Hale, who described the "rapid introduction of certain cultural elements, especially those associated with the horse and with the new mode of life which the animal made possible" (1846, 6:179).

Both dried salmon and eels were valuable trade items when transported to certain Plains groups east of the Rocky Mountains and traded for *buffalo robes* ($q^{w}spélx^{w}$) and other needed items not immediately available to the Spokan. Anastasio (1972:169) presented the most complete list of trade items throughout the Plateau and Plains: abalone, antlers, bark (tree unspecified), beads, berries, bitterroot, blankets, bows, buffalo bone beads, buffalo hides and meat, camas, canoes, catlinite, celts, copper, deer hides, deer nets, dentalia, eagle feathers, elk bone beads, fat, gathering and hunting privileges, goat hides and hair, hemp, horn spoons and ladles, horses, huckleberries, marine shell, marmot skins, mineral pigment, moose hides, pipes, pond lily seeds, rabbit skins, roots, rush mats, saddles, salmon oil and eggs, salmon pemmican, scent, sheep horn, skin bags, parfleche pieces, skin robes, slaves, snowshoes, soapstone, stone implements, tobacco, twine, wampum beads, wild carrot, and yew wood.

Reciprocal trade goods from the Plains were primarily bison robes, green and red catlinite pipes or blanks. Sioux-made feather bonnets were first traded to the Crow, who in turn traded them to eastern Plateau people. Teit noted the high value of tanned and decorated bison robes from the Crow: "The [Crow] buffalo robes [...] were of the softest tan, and ornamented with a band of beadwork across the middle [...] Often a horse [... or] a well-made leather shirt, was paid for one of the best robes" (1930:114). The Walla Walla, living in essentially a treeless area, traded for dugout canoes from the Spokan (Gibbs 1855, 1:403). Trade was also maintained with the *Sinkaietk* [southern Okaganon] (Walters 1938:75-6), probably for horses, hematite, and clay. This mutual dependence upon such reciprocal trade items was the primary reason to maintain peaceful relations. When speaking of the effects of these intergroup relations, Ray noted, "Common utilization of hunting, berrying, and root digging grounds by members of several villages serves as a cementing bond [...] The particular grouping is determined by various social factors together with geographic conditions. During these activities village affiliation is more or less forgotten and all mingle freely" (1939:10).

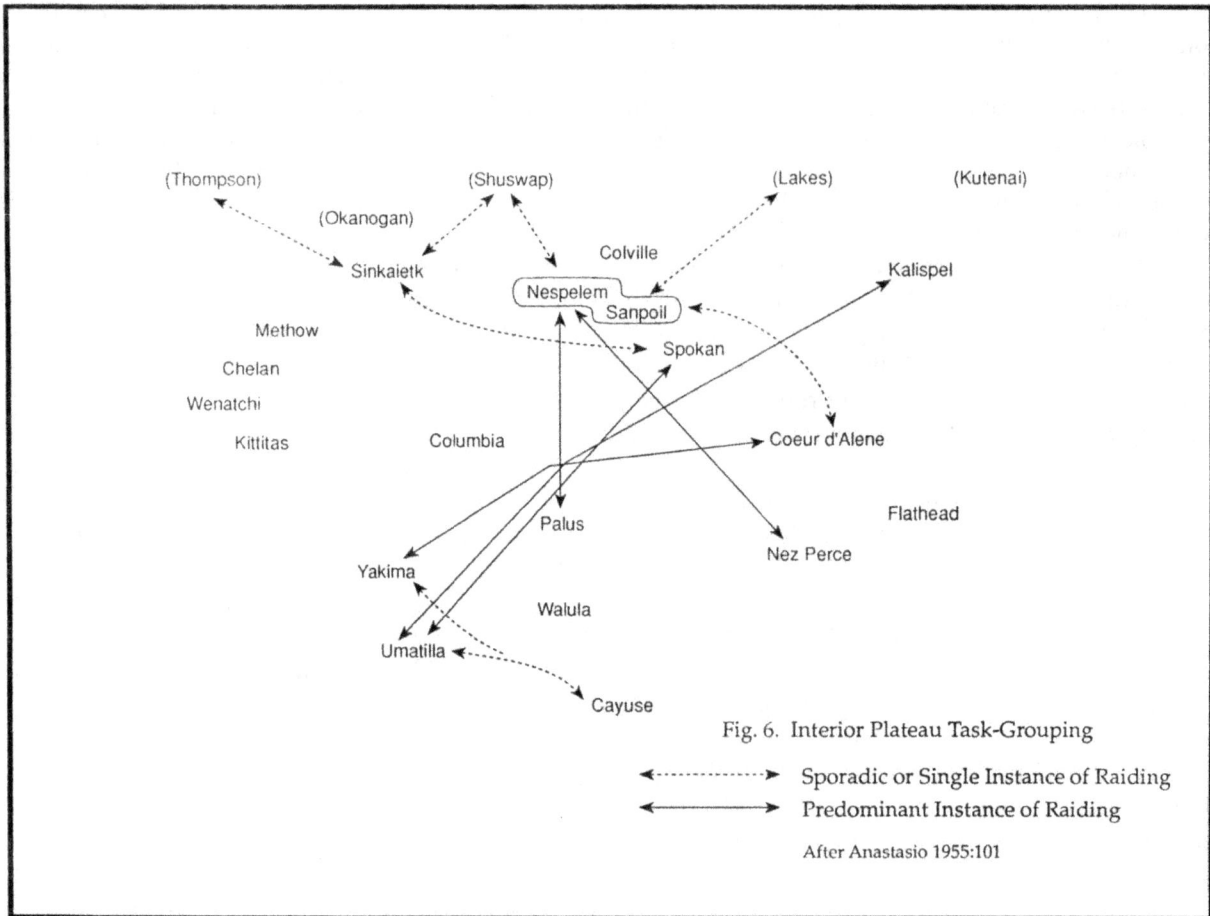

Fig. 6. Interior Plateau Task-Grouping

←------------→ Sporadic or Single Instance of Raiding
←—————————→ Predominant Instance of Raiding

After Anastasio 1955:101

Figure 6. Interior plateau task-grouping

"Among more distant tribesmen, with friendly Plateau neighbors, exchange might be expected to follow the lines of 'balanced reciprocity' [...] with a fair, but somewhat impersonal, calculation of values" (Stern 1998:647). Not only did these peaceful and regular gatherings facilitate intergroup trade relations, but they also encouraged numerous inter-village and inter-ethnic marriages, as noted by Teit: "The Spokan probably had most intercourse and marriage with the Coeur d'Alene, considerable with Kalispel, less with Colville and Sanpoil, and rather little with other tribes" (1930:323).

Given the availability of salmon within the Spokan and Kettle Falls area, Stern described the extent of their trading, claiming how the:

> Major middlemen from the northeast were the Spokane, who carried from the fishery at Kettle Falls, a trading center of great importance in the northeast, and the Southern Okanogan, west of them, both of whom carried down to the mouth of the Snake [...] Almost annually, the Spokane descended to The Dalles, while later they would make their way to Fort Vancouver (1998:643).

Historians and ethnographers have pondered why, "In spite of the proximity of the territory of the Spokan, it would appear that the Sanpoil carried on but little trade with them" (Smith 1941:299). Yet, "Some

34

horses and buffalo skin were procured from the Spokan chiefly by the Sanpoil; but there was not much direct trade with this tribe, although [the contiguous] Sanpoil visited the Lower Spokan" (Teit 1930:254). Curtis claimed the Spokan obtained their first horses "in the first decade of the eighteenth century, and guns were acquired a few years later, for the traders were in their country at an early date" (1911, 7:56). Teit claims they were first acquired from the Kalispel (1930:351; Cox 1957 [1832]:115-116 and 239-40).

Interior Salish intergroup relations were strongly influenced by two major trade routes that traversed the Plateau: one from east to west, and one from north to south. Griswald (1970:42) wrote that the north-south route was older because of the Columbia and Spokane River systems. The area of the Spokan was thus affiliated more with the east-to-west route, which involved these peoples as effective carriers of differential resources and manufactured resources and goods. As attested by the distribution of Chinook Jargon as a trade language along the Columbia River, including the Spokan area, Smith wrote, "The Columbia [Indians] enjoyed an important commercial contact with the Spokan, presumably the lower Spokan" (1936-8:291), Teit noted earlier (1928:110).

Lewis (1906:183) commented upon the systematic work of Hale, who spoke of the Flathead Group's dependence upon bison. "It is not likely [...] they formed any considerable part of the food of the natives of that region until the advent of the horse" (1846, 4:185).

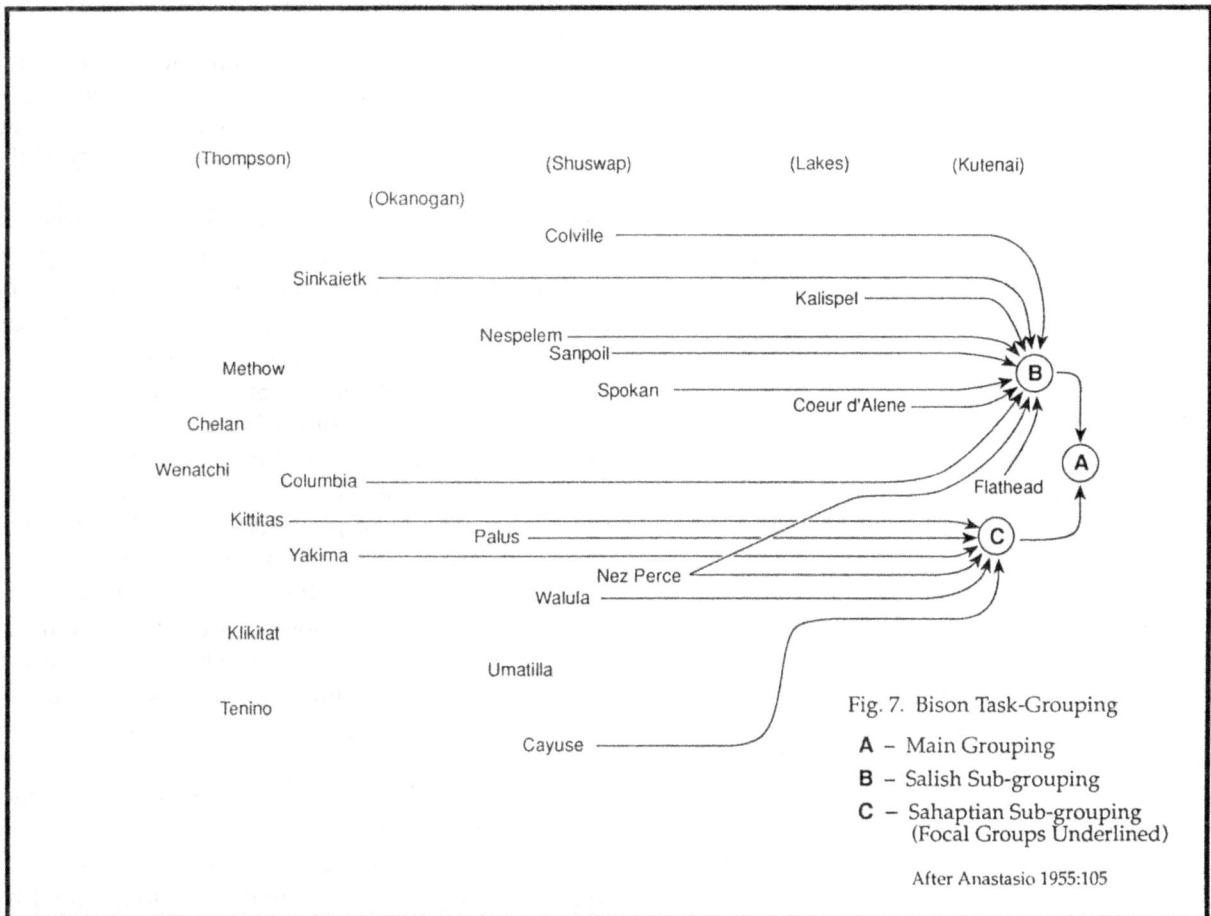

Fig. 7. Bison Task-Grouping

A – Main Grouping

B – Salish Sub-grouping

C – Sahaptian Sub-grouping
(Focal Groups Underlined)

After Anastasio 1955:105

Figure 7. Bison task-grouping

During the pre-contact period, there were some bison on the Plateau (Teit 1930; Schroedl 1973; Anastasio 1974), but not in any number that could give rise to or sustain any economic significance or a substantial predation specialization. Thus, after the advent of the horse, bison hunting became an annual journey, sometimes lasting two or more years. "Bison hunting would have required expeditions beyond the Rocky Mountains into grounds marked by hostilities between the Indians of the Plateau and those of the Plains" (Anastasio 1974, 4:3). As a result, the Spokan, Sanpoil, Nespelem, and Sinkaietk formed collective task-groups for protection prior to venturing onto the Plains for bison-hunting (Anastasio 1972:164).

Anastasio's method for examining early intergroup relations and task-groupings in the Plateau was to select a specific feature and trace its working among the various groups. This technique, which most contemporary ethnographers employ, was first used by Allan Smith in his 1941 PhD dissertation, and was probably responsible for Anastasio's later use of the existence of two definite networks of intergroup relations:

> One is a network of dyadic relations between adjacent groups. Each group was linked to its immediate neighbors by predominantly friendly and cooperative ties. Another network is one of polyadic relations, varying according to a number of conditions. This network was manifested in the joint performance of various activities such as bison-hunting, trading, and warfare. These groups were of comparatively short duration and the groups which participated varied (1955:6).

More specifically, Anastasio, in a major analysis of socioeconomic relations within the Plateau, discussed what he called the Spokan task-grouping, and how:

> [The] Spokan territory was well suited as a focal site for fishing and trading. The salmon season [on the Spokane River] began about the same time as at Kettle Falls (mid-June) and produced adequate supplies of salmon to permit a large gathering of people. The area in addition was a communication crossroads in all directions. The site was overshadowed by the closely located Kettle Falls, which lessened the possibility of the Spokan developing a major trading center (1972:155).

According to Anastasio (1955:91), the mechanisms regulating intergroup relations conferred many advantages: the relatively peaceful settlement of disputes; co-utilization of resource sites; peaceful congregation of large multiethnic groups; group responsibility guaranteeing the welfare of others and the property of visiting members of other groups; formalized trading and *gift-exchange* (*lmmštw'é?xʷ*) between ethnic groups; and the extension of kinship relations through marriage between different groups.

An important distinction existed in the aboriginal Plateau between the Interior Salishan and the Sahaptian peoples, but after the arrival of the horse, socioeconomic cooperation was more prevalent within the Plateau (Teit 1930:351; Haines 1938a:434-5). Although our understanding of the effects of language differences upon intergroup political relations is not complete, ethnocentrism was likely, as with all groups, universal—as it is to varying degrees within different language groups, despite the existence of polyglotism and the ameliorating effects of a trade language or *lingua franca* language. This was frequently demonstrated by what name one Plateau group would use for another—sometimes with an emphasis that implied a derogatory designation. Anastasio noted, "The Nez Perce, if not their Sahaptian neighbors were quite hostile with the western Salish, the Sanpoil, Nespelem, Colville, Sinkaietk, and probably the Methow and Spokan. These groups are even hostile today" (1955:40), and with on-going various intertribal litigation, which to some extent is presently true. After the Spokan received the horse—probably from the Nez Perce circa 1730— peaceful relations were maintained between these two different language groups.

The Spokan's traditional land, with its plentiful supply of fish and proximity to extensive root-gathering areas, facilitated intergroup trade between the Plains and the middle Columbia (Wishram-Wasco-Tenino area) (Teit 1930:356). During the pre-contact period, there were some bison on the Plateau (Teit 1930; Schroedl 1973; Anastasio 1974), but not in any number that could support or give rise to a real predation specialization or sustained economic significance. More specifically, Kingston (1932, 3:170) cited Duncan McDonald, who recalled several elderly Spokan Indians saying "that a number of buffalo were once killed north of Moses Lake or the Grand Coulee." Anastasio explained how:

The hostilities existing with the plains Indians tended to make bison hunting of the Plateau a specialized activity compared with that of the Plains Indian. The Plateau expeditions were stripped for mobility and defense. There was a selection of personnel, with the old, ill, small children, stores, equipment and spare horses left behind with a home guard when necessary (1972:24).

Kingston also quoted W. S. Lewis, a local amateur historian and newspaper reporter who worked extensively on early Spokan Indian history and trapper-trader activities at Fort Spokane: "Years ago in talking with some of the older Spokane Indians, they told me that their fathers had surrounded and killed the last buffalo in the Spokane Valley somewhere near the Idaho line. I figured that that was sometime along about 1810 to 1820" (Kingston 1932, 3:170).

The fact that the Spokan groups went onto the Plains in quest of bison is attested by Stevens, who, in 1853, observed a large number of Spokan on "their way to the Hunt" (1855, 12:134). The Spokan characterized peoples of the Plains *as our enemies* (*šimnm'sči?nti*), specifically the *Blackfoot* (*sčq'ʷišnI*) and the *Sioux* (*n?ixʷt'usm'*) (Elmendorf 1935-6, 2:6). Government Indian Agent Paige noted how the Spokan made "annual trips to the buffalo ground, east of the Rocky Mountains, and occasionally join war parties of the Flatheads and Upper Pend d'Oreilles, against their common enemy, the Blackfoot" (1868:52).

According to Elmendorf (1935-6 1:21), until approximately thirty years ago (1900s), some elders could recall stories from their great-grandparents of hunting bison during July and August in the general area of present day Helena (in western Montana), and how sometimes men moved there in the fall and winter to engage in horse-stealing and warfare against the Blackfoot. Oral history established that the Spokan ventured to the Plains in small groups for a *spring bison hunt* (*swíq'łc'e?*), as well as a *winter bison hunt* (*smšlwís*) (Egesdal, pers. comm.).

DeSmet (1843:196) also commented upon the dangers of bison hunting when the Flathead Group went annually onto the western Plains and were often confronted by the Blackfoot: "The buffalo hunt is attended with dangers, but the greatest of these does not exist in the mere pursuit of the animal, but rather from the hands of Black Feet, who constantly lurk in these regions, especially when there is some prospect of meeting with the larger game, or stealing a number of horses."

Anastasio (1972) further contended that the Spokan and Coeur d'Alene had little surplus in hunting and probably experienced dietary deficiencies, since those expeditionary forces were sometimes curtailed by inordinately severe winters and the subsequent loss of horses—such as in the winter of 1846-1847, when most of the Spokan horses died (Eells 1894:119-120).

Horse trading as a form of intergroup conflict existed in the Plateau as it did in the Plains. On the subject of horse raiding in general, Haines (1938a) and Ewers (1955) advance the hypothesis that in order for the horse complex to spread, peaceful relations were necessary, since it is likely that the prevalence of peaceful relations in the area was of some antiquity. The horse spread rapidly, and soon after, raiding began. However, horse raiding in the Plateau can hardly be compared with that of the Plains or that between the Plateau and its eastern and southern neighbors. A balance in the distribution of horses was soon reached and limited the intensity of raiding (Anastasio 1955:36-37).

As noted, the horse had a complex if not dramatic effect on Interior Plateau intergroup relations, and initially increased warlike activities among the eastern Interior Salish (Spokan, Coeur d'Alene, Flathead, and to a lesser extent with the Kalispel), but was later ameliorated by the need for task-grouping (Smith 1941; Anastasio 1955, 1972). Ultimately the horse reduced warlike activities among the eastern Salish by forcing them to cooperate politically and militarily. As Anastasio concluded, the horse facilitated their joint efforts to effectively exploit resources, in groups composed primarily of the Colville, Spokan, and Wenatchi (1955:37). It also affected the Spokan in terms of warfare. Spinden, in his early studies of the Nez Perce, commented how "the necessity of united defense against invading war parties from the Plains which probably brought about [inter] tribal integrity" (1908:271).

37

Warfare

The Spokan possessed the technology, strategies, ceremonies, and offices of warfare, and were quick to engage unwelcome trespassers, and when on the plains hunting bison and stealing horses. Raiding and ambush were the most common tactics when the Spokan engaged in *warfare* (*splstw'e?x^w* or *sk^w̓xu* or *n̓xcél'stis*) against the Blackfeet, Sioux, or other hostile groups (Elmendorf 1935-6, 2:6) when traveling on the Plains in July and August. Aside from conducting warfare with traditional foes, these travels were to *trade* (*n̓ey'x^wew'sm*), hunt bison, to *steal horses* (*x?i?lš*), and fight against tribes east of the Rocky Mountains, who collectively were called *šmenm'sči?nti*. The Spokan never ventured beyond Blackfeet territory, but did make incursions against the Yakima (Teit 1930:360; Ruby and Brown 1982:52).

Charles Wilson, during his four-year stay (1858-1862) in the interior eastern Plateau, kept a daily journal describing and painting many of his now valuable ethnographic observations of the Spokan and Flathead. One account, by the artist Stanley, provides an explanation of how:

> [...] Indians on this side of the Rocky mountains annually go over to the plains on the other side to hunt buffalo & lay in their winter stock of meat, & as the Indians on this side are in a state of constant war with the Indians on the other, frequent collisions take place; of all the Indians of the great plains the fierce Blackfoot [...] is the most dreaded both from his fierce & warlike nature & the great number of the tribe (1970:137).

Consequently, the Coeur d'Alene generally went with the Spokan, and both often joined with the Kalispel and Pend d'Oreilles, yet maintained economic relations with certain Sahaptian-speaking groups:

> The Spokan very rarely had wars with the Coeur d'Alene, Kalispel, and Nez Percé; but at one time they warred a great deal with the Yakima-speaking people, and raided down the Columbia to The Dalles, and even below. Spokan parties occasionally crossed the Wenatchi country and raided on the coast, and once or twice war parties of Spokan went as far as the Willamette. The Yakima-speaking people sometimes named the Spokan "robbers" because of their raids against them. There were no wars with the Colville or any tribes of the Okanagan group (Teit 1930:360).

Prior to acquiring the horse, warfare with western Plains groups, particularly the Blackfoot, was almost nonexistent:

> The horse provided an increased incentive to engage in warfare. Mounted parties could strike enemies at greater distances and with greater force than ever before. A war party on horseback could easily *defeat* [*šƛ'pnúntm* - to win a contest"] a much greater number of men on foot (Walker and Sprague 1998:139).

When referring to pre-horse warfare, Lahren (1998:284) noted, "Prehorse warfare could be caused by infringement on economic rights, murder or injury, itinerant raiders, or by insulting a chief. War associated with economic infringements could be avoided by compensation." Walker, speaking of the Nez Perce, also noted, "Horse culture brought an increased emphasis on warfare and exploitation of the buffalo" (1969:248; Walker and Schuster 1998:501).

When discussing pre-contact with Euro-Americans, several Spokan elders were recorded as saying how they "safely travelled down into New Perce country always. The Palus were friendly, as was the Cayuse, but the Walla Walla were not so friendly, they occasionally skirmished. All the tribes to the west were said to be friendly with the Spokanes" (STHC).

The Middle Spokan were known to have fought against the Coeur d'Alene (Cox 1831:151-52), but presumably never against the Kalispel or the Chewelah-Spokan Group. Also, "The only time when the Kalispel and the Coeur d'Alene fought was when the Spokans asked the Kalispel to help them fight the Coeur d'Alene. The Coeur d'Alene were so much bigger than the Spokans" (Smith 1936-8:924). Also, according to Smith, "warring between the Spokans and the Coeur d'Alene was stopped when the Spokan chief's son married the Coeur d'Alene's daughter" (1936-8:1173). Cox, however, provided an incident that lead to a further example of warfare between the Spokan and Coeur d'Alene:

> About twenty years before our arrival [circa 1790], the Spokans and Pointed Hearts were at war, caused by a kind of Trojan origin. A Party of the former had been on a hunting visit to the islands of the latter, and were

38

hospitably received. One day a young Spokan discovered the wife of a Pointed Heart alone, some distance from the village, and violated her. Although she might have borne this in silence from one of her own tribe, she immediately informed her husband of the outrage. He lost no time in seeking revenge, and shot the Spokan as he entered the village. The others fled to their own lands, and prepared for war. A succession of sanguinary conflicts followed, in the course of which the greatest warriors of both sides were nearly destroyed. At the end of a year, however, hostilities ceased; since which period they have been at peace. The two nations now intermarry, and appear to be on the best terms of friendship (1957:263).

The aforementioned incident illustrates how over the years peaceful Spokan relationships with other tribes were maintained by reciprocal economic exchange, intermarriage, and task-grouping when venturing onto the Plains. However, elders recalled hostile relationships between the Spokan and the Blackfeet, a traditional *enemy* (*ʔewtus* or *šmén'*). Before a group of Spokan men ventured forth with the intention of going to war or stealing horses from the Blackfeet, a ceremonial song and farewell to men before leaving for *war* (*nqaqʔaqsm*) was staged when the *leader* (*sisiúcménʔ*), who invariably was the instigator, received a dream of success in leading the pending expedition. During these conflict ceremonies, the leader might use a *special rattle* (*c'aʔaλá*) associated only with warfare.

A war party often contained boys who did not engage in battle, but attended to the logistical needs of the warriors, in squire-like roles. Young boys felt honored when asked to participate in a war or horse-stealing expedition. They provided valuable assistance in policing the temporary camp, procuring firewood, securing water, picketing horses, and serving as sentinels. The number of warriors varied from three men to several dozen, depending upon the intent and circumstances. If a group planned to spend several months on the Plains hunting and trading, it was common for wives to attend their husbands, to perform domestic chores, such as cooking, and to dress and tan the hides of antelope, deer, and bison. Franchère (1854:269), when speaking of combined Salish and Sahaptian task-grouping, provides no numbers of people, only that "the cavalcade often numbers two thousand horses."

Large groups of Interior Salish men would often publicly demonstrate their equestrian skills just prior to leaving for warfare. Alexander Ross first described how a rider gave the same care and time in painting a war-horse as he did to painting himself. Ross witnessed a pre-battle demonstration of some five or six hundred mounted and armed warriors:

> One of the principal chiefs, at the commencement, mounted on horseback [...] while at the same time the whole troop, mounted in fighting order, assembled in a group around him. After this chief had harangued them for some time they all started off at a slow trot, but soon increased their pace to a gallop, and from a gallop to a full race, the cleverest fellow taking the lead [...] During all the time silence prevailed within the camp, while the horsemen continued shouting or yelling, and went through all the attitudes peculiar to savages.

> At one moment they threw themselves to the right, the next to the left side of the horse, twisting and bending their bodies in a thousand different ways, now in the saddle, then out of the saddle, and nothing frequently to be seen but the horses, as if without riders, parrying or evading, according to their ideas, the onset of their assailants. I could very easily conceive that the real merit of the maneuvers was not who could kill the most enemies, but who could save himself best in battle. So dexterous and nimble were they in changing positions and slipping from side to side that it was done in the twinkling of an eye. As soon as the maneuvering was over they were again harangued and dismissed (1904:299-300).

Dogs were never taken on a war party for fear of alerting the enemy. The men ate only pemmican and dried meat, never stopping or sleeping at night or ever making fires once near or in Blackfeet territory. A *man* (*sql'tmixʷ*) always took several pairs of moccasins. Many years ago, an elderly woman, speaking of her great-grand parents, explained why:

> Going to the Plains for buffalo took seven pairs of moccasins. They often left here in early March and went to the area of Browning, Montana. But before they'd leave, they'd have a special dinner with all the travelers coming together; the men talked about the route, and the women discussed food, clothing, and about the young children. Once they were over the Rocky Mountains, they had to be very careful about making smokeless fires so they wouldn't be seen. The men would smoke their pipes under a cape or blanket. Going over ridges was also

dangerous and they would move quickly, always keeping low and out of sight if possible. If a[n] unknown man was seen, they worried how to reach him before being seen. The best [technique] was to crawl past him. If he was near his people, he was grabbed by a man who would cut open his throat and take his scalp. After the buffalo hunt, they returned always by fall and had many celebrations. Also, stolen horses and blankets were handed out. One brave man changed his name to *sčók*ʷ*oɫmic'* ("Indian tail" or "enemy scalp") (Ross 1968-2008).

As a precaution, it was customary for a war party to practice name-changing, which involved a warrior's horse as well as the man, and always:

> [...] before a man goes to fight he might change his name - the warparty leader does this always & any other man in the party may do this - their *su'me'c* tells them just before they go on the warparty what name to take - not the name of that animal, but an animal name - use these names only during the raid to protect themselves (Elmendorf 1935-6, 4:7-8).

When the war party approached the home area of the enemy, the *war party leader* (*cwénc*) always appointed two of the fastest and strongest distance runners to separate from the main group, always remaining in sight of one another as they advanced, and always using gullies and avoiding ridges while surreptitiously locating the enemy. If, while en route, the Spokan came upon an enemy war party, and were seen, the warriors would immediately separate and form a circle around their leader who gave hand directions, but if they saw the *enemy* (*šmnm'ʔesči ʔ nti* - "enemy people") first, they would spread out, forming a large concealed circle with hopes that the enemy leader would ride into the circle, where the Spokan would kill him, hopefully by *ambush* (*χle*).

Most frequently a raiding party was more concerned with stealing horses, and just prior to leaving for an engagement with the enemy, they often engaged in a ceremony called *snka'ka'a'*, during which there was no dancing. Warriors would call upon their guardian spirits to ensure their bravery and a safe return from battle. Before battle, the warriors painted their faces with *war paint* (*sk'ʷplstwexʷ* or *red paint* - *tulmn*). The first time a man went on a horse-stealing or war expedition, he was called *χʷy'áqeʔ*.

Once in enemy territory, and when *enemy peoples* (*šmnm'ʔesčiʔnti*) or their encampment had been sighted, the *scout* or *spy* (*sxʷč'tč'ítš* or *suxʷxʷaléxʷu*) would return to his leader with the news. Once informed of an enemy village or encampment, the leader would strategically situate his men approximately two km downwind from the enemy, where they would sleep briefly, except for several sentinels, who would awake the rest an hour or so after midnight.

The Doctrine of Signatures is an archaic notion that there is a functional relationship between cultural or natural objects similar in color, smell, sound, consistency, or shape. For example, red foods are beneficial for the blood; a walnut looks like the brain and thus can cure headaches or migraines; and the phallic shape of carrots, camas, and some animal horn were considered aphrodisiacs; to rope cattle would cause the man's pregnant wife's baby to be born with the umbilical cord around its neck. Adhering to this doctrine, some Spokan shamans who possessed certain powers were better able to elude or confuse an enemy by their spiritual transformation into a small mammal, bird, or reptile—one indicative of certain abilities to be a successful warrior. For example, a man with prairie chicken power could conceal himself in a sagebrush; when an unaware enemy approached, he could quickly leap up and transform himself into a warrior, killing the confused enemy. Men possessing coyote power were chosen as forward scouts, because they had the visual acuity of their guardian spirit for seeing great distances and discerning any concealed enemy. A warrior whose *tutelary spirit* (*suméš*) was a rodent, had exceptional powers for concealment. One with bear power possessed great strength and prowess for close combat.

When a man transformed into his guardian spirit form, and later when he resumed his human form, he always was careful to do so in private. Regardless of one's tutelary animal, a warrior would always be complemented by the physical abilities and characteristics of his guardian spirit. A warrior never needed magpie power, which was useful only for stick gaming; it was better to have wolf power for warfare and coyote power for stealing horses. A warrior's belief in his *suméš* must have been more important than any weapon, and in many respects was the most powerful aspect of his strength.

The particular guardian spirit of a warrior often determined his tactics when fighting. A guardian spirit with symbolic fighting abilities could also help a man allude a dangerous situation—particularly certain types of guardian spirits, even a small animal, such as a rodent. The significance of such a guardian spirit was cited by Elmendorf:

> [...] something small & hardly visible [was] good for war *suméš*—mouse—chipmunk—if surrounded by enemy (*sisiús*) with this *suméš* could change himself into a chipmunk and escape that way [later] turning back into [a] man—if any man (*sisiús*) is pursued he runs behind [a] clump of bushes & come[s] out [as] a chipmunk—or a wolf or whatever is his *suméš*—only do this when in real danger—must do this out of sight—also out of sight when changing back again (1935-6, 1:37).

This was apparent when, prior to battle, warriors were always careful to prepare for *warfare* (*ʔec xʔilši* - "a party preparing for warfare") by propitiating and seeking counsel from their tutelary spirits, who would give them greater powers of strength, bravery, and discernment. Just before an armed engagement, a man might be told by his guardian spirit to paint all of his exposed body with clay of a certain color. A Spokan typically used "red [hematite] on his forehead; or [painted] his entire face red or black, or yellow, [which was] removed before returning home" (Smith 1936-8:774).

George Catlin, an early painter of the American west, observed the universal use of each warrior carrying a medicine bag into battle, as practiced by the Spokan:

> An Indian carries his medicine bag into battle, and trusts to it for his protection, and if he loses it thus when fighting so bravely for his country, he suffers a disgrace scarcely less than that which occurs in case he sells or gives it away; his enemy carries it off and displays it to his own people as a trophy, whilst the loser is cut short of the respect that is due other young men of his tribe, and forever subjected to the degrading epithet of "a man without medicine," or "he who lost his medicine," until he can replace it again, which can be done by rushing into battle and plundering one from an enemy whom he slays with his own hand. This done, his medicine is restored, and he is reinstated again in the estimation of his tribe, and even higher than before, for such is called the best of medicine or 'honorable medicine' (1846:441).

Horse-Stealing

Prior to initiating a horse-stealing expedition, the Spokan conducted the same rituals as when going to war: they observed the same prohibitions, and also sought solace, advice, and, when in the act of horse-stealing, assistance from their tutelary spirits. Once the expedition reached the enemy camp, the raiding party would picket their horses, guarded by one or more older boys. Then the men would quietly steal into the camp, separate from one another, and cut each horse's rope (composed of individual braided horse hair). Or, if the horses were corralled, the men would open or release any barrier. Each man would then leap onto his stolen mount *bareback* (*nʔem'tičn'*), and ride it. Often colts would follow the lead mare with no persuasion. Schaeffer explained how "Every herd of horses had a mare lead horse [*sm'um'cšn'*] and they would follow her [...] When this mare was taken out of camp, the other horses would follow without neighing or making any noise" (1934-37, I-164:35). When racing through their own bivouac camp, the men would be joined by the sentinels riding and leading the horses they had been guarding. The entire party often rode non-stop for three days and three nights before resting and watering their horses.

It was known that within an enemy village, the chief and his sub-chiefs were the owners of the finest horses, which were typically stabled in special large tents for protection. The primary object of a war-raiding party was to first locate these horses and, if possible, steal them. "The leader would then proceed to divide the horses up among the members of his war-party, horse-stealing party. The leader usually got his first choice and would take at least two more horses than anyone else got. This was his reward for successfully planning the affair and [it was] considered proper" (STHC).

41

Any man who distinguished himself with outstanding guile or bravery—when fighting an enemy, or during a horse-stealing expedition—was made a chief and given the title *ʔilmíxʷm*. If a man distinguished himself through extreme effort and bravery, then he became a *war chief* (*łmíxum* or *pieλxáλ ʼλqs* - "white shirt") (STHC). This naturally was quite an incentive for maximum courage.

Elmendorf's field notes provide the most complete description of the Spokan pre-war party and individual preparations. Each warrior assiduously cleaned his weapons; he performed prolonged sweating and propitiation to his guardian spirit. Also, the group discussed the logistics of traveling and possible surprise tactics. Battle strategies were often presented by a man's *sumés̆* while sleeping, in a dream that told him of success and his later participation in the Victory Dance:

> If *sumés̆c* wants to speak to owner—he falls in a faint—Spirit goes out & comes back—*sumés̆* speaks to him [and] warns him near to [the] enemy—then he comes to & tells the party—[his] *sumés̆* comes to him all of a sudden—takes care of them all the time [and] and may visit the leader anytime—just the leader [and] gets them on the war path—before the party leaves at dawn [they] take sweat bathes—carried dry meat with them—[and] ate on the move—two men (who were fast runners) [went] ahead as scouts in daytime (appointed by leader)—if anyone came of the enemy they spread out and formed a ring & killed him after allowing him to come onto their midst—all men on party are scouts—if they meet with enemy they fight it out—the 2 scouts sight the enemy village first—then move back about 8 mi. & stay there until midnight—then creep up on camp—leader went first—they had planned the attack by observing the camp from a distance—stole into camp and cut all the braided horsehair ropes the horses were with—opened gate & herded them out if in corral—try to get out of camp without waking anyone—drive the stolen horses off [for] 3 days & nights without rest—[they] boast about it if he has gone near the chief's tent to get a horse because [this was] more dangerous—[chief had the] finest horse out of that he was very highly thought of—scalp slain enemy—try to get as many scalps as possible—step on neck [and] cut around [the] forehead and [pull the] whole scalp [until it is] torn off—[and would] try especially to get chiefs & [a] good warriors' scalps—after return [they] divide [the stolen] horses among the members of the party—[the] leader got pick of them—about 2 more than [the] other men—he divided them up among them—[they] take the scalps & dance[d] about it and [they] were glad when close to camp upon [their] return each would tie [the] scalp to [a] stick like [a] flag and wave it as [they] rode into camp—[and] chanted—every body handled the scalps & were happy about it all (1936-37, 1:35-7).

Franchère, who observed the conflict between the Flathead Group and the Blackfoot when going to hunt bison or scalp-taking, wrote of how large a task group of warriors would:

> [...] set out with their families, and the cavalcade often numbers two thousand horses. When they have the good fortune not to encounter the enemy, they return with the spoils of an abundant chase; they load a part of the country, they [were] so harassed by the Blackfeet, who surprise them in the night and carry off their horses, that they are forced to return light-handed, and then they have nothing to eat but roots, all the winter (1854, 6:269).

Scalp-Taking and Counting Coup

Once a raiding party met the enemy on a *battlefield* (*snt'apnwexʷmn*), often the encounter quickly developed into individual fighting—the primary intent being to take an *enemy scalp* (*soqʼqn*) or to *count coup* (*spʼentm* or *spʼntn* - "touching a man with a stick"). In a surprise night attack on a village, a war party would make every attempt to take the scalp of a chief and his best warriors, as they knew from earlier surveillance where these men dwelled (STHC).

As the Flathead Group (comprising the Spokan, Coeur d'Alene, and Kalispel) and the Nez Perce increased contact with western Plains groups, through trade and warfare, there resulted classification of bravery in fighting, as cited by Schaeffer:

> The greatest feat was that of vanquishing an enemy in a hand-to-hand fight; second, seizing a gun from a dead foe in battle; third, stealing a horse or gun from an enemy camp and lastly, striking the wall of an enemy barricade. Four men were privileged to count coup successively on the same foe, each one in doing so taking some object from the latter's body. The first two warriors thereafter formed an intimate friendship, or became "comrades," as did the third and fourth (1937, 3:241).

42

Scalp-taking signified a personal proof of ordeal for the warrior, which involved ringing the *skull* (*xxstéy'e?*) of the slain enemy with a knife just above his ears, placing one's foot on the neck, and tearing the scalp free, which became a trophy. It was similarly explained to Elmendorf how "scalps are cut around the hair line and jerked off by putting [the] right foot on [the] base of [the] neck—[the] man brings the scalp back just as it is—they never stretched it on a frame—[they] bring it back to prove that they did the deed they tell about" (1935-6, 4:19).

Just before returning to his village or camp, a successful warrior would tie all of his scalps onto the end of a *pole* (*čłšt'éne?tn*) before riding into camp—waving them like flags. Later, the people of the camp or village would dance around the pole, displaying the scalps, which were then handed around to all present (Elmendorf 1935-6, 4:19). During this welcoming ritual, any warrior who had taken a scalp was encouraged to describe the battle and his scalp-taking in great detail—often a lengthy and dramatic presentation:

> [...] he tells about it from [the] beginning to [the] end—this is *sqqʷlúm't*—this is at *swénc*—when he has finished he puts up a horse or [a] blanket—gives this away at the dance to any one—just gives away the one thing—this is to demonstrate that he is telling the truth [...] He doesn't try to give away as much as possible—people who have lost relatives from the enemy take the scalps & dance around with them & sing, "may be this is the one who killed my brother, etc." (Elmendorf 1935-6, 4:18-9)

Once the *swénc* was over, the scalps were often buried or burned, or the scalp-taker would put the scalp away and never bring it out again (Elmendorf 1935-6, 4:19). Smith states how the practice of taking scalps commenced once Plateau groups began periodically venturing onto the Plains, and taking scalps only from Plains Indians—notably the Blackfoot. The Kalispel were probably also influenced by the Flathead, who:

> [...] never used them [scalps] for decoration on their shirts or shields. They kept them put away. Once or twice a year, whenever they felt like it, they would take them out and tie them on a pole and stick the pole in the ground and then dance around it. They blackened their faces with charcoal. It was a victory dance. All the scalps were tied on one pole. Men and women do this dancing together, mixed up any old way, not alternating, in a single line forming a circle around the pole. They do not move but they dance in one place all the time. They are all facing in. They do not hold hands or anything like that. Some of the men and all of the women are all dolled up in their best clothes. A few men wear only clouts, but only their faces are colored black. They only dance this in the summer time, never in the winter (1936-8:936).

Teit described how the Spokan had war or scalp shirts. Some were edged with scalp locks. Also, "A scalp shirt which I saw among the Spokan had the leg pieces cut short, and this is said to have been customary with some" (1930:335), which suggests the Spokan shirt was long—almost to the knees—which is Plains style. Given the effort to make such an item, it is unfortunate that there is no information of whether—and how—the shirt was retired, discarded, or buried with the owner upon death. (See the later section on war shirts.)

Scalp-taking was understandably done less frequently after the introduction of the repeating rifle, which changed many aspects of warfare and hunting, since firearms prevented fewer encounters as hand-to-hand combat. Though there is no accountable data, firearms likely resulted in increased traumatic and seemingly indiscriminant wounds—ones that killed the victim immediately by severe trauma or later through infection or lead poisoning. When sustaining a wound within a *war zone* (*snplsqélxʷtn* - "a place to kill"), a wounded warrior sometimes painted his face with red hematite to help him recover from a bullet or arrow wound (STHC). Traditional shields were of no protection against rifled bullets, though some Spokan claimed that a proper green rawhide Plains shield made from the bison's hump could repel a smooth-bore musket ball.

Counting coup consisted of touching an enemy warrior, with the hand or a coup stick, and then escaping without harm. It could also involve stealing items from the enemy or recounting stories about battle exploits (Schaeffer 1937, 3:241). The term originated from the French verb *couper*, which means to cut, hit, or strike. It took swiftness and dexterity to avoid death or injury, should the enemy respond violently. Thus, especially among the Plains tribes, it was considered an act of bravery viewed more important than killing an enemy in close combat. With increased contact with the western Plains tribes, the Nez Perce, Spokan, Coeur d'Alene, and Kalispel increasingly adopted this form of warfare.

While visiting a village near Kettle Falls in 1847, Canadian artist Paul Kane (1810-1871) did a dramatic oil painting of approximately fifty Spokan men and women performing what he called "Scalp Dance by Spokane (?) Indians" (Kane 1859, Fig. 129), now in the National Gallery of Canada (103; crIV-329).

The central figure is a widow whose husband was killed by a Blackfoot warrior two or three years earlier, and immediately behind her are eight women whose faces are painted with white clay and charcoal. As the widow dances, she holds a Blackfoot scalp attached to a small hoop on the end of an upright stick. [Accordingly, it was stretched upon a small hoop, and attached to a stick as a handle, and thus carried by the afflicted woman [...]] (Kane 1859:220)

Figure 8. "Scalp Dance by Spokane (?) Indians"

Kane described a variation on the aforementioned Spokan Scalp Dance: A shaman wearing only a loincloth, whose entire body was covered with near-vertical white clay strips, held what appeared to be a scalp, but on a much shorter staff. During the scalp dance, the afflicted widow "commenced dancing and singing, swaying the scalp violently about and kicking it, whilst eight women, hideously painted, chanted, and danced round her and the fire. The remainder of the tribe stood round in a circle, beating drums, and all singing" (Kane 1859:220).

Slavery

There was confusion and even misinterpretation of the term *slave* (*sk^{w}ánxn* - "a captive" or "a person seized by the arms") by earlier travelers and writers within the Interior Plateau. A recent study of secondary material on Indian slavery in the Pacific Northwest, correctly questions the statements of some 19th century non-Indian observers:

> [...] their observations with varying degrees of accuracy. Although numerous examples of such may be cited, those of two American Board missionaries may be noted. One of these was the Reverend Elkanah Walker, who labored among the Spokane Indians from 1838 to 1847. He understandably evidenced greater concern for their spiritual welfare than for their social structure. This is seen in his statement [...] that their morals were "debased as any heathen people," adding that " [...] the more wives they have, the richer they consider themselves." He concluded that "their wives are to them what slaves are to the planter as it is their business to provide the provisions" since "a man without a wife is in great danger of being hunger [sic]." (Ruby and Brown 1993:228)

Universally, among highly mobile hunting and gathering peoples, slavery either did not exist or was relatively infrequent, due simply to the logistical disadvantages of overseeing adult slaves—specifically, trying to prevent men from escaping. Consequently, slaves were often young boys, girls, or women who, if not traded to other groups or bartered back to their parent group, invariably became socially incorporated through marriage to their captives, and were often well treated, and in some instances greatly depended upon for domestic chores. Wilson—undoubtedly referring to women slaves—was told: "Prisoners taken in war are generally enslaved, but are not treated so harshly or made such a common article of barter as amongst the coast tribes" (1866:303). When comparing Nez Perce slavery to other Interior Plateau groups, Hunt, citing Spinden (1908), claimed the Nez Perce [...]

> [...] did not buy slaves, merely using as such the male prisoners of war. The women taken in war became the wives of their masters. Slaves were the personal property of their owners and could be traded or even killed at will. As a matter of fact, they were treated kindly. It is said that the women could gamble away their freedom, but the men were not allowed to do this (1918, 4:281).

Hunt (1918, 4:283), using secondary research, and not identifying his sources or tribal affiliation, concluded "that many of the Indian tribes of the Northwest had the custom of flattening the heads of their infants by pressure. The flat head was the mark of the freeman in these tribes."

Gabriel Franchère (1854:137) once had the occasion to use his linguistic skills to restore the freedom of three of Astor's employees who had deserted and were later caught by Chinook speakers of the lower Willamette River. Unfortunately, Franchère often *speaks* (*sy^{2}ƛ'^{2}qn*) rather critically when generalizing about customs and speculating about the Indians' comparative intellectual and moral development (without mention of prejudices and practices of European slavery at the time):

> The natives of the Columbia procure these slaves from the neighboring tribes, and from the interior, in exchange for beads and furs. They treat them with humanity while their services are useful, but soon as they become incapable of labor, neglect them and suffer them to perish of want. When dead, they throw their bodies, without ceremony, under the stump of an old decayed tree, or drag them to the woods to be devoured by the wolves and vultures (Franchère 1904, 6:324).

For a given captured individual, it was not always clear as to whether he would become a slave, or be bought back by his people, or be incorporated into the capturing group:

> Another slave-holding people were the Spokanes in the watershed of the Spokane River, many of whose slaves were captured in war or acquired in trade at the Dalles. Like other Interior Salish peoples like the Flatheads and Okanagons, they preferred female slaves, and like that of many Plateau peoples their slavery fell off well after contact as noted by the Reverend Walker in 1841, who found but one "genuine" slave among them (Ruby and Brown 1993:246).

Teit (1930:380) described how the Flathead regarded age and gender, which once was considered important prior to securing a slave:

> Long ago the only slaves were a few captives of war, consisting of young women, boys, and girls, who were adopted into the families to which they belonged, and were treated well. Some of them were Blackfoot and

Shoshoni. In later times, it is said, there were no slaves of any kind, as the Flathead and Pend d'Oreilles did not trade in slaves, and never took captives. They preferred to kill rather than take prisoners; and members of enemy tribes at their mercy after a battle were either killed or allowed to escape [č'łnóq'ʷmist]. It is said that the Spokane, however, had a number of slaves at one time, some of them captives of war, and others procured in trade [...]

The reason for mounting a war party was not always to steal horses. Given the situation, the purpose was sometimes for revenge or to capture slaves. There is little evidence the Spokan kept adult male slaves, though young women were captured as slaves, being carefully protected by an older woman (Elmendorf 1935-6, 1:36):

[...] a coveted prize was to be able to kidnap a young girl, if they happened onto one all by herself. She was then sold to the chief, who in turn sold her to the highest bidder. The buyer was required to marry her, the kidnapped girls were never abused and were watched, taken care of by an old woman, so no harm would come to her, or that she wouldn't be stolen back or run away. Nearly always, it was a rich man who could afford her. (STHC)

Teit's extensive fieldwork in this area revealed that the Spokan did have slaves; he explained how and where some were procured:

Long ago a very few slaves were bought from the Spokan and Paloos [Palouse]. They were nearly all young boys and girls, and according to tradition, were chiefly Snake and Ute. Occasionally young slaves of Umatilla and Paloos extraction were also bought from the Spokan. Sooner or later these were bought back again by their relatives. Sometimes the Paloos would come and buy them back directly, but oftener the Spokan who sold them would buy them back and sell them to their Paloos or Umatilla relatives who wanted them (1930:113).

Smith provided a description of slavery within the Plateau, noting the Spokan once had numerous slaves of Northwest Coast origin (1941:119). He concluded that the data secured independently by Ray (1930:30) is correct, who stated, "The Spokane held no slaves in recent generations but may have had a certain number in earlier times." Ray also felt this was true as well for the Sanpoil and Nespelem, when he wrote how the "Sanpoil insistence upon the equality of men was of an impressive order. Class distinctions were unthinkable. Slavery was an unaccountable custom of foreigners" (Ray 1932a:25). Lewis (1906, 1:179), in concluding a cross-culture survey of slavery, and quoting Cox (1832:309), claimed slavery was the basis of chieftainship among the Northwest Coast and the Interior, and quoted Alexander Ross as saying:

There were no [socioeconomic] classes as on the coast. Prisoners of war were commonly held as slaves, but they were usually well treated and frequently adopted into the tribe. Slavery seems to have been an incident of war, rather than a recognized institution as in the Columbian River areas. Prisoners were sometimes subjected to torture, but were seldom put to death by this means, as was common farther east, even among the Flatheads (1904, 7:179).

Various cultural changes increased intermarriage between eastern Plateau peoples and even some Great Basin groups, such as the advent of the horse and subsequent alliances of tribes for bison hunting. Through these alliances, there was more intermarriage with other Plateau groups, both Salish- and Sahaptian-speaking peoples. There were no marriages between the Crow or other Plains tribes (Ray 1939:30-1).

Though intergroup relations effectively facilitated the distribution of food and goods throughout the Plateau, this cooperative socioeconomic network unfortunately was responsible for another change—one that was disastrous to all Plateau peoples: the introduction and spread of epidemic and pandemic contagious diseases.

Population

It is now impossible to arrive at an accurate population figure for the Amerindians who inhabited the Interior Plateau over a period of approximately 11,500 years (Galm, pers. comm.). Even estimations of Spokan population during the initial phase of Euro-American contact are questionable. The arrival of appreciable numbers of Euro-Americans created deculturation and a concomitant disruption of the indigenous medical and nutritional profile, in which people's health deteriorated and their population declined, not only from pandemics, but also the loss of traditional root fields and reduced salmon runs. Various psychological and physiological problems were exacerbated by access to alcohol. Unfortunately, Euro-American prejudice and socioeconomic deprivation eventually completed the deculturation of the traditional Plateau Indian culture.

Although the Lewis and Clark expedition (1804-06) did not traverse Spokan territory, they did provide the earliest historical estimate of the Spokan, at six hundred individuals living in approximately thirty dwellings. Alexander Ross (1783-1856), a Scottish observer married to Sara, a great-aunt of Okanogan chief Timentwa, "had ample opportunity to learn their customs; he seems to speak wholly from observation" (Holder 1958:n.p.):

> This expedition [Lewis and Clark] proceeded British and American fur traders who from 1811 to the mid-1840s had less effect upon the Indians than the later settlers, missionaries and military who were in direct conflict with those Indians whi[ch] were vainly attempting to retain their lands and maintain their way of life. From 1859 until [...], the Indians suffered severely from disease-reduced population, loss of territory, and deception and fraud once they were eventually confined to a reservation system with forced mission and government schooling (Thwaites 1904, 7:283).

In 1829, Work stated the total population of the three Spokan macro bands as 704, including children. In 1845-46, DeSmet (1853:38 fn.) estimated the Spokan population as 800, which correlated with Reverend Samuel Parker's findings, who earlier had surveyed the Plateau for the American Missionary Board (1836-37). He also estimated the Spokan population at 800 (Parker 1838:37; Franchère 1854:166; Hale 1846, 4:255-6). In 1841, Wilkes estimated the Spokan, whom he called *Sar-lie-lo*, to be 900 (1845:414). Dart's 1851 survey of the Oregon Territory, claimed the Spokan, whom he called *Sin-ha-ma-mish*, to be 232 (Gibbs 1855, 1:418). Whereas Gibbs—who later joined the Northwest Boundary Survey in 1857, serving as geologist and interpreter until 1862—estimated the Spokan population to be 450 (1855, 1:418). By 1882, the general Spokan population was estimated by the Colville Agency to be 685 (Simms 1882:342).

By 1872, the peoples of this region suffered severely from a series of Euro-American introduced pandemics, the most devastating of which was smallpox, according to Teit (1930:212, 315-6; Ray (1932:21-2) and Boyd (1985). Bouts of influenza and measles further complicated the medical problems (O'Neill 1962:3). Mooney (1928:444) estimated that as early as 1789 there were 1,400 Spokan, and that the 1782-83 smallpox epidemic destroyed approximately one-third to one-half of the area's indigenous inhabitants—a situation termed *č'łqʷumptin* ("when many people die at one time"). Smith (1983:294) agreed with Teit (1928:97) and Mooney (1928:13), who estimated that the first pre-contact epidemic of smallpox in the Columbia Basin area occurred in 1780, when the Spokan may have lost fifty percent of their population (Ruby and Brown 1982:29; Hewes 1998:635). There was a fourth major pandemic among Columbia River tribes in 1830-32. "This may have been the measles, which killed so many Spokane" (Smith 1991:8.97). Scarlet fever and other Euro-American communicable diseases also proved disastrous to all Amerindian groups—particularly to children and *elderly* (*p'x̌ʷp'x̌ʷut*) people. Anglo inhabitants also suffered from the diseases—again, notably children, who were more susceptible to so-called compulsory diseases, such as measles, chickenpox, whooping cough, scarlet fever, and mumps (Drury 1940:152).

Scott (1928, 29:146) discussed the effects of these diseases, which he and others contended were far more devastating than indigenous inter- and intra-warfare, as well as battles fought with whites. The Indians often acquired these pathogens through the acquisition of often-infected European clothing. "The wars among the tribes, the wars between the tribes and the whites, were the merest bagatelle in comparison with these desolating influences which sapped the vitality of the people" (Chittenden 1902, 2:619). Henry Schoolcraft (1793-1864), ethnologist and geologist, and former Indian Agent, spent thirty year gathering relatively extensive data on Amerindian language and demographics in the Plains, and wrote a most poignant description of the effects of smallpox, which affected many Indian groups:

Languages, however forcible, fails to give an idea of the reality. On every side was desolation, and wrecks of mortality everywhere presented themselves to the view. Prominent among these was the tent and wigwam: no longer did the curling smoke from its roof betoken a welcome, and its closed door gave sad evidence of the silence and darkness that reined within. The prairie wolf sent up its dismal howl, as it preyed upon the decaying carcasses; and the lonely traveler, as he rapidly passed through this scene of desolation and death, was frequently startled by the croaking of the raven, or the screams of the vulture and falcon, from trees or crags commanding a view of these funeral services (1857:487).

Major smallpox epidemics reoccurred in 1846 and again in 1853-4. Unfortunately, indigenous *materia medica* and traditional medical procedures for combating previously unknown communicable diseases, proved ineffective. For some diseases, the traditional cures proved swiftly disastrous, such as when the stricken resorted to the time-honored therapeutic cure of sweating. Yet, Spokan oral history cites that during the devastating 1852-3 smallpox epidemic, a powerful shaman, who had survived an earlier siege of smallpox, successfully 'inoculated' his group with blessed waters and by practicing unrecalled prophylactic rituals (Ross 1981).

In 1855, I. I. Stevens estimated the Spokan approximately at 600, as opposed to Gibbs's total of 450. However, "Stevens' figure included the Sanpoil and Nespelem. Except for a few changes in spelling Indian terms, Stevens' data on the Spokan are identical to those recorded by Gibbs" (Chalfant 1974:60). Indian Agent A. J. Cain (1856) also noted that the effects of disease and famine upon the Spokan were devastating, greatly reducing their numbers. He urged that the survivors be placed on a temporary reservation, and "that the government may acquire a title to their lands" (1860:413-17). In an 1880 report, Indian Agent Simms recorded a population of 685 "Spokan living along the Spokan River and vicinity from Spokan [sic] Falls to the junction with the Columbia [River]" (1880:153); in 1882, he again numbered the population at 685 (Simms 1882:342). The Indian Affairs Report of 1889, and the U.S. Census Bulletin of 1890, estimated the Lower Spokan at 417, and the Upper Spokan at 170 (Powell 1891:105), but listed no figures for the Middle Spokan.

Teit, in discussing the effects of warfare upon regional populations, stated, "The Pend d'Oreille, Spokan, Colville, and Columbia all suffered; but the disease is said to have been worse among the Spokan, whole bands of whom were wiped out [...] so many people died in some places that the lodges were full of corpses" (1930:315-6). This situation was reiterated by the same ethnographer when writing of the Spokan population in 1850:

[...] the Upper division is said to have been most numerous. The Lower Spokan were not so many; while the Middle Spokan were always a small body, numbering only a few hundred. The whole Spokan tribe is said to have numbered more than the Coeur d'Alene, immediately prior to the advent of the fur traders; the Kalispel about the same as the Spokan (Teit 1930:314).

Hale, who after taking leave from the Wilkes Expedition (Meany 1925, 1:49-55) with other members and two Indian guides, made "the first major organized exploration of the interior [Plateau]" (Chalfant 1974:43). During four years, surveying this region, including the Spokan, he concluded, "Northwest of the paloouses [sic] is found a nation of the Spokans. They are nearly 800 persons. Several small tribes, who may be considered as belonging to the same nation, stay in that neighborhood [...] They call themselves the Children of the Sun, which in their language is Spokani" (1846, 4:439).

Anastasio (1972:202) considers the effects of numerous pandemics, epidemics, and diseases brought to the Plateau by Europeans:

Group	1805	1835	1845	1853
Colville	2,000	600	600	500
Kalispel	2,500	2,000	1,200	700
Sanpoil & Nespelem	1,600	1,500	?	?
Spokane	1,300	800	700	600

Figure 9. Estimated populations of plateau groups

In a letter to J. W. Nesmith, Superintendent of Indian Affairs Oregon Territory, Indian Agent B. F. Yantis for the Colville and Spokan wrote, "Southeast of the Okenagens [sic] is the Spokanes numbering about Six or Seven hundred including a small tribe living near the mouth of the Spokane River called by different names but generally known by the name Isle depers [sic] or Rock Island" (1857:3).

Wilson (1866:292) numbered the Spokan at 350. Similar figures of Spokan population were noted by Agent George Paige, who estimated a total population at 750, with the Lower Spokan as 177, and the Middle and Upper Spokan having a combined population of 663. Later, in 1867, the same agent reported that the Spokan and contiguous groups depended upon salmon for approximately five-eighths of their diet, and went on to write:

> [The Spokan] was divided into three bands, Upper, Lower and Middle, and number, about 750 souls. From the sterility of their country, little is done by way of farming. They derive their subsistence, in the main, from the salmon fisheries of the Columbia and Spokane [Rivers], and from roots, berries, and the chase [...] They [Spokan] make annual trips to the buffalo ground [...] and occasionally join war parties of the Flatheads and Upper Pend d'Oreilles, against their common enemy, the Blackfeet (Paige 1868:52).

In 1870, Indian Agent William P. Winans (1836-1917), Farmer in Charge to the Colville and Spokan (1870-71) and other non-treaty Indians residing east of the Cascades, provided a seldom cited, unpublished population census of the northeastern Washington non-treaty Indian tribes—including the Spokan. Figures for the Spokan were a total of 716: 176 men, 174 men, and 366 children. Winans later (1871) reported that all three macro bands of 725 Spokan resided on the Spokane River. Later, in a letter of 8 April 1872 to the Office of Indian Affairs, the Spokan population was again estimated at 725. Winans, in addition to meticulously producing hand-drawn maps of the area, assiduously recorded the names, genders, and household composition of each family. He also accumulated a detailed list of the number of acres each family had fenced and cultivated, as well as the number of all farm animals, type of crops being grown, and the tools used in food production and storage (Avery 1956:17).

Government Agent M. C. Wilkinson estimated the total Spokan population in 1877 as 901—numbering the Lower Spokan at 200, the Middle Spokan at 200, and the Upper Spokan at 388. By 1892, the number of Lower Spokan was thought to be 443, and the Upper Spokan had 170 members. The succeeding population numbers for the Spokan varied for several reasons, but mainly that some 407 Spokan decided to remain on the Spokane Indian Reservation, while some Upper and Middle Spokan elected to live on the Coeur d'Alene Reservation. Nearly all early population studies of highly mobile indigenous peoples were at best approximations. For instance, Joseph Lane, in an 1849 survey of Indians in Oregon, estimated the Spokan population at 1,000 (Schoolcraft 1857:701). Whereas Stevens, in 1853, wrote that the Spokan population was 600 (Schoolcraft 1857:700). Exact population figures were always difficult to attain, largely because intertribal socio-economic ties were an integral part of the rules of marriage and subsequent residence. These ties caused the relocation of some Spokan on the Kalispel, Flathead, and Coeur d'Alene Reservations (Hodge 1912:625).

Anastasio performed research of Spokan population figures and epidemic dates, based upon extensive ethnohistorical data. He estimated that the Spokan population was reduced from the time of contact until 1855 by approximately fifty-four percent (1974, 4:72-93). Such a drastic reduction must have had serious consequences upon their social organization, subsistence logistics, and religion. Thoms, in discussing the major effects of Spokan depopulation, deculturation, and Euro-American suppression during the early historical period, described this impact upon general Plateau culture when he summarized depopulation figures for the area:

1. Loss of 30-100 percent of group populations within periods of time ranging from 1 to 100 years.
2. Abandonment of communities and geographic areas by traditional groups, and sometimes subsequent reoccupation by different groups.
3. A breakdown of traditional kinship patterns, coupled with development of new alliances, and perhaps formation of entirely new groups from the survivors of severely decimated groups.
4. Starvation and famine as a result of losses in the labor force.
5. Coalescence of small groups into larger ones, with fewer villages located in the most favorable settings with regard to access to food resources (Thoms 1983:19-20).

The difficulty in estimating populations was exacerbated by the introduction of the horse, which provided greater mobility and even longer times of absence. Also, intermarriage between the Spokan and other ethnic groups, and exchanges of residence, made such studies questionable. Few Euro-Americans spoke Spokan to fully appreciate the periodic travel and logistics required by an annual subsistence round, which necessitated a highly mobile hunting and gathering culture.

Chapter II: Euro-American Contact

The earliest recorded histories of the original inhabitants of the Northwest were made by Euro-Americans who ventured westward onto the Plateau from the east, circa 1801. Unfortunately, these histories are often incomplete and lack objectivity. There were probably several reasons for this, but perhaps the underpinning factor was the primary intent of those Anglos, namely, to colonize the territory of the Plateau Indians. Euro-Americans often held deprecating opinions of the Indians, whom they felt were savages and heathens with little or no religion. Moreover, whites generally believed that the Indians were not utilizing their environment and the resources in a more productive fashion to better themselves economically. (These critics failed to appreciate the sustainability of living synergistically with the ecosystem.) Fortunately, there were many exceptions. Some whites learned, to varying degrees, the indigenous languages, and also came to appreciate the egalitarian social and political organization, sense of justice, and necessary adaptations of indigenous groups.

The first trappers and traders became somewhat acculturated—much more so than the majority of the later Euro-Americans. Pickering, of the Wilkes Expedition (1838-1842), wrote, "The Canadians on all occasions termed them 'savages;' and they had adopted the epitaph, unsuspicious of the implied approbation" (1895:21). It is not known, however, what term may have applied to an Indian couple Pickering met on his visit to Fort Lapwaii. The couple had taken on the trappings of the whites, by building a log house, and the wife dressed in European fashion. Pickering remarked at seeing the homestead, "The little valley seemed, in fact, an earthly paradise, which I could not quit without misgivings as to the future"(1851:29).

Numerous explorers, trapper-traders, missionaries, military men, and settlers commented upon the physical characteristics, cultures, and character traits of eastern Plateau peoples. There was a general consensus—with some exceptions—that during the time of early contact, the aboriginal cultures were more stable and more adaptive, prior to Euro-American incursion and occupancy. As late as 1849, Captain B.L.E. Bonneville (1796-1878) wrote:

> During the time I have been with them [the Flathead, a term which frequently included the Spokan and Kalispel], I have never known an instance of theft among them: the least thing, even to a bead or pin, is brought to you, if found; and often, things that have been thrown away. Neither have I known any quarrelling, nor lying (Irving 1851, 10:390).

Even more laudatory were comments of indigenous values by Bonneville, in 1832, who was lamenting the effects of Christianity and the concomitant increased severity of punishment by Christian Indian leaders:

> Simply to call these people [Flathead] religious would convey but a faint idea of the deep tone of piety which pervades their whole conduct. Their honesty is immaculate, and the purity of purpose and their observance of the rites of their religion are the most uniform and remarkable. They are certainly more like a nation of saints than a horde of savages (Swanton 1909:94).

Irish-born Henry Thompson Cowley (1871-1917) was a Presbyterian minister, etymologist, and teacher who learned to speak Spokan, and was totally committed to their welfare. He described Spokan Indian character and disposition, which historian Drury recorded in his 1916 autobiography, *Early Times in Spokane Country*:

> I found the Indian nature totally different from what I had conceived it to be in my youth. In general they were just as reliable as white people, honest and regardful of their worth. In my entire experience I lost only two articles by theft—a halter and a water melon. They returned the halter, and the Indian who took the watermellon [sic] stood up in church and made open confession. I felt as safe among them as among the same number of whites. Once you get their confidence, they are loyal to the core (Drury 1949:150; Durham 1912, 1:110-1).

Historian Herbert Gaston presents a similar account:

> The Indians with whom we dealt were many of them really strong characters and all had a rather high moral sense. We found them peaceable, friendly and honest. My father says that in all his years with the Indians only

twice did he have anything stolen. One man took a bridle repented and brought it back. Another who yielded to temptation and stole a watermelon confessed the wrong in church and asked for forgiveness (1914:76).

A further example of Spokan character was experienced by Reverend Parker (1779-1866), while traveling between Walla Walla and Colville. His party became uncertain of the correct route, and engaged a Spokan man to guide them. After an hour or so, the guide pointed out the proper trail and direction, to which Parker offered a larger compensation. "His only, and unvarying answer was, that he had done for us all that was needed, and why should he perform any unnecessary labor for us and take pay. I was astonished at the honesty of this heathen, and his steadfast adherence to it" (1840:286).

Explorers

The first known mention of the Plateau inhabitants is found in the journals of Lewis and Clark, from their travels of 1804-1806. Their description (1814), like many early accounts, is fragmentary and enigmatic, and thus does not give a clear picture of the intergroup relations of the ethnic groups of the Upper Columbia Basin. As for the Spokan specifically, Lewis and Clark were aware of reports concerning the Spokan—a people and territory they never visited. The earliest reports of the Spokan were from trappers and traders, who were the first non-Indians to contact the Spokan.

Yet the published information by Lewis and Clark must have been appreciated by a growing nation ready to expand westward. They described a territory of seemingly unlimited resources, which made difficult the writing of an unbiased account. Frontier people, attracted by the news, came seeking economic gain, as reflected in their own histories. Due to logistical restrictions, various areas were explored more intensively than others, and some remained almost unknown. In addition, the explorers' accounts evidenced the common notion that most indigenous groups were in many ways inferior to Euro-Americans. This belief provided a rationale for exploitation of the explored areas and abuse of its aboriginal inhabitants—a New World social Darwinism.

The earliest Anglo diseases perhaps arrived with the Iroquois, from the northeast, but it cannot be known with certainty, given Amerindian mobility. But it is known that the most psychologically and physically destructive pandemics resulted from sustained Euro-American contact. Trimble (1914, 1:32-33) states how Mullan contended, in the final Mullan Road Report, that "The Indian is destined to disappear before the white man, and the only question is, how it may best be done, and his disappearance from our midst tempered with those element calculated to produce to himself the least amount of suffering, and to us the least amount of cost" (Mullan 1862:52).

Trapper-Traders

Information gathered during Captain James Cook's third and final voyage to China in 1776 made apparent the potential for huge demand for furs in the Orient. But only decades later, Scottish-born Alexander Mackenzie became the first published explorer and fur trader in the region. In 1801, his book was read by William Clark, who encouraged Thomas Jefferson to form the now-famous Lewis and Clark Expedition, which was launched twelve years later (Wallace 1999:106). Recognizing the wealth to be gained, the United States government and several private trade companies expended considerable time and money to secure the Northwest politically and economically. Mackenzie as well realized the future potential of the area, and urged Britain to assert control over the Pacific Northwest. One of the earliest transcontinental expeditions to the Pacific Ocean was that of David Thompson (Sperlin 1913, 4:3). He is credited with establishing the first trading post on the Columbia River, the Kootenae House, in June 1807. As "the chief surveyor, geographer, and astronomer of the Northwest Company of Canada" (Walker and Lahren 1977:44), he was well qualified to survey the area for the North West Company, intermittently during 1809-12. In his extensive research of Thompson and his travels, Elliott (1862-1943) magnanimously described him as "the greatest land geographer the English race has ever produced" (1915, 6:4), and also cites Thompson as one who "ranks as one of the most remarkable men known in connection with the history of the Columbia River" (Elliott 1918, 2:103).

"Gradually the Northwest Company of Montreal had pushed over the Rockies under the leadership of their great explorer, Thompson" (Sperlin 1917, 8:103). Interestingly, he courageously and strictly forbade liquor to be transported west of the Rockies by any of his employees. Edward Meany (1862-1935), a professor and early publisher of the Washington Historical Quarterly, and interviewer of Sioux Indians for Edward S. Curtis, quotes Wilkes: "Too much cannot be said in praise of the Company [HBC] in having done away with the trade in spirits" (Meany 1925, 4:290).

The ownership claims and boundaries of the resource-rich Plateau were naturally of great interest to colonial powers. "The international border was unsettled in 1844 and the British government dispatched spies and surveyors to assess their claim to the Oregon Country" (Kohnen 2007:5). Two of these spies were Royal Engineers Lieutenants Henry J. Warre and Alfred Vavasour, who conducted a military reconnaissance of the Hudson's Bay Company (HBC) facilities, and mapped the mouth of the Columbia River (Schaefer 1909, 10:1-99). A war between Britain and the United States was averted by the diplomacy displayed by Warre to the Americans, and Britain yielded the area between the Columbia River and the 49th parallel. Most American diplomats and historians agree that the work of Thompson "gave a considerable degree of fairness to the British demand for that boundary to follow the line of the Columbia River south from the 49th parallel, which is the most Great Britain ever seriously claimed" (Elliott 1925a, 2:201).

During their tour and exploration survey of the U.S.-Canadian border area (1839-1846), Warre and Vavasour became concerned with the effects of alcohol upon indigenous populations, and advocated the continuous restriction of alcohol:

> The total abolition of the sale of intoxicating liquors has done much for the good of the whole community, white as well as Indian; and so long as this abstinence (which can hardly be called voluntary) continues the country will prosper. When this prohibition is withdraw, and the intercourse with the world thrown open, such is the character of the dissolute and only partially reformed American and Canadian settlers, that every evil must be anticipated, and the unfortunate Indian will be the first to suffer (Warre and Vavasour 1845:57; Schafer 1909:57; Sperlin 1917, 8:110).

American frontier whiskey was a vile compound of water, flavoring, and raw alcohol, whereas the HBC issue was rum, which "was sold by the company in small quantities and to reliable persons, never to Indians or to the vicious riffraff element of the frontier community" (Lewis and Meyers 1925, 3:199). However, by 1832, a total prohibition was in place on the use of and distribution of alcohol in the fur trade (Wishart 1979:70).

In 1811, at the *junction* (*sčilíp*) of the Columbia and Okanogan Rivers, Alexander Ross and David Stuart—both of the American Fur Company—founded Fort Okanogan (Parker 1840:298). After six months they "took in some 1500 beaver skins as well as other pelts, for which he gave trade goods estimated at about one-sixth the value of the furs" (Walker and Lahren 1977:44). The first Euro-Americans to penetrate this area for purposes of exploitation, and to maintain sustained Indian-white contact, were the fur trappers and traders. To maintain their economic objectives, they were not only dependent upon trapping fur-bearing animals, but also upon establishing peaceful relations with the indigenous population. When commenting upon those relations, Gibbs claimed, "The Spokanes are a noble specimen of their race, and are as yet too proud to beg" (1855, 1:256). Much earlier, Cox mentioned how "Their country did not abound in furs, and they were rather indolent in hunting" (1832:104). Trapper-traders soon found that the best way to exploit resources was to recruit Indians as inexpensive but skilled labor. Indians assisted Work's party in all chores—particularly gathering fire and construction wood, gumming canoes, working as sawyers, making charcoal by working coal pits, melting tallow (Elliott 1925, 4:270), and re-barking canoes. Most gum and tallow was acquired by trade from the Indians, some of whom also assisted in making pemmican. The loss of canoe paddles was a major inconvenience, and Indians made those as well (Elliott 1914, 4:265 and 4:270; Sperlin 1915, 6:41).

53

The lithograph below, by John Mix Stanley (1862, 12 (1):142-143, Plate XXXVII), illustrates what is now known as Fort Okanogan.

Figure 10. "Fort Okinakane"

Though little has been written about the trapper-traders' preferred watercraft for carrying heavy loads in waterways of sufficient depth, it is known they developed a type of unnamed barge, with a keel, oarlocks, and sometimes an aft deck and rudder. John Work wrote, "The River [Spokan] is very shallow & it is difficult getting it [a planked barge] down the river" (Elliott 1914, 5:171). Work provided the dimensions of such a craft, made using planks that were most likely pit-sawn: "The sawyers finished the wood for three boats, in all 73 boards 6 inches wide and 40 feet long & 3 board pieces for keels 40 feet long & 14 inches wide, and 6 pieces for gunwales 40 feet long & 2 inches wide in 15 days" (Elliott 1914, 5:175). Because of the lack of cedar and other straight-grained woods, the Hudson's Bay Company apparently "made all the Columbia boats of the native Yellow pine" (Howay *et al.*, 1914, 8:198). With the barges came the rough but inspiring music of French-Canadian boat songs (*chansons l'avirons*) (Durham 1912, 1:39).

Through intermarriage with Indian women, and living in close contact with the Spokan and other Plateau peoples, trapper-traders became acquainted and often knowledgeable of the Salish language and the respective cultural customs and beliefs. The influence of the French-Canadian trappers and *voyageurs*, and their language, is reflected in the naming of several Plateau Indian tribes. For example, the designation Coeur d'Alene means "hearts of awls," and Pend d'Oreille means "ear ring."

Bonneville also provided an appreciative explanation of the fur-trapper's method of roasting beaver meat:
When they take any beaver, they bring it home, skin it, stretch the skin on sticks [hoops] to dry, and feast upon the flesh. The body, hung up before the fire, turns by its own weight, and is roasted in a superior style; the

54

tail is the trapper's delight; it is cut off, put on the end of a stick, and toasted, and is considered even a greater dainty than the tongue or marrow bone of a buffalo (Irving 1836:383).

Regarding the role and appearance of the horse, Caywood, who conducted extensive archaeological excavations of Fort Spokane, mentioned Governor Simpson's more economically-sensible plan to use boats rather than horses for transporting furs and supplies, and cited alternate uses of the horse by the trapper-trader:

> This would eliminate the time spent, and extra supplies used, in gathering the large herds of horses heretofore required for transportation. The horse trade always led to quarrels with the natives regarding horse thieving. From the number of horse bones found, horse meat must have been part of the diet of those living at Spokane House. Many a good horse probably appeared on the dinner table when hunting was bad and meat supplies were low (Caywood 1956:46).

Revealing are the types of trade goods chosen by the HBC:

> Mr. Astor's stock, selected especially to appeal to Indian nature, included guns and ammunition, spears, hatchets, knives, beaver traps, copper and brass kettles; blue, green and red clothes; calico, beads, rings, thimbles, hawksbells, and gew gaws (Durham 1912, 1:12).

The Indians' acceptance of the trapper-trader—and other Euro-American agencies of acculturation—was a gradual process of socialization. For example, "The Spokans and the traders shared horse races and festivals and [some] were soon bound by ties of marriage" (Cebula 2003:129). Consequently, after a period of contact, trapper-traders instituted a reciprocal, albeit economically unbalanced, relationship with many of the Plateau groups. Later, during the major fur trade period (circa 1808-1842), they developed with the Indians a most lucrative and competitive business.

The trapper-trader presence and their introduction of trade goods, promoted peaceful relations within the Plateau, because its inhabitants desired *iron* (*ʔululím*) tools, cloth, needles, European-made beads, and other items—particularly firearms, because the firearms, in conjunction with the horse, facilitated the eastern Salish to form task-groups for hunting bison on the hostile Plains. One steel trapper commented, "We made an enormous profit on the Indian trade [...] Since the object of every male Indian was to obtain a gun, we played upon this desire to persuade the red man to search diligently for beavers" (Dryden 1949:43).

An early and major figure in opening the Northwest fur trade, was John Jacob Astor (1763-1848), a German immigrant who became a rich merchant and fur trader. He founded the American Fur Company in 1808, with a subsidiary, the Pacific Fur Company.

The first two North West Company clerks in the Spokane area were Finan McDonald (1763-1848), who had lived earlier with the Spokan and had married a chief's daughter, and Jacques "Jaco" (Jocko) Raphael Finlay (circa 1768-1828), a Canadian *sauteur* (leaper or jumper). Finlay was one of the first white men to see Spokane Falls, and he felt that an establishment on that location might extend and control the fur traffic of the Interior Plateau. To Finlay "probably belongs the credit for selecting the site and erecting the first buildings at Spokane House [...] On this sheltered, flat peninsula between two rivers [where] Indians were accustomed to gather in great numbers to dry their fish" (Elliott 1917, 4:249).

David H. Chance, who conducted extensive secondary research on trappers-traders based on the original readings of Kennedy (1823) and Work (1829), wrote, "Geographically, the Spokan were located at a sort of crossroads, a factor that probably influenced the location of the Spokan House near the place of modern day Spokane by the Northwest Company in 1810" (Chance and Hudson 1981:115). Sperlin's earlier studies led him to state that "Spokane was always the most important trade emporium of the North-West Company this side of the Rockies" (1917, 8:103). Later, Spokane House became one of three posts, and "Such were the six primary posts: Spokane House, Okanogan, Nez Perces [sic], Vancouver, Colvile [sic], and Nisqually, ruled by the Hudson's Bay Company" (*vide supra* 1917:109).

The first buildings at Spokane House formed the first Anglo settlement, built in 1812, in what later became Washington State (Sperlin 1917, 8:103; Meyers 1919, 10:165; Elliott 1915, 1:7). It was fortuitous for the North West Company that Thompson, in 1810, sent Finley to establish Spokane House (Elliott 1915, 1:9). "In 1814, when the Pacific Fur Company was forced by war to relinquish its Northwest fur trade, they sold

Fort Spokane to the Canadian traders of the North West Company, who then transferred their goods and personnel to the 1812 fort" (Caywood 1981:5).

Realizing the potential of the region's resources, the traders of Astor's American-owned Pacific Fur Company erected Fort Spokane in 1812 with the assistance of Alexander Ross. Only a few hundred meters away from Spokane House, it was intended as a competing and more substantial post, but business failed with the advent of the War of 1812. The North West Company's choosing to establish a trading post on the flats near the confluence of the Spokane and Little Spokane Rivers, reveals their assessment of the logistical importance of pre-contact activities (Lavender 1964:139). It was at this post, now called Spokane House, where Thompson, a partner in the company, came in March 1812 and commented in his journal on this "bold wooded land" and abundance of fish:

> The Spokane Indians were delighted to have Spokane House in their midst. It made it easier for them to secure guns for their traditional warfare against the Indians east of the mountains, many of whom had been able to secure fire-arms much earlier and who, with their guns, made it difficult for the Spokanes to procure greatly needed buffalo meat and hides. In the second place, it made the Spokanes comparatively wealthy because of their position as middlemen, obtaining furs from surrounding tribes at low prices for resale to the traders, much to the disgust of the whites. The Spokanes showed their appreciation by demonstrating an uncommon friendship which was evidenced by the fact that the gates at Spokane House were seldom closed at night, a lack of caution which would have been costly in most places. The two cannon in the bastions of the stockade were never used except as festive noise-makers (Becher 1965:21).

Cox commented upon the general attitude of the trappers toward "the Spokan [who] we found to be a quiet, honest, inoffensive tribe; and although we had fortified our establishment [...] We seldom closed the gates at night" (1832, I:17-18). Alexander Ross, a fur trader in the area from 1811 to 1821, spoke of the relations with the competing groups, including:

> [...] the sly and underhand dealings of the competing parties [Fort Spokane and Spokane House], for the opposing post of the Northwest Company and Mr. Clarke were built contiguous to each other. When the two parties happened to meet they made amplest protestations of friendship and kindness, and a stranger, unacquainted with the politics of Indian trade would have pronounced them sincere; but the moment their backs were turned, they tore each other to pieces. Each party had its maneuvering scouts out in all directions, watching the motions of the Indians and laying plots and plans to entrap or foil each other. He that got the most skins, never minding the cost or the crime, was the cleverest fellow; and under such tutors the Indian were apt disciples. They played their tricks also, and turned the foibles and wiles of their teachers to their own advantage (1855, 1:306-307).

The often-outspoken Alexander Ross visited Spokane House in 1825, and adamantly "indulged in his usual disgust as to the site of Spokane House" (Elliott 1913, 4:43-44), for good reasons, lamenting the major economic and logistical problems. As for the matter of not locating it at Walla Walla or Grand Forks, he maintained there "were ostensible reasons, but the real cause lay deeper beneath the surface" (Ross 1849:126):

> Spokane House was a retired spot; no hostile natives were there to disquiet a great man. There the bourgeois who presided over the Company's affairs resided, and that made Spokane House the center of attraction [...] there were handsome buildings. There was a ballroom, even though no females in the land so fair to look upon as the nymphs of Spokane [...] Spokane House was not celebrated for fine women only, there were fine horses also [...] (Ross 1855, 1:126-7).

Cox concurred with Ross concerning the location of Spokane House, saying it would "be in a rather out of the way location, 150 miles from the better fur regions, furs being scarce in the immediate neighborhood, and the Indians being but indolent hunters" (Durham 1912, 1:51). Ross emphasized the inaccessibility and inconvenience of the *location* (*lčen'*) of Spokane House, which had been the view of Donald MacKenzie (1930, 1:6). Ross contended, "Spokane House, of all the posts in the interior, was the most unsuitable place for concentrating the different branches of the trade" (1855:95). In 1824, Ross reiterated his loathing of the location (Elliott 1930, 1:6): "Spokane House is the most singular: far from water, far from Indians and out of the way" (Elliott 1913, 4:388). He argued against both the "Spokane and Flathead House as a base for the Snake River Country operations" (Elliott 1909, 4:332). Governor Simpson contended that, even when replaced by Fort Colville near Kettle Falls, "no food supply from Vancouver would be transported to a post [Spokane House] so distant" (Sperlin 1917, 8:108). Simpson and McLoughlin (HBC's Chief Factor at the time), agreed "the location was impracticable, being sixty miles off line of travel and transportation by water up and down the Columbia" (Elliott 1930, 1:6). Consequently, Spokane House "was never reoccupied except occasionally by Indians and hunters" (Sperlin 1917, 8:111).

Despite the criticism leveled against Spokane House, Durham, quoting from the observations and notes of others, particularly MacKenzie, described it as:

[...] a popular rendezvous for the different posts and detached trading parties operating all over the Inland Empire. Many a gay gathering and many a lively social diversion could the sentinel pines and downlooking mountains narrate today if they had the power of speech. The establishment boasted a ball-room, and there on wintry nights, to the strains of flute and fiddle, the vivacious French-Canadians and some stolid young Scotch chaps trod a measure with the copper-tinted belles of the Spokanes (1912, 1:19).

Realizing that the activities of the Euro-Americans were primarily exploitative, some trapper-traders felt a genuine concern for the welfare of the Indians, and made considerable efforts to maintain peaceful relations. They sought to reduce Indian intergroup hostilities because, if pursued even sporadically, such conflict would prove detrimental to trapping and trade. Many of the trapper-traders were well aware of the disastrous consequences of whiskey to the Indians. Cox cites, "We never brought ardent spirits among them for the purposes of barter [...] the few whom we knew to have tasted any did not seem to relish it" (1832:235). Cox entered into a contract with James McMillian, head of the North West Company station at the junction of the Pointed Heart and Spokane Rivers, "to abstain from giving the Indians any spirituous liquors to which both parties strictly adhered" (1957:114). Peltier noted, "During the early days in the Pacific Northwest, the HBC representatives had a policy of not introducing liquor as a trade item" (1990:9). David Thompson too was very against the introduction of alcohol, and declared that no liquor would pass the mountains in his company (Holbrook 1956:41-2). Another trader exhorted, "It is needless to dilate upon the disastrous and demoralizing effects to the Indian of the whiskey trade. Robes, blankets, horses—everything—is sacrificed to whiskey, and when reduced to utter poverty the Indian steals, the result is war with the whites" (Viall 1871:409). The missionaries often condemned the practice of exchanging a gill of whiskey for a beaver pelt, and stated that "The HBC does not belong to this class of traders" (Whitman 1843:117).

Thompson also understood how the Indians suffered from the effects of over-trapping by non-Indian trappers, who learned that an effective beaver lure for traps could be made from castoreum (beaver musk)—a thick, oily, creamy, bitter, brownish secretion of the beaver's pineal glands—mixed with oil of juniper and gum of camphor: "The large scent glands, present in both sexes, lie on either side of the midline between the anus and external genitalia, and may readily be mistaken for testes" (Forbes 1968:248). The indefatigable Wilson observed how the pungent odor of the castor "was most effective for attracting beaver" (1866:294), and "can entice beaver from as far as a mile away" (Hansen 1972, 8:2). With this knowledge, and the introduction of steel traps, trading increased and eventually brought about the near-extinction of the beaver. Somewhat prophetically, Thompson recorded the following conversation between two Indian trappers: "We are now killing the Beaver without any labor, we are now rich, but shall soon be poor, for when the Beaver are destroyed we [will] have nothing to depend on to purchase what we want for our families, strangers now over run [sic] our country with iron traps and we, and they will soon be poor" (Lavender 1963:124).

Trapping inevitably fell on hard times as beaver hats and military headdress went out of fashion. Even prior to this, Alexander Kennedy, the Chief Factor, was given a statement by George Simpson (circa 1792-1860) regarding the Spokan Indians and the location of the post, arguing:

[...] that the post is badly located for food animals and that the Indians monopolize the salmon so that all food must be conveyed at great expense from Fort George. He recommends its abandonment and that the post be established at Kettle Falls to take its place. He thus would seem to deserve the credit for the action taken by

57

Governor Simpson in ordering this removal in 1825 to the site recommended by Kennedy. The new post was named Colville (Clark 1938, 29:6).

Consequently, Spokane House did not last long as a center of fur trade, and as early as April 1825, Governor George Simpson warned John Work that "The Spokans will not be pleased at the removal of the Fort, you must secure the Chiefs with a few presents; besides fair words" (Lewis 1925, 2:103). In 1825, Simpson ordered all Iroquois HBC employees from the Columbia River to eastern Canada, and also cancelled HBC operations at Spokane House. During the process of closing Spokane House, Work recorded, "The Indians [had] much regret our going off, and frequently complain that they will be pitiful when the whites leave them" (Elliott 1914, 4:279).

The North West Company merged with the powerful HBC in 1821, and by 1825 the transportation network of trade had shifted away from the Spokane House. Alexander Kennedy stated, "Spokane House and property was sold to the Canadians for a band of Indian horses to be delivered the following spring" (Durham 1912, 1:51). Prior to leaving Spokane House, Work reported, "The Blacksmith and cook, the only two men we have now here, employed collecting all the iron about the place, stripping off doors &c" (Elliott 1914, 4:279).

Unfortunately, the archaeological and historical significance of this famous site is not fully known. Caywood contends the Spokane House location was where "the Pacific Fur Company, the Northwest Company (before 1813), and the Hudson's Bay Company were previously situated" (1956:45).

Given the decline of the beaver population, the British-controlled HBC replaced Spokane House in 1826 with the establishment of Fort Colville (1825-1871), near Kettle Falls (Drury 1976:202 fn). The location was a major fishing site on the Columbia River for *many tribal groups* ($x^we\text{?}úle\text{?}x^w$) in July and August, to fish sockeye, Coho, and Chinook salmon (Wilkes 1845, 4:474; DeSmet 1905, 2:481).

By 1840, the zenith of the fur trade had passed, and in 1841 Pickering recorded (1895:27-28) how, within the Spokan drainage, "beaver were [once] commonly in all these streams, and were caught by the natives by setting baskets; but owing to the introduction of [steel] beaver-traps, they had become almost extinct." Further pressure upon the beaver population occurred during a severe winter, which made traveling difficult, so the Flathead and Spokan Indians remained in their area and spent the winter trapping beaver for economic gain.

Three decades of fur-trading had changed the Spokan irrevocably. In addition to the acquisition of horses, superior guns, steel knives, axes, woolens, and other types of durable trade goods, it accelerated the depletion of fur-bearing animals. Sadly, the Spokan became quite dependent upon this trade, as described by an anonymous trapper-trader: "We reached the Spokan on the last day of August. Here we found the trading goods had been exhausted long before, and the Indians had been upwards of two months without ammunition. Our arrival, therefore, was hailed with great joy" (Cox 1832:163).

Many of the skills and tools for making log and plank cabins were acquired from the trapper-traders, who were assisted by local Indians in constructing their boats, dwellings, store-houses, and even fortifications. This included iron-working, plank-dressing, making adobe bricks, and the use of parchment for windows (Elliott 1914, 3:184). Often the final coverings of a structure's roof was fashioned from tule mats acquired by trading with Indian women. A constant problem during spring and fall was to replace or repair such roofing, prompting the cabin owners to send word out to Indian women to bring in tule mats (Elliott 1914, 3:188).

The Indians may have been overjoyed by the whites providing them with the trade goods they desired, but the overall effect was a weakening of their independence and culture, and further overexploitation of their natural resources, which declined past the point of sustainable self-restoration. But resource recovery takes time and an appreciation of the ecosystem, which few whites had. Not only did the Indians receive inadequate compensation, but they lost more than they realized.

The appearance of the trapper-trader had unseen effects on the indigenous occupants of the eastern Plateau, because it created conditions that made the Indian economically dependent upon the white man, and changed the indigenous intergroup relations by altering their material culture and subsistence orientation. Also, "it is very probable that the much publicized interest of the Plateau peoples in Christianity was promoted by an interest in Euro-American material culture" (Walker and Schuster 1998: 501).

A number of other effects resulted from the introduction of Euro-American trade networks into the Plateau. The exploitation of fur-bearing animals increased, intergroup trade intensified, and certain established traditional subsistence activities diminished—and in some instances virtually disappeared or were greatly modified. These changes placed new demands upon the division of labor. In many instances, women became active members of the Indian-trapper-trader relationship, as evidenced by the many liaisons and marriages between the once-distinctly different groups (Ross 1967:32). It has been suggested (Elmendorf, pers. comm.) that polygyny increased, as it was advantageous to a trapper who engaged his multiple wives in processing hides—as happened elsewhere further to the north.

Gottfred wrote of the socioeconomic benefits of Canadian fur trapper-trader Indian conjugal relationships, which were the same with Indian-Americans: "In Native cultures, women usually set up camp, dressed furs, made leather, cooked meals, gathered firewood, made moccasins, netted snowshoes, many other things that were essential to daily life for both Natives and fur traders, yet were unfamiliar tasks for Europeans" (1995:1).

The social, domestic, and political importance of the older female was further increased through the sometimes long absences of the Spokan men, when they ventured to the Plains to engage in bison-hunting and trading. Older women seldom accompanied the men on these trips, because of hostilities with the Blackfoot. Yet this is not meant to suggest that, within some groups, the women's rise to eventual political power followed the arrival of Euro-Americans in the Plateau (Ackerman 1982).

Numerous Scottish-born trappers in North America married Indian women. Some remained married and in residence with their Scoto-Indian wives, whereas others returned to Scotland (Szasz 2000). Examples of Scottish trappers include Alexander Ross, Angus McDonald, Donald A. Smith, John McLoughlin (a plant collector for England's Horticultural society), and George Barnston of the North West Company, who married "a mixed blood [*Brulé*] daughter of an American Fur Company employee" (Brown and Van Kirk 1966:1). Sleeper-Smith (2000, 2:441) held that the fur trade was "clearly much more than the simple economic transaction of a market place economy; instead, it was defined by kinship and friendship." Therefore, multilingual Scoto-Indian wives "repeatedly served as godmothers to numerous children of mixed ancestry and were 'negotiators of change'" (Sleeper-Smith 2000, 2:424). Sleeper-Smith wrote that the "exchange of trade goods for peltry occurred on a face-to-face basis, along a kinship continuum" (2000, 2:428), and for the trapper to have "abandoned her would have resulted in the inevitable loss of her female congregation" (2000, 2:428).

Van Kirk, in a thoroughly-researched monograph, summarized the unique socio-economic relationship (*à la façon du pays* - "custom of the country" or "country marriage") between trapper-traders in western Canada, which was similar within the Columbia Plateau. Wives of fur-traders were frequently polyglots (French, English, and of course their own Indian language). More importantly, they taught their husbands their native language:

> The economic role played by Indian women in fur-trade society reflected the extent to which the European traders were compelled to adapt to the native way of life. The all-encompassing work role of Indian women was transferred, in modified form, to the trading post, where their skills not only facilitated the traders' survival in the wilderness but actual fur-trade operations (Van Kirk 1980:29).

Alexander Ross, during his stay among the Columbia Salish, had considerable personal experience with Scoto-Indian wives, whom he obviously held in high respect. He recited how close and supportive those wives were:

> The vigilance of these women had often been instrumental to the safety of the forts when the most diabolical combinations were set on foot by the natives [...] When they rejoin their tribe, the whites find them friendly, and

they never fail to influence their connections to the same end. By these means a close alliance is formed between the traders and the aborigines of the country (1855:287).

Sir George Simpson provided an excellent account of the variety of language often found in a single boatload:

> Our bateau [boat] was curious a muster of races and languages [...] Our crew of ten men contained Iroquois, who spoke their own tongue; a Cree halfbreed of French origin, who appeared to have borrowed his dialect from both his parents; a North Briton [Scot], who understood only the Gaelic of his native hills; Canadians who, of course, knew French; and Sandwich Islanders, who jabbered and in their own vernacular jargon a medley of Chinook (Eratinger 1914 3:192).

The mainly Montreal Iroquois were often French-speaking and of Catholic faith, and constituted approximately one-third of the voyagers employed by the HBC on the Columbia and within the area of the Spokan. They were:

> [...] expert voyagers, and especially so in the rapids and dangerous runs in the inland waters, which they either stem or shoot with the utmost skill. The object of intruding them into the service of traders was to make them act in the double capacity of canoe-men and trappers. They are not esteemed equal to the ablest trappers, nor the best calculated for the voyage they are not so esteemed (Ross 1855:286).

Cox noted the numerous advantages and superior comforts enjoyed by such marital unions, which reputedly motivated some Spokan women to marry *voyageurs*. "Given the Indian view of marriage, a trader's alliance with the Indian woman served the important public function of cementing trade ties" (1957:148).

Commercial fur trapping and trading had another deleterious effect on the Plateau: The Indian's economic subjugation was brought about primarily by the Euro-American mercantile groups, whose trading outposts were often the scenes of prostitution, gambling, and drunkenness. The Indian bringing in pelts was readily persuaded to trade them for such inducements. Then, by being advanced his winter's food and supplies, he was placed in debt until the trading station.

Chance (1973) gives a succinct overview of the effect of the fur trade, the incorporation of the horse into a hunter-gatherer system, the introduction of firearms, etc.—all of which ultimately resulted in the depletion of game resources, especially around sites used to overwinter, which in turn forced changes in patterns of resource exploitation. "The coming of the American settlers, the Indian wars consequent upon this influx, the placing of the Indians upon reservations by the Americans—these were important factors in bringing to a close the fur-trading epoch" (Oliphant 1925, 2:89). By 1854, when most Northwest Indians were confined to "reservations, their fur trapping days were virtually ended" (Mitchell 1963:402).

Missionaries

Yet the source of the most enduring changes upon indigenous groups was the missionary, who began the second phase of Anglo contact (Ross 1967:35). Well-meaning Christian missionaries dramatically and irrevocably devastated the once-receptive Spokan culture, which in turn had other long-term effects. Basically, the two belief systems—Christianity and animism—were diametrically opposed. Traditionally, Indians never fought about another's spiritual beliefs—at least not until the forced introduction of Christianity and the factionalism that it introduced (and continues to this day).

There were numerous missionaries—most notably the Jesuits—who studied and wrote of Indian culture. Some missionaries learned by necessity to speak, to varying degrees, the languages of the people whom they proselytized. In fact, Reverend Elkanah wrote a Spokan primer, *Etshiit thul sitskai*, published in 1842.

Long before organized missionization, there were numerous accounts of encounters with Indians—then considered a previously unknown race of people. Possibly the earliest account is a recorded meeting with a small group whom Bonneville described as "the remnants of a party of Iroquois hunters [trappers?], that came from [eastern] Canada into these mountain regions many years ago previously in the employ of the Hudson's Bay Company" (Irving 1843, 1:115). Iroquois trappers—essentially Catholic *voyageurs*—were quite

60

cognizant of certain elements of Christianity long before actual contact by missionaries with indigenous people in the Columbia River area. The Spokan were no exception:

On his *"Journey of a Summer Moon"* in 1811, Thompson learned that Indians of the Columbia River acknowledged a Great Spirit dwelling in the clouds, who was master of everything and the Maker of lightning, thunder, and rain. It was to him that their souls went to on their deaths. In contrast to Christian believers they recognized as solar deities the sun, moon, and stars, of which the greatest was the sun. At about the time when George Simpson visited the Spokanes they held religious services in their chief's lodge, kneeling before a religious picture obtained from some white traders and praying to *Quilentsatmen* (the Maker or literally, He Made Us) to prevent and rescue them at last from the Black One below (Ruby and Brown 1982:54).

The original explorers and trapper-traders made no effort to change the Indians' religion, social structure, or subsistence activities. But once the missionaries arrived and became established within the eastern Plateau, their socioeconomic effects upon the different tribes were disastrous. "This Anglo-Protestant approach was overwhelmingly ethnocentric" (Prucha 1988, 4:131). Even worse, for the Protestant to consider it a success, "a total and external transformation conversion was deemed necessary, and the Anglo-Protestants demanded ultimately the obliteration of Indian culture in its entirety—language, religion, ceremonies, social patterns" (Prucha 1988, 4:134). This conflict was exacerbated by competing religions: "One major source of dissonance was the tension between the Protestants and Catholic missionaries" (Miller 2003:92), as is presently. Another factor was the difficulty that the missionaries had with the Spokan language.

The initial reactions of the Spokan, and the tragic results of missionization—Catholic and Protestant— were best stated by ethnohistorian Larry Cebula:

The Spokans, like many Plateau Indians, greeted the first missionaries with enthusiasm in the late 1830s. But the creed of these white shamans proved more difficult and less useful than any had imagined. These shamans demanded that Indians give up their ceremonies, have only one wife, and pray in very specific ways. They took land from the Indians with little or no compensation. They did not share manufactured goods with the Indians as the fur traders had. And the white shamans argued among themselves, disparaging one another's teachings. Disease returned to the plateau as the shamans arrived, and to some there seemed a connection. Clearly the white religion was less useful than hoped (2003:129).

Drury's research of missionary-Indian relationships indicates that the missionaries presumed that if the Indians adopted agriculture, it would encourage them to remain in one location. Consequently, missionaries encouraged the Indians "to give up their semi-nomadic habits and accept a settled life" (Drury 1973, 1:253). But this counsel from the missionaries was not out of misguided concern for the diet of the Spokan. Rather, the missionaries encouraged the "Indians to remain in one location, [since] agriculture would also make them more susceptible to missionary influence and, indeed, control" (Coleman 1985:98).

Henry Cowley complained in 1876 how the:

[...] "poor" Spokan could not understand that their condition would be improved if they occupied less territory, and were obliged to gain the principal part of their livelihood by cultivation of the soil (Coleman 1985:98).

Later, Drury (1976:8) described how Eells and Walker agreed with Whitman and Spaulding "that unless the natives abandoned their seminomadic habits and settled down on farms, they would perish. The Spokane were cultivating potatoes to a limited extent before the missionaries arrived but were still depending upon hunting, fishing, and digging roots."

Yet the Spokan were not willing to adopt farming wholesale (Drury 1976:8), partly because they lacked an appropriate climate, as well as fences, and would have had to contend with free-roaming horses and cattle. Schaeffer's extensive linguistic and ethnographic field studies with the Flathead lead him to several explanations for the general retiscence of Indian men to forego hunting and take up the plow: The farmer's life, limited to a specific area, conflicted directly with the annual subsistence round and hunting. Plant gathering and digging were considered women's work, "and its general resemblance to the harvesting of cultivated crops stamped the latter activity unsuitable for men" (Schaeffer 1937, 3:243). "Agriculture, as introduced by the Jesuits, lacked a body of ceremonial practises appropriate for the expression of these values" (*vide supra* 1937:243). The same was true of the Protestant missionaries at Tschimakain Mission. When agriculture was practiced, some men refused their sons, who were attending the mission school, to do "women's work" in the fields (Palladino 1894:167-168).

Reverend Eells was quite concerned with the increased number of settlers and their effects upon the Spokan subsistence base and their proposed permanent settlement. Durham (1859-1938) quoted him: "They [the Indians] foresaw the coming of the changed conditions growing out of the settlement of their country, and took to the cultivation of the soil and raising of cattle, and wanted schoolhouses and churches" (1912, 1:111). "Walker and Eells kept a few cows, and the former's diary shows that no small part of the missionaries' labors consisted in searching after persistently straying cattle" (Kingston 1932, 3:177).

Other Indian groups in the Pacific Northwest were equally devastated. On the Walla Walla River, at Waiilatpu, where the Cayuse Indians lived successfully, Samuel Parker surveyed the area for a Protestant mission in 1835. During the next year, Marcus and Narcissa Whitman established the first Presbyterian mission in the area, at Waiilatpu (Drury 1976, 1:62). What relationship the missionaries may have had with the Indians was destroyed in 1847 by a devastating measles epidemic that struck the Cayuse, who claimed the missionaries were killing their people to acquire their land and horses. In fact, the Cayuse claimed that only Indian children were dying—not Anglo children. In response, the Cayuse attacked the mission on 29 November 1847, killing Dr. Marcus Whitman (1802-1847), his wife, and twelve other members of the mission (Coone 1917, 8:15). Reverend Cowley, who worked earlier among the Nez Perce, correctly described in his diaries how one traditional form of therapy, the sweathouse—with its intense heat and later plunge into cold water—"frequently brought death to those afflicted with white men's diseases. This measles epidemic with its heavy toll of lives was certainly one of the major causes of the Whitman massacre" (Drury 1949:26).

Two other Plateau groups were similarly affected: "The Chinooks were devastated and dispersed by European diseases by 1839, and the Sahaptians, as a consequence of an 1855 treaty, were forced to relocate to the Yakima Reservation in Washington or to Warm Springs and Umatilla reservations in Oregon" (Miller 1990:XXVI - XXVII).

Within the Spokan territory, the first permanent Christian mission was established in 1838 by American Board Protestant Congregational ministers Reverend Elkanah Walker, Reverend Cushing Eells, and their wives. It was located at Tschimakain ("Plain of Springs") on Tschimakain Creek, which flows into the Spokane River (once called *Skeetshoo* by traders). "The streams lose themselves in the earth, and after passing underground for about five miles, burst out again in springs" (Hale 1846, 4:438). The principal objectives of these missionaries were massive cultural changes:

> [...] the Indians were many: law must replace what the whites conceived to be Indian anarchy, hard work must replace the hand-to-mouth existence of the Indian, individual ownership of property must be substituted for communal ownership. Indians must change their external appearance to look like Europeans, and Indians must be educated. Conversion was accomplished when the above five objectives were accomplished. An important point made is that conversion to the Protestants meant the Indians were to become civilized and Americans. The above objectives coincided with the policy of the American government and the Protestants and government worked in concert (Prucha 1988, 4:131-2).

When describing the missionaries and the Spokan at the Tschimakain Mission, Hale was impressed with the village members' self-control and conscious of public opinion (aside from his unfortunate use of the term "savage"):

> The missionaries represent the Indians as being as very easily actuated by impulses, and impatient of restraint; but that, though quick-tempered, they are not sullen: a revengeful spirit is always discouraged—indeed it is esteemed a merit to be patient under injury. Public opinion has a very powerful influence upon them, and few savages are more susceptible of ridicule, to the utterance of which their language is particularly adapted. Although there is but little government in families, they are well behaved; and it is proverbial that they seldom

quarrel among themselves. Generosity and wealth are the two qualifications that give most consequence; after these comes noble blood (1846, 4:455).

The Tschimakain Mission was visited years later by Fathers Pierre J. DeSmet, S.J. and Nicolas Point, S.J., who had also visited the Spokan and Coeur d'Alene Indians in the spring of 1842. This meeting presumably created considerable consternation with the Tschimakain missionaries, since they knew DeSmet was an aggressive leader of the St. Mary's Mission and St. Igantious in the Bitterroot Valley, founded in 1841 for the Flathead Indians. DeSmet's colleague, Father Point (1799-1868), built the first Catholic church in Idaho, on the St. Joe River. He was an accomplished historian, artist, and cartographer, and spent six years in Montana. After traveling through the Tschimakain Valley, DeSmet, also an excellent artist, noted in his *Letters and Sketches* a rather critical description of the Protestant missionaries, which reflected the conflict between the Catholic and Protestant missionaries:

> Here, on a gay and smiling little plain, two ministers have settled themselves, with their wives, who have consented to share their husbands' soi-disant [self-styled] apostolical labors. During the four years they have spent here, they have baptized several of their own children. They cultivate a small farm, large enough, however, for their own maintenance and support of their animals and fowls. It appears that they are fearful that, should they cultivate more, they might have too frequent visits from the savages. They even try to prevent their encampment in their immediate neighborhood, and therefore they see and converse but seldom with the heathens, whom they have come so far to seek (DeSmet 1843:212).

Despite the number of baptisms, it is doubtful whether the missionaries had any Spokan converts, for as Mrs. Eells described to a friend in a letter dated 23 April 1846, "We have been here about seven years & I don't know that we have reason to think one soul has been converted to God" (Drury 1976, 1:336). A quote taken earlier from the letters and diaries of Spaulding and Smith, stated how Walker "had labored at Tschimakain for nine years without the joy of having a single native join the Mission church" (1958:351). Drury further stated, "The tenacity with which the Indians clung to their medicine rites continued to be the main reason why the missionaries were unable to win converts" (1976:265). Mrs. Eells's diary entry for March 1847 lamented, "We have been here almost nine years, and have not yet been permitted to hear the cry of one penitent, or the songs of one redeemed soul" (Snowden 1909:130). Drury also noted, "The Walkers and Eells labored among the Spokanes for nearly nine years without being cheered by a single convert" (1949:105). "The experience was heartbreaking for the Walkers" (Richardson 2006:7).

In essence, the Tschimakain missionaries were unable to successfully proselytize any Spokan, and:

> It is clear from their journals and letters that as the Indians refused to accept the severe puritanical restrictions demanded at Tschimakain, the mission families increasingly found it almost unbearable to have the Indians around. This lack of rapport doomed them to nine years of cultivating alone, praying among themselves, and baptizing none but their own children (Meinig 1968:137).

Legislation introduced by President Ulysses S. Grant in 1871, to delegate and regulate the activities of Christian missionaries working with Indians, was called a peace policy, but was intended to correct the flagrant abuses in the administration of Indian affairs. "Under this policy, several of the larger religious denominations of the nation were given the right to nominate the agent and teachers for specific reservations. Under this plan, the Presbyterians were given the responsibility for the Nez Perces and the Roman Catholics, for the Spokanes" (Drury 1976:500).

During this period of Spokan history, the Middle Spokan chief, *Illeeum* or *Illim-Spokanee* (d. 1828), was a most important and influential tribal member. His son was given the name Spokane Garry (1811-1892) by Governor Sir George Simpson. Some time in 1825, Simpson sent Garry to the HBC Red River school, an Anglican missionary school and settlement near Winnipeg. One other boy, Kutenai Pelly, accompanied Garry. Garry proved to be a bright and dedicated student, and learned to speak fluent English and French. He returned to his home in 1831 with a bible and a knowledge of Christianity, and began preaching to and teaching many Indians. His pronouncements and examples of faith were similar to the teachings of the shamans and the prophets. Gary became disillusioned with Calvinistic revivalists Cushing Eells and Elkaha

Walker, as well as their establishment of Tschimakain Mission (1838), which increased religious factionalism (Ross 1999c:118). His efforts in teaching Christianity, and even the value of horticulture, were summarized by Walker and Lahren:

> After 4 yr in the mission, the boys returned home wearing short hair and coats and ties and ready to teach Christianity to their people. Spokane Garry built a little tule-mat sanctuary and began a zealous preaching career which eventually spread Christianity to many Plateau people [...] He even taught the Spokane to say grace before meals. The concepts of prayer, hymn, and giving thanks for meals fit in very well with the habits of these people whose lives had always been rich in ritual. In addition to religious concepts, Spokane Garry taught various practices adopted from white culture, such as the use of the hoe and the planting of garden vegetables (1977:48).

Because of his strict Protestant education during his five years at the Red River school, Spokan Garry became a life-long ardent anti-Catholic, and on 27 March 1873, wanting to further extend his convictions and proselytizing, he "wrote to [Reverend] Spaulding inviting him to visit Spokane 'to baptize his people and marry them according to laws'" (Garry 1873:np). He later cited:

> The most active and influential chief of the first five tribes [...] He is about fifty eight years old [...] He was at one time employed as Interpreter by Governor Stevens. He speaks English fluently, is quite intelligent, but has the reputation of being treacherous, and keeping a smart look out for the main chance (Avery 1956:17).

Winans described Garry as "strongly anti-Catholic and succeeded in keeping the Catholic priests from obtaining a foothold among the Middle and Lower Spokanes" (Drury 1976:244 fn). "Garry had preached bitterly against Catholicism and priests to the Flatheads. He never lost this sustained animus" (Burns 1966:183). Though Garry and his people "were not treated justly by the government and by many white settlers" (1925:100), he continued to work toward better Indian-white relations, making use of his respected honesty and oratory skills. At a two-day conference on that very topic, he spoke to Stevens:

> When you look at the red men, you think you have more heart, more sense, than these poor Indians. I think the difference between us and you Americans is in the clothing: the blood and body are the same. Do you think, because your mother was white and theirs dark, that you arc higher and better? We are dark, yet if we cut ourselves, the blood will be red, and so with the whites it is the same, though their skin is white, I do not think we are poor because we belong to another nation. If you take those Indians for men, treat them so now. If you talk to the Indians to make peace, the Indians will do the same to you. You see now the Indians are proud. On account of one of your remarks, some of your people have already fallen to the ground. The Indians are not satisfied with the land you gave them. What commenced the trouble was the murder of Pu-pu-mox-mox's son (by miners in California) and Dr. Whitman, and now their [Nez Perce] reservation [is] too small. If all those Indians had marked their own reservation, the trouble would not have happened. If you could get their reservation made a little larger, they would be pleased. If I had the business to do, I could fix it by giving them a little more land. Talking about land, I am only speaking my mind. What I was saying yesterday about not crossing the soldiers to this side of the Columbia is my business. The Indians have gone to war, and I don't know myself how to fix it up. That is your business! Since, governor [Stevens], the beginning of the world there has been war. Why cannot you manage to make peace? Maybe there will be no peace ever. Even if you hang all the bad people, war would begin again, and would never stop (Durham 1912, 1:208).

Apparently, after this lengthy meeting with Garry, Stevens believed this exchange with Garry:

> [...] dissipated at least for the time, the growing hostile feelings of the Spokanes, [... and] expressed friendly sentiments and willingly exchanged their fresh horse for the travel-jaded animal and an ever increasing competition among Euro-American Christian sects and denominations for Spokan souls was to bring intra-tribal disharmony (Thoms 1989:41).

The historian Deutsch discussed the comparative principles of animism and Christianity:

> [...] there is abundant evidence to establish the fact that the Indian was responsive to Christian tenets and that the native faith was not out of tune with the white man's creed. It is even more apparent that denominationalism, regardless of how essential it may be in a free society, not only militated against the Indian's integration into the Christian community but fragmented the ranks of the natives at the very time concerted action was essential in the struggle for their survival (1976:5).

Consequently, some missionaries understood the ambivalence, even conflict, among the Spokan and the various Christian sects—which caused some missionaries to relocate. For example, Drury provided the following account of Cowley, who moved to work with the Spokan in 1874: "Thus after twenty-six years, the Lower Spokanes again had a Protestant missionary but, to their disappointment, Cowley chose to live with the Middle Spokanes at Spokane Falls" (1976:501).

Some missionaries were exceptionally dedicated—notably Cowley, who eventually learned to speak Spokan after being posted to work and live with the Middle Spokans. He established "two [Protestant] missions; one in Spokane and one at Deep Creek" (*Spokane Daily Chronicle*, 1917), "approximately six miles below Deep Creek Falls, which was known as Indian Prairie" (Drury 1949:165). This small Indian community was nearly all Protestant, and later "suffered severely from the intimidations of their new white neighbors" (Deutsch 1956:47).

The Spokan group of nineteen families settled on fifteen acres at Deep Creek in 1878, under the leadership and guidance of the highly respected and acculturated Spokan chief, William Three Mountains (Lewis 1926:19). He once "was a member of the Elkanah Walker household" (Drury 1949:145), and was considered by all who knew him as "exceptionally Christian."

Cowley repeatedly wrote to government agent John B. Monteith of the Office of Indian Affairs, in 1875, urging the government to purchase farm equipment needed by the Spokan. Monteith, who always expressed great sympathy and support for Cowley's commitment to the Spokan, passed on Cowley's request, recommending:

> The Spokans are very much in need of some assistance in the way of Harness, Plows, Shovels, Axes, Hammers, Nails &c, to enable them to support themselves. If there is any money that could be used for such a purpose, I would respectfully recommend that Six hundred or Eight hundred dollars be expended in the purchase of such Agriculture implements and tools as may be needed to assist them in their efforts to live a civilized life. This people show such a willingness to help themselves that I think the Gov't. ought to assist them a little (Drury 1949:135).

In August 1879, the indefatigable Cowley wrote to the Indian Agent Charles D. Warner, requesting funding. His plea demonstrated his commitment—and that of many others—to the agricultural program and overall welfare of a people forcibly removed from their traditional land. He noted William Three Mountain's:

> [...] colony on Deep Creek have an exceptionally fine crop, but are anxious to have a school, and unless some provision is made for the permanent residence of a teacher among them they are liable to discouragement and abandonment of their enterprise. I have some difficulty in persuading them to have patience assuring them that Gov't will not desert them. They are very much in need of the scythes and cradles promised them last spring. How can they be had? (Drury 1949:166).

Despite Cowley's efforts, few monies were forthcoming, because of a previous arrangement whereby the Protestant bands of Spokan Indians (Anon. 1881:22) had been placed under the representation of Dr. Araron L. Lindsley, pastor of the First Presbyterian Church of Portland. Cowley had had an earlier (January 1872) disagreement with Lindsley, who essentially denied Cowley and another missionary from learning Nez Perce (Drury 1949:46). After nine years (1838-48), the American Board closed Tschimakain Mission.

Prior to the Catholic and Protestant missionaries, the early fur traders were responsible for introducing Christianity. Josephy stated:

> On the other hand, a Christian impact that led to a profound change throughout the area came eventually from Anglicans connected with the Hudson's Bay Company [...] By its 1821 license from the British government, the company had accepted a[n] obligation to provide for the religious instruction of natives within the territories it controlled (1965:82).

Ruby and Brown identified the major problem confronting the missionaries:

> While the missionaries wished to have the Indians accept their teachings, the former knew they would have to adapt their own efforts to the latter's modes of gaining a living. Tschimakain was the center of a circle whose radius extended sixty miles and included some two thousand souls, many of whom seldom broke out of the circle.

65

The Indians migratory patterns made it difficult to hold services in the various camps. Lying as it did between the camass [sic] grounds and the fisheries, the site of the mission had been wisely chosen (1986:66).

Reverend Walker wrote of his missionary efforts to convert the Indians at Tschimakain Mission to Christianity, and to convince them to adopt a sedentary lifestyle based on agriculture: "No influence, however, seems to be able to make agriculturalists of them, as they still pursue their hunting and fishing, evincing the greatest dislike to anything like manual labour" (Drury 1976:414). Walker continued to express his frustration with attempting to persuade the Spokan to plant crops and become farmers, forsaking their traditional foods: "One of the great hinderances [sic] to their settling & cultivating the soil will be their extreme fondness for their native roots. Give them as much food as you say & the best kind & they will not be contented unless they can have some of their native roots" (Drury 1976:114).

According to historian Robert Berkhofer, the early missionaries perceived the profound effects of further Anglo incursion, deculturation, and spiritual conversion of the Plateau peoples. He paraphrased certain philosophical assumptions tenaciously held by missionaries:

> Let then, missionary Institutions, established to convey to them the benefits of civilization and the blessings of Christianity, be efficiently supported; and with cheering hope, you may look forward to the period when the savage shall be converted into the citizen; mechanic; when the hunter shall be transformed into the mechanic; when the farm, the workshop, the School-house, and the Church shall adorn every Indian village; when the fruits of Industry, good order, and sound morals, shall bless every Indian dwelling; and when throughout the vast range of the country from the Mississippi to the Pacific, the red man and the white man shall everywhere be found, mingling in the same benevolent and friendly feelings, fellow citizens of the same civil and religious community, and fellow-heirs to a glorious inheritance in the kingdom of Emmanuel (Berkhofer 1965:10-11).

The influence of the missionary throughout the Interior Plateau was broad and deep:

> From the standpoint of physical contact, the missionaries had closer and more prolonged relations with the Indians than any other white except traders. Only these two groups lived constantly in the Indian villages. Even more important was the psychological concomitant of contact, for the missionaries demanded more change in the Indian way of life than any other whites. Most other Americans wanted only minor changes in Indian customs, but the missionaries sought nothing less than a revolution in social relations and basic values (Berkhofer 1965:106).

Unfortunately, these attitudes were explicitly held by the Board of Foreign Missions of the Presbyterian Church, who, from 1837 to 1893, sent four hundred missionaries to many Indian tribes:

> The rigid cultural assumptions [...] produced a near-absolute ethnocentrism, the intensity of which can only be suggested here. Missionary after missionary drove home the utter worthlessness of Indian ways. Indian religions, kinship system, living habits, patterns of subsistence, leadership, sex roles, styles of clothing—all were subjected to a barrage of denunciation in the stock evangelical vocabulary of heathenism and darkness. An almost paradoxical picture of Indian society emerges in which wild, sinful, self-willed men and women lived imprisoned by chiefs, customs and kin (Coleman 1980:45).

Justifiably, some Indians regarded Christianity as a threat to their way of life, because the missionaries, with few exceptions, never really understood or appreciated Indian culture or their *Weltanschauung*—particularly since the Christians were encouraging a sedentary way of life that would drastically alter the Indians' culture. Undoubtedly, some Indians greatly appreciated certain aspects of the white man's material culture. The Indians naturally associated the religion of the mercantilists with material benefits. Lt. Johnson, of the Wilkes expedition, noted how "The missionaries have succeeded in inducing many of the Spokane tribe of Indians to reside near them, which affords an opportunity of attending their temporal wants, as well as of giving then instruction" (Wilkes 1845, 4:456). But that same culture demanded that the Spokan forego a way of life predicated on hunting, gathering, and fishing—which ultimately contributed to the eventual destruction of their aboriginal culture.

Historical records do not show the full gamut of reactions of the Spokan to missionaries, and to their teachings and claims of miracles—certainly those of soul-saving and curing. Yet some Indians were perplexed by some Christian behaviors, namely vices. For example, in 1881, a Spokan chief complained of hypocrisy to Rev. George L. Deffenbaugh (which Coleman quoted): "'You put on long faces and worship God[.] Then turn around and steal, tell lies, drink whiskey, play cards, etc. - What good is your religion?'" (1985:44). As one elder said, "You *suyápi* pray only with your mouths, and long before horses, we used to pray with our heart."

The missionaries' intentions to convert the Indians to a sedentary lifestyle, involved making the Indians dependent upon a market economy and urban centers for acquiring farm and household goods, which are based on a monetary system. This, along with prevailing antagonistic attitudes by whites, greatly limited the logistics and movements of the Spokan away from traditional areas of subsistence. As a result, numerous eastern Plateau polyadic relationships were disrupted. Other harmful long-term factors included ever-increasing encroachment of Anglo agribusiness, as well as tribalization, the reservation system, and the accompanying religious and political factionalism (Ross 1967). At one time, "Religious bigotry and friction were so prevalent that the Protestant Spokanes kept aloft from the agency, and refused the scant government aid provided for them" (Cowley 1916:48). Prior to Anglo incursion, there was of course no religious factionalism within the Plateau. But once Christianity was reinforced, certain denominations received differential government support: "The Spokane tribe had been assigned to the Roman Catholic, even as the Nez Perces had been to the Presbyterians" (Drury 1949:133).

Settlers and Farmers

By the 1840s, the final phase of Anglo contact began with the arrival into the region of homesteaders, farmers, miners, and other settlers in great numbers. Their main objective was to realize the economic potential of the Plateau:

The trapper-trader wanted to exploit a resource of minor importance to the Indian, namely fur-bearing mammals. He required no permanent tracks of land. Nor did the missionary, who wanted to transform the inhabitants rather than the land itself. Furthermore, these early Whites were more dependent on and more personally involved with the Indian than the later arrivals who saw the Indian as an obstacle to the successful settlement of the region. The threat posed by the early Whites was minimal by comparison to that presented by the miner and homesteader, with their military adjuncts. The success of their enterprises depended upon removing the Indian from his aboriginal territory and placing him permanently on greatly reduced reservations (Ross 1967:43).

These ethnocentric attitudes are clearly reflected in the following statement by an early settler, which represents a philosophy of social Darwinism:

When we, the American emigrants, come into what the Indians claimed as their own country [Oregon Territory] we were considerable in numbers, and we came, not to establish trade with the Indians, but to take and settle the country exclusively for ourselves. Consequently, we went anywhere we pleased, settled down without any treaty or consultation with the Indians, and occupied our claims without their consent and without compensation [...] Every succeeding fall they found the white population about doubled, and our settlements continually extending, and rapidly encroaching more and more upon their pasture camas grounds (Burnett 1904, 4:97).

Introduced food-getting practices—mainly agriculture and cattle—eventually lead to an unfortunate deterioration of the environment, including the destruction of numerous types of needed off-reservation flora. Fish stocks were reduced by Euro-American commercial fishing and water contamination (Scholz *et al.* 1985). Even worse, the Spokans' access to what natural foods were left was terribly reduced: Firstly, confinement to a reservation greatly diminished their ability to fish. Secondly, the Spokan were restricted in mobility for deer hunting. Thirdly, they were often prohibited from visiting and harvesting from traditional roots fields. Even today, some off-reservation ranchers refuse to permit the few root-digging Spokan from visiting root fields. All of these unconscionable policies combined to force the Spokan to be largely dependent upon agriculture. Yet even in that regard they were much abused: "The Spokan lands are sandy, gravely, and badly calculated for agriculture" (DeSmet 1843:211). In essence, Euro-American agrarian reform undercut Indian access to traditional resources (Ross 1995h, 3:672).

Indian hunting of deer was restricted by encroaching white ranchers and farmers, few of whom ever gave permission for hunting or gathering. The locations and activities of white settlements had various damaging effects upon aboriginal fisheries. Commercial activities—such as mining, logging, livestock-raising, agriculture, and general modification of streams through blockage and divergence—wrought disastrous effects upon the fish populations (Ellis 1937; Scholz *et al.* 1985). Prior to this Anglo invasion, it is believed that fish constituted approximately fifty percent of the indigenous diet, based upon Walker's (1967:30; Schulz *et al.* 1985) critical analysis of mutual cross-utilization of anadromous and aquatic resources in the eastern Plateau. Given annual fish population fluctuations and cycles, this shows the importance of salmon to the local diet in pre-contact times (Hewes 1973). But in the historical period, the creation of dams for generating electric power and for irrigation, wrought immediately destructive and essentially permanent results.

Parker noted the economic potential of hydroelectric dams: "No country in the world furnishes better opportunities for water power to be applied to manufacturing purposes; every river and stream having falls, cascades and rapids" (1840:225-6). Dams became the primary factor in the large-scale decline and eventual demise of the once-tremendous production of fish in the area of the Lower, Middle, and Upper Spokan. By late 1935, construction of Grand Coulee Dam brought an ignominious and tragic end to all anadromous fishing by the Spokan on the Spokane River. "Grand Coulee Dam, 350 feet high, has eliminated at one stroke some 1200 miles of salmon streams in the upper Columbia Basin" (Hewes 1973:147). As an elder said of the dam's construction, "Your houses are filled with light, but our stomachs are now empty."

Drury, a dedicated scholar and historian of Spokan history, had great empathy for these people:

> The natives had not asked for the white men. The Indians found the white men cruel and heartless. With cold insistence upon legal rights, the white men staked out their homesteads on the Indians' favorite camas grounds; they built fences around the lush meadows where the deer were accustomed to graze; and constructed dams across the streams with but little consideration of the spawning habits of the fish. What did an Indian care about a mere quarter section of land when he was accustomed to roam at will throughout the whole country? Just why, why was it necessary to give up the age-old customs of hunting, fishing, and digging roots? (1949:164-5).

The gradual transition to agriculture and animal husbandry dramatically changed Spokan culture. Both the Coeur d'Alene and Spokan Indians proved adept and eager in pursing these new paradigms of subsistence, as attested by the Jesuit missionary Father Alexander Diomedi, S.J. (1843-1932):

> In 1881, I think it was, that little tribe [Coeur d'Alene] raised fifty thousand bushels of wheat and sixty thousand of oats [*Avena sativa* - *lewén*] besides poultry, vegetables, and swine. They hire white labor; frequently during harvest time several whites have been seen working for Indians for monthly wages. They hired a sawmill to provide the lumber for building frame houses, and they sawed over a million feet of it. Their roads are good, and over Latah's Creek they have built two substantial bridges. One piece of swampy ground has been drained, and bridged on several places with a corduroy road between, and all this is the fruit of their own labor without assistance from anyone [...] The help they have had from anybody is not worth mentioning (1978:79).

In Agent Winan's report of 1873, he stated how "Indian farmers who live among the whites cultivate their land much better, have better fences, and raise better crops than those [non-Indians] engaged in the same business surrounded by Indians" (1873:357). He requested that "the purchases and distributions be largely of agriculture implements, as one plow will do more toward civilizing these Indians and making them self-sufficient than five hundred blankets" (Winans 1873:357).

Unfortunately, in some instances these agricultural practices devastated several extensive root fields that aboriginally had proved critical to the Spokan subsistence base. For instance:

> The callous settler busily broke the sod while the redmen stalked along the furrows, noting the destruction of the grass and muttering threats. It was a situation destined to recreate the recent troubles and prompt action was required. Lou Magers, abetted by son Bill and several neighbors, formed a delegation that called on this settler,

offering him the choice of paying the Indian couple a sum that met their approval or moving off, with or without assistance from the delegation (Reimers 1993:4)

Some whites commented upon the destruction of the root fields (Franchère 1854:270). However, the effects of the plow upon the Spokan subsistence base was far exceeded in damage by first religious and then political factionalism among the peoples of the Interior Plateau (Ross 1968). Also, sustained white encroachment within the Plateau proportionally increased the damage caused by the socioeconomic and political policies of the Euro-Americans. As French summarized, "The categories of Whites who were of the greatest significance during this period in the following order: (1) Lewis and Clark's party, 1805-6; (2) fur traders of the nineteenth century; (3) missionaries of the 1830's and after; and (4) immigrants or settlers" (1961:349).

Miners

Prior to military intrusion and established army posts, in the 1840s, the final phase of Euro-American contact began with the arrival of miners—including Chinese immigrants—and settlers in relatively large numbers. Though Cook failed to discuss the often severe relations the Chinese had with the whites, he did mention their relationship with the Indians, and how:

[...] 500 to 700 Chinamen mining on the Columbia River [...] as high as the mouth of the Spokane River [...] have been greatly interrupted and annoyed for several years past. So great has been the devilment done by the Savages that many have been driven from their work and out of the territory (1925:27 fn).

Some of the white miners and settlers had retired or been discharged early from the military or, in time, the Bureau of Indian Affairs. Their goals differed considerably from their predecessors (the explorers and trapper-traders). Resources sought by the settlers were timber, fish, minerals, water, establishment of orchards, and procurement of farm and grazing lands—all of which were exploited with success, but required permanent settlements and the acquisition of vast tracts of Indian lands, which limited indigenous exploitation of traditional sources of food and water. There was "a time when Indians could homestead the same as white settlers, if they could pay the filing fee. Some [Spokan] families stayed and worked with colony members; others more independent claimed land near springs of surface ponds" (Reimers 1993:6).

After acquiring lands, the settlers hoped to maintain peaceful relations with the soon-to-be disposed Indians. By government decree and use of the military, sometimes involving armed conflict, settlers and miners successfully implemented these various enterprises—removing by force the indigenous inhabitants and placing them on considerably smaller and poorly-located reservations with land often ill-fit for agriculture.

One of the main causes that precipitated warfare between the Indians and whites was the 1850 Land Donation Act, by which "married women were allowed to own their own land on their names" (Luttrell 1994:7.2). This served to increase uncontrolled Euro-American encroachment by miners and other settlers upon the lands of the Spokan and other Indians:

A rush of white gold miners to Colville in 1856 (?) and later, without any regard to Indian authority and rights in the country, made the Spokan and others resentful. They had not yet received any payments for their surrendered lands and no reserves had been set apart for them. They believed that the whites were playing them false and that the treaties and agreements meant nothing. By 1858 they had become of the strong opinion that the whites did not intend to keep their promises. In that year the Spokan and Coeur d'Alene made an alliance for defense and war (Teit 1930:369).

Chalfant noted how the "incursion of miners in Colville and the military expeditions of Colonel Steptoe, resulted in the war between American forces and the Spokane, Coeur d'Alene and other group[s] of the Plateau in 1858" (1974:163). While in the Colville area photographing and collecting ethnographic data, Curtis became aware of local history and the existing conflict between the Indians and the whites whose mining, agriculture, and orchard claims displaced many of the indigenous population and limited access to traditional resources. The astute Curtis wrote, "One of the immediate causes of the outbreak was connected with the discovery of gold in the Colville district in northeastern Washington, by which a sudden swarm of prospectors was attracted to that quarter. Inevitably there was friction with the Indians" (1911, 7:57).

With the "rediscovery" of Curtis in the 1960s, he sadly gained some non-Indian critics, including anthropologists (Makepeace 2000), and even one of his descendants, Marianne Wiggins (2007:11), who in a biography was critical of his accomplishments. This is also true of some anthropologists who still deprecate his "staged" photographs, without which we would be devoid of considerable ethnographic and photographic data.

In the Spokan territory, there was some mineral exploration, and by 1902 Congress permitted exploration and claims for minerals on the Spokane Indian Reservation. Fortunately, there was little subsequent mining, likely because there is no record of any such mining ventures being profitable, despite accounts of stream deposits of gold being found. Yet intense gold and silver mining was conducted for many years to the east, in the Coeur d'Alene area, as well as to the north in the Colville area. As late as the mid-1960s, there were several accounts of how in the late 1800s, an unknown number of Chinese mined and panned for gold on the southern and western edge of the present Spokane Indian Reservation. As testament to the influx and residence of Chinese miners, there are remains of at least one unmarked Chinese cemetery on the Spokane reservation (Ross 1993). Elders recalled their grandparents saying how honest the Chinese were in any of their dealings.

With the later usage of nuclear energy, exploration for uranium became a public issue on the Spokane reservation—particularly along a once-traditionally used section of *Blue Creek* ($q^{w}i\?q^{w}iy\acute{a}tk^{w}$ or $q^{w}i\?q^{w}iy\'etk^{w}$ or *snur'ur'šictn* - "blue water"). In the early spring of 1954, two Spokan brothers—Jim and John Lebret—using a Geiger counter, discovered radioactive autunite, a secondary uranium-bearing mineral (Ruby and Brown 1982:281). The original location of uranium was not on tribal land, as was erroneously thought, but on allowed land (Galbraith and Arnold Wynecoop, pers. comm.). The main part of the mine was located on eighty acres of the Boyd allotment, called Midnite Mine. By 1955, three more promising deposits were discovered, and by 1957 a non-tribal mining company (Newmont) joined with Midnite Mine to form Dawn Mining Company. Newmont owned fifty-one percent of the stock, and the original Midnite retained the rest. By 1957, three additional deposits were discovered, and two more large ore deposits of coffinite and uranium. From 1957 to 1967, the mine was profitable. However, in 1989, it was proposed that the tribe itself extract and manage the ore, but Spokane Agency Superintendent Jim Stevens rebuffed the sound advice and experience of Glen Galbraith and Claire Wynecoop. Unfortunately, these mineral discoveries led to many years of acrimonious conflict within the tribe as to ownership and distribution of profits (Galbraith, pers. comm.). Because of chronic intertribal dispute, plus the Three Mile Island catastrophe, the demand for uranium declined, which forestalled further development of uranium mining on the reservation.

Military

Although not known as an aggressive people (Ray 1939:35), the Spokan did conduct warfare, particularly when venturing forth onto the Plains for bison and, later, against "intrusion by the Hudson's Bay Company, the Walker and Eells Mission, the U.S. Army at Fort Spokane, and the Henry Cowley Protestant Mission" (Chance *et al.* 1981:131). There are numerous accounts of the Spokan engaging in warfare with other indigenous groups and with Euro-Americans (Nesmith 1858; Owen 1858; Mullan 1861; Dunn 1886; Manring 1912; Teit 1930; Elmendorf 1935-6; Chalfant 1974). Of the three aboriginal Spokan macro bands, the Lower Spokan were presumably more peaceful than the warlike Middle and Upper Spokan (Ruby and Brown 1982:125), who frequently joined forces, both before and after white first contact.

The encroachments by miners and settlers continued, and ultimately led to armed conflict. In 1858, the first military engagement on the Spokane Plains occurred when the United States Army defeated a mixed group of approximately one thousand Coeur d'Alene, Palouse, and Spokan—who were not parties to the Walla Walla Treaties. Some have called this well-documented (Hunt 1966) battle "The Coeur d'Alene War":

[...] an army column numbering 150 men commanded by Lt. Col. Edward J. Steptoe left Fort Walla Walla for Colville, Idaho, to investigate reports of Indian conflicts in the area and to satisfy miners' demands for army protection. Steptoe anticipated this would be an exercise in simply impressing the enemy, and so he failed to equip his column for serious trouble. He was apparently unaware of Indian anger at the development of the Missouri-Columbia Road, over which his command was now marching (Keenan 1997:50).

When Steptoe met the much larger Indian force, who angrily demanded that Wright should leave the area, he agreed. But during his withdrawal, Indian attackers forced the army to take defensive positions on Steptoe Butte—an area near Rosalia, Washington. The army of 570 regular troops, 100 packers, and thirty Nez Perce guides and interpreters were equipped with the new rifled muskets, which had an effective range of 400 m. The Army also had two horse-drawn field mountain howitzers. Yet Wright failed to subdue the attackers. Realizing his predicament, Wright and his command managed to escape during the night and return to Fort Walla Walla. Learning of Wright's defeat, the area commander, Brigadier General Newman Clarke, was "furious over the humiliating incident, [and] promptly directed Colonel George Wright to launch a reprisal campaign against the tribes involved. 'You will make their punishment severe,' Clark instructed Wright" (Keenan 1997:50). He did just that, by hanging seventeen Indians at *Latah Creek* (*sntuʔtʔulim*), after which the Indians agreed to return to their reservations.

An early account of this tragic conflict is given by Lord, who failed to mention the horror that confronted each Indian before he was hung: the belief that his breath-spirit would never properly leave his body, and that he would always wander as a ghost:

This large tribe had been carefully crippled by Colonel Wright, previously spoken of as commanding the United States troops at Walla Walla. The [approximately 1000] Indians made a cowardly attack on some unarmed dragoons exercising their horses. Colonel Wright, in retaliation, marched into their stronghold, and after a brief skirmish, routed them, taking several of the leaders prisoners, and with them a celebrated chief. These were all hung where the fight took place. Then all of the Indians horses that could be collected were driven together by order of the Colonel and shot; 700 were thus killed; three days were occupied in shooting the poor beasts down. I state the fact as it was told to me (Lord 1866, 2:157).

A sad postscript to Wright's devastating and demoralizing retaliation, was reported later by Oliphant:

The spirit of the Spokanes was broken when Colonel Wright came to punish them for the Steptoe massacre, and had subdued them after shooting down 900 head of their horses at one time. They never got over that, and kept out of all the subsequent wars.

The old men of the Spokanes used to tell me about their former condition of happiness and prosperity, and the tears would run down their cheeks. Before the coming of Wright, they said, they had been well fixed, with plenty of horses and much wealth. Now they were poor and unhappy (1927:123)

A detailed and unusually objective account of the military encounter with the Spokan and later military occupation by the U.S. Army, is contained in the reports of Winans (1873;15-22), which interestingly question Wright's reasons and even procedures involving the Spokan.

Spokane Indian Reservation

The 1850 Homestead Act permitted settlers to occupy and claim land where Indians lived, creating further tensions and armed conflict. "Indian lands reached a peak of 150,000,000 acres in 1873" (La Farge 1940:30). Later, under the Indian Homestead Act (3 March 1875), Indians were permitted to improve individual sections of land by farming or grazing—thus severing tribal control. But this legislation also opened Indian land to white encroachment. Even as late as 1889, Indian lands were being illegally confiscated by the Northern Pacific Railroad. Gibbs foresaw that many problems, for both Indian and white, would result from the taking of Indian land:

No conventional arrangements strictly so speaking, are known which need action on the part of the government; but the assurance has everywhere been given by the whites, settling among the Indian tribes, that Congress would compensate them for the lands taken. Those among whom establishments have been made for any length of time, finding themselves crowded out of their houses, and first dwindling away, ask often when the promise will be fulfilled, for they have but a little time left to employ it, and they leave no children behind. Distrust thus attaches to the country, and the advance of settlement into new districts is looked upon with suspicion (1855, 1:423).

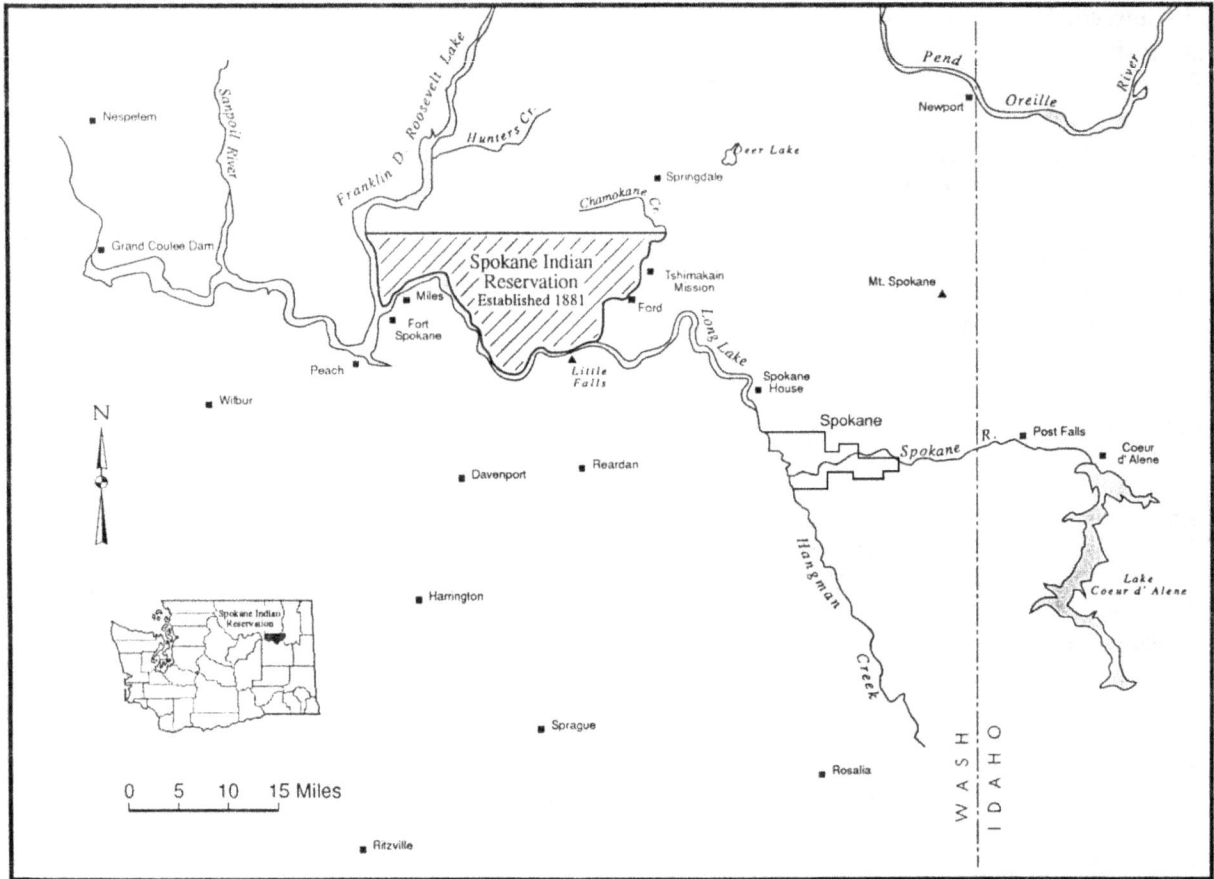

Figure 11. Spokane Indian Reservation

Haines, when writing of the numerous Indian problems of acculturation, contended that "Some groups have worked to exterminate the Indian people, while others have tried to assimilate them. Some say we should teach them to be like the white man, others want to keep the remnants of the tribes as separate cultural entities" (1955:203). Davenport, the Umatilla Indian Agent, stated that Indians were "put upon reservations, where goods and rations are occasionally doled out to them, for the reason that it is cheaper to do that than to fight them" (1907:5).

One of the early settlers, a homesteader during the late 1800s, commented on the problem of the Spokan retaining their traditional territorial rights:

In early days, an Indian had about as little chance of hanging onto a homestead of good land in a white settlement as a snowball has of remaining unmelted in the devil's capital. None of us in those days thought that an

Indian had any rights that a white man was bound to respect. We all thought that we had a superior right to the lands to any claim that the Indian had or could make. A great deal of the best land around here was actually wrestled from the Indians. They had lots of land and naturally when they wanted to cultivate a little garden or a small field of grain they picked out the best lands, where their truck [crops] would grow with the least risk of crop failure and the least effort to themselves. These, naturally, were the places the white men picked out. The Indians didn't know anything about the homestead laws and regulations and no one was anxious to put them wise. There were always little technicalities which one could raise against the Indians claim with a good prospect of winning out against the Indian in the land office, in case he showed fight and persisted in trying to hang on to the land wanted. Looking back, it is possible that we weren't always quite fair to these Indians (Lewis 1925:12-13).

Despite the aforesaid grievous actions of Governor Stevens, on 16 September 1854 he advocated some constructive principles the government should exercise in determining Indian policy. Coan, when speaking of the reservation policy in the Northwest, cited those proposals:

- The aim is to prepare the Indians to become citizens of the United States.
- The reservations should be good lands and "allow each head of a family a homestead."
- "The Indians should be supplied with farms to instruct them in agriculture."
- "Many bands should be concentrated on one reservation in order that the control of government over them might be more easily effected."
- "The Indians should not be excluded from the fisheries and hunting grounds."
- "The authority of the chiefs of the tribes should be increased so that they could be held responsible to the government for the conduct of their bands" (1922:14-5).

Coan's research of government reservation policies led him to conclude that even those who had worked with Indian people failed to properly understand the emotional significance of Anglo policies. The plan of concentrating the Indians was probably the best, but difficult to effect without the use of force, as Stevens must have known. In the previous year, while among the Pend d'Oreille, he learned of the Jesuit missionaries' attempts to persuade the Indians to move to a better region, and their refusal to leave because of ancestral ties to their own country (Coan 1922:14-5).

The conflict with Steptoe and Wright exacerbated tensions between the Spokan and the military-backed settlers. After Wright's 1858 defeat of the Spokan and their allies, negotiations began for establishing a Spokane Indian Reservation, but with no success, because "between November 1854 and January 1856, fifteen treaties were made which extinguished the Indian title to all of the Pacific Northwest except southwestern Washington, the Okanogan, Spokane, Coeur d'Alene region and the Snake" (Coan 1922:14-5).

In the 1880s, encouraged by the Indian Removal Act of 1830, settlers migrated in increasing numbers to remaining Indian lands, determined in 1873 to be approximately 150,000,000 acres. Though not immediately affecting the Spokan, the following policy and rationalization would in time:

> As with the removal policy, ethical justification was soon found for the enactment of laws which would reduce the Indian land holdings and also achieve the new objective of the rapid assimilation of the Indian. A popular theme, the white man's burden to uplift native people, was given a theoretical base by interpretations of Darwin's view of the evolution of man and Spencer's of the evolution of society (Hass 1957:12).

Prior to the establishment of the *Spokane Indian Reservation* (*sqelixʷulexʷ*), a large tract of land in Idaho was set aside on 8 November 1873 as a reserve for the Coeur d'Alene, the southern Spokan (Upper Spokan), and other Indians. The area, according to Royce, included the upper reaches of Latah Creek, an area originally claimed by the "Coeur d'Alenes, the Southern Spokane who had two villages on Latah creek in Washington [...] and villages extending east along Spokane river as far as Dishman" (1899:866-9). Later, some Spokan did take up residence on the Coeur d'Alene Indian Reservation, remaining as enrolled Spokan after the establishment of the Spokan Reservation. The Coeur d'Alene "admitted about one hundred Spokane Indians as enrolled members of the Coeur d'Alene Tribe" (Palmer 2001:44).

Spokane Garry, chief of the Middle and Upper Spokan, was not only responsible for bringing Christianity to the Plateau (Miller 2003:112), but was key in the creation of the present Spokane Indian Reservation (Drury 1949:166):

> With the dissolution of his tribe and loss of their lands to white settlers, [Garry] became anxious to secure a reservation for the Spokane. With the expected arrival of the Northern Pacific Railroad creating incentives on both sides [...] Garry's eloquence was a factor in convincing the government of the legitimacy of the Spokane Indian's claim for adequate territory (Nicandri 1986:89).

In 1887, Spokane Garry and 92 tribal headmen ceded their aboriginal territory of approximately 3,140,000 acres to the United States for a total sum of $95,000, or thirty-three cents per acre. That pittance was then greatly reduced by an executive order, signed on 18 January 1881 by President R. B. Hayes (Kappler 1904-1941, I:924-925). It set aside 154,898 acres of so-called public land for the Spokan, thereby establishing the Spokane Indian Reservation in 1892 by government ratification, with a loss of 164,898 acres:

> It is hereby ordered that the following tract of land, situated in Washington Territory, be, and the same is hereby, set aside reserved land for the use and occupancy of the Spokane Indians, namely: Commencing at a point where Chemakane [sic] Creek crosses the forty-eight parallel of latitude; thence down the east bank of said creek to where it enters the Spokane River; thence across said Spokane River westwardly along the southern bank thereof to a point where it enters the Columbia River; thence across the Columbia River, northwardly along its western bank to a point where said river crosses the said forty-eight parallel of latitude; thence east along said parallel to the place of beginning (Kappler 1913, 1:570, 754, I:925).

A major problem in establishing this reservation was the division between those Spokan who were—even nominally—Catholic or Protestant. A majority of Catholic Spokan, particularly of the Upper Spokan, "refused to go to the new reserve and instead remained on the outskirts of the rapidly growing village of Spokane" (Deutsch 1956:45). The Lower Spokan moved onto the newly formed Spokane Reservation in 1881. "The Lower Spokan are now Protestants, the rest are Catholics. They formerly owned the whole basin of Spokane river in Washington and extended into Idaho. They are now on [the] Spokane reservation in Washington and the Coeur d'Alene reservation in Idaho, and number in all about 900 or 1,000" (Mooney 1896:732).

Initially, the Spokane Indian Reservation was "considered by Simms and others the lower Spokan reservation" (Chalfant 1974:79), since the Upper and Middle Spokan bands had not signed the agreement of 1877, and remained living off the reservation until 18 March 1877, when the Upper and Middle Spokan ceded "all right, title and claims which they now have, or ever had, to any and all lands lying outside of the Indian Reservations in Washington and Idaho territories, and hereby agree to remove to and settle upon the Coeur d'Alene reservation in the territory of Idaho" (Kappler 1904-41:446, 449, 453).

The reservations created many difficulties, and renewed public concern over the welfare and rights of Indians on reservations, since many non-Indians demanded full citizenship and the right to own their now-designated land, and to achieve acculturation by encouraging the Indians to give up their traditional ways and beliefs (Haines 1950:211). To achieve these objectives, the government passed the Dawes Act (8 February 1887), or General Allotment Act, which was in effect from 1887 to 1934, and gave each enrolled tribal member title to reservation land as private property, in the hope that the new owners would improve their economic situation by pursuing farming or grazing. "The head of a family was to be allotted 80 acres of agriculture land or 160 acres of grazing land; and a single person over eighteen or an orphan child under eighteen, one-half of this amount" (Haas 1957:13). These so-called "surplus" lands "were then opened for homesteading and were paid for at $2.50 per acre, as and when the lands were taken up by homesteaders" (Haas 1957:13). As one would expect, the "Dawes Act did not solve the Indian problem" (Haines 1950:211).

> Thus the suspicion expressed in the Dawes Act. The General Allotment Act's safeguards to protect and preserve the Nations' Americans' last remaining birthright failed most Indians [...] When Congress repealed the General Allotment Act in 1934, Indians were in possession of less than one third of their original allotted lands (Gibson 1980:506-7).

Ultimately, the suspicion expressed in the Dawes Act Minority Report was confirmed: Truly the General Allotment Act's "real aim [was] to get at the Indians' land and open them to settlement" (Gibson 1980:507). This legislation was intended to turn Indians into models of Euro-American productive land-owners, along the lines of Hick's Peaceable Kingdom—a concept promulgated by the prominent Quaker Edward Hicks to maintain peaceful relations with Indians by treating them with respect. Unfortunately, Zimmerman, Commissioner of Indian Affairs from 1933 to 1970, believed, "The whole history of the legislation is another example of what John Collier has called the 'bi-lateral mutually consulting, contractual nature' of the government-Indian relationship" (1957:32). Collier also stressed the "real solution was not to tear down the tribal ties and the community property system but to build them up" (Haines 1950:211).

Farming and raising cattle in the Northwest, despite the legality of the Dawes Act, created insurmountable logistical difficulties for many Indians, including the Spokan:

> This is a fact; however heartless it may be. To say that the Indians who were put upon these reservations got little enough for what they gave up is to utter a truth that is practically unimportant. In the long run, the white man, not the Indians, determined what was just for the Indians. Accordingly, the Indians retained, willingly or not, only so much lands as the white men were willingly to keep (Oliphant 1950, 1:53).

Between 1880 and 1890, the failure of the Office of Indian Affairs to protect Indian reservation land from encroachment by ruthless non-Indian cattlemen, drastically reduced the allotted Indian land in eastern Washington, leaving only 3,777,820 acres (Oliphant, 1950, 1:43; 1:58).

The plan failed when the government sold Indian land to whites—land forbidden to Indians, thereby "further decreasing Indian land" (Garbarino and Sasso 1994:43). Even as late as 1902, both the Colville and the Spokan shared a government agency. The annual report from the Indian Agent Albert Anderson delineates some of the problems confronting the Spokan as well as the various groups on the Colville Indian Reservation, and which until recently continued through litigation:

> [...] the Spokane Indians who are territorially and otherwise comparatively poor, seem to be in danger of losing a large part of their reservation. This is the result of an act passed by the last Congress which provided land comprised in the reservation shall be thrown open to mineral location and entry after the Indians shall have received allotments in land severalty. At least on the face of the facts it would seem that the Indians are fully protected until they shall receive such allotments [...] (Anderson 1903:334)

After the allotment survey in 1916, the importance of the Columbia River to contiguous Indian groups—including the Spokan on the Spokane River—was recognized by Clair Hunt, chief government surveying agent: "It [the Columbia] is of great use to the Indians. It brings them fish and waterfowl for food and every year distributes an endless variety of driftwood along its banks now used for fuel, fences and buildings" (1916a:n.p.).

During the late 1800s, numerous Spokan individuals and families assumed residence in other Salish-speaking reservations. In 1893, "the Flathead, Pend d'Oreille, and Kootenai leaders agreed to allow the removal to the Flathead Reservation [... of] over 100 Spokanes" (Malouf 1998:308). In 1907, the Bureau of Indian Affairs gave full agency status to the 600 Spokan (Ross 1994; Ross 1995b). In 1924, Congress approved the Citizenship Act (43 Stat. 253), giving citizenship to all on- and off-reservation Indians who were twenty-one years and older, and "enfranchised them for federal elections. Most states soon after gave Indians the vote" (Garbarino and Sasso 1994:435). The Citizenship Act for Native Americans was partially in response to the heroic service of many Indian veterans in World War I.

Yet myths about Indian citizenship persisted into the 1950s:

> One of the oldest living legends in American life is the idea that Indians are not citizens. Behind this legend lie two popular fallacies: the idea that Indians are wards under the guardianship of the Great White Father, and the idea that a ward cannot be a citizen or, at least cannot exercise the rights of citizenship. Both these ideas are mistaken (Cohen 1953:8).

The reservation consisted of 154,898 acres, but a joint congressional resolution was passed in 1902 to allot the reservation. The Secretary of the Interior "was authorized to sell unallotted surplus lands in 1908, and was opened for homestead entry in 1909. The Middle and Upper Spokane signed an agreement in 1887, ratified in 1892, to be removed to the Coeur d'Alene Reservation" (Lahren 1998a:494). After the establishment and settling of the Spokan Indians (and others) within the boundaries, Durham wrote:

> It saddens me to think of the way the American people treated the Indians. They drove them from their hunting grounds, they cheated them and despoiled them and finally cooped them up on the reservation. The white man brought them disease, and drink, which cut them down faster than they were killed in war (1912, 1:123).

Government and Mission Schools

In later years, only a few elderly Spokan men and woman were knowledgeable of their language, ethnomedicine, and ethnobotany—mostly because they had never attended an off-reservation government or missionary school. Most elders who had been sent off-reservation as children, deeply regretted not being socialized by parents, grandparents, and older siblings, who had remained at home. Egesdal (pers. comm.) summarized how "the boarding schools separated an effective didactic method of learning oral history. One such elderly woman who was forced to attend the government school Chemawa, said how formal schooling had, 'Taken away from me my roots and memories of freedom.'" From the very beginning:

> [...] the Indian boarding school was an Anglo-American machine, designed to consume, remold, and temper young Indians and to create Christian yeoman. As part of the government's assimilation efforts, off-reservation boarding schools were especially damaging to Indian cultures, often separating children for years from their families and tribes (Reddick and Collins 2000:442-443).

The first of two attempts to establish schooling for Indians in the Inland Empire was undertaken by Spokane Garry, and later reported by Winans (1871:292-5). However, Coleman believed that "The Protestants supported the public education system free from sectarian control" (1985:44).

Construction of the first mission day school among the Spokan commenced on 22 December 1841, by the Walkers, who erected a tule mat pole structure, with a fireplace and adobe chimney. It also served as a *place of (snłq'ilštn)* worship.

Prior to establishing a schoolhouse at Spokane Falls in 1875, Cowley first taught Indian students in a "long lodge," using a few government-furnished primers. His first students were children, parents, and even some grandparents, using an effective pedagogical technique—one that helped him learn Spokan. In his assessment, "Considering the difficulties we had to contend with, they made rapid progress. They wanted to start the lessons [at] daybreak and keep up the instruction until dark" (Durham 1912, 1:109).

As a young girl, Cowley's daughter, Grace, once wrote a perceptive and understanding article entitled "Indians at School," saying how the Indian students had not:

> [...] behaved in school any better than we do, for they pinched, whispered and stuck pins through the cracks of the door and pricked people on the other side. Just normal humanity, perhaps more keen eyed, more sensitive to sound, but with a finer sense of humor, as they understand it, than the white people (Drury 1949:137).

Cowley was very concerned about the welfare of Indian children, and was troubled that only a few Spokan girls attended his classes: "Like all ignorant people these natives hold their women to be inferiors and their education is not regarded as essential" (Drury 1949:140-1).

Every early spring and summer, at the mission and some government schools, the attendance of both Indian boy and girl students ceased due to the demands of their parents, when the children helped to dismantle the tipis and move to resource areas to pursue food-getting activities. Apparently this problem was not so severe with the establishment of Camp Spokane by John Clarke of the Pacific Fur Company in the fall of 1880 (Peltier 1990:3), which was located at the confluence of the Spokane and Columbia Rivers—in an area once known by the Spokan as *č'łyaq'*. According to Sperlin:

> [Clarke] had [the] daring to establish Fort Spokane alongside the Spokane House that David Thompson's men had built two years before the North-West Company. This opportunity led to a very lively trade war, which was certainly not diminished when the United States that same year, 1812, declared war on Great Britain (1917, 8:104).

Another explanation for Camp Spokane was that the site remained as a camp until 1882, when the Army established it as Fort Spokane—after being first suggested by Lt. Col. Henry Clay Merriam. It was the last frontier army post in the Pacific Northwest, and was maintained as a garrison until 1899. On 2 April 1900, the fort was abandoned, because the Indian Service chose the buildings as a favorable site for a federal boarding school (Kappler 1913). The War Department turned the facility over to the Department of the Interior for the establishment of an Indian boarding school for Colville and Spokan children, under the direction of the Indian Service. The buildings were occupied by employees of the Colville Indian board, while the school superintendent lived in the former post commander's residence (Gilbert 1984:18-19). Once opened, the boarding school accommodated approximately two hundred Indian children per year. It was closed in 1908, largely because of a decline in Indian enrollment and increasing government expenses. Some Spokan children were sent to on- and off-reservation schools elsewhere.

In 1889, a federal boarding school opened at Fort Spokane. The Bureau of Indian Affairs, prior to its director John Collier and the New Deal (Collier 1938), sought to change the indigenous sociopolitical system of the Spokan and other Amerindian groups by promoting tribalization, agrarian reform, mission and government schooling, and missionization—all to bring these peoples out of the *vacuum domicilium* (wilderness). Collier "held that the real solution was not to tear down tribal ties and the community property system, but to build them up" (Gunther 1950:211). But the government's primary goal, to "'break down the prejudices of tribe among the Indians; to blot out the boundary lines which divide them into distinct nations, and fuse them into one homogenous mass'—was not met as the assimilationists had planned" (Reddick 2000:464).

Earlier government policies invariably lead to the destabilization and deculturation of indigenous peoples by enforcing monogamy, forbidding the use of "native" language and religion, implementing compulsory schooling, and eventually the appropriation and fencing of land to discourage the further pursuit of a traditional annual subsistence round. Collier (1938), however, continued his new policy to proclaim the principle of religious freedom, by forbidding forced attendance of boarding school students at Christian services, halting the sale of allotted Indian lands, canceling debts against tribal treasuries, and abolishing the ineffectual Board of Indian Commissioners. He viewed Spokan autonomy as important:

> Indians were to be trained to handle offices and agencies. Promising students were to be encouraged in suitable professions and vocations. The system [became the] property of the tribe. Additional tribal land could be purchased, and government loan funds were made available to aid in establishing the new plan (Gunther 1950:211).

By 1910, despite government and mission schooling, of the 512 Indians aged ten and over living on the Spokane Reservation, 38 could not speak English (Reddy, 1993:188). Twice as many women were non-English speakers—reflecting the occurrence and necessity of men pursuing off-reservation employment. Resident women, in most families, maintained the Spokan language and traditional roles of gathering foods and meeting domestic needs. With many men absent, matrifocality was critical to the care and enculturation of children, as well as care of the elderly. Among the Spokanes, "a man marrying out of his own tribe joins that of his wife, because she can work in a country to which he is accustomed, and in the same nation all the household goods were considered the wives' property" (Bancroft 1875, 1:14; Edwards 1900:14).

Aside from the dire effects of infection and parasites contracted by many Indian children while attending boarding and mission schools, even more damaging was the derogatory and deterministic attitudes of many government employees. An example is Mr. C. E. Hale, Superintendent of Indian Affairs in Washington Territory, who instituted a project that Captain John Mullan endorsed:

> This is to take the children and educate them under a proper system; for it is as difficult to mould the ideas and acts of an Indian, after he has passed the age of twenty-one, as it is those of his white neighbor; and it is only by taking the children, and rescuing them from sloth, ignorance, and savage propensities, that any decided improvement can be attained (1863:50).

Chapter III: Social and Political Organization

Social Organization

For most Indian groups of the Interior Salish, their sociopolitical organizations have been termed "tribes." Yet, strictly speaking, they were not tribes, but rather groupings of composite macro bands sharing the same language and territory—often without strict central political authority (Ross 1991:5.28). Bands were ethnocentric composites of kin-related residence groups that shared a common living site, namely, a winter residence. Their populations annually expanded and contracted to optimize their ongoing subsistence quest, and were typically composed of 50 to 250 people. These hunting and gathering societies had to develop a flexible form of sociopolitical organization—one whose internal and external socioeconomic relationships adapted to seasonally variable environments.

After adopting the horse complex, and prior to Euro-American contact, the Flathead Group and the Sahaptian-speaking Nez Perce had sustained contact with the western Plains tribes, whose sociopolitical structures began to change. But for the Spokan, a sociopolitical structure of autonomous macro bands persisted until they were prevented from utilizing off-reservation resources and were further disenfranchised by being confined to on-reservation land allotments.

Prior to Euro-American contact, the two primary facets of Spokan social life were religion and kinship. Religion became estranged from traditional beliefs with missionization, resulting in a syncretic belief system that combined elements of the old and the new. This belief system became further factionalized as the Upper Spokan subscribed to Catholicism, while the Middle and Lower Spokan tended to subscribe to Protestantism. The traditional obligations and rights of kinship were greatly altered when some Spokan went to the Colville, Kalispel, or Coeur d'Alene Reservations—resulting in more off-reservation residence. Christianity, with Christ as the authority figure, replaced the institution of patripotestal persuasion and concomitant obligation. As a result, some contemporary Spokan use abbreviated kin terms for *grandparents* (*t'pt'upye?*), but nowadays mostly use Euro-American designations.

Kinship

The most complete study and explanation of Spokan *kinship* (*ntméw'stn* or *n'ełnasqelix*[w] or *n'al'uye?* - "person's relatives") was made by Elmendorf, who claimed the original proto-Salish:

> [...] was of neither lineal nor bifurcate collateral type, but developed into two types in coastal and interior regions, respectively, as a result of linguistic and cultural separation of the proto-Salish community [...] Proto-Salish terminology was of linear type, which has been preserved among coastal groups, while Interior Salish peoples have innovated in developing bifurcate collateral terminologies (Elmendorf 1961, 4:367).

The Spokan had a type of bilateral descent (Elmendorf 1961, 1965), yet they also recognized a definite patripotestal system. That is, privileges and decisions were exercised by the husband, at least publicly. When speaking of the Spokan kinship descent system, in a more universal and comparative analysis, Elmendorf concluded that the Spokan were like the Nez Perce and Okanogan, but differed from the northern Plateau Salish of the Shuswap, Thompson, and Lillooet. The last were similar to coastal systems, which are consistently lineal, rather than bifurcate collateral (as all southern Plateau systems seem to be, Salish and Sahaptian). Yet these southern Interior Salish systems shared fundamental features with those of Coast Salish groups. There is systematic and linguistic evidence that the Coastal systems were derived from earlier ones like the southern Interior Salish ones (Elmendorf 1963:46).

The social organization of the aboriginal Spokan remained bilateral in descent, whereby an individual considered all of his or her kinspeople as extended kin. An individual recognized both maternal and paternal kinspeople with relatively equal responsibility and reciprocal claim. But there was some emphasis on "patripotestal authority," whereby one felt a greater socioeconomic allegiance to one's patrilineal kinspeople. After marriage, a woman often took residence with her husband's people (patrilocal), though neolocation of residence did occur when the newly-married couple lived away from both families.

Patrilocal residence was favored due to male-oriented fishing and hunting groups, especially as hunting required intimate knowledge of the terrain and resource areas. Also, strong male affiliations were based upon the sweathouse complex and the mutual sharing of a hunting-decoying language. Women's knowledge of plant availability was general within the Southern Plateau, and hence was not a consideration for restricting a patrilocal residence, but rather in recognizing personal motives for post-marital residence.

Bilateral descent was unique in its flexibility for expanding and contracting populations according to subsistence availability and exploitation. This social structure was further maintained through mutual intelligibility of various dialects. In addition to consanguineal and affinal relationships, the adult male was usually dependent upon fictive roles among other adult men from whom he received and gave support and status. These propinquity associations were intensified by joking relationships, and reinforced by joint sweat-bathing and various male activities that required an intimate knowledge of another's skill, temperament, and even courage (Ross 1991:5.28).

The most significant grouping was the autonomous residential household (neolocal), some of whose members might be related only affinally. Elmendorf (pers. comm.), in speaking of the extended family, also included within this realm those more immediately-related consanguineal people, termed *stm'e?l'is* or *sntr'?em'ep* ("one's heirs"). All consanguineal kinspeople were called *stmé?l'is* ("they are blood relatives") or *snkʷskʷsíxʷxʷ* ("blood relative").

For a complete chart showing Spokan consanguineal kin terms, see Appendix E.

Social Interaction

From an early age, children were constantly taught by example, that respect, in both words and deeds, was the most important aspect of any social relationship with kinspeople and non-kinspeople. Additionally, children were instructed to always accept and tolerate the physical and behavioral differences of others. Parents would usually not verbally instruct their children in these matters, partly because those adults were absent much of the time—especially the father. Rather, a boy would be told by his grandfather, and a girl by her grandmother.

For the Spokan, the acknowledgement of courtesies within families and between friends (*sl'áxt* - "friend") and acquaintances is quite different from Euro-American people. Traditionally, one never verbally acknowledged something done by a wife, husband, kinsperson, or friend. On the contrary, such acknowledgement could be taken as an insult, because one recognized the deeds of kin and friends with unscheduled or apparent reciprocal behavior. One elder said, "If I thank you, as a friend, I've then finished our friendship, which we must start over again. My thanks would be a payment, which is only for strangers, for you would know my feelings—what is in my heart, which is often difficult to explain." Clearly, there could easily arise a misunderstanding between a non-traditional person thanking a traditional elder, regardless of sincerity. However, certain acts of kindness or expressions of friendship might be acknowledged by a small gift, preferably one made by the giver. A husband might give a special gift to his wife after being away for an appreciable time.

When a younger man greeted an older kin or *non-kinsman* (*nk'ʷélixʷ*), he would never ask how well the elder felt, whether he was enjoying his health, whether his winter wood was cut, or whether his horses were ready for winter. Rather, the younger person—out of respect—would say he had come to hear the words of the elder, thereby acknowledging that the elder's enunciated wisdom, stories, and many experiences were more valuable to the younger person—more than anything "in his pocket" the elder could give. In fact, those thoughts and memories were all the elder could give. "My words have more strength than my hands."

Washington Irving quoted some of Captain Bonneville's observations of Flathead social interaction, which most likely were similar to Spokan behavior during the early time of Euro-American contact:

> They have a mild, playful, laughing disposition; and this is portrayed in their countenances. They are polite, and unobtrusive. When one speaks, the rest pay strict attention: when he is done, another assents by 'yes,' or dissents by 'no;' and then states his reasons, which are listened to with equal attention. Even the children are more peaceable than other children. I have never heard an angry word among them, nor any quarreling; although there were, at least, five hundred of them together, and continually at play. With all this quietness of spirit, they are brave when put to the test; and are an overmatch for an equal number of Blackfeet (Irving 1836:391).

Gift-Giving

As with all Amerindians, the Spokan practiced different types of *gift-giving* ($sx^w\acute{i}c\,'c\,'\check{s}$) between kinspeople, friends, persons with joking relationships, and acquaintances. These items were self-made or acquired through inheritance or warfare. Gift-giving—whether spontaneous, premeditated, or delayed—tended to establish a new relationship, maintain an existing one, or even re-establish a disrupted relationship that was necessary for social, political, or economic reasons. Whether public, private, or ceremonial, there was considerable protocol—even symbolic nuances—in the giving and in the acceptance. A gift was frequently a vehicle for expressing the feelings or intent of the giver, both symbolic and articulated by the presenter making an eloquent and sometimes emotional speech proclaiming his feelings and concomitant relationship with the recipient. Such a gift was never given away or traded.

The giver invariably held the gift—which often served as a mnemonic device—until he had finished explaining, in often considerable detail, the conditions under which he had attained or made the item. An elder once explained how such a gift story could easily take the better part of a day, or even all night, before the item was handed to the recipient. Conditions were never placed upon the recipient, who was always cognizant of her responsibilities to the care of the gift and her relationship to the giver. As was said, "When you see or touch my gift, you will hear my words."

Many years ago, the author was the grateful recipient of an unusual gift from an elderly Spokan man. The item was a power gift, wrapped in an old hematite-stained bundle of buckskin. As he unwrapped it, the man told his story, occasionally shaking the bundle carefully, producing a clinking sound. Much later, he sang over the bundle, and then explained that within the bundle were four crystals—two big and two small. Finally, he reverently opened and spread the bundle to reveal them. He removed the two small ones, and wrapped the two large ones in the buckskin, which he placed under his left axilla. When taking the bundle to the sweathouse, he announced his intent to his tutelary spirit, how the two large adult crystals had two more children, which he could give away—which he did (Ross 1964-67).

There was a type of gift exchange, $snk\,'\acute{e}\acute{t}x^wc\,'\check{s}twex^w$, that occasionally represented what is termed "delayed gift giving." It established a reciprocal relationship that was seldom understood among non-Indians, and often lead to conflict if the recipient was not Indian or was unfamiliar with the protocol. Consequently, the disparaging remark of "Indian giver" became popular. Such gift giving could occur between two good friends:

> Upon meeting each other, they either exchanged gifts of clothing (which they are wearing), blankets, horses, etc. Sometimes, one man has several horses, [and] he will bring one to his good friend—as time goes on, the horse-receiver will bring something of equal value to his good friend. This practice continues until one dies (STHC).

Any item made by a man and given to his wife, was her property to do as she pleased.

Social Control

The Spokan had definite rules of behavior and strict concepts of what constituted permissible versus antisocial behavior, as defined by a group's established norms, which were based upon religion and reiterated through oral history as a proven way to ensure group harmony. Admittedly, behavior in warfare and intergroup theft, could differ dramatically; in fact, a person could acquire status by violating the property of an antagonistic individual or taking the life of an enemy.

As with most unicentric political and legal systems, social control was exercised within the kin group and through face-to-face relationships with other village and band members. However, once *a conflict* or *dispute* (*q'ey'uʔsntm*) escalated and became public, the village or a council would intercede in an effort to resolve the problem or at least ameliorate the situation. Some individuals had a reputation as *litigious* (*sčeeʔneple ʔ*)—quick to be contentious and quarrelsome over matters of little consequence. Social cohesion and stability were favored, and instances of in-group antisocial behavior were deemed dysfunctional, because such actions could interrupt basic survival tasks, or lead to ongoing conflict.

Despite group adjudication being favored, there existed the option of direct reprisal—typically in response to murder, wife-stealing, or adultery. For example, a story was told of how a brother plotted to gain his brother's wife:

> Two brothers once lived near here [Chewelah], when most of this was Indian land [1890], but now all the Chewelah people have lost their land. Only one brother was married, to a very attractive and hard working woman. Well, one day the single brother asked his brother if he'd join him in the mountains to hunt eagles who lived in a large vertical cave. On getting above the cave, the eagle flew away. But the two men waited, knowing the eagle would come back. The single brother took his rope and told the married one he would lower him into the opening. So later he could kill the eagle when it came back. After lowering his brother, the single brother pulled the rope up stranding his brother in the cave. The single brother then ran off and returned home to claim his *brother's wife* (*seʔstem'*)—a reciprocal term, saying her husband had died in a fall. After a while the eagle returned, not knowing a man was there. The trapped man grabbed the eagle's legs, forcing the eagle to fly out of the cave with the Indian hanging on. After the eagle tired, he got on the ground and went home to reclaim his grieving wife (Ross 1968-2008).

Political Organization

Although the term "tribe" has and continues to be used when describing Amerindian groups as political units in the Columbia Basin, they were cultural and linguistic entities (Anastasio 1955, 1972, and 1974). Since the Spokan had no true tribal organization, the highest level of governance for intergroup politics was the individual *village* (*nkʷélixʷ*) (Burns 1966:7), whose members made decisions through often lengthy discussions to achieve *consensus* (*hec yaʔ scntels*). The next level of governance was the family or extended family group.

Typically, each village or band was politically autonomous. The ties which bound small groups into territorial units of significant size were of a more tenuous nature: the possession of a single dialect and common culture, and the observance of a relatively high level of social intercourse (Smith 1953:87).

Consequently, each Spokan winter village was completely autonomous, as were some larger non-winter resource camps. According to Ray, the dominant concern was equality: "The equality of men was a principle impressively emphasized. Much of the remarkable oratory that characterized public occasions was devoted to this ideal. Likewise, the principle was emphasized over and over in the education of the children" (1977:22).

The proto-historical period is defined as "the first introduction of non-aboriginal influences and the first recorded historical contact with non-Indian people" (Walker and Sprague 1998:138). During this period, the Spokan customarily moved in small bands, except during occasions for mutual support, such as venturing into

Blackfoot country. Horatio Hale, an anthropologist and philologist who was "fascinated with languages" (Wilson 1866:211), described the Spokan:

> This tribe can scarcely be said to be under general government; at least it is certain that none is regularly organized or acknowledged. They appear now to roam in small bands, as may best suit their temporary convenience, but these join for mutual support against their more powerful enemies, the Piikiani or Blackfeet [...] There is no authority recognized in their chief, at least so far as the power to inflict punishments for crimes or disorders in concerned. There is, however, often a principal man, who, from the circumstance of possessing wealth, intelligence, and character and sometimes from birth, united a sort of control or chieftainship, and exercised an authority over others from his personal influence, ruling more by persuasion than by command through sanction of law. The extent of his authority must of course depend upon the individual's own temper: if he were a determined character, he might no doubt exercise considerable authority (Hale 1846, 4:437-9; 447-8; 455-6).

Chalfant agreed with Wilkes's early observation (1845) of the ongoing change in Spokan political organization: "That the Spokan showed an inclination toward tribal organization is not denied; however, local rule, usually on the village level, was the rule, and tribal tendencies were late in formation" (1974:46), which was critical for facilitating greater mobility, task-grouping, and trade with certain Plains groups.

Euro-Americans had erroneous views of Salish polity; they believed it to be, at best, an incipient form of political organization. Euro-Americans were not able to understand a polity without social stratification, and hastened to change the autonomy inherent in the Spokan system (Ackerman 1987). Alexander Diomedi, S.J., an early priest in the Chelan area, "believed that the lack of authority was the cause of wars and even of polygamy. He made attempts to persuade a chief to exceed his powers by intervening in an impending feud" (1878:22-3).

Pertinent are later ethnographies, such as Teit's 1930 discussion of the Spokan, Ray's 1933 ethnography of the Sanpoil and Nespelem, Anastasio's 1955, 1972, and 1974 work, and Chalfant's 1974 comprehensive summary of Spokan ethnohistory and eastern Washington Salish. Anastasio, following the earlier work of Ray (1933) and Smith (1941), stated that the Plateau political organization was not without structure and authority, and:

> [...] was not disorganized and understandable only in the perspective of each local group; rather [...] it had an areal organization which was flexible and shifting within a certain range of variability [...] Intergroup relations, even those which are predominantly hostile or neutral, necessarily involve some sort of agreement (1974, 4:4).

Among the Spokan, the village was the major political unit:

> From Alaska to California there does not appear to have been a group that could be designated as a political unit, other than what it is usual to call the village; that is, each other, or linked by peaceful trade, inter-marriage, and participation in each world, whose intercourse, however intimate, friendly, and long enduring, is always [...] a condition of suspense, because built on nothing more than the occasions of the moment, the states being irreconcilable units (Kroeber 1939:396).

Conditions of political organization and control among the Spokan was probably comparable to that of the Sanpoil and Nespelem:

> Though theoretically every village, large or small, was autonomous, there was some modification of the principle in practice. A very small village, especially one of only two or three houses, often affiliated with the nearest large settlement to the extent of attending the assemblies and soliciting the advice of the chief of the latter. This was a volitional procedure, however, for the sake of convenience. The small village in such a case did not recognize a chief but named a head man to represent it at the political meetings of the large community. But even under such an arrangement the acts of the large village were never binding upon the other. Decisions which were thought wise were respected, others were ignored [...] Village composition was very fluid. A person was bound in no way to any particular village. He was privileged to change his residence at any time, selecting as his new home any village or group. Families often lived for a few years at one location, tired of it or became dissatisfied, and moved to another settlement. This might be continued in their respective villages throughout life but this sedentary group was always in the minority (Ray 1939:6).

Plateau groups shared long-established rules of cooperation that differentiated them from other groups, because their need to interact successfully during the annual subsistence round, and to mutually exploit predictable resources located differentially for brief periods of time. Knudson noted a universal principle of usufruct:

> The need for flexibility in Plateau adaptations underlies some of the most basic values shared by all groups in this region. Primary to these adaptations are the concepts of cross-utilization and stewardship. Cross-utilization refers to the right of any individual to exploit any resource needed, whether or not within the territory of one's own group. Thus, there was no exclusive "ownership" of any resource area, but relatively open access to all (1978:33).

Chieftainship

Political authority and control among the Spokan were maintained under the jurisdiction of each chief and his council, whose decisions were reinforced by the consensus of those who acknowledged this authority. Every Spokan village was headed by a *single chief* (*xʷistp'úsmn*), who retained office through building consensus, being a *generous and compassionate person* (*peʔpeʔt*), having a reputation for making deliberate and wise decisions, and possessing a *religious power* (*sumèš*). A medicine man would not serve as a chief (STHC).

Horatio Hale, one of the earliest observers of the Spokan, spent considerable time with them, and set aside his Anglo-European mindset when reporting that:

> In every band there is usually one who, by certain advantages of wealth, valor and intelligence, acquires a superiority over the rest, and is termed the chief. But his authority is derived rather from his personal influence than from any law, and is exerted more in the way of persuasion than of direct command. But if he is a man of shrewdness and of a determined character, he sometimes enjoys considerable power. The punishment of delinquents is, of course, regulated rather by circumstances than by any fixed code. Notorious criminals are sometimes punished by exclusion from the tribe or band to which they belong (1846, 4:205).

Although the chieftainship within the Spokan political structure was essentially hereditary, a qualified individual outside the family could assume the office. "When it became necessary to select a chief from a new lineage, any man was eligible. The selection was made without regard to any quality suggestive of class" (Ray 1977:23). A viable candidate was typically respected and known for his oratory skills, generosity, patience, and wisdom. This office was never based upon accrued wealth (in the form of material possessions), since a leader's principal obligation and concern was to maintain group tranquility by resolving differences of opinion, and making final judgment in cases of arbitration.

With the death of a chief, his oldest son might succeed him if he had the necessary abilities and qualities. If there were no such son, then the office might be assumed by the eldest son of the chief's eldest brother. The role could be accepted, or refused, or passed onto a younger brother, or given away to a reputable consanguineal male in the family if none of the chief's family wanted the responsibility. Through exceptional personal skills and perseverance, a man could achieve chieftainship, such as distinguishing himself by *horse-stealing* (*ʔilmixʷm*).

A reason for rejecting chieftainship was because the office was quite *demanding* (*kʷulst*) in terms of the commitment of time and responsibility. Also, an individual might feel that he was not worthy of such an important position. If a chief's son were likely to eventually hold the title, then, during the boy's maturation and formal enculturation, he would be given special tasks that required considerable discipline—particularly those intended to develop leadership.

There was no memory of women inheriting this office (Elmendorf, pers. comm.), though a leader's wife could provide meaningful counsel to her husband, and could influence other women. A chief's authority was extended to his wife or wives, whom were called *pu'ilimáxʷm*. Within the chief's family, one wife would have greater authority and "some chiefs had 5 or 6 wives [...] and the first or head wife [...] has charge of things—she can order the other wives around" (Elmendorf 1935-6, 4:10). In addition, she was in a sense the "chief" of all the women in the group.

A chief's principal obligation and concern was to resolve quarrels or conflicting claims that may be detrimental to village *tranquility* (*hi nqimls* - "be at peace"), make final judgement in cases of arbitration or violation of conduct, select camping sites, decide when to move to new resource areas, and be generous with his time and concern for the village's welfare. He chief was essentially a counselor and a leader who was concerned with maintaining amicable intra- and intergroup relations. A chief's authority was never questioned, and seldom was the authority of any sub-chief questioned by a non-council person. He invariably *possessed powers* (*k'ʷx̣'einm* - "man with power") that were of benefit to the group.

Situations of potential conflict were avoided or frequently ameliorated through the dynamics of intermarriage, as many Spokan traditionally intermarried with the Coeur d'Alene, Kalispel, and other contiguous Salish speakers. The title of chief was often without real authority—though his influence was respected—because he governed with the advice and consent of a chosen council or assembly of elders (even as late as the early 1900s).

As needed, he would call together the sub-leaders and elders to discuss important issues:

> The Council, consisting of the elder men and the younger ones of proved ability, met to select the successor of the deceased chief, but by custom their choice was limited to the men of his family; and as a rule his eldest son was named. If more than one relative was available, there might be some *discussion* [*sq'mq'mil's*; italics added]. Speeches were made in favor of the various candidates, and, as a Spokan informant said, " [...] after all the speeches were made, everybody all at once came to the same opinion." As occasion arose he would summon by name the old men and the subchiefs either for discussion of important questions or merely for a feast. One of the duties of a chief was to bear a present to the lodge of a dying person, and there to offer good advice and consolation (Curtis 1907-30, 7:73).

A chief of one band had authority over everyone living within his band's territory, and not just the members of his band:

> "A chief has no authority over members of another village group, even if they are sojourning in his village." If an outsider takes up residence the chief has authority over him then, since he is like [a] member of the tribe. Such an outside resident is under the authority of the chief of the village in which he is staying, and if he gets into trouble he will have to reckon with the local government (Elmendorf 1935-6, 4:10-11).

Among the three Spokan bands, the chief of the Upper Spokan had the greater authority. Teit noted how the political structure of the Spokan was influenced by the Flathead:

> I did not obtain any list of Spokan chiefs. It seems that each division of the Spokan had a chief and some small chiefs. Long ago there was no head chief proper, although, according to some, the chief of the Upper Spokan was considered the leading chief of the three divisions. After the tribe took up buffalo hunting the Upper Spokan had a head chief, a subchief, and small chiefs like the Flathead, and it was customary to recognize the head chief of the Upper Spokan as head chief of all the Spokan. When the divisions were combined in hunting, travelling, and war [and after the establishment of the Spokane Indian reservation], the divisional chiefs of the Middle and Lower Spokan and the subchief of the Upper Spokan were all cased as subchiefs, and ranked in the same way. Each tribe on the reserve continues to have its own chiefs. Besides the regular chiefs, there were a number of war chiefs and dance chiefs in each tribe. Sometimes, at least, there was a head war chief and a head dance chief. In some cases the regular chiefs were also war chiefs and hunting chiefs, and some of them were also sometimes dance chiefs. There may also have been some men who were special chiefs or permanent captains of companies or groups of various kinds, but I did not obtain sufficient information on this point (1930:378-9).

Chiefs treated one another with respect, while maintaining autonomy. This was similar with the Sanpoil, who had "the sense of equality of men and the idea of personal autonomy" (Spencer, Jennings, *et al.* 1965:221). Interband matters were discussed by all the assembled band chiefs and sub-chiefs representing the three macro bands; this was called *sq'mq'míle* ("conversing" or "discussion") (Elmendorf 1935-6, 1:50).

A Spokan chief is illustrated in a painting by Paul Kane (1847) titled "Spokan Chief Spokan River" (Plate XXXIII. Tum-se-ne-ho or "The Man without Blood" in Stark wwc43; crIV-337). The subject is carrying a combined bow case and quiver, as well as a second bow—a custom common among the Spokan.

Figure 12. A Spokane chief

Every resident band and territorial band (Rice 1970) had two or three petty chiefs (Gibbs 1855). "Each tribe had several chiefs, members of a sort of royal strain among them, and each chief exercised what authority he could without much regard to his fellow chiefs" (Manring 1912:123-4). Even with macroband political structure, and multiple chiefs, each village had its own chief, who always stayed in residence—never going on a warparty or horse-stealing expedition. Only with the establishment of the reservation was there one chief over the Spokan. By that time, the U.S. Government viewed the Spokan as *one people* (*tsq'aistsɫmi*), as did many of the Spokan themselves.

During mutual resource exploitation, a leader was an individual who possessed the power necessary for exploiting a particular resource. *War leaders* (*sisiúcménˀ*) were commonly self-designated, and exercised only temporary authority (Elmendorf, pers. comm.). After dreaming of the pending event, a war leader would organize and supervise a war party or horse-stealing party. An important function of a war chief was to achieve a consensus of proposed military tactics, by soliciting advise and consent only from older experienced warriors.

As a result of Anglo-European impatience, language barriers, misunderstanding of villages (rather than tribal autonomy), and ethnocentric views on sole leadership, Governor I. I. Stevens (1818-1862) and others, gave the title of chief to Spokane Garry. Stevens and other governmental representatives after him knew that Garry spoke English and possessed a keen mind (Ruby and Brown 2006:267). Some Spokan, to this date, claim the Spokan themselves never chose him for this position. This was a common occurrence in early Indian/white relations in eastern Washington, in which whites named certain men as "leaders," assuming their right to speak for the entire tribe.

Councils

Each band had a *head chief* (*sši?íti ilmixum* - "oldest chief"), as well as secondary chiefs, or sub-chiefs (*ilmixʷm*). They had equal rank, and exercised authority during collective subsistence activities, and during certain rituals, deliberations, and decisions affecting the village or camp. Sub-chiefs served as the *chief's advisory council* (*illilmixʷm* or *skʷakʷa'él* or *sq'mq'ilš* - "conversing" or "discussion") (Elmendorf 1936-36, 1:50). They sometimes also offered advice and consent, particularly in difficult matters concerning external relations with other groups. Thus a chief usually had sub-chiefs with specific powers or skills that were ultimately of benefit to his office and the general welfare of the village or camp.

Based on the advice and consent of the group's elders, a chief chose as his sub-chiefs individuals who had demonstrated thoughtfulness, consideration of others, bravery in warfare, oratory ability, charisma, energy in accomplishing tasks, success in hunting and fishing, leadership abilities, and generosity with their time and efforts for less fortunate individuals. Honesty and dependability were essential traits. According to Egesdal, the Indians "have a word for that virtue, one far better than anything centuries of well-crafted English have to offer: *?eswnéxʷisti* in Flathead, and *hecwnéxʷisti* in Spokan. It means 'what he thinks, says, and does are the same—truth'" (pers. comm.). Often, one or more much older, former council members—each called *p'xʷut* ("head old person of a large extended kin group")—would be invited by the chief to attend a session so the council could hear their opinions, thereby benefiting from their long tenure and experience.

Some Spokan elders recalled that each sub-chief had an exceptional power-based skill or ability that was different from those of the other sub-chiefs. Consequently, a man could never be a council member if he lacked *suméš*, such as a demonstrated knowledge and skill in "hunting or healing—did not have to be married, and if a boy refused to take training [vision quest, he] was finally driven out—'outcast' (*sxʷélmn*)—couldn't marry—[he was then a] burden to his people" (Elmendorf 1935-6, 1:20).

Council membership was eventually determined by village consensus, but always with the approval of the head chief, who frequently functioned as a war chief since the Spokan apparently had no person with this singular power. Some elders, however, have debated if a chief ever was a war chief.

Every responsible adult in the village could attend the council meetings (Elmendorf 1935-6, 1:20). During such a meeting, there was no recognition of status or formal order for any adult who chose to speak and give his or her opinion. Nor were women excluded from expressing their views, regardless of a husband's position or opinion.

Throughout the winter, councils met every evening (Elmendorf 1935-6, 1:77), to discuss any important matters, often in *lengthy sessions* (*?ec q'mq'milši*). During such sessions, only the principals would pass around a *council pipe* (*snmán'xʷtm* or *snmen'xʷtn*) and smoke. The group, called *ilsmíkʷm*, would sit in open conference—sometimes for several days, depending upon the magnitude of the matter at hand. Each band chief was equal in rank; no one would dominate the course of discussions, but rather each one exemplified the notion of "many people, but one voice."

A council's decision was usually unanimous, and represented the opinions of all attending adults. Voting was by acclamation (Ray 1977:33). Once a council decision was made, a *crier* (*skʷlskʷlstí*) would go through the village or camp announcing the news (Elmendorf 1935-6, 4:23). The appointment of a crier was a life term, always made by the chief to an individual with a loud and authoritative voice. This person was an active member of the chief's entourage, and upon his death, the chief appointed a replacement.

Crime and Punishment

Culturally-defined dysfunctional behavior, within the confines of an extended family could, if not resolved, become a serious concern for the entire community whose very survival depended upon adults coordinating their efforts to obtain resources and neutralize threats confronting the group. Unresolved private conflict—once it became public—could reduce the group's cooperation and fulfillment of their immediate economic tasks, especially if people took sides.

Both private and public social control were maintained through familial or communal excommunication, gossip, protocols of age, division of labor, humiliation, council censure or ridicule, consensus of opinion, public whipping, corporal punishment, and even threats of serious illness or spiritual death through sorcery or *social isolation* (*ča-na-qes*). Another deterrent was public threats of the physical punishment, such as whipping of adults and even children (Ross 1995g, 2:602).

Serious intrafamilial strife was typically prevented by the father—by example or word of authority—or, in his absence, by his wife or a resident consanguineal elder. Any unresolved problem—such as an accusation or a grievance—would be brought before the group's council, in the hope that the offender would confess the wrongdoing and, if appropriate, offer restitution.

Public crimes considered detrimental to a group's welfare and tribal authority, were adjudicated by a council headed by a chief, typically advised by a consortium of elders who gave advice in resolving moral transgressions and secular crimes. A leader and his advisors relied upon their office and prestige for settling transgressions and grievances, and serving as mediators without coercive prerogatives (Ross 1995i, 3:731). Legal decisions thereby reflected *consensus* (*hec yaʔ scntels*).

A priority was the prevention of family feuds, which could be socially, economically, and politically damaging to the individuals and possibly the group. Gossip was likened to a meadowlark: *kʷ eʔc w'aw'ickʷl'eʔey'* ("you are just like a meadowlark"), i.e., you are always carrying tales (STHC). One elderly lady recalled how she was always reminded by her grandmother, "What comes to your ears shouldn't go to your heart. One should not be a *meddlesome person*" [*suxʷšt'elt* or *suxʷšt'im* or *št'incutn*]. The Spokan also believed that certain illnesses were the result of moral transgression that could occur without intervention by a sorcerer.

Children were *enculturated* (*ʔas čc'x̣ʷx̣ʷepl'eʔ*) with a strict moral code, comprising rules of proper behavior—ones presumably exemplified privately and publicly by family members and society at large. Such pronouncements were reinforced almost daily by traditional stories that included dramatic accounts of mischievous children who committed transgressions, as well as people who were role models worthy of emulation. Threats of the whipper man, or being taken away by a regional nocturnal *monster* (*sqélixʷtn* or *sxʷq'ixʷtn* or *nʔaɫi*), were usually sufficient to correct the behavior of a recalcitrant child. The first admonishments to a child were for a falsehood, theft, or disrespect for elders. Shame of such a *violation* (*mawɫ cnč'x̣ʷepl'e*) was greatly feared, even by small children, but more by an adult.

Many of the established traditional customs—despite being critical to Spokan adaptation—were incompatible with Christian teachings and a Euro-American *Weltanschauung* ('worldview'). For example, polyandry (woman with more than one husband), apparently long practiced, was unacceptable under church dogma. Reverend Cowley spoke Spokan, and consequently was quite observant of Spokan culture. This is evidenced in a 1875 letter (Kingston 1950:n.p.), in which he explains to a Presbyterian missionary colleague how the values and accepted practice of polyandry (which the missionaries called "adultery") among the Lower Spokan had been drastically altered by Christian teachings:

> The abhorrence they [Christians] show against adultery was exemplified in the severe whipping of a woman who had two husbands, the latter of whom she left but a short time before coming to camp, and the punishment was made lest she might be tempted to offend again [...] There is strong public sentiment against adultery, theft, drunkenness, gambling [...] (Drury 1949:140).

The practice of public whipping by the Spokan is debated, as is the degree to which it was modified or encouraged by Euro-Americans (Smith 1936-8). Spier contended, "Punishment of crime has become much more rigid since the advent of the Catholic priests" (1938:94).

A man accused of a crime was judged at a *council meeting* (*sq'mq'milš*), always held in the *council house* (*snq'mq'milštn*). Similarly, for a dispute between two or more people, the parties would present their grievances and any counterclaims, before a council assembled by the chief, to establish the validity of the plaintiff's claim. The council members, led by the chief, were sartorially attired in their full regalia—wearing their headdresses of feathers, and faces painted with red hematite. A chief's regulatory authority was illustrated in how, each morning, one of his minor officers would beat on a piece of canvas while singing a special song to awaken everyone—a ritual called *snqaqaʕaqsn* (STHC).

The alleged offender would be brought before the council for an *explanation* (*sq'mq'milš* - "to talk"). If either the complainant or the defendant refused to tell his case or explain his actions, he was assumed to be guilty. During the inquiry, the *examiner* (*suxʷsuɫyúmc* or *suxʷsuʕɫtumš*) would conduct the cross-examination of both the defendant and the plaintiff. He was permanently appointed by the chief, having demonstrated his abilities and knowledge of village affairs. Regardless of age or gender, a person deemed guilty represented him or herself before the council—never through a spokesperson, for "truth has its own legs." A chief's main role in judicial matters was to resolve conflict as quickly as possible, and to expedite a decision of guilt or innocence. He often questioned the litigants himself, but otherwise relied on the examiner, who would skillfully question the plaintiff and defendant until there was consensus as to their guilt or innocence.

The assembled court would hear the accounts of the defendant and his accuser(s), as well as any pertinent information contributed by the community, because its members, through daily social interaction, knew each individual's health, stress, conflict, and even sexual liaisons. The council would be particularly attentive to the reactions and comments of the attending individuals, some of whom may have had knowledge of the alleged crime.

After consultation, the chief rendered his decision of guilt or innocence, in hopes it would restore village tranquility. However, in cases of denial or extenuating circumstances, the chief could sequester a council of sub-chiefs, with whom he would confer before making a final decision of guilt (Elmendorf 1935-6, 2:51). If the accused failed to acknowledge a known guilt, or refused to confess to the transgression, he was *judged* (*čc'xʷepl'eʔm's*) guilty and punished. In all cases, the severity of the punishment was decided by the council (STHC). When speaking of punishment, Johnson (1969) contended the Spokan recognized no judicial authority or power in their chief to administer punishment for crimes.

Within the chief's council, there were usually three or four men designated as *whippers* (*sxʷukʷném* or *suxʷɫc'im* - "official whipper"). Each was a *man who had been permanently appointed* (*sxʷɫc'im*) by the chief, and passed along to him any gossip relevant to the case. They were instructed by a person called a *sxʷsuɫtúmš*, who was designated by the chief to conduct an interrogation of the accused (Elmendorf 1935-6, 2:51). If the accused registered sincere remorse for his transgression, the punishment could be reduced. But if he were unrepentant, his punishment would be in full.

The sentence was administered immediately after pronouncement, in the council house. Whippers and *grapplers* (*sk'ʷmén*) would force the guilty individual into a prone position on a blanket or hide on the ground, without a shirt, and firmly restrain him. In some cases, one of his own blankets was spread over him. A publicly administered whipping was not only humiliating, but could be extremely painful. According to some sources, the whip had three leather thongs attached to a wooden handle, or consisted of three stout willow rods. The only detailed description of this instrument is provided by Smith:

> The whip had a wooden handle and was [covered with] heavy tanned-soft hide—probably off a deer's neck. The strands were about as big as the finger; it was one broad strip rolled up and sewn into a smooth roll. They were about 3 or 4 feet long and the handle about 1½ feet. Sometimes, though not very much, there were two strands attached to the handle. This latter is not as severe as the one because they get in the way of one another.

Sometimes it has a strand made by braiding narrow strips into 4 braid round, not square. (The Colvilles have square 4 braids, 4 or 5 inches long on the end of round 4 braids; the Kalispel did not have these which were probably got from the missionaries.) The braided one was not used by the Kalispel so much; but they had both the single and the double strand ones of this type. Women were lashed as much as the men, but no children were lashed (1936-8:889).

After the punishment, the guilty individual stayed down (Smith 1936-8:888) as the chief admonished him and told him how he would make restitution. Only after this was the convicted allowed to stand. If he was truly repentant, he was expected to *shake hands* (*t'emčsm* - "a greeting, acknowledgement") with all those of the court while pronouncing his shame and enunciating his good will to all those present. But if he failed to express remorse and verbally ask for forgiveness, or was defiant or disrespectful, or "acted cranky after punishment, they threw him back on the blanket and whipped him some more" (Elmendorf 1935-6, 2:45). Elmendorf, when speaking of whipping and public confession, wrote that several of his informants felt that:

> [...] if a man has done wrong in any way he should come before the council & make [his] confession—if he had interfered between a man & his wife or if he had stolen anything—the idea of confession—antedated missionary influences and Mrs. W[ynecoop]. thinks the early Catholic influences was due to the people having already had this idea—when a man confessed before the council he was exculpated if he did not confess then [he was] brought before the council [and] charged with [the] crime [and] he would be tied a while until he confessed—whipped only for stealing and adultery—[a] man might beat his wife in [the] case of adultery or if he didn't care for her much he just discarded [her]—adultery [was] one of the worse crimes—the council never seemed to have exercised [the] death penalty—cases [were] usually decided on the spot after hearing [the] evidence from plaintiff & defendants and opinions from any other adults in the tribe—then the council discussed [the case] until they arrived at a unanimous decision—punishment [was] allotted right then—[the] attitudes of [the] person being judged were taken into consideration—a frank confession and regret were the best defense (1935-6, 1:77-8).

There was a critical reason why the punishment should engender true remorse in the accused, because within a small community, it was paramount to prevent any feelings or acts of revenge, which would be detrimental for the entire group. That is why the grievous person, after being whipped, would ask for forgiveness from the chief, the sub-chiefs, and community at large. The transgression and the punishment were never discussed again. Even if a friend of the punished believed that he was innocent or that the punishment was excessive, he would never say, for instance, "I disagree with what was done to you." Similarly, parents would never tell a misbehaving child something like, "I've told you this before!" At a recent *sorrow* or *remembrance ceremony* (*xʷulsiłni*), a Spokan elder stated, "Things that are bad, you leave them in the past."

Apart from Elmendorf's account, there are few reports of whipping as punishment by the Spokan, though Curtis explained its purpose and proliferation: "Whipping as a punishment for various offenders, such as adultery, theft, drunkenness, murder, was introduced and gradually spread among many of the Salishan tribes of the interior, and is still in force among the Kalispel" (1911, 7:75). Turney-High "likewise found whipping equally old among the Flathead" (1937:46-47). According to Smith, the frequency of whipping and the role of the lashers became more pervasive and important among both the Kalispel and the Kalispel-Spokan groups with the arrival of Catholic missionaries. "After they got religion, the whipping turned into a religious practice and it was done to redeem the sinners from their sins as Christ was," and "Before that it was only a punishment" (1936-38, 8:888).

"Social control and punishment, depending upon the offense, was achieved mainly by public ridicule, excommunication [*čq'mnčnełxʷ* - "to be driven out"], and whipping, which was also a mode of social control" (Garth 1965:156). Whipping was the only type of physical punishment merited by a guilty person. Although children were threatened with whipping, they seldom were whipped, but instead privately or publicly humiliated. Regardless of age or gender, this was the most severe punishment, because a whipping would heal, but a memory of shame would endure. "The greatest fear wasn't a whipping, but the threat of angry

89

words and humiliation, which little kids didn't understand. The mood or angry expression of a parent was never forgotten." But punishment was not excessive, for "You shouldn't ever break a kid's spirit; it'll never come back."

Desire for contrition was fueled by many factors, notably: missionization, the fear of being doomed to hell, and occurrences of natural disasters. During a severe earthquake and the eruption of Mount St. Helens in the 1800s, huge cracks opened in the earth, and the sky darkened. This prompted many people to make public *confessions before the council* (*sq'mq'amílc*) (1935-6, 2:45). Gibbs was told about certain reactions of the Spokan during and after the violent coastal eruption (Holden 1898:88-92, 96). Gibbs believed such natural disasters were later leveraged by religious millennium movements, and influenced the teachings of missionaries, who eventually relegated public whippings to Sundays after the religious service.

Dr. Suckley presents a similar observation of the earthquake and eruption:

> A few inches below the surface of earth can be found the ashes and cineritious deposit of a volcano. The stratum is about one-third of an inch thick. As you proceed in a north-easterly direction, it becomes thicker and thicker [...] The inhabitants have never seen it. They do not travel from curiosity [...] In the tribe there are men and women still living who remember the eruption. They say that it came during the afternoon and night, during which it rained cinders and fire. The Indians supposed that the sun had burned up, and that there was an end of all things. The next morning, when the sun arose, they were so delighted as to have a great dance and a feast (1855:298).

Rape was considered the most serious and heinous crime. Any man or boy convicted of rape might suffer a severe public whipping or even *castration* (*nq'ʷq'ʷepl'e?*). Even purposely trespassing near the women's bathing area, or where several women often had a palisaded or fenced secluded area, could result in a whipping; a repeat offender was castrated. (Elmendorf 1935-6, 1:70).

Aboriginally, theft was a rare occurrence. Oftentimes, before children would retire for the night, their father would explain the consequences of lying, cheating, stealing, and other anti-social behavior; he would tell of the shame and disrepute that would forever accompany the perpetrator, as well as his family. When a child or young adult was first accused of stealing, he was counseled by the chief, who explained the consequences if he ever stole again. Theft was condemned to such an extent that an incorrigible thief could be killed with no fear of retaliation. Yet vengeance was rare, and usually the offended family accepted the communal decision, such as punishment. The family would never go against the group's consensus. At the least, theft warranted public whipping.

A person might suspect or actually know the identity of the *thief* (*suxʷnaq'ʷm*), but rarely would he confront the person directly, for fear that he might be wrong in his judgment. Rather, such a charge was judged and resolved publicly. Any accusation would be first made to the chief, who would arrange for a public hearing. Apparently for the Spokan, "property rights were vague and ill defined—little conception of property—theft [being a] mere aberration—criminal perversity" (Elmendorf 1935-6, 1:70).

Prior to Euro-American incursion and missionization, the incidence of theft was rare, partly because a thief would be unable to use or trade away a traditionally-made item he had stolen, since most people recognized the manufacturer and thus proper owner. Unfortunately, as a result of deculturation, a shift in certain values, and more means of concealment, theft increased. Some elders claimed the behavior of whites taught the Indian to steal.

The causes, frequency, and punishments for murder—like many crimes—has changed over the years, due mainly to deculturation and missionization, as well as the adoption of judicial law as interpreted and administered by the Bureau of Indian Affairs, and more recently the federal legal system. Aboriginally, the concept of murder had different meanings and consequences. There were cases in which the group ruled that the killing was justified—notably for adultery. There are no known instances of patricide. Murder of an innocent was apparently a rare crime, partly because such an act could spark retribution and then feuding.

Consequently, in the case of murder, the chief, council, and concerned families made every effort to compensate, in order to ameliorate hostile feelings and achieve peace between the parties.

When a murderer was brought before the chief and his entourage, the accused explained why he had murdered, relating the circumstances. As with many judgments, the chief was cognizant of the community's nuances of guilt or innocence. Before final judgment, the chief would solicit advice from those elders of the community whom he respected and felt would be objective and fair in their final appraisal of the punishment. The murderer might be whipped or ostracized, but permanent excommunication from the group was considered the most *severe (čč'essis)* punishment:

> Punishment for crime is generally inflicted by the tribe, and frequently goes so far as to expel the delinquent; but I understand that the circumstances under which the crime was committed, have great influence in their decisions, and that they are for the most part just (Hale 1846, 4:448).

If a man were caught having sexual relations with another man's wife, the offended husband could kill the guilty adulterer without any retribution from the guilty man's kin. The guilty woman would more likely be publicly whipped by a member of her consanguineal family as a demonstration of their shame. An adulterous wife was seldom killed by her husband, but rather by one of his family—usually his brother (Elmendorf 1935-6, 1:18). Adulterous men and women could be whipped or stoned. When a person was found guilty of a moral transgression, but not killed, then the man or woman—after their respective punishment—would ask forgiveness from the chief, who invariably gave it.

Years ago, it was believed that excommunication was the most serious non-corporal punishment given for crimes such as publicly humiliating a person, being drunk, hitting one's wife, being excessively cruel to a horse, being *stingy (y'ey'úkʷe?)* or mean, and not helping others. If a person did not correct his or her behavior, then the chief, prior to threats of excommunication, might decide that the village would *ignore (ta-sčq'els)* the individual for a given period, or until the guilty person was considered rehabilitated.

The Spokan practiced what Smith (1936-8:878) called the "rights of ferriage," whereby any person without a canoe or raft who announced his or her need for transport across a stream, would thereby oblige any adult who heard the request. If no man heard the announcement, then a woman would fulfill the required courtesy. Anyone who failed—by denial or purported ignorance—was later disciplined by the chief, who reminded the entire group that such inhospitable behavior reflected badly upon the good name of the tribe, and their obligations to strangers.

The traditional Spokan legal system changed drastically with deculturation, confinement to a reservation system, Euro-American religious and sociopolitical factionalism, the replacement of traditional leaders by the Bureau of Indian Affairs, and general dominance by a multicentric European legal system. The aboriginal Spokan legal system was observed by many early explorers, including Alexander Ross, who provided an insightful and comparative summation, in which the term "savage" is used in the Rousseauan sense of the noble savage:

> [...] the white man does not always observe the golden rule of forbearance and even-handed justice, but often arbitrarily abrogates the right of domineering over the natives; and yet these, in almost all cases, yield without a murmur. And to our shame be it said, that reason and right, humanity and forbearance, are as often to be found among the savages themselves as among the whites, who live by sufferance among them. The Indian in his natural state is happy, with his trader he is happy; but the moment he begins to walk in the path of the white man his happiness is at an end. Like a wild animal in a cage, his lustre [sic] is gone.
>
> However strongly we may abhor heathenism, and deprecate the savage character in its natural state, as compared to civilized humanity, yet we ought not, in our zeal for the one or abhorrence of the other, to suppress the truth, therefore, compels us to admit that there are many traits of virtue to be met with in the Indian character. They are brave, generous, and often charitable; and to their credit be it said, that there is less crime in an Indian camp of five hundred souls than there is in a civilized village of but half that number. Let the lawyer or moralist point out the cause (Ross 1849, 7:328-9).

91

Chapter IV: Life Cycle

Rites of Passage

The life cycle of every Spokan—from birth to death—comprised a sequence of distinct roles that were established by corresponding rites of passage. Upon completion, these rites acknowledged the individual's change from one status to the next. The major rites of passage were birth, naming, puberty (culminating in a vision quest), marriage, and death.

Every rite of passage had essentially three successive phases: separation, transition, and incorporation (Van Gennep 1969). Separation—including physical separation from others—was a departure from a (previously profane) role/status. Examples include: birth, menarche, acquiring a guardian spirit, marriage, and death.

Transition, the second phase, was a time of solemn reflection and anticipation, often spent in solitude, performing onerous tasks that were deemed necessary for acquiring the esoteric knowledge and skills integral to the desired role. Transitions were usually long, arduous, and sometimes quite stressful, as participants engaged in physical training, confinement, and strict supervision, to condition themselves for the pending ordeal. The neophyte was oftentimes uncertain and apprehensive as to whether he would maybe fail to complete the physical training. The risk of failure was increased since such individuals were in a liminal state of having "no status, nothing to demarcate them structurally from their fellows. Their condition is indeed the very prototype of sacred poverty" (Turner 1966:99). During the stressful transitional period of semi- or total-confinement, a candidate typically experienced considerable fear that the necessary physical, spiritual, and psychological transformations would not occur—thereby barring successful incorporation into the desired role. Consequently, transition was the most difficult phase of every rite of passage.

In the ritual of reincorporation, the final phase, the group recognized the male or female initiate as having successfully fulfilled the culturally-prescribed ordeals of the transitional phase. This reincorporation brought not only a change of group-acknowledged status for the individual, but also demonstrated the person's ability to assume more demanding responsibilities and behavior.

Most rites of passage served important functions for the individual and the group. These rituals reduced role confusion, promoted a strong sense of individual identity, and formalized an individual's obligation to family, kin group, and community. Moreover, this recognition of the different spiritual and occupational skills helped define the uniqueness of a Spokan man or woman, which in turn perpetuated group integration, fostered a significant sense of consciousness of kind, and acknowledged an individual's acceptance and eagerness to participate in her new role. A person's successful transition legitimized—in the eyes of the group—her newly-acquired status in the group.

The Spokan recognized other, less formal status changes, such as incipient-named male and female age-grouping: An individual, during his lifetime, occupied different categories, based on biological changes. "A boy or girl just learning to creep was called *pút u stišlwís*" (Smith 1936-8:839). Commencing at *birth* (*k'ʷl'l'l'elt* or *k'ʷl'el'elt* - "to give birth"), until she was able to imitate some of her mother's domestic duties, a girl and her peers were called *šéšuʔt'm*. Between the ages of seven and eight, her age-status was called *smiʔłšéšuʔtm'*. From nine to fourteen (or until her menarche), the term was *sxʷiʔtm'iʔš*. Girls seventeen to eighteen years of age were known as *smiłšéw'tm'*. From age twenty, she was known as *smʔém*. At approximately age seventy, she became a *sy'oʔpsčin't*.

Throughout the life cycle, nearly all rituals of personal change were based upon the Doctrine of Signatures. A common notion from the Middle Ages, it is now an anthropological label for the cultural assumption that there are significant functional relationships between rituals and a person's behavior, between colors and feelings, and between the changing of physical properties and the correct ritual. For example, to imitate a person's physical disabilities or behavioral peculiarities would bring the same conditions to the imitator, regardless of the latter's age. To the Spokan, both beneficial and detrimental change was inextricably related to their rituals, including profane matters in one's daily life—even the mundane activities of domestic chores.

Pre-Birth

Conception and Fetal Development

How the pre-historic and earliest historic Spokan explained conception (*npupéwlštn* or *čšʔel't* - "breathing" or "life") and the eventual development of the fetus, can only be partially reconstructed from oral history, comparative studies of contiguous groups, and linguistic studies concerned with obstetrics (Egesdal, pers. comm.). In the late 1960s, there were few elders who could recall traditional Spokan explanations regarding conception and fetal development—explanations that differ totally from contemporary beliefs and postpartum practices. Some anthropologists refer to the traditional explanation as "accumulative pregnancy," which is the belief—based on the Doctrine of Signatures—that the growth of the fetus is an ongoing accumulation of sperm and catamenial blood. Specifically, the bones, brain, lymphatic and nervous systems, and later the teeth were contributed by the father's (white) semen; whereas the blood, hair, and certain organs were constituted from the mother's (red) blood. A woman became aware of her condition when she *missed her menstrual period* (*čxʷxc-núxʷ* or *ʔec-čxʷc-núxʷ-i* or *xaʔxaʔéyxʷxʷ*) and experienced the first trimester of nausea or *morning sickness* (*ʔecčpxʷpqnéltni* or *čč'essis*), as similarly believed by the Flathead (Ross 1964).

The Spokan believed that, at conception, the *fetus* (*ʕesnt'úk'ʷ*) gained the life soul (the spirit) from both parents, and derived its identity from them, as well as some behavioral *characteristics* (*tr'eʔw'y'eʔ*) and physical traits of a previous bilateral *ancestor* (*p'xʷp'xʷút* - "ones who were before"). This principle necessitated strict adherence by the *pregnant woman* (*čxʷcnúxʷ* - "menstrual flow has stopped") to observe many familial dietary and *behavioral prohibitions* (*sčxeʔnépleʔ*). It was believed that, throughout its gestation, a fetus was directly influenced by the behavior and diet of both parents—including whatever the expectant woman ate, drank, dreamed, heard, said, or did. For instance, misbehavior that frightened a pregnant woman could result in the baby being always nervous, even as an adult.

Low fecundity could be caused by psychosomatic etiologies, such as fear of pregnancy. Possible physical explanations include periodic protein deficiency, due to insufficient caloric intake as a whole or inadequate protein foods in particular. Low body fat, due to insufficient protein intake or excessive physical activity, can reduce a woman's fecundity. Other possible reasons are infection and abortion-caused physiological debilities.

The rates of mortality and morbidity during the pre-contact period, are not known exactly. Yet the evidence suggests that, prior to white incursion, pre-historic Indian populations rarely experienced rapid changes in their numbers. But with the introduction of Euro-American pandemics, the total Columbia Plateau population suffered a drastic decline of 48 percent between 1805 and 1870 (Boyd 1985:520). Various theories have tried to explain the long-term declines (Dixon 1962:325; Thoms 1983). Population density was relatively low within the Plateau, but "how much Plateau population declined between 1774 and 1805 is uncertain" (Boyd 1998:470). Several reasons can be posited as to why small population fluctuations occur among foraging peoples, such as the Spokan and other Plateau groups (Boyd 1985; Boyd and Hajda 1987). Boyd (1998:470) cites Stern (1993:43), who argues that the population changes were due to groups being absent while hunting bison on the Plains.

Despite the devastating effects of pandemics (Boyd 1985), missionization, the introduction of Euro-American medicine (Ross 1991a), and the inevitable deculturation of the Spokan, obstetrics was an area of traditional belief, behavior, and ritual that was relatively successful. Spokan women were key conservators of traditional culture, notably because of their knowledge and practice of obstetrics and the gathering of medicinal plants—activities once considered sacred.

Prenatal Prohibitions

There are some ethnographic explanations (Ray 1933; Teit 1928; Turney-High 1937; Elmendorf 1935-6; Smith 1936-8; Ross 1968-2008) of how pregnant women in the Plateau once observed the various taboos of behavior. The use of the term "taboo" in this monograph is best clarified by Steven Egesdal (pers. comm.):

> The word combines the English nuances of taboo (but that word is too strong) and sacred (perhaps a closer fit, without the religious overtone). It is something that deserves respect as having ultranatural powers, using the unnatural instead of supernatural, because the power of the item is natural (i.e., part of nature). That quality may inhere in, for instance, an artesian well, menstrual blood, or bird's eggs, and so on. It is an old word. Thompson River Salish has *xaʔxáʔ*, which describes the same notion. Elders would utter it in a whisper to describe something. It is signaled that one had to beware not to upset the natural order of things by disturbing (and therefore offending) something *xaʔxáʔ*. Offending the sacred asked bringing adverse consequences. Telling Coyote stories out of season risked an attack by rattlesnakes or bears. Talking about Coyote in summer risked bringing cold weather.

A woman's *pregnancy* (*hescšt'mí*) was the most dramatic change in her life and in her relationship with her husband. Even though a pregnant woman had to observe many strict dietary and behavioral taboos, she was expected to work industriously throughout her confinement, to strengthen herself for the impending ordeal, to ensure a less *painful delivery* (*ʔesnčʔaʔlénči* - "she is aching in her stomach"), and for the child's well-being (STHC). She would be subjected to a strict regimen of physical conditioning, which involved running, swimming, and bathing daily, regardless of the weather or season, and always in private.

It is difficult to reconstruct traditional attitudes about when a pregnant woman would abstain from sexual relations with her husband. But elderly female Spokan informants generally agreed that abstinence was determined not so much by custom or rule, but rather mutual agreement between husband and wife. Abstinence usually commenced in the first weeks of the third trimester. It was once believed that sexual relations beyond that could cause a premature birth or a baby so large as to cause a painful delivery (again, accumulative pregnancy).

Exercise and natural care were observed throughout a woman's pregnancy, and were beneficial to both mother and child. Contemporary physicians and health workers agree that such practices are probably the main reason why, among Indians prior to the early 1900s, there were low rates of toxemia—including preeclampsia and eclampsia—and other pregnancy disorders.

A pregnant woman was guided by *taboos* (*sčxeʔnépl'eʔ* - "restrictions"), which were monitored by her older consanguineal kinswomen, who frequently reminded her that violations of diet or behavior could result in congenital deformities in her child or later aberrant behavior—even though there were few birth defects. For example, she was admonished to never speak ill of others, and to avoid any extremes of social behavior or physical activity detrimental to the child's well-being and character development. If a child *stuttered* (*nslépcin* - "to stutter"), then the mother, while pregnant, had spoken ill of another.

Older women would warn a young *expectant mother* (*hescšt'mí*) that violations of any *pregnancy taboo* (*ncʾxʷél'tis* or *sčsmtél't*) could result in the death of both the woman and her unborn child, or result in *congenital defects* (*ʔec ʔul'm'wʾíl'm'* - "deformed baby"). For instance, looking upon a dead person—even a deceased member of her family—was a serious violation. In his earlier work with the Sanpoil and Nespelem, Ray similarly reported, "the child would be cross-eyed and open-mouthed, like a corpse" (1933:124). The viewing of a *dead domestic animal* (*sƛ'llsqáxeʔ*) was considered not dangerous, which was economically practical. A *miscarriage* (*heɫxʷúp*) was explained differently, depending upon the woman's generation and family. Traditionally, a woman known to be pregnant was forbidden to attend any mortuary rituals, because this was the most common explanation for a spontaneous abortion—usually during the second or third month

94

of pregnancy. Until recently, some maintained that a pregnant woman, when attending a burial ceremony, could possibly abort if she failed to protect her abdominal area by placing a section of buckskin around her waist—a practice no longer followed. But, to be cautious, a pregnant woman would not clean or process any of a dead animal's by-products, such as tanning hides.

Many of these behavioral prohibitions were consistent with the Doctrine of Signatures, even though not related to congenital defects. For example, a pregnant woman was admonished never to stick her head out of a window, nor to stand inside a doorway, but rather to pass either completely through the doorway or not to enter it at all. This taboo reflects the concern that the baby, during delivery, might become lodged partway in the birth canal.

A pregnant woman's diet was carefully monitored by older female relatives, since it was believed that the amount and types of food she ate could influence the physiological character of the baby. For example, if she ate greasy foods, then her child would have a greasy head throughout its life. Or if a pregnant woman ate any ground-nesting bird, then her baby would frequently cry.

An expectant mother increased her daily intake of water in order to *wash* (*čy' ecxʷúk'ʷ* - "I am washing") the fetus, thereby removing any physical contaminants that may have been inadvertently ingested by either the mother and passed to the fetus. Prior to the raising of the Spokane River (with the construction of Grand Coulee Dam), there were two sacred springs that produced waters noted for their *sweet taste* (*nt'iškʷ*). They *never froze* (*sw'ey'tn'*), and thus were presumed to contain curing properties, which, if drunk by a pregnant woman, would cleanse the unborn infant—a process called *skʷlétkʷ*.

A pregnant woman was compelled to observe prohibitions against eating certain animal foods, since the appearance or behavior of the *animal* (*xʷyxʷey'úł*) would be transferred to the fetus. Rabbit meat was avoided lest the child be born with a hare lip, weak legs, or a timid character. If the woman saw a cottontail rabbit, her baby might be born with a cleft palate (Egesdal, pers. comm.). A relatively recent variation involved the malicious treatment of a rabbit: "A Spokan woman [had a] hare lip due to her father's catching in a steel trap and kicking to death a rabbit that was stealing his garden and he was mad at it for stealing in his garden; he did it while his wife was pregnant with his girl" (Smith 1936-8:1106).

Eating predatory birds meant a child would likely be *greedy* (*čm'e?šm'cín'*) and unlikely to share food as an adult, e.g., she would eat before coming home from berrying. Eating the meat of a lynx could result in the baby having a round face, replicating the animal's characteristic short face. Otherwise, the white meat of lynx was considered good eating. A pregnant woman and her husband both avoided killing or molesting any *snake* (*titišúle?xʷ* - "creature that crawls on the ground") for fear that their child would have the markings and rough skin of the snake, or that the umbilical cord would be twisted around the baby's neck. The couple avoided touching the *shed skin* (*sn?awc'?encút*) of a snake, lest it cause the baby to be born with rough skin. If a pregnant woman's husband ever bound his feet together, the child would be born with its *feet wrapped in its umbilical cord* (*tému?* or *?eclč'lč'šin* or *lč'lč'e?čst* - "hobbled, fettered front legs and feet"). Nor would a woman eat lamprey or other types of anadromous fish in her third trimester, since this could cause the fetus to slip prematurely from the *womb* (*snč̓ɫ?sqaxe*).

A pregnant woman avoided certain parts of dead animals, lest her child later have behavioral characteristics of the offended animal. If a pregnant woman ate a fish's tail or the hooves or detached legs of a deer, then her child, like a twitching tail, would never be able to settle in one place—a behavior called *čsc'q'smnúpsmntm*. The person would never be able to sit still, or remain in one place, or be able to concentrate, or attend to responsibilities; rather, he would wander aimlessly, known as *one who drifts* (*člaʕpmɫk'ʷu?* - "wanderer"). Similarly, a child who played with the *detached tail of a deer* (*čxʷxʷtéptn* - "cut tail off deer hide") would suffer the same affliction. Children and adults knew they should never play with the parts of any dead animal, except hairballs from deer hide or the stomach of ungulates (used to make game balls).

A pregnant woman knew to not split the skull of any animal—even a deer to get the brains for tanning, or that of the (non-indigenous) *cow* (*sqáxeʔ*)—or to cook any animal's skull, else her baby's fontanel would take several years to close. "A white butcher [who] lived with a Spokan woman and all of his children had split heads from front to back [...] believed to have been the result of his splitting cow heads" (Smith 1936-8:1106). This was also an explanation for a child later appearing *demented* (*qʷoʔqʷawʼw*).

An expectant mother was continually reminded to never overeat or gain excessive weight, for fear the unborn child's head would be abnormally large, complicating the baby's delivery and causing excessive pain.

Certain foods were believed to result in certain types of physical characteristics or behaviors. Great importance was attached to dietary taboos, and many of the Spokan dietary prohibitions were similar to those that Ray cited for the contiguous Sanpoil and Nespelem:

> If pheasant [which had been imported] were eaten the child would cry until out of breath, then have convulsions. Meat in general was not eaten for an indefinite period preceding childbirth, and at no time during pregnancy was any meat eaten which was not strictly fresh. Eating of the fool hen was prohibited; else the child would be foolish (1933:124).

However, some elderly Spokan believed that both the pregnant woman and her husband could and did eat fool hen or spruce grouse, so the child, during infancy, would not fuss or cry.

Further examples of the Doctrine of Signatures are as follows: If the pregnant woman heard a *crow* (*Corvus brachyrhynchos* - *scʔqʼaqʼ*), raven (*C. corax* - *mláqlq*), or a *magpie* (*Pica pica* - *ʕánʼnʼ*) at night, the child would likely be a thief, emulating the behavior of such birds who stole bright and unusually shaped objects of human origin. If the mother heard the song of a *Western meadowlark* (*Sturnella neglecta* - *wʼewʼʼíckʷlʼeʔ*) during her delivery, the child could later become a sorcerer. At any time during her pregnancy, a woman was careful to never *step over* (*čłkʼʷtʼšlšénʔis*) or under her husband's projectile-type weapons, for they would never again shoot straight. This fear of the weapons being contaminated by menstrual blood, is another example of the Stigma of Femininity. The same precaution included firearms, particularly the rifle.

A pregnant woman who stepped over any type of spilt blood might have a spontaneous abortion, or experience a hemorrhage while pregnant. Particularly dangerous would be contact with another woman's menstrual blood, which was believed to cause the fetus to immediately abort, and prevent the woman from ever conceiving again. A child would experience frequent *fainting spells* (*qʷnʔíw* - "to faint") if her mother had looked upon a *corpse* (*tmtmnéyʼ*) while she was pregnant.

Nearly all Spokan notions of diet and behavior during pregnancy reflect the Doctrine of Signatures, including the selection of meats and animal organs. For instance, deer marrow was eaten by the pregnant woman so her *baby* (*ʔoʔxʷtélʼt* or *łoʔxtélʼt*) would develop strong bones and be an outstanding foot-racer ("fleet as a deer").

Some behaviors would result in the umbilical cord encircling the baby's head upon delivery and the baby being *strangled* (*čʼłpʼeʔcín* - "I choked him"). A pregnant woman never encircled her ankles or legs with any *binding material* (*ʔeclčʼlčʼšín*). She would never reach up high or lift a heavy object above her head, such as placing a large salmon high on a drying rack. She refrained from sewing or long-stitching, and from making any cat's cradle figures when telling a story.

Husbands too were required to be mindful of the consequences when working with material things. He would avoid setting traps or snares, working with cordage, tying knots, throwing a lasso, line-fishing, using a dip net when fishing, *placing a lariat over the head* (*łxʷpús*) of an animal, or making circular stretchers when processing beaver or muskrat pelts (STHC). Both the *husband and his pregnant wife never wore any cord about their necks* (*ta qeʔs łxʷpústxʷ*) during her pregnancy. Even young boys, whose mothers were pregnant, were *warned* (*xʔistéʔm*) to not *throw a rope around a horse's neck* (*ts qeʔcs łuxʷpústxʷ*).

A pregnant woman would never eat, clean, or even touch the intestines of fish or mammals, lest the umbilical cord become twisted or strangle the unborn fetus. A baby's stomach pains or cramps were attributed to one of the parent's aforementioned transgressions, or if either parent had thrown sinew or rawhide strips into a fire, or if the father had cinched a horse's saddle too tightly during his wife's pregnancy. Even after westernization, a pregnant woman's husband would avoid setting choker chain or any type of cable when logging, or replace an engine's fan belt.

Elders always cautioned a pregnant woman to never go too close to a fire, or perspire unduly, or over-exert herself, since overheating the body could cause her blood to clot and in turn cause severe leg pains during her confinement, sedulous abdominal cramps during early pregnancy, and even threaten the unborn infant. Heat exhaustion was thought to be responsible for a pregnant woman's persistent headaches or undue eyestrain. Similarly, a pregnant woman's nearness to excessively hot cooking pits, and later *iron stoves* (*snkʷ'l'sncútn* - "place to prepare food") and space heaters, was reason to have a clinical condition now termed an ovulatory bleeding. The taboo against excessive body heat or perspiration was recognized as a precaution during her menarche or menopause, as well. If a husband and his expectant wife became overly fatigued, she was likely to experience a difficult labor.

Until recently, a few Spokan depended upon these traditional beliefs to correct the behavior of children. For example, in the 1970s, a concerned grandmother cautioned her pregnant granddaughter to avoid watching television, as this could cause her child to be born *cross-eyed* (*np'lp'lč'ús*). The condition of a person born with a *white eye* (*píqs*), due to physical or pathological damage to the cornea, was called *hi čpáqs*, and was thought to have been caused by the mother looking at something forbidden during her pregnancy.

In all cultures that experience dramatic changes in lifestyle—usually deculturation—certain introduced foods and mechanical devices serve as explanations for societal dysfunction, especially if they are quite technological. Some elderly Spokan women would reinforce traditional taboos to pregnant grandchildren, and to existing grandchildren and great-grandchildren, by explaining how some modern mechanical devices are capable of causing specific illnesses or disabilities in the youth and congenital defects in the unborn. For example, the most common explanation for ocular problems was the watching of too much television, or simply staying up late while using electrically-powered lighting. The ultimate deleterious medical and physiological effects of excessive television, fast foods, and other unnatural behaviors, cannot be denied.

A pregnant woman would be quickly and severely reprimanded by her mother or mother-in-law for loss of temper or any other contemptible behavior, because, if not corrected, such misbehavior could lead to a difficult and *painful delivery* (*ʔesnc'aʔlénči* - "painful delivery").

The husband would also comply with *behavioral restrictions regarding an unborn child* (*nc'x̌ʷél'tiʔs*). These became more pronounced with the progression of his wife's pregnancy. When the woman first felt movement of the fetus, then he would stop hunting with a bow and arrow, or fishing with spear or leister. He could, however, accompany other fishermen or hunters, but would avoid touching fish or animal entrails. A man's less-than-ideal behavior, a *mean disposition* (*nč'sels*), or cruelty toward any domesticated or wild animal, would be later recalled as an explanation as to why his child manifested aberrant behavior. If an expectant woman's husband *beat his horse* (*plsqx̌ʔencút*) or exhibited any other abuse of an animal, then his child could later be unsuccessful in securing an animal as a tutelary spirit. The interpretation for an unsuccessful collective hunt could be that a participant, or even his father, had once been cruel or unreasonably disrespectful to a large and economically significant animal, particularly any wild or domesticated *pregnant animal* (*ʔecnt'k'ʷélt* or *nt'k'ʷélt*).

During a wife's pregnancy, the husband was careful to never mistreat *domesticated animals* (*tx̌ʷóx̌ʷ*) or disturb any type of hibernating or sleeping animal, lest his child be stillborn. When in the woods, he had to be cautious where he stepped so as to avoid touching any animal or bird bones—especially an animal's skull, for fear the baby would be deformed. Even removing a *bird's egg* (*ʔuʔúseʔ*) from a nest would be sufficient cause for his wife to have a spontaneous abortion. Stepping upon an egg of a turtle, snake, or ground-nesting bird could cause damage to his child's skull during the delivery. One elder remembered her younger brother being told by her great-grandmother that, when in the woods, he should never destroy the nest or *eggs of fire ants* (*sxʷúxʷy'e?* - "ants"). Similarly, pregnant women, when collecting punk wood, were careful not to disturb downed trees that housed termite eggs.

Any pregnant woman was continually reminded by her family and kin group to be exceptionally polite—never arrogant, loud, or boisterous—as these *undesirable traits* (*n?eccšt'im*) would be endowed in the unborn child. Violations of this principle by either parent could cause congenital defects, such as *deformed limbs* (*čq'ʷaq'ʷu?secst*), and later *psychological* (*síl'sl't*) or *behavioral problems* (*me?mé?t* - "annoying"). If the pregnant woman spent too much time looking out of her dwelling at other people, "with the eyes of an owl," so too would her child always be involved in other people's affairs, and would gather, like tough and inedible roots, the rumors of others. One elderly lady extended this metaphor by saying that rumors would eventually "plug and even distend a pregnant person's intestines, so she appeared as though she was going to give birth to twins." A pregnant woman who did not keep her counsel, could have a difficult delivery during which her baby's head would presumably appear in the birth canal and then withdraw several times, until eventual delivery. If a child, at an early age, was reticent to talk, or had difficulty speaking, then these lamentable traits were explained as being the result of the mother's endless chatter or unfounded rumors of other people.

During an expectant mother's third trimester, she was warned to not sleep too much, but rather *rise* (*nwisslš*) early in the morning, before the other occupants of her dwelling. Otherwise, she would experience a difficult and protracted delivery, and her child would be lazy. Similarly, she would never remain in bed after sunrise or go to bed before sunset, otherwise the fetus would become too large and the delivery would be difficult. Furthermore, the child would later sleep too much, and never be an active or an industrious person. Likewise, the expectant woman's husband would arise early for the same reason; failing to do so would diminish the later ambition of the undelivered child. There were numerous explanations as to why a child or woman was lazy, which was the most undesirable trait in a woman. An elderly woman said:

> [...] a pregnant woman should always get up early, before everyone else, and not lay in bed. When I had my first child, I was visiting my grandmother, who was not home, so I laid on a small patch of grass and went to sleep. When my grandmother returned she woke me and gave me a terrible scolding, telling me that if I slept during the day, I'd have a very difficult and painful delivery, which I did. Yet it was also my husband's fault because he would lay about in bed in the morning (Ross 1968-2008).

Personal cleanliness and the condition of one's home were given considerable attention. This proscription was followed partly because, if ignored, this undesirable characteristic would later be acquired by the unborn child. The "loose material" (*qʷpswéyn*) with which mice lined their nests was a metaphor for any woman's home that was *littered* or *unkempt* (*loqʷ*).

There was a recorded account of a woman who was an accomplished hunter of small game and birds, using the popular .22 Winchester rimfire rifle *cartridge* (*t'm'ayóye?*). One day, when she was pregnant with her daughter, she came too near to a ruffed grouse, a bird known to protect its nests when humans or other animals come too close—particularly the male grouse after the chicks are born. Consequently, when the woman approached the *bird's nest* (*himéne?*), the frightened bird flew up, attacked her, and fell to the ground in front of the woman, fluttering its wings, spreading its tail feathers dramatically, making a *tukʷtukʷtukʷ* sound by violently flapping its wings, and producing a threatening *ur'ur'ur'* sound in its throat, which frightened the woman. Later, her child often became excited, flapped her arms, and imitated the sound of a defensive grouse (STHC).

Any complication of birth, congenital defect, or later psychological difficulties, were always attributed to a moral transgression committed by either the newborn's uterine mother or jural father during the gestation period. For example, a pregnant woman and her husband would avoid criticizing a *deformed* (*?ul'm'w'íl'm'*) person, else the same condition would characterize their unborn child. A child with a *long misshapen head* (*kʷossnáy?a?qn*) indicated that the parents had made an unkind judgment of a person so afflicted. Parents of a baby born with an *abnormally opened frontal fontanel* (*sntqʷ?máw'a?sqn'*) were considered guilty of killing

98

or injuring a pregnant domesticated or *wild animal* (*ʔuw'q'ʷuʔt* - "wild"). The Spokan never attempted to flatten a child's head.

Yet some prenatal difficulties were unavoidable. Discomfort, most commonly morning sickness, was treated with family formulae, such as tea infusions made from the small branches of chokecherry or diluted clay, taken before the morning meal. Solutions made with powdered wood or ground deer bone charcoal were apparently an effective medicament for this malady. (Other pregnancy-related medicines are discussed in greater detail in Chapter XVII.)

Young married women were apprehensive, if not fearful, of becoming pregnant, because of their lack of experience and their concern for the many social, physical, and dietary *restrictions* (*cnč'xʷepl'e*). They were unavoidable—due to the near-constant familial and group surveillance—and would effectively control the woman's life throughout her pregnancy. Moreover, she had no assurance of the eventual outcome of the birthing process. There was always the possibility of an interruption of her pregnancy, due to unexpected physical trauma or, it was believed, some moral transgression on her part. A pregnant woman was always at risk of malevolent sorcery, or any other explanation for an unwanted abortion. Another explanation for a spontaneous abortion, or for premature labor, was that the pregnant woman had seen a ghost. Usually the ghost was from a deceased child of the area, and was lonely, causing it to remain in a liminal state waiting for a soul mate to mitigate its loneliness.

Expectant parents were urged to never insult or malign another person, for fear of sorcery, as retribution to the unborn. They were cautioned to be particularly humble and respectful to others during the time of gestation and delivery. If anyone took anything for granted, in thought or speech, their desires could be denied. Clearly, among the traditional Spokan, arrogance was not considered a quality character trait, but rather would "cloud a person's vision to not understand what you see; close your heart and not really feel things; and to not hear what is in the wind." An elderly sage offered a Zen-like aphorism: "To see a leaf fall, one must first hear the leaf leave the tree." Some claim that there were words that resembled the actual creaking sounds of branches (T. Wynecoop, pers. comm.).

Couvade

During a pregnant woman's confinement, her husband practiced the couvade syndrome (Fr. "to brood"), which was a universal expression of sympathetic magic, in which the husband adhered to strict dietary and behavioral prohibitions, for mainly two purposes: Firstly, by observing specific *traditional taboos* (*nčxeʔn'eʔpleʔtis*), he publicly indicated his paternity (i.e., that he was indeed the jural father) and his commitment to assume all paternal obligations. Secondly, it was believed that lack of such adherence could be injurious to his unborn child if it were a boy (Ross 1991a).

Strict moral prohibitions were more pronounced when the man's wife was in her third trimester, and even more so when nearing her delivery. Ray observed the same in his work with the Sanpoil and Nespelem (1933:124). Several months before delivery, a wife might leave her husband and remain with her mother until her delivery.

Several elderly women said how, in the past, a man might demonstrate sympathetic behavior by complaining of a stomachache when his wife was experiencing morning sickness. It could not be recalled if a Spokan man actually confined himself during his wife's delivery, or went through any unusual ritual of symbolic delivery, as was done in some cultures (Ross 1964:n.p.).

It was prescribed that, during his couvade, the man should never exhibit mannerisms of a woman, even jokingly, as these could be transferred to an unborn male, who might later in life emulate characteristics unbecoming a man, such as becoming a berdache. Throughout the Plateau, there were men and women—each termed a "berdache"—who could possess the power, skills, mannerisms, and dress of the opposite gender. As will be discussed later, these abilities were not actively sought, but were considered of value to the group.

When an expectant woman's husband was telling a story, he never imitated a woman's voice, or the sounds of those birds that were considered weak.

During his couvade, he might be assisted by those age-mates with whom he had a joking relationship—certainly his *sweathouse partners* (*npλ'áceʔ*). They would be solicitous about him when in public, but privately they would subject him to intense joking (*xʷtpaw'sqn* - "verbal repartee"), suggesting he had required assistance in creating the unborn child, and its true paternity would be jokingly accredited to a decrepit and unlikely *man alone* (*ql'tm'xʷm'ís*), such as a bachelor or an old debilitated man. An elderly gentleman related to me how his great-grandfather told his father how a pregnant woman's male kinsmen assisted the expectant husband during his couvade by assuming his domestic and food-getting chores. Although this was an account of a single instance, it was likely a common practice.

After the child's birth, the father was not expected to observe any further couvade taboos. As to the potential grandparents, there is no evidence that they were committed to any similar changes in their behavior at any time.

The active participation in the couvade was less apparent by the time of the establishment of the Spokane Indian Reservation, since the unfortunate effects of deculturation were already drastically altering many aspects of traditional Spokan culture, including the economic roles of husbands, who often lived off-reservation for wage-earning. Another possible factor is that the Spokan believed the couvade was of lesser significance than was practiced by other groups—particularly western Plains groups (Benedict 1932:14).

Gender Determination

There were different ways of presumably predicting the gender of an unborn child. The most common was for the pregnant woman to dream of it. The second most common was when an elderly woman *wise in these matters* (*č'éw'lč'exʷ*) would visit the pregnant woman three times during her last trimester. A grandmother—usually the matrilineal grandmother—would be the first to know of her granddaughter's pregnancy because of recurring prophetic dreams she had of her granddaughter's condition. Just prior to the delivery, she would sometimes profess to know the unborn grandchild's sex.

The shape and hair distribution of an older sibling was presumably indicative. Elongated hair that descended onto his or her neck, indicated a male baby, whereas a wider hair distribution predicted a female. For an unborn *primogenitary child* (*šʔitmíšlt* - "first child" or *sciʔíti*), a *midwife* (*n-n-ʔec-čt-'ím* or *sxʷkʷénlt* or *sxʷčšt'-ím* - "nurse") might lift the pregnant woman's hair at the nape of the neck and interpret her hair configuration—again, the Doctrine of Signatures.

A stranger approaching a camp would know there was going to be a birth if a rainbow was observed; but it is unknown whether the phenomenon indicated the sex of the *baby boy or girl* (*ʔoʔxwtél't*). It was believed that if a boy always wanted to be at his pregnant mother's side, then she would deliver another boy.

The appearance of a *Great Horned Owl* (*Bubo virginianus* - *snineʔ*) for three nights during the first trimester predicted that the unborn would likely be a male. This was perhaps, as one elderly lady explained, an interpretation of phallic symbolism because of the owl's long tufted ears. A woman in solitude could be informed of her unborn child's gender by a yellow-tailed chipmunk (*Eutamias ruficauduss* - *q'ʷq'ʷc'w'éy'eʔ*) or a hummingbird. When a pregnant mother had repeated dreams of either a male or female animal, it was an accepted prediction of her baby's probable sex.

Other procedures were not predictive, but rather meant to influence, if not altogether determine, the child's gender. Internal medicaments would be given to the pregnant woman. Or a grandmother might massage her granddaughter's extended abdominal region during the third trimester. Some felt that the dominance of a particular parent's personality, if pronounced or unique, could determine the child's sex. A few elders contended that an individual's appearance and behavior was more similar to either a father or mother who was thought to be more dominant in behavior or possessed certain physical features.

100

Birth

One can only speculate as to the success of the average Spokan woman's full-term pregnancy and the eventual birthing process, because there is limited archaeological evidence of fetal mortality (Galm, pers. comm.) or of death during birthing (Sprague, pers. comm.). Yet most likely there was relatively little fetal or post-natal procedural mortality. Few of the contemporary elders could recall a woman dying during *childbirth* (*nt'k'ʷmnqín*).

There was no recollection if sorcery was ever believed the reason a child was *stillborn* (*ʔesλ'líl*).

Birthing

When *parturition* (*č'iʔtmnúʔxʷ* - "about to give birth") became imminent, the pregnant woman made every effort to be with her mother *before labor commenced* (*n-ʔecʔ enwncúti*), since the potential grandmother was preferred to assist in the delivery. Elderly women maintained that the assistance of a mother or grandmother would provide for an easier and safer delivery, and thus the expectant mother would be less apprehensive.

Cline (1938:120) noted that the *Sinkaietk* (*sʔučn'aʔqíni* or *sučnaʔqíni*), the southern Okanogan, used the menstrual hut for birthing. Ray also reported (1933:125) how the Sanpoil and Nespelem did the same, or used a partitioned part of the house. Some contemporary younger Spokan, when trying to reconstruct accounts of obstetrical procedures, claimed that the menstrual hut was used by the Spokan for delivery. However, linguistic evidence and ethnographic agreement within oral history from elderly and more *traditional women* (*čnp'xʷtl'šéw'si*), indicate that the Spokan never used the menstrual hut for delivery, lest a *male child* (*ttw'it*) develop female behaviors or become a *transvestite* (*st'ém'y'eʔ* or *meʔmútm*), or that a *female child* (*šéšuʔtm'*) have *questionable morals* (*č'słcúwt* - "bad habits") as an adult.

The Spokan typically used a small, temporary, *tipi-like structure* (*tq'éłpntm*) covered with brush. Elmendorf (1935-36, 2:61-2) described how occasionally a woman, preparing for a delivery, would retire to a birthing place having a small enclosure of pre-fashioned vertical tule mats, adjacent to running water. In preparation for a delivery, the attending *mother* (*tum'*) or midwife would dig a *shallow trench* (*nciqleʔxʷm*) inside the birthing lodge. The earthen floor was completely covered with grasses or with plants, such as sage, sweet grass, various species of *Festuca*, or the (preferred) soft, broad leaves of *mullein* (*Verbasecum thapsus* L. - *smén'xʷ* - "tobacco"). Even though mullein is a weed introduced from Eurasia, it became used throughout the Plateau. Around the birthing trench, and atop the layers of grass (*skʷeʔr'úleʔxʷ* or *skʷrúleʔxʷ* or *supúlexʷ*), several new tule mats would be placed.

Two *large stakes* (*úleʔxʷ*) or two *digging sticks* (*péceʔ*) were driven either side of the birthing trench, against which the puerperal woman positioned her knees for stability while squatting, and which she could grasp during a *delivery* (*ʔest'k'ʷelti* or *n'e t'k'ʷul'l'*). However, some elderly women contended that digging sticks were never used for this purpose; rather, the expectant woman would push both her feet against two additional horizontal stakes firmly implanted at her feet. The other two connecting birthing stakes were sometimes reinforced by a horizontal cross member secured to the top of each stake, giving her further support. Some women preferred a large loop of twisted smooth Indian hemp or *braided* (*q'ic'*) *horse-hair rope* (*c'iqp*), secured to the apex of the structure's *poles* (*čtíléneʔtn* - "multiple poles"), providing support as she squatted on her heels during delivery (Elmendorf, pers. comm.). The expectant woman could receive extra support by partially sitting back on the knees of the midwife, who knelt behind her and held her.

A *squatting position* (*q'ʷq'ʷišénm*) facilitated the pregnant woman's breathing as well as circulation in her *peritoneal area* (*sctk'ʷé*). This position allowed a more natural gravitational delivery. These practices, plus the prenatal physical conditioning, negated any need for an *episiotomy* (*nnič'psntm* - "she was cut at her perineum"). That invasive surgical procedure was not needed by Indian women until western hospitalization and use of the *supine* (*cql'ʔut* - "lie on one's back") birthing position, which increases the likelihood of staphylococcus infections and other communicable iatrogenic diseases when *her knees were up* (*c'l'c'l'qin'šn'*).

In discussing the deculturation of the Flathead and the resulting degeneration of their medical profile, Father Palladino, S.J. contrasts the comparative ease of aboriginal parturition:

> The Flat-Heads are well built and were in earlier days a strong, healthy race, subject to few diseases, but their present physical condition is greatly deteriorated. An unequivocal proof of this may be found in the fact that the wonderful facility with which the Indian women of former days were wont to bring forth their children, had entirely ceased to be. Whereas, at an earlier date, parturition among them was attended with scarcely the disability of an hour's delay to take again to their horses and go to work, it is now just as difficult, long and laborious as with the whites. Until more recent times, death in child-birth was a thing unknown among those Indians, whose former power of endurance, due no doubt to their remarkably sound and robust constitution, could scarcely be credited at the present day. This benevolent gift of nature exempted the Indian women from pains which their savage state would have rendered doubly grievous and unendurable (1894:5-6).

A woman knew she was *close to birth* (*č'iʔtmnúxʷ*) when her *amniotic sac broke* (*nt'k'ʷmnqínm* - "water breaks"). When she sensed the onset of labor pains (*ʔenwncúti* - "hurting" or *čʔer'nči* - "aching at the womb"), the attendant helped position her over the trench by securing her arms in the suspended birthing loop. Once positioned and settled, she was given warm water to drink, and the attendant applied either a handful of warmed green *ponderosa needles* (*sčč'č'ewečst*) or a warmed mat of black moss to her extended *abdomen* (*ʔur'in* - "stomach"); this was believed to encourage the birthing process by stimulating the woman's insides. During the first and *second stage of delivery* (*c'ʔer'mí* - "to hurt"), the expectant mother was instructed not to *scream* (*c'ew'lš*) or *call out* (*nyáʕʷyolsm*), but to *be brave* (*k'ʷaʔqnéysm* - "bites her top lip to fight back pain"), because it was believed her stoicism and courage would positively influence the child's character. A woman who did not scream was later complimented when asked by neighbors and friends, "When did you deliver?" If the midwife thought the delivering mother was about to *cry* (*c'qʷaqʷ*) out or scream, she would reach around, cover her mouth, and make soothing noises to calm the woman. Each practitioner had a unique repertoire of comforting euphonic sounds.

During birthing, the woman was told how and when to contract her breathing, as her mother or the midwife alternately massaged and *pressed down* (*čtqqapqntm*) on the woman's abdomen with each contraction, eventually pushing the baby out onto a tule mat. If the birthing process became prolonged, the woman could drink an infusion of boiled *smooth sumac* (*Rhus glabra* L. - *t'lt'ltéɫp*); the red infusion was believed to help turn the baby, to facilitate delivery.

As recently as the 1960s, most elderly women were able to recall an occasion when, prior to the reservation system, a woman in their respective group had delivered her baby by herself when traveling alone, or when separated from the group—collecting berries or gathering roots. Even in a group, a woman would deliver her own baby when there was no experienced woman in the party. Many years ago, an elderly Sinkaietk woman—who had married a Spokan—related with considerable pride how her mother, while traveling during a severe snowstorm, had delivered her in a makeshift tree-well shelter, where she and her newborn then spent the night. The next day, the mother wrapped her baby in a blanket and rode two days before reaching *Wellpinit* (*sčecw'ešuʔs*). Indeed, elderly women often related how most women preferred to perform the delivery themselves if they were without support from a close female kinsperson (STHC). In his early cross-cultural survey of the Columbia River upper Cascades, Townsend reported a solo birthing:

> The tent in which she was lying was within a few feet of the one which I occupied, and we had no intimation of the matter being in progress until we heard the crying of the infant. It is truly astonishing with what ease the parturition of these women is performed; they generally require no assistance in delivery, being fully competent to manage the whole paraphernalia themselves. In about half an hour after this event, we got under way, and the woman walked to the boat, carrying her new born infant on her back, embarked, laughed, and talked as usual, and appeared, in every respect, as well as if nothing had happened (1839:242).

102

Wilson's descriptions of a woman's postpartum confinement, and her preparation for childbirth, form one of the few known accounts:

> After childbirth, the women have to live apart for about thirty days, frequently washing themselves, and, before joining the others, they have to wash all their clothes and undergo general purification. A small lodge is erected about ten or twelve paces from the large or family one, and in this the woman lives during the period of her seclusion, which is kept with great strictness, notwithstanding the close proximity of her friends and relations. When the time of childbirth is felt to be approaching, the woman goes out and plucks a sprig of the wild rose, which she places upright in the ground of the lodge and fixes her eyes upon it during the pangs of labour, which it is believed are alleviated by this ceremony. The rattles of the rattlesnake are also frequently used as a medicine to procure ease in the same cases (1866:294).

An early account of a delivery is unique in that the Spokan woman apparently delivered after escaping her captives:

> [...] a woman was taken in labour whilst escaping on horseback from the Blackfeet; hastily dismounting, she removed behind a bush and gave birth to a female child, at which moment some of her pursuers came up, but filled with admiration at the courage of a woman who would attempt an escape under such circumstances, with unexpected gallantry they allowed her to pursue her way; and after several days solitary, she reached the camp of her tribe, with the baby wrapped in a shawl at her back, neither of them the worse for the hardships they had undergone (Wilson 1866:295).

In instances of a difficult delivery or a prolapsed uterus, a female shaman would make beneficial plant concoctions for the expectant woman to drink. After a difficult delivery, a major concern was the danger of *large clots of blood* (*mɫč'éye?*), which could lead to cardiac arrest or a pulmonary embolism later. If the baby experienced an excessive subdural *hemorrhaging* (*hensxʷmmi*) due to a traumatic delivery, then death was inevitable—though some claimed this never happened.

Though seldom discussed, elderly Spokan women have suggested that sorcery was once considered a potential complicating factor in a delivery, and could result in later physiological or psychological defects in the child. Even several decades after deculturation, elderly Spokan women would encourage a pregnant granddaughter to deliver at home—not in a hospital—for fear of contracting postpartum infection and other iatrogenic diseases, particularly in obstetrical wards. This reasoning was based on their experience and observations that hospitals are where "one goes to die," and where one's organs—during surgery or at night—are surreptitiously removed or replaced. Even a *healthy* (*meɫ*) visitor could be afflicted with illness when *visiting* (*čxʷimsqélixʷi*) a sick kinsperson in a western medical facility.

We have no information regarding pre-contact intrauterine death or septic abortions, but there were oral accounts of both a mother and her newborn child dying during delivery in the early historical period (Ross 1994), and several recorded archaeological burials of such tragedies (Ross 1984a). Also, there are some excavated Spokan sites where a mother was buried with her neonatal baby, including a (river-eroded) burial that contained a mother and *prenatal twins* (*sn?éƛ'ƛ* or *sn?es?essél'*) (Ross 1993). In the few instances of known "delivery death" and multiple burials (with in situ evidence), death was not necessarily a complication from the birthing, but instead likely due to Euro-American pandemic communicable diseases. Given the demonstrated advantages of traditional prenatal care and birthing procedures, postnatal morbidity and mortality were probably infrequent.

Parents felt particularly blessed to have twins (Teit 1930:166; Elmendorf 1935-6, 2:10). However, no special ceremony marked multiple births, and no special rituals or twin songs were known to have existed (Teit 1930:38). In fact, twins did not have any special power or tutelary spirit. If, during her first trimester, a pregnant woman happened to *dream* (*qéy's*) of one or more bear cubs—especially in a recurring dream—then it was believed she might have twins. Oral history tended to confirm Lord's early observation that "Twin-births are rare" (1866, 2, 232).

Upon delivery, the *newborn* (*sic-ɫo?xʷtél't* - "new baby") was either immediately plunged into a basket of cold water for washing and to stimulate the baby's breathing, or the midwife or woman's mother would breathe into the baby's mouth with several rapid strong breaths. Afterwards, the attendant rubbed the infant's body and extremities vigorously with soft tanned deer hide or the top sides of mullein leaves, to strengthen the baby and to remove birth lines. She would then wash the newborn, and massage the infant's nose, and sometimes the arms and legs. Some elders remember their mothers saying how the baby was then wrapped in a pre-warmed horse or saddle blanket, to prevent it from becoming deformed. Prior to the availability of such trade goods, the baby was wrapped in rabbit skins or soft kneaded buckskin. Attendants were careful to not touch the soft area of the baby's skull, the *frontal fontanel* (*sntqʷm'áw'a?sqn'*), for fear of injuring the newborn.

To facilitate expulsion of the *afterbirth* (*ntxʷúsm* or *ntxʷséltn* or *sc'síkʷlt'n*), if necessary, an attendant *gently* (*k'ʷkʷen'ist*) applied steady downward pressure each time the fundus contracted. If the placenta was not being expelled, an attendant would wrap handfuls of warmed green pine needles in a piece of *tanned deer hide* (*sip'i*) and apply it the woman's abdomen, in the belief that warming the abdominal area thins the blood. The procedure was repeated until the placenta was expelled, sometimes after drinking a tea made from mashed *uncooked* (*xʷel'-?ek'*) *wild licorice root* (*Ligusticum grayi - ?eyút* or *k'ʷaxt*).

To prevent bleeding, the attendant would carefully fold the umbilical cord back upon itself and tie off the remaining appendage with prepared deer leg sinew. Only then did she sever the umbilical cord, approximately 10 to 12 cm from the child, using her teeth or sharp obsidian. After expulsion of the placenta, rabbit skin was placed between the mother's legs to absorb any moisture, such as further discharge or blood. The material was replaced as needed with a clean rabbit skin, and the soiled pad was washed and dried for later reuse.

Several medicaments were believed helpful to a woman's post-natal recovery: When available, the fresh leaves of pasture wormwood were crushed and steeped in warm water and drunk by the new mother as a tea, to "cleanse" her. It also served as a post-natal washing solution, applied to her *forehead* (*sčč'méssn'*) to cure any headache. A leaf could be placed on the genitalia to *relieve pain* (*c'?ermís* - "it caused her pain") and to heal (contract) her uterus. Another type of bitter but cleansing tea was made from leaves and stems from the upper reaches of immature *mountain alder* (*Alus tenuifolia* Nutt. - *č'ič'i?tn'é4p*). The new mother would drink this concoction daily for at least one week. A similar tea was brewed from both red willow and alder. Red willow tea was drunk in great quantities on a daily basis, as it was believed to clean out the womb and help restore the woman's lost blood. The entire stonecrop plant (*Sedum lanceolatum* Tott.) was crushed and steeped in hot water as a medicinal drink by women after delivery, to cleanse the womb.

The baby's *navel* (*č4xʷéw's*) would be thoroughly rubbed with the *tallow* (*sq'ʷuct* - fat or grease, or *snlóqʷ*) that covers a deer's kidneys. Some grandmothers recommended applying a mixture of deer tallow and powdered dry fresh lichen to the navel. After removing the spiny exoperidium of the edible pear-shaped *mushroom* (*Lycoperdon echinatum*), some women mixed its contents with deer fat to gently and thoroughly rub into the healing navel. The attached umbilical cord was dressed with a folded patch of tanned deer hide, or a small, beaded buckskin pouch, and held in place by a stricture of rawhide or twisted Indian hemp encircling the baby's body. Deer fat was used specifically for dressing a *baby's umbilicus* (*temu?*), sometimes called *?ulíkʷ4* or *č4xʷew's*.

The *placenta* (*snxʷúl'l'tn* cf. *k'ʷúl'l'* - "it was born," or *snč4?emútn* or *sntxʷústn*) and detached umbilical cord could each be disposed of in one of several ways, and there is disagreement as to which methods were most commonly used, if at all. Yet the primary concern was to keep them away from animals and malevolent humans.

The detached umbilical cord could be placed in a small buckskin bag and attached to the infant's cradleboard, until the child was ambulatory, at which time the mother or grandmother might ritually dispose of the cord by burial. Or, in a more frequent practice called *?élk'ʷis 4u tému?* ("dispose of the umbilical cord"), the cord was placed in a *small buckskin pouch* (*snému?tn*), which was buried under a rosebush by the midwife or mother, to discourage recovery by an animal or sorcerer. The hole could be hidden by walking over the area with a horse. Also, stones could be placed on top to discourage animals from excavating. Or the grandmother or mother would "bury this dried up navel (umbilical cord) right outside the door [of the birthing hut], so it will continually call the child home!" (STHC). Teit noted that "Navel-string pouches were in common use" (1930:381).

The placenta and (still attached) umbilical cord could instead be placed in a closed cedar bark container, and tightly wedged or otherwise secured high in a tree by the new father. However, several elderly women explained that the cord was kept in a small buckskin bag until the owner's death, and not disposed of as reported for the Flathead by Turney-High: "It was never thrown away or discarded. After a boy arrived at puberty and was ashamed of this ornament his mother preserved the token for him. Girls, too, wore theirs until they were ashamed of it, such being a mark of childhood" (1937:68).

Any blood or materials associated with the birthing blood could be contained and buried with rocks atop a disposal site, in talus, to prevent detection by humans or animals. It was feared that a potential sorcerer could manipulate the blood to harm the mother or her child, and if animals dug up any disposed birthing material, the woman could become barren. The placenta and umbilical cord were never burned, nor was the placenta considered to be an undeveloped baby. A grandmother might throw her daughter's placenta into a moving stream, which was believed to prevent her daughter from having any more babies (STHC).

Contact with missionaries affected the once-traditional rituals associated with an individual's placenta and umbilical cord. However, it is not known as to what extent, if any, the practices of the Spokan were influenced by Protestant missionaries, nor how these practices varied over time. But it is known that the original practices of the Flathead regarding the care of the placenta and umbilical cord was altered by Jesuit missionization. In essence, the Christians taught the native Americans to not preserve body parts, and that such items should not be ritualized or worn as amulets.

The so-called Stigma of Femininity (the fear of being contaminated by menstrual blood) was always present. After the birthing, the attendants conducted their own purification in a specially-built and secluded sweathouse, to remove any of the mother's or child's blood. Afterward, the structure was dismantled; the willow frame was carefully burned in the existing fire; and the vesicular basalt sweathouse stones were buried and never used again.

The newborn's umbilicus was intermittently aired daily to encourage drying, and the greased patch was replaced. Once the child's navel had healed, the new mother resumed most of her domestic duties. She ate certain foods believed to assist her lactation and to give strength to the child's bones. Several elderly women maintained that a husband and wife refrained from sexual intercourse for approximately three months from the time of the child's delivery; whereas others claimed that the parents resumed *sexual intercourse* (*skʷénuʔs*) once the child's navel had *healed* (*p'ʔáx*).

To induce *sleep* (*sʔíts̆*) in a restless newborn, the edible *dark-colored mushroom* (*Lycoperdon umbrinum* - also *sʔíts̆*) was utilized. Or the mother might collect its dried spores in her hands and rub them on the child's eyelids and cheeks, until *he sleeps* (*ʔíts̆*) (Egesdal, pers. comm.). Some elders believed that rubbing the spores on the child's temple produced the same results. During such treatments, the mother or *maternal grandmother* (*čč̆y'éʔ*) would sing a soothing child's melody, or imitate the sounds of a contented animal.

When a child lost a deciduous tooth, it was surreptitiously buried by the grandmother to prevent the child being harmed by a malevolent sorcerer. It was believed that a sorcerer in possession of any part of the intended victim's body—particularly one or more teeth—could cripple or kill the child. This fear of contagious sorcery prompted the Spokan to conceal all detached or rejected body parts. Some elders recalled their grandparents placing a child's deciduous tooth in a piece of meat, which was fed to a dog, so the child would develop strong teeth, and because the dog later defecated the tooth away from people (Elmendorf, pers. comm.).

Lord, Wilson's colleague, observed a ritual that tended to integrate the extended family of a newborn:

Amongst the 'Salish,' mis-named Flatheads, and the Kalleespelem [Kalispel], it was in primitive times the custom, amongst the wealthier families of a tribe, for the paternal relatives to present the mother on the birth of a child, such things as the child would need. The maternal relations made return of clothing and other valuables, but not of food (1866, 2:231).

Midwives

An expectant woman, whether by herself or aided by a kinswoman, usually had the option of being attended by a midwife. A midwife was typically not of the same kin group as the expectant woman, because a non-related person was believed to have greater empathy than a kinswoman. For group harmony, a midwife was always circumspect regarding personal problems and sensitive matters. An *unwed elderly* (*m'e?m'íst* or *m'm'e?míst* - "old maid") midwife was considered as competent as one who had borne children. But several elders felt that, in the past, there was concern that a baby girl being delivered by such a woman would later not be able to conceive.

In addition to being knowledgeable in birthing, only female midwives knew how to perform abortions, possessed esoteric knowledge of women's aphrodisiacs, and on occasion performed love spells to enable a woman to capture the attention and affections of a man. There is a recorded instance of a 105-year-old woman who explained how the most powerful love songs of her generation (1840s) were composed and owned by an elderly midwife who, as proof of her ability, had once lived with a much younger man.

Some older women were known for their knowledge and skills of *midwifery* (*n?eccčšt'im*), and were compensated with small gifts, but never with traditional forms of wealth. During the reservation period, some midwives would accept more substantial compensation, but seldom in the form of money. Some elders maintained that, in the past, it was believed that an exceptional midwife received her obstetrical powers from supernatural sources, which thus forbade her from being materially compensated for her services. Yet she would be rewarded in the form of communal reputation and status, and occasionally a role of leadership among the women of the village. Elders recalled that although a midwife would not gain wealth or possessions, she was able to sustain a relationship with a supernatural power—usually a guardian spirit.

The older midwives of a settlement, as an informal cadre, helped and shared their knowledge with any younger woman who had assisted with at least one delivery and was willing to learn obstetrical skills— including the identification and use of botanical medicaments. Yet they never shared their knowledge of such medicaments with non-kinspeople. A younger woman aspiring to be a midwife was always assisted during her first deliveries by one or more of the established midwives, or until she acquired confidence and had demonstrated her ability.

Interestingly, not all Indians looked favorably upon midwifery. While at the Tschimakain Mission, the wife of Reverend Eellis told Angus McDonald that:

> [...] once a physician was sent for her by her own permission, but she freed herself before he arrived. She said that the old Indian mothers held, children brought to the world with the help of mid-wives were not so self reliant and brave as those born with no help but that of the laboring mother (Howay, *et al.* 1907:204).

If a *difficult delivery* (*n'e tl'xʷmíst* - "it will be difficult") was anticipated, an older woman with obstetrical experience would assist, particularly in the case of a *breech baby* (*?esčwupm'ús* or *?o?xʷtél't* - "feet first").

A male shaman—often a male berdache—would on occasion be asked to assist. Despite their presence, men were reported to have never physically assisted; rather, the shaman would relax the mother-to-be by singing obstetrical breathing chants, offering advice, giving reassurance to her, and, if necessary, acting as a liaison between the woman and her family regarding her progress (Ross 1984). Some Spokan elders claimed that a male berdache was never allowed to look upon the congenital area of the expectant woman, nor could he have physical contact with either the expectant woman or any delivering woman. Besides, the birthing hut would be closed and thus fairly dark, lit only by a low fire, made of dry wood to minimize smoke. Some informants stated that the male attendant vacated the lodge when birthing was imminent; otherwise he could lose his power. But when asked about male midwives or berdaches attending a delivery, one elderly woman stated that, despite contrary memories, this never happened because the baby boy might later become a berdache.

Despite the recorded (and oft-cited) objections and disbelief in shamans by Walker and his wife Mary, she recorded a birthing by the wife of Mevway Mungo, a young part-Hawaiian who spent the winter of 1841-42 with the Walkers at Tschimakain Mission:

> Mungo's wife had a difficult delivery [...] "The jugler [sic] or medicine men kept up their business till about midnight when they rested. About 9 A. M. [Dr. Walker] gave her cathoric [cathartic] pills. About noon [he] tried to administer an injection but did not succeed well. After dinner [he] gave more pills [...] This evening they commenced their medicine again. I went out determined to induce them to stop [...] After a little time the medicine men commenced again, rather still at first but became louder as the dead of the night came on. In the morning [...] a child was born. The safe delivery was all the result of their ridiculous jugling [sic]" (Drury 1976:254 fn).

Admittedly, some of the information above concerning midwives is conflicting. Hence, it is difficult to draw definitive ethnographic conclusions, particularly since more recent elders believed that the skills of midwives were founded on experience—never any special power, nor a dependence upon a respective tutelary spirit.

Birthmarks

The shape, color, and body location of moles and birthmarks were culturally significant—evidenced by the different terms for them. There were numerous explanations for congenital nevi. Yet the underlying belief was that one or both parents had violated a particular taboo prior to their child's delivery, or that the mother had an unusual experience during her pregnancy, thereby adversely affecting the fetus by *creating birthmarks* (*čsy'úm'tm'y's*). Failing to observe even a minor pregnancy taboo could result in a large and sometimes suggestive zoomorphic *xʷa sčsyúmts* ("his birthmark").

The most common explanation for nevi was that the pregnant woman had dreamed of or consciously thought of having sexual relations with a different man. An *unusual birthmark* (*ʔčsy'úm'tiʔ*) was believed to have been caused by one or both of the parents ridiculing a disabled person, or being psychologically disturbed or frightened by a horrible sight, such as *bad dreams* (*č'sč'sqéy's*)—specifically, a nightmare in which family members were seen experiencing considerable pain.

In response to unpleasant nighttime thoughts and to *prevent illness due to bad dreams or loneliness* (*čɬxʷcxʷécn'eʔstm*), the pregnant woman could place crushed licorice root near her head or tied by a small piece of buckskin or hemp around her neck at night. This root—sometimes called Indian marijuana, wild celery, wild ginseng, sweet root, or *Canby's Lovage* (*Ligusticum canbyi* Coult. & Rose - *xásxs*)—was the most important plant in the Spokan pharmacopoeia. It is an adaptogen, containing sweet-tasting triterpenoid saponins, notably glycyrrhizin and glycyrrhetinic acid, as well as flavonoids, useful for treating sore throat, laryngitis, gastritis, depression, and other maladies. It was said that a woman never forgot where she found the best and strongest wild licorice root, because she never forgot the unique aroma of the first plant she harvested. "All its sisters in that area will have the same smell."

Breast-feeding

Nurturing began immediately after the child was washed and wrapped in a fur-lined robe. The baby was not presented formally to the village just yet, as the mother and child remained secluded in the temporary birthing lodge, sometimes for several days. The two were closely attended by the woman's mother, who continued to enforce the observance of her daughter's postnatal dietary taboos, which were believed to ensure

107

an easy flow of *breast milk* (*sqʔém*). *Breast-feeding* (*qeʔmélt* - "nurse a child" or *ʔoʔxʷtéit* - "baby") was thought to contract the *uterus* (*snsíxʷltn*) and prevent later *hemorrhaging after giving birth* (*hecʔ čsnyllmétxʷtni* - "blood coming out"). A woman never breast-fed her baby in public, nor did she ever expose her *breasts* (*sqaʔqʔém*) or *genitalia* (*teλ'čey'*), even to her husband (Elmendorf, pers. comm.).

To encourage the young mother's post-operative recovery, the older women of each family utilized common as well as esoteric family formulae for medicinal plant concoctions and infusions, which the postpartum mother drank to regain her strength, replenish her blood, and to maintain and encourage lactation. When there was an inadequate flow of breast milk, the young *mother's mother* (*ččiy'eʔ*) or a visiting midwife encouraged the new mother to drink hot soups and broths made with meat. If the condition continued, a gruel was made by first boiling mashed bitterroots into a farinaceous jelly, which was eaten several times a day until lactation commenced. Fish broth was never used as a remedy, since both fish and fowl were considered 'cold' foods and avoided by lactating mothers. Another treatment was to place on her *breasts* (*sqaʔqʔém* or *sč'mč'semxʷ*) and *nipples* (*qʔemtín*) a warm poultice of sliced bracket fungus, and then wrap her in a preheated robe.

Prior to the child's first tooth eruption, a nursing mother occasionally placed a small amount of deer bone marrow on her finger for the child to suck. Apart from the unknown nutritional benefits, it was believed that male babies would later be better conditioned for running, jumping, and deer hunting—another case of the Doctrine of Signatures. When the first deciduous tooth erupted, the child's diet of only breast milk was then supplemented with small amounts of carefully premasticated deer meat, crushed huckleberries, and mashed boiled roots.

A mother administered warm medicinal solutions or meat broth to a *sick* (*ččq'méλtn*) child by intermittently dipping a finger for the baby to suck upon, or by dripping the solution behind the baby's lower lip. Past accounts of a child sucking saturated pieces of buckskin were mentioned, but few details were remembered. According to the particular mother or grandmother, a child experiencing prolonged abdominal pain was treated in a variety of ways, but most commonly by sucking pieces of twisted buckskin saturated in mild solutions of warm water and powdered red willow bark or powdered fresh western yarrow root. If a breast-feeding baby experienced prolonged abdominal discomfort, a common reason was that the lactating mother was eating a prohibited food or violating a behavioral taboo.

If a woman was unable to nurse her newborn because of deficient milk secretion (agalactia), or if she died in childbirth, then another woman would *breast feed* (*qeʔmél't* or *tatam'eʔ*) the baby. This role was filled by a blood-related woman or a *wet nurse* (*sxʷqeʔmélt* or *snkʷeʔsqʔem* - "to share another's milk"), whose services were immediately discontinued if the birth mother commenced lactating. After weaning, the child would not be returned to the uterine mother if she felt the change would be emotionally disruptive for the child, and in such situations the wet nurse would visit the child's home whenever possible.

It was reported that a lactating woman could, if necessary, nurse two unrelated babies at the same time. If fact, it was recalled that one mother with nursing twins also nursed another friend's baby (T. Wynecoop, pers. comm.).

Based upon his fieldwork with the Kutenai and Flathead during the late 1930s and early 1940s, Turney-High described surrogate care by wet nurses, which was essentially the same for the Spokan:

> If a mother was too sick to nurse the child, or was milkless, a baby was given to another woman to suckle. A permanent relationship was then set up between the child and its wet-nurse which was to last throughout life. The woman had saved the child's life and was given it of her flesh through milk. The child was told of this relationship as soon as it could understand (1941:115).

It was believed that a child who required a wet nurse could never marry any of the woman's offspring, for this would have been viewed as incestuous behavior between *milk siblings* (*snkʷíxʷxʷ* - "sibling"), since each biological child of the wet nurse was now considered a *younger sister* (*łčíčšeʔ*) or a *younger brother* (*sísnceʔ* - "when a child"). Throughout the child's life, he always acknowledged a special fictive relationship

108

with his wet nurse, who was addressed with a kin term that implied *mother* (*túm'* - "mother's mother"). Consequently, a Spokan child, upon learning to speak, always used modified kinship terms for the wet nurse and any of her children.

Methods of weaning babies varied between families, as did the circumstances which encouraged or delayed this biological and emotional transition for the mother and child. *Breast-feeding* (*qe?me'y'ɫp* or *yq'ʷe?il* - "breast fed") continued for approximately two years, at which point the child was *weaned* (*xʷl'síxʷm* - "pour" or "spill"), usually by applying to a nursing mother's nipples an oil-based, ground paste from the black, mature mycelial tuft of a mature mushroom. The paste was repulsive to the baby and quickly discouraged the baby from further nursing. Elders stated that other substances achieved this same purpose, including ground, moistened tobacco leaves. Just prior to weaning, a mixture of berry juice and boiled black tree lichen was administered by a mother to her nursing child, to prepare the baby's digestive system for adult foods. This is similar to what was reported for the Okanogan (Gabriel 1954). The Spokan are not known to have forbidden a pregnant woman from eating black tree lichen for fear of darkening an unborn baby's skin, as cited by Lerman (1952-54) for the Okanogan.

Several elderly ladies remembered their grandmothers stating how—during the time of breast-feeding—a woman abstained from sexual relations to prevent such infant maladies as colic, diarrhea, and constipation. Some elders felt that to delay weaning was discouraged by the mother's husband, but stated the decision was invariably made by the woman's mother. All agreed that it was considered normal for an ambulatory child to be weaned. Some older men would joke with a new father by using the expression for a boy's first steps, "He has his father's feet"—meaning that he is now weaned and the parents can resume sexual relations.

Cradleboards and Bundling

Prior to a baby being placed in a cradleboard, the infant was first confined to a *buckskin sack* (*mxʷlílt*), sometimes decorated with beads (Glover 1985:30). Glover described the impressive beaded design work of men's and particularly women's moccasins, noting that "The pouches in which the women carried their younger ones also were decorated in this way" (1927:100).

Several weeks after birthing, the baby was placed in a flat cedar or birch bark carrier filled with powdered punk, or with any of the materials used to line the cradleboard.

It was not until *after delivery* (*n'qʷíc'yn*) that an infant's *cradleboard* (*mxl'éltt* or *mxʷúl'* - "baby basket" or *sq'ttéwɫ* - "hide canoe-like vessel") was constructed (Egesdal, pers. comm.), often by the *father's brother* (*smé?ɫ*) or any close agnatic kinsperson. But it was not used until the end of the three-month postpartum, because the parents would not be so presumptuous as to assume a healthy baby.

Ray (1933:128-130), Smith (1936-8:581-590), and Teit (1928:166-167) provide the most complete descriptions of the Plateau cradleboard. However, Spokan cradleboards often varied slightly in shape from those of the neighboring Sanpoil and Nespelem. The Spokan also made a buckskin bag. They constructed essentially an oviform or trapezoidal shape on a rigid composite wood frame that secured the infant when closed with buckskin flaps further secured by buckskin ties. Some cradleboards had a hand-size opening near the top of the frame for carrying—called a *snɫa?máya?qn*. When traveling during inclement weather, a mother would cover the *cradleboard with a cover* (*?epɫm'm'xʷúl'* - "he/she has a small cradleboard") made from tightly woven cattail leaves. Pickering's notes of 1841 cited, "Infants on the boards [were] suspended to the flanks of the horses, a practice said to be derived from the eastern side of the mountains" (1895:28; Barry 1929:60).

Alexander Ross, an erudite Scottish fur-trader, spent time with the Spokan and understood the necessity of certain customs—not always apparent in the writings of missionaries. He creditably stated:

> Tacitus found fault with the Roman ladies of his day for giving their children to Grecian women to nurse, and thus depriving the infant of maternal tenderness. What would the historian have thought had he seen an infant

of the savage race, as practiced in these parts, tied naked on a hard board [cradleboard] and allowed to tumble and roll about as it best could? and yet this very race, or portion of the human family, is as perfect in form, as healthy and vigorous, as any people on the face of the earth (1849, 7:329).

He described the components and use of the cradleboard, as well as prohibitions against the mother assuming that her newborn would survive, which would have been interpreted as arrogant:

> Custom here constitutes law, not only in reference to the great affairs of the nation or tribe, but in tribal things also. A mother is not allowed to prepare swaddling-clothes for an unborn infant; and, indeed, but little preparation is required, for the whole paraphernalia consists of but four articles—a rude piece of board, which serves for a cradle; a bit of skin, which serves to wrap the new-born babe in; some moss to lie on; and a string to lash the whole together. Thus secured, the bantling is carried about on its mother's back, or allowed to sprawl on the ground, in all weather and all seasons (1849, 7:308-9).

Cradleboards were, by availability and choice of material, *lined* (*nq'ʷuλ'šn* - "sock") with dried tamarack, cambium, moss, or dry pounded *cheatgrass* (*Bromus tectorum* L. - *hi t't'óqʷ*). Common barley or bromegrass served the same purpose (STHC). Rotten wood, used for smoking tanned hides, was crumbled into a fine dust and used as an absorbent of urine. The fragrant menthol-smelling leaves of dragon sagewort or pounded sweet grass were used during hot weather to cool the child and mask the odor of urine. Freshly-gathered green mullein leaves were a common and readily-available material for lining a cradleboard. Small pieces of buckskin and *cattail fluff* (*sq'ʷsq'ʷastqín*) often served as diapers, as did various species of soft leaves—particularly the ubiquitous mullein, which also served as *toilet paper* (*nʔip'pstn* - "to wipe anus with") for all ages. Another plant used as a diaper or for cleaning *excrement* (*mneč*) from the buttocks was the large, soft, velvet-like leaves of wild ginger. Soiled diaper materials were buried after use, for fear of sorcery and to prevent animals from distributing the materials in living areas. Mothers were extremely careful to bury the feces of a baby or young child, for as Ray reported for the Sanpoil:

> A baby's excrement was always deposited in the same place, a hole in the ground. If this were not done the child would become mischievous and later refuse to obey. Diapers were pieces of buckskin. They were washed and used repeatedly. Sometimes they were lined with grass (1933:128).

A baby's continuous confinement to a cradleboard could cause hygiene problems for the baby. The Spokan dealt with them the same way the Sanpoil and Nespelem did:

> If an infant urinated too frequently it was made to urinate on a piece of granite schist which had been heated over the fire. This treatment was usually successful, but if not, gopher manure was rubbed on the buttocks and abdomen. Another alternative was to clean and cook a mouse and feed it to the child if it were old enough to eat. Still another method was to break open a puffball and rub it directly on the buttocks (Ray 1933:128).

It was reported (T. Wynecoop, pers. comm.) that some Spokan cradleboards had a simple yet ingenious funnel-like trough or tube attached to the board's covering, designed to carry a male baby's urine away from him and his bundling material.

Despite such care, infants still developed skin irritation, which was treated with dry powdered clay, applied as a moist paste. An older and more traditional lotion for baby rash was to mix powdered clay with bear grease. Adults used the same treatment as remedies for their own skin irritations and dermal eruptions, sometimes thought to be caused by sorcery. Application of clay was continued until the child was ambulatory, and not crawling naked on earthen floors. Another medicament for treating a baby's skin problem was fish oil, preferably that of sturgeon. Grease from the neck area of a lamprey, if available, was also used. The spore powder from the *puffballs* (*Calvatia gigantea* Batsch: Pers or *Bovista oila* or *Lycoperdon* spp. - *sʔitš*) was dusted on a baby's *rump* (*soq'ʷémep*) to prevent or treat diaper rash. The spores of alum root puffballs were an effective treatment for urine rash. Some mothers preferred to treat *diaper rash* (*st'aʔxawí*) with a strong solution made by boiling both the branch tops and attached leaves of snowbush, and then saturating a piece of tanned buckskin, which was placed upon the areas of irritation. In post-contact time, wheat flour mixed with water was heated in a skillet and administered upon cooling to treat diaper rash (T. Wynecoop, pers. comm.).

The child spent much of her time secured in a cradleboard, being removed several times a day to be washed with warm water and then thoroughly rubbed with fish oil. In addition to being diapered with buckskin, the Spokan used, when available, what is commonly called buckskin tamarack, a soft pliable growth of vegetative mycelium felt-like membrane referred to as *nqaʔqeʔmín*, which may encircle an internal annual growth ring of a diseased tamarack (Hensold, pers. comm.). The *peeling* (*lqʼntén* - "it was peeled") of the membrane, known as *ƛáwm*, appears in color and texture like buckskin.

Once the child was confined to a cradleboard, it was carried by a *tumpline* (*ƚqwqíntn* - "headstrap used to carry cradleboard") when the mother was walking (Teit 1928:166), or suspended carefully from the side of the saddle when the mother was traveling by horseback, as seen in old Spokan photographs. When a mother was preoccupied, she would often suspend the cradle from the frame of the dwelling, in a *cradle hammock* (*snqʼetewá*), which was a flexible structure made from willow, which assumed a boat-like shape with the ends tied together.

Elmendorf fortunately provided a detailed description of the Spokan cradleboard:

> [...] sewed up about 6 inches from [the] bottom and from there on up holes or loops to be laced up - [the] buckskin band for [the] navel simply folds across [the] infant's abdomen - [the] bottom of this cradle is filled with cattail down - packed around [the] lower end of [the] baby - [the] *mxʷlʼélt* might be lined with rabbit fur [for] in [the] winter - [the] top [is] folded over [the] baby's head and tied with leather string - [the] infant [is] never taken out of [the] cradle except when necessary - [baby is] oiled with goose oil & washed frequently - [then its] arms, legs & back [when] frequently massaging [is] done at frequent intervals - [the] buckskin thong stuck through [the] back of [the] baby-sack - [it] could be carried on [one's] back or in [one's] arms - [a] woman usually worked around [the] house for some time after [the] birth - at about 4 mo[nths] the baby was transferred to a larger sack on a buckskin-covered board - [with] soft furred skins used as padding between [the] sack & board - in summer time a hoop frame projected from the top of [the] board and was covered for shade - [it could be] hung on [a] branch by thongs or end set on [the] ground & rocked in one hand - most of the time after [the] first few weeks when he [could] lay on a pillow the baby was in an upright position on [the] mother's back or hanging by the cradleboard - between one & two years old the child is weaned - any kind of boiled or cooked food [was] fed to children while weaning - [the mother] attempted to wean a baby as early as possible (1935-6, 2:62-63).

On the vertical frame of the cradleboard, various prophylactic amulets would be placed to protect the child's spirit from being stolen by *malicious spirits who could jump into your baby* (*nʼe m čxʷtʼpmíƚts*). Though these devices varied by family tradition and individual choice, it was common for the child's grandmother to make a *small pair of moccasins* (*sqqélʼixʷšnʼ* - "little people's shoes"), with holes pierced in the soles by sharpened deer horn, bone, or a stone awl, and hung from the *cradleboard handle* (*nƛʼamʼápaʔqnʼ* - "sharp point") so the baby could say to a malevolent power that he could not go with the theriomorphic creature because there were holes in his moccasins, which would hurt his feet. Wilson also recorded how the Spokan adorned cradleboards: "The cradle [board] is adorned with various ornaments and medicines, or charms, such as beads, the legs, heads, etc., of birds or small animals, and at the top is invariably fastened a portion of the umbilical cord, which is cut off at birth, sewn up in [a] piece of cloth, and tastefully ornamented with beads" (1866:295).

Another powerful prophylactic device—suspended from the cradleboard—was a piece of *buckskin* (*sípʼiʔ*) that had been dipped in menstrual blood, which, because of the Stigma of Femininity, no spiritual force would approach. These and other types of prophylactic devices were intended to protect a baby from any *evil spirit* (*nʼem čxʷtʼpmíƚts*) that could otherwise enter the child and gain control of its soul. Traditionally, the cradleboard was never used again for a second baby or given as a gift, but instead was discarded. It was best recalled by elders that the contemporary practice of using the same cradleboard by successive generations, and loaning it to other families, commenced in the early 1900s.

When not restricted to a cradleboard, the infant was placed in a loosely padded *night sack* (*sqqtté*), which confined the child, reassuring the mother of the baby's whereabouts. A constant fear was that a crawling baby could wander into an open fire pit. Elderly Spokan women repeatedly instructed their granddaughters to place a baby on its back when removed from the cradleboard, so the child was less likely to suffocate or crawl into a fire pit. It has been reported that some Salish peoples used restrictively tight night sacks (Mandelbaum 1938:107) when the mother was sleeping.

While the baby was awake, it received near-constant attention from the mother, a grandmother, or older siblings who would *pacify* (*tetew'eéltm* - "to pacify") a crying baby by *stroking* (*čixʷntm*) its cheek or neck with an eagle *feather* (*sqpúsl'*), or by imitating a songbird or other small animal. An old method for treating a baby who cried often was to smudge the child with smoke from burning shaven bits of dried rosehip bush, sometimes mixed with fine shavings of dogwood bush. Or smoke from the aromatic leaves of either *sagebrush* (*Artemisis tridentata* Nutt. - *k'ʷel'k'ʷmnílhp*) or *Western sage* (*A. ludovicana* Nutt. - *n'w'nq'etełp*) would be used in a small tent to smoke the baby and its bedding (STHC). A method to induce sleep in a restless baby was to rub the contents of a *puffball* (*sʔítš* - "get sleepy") upon the baby's temples. Another treatment for a fussy or crying child was to place fresh rosehip shavings under the pad of the baby's cradleboard. Fresh leaves of the fern-leafed biscuit root (*Lomatium dissectum* Var. multifidum [Nutt.] Math. & Const - *sp'xʷenč*) were used as a padding in the baby's cradleboard to encourage sleep.

To pacify a crying child who was briefly left alone, the mother might present the child with a small gift to forget its loneliness—an act called *młmálxšn*. A mother might sing a *song* (*čt'eskʷépi*), often reciting humorous accounts of small animals with their babies. When awakening their infants or small children, mothers softly imitated certain animal sounds or skillfully rendered birdcalls. Older siblings were cautioned to never quickly awaken any baby or sleeping adult because the sudden shock or *fright* (*nxeł* or *qʷisasus*) could kill the awakened individual if his or her soul had been on a journey away from the body (as attested by one's dreams) and not able to fully return to the host's body.

The Spokan are not known to have practiced any form of head deformation during the child's early life, nor later while the child was restricted to a cradleboard, where it spent much of its perambulatory life. There is no evidence that the swaddling of Spokan babies in cradleboards ever resulted in plagiocephaly (misshapen head) or hip dysplasia, which has been reported for some other North American peoples (Wynne-Davies 1972). Wolman's (1970) and Coleman's (1968) studies of this practice conclude that cradleboards were a factor in preventing cases of neonatal hip dislocations from self-correcting. A subject long debated, and acknowledged of the Flathead, it was not resolved by Townsend's statement that "The tribe called Flatheads, or *Salish*, who reside near the sources of the Oregon, have long since abolished this custom" (1839:175).

Yet it appears that these Indians never adopted the practice of flattening the heads of their infants. Certainly they were not given to the custom when the white man came into the country. Perhaps the name was bestowed in derision or anger, since the term "*tépe plate*" or Flathead had long been used among the French as a term of reproach or vilification (Durham 1912, 1:17). Bancroft also maintained that "The Salish family do not flatten the head" (1875 1:256 fn; Hale 1846, 5:214). In his annual Bureau of Ethnology report, Dart maintained the Flathead Indians "received the name of Flat Heads from the fact that their heads were not sharpened by pressure on the forehead; as the Chinooks" (1851:216). But the following was cited by Burr Osborn:

> Their way of making a flat head was to place the papoose in a box and lash a board over the forehead in a slanting position and keep the papoose there for twelve months. The forehead would become flat and the head run up to a peak. The box was fastened to a pole about six feet long, and when they wanted to sit the kid down, they would stand it up against a tree (Himes 1913:361-2).

Teit described how "All the tribes except the Coeur d'Alene claim that no head flattening was practiced in early times, for it was impossible with the old-style board carrier." Teit described how the Coeur d'Alene once used "a pad of stiff skin attached to the corner, which was tightened over the baby's head when it sleep to keep the head from moving. This is said to sometimes have caused slight flattening of the head" (1930:381).

Franchère (1854:324) also claimed to have seen flattening of the head among unnamed tribes of the Columbia. Upon inquiry as to the reason for this practice, he was apparently informed that "it was only slaves who had not their heads flattened. The slaves in fact have the usual rounded head, and they are not permitted to flatten the foreheads of their children destined to bear the charms of their sires" (Hunt 1918, 9:283). Speaking of this practice, Parker stated that he observed among the Flathead and Nez Perce how they would flatten the heads of babies as well as pierce the nasal septum: "The flattening of their heads is not so great a deformation as is generally supposed. From a little above the eye the apex or crown of the head, there is a depression, but generally in adult person very noticeable" (1840:140). Yet Parker, at an earlier date, refuted the belief that the Flathead practiced plagiocephaly: "I was disappointed to see nothing peculiar in the Flathead Indians, to give them this name. Who gave them this name, or for what reason, is not known" (1840:79). Parker was also emphatic that the Nez Perce never pierced their noses (1840:79).

Some art critics feel that Paul Kane's field sketches and watercolors were often more accurate than his oils, some of which were dramatic and even embellished. One field sketch of a Flathead woman and her cradled child (*Caw Wach Ham*, Fig. 171, CRIV-492) with head-binding, is actually a combined sketch of a Chinookan baby undergoing the process of flattening the head in a cradleboard (CRIV-290), and a Cowlitz woman who had a flattened forehead, and may not prove or disprove the argument of plagiocephaly among certain Salish groups. Ermatinger (1796-1833), once a clerk and fur trader for the HBC, contended that Kane "was regarded as a great 'medicine man' by the natives, who sometimes gathered in great numbers to watch him manipulate his supposed implements of magic" (Ermatinger 1914, 3:201). In fact, Kane:

> [...] spent nearly four years in these wanderings, to and from the Pacific, sketching portraits of chiefs, medicine men, warriors, their wives and daughters—also fishing, hunting and other scenes, illustrations of the customs, occupations and amusements of the red men and the physical features of the country (Ermatinger 1914 3:201).

Infertility

Women who were presumed *barren* (*čstmélt* or *kʷhóylt* - "stopped having children")—husbands were never considered sterile—could take various medicines to become fecund. These medicaments were obtained from an elderly woman or midwife who had esoteric knowledge of their use and who knew local sources. Elderly women contended that plants for this purpose were never acquired through trading. Such medicaments were reported for the Southern Plateau (Mandelbaum 1938:119), as were plants taken as aphrodisiacs, presumably for both men and women (Elmendorf, pers. comm.). Though men and women ate boiled or raw deer testicles as a food, there is no evidence they were considered an aphrodisiac.

Barrenness was believed to have been caused by multiple self-induced abortions, ignoring a mother's *warning* (*xeyɬtumš*) to eschew masturbation, being a victim of malicious sorcery, or being 'sung against' by a sorcerer. It could also be attributed to her unnecessarily killing the offspring of a land mammal, such as drowning a domesticated cat's litter. While confined to the menstrual hut, she may have purposely imbibed a strong solution made from boiled Indian hemp roots.

Anything regarding infertility in men and sperm counts is only conjectural, though it is now known that excessive testicular heat in daily sweating sessions—external temperatures often above fifty degrees centigrade—could result in oligospermia (low sperm count) and impaired spermatogenesis. Unusually high environmental temperatures were also endured during summer months. The average family had two to three children, and their ages were commonly two to three years apart. Boyd, in speaking of increased sedentariness, cites Suttles and Chance on how an increase in cultivated foods—introduced by Euro-Americans—may have caused an increase in fecundity (ability to reproduce) and fertility (actual live births):

> Increased sedentism is apparent in many areas, arising from a number of changes relating ultimately to the food base. The widespread adoption of the white potato into Northwest economies (Suttles 1951) not only added a productive source of carbohydrate to native diets, but also allowed natives to stay closer to home. Both changes

may have encouraged greater fertility. Concentration of Plateau peoples (in particular) around trading posts, with their more reliable food supplies, may have had similar effects (Chance 1973). And it is also possible that depopulation through disease, by decreasing the population pressure on the land in certain native territories and leaving adequate wild foods supplies within a narrower circumference, promoted sedentism, increased fertility, and population rebound (Boyd 1985:184).

Feticide and Infanticide

There is an unfortunate paucity of ethnographic data regarding *abortion* (*č'ɫplsténčntm* - "killed in the womb") and *infanticide* (*plsqelixʷ*), partly due to the Spokan women being understandably reticent to discuss such personal decisions, yet mostly due to the limited contact with or disclosure by missionaries, and (later-assigned) government medical personnel—nearly all of whom were male. Recognizing the nature of this behavior, Spokan elders said it did occur, but certainly with less frequency than clinical or illicit feticide (abortion) nowadays. When societies enjoyed the support of closely-knit extended families and extended kin groups, infanticide was probably not common since an unwanted baby was invariably adopted by a kinsperson or given conditionally to foster parents—thus fulfilling the emotional needs of the surrogate parents and those of the unwed uterine mother. A woman who gave up a child for adoption or foster care was recognized by the community to have made her decision based upon legitimate reasons, whereas a woman known to have *aborted* (*č'ɫplstnčscút* - "she aborted it") was held in poor regard, but over time could recover her status. Numerous elderly women, as late as the 1960s, said that the practice of holding a woman in poor regard for abortion was universal, and no elder could recall an example of prolicide (killing one's offspring)—infanticide or abortion.

Yet we cannot ignore the use of these solutions to unwanted pregnancies or births. It is understandable why many contemporary people claim that—during the pre-contact period—abortion, infanticide, prostitution, incest, and other illegal and abnormal behaviors did not exist, and rather these universally antisocial practices were introduced with Euro-American contact, and became exacerbated by the deculturation, deprivation, and resulting alienation of young Spokan men and women. Most contemporary Spokan erroneously contend that they did not have words for such acts, nor did they presumably have access to any type of abortifacient. Those informants who denied that these acts took place, said that they had forgotten the linguistic designations, which in most cases is true.

Abortion was invariably in response to an unwanted pregnancy from premarital sex or either person being an *adulterer* (*sxʷw'el'scút*) or *adulteress* (*sxʷw'el'mscút*). There was agreement that abortion was probably less frequent prior to the late historical period, because traditional beliefs and practices placed considerable value on the premarital chastity of a *maiden* (*st'ič'míš* or *sk'ʷmélt* - "top person"). Virginity thereby brought many benefits to courtship: The maiden increased her likelihood of marriage; warranted a more valuable bride-price (or a quasi-form of bride service); was more able to attract and marry a man of greater status and means; and reduced the fear that a premarital pregnancy would bring shame to her family. On occasion, a single woman was *sorcerized* (*pɫaxntm*) by a person who had been contracted by a man desirous of marrying her; but those advances were rejected. The reasons for the sorcery were numerous; even a slight affront to a person not known to be a sorcerer could result in retribution against the offender.

In preventing pregnancy—apart from *coitus interruptus*—little is known of contraception by physical or chemical means, except some basic techniques: Impaction of the vagina with moist plant material created a septic solution. The woman could ingest a solution of mashed *white clematis* (*Clematis lingusticifolia* Nutt., ex T. & G. - *q'ic'esníneʔ* - "owl's braids"), which was an extremely dangerous contraceptive if the decoction of boiled leaves was too strong. She could boil the roots of Oregon grape and drink the resulting decoction once a week to prevent conception (Ray 1933:219). Roots of false Solomon's Seal were mashed and steeped to regulate the menses and prevent contraception, if drunk daily for one week.

114

Another woman's contraceptive was an infusion of mashed roots of dogbane or "false hemp" boiled in water, drunk several times for at least a week prior to ovulation. Ray's material (1933:219), however, states that this solution was drunk about once a week by the Sanpoil. The mashed roots of Indian hemp were boiled and, upon cooling, drunk throughout the woman's menstrual period to prevent pregnancy—a practice some claimed could cause sterility.

Turner, citing Lerman's earlier inquiry (1952-1954), wrote that "barrenness from any other cause could be counteracted by eating the leaves of the female plant *False Box* (*Paxistima myrsinites* [Pursh] Raf. - *skʷlkʷʷlseɫp*). The point of the leaf was opened with a sharp twig, and the leaf was then blown full of air and swallowed. If the leaf could be blown up without bursting, the woman would conceive. "Some women could never blow up a leaf without bursting it; they would always be barren" (Turner *et al.* 1980:96).

However, unwanted pregnancies occurred despite the sanctions, the known consequences of violation, and a strict system of chaperoning that dominated a young woman's actions and associations until her marriage. Chaperoning was usually performed by the girl's mother, and seldom by a grandmother, for as a Spokan elder said, "A young girl may not outwit her grandmother, but she could *run faster* (*sƛ̣xaƛ̣xxšn*) than a much older woman."

Young women who avoided being chaperoned were cognizant of the social and physical consequences— in the form of public announcements, condemnation, innuendo, *gossip* (*sxʷwékʷcn* - "one who hides one's talk" or *m'ey'm'l'w'ís* - "tells news here and there repeatedly") (Egesdal, pers. comm.). Even after marriage, except when residing in a menstrual hut, a young married woman would often be chaperoned, for reasons of moral safety and the prevention of scandal and gossip.

Regardless of these precautions, an unmarried woman could become pregnant, and possibly *commit suicide* (*ši?čstmíst* or *plscút*), run away, give her infant up for adoption, or resort to abortion. Given the social and physiological difficulties of abortion, a woman not wanting a child could, just prior to delivery, go off by herself to deliver. Ray wrote of the same situation for the Sanpoil and Nespelem: "If the woman did not want the child she was about to bear, this seclusion gave her an opportunity to return to camp with the baby dead and declare that it had been born dead. If this were not true and the facts were discovered the woman was subjected to severe lashings upon order of the chief" (1933:126).

However, since abortion was considered a serious moral transgression, it was always done in secrecy, either away from the camp or village, or self-performed in the menstrual hut. A woman's family never knew if the confined person was truly menstruating, or was pregnant and *without her menses* (*hesčxʷcnúxʷi* - "she's in the state of having passed it by [her menses] without her control").

A married woman who wanted to terminate her pregnancy could abort in her first trimester without her family or husband knowing, since any *menstruating woman* (*so?c?ócqe?* - "one who is outside") was always confined to a menstrual hut for five to seven days, and no one, not even her husband, would approach such a structure when occupied, because of the Stigma of Femininity, i.e., a fear of menstrual blood. Consequently, the confined woman was the only one aware of her pregnancy, and her physical isolation gave her the opportunity to abort herself.

When a woman chose to terminate her pregnancy during the first trimester, the common method was to drink a variety of plant infusions that often induced severe abdominal and intestinal peristalsis, which usually aborted the fetus. For example, the needles of lodge pole pine were boiled to make a strong tea, which could be drunk in quantity, or she could chew and suck the juice from their green buds. If she were unattended, then this method could be dangerous at any time because of resulting severe dehydration. So the most common abortifacient was created by crushing the leaves and stems of western yarrow, concentrating them in a solution of warm water, and drinking it three times—in the morning, afternoon, and evening. For the Sanpoil, chewing several fresh Oregon grape leaves was claimed to have been a bitter but an effective abortifacient (Moerman 2009:430). It is unknown whether a decoction of steeped mashed goldenrod leaves or crushed seeds was ever used. She could make a concoction from any one of several types of tree bark, causing severe contractions—a method normally used to treat constipation. For instance, usually during her second menstrual hut confinement, she could make a strong tea by boiling shredded *ponderosa pine bark* (*č'i?lex*ʷ) and, upon cooling, drink a quantity sufficient to create severe vomiting and, in turn, severe peristalsis.

Any woman experiencing a painful or otherwise *abnormal menses* (*čsnylmétx*ʷ*tni*) might fear she was the victim of sorcery. She could counter it by removing the inflicted evil and by modifying her diet. As part of the latter method, a decoction of steeped yarrow was considered the best treatment for *difficult menstruation* (dysmenorrhea) (*n'e tl'x*ʷ*mist* - "it will be difficult, trying"). Or, in the case of amenorrhea, yarrow tea was drunk to induce menstrual flow. One woman was instructed to eat any freshly butchered raw meat, sometimes supplemented with small amounts of the *animal's blood* (*mɫč'éye?*) to stimulate menstruation.

Another method of intrusive abortion during the first phase of the second trimester, was for the woman to *pierce* or *stab* (*ɫu?úntém*) the amniotic sac with a sharpened stick or antler shaft. Such a procedure unknowingly could cause a fallopian infection that could cause either later insufficient fecundity, or a septic abortion that could result in massive if not fatal bleeding. There were several instances of a pregnant woman desperately resorting to a traumatic abortive procedure by simply dropping herself onto a log or a stump, which was dangerous because of induced internal bleeding or even uncontrollable hemorrhaging (*?ocqeɫ-snx*ʷ*ul* - "internal bleeding"). As with any self-induced abortion, there was the possibility of infectious complications, and even death.

Despite the relative infrequency of infanticide during traditional times, the Spokan—like all cultures—had procedures for terminating a new and unwanted child, usually by *smothering* (*n'tk*ʷ*páqs* - "confine the nose") the infant by blocking the nasal passages (Egesdal, pers. comm.). A reasonably accepted situation would have been when the mother or group was forced to endure extreme environmental conditions.

There was considerable debate among some elders as to whether the Spokan resorted to infanticide when there was an apparent severe congenital disability of the newborn or when the group was confronted with starvation at the time of a woman's delivery. It was more likely for a family member or someone in the village to *adopt* (*k'*ʷ*l'sx*ʷ*six*ʷ*lt*) an unwanted baby. A child born with a deformity, or who developed one as a result of disease or accident, was never killed for that reason alone. Instead, he or she was cared for and treated with kindness. This also applied to adults. It was unfortunate when a woman (married or unmarried) chose to abort unintentionally due to a traumatic or occupational related *accident* (*čn-x̲nnúmt* - "I had an accident").

Adoption and Fostering

When both parents of one or more children died, for whatever reason, close kin of either parent would assume all responsibilities of adopting the orphan (*čšt'élt* or *stmél'is* or *čttm'ápl'e?* or *sk'*ʷ*l'scix*ʷ*lt* - "little orphan" or "child taken care of"). Elmendorf wrote, "no stigma whatever [was] attached to the word, or the concept of orphan" (1935-6, 3:30-31). If the orphan was without any kinspeople, a family in the community would care for the child as their own—a status known as *stm'el'is*, meaning one with all consanguineal rights. The term also denoted all of one's consanguineal and affinal kinspeople. Assuming responsibilities gave the parent adoptive rights, and the child was given the name of one of their known *deceased consanguineal relatives* (*snt?er'mep*), or the name of a deceased relative from the adoptee's new family, or preferably one of the orphan's *deceased parents* (*čtmáple?*) (Elmendorf 1935-6, 4:16). A family would often adopt the *children of a deceased friend* (*?el?elk'*ʷ*melt* - "keep-sake children") if the children were without consanguineal kinspeople. A deceased son's daughter or son was called *č'ewe?*. When both parents died, orphaned children were known as *čtitm'apl'e?*.

If a widow found herself with too many children, she could give one or more of them to married relatives, or to a *close friend* (*lax̲eɫ'iš*) who was childless and a widow herself. The term *sl'áx̲tnqép* referred to any man or woman you could depend upon and who was always at your side in the most difficult times (Egesdal, pers. comm.). A widower experiencing considerable difficulty in caring for his baby or young children, could arrange for their *adoption* (*k'ʷl'sxʷlt*) by his wife's family or by a married family of his kin group. Most childless couples were eager to adopt an 'abandoned' child. In all instances where only the mother had died, the jural father was expected to hunt and provide for his children until they were of age to support themselves, or when a daughter married (Elmendorf, pers. comm.).

Grandparents who had adopted orphans from outside the family always maintained emotional ties, by visiting and providing gifts, and thereby enjoyed intense and enduring relationships with their *grandchildren* (*čkʷeʔr'éčt* - "roots" or *st't'ʔac'* - "seedling"). If the adoptive parents relinquished their parental claim, or neglected a child in any way, the child would be taken and given to different surrogate parents (Elmendorf, pers. comm.). When an unwed mother was unable to keep or manage an infant, adoption was preferred over infanticide. Nor was it unusual for the newborn to be adopted by people other than grandparents, even distant kinspeople of the child. The mother keep the child until it was properly weaned, and then give the child up for adoption to a woman of her choice.

In the infrequent case of *multiple births* (*qqmn'él'tm'*) by an unwed mother, both of the twins were given to different *childless couples* (*čnƛ'llélt*). There was never any ceremony (Elmendorf, pers. comm.), for it was understood that the foster parents would raise the foster child as their own—never failing to recognize and praise the kindness of the child's uterine mother and jural father. The term for a foster child whose parents who have left it, for any reason, was *sɫuwélt* ("child whose parents have left it, gone away, are absent") (Elmendorf 1935-6, 3:30-31). The new surrogate parents never changed an adopted child's name. Depending upon the composition of the *household* (*nk'ʷeɫxʷ* - "one house"), if the mother of twins had her sister or sisters living near her, the mother could temporarily give them one of the twins. The difficulties for the mother included breastfeeding, performing daily chores for food-getting, and other demanding domestic obligations.

An unwanted child was never neglected by the larger kin group, and was ultimately adopted by a kinsperson or unrelated couple. An *illegitimate child* (*scsl'éčst* - "product of a mistaken act") (Egesdal, pers. comm.) who survived infanticide usually had little status within the community. As a consequence, an illegitimate child would typically leave when old enough to move to another tribe—the Coeur d'Alene or Kalispel in most cases. Despite the illegitimate person's relocation, their status preceded them, because knowledge of other people's kin affiliations was shared among these contiguous groups. As a result, the person's lack of knowledge regarding the identity of his or her jural father persisted. One of Elmendorf's principal informants described how illegitimate children were often physically abused by known kinspeople, and later an enemy would publicly flaunt this knowledge before the grown person, often in battle (1935-6, 3:42).

Occasionally, an *older unwed woman* (*memist* or *sʔámtsʔem* - "one who sits in one place" or *č'en'itw'iɫ* - "bachelor lady") would adopt and name an orphan or an illegitimate child. Such an act accorded the woman considerable status within the community. It is not known if such an arrangement ever ameliorated the negative status of the illegitimate child, nor is there any known ethnographic data or oral accounts concerning the status of *children* (*sccm'el't*) born of such a person.

If a baby's mother died, and the father agreed, adoption was the prerogative of grandparents or the deceased woman's married sister, or even one of the child's father's siblings. Some childless married couples could adopt an orphan, and were so chosen if they had what was considered a good marriage. An orphan who had *lost both parents* (*čtmtmáple ʔ*) was, if possible, adopted by a close relative of the same generation as the parents—often a married sibling of the father or mother (Elmendorf 1935-6, 3:30). Assumed surrogate parents used a general term when referring to a *step-child* (*sɫwéltn*).

Within the oral history, there are several mythological accounts of a parentless child being adopted by a bear, the most humanoid of all animals (see Appendix F). No one could remember ever hearing of a parent

117

disciplining a child by threatening to leave the recalcitrant child in the care of an animal, albeit small children were known to talk to and understand certain animals—usually a dog.

Joking Relationship and Fictive Names

Between any two or more older children and adult individuals there often existed a *joking relationship* (*snkʷłčpoʔsčštmnwáxʷ* - "co-reciprocal practical jokesters"). It was a privilege that recognized the intensity of one's relationship with non-kin, but could be established to a lesser extent with affinal or consanguineal people. In the past, this type of relationship was apparent between a man and his mother, but seldom with a father and his daughter. In such a relationship between an elder and a much younger person, the *elder* (*p'xʷp'xʷút*) initiated and essentially controlled the intensity of the verbal exchange.

One of Smith's informants claimed there was no joking relationship among the Kalispel. Yet Smith correctly speaks of joking friendship, or a joking privilege, and provides the Kalispel terms for such a relationship (1935-6:856). This is interesting, since the Chewelah-Spokan Group were known to maintain a joking relationship.

The intensity of the expressions used in this relationship were influenced, even regulated, by the social setting, whether private or public. The latter behavior was usually between non-kinspeople. For example, a sweathouse partner, or the wife of a man's *best friend* (*stúm'čst* - "mother finger" or *qép* - "partner"), could be a *joking friend* (*l'xtéw's* - "they two are friends"). A man could have a private joking relationship about sexual matters with the wife of a close friend, but never in public.

Some elders recalled how as children they had open or public joking relationships with acquaintances, and private and more personal relationships between trusted age-mates. Some men enjoyed a special *reciprocal relationship* (*sumét*) based upon a shared religious experience—which may have occurred in the sweathouse—or a shared near-death occurrence during warfare.

Joking and inferences of anticipated sexual behavior between an unmarried man and woman could be public, but never in private, particularly since this type of relationship was often considered—or could be misconstrued—as a verbal prelude to dysfunctional behavior or conflict, such as divorce.

The use of fictive names by older boys and men was often the basis for intense joking relationships, which established reciprocal obligations and loyalties. Only such participants knew of and were permitted to use otherwise seldom-used or restricted name. Though not always apparent to an outsider, a joking relationship evidenced in public was more personal and demonstrative when attempting to *tease* (*heʔtim'*) or *humiliate* (*qʷn'čstmnwéʔxʷ*). In private, however, a person was more circumspect when joking with another. The only unspoken restriction was for the older person to initiate the repartee—never the younger person, which would be considered disrespectful and unforgivably arrogant. It was believed that a younger person who was disrespectful or giggled in the presence of an elder, would be punished for such a transgression by being bitten by a yellow jacket.

A private joking relationship usually existed between close and sometimes distant relatives, but more frequently between siblings. Distant or more older kinspeople seldom engaged in joking relationships. Despite the levity of such relationships, more socially important protocols were not violated. For instance, personal characterizations of siblings and other relatives never referred to sex or other close intimacy. Between a middle-aged man and his mother, frequent joking always reflected the man's respect for her. This respect restricted the extent of his public display of such humor, but did not inhibit her humorous characterizations of her beloved but tolerant son.

Joking relationships could establish, maintain, and intensify ties with people who were otherwise not involved socially or economically. While helping to maintain social solidarity, joking relationships served as a catharsis to ameliorate conflict—particularly when engaged in hunting, warfare, and other stressful activities. Also, joking gave participants an opportunity to discover one another's psychological limitations, such as their ability to tolerate criticism. Such episodes could go on for more than an hour, and become quite intense, particularly if other people attended the *performance* (*x̣ac'iscut*). Yet it was critical to never truly anger another with one's joking, because he or she could lose face. Moreover, in situations where decision-making was paramount, such anger could prove dangerous to the upset individual or to the group as a whole, because few people can make effective decisions when angry. To lose one's temper was to lose one's judgement and emotional strength, and any person—young or old—who lost his or her temper, could not be trusted.

In addition to the verbal repartee, joking relationships were sometimes demonstrated physically, for trust among friends allowed for liberties of inciting nominal physical pain or even humiliation—to a point. It was an exchange of sometimes near-violent, yet trusted intimacy—publicly demonstrated and valuable. For instance, a man might hit a friend firmly but not painfully in the stomach, or toss a hot coal or stone to *one who is* (*suxʷɬq'ilš*) crouched down and thus scarcely able to avoid being hit. Such adult horseplay helped the participants to learn the physical capabilities and limitations of the people whom they hunted with and relied upon.

Women also engaged in joking relationships with close friends, but primarily in one's own immediate group or certain non-kinspeople, but not always older consanguineal people. This behavior intensified their social and emotional relationships. Young girls engaged in joking relationships with those of their age, but most frequently between close friends.

Joking relationships also provided an appreciated form of entertainment—valuable in any culture that does not have the blessings and curses of passive entertainment, such as television. Even in the modern era, joking among native Americans tends to be more clever and insightful than that of most Euro-Americans.

A man had support from the parents and kinspeople of those with whom he had a joking relationship—sometimes addressing them in surrogate kin terms. Relationships between fictives were encouraged and reinforced when one man purposely married a sister of his *friend* (*sl'áx̣t*). Unrelated women who were friends—particularly those who joined in the daily sweathouse—maintained joking relationships. Elder women were known for possessing the most original and often intense humor when in the sweathouse with younger women. Women of comparable age often used endearing nicknames when addressing one another in the sweathouse, or when socializing in private. Some women said that fictive names were never used in the company of men, even male kinspeople. Women's fictive sweathouse names were once generational, with older women always designating sweathouse names to younger women, whether related or not. Until recently, elderly women would say that what one called another person always indicated one's rights and responsibilities to that person, as well as reciprocal responsibilities.

Men who enjoyed joking relationships would use analogies, such as comparing the length of the speaker's genitalia and his sexual performance with those of a horse. A man might make deprecating descriptions of a friend's athletic or hunting skills that were dependent upon the person's speed, sight, hearing, and physical coordination. Participants enjoyed the detailed, lengthy, clever, and often exaggerated accounts. Other close friends might contribute obscene sound effects, which could elicit a more dramatic response from others present.

Many years ago, during the social sweat, and within each sweathouse cadre, there might be one man who enjoyed a reputation for "making the stones laugh, the ground shake, and the stones send sparks" when he satirized the behavior of fellow members of the group. After a particularly humorous joking of a close friend by his partners, and just before disbanding, an expression sometimes heard was, "That was a good deer stew, but so-and-so got only gristle and bone."

Enculturation

119

It was believed—and practiced—that the mother, father, resident grandparents, and extended family were all responsible for the caring and enculturation of their children. It encompassed respectful behavior, general manners, and etiquette specific to certain events and rituals. Yet a child's early life, socialization, and welfare was predominated by one or both grandmothers. This nurturing by a grandmother permitted her son or daughter the opportunity to pursue their own economic responsibilities. The matrilineal grandmother in particular devoted inordinate amounts of time to her grandchildren—conversing in baby talk, singing a favorite *lullaby* (*ʔemím* or *emm'eʔhi*), and sparing no effort to fulfill her grandchildren's physical and emotional needs. To placate the baby or induce sleep, a grandmother would sing a lullaby— one composed by the mother, and never acquired through dreaming or a vision.

A child at four to six months was thought to be able to recognize family members. When a child began to walk, up to the first three to four years, he was frequently cared for by older siblings and consanguineal female elders (Elmendorf, pers. comm.). Older siblings, particularly an *older sister* (*ɬčičšeʔ*), had the right and responsibility to advise or correct a younger sibling's behavior, but always in private. Older siblings would judiciously counsel the child and demonstrate what was considered correct behavior, particularly toward any elder. On occasion, they could rightfully enact an appropriate measure of discipline. An older child was also responsible for the welfare of any *younger child* (*stʔéwti*) within the group, regardless of their relationship. Some claimed that older girls, but rarely boys, assumed these surrogate parental roles. Older non-kin children were expected to attend to certain needs of younger children, such as warning them of dangerous situations. Similarly, an adult, even a stranger, could give a child a warning of what to *forbid* (*ʷʔentém*) if she felt a child was liable to commit a transgression.

After a boy became ambulatory, his father assumed most of his upbringing, and the boy was discouraged from spending time with his mother when the father was home. Mourning Dove, a Sinkaietk Indian, stated, "The training of the boys was given in strict confidence by the men in their own quarters. Just as soon as a boy was able to walk [without assistance], he drew away from his mother and any feminine associates, to be literally absorbed into manhood" (Ward and Maveety 1995:19). Gender difference began early in a child's upbringing.

If a boy asked his mother a question, she would refer him to his father, as it was believed that her answer could make the boy feminine (Elmendorf 1935-6, 3:6). If his father were away, the child would be told to ask the question of an older agnatic kinsman. "a mother was not supposed to instruct her son if he asked her questions. Rather, she referred him to the men's department—she didn't want to make a squaw out of him" (Elmendorf 1935-6, 3:6). A boy would be cautioned against dressing in girls' or women's clothing, lest he later become a berdache or homosexual—statuses which were respected, but not sought.

Elmendorf's early fieldwork clarifies certain social and familial relations not discussed elsewhere:

[...] his father would even feed him—[the] boy might refuse food from the women folks if they offered it to him, but [he] would eat it if his father gave it to him—[who] impressed [the boy] with the idea of male superiority at a early age—[that] he was man—when [on] big hunts [little boys] were [left with] the older men in camp [who] looked out for the little boys [...] Fathers might start sending [a] boy out alone on errands & to perform set tasks alone in the woods when they were only 7 or 8—taught them not to be afraid—the age varied with the lad's ability—boys had little traps of their own off in the woods (1935-6, 2:58).

After an orphaned boy had moved to the men's area of the long-house, he received considerable care and attention from his grandfather and other male elders. Likewise, an orphaned granddaughter would be cared for by her grandmother and other older women in the women's end of the long-house. Any elder man or woman, with no affinal or consanguineal grandchildren, was happy to adopt an orphan in both name and care, assuming all logistical and emotional responsibilities.

The Spokan recognized numerous behavioral traits that distinguished a good man or woman. The most esteemed quality was respect for anyone older, regardless of age. A personal example of this occurred years ago when I visited a Spokan family to meet its eldest male, and speak with him, even though I knew he intensely disliked *whites* (*suyápi*). While waiting for him to enter the house after his sweat, I sat in the only vacant chair. When the old gentleman entered the room, I stood up to give him my seat. He immediately looked around the room at his sons and the other men—all still sitting comfortably in their chairs—and said, "I'll speak to the *suyápi*. At least he respects older people."

Young boys and girls strictly demonstrated their respect for both family and non-family older people by always walking behind them. Similarly, a person, regardless of age, would always face the sun when speaking with an older man or woman. If a young man stood with his back to the sun when speaking with an elder, the community concluded that he had 'no shadow'—no respect—a terrible insult to his parents. Children were taught, primarily by example, to respect elders. A boy might ask permission to walk behind his grandfather. A girl would assist in performing a domestic task after she first gained permission from the responsible mother or grandmother. The principal lessons were to always be respectful and courteous to all kin and non-kin elders. Years ago, an elderly woman noted:

> I can still recall when I was a small girl [1880], my parents always made me go to all the ceremonies, a time when all the old men and traditional leaders explained the different responsibilities of young men to the village to always provide food to the young, the widows, and old people. [They] told how one day the young men and women [would] be old and need help. Today you might see an old and lonely person living alone, with no family and no one to help them. This is because when they were young, like some of you, they never helped or shared with the elders (Ross 1968-2008).

Most children were ambulatory by the age of one year, and by age two could converse with an adult in a limited vocabulary. Even at such an early age, a child was warned to be extremely careful when around elders and in large gatherings. Children were taught to never laugh or speak loudly in such situations, and to avoid bumping into non-kinspeople, because if a child were to accidentally insult or bump into a sorcerer, he could take revenge by causing the child to *be sick* (*witúsm* or *hec wéyti*) and possibly die. Even an indiscrete expression, or staring too long at one suspected of being a sorcerer, might be a later explanation for a child becoming inattentive or careless.

Boys, particularly at age three or four, were warned to never look upon their mother's or sisters' nakedness, as this was *shameful behavior* (*c'ešc'št*), and violations of this prohibition could result in the boy becoming totally *blind* (*hesčn'mpqíni* or *čnmpqín*), *cross-eyed* (*np'lp'lč'ús*), or *deaf* (*hesntqtqéneʔ*). The term for a person who was sightless from an accident was *nλ'qʷλ'íqʷs* ("eyes were removed"). Pointing a finger at another person was a major breach of etiquette, for it was believed to be a form of projective magic that could cause *illness or even death* (*q'ʔéwi*).

As a child became older, enculturation became more apparent, as did the social consequences to any boy who was routinely rebellious, uncommunicative, or deceitful. A child's behavior, particularly when in public, was always a concern for the parents. Likewise, parents and grandparents were always extremely proud upon receiving approbation of their child or grandchild.

As a boy or girl became older, a grandparent frequently supervised the youth's initiation into adult activities. A grandmother invariably served as a child's closest confidant—a cherished relationship that was maintained by men and women until *her death* (*łu nλ'lltín*), at which time they were the most demonstrative of their *grief* (*ʔecpupuʔsénč* or *nč't'pmí*), regardless of age or gender. Elderly men and women often emotionally recalled the wonderful relationships they enjoyed with one or both grandmothers, who had given them love, trust, support, and understanding. "All relatives should hear their children's laughter, but only grandparents can understand their grandchildren's sorrow." The four grandparents were collectively known as *čmúspleʔ* ("four roots" - "four handles") (STHC).

A young girl would accompany her mother or grandmother on one-day berry- or plant-gathering excursions, which were opportunities for the child to be taught the names and uses of certain plants. If possible, a father similarly taught his son knowledge of animals, their calls and habits, and the skills needed for hunting them—including how to read *animal tracks* (*nʔucšnms*).

121

Parents instilled in their children a respect for the environment and for all animals. For instance, children were told that if they played with or, worse, destroyed a bird's nest or broke bird eggs, *thunder* (*st'rt'ré?m*) could cause a severe storm that might even kill the offending child. If a storm arose, the guilty child or children were made to dive into water fully clothed to prevent their being harmed. It was also believed that children who acted maliciously or mutilated any caught animal, would suffer muscular spasms, temporary physical paralysis, or a physical injury.

When learning to walk, children were cautioned—by all adults of a village or encampment—to avoid hot stones, open fires, and snakes. They were also instructed to avoid bathing in swift water, and to never go under a tree in the presence of lightning, which was a *dangerous practice* (*λ'ik'ʷlqʷm*).

The explanations given for an *irritable child* (*nčn'n'xʷél'sm'*) or a *naughty child* (*če?čé?t*) who had a *temper tantrum* (*sn'č'máw'sqn* - "loud enough to rip off the top of the head" - *?ec ?óqʷ'?ey* or "moon struck" - *lalamíst*), were rarely related to a child's socialization, but more to the nature of the parents or their violation of behavior or dietary prohibitions during the pregnancy. The same was true for a less objectionable *tantrum* (*cácácqʷ*). A *misbehaving child* (*qʷqʷáw'qʷu?t*) was admonished "to keep quiet" (*x?encíntxʷ*) by anyone present. If such admonishment only increased the child's unpleasant demonstrations, she would be ignored by those present. An *only child* (*č'n'qsl'tél't* or *scsixʷl't* or *ši?miš scsixʷlt*) was thought to be more susceptible to such behavior, due to excessive attention from the parents, and more likely to be a *cry-baby* (*c'qʷqʷemn*). Such a child might have a *stubborn disposition* (*qac'Síc'ac't*), or even be *mean-tempered* (*nlč'lč'ene?* or *nč'sels*), and usually displayed *bad manners* (*č'sɫcut*).

If a small child misbehaved in public, and his family were absent, it was acceptable for an unrelated adult to discipline him. The humiliation from being spoken to directly—often through allegoric example—normally precluded any need for further disciplining when it became public knowledge. The corrected child would later demonstrate respect toward the disciplinarian by publicly presenting a small gift or performing a chore. Thereafter the incident was never mentioned, for, if spoken of by an adult, it could be repeated by any child who overheard it. An example of this form of rehabilitation was told by an elderly man who, as a young boy, used without permission a non-kinsman's horse to look for and bring home a truant *older brother* (*ɫqáqce?*). Upon completing the task and returning the horse, the boy was accused of *horse-stealing* (*?ilmixʷm*) by the owner. The boy said he only borrowed it, but the owner argued that it was the same as horse theft, since the boy had not sought permission, and that one day he might become a *horse thief* (*nawq'ʷ sqaxe?*)—a serious and unsettling prediction. The man continued, "A good man works hard, and a hardworking man curries horses. Horse thieves don't." The rancher handed the boy a brush, saying, "[If] done, you'll be a good man." The old man said that whenever he picks up a *curry brush* or *curry comb* (*w'u?šul'e?xʷtn'*), he thinks of the now-deceased rancher.

Observed adult behavior generally proved the most effective pedagogical method. For young girls, a mother would counsel her daughter to "keep in the stream, avoid eddies, etc.—legends and myths were extensively used for enculturation—to illustrate morals" (Elmendorf, 1935-36, 3:6).

The near-constant attention and socialization continued until a child was four or five years of age, when she began to demonstrate physical independence and a greater range of expression to indicate her physical and emotional needs. A child's chosen activities were usually limited only by physical ability, as well as the judgment of older siblings. Children were told to always be home before dark, for several reasons: Animals, malevolent spirits, ghosts, and various theriomorphic creatures were afoot during the night. It was believed that one was more likely to become sick then; for instance, a *bat* (*Eptesicus fuscus* or *Myotis califirnicus* - *t'enw'éy'e?*) might nest in the child's hair, resulting in illness—usually a fever and night sweats.

Elders related how grandparents would recall with fondness their carefree childhoods, roaming, often en masse, like "great hordes of grasshoppers from people's homes, eating what they wanted, spending the night listening to *wonderful stories* (*m'ey'štw'e?xʷ*), and always being well cared for." A child might do this for several days before returning home, usually accompanied by an entourage of other hungry children. When in a sweathouse, elderly women discussed with delight their recent experiences while *babysitting* (*čšt'eltm* or *čƛ'elt*) their charges, and enjoyed the admiration of the other women. All such women agreed that the best times in the sweathouses were when relating stories of their grandchildren. The stamina of a devoted grandmother was revealed during long sessions of *baby talk* (*p'ep'n'em'* or *tetéwe?* or *yem'e?* or *?u?úpe?* or *tatam'e?* - "children's speech"). An example of baby talk was the word *cčiči* or *čiči* for an *older sister* (*łčičše?*). A man called his younger sister *łcc?ups* until she became an adult, and then he called her *sntxʷus*. A woman also called her younger sister *łcc?ups*, even after maturity. Adults and older siblings often used baby talk prior to a child's speaking, such as *wawá?* for "little baby" (*?o?xtel't*), *?iitš* for "go to sleep" (*?itš*), or *teté* to tell the child to "eat" (*?iłn*).

Young children were indulged and given much attention by older siblings, who nurtured them and instructed them in their obligations. Grandparents, particularly grandmothers, carefully monitored their diet, play, and other childhood activities. Adults were primarily concerned that a child learn all environmental dangers and was always courteous to elders. A sister of a child's father was often referred to as *little mother* (*sk'úk'ʷi?*) by the child, because of her supervision and care for her brother's children.

The time of adolescence was an enjoyable period for most children. Yet between the ages of eight and twelve, they participated in certain domestic and subsistence-getting activities—which parents were quick to favorably acknowledge. These efforts utilized the *child's first toys for hunting* (*t't'a?pm'ín'* - "little target"), which were prototypes of adult tools for hunting, gathering, and fishing. Such implements were made and given by a parent or grandparent, who would patiently explain to the child how it was to be used and cared for. The father or an *uncle* (*sm'e?ł*) taught a young boy how to trap for small animals using a noose—never failing to praise a boy's success. A major accomplishment was when the young hunter first *pulled the hide off all together* (*n?awepsc*) of a *jack rabbit* (*Lepus townsendii* - *ʕʷananiče?*) or a *snowshoe hare* (*L. americanus* - *sqʷáqʷci?*), which was quite a feat for a youngster because of the animal's thin skin. Skunk, having a pork-like flavor, was eaten, but boys were warned to avoid skunks for risk of being sprayed. If sprayed, the youngster had to endure lengthy and repeated washings, which were less painful than the humiliating jeers from his friends suggesting the boy had found a new friend. Skunks were hunted by both men and boys, and killed by throwing a club, or by repeatedly hitting the animal with a long pole from a safe distance. Porcupine meat tastes like deer meat, and was taken by small boys using clubs. Thus an important ceremony for a young boy was his First Kill Ceremony (*eminš*), after he had killed any animal, including a bird, regardless of size or method. The boy already knew how to properly dress the game, and afterward he would gift the game to an elderly non-kin person in the camp or village.

Children received considerable recognition from adults for their contributions of even small animals and firewood, because they were economically significant to the household and the immediate residence group, if only symbolically. Using metaphor, elders would say that by age eight a *boy* (*ttw'ít*) or *girl* (*šéšu?tm'*) was like a tree, and one could tell how she would grow—i.e., what direction her life would take—by how she behaved and helped elders. As Turney-High noted in his study of the Kutenai:

> [...] by the age of six he was supposed to accompany his father on easy deer hunts to learn what he could. A little bow was made for him at two, and by three he was supposed to be able to hit prairie chickens. At six he was supposed to kill birds regularly and to furnish part of his food. The motivation here was one of education and discipline, of 'making a man early,' instead of being truly economic, as the child was led to believe. At the age of ten such parental pretense was over (1941:117).

When possible, boys were required to perform *onerous tasks* (*?ay'?ay'xwi?l'š*) that would strengthen them, such as gathering water in buckets for horses from ponds covered with *green-yellow pond algae* (*Spirogyra spp.* - *nmtr?etkʷ*) (STHC). A young boy was also required to serve as a *messenger* (*sxʷqeclš* or *suxʷmimimist* - "runner")—not only for his parents, but also for older siblings (STHC) and village elders.

As boys and girls began to *attain the age of puberty* (*ƛxʷúm'e?*), they were continually instructed—or admonished, if warranted—by their families on proper private and public behavior. For example, "Silence was strength. Being boisterous or loud was weakness." More than one boy was told how "Animals run before noise. Only crows and magpies look to those who make loud noises." An *insult* (*lxʷpsqelixʷ* - "hurt someone's feelings") to a young person was to say that his words were like the *flatulence* (*sp'u?*) of a constipated elk. Prior to a youth's initiation into the sweathouse, he was reminded to always control his temper and his actions, no matter what was said or done to him, and to conceal any disrespectful feelings. The worst public insult was for a man to slap a man or strike a person with a quirt (Elmendorf (1935-6, 3:26).

Spokan people were never known to swear. When referring to human waste, an individual spoke euphemistically or indicated it by simply fluttering his or her right hand.

Children were encouraged by their kinspeople and community to emulate the domestic and food-getting activities of adults. The efforts of youngsters who worked diligently and cared for their elders, were often reinforced by public approbation. For example, adults would recognize a boy as he walked through the village or camp with an animal he had trapped or shot: "Look at that boy. What a great hunter he will be when he is a man. His family will never hear their stomachs groan," or "I have never seen such a large gopher," or "I wonder if we should help him carry such a large animal," or "I wonder if the boy knows he caught a bobcat." The greatest accolade that recognized a young man's hunting success, however, was for the elderly men to say, "That boy's skill and courage will make his grandfather proud."

Young girls were encouraged to *work industriously* (*sisyús*) and to learn the various skills necessary to be a good wife. If a young girl were lazy or *unskilled* (*šéššís*), she would be told that no man would marry her, or she would later be abandoned, and her life would be a lonely existence without a family and children to support her when she was old. A girl was recognized for her accomplishments and encouraged to work hard. For example, upon returning from a root field with her mother and other women and children, a girl carrying roots would warrant similar adulation of her skill and efforts, and what a good wife she will be for some fortunate man. Most complimentary would be when an elderly lady announced publicly, "That young girl with the heavy root basket must have listened carefully to her grandmother. Like her grandmother, her digging stick (*péc'e?*) will always catch the sun's first rays." (When metal shafts replaced traditional fire-hardened wood shafts.)

An *elder* (*p'xʷp'xʷut*) would publicly recognize the assistance of even a young non-kinsperson who had helped, even by simply sitting patiently and attentively listening to the elder's stories. Inhabitants of a village or camp always gave a complimentary nickname to a helpful young person—one that indicated unselfishness and humility to elders. Respect and physical assistance afforded to elders by children reflected well upon their extended family, and was the greatest gift a child could give to the child's parents and grandparents. Elderly widows, widowers, the infirm, and the *senile* (*n'ew'm'*) frequently received special attention and care from children, who fulfilled essential daily chores, such as hauling water and collecting firewood. Respect for elders was reinforced by the common practice of unrelated children visiting lonely elders, who would address them with terms of endearment and occasionally give small handcrafted gifts.

Punishment and Discipline

Social control of children—and adults—was inextricably related to the perceived feelings of the community, as well as those of deceased kinspeople, supernatural forces, and spiritual beings—all of whom presumably would be offended by any moral transgressions of humans.

The Spokan believed a *child's temperament and mannerisms* (*tr'e?w'y'e?*) were inherited from one or both parents, but could be influenced by anyone's observed behavior—even a non-kinsperson. Yet the most effective social control of children was accomplished through instruction during the winter months by grandparents reciting deeds of bravery and generosity by past culture heroes.

Social control of children was also attained by use of character stories—dramatic accounts of local or universally acknowledged theriomorphic creatures, which would *punish* (*xʷey'stm* - "to punish") an offending child for any infraction to the group, or to nature. Misuse or disrespect of natural resources by children was prohibited, and warranted immediate discipline.

Parents told their children of the dangers of *zoomorphic creatures* (*čxltsqélixʷ*), such as dwarfs, *little people* (*sncmasqélixʷ* or *smtéw'si* - "mythical race of foolish people"), and *monsters* (*n'atisqélixʷtn* - "man eater"), who were attracted by—and would devour—delinquent children. In 1843, Reverend Walker noted that, during an afternoon worship, "I heard one cry to his son to keep awake or he would get the medicine put upon him" (Drury 1976:229), which he speculated was "A reference to their belief that the medicine man could snatch away the child's spirit" (Drury 1976:229 fn). Egesdal (pers. comm.) cites how children who were naughty, or noisy at night, could be influenced by stories of Coyote, and by the story of Owl (*sty'táye?* - "mottled one") putting such children into a large covered watertight basket (*yámxʷe?*) made of woven cedar root and filled with snakes and other biting creatures. The origin of the mottled feathering of the Great Horned Owl (*snine?*) is noted by Egesdal (pers. comm.): Long ago, there was an evil *snine?* that was a cannibalistic monster (*n'atisqélixʷtn*). Coyote tricked her into putting pitch all over herself, and then, during a dance around a fire, he pushed her into the fire, which ignited the pitch, burning her.

A recalcitrant child could be threatened with a visit at *night* (*skʷkʷ?éc*) from a *whipping man* (*sxʷtc'ím*), who would whip the child with a *switch* (*syél'u?* - "a twisted stick") if the child did not correct his behavior. A village chief would occasionally appoint a man to run through the village or camp at night, striking dwellings with a whip made of "thongs braided over a stick into one thong" (Elmendorf 1935-6, 2:45). Such sticks were sometimes used in lieu of whips. A few elders recalled how excruciatingly painful it was to be switched on the legs by a freshly-cut length of willow. By prior arrangement, a number of men might enter the camp or village at night, striking the dwellings with sticks and calling out the punishments they would administer to children who misbehaved. Children, frightened by the hollering of apparently *wild* (*u?w'áq'ʷu?q't*) creatures, were reminded of the value of good behavior. Despite these visitations, there was invariably a child who warranted being *scolded* (*he?h?éne?stm*) or, as a final measure, whipped. Another nondescript theriomorphic creature that served as a disciplinary force, was *sti?tá*, a monster owl that was a frightening and malodorous humanoid. It would presumably kidnap and eat any recalcitrant child, or turn him into a *northern leopard frog* (*Ran apipiens* - *tmtám'áye?*).

Children were warned that if they misbehaved they could be harmed during lightning and *thunderstorms* (*st'r't'r'e?m*), or that a *whirlwind* (*hecnéw'ti*) would carry them away or create enough confusion so they would get lost. As a more immediate punishment, a father might throw a container of water on a recalcitrant boy; eventually he needed only to place his hand near the water-filled basket to gain the boy's attention (STHC).

Elders assiduously maintained that although an adult could administer corporal punishment, children were rarely severely whipped—for if a parent had to frequently resort to physical punishment, then he or she

125

was publicly viewed as weak, incompetent, and perhaps undeserving of the parental role. Similarly, a whipper appointed by the village chief could punish a child for any reported misdemeanor.

Due to the frequent attention and physical contact given by adults to their children—particularly the *youngest child* (*st'éwti* or *stt'ew'ti'*)—the older children quickly realized when one or several of them were in trouble for a remark or deed, and were consequently being ignored. Like children everywhere, they would be more embarrassed to be disciplined in front of siblings. Given the offense, sometimes adults would ignore a misbehaving child until he made amends to those whom he had offended. It was believed the *youngest son* (*st'ewti*) was always smarter than his older siblings, because as the youngest, he had received the most powerful *sumés*, and was most likely to become a curing shaman (STHC).

From an early age, children were constantly warned to always tell the truth. Lessons were occasionally reinforced through examples from nature, often based on the Doctrine of Signatures. For example, a parent might give a dramatic account of how a mendacious child's lips could be sewn shut by a *dragon fly* (*Anax junius* or *Calopteryx spelendens - xʷatqín'e'* or *xʷatqán*). A child who disregarded her appearance might be warned that a *Lewis's woodpecker* (*Asyndesmus lewis - č'ƛck'ʷá* or *cíwcu*), or worse, a red pileated woodpecker would nest in her hair—the latter bird causing greater pain.

Yet some elders recalled, with obviously fond memories, of how tolerant and less outspoken their fathers were in matters of discipline. When a father was contemplating an appropriate measure of punishment, the ultimate threat by a young son was to declare, "I want to go live with my grandparents who live in Idaho."

Elders believed that speaking too harshly—and thereby possibly humiliating the child—or using corporal punishment, could break his spirit. Also, the *ancestors* (*ši'š'í't* or *ši'tmasqélixʷ*) of the child could retaliate, causing the disciplinarian to have *bad dreams* (*c'qeys*), or worse, interrupting his or her life with unexplained misfortune. It was believed that children should not be pushed, but rather lead by example. Elders thus contended that a child was best taught with praise and by an adult's correct behavior, and that praise is more conducive to socially accepted behavior. Elders also claimed that it was rare to *spank* (*t'qʷéplentm*) a child, for it was better to use a "tongue" first rather than a hand.

Most verbal disciplining took the form of parables—told to all the children present, and not just the transgressor. This allowed each individual child to take from it according to their guilt, which each child would realize. Given the great importance most individuals placed upon being accepted by their social groups, sometimes the most severe discipline, particularly for an adult, was the threat of excommunication—being sent away from kinspeople.

An example of adults using instructive metaphors from nature occurred in the mid-1960s, when I was assisting a family bring in their cattle for winter branding. The youngest boy was throwing stones at the cattle as they came through an enclosure gate. Typically, an older boy was not reprimanded in public. But late in the afternoon, when all the men and the boy were in the sweathouse, an elder man told the *story* (*sm'e'm'í'*)—here considerably condensed—of a young boy whom he once knew who would throw stones at horses:

When the boy *became a man* [*qlcm'x'il'š*], he couldn't kill deer. Everyone said he was a generally damn poor hunter, and it all started because he was always throwing stones at horses and even cattle, so that every time he tried to hunt for deer or other animals, he failed because his arm had grown so long that it would always drag in the dust, or in the leaves in the woods, therefore warning the deer and other animals, who ran away to safety. When the boy was older, and became a man, he was called the "long armed man" because his arm was so long. Finally the poor man realized he needed someone to get food for him because his parents had "moved on," and so naturally he decided he should marry. He knew a widow woman who was about his age, and thought she would be a good wife—one who would care for him. And yet it was sad because no matter how much he tried, the man couldn't get to the house of the woman he wanted to marry. He tried and tried, but he couldn't ever get even near to her home because the horse always traveled in huge circles since the man's arm dragged on the ground like a great rock (Ross 1964-1967).

126

Children were also warned about the consequences of disregarding the advice of one's parents and elders, and were admonished to never walk or run too close behind an elderly man or woman, who in retaliation could place a curse upon the unthinking child. Such an act of evil retribution was called *ta qeʔcnxʷčičiʔstxʷ* ("you should not cross the back of someone") (STHC).

Through example and spoken word, children were taught to respect and honor their parents and other elders, and that to become respected adults themselves and avoid punishment, they must honor their elders and even hold them in awe. This concept was extended to all occasions when a child was asked to do work; they were told that their efforts should fulfill the expectations of parents and grandparents. For instance, several older women told the story of a young girl—a playmate of their great grandmothers—who always tried to evade her domestic responsibilities. Instead of filling her basket with huckleberries, she would:

> [...] stuff the bottom of her cedar-root gathering basket with dried leaves, and she'd cleverly add some stones so the basket seemed heavy to other women in the camp. The girl was smart enough to cover the stones and leaves with stiff pieces of willow so when she emptied the basket, only the few berries she had picked would fall out onto the tule mats. None of the other women knew what she was doing, because at the end of the gathering day, the berries collected by the women of her family were spread out on tule mats to dry, so they wouldn't be too heavy to carry back to the village, and the girl would add her collection to the piles. She did this for many years, and was never found out. But when she married, and she moved to her new husband's place, and had a couple of nice children, everyone noticed how skinny her children were, but never knew why. The lazy woman's secret was finally discovered when her young daughter borrowed her mother's berry basket to play berry picking with her little friends. The little girl, being so underfed and weak, happened to drop the basket because it was too heavy with the stones, and the stones rolled out and revealed to everyone her mother's secret (Ross 1968-2008).

Prior to becoming *teenagers* (*ʔawtmasqélixʷ*), children generally found childhood to be an enjoyable and memorable time, because of the security and attention provided not only by the extended kin group, but also by the general community. As noted earlier, the principal individuals involved in the socialization and care of children were the grandparents, and occasionally a great-grandparent. One old man referred to his childhood, and that of his ancestors and other kinspeople, as being like a towering ponderosa tree that grew straight because of what was given him by his family, larger kin group, and village. On becoming an adult, he would be like the great tree, for the sun was the laughter; the night was the time to dream of future things, but always being brave; and the winds would strengthen its roots, like the words of caution by his elders.

Naming

With the establishment of the reservation system—certainly by 1904—the Spokan no longer controlled the allotment of land or formal enrollment. Also, the practice of *naming* (*qeɫ tixʷɫ skʷest* - "name change")—or renaming—a principle adult married individual, who had an existing Indian name, was, in many instances due to association with traders, trapper-traders, and of course with Christian missionaries. There were many instances when a Spokan assumed an English name, one that was a translation of his or her Indian name. The practice of assuming English Christian and sir names was encouraged with the introduced practice of land allotments. These were names that non-Indian speaking Euro-Americans could pronounce.

This forced naming weakened the once-traditional use of supernatural sources that were often revealed to the pregnant woman as a name for her child—provided by a dream, a vision, power-based occurrences, or an animal. The new system made name change impossible, except for a woman taking her husband's last name in marriage. An individual's designation was only a secular name, devoid of sacred entities and powers, or public recognition of previous achievements or intimate relationship with a supernatural power. Prior to tribalization, the Spokane never subscribed to patronymic or matronymic designations.

After the death of a first child, it was believed that a second child, if any, possessed the deceased child's life or breath-spirit. However, parents recognized the second child to be different, and the child was never given the name of a deceased sibling for fear the surviving child would, as a result, also die prematurely.

Prior to Euro-American contact, an important rite of passage was the required naming ceremony (*qs tix*ʷ*ɫ skʷest* - "getting name") and *feast* (*sk'ʷl'cncút*), held within several days of an infant's birth, when it appeared that the baby would survive the trauma of birth. There were, however, several remembered accounts of a child being named at birth. If the designated name was that of a *deceased kinsperson* (*sntr'r'm'ép*), then the selection process warranted considerable attention, and all of the baby's living relatives were consulted as to whether it would be appropriate to name the new baby after the chosen decedent. Some babies were named after a *grandparent* (*nkʷescn*)—usually was a grandmother. This both recognized and reinforced the young person's life-long special relationship to that grandparent.

As a boy became older, his parents could change his name to that of a deceased kinsperson (Elmendorf 1935-6, 2:66). Some Spokan considered it important—an indication of ancestral respect—that a person's name be remembered by succeeding generations, albeit the name might skip one or more generations. Yet such lineal recognition of a deceased never went beyond seven generations.

Before changing his name, the boy would ask his older relatives for the names of *deceased relatives* (*snqʷmíp*) from whom he could make a selection. But it was considered indecent and disrespectful to use a dead person's name in conversation, so that person would instead be referred to as "son of so-and-so" or a similar circumlocution (Elmendorf 1935-6, 2:66). Some believed that to not name a child after a consanguineal relative who had recently died, was an explanation for the appearance of the decedent's insulted ghost.

Traditionally, a person had to demonstrate the specific kin affiliation he had to the deceased person before being given the person's name. Changing one's name depended upon a number of circumstances, and was more circumspect than alluded to by an early observer:

> Their adoption of names is arbitrary, and a fortuitous circumstance is frequently seized upon to gratify the passion for a change. The first name they bear [sic] is generally taken from some circumstance at the child's birth, and in later life others are added to the first, and there are few individuals but are well supplied with them (1846, 4:456).

A boy could change his given name *prior to puberty* (*né ʔi' sppxép* or *čtmtmá ploʔ*), taking a name he simply liked—one that represented a favorite type of animal, an unusual aspect or event of nature, or a unique experience called *kʷéstmis* ("he takes that name"). In return, the boy would give his parents a gift for the new name, usually a *buckskin robe* (*sp'y'álqs*). Or he could buy another's name, by giving the owner a blanket (Elmendorf 1935-6, 4:9).

During the naming ceremony, people who knew the deceased (whose name was going to be used) would stand and provide often lengthy and dramatic accounts of that person's particular traits, unique accomplishments, or adventures that demonstrated bravery and generosity. Such laudatory accounts were delivered by kinspeople, as well as non-kinspeople who had regularly shared the sweathouse, or spent time in hunting and other activities while away from the family of the person named, and had once enjoyed a joking relationship with the deceased. In naming the child, it was believed—or at least hoped—that these desirable traits or abilities of the deceased would eventually become manifest in the recipient later in his or her adult life.

At a naming ceremony, after someone described the qualities of the decedent, the sponsoring family would present to the speaker a gift—its value dependent upon the narrator's eloquence or status. Acceptance of a naming gift further legitimized the child's existence by that individual, as well as the group. Thus, this exchange of gifts tended to further integrate the community. A gift could eventually become well known, especially if it had been previously given many times, or had an unusual origin or value. It could serve as a mnemonic device, when participants recalled with emotion when a parent or grandparent received the gift. Some gifts even received special names, and were always referred to in awe. For instance, elders might recognize an old Pendleton or Hudson's trade blanket as having been passed "over the laps of eight remembered babies." As a woman passed a folded blanket (to the person on her right), she would gently and slowly rub a hand over the 'memory blanket' as she quietly recalled the words of sorrow and kindness that over the many years had been spoken at the naming ceremonies of the earlier recipients. These blankets were always kept neatly folded so the kind words would never be lost or swept away. Other gifts were typically utilitarian objects, such as *quilts* (*st'aq^{w}íc'e^ʔ*), bedding, cloths, saddle blankets, or shawls—but were seldom used, instead being carefully stored away for the next naming ceremony.

When naming a newborn, the ceremony served primarily to recognize the baby's existence, and to establish the inherited prerogative rights and responsibilities of the child as she matured within the kin group. Giving her a name also tended to thwart infanticide. If the name was that of a deceased kinsperson, then the recipient was treated with more respect—representing the spirit of the deceased. It was believed that the specific name of a person could influence personal skills, similar to a person's tutelary spirit. For example, a designation for an adept fisherman was *nk'$^{'w}$nk^{w}e^ʔ* ("skilled in taking things from the water"). A small child might receive a name from some trait he displayed or an event, such as when he took his first step and someone threw a moccasin between his feet, hoping that the omen would make him an outstanding foot-racer (Elmendorf 1935-6, 2:54).

Names could also be inspired by a unique experience or dream that the father or pregnant wife had prior to, during, or immediately after their child's birth. During pregnancy or delivery, the woman might hear a name spoken to her by an animal, or in a dream she might hear a name recur at least three times. There were instances when a name was stolen by an adult, claiming it was given during a dream, usually from a deceased non-kinsperson noted for major accomplishments. It was hoped that the name would be of assistance to the child later in his life. More commonly, the name would be purchased by the *family* (*sx^{w}sx^{w}lt*) if it was from a non-kinsperson (Elmendorf 1935-6, 4:9).

A baby might be given the name of a person—even a non-kinsperson—who dreamed what the sex of the unborn child would be; this acknowledged the dreamer's power and presumed empathy with the unborn child. Unfortunately, the term for the special relationship between the child and the dreamer, has been forgotten. One elder explained how her grandmother had received her name: "If an old lady has a dream, and then tells the pregnant person the sex of your unborn child, and if the dreamer is correct, the mother might give the child the dreamer's name. But you know, the important thing is a woman can't change a baby's name, no matter what, because if she does the baby will die."

During a person's life, she might acquire several names, such as upon surviving a serious illness, or a child's repeated dreams of a changed identity, or a man's success in warfare. It was common for a man to take the name of his dead father, during a *name-changing ceremony* (*sk'$^{'w}$l'cncút*). Similarly, he could take the name of his dead son. Sometimes an individual wanted simply to change his name for no apparent reason, as was related to Elmendorf (1935-1936, 4:7). A man might change his name four or five times during his life, each time announcing his decision publicly at a name-changing ceremony and feast, to which he invited *friends* (*l'x̣téw's*) and villagers. He gave them gifts, thereby recognizing them and acknowledging their acceptance of his new name as they audibly recited his new identity. He might give his old name to his son, as a "gift name." Yet before a person died, she typically would take back her given name, because the first ancestral name was thought to provide a connection with deceased kinspeople in the spirit world.

When assuming a new name, the former name was no longer used. In the case of a *first born* (*ci^{ʔ}ít* - "head first") being named, but then dying, no successive children took the deceased child's name since it was believed that a child named after the deceased sibling could possibly suffer the same fate.

Unfortunately, there are no accounts by earlier ethnographers as to whether the Spokan practiced teknonymy (when a father took the name of his newborn son), but there are several accounts that suggest this did happen just prior to the time of the reservation, as well as during tribal enrollment. This resulted in boys inheriting quasi-patripotestal rights with the forced practice of surnames (Elmendorf, pers. comm.). A man whose son had died could permanently take on the *same name* (*snkʷeʔpskʷést* - "co-named") of his deceased son. A modified form of teknonymy for women was when the mother would take the child's name. This was typically done by non-kinspeople, thereby recognizing the new kinsperson. It was manifested when a person referred to the baby's or child's mother as "the mother of so-and-so," not using the mother's name.

A man was able to assume the name of an older deceased agnate (affiliative kinsman), but there is no evidence that a woman could change her name if her daughter died. It was unusual for a person to take or give the name of any recently deceased member of an extended family, because it was believed that the deceased child would never be incorporated into a life hereafter, and would return upon hearing his name spoken. The practice of not naming (*nescio nomen*), according to some elders, was practiced if the newborn appeared too fragile to survive.

The selection of a long-deceased kinsperson's name was an extremely involved and sometimes protracted process, because it always required asking every known consanguineal and affinal relative for his opinion of several names presented for consideration. It is even more difficult nowadays, when one's relatives can be demographically dispersed. In some cases, the logistical costs are less than the social costs of dissenting feelings created by factionalism, divorce, and the renewal of long-standing antagonisms when distant kinspersons are not considered. After a person's *death* (*nλ'lltn*), the immediate members of both families seldom said the name of the deceased (Elmendorf 1935-6, 3:34).

Temporary name change sometimes preceded warfare if during the prior preparation and intense sweating, or in a dream, the warrior was instructed by his tutelary spirit to assume a temporary identity. The reasons for a temporary name change varied, as Elmendorf recorded:

> [T]he war party leader does this always [...] their [*suméš*] tell them just before they go on the war party what name to take[;] not the name of that animal [their] *suméš*, but [another] animal name. [They use] these names only during the raid to protect themselves—[it] gives them power to protect [*č'łqixʷntm*] themselves and when they return they take their former name back (1935-1936, 4:7-8).

A man would presumably never sell or give away the name his guardian spirit had bestowed (Elmendorf 1935-6, 4:9). Prior to the reservation system, a man might want to change his name by purchase, which often obligated him to give a *name-changing feast* (*sk'ʷul'tcintsút*). A man could buy a new name from another who was not related to him, with a blanket. He would ask the owner if would give him the name; if agreed, then the new owner would tell people his new name, but would not give a feast (Elmendorf 1935-6, 4:9).

Similarly, "women change their names just as men do—their names also are from ancestors [and] in the family—women gave [a] *sk'ʷul'tcintsút* when taking a name" (Elmendorf 1935-6, 4:9). There are no known instances of a Spokan ever changing his or her name due to change of marital status when losing a spouse, or after rehabilitation from a serious illness to prevent further illness—as was once common in some Plateau groups. However, Curtis recorded how Interior Salish burial practices were occasions when a widow could change her given name: "The practice of giving away all of one's possessions when a close relative died was sometimes observed, and on such an occasion a woman also 'threw away' her name" (1911, 7:76).

A Spokan never addressed a kinspeople—including one's parents—by their proper names, but instead used kin terms, such as 'mother of my mother' (Elmendorf 1935-6, 3:2). Children were *forbidden* (*xʔentém*) to use given names, especially for one's grandparents. However, a full name could be used to address a friend whom one had not seen for some time, and yet not imply formality (Elmendorf 1935-6, 4:35). In other words, all of one's kinspeople were addressed in third-person kin terms or relationship terms with personal pronouns. Full names were always used when addressing non-relatives or people whom one did not know well. Given names were always used in political council or during any formal business or social transaction. This importance of kinship is reflected by the general term *čtámmqn* ("ultimate lineal kin [plural head]"), which usually refers to one's kin (Egesdal, pers. comm.). The manner of addressing a person indicated respect, status, and even obligations. Elders said that "kinspeople have no pockets, but strangers do"—which meant that strangers could conceal things, being more formal, whereas kinspeople should not hide things, but rather should be forthright.

Agnomens

The Spokan traditionally used agnomens, i.e., *nicknames* (*saʔw'stéy'eʔ* or *ʔaw'stéy'eʔstm'*). But because these designations often reflected an unpleasant social or physical trait, they were seldom used in the person's presence, for such a designation would be considered a serious insult. A most humiliating and deprecating nickname was one that suggested the person was *stingy* (*q'iẋt'mn* or *y'ey'úkʷeʔ*)—a behavior considered detrimental to community harmony. There is no memory of a person being addressed with a derogatory adjective or a gross profanity—as may happen today—for elders believed that any vocal condemnation, even in *absentia*, would eventually result in the deplorable characterization befalling the accuser. It was once claimed that a stingy person who had no heart or compassion, would steal from his neighbor, hide food from the needy, and share only his grief with others. Presumably, children never assigned nicknames to elders.

In addition to a given name, any person or domesticated animal noted for an acquired and unusual behavior, could be given a corresponding sobriquet. For example, any animal considered *lazy* (*ʔsẋéyti*) or generally found lying on the ground in an indiscriminate heap, was referred to as *łuqʷʷtul'eʔxʷ*. Many years ago, an elderly man earned that nickname because he was very often seen lying down when in public (STHC).

Among peers, a man might enjoy an agnomen that recognized his physical strength or ability in a particular sport or subsistence-getting activity. A person with exceptional hearing, sight, smell, or other physical attribute, would not be given an agnomen, but often rather an anthropomorphic approbation, e.g., "he has the eyes of an eagle" or "the strength of a bear." A girl's agnomen was commonly named after a songbird, a mouse, or a butterfly—most commonly the *monarch* (*Danaus plexippus* - *k'ʷhúleʔ*). A boy's fictive identity was typically associated with a land mammal. Young children were sometimes given nicknames by playmates, but these were usually discarded when the child approached puberty.

Nicknames given by grandparents were never forgotten, and used only in private with the grandchild. Hale (1846, 4:456) noted that, during one's childhood, boys and girls were sometimes bestowed different *endearing children's names* (*ʔaw'stey'eʔstm'*), conferred in fun by both grandmothers—appellations that emphasized certain physical traits or behavioral characteristics of birds or land mammals. Elders could not recall children being named after fish, insects, or reptiles. A young boy or girl knew that a displeased parent or grandparent could quickly substitute a favorite nickname with that of a predator bird or one of the few unfavorable animals. A child's best hope was that the favored nickname would be restored once he corrected his behavior. Though a grandparent might address an adult grandchild by his childhood name, one's adult friends never exercised such a privilege.

The Spokan are not known to have ever used secret names. As an individual became older, she acquired numerous informal names, used according to that person's consanguineal (related by blood), affinal (related by marriage), or fictive relationship to the speaker. For example, only a man's sweathouse partners used—or knew of—his sweathouse name, one that usually epitomized particular physical attributes or unique psychological abilities. These male-given personal designations or agnomens were often gross exaggerations of women's genitalia, or suggested the potential or reputed aberrant behavior of the person named—even of unnatural sexual relations with an 'unusual' person or thing. A man took not only considerable pride in the verbal accolades that suggested libidinous and licentious behavior, but also understood that the recipient had been accepted by males of comparable age. It was not unusual for a man to have several sweathouse names.

Puberty

A major individual rite of passage was the puberty ceremony, which required both males and females to spend this liminal time in solitude, fasting and praying (Hocart 1952:160). Prior to puberty, both sexes underwent daily strenuous regimens of training, to condition themselves physically and psychologically for *puberty* (*ɬx̌ʷúnʔey* or *né ʔi sppx̌ép* - "acquires powers of reasoning"). The most dramatic change in an individual's life occurred with the ritual's successful completion, because it delineated the role separation when the boy or girl was forced to *abandon* (*čsuʔx̌ʷx̌ʷ*) the relatively easy life of a child and assume an adult's responsibilities. Also, certain moral prohibitions, personal relationships, and activities would be different.

Boy's Puberty Ceremony

A young male's rite of passage to adulthood was invariably demonstrated by his participation in a vision quest. These rituals of transformation terminated his leisure of youth , and began the time when the responsibilities and known difficulties of adulthood were acknowledged.

Prior to receiving his tutelary spirit, a boy was called *sisyus*, and often during this time he would receive some indication of the type of his future tutelary or guardian spirit. In fact, each stage of a man's life was named: Boys, from birth until they could walk, were called *ttw'ít*. From two to three years of age, they were known as *mqipšin* ("on the feet" or "learning everything"). From seven to ten or eleven, their status was known as *misɬttw'it*. Boys aged twelve to thirteen were grouped as *ɬx̌ʷúm'š* ("puberty"). Young men seventeen to nineteen constituted a group called *swiʔn'úm'ti* ("becoming handsome") or *k'ʷck'ʷac't* ("becoming strong, stiff, muscular"). Men from twenty to their late forties were known as *sx̌estm* ("at his best"). A man in his fifties was of a status called *čy'eʔk'ʷšin* (*y'ek'ʷ* - "to cross over") (STHC). Those in their late fifties were generally classed as *čx̌ʷú x̌ʷp'x̌ʷut* ("becoming old and wise") (STHC).

A young man's transition from childhood to adulthood was not an issue only of biological change—usually when his voice began to change—but also a decision by his father and other close male consanguineal and agnatic kinsmen, when the boy demonstrated maturity and decision-making. He was called *sɬx̌ʷúmeʔ* during his puberty change.

This ritual of transformation not only terminated his leisure of youth, but commenced his adult life and their associated responsibilities and difficulties. Yet despite considerable apprehension of the actual ritual, boys generally looked forward to this rite of passage, despite the ramifications of the vision quest.

The actual puberty ceremonies was preceded by a rigorous program of daily running and swimming, to physically and psychologically prepare the boy for the anticipated vision quest. Every morning at first light, boys would fill their mouths with water and run to the top of a steep hill and spit out the water near an elderly man who stood, supervising his charges. If a boy prematurely swallowed the water, he had to repeat the exercise.

Acquiring a power during a vision quest was accomplished only in strict isolation from one's family and community, since it was believed that only through solitude and focused propitiation to a desired guardian spirit could the novice be recognized by that spirit. If successful, the novice gained esoteric knowledge of his newly-acquired role, its associated status and power, and the rituals for fulfilling that role. While the boy did gain such knowledge from his sponsor—a kinsman, often his father's brother—the most significant and unique knowledge was learned from the initial encounter with the tutelary spirit, and was bolstered during special individual and group rites of intensification. Similarly, the novice was instructed to heed his mentor and even more the instructions of his tutelary spirit.

Lewis noted that:

> In main morality religions, an initial experience of disorder and its mastering through controlled possession are particularly emphasized in the case of those candidates who lack hereditary qualifications. For such outsiders

132

in the quest for shamanistic office, personal peculiarities and anomalous experiences which society recognizes as expressions of spiritual attention may indeed be exploited with advantage. But they are of no value at all unless they can be conspicuously mastered. The ability to contain and control the grounds of disorder remains the essential requirement; and obviously the greater the apparent trauma which is to be mastered, the greater the authority and power of the new shaman (1971:191).

During his vision quest, the novice fasted in seclusion for no longer than three days and two nights in an isolated area—the *place of vision quest* (*snwčsuneštis*)—waiting for a guardian spirit to appear. If the boy was successful in being visited by a specific animal, then this tutelary spirit would give him a power, and possibly present him with a power bundle and a song. He would be referred to as *sisyús* after having received his *suméš*, a spiritual revelation or epiphany called *tłákʷílx*. However, he would also be referred to as *titʔuw'it* anytime "his guiding spirit has come upon him" (*ʔec čicnm t suméšs*). A boy's sponsor might acknowledge his avuncular role by giving the boy a *keepsake* (*sʔélk'ʷmn*) upon the successful completion of his vision quest (see Appendix G).

Later, during the late Mid-Winter Ceremony, the boy, when alone in the sweathouse, would assume the behavioral and physical characteristics of his new guardian spirit—most of which were animals. There were certain behavioral traits of each animal. For instance, a magpie collects things, so the name might provide a person gambling skills. A mole was skilled at concealment; hence a person possessing a mole tutelary spirit could be an excellent warrior, if only for concealing himself when in danger. A wolf spirit would convey fierceness. Consequently, within a warring or hunting party, there may be a dozen or more distinct powers representative of the individual's various abilities.

A young person's future *suméš* could be any one of a number of skills, such as hunting, fishing, gambling, love-making, or curing. With this revelation, the young boy had *become a man* (*qltm'xʷil'š*), and during his life might acquire different powers and familial spirits. Despite the lengthy training, the physical and mental conditioning, and the long vigil, some boys never acquired a tutelary spirit. In essence, "Power [was] a supernatural force conferred upon an individual by a spirit who becomes the protector and ally of that individual always carried by a person [in] a power bundle or item representing his *suméš* " (Randolph 1957:140). Elders claimed there was no stigma if a boy failed to receive a tutelary spirit. However, a boy was never considered a man until he received a tutelary spirit, but he could marry.

During the sometimes traumatic experience of the vision quest, a neophyte—when confronted with a tutelary spirit—might not want to receive an apparent *suméš*, particularly if it is an inherited endowment. Thus, if the "successor shows reluctance in assuming his onerous duties, the spirits remind him forcefully of his obligations by badgering him with trials and tribulations until he acknowledged defeat and accepts their insistent prodding" (Smith 1971:66). "Under these conditions, all that a shaman can bequeath to his heirs is a body of technical expertise which may help a successor to gain privileged intercourse with the gods [spirits], but cannot guarantee that this will happen" (Lewis 2003:156).

Of interest is Ray's work with the Sanpoil, who adamantly claimed that after a boy first experienced the presence of his tutelary spirit, it was completely forgotten, until a later age:

> The visionary [...] was completely powerless to recall any details of the incident until he was again visited by his spirit. This did not occur until many years later, usually when the person reached twenty-five or thirty years of age. This repression for many years explains many aspects of the guardian spirit complex. By the time the spirit returned the individual had more or less definitely found his place in the community. His talents were known to himself and to others, and his character likewise (Ray 1933:186).

There were numerous ways for a man or woman to receive a *suméš*, oftentimes when the young novice commenced to learn the unique ways and powers of animals. A young girl might have a guardian spirit appear in recurring dreams and later, after her menopause, receive a power. A person who became seriously ill would often, upon recovering, know that he was bequeathed with a tutelary spirit—thenceforth having the power for curing individuals with a similar malady. During a vision quest, if a boy were left near water by an older

133

sponsor, the boy might be enticed into the water by a weasel, where the boy would live with the animal underwater for three days. Upon his return, the young man would be recognized as having acquired the animal's unique power (see Appendices H and I). Every occasion of acquiring a tutelary spirit was different, and thus reinforced the aspects of personal power and uniqueness of the experience. All guardian spirits could transform themselves into human form.

The completion of either the male or female puberty ceremony brought an immediate change in the individual's life. This important rite of passage, if successful, meant that the person was now publicly recognized as an adult—as a man or woman prepared for the rights and responsibilities of a *mature* (*p'x*ʷ*x̣*ʷ*tw'ilš* - "to age") adult, and expected to make significant contributions to the community, particularly after marriage.

Girl's Puberty Ceremony

Unlike boys, Spokan girls did not go through a vision quest. Traditionally, a girl would receive her tutelary spirit—her guardian spirit—in one of several ways: by inheritance from an elderly female kinsperson; during an unusual event, such as the Mid-Winter Ceremony; from an unusual dream, during which a guardian spirit would appear to her when she was alone in a unique situation; or in a dream that an elderly kinswoman would later interpret, explaining the significance of the girl being "gifted" with a power. A girl might receive her tutelary spirit anytime between early adolescence and adulthood, but this never occurred during her time of monthly confinement in the *menstrual lodge* (*snłx*ʷ*umxtn*).

As part of their physical training for their puberty ceremony, *young girls would fill their waist aprons* (*čłpk*ʷ*álqsntm*) with old sweathouse stones and climb a *hill* (*šrutm*)—away from any boys—and drop their heavy burden before an *old woman* (*sy'o?psčín't*), who supervised this daily exercise. The piled stones were never removed, but remained and were called *sq*ʷ*llúmt* ("traditional stones"). A few elderly claimed this ritual signified easy delivery of any future babies. Afterward, the girls were encouraged to swim and run daily—as were boys.

Apart from a girl's change in behavior, a mother or maternal grandmother could presumably tell when her daughter was approaching her menarche, by observing that her skin was a bit paler and she had shadows under her eyes. These biological changes would prompt the mother—and other older female relatives—to explain to the girl how she was entering a new life, which demanded that she strictly adhere to menstrual prohibitions, avoid sexual relationships, be active and industrious (partly to avoid becoming lazy), and observe the needs of elderly people (Ross 1965:423).

Even prior to a girl's menses, she was confined and isolated once a month—a time called *stsm'améy'a* (Elmendorf 1935-6, 1:38)—and her mother or grandmother would tell her about her impending menarche, including rules of behavior and associated taboos. A woman's menarchial confinement, during which she was forbidden to gather or prepare food, was considered by some as a time of welcomed leisure.

Despite the restrictions of diet and behavior—which lasted until menopause—all women agreed that the menarche was greatly anticipated, though often with apprehension. During a girl's puberty, she was known as (*słx*ʷ*úmš* - "first onset, first day"). Most elderly women agreed that their *puberty ceremony* (*słx*ʷ*úme?*) was when they became women, because afterward they were eligible for marriage and for having a family. If a girl was not already obligated by a prescribed marriage, then usually her mother would determine when her daughter could be courted, and when she was capable of handling the social and domestic responsibilities of marriage. From the time of her menarche to her marriage, the young woman was always chaperoned by an older woman, to prevent her from falling under the spell of a man's love magic and in turn having sexual relations or eloping. When not confined, an unmarried woman, regardless of age, always wore a long buckskin dress that hung below her ankles, so no male could see her ankles. She was careful when she walked

134

or sat, and never stepped over any object on the ground that might expose her ankles. Even an older unmarried woman, who choose to *remain at home with her parents* (*č'em'tw'íi*), had to abide by this custom.

The long-anticipated puberty ceremony brought a distinct transformation of status from carefree youth to the responsibilities and difficulties of adulthood. When a *girl changed to being a woman* (*ʔesłxʷúm'ši* or *n'e ʔi sppxép* - "female puberty") was largely determined by the occurrence of her *menarche* (*sxʷey'míš* or *hec łq'ʷew'si* - "she is experiencing her second period" or *słxúmš*). Upon the onset of a girl's first *menstrual period* (*xaʔxeʔéyxʷxʷ*), her mother or grandmother became her *instructor* (*suxmáiam* - "person who instructs or speaks") (Elmendorf 1935-35, 1:79). She was given esoteric knowledge concerning women's matters, such as personal sanitation, sexual prohibitions, pregnancy, dietary restrictions, and the use of certain medicines.

Upon her *second catamenial discharge* (*łq'ʷew's*), a girl was reminded of the rituals and prohibitions of her strict confinement. There was disagreement among informants as to the length of time a girl was first confined in a menstrual hut, but five to seven days is cited. Yet Wilkes claimed, "At the *first menstruation* [*łxʷúm'š*] the Spokane woman must conceal herself for two days in the forest, for [if] a man were to see her [it] would be fatal; she must then be confined for twenty days longer in a separate lodge" (1845, 4:456).

Menstrual huts could be made of cattail mats supported by bent willow, and covered with fir or balsam boughs and grass. A more sturdy type was a small four-pole tipi-like structure covered with the same materials. Other structures had a low, small entrance that always faced west, to better catch the first rays of sun. *Balsam fir* (*Abies balsamea* - *mrinłp*) boughs were preferred for covering the earthen floor, because the overturned boughs laid flat and produced a pleasant scent. When fir was not available, grass or mullein leaves were used. There were varying opinions of whether tule mats were ever used.

A girl's mother was careful to locate and construct the menstrual hut away from the village or camp, primarily to minimize the chance of her daughter intentionally or accidentally seeing others—particularly males, of any age. A menstrual hut was never used by women outside the family. Traditionally, the entire menstrual hut was burned after a girl's first confinement—a practice presumably discontinued in the early reservation period.

The first time a *menstruating woman* (*snilmélxʷtni* or *sč'mtč'en'é* - "sitting inside") entered the structure, she was called *sxʷétmí*. During her isolation, the young girl was put through:

[a] series of physical tests & tasks to develop hardihood & endurance [...] in retirement are not suppose to come in contact with food while it is in preparation [but] could dig camas or bring stones for [the] fire—but not to come near [the earth-oven] when [the] pit [is] open [...] Older women were always with them secluded them in training until marriage—[in] servitude to their relations & [the] family engrained in them at this time—[that they] must anticipate their wishes—must always [be] ready to serve (Elmendorf 1935-6, 1:38).

All young boys were taught to respect a menstruating woman's seclusion, and were warned of the severe consequences if they approached a menstrual hut or, worse, if they had physical contact with a menstruating woman: partial or full blindness, periodic psychological disorientation, loss of speech, and a reduction in their hearing and physical endurance. All males avoided the area of a menstrual structure for fear of *contamination* (*čnil*), which could result in any of the aforementioned consequences. Catamenial blood—the universal Stigma of Femininity—was greatly feared by all males, regardless of age. During confinement, a woman wore a menstrual *pad* (*n'łq'ʷéw'stn*), usually fashioned from several folded mullein leaves, which was later burned.

There was a second reason to avoid social contact: *puberty aged girls* (*sxʷiʔm'íš* or *słtiʔčm'íš* - "girl at puberty") were considered ungroomed, unwashed, and unskilled (STHC). Parents and other older family members anticipated a girl's approaching menarche by a pronounced *puberty laziness* (*sxʷéyti*), sometimes evidenced by her neglecting her appearance. To counter this, a girl was exhorted to follow an intense regimen of physical exercise and grooming, while elderly kinswomen explained the numerous dietary and behavioral restrictions she had to observe until her menopause. In addition, the young woman was required to perform chores for older people within the community. During the second year, her training intensified and her chores became more demanding, e.g., she was expected to contribute to older people greater amounts of berries and firewood.

To warn every man against a chance encounter with her, a menstruating woman was required to wear a confining ankle-length *buckskin dress* (*sp'iy'alqs*) with a narrow red ochre strip painted around the *dress hem* (*sč'mpál'qs*) to symbolize her condition. Otherwise *naked* (*čtméƛxʷ* or *sčtmelxʷ*), she wore no type of undergarment during her confinement. Before leaving the menstrual hut to resume her residence and domestic obligations, a woman—married or *single* (*sntxʷsncút*)—was always careful to bathe using water from a watertight, split cedar-root basket, but never in a stream.

Any menstruating woman was forbidden to touch or cook food, go near water, gather wood, or engage in any tasks associated with others that involved their contact. During confinement, she was forbidden to *scratch* (*aẋʷ* or *c'lẋiw'm*) any part of her body with her nails, for fear of later contaminating other persons. Instead, she used a special *wooden scratcher* (*nqsqíntin*), or a small piece of sharpened deer antler that was always kept in her hair during confinement and when she was outside at night doing her prescribed chores. Nor could she use a comb or *braid* (*sčtɫt'ɫpé* - "braid a woman's hair") her hair, though some elders say she was permitted to do so the last day of her confinement by using a discarded huckleberry-gathering comb that always remained at the site. Girls were told, "Do not touch your hair, for you are unclean. You will stop its growth. Use a stick when you want to scratch your scalp." (Miller 1990:42-43). During the first year's confinement, the mother braided and tied her daughter's hair up in a tight bun atop her head, or into two side buns—on each side of the girl's head—to prevent loose hairs from falling. The mother braided her daughter's hair, working beaver castor oil into it, which was believed to encourage growth of the girl's hair. Some contended that a menstruating woman could wear, when outside the menstrual hut, a *coiled basket cap* (*snq'qay'ámxʷqn'*) made of coiled Indian hemp and decorated with wrappings of cedar root or bear grass. The hat was left at the menstrual hut until her next monthly visit (STHC).

A taboo with serious implications, was that a menstruating woman not *contaminate* (*scwekʷ*) a stream or other source of water, particularly if it contained any fishing weirs. Hence, she was not permitted to approach waterways, nor ever drink directly from a stream. It was believed that a menstruating woman could contaminate a seep, a *spring* (*sʔocqʔétkʷ* - "water coming out" or *p'p't'ič'* - "gurgling sound of little spring"), a stream, or a standing body of water through her physical contact. If contamination occurred, then the animals—notably *male animals* (*sql'tmsqáẋeʔ*)—in the immediate area would not be hunted or trapped for some time, if only because those animals presumably would leave the region. To avoid this, every confined woman drank from a gummed water container. To prevent her touching the water with her lips, she sucked the water through the leg bone of any large wading bird—preferably a *greater sandhill crane* (*Grus canadensis* - *sʔétw'l'* or *skʷršín* - "yellow legs")—or a section of hollowed elderberry stem.

In winter, a confined menstruating woman had little protection from the cold, except what was provided by her clothing, the shelter, and a small fire outside her hut, since fire was forbidden within the hut regardless of weather. During the summer she was not permitted any fire. Wood burned in any such fire was always gathered by the woman in *early morning* (*kʷekʷst*) or just before dusk. As she collected her firewood— preferably *fir wood* (*cq'éɫp*) or tamarack—she always prayed to and gave thanks to the source of this warmth. These types of wood make cracking or popping sounds when burned, and she would pray for the fire noises to speak and bring her strength and good wind to accomplish her daily and sometimes nightly chores. The singing of wind in the trees was called *swáwlqʷ*, and was invariably of significance to the listener—often from one's acquired or intended *tutelary spirit* (*suméš*), which was occasionally called *n'e ʔis ppẋep*.

Whenever a girl was doing a chore, she prayed for a long and industrious life, and to never be lazy—a condition that was most feared by all women. She was told she must always rise before the songs and flight of birds. This fear of being lazy was somewhat allayed when old women would give her mother baskets for the girl to repair. During the first year, she never did any hide work or sewing, but could do minor chores during her second year. A confined girl was continually provided lessons of industry and reminders to always remain physically active. To prove to her mother that she had gone to a particular area (near the site of her confinement) as instructed, the girl would tie *small immature ponderosa saplings* (*sʔáʔtkʷɬp*) in a knot. To this day, one can find large mature bull pine trees whose lower trunk sections are tied in a knot—done many years ago by girls during their menstrual seclusion.

In late summer and fall, a girl would collect berries, which her mother would give to postmenopausal women of the camp or village. Parents knew this was the first time that the girl was so isolated, and keeping her occupied helped to keep her mind calm and not frightened by the sounds of the wilderness that she was familiar with, but could be frightening because of her isolation. A stick could break in the *forest* (*č'súleʔxʷ* - "bad, rough terrain") due to the wind, but could sound like a theriomorphic monster—usually a so-called Stick Indian. As an old Spokan woman once said, what is most fearful, "is what you can hear, and can't always see."

The only food eaten by the confined woman, *sč'lúxʷm* ("her evening meal"), was brought to her by her mother, usually just before dawn. The fear of contaminating food and utensils required her mother to *bring her food* (*nʔukʷcíšts*) on a wooden tray covered with a large mullein leaf to prevent the girl from touching the tray with her fingers. An elderly woman recalled an account of one woman, who had married into the village, and not having immediate consanguineal kin, was brought food by her husband during her confinement, but always left at a distance from her place of confinement.

When a young woman was experiencing her first menstruation, she was not given food for four days, so that her insides could be properly cleansed. Before retiring, and immediately upon rising, she would perform ablutions outside her hut by pouring small amounts of water over her *vagina* (*sxʷúʔt* - "female genitals"), being careful to not touch her body with her hands, particularly her genitalia. Upon completion of her daily ablutions, her mother made for the girl a medicinal tea from shredded yew tree bark, to cleanse her insides.

After her confinement, all of the sweepings, black moss, mullein leaves, and other materials used as absorbent pads, as well as any loose accumulated body hairs, were burned by her mother or one of the women who attended her daily needs. An older menstruating woman would dispose of her own materials before returning to her family.

During her confinement, a woman was given only certain types of foods. This generally did not include meats, particularly those which would be offensive to certain animals and detrimental to the woman. For instance, the meat of an unborn *fawn* (*spapičaqn*) would presumably cause the woman to later abort a pregnancy. Land mammal meats were considered too bloody, and were avoided lest she experience a hemorrhage or prolonged periods of bleeding, such as hypermenorrhea or menorrhagia. Even fish, lamprey, or turtle in small amounts were thought to be sufficient to cause dysmenorrhea. Some elders claimed that certain, but now unknown, types of white meat were permitted—a custom that might have begun well into the reservation period.

A menstruating young woman slept intermittently throughout the night, and only for brief spells—and never during the day. She was not permitted to leave her menstrual hut during the day, except to do chores, and to urinate or *defecate* (*mn'eč*)—always careful to bury excreta and any cleaning material. However, some elderly women remembered their grandmothers telling how, during the night, a confined young woman was required to travel to a designated talus pile to collect three round vesicular basalt stones, which she carried under her garment, depositing them in a pile near the menstrual hut. There was not agreement as to whether dropping the stones to the earth symbolized an easier delivery when later pregnant. The stones were not known to fulfill any utilitarian or aesthetic function, but were only a proof of ordeal that she had been active.

It was believed that the menses made a woman lazy, and thus a major concern of the girl's family was to prevent laziness. She was instructed to always run when performing chores, never walk, and even required to increase the distance and sometimes the elevation. Another onerous but required task was to collect firewood at night for elderly non-kinswomen widows, who would find it deposited in a prescribed location distant from the menstrual hut.

Every morning at sun up, following her mother's instructions, the confined girl would dutifully go outside her shelter and jump up and down while praying for a long and happy life—one with a kind husband and respectful children. Some girls were instructed to face the rising sun and dance by jumping sideways from one foot to the other, all the time singing a prayer to the sun for a long and happy life. Later, just as the sun was setting, she repeated the dancing and praying, now facing west. This was the most important of the cardinal directions since west was considered female, while east was considered male. Some elders maintained that the girl would cover her face with ochre in the morning when she first saw the rising sun. Other collected sources indicate that a young woman never covered her face with ochre during the morning and evening ritual (STHC). But several elderly Spokan women remembered accounts of how a confined woman always smeared grease-based ochre under both eyes, for now unknown reasons.

A woman never processed or tanned hides, nor engaged in menial chores, when confined to a menstrual lodge, since her family tended her immediate domestic responsibilities. If a woman experienced her menses when traveling, a *small tent-like structure* (k'ʷšqsústm or k'ʷk'ʷl'č'étxʷ) was made for her confinement. It was often made from large slabs of dead bark, supported by three or four upright poles. Yet during the last years that the menstrual hut was still used, in the 1930s, the woman's husband could deliver food, leaving it a short distance from the structure, and always being careful to never approach for fear of going blind if he saw his menstruating wife. Several elders cited an example of a renowned male berdache who became blind at a young age because he had spied upon his older menstruating sister.

With the deculturation from Euro-American contact, the practice of confinement diminished until it was abandoned—lastly by more traditional women—probably in the late 1930s. The following early account of the Spokan menarche ritual is unique, since so little has been recorded regarding the subject, because it was rarely discussed with men—particularly men one did not know—and because the conflicting number of seclusion days is not consistent with other accounts:

> The customs of the Indians, in relation to the treatment of females, are singular. On the first appearance of the menses, they are furnished with provisions, and sent into the woods, to remain concealed for two days; for they have a superstition, that if a man should be seen or met with during that time, death [of the man] will be the consequence. At the end of the second day, the woman is permitted to return to the lodge, when she is placed in a hut just large enough for her to lie in at full length, in which she is compelled to remain for twenty days, cut off from all communication with her friends, and is obliged to hide her face at the appearance of a man. Provisions are supplied her daily. After this, she is required to perform repeated ablutions, before she can resume her place in the family. At every return, the women go into seclusion for two or more days. When in childbirth, they are still more hardly treated, being required to keep strictly to the hut, whence they are not suffered to be moved, however ill they may be. Death often ensues in consequence (Hale 1846, 4:456).

This ritual is no longer practiced or recalled with detail in the oral tradition, as are the Bluejay Ceremony and certain curing rituals. However, a few elders disclosed what they could recall being told to them many years prior by their elders. Given the seclusion of the menstrual ritual, it is not astonishing that those few non-Indian recorders cited differing durations of confinement and whether it was the first or subsequent confinements. Few if any traditional women would likely have discussed the menstrual ritual with a non-Indian male.

The following statement by Curtis is probably correct when describing certain aspects of a girl's first menstrual ceremony, a statement that incidentally verifies the use of red ochre. However, the ceremony was maintained by some Spokan until the early 1900s:

> Among the Spokan a girl just arrived at puberty was sent to a small, rude shelter erected especially for her. At sunset she painted her face with red ocher, and then after darkness had fallen she went into the hills and at various points piled up stones, and returned late at night. This was intended, by supernatural powers, to give her strength of body, and to afford her their protection. During the day she gathered wood, which the old women

carried from her lodge to their own. The girl remained apart from her people for the ten days. The custom fell into disuse about 1850 (Curtis 1907-30, 7:75).

When asking elderly men about a woman's child-bearing, menstruation, anatomy, or personal taboos, an interviewer would be told that such matters were never discussed by men, and could be answered only rightfully by elderly women who might to willing to respond to such unusual inquiries by a man. Yet elderly men and women would explain, often in memorable detail—what they claimed would be for the 'last time'—rituals and beliefs that years earlier were even unmentionable, particularly to a non-Indian man. Their explanations and memories afforded them, if only briefly, considerable pleasure from their past.

In the late historical period, deculturated families did not adhere to the ritual of confinement, partly because the extended family was often dispersed by off-reservation labor opportunities (such as cash-cropping by fruit-picking in orchards, hop-picking, and periodic domestic work with urban white families). However, when in residence with her family, a menstruating woman had to cook, but never used metal utensils. This verifies that within the early reservation period, not all menstruating women were being confined to a menstrual lodge. Yet the practice of menstruating women never preparing foods that were to be stored, or to dress any game or fish, was continued. Some very elderly women recalled their great-grandmothers explaining that 'in the time before horses,' a woman occupying a menstrual lodge was never permitted to eat any type of food, instead fasting to cleanse herself. But she could, as mentioned, drink water brought by her mother. Such dietary prohibitions were presumably not practiced once a woman was married and with children, though before that it was strictly adhered to.

Any dressing material that had been soiled with catamenial blood during confinement, and not properly destroyed by burning, was carefully cleaned by an elderly postmenopausal kinswoman, by *rubbing (qe^ʔ yutmⁱlt* - "we rub it") the garment with diatomaceous earth (dry, white clay). This cleaning material was absorbent and effective in ridding any buckskin garment of blood, grease, or general soiling. The women of every family always kept a generous supply of this anhydrous material on hand, and also used it for tanning as well as internal and topical medicinal uses. The material was worked into the soiled spot with the pre-chewed end of a thick piece of red willow stripped of its bark. After use it was immediately burned with any other contaminated materials. Once woolen items were introduced, any soiled wool blanket or clothing was cleaned by whipping the woolen upon dry, crusted snow—an old technique called *čⁱtc'i^ʔčči^ʔs* (STHC). However, all other clothing used by a woman during confinement was burned after use, by her mother or the woman herself when older. Some claimed that the soiled garments might be given away after being washed. Before the girl terminated her confinement, the mother would bring her daughter new clothes to wear before returning to the village.

If her daughter experienced an infestation of head lice, a mother *would feel around and search for head lice (hecm'a m'ósqn'i^ʔ)*. This apparently was rare, since a confined woman would daily collect a small bundle of fresh green ponderosa needles, to be inserted into her hair to prevent lice, and if needed to scratch her scalp. The pine needle bundles were renewed and burned every morning by her visiting mother, for if any contaminated item was accidentally left outside, it could be dangerous if retrieved by a sorcerer, and could cause game to leave the area. It was believed that any sick, infirm, or weakened person could die of internal bleeding if they had contact with a menstruating woman. It was understood that the reason for a person to suffer from an open wound that never properly healed—rather always bleeding or seeping—was from being accidentally contaminated by menstrual blood.

There were varying opinions regarding the disposal of contaminated vegetative material used for personal hygiene while confined. Several elderly women said the woman would *dig a hole (nciqm)* inside the structure and bury any human waste. Others claimed that any items contaminated with catamenial blood were never buried, because animals might detect the odor, dig them up, and distribute them, thereby contaminating the environment. There was also the fear that the buried items could be recovered by a sorcerer. But given a

139

woman's sometimes wide range of travel while gathering food, one possible means of safe disposal was to bury the contaminated materials far away, and cover the site with rocks.

When a woman left the menstrual lodge to resume her domestic duties, she would scrape her body with a doe's deer rib, and then rub her body with moss, soaked yarrow, or mullein leaves, to remove any residual catamenial blood. If she were unmarried, this cleansing ritual would be supervised or conducted by her postmenarcheal mother or another older woman of the family, which displayed support and caring. To ensure thorough cleansing, the woman also performed a sweathouse ceremony, in a small lodge erected near the menstrual hut, and disassembled after confinement, but not destroyed. Due to lapse of memory by informants, there remains debate as to whether the menstrual hut was burned after each use, which is reported to have been done by the Chewelah-Spokan Group (Smith 1936-8:1140).

Marriage

Marriage (*snk'ʷłk'ʷul'l* - "the one you marry") was in some ways an even more critical change of role and state for the individual than the vision quest, for it legitimized the birthrights of any offspring as well as one's being incorporated and maintained economic and social relationships with other individuals and groups—which could be distant. Both women's and men's lives were in many respects more demanding by both private and public responsibilities.

Marriage served important socioeconomic functions for the newlyweds, their families, their respective kin groups, and occasionally other bands or contiguous ethnic groups. It thereby created or renewed extended webs of social relationships, which were important for maintaining necessary intergroup socioeconomic ties. Exogamous marriage rules maintained and extended webs of social relationships, by permitting a mutual exploitation of common resources and maintained polyadic task-grouping (Anastasio 1972). Economic relationships between other dialectic or language groups were also encouraged and fostered by polyglotism, which helped to facilitate trade and other types of cross-utilization of resources necessary for fulfilling both economic and political needs. Teit (1930:323) acknowledged, "The Spokan probably had the most social intercourse and intermarriage with the Coeur d'Alene, considerable with Kalispel, less with Colville and Sanpoil, and very little with other tribes." The Spokan also married freely among Flatheads (Fahey 1974:22). A son or daughter who married out of his or her group—usually in a different tribe, was referred to as *słxmélt*. Some Upper Spokan and Kalispel occasionally intermarried, but not often as the Kalispel did with the Chewelah (Smith 1936-8:118).

The general impression of marital commitment by the Spokan women was cited by Cox, "The women are good wives, and most affectionate mothers: the old, cheerful and complete slaves to their families; the young, lively and confiding; and whether married or single, free from the vice of incontinence" (1832:105; 1957:115).

One elderly lady explained, "Before puberty, you're only half. With marriage, you're whole." In fact, there was consensus that both men and women looked forward to being elders, a time when their hair had turned white.

Marriage was performed when the man was about eighteen years of age, and the woman between puberty and twenty years of age. As in many cultures, a virgin was a potentially more desirable *wife* (*nóxʷnxʷ*). A younger woman who was reputed to not be a virgin had little chance of marriage, but often agreed to such an arrangement with an older widower (Elmendorf, pers. comm.). There were no restrictions of marriage between people of notably different ages, and there existed no strict practice of territorial exogamy or non-kin exogamy or endogamy.

The first recorded description of general Spokan life and marriage was made by Ross Cox, "who was a very bright & highly educated young Irishman" (Brown 1911:21), but not fluent in the Spokan language, and whose principal informants were, as he wrote, *voyageurs*, which probably explains the following:

140

The Spokans are an honest friendly tribe. They are good hunters, but somewhat indolent, fond of gambling, despotic husbands, and indulgent fathers. Their women are great slaves, and most submissive to marital authority. They do not exhibit the same indifference to the superior comforts of a white man's wife as that displayed by the Flat-head women, and some of them consequently became partners of the voyageurs. They made excellent wives, and in general conducted themselves with propriety. Although the Spokan men are extremely jealous, and punish with severity any infidelity on the part of their wives, they are themselves not over-scrupulous in their own conduct (Cox 1831, 2:129-30).

It may be of some interest that after years of Spokan deculturation, Wilson, who resided for eighteen months with the Spokan, made a similar description about the Flathead Group, whom he considered to be inveterate gamblers, but, "they are, however, brave, honest, polite, unobtrusive, and dutiful to their parents" (1866:293).

In most instances, marriage was by mutual consent. Then a couple wanting to *marry* (*sntxʷuʔsncuʔt*), they would secure the permission of their parents as well as the chief of their group, who reciprocated the courtesy, and who always supported a family's request. If a man *had no parents* (*čtmtmápleʔ*), he would engage the services of a woman who acted as a *go-between* (*nsucnmist*)—usually an older woman who was known among the group for her skills in negotiating. Or the man would have a male friend negotiate his proposal (Elmendorf 1935-6, 4:9). In 1853, during an extensive government survey, Major Benjamin Alvord referred to the practice of how, "The suitor never in person asks the parents for their daughter, but sends one or more friends, whom he pays for their service" (1857:19). Bancroft cited, "the Spokane suitor must consult both the chief and the young lady, as were as her parents; indeed the latter may herself propose if she wishes" (1875, 1:247). John Keast Lord also spoke of a chief's authority:

Regardless of the method of proposal, the chief had to give his consent. If the intermediary was successful, then the man would perform certain services, a minor form of bride service, or by the presentation of a gift, such as several untanned deer hides to the parents of his intended wife. Among certain tribes a kind of apprenticeship is enacted, in hunting or, otherwise from the groom (1867:233-4).

However, if a man had been secretly courting a young woman, and was responsible for her pregnancy, the parents of the respective families might insist upon the couple's marriage. Parents of status could exercise considerable pressure upon their son or daughter to marry someone of similar position, such as the son or daughter of another family that was of equally well-to-do status. Couples of different socioeconomic backgrounds could and did marry; and, as in all cultures, any children were welcomed by both families.

Courtship

Marriage was most often preceded a courtship for a period deemed appropriate, requiring an exchange of favors, and hopefully the acceptance of both families. Courtship was a pleasant experience as a young *bachelor* (*qlʼqłtmʼxʷmʼíst*) devoted considerable time and effort in gaining the attention of a young woman, one who might indicate her receptiveness. If a young woman appeared uninterested, a suitor could attempt to improve his chances by surreptitiously securing supernatural assistance, in order to influence the affections of his love, through the use of specific plants or symbolic parts of animals. A young suitor might make, but more often borrow a particularly successful *love flute* (*člmšqíntn*). After learning one of the mournful love songs from an older man, who was known to have been previously successful in amours because of his songs and ability to make the flute "speak or sing of love, the suitor would, in the evening after birds stopped singing, serenade his love from a distance where she could still hear him.

A more expressive and creative young male suitor could compose a new *love song* (*člmʼšqʼíntn* - "that is his love song"), always singing it when just out of sight of a young woman, and, if possible, away from the seemingly constant attention of his love's chaperon. If a man were unsuccessful in his attempts "to gain the attention of a young lady, he could pay a shaman to *put a spell on her* (*płáxntm* - "someone cast a love spell on her"), usually with a certain *powder* (*płáxt* - "potion") (Egesdal, pers. comm.). Dried and powdered roots of arnica were "mixed with a robin's heart and tongue and with ochre paint, then dried and powdered the mixture" (Turner *et al.* 1980:75). Then the male suitor would wade into a stream, face east, mark his face with ochre, and mention the name of his love. The roots of *Coyote's strawberry* (*Genum triflorium* Pursh - *spilye? q'it'q'm's*) were mashed by a married woman and steeped in boiled water as a love potion to regain the attention of her husband. The stalk of mountain valerian and hummingbird heart was crushed and consumed during courtship. A young woman could be alerted to the nightly presence and intentions of her lover when she heard his 'love call' or signal—a rather distinct sound he made by blowing on the knuckles of his thumbs joined over both cupped hands, which made an effective resonating chamber. The sound was a distinct and agreed-upon melody or previously arranged imitation of a specific animal. This method of projecting sound was also used between hunters when communicating with one another. The success of a courtship, but more often a brief daytime rendezvous, was sometimes dependent upon one of the man's sweathouse partner's skill in creating a diversion to draw away the attention of the girl's mother. The young man would reciprocate his friend's efforts with a deed or gift, in a manner that was dependent upon success or failure.

It was not unusual for a young girl to attempt to gain the attention and affections of a young man by using different rituals and medicines, which were often acquired from a midwife who had such knowledge. If she managed to acquire a small article of the young man's clothing, the young girl would place it under her pillow—practicing what may be termed contagious or projective magic, for it was believed that if she dreamed of him for three consecutive nights, they would later wed. A girl might also entice, or at least attract, a young man's attention with the pleasant scent from a type of necklace made by wrapping and stitching a small rectangular piece of buckskin around three pieces of sweet grass, which was worn about her neck, called *siyaλk'ʷ*. Some people wove strands of dried *x̣ásx̣s* in with the sweet grass to enhance the desired effects of attracting the favors of another when it was burned.

To prevent and safeguard a young woman from the attentions of an unwanted man trying to make a surreptitious nocturnal rendezvous, the mother often tied to her hand a long narrow section of buckskin that was then attached to the girl's ankle, a type of *ankle leash* (*k'ʷłʕccinštn*). When the girl attempted to move any distance, her mother was alerted to her daughter's intentions. The father, on being alerted, hastened to build up an already banked fire in hopes of learning the identity of the suitor before he got away (Smith 1936-8:1185). If the man was then identified, the father would the next day inform the chief who would instruct his whippers to publicly administer the chief's judgment upon the guilty interloper. If a couple was discovered in *flagrante delicto*, by rights the girl's mother could whip her daughter without the chief's permission. As mentioned, the young man was often judged and punished by the court if the offended parents chose to make public what was normally considered a family disgrace.

Couples (*sx̣mnčew's* - "lovers" or *sntx̣ʷu?sncu?t* - "fiancées") were generally not required to practice prescribed marriage (in which parents determined with whom their son or daughter should marry). Parents did, however, influence a young person's choice in marriage. Prior to courtship, a father might indicate to his son the skills of a young, unrelated, and marriageable woman, and point out how properly her family had raised her. The parents of a young lady could similarly encourage their daughter to marry a young man whom they knew she was interested in by identifying the man's abilities to provide for a family. After individual parental agreement of courtship, the parents of both families would mutually meet to acknowledge their acceptance, and would continue to encourage the proposed courtship (Bancroft 1875, 1:277). Prior to asking a chief for permission to marry, whose consent was invariably given, the parents of the couple would present their intentions before the council. "The Spokane suitor must consider both the chief and the young lady, as well as her parents, indeed the latter may herself propose if she wishes" (Bancroft 1875, 1:278 fn).

Until a woman married, she was never permitted to be left alone outside her immediate family; indeed, an older woman would always accompany her when she went root-digging, berry-picking, or was engaged in any public activity. As previously mentioned, a young unwed woman was required to wear an ankle-length dress as she was aware of the custom that, if a man saw her *bare legs* (*čɫtmélxʷ*) or (*qʷu čqʼʷčqʼʷqʼʷíčqscšntxʷ* - "you have seen my bare legs"), she must marry him (STHC).

Love Charms

Both men and women had access to a wide variety of love charms and potions acquired for payment from a shaman, a midwife, or by using a known family formula. Most commonly, an individual desirous of maintaining, establishing, or reestablishing a relationship, would attempt to surreptitiously acquire from the other person an article of clothing or a bit of hair. If successful, the item was sung over or manipulated in a prescribed fashion that would hopefully gain the attention and love of the other individual. Elmendorf's field notes provide several examples of contagious magic, describing how certain charms were used to gain another's affection, or to disrupt an existing relationship. His use of the term scapularies refers to a small bag a man or woman on their shoulder under a garment, one that hung in the person's left axilla:

> [...] roots used in *scapularies* (*pɫáx*) - a woman's secret - if a man is not treating his wife right she brings out her love charms and it is in the form of a powder and they are sprinkled a little on his coat or on his moccasin or mix[ed] it in some of the vermilion paint and [she] puts a speck of it on her face & put[s] a little bit of it on her children's hair-part or back of their ear[s] - [or] put a little of this in between the two layers of her husband's moccasin tongue - this will retain his affection - [a] mother-in-law can use this on her son-in-law if he is not kind to her [daughter] - [and] promoted [a] friendly relation [...] if a man takes a second wife & [his] first wife is [still] attached to him, the first wife takes some near possession of the other woman - something she had chewed on or worn or been in contact with - the herb used for this is something like wild morning glory - [which grows in matted beds from shoots] - the woman will take a single plant from this and parch the whole thing [is powdered] place and [the] powder it & mix it with vermilion to make it look like any other charm [and] it in separate bag [and] then she'd put the possessions on a piece of bark and sprinkle the powdered plant - all of it - on the possessions and even put the bag it has been in with this stuff and even the stones it was powdered with - then [she] either burns it or sits it adrift on a stream - some believe one way more effective, some [believe] the other - if she does this right the other woman & her husband will break up - this [malevolent] charm [is] called *p'áumn* ("discarding").

> [A] person well informed about these charms will [have] paid for [these] services - [and] must not leave anything of themselves on the bark or they will cut themselves - the same herb is dug - the whole root complex for the charm to hold [the] family group together - the whole bundle is parched and powdered and mixed and a portion [is] taken and the rest [is] thrown away - [and is] used to keep a family group together in accord - prevents desertion - [a] small plant used for keeping newlyweds together - [is] one root & one flower [and] the top leaves [are] fuzzy & sticky - sort of a milkweed - gray-green with white spines - [the] shaft [is] shaped like [a] rat tail - [with] one blossom stem on [the] plant - two leaves are taken & and stuck together [Doctrine of Signatures] - this [is] parched and made into a powder & the wife keeps it with her - [the] man might occasionally use this too but usually it's the woman who has to look out for these things (Elmendorf 1935-6, 1:74-76).

Though not a love charm, a woman having conflict or an ongoing disagreement with her daughter's husband would, to gain the affection of her son-in-law, surreptitiously wear a small neck bag containing various currently unknown species of crushed roots (Elmendorf, pers. comm.). To gain the woman's attention, a man might have acquired love power which was complemented when he played a special love flute and sang songs that enabled his amorous ambitions to influence, and possibly be accepted by a woman. If a man's musical abilities failed, he could aspire to gaining a woman's attention with a love potion. One type of love potion consisted of powdered roots of *common dandelion* (*Taraxacum officinale* Weber) or *yellow agoseris* (*Agoseris glauca* [Pursh] Raf. var. *dasycephala* [T. & G.] Jeps. - *snlekʷús* or *snlqʷ* - "pale dandelion"), which were mixed with a mashed robin's tongue and heart and powdered red hematite. Some of this concoction was drunk, and some painted on the hopeful lover's face while wading in a stream facing to the east, all the while reciting the name of his affection (May, pers. comm.). The mashed roots of either *heart-leafed arnica* (*Arnica cordifolia* Hook.) or *broad-leafed arnica* (*A. latifolia* Bong. var. *latifolia - čenłemłemeqeʔeneʔ*) also served as a love-medicine. Presumably the young lady would have favorable dreams of her suitor.

The most effective love charms were made by elderly women, often midwives who would sometimes 'renew' the charm's power. It was believed a love charm, such as a unique fossil, unusual crystal, incised flat stone, often carried in a small buckskin suspended neck bag—had power only for the finder, and could not be used effectively by anyone else, even if it was gifted.

Bride-Price

As with some immediate or *delayed* (*qʔemin'cut*) reciprocal exchanges of items, there were seldom few conclusive non-Indian statements, particularly with the practice of bride-price among the Spokan, which may be further confused by an observer's notion of gifting. Among the Spokan there were few documented examples of an institutionalized bride-price in which gifts were ostensibly given primarily to the bride's family at the marriage ceremony, which would be later returned or some amending retribution made if the couple dissolved their marriage. Curtis noted that, "Among the Flatheads and the Spokan there was no payment of exchange of presents" (1907-30, 7:73) as a bride-price. However, there were numerous examples of a quasi-bride-price whereby a future husband would prove his ability to support a family by demonstrating his hunting skills. As a form of suitor service, the results of his efforts were given to his intended in-laws as a form of suitor service.

An early observation of marriage customs was made by Hale who provided a rather general yet interesting account of marriage, divorce, infant betrothal, bride-price, and polygamy, as practiced by the Flathead Group:

> The men may take and put away their wives at pleasure, and both parties may marry again. The greatest requisition sought for in a wife is her capability of providing food. Polygamy was and is still practiced. Where this is the case, or where many families reside in the same lodge, each family or wife has a separate fire. In marriages, permission is first asked of the chief, then the consent of the parents is sought for, and afterwards that of the intended. If she objects, it is conclusive; if acceptance takes place, the groom gives from one to five horses to the bride's parents, they have a pow-wow, and the marriage is concluded. They are often espoused in infancy, but it is not considered as binding on either side. The squaws sometimes make proposals to the men. In other cases, young girls are contracted for, and the price paid down, some years in advance of the marriageable age (1846, 4:457).

However, elders contended that when asking the parents for their permission to marry their daughter, a young man presented gifts to the parents, but only when he was assured he had their permission. Otherwise, to anticipate their agreement by gifting could prove embarrassing to all concerned. The acceptance of him as a future *son-in-law* (*snč'łxⁿ'eyeʔ* or *sneč'łxʷ*) may obligate him to meet certain obligations associated with being a successful husband and provider, namely hunting. Traditionally, the meat from a deer considered sacred was given to the parents of a man's fiancée. An elder once explained the procedure and identity of a sacred deer:

> Near my home is a sacred area—about one acre—where sacred [mule] deer used to live. One adult deer would always present itself only to a young man just before he was about to get married. But only to a man who, before starting his hunt, had for three days sweated while singing his power song, of course fasted, and being careful to not do any wrong things. Three days before the naming or wedding ceremony, the hunter would kill only one deer no matter how many were there—a deer who would come right up near to the hunter, so he couldn't miss. The deer was bled but never dressed out until the hunter returned home. He carefully removed the hide, and later the hunter's wife, or mother if he wasn't married, would tan and later smoke the hide. The meat was cut up into small chunks, and then given to his intended wife's mother who *redistributed the meat to the guests (ʕaʔ ʕłcwe'mn)*. The smoked buckskin was given to the new wife or to the babe getting a name. This ceremony hasn't been done for many years, and the sacred area of the special deer was logged twice many, many years ago. I

144

know those special deer are long gone from this special area, and none of us ever see any there anymore (Ross 1968-2008).

Only a woman older than her intended husband could ask a younger man to marry her, but a younger woman could never ask an older man for marriage. A woman older than her intended husband may give him a present of her choosing, such as a horse or rifle, and if he accepts he must marry her. Ross Cox (1957 [1932]:209-10) also mentioned the subscription of a bride-price by one of his young clerks, who made inquiry among the Spokan if there was an *unwed woman* (*me?mist*) whom he could marry, and in brief time:

> A pretty-looking damsel, about seventeen years of age, immediately became a candidate for the prize. As her father had died some years before, she was under the guardianship of her mother, who, with her brother, settled the terms of the negotiation. Blankets and kettles were presented to her principal relations; while beads, hawk-bells &c., were distributed among the remaining kindred. Unfortunately, for all concerned, the young clerk's wife, unbeknownst to her new husband, was already the wife of a Spokan man. When he returned from a hunting expedition with his friends, he immediately demonstrated his displeasure, demanded the return of his wife, and admonished the whites for their apparent lack of decorum and violation of Spokan hospitality and assistance.

By the late 1860s, Lord interviewed a HBC employee regarding the practices associated with marriage, and wrote of the existence of bride-price among the Spokan and how the, "Interchange of presents chiefly and a purchase-money occurring to the father of the bride" (1867:233-234). It should be noted that upon the death of a married woman—one without children, her parents, if living, could reclaim any belongings their deceased daughter had made, ones given as gifts, or acquired through trade or barter. In the winter of 1814-15, one of McDonald's junior clerks negotiated with a young lady's mother and brother for her hand in marriage.

During his stay (1810-1813) among the Okanogan, Alexander Ross observed numerous marriage ceremonies, and concluded that:

> When a marriage alliance is thus entered into between on behalf of their infant children, reciprocal present exchanged immediately between them serve as a seal to the marriage contract. These presents are occasionally repeated afterwards; but not by both parents, as in the first instance. The friends of the young couple cease to give, but are always ready to receive what the friends of the young man may from time to time choose to give, until the parties come of age (1904, 7:247-248).

Elopement

In the rare instances of a man and woman being forced to marry, particularly if the woman's parents remained obdurate, it was often the case that the young woman would, against her parents' wishes, *run away* (*xʷit'pstwexʷ* - "to elope") and marry a different man. Whereas, a woman who *ran away* (*č'łn'qʷmis* - "eloped"), and married without her parent's permission, was called *xʷt'ip*. A girl who ran away without permission to marry was forbidden to return to her home, a decision referred to as *wéšiš*. If a couple ignored the censure of their parents, and ran away against the parents' wishes, they often returned after several months, knowing that they would remain together as they were considered married (Elmendorf 1935-6, 3:17). And yet for obvious socioeconomic reasons, elopement was considered a weak marriage—seldom receiving general support of either kin group. However, Ross stated it was not common, and "sometimes happens that the plighted virgin rejects the parents' choice. The parents themselves also change their sentiments in this case; and the young woman marries, not the person she was betrothed to, but another" (1904, 7:285).

However, if the eloping couple became married, the girl would often *have to remain living with her husband's people* (*wéšš* - "dwell"). But when an unmarried couple lived together neolocally, the man's mother would refer to the woman living with her son as *spn'éy'e?*, meaning "pretend-daughter-in-law" (Elmendorf 1935-6, 3:17). Usually, through time, any initial disagreement of the elopement by the parents would be ameliorated, if not completely dispelled when they became grandparents.

Marriage between so-called first cousins, particularly parallel cousins (*mother's sister's - qaxqaxeʔ -* child or father's brother's child), was absolutely forbidden. But in the memory of some sources (Elmendorf 1935-6, 3:18), there were rare instances of first cousins being in love and actually eloping. If the married couple chose to return, both families would ignore them, nor would the village help them or even agree to their presence. Father's sister was called *tetikʷeʔ* or *sk'ʷukʼʷiʔ*, a reciprocal term meaning "little mother" (Elmendorf, pers. comm.). During the historical period there were some changes to the strictures of marriage. Generally, marriage to a second or third cousin was forbidden, but several sources indicated that there were some instances of this arrangement happening.

Preferred Marriage

The earlier discussion of general marriage varies only slightly from preferred marriage in that preferred marriage always had the encouragement and blessings of the couple's parents, varying more by consensus of the parent's attitude than with ritual. Consequently, the most common marriage arrangement was preferred marriage. After a young couple decided that they would like to marry, the parents of the couple were informed. Usually the young man's mother approached the mother of the young lady, explaining the couple's intentions. If they had the consent of the parents, the couple commenced a period of chaperoned courtship. During the courtship there were usually different forms of gift-giving by the young man to his intended bride and occasionally to the bride's parents. Eventually discussions between the couple's parents were conducted until both families gave their consent. This consensual arrangement was an occasion when the girl's father would actively proclaim to her future husband's family the good qualities of his daughter, as well as her skills, traits, and abilities thought necessary for a successful marriage.

Preferred marriages were always attended by a chief who would make a speech that invariably involved giving perfunctory permission and advice to the newlyweds, and he also used this opportunity to reiterate their responsibilities to each other, their kin group, and to society at large. The chief's speech was often dramatically delivered, and publicly demonstrated the man's awareness of past events of both families, which through time had also been important to the entire tribe. This performance was thus, a form of omniscient narration. During the feasting, the *potential husband* (*sntxʷuʔsncút* - "husband-to-be") was again reminded by the chief and attending elders to always be *resourceful and dependable* (*q'ʷiłq'ʷłt*) to his new family, and to be attentive to his newly acquired affinal kinspeople. Preferred marriages tended to function primarily to reinforce already established economic relationships between kin groups and, in some instances, establishing extended relationships with more distant groups.

Prescribed Marriage

Though no word could be recalled for the custom of prescribed marriage, there were remembered instances of this type of marriage, in which the parents of the young man and woman required, for various reasons, that their son or daughter marries one another. Such a prescribed arrangement often ended in disaster if one of the couple eloped with someone else, or, worse, the young woman committed *suicide* (*plscút*) to avoid the parentally imposed obligation. Even the sororate and levirate were not required forms of marriage, but rather a preferred form of marriage. The only instances of prescribed marriage were in the form of infant betrothal, as will be discussed later.

The stated purpose of prescribed *reciprocal marital arrangements* (*uł ntxʷtxʷsnwéxʷ*) was to reinforce the mutually congenial relations that existed between non-related families, which became socioeconomic extensions of kin ties. The importance of marriage-established ties, and even in the instance of divorce this was apparent when in-laws regarded a son-in-law as a son, and conversely with a daughter-in-law by her former husband's parents. A woman called her father-in-law (*sxaʔxéʔ*) and her *mother-in-law* (*łcécč*), and the woman's parents called the *son-in-law* (*snéč'łxʷ*).

146

Reciprocal feasting accompanied the marriage ritual, and often included a *marriage dance* (*sq'ʷimncút* - "worship dance") with the couple being joined by the family and guests, and was accompanied by music and singing. Participants formed two circles, one inside the other, with the groom and his kinspeople outside facing the backs of the bride and her kin group—both circles moving counterclockwise, always with the groom behind his bride. The marriage ritual culminated when the groom's kinspeople gave the bride's family dried salmon, dried camas and other root products, baskets, and buckskins. Such goods and commodities were considered a quasi bride-price.

Infant or Child Betrothal

Infant betrothal was actually a form of prescribed marriage, the main distinction being when *younger children become betrothed* (*sntxʷtxʷsncút*). Though *arranged marriages* (*hesntxʷsnwéxʷi* or *uɬ ntxʷ tuxʷsn'wexʷ* - "betrothed to each other") involved predetermined arrangements between adolescents, and though no longer practiced (Elmendorf 1935-6, 3:17), they did occur in the past between families of higher political status, and to some extent between families to ensure a couple's later socioeconomic success. At any early age, two young children could be betrothed and required later to marry one another. But such a marital arrangement was not common.

Prior to such an arrangement, and after lengthy discussions, the parents of two families might decide to *betroth two of their children* (*sntxʷtxʷsncút* - "fiancées" or *uɬ ntxʷsnwéxʷ* - "the reciprocally betrothed") (Elmendorf 1935-6, 3:16). Between mutually congenial families, this was seen as an effective way of reciprocally extending socioeconomic ties.

Even prior to puberty or marriage, the young boy designated for such a marriage would give small animals he trapped to his future in-laws and do favors for his future wife, who might cook for the boy and make him clothing. During their childhood years, the boy would live for a while with his future in-laws; girls did the same. As a result, by the time they married they were well acquainted with each other and their respective in-laws. Upon reaching puberty, they were called *sntxʷsntcút*, and were recognized as each other's fiancées.

The father of the infant male or small boy was the one who would commence the negotiations with a girl's father for the future marriage; eventually all four of the respective parents came to an agreement (Elmendorf 1935-6, 4:1). Presumably the mothers of the children were responsible for the negotiations of establishing the infant betrothal. However, the parents could in time disagree with such an arrangement, or the two children could later—at the time of the marriage, not consent because of some previously recognized incompatibility. If they were eventually married, there was the usual *marriage feast* (*nlémtn* - "joy feast") with the exchange of gifts between the two principal families. After being married for one year, the couple usually sponsored another feast with invited *distant relatives* (*čtám'm'qn*) and other couples who had been married for approximately one year; gifts were again exchanged between the participants.

The only difference between infant and child betrothal was the age of the children when arrangements were negotiated for their future marriage. The following is an unedited account from Elmendorf's field notes of child-bride selection:

> [The] father usually pointed out a certain girl [and] told his son she had been brought up right and he ought to marry her—then he started courting her & soon they got married [and] parents met each other & talked it over and agreed that their son & daughter would make a good marriage—but couldn't force them to marry—must be according to their wishes—[The] girl's family might make the overtures if they had their eye on some fine young hunter or capable young man—but if the parents betrothed their son & daughter while they were children they had to get married when they grew up—they almost never disagreed with this as they were told from infancy they must marry each other—didn't have to have *sumés* to get married (1935-6, 2:7-8).

Both sets of consanguineal in-laws were known as *ntétm'tn'*; albeit two affinally mutual families of in-laws were called *ntetm'tn'éw's* ("related by marriage"), a term used when addressing one another. If one of the couple dies, the relationship and obligations between the in-laws were terminated. The *parents-in-law* (*sč'ʔélp*) generally accepted their *children-in-law* (*tétm'tn'*) much as their own children, even if, as noted earlier, one of the in-law children later divorces and marries outside the kin group (Elmendorf 1935-6, 3:19). Elmendorf was told that infant betrothal was not a binding arrangement, and that a promised marriage sometimes failed. Despite this marital disruption the couple's parents who instigated the marriage still remained supportive, "if the husband was unsatisfactory, even after the couple had children, the father-in-law might take her back—a son-in-law was regarded by her parents as a son, if he was unreasonable or cruel to her she would go back to her parents and take the children" (Elmendorf 1935-6, 3:19).

In the past, the Spokan, Chewelah-Spokan, and Kalispel conducted, separately from one another, a summer ceremonial dance once a year in which prepubescent boys and girls would make a selection of a future mate, or, as Smith explained, how if the boy and girl were too young, the parents would make such a decision, "In this dance men [boys] have a little stick, about 3 feet long. He lays it on the shoulder of the girl which he wants to marry. If she accepts him, she leaves it lying there; if she does not want him she knocks it off. This amounts to a marriage ceremony; the parents cannot do anything about it" (1936-8:1204).

Polygamy

Multiple marriage (polygamy) was a universal practice, or at least the opportunity existed for either form of polygamy, polygyny (man with two or more wives at the same time) or polyandry (woman with two husbands at the same time). However, the opportunity of a man having more than one wife (polygyny) was lessened by economic responsibilities, the logistics of multiple domiciles, and marital demands. As for any culture at any period in history, supporting a *second wife* (*xʷl'xʷúl'yeʔ*) incurred additional economic burden. And yet among the Spokan and other ethnic groups during the time of extensive commercial trapping of beaver, otter, red fox, fisher, martin and mink, a man with more than one wife enjoyed an economic advantage in being able to process more hides. Normally, only a few men of political office, or ones having gained status through hunting or warfare, could support more than one wife. The preferred form of polygamy was sororal polygamy, a type of marriage when a man married his wife's younger sister, which tended to reduce some of the aforementioned difficulties. A man called his wife's sister *seʔstem'* and her brother *sc'éšt*.

Of interest, was Wilson's observation and comment how many Salish marriages were being performed by Roman Catholic priests, most notably among the Coeur d'Alene and Flathead, claiming, "Polygamy does not exist amongst the 'Selish' [Flathead], and the wives, when not in the neighborhood of a white settlement, are faithful to their husbands and affectionate mothers" (1866:296). The influence of both the Protestant and Catholic missionaries, and the demands of the Catholic and Anglican church to recognize only monogamous marriages, might be said to have reduced the number of polygamous unions; but certainly not completely. The early missionization of the Spokan was largely by Protestant missionaries, who had less effect upon reducing the opportunity for multiple marriages than the Catholic missionaries.

A major problem for DeSmet, from the very beginning, was the practice of polygamy—connubial unions which he felt were invalid, saying, "Many even have several wives at the same time. We are then agreed on the principle, that among them, even to the present time, there has been no marriage, because they have never known well in what its essence and obligation consisted" (O'Hara 1909, 3:248).

Hale further cited some of the effects created by missionaries upon multiple marriages, saying how, "The missionaries had, as I understood, adopted the following rule in relation to these connections: all who already had wives were required to maintain them, but no new ones were to be taken. In consequence of this regulation, there have been no new instances of polygamy" (1846, 4:457). Alexander Ross was more critical of indigenous polygamy:

> The greatest source of evil existing among this otherwise happy people [Okanogan] is polygamy. All the
> chiefs and other great men have invariably a plurality of wives: for he that has not one is neither chief nor great

man, according to their ideas of greatness, and he is looked upon with contempt. Many have two, three, four, or five according to their means and influence; but those wives do not at all times remain together, that would be utterly impossible, but at different camps where their relatives are; so that the husband goes from camp to camp occasionally to visit them, keeping seldom more than or two at a time with himself. The greatest favor is of course his constant companion. Indeed brawls, and squabbles constantly ensue when several wives meet; and what is still more revolting, the husband of the eldest daughter of the family is entitled by their laws to take wife all her sisters as they grow up, if able to maintain them (1904, 7:280-282).

According to Drury, who relied upon the 1839 diaries of missionary Elkanah Walker, who despite having spent nine years with the Spokan, was always very contemptuous of native beliefs, rituals, and marriage customs, particularly polygyny when he wrote a particularly unfortunate and untrue statement that indicated he obviously never really understood the socioeconomic and political significance of Spokan polygynous marriage customs:

As regards their morals, they are as debased as any heathen people. The more wives they have, the richer they consider themselves. Their wives are to them what slaves are to the planter as it is their business to provide the provisions. A man without a wife is in great danger of being hungry [...] They are continually changing their wives—throwing away one and taking another [...] The course we have pursued is that they ought not to throw away their wives, let them take as many as they may [but] that they should not take any new ones so long as one of their old ones was alive & all their young men should take only one. Our reason for this course to them is that they took them when they did not know that it was wrong for them to have more than one wife. But now they know better for we have told them (1976:113).

Regardless of the type of polygamous marriage, there existed numerous important benefits to the children of such a union, which tended "to perpetuate the alliance between two families and protect the children of the previous marriage from trauma" (Miller 1990:206). Polygamous intermarriage between different groups also invariably served to extend economic ties by integrating otherwise separate families. To reduce domestic conflict, each wife and her children enjoyed different dwellings or occupied a separate section when in a large dwelling, and of the two types of polygamy—polyandry and polygyny—the latter was the most common form of plural marriage.

Curtis described how among the Spokan and other Salish groups, the practice of polygamy, and even sororal polygyny existed, "Polygamy was practiced by those who could support more than one wife, and the younger sisters of a man's first wife, on attaining the marriageable age, usually became his wives as a matter of course" (1907-30, 7:74).

Ray's *Cultural Relations* study (1939) also recorded the importance of polygynous intermarriage that established and maintained extended consanguineal and affinal ties with more distant kin groups, thereby maintaining often necessary intertribal relations:

[...] intermarriage is extremely common among members of friendly villages not far separated, though this is not made necessary by any system of exogamy. Walters [1938] feels that blood relationship is the principal factor leading to social unity among the various villages of the Southern Okanogan [Sinkaietk] and observes that constant intermarriage and the practice of polygyny results in almost every man having relatives throughout the group (1939:10).

Polygyny

The patterns of Spokan kinship were basically bilateral (Elmendorf 1961), and formed a patripotestal system whereby certain privileges and decisions were executed by the *husband* (xélwiʔ), at least publicly. Though monogamous marriage was the most common form of marriage among the Spokan, polygyny did exist and was practiced only by those few who were wealthy and in a position to support two or more wives. In the past, a few men were known to have as many as four or five wives if they could afford to support them—some chiefs had five or six wives. Schaeffer acknowledged how during the early nineteenth century the socio-economic importance of polygyny became more popular due to, "The increased quantity of furs and dried meat required by the traders made necessary the efforts of greater numbers of women in the households" (1937, 3:244).

In polygynous marriages, the custom was for all of the wives to share the different areas within the same dwelling when performing domestic tasks according the directions of the *first wife* (*nóxʷnxʷ*) who was always considered as the *head wife* (*puʔsšʔit* or *puʔ seiʔita*). Elmendorf noted, "all a man's wives live in the same house & the first wife [...] is called 'head wife' & she has charge of things—she can order the other wives around" (1935-6, 4:10). With such a living arrangement, the husband spent one or several nights with each wife, an informal arrangement, which presumably reduced marital conflict.

Similarly with polygyny, a second wife was addressed as *nqʼʷíctn* (death replacement term) (Egesdal, pers. comm.) even if she was not related to the first spouse. The husband called her parents *sčʼʔélp*. If a man remarried after his wife left or divorced him, the man's new wife would call the first wife's children *słwéλt*. The children, if they remained with their father, accorded their new mother the respect and courtesy as they did their uterine mother. One can appreciate the value of bifurcate merging in sororal polygyny because, in the case of their uterine (biological) mother dying, the children, regardless of age, would still have a "mother."

When a man wanted to take another wife, he would send a good friend to negotiate his wishes to the woman. If she agreed, then they both were required to present their intentions to the chief who interrogated the man as to whether he had left his wife, and if he intended to live separately with the new wife, or have her live together with his first wife in the same dwelling. It was not customary for a man to give a wedding feast when he took two or more wives. Some elders recalled accounts of how a man's multiple wives worked well together in sharing social and domestic responsibilities, even becoming close friends. Elmendorf explained how there were numerous types of marriage arrangements:

> If a man is married and wishes to take a second wife he doesn't give a marriage feast—he sends a go-between to ask the woman—they have to go & ask the chief about it & he asks him if he has left his wife & and if he has they simply go & live together—if he doesn't want to leave his first wife she asks the woman to come & live with him & and they are man & wife—all a man's wives lived in the same house [...] (1935-6, 3:38b).

In some instances of considerable age difference, the older wife became dependent upon a younger wife. One elderly woman remarked how in public, when as a girl, she witnessed a man who had several wives, and the wives walked more or less in a staggered line behind their husband. But her mother later explained (in the privacy of the girl's and mother's home), that the man was on "the end, not out in front."

Sororal Polygyny

There is consensus among anthropologists that sororal polygyny creates less conflict, particularly when the principles of bifurcated merging exists (merging one consanguineal kin under the same term), whereby the children of the first and oldest call their uterine mother as did the children of their father's second wife. The boys call one another 'brother' and the girls call one another 'sister.' All such children might say that, "My sisters' and brothers' mothers are married to my father." For example, in polygyny all of the children, regardless of age, called their father's wives "mother"—both their affinal (related by marriage) and consanguineal (uterine) mother. If a woman or man marries again after the death of a spouse, the children called the step-parent *łwestn*, giving their attention and respect to the parent's new spouse. When a polygamous man died, his wives would share equally in the distribution of his property, and always continued their parental responsibilities. Understandably, sororal polygyny was of course a preferred form of marriage:

> Of polygynous marriages, the most common and preferred was sororal polygyny (*qsnqʼʷícʼtni*), whereby a man married his wife's younger unwed sister—but never at the same time, and the multiple wives commingled and shared domestic responsibilities and the same dwelling. And yet the first and oldest wife enjoyed greater authority (Elmendorf 1935-6, 4:3).

Allan Smith, in speaking of sororal polygyny among the Kalispel, described that, "When a man dies, his brother (older or younger, either one) could take the widow as his wife. He does not have to take her - he can do it or not; if he wants her she has to go. He never does this until after at least 2 years have passed. A man never takes such a widow unless he is unmarried" (1936-8:1202).

In cases of sororal polygyny, the co-wives invariably lived together or in close proximity for logistical and emotional reasons. They could share the same cooking fire, but recognized a quasi division of labor. This was the case, despite a once heard expression that, "*wives can share the same bed (snɫqʷútn)*, but not the same cooking fire." Alvord, however, observed that the husband, "seldom has his wives in the same lodge. Their lodges are sometimes in different villages, but they are generally in the same camp" (1857:19). A married man would acquire status if he took a widow as a second wife—one who had demonstrated certain skills, particularly hide-processing. Hunn succinctly described how in the Plateau:

> The equation of cousins with siblings may have been reinforced by the widespread practice of the levirate and sororate and the preference for sororal polygyny reported for a number of Plateau groups. The cultural expectation was that following the death of a spouse, the deceased spouse's family would replace the spouse with a "sibling" (whether a "true" sibling or expected though not required) to marry one of his wife's sister or female cousins. If a woman's husband died, she would be expected to marry one of her husband's brother or male cousins. In this way the enduring bond established by marriage between two families would not be broken by death (1990:371-372).

The notion that sororal polygyny usually created a peaceful, or at least tolerable domestic atmosphere is not universal; for expressions and even violent demonstrations of jealousy did occasionally occur in such marital situation, as was described to Kane while visiting Kettle Falls, "A curious case occurred, about a year before my visit, of two sisters, wives of one man, each jealous of the other, who went into the woods and hung themselves, as was supposed, unknown to each other, as they were found dead a long distance apart" (1971:123).

For socioeconomic reasons, sororal polygyny was a preferred form of polyandry when a man's wives were sisters, thereby reducing jealousy and conflict and providing a more stable marriage. The term 'squaw', which currently is considered offensive by some historians, anthropologists, and American Indian activists, may be the result of the erroneous contention by some that the term originally meant prostitute in Algonquin, which was not true (Egesdal, pers. comm.). Marge Bruchac, a traditional story-teller, historical consultant, and member of the Institute for the Advancement of Aboriginal Women, noted that the word 'squaw' is actually not a pejorative word but rather one that "traditionally means the totality of being female, not just the female anatomy" (1999:1). Anyone doing a thorough reading of early authors of Amerindian cultures, would clearly see that this term was not always used in a derogatory sense at that time, and once was an acceptable description of Indian women by some authors (Egesdal, pers. comm.).

Polyandry

The practice of polyandry—when a woman was married to two or more husbands at the same time—was indeed rare, and only a few Spokan could recall it ever happening (Elmendorf, pers. comm.). Moreover, there were few memories that the Spokan practiced fraternal or adelphic polyandry—when a woman was married at the same time to two or more husbands who were brothers. If a man perished, his widow might be taken as a second wife by his brother. An informant explained to Elmendorf a hypothetical situation:

> If I have a married brother and that brother dies, I think, that's my sister- in-law [seʔstem'], then should I marry the widow. If some other man takes her away then I would be mad and would wait until I met up with him and then would take his horse and blanket. If he fought I would kill him or I might whip him with my quirt as an extreme insult (1935-6, 4:26).

There was consensus among contemporary elderly women that a woman would not want more than one husband, always remarking—sometimes facetiously—how, in addition to caring for their children, it would take too much of their time and effort to tend to more than one husband. In the few instances of polyandry, when a woman had more than one husband, the first husband practiced the couvade for the primogenitary, and if the woman had a second child, the next husband followed the restrictions and behavior of the couvade. Some contend that the reason polyandry, even fraternal polyandry was so rare, was that one brother, or both, would eventually become *jealous* (*sm'l'l'x^wéw'se?i*) and possibly kill his brother.

Fraternal Polyandry

As cited, and apart from Elmendorf's field notes (1935-36, 4:26), there were few memories of the Spokan practicing fraternal or adelphic polyandry, a practice when a woman was married simultaneously to the same brothers. When inquiring with elderly women about such an arrangement, there was no acceptance or sense of belief that any woman would want more than one husband, summarily stating, "To carrying and care for one husband and his brother would be enough trouble without doubling my work and tripling my worry."

Sororate and Levirate

The Spokan practiced the sororate a form of monogamy in which a widower marries a sister of his deceased wife. A man's second wife, after his wife's death, was called *nq'^wíc'tn*, and she called her new husband *se?stém* ("woman's sister's husband"). He continued to call her parents-in-law *sč''?élp* ("reciprocal term for parents-in-law vis-à-vis children-in-law") (Elmendorf 1935-1936, 3:18; Egesdal, pers. comm.). The sororate tended to reduce any trauma to the children, since prior to their mother's death they called their *mother's sister* (*čičíy'e?*). The new wife and mother treated her husband's children as her own, always assuming on-going daily tasks and requirements for the family's survival.

A senior sororate was when a man married his deceased wife's *older sister* (*łčíčše?*), while in a junior sororate he would marry a *younger sister* (*łcc?ups*), which some say the Spokan did not practice (STHC). Elmendorf claimed, "the Spokan had neither the junior or senior sororate" (12035-36:3:18). Therefore, no terms are known that even suggest a linguistic difference between the junior and senior sororates. However, it was preferred, but not prescribed, that the man marry the younger and unwed sister of his deceased wife.

Smith described the sororate as an important obligation; even a right that was practiced by the Kalispel, which was also recognized by the Spokan, "When a married man loses his wife by death, he has no right to claim her sister but she has a right to claim him because she is related to the dead woman and he is only related by marriage. Either one can suggest it to the other, but she has the right to push it" (1936-8:1203).

Though the levirate and sororate existed, but was not obligatory (Ross 1998:275). The *levirate* (*nq'^wíc'tnm*) was an accepted form of marriage, whereby a woman married the brother of the *deceased husband* (*nq'^wíc'tn*) (Elmendorf 1935-6, 1:17). If the deceased brother had no sons, the surviving brother was obligated to marry his brother's widow. Yet, this practice was less common than the sororate, for a widow usually had a choice of whom she could marry, not being compelled to marry a brother of her deceased husband. All children called their stepfather *łwéstn*. In some instances, the levirate was, "the rule among the Spokane, either his elder or younger brother, if she did not marry; thus, the deceased husband's family could make trouble [...] If she did not marry husband's bro[ther], his family, if she had any possessions they would take it all" (Elmendorf 1935-6, 1;16-7).

A Spokan widow, not wanting to marry her deceased husband's brother, had a right and practice similar to the Flathead, whereby, as Schaeffer cited:

> If a woman, preferred to marry someone else, refused the younger brother of her dead husband, it was considered an affront to the latter and to his relatives and was punishable in the same matter as adultery. The rejected man was privileged to shoot the woman in the leg or kill her favorite horse of his rival. However, if none of her brothers-in-law care to marry her, the widow was given permission to go elsewhere (1937, 3:249).

Despite the often intense fictive filial relationships between male sweathouse partners, there is no recollection that when a close friend died, that anyone other than the deceased man's brother could claim the rights of the levirate, which apparently was true with the Flathead (Turney-High 1937:93). The levirate may be said to have personified intense male bonds in war-centered societies, as was happening with the Flathead.

The woman called her deceased husband's brother's children *sɬwéƛt*, but only if their father was dead, not divorced. A woman would call her deceased husband's wife *seʔstém*, as in the sororate. Within the levirate, a widow was still called *sč'iʕelpp* after marrying her deceased husband's brother, a reciprocal term also used by her parents-in-law:

> In the past, a man whose offer of marriage was rejected by his brother's widow had the *right to break her leg* (*nqʷúsčstšnc*). If a woman refused marriage, the deceased man's family might demand a horse, and in some instances the woman's property. Neither the sororate nor levirate was obligatory (Elmendorf, pers. comm.).

Bigamy

Traditionally, *bigamy* (*puʔč'sél'* - "two spouses" or "bigamist" or *puʔčsée*) was not a frequent occurrence among the Spokan, or later after being confined to the reservation. Primarily for economic reasons, it did exist with men who annually would travel to trade with Plains groups, whereby for logistical reasons the man may live with a second wife for months at a time, often on an annual basis. Years ago, one heard stories of husbands who had second wives "east of the mountains"—wives whom they spent time with when bison hunting or trading. At one time the practice of bigamy probably increased with beaver trapping and the sale of hides to the HBC, an endeavor that encouraged a man to have a woman who resided with another group or close to his trapline, a person who would process the valuable hides.

In such situations, the second consort of a bigamous man may remain living with her more distant group, and in time be considered a *co-wife* (*sƛxu'tsélp*), a term that also described wives of a polygynous union. The children called their non-maternal mother *spuxʷuʔselp*; not by a relationship term. Spokan elders contend they never practiced "wife swapping," even between long established and often distant trading partners (STHC). In the case of bigamy, residence for the man was basically duolocal, with the husband alternating his residence between his first wife and his consort, a practice usually influenced by his economic pursuits.

Bride Capture

When the Spokan went onto the Plains for stealing horses and warfare, they conducted forays mostly against the Blackfoot who were traditional enemies, and against whom they choose to practice *bride capture* (*puʔkʷném*). During midnight raids on small Blackfoot encampments, *any girl captured* (*skʷánxn* - "seized by the arm," or "prisoner") was eventually taken back to a Spokan village or encampment and sold to a chief, who in turn could sell the captive to anyone who wanted to marry the woman. Such a woman was never abused, but was watched over carefully by the older women, and was described by Elmendorf:

> [... if they had] take[n] any girl captive if they catch her alone—they took her back to the chief and sold [her] to [the] chief & he sells her to anyone who wants to buy her to marry or [she was] sold for whatever was [a] good offer—[she] was never abused—[and always] watched by [an] old woman—nearly always a rich man who gets her (good thing to marry her)—[the] man might go out alone to look for [an] enemy girl—[the] girl's tribe often tries to kidnap her back (1935-6, 2:69).

However, a wife captured from another tribe might be *sent back by her husband* (*c'éšc'št* or *c'ér'c'r't* - "bitter emotional pain") for any one of many reasons—usually social pressure from his kinspeople, or simply that the wife grieved for her people. The desire of a daughter or son who wanted to marry into a distant village or tribe was by consensual behavior, a relationship termed *sɬxmelt*, which was not uncommon since the union served to implement and extend economic ties.

Wife and Husband Stealing

Stealing a wife differed from bride capture since it generally happened within or between a Spokan village or band or other similar dialectic group, not necessarily between hostile groups. Force was rarely used in wife or husband stealing; rather, it was accomplished through the machinations of guile or sorcery. A man might be called a *wife stealer* (*sxʷpxʷuʔsélp*) if he was able to entice a woman away from her *husband* (*x̌élwiʔ*). Likewise, a woman might steal another woman's husband way. Using the same methods of enticement, a captured married mother would always attempt to take her children with her if possible

The marital union that resulted from wife stealing seldom endured; being not only disruptive if there were children of one or both marrying people. Additionally, such behavior was censored by their families and respective village. Wife and husband stealing usually resulted in the couple being forced from the village or camp—a situation called *puʔkʷéntm*.

It was not always known if a husband or wife was stolen from his or her spouse, because sometimes it was suspected that a woman was deserted by her husband or a woman had surreptitiously left her husband. It was suspected that a woman deserted by her husband, was termed *stsaʔám*. A man whose wife ran away with another man was termed *puʔkʷéntm* (STHC). In a case where a married man and women simply left their respective spouses, they were classified as *kʷntuwéxʷ* ("they took each other") (Elmendorf 1935-6, 4:6). A spouse, particularly a male, was not always forgiving about being deserted, for as Elmendorf noted:

> If a man's wife runs away with another man - the husband might kill the man if he caught him—the husband's family would then try to smooth things over with the dead man's family with gifts etc.—the man is said to be *pu'ʔkʷéntm* (wife "is taken away") [...] If another man takes his wife he might steal one of that man's horses & fight if the man tried to get it back. [A] woman might be deserted by her husband—she can't do much of anything but if she runs across the other woman she gets into a fight with her & when she's half-killed her she is satisfied (1935-6, 1:17).

If there were two or more women deserted by their husbands, then they could band together, and share the chores of maintaining themselves. Such a group—known as *meʔmeʔmist*—often remained a viable economic and social unit, since an older deserted woman had few opportunities for remarriage (Elmendorf 1935-6, 1:15).

Marriage created a beneficial situation for the *married couple* (*nxʷnxʷéw's*) as well as their extended families and kin group, partly because this rite of passage brought together families and supporting groups for the benefits of trade and usufruct of otherwise unavailable resources. As previously noted, marriage also functioned to integrate once unrelated groups by effectively expanding their kinship base and creating what has earlier been termed polyadic intergroup task-grouping. Moreover, it provided better protection against hostile Plains groups (Anastasio 1972). Another benefit, not always identified, is that the rules of exogamy served to create a condition of polyglotism, and permitted more effective communication among dialectically different groups—even for which the marriages were not always sustained (Elmendorf 1935-6, 3:23).

Post-Nuptial Residence

There were no definite rules of post-nuptial residence for a couple after marriage, but usually they resided with either the husband's or wife's parents for a brief period, though more often the *bride* (*nóx̌ʷnx̌ʷ* or *sntx̌ʷuʔsncút*) lived with her husband in his parent's home—a form of patrilocal residence. Patrilocal residence best accommodated a husband's economic and subsistence activities that required a man to remain in an area he was most familiar with, and maintain a relationship with a male cadre—one based on a familiarity and trust with his peers. It was established that a woman could live in any location and maintain her subsistence responsibilities, given her general knowledge of predictable subsistence resources. However, a woman's extensive range of knowledge and command of skills that were applicable to any environment also encouraged patrilocal residence, which was of benefit to the bride's mother-in-law in many ways. An account of a newlywed bride in a patrilocal residence is provided by a Lakes woman, which was consistent with the Spokan, of the bride's:

> [...] first morning in the tipi of her in-laws marked the start of intensive training in the domestic activities that would determine her standing for the rest of her life. Her mother-in-law was first up to stir the coals or built the fire for a new day. Then she shook the new bride awake to have her take a cold bath and bring back a basketful of water for the morning meal. If the bride appeared to be lazy or refused to arise cheerfully, her mother-in-law used the firestick on her shins, saying, "Get up and take care of your husband's food and clothing [...] The mother-in-law was relieved of heavy duties and spent her time at more leisurely activities like basket making, skin decoration, and advising the family. She remained the supreme head of the family, ruling her husband, son, daughter-in-law, and children when they arrived (Miller 1990: 60-61).

Not every daughter-in-law was treated so sternly, and some mothers-in-law were known to be, "more considerate than others and would help a daughter-in-law to lighten the work or allow her other considerations" (Miller 1990:66).

If after marriage, a couple established patrilocal residence (man's wife resides after marriage with her husband and his kin), and if the wife was *unhappy* (*nč'isls* - "unhappy person"), her parents may insist upon the couple establishing *neolocal residence* (*nk'ʷéʔɬxʷm* - "they live together in one house"), whereby the couple lived independent of both families (Elmendorf 1935-6, I:18, 3:23). For various reasons, it could happen that a couple who married with mutual *consent* (*sɬxmelt*) might decide to establish a neolocal residence with a different tribe, and both the husband and wife would be called *sɬxmélt* by their parents and other members of their tribe (Elmendorf 1935-6, 1:17). In both neolocal and patrilocal residence, there were instances of a dissatisfied husband sending his wife back to her tribe of origin, a practice that was considered *c'éšc'št* - "shameful" or *c'ér'c'r't* - "painful" (emotionally) Egesdal, pers. comm.).

A temporary form of residence was if both the married couple practiced what was essentially ambilocal residence, whereby the couple alternated residence between the parents of the husband and wife. "Ambilocal residence was most common when a man and his pregnant wife would reside with her family during her third trimester, who best provided his wife assurance and assistance with domestic chores, and even her delivery. With ambilocal rules of residence in the Plateau, a young couple often switched residence back and forth between his parents' winter residence and hers" (Ackerman 1994:298).

Schaeffer's keen observation of the Flathead residence pattern of a woman who delivers her first child was the same as the Spokan, when:

> After their marriage the young couple continued to live with the man's parents until the time approached for the birth of their first child. They then returned to the bride's family, so that [...] the young mother might receive the proper care and attention from her own people. After the child was born, the young parents usually set up a separate lodge of their own [neolocal residence] (1937:246).

With matrilocal residence, the couple resided with the wife's family, particularly when the man's wife was approaching the time of her delivery. In such instances, they lived with the pregnant woman's mother and father for a time determined by the new mother. Speaking of matrilocal residence, Scott quoted Bancroft (1875, 1:195): "Among the Spokanes, women were held in respect, and an outside husband joined the wife's tribe; women are held in great respect and much affection is shown for children" (Bancroft 1875 1:278 fn; Scott 1941, 3:209). There were, however, undoubtedly instances of the couple living with her people for indefinite periods of time. Pickering (1895) considered how matrifocal residence tended to reduce intermittent warfare with local groups. Hale felt matrilocal residence was very common and beneficial with intertribal marriage: "the husband almost invariably joins the tribe to which his wife belongs, under the idea that among her own family and friends she will be better able to provide for her husband and children's wants" (1846, 4:447).

155

In-law Avoidance

The practice of in-law avoidance by the Spokan was not formalized in any fashion, such as using indirect-speaking, whereby a man addressed his *wife's mother* (*łcecč*) when speaking to an inanimate object or a child in a cradleboard, or by referring to her in the third person. However, mother-in-law jokes involving humorous and often distorted and exaggerated accounts of one's mother-in-law's behavior were common when men gathered, usually in the privacy of the sweathouse or during long hunts.

Despite the occasional innuendo and attempts at bravado regarding one's mother-in-law, it is not an idealization to state that a man was generally respectful and helpful to his wife's mother, particularly since the son-in-law was reputedly treated as a son (Elmendorf 1935-6, 3:18-19, 4:6). There were presumably no mother-in-law taboos, "[a] man behaves toward his mother-in-law just like his mother, respects & treats her just like his mother" (Elmendorf 1935-6, 4:6). As a consequence, there was no apparent established mother-in-law avoidance, and a wife was respectful of her mother-in-law, and she usually would tend to her until she died (Elmendorf 1935-6, 2:59).

Yet, if the husband had conflict with his in-laws, he would speak in third person when addressing his wife's mother, or speak through an inanimate object while addressing his concerns or needs that involved participation of an in-law, usually the wife's mother. One man claimed to have restored some semblance of decorum when being admonished by his wife, by saying, "You are starting to sound like your mother."

There were no known established forms of *father-in-law* (*sxaʔxéʔ*) avoidance (several elders noted that there was a now-forgotten word for such behavior). Yet it was acknowledged that a few instances of father-in-law avoidance did occur—particularly in rare cases of matrilocal residence, or more commonly postnuptial virilocal residence. The following is a case of such a situation:

> Some power is really bad. I remember when I was young [in 1923], a man our family knew married a young woman, and after their marriage, the bride went and lived with her husband and his people. They were now about 30 miles from her family. Once the husband and his new wife went back to her people to visit. However, after their visit, the mother-in-law said: "I'm going to stop my son-in-law from taking my daughter away again. I'm going to dig roots and put on his clothing the powder [ground roots] and he'll turn crazy." She did and the man seemed to turn nuts, so much so he was taken to the sanitarium at Medical Lake. But he kept saying he wasn't really crazy. Finally the father-in-law came to the hospital and got him released, and took him home to be doctored by his own people. Well, they got a powerful shaman to come and look over the young man. The shaman, after some time, said he saw the patient walking along a path and without any head. The shaman said he knew who had sorcerized the young man, who answered: "I don't want to know." [The] shaman told him he was going to know, so the name of his mother-in-law was said. Eventually the mother-in-law said "yes" she had someone [sorcerer] who "worked against" the young man, but that she never wanted to hurt him. [The] young man got better, but the mother-law was never the same again (Ross 1968-2008).

Husband-Wife Relations

Definite prescribed customs and expectations of behavior existed for a married couple, though apparently more for a married woman's domestic and private life than for her husband. For example, a married woman always arose early before her husband, and retired only when her domestic responsibilities were completed. A woman would comb her husband's hair in the morning and immediately before he went to bed at night, always being extremely careful to collect any loosened hair and burn it, lest the hair be used by a sorcerer to harm the man, or for controlling him from afar in ways that were detrimental to their connubial relationship. A wife always assumed the increased domestic responsibilities that accompanied the needs of her husband's friends, who might stay for several days—or longer in the family residence, before leaving for a male-oriented activity, such as a hunt. Until recently, the obligations of accepting and tending to the needs of a *visitor* (*sčiccn*) were always demonstrated by a family's hospitality—never asking when a person, even a non-

156

kinsperson, would be leaving. Historian and Judge George Wilkes (1817-1885) observed, "Although there is but little government in families, they are, still, well behaved; and it is proverbial that they seldom quarrel among themselves" (1845, 4:455).

Whether single or married, an individual or family's pride was predicated on their overriding concern and concomitant ability to provide hospitality to a visiting kin or non-kin guest. Regardless of the amount or quality of food, a host or hostess never credited the skill of the provider, but would be somewhat deprecating of the quality that was seemingly lacking for such a guest. Nor did a person ever boast of his or her success in food-getting activities. A lack of humility was believed to diminish a person's skill and ability in providing for one's family, and of course service to one's guests. Upon leaving, guests were always given food if their journey was any distance. An enduring compliment to a host was, "The memory of my stay will always be with me, long after the good taste of your food." One seldom directly thanked another for a favor or effort that benefited the recipient, for to maintain a balanced reciprocity, "One thanks strangers, but not friends."

Hale, when speaking of husband-wife relations, noted the instances of tribal exogamy and matrilocal residence after marriage:

> This may also proceed from the fact of the influence the women possess; for they always assume much authority in their tribe, and are held in high respect. They have charge of the lodge and the stores, and their consent is necessary for the use of them; for after coming into their possession, these articles are considered the women's own. Where such a state of things exists, it may readily be inferred that the domestic ties are not very weak; and they are reputed to have strong affection for their children and nearest relatives (1846, 4:447).

A woman took considerable pride when her husband was recognized for his occupational skills and his ability to maintain his role as a consistently excellent family provider. Many years ago one could hear a woman say of her husband, "He has strong hands, a gentle heart, but a firm voice." Similarly, a man acknowledged his wife's care and love for their children, as well as her knowledge of hand skills and keeping food in the larder. A man often paid the ultimate respect to his wife by saying she was his *big toe* (*stúʔúmšn* - "mother toe" or "friend"), a metaphor referring to the known fact that a man can hardly walk or stay balanced if he loses his big toe. And yet, when in public, a man was not always known to demonstrate uxorious behavior. *Some have said* (*q'iλ't hec cuti*) that a man could never live for any length of time if he was alone in the woods without his male friends, nor could he maintain a successful domestic existence if he had no wife.

A woman contributed considerable time and effort to her family and often to the extended family. And yet given the difficulties of cultural relativism and comparative values held by some early writers, as well as faulty conclusions based upon limited observation and linguistic problems, it often is difficult to evaluate recorded comments upon past logistics of certain marital relationships among the Spokan. A statement by Cox regarding marital division of labor is noteworthy:

> The treatment of the women differs materially among the various tribes. Where food is principally obtained by the exertions of the men (as among the Cotton's [sic], Flat-heads, Spokans, &c) the women are condemned to great drudgery. When a hunter kills a deer, he merely cuts out the tongue, or takes enough for a meal, and on returning to his lodge dispatches his wife for the body. She is guided to the spot by notches which he has made in the trees. She also collects firewood, carries water, cooks, makes and cleans his shirt, prepares the meat and fish for curing, &c. They possess little or no influence, and, notwithstanding their laborious duties, seem perfectly contented (1831, 2:159).

Children were first aware of the strict relations between gender by observing their parents, older kin, and other adults. Adolescent children were instructed about the correct behavior, both public and private, including the different responsibilities a man had to his wife, and a wife to her husband. Once the child became older, particularly the girl, lecturing gave way to actual participation with responsibilities and behavior that later would serve as conducive roles of adulthood and marriage. This enculturation and training was the basis of a strict division of labor that was believed necessary to regulate and prescribe the duties and logistics for maintaining the household.

[...] yet [the] man's training enforced certain male duties - always have meat at [the] door - he must be indifferent to his own possessions - not ask about them or what becomes of them [...] meat brought in belonged to the woman of [the] household - all things he gives - "must be unstinted" - [a] wife's expression [was] "in my adornment" to her *in qcncútn* - [a] wife's whole thought is to [her] husband's comfort - his clothing & possessions [are] her s[pecial] care - combing his hair - no one would ever ask outright of [anything from] anyone - "will you give me such & such of yours" for this would (imply beggerliness on the part of the askee) - [a] woman who goes to another's home to ask for something [...] they simply come in and on leaving are simply given something but they never ask for anything - a *skítstsn* [Colville] or *sčieen* ("visitor") usually bring a present [and] might stay several days (Elmendorf 1935-6, 1:39).

Cox when speaking of the Flathead observed that, "The women are excellent wives and mothers, and their character for fidelity is so well established, that we never heard an instance of one of them proving unfaithful to her husband. They are also free from the vice of backbiting [...] and laziness is a stranger among them" (1831, 1:219). George Wilkes (1817-1885) observed, "Although there is but little government in families, still they are well behaved; and it is proverbial that they seldom quarrel among themselves" (1845, 4:455).

In the 1880s, A. J. Williamson explained his understanding of Spokan division of labor, and how:

[...] the Indian women did most of the work about the camp. They were the ones who gathered the fire-wood, sometimes carrying it a considerable distance on their backs; they brought the water and did the cooking; when camp was moved; they dismantled the lodges and packed the horses; they dug the camas and dried it; or smoked the salmon. What did the men do? They did the hunting and fishing. In case of tribal wars, they did the fighting (Drury 1949:151-2).

Elmendorf noted that a man never asked another—even a close friend—how his wife was doing, since this was such a private matter (1935-6, 1:38). Upon his leaving the dwelling, a man's wife would not always be certain where he was going, or when he would return, unless she had some indication by the tools or weapons he took with him. A man had near-complete authority—at least over his wife—but was extremely careful in exercising such rights, and then usually from concern for his wife's welfare:

[...] if a man in his dreams sees danger he may tell all his women folks to stay in the house & not to go out that day—Mrs. W.'s grandmother was once told thus by her husband but another woman persuaded her to go & dig a certain kind of camas—[she] took her first child a little son and went—the child was drowned & when she came home her husband dashed a paddle of water in her face—she always attributed this loss to her disobedience [...] Good men were not inclined to be bossy however—a man might beat his wife if she needed it—a woman could always take refuge from an angry husband in the women's quarters (Elmendorf 1935-6, 2:58).

The extent of respect a married man and woman had for each other was not always apparent, at least publicly. Connubial communication was not regulated by tradition—even when wanting to speak with his wife regarding about domestic and non-domestic matters. This is not the case today, nor is it really understood by younger Spokan. Some elders recalled how they seldom heard their parents speaking, even at the dinner table, which is certainly not saying they did not communicate, but:

[...] if [a] man wanted to talk pleasantly to his wife even he met her away from camp—[when he] said "there are good berries [at] such & such a place"—and naturally men had [a] private path for going out on [that trail]— women were supposed to—die if they were found on that trail—if a woman lifted the curtain on the man's door of the house she was in danger of being killed—in the home a man could sit & talk with his wife—boys & girls of 'teen age [were] strictly segregated (Elmendorf 1935-6, 1:65-6).

The wife tended to be more committed than her husband to maintaining a peaceful domestic environment, and was more devoted in her efforts to sustain the *nuclear family* (*nkʷsuxʷteʔl'is*). Should her husband die, desert her, become incompatible, or take another wife, she would retire to a place of *seclusion* (*kʷlkʷéle*) and *retirement* (*snq'uqntsútn* - "a women's place of isolation"). This site was like a community where every woman had a place of her own. There were individual lodges and large tipis for several usually related women. Outsiders were freely admitted to such a communal group. The living quarters were in the open and surrounded by a palisade of poles or tripod post with branches interwoven to form a privacy wall. If her husband takes another wife she may marry again after a certain interval, but this was not often practiced. Should the husband die or desert her, then she is free to marry again (Elmendorf 1935-6, 1:69-70).

The woman's role within the family unit, though not always verbally expressed by male members of the family was important. A small group of elderly men would sometimes joke among themselves about their wives; whereas in private, each of the elderly men made certain that the author understood what his peers knew, that their wives had more often been superior to them; physically, morally, intellectually, and in their knowledge of the past. One elder woman said that, "Women are like trees bending in the wind, but their roots are always there. Men are like the winds, blowing in different directions; sometimes hot, sometimes cold, and blowing great clouds of *wind-blown dust* (*sqʷʔuɬ*) and debris."

It was considered impolite to maintain sociability between adult men and women when in public. Elmendorf noted: "if a man wanted to talk pleasantly to his wife even if he met her away from camp—[he may have] said 'there are good berries at such & such a place'" (1935-36, 1:66). He further described how "boys & girls of 'teen age [were] strictly segregated—individuals were never married against their choice—if as [sic] man's wife proves disagreeable & impossible to get along with, her husband could set her aside after [getting] the permission of the men's department [men's area of the long house]—he could then take a second wife & bring her into the house with the first wife—he had always to support the first wife—even if she moved away" (1935-36, 1:66).

Divorce

Divorce (*xʷlʼ ntlpséwʼs* - "broken apart" or *xʷoqʼpewʼs* - "divided") was considered dysfunctional to all concerned. Thus, when it happened, every attempt was made to restore amicable relations between the divorcees and their families. Most divorces were based on mutual consent by both parties. However, reasons for marital disruption varied, but usually a husband's most incriminating accusation was that his spouse was *lazy* (*puʔxʷúpt* or *xʷupt* or *ʔecxéyti*) and generally unproductive; providing sufficient cause for dissolving the union. Similarly, a woman could leave her husband if he did not provide for his family. A few elders recalled that a common reason for a wife to leave her husband was if, "he was unreasonably cruel" (Elmendorf 1935-6, 3:113). Some claim that traditionally a man seldom beat his wife, particularly when her kinspeople resided in the immediate vicinity. Divorce was communally justified if the husband was accused of continuous adulterous behavior, and the marriage could be terminated, but the children remained with their mother. It was not uncommon for a marriage to be temporarily or permanently disrupted when another man or woman resorted to using love power to enhance the desires of another married man or woman

A chief did not have to give his consent for a couple to divorce. A marriage could be dissolved, though not through divorce, *when a married woman was stolen by a man* (*puʔkʷném*) from another village or group. If a displeased wife ran away from her husband, she was now known as a *puʕkʷéntm*, and would likely return to her family of orientation.

If a married couple *separated* (*nʼe m xʷqʼʷpéwʼs*), the father was always held responsible for the continued support and maintenance of his children, not only by his conscience, but by the demands of his father, mother, and public opinion. The pressures from the grandparents for a couple to not disrupt their home life by divorce were considerable, for they recognized that marriage stabilized the lives of their grandchildren. A *man who left his wife for another* (*xʷláɬq* - "abandoned wife") was invariably censored by both kin groups, as well as by the community. If a divorced or widowed woman married again, her children would refer to the step-father as *ɬwestn*, the same designation for step-mother. A step-son or step-daughter was known as *sɬuwélt*—a man or woman who marries after a spouse's death.

The reasons for divorce varied with circumstances. Nearly all older adult males had been married at least twice (Elmendorf, pers. comm.). Yet there were instances in which a husband left his wife for a long period of time—weeks, months, even years—before he returned after wandering about. During the late historical period, it was not unusual for a man to be away, sometimes intermittently from his family, or even for many years pursuing logging or other seasonal cash-cropping endeavors. It was remembered how in the past only a few men, because of long occupational absences, remained bachelors.

Elders have maintained that an adulterous man was often the reason for a woman to commit suicide, and that such a man was always conscious of his misdeed, often causing him to leave the area, sometimes permanently. A *divorced man or woman* (*sce?ém*) apparently seldom suffered any loss of status from their kin group or friends if their disunion was for incompatibility. Amicable relations were said to have been maintained, if possible, by the parents of a divorced couple, especially for the benefit of any grandchildren. "Many Plateau individuals feel more obligation to and affection for their consanguineal kin than they do to or for their spouses" (Ross 1968-2008).

"Marriage ties may be severed, but a blood tie always remains in tact" (Ackerman 1994:293). And yet, among the Spokan, there is considerable evidence that after divorce, some men and women maintained close relationships with one or both of their former in-laws, by linguistic designations and even fulfilling certain socioeconomic responsibilities. One man said how he favored his former *wife's father* (*sxa?xe?*) to his present father-in-law. Even after remarrying, it was common for both the man and wife to maintain close relations with their former in-laws. Given social and kin pressures, they continued to fulfill most if not all of their previous economic responsibilities; and in some situations the daily care of the in-laws, particularly if they were debilitated and had few supporting family members.

After separating, a couple could renew familial obligations through negotiation and kin influence. If such efforts were successful, then they would live together, resuming previous socioeconomic obligations and connubial rights. The reestablishing of marriage was called *?ihemtwéx^wi*, a term which denoted the occasion and ritual when two previously warring tribes agreed to bring a cessation to conflict, and live in peace (STHC)—and hence could be considered a well-chosen term by all married readers. A divorced woman always took any horses that belonged to her.

Remarriage

An extended family always attempted to fulfill its social and economic responsibilities to any adult members who were widowed or divorced. Most of these single adults typically did attempt to *remarry* (*hełnt'q^wuq^waméw's*). In a culture that required a high division of labor to fulfill individual and group economic needs, a single once-married adult placed certain stresses upon the extended family. Some people, given certain situations, never remarried—particularly the older widows, widowers, and divorcées. An older unmarried woman who was unable to marry was known as *ma?amíst*.

Aside from the occasional demands of a sororate, and in rare instances of a levirate, a young widow(er) would make every attempt to remarry for personal and socioeconomic reasons after the prescribed period of mourning. Such unions were seldom manipulated by their elders or family members. In some respects, a remarried couple thereby assumed an even larger extended family. Alvord observed, "After the death of a wife, a man will not take another wife for one or two years, even if he has no other woman with him in the same lodge. He helps to take care of the children, who will go into the immediate charge of the wife's mother" (1857:19).

It was logistically difficult for a typical older single man to maintain a household if he lived alone, regardless if he was divorced, widowed, or never married, even though kinspeople, neighbors, and even young children assisted him in various ways. One elderly Spokan man reverently maintained, "It's not natural for a man to live alone. Only sorcerers and wolves can do this." Thus, it was not uncommon for such a person to marry, often another single person who was established and respected within the community. Older women tended to not remarry, for it was generally believed, and demonstrated, they were more self-sufficient than men.

Censored Sexual Relations

Determining what sexual relations should be considered illegal or abnormal is a matter of cross-cultural interpretation, based upon the reviewer's individual and cultural beliefs. It is one area in which cultural relativism is often a determining factor in making such distinctions and conclusions. For Native American cultures, what was condoned prehistorically—certainly with the influence of Christian missionaries—may nowadays be seen as *immoral* (*č'słcut*). All Plateau people recognized strict prohibitions against illegal or abnormal sexual relations, and held definite notions of punishments for those individuals found guilty. Yet despite these strong moral prohibitions, contemporary male and female elders acknowledged the past and present occurrence of culturally prohibited and abnormal sex relations. However, many Spokan were often understandably reticent to discuss individual instances of culturally defined following aberrant sexual behavior.

Male and female Spokan elders pointed out that premarital sexual relations were probably not as frequent prior to the early reservation period, given the strict chaperoning, as well as the fear of out-of-wedlock pregnancies.

Adultery

Apart from incest and rape, adultery was the most commonly condemned sexual behavior. If a married woman were to be publicly found guilty of adultery, her husband would administer one of several types of punishment. He could beat his wife or administer a whipping with a hand quirt or whip, but always with the consent of her parents. Or a man could kill his unfaithful wife without anyone's consent (Elmendorf 1935-6, 2:45). One elder remembers the telling of a case many years ago in which the group's women quickly and publicly stoned an adulterous woman. An offended husband had the right and support of the community—if he chose—to destroy valuable personal property of the guilty party. Yet most informants agreed that, in time, people would never publicly mention the transgression of either the man or woman. It was possible that after a period of time, a man might marry a woman who had been *judged* (*čcx*ʷ*epl'e?m's*) by the community as having been an adulteress.

The sanctions against an adulterous woman were severe and warranted derogatory epithets—sometimes public—that compared the woman's behavior to presumably licentious animals, or even those few anthropomorphic creatures believed to have no *shame* (*sc'ešt*) or conscience. It was not unusual for adulterers to be publicly whipped or even stoned after such a judgment by the village council (Elmendorf, pers. comm.). Nor was it unusual for a condemned woman to leave her village or group, returning after what was considered a period of redemption. Regardless of the allotted punishment, the community and the families of the ostracized pair wore their shame in public, sometimes for many years. Consequently, some guilty persons succumbed to social pressures and relocated to a different community.

Though adultery was considered disruptive to the social tranquility of a village and respective kin structure, it is probably true—as most elders maintained—that young men would try to surreptitiously secure a paramour with a single or married woman. In a small private gathering of young men, it has been said that the "warmest log on a fire" was a man giving a graphically detailed and lengthy account of his sexual success with a single or married woman. Some young men were known as being *flirts* (*nw'íw'x*ʷ*n'e?*), albeit some had reputations for their "sexual prowess" and were called *salapáya?qn*. When speaking of adultery, one may question Franchère's understanding of private familial relationships, when he wrote:

> [...] once the marriage is contracted, the spouses observe toward each other as inviolable fidelity; adultery is almost unknown among them, and the woman who should be found guilty of it would be punished with death. At the same time, the husband may repudiate his wife, and the latter may then unite herself in marriage to another man (1904, 6:332).

A man who enjoyed success during his sexual liaisons may have a special sweathouse name—one that indicated his alleged sexual prowess, particularly with married women. Sexual relations with an unmarried woman were invariably more difficult because of the constant chaperoning by her family, for if she were caught, her misbehavior would reduce her value in later marriage. The reputation of a young man who was accused of adultery with a married woman seldom suffered, whereas the married woman was not so fortunate, being ostracized by the group and the community.

The publicly revealed extramarital pursuits of a husband could have dire consequences, as witnessed by Cox, whose unfortunate and generalized characterization of the Spokan woman do not lessen the following description:

> Slavish and submissive as the Spokan women are, they do not all tamely submit to the occasional lapses of their husbands; an instance of which occurred in the summer of 1815, while I was at Spokan House: One of the tribe named *Singhelsasscoghaght* (or the horse), from his great swiftness, and dexterity in riding, was a tall and rather handsome Indian. He was remarkable for his gallantries, and it was also whispered among the females that he never spared a woman whom he caught unprotected in the woods. His wife had for some time suspected him of carrying on an intrigue, and, being constantly on watch, she soon discovered that her suspicions were not groundless. The very night of the discovery, while he was in a profound sleep, she inflicted on him a dreadful injury, of which he died before morning. On the intelligence becoming public, a crowd of his relatives assembled round his lodge, to whom she openly avowed herself as the author of his death, stating at the same time the reasons for committing the dreadful act; but she had scarcely finished, when an arrow from her husband's brother quivered in her heart. Her relatives instantly collected. Guns, arrows, and tomahawks were in immediate requisition, and before long we could arrive to check the bloody conflict, two men and two women had fallen victims [... eventually] each party rested satisfaction with its respective loss (1832:231-2).

Rape

Daily, except during her menses, a woman had to make often solitary expeditions to collect firewood, roots, and water, and to perform other domestic chores. This exposed her into unprotected situations, and exposed her to being compromised by a malicious man, which was noted by Cox:

> We learned from the wives of the *voyageurs*, that female violation is by no means uncommon among them. The frequent journeys which the women in the execution of their laborious duties are obligated to make alone into the woods in search of fuel, roots &c., afford great facility to the commission of this offence; and the ravisher demands on impurity from the well-known fear of the women to tell her husband, who might either abandon her, or by taking the offender's life, embroil their respective families in a sanguinary contest (1831, 2:129-130).

The accusation of *rape* (*ckʷn'té* or *ckʷmí* - "drag her") was a serious crime. If the guilty man was identified, judged, and convicted, he was severely punished, usually by receiving a public lashing. Some elders said that an older man accused of raping a much younger woman would be lashed, excommunicated from the village, or even stoned to death by the community. If a girl's family suspected that their unwed daughter had been raped, she would undergo an intense interrogation—one that often involved questioning by the chief, who would attempt to determine the identity of the rapist. Consensus could preclude any action by the chief and his *advisors* (*sxʷč'ɫpaʔxém*) when the women—most notably the grandmothers—of a village or camp came together and dispensed often severe retribution to the male culprit. Given the circumstances of the girl's age and family, prior to being excommunicated, the guilty male could be *castrated* (*nqʼʷaʔqʼʷʔ* or *nqʼʷaqʼʷʔʔéplsntm*). This occurred many years ago on a neighboring reservation, when the guilty male was "stumped" (a radical bi-lateral orchidectomy) with a Hudson's Bay cruising axe on a tree stump by the agnatic kinsmen of the raped woman.

A girl who had been raped could be whipped if it was determined she had been careless or had gone against her family's strict training and threatened admonishments. Despite what must have been a humiliating ordeal, the girl did not always identify the man who was guilty of bringing such shame to the woman, her family, and her kinspeople. A married woman might resort to suicide if the crime of rape became public.

Ray's writing on the neighboring Sanpoil (1933), and Elmendorf's work with the Spokan (1935-6) described how women, having conceived a child from rape, were not expected to marry the man responsible. This was partly because the woman's family and village simply felt that the male rapist was unworthy of marriage to their daughter. If the child was born out of wedlock, the raped woman could keep the child, who was never referred to as a *bastard* (*scsl'éčst* - "lost" - "product of an unnatural act"), at least publicly. Yet privately, the child's peers might refer to him in derogatory terms or make disparaging remarks. It was agreed that a raped woman whose child was born out of wedlock never suffered a loss of status. However, in certain instances, if a woman wanted to give up her child, then a *childless couple* (*čtmé?lt*) would make proper arrangements for the child's adoption.

Incest

Incidences of a woman being raped by a kinsman—particularly among members of a small and homogeneous Plateau community—was seldom publicly acknowledged as incest. The Spokan were no exception, even though it did occur. Ethnographic data dealing with late historical accounts of incest within the Plateau are found in Ray's comprehensive ethnography (1933) of the Sanpoil and Nespelem. The fieldwork with the Spokan (Elmendorf, pers. comm.) offers no significant differences from what has been recorded by Ray (1933). Several Spokan elders remember their grandparents describing siblings who had been accused of intergenerational sex within the family, and how they were stoned by the community, sometimes killing one or both parties. If this societal punishment was not enacted, the offenders were summarily excommunicated from the village and kin group.

Accusations (*čtmłtúmš*) of incest between siblings or between parent and child were sufficient reasons for one or both guilty parties to commit suicide, particularly the accused woman. A man or woman was strictly forbidden to marry a half-sister or half-brother. The fear of incest through marriage was so strong that prohibition included even a fifth generation, but was not always observed since few persons could remember or name five preceding generations (Elmendorf, pers. comm.).

The initial condemnation of an incestuous pair lead sometimes to their being ridiculed or, more dramatically, being publicly lashed by rawhide or whipped with soaked willow branches. Shame was even more grievous for the parents, who felt that any child of such a wrongful union could be born deformed. It was believed that any adults who had engaged in sibling incest would likely have children who would possibly commit incest or other grievous moral transgressions. A commonly held notion was that what one did as a parent would be passed on to the child, a notion acknowledged by physical defects and sometimes by what were considered deficiencies of character.

The prohibitions of illegal and abnormal sexual relations were well defined and often reiterated by stories during family gatherings. Some legends, even *little legends* (*sqʷqʷell'um't*) of animals, particularly the mythical Coyote, dramatized the consequences and problems of incest. Some elders had early memories of great or grandparents telling stories of his aberrant sexual behavior with other animals, even with unusual and anthropomorphic creatures. What might be interpreted as the intended sexual advance by an animal of different species was considered incestuous. These stories always illustrated a moral standard intended for the attentive audience—accounts that were usually dramatically recited by an elder at considerable length during winter confinement. The obvious moral *message* (*smemi?*) to young listeners was that the *rules and ethics* (*sm'y'e?łtú?m'šs*) of incest prohibition were created essentially to prevent role confusion, and that a woman was not to be violated or sexually dominated, certainly by male consanguineals. On the south boundary of the Spokane Indian reservation, adjacent to the river, there are three standing and one fallen basalt columns. In the following condensed account, they explain the dire consequences of incest:

[...] how before the time of horses, a man's four daughters were turned to pillars of stone [sandstone columns] as a visual warning and explanation to anyone who travelled the Spokane River. These tall columns were the consequence of incestuous behavior of a father who had repeatedly committed incest with his daughters, and after each violation the daughters cried incessantly until they realized their bodies were gradually "drying up". All the while, the daughters, in their shame, wished that they would eventually become pillars so as to warn other fathers what would happen to their daughter if they violated the laws of their people (Ross 1968-2008).

Berdache, Transvestism, and Homosexuality

The term 'berdache' is thought by anthropologists to have originally been an Arabic word, "meaning sex-slave boy, or a male child used sexually by adult males" (Allen 1986:31). The now accepted term 'berdache'—as used universally by anthropologists—was, according to some scholars, later used in the 16th century when Catholic missionaries gave the term *bardag* to describe male aborigines who dressed as women and presumably practiced sodomy. However, because of certain contemporary prejudices, misunderstandings of cultural practices, and even linguistic confusion, the ethnographic record does not always make a clear distinction between a berdache and a homosexual, albeit there are known instances of berdache who were not homosexuals. Fulton and Anderson (1992:609) propose that the Amerindian 'man-woman' (a feminine male) "was an intermediary role that bridged aboriginal conceptions of "female" and "male", and as such presided over what Victor Turner (1967:95) calls the transitional-being or "liminal *persona*". Nor was it axiomatic that a berdache was a homosexual or a shaman. There was, however, some agreement among the Spokan regarding men who assumed the attire, public behavior, and assumed occupational roles of women; but it was believed that like other shamans, the man-woman possessed a unique "power to mediate with the supernatural" (Fulton and Anderson 1992:609). Though there were no recorded or spoken occasions that when during a young man's vision quest, if he ever dreamed of a woman's digging stick or any woman's clothing or paraphernalia, that he would later assume the role and behavior of a berdache as Victor Turner's fieldwork (1964:100) with the Omaha suggests.

A berdache could be taken over by his or her power (of the opposite sex) voluntarily or otherwise. A male berdache having woman's power may have dressed, acted, and performed the skills of a woman. Conversely, a woman possessing a man's power could have exhibited the same powers of a man. Both were assumed to be berdache. Berdaches were not necessarily homosexual.

Certain inherent problems of classification regarding, "Berdaches were often confounded with intersexual persons" (Callender and Kochems 1983:444), and, "other cultures blurred the line by assigning berdache and intersexes to the same status" (Ray 1932:148).

> There were few cases of men dressing and acting like women. As a rule, they became shamans, and cured sick people. They lived along, did not marry, did not go to war, dressed in poor clothes, and never bedecked their persons gaudily. They dressed and did their hair up like women. They did all kinds of women's work, and no man's work. Young men sometimes visited them and joked with them, but they held no familiar intercourse with the other sex. Occasionally, to please the men, they would dress in men's clothing for a day and then resume their ordinary clothing. It is supposed that they were told by their guardian spirits to live as women do (Teit 1930:384).

Turney-High (1937:156-7) provides the Flathead words for a berdache, *lesbianism* (*ntałá*), and the words for homosexuality in men and women. One can only surmise that this notion represents the influence of Catholic missionization which actively condemned berdache, plural marriage, animism, and many other traditional religious rituals.

Failing to make any meaningful distinctions between a berdache and a homosexual—admittedly very difficult in some instances—by missionaries and other early settlers, who unfortunately condemned behavior what was sometimes erroneously perceived as homosexuality among indigenous peoples of the Plateau, individuals who in some cases were berdaches. There are some ethnographies (Cox 1831, 1832; Holder 1889; Teit 1930; Ray 1933; Turney-High 1937, 1941; Schaeffer 1965; Thayer 1980; Ross 1984) who provide some explanation of homosexual behavior, and the benefits to the particular individual and Spokan group of

164

accommodating so-called aberrant behavior (as judged by non-Indians). Though the berdache was a marginal figure, "[he] was interstitial" (Douglas 1966:123 fn), because, as Thayer described:

[...] he was both male and female by virtue of his physiological maleness and cultural femaleness, and at the same time he was neither male (e.g., with reference to sexuality of paternity) nor female (e.g., with reference to marriage or maternity). It was from this interstitial character that his mediating powers spring: as half-man/half-woman he had powers to mediate cross sexual boundaries and roles and, since he was a creature of vision like other shamans, he mediated as well between the divine and human worlds (1980:291-3).

In most groups, either a male or female shaman could be a *berdache* (*st'ém'y'e*ʔ or *hecm'e*ʔ*m'útm'* or *mʔmí* - "capable of being a woman" or *hecm'e*ʔ*m'éy'*ʔ*i*ʔ - "he's pretending to be a woman"). In the case of men, a berdache was a *man who possessed a woman's power* (*m'e*ʔ*m'ín'st*) and was not necessarily a homosexual. Unfortunately, among the Spokan—probably due to the loss of traditional knowledge—there are several inconclusive accounts of a *female berdache* (*sšʔém*), a woman with man's power. But there are numerous accounts of male berdaches, as was more common for Plains groups.

Several early explorers recorded the remarkable attire and behavior of a woman who was living as the wife of a Canadian employee at a North West Company post on the Columbia River. This behavior was cited in a letter to the once-famed but tragic Arctic explorer, Sir John Franklin (1786-1847), by John Stuart, as well as John Work (1825:190), and acknowledged by Franchère (1914:305-306) who was translated and edited by Huntington (1854:118-119). Elliott (1914, 3:190) and Alexander Ross (1966:85) wrote of this unusual woman who had:

[...] formed a sudden resolution of becoming a warrior; and throwing aside her female dress, she clothed herself in a suitable manner. Having procured a gun, a bow and arrows, and a horse, she sallied forth to join a party of her countrymen then going to war; and in her first essay, displayed so much courage as to attract general regard, that many young men put themselves under her command [...] under the designation of "Manlike Woman." At a period of her life, our heroine undertook to convey a packet of importance [...] which had not, at that time, been passed by the traders, and which was known to be infested by several hostile tribes. She chose for her companion another woman, whom she passed off as her wife. They were attacked by a party of Indians, and though the Manlike Woman received a wound in the breast, she accomplished her object, and returned to the Columbia with answers to the letters (Sperlin 1930, 21:125).

Schaeffer's work with the Kutenai and Flathead, and cross-cultural surveying of interior eastern Plateau tribes, lead him to conclude that, "Women who liked to hunt and were not interested in marrying, were not called by the same term as the berdaches. Such were known to exist. In neither case did the community consider the disturbance to be sexual" (1965, 3:2190).

Angelino and Shedd defined a berdache as "an individual of a definite physiological sex (male or female), who has *suméš* the role and status of the opposite sex, and who is viewed by the community as being of one sex physiologically but as having assumed the role and status of the opposite sex" (1955:125).

The apparent lack of understanding of the berdache, and the ensuing prejudices, are often reflected in the attitudes and writings of many Euro-American observers. Thayer correctly noted that too great "an overemphasis has been placed on its sexual aspects" (1980:293); Laurie stated the same when speaking of the Winnebago. It may be presumed that "transvestites who conducted themselves as women were not always true berdaches" (1953:710).

Unfortunately, the role of the berdache and the homosexual, and their adaptation to a changing way of life, were made difficult by increasing Euro-American-induced conflict, deculturation, and missionization. These sociocultural conditions lead to the eventual loss of status, as well as the humiliation and ostracism of berdaches and homosexuals—most acutely among some presumably acculturated indigenous people.

One of the earliest accounts of a woman dressing and acting as a man was given by Thompson (1962:366-7) when he was at the Spokane House in 1811. He described two letter-bearing Indians who, by dress and behavior, gave the impression they were husband and wife. The historian David Lavender, using Thompson's writings, described the situation:

He [Thompson] was dumbfounded. Man and wife nothing! The "husband" was a Kootenai squaw. Three years earlier she had been living with one of his voyageurs and he had thrown her out of camp for her loose morals. Her tribe refused to have her back, so she wandered off to other bands. Somehow she had set herself up as a prophetess. Declaring her sex changed, she adopted male clothing and took a "wife" (1964:143).

The existence of hermaphroditism, was defined by Egerton as being characterized by "persons possessing some degree of anatomical or physiological sexual ambiguity" (1964:1288), and cannot be determined simply by behavior or dress. This compounds the difficulty in assigning specific categories to explain perceived sexual incongruity. Schaeffer is undoubtedly correct when discussing instances in which there was "perhaps less social recognition of [sexual] deviancy in the Plateau than among certain Plains Tribes" (1965:217). This supports Ray's (1933:114-5) earlier conclusion that men in the eastern Plateau, experiencing less of an emphasis upon warfare, were better able to conform to more accepted traditional male roles. Thayer, when speaking of the diversity of the berdache's role, and why it fulfilled a variety of functional roles provides a universal explanation of why such a role and its public performance was generally accepted as being normative, and cited how:

[...] the berdache's power was from outside the ordinary realm, and was located within the sacred realm of the vision quest—guardian spirit complex, it did not threaten, abuse, or collapse pre-existing social and sexual categories (e.g., male-female, normal-abnormal, rational-irrational). In fact; such power as that of the berdache may have enhanced normative sexual categories, at the same time it served to mediate between the symbolic or social categories of male and female. By his supernatural ability to be half-man/half-woman, the berdache could simultaneously violate and reconcile the categories of male and female (1980:292-3).

Turney-High's later work with the Flathead agreed with Teit's findings regarding the characteristics and behavior of a berdache: Living people deny any supernaturalism to these men [berdache], either in their powers or in the causes of the phenomenon. Turney-High stated:

[They] were decently treated [although] they were the source of fun and ridicule behind their backs. Informants say that they became berdaches because they were cowards, not wanting to indulge in the male activities of hunting and fighting. They always lived in lodges by themselves and did all the traditional female work. Flathead berdaches did not indulge in male economic occupations, and were not therefore rich men because of bisexual skills. They preferred female society, always going with the women to the berry-picking grounds where they were mildly tolerated. They walked with an imitation of swaying female hips and tried to speak in falsetto (1937:85).

Much has been written about berdaches, homosexuality, and gender roles among North American Indians, particularly the Plains and Plateau Indians (Cox 1831, 1832; Teit 1930; Turney-High 1941; Angelino and Shedd 1955; Schaeffer 1965; Thayer 1980; Roscoe 1987 and 1988; Murray 1994, to name but a few). And yet, Ray (1933:148) claims there were no instances of male homosexuality among mature Sanpoil males, even though they possessed terms for both male and female homosexuals, which one may say suggests the existence of such behavior. There is, however, consensus between Turney-High (1937) and Teit (1930), both of whom worked with the contiguous Flathead, that being a berdache—by dress and behavior, might suggest but did not necessarily imply homosexuality.

The Spokan emphasized a strict division of labor, and ritual separation of the sexes in different occupations and roles, thereby accommodating people of different sexual persuasion and placing greater importance upon acquired skills, not just gender. It was understood that a person did not actively choose to become a homosexual, and yet on occasion homosexuals were publicly teased and privately ridiculed.

The most detailed known account of a Spokan berdache was made by Cox, who resided in the area from 1810 to 1818. Cox spent nearly a week visiting a Spokan-speaking berdache, who resided in a small village of approximately fifteen Chewelah-Spokan families located between Kettle Falls and Spokan House. This description not only acknowledges a berdache, but illustrates the covert consternation of the berdache to others in the community:

We visited a small tribe, consisting of not more than fifteen families, who occupied a few hunting lodges about midway between Spokan House and the Chaudière falls; their language is a dialect of that spoken by the natives of the above places, but approaching more nearly to the Spokan. Their immediate lands consist of beautiful open prairies, bounded by clear woods, and interspersed with small rivulets and lakes. The latter are visited in the autumnal months by numbers of wild geese and ducks, and their hills are well stocked with grouse. They are an inoffensive race, and received us with every demonstration of friendship. We remained a week among them, during which period we had excellent sport. The aquatic birds were large and fat; and the grouse much beyond ours in size; and so tame, that they seldom took wing until we approached within a few yards of them (1831:327).

Given Work's brief mention of the Salish berdache (1825:1), and using Cox's writings (1957), which provide some descriptions of the social and economic roles of a berdache that emphasized that how a berdache may or may not have been a homosexual, but was often the case, and was sometimes a person who played a significant role within the community. Concerning the aforementioned Chewelah-Spokan individual, of which there are several other recordings because of the confusion of gender created by dress and costume, perhaps the best description was by Cox. His definition not only acknowledges a berdache, but illustrates the covert consternation of the berdache role to others in the community. Consequently, the following lengthy and detailed account is truly quite noteworthy, and is a testimony of Cox's fine sense of cultural relativism, astute observations and forté as an ethnographer:

They [Chewelah-Spokan Group] are an inoffensive race, and received us with every demonstration of friendship [...] The chief of this tribe is an extraordinary being. The Indians allege that he belongs to the epicene gender. He wears a woman's dress, overloaded with a profusion of beads, thimbles, and small shells: add to which, the upper part of the face and manner of wearing the hair are quite feminine fashion; but these appearances are more than counter-balanced by a rough beard and a masculine tone of voice, which would seem to set his virility beyond dispute. He never gambles or associates with either sex, and he is regarded with a certain portion of fear and awe by both men and women, who look upon him as a being more than human. He has a calm and rather stern countenance, and I never observed any tendency towards relaxation of his visible muscles. He is usually attended by two or three children, to whom he paid great attention. Their chief occupation to catch his horses, collect provisions, make fires and cook his meals. When they attain a proper age, he gives them a portion, gets them married, and dismisses them; after which he selects from the largest and poorest families a fresh set of juvenile domestics. Their parents make no opposition, and are glad to have them so well provided for.

The chief possessed a large number of horses, some of which are the finest in the country. We purchased a few, and found him liberal in his dealings. He is free from the canting hypocrisy so common among Indians; and if he finds any of his young attendants tell a lie, or prevaricate in the least, the offender is punished by a flogging and sent home, after which no consideration whatever would induce him to take back the delinquent.

He seldom visited our fort; but whenever we called on him we were received with a degree of courteous hospitality which I have never experienced elsewhere. He was communicative, and inquisitive, and ridiculed the follies of the Indians in the most philosophical manner. Of these he inveighed principally against gambling, and their improvident thoughtlessness in neglecting to provide, during the summer and autumnal months, a sufficient quantity of dried salmon for the spring, which is the season of scarcity; by which neglect they have been frequently reduced to starvation. He had heard of MacDonald's quarrel with the Indian, which he adduced as one of the bad effects resulting from gambling, and added, "had the Spokan been mad enough to follow the foolish custom of your countrymen, it is probable one of you would have been killed about a foolish dispute arising out of a bad practice, which every wise man should avoid."

He inquired particularly about our form of government, laws, customs, marriages, our ideas of a future life, &c. Our answers proved generally satisfactory; but the only two things he could not reconcile to wisdom, was the law of primogeniture and the custom of dwelling. The first, he said, was gross injustice; and he thought no one but a man bereft of his senses could be guilty of the latter.

He is fond of tobacco: and the Indians say they often see him sitting late at night, enjoying his calumet at the door of his tent, and observing the various revolutions in the firmament. On all subjects therefore connected with the changes of weather his opinion is deemed oracular, and I understand he is seldom or never mistaken in his prognostications.

Although clothed in the garment of a female, I have hitherto classed this uncommon being among the masculine portion of the human race; and from his muscular frame, bushy beard, and strong decided tone of voice, I conceive myself justified in so doing. I never saw him angry but once, and that was occasioned by observing some private whispering and tittering in his presence, which he suspected had some allusion to his doubtful gender. His countenance instantly assumed a savage fierceness; but he quickly regained his composure on finding that the supposed offenders had changed their conduct. His dwelling was covered with large deer-skins, and was completely water-proof. The interior was remarkably clean, and spread over with mats. In one corner he had a stock of dried provisions, stored in leather and mat bags, which in periods of scarcity he shared liberally among the tribe; in fact he wanted nothing that could add to his happiness or comfort, and possessed a degree of calm contentment uncommon among savages, and which would put to blush much of the philosophical wisdom of civilized man (1832:190-2).

Despite contemporary interpretations that are sometimes ethnographically incorrect, both berdaches and homosexuals possessed valuable, unique, and specialized skills that benefited an entire community—which was acknowledged by some early observers. A few elders recalled how presumed homosexual berdaches excelled in their knowledge and practice of medicine, as well as domestic skills:

Yes, there were some old men who could really do fine sewing and good hide work. One man could make a hide whiter than any of [my] grandmother's women friends. I can't recall what in Spokan we called them, but I do remember hearing how all those men who were that way, could sing very high, just like women (Ross 1968-2008).

Again, Schaeffer (1965) justifiably states that it is difficult to draw conclusions from non-Indian verbal accounts or from presumed observed instances of homosexuality, transvestitism, or simply *feminine characteristics* (*me?mútm* - "he could be a woman") of appearance or behavior (*me?mín'st* - "does woman's work") exhibited by a few Spokan men. Some berdaches would on occasion *pretend to look like a woman* (*mem?éye?ey*), which probably lead to certain confusion among some early anthropologist and historians (Teit 1928; Spier 1936; Cline *et al* 1938) regarding a berdache's roles and behaviors. It should be noted that when using the classification of transvestic fetishism (TF), it is the practice of heterosexual males dressing in female clothing, but it should be noted that, "There is no empirical evidence that TF is problematic, let alone a mental disorder" (Moser and Klemplatz 2002, 56, 2:17). Thayer, speaking generally of the North American berdache, succinctly explains how "the berdache served as a mediating figure between sexual categories and roles, as well as between divine and human categories" (1980:287).

Transvestitism existed among the Spokan, and "is assumed to be part of the role structure taken on by the individual, and the erotic object, if noted, is designated by the appropriate adjective (homosexual, heterosexual, etc.)" (Schaeffer 1965:231). There are, however, no known accounts of Spokan who were hermaphrodites during the historical or late historic time, though the term was known. Of interest is that one of Ray's Sanpoil informants described a Coeur d'Alene whom he knew and whom the Spokan would have called a *hermaphrodite* (*st'ém'y'e?*):

This person, whose characteristics were preponderantly female, had much hair on her upper lip and chin. She assumed male dress, however, and associated more with men than women but stayed alone a great part of time. She was slow in speech, staring at a person for some time before speaking, and talked very obscenely. She did not marry, but lived alone much of the time (1933:148).

Male and female homosexuals were not considered by the community to create sexual disturbance, and assumed such a status for a variety of established reasons. Given the disregard and even ignorance of Indian culture by many Euro-Americans, recorded accounts are more likely incomplete observations and erroneous speculations, based prejudicially on the observer's misinterpretation of an accused Indian's proclivities. There continues to be numerous misunderstandings of the meaning and significance of many rituals and certain public behaviors. Unfortunately, this is true with some younger members of the Indian community regarding certain revitalized traditional rituals, or of ones that are now no longer practiced. Blackwood summarized the problems of misinterpretation and lack of understanding of transitional gender roles in Amerindian societies, most obviously because, "Western interpretations dichotomize the gender roles for each sex, which results from erroneous assumptions about, first, the connection between biology and gender, and second, the nature of gender roles" (1984:40).

The Spokan had numerous reasons explaining why an individual had become a berdache or a homosexual. Sometimes a man or woman assumed such a role because of a recurring dream, or when acquiring their power during a vision quest, or violation of taboos by the parents during the gestation period of the individual. Some male berdaches assumed the role and duties of a woman because of physical disabilities that precluded pursuing many often male activities. Thus, being a shaman provided a means of adapting to an otherwise untenable predicament. Conversely, and for a myriad of reasons, there was the occasional woman who did not want to marry, but preferred to participate in particular male activities. But it is not known if these women were viewed as berdaches (Elmendorf, pers. comm.). Spokan elders felt that it was not the intent of an individual to become a homosexual, but that gender transition was given to one by his or her tutelary spirit.

Some elders said that a male became a berdache due to a physical injury the boy might have sustained in his youth; others said that it is inherited from either the father's or mother's side of the *family* (*sxʷsxʷltél'is* - "the family"). One account was of how an unmarried man once made a passing but derogatory remark in private about a man who was a known berdache. Years later, after marrying, the man had several boys, one of whom later became a berdache. The reason given was that it resulted from his earlier comment. Another source recalled an instance of a male berdache who was thought to have received this power from his *mother's father* (*sl'sil'eʔ or sileʔ*).

Prostitution

There is no evidence that the pre-contact Spokan practiced prostitution, though the Spokan later acknowledged the role of a *prostitute* (*suxłqʼilš* - "one who is" or *snłqʼilštn* - "place of"), which many elders contended was a late historical phenomenon, introduced by Euro-Americans.

However, one can only assume that prostitution, by contemporary definition and practice, did exist among some post-contact indigenous Spokan, if one accepts the notion that traditional wealth was given in exchange for sexual services. Admittedly, Ray (1933) and others (Walters 1938, Cline 1938, Mandelbaum 1938) have used the term prostitution, but without being specific as to the promiscuous deeds and remuneration, if any. Depending upon circumstances, even in English usage, being sexually unfaithful is not always prostitution. Ray, when speaking of the Sanpoil and Nespelem, provides the most definitive description of prostitution in the Plateau. Unfortunately, it is based on an erroneous assumption that prostitution was probably common because of polygamous rules of marriage. Yet, the attitudes of older male informants toward what Ray calls "prostitution" are substantiated by his informants, who agreed that:

> The common objection to marrying a prostitute was not a moral one, but the fear that she would not remain faithful. Although prostitutes were not ordinarily molested, their profession was not openly recognized. If concrete evidence were obtained against one and brought to the attention of the chief she was lashed. The men involved might be punished as well (1933:146).

It is unfortunate that Ray does not state explicitly if a promiscuous Sanpoil woman received some form of remuneration, for one can perhaps assume that he realized his term "prostitution" was inappropriate when describing what is currently understood as prostitution.

Death

The basic concept of death was when a *breath-soul* (*nxʷlxʷlscútn* or *npopéwlštn*) or life-spirit (*nxʷlxʷlsctnt*), or a non-specific life-force permanently left one's body, never to return. For as an old Kalispel man told Allan Smith, "In the old days, they did not know that a person was composed of a soul" (1936-8:1220). In some cases of sorcery, certain illnesses or acts of ghosting did not mean the person could not be revived and brought back to life. The death-rattle a person sometimes made when dying, was said to have sounded like a *decaying carcass* (*l'óqʷm'i?st*) or *like someone crawling under a log* (*č'ɬ?ošxʷalqʷ*) (STHC). Aboriginally there was only a vague notion of an afterlife or a pantheon of benevolent or malevolent forces, for as was explained to Elmendorf, "there is no definite land of the dead" (1935-6, 4:26). The teachings of missionaries were apparent when McWhorter claimed, "The Indians believe that the dead people go to a place called 'Country of the souls' and that certain medicine men have the power to go into that country and bring back souls of sick people" (1904-10 [Folder 349]:7). Given the time of interview and age of his informants, Teit's published comparative and extensive fieldwork is important in many ways; certainly regarding the future state of souls and ghosts, which obviously reflected indigenous ambiguity based upon a prescribed Christian-taught explanation of an afterlife. Teit recorded how he:

> [...] obtained very little information about beliefs regarding the soul and the future state. My informants said that long ago the Indians had no knowledge of what the whites call the "soul." Besides the body, people knew nothing else belonging to a person except [a] shadow, which they believed survived after death. Some thought there were two of these, one of which remained near the body, the other going off to some other place, they knew not where, to a land where all shades finally lived together. Many however, believed in one shade, which became a ghost after death. It remained near the grave, or wandered about places where the person had been in his lifetime. After a greater or lesser length of time it disappeared altogether and no one knew where it went (1910:183).

As the aforementioned quote by Teit suggests, until recently there were only a few contemporary Spokan elders who knew anything about the past significance of a person's *shadow* (*sm'el'k'ʷéy'e?*). They did say, however, it was once believed if a stranger stepped on a person's shadow, that s/he may become ill or possibly die. The rational being that a stranger could—unknowingly—be a sorcerer. Yet in the course of events, a friend or small child may inadvertently step on another's shadow and not cause harm. A complication of this once-traditional taboo was when a younger person was speaking with an elder, it was proscribed that the young person always faced the sun so the older person had his or her back shaded from the sun. Even then, the younger individual was forbidden to step on the other person's shadow. Consequently, some remaining courtesies are based upon a few past strict moral prohibitions, though remembered by only a few.

The presumed translation and connotation of the term 'soul' was introduced by missionaries. Walker noted that an elder (Teacher, an old chief) "seemed to understand very well about the people & said they did not have the least concern about their souls & that he was just like them" (Drury 1976:184). "The word 'soul' was singularly translated to the Indians, by one of these [missionaries] telling them that they had a gut that never rotted, and that this was their living principle or soul" (Durham 1912, 1:120).

Nor did there exist concepts of a purgatory or a *devil* (*sxʷélmn*). Howard asserted that the Spokan "had no definite conception of a future world, [but] believed that all objects and living things possessed supernatural attributes" (1980:319). Hale wrote, "As respects the belief of these Indians in a Supreme Being, they had a very confused idea" (1846, 4:448). Local historian Jerome Peltier recorded an elderly Spokane woman's interpretation of heaven and hell:

> There is no heaven or hell in Spokane beliefs! We believe that those people who live an honorable life will go to a spirit land where there is no pain and where all is happiness. Those who are bad are sent to earth where they assume the life of an animal, with all of its fears and pains (1975:47).

This was reiterated by a number of older Spokan who maintained that those who are bad to other people, and to themselves during their lives, will remain here on earth as ghosts, and all of their lives will be spent *roaming endlessly* (*xʷilwisi*) in pain as ghosts. Like the great and inevitable circle of birth and death, it was believed—long ago—that after all of a person's siblings had died, then the sole survivor had reason to die so s/he could go to where family and friends resided.

With few exceptions, some archaeologists finding so-called grave goods apparently agreed with Spokan elders who maintained that there was always a belief in a life hereafter; a place where one's life/breath-spirit [soul?] went after death. Whereas some elders were adamant that the notion of a life hereafter—or a resurrection—was a concept introduced by Christian missionaries. Yet despite the many years of Christian missionization with the Spokan, their explanations of the different causes of spiritual and sorcery *death* (*łu nλ'lltín*), the protocol of mortuary rites, and the beliefs of a guardian spirit, tended to remain more traditional for those less-acculturated Spokan-speakers until probably the early 1900s.

Sorcery-Induced Death

The Spokan never subscribed to witchcraft, but believed and practiced sorcery for many reasons; mainly as an effective means of social control and revenge. Sorcery was also sometimes an explanation for illness or death. There existed many reasons why one became a victim of sorcery since a potential victim was often one who was too perfect or pretentious, or who had publicly humiliated another, was greedy or stingy, or had spoken ill of another. Yet, the reason to sorcerize an individual was not always certain; because it was acknowledged some sorcerers were by nature extremely maliciously evil. Nor was it always certain who a sorcerer was; despite seldom publicly expressed opinions. There were both male and female sorcerers; often persons possessing different types *of sumés:* ones for benevolent acts—particularly curing, and powers for malicious deeds. Years ago, it was believed that the most effective sorcerers were women because of their knowledge of plants, which invariably constituted a greater source of their poisons. It was also generally believed that with deculturation, women became the natural conservators of traditional culture, not only because of their knowledge of plants; but obstetrical procedures. This became more apparent with restrictive treaties and the reservation system where by necessity men tended to be more acculturated and mobile pursuing off-reservation seasonal employment.

The multiple malevolent powers of a sorcerer varied according to which designated *sumés* would be used for a particular deed. Consequently, a person may seek a sorcerer's power for a variety of reasons, but usually to kill an antagonistic person, or simply because of envy. It was believed that a sorcerer could only purposely sicken a designated individual as a warning, thereby demonstrating his or her powers and creating considerable fear within a group. A sorcerer might kill or debilitate domesticated animals, gain control of another's spouse, or be recruited by a grievously offended person to harm or kill his offender.

Suicide

The Spokan did not believe that certain burial practices were necessary for a man or woman who had committed *suicide* (*ši?čstm'íst* or *plscút* - "he killed himself"). Reasons for self-aggression varied. For example, a distraught young man who had been rejected by a marriage proposal may choose to mount his horse and ride against an enemy—without any weapons—flaunting the enemy force by riding in circles before them, or—on foot—*he would run into the enemy's defense* (*n'łxʷp'm'éw'si?*); and if for some reason he was not killed, his escape from death was interpreted as a sign that the individual was meant to live (STHC). A man so disposed to commit suicide could wear a *feather in his hair* (*sn'acáw'sqis*) to signify his intentions to everyone, and ride into battle unarmed to show his disdain of his opponents. It has been said that men committed self-aggression by directly using a knife or by repeatedly shooting arrows into the air, being purposely impaled while standing beneath an arrow's downward trajectory.

A young woman might commit suicide if the man whom she loved was killed during warfare—a practice called *nš?im'qín* (STHC). Paul Kane witnessed a young man at Kettle Falls who committed suicide after losing everything at gambling (1859:309-310). Kane commented earlier that, "Suicide prevails more among the Indians of the Columbia River than in any other portion of the continent which I have visited" (1859:282-3, 1971:123).

It would have been extremely difficult—even impossible—for a non-Indian to determine the number of suicides among such mobile people, particularly by a person who was not fluent in the language. Yet in a letter dated 1841, Elkanah Walker wrote, "There is one thing I have neglected to say, that is the practice of committing suicide. This prevailed to a great extent formerly. There has been only one case [...] since we have been in the country" (Drury 1976:256 fn). Walker cited another example of suicide when a young Indian girl hung herself, but he never stated the reason (Drury 1976:256 fn).

An elderly man or incapacitated *widower* (*sɬwélmt* or *sčʔelp*), however, could commit suicide when alone in the sweathouse by pouring a large split cedar-root water tight *container* (*yámxʷeʔ*) of water upon the heated stones, thereby dying of self-induced cardiac arrest from the intense heat. There are however no written accounts or memories of a woman using this method to commit suicide.

It is interesting to note, that Pickering observed a Sinkaietk (?) clay-covered sweathouse on the bank of the Okanogan River near its confluence with the Columbia River, "It was low, rounded, and covered with clay, affording scarcely room for more than a single person; and it might readily have been mistaken for the work of a beaver or some similar animal" (1895:26). Though it may be an unwarrantedly facile aside that such a small, single occupant, air-tight, clay-covered sweathouse would have been used by an elderly man committing suicide. Yet many years ago, a Similkameen elder on the Colville Indian Reservation said he knew of several instances of men constructing such a clay-covered structure for this purpose.

When an older man's wife ran away with another man, the *grieved husband* (*puʔkʷéntm* - "someone took his spouse" or *scʔém* - "grass widower"), suffering severe and inconsolable grief may commit suicide. The grief of the widower was apparent when he would annually, or more frequently, revisit and nostalgically reminisce at places he and his wife had shared happy experiences, a practice known as *hecnʔucʔucšncuti*.

Familial and community sanctions against an adulterous woman were very severe and warranted derogatory epithets, sometimes given publicly when relating the woman's behavior to certain animals—more commonly a dog, or even an anthropomorphic creature believed to have no shame or conscience. In the past, if an adulterer did not commit suicide, it was not unusual for adulterers to be publicly whipped or stoned after such a judgment by consensus or by the village council. An offending couple was always ostracized by the community and their families. Depending upon circumstances, some guilty persons succumbed to communal pressures and would attempt to relocate to a different and distant community. Adultery was often a reason for suicide by the publicly acclaimed guilty spouse—usually a man's wife.

To escape the opprobrium of severe humiliation or rejection, suicide was an accepted course of behavior. There are no accounts of *men hanging* (*čacuʔscû*) themselves as reported for women who would occasionally erect a tri-pole structure that supported from its apex a hemp rope with a noose (STHC). Public humiliation caused by a person's moral transgression was sufficient reason for suicide, which reflected badly upon the perpetrator who had no recourse. To be wrongly accused of infidelity; certainly publicly, was reason traditionally to commit self-aggression. Yet most suicides were spontaneous—often in reaction to an individual's extreme jealousy or humiliation. Beside the private sorrow and shameful disgrace by a family who had lost a member through suicide, there was often the burden of guilt for not preventing such a loss.

Apparently suicide was more frequent with women than men, but its trauma to others was even greater in the case of a married woman with children. The increased pressure upon a family was noted by Elmendorf, who recorded that a widower "would abstain from hunting and fishing for a week or more after the death of his wife" (1936-8, 4:25), but not commit suicide himself because of his familial responsibilities and obligations to his children. It was said that a man contemplating suicide would isolate himself and sing a *death chant* (*hi w'ésteʔtnʔ*), one which lamented his wrongdoings and asked for forgiveness by his family and community, and asked for care of his family by his kinspeople after his death.

Apart from hanging, the methods for a woman committing suicide varied: such as leaping to her death from a great height, or throwing herself onto an up-ended implanted digging stick. The most common reason for committing suicide was the shame a woman felt upon being *deserted* (*xʷláɬq* - "he deserted his wife"), particularly if her husband's desertion was due to another woman—usually one younger. A deserted woman was called *scʔém'ɬ*. Some elders said that a woman would threaten a husband with her suicide to control or defer him from a potential liaison with another woman. Ray reported (1933:149) that among the contiguous Sanpoil and Nespelem, if an eloping couple was captured, the woman may kill herself.

There were several oral accounts of Spokan women committing suicide by leaping from a well-known, high, near-vertical, yellow lichen-covered basalt rock face called *yellow face* (*skʷrʔúseʔst*), a site just northwest of Little Falls and used for this purpose well into the historical period. There were recalled instances of deserted women quietly leaving their group and never being heard of again. This does not imply that the women did not affiliate with other groups or had committed suicide. If a woman had been wrongly accused of a severe moral transgression by her husband or family, she might commit suicide in her frustration and inability to prove her innocence. Mothers were known to commit *self-aggression* (*šiʔdstmist*), especially when the person felt too much pain and grief with the loss of a child.

A subject not often spoken of was when a person would *will him or herself to death* (*čičpel's* - "a moth-like experience"). This was usually an elderly widower—one who was living alone. Interestingly, this was not considered suicide by the elderly Spokan. One particular occasion of psychologically self-inducted death was an elderly widower in his late nineties who lived alone, and with whom the author spent considerable time over many years. On what was unknowingly to be the author's last visit, the elderly gentleman explained how that morning he had received his annual physical at the Wynecoop Memorial Indian Health Service Clinic, and was informed of his excellent health, being told he had good *lungs* (*spéw'puʔ*) and the heart of a young man. Before leaving him, the elder confided that this was the anniversary of his wife's death, whom he obviously still loved and missed greatly, and felt *abandoned* (*ɫuwént* - "left alone"). He proceeded to explain how he was going to 'go away.' Asking him why, he lamented, "Oh, to be with my wife and all my old friends and family. I want to hear people who know how to properly speak my language and where there are deer and clean water: I want now only to sleep." He died about two hours later. There was one memory of a woman dying of grief after the accidental death of her child, *nčn'pečstmntm*.

To become an *old person* (*p'xʷp'xʷútm*) was not an issue per se, but for a married man, it was a great concern to lose his wife, because she cooked, washed, generally supported him, and was someone with whom he could *converse and exchange ideas* (*m'ey'štw'éʔxʷ*). Elderly widowers and widows living alone often said how they received better solace, care, and attention from a non-kin age-mate—one who was either a widow or widower of the same gender, because they could share memories, discuss intimate experiences, and speak only of certain things. This type of relationship and exchange was known as *č'xʷ-m'tw'éʔxʷiʔ*. When such a close friend died, the other in many cases soon followed.

Santora and Starkey, who paraphrased Bullough and Bullough (1972), identified some of the unfortunate issues surrounding contemporary suicide with native peoples of this region, and have perhaps identified an aspect of what is a major contemporary problem, stating that they:

> [...] attributed the suicide attempts to cultural transition and the changing of the old organization of values held by the tribal [elder] members. Conflict resulted because the old and new values were not always congruent. This conflict was most evident in the young because they were not able to identify with their Indian heritage or with Anglo values. The young were unable to use their parents as role models for existing in an Anglo world [...] The concept of cultural integration encourages isolation, but economic and social needs have required the Indians to interact with the Anglo society. Conversely, the concept of integration places a premium on the Indians' ability to conform to the Anglo culture and to reject their own (Santora and Starkey 1982:27-28).

There were no oral or written accounts of senicide, regardless of a person's age or if severely *crippled* (*tl'xʷncút* or *hecw'íl'm'w'il'm'* - "he's a cripple"). Disabled people, regardless of age, were cared for as all elders were greatly respected. Apparently, among the Nez Perce, a person who had committed suicide by drowning was buried near the water where the body was recovered (Sprague, pers. comm.). It was said that the survivors always felt the deceased individual had acted according to his or her interpretation of a situation that had gotten beyond their control. A person who committed suicide rarely had his name later given in a naming ceremony to a baby or small child, for fear the same tendency or consequences would be passed on.

Confession

Nearing the time of his death (*č'i'tmnúxʷ*), a dying person who had the opportunity to *confess his sins* (*snt'éye'tn* - "bad things"), for whatever reason, would ask a trusted non-kinsperson to hear his life's *confession* (*nmipmíst*), since a kinsperson would be unsympathetic, embarrassed, or even emotionally unable to discharge the responsibilities incurred by taking a relative's confession. Lewis, when speaking of the stress of private or public confession, feels it would appear to be, "as a direct consequence of the importance of moral obligation [...] where illness is a sin" (1971:197). During the confession, the confessee might be asked to assume certain social and economic responsibilities that occasionally entailed making necessary amends for certain social transgressions and debts incurred by the confessor during his or her life.

The person who heard the confession usually stayed with the dying person until his or her death, closing the eyes of the deceased, and might later assist the *family* (*sxʷsxʷltel'is*) with the distribution of the dead person's belongings. Often it was the confessee who would *wash the face and hands of the dying person* (*xʷk'ʷncúti* - "he cleaned himself"), and, if requested, the confessee would prepare a *special last meal* (*n'ukʷm'e'scíni*) for the individual, particularly when the dying person had not eaten for some time. It was also expected that the person hearing a male friend's confession would assume responsibility for the initial burial preparations, and even direct the digging and preparation of the grave in an appropriate *place of the corpse* (*sntmtmnéy'tn*).

The pending death of a person, even for one *who dies in his sleep* (*č'ɫyíkʷ'em'tm* - "never wake up") or *unexpectedly* (*qe' č'ɫk'llmíɫs* - "he died on us") was announced in different ways, such as the man's dog howling immediately before his owner's death. Or just before death, a dying person would sometimes give a sigh followed by a *death yawn* (*héwnt*). The *persistent howling of a coyote during the day* (*'uw'hencúti* - "howl"), was considered to be a definite harbinger of death, as was the appearance of an owl—usually the great horned owl—or being told at night by a mouse of pending death, or through a friend's or acquaintance's *dreams* or *premonitions* (*č'ɫxaqlstn* - "a feeling to help you get out of the way"). A kinsperson's repeated dream of the *pending event* (*nqʷ'ic'ɫn*), or by the individual being *suddenly startled* (*kʷssús*) by any animal may bring death.

Prior to death, an individual might make *unusual sounds* (*l'óqʷm'i'st*), *labored breath* (*hac'pmɫtem* or *stspá'ulc* or *ntk'ʷels*), but most notably the *death rattle* (*nt'k'ʷels*), indicating the inevitable. An individual who experienced any persistent twitching of his nose, ear, or eyelid, knew that someone was going to die. A person with twitching feet had the same realization. Even more specifically, if a person's feet are *twitching* (*siwést*), this was a prophetic sign he would soon be standing in a *graveyard* or *cemetery* (*sntmtmnéy'tn*). The belief was that any person who knew death was imminent, would usually first experience a feeling or sensation that death had commenced in his or her feet and would gradually work its way up their body until the person took his or her *last breath* (*npupéwšltn*). These cultural signs were apparent even when the person experienced an *unexplainable death* (*čs'ololqncút*), which may be interpreted as the result of sorcery.

Death could occur when an antagonist wished another's death, or if the person mocked an already *dead person's voice* (*sk'ʷsč'e'c'ínm*). As a result, it was not uncommon for an individual to have a temporary loss of voice or hearing after maligning a deceased person. These incidents were understood to have had nothing to do with being sorcerized, but were considered to have been caused by an inappropriate verbal expression against a deceased or surviving kinsperson of the deceased, one whom the individual had offended. Also, an *aged* (*č'éw'lši*) man who had selfishly refused to ritually *release his tutelary spirit* (*tr'mí'l'š*) might, after first being warned, be killed if he then did not relinquish his *power spirit* (*sumés*). At any age, a child could have a dream that might foretell the premature death of either his father or mother. Of course it was sometimes possible for someone who had been forewarned of death, to perform penance, make a sacrifice or confession to prevent or at least forestall his or her predicted death.

Until recently, when a Spokan person died in a *hospital* (*snwitéłx^wtn*), a close friend of the family who was present may be asked to close the person's eyes, prior to the cleansing ritual. From personal experience I know that when a family realizes a family member is dying, a friend may be asked to privately listen to the dying person's confession.

Cleansing Ritual of the Deceased

The body of the deceased was prepared by a non-kinsperson, often an elderly woman or widow of different gender who had experience in these matters, and who would less likely be attacked by *malevolent spirits* (*sx^wqíx^wm*), an offended spirit, or the *ghost of the deceased* (*sk^wússč'e?* - "ghost"). Older Spokan explained how these so-called designated *specialists* (*x̣^wk'^{'w}nénti*) enjoyed greater assurance of not becoming spiritually contaminated because of their extensive experience, thoroughness of purification, and protracted prophylactic rituals. It was not recalled if a *x̣^wk'^{'w}nénti* ever possessed a specific *sumés̆*. The older unwed woman or widow who conducted the *cleansing ritual* (of the deceased) (*x̣^wuq'^{'w}incut*) was compensated with gifts for her services by the family and kinspeople of the deceased whom she had prepared for burial. Curtis, however, made further clarification of the gender of a *sk^wnénti*, noting that "the deceased was always [...] cleansed and prepared by one of the same sex" (1907-30, 2:6). Pickering (1895) also recorded the ritual, and Hale observed how:

> Prior to the usage of the services of contemporary morticians, the deceased was thoroughly washed in private by an elderly widow, known to perform such ablutions, thereby sparing the family further grief—even embarrassment. After removing the clothes, any after death waste [*mneč*] would be gathered, taken outside, and burned. The corpse is washed, wrapped in skins, with the legs doubled up, and then put into a grave three feet deep, which is surrounded and covered with stones and sticks, to prevent the wolves getting at it (1846, 4:456-57).

Upon removing a person's death waste, if there was any observed *blood* (*snx^wúl*) clots or foreign objects in the *feces* (*sm'n'čsqax̣e?* - "cattle feces"), then it was concluded that the person died from internal hemorrhaging brought on by sorcery. At the completion of the cleansing ritual, it was common for sprigs of rosehip bushes or stinging nettles to be suspended in the corners of the rooms of the dead person's dwelling; particularly the sleeping room to prevent a *malevolent force* (*sx^wqíx̣^wmix^wm*) or theriomorphic creatures from occupying the dwelling. In lieu of rosehip bushes, branches of Oregon grape were similarly hung in dwellings or upon a favorite chair of the deceased to prevent the return of his ghost. As recently as the late 1960s, some elders practiced this prophylactic ritual. In addition, or separately, suspending a large, inert hornet's nest from a ceiling corner in the main room of the house also served as a prophylactic device against malevolent forces. Depending upon the cause of contamination, rosehip water was, until recently, used to wash the walls of the house or room where one had died. The same procedure was closely followed to prevent a wandering spirit/soul from returning to the dwelling.

Immediately upon dying, a person's spirit/soul might precede the corpse to the intended grave, usually in the form of a large *blue horsefly* (*Calliphora vicina* - *q'^{'w}q'^{'w}atn'* - "one that made a loud and unusual buzzing sound") (STHC). Another harbinger of death that might not appear to a person in a dream, but during the day or early evening was, until recently, the much-feared large *polyphemus moth* (*Antheraea polyphemus* - *cqcqósx̣n* or *slsláx̣n* or *k'^{'w}e?lúle?x^w* or *qcqqo?sax̣n* or *palw'íty'a?* - "bad luck moth" or "death moth"). This impressive creature was so designated because of the varying colors in large circles on its wings that looked like two huge eyes, and were interpreted as being prophetic of either an impending serious illness or the observer's death. If the wing circles were gray, a person knew that there would be news of an acquaintance or friend's serious illness, or even that of himself. If the wing circles were red, then s/he or an unknown person would soon bleed severely, even bleed to death internally (Egesdal, pers. comm.). When seeing this moth, a person fainted or went into a deep coma, and required treatment as soon as possible from a curing shaman

175

who would perform a special prophylactic ritual, one that involved the patient to first drink a tea—actually a placebo made from scraping and steeping the crushed inner bark of either black or red thornberry. The shaman then performed a special cleansing ceremony to hopefully remove the poison. This moth was called *palw'icya?* by the Colville; a near-sounding name of *pal'wítt'ya?*, identified as the orange sulphur butterfly (*Colias eurytheme* Boisduval) (Egesdal, pers. comm.).

Until recently, another common prophylactic ceremony for purifying a dwelling after death was to simmer hemlock needles or subalpine fir needles in an open metal can of water on a low-burning *wood stove* (*sn ?ur'šictn*). Sometimes the solution was supplemented by scraping the dried bark of aspen into the container, along with mashed hemlock or subalpine needles, which, when combined and warmed into a vapor, protected the dwelling and inhabitants from any ghost or *yellow-pine chipmunk* (*Tamias amoenus -q'ʷq'ʷatn'*) which might assist different ghost forms to perform malevolent acts toward the living. It was agreed that chipmunks could recount the doings of humans changing into ghosts and even evil spirits to a sorcerer's guardian spirit.

Long-house Reception and Wake

The traditional wake served numerous social and psychological functions, as described many years ago by an elderly Spokan man who explained how in the past all renewal and intensification rites *united* (*xʷtéłp*) even distant kinspeople and friends, provided an opportunity to exchange news, renewed or reinforced relationships, and demonstrated collective support for those in need. For younger people, mortuary gatherings provided an opportunity to see and learn of people whom they had sometimes only heard described in oral accounts, as well as learn from others about the unique history and accomplishments of the deceased, which were recited during the eulogies made public to the family for the first time. As an elderly man said, "My grandchildren will know more about me after I die when stories (eulogies) are told of me. You know that all a man really ever leaves—after his footprints which are blown or swept away with rosehip branches—are memories of him told by his friends to his grandchildren."

During the long-house wake, and throughout the entire night, spontaneous public behavior often tended to exclude any formal prescribed ritual, varying according to one's consanguineal, affinal, fictive, or other considered relationship with the deceased. Usually in the evening—at one's volition, any individual may stand and present an impromptu eulogy or testimonial, enunciating certain memories of significant events s/he may have shared with the deceased. These sometimes lengthy and often dramatic oral accounts identified the particular social or physical skills, moral character, and contributions the deceased possessed and shared with the community. Such extemporaneous testimonials were not only an individual catharsis and even therapeutic for the speaker, but served as examples of exemplary behavior to be emulated by the youth.

Once assembled, friends and kinspeople begin a vigil after greeting and giving their condolences to the bereaved, and offering any assistance that might be required by the family during their time of mourning. During the wake, family and relatives openly expressed their grief, often remaining awake for twenty-four hours. Traditionally, close friends of the deceased functioned as *watchers* (*č'emtuw'il'i?*) to make certain that the body was not disturbed, and to perform domestic chores for the family and guests.

It was common for one or more prayer leaders to be present, men who periodically lead the assembled mourners in traditional prayers. At any time during the wake, a person could stand up and speak of their respect for the deceased. A close friend might sing praises honoring the deceased person. Leaders also paid their respects by speaking of the individual's worth and contributions to the tribe, saying how younger members of the family should emulate the deceased person's service and commitment to elders and the needy, thereby giving solace to the survivors.

The traditional wake served numerous functions, as cited by an elderly Spokan many years ago, who explained how in the past funerals *united* (*xʷtéłp*) distant kinspeople and friends, thereby providing opportunities to exchange news, renew and reinforce relationships. Funerals demonstrated mutual support for those in need.

In summary, prior to missionization, it was a matter of concern to protect the corpse from an enemy, especially if the deceased was a chief, sub-chief, or medicine man who had angered some other dignitary from a hostile tribe. Therefore, the relatives sat up with the body throughout the night to ensure that it would not be stolen or mutilated, and to prevent anyone from stealing the medicine man's paraphernalia, profaning it, or otherwise trying to adapt it for his or her own devious intentions. If it were discerned that evil spirits might attend the deceased, this required the survivors to guard the dead person's body in order to keep such spirits from stealing the deceased's soul. This concern that no one should tamper with the body exists for some elderly Spokan today, who believe that if any organs were removed, the spirit of the deceased would never rest. Until recently, some elders deemed the giving or receiving of blood or organs an abomination, often even refusing to discuss such a distasteful subject. Yet, some conceded that a relative in need could be a recipient from a close relative, but never from a stranger. Given the revitalization of many aspects of contemporary mortuary rituals, it is not surprising that the practice of embalming has become distasteful to some Spokan.

Eulogies

Eulogies were traditionally given by both kinspeople and unrelated friends at the open grave, or today at the open (or closed) coffin while in the long-house. Although the grieving kinspeople had previously required a person from the family to present eulogies, anyone could step forward and say whatever s/he wanted regarding the deceased. During this occasion, there would appear a *man known for his unusual humor* (*čłm'n'eʔšict*), one who had been a good friend of the deceased. At an appropriate time during the wake, the *čłm'n'eʔšict* told humorous stories of his deceased friend, and experiences that they had shared. Some men were known for their ability to present eloquent and dramatic eulogies, ones that often included detailed accounts of extraordinary accomplishments by the deceased in warfare, trading, gambling, hunting, fishing, or travel to distant lands—eulogies that were recalled many years later. The speaker seldom failed to elicit from the appreciative family and attending mourners a range of emotions of humor and sadness. The grieving kinspeople and friends welcomed these often moving and eloquent eulogies as being therapeutic for the family and those attending.

Anyone could speak during a wake—even an unrelated person, possibly from a different village, or a local person known and respected for his skills as an *orator* (*sxʷqʷlqʷéltm*). In the past, the friend of a deceased fellow warrior may give a dramatic and stirring eulogy of his friend's exploits and bravery: a presentation called *qʷllúmtntm'*. Also, there was consensus that the principal and most useful *message* (*sm-me-miʔ*) enunciated during a *eulogy* (*suw't*) was when the speaker impressed upon the gathering that the material things a man left behind were not important or really accolades to his life; but rather his remembered deeds of charity and humility were paramount. This message would be illustrated with explanations of the deceased person's integrity, honor, generosity, kindness, and support of his family, friends, and community.

Today; however, it is unusual to hear a eulogy presented entirely in Spokan. Occasionally one hears certain phrases or a concluding remark in the traditional language thanking people for their support and attendance. And yet the reading of the eulogy is still considered an honor and an obligation and opportunity to emotionally and even dramatically—by inflection and choice of words—to summarize those beliefs and behaviors that once characterized the deceased, and which were responsible for the deceased leading an exemplary life. Today, one will rarely hear the phrase, "What I have in my heart I cannot hold in my hand" (*łu hec kʷestn n mi spʔus taqs kʷestn łu n hin čelč* - "I cannot adequately show my grief").

Mortuary Feast

After the burial, all participants returned by custom to the long-house to partake in a *mortuary feast* (*xʷls ʔíɨn* - "throw, give, share food" or *šxʷsi ʔíɨm* - "giving away food"), also called a Memorial Feast, was an occasion to continue discussions of past memories with renewed acquaintances and friends, many of whom they had not seen since the last funeral. Among the different small groups of separated men and women—commonly by age, it was common for one to hear, prior to departure, "I hope to see you at the next one." Several important functions of this public rite of intensification—or *celebration* (*y'aʕ'pqín'i ʔ*)—was the *distribution of food* (*pxʷmstés*), and the public recognition of the community's generosity and support of the grieving family, creating and reinforcing of social ties. It was an opportunity for guests to quietly demonstrate their emotional support, and sometimes, and even more importantly, to pledge their emotional and economic support to the family. This was and continues today to be an important contribution with the change in kinship patterns and often distant dispersal of kin groups, made all the more important if a contributing male had died.

Before eating, several friends would alternately stand and eulogize the deceased, relating a private event, such as a brave or kind deed by the deceased, or even a humorous account previously unknown to the family, one that acknowledged the person's *good character* (*xsɨ-cut*). A person might commence his eulogy by saying, "I want to tell the children and grandchildren what only I know, what they should know to better remember this person, what he did for our community."

The last person to speak was the chief, who would pick up a piece of property belonging to the deceased, and give it to one of the distributors to dispense to a recipient who had been determined by the person's survivors. Then the chief then made a brief but poignant speech, and the survivors of the deceased were naturally heartened by such comments, which were reiterated acts of kindness to others by the deceased—thus, a type of *keepsake* (*ʕukʷam'e ʔcinm*) that helps in one's sorrow. Today the final closure is a prayer (Elmendorf 1935-6, 2:48).

Give-away ceremonies were dramatic events—times when the various qualities and virtues of the deceased were publicly enunciated to the gathering, often by a *non-kinsman* (*nk'ʷélixʷ* - "from another tribe"), or one who had given the major eulogy or *memorial speech* (*so ʔsow'tm'*), or by a distant kinsperson through prior arrangement by the family. Over the many years, some very old and still recognized blankets and shawls were given away on numerous give-aways, and elicited audible and appreciable comments from former owners. Though these gifts were intended to be used according to their nature, but seldom were; rather they were carefully stored until a future give-away. When receiving a gift, the receiver expressed his or her gratitude and may speak briefly of the deceased, but was not required to do so. Even today, the give-away is an integral part of the Memorial Feast.

The following quote from Elmendorf (1935-6, 1:46-8) provides the most definitive ethnography of the memorial give-away ceremony:

Some time after preparation for burial– deceased's relations—not by marriage—prepare for the feast—accumulated a quantity of food—the deceased clothes & belongings—everyone in [the] tribe [is] invited by word of mouth—usually begins at noon—held outdoors under shades in summer or in long-house in winter— [...] guests were served by volunteer cooks—everybody ate what they wanted & when they were done all the remaining food was given away - *sxʷqʷlqʷélt* = "crier"—chief usually acts as this—or appointed another 2 young men appointed as *suxʷíts'c* [*sxʷxʷíc'š*] to deliver the property to those to whom it is given—one for men & one for women—the *suʷqʷlqʷált* distributed the property—two or three speakers (*suxʷqʷlqʷált* or *suxʷqʷlqʷeltm*) appointed before the feast day by the chief—men appointed to look after the food & see that everyone is served (*sxʷčn'šíš* = "servers")—the speakers sit down with the others at the food—each speaker then rises & recounts some incident or memory in connection with the dead person, eulogizing him—chief speaks last—then they eat—after the meal some gather the food and distribute it while others just tell the guests to help themselves to what is left—servers then cleared away food & remains & the gifts are distributed—[the] chief picks up the property and makes a little speech about the dead in connection with the object & gives it to one of the distributors & names the person to whom he shall carry it [to]—the recipients of each article have been determined beforehand by the deceased's father or mother or whoever of his relations gives the feast—some relatives gave away much of their own possessions at such a feast if they thought much of the deceased. This ceremony is still carried on with the addition of a prayer meeting to close.

The give-away ceremony undoubtedly served numerous spiritual and psychological functions for the family and friends of the deceased: to recognize the deeds and words of the deceased person's friends; to make a public display of the family's generosity; to fulfill any obligations of debt contracted by the deceased; to reduce inter-family conflict by publicly distributing some of the deceased person's possessions to non-kinspeople. It was not unusual for the family of the deceased to give away *personal mementos* (*sʔélk'ʷmn* - "keep-sakes") to close family members and friends. On occasion, friends and kinspeople of the deceased would also *give away* (*qspux̌ʷm'íl'š* - "give-away items"), some of their own possessions to *special guests* (*sčičicn*)—particularly those who held the deceased in high regard, sometimes reflecting the pre-death wishes of the deceased. Great care was given to recognized close friends of the deceased by gifting; otherwise it was reason for the deceased to later appear before the offender as a ghost. A more common reason for the deceased to visit his family as a ghost, was his displeasure over an uncompleted task, or a valuable that was not properly given at the give-away or donated to a needy person. Once this was corrected, the visitation would cease.

Prior to the distribution of the deceased person's belongings to those attending, all of the items were scrupulously cleansed in rosehip water (a concoction of crushed rosehip flowers) to remove the owner's finger prints—signs of ownership—and to rid them of any malevolent spirit contamination. People receiving articles of the deceased kept their gifts carefully wrapped in rosehip bushes for several months to rid the items of *evil* (*t'éyeʔ*) that may have inadvertently accompanied the items. Prior to the distribution of the items, an older member of the family would wash the objects in rose water to rid them of bad fortune.

After a death there were instances of the deceased individual's belongings being stolen, or "leaving young children who are not able to defend themselves, his other relatives seize upon his property, and particularly the horses, which he may have left" (Hale 1846, 4:448). On occasion, wives specifically designated the recipients of their deceased husbands' properties to close friends—usually tools or weapons, knowing that certain items were cherished by particular individuals. Oral history indicated that certain possessions were secretly buried away from the body in order to protect their ownership, and reduce conflict of distribution to a specific person or people, as well as protecting the goods from being sometimes stolen by friends and relatives. There was no prescription of primogeniture (first born) inheritance, nor the practice of *ultimogeniture* (*sttʔéw'tiʔ* - "the last born") inheritance—customs practiced by some cultures to reduce familial conflict.

Anthropologist-historian Rodney Frey, writing of his experience with the Coeur d'Alene, explained some of the functions of the ritualized give-away:

The spirit of the deceased is released. In sharing the gifts of the deceased, the tremendous sorrow associated with an individual death is widely diffused among the many, and not left to be shouldered by a few. And in the sharing of gifts, the kinship ties between the living and dead are remembered and vitalized. Each time a particular piece of clothing is worn, rifle held [...] Something special about the deceased is recalled. His or her memory lives among the living. Gifts are often distributed to individuals who were not necessarily closely related to the deceased, such as friends, or even acquaintances, and "those who have travelled a great distance to help honor the deceased." The circle of the family is thus expanded (2001:248-9).

With the death of a woman, a female relative or close friend of the deceased would be responsible for the redistribution to the attending women. Close friends who had not seen one another for some time, on occasions other than funerals, would exchange gifts upon *greeting* (*t'emčsm*) one another. One might give a particular item of clothing, or even a horse if the giver had two or more horses at the time of meeting. Such relationships continued to be reinforced by the exchange of gifts until one of the friends died. The importance of *interpersonal relationships* (*tm'ew's*) with non-kinspeople was similarly expressed by the special term of

179

lmmštw'é?xʷ, which also defined the exchange of gifts between people who were happy to see one another. Exchanging of gifts could occur at any time, not always during a give-away.

The grieving family was never expected to contribute, prepare, or serve food to attending guests. The entire camp or village would bring a wide variety of fresh and stored foods, often supplemented with fish and fresh deer meat. During the feast, those who had been designated by the chief as *servers* (*sxʷčn'šíš* - "helper") were people seldom related by marriage to the host family, and were appointed as principal speakers during the dinner. Following traditional custom, the feast is prepared and organized, as is the preparation and gifting of food by *non-kinspeople* (*sxʷčn'šíš*) who served the food and later washed the dishes and cooking utensils.

Because of changes in dietary preferences, and the seasonal unavailability of certain traditional foods, it is no longer the practice for only *Indian food* (*sqlixʷs?íƚn*) to be served at the mortuary feast. Nowadays, the selection usually includes foods such as the ubiquitous *fry bread* (*sncaxle?x*), canned fruit, potato salad, cake, juice, and coffee—served first to the elders. Whenever possible, traditional foods are served, but most foods served today are so-called *white man's food* (*swips?íƚn*).

After the traditional mortuary feast, the custom was to equally distribute *any food that had not been eaten* (*sčma?wá?qs*) to guests. Those who had travelled great distances were given additional *goodbye food* (*sxʷls?íƚn*) to help sustain them and to recognize their sacrifice of time and effort in attending. Regardless of when the mortuary feast was held, it always signified a final *farewell meal* (*n?ukʷme?scínm*) to the deceased. Many families today delay this rite of separation until after the headstone has been erected, which could be a year or so later.

During a wake, the public display of grief and respect for the deceased was always a moving and collective sentiment, and yet there is occasionally a solitary but unique expression of one's loss. Though there is no organized syncretic religion on the Spokane Reservation, there is a Nez Perce Seven Drums religion on the Colville Indian Reservation (Walker 1985:18; Walker and Schuster 1998:499), referred to as *wáašat* ("dancers" or "dancing"), "a reference to a characteristic circling and spinning form of worship" (Walker 1963-64, 18:24-25). These men may be invited by a member of the deceased family to participate during the Long-house wake, particularly if the deceased is even nominally Nez Perce in blood degree. During the ceremony, women sit to the right of the casket and the men on the left side. If possible, the casket is normally oriented to the north. Great respect is afforded the seven drummers and the group's leader. In the evening, when the drumming creates an often intense psychodrama, this is reflected by a heightening of the congregation's attention and sense of involvement.

An example occurred years ago, held in a high school auditorium that was not large enough to accommodate all the mourners. An adult son of a deceased but once-important spiritual person and powerful political leader, dramatically displayed the extent of his sorrow during his father's wake. At one point, seven Nez Perce drummers of the Seven Drums Religion (referred to as *énpšlut* or *?ipnú-cililpt'*), commenced a death song while first beating their drums very softly, then gradually intensifying their beating. All the while, the middle age son of the deceased, wearing beaded moccasins, old Levis with a Brahman bull belt-buckle, and neck scarf, gracefully moved his feet in time with the increasing drum beat—all the while bent low as he executed ever-decreasing clockwise concentric circles while he sang his *song* (*nkʷenm'éy'e?*). His *death song* (*λ'ƚq̓ʷelem'*), first heard as a *whisper* (*su?sw'íls*), later became louder—with the drumming—until his voice was an audible *lament for the deceased* (*c'ewplsmist*). Such songs are always sung in Indian. Eventually nearly all the dancers left the floor out of respect, and it soon became apparent to everyone watching this dancer, how in a very subtle yet dramatic fashion he was displaying his sorrow when seeing his *long parted braided hair* (*čq'cq'cpen'e?*) at an obvious angle, giving everyone the distinct impression that the top of his head had been painfully twisted and bent out of shape by his extreme grief, a condition known as *p'i?xus*.

During the dances and testimonials associated with mortuary rites, the participants always turn counterclockwise, a precise movement that metaphorically symbolizes the transition of time as well as leaving one's sorrow behind and a commitment to not turn back on a pledge. Testimonials are of varying length, and usually in Sahaptian, which after delivery the speaker may paraphrase his praise and recognition of the deceased in English. In lieu of a testimonial, an individual mourner may choose to sing any one of the many death songs, eventually being joined by the entire group. These individual unharmonized melodies in free rhythm often commence softly and become dramatic as other participants join in singing. This particular ceremony is usually approximately four hours in length, finishing at midnight.

Burial Areas and Cemeteries.

Despite certain minor linguistic differences and variations in fishing technology within the Spokan, they tended to locate their graves, if possible, in areas of sandy loam riverine terraces. This was borne out by the extensive exhumations of 1388 burials by Collier *et al.* (1942:39) within the region to be impounded by the Columbia River waters after construction of Grand Coulee Dam. "Indians leaders then indicated the discovery" (Petzer 1994:221) of many other burials. Elmendorf sites how the Spokan preferred to dig graves in rock slides, "The majority of burials were found in sandy river banks one and one-half to four feet below the surface, with heads of the deceased oriented downstream. Other preferred sites were most frequently within riverine terraces along the Spokane River, or in often adjoining *loose basalt talus slopes [ipulyn]*" (1935-36, 1:46).

The *grave-diggers* (*sx̣k'ʷƛcl'qam* or *nciql'e?x^wi* - "digging to bury something") were never members of the deceased person's family, but instead were usually friends who volunteered out of respect for the deceased. After being wrapped in deer hide or a blanket, the corpse was deposited within the grave on its side or back, the head oriented predominantly to the west. Several early historical graves were found by Douglas in 1826 (1904, 5:20) with the corpse in an orthograde or seated position.

If a Spokan man died in enemy territory, then the body would be buried not far from the place of his death. In such a situation, a fire was built over the covered grave and the war party would ride their horses back and forth over the grave site to further conceal the burial, which would appear as an innocuous campfire site. This common practice was when "horses trampled earth graves to prevent desecration by the enemy" (O'Neill 1962:13). Teit verified this practice:

> If the burial took place in a strange country no stones or poles were used, and all marks of the burial were obliterated. This is said to have been chiefly so that no enemy might find the grave and desecrate it in any way or take the scalp of a person lately buried. To deceive enemies, horses were ridden and driven back and forth over the grave, as well as over the ground for a considerable distance around; so that it became difficult to tell the exact spot of the burial [...] Another method was to bury in the camp circle [*snq'éytn*] and to light a fire over the grave, so that it had the appearance of one of the ordinary fires of the circle. A number of small camps were also made to deceive enemies. On examining the place people would think a party had rested there for a short time, judging by remains of small fires, cut wood, and tracks (1930:382-383).

Circumstances determined the site location and burial ritual, and yet there is no evidence the Spokan ever used tree or platform burials despite an article that appeared in the *Spokesman-Review* (23 July 1911, Pt. 4:2), showing a photograph and account of two tree burials near *Indian Canyon* (*?uɫx^wétɫk^w*) in present-day Spokane. The anonymous reporter suggested the burials were probably Spokan, but not yet interred, despite the reporter's claim that this was once their prehistoric method of burial. Oral history, along with several early accounts of Spokan burial, do not support the practice of tree or suspended burials. However, Teit maintained that the Flathead and Interior Salish tribes would temporarily place a corpse on a platform or in the branches of a tree while they excavated the grave (1930:346).

Yet, *human bones* (*sqlix^wsc'om'*), when later exposed by animals or erosion, were placed or tied in tree branches by any married person finding them, since a single person would have been too fearful to handle human bones. If several people found human skeletal material, only one person—usually the oldest—would properly bury the bones, after which each person in the group would assiduously conduct a ritual of

181

purification by smoking their hands before building a sweathouse for further purification. Hunters, when they found animal skulls, often placed them on the branches of trees (Teit 1930:174).

"The Spokanes were not given to the practice of tree burials, although their neighbors were" (Ruby and Brown 1982:31). However, a number of such graves were found near the mouth of Okanogan River soon after whites came to this area. Learning of two tree burials in 1911 in Greenwood Cemetery, Ruby and Brown speculated, "They could have been placed there by visiting Nez Percés, who sometimes laid their dead to rest on scaffolds in trees, or they could have been placed there by diehard Spokanes who wished to spare their dead embalming and interment in vaults and caskets" (1982:31).

Teit (1930:346) maintains that the Flathead and "interior Salish tribes" would temporarily place a corpse on a platform or in the branches of a tree while they excavated the grave. More specifically:

> Burial was the method of disposing of the dead among the Interior Salish tribes. The corpse was sewed or tied up in mats, skins, or robes, and placed outside on a scaffold or in the branches of trees until ready for burial. As soon as the people had gathered and a grave had been dug, it was buried in the ground, preferably in sandy knolls, or in the base of a rock slide. In the olden times stones were piled on top of graves (1930:382).

Late historical and contemporary Spokan burials are in either the Catholic or Protestant cemetery in Wellpinit, and less frequently in several small established private family plots, some of which are very old. A comprehensive account of Spokan burial sites is provided by Sprague (1959, 1967, 2006; Sprague and Birkby 1970).

Burial

Immediately upon *death* (*ɫunx̣lltin*), the *corpse* (*tmtmnéy'*) was traditionally removed from the dwelling, sometimes *flexed* (*čɫčɫqinšn*) and sewn in deer hide, or wrapped in a red cedar bark mat or old tule floor mats, and buried without delay (Hale 1846, 4:456; Elmendorf 1935-6,2:46; Sprague 1967). This practice has been replaced by holding a wake, a delayed burial to provided friends and kinspeople the time and opportunity for attending the burial ceremony. A deceased small child or baby was sometimes first placed in a parfleche before being interred. There are *oral accounts* (*sm'em'i?*) from the early historical period of the body remaining in the dwelling for one day before burial, but no specific reasons for such delay were ever stated, apart from accommodating the arrival and gathering of kinspeople. Pickering, however, wrote in 1895 that, "after death burial takes place within hours, and how the corpse was washed, wrapped in skins, with the legs doubled, and then put into a grave three feet deep, which is surrounded and covered with stones and sticks to prevent the wolves getting at it" (Hale 1846, 4:456-7).

Several other minor variations of this ritual have been reported by elders and later anthropologists who maintained the body had to be cold before any burial—the feet and lower extremities becoming cold first, and then spreading up and through the body until reaching the head. What is known about Southern Plateau burial practices suggests that immediate burial was most common, but with the occasional exception when burial was delayed for one or two days, particularly in winter (Curtis 1907-30; Teit 1930; Ray 1933; Mandelbaum 1938).

Prior to any burial, the Spokan followed certain procedures and sacred rituals to ensure that the deceased was actually dead, not in a liminal state or a coma. Aboriginally, and until the early 1950s, the Spokan recognized the services of a *sx̣ʷnwé?n?em* ("one who hollers in one's ear") or *nx̣ʷé?n?em* or *sx̣ʷnqíx̣ʷle?x̣ʷm* ("dead awakener"). There were usually several such individuals within any winter village and often—depending upon population size—within a resource camp. If a person was thought to be dying, or was presumably dead, the family always sought the services of a *sx̣ʷnwé?n?em* who would make a determination. To determine the condition of any unconscious individual, the recognized procedure was for the *sx̣ʷnwé?n?em* to first lay his ear on the presumed deceased or unconscious individual's chest to ascertain the person's condition by listening for any diagnostic *pneumatic 'rattling' sounds* (*cos* or *čɫ?ošx̣ʷálqʷ*). Several elders explained that their grandparents and great-grandparents had been told how with the introduction of metal and glass mirrors, the *sxʷnwéʔnʔem* would sometimes position the device near the person's lips and looked for pneumatic condensation. There are no indications that physical intervention—such as prodding or manipulation—was ever used to determine death or as an attempt to reinstate life. The circumstances leading to a person *dying instantly* (*čsnt'tʼwʼé*) were almost always due to a traumatic event that seldom suggested sorcery.

The main responsibility of the *sxʷnwéʔnʔem* was to determine if an individual was alive or dead by shouting loudly or *hollering* (*čoším*) the name of the deceased in the ear of the presumed dead person. A revival session could last for as long as thirty minutes; after which time—if there was no physical response, then group *consensus* (*cʼx̣ʷɫcʼx̣ʷmʼeʔštwʼéʔx̣ʷ*) declared the individual was dead. Once a person's death had been determined, a period of time commenced when the deceased person's name could not be mentioned, which may have brought the spirit to the living area. Any mention of the person's name could create confusion, even empathy for the wandering ghost, which might then attempt to remain on earth, thereby preventing an immediate transition and incorporation into the hereafter.

Several accounts were told of people who thought they had died, and upon recovering described their *temporary* (*iššeʔ*) experience in which they had travelled to a "life hereafter," which they described as a place like heaven—with a pleasant climate, plentiful clean running water, lush meadows, and woods abundant in game—a place without social strife or sorcerers. Upon recovering from such a liminal experience, the person may explain how s/he heard their name being called: at first only a slight indistinguishable sound, which became more clear and louder until s/he *regained consciousness* (*nčʼeʔʔspʔus*), or until there was no doubt as to his or her identity. Despite the beauty and serenity of the hereafter land, and one's usual reluctance to leave, the *deceased* (*ɫutʼɫíl* or *ɫuλʼlil*) realized his or her familial obligations, and the fact that s/he was being called to *return* (*xʷlxʷílt* - "alive"), which was reinforced as s/he began to focus upon those at the bedside.

People who died by *drowning* (*nλʼllétkʷ* - "die in water"), or who were *struck by lightning* (*sʔuwʼéčnʼt*), were afforded no special ritual or any observed variation of the mortuary ceremony. Despite being excellent swimmers, of these two causes of death, more people invariably died from drowning, which, regardless of age or sex, was believed to be the direct result of a moral transgression against a particular body of water or a water-dwelling spirit.

An example for reasons of drowning was told—really a *pitiful story* (*nqʷnʼqʷnʼáplʼqs*) of a mother who, in the 1890s, continually warned her young son against throwing stones onto the lofted *ice* (*sxʷuyntkʷ*) of the slow-flowing Spokane River. The stones hitting the ice created a loud booming sound, since the water level had receded below the ice cove, thereby creating a resonating chamber. Finally, even the grandmother told the boy that these noises were disturbing and even frightening the water-dwelling spirits who spent the winter sleeping, and that during the spring thaw they would take him away—under water—if he persisted in this wrongful behavior. Regardless of his mother and grandmother's repeated warnings, the boy continued throwing rocks. During the *spring breakup of ice* (*nlóqʼʷqʼʷ*), the boy went beyond the shore, broke through the *thin ice* (*nλletkʷ*), and *drowned* (*ʔu čʼɫcmʼóqʷ* - "the ice gave away under him like an egg shell"). Therefore, village agreed that the boy had been *naughty* (*čeʔčéʔt* or *orpseyé* - "vulgar") in offending the spirits and had been rightfully punished. "*An accidental death of a child may cause the mother to die (nčnʼpečstmntm) from extreme grief*" (STHC).

Burial ceremonies were, if possible, attended by the entire family and resident group and by an officiating shaman who would carefully sweep the grave site with bundled dry rose bushes to clear away any malevolent spirits that might interrupt or prevent the transitional of the deceased person's soul to the life hereafter. Nor was it unusual for the shaman to carefully sweep away with bundled rosehip bushes any noticeable *footprints of the deceased* (*nqlʼwetšnm* - "he made a footprint") that remained in the immediate area, thereby discouraging the soul of the deceased from remaining among the living. It was believed that after a person's burial, the footprints of the deceased that had not been swept away would create small dust devils to indicate his displeasure for the survivors' lack of respect.

The survivors' major objective was to facilitate and hasten the spirit's transition and incorporation in an afterworld. It has been said that in the past a family present at a person's death knew when the breath-spirit left because it sounded like the fluttering and buzzing of a large blue horsefly or a hummingbird. It was critical that the ghost of the deceased should never be offended by improper observance of burial ritual, which was cause to remain to torment offenders.

There were a few accounts that suggested that an inquest would be held if an individual was believed to have died from sorcery, or if such a claim had not been resolved during the group medical inquest before the patient died, or if no one was detected removing a malevolent power from the deceased before burial; assuming the person died from being *sorcerized* (*płaxntm*). Those attending could use this opportunity— through confession—to be healed if their self-proclaimed malady was not too serious.

Another ritual of purification of the grave—discontinued in the early 1960s—was performed by a special shaman called *sxʷnqíxʷleʔxʷm* ("one who gets in empty grave and chases evil away"), and possessed a patrilineally-derived special power who had been called upon by the relatives of the deceased to *purify* (*xʷuqʼʷncut*) the grave before the body was lowered into place. The *sxʷnqíxʷleʔxʷm* would leap into the open grave with a large bundle of dried rosehip branches, thoroughly *sweep and whip the walls of the grave* (*sntmtmnéyʼtn*), always doing this in a circular, clockwise fashion three times (Quintasket, pers. comm.). Upon completion, and not hearing voices or *ominous crying* (*čowowpus*) moaning sounds, or sometimes screaming, the sweeper would dramatically leap without assistance from the grave. Then, he might report to the attending kinspeople of the deceased that initially he heard voices of *deceased kinspeople* (*ʔasnqʷmíp* - "your dead people") who *wailed* (*cʔót*), moaned, and sometimes screamed of their deaths—indicating that their graves had not been properly cleansed, and that those attending—who were at fault for such a violation of protocol—would die prematurely if the open grave was not properly cleansed. In the past, the *cleaning of kinspeople's graves* (*čłxʼkʼʼʷénʔey* - "cleaning over the graves") was a serious and dedicated responsibility. By first jumping in and later out of the grave, the *sxʷnqíxʷlʼeʔxʷm* was also demonstrating his religious power and skill by avoiding touching the walls of the grave with his body, and thereby avoiding becoming contaminated by any residual malevolent forces that might have wandered in from previously improperly prepared graves, or from forces looking for new company and contact with the spirit of the deceased.

Many years ago, the author remarked to the last known *sxʷnqíxʷleʔxʷm* how he must have been an excellent athlete to perform such a *grand jetté* at his age. Upon some reflection he responded that he had rheumatism much of his adult life, and that it was his *suméš* which permitted him to perform such seemingly athletic feats.

The *sxʷnqíxʷleʔxʷm* was a highly respected and gifted man, one who had dramatically demonstrated his powers in many previous mortuary ceremonies and public ritual gatherings. During the mid-winter Medicine Dances, the *sxʷnqíxʷleʔxʷm* was the first to dance, always holding in each hand a long bundle of rosehip branches to *chase away* (*qíxʷ*) any resident evil spirits or forces that had been released by an occasional malicious sorcerer. If the dance area was not properly cleared of malevolent spirits, the participants could later suffer misfortune or become debilitated with illness or disease. Always dancing in a clockwise fashion, the recognized leader would switch the tied rosehip branches in the air and along the ground before his path, always displaying great effort and concern as he carefully switched the corners of the room or ceremonial structure. Even prior to living in lumber dwellings, it was known that *evil spirits* (*sxʷ qíxʷm*) were most likely to dwell in the recesses or corners of a room or ceremonial structure. An appointed shaman, called *sʔec čłλʼuʔλʼuʔsmisti*, was always present at the main entrance to restrict entrance of individuals. The last *sxʷnqíxʷleʔxʷm* to assist the Spokan was Charlie Quintasket, a most knowledgeable and gentle Lakes Indian, a WWII veteran who fought on the infamous Kokoda Trail.

In the past, a *sxʷnqixʷl'e?xʷm* would gift this unique *sumés* to his oldest son, who had demonstrated a sensitivity and ability to assume such an important communal role. However, if the first son, or any of his successive sons, did not want such a responsibility, the *sxʷnqíxʷle?xʷm* could pass on his knowledge to someone outside the family, serving as a mentor to anyone he thought deserving—invariably a younger man who was a shaman.

During the ceremony of interring, which took place just after dawn or late in the day, both men and women would express grief in different ways—the woman often by *wailing* (*snixʷpéls*) and high pitch *keening* (*q'xtsqelixʷ*) after the grave had been respectfully filled in with earth by those attending. As in the past, people would frequently say a few words of respect and farewell to the deceased as they placed a handful of earth on the body or coffin.

Caution was observed where an already *open grave* (*nt'ipúle?xʷ*) was left unattended, since there was universal agreement that if a person—usually someone not familiar with the situation should accidentally fall into the grave, their spirit would remain in the grave, and they would eventually die of spirit loss (STHC). There are no remembered accounts of this happening, because traditionally a grave was excavated on the day of burial and filled before the mourners departed. Benedict, using the Flathead Group as an example, described the belief "that the soul of the living may fall into a new-dug grave" (1923:110 fn.).

The most lengthy description of burial practices and mortuary rituals was fortunately observed and recorded by Curtis, whose accounts of the Spokan, Sanpoil-Nespelem, and Kalispel are important ethnographic contributions regarding certain behaviors associated with funeral feasting, ceremonial leadership, and the sacrificing of the deceased person's horse:

> A corpse was deposited in a grave just large enough to receive it, or was laid at the foot of the hills and covered with stones, the place being marked with poles. When anyone died, the chief announced the fact to the camp and directed that all preserve quiet and remain as much as possible within their lodges until the burial had taken place. The relations and friends assembled in the [main] lodge, wailing, and one of the same sex as the deceased was chosen to prepare the corpse for burial. After he had washed the body from head to foot, and painted the face red, it was raised and made to assume a life-like appearance, while the relatives and friends bore, as tokens of affection, usually some articles of their own personal apparel. In as many of these articles as could be used the body was then dressed, and a blanket spread over it. Thus it was carried to the grave by the chief and some assistants, and the interred reclining on the back with the head to the east. The gifts not already used in clothing the body were placed in the grave with it. Horses were sometimes killed at the grave and skinned, the hide being hung on a near-by tree and the meat left lying on the ground. It was not believed that the spirits of the horses accompanied the soul, for there was no definite conception of the future world, but the animals were killed as a mark of respect for the dead: he had liked them, hence no one else must use them. When a woman was buried, the thatching [tule mats] of the lodge was rolled up and tied in a tree near the grave (1911, 7:76).

David Douglas presented a detailed description of an Upper Spokan burial site that explained the offerings and makings of a grave in 1826. Also, significant are his posited ethnological interpretations:

> Near this spot was an Indian burying ground, certainly one of the most curious I had yet seen. All the property of the deceased was here deposited near their graves, their implements, garments, and gambling articles. Even the favourite horse of the deceased is not spared; it is customary to shoot the animal with a bow and arrow, and suspend his skin, with the hoofs and skull, just above the remains of the master. On the trees, which are around the burying place, small bundles may be seen, tied up in the same manner as the provisions, which they carry when traveling. I could not learn whether this was intended as food for the dead or propitiative offerings to the divinities. Within the grave the body is placed in a sitting posture, with the knees touching the chin, and the arms folded across the chest. It is difficult to gain any information on these people on these subjects, as nothing seems to hurt the feelings of these people as much as alluding to their departed friends (1904, 4:339).

Isaac Stevens, a person who was responsible for establishing several regional *Indian reservations* (*sqlixʷúle?xʷ*), made the following observation in 1853 while traveling through Spokan territory:

> In view of this camp [*se-clue-eel-qua*] [near a small lake on the Spokane Plain] were the graves of a number of Spokane Indian position by the stone designated to protect the bodies from the wolves, and by poles supported

in an upright position by the stones. It was the usage, until within a few years past, for the Spokanes [sic], and other northern tribes toward the Pacific to slay horses and cattle of the deceased at his grave, and also to sacrifice his other property; but they are gradually relinquishing this pernicious practice, under the influence of the counsels and example of the white man (1855, 1:150).

Following the interment of a parent, and before filling the *grave* (*člplsten'e?ntm*) with earth or rocks, a *ceremony* (*čłx*ʷ*cx*ʷ*écn'e?stm*) was conducted by two men, one on either side of the open grave, who would pass between them three times any *young children* (*sk'*ʷ*uk'*ʷ*iml't*) of the deceased. In the past, even a *small baby* (*?o?x*ʷ*téit* or *q*ʷ*o?ywtelc*) was similarly passed over the deceased, particularly if the deceased was a parent or grandparent. This was a prophylactic ritual to prevent the child from having *nightmares* (*č'sč'sqey's* or *č'sč'ss?itš*) or experiencing excessive grief or anxiety, and so the small child would forget the actual death of the deceased family member, but would remember the deceased in a favorable way. Not to pass young children over the casket of a deceased person was considered disrespectful to the deceased, and may even cause the young child to become sick. Or, the young child would die if the older sibling had not been passed over the casket or grave of a *deceased relative* (*?es?óq'*ʷ*?ey* or *čx*ʷ*ecti*). In addition to this aforementioned prophylactic ritual, it was believed that failure to do so was an accepted explanation for the oldest family member to be *ghosted* (*c'el'čtm'n'tm* or *k'*ʷ*usč?em* - "it ghosted him") (STHC). This practice is still followed by some Spokan when burial is on the reservation.

> After the burial the people returned to the lodge, and the chief brought food, calling out, "We will waste our food for the dead person!" It was divided among the old people, who took it to their respective lodges. He then commanded all to paint their faces for four days, nor to permit children to play noisily. In earlier times men and women in mourning cut the hair at the level of the ears and refrained from painting their faces until the hair had grown to its normal length. Men also docked the tails of their horses. Mourners frequently went alone into the mountains to fast and weep. The practice of giving away all of one's possession when a close relative died was sometimes observed, and on such an occasion a woman also "threw away her name" (Curtis 1907-30, 7:76).

After the interment ceremony, the men and women divided into small separate groups and respectfully exchanged local news and from afar. It was not unusual to hear someone acknowledge a person's eulogy, commenting on how pleased the soul/spirit in transition must be to have been so well remembered and honored. Family members and other close friends often thanked and appropriately made remarks that recognized a speaker's feelings and skill in speaking so well and for kindly holding in his "hands" the grief and feelings of those attending. "Our history is only in the words and memories of the living."

Grave Goods

An important part of the burial ceremony was placing the deceased *shaman's medicine bag* (*s?elk'*ʷ*lscút* - "with his body"). However, if the shaman had given up his power before death, his bundle would not necessarily be placed with him. No longer practiced was the once traditional custom of prior to interment, the exposed corpse was carefully guarded throughout the night against a sorcerer from surreptitiously removing the sacred buckskin neck or hand bag, which could disrupt or even prevent incorporation of the individual's breath spirit in the life hereafter. Strict vigilance was also maintained so the retrieval of a power-charged object, one that was responsible for the demise of the individual by the sorcerer, might be observed and charges made against the evil-doer. If the deceased were a shaman, all of the man's paraphernalia would be buried with him to prevent their theft and ultimate malicious use (STHC), particularly if the deceased was a suspected sorcerer. Johnson remarked how upon death, "The Spokanes require all garments, etc., about the death-bed to be buried with the body, hence few comforts for the sick" (Wilkes 1845, 4:456).

Although rarely substantiated by archaeologists, there existed, certainly within the early historical period, a traditional ceremony in which a close *sweathouse friend* (*nλ'áce?*), usually a non-kinsman with whom the deceased enjoyed an intense joking relationship, would be charged with the responsibility of preparing a *death journey bag* or *buckskin bundle* (*č'łt'uk'*ʷ*wč'ép*) that was placed beneath the neck of the deceased man.

186

Making such a bundle was an obligation usually fulfilled by the man who had taken his friend's *death confession* (*n'mípmist*). The bundle contained special items and medicinal plants (usually *x̣ásax̣*) for use by the deceased in the afterlife, items that were probably in some instances traditional grave goods, and were replaced in the historic period by representative contemporary counterparts. The use of grave goods suggests utilization during an afterlife by the deceased, for as Caywood described the contents of an historical Spokan grave that "was rich in burial goods: copper kettle, three flintlocks, a mirror in a wooden case, numerous dentalia and blue glass beads, a bear tooth, a miniature bow, two bows, stone pipe fragments, brass butt plate, and a birch bark box with three bone tubes" (1954:30-31).

For example, a .45-70 shell in lieu of a projective point and a small steel knife—not a lithic example. Within this small and often undecorated buckskin bag would be three items that were symbolic of one's needs after death. In another personally-witnessed situation, the *dying man* (*šels-ƛ'lil*) requested that a .32-20 bullet, a small nodule of ochre, and a red-tailed hawk's three large tail feathers be placed in the bag—items thought to be necessary in the afterlife. Within the archaeological record, there appears to be only one citation for this practice of interment with a neck bag, when Caywood found that "directly beneath the skull was what appeared to have been a bag decorated with dentalia and blue glass beads" (1954:30).

The giver would make the special gift bundle at the time of the receiver's death, purifying it by taking the bundle into the sweathouse three different but consecutive sessions. During the first sweat, the man would open the bundle and lay it on a nest of white sage, while physically and spiritually purifying himself by placing small bits of dried *x̣ásx̣a* on the heated stones. The second sweating session was devoted to praying over the bundle as it was 'smoked' by passing it back and forth three times over the replaced hot stones after being *sprinkled* (*łil*) with dried *x̣ásx̣s*. During the third and always solitary sweat, the bundle was carefully wrapped and closed with a buckskin thong. The final act of purification was when the friend sang his personal *special power song* (*nƛ'e?kʷlšscútn*) over the bundle. Before burial, the maker would place the death journey bag under the neck of the deceased, or in some instances on the waist of the deceased. There was no recollection of this ritual being done for a woman, for presumably the rationale was that a woman's grave-side digging stick was sufficient for her travail in an afterlife.

As cited, there is no agreement, either among contemporary Indians or among anthropologists, on whether the Spokan believed in an afterlife. Unfortunately the following quote from Elmendorf's Spokan-Lakes field notes does not resolve the issue, and mentions only that the grave goods were the deceased's "our little belongings"—nothing of a utilitarian nature that might suggest a future use:

> When a man died—they put on his best clothes—take him out among [the] rocks and dig a little hole—[they] put a blanket in and put the [deceased] in—some times in a crouching position, sometimes lying stretched out—[they] pile the rocks over them & erect a memorial pole over the grave—the Nespelem killed a horse on a man's grave—before they laid the corpse in they put grass in and then a blanket—never swept it [grave] out—[person's] own little belongings were put in with him but nothing else—no particular time for burial—no special medicine man—never asked one to come—one can go if they want to—man's property divided among his family—parents—brothers—sisters equally—if he had a wife & children [the] property went to them (1935-36, 2:7).

Personal possessions (*tem'tn'*), such as weapons, implements for hunting and fishing, and articles of sacred significance were on occasion placed with the corpse—again, suggesting future usage. What may have been one or more prized belongings could also be funerary offerings (Caywood 1954; Combs 1964: Ross 1993). During the late historical period, and until the late 1940s, it was not unusual for a widow to conceal from her family certain trade-acquired goods, such as rifles by burying them to prevent conflict of ownership by her sons during the ceremony of redistribution.

A dying person, if possible, could attempt to avoid or at least reduce conflicting claims of property within a kingroup by stating to a close friend his wishes to whom his belongings should be *distributed* (*px̣ʷmstés* - "he passed it out"). The person selected was invariably not a kinsperson, and consequently not obligated by any demands of kinship. Other belongings of the deceased that were not to be destroyed or distributed, were often designated as grave goods by the principal survivors.

Ruby and Brown, citing the works of Hale (1846) and Curtis (1911, 7:30), wrote about burials during the time of *epidemics* [*č'łq*ʷ*mptín* - "that killed many"], and that many funeral customs must have gone unobserved in that time of sudden mass death (1982:29-30):

> Many funeral customs must have gone unobserved in that time of sudden mass death. Normally, the deceased would have distributed their possessions before death had they an indication that they might die. Sometimes their possessions were distributed after their burial during celebrations in their honor, in the donation feasts or potlatches. Even after white contact, until the state laws forced on Indians, their possessions were handed down through no regular descent pattern and without benefit of anything resembling a will. Wives designated the recipients of their deceased husbands' properties, knowing that certain items were cherished by others. Sometimes friends and relatives stole the deceased's property, usually horses. In later days, speakers at feasts lamented the dead, a practice of native origin reinforced by the Christian practice of eulogizing at funerals. After feasting and celebrating, no one mentioned the names of the deceased, for to have done so would have brought their spirits close by. Even wives on these occasions changed their names (1982:29-30).

Cox trapped along the Upper Columbia from 1812 to 1821, and in writing of Spokan burial practices and grave goods, observed:

> When a man dies, several horses are killed, and the skins are attached to the end of long poles, which are planted in the graves: the number of horses sacrificed is proportioned to the wealth of the individual. Besides the horse-skins, buffalo and deer robes, leather shirts, blankets, pieces of blue, green, and scarlet cloth, strips of calico, moccasins, provisions, warlike weapons, &c., are placed in and about the cemetery; all of which they imagine will be more or less necessary for the deceased in the world of spirits (1831:105).

In his discussion of grave goods and markers, Cox was presumably speaking of the Chewelah-Spokan Group in a much later variation of his aforementioned quote:

> When a man died, several horses were killed and the skins, attached to long poles, were planted on the graves. Besides this tribute, buffalo hides and deer robes, leather goods, food weapons for warfare were placed in & about the cemetary [sic]. It was thought that all this would be necessary for the dead man in the world of spirits (Dryden 1949:44).

There is no evidence that dogs were killed for an owner's burial. Until recently, however, there was disagreement whether the Spokan ever killed horses for an owner's interment, some stating how valuable horses were to facilitate load-caring and for traveling to the Plains. Elmendorf (1935-6, 2:46) also states the Spokan never killed a horse to be placed on the grave of its owner. But some elders described the custom of *killing a man's favorite horse over his grave* (*hesčłplsténʔem t x̣łcíys* - "his horse is killed over him") (STHC). It should, however, be noted that this occasional practice was also mentioned by Elmendorf's oldest non-English-speaking Spokan informants, who recounted how the practice of killing the horses of a deceased man may have been adopted from a Nez Perce burial, located near Little Falls where a stone cache still remains (Ross 1993):

> [...] killed horses around a man's grave, but the Spokane [informant] remembers a Nez Perce's grave a little way from [Little Falls ...] This man died and his people buried him on a sidehill stretched out with a post at his head & feet and a cross bar over which was hung the hide of the horse—called "his horse [hide] is hung over him - immediate relatives take the deceased's possessions and give them away" (Elmendorf 1935-6, 2:46).

Another example of Spokan grave goods and body position of the deceased was cited in the *Spokane Chronicle* after a grave had been uncovered by road construction near the mouth of the Little Spokane River:

> The Indian was buried near an old salmon fishing pool of the Indians near an old blockhouse, which is now under the surface of the river. This was an old Indian rendezvous and landmark. The Indian was buried in a sitting position with his knees under the chin [...] The skull of the skeleton has been crushed in and from the appearance of the wound it had been inflicted by a stone ax or some similar instrument. Within the kettle was the head of an Indian wrapped in buffalo skin. The copper was so old it had turned to copper carbonate. The skull, a part of the

scalp and the buffalo skin, which had served as a preservative, had absorbed this chemical compound. A buckskin shirt was also within the kettle (Anon. 1922:4).

Post-Burial Purification

The last collective formalized expression by participants attending the burial ceremony was to conduct a special purification sweating ritual with separation of the sexes, to cleanse themselves of any physical or spiritual contamination that may have occurred during the burial ceremony. During the cleansing sweat, participants vigorously scrubbed their bodies with the upper side of young fir boughs, which also covered the floor of the sweathouse. This patulous covering that was replaced weekly. The water for the hot stones was a mixture made by boiling small sections of branches of rosehip, fir bough, and cedar. Those men who had dug the grave and attended to the deceased would conduct a compulsory cleansing sweat, and afterward their clothing would be burned, along with any wooden grave-digging tools that may have been used. Again, these behaviors demonstrated the fear of contamination that existed as well as a clear concern for the living and any possible, sometimes even inevitable, repercussions if they committed any transgressions that would have attracted unfavorable attention by the deceased's spirit.

Even after a kinsperson's *death* (*łu nλ'lltín*), spiritual *contamination* (*q'éw'ntm* - "he was sorcerized") remained a concern, thereby necessitating the use of dried rose hips, which among the Plateau tribes was universally associated with medicines, death, and purification (Teit 1930; Cline 1938; Mandelbaum 1938). After a person died—particularly one who had been unhappy or grieving prior to death, they could return as a ghost to haunt the survivors' kinspeople or anyone else in the area. The ghost could also return if his or her memory or reputation had been slighted during the mortuary ritual, or if the ceremony had been somehow improperly conducted, or if personal possessions of the ghost remained in the dwelling. For this reason, it has been assumed that a dwelling was often deserted or even destroyed by fire. Even if the person died in a temporary structure, it would be burned after the funeral—a practice of the Chewelah-Spokan Group (Smith 1936-8:508). It is personally known that sweathouses thought to be contaminated for any one of several reasons, were burned. It should be noted that once the Spokan commenced to utilize dwellings of logs, and later lumber, the burning of structures was rarely practiced.

Although this is conjectural, the destruction of a multi-family winter pit house after the death of an occupant would indeed have been a dramatic indiscretion, one with particularly devastating consequences. Destroying a dwelling was certainly not the practice after carpenter-built allotment houses were constructed (1904-07). In some instances, they were temporarily deserted by survivors of the deceased, but apparently never purposely burned.

It is not known if the Spokan, after removing a corpse, disassembled movable structures, such as mat or hide tipis. It is more reasonable to assume that rather than permanently deserting or burning the structure, the survivors of the deceased followed the traditional custom of arranging for a *sxʷnqíxʷleʔxʷm* to sweep the inside of the dwelling with rosehip bushes before sprinkling the walls and floor surfaces, as well as house possessions, including food containers with a solution of rosewater, as has been personally observed with recent post-burial purifications when a person died within his home. Whipping the walls with rosehip branches and washing the walls was also believed to prevent the deceased from returning as a ghost, and traditionally was accomplished by a shaman—known as a *sxʷqíxʷm* or *λ'ak'ʷílš*—who had the power to cleanse an area of ghosts or malevolent forces.

Further precautions were taken by using a rosehip solution to thoroughly cleanse the weapons and tools of the deceased before they were distributed in a give-away. Such precautions were taken to protect the new owner from any designs that the deceased might have placed upon his former possessions. A widow or widower might seek further protection from the *ghost* (*k'ʷsk'ʷsxč'aʔsqé*) of a deceased spouse by hanging an eagle feather over the bed while sleeping to provide protection. The feather served to warn of a ghost's presence by whirling and produce a warning sound.

Grave Markers and Headstones

The earliest ethnographically significant account of a Spokan burial area, one located at Spokan House, was provided by Work, who first described an encampment of both round and oblong tule mat houses covered with mats made of rushes:

> There is also an Indian burying ground here, the graves are generally marked with a few poles and boards rudely ornamented with some red paint or ochre, the trees are loaded with the skin of horses which have been sacrificed to the masses of the dead, buffalo robes, shirts, pieces of flannel, calico, &c. With kettles, and other utensils are also hung up as offerings to the spirits of the departed. The kettles and other vessels have generally a hole in their bottom and a pole drawn through it, as if the dead did not require them to be whole or to prevent the needy living from stealing them (1823:24-5).

Upon completion of a burial, the grave would be quickly covered to keep out any malevolent spirits and marked with one or several split cedar stakes placed vertically at the head as grave markers, that were once covered with pine pitch. Howard T. Ball, a Spokane funeral director responsible for the re-interment of Spokan burials of the 1939 pre-Grand Coulee Dam construction (Ball 1941:35-8; Gibby and Ball 1997:54) wrote, "All together, 1388 graves were removed and carefully put into four new cemeteries above rising water." Ball further noted that, "at the head of every soil inhumation there was, without exception, a cedar stake probably until the historical period" (Sprague 1967:123). Ball also said that another 10,000 were "lined up to excavate when shut down by the Corps (sic)" (Sprague 1967:123). Burial sites within the confines of Spokan village and camp territory tended to be indicated by a number of means, such as cedar cysts marked off with a stone ring (Collier, Hudson, and Ford 1942:39). Stevens mentioned how there were "stone mounds over Spokane graves," and the use of vertical sticks as grave markers (1855, 12, Part 1:150).

Some individuals had their *rock graves* (*c'l'púle?x^wtn*) marked with stone piles of varying size, or by placing vertically a long section of lodge pole used to carry him to his grave, and often with a *stick covered with pitch* (*čšt'en'e?tn*), but no reason could be given (STHC), except the pitch knowingly presumably helped keep scavenging animals away from the grave. Shallow grave sites were also covered with piled rocks or short stakes as markers for protection from scavenging animals. The use of *stone cairns* (*pk^wpk^wu?súle?x^w*) as markers for Spokan graves was observed by Stevens (1855 1:400), Hazard Stevens (1900:150), and Teit (1930), who explained that among interior Salish groups, the pole used to transport the body to the burial area was often placed upright as a grave marker. Elmendorf's (1935-6, 1:74 and 2I:46) informants stated that during the late1800s, the Spokan used a *single pole* (*čšt'éne?tn*) or *multiple poles* (*čc'léne?tn*) to mark the grave, and that during the early 1900s a cloth was sometimes tied to the top of the pole as a *grave marker* (*čc'l'én'e?tn*). Elmendorf (1935-6, 2:6) termed this a memorial pole. Teit also provided a description of how the pole used to carry a body to the grave was, "Sometimes also one or more small poles in form of a tripod were erected to mark the spot. Offerings were tied to these poles" (1930:382). As previously mentioned, some burial markers were marked with *pitch* (*sλ'λ'úk'^we?*). This method was used sometimes for marking a man's grave, but apparently not a woman's. On some of the river terraces there are several prehistoric gravesites which have been encircled with grapefruit size rocks, clearly identify their location (Ross 1993a).

Burials were located most commonly within talus slopes and marked in various ways depending upon whether the grave was of a man or a woman. In the case of a woman, one or two of her digging sticks marked the grave; one was always at the head of the burial. Some graves have been found with a digging stick accompanying the woman's body within the burial, or a small digging stick on or in a girl's grave site (Ross 1993).

Sprague (pers. comm.) explained how the practice of using coffins was introduced to the Spokan between 1853 and 1879, citing Guy Haines (1879), the Indian Agent at Fort Colville, who wrote of the Lower

190

Spokan requesting "lumber, nails, cotton for shroud, etc." for a burial. Whether one can conclude the use of coffins was encouraged by missionaries is unknown, but seems quite probable as Williams (1922:110) stated that graves were "decorated with horse hides, cloth blankets, etc, a custom which disappeared with the teachings of the missionaries." A further account of the use of coffins was recorded in The Morning Herald (1887), a Spokane newspaper, "A couple of Indians were seen yesterday moving down toward Latah Creek with a large sized coffin swung on a pole between them. The box was for Indian George, who was killed in a row the night before."

Gibbs (1855, 1:405) also noted the existence of traditional burial practices in 1853 when he wrote of Spokan interment, "but without any attempts at *coffins* (nt'k'ʷmín), the body was merely wrapped in its clothing." Elmendorf (1935-6, 2:74) recorded how the "deceased was always attired in his or her finest clothing, wrapped in a robe, and placed in a crouching position with all their immediate possessions." While on the Wilkes Expedition, Pickering noted "the graves being marked by a heap of stones surrounding an upright post" (1895:24).

There are reported instances of artifacts having been placed immediately atop the burial, and thought by some to be grave goods. In the case of earth exhumations, there probably were artifacts from adjacent living sites. Such incidents can be confusing, making interpretation difficult. Partially burned osteological material has been discovered in some burials; but there is no archaeological or ethnographic evidence that suggests the Spokan ever practiced cremation. It has been posited that grave goods may have on occasion been burned (Sprague, pers. comm.).

Caywood conducted excavations of historical burials at Fort Spokane in the early 1950s, and found grave goods in many of the graves, noting one burial with "the fragment of a pair of spectacles, the remains of an iron cup or mug, and three metal buttons. A few fragments of cloth were indistinguishable which probably were the remains of a coat on which buttons had been fastened" (1954:23). The same archaeologist (1954:32) also cited an interesting array of grave goods excavated in the same area, which:

> [...] included a glass mirror [sʕac'xsn'cútn or šuxnweʔnʔem] in a wooden case, several strands of dentalia and blue glass beads, a birch bark box containing three bone tubes, a bear tooth with three round drill marks, a small article made of wood which resembled a miniature bow 4¼ inches long, a fragment of finely worked stone pipe, and a brass butt plate of a trade musket which had been straightened. Two very finely decorated short bows found between the knees.

Foote recorded how, after the arrival of Euro-Americans, the Spokan—like their neighbors the Chewelah and Coeur d'Alene—altered their practices:

> With the advent of the white man, some Spokanes, like their close neighbors the Chewelah and Coeur d'Alene, began covering their dead with small logs and later, frame houses capped by flags, pennants, and sometimes timber crosses. These structures occasionally covered five or six bodies. The Spokanes seem to have built such burial shelters to cover the dead before they built them to cover the living (Ruby and Brown 1982:31).

Burnett recalled in the *Spokesman-Review* of a large burial area:

> [...] about an acre in extent. The graves were enclosed by fences made of pole or small logs laid out in the manner of the walls of a log house. It had the appearance of an old graveyard. Most of these log fences surrounding the graves were old and most of the graves were sunken. I think that there were from 75 to 100 enclosed graves we tore down these log enclosures, hauled the logs away and cultivated the grounds (Lewis 1925:15).

Mourning

Often the parents of the deceased established the duration of mourning for a widow or widower. In-laws usually determined the length of mourning for a grieving daughter-in-law. In some instances, close relatives of the deceased spouse recognized a long period of mourning; sometimes for as long as four years, when the widow and her children were economically assisted by her kinspeople, particularly if she and her husband had lived matrilocally.

Upon the death of her husband, the widow might demonstrate her grief publicly by *wailing* (*hescʕʼʷóti*), *sobbing* (*čawawpús* - "tears on the face" or *nyixʷyxʷéls* - "to sob"), and even *crying out loudly* (*cʼqʷáqʷ*). Her *sorrow* (*snixʷpéls*) is sometimes termed a *death wail* (*scʕʼʷót*).

Many years ago, it was said (Elmendorf, pers. comm.) that the widow privately performed self-mutilation on her *flesh* (*sqeltč* - "meat, body") by using an obsidian utility knife or quartzite skinning knife to painfully lacerate and gouge herself. These wounds were never shown publicly. A grieved (*cʔótm* - "to mourn the dead") widow was often closely watched by her mother or mother's sisters to prevent the widow from excessively lacerating her thighs or her torso.

In extreme grief, a widow might perform self-mutilation on her *flesh* (*sqeltč* - "meat, body") using a large sharp obsidian flake, quartzite skinning knife, or later with a steel knife (Elmendorf, pers. comm.). She could lacerate her arms as a public display of grief, and even mutilate her thighs, though these latter marks were never made public. Lacerations of the arms were not obvious because of the long sleeve mourning garment she wore. Since lacerating with obsidian caused little pain, the procedure could, however, result in excessive bleeding if openings were near or on an artery or large vein. A newly grieved (*cʔótm* - "to mourn the dead") widow was often closely observed by her mother or *mother's sisters* (*čičíyʼeʔ*) to prevent the widow from excessively lacerating herself.

All widows disfigured themselves by cutting off all their long-braided hair so that only ragged remnants remained (STHC). These were carefully gathered and burned by a female relative, to prevent any malevolent use by a sorcerer (Teit 1930:174).

In the past, a widow, upon the death of her husband, would rub her entire dress with charcoal, all the while softly chanting repetitious sounds to indicate her grief. But there was no memory of a woman blackening her face or hands, nor of women in mourning ever lacerating their faces (Elmendorf 1935-36, 4:4).

Prior to reservation settlement, a widow might wonder off into the surrounding hills by herself, sometimes prior to the actual burial, further mortifying her flesh, all the while wailing and periodically shouting her grief. This *unkempt appearance* (*nʼɬátmʼilʼáʔst*) was also dramatized by not washing during her period of bereavement. A *widow* (*sɬwélmt* or *sčɬelp* or *ncʼliškʷeʔ*) wore the same attire throughout the period of mourning—one year (Wilkes 1845,4:457). A widow's deliberate unattractiveness and lack of self-grooming served as a catharsis as well as physically emphasizing her grief, asocial state, and lamenting her loss. There have been several noted instances in which a *widow* (*sɬwéllmt*) continued to wear her "weeds" until she died (Quintasket, pers. comm.).

A widow who had *inconsolable grief* (*nčʼtʼpmí* or *nixʷpélsi* - "lonesome for the deceased") might eventually *die from a broken heart* (*ʔumsčyʼeʔ*). The parents of a deceased son or daughter might express their deep sorrow—as could the surviving widow or *widower* (*syuwʼélʼinʼ* or *sɬxʷélmʼt*)—by lying crossways upon their tule bedding mat with their backs to the entryway; an indication they wanted their solitude (Elmendorf 1935-36, 3:63).

Mourners were careful to never express themselves in a frivolous fashion, always conducting their personal lives in a *somber manner* (*ninčʔéy*) while honoring their memory of a *dead relative* (*ninčeʔ*) in speech, dress, and behavior. For example, a man who war danced too soon after his brother's death might be accused of violating a *mortuary taboo* (*ninčʔem*). Also, the behavior of the immediate family was restricted and carefully monitored by the community. A recently deceased person's ghost might return if he had not been happy in their marriage, or if he had not completed an important task, or had hidden something of value that his family might find for his give-away ceremony (STHC).

A common cause for a recent widow or widower to experience frightening dreams was that the person had either thought poorly of the deceased husband or wife, or the survivor was prematurely contemplating an inappropriate relationship before the end of the prescribed mourning period. It was during such a prophetic dream that the deceased could warn the living of dire consequences if the widow or widower persisted in not recognizing his or her obligations of thought and behavior. If they heard an owl at night or coyote during the day, a friend or family member might die the next morning (Ross 1983c).

Upon the death of a spouse, the widow or widower would sometimes be visited by an *apparition* (*sčíccn* - "visitor") of the deceased—one that may or may not speak; but regardless it would be discomforting if not frightening. Various explanations for this were given by an attending shaman. A frequent explanation was that the collected hair of the deceased man or woman had not been properly disposed of before death, and therefore the dwelling would be thoroughly searched. When found, the ball of hair was carefully burned outside, away from the dwelling, so that no one was contaminated by the smoke. After the death of a kinsperson, the adult survivors would drink a mild tea made from the fresh leaves of *rabbit brush* (*Chrysothamnus nauseosus* [Pall.] Britt. - *k'ʷeík'ʷeík'ín*) to prevent apparitions of the deceased. After a man's wife died, he moved with his bedding to the men's end of the dwelling (Elmendorf, 1935-6, 3:6).

During a one- to two-year period of mourning, the widow or widower never mentioned the deceased person's name to prevent dreaming of the person. Otherwise, the violated spirit of the deceased might be encouraged to *return* (*xʷlxʷílt* - "alive") and disrupt the survivor's mourning period. Occasionally a widow's husband's spirit would appear in a *dream* (*sqey's* or *snspsúpps*), in person, or in the voice of an animal—usually a rodent to warn the woman of impending danger to her family. The spirit of a deceased husband or wife could appear when the surviving spouse was alone in a sweathouse, usually to advise or warn the person of matters that could be avoided or *resolved*. Immediate *dead relatives* (*ʔa snqʷmip*), or those *long deceased relatives* (*ši ʔš ʔi ʔt*), could appear in the dreams of a widow or widower for reasons of concern for the survivor. It was common that after one to two years when the living would cease to have spiritual contact with a *deceased kinsperson* (*nƛ'lil*), but would continue to dream of a deceased spouse.

The grieving woman was always properly addressed by the resident group and visitors as widow until the end of her mourning period. The mourning period for a widower was sometimes less restrictive in time and behavior, and was often terminated by choice. Nevertheless, there was always a period of time that was considered respectful to his dead wife's kinspeople.

Widows and Widowers

The transition from mourning to resuming a more normal life was often clearly delineated by not only different social behavior, but certainly when either the widow or widower had 'put away their weeds'. "Widows are not allowed to change their dress for a whole year" (Hale 1846, 4:457). At the termination of mourning, the woman was reincorporated back onto her village, and would assume her new status by *decorating herself* (*nc'l'iáškʷe ʔ* or *nt'slíckʷ* - "dressed up again") and wearing *new buckskin clothing* (*sp'y'álqs* or *sip'iálqs*)—always a recently made long buckskin dress. Such an occasion was a joyous event, often recognized by a communal feast given by her family and relatives of her deceased husband—indicating that she was again *eligible for marriage* (*ʔecnc'liškʷš ʔey*) (Elmendorf 1935-36, 3:20, 4:3). As noted, the time of mourning for a widower was less in duration and was, reasonably, contingent upon various economic and social responsibilities.

When a widow or widower married too soon after a spouse's death, dire events might ensue because this demonstrated disrespect not only to the *dead spouse* (*hi spu ʔlíl*), but also to the family of the deceased

193

(Elmendorf 1935-36, 1:16-17). There was still remembered an account of a woman being ghosted while picking berries many years ago, just north of Wellpinit:

> The young woman had married a widower who hadn't observed the prescribed time of his mourning period for his recently deceased wife. One late summer day his young wife was out away from the camp trying to locate huckleberries, and before her appeared a woman with a burden basket laden with huckleberries. At first glance the new wife noticed the older woman beckoning over her shoulder for her to follow, which she did for a long distance. After several hours, the older woman turned around and showed who she really was. It was her husband's dead wife. At first light the next day, her husband and others in the berrying-camp searched for the new, young wife, and when finally finding her, she was able to tell them what had happened. After suffering a slow and painful ghost illness, she finally died (Ross 1968-2008).

All elders agreed that the period of mourning was of considerable benefit to not only the survivor, but also for the family of the deceased. It was time when important social and economic decisions could be made with reason and to the benefit of both families. Additionally, a survivor's temperance and restraint was an important public display of respect for the deceased, the family of the deceased, and the widower or widow's communal reputation. It was said that, "One who mourned well was respected and honored by her immediate family and kin group."

After a prescribed period of grieving, a deceased man's close friend would visit the widow at her home, a custom called *nc'llelpntm*, and if necessary to perform tasks and help instruct her sons in necessary hunting skills. In time he might marry the widow or take her as a second wife, if he was already married. These preferred forms of marriage were conducive to maintaining necessary socioeconomic responsibilities between newly established kin groups, as well as ensuring continuing support for any children or grandchildren.

A further responsibility of friends and kinspeople of the grieving family was to provide protection for the survivors from malevolent creatures and forces:

> After my husband died, I was told by a friend of mine that she had a dream after the funeral that something bad was going to happen to me in the house—in my bedroom. So my daughter and me put up fresh rosehip bundles in each corner and hung a brand new eagle feather over my bed. But then my old friend told me to spray the room with white man's cleaner, so I sprayed the walls and furniture with Raid. It all worked, because nothing bad has happened (Ross 1968-2008).

It is sometimes still apparent at funerals that some widows tend to sit together—often along the two side rows of chairs, and quickly identified by their head scarves. A further expression of consciousness of kind was also apparent with widows who were not expected to marry again. This independent and often of a symbiotic relationship was reinforced by widows sharing the same sweathouse and forming small congenial task-groups when berry-picking, root-digging, and even sharing the same structure for smoking hides. It was said that such a group would readily adopt a widow, but more likely if she were a kinsperson. Each elderly woman was responsible for her own domestic maintenance, but periodically accepted assistance from younger women. Some single men assisted by having these women tan, smoke, and make moccasins, which when worn were said to 'always know their way home.' Once a very elder lady lowered her head, and while smiling, claimed that such moccasins had thick neck-hide over the toes so a man crawling from tipi to tipi would not wear holes in his foot wear.

A mourning widow could continue to breast-feed her child, but was discouraged from breast-feeding any child not her own, nor could she hold a child not her own during her period of mourning. The bed s/he had shared with a spouse was burned, and s/he was careful to never leave the dwelling at night, lest s/he attract the deceased partner's soul, spirit or ghost, which could protract the survivor's grief and period of mourning. A widower was also subject to publicly-observed *prohibitions* (*sčxeʔnepleʔ*), *especially regarding food-getting activities*. Given individual circumstances, a widow or widower was economically supported in varying degrees by the deceased's kinspeople and friends during the prescribed period of mourning. It was said that a widower could not fish or hunt for at least one year, for fear that fish or game would leave the country (Ray 1933) because of possible contamination and disrespect toward these resources.

194

Once the widow was released from her mourning by her in-laws, it was said that the widow is *on the prowl* (*nc'lišk^wᵉʔ*), a time when she could commence to wear new clothing and decorate herself to indicate the possibility of courtship. This change of status acknowledged the agreement by the widow and widower's family, as well as members of the deceased spouse's family. The widow could now commence to find a new spouse and prepare to set up *housekeeping* (*nc'lišk^wʔem*). Prior to *remarriage* (*heɫn't'k'^wk'^wméw's*) she was known to the community and her family as *nc'lišk^wʔem* ("she is now marriageable"). A widow or widower would terminate their *time of mourning* (*ninč'ey*) by war dancing or "other forms of merry-making" (STHC). After mourning, the widow was no longer referred to as *sɫwelmt*, but rather as *nc'lišk^wᵉʔ*. If the widow or widower had children from a previous marriage, the children called their new *step-parent* (*sɫu'wélt*). According to Curtis (1911, 7:76), Spokan women, on becoming widows, could change their names if they wanted.

Only when the widow's self-inflicted wounds were healed, and her hair had grown a proper length (just below her shoulders) (Ray 1932; Elmendorf 1935-36), was she permitted to remove her mourning dress and properly cleanse herself in a special sweat given by her sweathouse companions who carefully oiled and then scraped her body with deer ribs, followed by rubbing the women completely with pads of pounded, green ground moss. Later, after these ritual ablutions, her kinspeople and those of her deceased husband, along with the village or camp, collectively acknowledged the termination of her period of bereavement—always a major change of status.

A widow was always properly addressed by the group as a widow until the end of her proscribed mourning, for a widower was sometimes less restrictive in time and behavior, being terminated often by choice; nevertheless, there was always a period of time that was considered respectful to the kinspeople of his dead wife. There was always consensus that a long mourning period served different functions, not the least being it afforded the widow an opportunity to make a proper choice of a future husband, assuming there was not an occasion for the levirate.

Memorial Feast and Give-Away Ceremony

Approximately one year after a burial, the immediate kin group sponsored a memorial feast and a give-away ceremony, which tended to serve various therapeutic functions for the grieving family, kinspeople, and attending friends. Formally announcing or using in conversation the name of the recently deceased served to elicit fond memories of the person. To forget the deeds of a deceased person was considered disrespectful, and it was, therefore, incumbent upon older survivors, when possible, to acquaint younger kinspeople—as they matured—of the good deeds of the deceased. During this ceremony, the greatest demonstrations of respect—more than words—were expressions of grief and sorrow, which often were audible during this rite of passage. On occasions, a person was unable to express his sorrow, as indicated by a person being unable to speak. "It was believed that men's sorrow was more deep, as they were silent, while the women were more expressive" (STHC). The elders believed that the greatest respect one could show for a deceased person was through sorrow. In addition, it was not considered masculine to express sorrow, especially publicly. This was particularly true of the earlier periods. In essence, silence was a form of *stoicism* (*nyáʕ^wyolsm*) and projected strength. One's greatest sorrow was when one could not even make any reference to the deceased.

Following traditional custom, the *memorial feast* (*sx^wlsiʔɫn* - "giving away food" or *x^wlsʔiɫn* - "goodbye meal") would be celebrated approximately one year after a person's burial and was an occasion for the *distribution of possessions* (*sux^wq^wlq^wélt* or *px^wm'ɫcút*) of the deceased to kinspeople and friends (Elmendorf 1935-6, 1:46-7). After the date was set for the give-away, the consanguineal family would gather the clothes and belongings of the deceased. This *ceremony of distributing the deceased person's possessions* (*pux^wm'sm'* - "the one who speaks") among the assembled company typically commenced at noon. In warm weather, it was preferably held out-of-doors in the *shade* (*čɫč''éynetn*) or under pole-erected awnings of hide, tule mats,

195

or more recently, canvas. During winter or inclement weather, the ceremony was conducted in the long-house. All those in attendance would partake of the great quantities of food put together by the *consanguineal family* (*stm'elis* - "all blood relatives").

The memorial feast was organized by non-kinspeople who would collect and supervise all the preparation and distribution of food by the servers, and the later distribution of any left-over food. Any remaining food was most often given away by the *crier* (*suxqʷlqʷelt* or *skʷlskʷlstelt*), mostly to those who had travelled an appreciable distance. Non-kinspersons would also clean any of the deceased person's clothes that were to be given away at the Sorrow or Remembrance Ceremony held just before the dinner, always a *sad* (*ʔespuʔpuʔsénči*) and emotional time.

Recipients of *memorials* (*sʔél'k'ʾʷmn*) were determined by the family prior to the ceremony, but in some instances the person in charge of the ceremony would make such designations, even a chief. To the on-looker it would appear a sorrowful ritual, one with considerable pathos as the grief of a widow was demonstrated by her keening and *wailing* (*scqʾʷóti* - "wailing") at the wake, or the give-away when clothing was brought out and distributed to those attending. The ritual was essentially a psychodrama in which many of the deceased person's belongings were held up for all to see, and the *presenter* (*sxʷxʷíc'š*) may say, in effect, "you will never see this person again in these clothes when you came for help or advice, nor will you hear his laughter." Or, "when you wear his hat or jacket, remember all he did for you, and ask yourself what you did for him or his family."

Just as gifts given at the mortuary feast were cleansed with rose water and wrapped in rosehip bushes, so too were gifts given at a memorial feast. For example, a rifle would never shoot straight or kill game if it had not been completely disassembled and thoroughly washed with rose water, before oiling and reassembling. Any gift received at a memorial feast was called *sʔélk'ʾʷn*.

Clothing worn by the deceased, when approaching the *time of death* (*š'iʔtmnúxʷ*)—non-ceremonial clothing, once worn by the deceased was gathered and invariably later burned to prevent it from being worn, which was a serious offense or insult to the deceased person's ghost. During the Memorial Feast and Give-away Ceremony, and out of respect and possible fear of retaliation by the dead, individuals never spoke loudly nor wore any sort of ornamentation or *fine clothing* (*siʔáʔ*). Through advice and consent of the deceased person's family, the individual conducting the give-away respected the family's wishes by giving certain gifts to specific people. The person conducting the give-away was often the individual who took the deceased person's last confession and had; consequently assumed this responsibility, and hence, was one who could *distribute* (*px̣ʷmstés* - "he distributed it") the deceased person's belongings. A guest may stand and dramatically relate his own heroic accomplishments to the group with an accompanying give-away to honor his own deeds, a procedure termed *ʔec qʷqʷl'úm'ti* - "to tell traditional stories" (STHC).

Contemporary Mortuary Ritual

With current attempts at revitalizing certain past rites of passage, by both younger and older Spokan, there are greater variations in rituals of birthing, naming, puberty, and marriage. Some Spokan have said that these particular rites of passage are less complex and with little, if any, of the once traditional beliefs and associated behavioral taboos that were once believed to be critical to the individual and the stability of the community. Perhaps the most apparent changes are seen with contemporary mortuary and burial ritual.

At the pronouncement of death, the deceased is often taken immediately from the hospital or home to a mortuary where the body is embalmed. If possible, autopsies are discouraged, and the donation of organs is not always agreed upon by the family. Also, unless legal circumstances prevail, cremation of the body, even after death, is abhorrent. Upon notification of death, family and friends will usually bring funeral attire for the deceased to the funeral home, and after embalming and preparation, the body is taken to the deceased person's home. In some instances for those enrolled Spokan living off-reservation, and who may have preplanned burial in one of Spokanes many cemeteries, it is customary to view the deceased at the funeral home.

From this, it is only too apparent that many aspects of contemporary burial practices, and associated mortuary beliefs, have changed in complexity, duration, and even order of occurrence, and, it is posited, the functions. The present *wake* (*nč'méple?tn* - "kind of handle") differs little from the historic or, it is posited, the prehistoric rituals, mainly the size and construction of the long-house.

Another aspect of the present-day mortuary ritual and memorial ceremony that has changed only slightly is the Memorial Feast menu, which naturally varies with the availability of fresh fruits and vegetables. Even salmon is not caught locally, but fresh deer meat is always available. Once common fresh or dried traditional foods are gradually being replaced by home-made or store-bought foods which accommodate a preference for sweeter tasting commodities. Fry bread continues to represent a preference developed with the introduction and growing of wheat to the Indian diet.

The introduction of caskets brought change in mortuary ritual, which actually created the practice of a strict and continuous surveillance of the body after being placed in a casket while in the long-house for usually one or three nights; a duration depending upon the person's importance or the family's wishes. Due to contemporary religious revitalization and relative cost, the use of metal caskets has been replaced by the us of using wooden caskets. The deceased—regardless of age or gender—is interred in a horizontally tapered, break-sided, or straight-sided casket constructed from untreated ponderosa pine with two rope handles on either side. The interior of the casket may be lined with one or more Pendleton blankets with colored linear designs. In some caskets a type of shadow box is inset to display items and photographs important to the deceased or their kin. Such caskets are often constructed off-reservation by one of several casket-makers who apparently specialize in constructing "Indian caskets." There are, however, instances when an on-reservation male relative of the deceased will fashion a wooden casket for a deceased kinsperson.

When in the long-house, a casket is usually placed atop two sawhorses which are covered by one or more draped Pendleton wool blankets. For a deceased widow or widower, a large photograph of one's deceased spouse may be displaced behind or to one side of the head of the casket. Often commercial floral wreaths are behind or at the foot of the casket, which later will be transported with the casket to the *cemetery* (*tmtmney'tn*) by *pall-bearers* (*suxʷ-qʷnem*) or a hearse and later placed atop the filled grave mound. Long after the burial, plastic or real flowers may replace the withered funeral wreaths.

The deceased may be clothed in finely beaded or embroidered buckskin attire, and sometimes the individual may hold a *bald eagle wing wand* (*pql'qin xaustn*) in the right hand over his or her chest. Depending upon gender, other forms of adornment may be draped around the person's neck. For Catholics, *rosary beads* (*łiq'ʷ* or *slik'ʷ* - "prayer beads") will often be wrapped around the clasped hands of the deceased, or various Christian medallions may be pinned or placed on the body. Some family members will place within the casket small family photographs to accompany a loved one. Certain significant and even sacred plants, such as Canby's lovage or sweet grass may be placed in the casket.

Participating dancers will be dressed in their best traditional costumes, and many elderly women will be sartorially attired in either fringed shoulder shawls over long dresses or beautifully beaded-designed dresses that always cover the tops of their high, thong-wrapped buckskin moccasins. Older and more traditional women may carry large imbricated cornhusk bags or beaded twine or buckskin purses. Both men and women, and sometimes children, wear moccasins if they will be dancing.

Even today, on the last day of the wake—during the Long-house ceremony, an elderly woman may lead the congregation in singing Christian songs accompanied by a guitar or piano. Depending upon the deceased person's acknowledged faith, a priest or minister—sometimes jointly, will officiate and direct events as indicated in the burial announcement, reciting selected Christian prayers and reciting certain psalms.

Contemporary revitalization efforts of observing traditional and dignified burial ceremonies are also apparent in various ways, usually by a pre-ceremonial request that there be no playing of guitars and non-

197

traditional musical instruments. For instance, the deceased may make a pre-death request that guitars and other non-traditional musical instruments not be played during the service, that wooden caskets be lined with Pendleton blanket material, and that the vigilance of the deceased continue throughout the night. During the wake, one might see the adult son of the deceased publicly display his grief by softly commencing to *sing* (*nkʷenm'éy'ʔ*) his song; first as a *whisper* (*suʔsw'íłš*), and eventually as an audible lament. Fortunately, rarely does one hear a cell phone ring during the ceremony.

A major change in the burial ceremony, one that actually started during the late historical period, and of course now evident in cemeteries, is the erecting of a *headstone* (*št'eʔneʔtn*). Contemporary headstones vary in cost, shape, and type of stone. Since the 1960s, however, the general style of headstone art has evolved from the typical Anglo-American engraving of only name, birth-death dates, and sometimes a biblical passage. Many headstones now serve to express an increasing pride of "Indianness" with visible expressions of Indian art, particularly motifs that reflect once traditionally significant animals, particularly the bald or golden eagle. Many had usually edge- or surface-sculptured headstones to reveal the date of installation. The cemetery is usually attended by only the immediate or extended family. There are several gifted on-reservation Spokan stone-sculptors whose skills with free-form sculpturing are acknowledged locally and even internationally.

Headstones may have imprinted photographs of the deceased, and are frequently surrounded by grave goods, ones that often reflect the age and even gender of the deceased person. Perishable cloth offerings–such as dolls or stuffed animals—are simply left to deteriorate. More durable metal and glass objects such as religious crosses and rosary beads, often identify the religious commitment and pursuance of the deceased. The location of headstones commonly identify extended families. Rarely are wooden crosses or engraved headboards used, though some very old ones are, still, visible, especially ones fashioned many years ago from red cedar. On all on-reservation private and church cemeteries there are still a few of the once popular narrow, pressed metal grave markers, which may have a still legible identity and date of death.

Later visiting or conducting maintenance of grave sites will be done by personal preference, invariably in the spring; but always several days prior to the national Memorial Day. There is a long-standing tradition when the family will clean the grave and straighten flower containers on all the graves of immediate kinspeople. It is an annual tradition that common "unclaimed" graves be cleaned by tribal members. This cleaning ritual is an appropriate occasion for older people to recite and explain the various characteristics and accomplishments of the deceased to those attending people whom they often had never met, or simply to reiterate their former association with the deceased.

If the deceased had been a military veteran of any military organization, and had served in WW II, Korea, Vietnam, Desert Storm, or in Iraq, the local chapter of the members of the Veterans of Foreign Wars (VFW) will purchase and arrange for the engraving of a deceased veteran's headstone. It remains a common practice for the person's rank, serial number, and military unit—more often the army—to be engraved upon the headstone. During a veteran's funeral, members of the VFW will join the grave-side congregation, and after the Honor Guard, fire five blank volleys in unison from 30. Caliber WW II Garands. Then two of their members served as flag bearers, one carrying the American flag and the other a Spokane tribal flag. They will carefully fold the American flag with 13 folds, and present the flag to the widow or to a family member of the deceased. This occasion may or may not require the presence of a priest or minister, simply because the survivor's obligations have been fulfilled, and there is no need for apprehension or concern with the state of the deceased. If there is interment, however, after the earlier long-house reception and wake, a priest or minister, sometimes both, will attend the burial service. Until recently, a shaman would have been present to purify the grave.

Osteological material, found on and off-reservation are collected by qualified individuals from the tribe, "taken care of" then re-interred, with ceremony, in a designated cemetery on the Reservation. With the creation of The Native American Graves Protection and Repatriation Act (NAGPRA), a Federal law passed in

16 November 1990 [Pub. L. 101-601, 104 Stat. 3048] human remains in museums and universities are being returned to the federally-recognized tribes of origin in greater numbers. These individuals are also re-interred with honor, respect, and sadness for their being so long gone from their homelands.

Chapter V: Settlement Patterns and Structures

Prehistoric Spokan settlement patterns consisted of permanent winter villages as well as temporary spring, summer, and autumn camps to facilitate the exploitation and storage of different resources. This multiplicity of settlement types was a form of logistical adaptation in response to the varying location, elevation, and availability of plant, animal, and fish resources that were influenced by the seasonally semi-arid environment characteristic of the eastern Plateau.

Spring, summer, and autumn exploitation sites were associated with predictable plant food resource areas and less so with the availability of game populations that experienced periodic fluctuations in response to severe and long winters. Ray noted that "On the whole, Plateau life involved wintertime occupancy of [a] river village, and summertime camping at berrying and root-digging grounds" (1939:4). Root-digging areas were known as *snx̣éctn* ("place for digging roots"), whereas *snč̓łiptn* refers to "hunting grounds" (Egesdal, pers. comm.). In addition to certain resource grounds, Ray provided the most accurate locations and names of Lower, Middle, and Upper Spokan villages on the Spokane and Columbia Rivers (1936:133-5).

Several types of residence locations were used by the Spokan: permanent winter villages comprised of semi-subterranean lodges, temporary and permanent summer villages, and temporary resource extraction camps. The actual settlement types and their location emphasized the need for a highly mobile annual subsistence quest, one that involved specific tasks that facilitated the procurement of food resources from areas of differential productive occurrence. When summarizing band structure and social organization within the southern plateau, Boyd and Gregory stated:

> [...] the most effective social system appears to have been a central based band organization with a simple, fluid social structure capable of breaking up or coalescing into units whose size varied according to the particular task to be accomplished (2007, 1:39).

To appreciate the variance of the logistics of residence, one can read Smith's Plateau mesa study, which presents a useful explanation of *camp* (*q̓ey* or *snč̓luʕiʔsełx̣ʷtn* - "campsite") type and their use—an explanation that is applicable to the Spokan:

> Among hunting-gathering societies generally, it is possible to distinguish between two classes of technological activities: extraction, involving procurement of food, fuel, and other sources from the environment, the maintenance, or storage, processing and consumption of material already at hand. Generally, maintenance activities are concentrated in base camps, whereas extraction activities tend to characterize specialized work camps, such as kill sites, collecting stations, and quarries. Transient camps may combine both types of activities. The manner in which settlement types are functionally different and distributed within the territory of any specific society will define the settlement system of that society. Archaeologically, we would expect such a settlement system to be reflected in the variable and nonrandom patterns of distribution of artifacts, features, and other material within and among archaeological sites, as determined by the kinds of tasks performed, as well as by the size and composition of social units engaged in the tasks (1977:12).

Permanent Structures

With some exceptions in the Lower Spokan, areas of permanent structures, i.e., winter villages, were located on south or south-west facing riverine terraces on both the Columbia and Spokane Rivers, where they were best located because of lower elevation, directional orientation, readily available water, and proximity to fish, game animals, and food plants. With few exceptions, villages were located on lower riverine or *upper riverbank* (*nustcín* or *sx̣cin*) terraces, enjoying a southwest facing exposure to the Spokane River. Near the dwellings each extended family had large drying racks, storage sheds, and distant, large food storage pits. According to oral history, there was only one known exception to this, a small winter village located away from the river on a higher elevation, presumably once occupied by a small group of several extended families that had presumably been *excommunicated* (*šx̣ʷéłmn* or *wešiš*) "Before the time of horses" (Ross 1993).

200

Winter Villages

Permanent *winter villages* (*čnuyéłxútn* - "building houses") were the most dominant features within the cultural landscape. Despite what was an inevitable historical change in the architecture of winter dwellings during the late prehistoric and protohistoric periods (Nelson 1973), the structures used are described by the ethnographic reconstruction by Ray (1933) and Teit (1930), and more recently by archaeological finds (Ames *et al.* 1998), as well as by numerous other archaeological surveys. Elmendorf (1935-6, 2:32) states that, "all of the Spokan [winter] settlements were on the north side of the Spokane River," while some were located on the Spokane River at the confluence of both Little and Big Tschimakain Creek—the people were called *sč'č'm'qini*. Some permanent villages on both the Columbia and Spokane Rivers were inhabited during the major summer fish runs. The riverine orientation of winter villages afforded the occupants access to water travel, warmer conditions, driftwood, fresh water, fish and other riparian resources, game, and certain hydrophytes, including water cress (Ross 1989a:71).

The spatial location and types of dwellings differed between so-called winter and non-winter residence. Winter lodges were almost always arranged parallel to one another—side by side and spaced approximately 15 to 20 m apart, with each major entryway facing south or southwest toward the water. A ceremonial lodge was situated farther from the other dwellings, often farther away from the river, or, in some instances, in line with the main *winter dwelling* (*sn?ét'čéłx"tn*). Most outside storage facilities were in close proximity behind the village, often in excavated storage pits adjoining talus slopes, including tree storage platforms and raised storage houses. Sweathouses and menstrual structures were always strategically located away from the village.

All pre-contact architecture reflected a definite bimodal type of demographic existence—one in which residence fluctuated between permanent riverine winter dwellings and temporary summer dwellings situated at different resource sites. The exact construction of the earliest dwellings, particularly permanent winter structures, such as the semi-subterranean conical pit house, are sometimes difficult to reconstruct because just prior to the protohistoric period, the *pit house* (*sčláq'łxú* - "buried house") was replaced with a larger rectangular *tule mat lodge* (*siyiqssełx"* or *sušnełx"*). However, there has been no archaeological evidence to suggest significant changes with other types of structures during this transition, only with the permanent dwellings. Tule mat lodges were used primarily in the non-winter months, though tule mat tipis were used in certain situations.

Cox, while visiting the winter village at the confluence of the Spokane River and Little Tschimakain Creek, spoke of how "The oblong or cone-shaped houses were covered with mats or skins, according to the wealth of the owners" (Dryden 1949:43). According to Smith (1936-8:515), the Chewelah-Spokan settlement had both round and long lodges. As late as 1846, Pickering noted, "Some of the lodges were, as usual, of [tule] mats; and to my surprise I saw also buffalo robes, and conical skin-lodges, like those used on the Missouri" (Barry 1929:59). Hale described a camp of approximately 300 individuals, living in 20 lodges, "of which were conical, and of buffalo-skins" (1846, 4:458).

Winter villages were comprised of various types of structures, such as storage pits and platform structures for food, *winter long-houses* (*si?y'qséłx"*), sweathouses, and menstrual structures. Archaeologists have clearly determined the basic structure of permanent winter pit houses, which were outlined by postholes supporting *house posts* (*hecnšt'úle?x"*) for the walls and roof, suggesting that they could accommodate one or more extended families. Either due to presumed population increase, shifts in resource base, or changes in Spokan sociopolitical organization, the long-house was a second type of *permanent dwelling* (*sqql'ix"éłx"*)—one that served various sociopolitical purposes apart from inhabitation by a chief and his family, sometimes with multiple families. By the early 1800s, major changes in architecture and certain building materials of some temporary dwellings occurred due to the influence of the Plains Indian cultures, and later, with Euro-American contact which modified traditional permanent dwellings and certain temporary structures.

All villages had geonomic designations, which often indicated the location of a particular resource, a unique topographical feature, or even the nature of the water, such as unusual rapids (*sn?iw'lm'* or *snewlm*). For example, a former large year-round village located on a productive fishing area was called *č'lm'ł'm'el'mn* ("water came running over the meadow").

The term village may be confusing as it suggests a relatively large residential population. But for the Spokane there were usually only six to twenty extended families occupying a village during the winter months, some had even fewer dwellings (Ray 1936:133-137). Each village naturally differed in size and population, but usually comprised of approximately twenty to one hundred people, all of whom had a sense of territorial interdependence and unique identity, known as *nk'ʷusm* or *nk'ʷelixʷ* ("village group"). Winter villages located at highly productive fisheries had larger populations. Village territorial areas included traditional hunting grounds, certain tree resource areas, cambium groves, and sacred sites. Access to these resources was facilitated along lines of kin affiliation and recognized fictive associations, particularly among males. Highly productive resource sites—most notably fishing stations—were annually exploited by non-residents. Exploitation of resource areas was traditionally determined by recognized principles of usufruct or direct permission to gain access, often through established marriages among families distant from each other. Linguistic similarity tended to facilitate these usually brief socioeconomic reciprocal interdependencies.

Semi-Subterranean Pit House

Prehistorically there were essentially two types of permanent semi-subterranean *winter dwellings* (*s?ístčn* - "winter dwelling"). The earliest prehistoric winter dwelling was an earthen-covered semi-subterranean conical pit house, in existence by 2000 to 1800 BCE (Ames, *et al.*,1998:111). Just prior to the protohistoric period, semi-subterranean pit houses were replaced with larger rectangular tule mat lodges. Later, these larger *tule mat-covered* (*s'yi?qsétxʷ* - "tule winter home") double apsidal, multi-pole dwellings were large enough to house several extended families. The most reliable information regarding the size of both types of Spokan semi-subterranean pit houses comes from the remaining dwelling pit house sites located during recent ethno-archaeological surveys (Ross 1984a,1993) and archaeological surveys (Chance 1967; Rice and Ross 1980; Galm and Lyman 1988a:53-5; Galm, *et al.* 1994; Ames, *et al.* 1998). The floor plan and the construction of semi-subterranean dwellings, and the covering structure, have been reconstructed by the recent work of archaeologists who have documented how pit houses were:

> [...] roofed with a light framework covered with mats and earth. That any earth cover was light, however, is clear from the lack of heavy fill above the uppermost floor in most houses. The fill between superimposed floors in excavated houses, with each of them including three such floors, suggests that no roof inhibited the encroachment of the plentiful sand during periods of non-occupation. The conclusion is that the roof was light and was removed at the end of each season of occupation (Ames, *et al.* 1998:112).

Further information from comparative studies of dwellings and utility structures within this general area (Teit 1928, 1930; Ray 1933; Smith 1936-8; Turney-High 1937; Post and Commons 1938; Rice 1984) contribute to our knowledge of the structural configuration and materials used by the Spokan for their permanent structures. Some of the following descriptions of dwellings will rely upon the aforementioned ethnographic and archaeological works, and acknowledging certain physical constraints of building materials available to the Spokan. Without identifying the exact village, Hale spoke of, "The number of [winter] lodges was twenty, some of which were conical, and of buffalo-skins" (1846, 4:458).

Figure 13. Circular semi-subterranean tule mat pit house

Because of topographic restraints of certain sloping terraces, not all prehistoric semi-subterranean pit houses could be constructed on *level ground* (*šiƛ'leʔxʷ*). As a result, the construction of a permanent dwelling commenced with the excavation and leveling of the surface and subsurface of the desired site. When completed, an excavated circular pit measured 7 to 8 m in diameter, with a depth of approximately 50 cm to 2 m. The second phase of construction involved cutting, debarking, and transporting the required lodge poles to the proposed site, and were then erected in a standard conical shape. The main support frame consisted of three or four top-forked poles secured by binding them together at their distal ends with hemp at the apex, forming a tipi-like structure, using the most stout forked pole (*sxxcéyʼ*) as the main bearing frame. Additional lodge poles were supported by this frame, and were further stabilized by attaching additional smaller-diameter lodge poles, cut to length with each end connected horizontally at right angles to the main poles. Women then assisted the men in constructing a complex secondary frame of bound willow withes that were lashed to the main frame with hemp, stripped cedar, or long sections of spruce root. More willow withes were then secured at close intervals to later accommodate shingled slabs of bark or tule or cattail mats, and these overlapping layers of mats were secured in place by women using a 20 cm polished *hardwood tule mat needle* (*ƛ'áqam*) with an end-eye in the middle. Willow withes, with cedar strips or spruce roots, were then passed through the covering material and attached to the secondary frame. Approximately twenty woven tule mats were required to cover the structure. Each mat could measure roughly 3 m long and 110 cm wide. Once secured, the mats were then covered with 15 to 20 cm of earth, sometimes mixed with clay to increase the stability of the roof and help prevent the infiltration of rain. Ray has cited such a practice for the Sanpoil and Nespelem, and offers an excellent description of a single-center-pole, earth-covered semi-subterranean pit house, including the use of clay in roofing:

> The semi-subterranean earth lodge [...] consisted of a circular pit with a flat or conical roof. The depth of the pit varied from four to six feet; a deep pit was necessary for the flat roof type. The diameter ranged from ten to sixteen feet. The hole was dug with a sharp edged paddle-like tool of wood. In the conical roofed structure a single large log served as a center post, from the top of which radiated poles extending slightly beyond the margin of the hole. At the periphery the distance between the poles was about two feet. The angle of slope was approximately 22 degrees. The method used to secure the radiating poles to the center post is not clear; they were tied in some manner with willow rope. Cedar planks, split from driftwood, were laid as a first covering on the roof when such wood was available. In lieu of planks willow mats were used. A layer of grass and brush was then added to a thickness of about six inches. On top of this a thick layer of dirt was placed, usually a part of that which has been excavated. However, if clay were available the covering would be made of this, since it turned water much better than ordinary soil. A single hole in the top near the center post permitted entrance and egress

203

and allowed the smoke to escape. The ladder consisted of two vertical poles set a small distance apart upon which cross sticks were tied with thongs of willow bark. The ladder projected a foot or two out of the opening. The notched log type of ladder was not known. Only one fire was used, placed near the center of the room.

Though the semi-subterranean lodge and the winter mat house were used simultaneously the natives speak of the former as being the older type, and the only winter house known until fairly recent times. With the introduction of the mat type of winter shelter the earth lodge fell into disuse (1933:31).

In an earlier but brief description of entering and exiting a pit house, Curtis described how, "In winter an underground house with a single small opening in the roof was in general use for sleeping quarters" (1907-30, 7:75). All structures were manufactured from resources within the immediate area: dressed lodge poles, tule and cattail mats, bark, cordage, and spilt cedar or split tamarack planks. Larger and more permanent structures had double or triple layers of tule mats covered with earth that was packed before the lower ground areas were covered with sloped skirts fashioned from large, flattened slabs of bark—preferably black cottonwood. The upper ends of the bark slabs were situated under the lowest horizontal course of *tule mats* (*q'ucłxʷtn*) that extended beyond the structure to carry water away from the dwelling to down-sloping earthen ditches, which ran around the structure and were joined at the lowest elevation.

Subterranean Dwellings

There was no memory of any type of temporary or permanent subterranean dwellings or structures used by the Spokan; only one of several subterranean structures that were primarily high-riverine bank food storage caches has been noted, but not dwellings. Teit (1939:331), however, noted how the Kalispel and Lower Spokan utilized a semi-underground lodge, but with little detail. Rice makes an interesting distinction between semi- and subterranean dwellings, but was undoubtedly not referring to the Spokan when he claimed how, "The completely underground lodge is referred to frequently" (1984:97), which were, according to Spinden (1908, 71:198-199), Curtis (1911, 7:42-43), Teit (1930:62,114), Twaites (1969, 3:108, 4:280), and Kane (1971:189-191), structures once built by the Nez Perce, Methow, Southern Okanogan, Walla Walla, and Wishram. Fortunately, Ray did describe how the Sanpoil and Nespelem constructed a flat-roofed subterranean structure with a depth of 2 m:

> The entire room of the flat top earth lodge was *below* [italics added] the ground level [...] the opening leading outside was placed at the edge instead of the center, necessitating a corresponding change in the location of the fireplace. Although easier to build than the conical roofed lodge, this type was less efficient in the matter of drainage and consequently less used (1933:31-32).

A description of a Nez Perce subterranean flat-roof circular pit, with a side entrance (?), was first cited by Spinden (1908:198), and is undoubtedly the basis for Rice's uncited ethnic identification which he presumably acquired from Spinden (1908:62). Unfortunately, Spinden erroneously suggests that these Nez Perce structures served as either a male sweathouse or as a menstrual lodge. One can only conclude that Spinden (1908) and Rice (2005) assumed the reader would realize these particular subscribed activities of sweating and menstrual confinement were never conducted or condoned by the Spokan within the same structure; then even the dimensions of depth are questionable:

> Reportedly, lodges were dug to a maximum depth of 10 to twelve feet with logs, split timbers, planks, or poles, and then covered [the roof] by brush or grass followed by a layer of mud or earth. The entrance was a hole in the roof through which a notched log ladder protruded. Twelve to fifteen people could winter in one of these dwellings, which frequently was warmed by combined body heat of the occupants so that no fire was needed. In addition to housing family groups, special subterranean structures of various sizes also served as menstrual lodges for females and as sudatories or sweathouses for men and boys (Rice 2005:92).

Long-House

One type of winter dwelling, called a *long-house* (*sussnéɫx^w* or *sn²esštčéɫx^wtn* - "long lodge"), appeared by 1900 BCE (Ames, *et al.*, 1998:111). Traditionally, a long-house was not seen as a dwelling, but used more as a *place for celebrations* (*snpyélstn*), primarily because the interior capacity made them ideal for accommodating large groups of people. Long-houses required considerable supplies of wood to heat the dwelling throughout the winter. To appreciate the length of a long-house, Glover gave details, when speaking of opening a school for Spokan children in an Indian lodge that was, "about eighty feet long, covered with Indian [tule] matting, canvas, sheeting and a few buffalo robes" (Durham 1921, 1:109).

Long-houses were in use continually until being replaced—in the pre-reservation period—by different structures with certain advantages of construction and materials. Each *permanent winter village* (*nk'^wélix^w*), depending upon population size, had at least one long-house and sometimes two. Unfortunately, contemporary responses to questions of Spokan oral history regarding prehistoric and protohistoric ethnography, particularly of house type, are frequently based on earlier anthropological accounts gained from anthropologists during the late 1920s and the 1930s, and from the deceased elders of present-day Spokan. Explanations of the Spokan long-house are found in notes from Teit (1930:331; Elmendorf 1935-6, 1:28-30), Elmendorf's Spokan notes (1935-6), and Smith's descriptions (1936-8) of the Upper Spokan. However, the following partial quote from Ray's work with the contiguous Sanpoil and Nespelem provides the most complete description of long-house construction, one that would have been similar to the Spokan:

Construction began with the digging of slanting holes, about a foot deep, to receive the bases of the poles used in the upright frame. Sets of two poles, each eighteen to twenty feet long, were then tied together near one end to form a "V". These were raised to position in the holes, each pair separated by about twelve feet from the next one. The apex thus formed was approximately fourteen feet above the ground. No ridge pole was used. Beginning about one foot below the peak on either side transverse poles were tied to the uprights in parallel courses approximately three feet apart until the ground was reached. The poles were tied together at the intersections with small willow branches which had been twisted until flexible. The framework at the ends of the structure consisted of upright poles arranged in half-tipi fashion. The horizontal courses were carried around the ends by the use of flexible willow branches. The lower four or five feet of the framework was made of rye-grass. A covering of grass of any variety, a few inches thick, was added, then a layer of dirt, varying from six to eight inches thick at ground level to half that amount at the upper edge. The next row of mats overlapped this dirt layer by several inches. All mats except those forming the *bottom* (*č'-ɫni-šut*) course were of tule. Each section was four to five feet wide, as determined by the height of the tules, and ten to twenty feet in length. They were laid lengthwise, each course overlapping the last by three or four inches. Mats were attached from the inside by tying cords, previously secured to the mats, around the poles of the framework. The space above the uppermost horizontal pole was left completely open, providing an aperture about a foot wide along the entire length of the house for the escape of smoke and the admission of light. Entrances were provided in each end of the house, but never along the sides, and were double, each consisting of an outer and inner door. The outer opening was a space between two of the vertical poles, about three feet wide and six feet high, over which the covering of the framework did not extend. It was closed with a tule mat, stiffened at the top with a willow pole and fastened at each end on the upper side. This door opened in to a narrow passageway formed by partitions of cedar planks or mats on each side, as high as the door and extended to a point directly below the apex of the rounded portion of the end of the house. Here was the inner doorway; a mat was hung between the partitions at this point.

The space at the ends of the house between the walls and the passageway was used for storage purposes. Temporary food supplies were kept there, usually in flexible bags. The bags were hung on cross poles or simply laid on the ground. Platforms were not employed. Short sticks were sometimes thrust into the house mats and used as pegs on which to hang small articles.

A pathway about four feet wide ran throughout the length of the house from door to door. This pathway was marked off from the portion of floor space given over to beds by poles placed end to end along each side. Fireplaces were in the middle of this central alley, the number varying with the number of families. One fire sufficed for the two families living on opposite sides of it. A pit was purposely dug for holding the fire but frequent removal of ashes soon caused a depression to form. Mats covered the floor on each side of the passageway but the ground was left bare along the path itself. Bedding consisted of mats, robes and blankets. When mats were used as bed covering they were made of slough grass, not the course tule used for house covering (1933:32-3).

In cold weather, inhabitants slept at night with their feet to the fire, using bedding of hides, furs, and even tule mats. After the family rose in the morning, the mother would air the hide and fur robes, and then roll them against the *wall (nxlenč)* of the structure (Elmendorf 1935-6, 1:5). In the winter, she would periodically place the robes, fur side down, outside on the snow, and beat them with a staff to remove any vermin. Tule or cattail *wall mats (sy'ay's)* were not annually aired, but rather replaced in the fall prior to winter occupancy. These rolled mats were then sometimes used in burials if necessary, for wrapping the corpse. Durham quotes an early remark by Cox, who stated how the Flathead, "dwelling [are] pretty free from vermin, and are easily changed when the occasion arises" (1912, 1:13).

There was little difference between the Spokan and Sanpoil building techniques and required materials when building a long-house. The most complete description for the Spokan long-house is from one of Elmendorf's elderly informants who recalled seeing a *small semi-subterranean, earthen-covered long-house (ul'čín')*, which he said had a floor excavated to approximately 1.5 m, and measuring approximately 2 m in width by 3 to 4 m in length (1935-6, 2:28-32). The roof was built from a series of lodge poles, assembled as inverted "V"s that were then stabilized, by poles placed upright in holes as mentioned above by Ray (1933:32). Roofing was fabricated from mats attached to numerous parallel side poles, and covered with earth from the ground level to the ridge line.

An entrance was through two framed low doors, each located at either end of the dwelling. However, Teit maintained that the semi-subterranean lodge was used only by the Lower Spokan (1930:331), whereas surveys have recorded both the Middle and Upper Spokan using this type of dwelling (Ross 1993). Elmendorf (1935-6, 3:28) cited that the Spokan maintained strict protocol regarding the use of each entrance: the men's door faced upstream, whereas the women's faced downstream. A deceased person was never taken out through a doorway, nor was a dressed animal ever brought into a dwelling by a doorway, but through an opening temporarily made in one of the sloping side walls after first removing or lifting a section of matting (STHC).

A center passageway that ran the length of the structure was roughly one meter in width, and was first covered with wet earth, then pounded hard to prevent excessive dust. After pounding the floor flat with a flat-ended section of wood, it was covered with grass or inverted fir boughs and then covered with flexible cattail mats, upon which the bedding was laid. Each bed was bordered by stalks of ryegrass that were used to cover the mats. A large long-house had a raised earthen platform of pounded earth approximately 2 m in width for sleeping. This sleeping platform was covered with a *bearskin rug (m'l'k'ʷélxʷ* - "tanned hide with fur intact"), a favored choice for a family to *sleep (s?iyš)* upon or to share as a blanket in extremely cold weather. Because of its warmth and size, the most sought blanket was one of *bison fur (mulxʷ)*. A sleeping platform was often first covered with fir boughs to make a *fir bough mattress (t'aqélp)*, then covered with tule mats to support the bedding. Each occupant had his or her own *pillow (nč'?éne? or snéína)* made from a tanned inverted whole skin of an animal with the leg sections pushed inside and the openings stitched closed after filling the container with pheasant or duck feathers (Elmendorf 1935-6, I:66). An improvised pillow was quickly made from a folded blanket or garment, and called *nq'ʷq'ʷm'éne?*.

Each end of the lodge had an external slanting rectangular door frame that was attached to the main structure, and formed an interior and exterior doorway, providing a vestibule, each with a *partition (hec qal'éw's)*. This appendage was made by lashing two vertical lodge poles together and attaching them to the tipi-like structure by two separate walls, each extending approximately 2 to 2.5 m from the main structure. Every multi-pole dwelling had two of these vestibules, one at either side of each entrance, and was used

206

primarily for storing firewood, food parcels, tools, weapons, and materials needed when manufacturing baskets and other needed utilities during the winter. A vestibule also served as a place to remove snow and to hang wet clothing after entering.

A dwelling frequently had one or more additional outside structures near the entrance for storing firewood and kindling. Every long-house *firepit* (*ʔurʼšictm* or *snqʷlʼépmn*) had two large logs anchored in place by long, anchored pegs, and spaced in parallel fashion on either long side to prevent floor coverings from being ignited. Smoke exited through slight openings in the ridge. Yearly (before leaving the winter village and prior to commencing the extended subsistence round), or as needed, the top course of tule mats was removed from sleeping dwellings and cleaned of the accumulated soot for fear of fire from sparks the coming winter (Smith 1936-8:463); cleaning by brushing, scraping, or beating is not known.

In cold weather the entrances were closed with tule or cattail mats suspended at the top for ease of entry. Some elders recall hearing how shelves were located in each vestibule where dried meat was stored—always up high to keep the meat dry and beyond the reach of dogs, small children, and rodents. In addition, there were usually two or three cooking pits in the center aisle, depending upon the length of the earth lodge and the number of families in residence. "Even during warm weather, when occupants [were] cooking and eating outside their lodge, at least one fire was maintained to purify the main dwelling" (Elmendorf 1935-6, 1:5). According to Lyons (pers. comm.), the question of fashioning exterior tule mats for covering a dwelling was more functional than what has always been viewed as a style of manufacture. Every adult had within the structure a *personal storage place* (*snkʷmlscútn*) for small items such as tools, whereas a person's *hidden items* (*scʔelkʼʷ*) were concealed by burial under a *floor mat* (*tkʷtin* or *syʼayʼs*) or secreted in the roofing material (Elmendorf 1935-6, 2:28-30).

A long-house could accommodate five to six nuclear or extended families, each occupying a sleeping compartment made semi-private, if necessary, with suspended partitions of tule mats from the slanted ceiling on side-wall frames. An extended family comprised a married couple, their children, and often one or more grandparents—a residential unit called *nkʼʷʔétxʷ*. Two families situated opposite one another would share the same fire and responsibilities of gathering firewood. A chief and his family had their own long-house, large enough to accommodate visiting people concerned with *council business* (*nqʼmqʼmílštn*) and visitors.

Elmendorf provided the following description of how the occupants of multiple family structures observed a special occupancy between men and women during the day and evening:

> Men went & came through [a] special door in [the] house - one door for men, one for women [...] Men assembled in [the] evening in this end of [the] house [and] ate [their] evening meal there - women served them [and the] women cooked for them - [tule] mats [were] spread over [the] whole end of [the] house - [the boys gathered around & listened - [while the] men talked or told stories - men only smoked on ceremonial occasions - [and] visitors smoked with them - peace was [the] idea. A number of families lived in such a house - [and] each family brought [their] own mats & roofed over a section for itself - [anyone] might use [or] own [a] fire [pit] or share with another family - sharing & neighborliness [was] highly developed - [they] travelled often in groups - always someone in [from the] village (1935-6, 1:4-5).

Both types of winter dwelling roofs were covered with mats of tule, cattail, or willow; approximately 2 m in length and 1 to 2 m in width. The first layer abutting the ground was made of three layers of mats, the second row had two layers, and the successive layers comprised of single mats overlapping the preceding lower row of mats. Mats were secured to the secondary frame from the inside, with long split willow withes. Hemp was used for securing *cattail mats* (*pʼštpáxn*), which were heavier than tule mats. Once the dwelling was covered, the lower courses of mats were sometimes covered with large slabs of spread bark, outside of which a sloping ditch was dug to take water away from the structure. Space was left at the apex of the two *slanting roof* (*nčʼmqnelxʷ*) sections for the emission of smoke.

Though not reported elsewhere, Walker's diary briefly mentions a large building in the center of a village, "I should think 30 feet long & fifteen wide, covered with flags, woven" (Drury 1976:79), a plant which Drury believed was, "A wild iris plant with sword-shaped leaves which grows in moist places. The natives wove the leaves into mats which were used in the construction of their lodges" (1976:79 fn).

Pickering visited a large encampment of twenty lodges and approximately 300 natives, lining in conical skin-lodges and some with buffalo robe coverings, "like those used on the Missouri" (Hale 1846, 4:59).

Ceremonial Long-House

Elmendorf (1935-6, 1:31-2) and Teit (1930:331) provide excellent descriptions for the methods of constructing a ceremonial long-house (often called a medicine lodge), which, prior to the reservation period, was used primarily as a ceremonial structure for public gatherings, religious ceremonies, weddings, funerals, as well as socioeconomic and political activities. The construction of a ceremonial long-house required the intended floor area to be excavated to a depth of approximately 50 cm, leaving an excavated floor area approximately 6 m wide and 12 to 14 m in length, and pounded with a butt log to level and pack the earth. A large structure might require at least ten to fourteen double-pole "V" sections, besides the number required for the two entrances and the ends. The structure was founded on a succession of two long poles, each roughly 7 m in length, tied near their top ends. The bottom ends formed an inverted "V," and were further stabilized when placed against the base of the walls made by the excavation, spread to the width of the proposed dwelling, and anchored firmly in holes approximately 40 to 50 cm apart. As will be discussed later, ceremonial long-houses used for Bluejay rituals always had ridge poles, while others did not. Further stability was afforded by lashing split or narrow diameter lodge poles horizontally to the length of the structure, starting just above the outside ground level and repeated every 60 to 70 cm up to the apex of the dwelling.

Both slanting sections of the long-house were made by tying together the small ends of approximately six lodge poles, and spreading the base of the poles in a hemisphere, making a pattern not unlike half a tipi. A doorway was made in each of these ends by placing two main poles 60 to 70 cm apart. Each door was made from cattail mats, secured in place by braided hemp. The structure was then covered with either cattail or tule mats, sometimes both. Typically, the series of over-lapping mats were each 3 m in length, made by the women who would arrange the ground row of mats and secure them to the frame by willow withes. The bottom of each ascending course slightly overlapped the lower row of mats until both sides were covered. Either a cattail or tule *mat (sy'áy'qs)* was used in a winter *medicine lodge (sy'i?qséɫxʷ)*.

Every ceremonial long-house had a firepit situated in the back of the structure, permitting the smoke to be emitted through the apex of the roof where it escaped by the smoke's heat. When used for the Medicine Dance, three spaced fires were always built. It was common for a dance-house to have three, each fireplace was always tended by one of three men appointed by the dance leader (Elmendorf 1935-6, 1:24). Each medicine lodge had a *sacred door (sčɫnh?ép)*, used exclusively by Bluejays (Egesdal, pers. comm.).

Unfortunately there are no detailed ethnographic accounts or known photographic depictions of how the *ceremonial* or *dance-house (st'áx̣ʷa* or *str'qem)* differed from the first type of long-house, if in fact, it did. However, some elders said they were one and the same, differing only in use. What is known is that the term 'ceremonial long-house' was most applicable when the structure served as the primary facility for the Mid-Winter Ceremonies, which were primarily World Renewal Rites, and always required the use of the power pole for individuals to renew their power. Through time, the ethnographic nuances defining the use of such a structure are further complicated by the term *song-house (snkʷenm'eɫxʷtn)* or dance-house where the *?e n'ixʷmi* dance was held; this term, several elders recalled, was synonymous with dance or ceremonial house (STHC).

The present carpenter-built Spokan long-house continues to be the center for the aforementioned functions. At least once a year there is a general open council meeting when the tribe discusses political and socioeconomic issues, and sometimes votes upon pending legislation. The Spokan long-house is currently the place for certain Winter Ceremonies that are being revitalized.

Log Houses

Prior to having access to *lumber* (*scpíč*), and reflecting Euro-American influences, many Spokan adopted the use of dressed logs for *log houses* (*sq'c'ełxʷ*), horse barns, and storage structures prior to the reservation system. Several of these rather magnificent structures, attesting to craftsmanship and durability, were standing not too many years ago. One log dwelling, now burned, was approximately 10 m in length, 4 m wide, and side walls approximately 3 m high. Some elders recalled two-story dwellings of broad-axed, hand-adzed Ponderosa pine logs: none of which now exist. Such structures varied in dimension, but nearly all were rectangular with a hipped framed roof that was covered with long 50 to 60 cm tamarack or cedar shingles, hand split with an offset frow. In areas of cattle, long-deserted, partially excavated dwellings and barns were burned to prevent cattle from entering and possibly breaking a leg.

The walls were constructed of ponderosa pine logs fashioned to desired dimensions—usually 30 cm in width and 40 to 50 cm in height—by men using first a broad axe and finishing leveling with an adz. To prevent the dressed log from twisting, the center or heart wood was always off-center. Each end was given an inverted "V" notch on top and undercut with an upright "V" notch, thereby accommodating another; similarly, dressed log which was situated at right angles. The four bottom-most logs, forming the rectangular frame, were set off the ground by several flat granite slab rocks to prevent the log base from rotting the base frame and plank flooring. Prior to using planks, floors were made of pounded earth mixed with clay brought from stream beds. The vertical weight and end-notching kept the log walls in place, and were then finished by caulking the slight interstices with clay mixed with *dried grass* (*supúlexʷ*), and some builders first chinked large log wall interstices, "with sticks and moss and then plastered over with clay" (Bagley 1924:30) (1843-1932). No nails were used except when securing a door frame or occasional window frame of thinly dressed boards. The door was made of boards, some had leather hinges before metal hinges were adopted.

Prior to acquiring iron stoves, a log dwelling often had an inside *fireplace* (*nxm'élč* - "hollow burned out tree") and a chimney made of local slab granite held in place by chinking with blue clay, usually with a vertical height of approximately 2 m and a thickness of 35 to 40 cm. The Spokan log homes were often constructed with fireplaces of adobe bricks, which the missionaries Walker and Eells realized "would catch fire, usually in the coldest weather when a hot fire was needed. This often caused a part of the fireplace chimney to collapse" (Drury 1976:131 fn). Work was once present when, "One Indian lodge took afire and was burnt" (1820:111). Structures built by early trapper-traders had relatively large fireplaces, ones in which, "Firewood was cut in three-foot lengths and, as in most trading posts was burned vertically instead of being laid horizontally" (Bond 1971:85). Some log houses had an outside kitchen with one side against the dwelling with vertical wood walls protected by a sloping cedar or tamarack shake roof. Burnett recalled how roof timbers were secured with wooden pegs, and cedar shakes were, "also fastened on with wooden pegs" (Lewis 1925a:23).

Women's Winter Bathing Hut

Without providing any dimensions or structural details, Elmendorf provides the only known account of a women's *bathing pool* (*snáwlštn*) hut that was possibly a permanent structure in many if not all riverine winter villages; one that was located:

> [...] in [the] women's quarters [with tule] curtains set up between [the] main river & these [three] pools made of reed matting close to [the] river - dug oblong holes & lined them with rocks - fire lighted and rocks [were] heated. [The] pools [were] about 6' long - 3 of them - [and] lined with good sized rocks - ditches [were] dug from them to the river - [and] cold water [was] let in from [the] river by opening ditches - [until the] 3 pools [were] full - hot rocks and ashes for soap [were] put in [the] first pool - [hot] rock[s] [were placed] in [the first and] in the second pool & [the] 3rd was [for a] cold dip - if they had a dress or anything they wanted to wash they carried it along with them from pool to pool - after bathing in [the] first pool [they also] bathed in [the] second [pool] -

[they then] dipped in [the] third [pool] as [for a] rinse - [after they would take] little switches of [the] *t'sntsútn* bush or twigs and switched themselves dry by the fire (1935-6, 1:65).

Drury, using Elkanah Walker's 1840 diary, explained how the Tschimakain missionaries used both wood ash and caustic soda deposits located near Medical Lake to make soap, and suggests the missionaries taught the Spokan how to use ash and soda when bathing (1976:148-9 fn, 169 fn).

Temporary Structures

Temporary dwellings (*q'ey'xʷeyeʔ*), by their construction, size, and location, reflected the high degree of mobility the Spokan required when traveling during the annual subsistence round, searching for food and attending to the gathering of needed resources. These structures were built mainly for privacy, protection from inclement weather, and of course temporary storage of food. And yet the term temporary is not always valid; perhaps being used when considering building material and not ease or difficulty in construction. An example, as will be discussed, was the tipi.

An unusually productive *resource camp* (*snq'iq'eyitn*), usually at major root fields or berrying patches, at harvest was occupied by relatively large but temporary populations of several hundred or more inhabitants. Noted examples of such areas were located at Little Falls where the Coeur d'Alene, Colville, Kalispel, Palouse, and Sinkaietk people gathered in great numbers. A large heterogeneous gathering of different groups occurred further upriver at Spokane Falls, a feature often referred to as the Chutes by Work (Elliott 1914, 4:267 fn).

The mostly grass and wood materials used in construction were frequently acquired within the vicinity of the *camp* (*q'eyɬxʷm* - "to make camp"). Temporary structures, degraded by weather and general deterioration, were renewed each year of occupancy. Upon arrival at the temporary camps, it was common for families to transport rolled tule mats from winter villages. This was done when vacating the summer camp for the winter village, or when moving to another resource camp. Women were responsible for constructing and disassembling a dwelling, and, when traveling with men's hunting parties, would make an overnight hunting structure. When vacating temporary camps, lodge poles were carefully bundled and stacked vertically against nearby trees for use the following year, to prevent rot or warping of the poles.

The life of a pole was extended by first debarking and then rubbing and smoothing the entire length with deer *antlers* (*qxqxmíntn*), thereby making it more impervious to water and weathering. This process leaves the wood with a smooth, shiny surface that reduces water absorption. It is an interesting and excellent example of the Spokan learning from nature, having observed long ago how the wood that had been rubbed smooth by animals (for whatever reason) did not rot while the other parts of the same *piece of wood* (*l'luq'ʷ*) were often thoroughly rotted. For instance, near deer salt licks they observed how the bottom 2 m or so of a dead ponderosa tree would seldom rot, because of frequent rubbing against it (as indicated by the animal hairs stuck in it, and the lack of bark), making it as smooth and almost like stone.

Summer Mat Dwellings

When mutually exploiting resource sites for some duration, each nuclear or extended family was responsible for building temporary mat dwellings, even at major fisheries such as Little Falls, Spokane Falls, and Latah Creek. There were, however, permanent dwellings for those individuals who remained at these fishing sites through much of the year, usually men and their families who were responsible for stewardship of the area. For example, one powerful shaman, named *sč'uɬšmxe* ("climbing grizzly bear"), maintained a year-round residence at Little Falls and was considered by many to be the steward of this fishing facility.

A temporary dwelling located for purposes of fishing or hunting was called *snʔistčtn*, indicating a location usually protected from *wind* (*hi q'ʷúy'* - "it is sheltered"), and had access to water. These sites were occasionally used for hunting deer during fall and winter, and the structures built of loose materials were

210

referred to as *t'qéɫxʷ*. Some temporary summer dwellings at higher elevations were built by placing slabs of peeled red cedar or Ponderosa bark over bent or angular poles, the lower sections being anchored with earth, and the higher pieces of bark were secured by passing hemp or buckskin through pre-bored holes, and tied to the frame. During fall camping, the spring and summer dwellings were frequently slant-pole structures covered with tule mats brought from the winter village for this purpose. When in transit through known areas, temporary dwellings were located in sites called *λ'ʔeʔlpm* ("search for a place to sleep"), which referred to a camp-site that was ideal for bedding down during brief durations—having water and available building materials.

The surface remains of various structures used during summer and fall resource hunting, and other food gathering pursuits, can be examined only through archaeology, and occasionally located by existing geonomic designations. Structures at overnight camps, and short-term-use resource sites were temporary, made of available materials, and usually built in less than an hour. One example of such a dwelling was the *lean-to* (*č'k'ʷek'ʷl'č* or *snsč'tmế*), which was erected by easily removing slabs of *tree bark* (*č'iʔet'čl'éɫxʷ*) for a cover or temporary walls that were ideal for constructing fall hunting camp structures. As previously noted, it was common for temporary pole structures to be disassembled when no longer needed, and in all cases the poles were bundled and carefully stacked against a tree for protection from warping and rotting. Given distance and local resources, tule, cattail, or willow mats, as well as cordage and deer hides, were brought to a temporary *camping site* (*nɫxɫx*). Tule and willow mats were more durable and not as heavy as cattail mats, and, if properly *stored* (*ʔelk'ʷ''ntxʷ* - "to stash") off the ground, could last for two to three years before requiring replacement. Occasionally a tule or cattail roofing mat would have one or more leaks, and, if large enough, could admit rain. Leaks were sealed by plugging the hole with a fir cone or wadded leaves.

Regardless of the builder, there was no sense of ownership, and the use of buildings or acquiring new building materials was determined by the immediate builder's needs. Both men and women cooperated in the construction of short duration temporary dwellings. Unfortunately there is no record or oral history to suggest that men gave any assistance to women constructing and maintaining their temporary menstrual huts.

Traditionally, when constructing a summer tule mat lodge, there was a strict division of labor. The initial construction was commenced by men excavating a circular pit, approximately 12 cm in depth, the circumference being determined by the size and number of occupants. The bases of each of the three large poles were spaced equally around the structure's circumference, and secured at the top by hemp or buckskin. Poles smaller in diameter were then stood between the base poles and secured at the top in like fashion. Commencing at the bottom, a series of triple-layered tule mats encircled the structure, each mat being secured to the inside resting poles with hemp. At the top of the apex of each opposite *top course of tule mats* (*psúɫptn*), a small hole was left for the escape of smoke. The only dimension Curtis recorded was that of the height of the mat lodges which he estimated to be, "about fifteen feet in height" (1911, 7:75). Earth, turf, and slabs of bark were banked around the exterior of the lodge for stability and warmth. An east-facing doorway was protected with an attached cattail mat, being sturdier than one made of tules.

The earthen floor, as in nearly all types of dwellings, would be covered with layers of various species of available grass, and finished with a layer of tule mats. With several families of one or more, excavated fire hearths were situated roughly in the center of the lodge, and if necessary were shared with other families who would often share the cooking baskets, and kept alight by the women when occupied. This type of dwelling had two or three living areas partitioned with hanging tule mats, and each area would be occupied by an extended consanguineal family, whose women had manufactured the mats used in the construction of the dwelling. The entrances to all winter dwellings had *doormats* (*kʷɫcníl'xʷpnsutn*) made of either tule or cattail, which were turned over every day until being replaced. Outside *campfires* (*ʔur'seyʔútyeʔ* - "small campfire") were always extinguished after use for fear of grass or bush fires being ignited by wind.

211

Summer Hunting and Gathering Camps

Throughout the annual subsistence round, most hunting camps were *deer camps* (*hecq'éyi*) or *fall hunting camps* (*hes ec č²eymíi*) for deer. Summer and early fall camp sites were named after a certain plant resource gathered by women, nearness of water, or unusual topographical features. Resource camp locations were often traditionally occupied by the same resident group who were responsible for annual selective burning, when necessary.

After a successful hunt, deer meat was dried, pounded, and usually stored in grass bags before being transferred to winter villages for storage. The women, who accompanied men to hunting camps (STHC), scraped and tanned deer hides. A late summer or *fall hunting place* (*snčłptin*) was frequently one that the same hunters used year after year, and was typically in an area in close proximity to game and berrying areas, and known to be good for *bedding-down* (*λ'²élpm* - "looking for a camp"). The same families often congregated to gather subsistence and to enjoy the collective company after the women returned from berrying, and the men from a *hunt* (*sčłip*). In late afternoon, both children and adults played games, while some men gambled. After dinner, storytelling by one or more adults provided the children with accounts of the past.

Small hunting groups would form a temporary summer camp by building a tent-like structure using numerous long sections of bark or tule mats, which were layered over a series of parallel poles laid horizontally with each end secured to two inverted "V" shaped uprights.

Women's Semi-Subterranean Day Lodge

One of Elmendorf's elderly informants provided the only known description of a near-complete *women's semi-subterranean day lodge* (*ul'ečin'*) structure which would have probably existed at least until 1870. Elmendorf's diagram of the structure illustrates how a horizontal ridge pole was supported at intervals by five pairs of slanting poles that formed an A-frame:

> Dirt [was] piled [on the] sides to [cover the] top [and] dug down some into [the] ground—this was at *ntntúlm* or *sčláq'łx^w*—("buried house")—[and] dug out 3' or more in [the] ground—[and was] used for [a] cool retreat in hot weather—this place was used by women as a quiet place where they could sew (1935-6, 3:29).

There remains the question as to the actual construction of what the Spokan referred to as a *completely subterranean house* (*stclák'łx^w* - "buried house"). Several elderly women recall their grandmothers providing memories of such structures—a structure that was entered from the top. The conflict of informants giving different ethnographic statements is evident in Elmendorf's research on underground houses, which some younger Spokan say never existed, and yet others did provide plausible descriptions from oral history. As frequently happens in gathering oral history, or descriptions of past beliefs and rituals, and with loss of language and even concern with the past, it is common for a person to deny that the aforementioned events ever existed. The other assumption is that white people have no knowledge or should not be privy to the Indian past. Consequently, what are most valuable are Elmendorf's field notes and his linguistic ability.

Depending upon the size of a winter village, there would be at least one or sometimes several relatively small semi-subterranean structures, each used exclusively by women as a retreat during the day. Apparently women never slept in this structure, which may have been tempting since it was a cool retreat in the summer and warm in the winter. This was a place where women could sew, enjoy each other's conversation, or simply relax in peace and quiet. Such a structure afforded a nursing mother an opportunity to take her child for privacy from her family. Interesting that Teit cites how, "the underground house was not used by the tribes of the Flathead group, except possibly a very few by the Kalispel and Lower Spokan" (1930:331).

The roughly 2-by-3 m dwelling was built atop a deeply (?) excavated depression, over which the women placed a sufficient number of half-length poles that formed a series of inverted "V"s. These were then stabilized by laying and securing a long lodge pole lengthwise across, and connecting the tops of each section.

The structure was roofed with tule mats and finally with a deep layer of earth. A firepit was dug in the ground toward the back of the structure, and smoke exited through a small opening above the firepit.

In the summer, both wall-ends were left open for ventilation, whereas in winter only the leeward end was left open, which was impossible for a completely subterranean dwelling. Such a structure was usually located back and away from the main village, where men knew not to trespass, nor were children permitted near the structure, it being basically a women's retreat. Some smaller *rock house* (*sšn'šéłxʷ*) retreats were made by erecting dry walls of vesicular basalt around the edges of an excavated pit. The structure was completed with a slanting flat roof of lodge poles, and then covered with fir branches or tule mats that supported an earthen cover. The completed structure accommodated one to several women (McCarty, pers. comm.).

Women's Seclusion Structures

As a result of concentrated domestic living, most notably with several unrelated families in a single longhouse, it is understandable that women sometimes chose to temporarily segregate themselves from men in a secluded area or *secluded place* (*snq'áwqncútn* - "place where one can saying one's medicine song") (Egesdal, pers. comm.). This was often a woman's semi-buried dwelling, which Elmendorf (1935-36, 3:29) called *ntutuʔúlm* or *stelák'łxʷ*. It is significant that the term *meʔmeʔmíst* was applied to a group of several or more women, who, over time, had been deserted by their husbands. These women never dwelled together, but during the day collectively shared a special low-roofed structure that reputedly allowed each solitary woman emotional support from other deserted women who meet sometimes daily to sweat and confer with one another. However, even while secluded from men, they continued to complete their domestic tasks. Women who usually shared the same sweathouse would share in constructing and utilizing a secluded area or structure. On occasion it was used for a pregnant woman's delivery.

Another example of using a secluded dwelling was when a woman was unable to get along amicably with her husband, or when tension was created by his taking a second wife, which forced the first wife to retire temporarily to a place of seclusion in *a stump house* (*snquʔq'ntéłxʷtn*). Such a structure—often a tipi—would vary in size, but being somewhat larger if shared with one or more married women. Of course the number of these secluded retreats depended upon village or camp size. Any woman was free to enter such a retreat after seeking permission from the other occupants, though more often a woman was asked to reside by residing women who presumably were aware of another person's need for seclusion. The rights of a woman's privacy was apparent when bathing:

> [...] in the open this place would be surrounded by a kind of palisade of poles on tripod supports like a fish trap—[with] reed matting laid over that—sometimes branches [were] woven in this, or trees [were] used for support—same as [for] protection from [the] river side of [a] woman's bathing area (Elmendorf 1935-6, 1:69-70).

However, and not in conflicting descriptions within his unedited Spokan field notes, Elmendorf and some other ethnographers such as Allan Smith, and even historians acknowledge the variation of their written descriptions of past Indian practices and beliefs, probably due primarily to deculturation. For example, Elmendorf noted, when writing about semi-subterranean dwellings, that there was "no particular rule to keep men out" (1935-6, 2:31) of a woman's semi-subterranean lodge, whereas earlier he implies there was. One must of course define the term semi-subterranean, and if the structure was completely or only partially subterranean:

> [a] hole dug in [the] ground & a roof [was placed] over [the] top & smoke came out [through the] roof & the women would sit there in the winter time & sew [... a] very small fire in this would keep it warm. [The structure was] small, about 10' x 6' - [and called] *ulátcín'* = underground "house" like this—[but was] never slept [in] these [sic]—dirt [was] piled on the roof—[and there was a] hole in [the] roof toward [the] back for smoke and [a] door at one side of [the] fire—remembers hearing of a tribe using underground houses, but says the Spokanes never used them (1935-6, 1-31).

Winter Hunting Camps

Some winter camp sites might actually occupy summer camp sites, and were always situated to permit ready access to known deer areas, called *snʔiʔstčtis*. The location of a relatively high, temporary *wintering camp place* (*snʔis'tčn* - "wintering place") sometimes varied according to the weather, the deer population, and the resulting decision that ultimately determined the group's strategy, which often depended upon the group's mobility. Hunters at winter deer hunting camps were never attended by children, but often by the hunters' wives who fulfilled domestic chores as well as processing the deer meat and hides—tanning them later at the village. A woman's main chore was the gathering of firewood. If the winter camp occupied a previous summer camp, some ricked and bark-covered firewood may be present, having been gathered by earlier occupants.

Debarked and previously stored lodge poles were used year after year for the construction of tipis and of longer rectangular fir-covered inverted double-pole structures. As mentioned, poles were carefully stacked near-vertically against the trunk of a large fir tree. When possible, rectangular dwellings were usually sided with slabs of pine bark, for black cottonwood trees were never available at higher elevations. If caught in a snow storm without proper shelter, "the snow-trapped hunter would sleep in a fresh deer hide" (Smith 1951:82).

Given weather conditions and the fluctuation of deer population, it was sometimes necessary to find a new winter campsite, a decision usually made by several of the elderly men who had previous experience as to where to *search for a place to camp* (*λ̓ʔélpm*) and the location of game. All campsites were named according to a physical feature, resource, or an unusual event of a hunt, but *never* after a person.

Brush Shelters

Temporary fir bough shelters were common in hunting and other transient camps at higher elevations, ones requiring little effort or time to build. Often a similar *small dwelling* (*kʷʔukʼʷɫxʷntm* or *kʷʔkʼʷim'eʔɫxʷeʔxʷ* - "someone made a small dwelling") would be used to *provide shade* (*čɫč'éyneʔɫtn* - "they would sit in the shade" or "woven with tules") during hot weather, or to contain heat from a small fire in the late autumn or winter. Poles were erected to form a *low conical tule tipi* (*siy'ay'qs*), a lean-to, or a rectangular shelter with walls of tree boughs—preferably balsam-fir boughs—that were hung inverted upon smaller interwoven poles. A simple but effective small framed brush shelter afforded adequate protection when covered with *fir* or *pine boughs shelters* (*st'qéɫxʷ*), preferably the former. A small fire was made during cold weather, as smoke was not a problem due to adequate airflow. For longer occupancy, a more substantial shelter could be made using large sections of bark stripped from either dead or living trees. These sections were held in place by leaning each over-lapped end against a single slanting pole that was held higher at one end by a cross of two short pieces of wood.

When occupying a summer camp, a mother might comply with the wishes of her young children and construct a small dwelling for their play and replication of adult activities. The structure was made of fir boughs, bark slabs, or deer hide supported by a tri-pole frame. Fires were never permitted within such a dwelling, but built in an outdoor *camp-site fire site* (*snʔurʔur'šictn*). Likewise, inverted fir boughs were used as their *bedding* (*č'ɫqʼʷmqʼʷmncúʔtis*). Brush arbors were never disassembled upon vacating, particularly at *temporary camp sites* (*nɫxɫx*).

Trappers' Winter Dwellings

When exploiting established trapping areas, it was necessary to make near-daily runs of a trapline for fear that a trapped and debilitated animal would be destroyed by a predator. Consequently, a trapper constructed one or two line dwellings, each structure was strategically located at the extreme ends of his trapline, permitting the trapper to spend one night in one lodge, then the following day run his trapline and spend that night in the other dwelling. This strategy was repeated until he had exhausted his food supply or had to return to his winter village with a load of skins. A trapper's dwelling assumed various forms that were largely determined by the available materials, individual preference of design, and how extensive the trapline was since a trapline was often too distant from the village, and a trapper was dependent upon available site materials for building or repairing the previous winter lodge. Traplines and any associated dwellings were invariably passed on, if possible, to the eldest son.

The varying elevation and location of drainage systems that supported different fur-bearing animals, often determined the type of dwelling a trapper would construct. The dwellings were often one of two basic forms: a temporary tipi or a more substantial lodge pole structure. Of the two dwellings, one was a larger and more elaborate structure that was necessary to store trapping paraphernalia, hides, stretching frames, snowshoes, and other winter gear, as well as food. This more substantial dwelling—often at higher elevations—had a square or rectangular floor plan. The dwelling was constructed of a lodge pole frame with pitched and pole rafters, which supported a roof of secured fir boughs. A trapper's line dwelling had neither windows nor an integral door. The interior and contents were protected by a series of vertically lashed lodge poles, which could be easily moved by pivoting on one longer edge pole.

After acquiring the broad axe and adz, some trappers constructed log structures. Prior to the recline of fur-marketing, some elderly men recalled hearing how in the late 1800s and early 1900s a larger structure sometimes had a split tamarack or cedar shake roof if the owner had a Hudson's Bay cruising ax. Roofing shakes were held in place by a series of long lodge poles secured by looped wires over the external poles that passed through the roof and tied to interior support poles. Elmendorf (pers. comm.) spoke of an elderly man who once saw a trapper's log dwelling with a slanted roof of logs large enough to support snow weight.

When winter stream-trapping, the second type of structure was a relatively simple pole-frame hide tipi that was protected by large over-lapping slabs of black cottonwood bark. This type of structure was preferred because of the availability and ease of acquiring the necessary poles and bark. Regardless of the method of construction, no structure was safe from the ravages of a bear or a wolverine. Log dwellings were never disassembled after a trapping season.

A trapper often skinned the hides he obtained, but never tanned them while in the woods away from his line cabin. After cleaning a beaver or muskrat pelt, he then stretched each hide on a stout round wooden stretching frame, which later permitted the prepared hides to be more easily packed, being laid flat and not folded. Stretching frames were, if possible, hauled to his most structurally sound permanent year round dwelling. Otherwise, traps and equipment was left in a trapper's line dwelling until the next winter, and once the steel trap was introduced, a trapper stored his traps and bent wooded hoops used for stretching hides in the main line dwelling.

It was understood that any stored food or firewood in a trapper's line dwelling could be used as a haven by anyone caught in a severe snow storm. Given the length of a person's refuge, used supplies and firewood were, if possible, always later replenished by the visitor. There was no memory of theft, but damage by wolverine was reported.

Tule Mat Ramadas

Women used the shade of tule mat ramadas during warm weather while they performed sedentary sitting-chores or handiwork, often in company with other women who shared their company and gossip. The square, flat, tule-covered roof would be supported by a simple frame of four corner-connected poles, approximately 2 m by 2 m. Each corner was supported by an upright pole, each about 2 m in length. This type of temporary structure, called a *čłq'aʔq'iʔsc*, was always built by a woman who located it near the main dwelling to have better visibility of the camp doings and the activities of her family and any grandchildren in her charge. Such a structure apparently had no tule mat walls, which would have restricted air-flow and prevented the occupants' surveillance of the camp. When ramadas were used during summer fishing, the tule mat roof would be removed so that the structure could serve as a sun-drying rack for fish (Smith 1936-8:517). Smith described how during fishing season, all three Spokan groups would remove the covering tule mats and place horizontally a series of smaller diameter [but stout] willow rods across the main supports to dry fish (1991:8.53).

Bark, Hide, and Canvas Tipis

Ray contended that the Spokan never used the *tipi* (*q'ey'múty'e?* or *citx^w* - "gathered at the top"), particularly the early *buckskin tipi* (*c'?úlix^wéɫx^w* or *sp'y'eɫx^w* - "buckskin tipi") during aboriginal times (1977:39), which was probably acquired initially from the Flathead and further influenced by groups going onto the Plains. However, linguistic and ethnographic evidence, and existing old photographs prove that the Spokan used tipis. The *hide tipi* (*sp'y'eɫx^w* - "skin house") was later replaced by the *canvas tipi* (*sp'c'néɫx^w*),, presumably by the early 1800s when the Spokan commenced using bison hide, probably first acquired from the Nez Perce (STHC).

The earliest recorded observation of a Spokan tipi was by Cox in 1830, who observed a hide structure that was "a comfortable dwelling covered with deerskins" (1831:103). And as late as 1915, "Quite a few of the natives could boast of buffalo skin lodges, but principally the teepees were made of tule matting, and some could afford cotton sheeting" (Cowley 1916, 1:53-5). On the other hand, Drury quotes Cox as saying, "few of the Indian lodges were made out of buffalo hides. Some were constructed out of native tule matting and a few out of cotton sheeting purchased from the white man" (1949:139). The size of tipis varied according to the size of the *family* (*sx^wsx^wltel'is*), but oral and pictorial evidence indicates that the Spokan used both the earlier hide and later canvas tipis which could accommodate *several families in one tipi* (*k'^wnšqsustm*).

Years later, Pickering (1895:27), without providing specific location, visited a large Spokan encampment of approximately twenty lodges: "some of the lodges were, as usual, of mats; and to my surprise, I saw also buffalo robes, and conical skin-lodges, like those used on the Missouri."

From existing photographs, and the memories of elderly informants, it may be concluded that the Spokan used a three-pole foundation for the twelve to fifteen additional *lodge poles* (*čwatč'lew'stn* or *sqéy'mn* or *sxxc'ey'*), which, after *erected* (*?uc'lx^wnte?s* or *q'íq'e?yɫx^wm* - "setting up tipis") by women, gave shape and support to the covering. The skirt of the tipi material, where it touched the ground, was held in place with either heavy stones or *tipi pegs* (*sq'^wpeɫx^wtn* or *ck^wpéɫx^wt*) made from red osier dogwood, serviceberry, and other hardwoods whose sharpened ends had been fire-hardened for durability, but never of bone.

There are accounts that de-haired and tanned bison hides were once used for covering tipis (STHC) that had been acquired by trade initially from the Flathead and later on a more regular basis after the Spokan acquired the horse, venturing more readily onto the Plains. But it was not long after the arrival of the horse that canvas became the favored material when constructing summer tipis, eventually replacing tule mat construction.

The first tipi was probably a tule mat tipi, which was an excellent adaptation in warm weather since the mats could breathe, and when it rained the tules swelled enough and became 'waterproof'. This type of covering was eventually replaced by elk or deer hide tipis. The first skin tipi—probably used as a *summer home* (*sp'y'eɫx^w* - "hide tipi")—was made from elk hide or a series of patterned deer hides, later replaced by bison hide, a technology that the Spokan probably learned from the Nez Perce during the 1880s (Elmendorf 1935-236, 2:29; STHC).

Figure 14. Closed tule mat tipi

An elderly Spokan lady, Nancy Perkins Wynecoop (1875-1939), recorded many of her mother's experiences. She provided a description—probably observed when she was a child during the late 1870s—of her mother making cattail mats for covering tipis, as well as for bedding:

> There were different ways of weaving the grass mats. Circular mats were made for the round teepee. There were three mats for these. The one at the bottom was about four yards long, the others shorter. Cattail stalks were used, all the stalk ends together, making it narrower at one end. Other mats were woven by alternating the ends, first a small end, then a large. Pine boughs were covered with grass for beds. During the day, grass mats were laid over the beds. At night they were spread with blankets and skins (Wynecoop 1985:65).

The lower, middle, and upper sections of tipis were 'winterized' with three rows of such cattail mats, which essentially encircled the interior.

Opposite the entryway, in the *back of the tipi* (*nč'mpełxʷ*), was located a tripod frame-supported willow or silverberry woven mat *backrest* (*ntáqʼᵂčnʼ* or *sp;óqʷiʔ*) placed against the two forward legs for the oldest male. In the past, the backrest also served as a holder for medicine bundles (Schaeffer 1934-38, I-104). The

217

backrest was the only thing a man owned, since a woman owned all the food, even meat and fish, once it was brought into the tipi, and "was placed at the head of the married couple's bed" (Schaeffer 1934-37, I-78:5). On the other hand, the women, who made and erected the tipis, were the sole owners of the coverings, and it seems reasonable that they made any decisions as to their construction and appearance—which is given credence by comparative ethnographic reasoning afforded by Turney-High's work with the Flathead, which was also applicable for the Spokan:

> The women made and in theory owned the tents. This was most reasonable since there was no mean trick in the designing, cutting, and fitting, and the toil involved was considerable. Except for the bride's first tipi, which she rather ceremonially made by herself, a new tipi cover was made by all the women of the camp who would help. Ordinarily there was no difficulty in persuading six to ten skilful women to help since it was a fine time for gossip, exhibition of skill, and for eating liberal repasts laid out by the hostess. Cover designers were considered experts and were admired by all the village. This woman might direct all the work, although specialists in certain particular skills were usually called in; one for the ticklish job of designing and fitting the smoke hole wings, one for fitting the top, one known for her ability in sewing up the front, and so on. These specialists worked without fee, content with the adulation of the others, and the joy of bossing subordinates (1937:100).

When a *tipi liner* (*snč'ɫyel'xʷtn*) was installed in late autumn, the tipi was, according to elders, a warm and comfortable structure, even when heated by only a low fire. The liner, made of numerous stitched deer hides—later canvas—was sometimes retained throughout the summer because the extra layer made excellent insulation for retaining cool air and provided efficient ventilation when rolled up. Tipi liners were approximately a meter or more in width and hung just to the ground, the top edge being held in place at each tipi pole by ties. Smith's description of Kalispel tipi liners was the same for the Chewelah-Spokan Group and Lower Spokan:

> Around the bottom of the skin tipi, which was never used in winter, they put a 4 foot wide strip of skin around between the poles and the outer skin. It was just pinched here and was not fastened even at the top; it was not pegged at the ground but it just comes down and hits the ground; it does not bend over the ground. At the edges where it hit the two door poles, it was generally only one buckskin string threaded thru a number of holes at the top and tied around the door poles; occasionally there is one at the middle and the bottom but only rarely. The Chewelah [Chewelah-Spokan Group] also had this (1936-8:511).

Because of the problems of controlling open-ventilation, bark tipis were, if possible, rarely occupied in the summer—only during winter. Also, it was far more difficult to collect materials for erecting a bark tipi, whereas canvas presented none of these problems. Canvas was more flexible and withstood wind pressure better than bark, and was lighter and more transferable. After a heavy snow, a woman would carefully beat on the insides of the canvas to release the snow, or later she shoveled away the accumulated snow from around the base of the dwelling with her snow shovel or a bear-paw snowshoe to prevent any leakage or water infiltration from fire-melted snow.

In the summer, women would cut fir boughs that were placed against the outside of the tipi to afford a ramada for temporary shade. The fabric *ears of the tipi* (*t'nt'éne?*) (smoke flaps or smoke wings) were pocketed so the dog or *tipi ear poles* (*c'k'ʷc'k'ʷmín*) could be maneuvered to close the hole at the apex during torrential rains, or to catch the wind for better ventilation. Existing photographs illustrate how the customary ventilation or the two *dog ears* (*tn'ten'e?s*) of the *smoke hole* (*č'mqnéɫxʷ* or *snmatqnéλxʷ*) were supported and controlled by tipi ear-flap poles. Each tipi had a *large feather* (*sqpúsl*) from one of the supporting poles, a type of *flag* (*k'ʷɫy'il'xʷpncútn*) that indicated wind direction, often required when adjusting the dog ears for better ventilation. The translated term 'dog pole' came about from Plains Indian, since these two poles were used in the construction of each travois that was pulled by dogs—prior to the adoption of the horse. The dragging or butt ends of the two poles were treated in one of two ways: green hide from a bison's hump was used to cover the ends of each pole, or the ends were hardened by running deer horn back and forth forcibly to break the wood cells, giving it a smooth, hard surface. These measures were used to prevent the poles from being slowly worn down while being dragged along the rough ground, particularly since poles were so scarce on the plains, and resisted rot when placed upright on damp ground.

Located just inside to the left of the doorway was a *tipi storehouse* (*xaλéneʔ*) or *tipi pantry* (*xléneʔ*), made of vertical poles that reached the inclined wall and were covered with hide. One or more simple buckskin *storage pockets* (*nxlénč*) were stitched to either the tipi liner or directly to the tipi for storage of small items needed for daily house-keeping.

On a tipi, its *entry flaps* (*čʼłnyilʼxéptn*) or *entry flap door* (*čʼłnšrʼpncútn*) was closed with special *fastener sticks* (*čwtčʼlʼéwʼstn*) sharpened at both ends. The entrances to tipis always faced the water or when distant from water, they faced the main trail. Under certain situations, the tipis formed a circle with entrances to the center of the encampment. When grouped, each was immediately adjacent to the other on each side. Tipi doors were made of tule or cattail mats, and kept closed by a special *hardwood pin* (*čutčʼélʼuʔstn*). There are three excellent examples of partially earth and lichen-covered stone *tipi rings* (*qʼuclxutn*) at a once-traditional on-reservation summer fishing camp. Such fine examples of tipi rings are rarely found in the Plateau, and are undoubtedly another example of diffusion of the traits originating with Plain's peoples. Yet it is possible that some small dwellings used such stones to hold the circular base of a hide or cloth covering material, but not tule matting. In an on-reservation summer Spokane River fishing site, there are still two excellent examples of what appear to have been tipi rings.

When residing in a tipi, domestic responsibilities were strongly influenced by an established division of labor, one that acknowledged the constant concern and efforts of women who performed all the chores. During the day, and when not outside gathering wood or food, a woman was usually minding the fire, cooking, boiling water, or caring for children. Fires were started in a three-log fire place with the opening to the entrance. This *cooking hole* (*snłččíntn*) located to the right or left of the entrance used pitch wood, but the main wood was deciduous firewood, which did not impart a pine flavor or smoke as much as fir or pine. The fire-hole was lined with a woven bark bowl (*łččín*) or a coiled cedar basket (Egesdal, per. comm.). Firewood was stored in the rear of the tipi. Most tipis had an *inside drying rack* (*snsqiʔéłcʼeʔtn*) for meat or fish.

Smith (1936-8:473) described an occasional practice of *smoking up* (*hecqʼxʷúłm*) a tipi, which demonstrated dissatisfaction to an unpleasant in-law relegated to the rear of the tipi to endure a smoking fire—sometimes to the delight of knowledgeable neighbors.

However, when possible, an elderly woman often positioned herself near the entrance of a tipi to better observe the doings of the younger children or, if her eyes served her, approaching guests; one who was a 'sticky beak'. The man tended to occupy the back of the tipi, exchanging news and smoking with any male guests (Smith 1936-8:511). Photographs and oral accounts verify that hide tipis were often painted with curvilinear and geometric designs, undoubtedly using the same traditional organic paints used for painting other hide items. Once the Spokan commenced to use canvas in lieu of tanned deer hide, there was a renaissance in the *designs on tipis* (*nqʼiʔqnʷéłxʷ*) in color and configuration, particularly *floral designs* (*scʼʔékʼʷ sqʼéyʼ*). Unfortunately, it is not known if a particular Spokan motif or art style ever developed, though it is highly likely that visits onto the Plains had a considerable influence on Spokan artistic expression.

Canvas tents (*kʼʷlkʼʷlčʼełxʷ* - "upside-down homes") and log houses as winter dwellings were largely replaced just prior to World War I when people commenced to occupy government lumber-built houses during the Allotment Period. Most of the construction was done by Spokan men who had been trained as carpenters by the U.S. Government or at mission or government boarding schools. Only two of the original allotment structures presently remain partially intact. However, several elders recalled four government houses being first built in 1896, and most were constructed from 1904 to 1907. Summer tipis were common on the Spokane Indian Reservation until the early 1940s—used mostly for sleeping. They are still used during the annual 4th of July Powwow. A few on-reservation families have erected tipi pole structures, with only a few being covered with canvas in the summer.

Caves

There is no archaeological evidence or known ethnographic citations or oral accounts to show that the Spokan ever used a *cave* (*nɬxʷolexʷ* - "hole in the ground") for any duration, but presumably they were occasionally used for temporary shelter during storms during travels.

Outhouses

With the construction of permanent carpenter-built houses, an adjacent feature was an *outhouse* (*snʔóʔcqeʔtn* or *snmnéčtn*) for each family dwelling, which initially—and for some time—was often avoided due to the fear of being sorcerized if such a person was able to surreptitiously acquire any bodily discharge, particularly feces. Some recall elders who described an unspoken protocol, whereby non-family members were not expected to use a family facility. The outhouse served some individuals for disposing of objects in a personal privy. If not near a privy, one was careful to never leave feces on the ground, which was buried in a pre-dug hole to a depth of approximately 8 to 10 cm, then covered with earth, and if available, a manageable-sized rock was later placed atop the small mound of earth to discourage an animal from digging. As mentioned, the top side of mullein leaves, if available, ideally served as toilet paper. No such disposal precautions were observed when one urinated, but it was done always at a distance from dwellings and food storage pits.

Sweathouses

The sweathouse, known as *t'úpyeʔ* ("great-grandfather" or *sláq'ist* or *kʷil'stn* - "sweat bath" or *orláq'a* - "splash with water"), was either constructed temporarily for brief use in camps, or as a permanent structure located in close proximity to the winter village. The size of a sweathouse or steam lodge was approximately 1 to 1.5 m in height, and 2 to 2.5 m in diameter. The *dome-like* (*k'ʷlč'uleʔxʷ*) sweathouse frame was made with long bent sections of red osier willow, *Osage orange* (*Maclura pomifera* [Raf.] Schneid.), or *syringa* (*Philadelphus Lewisii* Pursh, var. *Lewisii* - *wáxiʔɬp* or *wuxʷáxiɬp*) (Hitchcock and Cronquist 1981:75). It was said how de-stemmed serviceberry plants were preferred for making the frame since they bent easily without breaking. The large ends of each piece were sharpened with obsidian, shoved into the ground, and then bent over and joined by overlapping and securing with hemp the loose, smaller ends.

Sweathouses were commonly covered with several joined deer or elk hides or sometimes overlaying tule or cattail mats, or even fir boughs on a temporary sweathouse when traveling. A permanent sweathouse would be covered in the same fashion, and the hides or mats covered with approximately 10 to 12 cm of earth. Elmendorf (1935-6, 2:29) described how some long-established, earth-covered sweathouses in villages were covered with earth and growing grass, and would be used for many years, or until the bent willow frame rotted and collapsed. Traditional covering materials were eventually replaced with trade canvas and blankets that were double-layered to contain the steam; after several years of daily sweating, the deteriorated covering materials were replaced.

When several men were traveling, the frame of the structure could later be used as a *domed tent* (*sk'ʷlč'eɬx*) by replacing the sweathouse cover with fir boughs after sweating. When traveling, a temporary and usually smaller sweathouse was made in a similar fashion, using available on-site materials. An even simpler structure was made with available thickly piled fir boughs, then covered with sod and earth—enough to seal the structure to sufficiently contain the steam. The door of a men's sweathouse always faced east, and was made with a section of hide, secured at either upper end by a long circular strip of rawhide that went over and around the top of the structure, so that it could be easily swung open or closed, and was kept in this position on top of the sweathouse by its own weight—when not in use.

Most sweathouses were 3 m in diameter and approximately 140 cm in height; large enough to accommodate six to eight men who sat in a circle. Such a structure was built just prior to conducting important ceremonies or before leaving for warfare. Given the size of the war party, several such structures would be built.

An important feature of a sweathouse was a *small, round depression* (*nɬxxʷúleʔxʷ* - "hole in the ground") of approximately 30 cm in diameter and about 15 cm deep, dug in the floor's center to accommodate the heated sweathouse stones. However, when a sweathouse was being used exclusively for curing, the heated vesicular basalt stones were placed in a similar excavation immediately to the right of the entrance (when viewed from outside), affording the patient enough space to lie in an extended pronograde position. If vesicular basalt was not available in a transit camp, then solid stones were used, which could possibly explode when water was placed on them necessitating their placement in a sunken depression. One was always careful when selecting any type of stone from a stream that was not vesicular, one that was never cracked possibly to prevent exploding when super-heated. Some elders claimed that, when not using vesicular basalt, or stones of other material, they always first banged them together to see if they would chip or break.

Stones used for generating steam in sweathouses were ideally naturally occurring round vesicular basalt stones the size of a grapefruit. Approximately twelve of these stones were used during the late afternoon sweat, and, after the men's sweat, they were reheated to be used by the women of the household who followed the same ritual. In the vicinity of a family sweathouse, it was, until recently, common to see numerous piles of discarded and fractured heating stones—ones that had been discarded after prolonged use, usually after four to six months. These discarded stones became lighter in color and in weight over time, and more likely to fracture if used.

Several hours before sweating, at least nine or more stones—preferably vesicular basalt—were placed between three or five side-by-side horizontal, parallel logs that were slightly elevated on each end by old, broken sweathouse stones, and covered with smaller pieces of wood. This setup resulted in an intense fire that burned for an hour or more, with an attendant adding wood as needed. The skill and experience of the individuals, and the condition of the wood, determined the actual length of heating until the stones began to glow red. After heating, at least three stones were removed from the firepit to the sweathouse in one of several ways. A piece of freshly cut red osier branch could be bent with the small end tied to the shaft, forming a loop much like a lacrosse stick. Or a stout piece of hardwood was tied off approximately one third from its lesser end, and then split and spread to serve as tongs with the flexible ends wide enough to accommodate a heated stone.

Traditionally, a leader of a sweathouse party would designate three men to each bring a stone to the entrance of the sweathouse. Then the leader would take each hot stone with his bare hands and place it in the center depression. Father Nicolas Point, S.J., who worked from 1840 to 1847 among the Salish and certain Plains groups, illustrated in one of his paintings how a man would demonstrate that he was "strong in medicine" (1967:60) by holding red-hot stones in his hands or between his teeth, and even plunging one or both arms into boiling water without feeling pain (Curtis 1907-30, 7:85). Persons who had the *sumèš* of any animal that lives in rocks, such as chipmunk or marmot, were best suited for this task. Only a person without sufficient power or temporarily doubting his *sumèš* would sustain burns.

The leader might ask only one man to individually pass to him the rocks, then placed them in the center depression. Some elders claim that in the past, when older women sweated together, the 'outside woman' would roll the required heated stones to another woman in the entrance, rather than carry them in her hands. The few who sweat today frequently use a shovel or pitch fork to transfer the heated stones; but elders once condemned this procedure, saying that metal would negate the power of the stones.

Another critical item in the sweathouse was the water container, usually a *water-tight basket* (*yámxʷʔ* or *snčtel'tn'*) woven from either cedar or spruce root or a *rawhide bucket* or *basket - aʔxéneʔ*) supported within a tri-pole frame. Cedar-root baskets were once preferred for this purpose. When sweating during hunting forays, the water container was a deer stomach pouch, easily secured within a tri-pole frame. Once everyone was in the sweathouse, the leader would ask who wanted to sprinkle the water on the heated stones. The *water man* (*sxʷŧílm*) then sang his *suméš* song—alone or with others singing their respective power songs. Sweathouse chants were always without a tune. Also, there were different ways to sprinkle the water. Some preferred to use only one hand, whereas another person might use a loop of bear-grass, sweet grass, or a sprig of cedar or fir bough for applying water to the heated stones. A shaman, when curing, usually sprayed the rocks with water held in his mouth, creating a fine spray. The sweathouse will be discussed further in Chapter XVII.

There are, incidentally, no citations or memories of the Spokan ever using subterranean sweathouses, as Clark once observed with the Nez Perce near Almota Creek, and wrote, "I saw a curious Swet [sic] house underground, with a Small hole at the top to pass in or throw in the hot stones, which in[side] threw on as much water as to create the temperate of heat they wished" (Twaites 1959, 3:108).

Chapter VI: Tool Making and Related Technologies

The development and maintenance of prehistoric Spokan technologies, prior to sustained Euro-American contact and trading, depended essentially upon locally available indigenous materials and resources. In some instances, the lack of natural resources were supplemented with finished lithic tools and certain raw materials, including native *copper* (*kʷkʷl'kʷil'ssn*), dentalium shell, and other items that were traded up The Dalles on the Columbia River from *Northwest Coast Indians* (*čsq'ʷtičn'i*), and from the northern Plateau (Stapp 1984; Stern 1998:650). Though the territory of the Spokan was included in the Columbia River trade network, it was not located on a major trade route, and never became a major aboriginal trade center, despite the high yields of their salmon fisheries. The Spokan people in essence acted as middlemen. "Almost annually, the Spokane descended to The Dalles, while later they would make their way to Fort Vancouver" (Stern 1998:643). Prior to sustained Euro-American contact, and the introduction of such items as brass, cloth, wool, iron, glass beads, and other goods, the technologies of the Spokan continued to remain partially dependent upon several indigenously produced commodities. Despite an increasing influx of trade goods during the Protohistoric Period (circa 1700s-1804), there remained a need for locally procured resources to *manufacture tools* (*k'ʷul'mn* - "to work with") and other products from stone, shell, wood, grasses, and minerals, as well as animal by-products, such as hide, antlers, bone, and hooves.

Tool-making and tool-use was a near-daily activity for Spokan men and women, all of whom possessed the ability to manipulate raw materials into functional tools and other forms of material culture. The Spokan never had what many called true craft specialization, although there were notable exceptions of some adults who possessed skills for manufacturing certain refined tool assemblages and hide products. And yet no one man or woman could sustain a family by solely pursing a single occupational specialization. There were, however, craftspeople who had attained specific knowledge and acquired exceptional ability that was often passed from one generation to the next. Elders recall how in the past a few individuals, those possessing certain presumed esoteric knowledge, were quite capable of achieving excellence in lithic tool-making, which was based on experience, but not possessing a certain *smuéš*.

Given the limitations of possible innovations with the materials at hand, there were not many revolutionary skills. A few examples of special skills were the manufacture of successful courting flutes that captured a woman's love, hunting bows that seldom failed, or fishing leisters that presumably claimed the *largest salmon* (*kʷen't smłič*), which weighed on "average twenty pounds each; some exceeded forty pounds" (Howison 1913:48). A woman could readily identify another woman's skill and technique in the preparation and bleaching of tanned hide clothing, or another's distinctive *beadwork* (*sčk'ʷúl'* - "to do beadwork").

Multipurpose Technologies

As cited, the survival of any highly mobile hunting and gathering people depended on their knowledge and skill in developing multipurpose technologies, and utilizing local and traded materials. Many Plateau implements of hunting were effective for warfare, which was certainly true for projectile, thrusting, and cutting implements. However, the gathering and manufacturing of material culture often reflected a high division of labor, whereby men invariably assumed sole responsibility for producing the technologies for warfare, hunting, fishing, and trapping. Similarly, women gathered those materials used in the final production of implements for procuring plant foods, manufacturing clothing, making basketry and tule mats, and processing and tanning hides. Women assumed the responsibility for nearly all food preparation and storage.

Technologies were frequently classified by the orientation of the task, rather than the materials involved, particularly multipurpose technologies. This was more apparent for certain prescriptions of protocol and prohibitions that tended to regulate a man's or woman's involvement, such as hunting, fishing, trapping, and plant gathering—leading to a fairly strict division of labor.

And yet some men and women, by desire or necessity, successfully learned technologies normally assigned to the opposite gender. As a consequence, it was recognized and accepted that certain men and women were quite able to achieve significant results in various tasks. As a result, any man or woman could acquire a status and reputation based upon his or her ability for not only gathering the needed resources, but applying their knowledge and skill in converting resources to needed material items.

Despite the presumed high division of labor by gender among hunting and gathering cultures in general, Spokan women frequently possessed the knowledge and skill not only to manufacture the tools associated with male-oriented pursuits, but to use such tools, and often with acclaimed success. Ethnographic data from older traditional Spokan (Elmendorf 1935-6 and Teit 1930) provide evidence that women were more likely to be successful in many male endeavors than men seeking accomplishments with women's skills. Yet there existed cultural stereotypes that tended to dominate all the members of this relatively homogeneous group as to their specific occupational and social roles, which were publicly recognized.

The manufacturing of tools and implements from different materials depended upon possessing adequate knowledge of an area's differential resources. Though the principle of usufruct prevailed among the Spokan, there were certain exceptions regarding resource utilization, such as an individual who claimed preferential rights to exploit a particular resource site. For example, a woman, through secrecy, might control a resource site for certain geo-floral medicaments and ochre. With few exceptions, permission to exploit resource sites within the Spokan territory was given even to those who were not Spokan. All Amerindian peoples had basically three types of economic reciprocity: generalized, balanced, and negative—ones that reflected a continuum of exchange that was associated with distance of kinspeople and unrelated people (Sahlins 1965). Members of immediate and extended kin groups enjoyed the privileges of generalized reciprocity, whereas non-kinspeople recognized various forms of balanced reciprocity in which goods of comparable value were exchanged. Negative reciprocity, however, was the theft or acquisition from people of different ethnic affiliation or language, and of course through warfare. Balanced reciprocal resource utilization and trade was, in part, the basis for the successful adaptation by the Spokan of what other Interior Plateau groups possessed.

Another factor responsible for assuring successful adaptation was that many *tools* and *implements* (*k'ʷúʔl'm'iʔs* - "their tools") were multipurpose ones, in that one tool could accomplish different tasks. For example, a bow could be used for projecting arrows, playing music as a mouth harp, enlarging a rodent burrow (after being unstrung), twisting wet rawhide to remove the water, scratching one's back, and other applications restricted only by the user's imagination. Tools were manufactured from stone and different *animal* (*xʷixey'úɫ*) by-products such as teeth, sinew, rawhide, horn, hair, fish blood, bones and skins, as well as the stomachs of larger animals. Wood and its many by-products were also often necessary in the making of various tools and implements.

Lithic Technology and Minerals

The conversion of stone to a usable product required various techniques, using either direct or indirect percussion, such as pressure flaking, pecking, as well as grinding, or sanding. The first phase of lithic technology was gathering the needed materials from known resource sites. Due to the total absence of most desired lithic materials within the Spokan area, and the differential availability of potential *lithic material* (*st'tqʷʼan'eʔ*), *trading* (*č'ɫk'ʷl'éysm* - "exchange") for the finished product or for the raw material was sometimes necessary. *Highly prized* (*nkʷtnáqsm*) obsidian was obtained indirectly through trade from quarries in central Oregon, and the occurrence of regional quarries and incidental finds of *flint nodules* (*snč'páxmn*) were exploited by usury rights. Most productive flint quarries, because of exposure, were on the edge of the Spokan River. Apart from various types of stone that were acquired by trade, most lithic materials were gathered from local quarries. Within the area of the Spokan territory there were three major lithic quarries, which, unfortunately, were destroyed or covered by the road-building of the late 1960s and even earlier, by dam construction and rising waters.

Argillite, nephrite, and greenstone came primarily from the Northwest Coast through a series of established trading routes. The most common trade materials were, "glassy volcanics (i.e., obsidian, vitrophyre, ignimbrite) and marine shell" (Ames *et al.*, 1998:118). The much sought jadeite came through trade from Canada (Sprague, pers. comm.).

Traditionally, the exchange of goods was based upon the established value of the item, which was frequently determined not only by need and availability, but also by the skill in manufacturing a finished item. Some materials, such as obsidian, were usually acquired as "blanks," and, thus, required finishing by the Spokan. Again, the techniques of manufacture were universal, but the final differences were based upon the individual worker's skill.

Lithic technology produced a number of implements and utensils, such as *arrow-shaft straighteners* (*x̣waqʾ'ʷƛstn*), mortars, knives, projectile points, lap rocks, pestles, and mauls. Stone was used in the manufacture of elbow and tube pipes, beads, fishing weights and anchors, axes, hide scrapers, bifacial scrapers, thumb and end scrapers, lenticular knives, cobble chopping tools, chisels, adzes, anvil rocks, and various cutting and thrusting tools. Stone hide *scrapers* (*sx̣ʷix̣ʷyé*)—illustrated in the figure below—were made from smooth stones and it required a minimum amount of time, skill, and effort to produce an effective tool; they were typically 7 to 8 cm in diameter. An imperfectly formed *shale rock* (*nscósl'eʔ*) made an excellent *hide scraper* (*ʔáqʾmn*) for softening buckskin. Despite a strict division of labor, men predominantly made stone tools, while hide discoidal scrapers and lenticular knives were often finished by women.

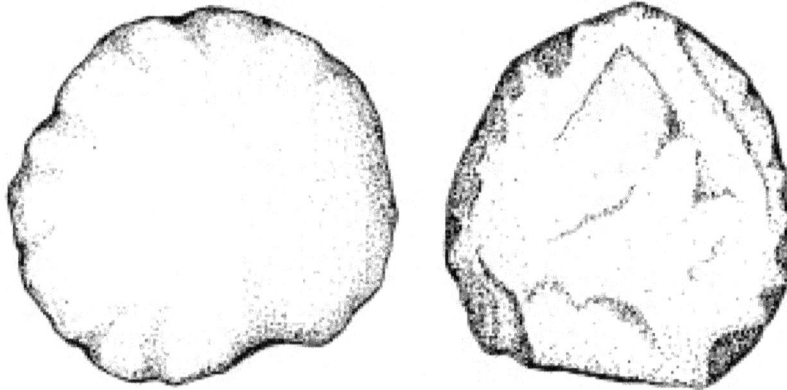

Figure 15. Discoidal hide scrapers

The *club* (*nčča ʔqʾín* - "a stick with something laid on top") was used primarily to *club* (*sp'im*) an opponent in warfare (Smith 1936-8:679), and occasionally for utilitarian purposes, such as driving tent pegs, removing tree bark, or breaking large animal bones for marrow. The striking stone was made smooth by grinding to prevent unnecessary fractures or chipping, and was usually the size of a man's fist. When completed, the stone head was attached to a handle made from mock orange, ocean spray, or western yew, varying in length from 20 to 25 cm, with a diameter from 2 to 3 cm. The stone head was covered tightly with several layers of sewn buckskin which extended part way down the handle to further secure the head. Such a weapon had a looped wrist strap that prevented the loss of the weapon when being used in combat. An *axe* (*šlmíy*) was an indispensable tool, usually hafting a stone to a length of hard wood or a modified deer antler.

Both sexes possessed the knowledge of converting lithic materials to serviceable tools, though some men and women had greater manipulative skills in working on stone. There was no religious power associated with lithic or hide-working skills.

Weir Anchors and Net Weights

Heavy stone weights were used to stabilize the often large and elaborate *fishing weirs* (*sqʷyóxʷ*) and attached *fish traps* (*ʔoléwltn*). Granite, because of its density and its presence on most stream terraces, was the preferred stone for making weir and trap anchors, weighing 15 to 30 kg. The shape of a selected boulder determined how it would be worked on. To reduce labor, and to ensure stability in utilization, the intended weight was prepared by pecking a groove with a depth of approximately 5 to15 mm around the end with less diameter. This was done in order to better accommodate a heavy, multi-strand hemp rope, which was later replaced with *horsehair rope* (*c'íqp*), commonly horsetail).

Placement of heavy weir anchors was accomplished in several ways, depending upon their weight and the available manpower. Since water provides no buoyancy, an exceptionally heavy stone anchor was rolled along the stream to the desired location where it was then lifted onto a raised *weir platform* (*xlússn* or *xaλússn*), or onto a weir's horizontal support brace by three or four men who carefully coordinated their efforts in positioning the anchor. Crude rafts, made of limbed logs lashed together with hemp rope were used to transport heavy stones to a weir. The raft was first loaded with one or more large stone anchors, and the burden was pushed or poled by several men to the designated location and off-loaded. In early spring, weirs were repaired, by relocating anchors and weir weights from previous years were reused, having served numerous generations of fisherman. It was once common for the larger and more spectacular weights to be named, never after a person, but based on shape, weight, or site of origin. Due to the construction of the Grand Coulee Dam (1933-42), and with the consequent flooding and fluctuation of water levels, many of these stone anchors can be seen at low water at former traditional fishing sites.

Another type of fishing weight was a relatively small, flat stone, usually a metamorphic stone made functional by pecking a center hole from opposite sides, and finished using a stone-tipped drill that was rotated in the maker's hands. This type of weight was for seine-netting, and was easily fashioned by striking a *sharp* (*xʷixʷíyt*) edged stone against a relatively flat, oval-shaped stone, thereby forming two or four indentations spaced opposite one another. Specimens show, in some cases, the weight was then turned, and the process repeated on the opposite side of each indentation. These small weights were approximately 10 to 15 cm in length and width, and until the mid 1930s were occasionally found in great abundance on stream terraces during low water. This type of small weight was used in seine-netting. All fishing weights were always left on the terraces of the fishing sites until next required.

Four different types of net sinkers are illustrated in the figure below. The two on top were typically 16 to 18 cm in length, and the bottom two were often about 9 cm.

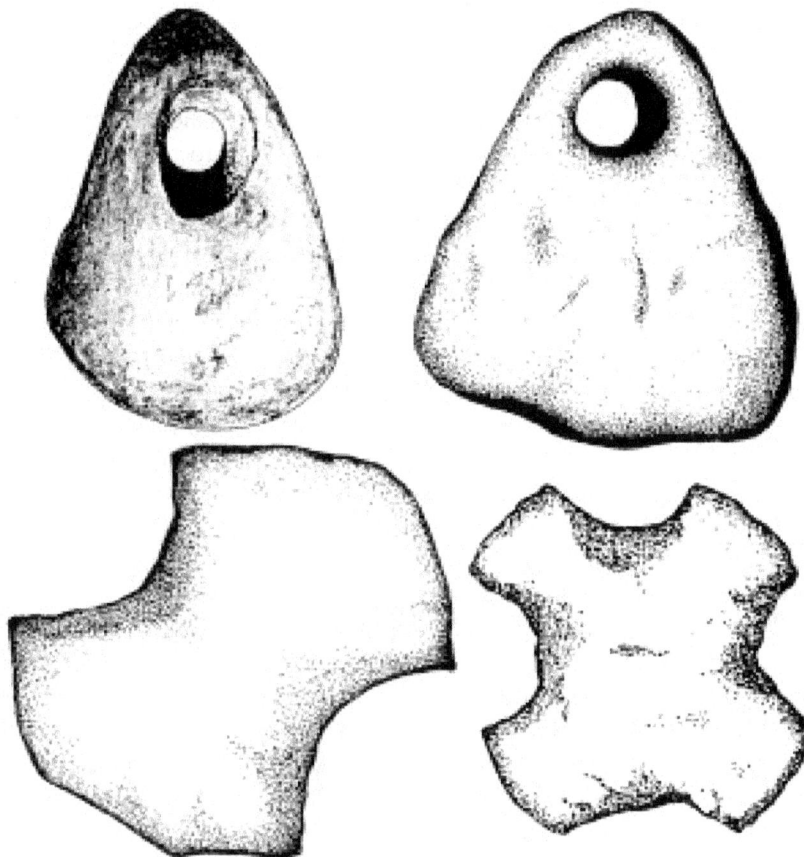

Figure 16. Set-line net sinkers

A common type of net sinker was, "of globular or oblong spheroid [granite] pebbles or rocks encircled by a transverse groove. Such articles are generally supposed to have been sinkers for fishing, both for nets and lines" (Collier *et al.* 1942:74). Smith suggested that this type of artifact was used as a hafted hammer stone, since there is evidence that sometimes both ends were pitted by battering (1900:30).

Mortars and Pestles

The Spokan shaped their mortars and pestles from wood, metamorphosed rock, basalt, and calcium carbonate. While lithic material was more durable, it proved more difficult to process than comparable utensils shaped from wood. Producing a stone mortar or pestle required considerable time to *shape* (*čl'aʔqʷʼessn'm* - "to work in stone") the item by pecking with an edged stone until the near-final form could be ground to achieve some degree of smoothness, which was accomplished by rubbing with sandstone. After prolonged use of pounding and grinding in a stone mortar, the striking end of the *pestle* (*snteʔmín* or *te'míntn*) was further smoothed, as was the inside of the *mortar* (*snteʔmíntn* or *łčcin'*) (the general term for all mortars). A shallow, metate-like, near-flat stone was called *snsteʔmín*.

227

Initially, the depression in a mortar was shaped by pecking the parent material with another stone, usually one of *greater density* (*pɫiɫt*), as explained in Teit's work with the Coeur d'Alene, "The pecking was first done in rings parallel to one another or in spirals, and then the intervening ridges were battered down, the process being repeated until the desired size and shape were attained" (1930:41). Over time, grinding with a stone pestle would eventually further enlarge the depression within the mortar. (A different kind of grinding also occurred when the stone particles and dust inadvertently became part of the food, and thus wore down people's teeth.) The finished shape of all portable stone mortars was not always round, particularly if the parent rock was too large and required a great expenditure of energy to move or transport when completed. Consequently, large stationary mortars tended to be located in the vicinity of a winter village or within the general vicinity of a major resource site. A regular stone mortar, as depicted above, would have a diameter of 10 to 12 cm. It would need to be large enough for a stone pestle, for crushing ochre, nuts, roots, etc.

It is debatable whether some small, concave, *stone dish-like* (*ɫčcín*) artifacts were not probably multipurpose since they may have been used as a food dish and as a mortar, whereas some small, hand-held mortars, approximately 3 to 4 cm in diameter, were used for *grinding small nodules* (*sčxʷáqʼʷsšnʼ* - "grind small objects") of ochre and other pigments, or in the preparation of medicines. One such stone piece in a private collection of early Spokan artifacts found on the reservation, is a relatively small mortar stained with red ochre—probably used to mix paints. With no way to date the artifact, one may assume that it served as a hand-held reservoir while the artist used reconstituted pigments when painting pictographs or for body adornment. This mortar was found in the loft of an allotment house built prior to 1908, with a radius of approximately 8 cm with a depth of 6 cm. Unfortunately, no accompanying pestle was found (Ross 1993).

Manufacturing a pestle from basalt or granite stone was a difficult and time-consuming process. Consequently, the Spokane sought concoidally-shaped stones, often found on stream terraces. Completed pestles varied in shape, but usually had a smooth top end and an enlarged base with a pounding surface. Some pestles recovered from Spokan sites have anthropomorphic forms, and some appear to have been acquired through trade from the Middle Columbia River. Several elongated cylindrical stones have been found with both ends worked to decreasing diameter, and these so-called "salmon-packers" were used to compress the salmon—thereby reducing the volume of the load—before transporting from fishing sites to winter storage areas. To reduce the chance of chipping or even breaking a stone pestle, the surface was commonly worked until smooth. A nearly straight-sided pestle used for crushing chokecherries had the upper two-thirds of the stone shaft covered with rawhide, called *qʼawʼísq*.

Wooden pestles were used with stone mortars to *grind* (*xʷáqʼʷis*) or pulverize small sections of *pounded dried meat* (*stʼeltnʼ*) or fish when preparing stews or soups. Powdered camas was similarly prepared with either a wooden or stone pestle for making soups. Often with dry aged meat, fragments that would fall off a larger piece were placed in a boiling cauldron for making soup or stew—a process called *sntʼaʔqetkʷ* (STHC). A typical length would be 22 cm.

Some mortars and pestles were made from wood, but less is known about them due to deterioration and fire, and because they are less durable than stone. However, wooden mortars and pestles were common, being easier to manufacture. *Wooden mortars* (*snteʔmí*), often larger than stone mortars, were typically fashioned from a standing tree stump, a large section of driftwood, or a fallen log that was hollowed by first *burning and then whittling out as a mortar* (*nxʷƛʼéɫcʼeʔntm*). The manufacture and use of wooden mortars are seldom recorded or remembered in any detail by present Spokan. Fortunately, they are reported for neighboring groups (Teit 1930:326; Turney-High 1941:78; Ray 1933:41) who lined the mortar with rawhide to prevent the mortar from splitting or fraying. One may assume, according to Elmendorf (1935-6, 2:14), that the Spokan did the same. It is known that the Spokan used rawhide-lined mortars—with the rawhide sides folded up and sewn in place—when crushing soft berries and cooked roots. This low-sided dish-like bowl was approximately 12 to 14 cm across the top. According to Ray, wooden mortars:

[...] had a comparatively short life because of the rapid abrasion of the grinding surface, a lining of rawhide was often added. This lining, which fitted tightly against the inside walls, was made in two parts. The bottom part, designed to take the greatest wear, was made of rawhide cut into thin strips and braided, then woven, cup shaped, to fit the contour of the bottom. To this were sewed sides of plain rawhide, which in turn were stitched at the upper edge of the mortar to the outside covering of hide, thereby completely enclosing the wooden portion (1933:41).

A small mortar for crushing seeded berries was easily fashioned by a woman taking a section of soaked rawhide and pulling it tightly over a rounded stone of appropriate size until the hide was dry. Because a rawhide mortar was small, lightweight, and *pliable* (*t'et'iy'm'*), most women occasionally carried this personal possession when berrying. The mashing of berries was done with a stone or wooden pestle, or with any fist-size rounded stone. Berries were crushed in a type of hopper-shaped *bottomless basket mortar* (*snte'mín*) which was placed on a flat milling stone and supported in place by attaching the stout rim of the basket with buckskin straps to several long hardwood sticks driven vertically into the ground at the edge of the milling stone.

Flat Milling Stones

Carefully selected flat stones of granite or vesicular slab stone—often called grinding slabs—required little if any modification. These naturally occurring shaped-stones measured in thickness from approximately 4 to 6 cm, and from 25 to 40 cm in diameter. With the loss of descriptive terms for many aspects of traditional technology, these stones have now been given the English designation of lap rocks because the worker usually held the flat stone on her lap when grinding seeds or nuts, and when breaking dry long bones for making implements or extracting marrow. Until recently, a few elderly women used flat milling stones to break open hazelnuts, though when ripe, the husk opens and releases the nut. However, one elderly woman contended that these grinding stones were not used to break fresh bones for marrow, since the residual fat would contaminate the stone. Therefore, some designated lap rocks were used to break bones for their marrow after first covering the flat stone with a section of buckskin. Fortunately, there exists a pre-reservation account: "Piles of dried meat and grease were taken care of while the bones were cracked to save the marrow. The mashing of bones was called *hecpłmá*, after which the bones were called *spáł*. The grease [and marrow] was of much importance because, like *lard* (*nsloqʷ*), it was preferred for the cooking of roots and sarvisberries [serviceberries]" (Wynecoop 1985:33). Every woman possessed a *flat rock with a depression* (*snte'míntn* - "place where something is crushed") that was laid atop a section of buckskin placed on a level section of ground or floor so that after grinding the ground pieces or bits could be easily picked up (Elmendorf 1935-6, 1:34).

Until recently, a berry-picker exploiting a traditional berrying camp would occasionally find a flat-stone that had once been used as a flat mortar or lap rock for processing berries. As mentioned earlier, large and heavy fishing weights were left in situ, as were larger mortars and grinding stones, and could be used by any passerby observing the rights of usufruct.

Hammers and Mauls

Every family owned at least one *stone hammer* (*q'aw'ísqn*) and several sizes of mauls, all of which were indispensable tools, being used by both men and women according to task. The major difference between these two tool types was that the stone hammer head was hafted by splitting one end of the *wood handle* (*čéple'tn*), inserting the hammer head, and then securing it by hafting either side of the hammer stone with wet rawhide to the handle. The hammer head was normally twice as long as it was wide, and hammer face had a relatively flat striking surface by selection or reworking or both.

A more elaborate type of hammer was made from a naturally-shaped elliptical or rounded, elongated, dense stone that was several times the length of the diameter. Around the center of the stone, a slight groove of 4 to 6 mm was fashioned with another dense stone, to which was attached a long strip of *split serviceberry* (*ɫqéɫp*) by looping over as much of the groove as possible. The slightly flexible handle was then held in place by tightly wrapping a sufficient length of soaked rawhide, which when dry held the handle in place. There are several examples of how the manufacturer wrapped a single piece of wet rawhide around the length of the handle that was then stitched the entire length, affording a better grip. A similar technique of stitching wet rawhide near the head of an axe or *maul* (*teʔmín*) is used today to prevent the less experienced borrower from shredding or otherwise damaging the handle of an axe or hatchet.

By necessity, both stone and wooden mauls varied greatly in size and shape. The hand maul illustrated here was about 17 cm in length. Some stone mauls, particularly splitting mauls, were similar to a pestle and sometimes given the same designation - *teʔmíntn*. But they were shorter in length and of greater weight and circumference than a hammer. Mauls were sometimes made from hard-wood, but more often of metamorphosed rock, basalt, or calcium carbonate. Mauls were used for driving ground tipi pegs, setting wooden stacks that pegged hides for stone-boiling, bruising tree bark to facilitate the gathering of cambium, breaking dead branches when gathering firewood, to *split wood* (*hecsáxʷslk'ʷpi or suxʷlʔk'ʷpm'*) for fire, and for breaking open the long bones of animals to recover the marrow.

Some workers preferred mauls made from wood—most notably thornbush, birch root, or red hawthorn—because they did not destroy *horn wedges* (*qxmín* - "something that is driven into something") as did stone mauls. Some stone mauls were large enough to require the use of both hands when driving large stakes into the ground or setting weirs on a river bed. Mauls drove stakes used to support a *large drying rack* (*sncqy'éɫceʔtn or snxw'íɫttn* - "place to dry fish on"), or as uprights for walkways at fishing stations, or for upright fishing weir pilings, or for breaking large fallen dead trees into *dry wood* (*č'éyeʔ*) kindling, or driving horn wedges when splintering green wood. Elk hide was preferred to deer hide for wrapping and securing the heavy *maul* (*teʔmín*) head to a handle.

Splitting Wedges, Bifaces, and Adzes

The archaeological data and ethnographic record provide evidence that some *bifacial stone splitting wedges* (*qaʔxmin*) and bifacial adzes were manufactured of materials found only on the Northwest Coast. The Spokan acquired these particular tools through trade that moved up the Columbia River corridor. Traded tools were preferred not only for their structural efficiency, but also for their shape and color when compared with those of local manufacture. If grave goods are any indication, ownership of certain traded stone tools might have added to an owner's status. Despite the desire for traded stone wedges, most splitting wedges were manufactured locally from readily available deer and elk antlers that were *stone-sharpened* (*sxʷxʷq'sel'stn* - "whet stone") and reworked when the bifacial edge became dull.

Different types of *wooden wedges* (*q'eʔséw'stn*) were part of the tool assemblage. *Wooden mauls* (*nsp'qíntn*) were almost always used when working with deer and elk wedges, since stone mauls could easily fracture the antler and bone wedges. When describing wedges, Lewis chose to use the term axe: "The axes first used by the Spokane Indians were of bone or deer horn—about 20 inches long and sharp at one end. This an Indian would stick into a log or tree and pry off slivers until they fell the tree or cut through the log" (1927:10).

All of the lithic bifaces and adz-like tools that exist in regional museums and in known amateur collections indicate that these particular tools were probably not made by the Spokan, but, as noted above, some were traded from the Northwest Coast. Contemporary Spokan refer to these two tool types as axes, and gave varying accounts as to how they may have been used. A review of so-called grave goods suggest that all types of Northwest Coast artifacts were highly prized, but one can only speculate as to their value, if any, in an afterlife.

Awls and Engravers

An indispensable tool for both men and women was a stone or *bone awl* (*λ'q*ʷ*úmn*) used for perforating rawhide or buckskin for stitching and when making tule and cattail mats. Stone awls were frequently refashioned by secondary chipping or flaking from broken projectile points or knives, work usually done by men, though a woman made her own bone awls. There are no existing examples or accounts of the Spokan making wooden awls, though bear penis bones—some decorated by incising—may have been used as awls (Collier *et al.*, 1942:92). Presumably the best awls were fashioned from a deer or elk's shin bone.

Women had a variety of both stone and bone awls which, depending upon their intended use, were either flat or rounded with one end pointed and the other somewhat rounded. Large bone awls, roughly 15 to 22 cm in length, were typically made from a deer's back tibia or the lower leg bone of a heron. Often the upper end of the tibia was retained in order to facilitate the user's grip and control of the tool. Some awls were fashioned from a deer's scapula, which, being flat, reduced time in manufacturing, and the epiphysis was retained as a handle for better control or when pushing through material. The diameter of the leg bone was gradually reduced by scraping with a sharpened stone—preferably obsidian—until a near-point was achieved. A sharp point was produced by rubbing the bone on a fairly flat abraded stone, whereas a medium-size awl was made from the tibia of a deer's foreleg. The medial malleolus or distal end formed the hand piece for manipulating and pushing the awl, and the upper extremity was sharpened to a long, gradual but sharp point. Smaller awls were produced by serrating longitudinal grooves in a deer's foreleg tibia, which upon being struck with a flat stone, made numerous small shafts, and were similarly fashioned by rubbing with abraded stone. Awls and engravers, unlike hide-sewing needles, were apparently not made from bear bone although this animal's bones were known to be the densest of all land mammals.

When making tule or cattail mats, an awl was used for presetting holes when threading with twisted hemp. Clematis bark and stripped lengths of willow bark were used for *thread* (*st'ópqs*). In some instances, the carefully shredded and plaited fibers of sagebrush were used when sewing baskets.

During the Historical Period (1804-1881) steel needles for stitching and beadwork were greatly appreciated, being the finest of gifts, particularly when given with spools of commercial thread and a decent size lump of beeswax.

The figure below shows four representative awls made from bone. (Their catalog numbers, from top to bottom, are 220C-6711, 222A-9-10-HC, 5, and 265.)

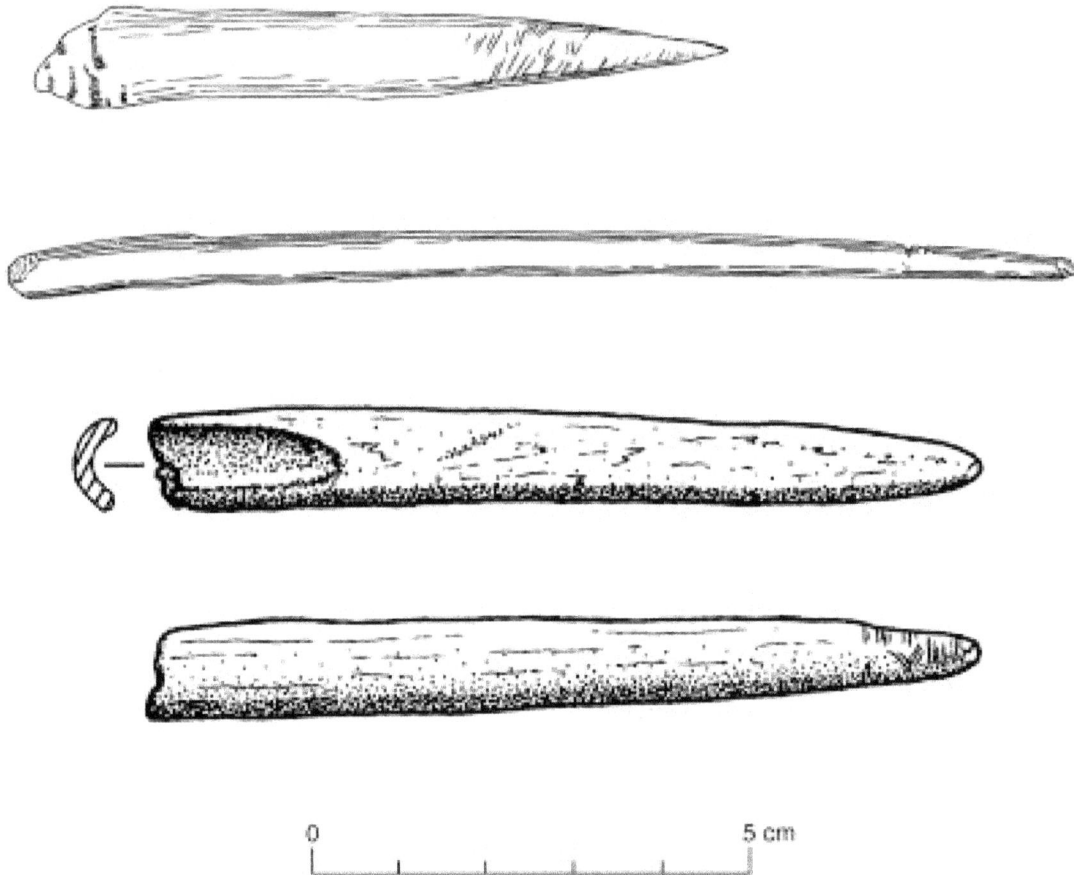

Figure 17. Bone awls

Tabular Knives/Spokeshave

Most of the hand-held tabular knives were bifacially flaked, and are believed to have been associated with scrapping tasks and for dressing salmon. "The term 'tabular knife' most likely encompasses scraping and cleaving as well as cutting tasks" (Galm and Layman 1988a:70). After prolonged use, the cutting edges of a tabular knife were dulled, then sharpened by working and flaking one side, then working the opposite side. Until recently, a number of elderly Spokan women continued using these relatively simple but effective implements for scraping hides prior to tanning, and were often found in profusion near the tanning area. When an elderly woman was asked about her scraper, she lamented that since her fingers no longer had the strength to tan hides, her grandchildren had used all of hers for skipping on the river.

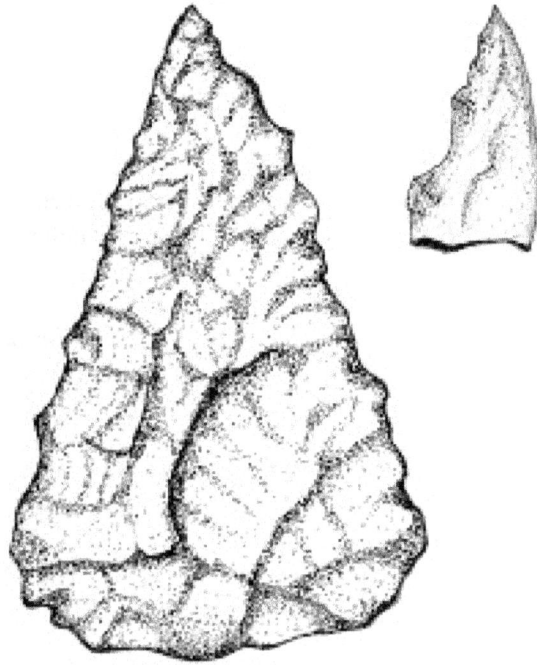

Figure 18. Bifacial lanceolate knife and spokeshave

The two lithic artifacts illustrated in the figure above are not in comparative scale: the knife is approximately 10 cm in length, with a maximum width of 5 cm; the spokeshave (scraper) is roughly 7 cm in length. The cutting or working edge of the scraper is on the left side, where there is an indentation shaped somewhat like a lunar quarter.

Quartz, Basalt, Slate, and Crystal Implements

Some types of rudimentary implements were manufactured from mudstone, metamorphosed slate, quartz, and basalt. Lithic projectile points, knives, and bifacial scrapers were manufactured from a variety of stones that could be ground or fractured with some degree of control by percussion, pressure flaking, or grinding. Locally quarried basalt, cryptocrystalline stone, such as flint and chert, were used to produce spear and projectile points. There are no oral records or ethnographic data that would suggest that the Spokan pre-heated cryptocrystalline material before making tools, or preparing a flint blank before fashioning a *projectile point* (*sc'c'l'ál'q*ʷ or *snc'l'él'stn* or *snlč'pel'* or *st'čw'an'eʔ* - "arrow head"), *awl* (*λ'q*ʷ*úmn*) or burin. Secondary chipping extended the use of most cutting tools. In addition, by products of chipping and manufacturing large tools could be used. For example, a large flake of any cryptocrystalline stone could quickly be made into a *thumb scraper* (*st'úm'čst* or *x*ʷ*ík*ʷ*mis*).

Given its unique physical characteristics, slate was an easily worked stone, but was limited to ornaments and tools that were essentially flat. However, small stone-bored ear pendants were rounded and sometimes incised with linear designs that circumscribed the object. Larger pieces of smooth slate were used in flattening tules to facilitate weaving if they had not already been flattened by drawing the plant over a rounded surface by using a debarked log. Crystal was another hard material that occurred naturally in various shapes and colors, and was modified for incising slate and other semi-hard materials. These unusual and highly sought stones were carried by some curing shamans in their medicine bags, because they were supposed to bestow

233

certain powers and abilities to the owner. One may still see many of these very old power stones and crystals that have all the ridges smoothened almost flat from years of rubbing.

Pictographs and Petroglyphs

Fortunately, there is ethnographic data on the types and use of paints and dyes in rock art, but limited information on the interpretation and significance of the many symbolic representations drawn by the Spokan (Boreson, pers. comm.). Colors applied to a flat stone surface are called (*sč'łq'ʔncút*) or *rock paintings* (*nq'iʔq'y'énč* - "writing on the wall" or "history rocks"), ones that were representative of either anthropomorphic or zoomorphic creatures, such as specific animal species, humans, insects, birds and celestial bodies. In fact, the largest area of existing on-reservation examples are found on rather dramatic vertical granite monoliths at a site called *nq'iq'iyénč*. Keyser identified characteristic Columbia Plateau motifs as "stick figure humans, simple block-body animal forms, rayed arcs and circles, tally marks, abstract spirit or mythical figures, and geometric forms" (1992:16). Pictographs were applied to granite rocks, some of which fortunately had an overhang, which has protected these depictions. Rock art varied in subject and size according to the artist. Some are as small as 3 cm, often seen in clusters, whereas a large representation may be approximately 5 to 6 m.

During his surveys of the Spokan territory, Stevens was told, "The Painted rocks are very high, and contain effigies of men and beasts, and other characters, made, as the Indians believe, by a race of men who preceded them as inhabitants of the land" (1860, 12, Part 2:150). Though many symbols obviously represented humans and animals, some are difficult or even impossible to be interpreted to discern what they represent. Ben Norman, an early settler, asked Spokan Garry, the meaning of the rock-drawings, but Garry said he could not provide any "meaning of these painted rocks" (Lewis 1920, 1:34). Yet Lewis, after interviewing some elderly Spokan men, was told how "It was a custom when a boy was sick to send him out to paint [a] certain rock as a charm of 'good medicine' for his recovery" (1920, 1:34).

Petroglyphs have both naturalistic and abstract figures of either open (outlined) or closed (solid) representation, configurations that probably served as mnemonic representations of an individual's unique spiritual experience with his or her guardian spirit. Many of these geometric and abstract symbols are now invariably indecipherable because of erosion or defacement, but mostly the uncertainty is as to their function, whether of religious meaning or *artistic* (*xsxséčst*) expression. Given the known locations of most, it has been posited by some that young boys visited these sites during their vision quests, perhaps making an individual symbol or animistic representation to influence a prospective tutelary spirit as a form of propitiation, or simply as proof to the sponsor of the neophyte's lonely vigil. In the past some elderly Spokan agreed that during their vision quests, boys probably made pictographs to substantiate their vigilance, whereas some elders felt that rock-art was done by men when propitiating and respecting a tutelary representative for assistance in fulfilling a certain quest.

The figure shows sketches of several pictographs. They are done entirely in red ocher, and are typically 8 to 10 cm in their longest dimension.

Figure 19. Pictographs

Petroglyphs are normally found on large stationary granite boulders, often near a stream, a resource site, or a permanent riverine village site. They were culturally-produced inscribed indentations upon stone, often similar to pictographic representations in shape. Spokan pictographs and petroglyphs are seldom seen on basalt. Because of the difficulty in producing petroglyphs, nearly all known Spokan rock-carvings comprise only one symbol or animistic representation. Unfortunately, many of those known and recorded Spokan petroglyphs have been either destroyed or buried by road construction, or covered by rising waters due to the construction of Grand Coulee Dam. It is known that the construction of the Little Falls Dam in 1911 blocked migratory fishes from the upper portions of the river (Schulz *et al.* 1985:20), and covered and presumably destroyed many culturally important features (Ross 1993). Some off-reservation Spokan rock art have unfortunately been obliterated or partially destroyed with spray paint, or defaced by vandals shooting .22 caliber *bullets* (*m'l'm'íl'q'ʷ*) at the representations. The latter form of defacement was caused by extensive pitting and flaking. An unfortunate example of this vandalism is found just north of *Long Lake* (*čɫišišut*) where one may still view a now-protected large granite monolith depicting various anthropomorphic and animal forms. Upon numerous rocks, several hundred meters above the protected site, are further examples of rock-painting. Below these there was a summer camp ground called *nšt'én'eʔ* that was strategically close to the *shore* (*ɫeʔʔcn'etkʷ*) of the Spokane River, and annually occupied during late spring and summer for fishing and root-digging.

There are no known examples of dendroglyphs—trees which have been carved, incised, or marked—within the Spokan territory, as there are on the Colville Indian Reservation. The twelve documented Colville dendroglyphs designated an area on the Sanpoil River where trapper-traders met with Indians to trade for furs in the early 1800s (Peltier, pers. comm.; Ross 1965-67).

The only known geoglyph in the area is located just east of the Spokane Indian Reservation where there remains an unusual depiction of an elk lying on its side; actually a bas-relief geoglyph made of mounded earth, and, until recently, it was approximately 20 cm at its highest point. The story was that three Spokan men in the 1880s were hunting elk on what is now called Lane Mountain near Chewelah (the site was previously called *čq'ʷc'wey'ʔm*), and one of the hunters wounded an unusually large elk with an 1886 Winchester .45-70 rifle. The hunters tracked the elk south, to the Spokane River where it died. In respect for the animal's courage and stamina, the men made the existing elk mound by creating a distinct outline with small vesicular basalt stones. Every spring, when going to Spokane Falls to fish, the site was visited for cleaning and maintenance and any stones that had been moved by wild life were then rearranged. Before leaving the site, women carefully swept the now seldom visited effigy. Children were never permitted to visit the site, and, "were kept behind a long and fairly high ridge (approximately 1.5 m). Only adults could go, work, and visit" (Ross 1993).

Clay

The Kutenai were the nearest known group to the Spokan who made molded pottery by using molds of sectional birch bark, and they also made molded (slab-ware) pottery (Schaeffer 1952:4). However, the Spokan are not known to have produced utilitarian pottery (Elmendorf 1935-6, 2:48), but used *clay* for manufacturing children's toys (such as small figures), pipe bowls, *cleaning hides* (*npawaʔn'eč*), and occasionally excavating earth that was lined with sun-dried clay for stone-boiling. Post and Commons (1938:69) noted how the area of the Spokan produced enough clay (usually in the form of dust) to be traded to the Sinkaietk.

Clay played a major role in the Spokan pharmacopoeia for treating internal and external maladies, but most notably for treating diarrhea (Ross 1993). In the past, moistened clay was used by both sexes as a protective skin cover when traveling in an area infested with mosquitoes or other insects to prevent being bitten. Elders noted that in the past, clay—diatomaceous earth—was put on the face of a person suffering from ghost illness, as it was believed to prevent further ghostly visitations.

Tanned hides that became soiled were traditionally cleaned by rubbing dry, absorbent, powdered white clay as a *cleaner* (*npaqʷánepcn*) into the garment, allowing it to thoroughly dry before brushing it off. *Yellow clay* (*np'úmp'umƛxʷ*) and *blue clay* (*sč'íłt*) were used for cleaning buckskin. In addition to clay, *black cottonwood ashes* (*qʷl'mín*) were used to clean soiled buckskin garments (Gabriel 1954:27). With the acquisition of trade cloth, clay continued to be used for removing grease stains or other organic materials from cotton and wool garments and blankets. Today, few women continue to follow these traditional methods for cleaning tanned hide garments; rather, they prefer to *rub* (*yílkʷ*) the soiled garment with dried bread or wash it with liquid soap, typically Ivory.

Ray (1932 and 1933) provided evidence that some groups near the Colville National Forest used clay for making a *child's toy* (*sm'l'm'él'čst*), such as doll heads and animal figures, and even for producing hand-formed, sun-dried, water containers, which were strengthened by enclosing the pot's interior with salmon skin. The Spokan are not known to have used clay for slab or coiled pots though some Plateau groups used clay pots for stone-boiling (Teit 1930). Collier and his colleagues stated that in all of the hundreds of pre-dam excavations, "No potsherds or other evidence of the use of clay were found" (1942:110).

Until recently, a few elderly women, who continued to use clay, would dig it from two existing and long-used stream bed *clay quarries* (*snpqʷan'ečtn*) on *Little Tschimakain Creek* (*č'čmqin'* or *nkʷiʔméteʔkʷ* - "small creek" or "head of the waters"), an area called *snkʷim'etekʷi* ("people who lived at this creek), and Big Tschimakain Creek where there remain several quarries of *gray clay* (*spaʔʷán'eʔčtn - npaqʕʷaneč*). Any large quarry of white clay was called *pawaneč*, whereas areas noted for white clay deposits were called *snpawanéčtn* ("a place of white clay") or *sppaw'an'eʔčtn'* ("place of little white clay"). Unfortunately, many traditional clay beds were destroyed or covered by the rising waters resulting from the construction of two large hydroelectric dams. On Big Tschimakain Creek was a large quarry where people had to wade, or in the spring dive, to secure clay—a site called *snpawanéčtn*. An undisclosed area of the Spokane Indian

236

Reservation produced a bright yellow clay, commercially called Spokane yellow, which was acquired through trade by contiguous groups for painting (Anon. 1981a).

Ochre

Due to the 1940 raising of the Spokane River with the construction of Grand Coulee Dam, three major *ochre mines* (*snyac'mn* - "place of ochre") were destroyed. All of these and other lithic sites were extensive and important to the Spokan economy, but are now mostly underwater and exposed only occasionally on river terraces during low-water. A few elders recalled how one of the principal ochre mine areas was called *red ground* (*kʷlúl'eʔxʷ*), that produced enough hematite nodules for trading with distant groups. Prior to WW II, some older women quarried both yellow and red hematite nodules which they sold in buckskin bundles to other Indians at pow-wows. At one time, dancers used only hematite for decorating their bodies—using salmon oil or bear grease as a vehicle for powdered hematite, but later adopted petroleum jelly. *Ochre* (*kʷkʷl'k'ʷil'sšn'* - "small red rocks"), i.e., hematite, was most often quarried by women who were ultimately responsible for its distribution, either by gifting or trade with other groups having restricted quarries. Ochre was indispensable for many decorative and sacred uses.

Wood, Fiber, and Bark Technology

Numerous species of *wood* (*lúk'ʷ*) and plant and plant by-products, such as cambium, bark, pitch, lichens, roots, leaves, mosses, sedges, bulrushes, ferns, and even mushrooms were effectively modified to fulfill numerous uses. These items were gathered nearly always by women. However, due to the limited durability of wood and an unfortunate paucity of data within the archaeological record, more is known about lithic tools than about implements manufactured from organic materials such as wood. Also, because of the ready availability and relative ease of manipulation, it was not unusual for wood to be substituted for stone when making certain tools and implements, such as mortars and pestles, splitting wedges of elk horn, and making mauls that were occasionally used as pestles.

Deciduous woods were used in making *serving trays* (*sxʷƛ'xʷúƛ'n'* or *snʔeščenm*), scoops, scrapers, and *dippers* (*snč'lmúlmn* or *č'lmulmn*). Trays were made from sections of birch bark (Wynecoop 1985:78) and black cotton wood—food being placed on the inside concave side. The dipper was a multipurpose tool for eating soup, broth and stews, spreading water on hot stones to create steam, and extinguishing fires.

An implement used by every household was the splayed front scraper, made by splitting a one meter length of yellow pine for a handle that was then attached to a yellow pine or tamarack blade nearly 30 cm long and 16 to 20 cm wide. It was basically a *shovel* (*ʔaxʷméčstn*) for clearing ashes from the firepit and for moving snow on walkways or low-lying slanting shed roofs. Some women had a *snow shovel*, a similar tool made by first tightly tying a short section of wet rawhide around the upper section of a stout hard-wood branch, approximately one-third from the feeble end. After the rawhide wrap had dried, the smaller end was then split open to the rawhide wrap, resulting in a split roughly 15 to 20 cm in length, and the split end was then spread to approximately 15 cm and held open with a short but stout piece of wood. Both ends were then secured by rawhide to the ends of the split fork. Finally, a connecting section of rawhide was wrapped and stitched to the sides of the forks and the spreader. The attached hide platform was given a concave impression by first soaking it thoroughly, and then pressing a rounded stone into the now-pliable hide until dry. A second type of snow *shovel was whittled from wood* (*č'axʷčstúleʔxʷtn*), usually using a prepared piece of white pine or cottonwood (STHC). Since cedar splits so easily, it was never used for making shovel for fire ash or snow.

Stems and Bark

Certain *stems* (*sčoxʷoxʷépleʔ*) and *bark* (*č'iʔlélxʷ*) were assiduously collected for immediate application or stored for later use. There was some specific knowledge possessed by those who harvested certain barks thought to be adscititious to the Spokan pharmacopoeia—ones which were collected, prepared, and administered by only those people possessing the necessary skills and knowledge of the desired medicinal effects of known simple and compound medicines.

Most bark medicines were gathered from trees common to the many streams and wet areas, particularly *Scouler's willow* (*Salix Scouleriana* Barratt. - *q'ʷq'ʷl'sál'qʷ*, paper birch (*Betula papyrifera* Marsh. - *yeswlš̌ʷ* or *lep'yálqʷ*), water birch (*B. occidentalis* Hook. - *qʷqʷt̓in'*), river or mountain alder, red osier, dogwood bush, syringa (mock orange), quaking aspen, or black cottonwood. The opened sections of bark from these trees were roughed with a *flat stone scrape*r (*xʷík̓ʷmn*), soaked in hot water, and then applied to ease a patient's arthritic joints or afflicted long bones. Cottonwood ashes, which contain *lye* (*mx̌ʷyúleʔxʷ*), were soaked overnight in water, and the upper half of the solution was decanted after boiling, and upon cooling was used for washing a person's hair.

Plant stalks or stems were used almost daily by men, women, and children to fulfill various tasks of necessity and pleasure, from making small humanoid figures, to fashioning trays or platters for carrying food, called *sx̌ʷx̌ʷƛ'x̌ʷuƛ'm'*, and were made by weaving certain stems of the willow family (*Salicaceae*). They were used for even larger items associated with fishing weirs, hunting blinds, dwellings, and baskets for subsistence gathering. Some elderly women once gained considerable notoriety—if only with children and the occasional anthropologist—by artistically rendering many identifiable creatures of the animal kingdom by deftly manipulating soaked red willow stems. Once, before a group of great grandchildren, a proud great grandfather had made a deer from pipe cleaners for the pleasure of his young admiring audience. His wife, with an appreciative and respectful smile, proceeded to sit next to the old gentleman, and after making the same animal with willow stems, she diplomatically covered her wide smile with a handkerchief and said to her husband, "My deer has life; your deer can only clean pipes."

Bark was used in a variety of ways: making plates for eating, covering small dwellings, making baskets and *food platters* (*snčɫʔeščeʔn'm'ismn*), securing tule mats that encircled the base of pit houses and long-houses, and for the outside bases of canvas tipis. Plates of decayed poplar wood were common. Another ingenious use of black cottonwood bark was for making *snake leggings* or *protective puttees*, (*snake leggings* (*sx̌ƛ'x̌éʔƛ'iʔšn* - "women's leggings" or *sčacacqínšn* - "men's leggings"), which were used by people when berry-collecting in late summer, and by men when logging to protect against snake bites. These activities increased the odds of encountering snakes, such as the venomous *Western diamond-back rattler* (*Crotalus atox* - *x̌ʔúleʔxʷ*), picking up wood ticks, and receiving skin abrasions from dense understory. Bark leggings extended from below the knees to the ankles, and were held in place by wrapping with strips of rawhide. The most preferred bark was freshly cut black cottonwood or, if available, the more pliable pine or birch bark. During the mid-1960s, an elderly gentleman laughed as he recalled various jokes regarding the use of such leg protectors. It was said that if a man intended a visit to his *mother-in-law* (*ɫcécč*), a close sweathouse partner would invariably and very audibly offer helpful comments such as: "Be sure to wear your snake leggings," or "Do you expect to see your mother-in-law?" As a further precaution prior to traveling through arid, bushy country, both men and women would take and mash the pungent, ill-smelling edible roots of valerian (tobacco root), and rub the mash on their ankles to prevent snake bites.

As previously discussed, the bark used for house construction was collected mainly in the spring when it was most pliable, since this facilitated the removal and flattening of the bark before drying that retained the desired shape. The bark was used primarily for insulating the lower outside perimeter of dwellings in winter, as well as for facilitating water runoff throughout the year:

238

Every dwelling was made warm by lining with newly dried hides and mats. Bark that had been stripped off during the spring was now made to stand up in the ground, overlap and rest on the cross boards of the pole frames. A ditch was dug along the wall and dirt poured on the bark (Wynecoop 1985:36).

Willow bark was an invaluable material that fulfilled numerous purposes. Long bark strips of soaked *white willow* (*Salix sitchensis* Sanson - *q'ʷq'ʷl'sál'qʷ* or *l'p'iy''alqʷ*) served to stabilize smaller pieces of willow with larger sections of willow when constructing a woven willow *fish trap* (*sq'ʷyóxʷ*). Though both men and women collected this material, men were responsible for manufacturing the large, open mats used in making fishing weirs and traps, as well as animal traps and snares. When constructing sweathouses and storage structures, men extensively used *willow branches* (*čq'ʷaʔq'ʷaʔl'ečst*)—one exception was when women erected menstrual huts.

Women often used willow in constructing various types of baskets, particularly their husbands' open-weave baskets for gathering fresh water mussels. It was not unusual for both men and women to use willow in making a variety of toys and musical instruments for their children. Bark peeled from fresh red willow shafts was used on special occasions in the sweathouse as an *emetic stick* (*nxʷwq'ʷɫceʔtn'*), and as a nasal cleansing device by chewing and shredding the end, and then soaking the willow to make it pliant before use. In the past, a man might decide to take two dry sections of red willow, and commencing at the feeble end he would make a series of cuts with a sharp obsidian flake before soaking the pieces prior to alternately inserting one at a time in each nostril until the feeble end was in his mouth, then, with his finger, he would grab the end and pull the length of willow out through his mouth.

Whenever women were traversing a wooded area, they would collect willow punk wood, which was preferred for smoking hides. When dried and shredded, willow bark was used for lining cradleboards. The dried, pungent bark of *rabbitbrush* (*Ericameria nauseosus* Britton, var. *albicaulis* [Nutt.] Rydb. - *papʕáyɫp* or *sncn'čtqin*) was used to tan hides. This plant was considered to be poisonous (St. John 1963:476); hence, the pulverized leaves were rubbed on horses to protect them from horse-flies (Turner 1979:186).

Some mats for sleeping and sitting were manufactured from materials other than tules and cattails—such as the, "bark of dead willow trees" (Teit 1930 327) and shredded sage bark, which made a flexible mat, as well as other items. A fine gift to an elder was a *split cedar mat* (*nšcnšcné*) made from old close-growth cedar that had been split into a series of one meter length strips approximately 5 to 10 mm in thickness, and serially attached at the ends and center with braided hemp, permitting it to be rolled when not in use. Silverberry has an oily bark, and, thus, remains supple and does not easily dry out when used to make mats, bags, and for *plaited rope* (*acsqáxen hecq'ic'*). Twined silverberry rope was favored for constructing *fishing stick weir* (*stem'ús* or *q'ʷyxum*), and for manufacturing *woven stick weirs* (*sxʷayxʷ* or *sq'ʷyxi*) and traps because it remained strong and did not deteriorate even when kept under water for an entire fishing season.

The Spokan used a method of twining that required the use of three strands of bast or willow bark, which were rolled back and forth over the worker's *thigh* (*t'upm*)—adding additional strands as the work progressed. Given a specific use, additional strands were plaited together for greater strength. The length of the rope was determined by its intended use, and when finished, the rope was not the property of the manufacturer if it was to be used for constructing a communal weir or fishing trap. It was said that women did not make rope intended for fishing activities for fear of contaminating the water, which would keep the fish from entering the area. Twining for basketry and other uses was done by women who would roll bast or bark between their hands. If alone, or with female co-workers, a woman would do the twining on her exposed thigh, but never in the presence of her husband or older son.

For the daily early morning cleaning of villages, a *man's large broom* (*čxʷk'ʷčn'éɫxʷtn*) was made from snowberry bush branches that had been bunched together and tied around a stout two meter stick, which served as an effective means to *sweep* (*hescɫʔáxʷlpi* or *čy escɫʔáxʷlpi* - "I am sweeping the ground"). Such a broom was used for sweeping large open *areas of debris* (*čxʷk'ʷčnéɫpm'*); usually a daily chore for any elderly man unable to participate in hunting or fishing. As will be noted, smaller snowberry branches were bound together for combing huckleberries off the bushes. If necessary, a person would sweep an area of debris using a *rosehip bush* (*snqixʷleʔxʷm*) used to rid a place of malevolent spirits and the footprints of a deceased person. After gathering wood, and upon returning to a living area, women would occasionally break off several branches of the snowberry bush and tie them together to sweep the pathway (Elmendorf 1935-6, 1:63).

Every woman would sweep the family's bedding daily with a *brush* (*xk’ʷélptn*), one made by her husband from the more stout lower section of the wing from a goose, eagle, or greater sandhill crane. When required, the brush served as a *fan* (*xaxaʕústn*) during exceptionally hot weather. Sleeping platforms and smaller items were often cleaned with a *feather brush* (*xk’ʷélptn*) fashioned from the detached wing of a hawk. The very pliable and plentiful rabbitbrush was used to make medicine bundles, and the dried leaves were sprinkled on sweathouse stones to purify participants. Interestingly, *elderberry stems* (*c’kʷkʷalqʷ*), with the pith removed, were used to *inflate* (*npéwman*) *animal intestines* (*stxénč*), and as *soft food containers* (*np’t’mán* - "to put soft things into") (STHC). Such containers were commonly used for storing fats as *winter provisions* (*stčeʔn’eʔs*) that had been heated until near liquid and then poured into the *intestine containers* (*np’t’man*) (Elmendorf, pers. comm.). Intestine containers were usually hung from exposed roofing poles within the main dwelling.

Sap

Tree sap (*lamnás*) was highly valued by the Spokan, serving as a wide spectrum *medicament* (*k’ʷułmr’yémistmstmn*). The importance of this product was noted since the month of August was called *slamp*, "the time or moon of running sap," when most of the *sap was collected* (*sč’mxcI* - "scraping something to eat") from *sap pockets* (*st’íqʷlqʷ*). However, depending upon the tree species, and given the purpose, sap was collected in late winter or early spring from both deciduous and evergreen trees. Because women were more active than men in the collecting and processing of sap, and in making the required collection paraphernalia, they retained all prerogatives of distribution. Though usury rights applied, more through courtesy, and often inherited rights to cambium groves, women could claim any number of "sap trees" simply by cutting and placing her collecting receptacle on those she had tapped. The amount of sap varied according to the age and species of a particular tree species, and a productive tree could yield at least 4 to 5 liters twice a year (Turner 1978:53).

Women collected tamarack sap the same way as they collected birch sap, by cutting a "V" into the cambium bark near the base of the tree, or at about shoulder level in late winter or early spring. The sap dripped into a *birch bark container* (*lúp’iʔ*) or one made of cottonwood that was held below the cut by either tying the basket to the tree or using several forked sticks supported by a forked branch wedged against the bottom of the container. Birch tree sap was always considered a delicacy—particularly water birch, and *Western paper birch* (*Betaula papyrifera* Marsh., var. *communtata* [Regel] Fern. - *p’y’álqʷ*) had a most favorable taste. The process of scraping sap was called *sč’mxcí*. Archaeological examples of sap and cambium scooping spoons have been found (Collier *et al* 1942:87), ones frequently made from mountain sheep horn. Ponderosa pine cambium was called *sc’xʷiʔ*.

Since it required considerable time and patience to secure a significant quantity of the clear, sweet liquid, sap was considered a thoughtful gift. This was particularly true for elderly people who exercised certain proprietary rights in its distribution—sometimes claiming that the best of stories could be recalled only after an adequate consumption of this delectable food. Some recalled how the sap was drunk as collected or carefully boiled by the collector until it was thicker and sometimes crystallized, which made for better storage.

Pitch and Gum

Pitch and *gum* (*t'aq'ʷéy'* - "hard, brown gum") are essentially the same; nearly always from fir and pine trees, but in some instances from deciduous trees, and were important by-products to different aspects of Spokan technology as well as the indigenous *materia medica*. A problem with these products was that if they were not collected in the late summer or early autumn, before prescribed burning, then they were likely to be destroyed by an *uncontrolled fire* (*sp'ap*).

People frequently extracted pitch with wooden spoons, usually for immediate consumption, or to be stored in closed bark containers made from stripped white pine, which was easily bent to a desired shape. Pitch was gathered and stored for caulking structures, as a glue for adhering porous materials, for starting fires, for repairing bark baskets, canoes, and other wood products, and as medicine. Solid or liquid pitch from pine and fir sap pockets was warmed and then worked, for example, into hemp lashings that secured *antler fish harpoon* (*łuʔmín* - "something to jab with") and leister heads to wooden shafts. When hafting composite knives, spears, and compound leisters, men used pitch as a *glue from white pine* (*t'áłqntxʷ*) to help waterproof and preserve the wood, and to secure the binding wraps—most notably covering the hemp with *pitch* (*péłiʔn*) on a harpoon. Warm pitch was applied to the wood joints before any wrapping with hemp or stripped cambium, and later thinly applied over the wrappings to protect and waterproof the bindings. "Cottonwood bud resin was used as a glue and paint base, spruce pitch as an adhesive, and prickly-pear cactus mucilage as a paint fixative" (Hunn, Turner, and French 1998:534). Work described the need and value of gum, which was used sometimes daily for the repair of canoes: "The Indians [sic] women were sent off to gather gum to repair one of the canoes to make another trip below if the weather continues favorable" (Elliott 1914, 4:264), and how this application was done only by men (Elliott 1914, 4:264). During an unproductive trapping session, he recorded: "Nothing going in the way of trade except a little gum [pitch]" (Elliott 1914, 4:271).

The *blisters on subalpine fir* (*st'íkʷlqʷ*) and the blisters of tamarack trees were used as an adhesive and as a glue. This was useful for creating makeshift *footwear* (*hahán'eʔ*) when traveling over rough terrain, or on a long journey when a person's moccasins wear out. When wrapping material for improvising foot cover was unavailable, survival footwear could be made by applying soft, *warm pine pitch* (*t'éłłtn*) to a person's *bare feet* (*p'piλ'ešn* - "bare foot") and then applying green ponderosa needles placed at right angles to the long axis of the foot. Alternatively, pitch could be applied to the feet and was then rubbed with fine earth or crushed grasses, which effectively glued the protective material to one's feet. Though not as durable, shredded sagebrush bark could be adhered to the pitch to make an effectively protective sole.

Deciduous *western larch* (*Larix occidentalis* Nutt. - *cáqʷlš*) and fir trees contain *partially dried form of* pitch (*čpkʷkʷálqʷ*) in small pockets on their bark. The pitch is similar to *pine gum* (*him'np'il'q'ʷ*) and was commonly used as a *chewing gum* (*t'aq'ʷéy'*). As a matter of taste, older men and women preferred to chew *tamarack gum* (*čpkʷpkʷálqʷ*) and *pine tree gum* (*t'aq'ʷy'*), always avoiding *hard tree pitch* (*t'aq'ʷáy'*). The Spokan knew that after approximately ten minutes of chewing any tree gum, they would have to remove the substance before it became hard, which would effectively glue their jaws together, at least until the mass eventually dissolved. When traveling in open grassland areas, chewing gum was made from dandelion latex.

Pitches were useful in caulking, for adhering materials, and for repairing bark and certain wood products. The manufacture of fish harpoon and leister heads was dependent upon this adhesive material, which, when applied warm, was bound and secured with hemp. Tanned hide glued to pitch could be used as an emergency foot pad.

241

Cambium

The *cambium* (*sc'éxʷíʔ*) of ponderosa, white fir, Douglas fir, and *subalpine fir* (*Abies lasiocarpa* [Hook.] Nutt. - *mriałp*) was gathered and eaten in early spring, when it was considered a delicacy—being quite sweet. In late winter, it served as a readily available starvation food to supplement depleted food larders. Most cambium was collected in early spring and stored throughout the year as a medicine and for hafting tools, making cordage and baskets. Dried cambium cakes were frequently used as trail food to supplement jerky.

Other types of trees which were used for their cambium were three species of alder (*c'k'ʷk'ʷálqʷ*), *Sitka alder* (*Alnus sinuta* [Regel] Rydb. - *pčłn'áʔ*), with the same Spokan designation as *A. incana* (L.) Moench, and *mountain alder* (*A. tenuifolia* Nutt. - *č'č'itnéłp*), white fir, *Douglas fir* (*Pseudotsuga taxifolia* [Lamb. qʷqʷłin'oir] rehder - *c'q'éłp*), white pine, and subalpine fir were also utilized. Only Cottonwood cambium was scraped and eaten, but after several days it would sour. When preparing cambium for storage, it was first soaked in water, then cooked in an earth oven until leather hard, and when needed the strips were pounded with a wooden hammer until softened.

Pine bark cambium (*sc'éxʷiʔ*) was typically gathered by women in areas designated as *cambium groves* (*n'ssʔátqʷłp*). Before collecting, the bark was first removed by making two horizontal cuts with a sharp stone—one around the top and the other around the bottom of a 40 to 50 cm section. These two incisions were connected with one deep vertical cut, and the entire circular slab was easily stripped or *peeled* (*łáum*) with a thin, flat wood spatula-like tool. The thin white inside layer was scraped to make it easier to pull off in long strips with the outside sharpened edge of a *deer rib* (*ʔáq'mn* - "rib knife"), a wooden spatula or a *special stick* (*sčłq'ʷálqʷtn*), or with a sharp uniface stone—tools that had been stored in the area. Some women favored a piece of worked long bone as a *stripper* (*c'éxʷiʔtn*), approximately 2 cm in width and 20 cm in length, with a fore-rounded end. After several years of use, this tool often became so thin that one could see the *shadow* (*sm'el'k'ʷéy'eʔ*) of one's hand when passed beneath the stripper.

A few elders remembered their parents and grandparents explaining how, during earlier times, people would scoop the cambium from the exposed tree with large metal spoons that would be hung for anyone's use. One elder recalled with considerable delight how:

> In the spring my grandmother [born circa 1840] was always had the able to find a "sweet" pine tree. Some people had to see which tree the porcupine had been chewing, but not her. When she found the right one, she'd have my father "throw the tree" [cut it down], then, with her deer bone knife, she'd carefully strip away the bark. Then she'd carefully peel the cambium for us children to chew. This was always a nice treat after eating stored foods of winter (Ross 1968-2008).

Once removed, the cambium was dried for future use—usually for manufacturing baskets—after cutting the material into narrow strips for stitching, often used to make two-ply strings or three-ply rope. Most cambium was harvested in strips approximately 10 to 12 cm wide. When gathering for the construction of conical fish traps, willow was cut in long strips from approximately 12 to 15 cm in width. These were soaked until supple, and used for securing weirs or netting to vertical stakes. Though somewhat flexible, cambium remained durable throughout its intended use as long as the material was kept wet by submersion, and proved capable of surviving periodic exposure to nature with occasional water level fluctuations. The only animals it was not fully immune to were hungry bears and porcupines. Top and bottom spans of corral nets were made by tightly braiding long sections of inner willow bark.

If necessary, cambium was consumed as a starvation food in late winter or early spring when food supplies were depleted and there was little or *nothing to eat* (*miʔš t sʔiłn*). In early spring, when both men and women were busy gathering foods, elders would take young children to the nearest cambium grove and collect cambium. After collecting, some cambium was spread and dehydrated (*č'exʷ*) on tule mats supported on horizontal drying racks, and then bundled and stored within the dwelling—never in storage sheds for fear of loss to marauding animals. The remaining cambium was stored for future use in bundles inside of bark containers, usually made on the site from stripped white pine bark which was easily bent into shape.

According to Lord, who observed how the most sought cambium was from young ponderosa trees:

[...] the young trees of this species are invariably stripped of their bark to a height of seven feet from the ground, or as high up the trunk as an ordinary person can reach. This is done in order to procure the inner bark, which the savages use as food; they eat it in the fresh state as peeled from the tree, and compressed into cakes, in which state it can be preserved for a long time, and is easily carried (1866, 2:188).

Lichens

Several types of tree and rock lichens (sčk'ʷrnéčst) were used as food, dyes, diapers, padding, medicine, and poisons. Tree lichens, such as black tree lichen (*Bryoria fremontii* [Tuck.] Brodo & D. Hawksw.), sometimes called *horsehair lichen* (*Alectoria fremontii* Tuck. - sqʷl'ápq or sqʷelapqen), are pendulous lichens once highly regarded as a food. A different variety of *black tree lichen* (*A. jubata* - šawtmqn or aw'temeqen) was collected. "If it was sweet and not bitter they would gather great quantities" (Turner 1977:461). There are numerous Spokan and English designations for the epiphyte—one being Coyote's Hair, *so named to explain* (ta? cn miy'áw'sqn) its origin when Coyote caught his hair in the trees while being pursued by swans. This preferred source of tree lichen was gathered from western larch (tamarack) and from *western tamarack* (*Tsuga heterophylla* [Raf.] Sarg. - p'ƛtené?) as it was less bitter than that from other trees, but sweeter than lichen harvested from other types of *gymnospermae*, particularly ponderosa pine or Douglas fir (Spier 1938). Lichens, as observed by Turner (1975:8), when collected from older, mature trees, are usually not as bitter as lichens from younger comparable species. DeSmet described how, "a piece of cooked moss [lichen] tasted like soap, and as black as pitch" (1966:363).

Yellow tree lichen (*Letharia columbiana* [Nutt.] Thomas. - sčkʷe?rnéčst) was collected from conifers at higher elevations, notably subalpine fir and white-bark pine (*Pinus albicaulis*), and used as a yellow dye. Only a few lichens that were once gathered, namely *Cetraria islandica* (L.) Ach., and the common *Parmedia sulcata* Tayla, were remembered by a few as having medicinal properties.

Spier (1938) observed there were two species of wolf lichens: *yellow-green lichen* (*L. vulpina* [L.] Hue - skʷalyo?álqʷ) and *wolf lichen* (*Letharia vulpina* [L] Wain. - sčkʷrnéčst). Wolf lichen was used by the contiguous Coeur d'Alene who steeped this ubiquitous tree lichen in hot water to produce a bright yellow dye, not unlike the dye from boiled Oregon grape roots (Teit 1930:44). The most common lichens used for making dyes were *Licidella euphora*, *L. glomerulosa*, *Acarrospora chlorophana* (Ach.) Mass., *Candelariella vitellina* (Hoffm.), *Xanthoria elegans* (Link) Th. Fr., *X. Fallax* (Hepp) Am., and *X. polycarpa* Hoffin. Rieber. Lichens are no longer utilized as a dye or collected as medicines by those few remaining craftspeople when working with traditional materials, nor did the few remaining elder women recall all the specific medicinal uses of lichens.

Wolf lichen, when steeped and decanted three times, made a concentrate of "poisonous lichen acid [now] known as vulpinic acid" (Turner 1979:50), which was poisonous to marauding dogs (usually placed in a small piece of raw meat). This is particularly true of *Bryoria fremonti* and *B. Abbreviata*, which were gathered at higher elevations (Vitt *et al.* 1988:248). Of the two lichens, *B. Fremontii* had the lowest concentration of vulpinic acid (Turner 1978:35), and was removed by proper leaching during the initial washing, preferably in running stream water. However, *Alectoria fremontii* Tuck. was similarly used as a poison, which was concentrated with repeated boiling. Turner (1977:463) states that *B. fremontii* is usually free of vulpinic acid, whereas *B. tortuosa* is high in vulpinic acid and potentially toxic (Turner 1977, 33:465).

The time and effort that women once expended throughout the year for collecting lichens reflected the utilitarian and dietary importance of this prolific *epiphyte* (šáw'tmqn). Men going hunting and to other resource areas and camps would, before returning home, collect different lichens—particularly *Bryoria*. Some elderly women recall hearing grandmothers discuss how they once gathered great quantities, usually while in small groups, and who looked upon these collecting expeditions as memorable social excursions that provided opportunities to exchange communal gossip.

Older children were encouraged to participate in lichen-collecting, being mindful of social pleasures and receiving praise when assisting elderly women in the group. Younger boys demonstrated adolescent nerve and skills by climbing trees when collecting and removing branches to be picked over later. Participating youngsters were praised and often given a deserving treat by the grandmother. Climbing tamarack trees was considered a challenge—even dangerous—due to the characteristically brittle limbs. Because this lichen grew in such abundance, it was more easily gathered in great quantities from low *branches* (*sč'č'šmečst'* or *čl'čl'šm'ečst*), whereas harvesting from higher branches required using a long, dry, pine *pole with a hafted wooden projection* (*ʔúp'čstn*), an instrument used for gathering tree lichens, or a *fallen limb with small protruding snags* (*nq'ey'uʔs*) and to pull down moss-laden or large clumps of *moss* (*mtrʔálqʷ*). In dense productive areas, gathering poles, 4 to 6 m in length, were always left leaning against a tree for future use by anyone. Before storing black moss in grass sacks, it was spread on several layers of dry pine needles and hit with sticks to remove any debris (Elmendorf 1935-6, 1:27).

After a large harvest, lichens were transported to the summer camp or winter village and distributed equally among the gatherers regardless of a person's individual effort. As cited, climbing a tamarack or pine tree to harvest lichens and moss was sometimes a dangerous if not fatal activity, certainly for a much older woman, as attested by the missionary Walker, who mentioned in his dairy (19 March 1841) of treating a woman who had injured herself while probably climbing a tree (Drury 1976:141), and later of a man breaking, "his collar & thigh bones" (Drury 1976:269) while gathering lichens. Young boys, being lighter and often more agile than older men, on occasions assisted women in gathering tree lichens.

Collected lichens were first carefully leached and cleaned by washing in the nearest stream to remove any loose bark, fir and pine needles, and wind-borne *dust* (*sqʷʔuł*). Time and logistics tended to determine the exact location for washing the harvest. Large amounts of tree lichens were cleaned by constructing a small temporary log or stone dam, which prevented any large masses of soaking lichens from being washed downstream. After returning to a camp or village, the women carefully spread their harvest to dry on "layered [tamarack] needles to remove foreign matter & to impart a bitter taste" (Elmendorf 1935-6, 1:27). Prior to placing the lichens in an iron cooking cauldron, the sodden mass of lichens was compressed before bringing the water to a boil, and upon *cooling* (*c'ʔéł* - "to cool down"), small moss cakes of cooked lichen were made and stored. Traditionally, this cooking process was best accomplished by using an earthen oven.

When cooking large amounts of lichens, they were first placed in an excavated pit lined with heated stones, then covered with various types of grass, such as *bear-grass* (*Xerophyllum tenax* - *šlč'éstéyeʔ* or *mlk'ʷtełt'iy'eʔ* or *sxʷq'ʷéłt* or *m'l'k'ʷt'est'y'eʔ*) and available flat green leaves. The closed cattail sacks containing the uncooked lichens were covered with grass or leaves, or with old tule mats. An adequate layer of roughly 16 cm of earth was laid and then firmly packed, and several holes were made by shoving several short poles completely through the earth, grass, and tule mat cover to the heated base stones. After the poles were removed, cold water was poured in to create steam, then plugged to contain the steam. The final stage was to cover the entire earth oven with another layer of heated vesicular stone, which was permitted to steam the rest of the day and overnight, or longer depending upon the amount of lichen being cooked. When there were only ashes, the pit was opened to reveal a blue-black congealed jelly-like mass that was cooled for immediate consumption or to be cut into thin sections and dried for storage. If kept dry, moss and lichens would keep indefinitely. During storage, the flavor of tree lichens was improved by covering the dry blocks or bundles with sunflower leaves, which will also make the lichen less sticky (Schaeffer 1934-37, I-34:13).

Around noon the following day or in two days, only women would open the enclosed oven under the direction of the oldest woman, while all of the participants sang songs in general praise of their harvest and their friendship, and for being together again with the elderly women who would conduct the ceremony and direct the harvest. By late afternoon, the soft mass of prepared lichens was distributed evenly among all participants, who in turn would redistribute lesser amounts to non-attending gatherers. Then the lichens were allowed to cool into a black *pudding* (*sp'at'qan*), and then pressed into tight flat cakes and wrapped in mullein leaves to maintain shape. Baked lichens were sometimes consumed immediately, or, as mentioned earlier, were stored separately as a winter food, often mixed with deer meat at the meal. Baked *Bryoria* was high in carbohydrates, and Turney-High estimated that the average Flathead consumed approximately 25 pounds per person annually (Turner (1977, 31:465).

Lichens were considered an important food in late winter when women would gather them in nearby wooded areas that had been purposely unharvested for such emergencies. Though it is not known how extensively the yellow-green lichen was cooked and eaten during a typical year, it was, however, a supplemental winter food. In addition to storing in mullein leaves, cooked lichens saved for winter storage were compressed as dehydrated masses into long cakes and kept in folded cedar bark-envelopes or grass bags. Alexander Ross provided a near complete description of collecting and preparing tree lichen for winter use by the Sinkaietk, one that basically duplicates procedures once used by the Spokan:

This moss is carefully gathered every autumn, when it has the appearance of dirty coarse wool. It is soaked in water, pressed hard together, and then cooked in an oven or furnace, from which it comes forth in large sheets like slat, but supple and pliable, resembling pieces of tarpauling, black as ink, and tasteless; and when cut with a knife it has a spotted or marbled appearance, owing to the number of small twigs of wood, bark, or other extraneous substances, unavoidably collected [...] This cake when dried in the sun becomes as hard as flint, and must always be soaked in water before use. It is generally eaten with the raw fat of animals, as we use bread and butter. It is viscous and clammy in the mouth, but with little taste. Thus prepared it will keep for years; is much liked by the natives, and sometimes eaten by the whites. It is called squill-ape [*sq'ʷl'ápqn*] (1849:299).

Army Captain John Mullan (1830-1909), in the mid-1850s, while railroad surveying for a route between Ft. Benton and Ft. Walla Walla, observed tree lichens being burned by a Coeur d'Alene Indian, who, when asked, stated that, "By burning the moss the deer are obliged to descend into the valleys for food" (Mullan 1861:152); thus, making them more available for Indian predation. During the Wilkes Expedition, Pickering also observed the harvesting of lichens while visiting Tschimakain Mission, and commented how the local Indians "cut down the pines for the sake of the black lichen [probably *Alectoria*] which grows upon them, and which is made into bread, or mixed with kamas [sic] in a sort of pudding" (1895:26), and later reported by Barry (1929:59).

After the year's first event of collecting and distributing lichens and mosses, and prior to cooking, an elderly lady would lead the participants and guests in a special ceremony of thanksgiving, an annual late summer ritual that attested to the importance of this food. The past importance of tree lichens was attested by an annual fall ceremony that the Spokan practiced, in which a sacred ritual attended the pit-cooking of great amounts of this food, and was last conducted and personally observed in the fall of 1981 (Ross 1981). During this particular event, it was recalled how in the past a certain elderly woman was noted for never assisting in the laborious construction of the earth oven, and yet she always somehow managed to appear when the other women were placing their uncooked food into the pit, and would somehow get her sacks in among the others. Such a person was called *l'el'éč'e?i*.

Collecting accumulated masses of lichens helped to reduce the chance of ground fires or lightning-caused fires, which potentially could create quite destructive crown fires. Elderly Spokan women remembered how, when berrying in early autumn at higher elevations, they would group together to collect with their hands and poles any accessible lichens to reduce fire danger as well as for food. Barrett stated that the Flathead people would gather lichen as food, and "to reduce the threat of wildfires which could ignite the lichen and spread in to the forest canopy" (1980a:152).

Lichens have not been seriously collected by the Spokan for any purpose since the late 1950s, and even then, when gathered as a food, adults and children would add sugar to make the dish more palatable. Prior to the reservation period, during the hottest weather, women would sometimes sweeten this food by collecting white crystalline sugar from Douglas fir. It is "a white crystalline sugar having a high concentration of a rare trisaccharide called melezitose" (Turner *et al.* 1980:34). Due to the bitter taste, black tree lichens were seldom eaten raw, being considered unpalatable unless baked in an earth oven.

Mosses

Prior to the late 1950s, most elderly women were able to make critical linguistic distinctions between the different lichens and mosses, whereas now most Spokan people simply include lichens with moss (*mtr?álq*). Until recently, a few contemporary elders could identify the different types of mosses that were collected many years ago, and several elderly women recalled how their mothers and grandmothers collected a wide range of mosses several times a year. During such occasions, it was said that when younger and older women gathered to harvest an area, the younger ones stayed together as did the elderly women. However, when a younger non-kinswoman left her group, and temporarily joined with several elders, it was known that the younger woman was seeking the experience and advice of her seniors, who would later respect her anonymity. To reveal certain problems with one's relatives could cause problems. A young man occasionally sought advice from a non-related elder. As was once said, "I learned more from strangers than from friends."

Though the Spokan made a linguistic distinction between *rock moss* (*Selaginella wallacei* Hieron - *čqʷsqʷspéssn'*) and *ground moss* (*nqʷsqʷspúl'e?xʷ*), they had different names for the same species. Despite the name, it also grows on some trees, and given its soft and elastic composition, it was used as camp bedding if dry when collected. For properties of absorption, the most generally used mosses were sphagnum moss, and it was "used for lining cradleboards and padding as baby diapers, and was said to last a full twelve hours without needing changing" (Turner 1979:58). All grandmothers carried a ready supply of moss when tending to grandchildren, and before the advent of tissue paper, a certain sign of a woman attending one's grandchildren was to stuff moss into her waist bag. Both men and women used moss to cleanse their hands after cleaning fish or dressing game. Dry *fire moss* (*Ceraatodon puroureus* [Hedw.] Brid. - *čqʷsqʷspessbn*) was used by hunters for removing excessive abdominal blood from a deer and when cleaning their hands after butchering game.

Despite the present abundance of cloth, and until recently, hunters recognized the absorbent qualities of moss and occasionally used this material, if available, for absorbing, as mentioned, the blood in the abdominal cavities of deer or elk when dressing such game. It was said that a serious hunter always carried a skin bag of dried moss for this purpose, and as a deodorant, and for sanitation purposes if there were no available mullein leaves. Sphagnum moss was mixed with clay or mud for caulking log structures.

The information of how and why some plants were formerly used as medicaments is now unfortunately inconclusive. Yet until recently, when asked, nearly all elderly women vaguely recalled their grandmothers boiling ground moss to make a tea when treating various stomach problems and dysmenorrhea. Even the once common practice of using dried moss, particularly *Claopodeium*, as an absorbent medicament when placed upon dermal eruptions, is now unknown or not known to be practiced.

Partly as a result of the deculturation and acculturation of the Spokan, there are few remaining reasons for them to identify, collect, and use the various species of lichens and mosses that once served as deodorants, medicines, and the material for boiling to make dyes, caulking dwellings, and for making padding in moccasins if winter traveling. In most instances, these once indigenous technologies have been replaced by readily available but expensive Euro-American products.

246

Leaves

Women collected leaves from an extensive variety of plants, primarily for producing beverages, as emergency camp bedding, toiletry, substitute diapers, dyes, cleansing pads, and medicines, for covering emergency or *small overnight shelters* (*k'ʷuk'ʷɬxʷn'tm'* - "small houses were made"), for lining pit ovens and berrying-collecting baskets, making small folded packets and cups, and for rubbing on items to mask human odors when hunting.

The *leaves* (*picčɬ*) from an extensive list of plants were collected at different times of the year according to their intended use, and almost always by women, primarily for making beverages and medicines. The most notable medicinal leaves were those from mint and a variety of field or *Canada mint* (*Mentha arvensis* L. var. *glabrata* [Benth] Fern - *xaʕxʕáyɬp* or *xaxaiɬp*, syn. *Mentha arvensis L. canadensis* L.), and a variety of a spearmint; all were made into teas to promote sweating for people diagnosed with fever or colds. This tea was made by boiling the entire plant after it had been washed. Either fresh or dried leaves of Coyote mint plants were used to cleanse human odor from spears, fish and animal traps, and fishing hooks (Ray 1932:105; Turner 1979:275) to make them again effective. The outer leaves of skunk cabbage were used, if available, to line and cover earth ovens.

Sedges and Bulrushes

Critical to the environmental adaptation of the Spokan people was an extensive knowledge of using sedges, bulrushes, and other types of grasses, which had a wide utility in the manufacture of numerous finished products, from thread to mat house coverings. One of their most important technologies was the manufacturing of mats that were produced in large numbers and served a multitude of uses. In addition, tules and cattail were used as flooring mats, small trays for serving and eating food, and as rain capes.

The principal types of hydrophytes or *sedges* (*Carex lenticularis* Michx. - *q'ʷq'ʷís*) used in mat-making were *tules* (bulrushes) (*Scripus validus* Vahl. and S. *acutus* Muhl. ex Bigel. - *t'kʷtín'* or *sy'áy'qs*) and *broadleaf cattail* (*Typha latifolia* - *šq'ʷastqín*). Any long so-called *waterweeds* (*snupl'e?xʷétkʷ*) provided material for small baskets and imbrication. On occasion, both red and green *willow withes* (*syel'u?* - "twisted stick") were used in making enclosure mats for fishing weirs and corrals, and for game fences and for channeling deer during collective hunting. The choice of materials and the shape of a *mat* (*p'šɬpáxn*) were typically determined on the basis of the availability of materials and its intended use.

A major activity of all women in the late fall was the laborious but often enjoyable activity of collecting great amounts of bundled tules and cattails from ponds, seeps, and mostly from shallow lake edges. Though not a starvation food, in early spring, when cattails had grown to a height of approximately 40 to 50 cm above water level, the plant was cut off just above the rhizome and the short developing clustered leaves were peeled back, revealing a white inner core, which was eaten raw. The principles of usufruct applied to all sites when collectively gathering tules and cattails, and not only facilitated any woman's access to those resource areas, but encouraged peaceful relations with distant non-kinspeople who mutually exploited any such resource site. Harvesting hydrophytes *always* occurred after a *killing frost* (*sxʷek'ʷt*) when the tules and cattails had turned a dark, mottled brown color. Prior to collecting, the period of maximum growth was known as *tkʷtín*. Tules collected when they were still green would shrink, thereby preventing the finished product from retaining its desired shape, and upon drying, they became brittle and would crack when bending or manipulating, whereas the post-freeze cattail remained more flexible. Older women have commented how pleasing the mottled brown and tan colors of tules were when gathered after a killing frost. Some stated that their mothers and grandmothers claimed how some women, when making tule mats, had the ability to select tules with certain color configurations and hues so that the finished product had appealing patterns. Such a mat could reveal a

247

story to an imaginative child, or at least when interpreted by a grandmother. There is no evidence that the Spokan ever made tule or cattail mats with any distinct designs by imbrication or by painting. Nor is it known if the Spokan decorated food and berry tule mats by cutting the edges of mats in varying lengths to achieve different patterns, as recorded for the Kalispel by Teit (1930:47) and Smith (1936-8:616). Tules woven into mats were called *sҙ́áy'qs* .

Smith describes but does not explain an interesting aspect of tule mat design attendant to residential structures that from a physics standpoint is rather rational and readily explainable. He describes that the distal margins of tule mats used in household coverings were crenellated in a pattern of two, seven, two with each grouping of two extending approximately three inches longer than the margins. Initially assumed to be an aesthetic feature when snow pack and household icing are considered, this feature may have functioned to promote ice melt on the structure. The crenellations provided an increased surface area relative to the mat's mass allowing for increased evaporation (Lyons, pers. comm.).

The most desired tules were ones with a long gradually diminishing taper, an acuminate shape that were best found with tules that grew in water that was intermittently shaded from the summer sun. Tules grew to a height of 2 to 3 m, but in partial shade they often reached 3 m or taller. Though cattails and tules were not always found together in the same body or course of water, they were harvested in the same manner. In spring, the long white fleshy rhizomes of both plants would be occasionally dug and roasted as food, being eaten raw, baked, or crushed and boiled to make sweet syrup. Cattail rhizomes were preferred for taste and quantity and were always eaten after ember or pit-cooking. In late spring the outer layers of young stalks were peeled, revealing a white inner stalk that was always eaten raw. In late summer the *small seeds (snλ'č'tesšn)* of tules—though difficult to harvest—were eaten raw or stone-ground and added to stews, both *meat* and *salmon stew (smłič snp'q'ʷetkʷ)*. The *duff (sq'ʷastqé)* of mature cattail spikes that survived were carried back to the village and saved, since the flowers were used as poultices on open wounds, or placed in cradleboards as *bunting (sq'q'tew't)* to absorb a baby's urine and feces. Every mother and grandmother carried a supply "of the cattail which [...] kept in a skin bag, and placed in her place on the pillow" (Ward and Maveety 1995:19).

There is only speculation as to whether people collecting cattail or tule shoots or *rhizomes (p'išłp sxʷéps* - "cattail roots") for food from still waters inhabited by beaver or muskrat, ever contracted giardiasis (*Giardia lamblia intestinalis*), often called beaver fever, from the beaver or muskrat feces in the water. The giardiasis protozoa, after collecting in the intestinal tract of the victim, causes diarrhea, cramps, dehydration, and sometimes vomiting (Blasser 2000:27).

The importance of tules and cattails to the Spokan was reflected in a ceremony that preceded the actual cutting and gathering of these hydrophytes. This ritual was led by an elderly woman who was recognized as being the most knowledgeable of such harvesting, and, prior to cutting and gathering, she would give an oration of gratitude for the resource as well as recognize the presence of all the women in attendance, knowing that some probably would not be there for the following year's harvest. Votive offerings were once given for each person's harvest, but prayers varied with each individual. While gathering tules, the women often sang songs, directed by the recognized elderly woman who was exempt from labor so she could instruct and help young girls with their first efforts. It was said that the songs told of the pleasures others would derive from their efforts when using the various finished tule and cattail products; old women would later be given the products of their labor in the form of finished mats.

Despite the high division of labor associated with women's work, it was not unusual for a male berdache (a man with woman's power) to conduct this ritual and physically assist the women in their labors. Certain berdaches possessed the skill to collect, process, and make sacred tule products sometimes used by other shamans. The last known living male berdache in the Spokan area, who was a healing shaman, possessed bear power, which included powers for locating and harvesting huckleberries and tules. One very elderly woman remembered a berdache with weasel power who assisted women when collecting tules and cattails. A male berdache—who had tule *suméš*—also had the power to locate water when occupying transitional camps in xerophytic areas. The person with such power would first sing his water power song, and then proceed to walk in a pattern of ever-decreasing circles until he would commence to shake as he increased the volume of his singing. Then, immediately adjacent to or between his feet there would be found a sagebrush, which he pulled from the ground to release the water. After fulfilling the needs of those in the group, the berdache would stop the flow of water by carefully replacing the bush, after which he would recite a brief prayer.

After cutting a tule from its base with a stone knife, it was laid flat on the dry ground or on a mat if stacking a harvest on damp ground. To make a bundle with each end of comparable circumference, the collected tules were positioned with each tule alternating, tip to base with the next. A bundle, when properly stacked, was as high as a *beaver dam* (*sqléw' cítxʷs or sqléw' st'qép*), and were tied—using *cattail leaves* (*písƚp*) or flattened tules—into tight bundles of approximately one to one-and-a-half m in circumference. Strips of rawhide could serve the same purpose. The individual collector determined the final weight and shape of her finished bundles. Each person carried, upon her head or across her back, the harvest to her respective winter village.

Before leaving a gathering area, the leader, in a *pro forma* manner, carefully instructed the cutters to burn over the unharvested tules to insure an abundant supply the following season. It was recalled how, before burning, a male berdache, one with water power, would direct a ceremony by first singing his power song, joined by all the women attending, and then loudly reciting a prayer of thanksgiving. Before burning the remaining tules, the women would gather the edible seeds from the *yellow pond lily* (*Nuphar polysepalum* Engelm. - *qʷúnmƚp*). The rhizomes were baked, then sliced and later applied to areas of rheumatism, or mashed as a poultice.

Several elderly women remember seeing their mothers, before leaving the tule bed, carefully detaching enough cattail leaves from the stalks to make several neat piles for the express purpose of offering them to squirrels for constructing nests in near-by fir trees. Every fall, it was observed how a squirrel would annually intertwine additional layers of cattail leaves, often increasing the outer diameter until the accumulated additional weight or a severe wind dislodged the nest. In one observed case, the near-spherical structure was approximately 40 to 50 to 60 cm in diameter, with an entrance on a southwest-facing side that gave access to a round chamber, approximately 15 to 20 cm in diameter. Of interest is the explanation given for this annual autumn practice, one that acknowledged the similarity of technologies between humans and certain humanoid-like mammals that included bears, beaver, muskrats, and of course squirrels for building winter 'homes'.

Because of the numerous uses of tules and cattails, these hydrophytes were referred to as the "bamboo of the Plateau" by outside observers. Unfortunately, many of the prime tule and cattail beds were destroyed with the introduction of *domesticated cattle* (*q'iʔq'y'elxʷ*) who were responsible for eating, trampling and destroying the rhizome beds. Major, even permanent, damage to tule and cattail beds was of course by the lowering of water tables and ground water for later irrigation. Gibbs was aware of the destruction to Indian land and plant foods created by introduced domesticated animals, "A drove of hogs belonging to one white man will consume the winter provisions of a tribe of Indians" (1855, 1:423). Unfortunately, Oliphant, when writing extensively of the Northwest cattle industry in the late 1800s and early 1900s, says little about the effects of cattle upon reservation land, but notes that such a study should be made (1948, 1:22). Historian John Fahey wrote how problems of non-Indian land use were leading to the destruction of many Indian resource areas, and "the 10th Census of the United States (1880) reported eastern Washington overstocked with cattle and sheep and homesteaders competing for better lands. Homesteaders filed on streams and waterholes, fencing them off so herders could not water their animals" (1995:176).

After gathering materials for the manufacture of the indispensable cattail and tule mats, it was necessary to spread and dry the raw material in the often late autumn shade. Later, some were made into mats straightaway while the rest were bundled and stored in the lofts of dwellings to be worked during the winter, when most mats were manufactured. Elderly women often said that more than half of all the mats produced were probably made by grandmothers when tending and entertaining their grandchildren during the winter months.

The process of making a *cattail mat* (*p'šłpáxn*) or a *tule mat* (*sy'áy'qs*) varied only slightly with the individual worker; the primary differences in manufacturing were in the dimensions of each mat. The more plentiful tule mats, and the less-used cattail mats, were actually quite different in weight, thickness, and their intended use. Tule mats were relatively lighter than a cattail mat for a given area, and invariably longer. Women made both types of mats while sitting on the ground, thereby maintaining greater control when plaiting or sewing the flexible stalks. *Sewing tules into mats* (*hesλ'áqi*) was always done by a solitary woman using a "[a] long wooden needle that had a hole in the center" (Elmendorf 1935-6, 1:28) to accommodate a sufficient length of Indian hemp that was then sewn through both ends of the tule. In fact, an arm's length of raw hemp, approximately 14 cm thick, was worth a horse (Spier 1938:77). Dwellings had no chairs or benches until they were introduced in the historic period, and even then some elders—until recently—continued this practice of ground-sitting despite having chairs and tables. It was common for several or more women to gather and socialize while making mats, particularly in the winter. Even when working with other women, a woman might *talk to the plant* (*č'i?tm'iłlt*) as she made a tule or cattail mat.

Cattail mats, when reinforced on one or more edges with sections of stout red osier dogwood, were used primarily as hanging doors to shelters, floor coverings in spring and summer dwellings, roof covers for storage sheds, and, occasionally as large flat food storage baskets. Floor mats were seldom used in summer. Unworked tules or finished products could be given later as gifts or for *bartering* (*n?ey'xʷéw'sm*). Prior to the construction of mats, the tules or cattails were laid out on the ground and sorted by length, with some attention to selecting similar base diameter of the tule or cattail stalks. Broken or loose stalks were put aside and not used. The cattail was usually first flattened by pulling it over a smooth rounded surface, or by rolling an elliptical pestle over one or more stalks. When discussing the Northwest Coast and its impact upon Flathead material culture, Turney-High provided explanation description of making cattail mats, which was done by the Spokan:

> The cattails were laid in parallel bunches on the ground. Care was used in sizing them so that the lower ends of the stalk were laid next to the smaller upper end of it neighbor. The twining was then begun by weaving and tying through the bunches with cords of twisted silverberry, beginning at the proposed top of the mat and working from right to left. When this top binder row had been completed, others were made just a few inches apart until the bottom of the mat had been bound. A wide selvage was produced by allowing some of the thinner ends of the cattail to protrude above and below the border. These were then bent back upon the mat and twined into it. The grass mats were made in a similar manner. Mats were made by the woman (1937:102).

A tule or cattail mat was threaded preferably with hemp, though sometimes either slough grass (*Beckmannia eruaeformis* L.) or *stringing needle* (*Urtica dioca* - *c'c'áxi?łp* or *c'cxiłp*) was used. A long sliver-bone or slender piece of hard *whittled* (*xʷeλ'im'*) deciduous wood with a hole served as a *weaving needle* (*čłłxʷépl'e?* - "hole in the handle"). Sometimes a woman preferred using a needle with a hole at the mid-point. A needle was usually 15 to 20 cm in length, and was threaded with two or three lengths of rolled, intertwined hemp. To prevent the hemp line from twisting or knotting, the woman would draw it through a large ball of pine pitch that had been carefully heated and mixed with black bear grease. The threaded needle was passed through the broad end of the *leaf* (*picčł*) and looped twice over the stalk. This was repeated successively with each adjoining leaf (stalk) until the desired width was achieved. Some women would dampen the ends of the tules so that they would not be brittle, which, otherwise, could misshapen or split the feeble end of the material if using a needle.

When stitching tule or cattail stalks, they were laid side by side with the smaller top (feeble end) of each stalk next to the larger bottom end of the next, and upon completion, both ends of the mat were equal in width and length. A series of successive parallel seams were made approximately every 15 to 20 cm. In addition, each short end of the mat was reinforced with one or two long pieces of red osier dogwood withes, which were used at each end of the mat as a stiffener. The so-called *end stick of a tule mat* (*táɫxn*) was always made from a stout section of red osier dogwood. Depending upon its intended use, a mat could measure from one meter to 7 m long, and could be 100 to 110 cm wide. When required, finished individual mats made specifically to cover slanting tipi-like pole structures were shaped roughly in a long relatively triangle shape; this required all of the broad tule base ends be stitched serially together, a process that was repeated when sewing together the smaller ends of the *tule* (*Schoenoplectus acutus.* syn., *Scirpus acutus* Muhl. ex Bigel. - *t'k'ʷtin*).

Tules, being pithy and light in weight, afforded good insulation. A tule mat, if not bent or permitted to get wet or weathered, could last for several years. Families would take twelve or more bundles to a summer camp, leaving the remaining mats carefully rolled and stored in their winter dwelling's loft or standing each rolled mat on end within the dwelling. The age and use of a mat determined its serviceability; older mats were used for lining food storage pits, drying foods, covering earth ovens, making bundle boats, or, as mentioned earlier, for wrapping a corpse.

Grasses and Cornhusks

Grasses, mainly the aforementioned sedges, were used to make hats, cordage, thread, fishing weirs, bags, storage containers, and dwelling partitions. *Barleygrass* (*Hordeum vulgare* L. - *nwawaqín* or *ʔopopqin*), sweet grass and bromegrass were used in a variety of ways: making thread, cordage, imbrication, trimming basket rims, making smudge fires for insects, lining earth ovens and food storage caches, as bedding, stuffing winter moccasins, and making boys' arrows. Dry, crushed sweet grass gave off a pleasant scent, and, in addition to feathers, was used to stuff pillows (STHC). Sweet grass is aptly known for, "The sweet, lingering fragrance [...] due to the presence of coumarin, a lactose glycoside" (Turner 1979:142). The long, dry leaves were used to make three-strand plaited bundles of varying length, which, when lit, gave off a pleasant scent when burned slowly, producing a smoke that was believed to purify by fumigating a person or dwelling. An unconscious person or one possessed by his *suméš* could be revived, if necessary, when inhaling the *fumes* (*k'ʷiʔ*). Some remember how this grass could be used as a substitute for tobacco.

Ryegrass was another important utilitarian plant, having long, dry, hollow stalks, and when carefully held upon a low rack over a hot ember fire, it assumes a light sand color, and after soaking made pliable, and was used to imbricate berry-gathering baskets. It is not known if the Spokan used these long hollow grasses as did the Thompson (Turner 1979:141), to ventilate food storage pits to prevent mildew and rotting. Pliable grass gathering sacks were often first soaked before gathering roots or berries to make the material more pliable, and less likely to break while filling with storage items. Ryegrass served as an effective *layer* (*t'qasq'l'*) to hold heat when spread directly upon both the lowest and upper layer of heated rocks when pit-baking.

Cut and washed *timbergrass* or *pinegrass* (*t'áqʷnɫp*) stalks were tied to make bundles for whipping crushed foamberries to make Indian ice cream. In the winter, damp pinegrass was stuffed in moccasins and shaped as an insole or additional matting for warmth. Pine grass was also used to line and even cover food containers being steamed in cooking pits.

Bear-grass was widely used for camp bedding, basket imbrication, and for making flexible grass bags for winter storage of roots and dried berries. After collecting various roots in different types of rigid baskets, particularly camas, the roots were placed in woven bear-grass bags for stream-washing. When available, *foul meadow grass* (*Poa nervosa* [Hook] Vasey - *suʔpúleʔxʷ*) was gathered by women and used for ground cover under bedding when camping. Later, with agriculture, the introduced mid-summer *alfalfa* (*Medicago sativa* - *ʔeslxʷicleʔxʷtn*) was occasionally used as bedding.

Prior to Euro-American contact, the Spokan received cornhusk bags from both the Flathead and Nez Perce who were also responsible for the introduction of numerous Plains culture traits, and even certain rituals into the eastern Plateau. Cornhusk bags, being relatively lighter, stronger, and more flexible than other types of indigenous baskets, replaced some heavier types of traditional bags and containers used for gathering and storing plant foods. Women mainly made flat *cornhusk bags* (*qqépeʔ*), and by the mid and late1800s, one of the first sources of monetary income for Spokan women was realized by selling cornhusk bags to non-Indians in Spokane, usually at fairs.

Cornhusk readily absorbs natural plant dyes, and served as a foundation for *beautiful* (*xssʕac'x*) and colorful *imbrication* (*q'q'ey'íl'xʷ*) of geometric designs of parallelograms, diamonds, stars, triangles, and horizontal bands. Some bags had realistic and slightly curvilinear patterns of nondescript plants. The colors black, blue, gray, and yellow were provided by local plants—save for certain hues of blue obtained from diluted *duck* (*sesƛ'xʷm*) excrement (Anon. 1974:5). The completed cornhusk bag had "the warp strands [...] turned in at the top and bound down by weaving with the weft. Often buckskin or cloth is bound onto the rim of the bag and sometimes a drawstring of rope or thong is run through this buckskin or cloth edge" (Anon. 1974:7).

A non-Indian and anonymous author, working with several collections of Nez Perce, Spokan, and Palouse cornhusk bags collected before the early 1950s, gave this description:

> Originally the flexibility of the bags made them extremely useful in harvesting and storing of roots, berries and such materials as hemp and grasses which were used for making new bags. The bags were also used to store household items. The Indians made an annual round within their tribal territories and used large bags to carry their household items and to store and bury part of their seasonal harvests in caches to which they could return later in the year. The small bags were used for carrying personal items (Anon. 1974:5).

Some elderly Spokan women stated cornhusk bags were not used for burying food, because ground-dwelling animals were certain to easily locate such a food cache and destroy the bag and its contents. Yet there are accounts of a woman being sent out of a ceremony because a shaman's *suméš* permitted him to "see" that her cornhusk bag contained dried camas.

The Nez Perce are reputed to have made cornhusk bags of the highest quantity and quality, and initially being relatively lighter than other types of basketry, as well as stronger and more flexible. Cornhusk bags became popular for collecting different non-staining plant foods. Some elderly women said how the cornhusk bag never replaced the more rigid and heavier traditional utilitarian and storage bag. Cornhusk bags eventually became associated more with ceremonial dress, sometimes replacing bags of traditional materials:

> Twining was the preferred method of construction when working with cornhusk, a plant fiber that readily absorbs natural plant dyes, as well as the later aniline dyes. In the hands of a skilled woman, beautiful and colorful *imbricated* [*q'q'ey'íl'xʷ*] geometric and curvilinear designs were added, which reflected personal skills and motifs. Porcupine quills were given a deep yellow color by soaking them overnight in a solution of mashed yellow moss. Both the cherry's fruit and bark were boiled, then steeped to produce a dye of distinct cherry-red color for staining plant fibers that served as *imbrication* [*skʷlíss*] for baskets (Anon. 1974:6).

An unknown author who had worked with several large eastern Plateau cornhusk bag collections, including the Dunning collection of 269 cornhusk bags, now at Eastern Washington Historical Society, described how "Originally the flexibility of the bags made them extremely useful in harvesting and storing of roots, berries and such materials as hemp and grasses which were used for making new bags. The bags were used to store household items" (Anon. 1974:3).

Hemp

The three most widely used plants for making cordage of different dimensions were smooth *Indian hemp* (*Apocynum cannabinum* L., var, *glabellum* A.D.C. - *sp'éc'n*), the spreading dogbane or false hemp (Spier 1938; Lerman 1952-54), and the introduced flax (*Linim usitatissimum*) (Barry 1929:45). The latter is similar to Indian hemp, and all three plants were gathered by women in the fall after the leaves had fallen or commenced to turn yellow. The collected stems were prepared by flattening them and drawing the stem back and forth over a horizontal smooth pole, after which the stems were split length-wise with a sharp stick or piece of obsidian. The outer husk was removed by hand and then bundled together to hang dry within the dwelling. When women collectively gathered this plant, they often made an *overnight camp* (*ccil'š*), and while exchanging stories, they would *peel* (*člq'ʷusm* or *člq'ésšn*) the bark, which later might be woven into a *closed peeled cedar-root berry basket* (*yamx̌ʷeʔ*). A second method of preparing hemp, after gathering, was to hang the material "upside down to dry. It was then placed on a piece of soft wood and pounded with a heavy stick to remove the 'outer bark'. After beating, the stems were rubbed together to remove the already-softened outer covering" (Bouchard and Kennedy 1975:14). The stems were then hung outside and dried for three weeks before storage.

Indian hemp, however, was the principal plant used, being central to Spokan technology for making thread, twine, and *rope* (*acmíntin*). Indian hemp was used extensively when mending or binding a wide variety of tools, and certainly those subject to moisture or being repeatedly submerged underwater, particularly when building or repairing fishing weirs, corrals, or fish traps. Hemp was first uncoiled and then thoroughly soaked often overnight and stretched taut and permitted to dry. To make the cordage more pliable and easier to manipulate, the material was again soaked for an hour or so before use. For the material to be effective and pliable, it must be able to stretch. A material comparable to hemp was the inner bark of dogbane, sometimes called red willow, which is durable and pliable. It was plaited into long sections for measuring distances for fastening weir pylon poles and for the placement of longhouse lodge poles for roofing.

Women carefully collected and stored adequate quantities of the inner fibrous layers of Indian hemp for winter production of various items. The extensive fieldwork of Turner provides an excellent description of where this plant was collected and later processed:

> Damp areas were said to produce the tallest, thickest plants. The branches and leaves were removed and the stems were then flattened by pulling them over a pole tied to a tree. They were then split open from bottom to top with a knife or sharp stick. The outer skin or "bark" was peeled off by hand and the inner fibrous parts were bundled together by the tops to dry in the wind. When dry, the stems became brittle and the pithy middle tissue was separated from the fibre by pounding the flattened pieces with a stick or twisting them with the hands. The fibres were then formed into twine by rolling them with dampened hands on the bare thigh or on a piece of buckskin draped over the leg, with one end of the fibre being held to maintain tension [...] To join the fibre segments together into a continuous length of twine, the thick end of one piece and the thin end of another were each split about one length of the stem and these were spliced together as an interlocking "V," then rolled together until they were intertwined [...] Even the thinnest of threads is difficult to break with the hands. When stored properly, Indian hemp fibre will keep for many years without deteriorating (1979:169-70).

The method of rope-making, by both men and women, as described by Turney-High (1937:110), was the same as that of the Spokan, and accomplished by using either hemp or horse hair hogged from the mane rather than the heavier and coarser tail. Horse hair was naturally stiffer than hemp. Turney-High further noted how "The simplest method of twining cords into rope is to *braid* (*q'ic''m*) three or more together as one would his own hair. Rope of two piles, or more than three, was ordinarily twined upon the thigh" (1937:11).

Indian hemp was the most satisfactory and the most extensively used of these materials. The plant was found in profusion in damp ground, where it grew to a height of about five feet. It was cut in the fall, cured in the sun for about two weeks, then tied into large bundles and stored for future use. The exact time that it was gathered depended upon the color desired. The fiber was light in color before the leaves fell, a dark-brown afterwards. In preparing the hemp for use it was split down the hollow center with the thumb nail and the flattened piece bent double. The fiber was then easily removed by peeling from the middle toward each end. The rough fibers were dressed by scraping with a sharp piece of flint and rubbing between the palms. When all coarseness had been overcome the fine strands were rolled and twisted between the palm and the bare thigh in to cord of the weight desired (Ray 1933:36).

The process of making fishing line by braiding, or rolling strands of hemp, with dampened palms, or on one's thigh was called *t'úpm*. These long sections of hemp varied in diameter according to task and were used for hafting fishing spears or leisters, securing fish corrals, fish traps, and weirs, and later in making lariats, bridles, and martingales. Hemp was indispensable to Spokan technology, and, as recollected by an elderly woman, "was collected in the fall by women. My mother had a special patch she always prayed over while attending it." Of interest is McWhorter's questionable suggestion that there were elderly women who could still "describe the spindle and the method of weaving" [blankets?] (1910-14:2, File 1-H). Franchère recorded, "The women at this camp [Kettle Falls] were busy spinning the coarse wool of the mountain sheep; they had blankets or mantles, woven or platted of the same material" 1854:349). Teit's description of the Sinkaietk method for collecting and making Indian hemp for stitching, which he observed, was the same process used by the Spokan:

> Whole families would move to the hemp fields to camp while the women gathered it. The harvest lasted about two weeks. During this period, women would gather enough for five bundles at a time (each bundle five inches thick, three four feet long) which took two or three days. After preparing fibers from this, they went to gather it again. Some of the hemp was reserved for their own use [...] The plants were soaked in water and the bark stripped away. The decorticated part was then separated into fibers by rubbing between the fists. The fibers were made into two long bundles, each half the thickness of the cord desired. These were rolled with the palm on the right thigh: the two bundles, separated by about an inch, were rolled toward the body; then by a sharp reverse movement without lifting the palm, they were made to twist about each other rolled with the right hand fed in new bundles of fiber. Various sizes of cords and rope were made for different uses. For most purposes, two strand cords were used (1930:68).

When properly stored in a dry area of the dwelling, the light tan color material will not deteriorate for many years. A few elderly women stored small quantities of dried, coiled, or round balls of Indian hemp—mostly in the hope of showing a young granddaughter how to make hemp articles.

Other plant fibers used were showy *milkweed* (*Asclepias speciosa* - *nt'i̓ʔxʷéyeʔ*), sometimes called *Coyote's Indian hemp* (*spilyeʔ* or *sp'éc'is*), which was, when necessary, a substitute for other types of hemp. The leaves and stalks of showy milkweed were boiled as food, and the dried latex was used as gum. Other fibrous plants, such as *Humulus lupulus*, *Cannabis sativa* L., and *A. androsaemifolium* L. were gathered and processed to produce a type of hemp. When available, the *vines* (*nt'št'šel'č'*) of white clematis were intertwined with hemp for weaving storage and picking baskets. Willow sage and even deer hair and both horsetail and mane were used to make continuous twine. "A good, several-ply Indian hemp rope is said to have the equivalent strength of a modern rope of several hundred pounds test weight. Even the thinnest of threads is difficult to break" (Turner 1979:170).

The most definitive explanation of Interior Salish rope-making is by Schaeffer (1934-37, I-187:11-15), who describes braided three, four, six, and eight stranded buffalo hair and horse mane hair to achieve—depending upon use—flat, square, and round short bridle length or full length of 10 m. Rope was made by twisting with a spindle or braiding strands of hair. Bison hair rope was soft, whereas "horse tail (hair) rope was too rough and bristly and when a rope made of this hair got wet, it became stiff and hard" (Schaeffer 1934-37, I-188:12).

The Spokan used hemp for more applications than any other plant, and its importance was reflected in the practice of never over-harvesting any stand of this valuable plant. The Spokan were quite cognizant that a clear harvest of plants in an area would bring about the demise of this valuable resource until it could be reestablished—but only through time. In this sense, many of their time-proven conservation practices were more advanced for maintaining a sustained yield than the policies of some contemporary forestry personnel and agencies.

Fungi

Both mushrooms and tree fungi were used in a variety of ways by the Spokan. The major forms of edible mushrooms, most notably *Morchella esculenta* and *Boletus edulu*, were assiduously gathered by women in known areas and were eaten *raw* (*xiw'*) by both men and women after removing the plant's hood or cap; they were never roasted (Smith 1936-8:195), and usually prepared for eating by women. When found by a man, *mushrooms* (*p'aλ'qén'e?* or *p'aλ'qin* or *λ'eqán* - "always bare-headed") were often presented as a favor for one's wife, or, if single, for his mother as a gift. An expression of an enduring friendship was, "We always knew each other's mushroom patch."

Yet as a food, mushrooms were not considered as being an important ingredient, contributing no discernable caloric intake to the Spokan diet though a wide variety were used as medicines, and gathered for their known medicinal effects. Important to the Spokan pharmacopoeia was the so-called puff-ball, used when treating certain types of extreme anxiety or for inducing sleep for a person experiencing a non-descriptive spirit illness. For example, a pregnant woman diagnosed with an intrusive spirit, or object-intruded illness, was treated by a shaman who would first manipulate the suspected area of entry to confine the malevolent force or intruding object body. He would next apply a warmed mushroom to the site, and after the malevolent force or object was extracted and absorbed by the mushroom, the shaman then displayed the object to the patient as proof of ordeal.

Certain mushrooms were administered either internally or externally, depending upon the curing shaman's diagnosis. An unidentified mushroom—no longer used—was claimed to have been used as an emetic when eaten by a man in the sweathouse, causing the person to later vomit ingested food or a *blood clot* (*ncxwúm*) suspected of being poisonous or any malevolent force, thought to be harmful or causing the illness. Another emetic for removing bile in the sweathouse, used sometimes in poison illnesses, required swallowing the black powder of the *mushroom Bovista nigrescens* (probably *p'áλ'qín* - "from above"), which, upon taking even small amounts, caused severe abdominal retching.

Both *Bovis pita* and *B. plumbea* were important medicinal mushrooms, and used primarily for infant care. Given the age of the puff-ball, which produces an olive-brown powder (spores) when released after breaking open the puff-ball, it was applied as a powder to a newborn baby's navel in order to expedite the healing process of the umbilicus. A related practice, usually done by the grandmother, was to rub the spores from either of these plants on the released umbilical cord as the mother prayed that her child would not later become *restless* (*hecme?m'í*) or become a wanderer. These spores were rubbed on the temples of a distraught child to induce sleep, and the spores were said to have been effective for preventing and treating diaper rash.

Unfortunately, little was remembered about the types and uses of fungi, partly because they are no longer gathered. Yet in the past, children collected bracket fungus expressly to etch various designs or animal figures upon the smooth cap with a sharp stone or stick. And yet women once collected numerous types of tree, rock, and ground fungi that were considered important in Spokan technology—mainly as pigments and medicines. For example, the fungus now known as *Echinodontium tinctorium* Ell. & Everh. (*yóq'ʷi?*), used with hematite and certain berries, was a source of red pigment for aesthetic and religious decoration. This fungus also "contains various alkaloids and tannin and may have been used as a medicine" (Pacioni 1999:311).

Ferns

Many species of *fern* (*čxtxitłp*) were remembered as once having multiple uses. For example, Wallace's fern was gathered for making bedding and as a general medicinal tea. The unfurled fronds of the *bracken fern* (*xʷey?tw'íl'š*) were eaten either raw or cooked by women as a pot green after placing the fronds in an earthen depression, encased with hot embers. The rhizomes of bracken fern were once used in winter as a means to transport fire (slow match), and presumably the rhizome produced a rather distinct greenish-yellow dye. In addition, bracken leaves, when available, often served as the final lining for pit-cooking. Classified as ferns, *Equisetum sylvaticum L.*, giant horsetail (*E. laevigatum*), and common horsetail (*E. arvense L.*) were used primarily as abrasives for smoothing slate, diorite, bone, and certain wood implements to produce a fine finish. Though wood horsetail (*Equisetum telmateia* Ehrh.) is unrelated to *Mare's Tail* (*snkʷeʔr'etkʷ*), both were used as abrasives., and *P. hesperium* Maxon for treating sores.

Swordfern (*Polypodium munitum* [Kaulf.] Presl.) was once a principal general purpose fern for camp bedding or as mats when laying out butchered game or when distributing fish. Licorice-flavored rhizomes of *Polypodium vulgare L.*, *P. munitum* [Kaulf.], and *P. hesperium* Maxon were occasionally used for treating sore throats. Fresh and dried rhizomes of the licorice fern (*P. glycyrrhiza* D. C. Eaton), called 'wild licorice' by some Spokan, were effective for treating sore throats and colds. Some elderly women recall collecting and eating the fresh but immature fiddleheads of bracken fern (*Pteridiumm aquilinum* [L.] Kuhn. [*Polypodiaceae*]), the small Rocky Mountain woodsia (*Woodsia scopuline* D. C. Eaton), and the *fiddleneck or maidenhair fern* (*Amesinckia intgermedia* Fisch. & Mey. - *sxʷixʷiyt*), an introduced plant, while the fragile fern (*Cystopteris fragalis* [L.] Bernh.) served medicinal purposes.

Hide, Horn, and Bone Technology

The various multipurpose uses of hide, horn, and bone were invaluable in nearly all technological aspects of Spokan adaptation such as clothing, shelter, predation and utilitarian tools as well as musical instruments, and for many recreational devices. With some noted exceptions, most of these materials were by-products acquired by men from deer, and most often processed and finished to final tools and products by women, who were quite capable of processing and finishing necessary hide, horn, and bone products. There was one account of two older blind women who were able to make tule and cattail mats in addition to tanning hides, and were noted for their skills.

Butchering

After killing a deer, the hunter exercised considerable care in *butchering* (*xʷcéłc'ʔem*) and *skinning the deer* (*čłckʷélxʷm* - "pulling hide off"), for fear that an act of disrespect would impair his future hunting success, or worse, keep the offended species away from the hunting range of his group. When in a group, the man who killed a deer would, out of respect, never skin it, but appointed a fellow hunter to *skin the animal* (*čłckʷelxʷ* or *nʕawep* - "pulling skin off smaller game"). Different types of hide scrapers often facilitated the removal of fat and meat. After skinning numerous small animals, a process called *nʕew'épmw*, a major acquisition of status occurred when either a boy or girl was given the opportunity by a parent to *skin a large animal* (*čckʷelxʷm*).

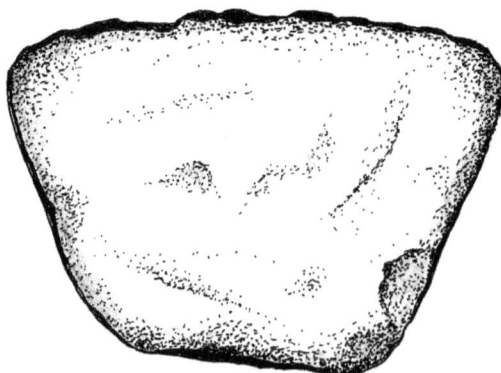

Figure 20. Hide scraper

One who butchers an animal (sxʷcim) was involved in a process termed *plsqaxeʔ*. A successful hunter would always retain the deer's back bone; the rest was *distributed (spxʷmsʔiłn - "distributed food")* equally among the other hunters (STHC). The consequences of disrespectful behavior, such as breaking a taboo or violating custom or protocol, were sufficient to cause the meat to spoil or 'go bad' (*č'stw''il'š*) prematurely, or for the hunter to temporarily lose his hunting abilities. A major concern of all hunters, particularly in warm weather, was to prevent the spoilage of meat or contamination by other mammals and birds if it were not properly and quickly dressed and dried.

Deculturation brought unfortunate changes into many attitudes and protocol regarding traditional rituals and approaches about what now are viewed as secular activities, such as the butchering and distribution of meat. Former universal beliefs and associated practices are believed to have changed due to missionary influence (Miller 1990:117). Regarding butchering, a Lakes woman, Christine Quintasket (Morning Dove), gave this report:

> Colville hunters always *strung up* [*ʕʷóxʷ*] deer heads on high limbs [*ponderosa limb - sččelšemečst*], with the nose pointing up so the deer could not smell the camp [and warn other deer]. They were never cooked or eaten until the hunt was finished. Only men and maybe a very old woman could do this. The same was true for the kidneys. Only adults, never children, could eat bone marrow. Were a child to eat marrow or fat, s/he would have weak legs and lungs. Only old people could eat unborn fawns, and they relished their tenderness. Children would be paralyzed (have dead bodies) in later life if they did so (Miller 1990:117).

Nancy Wynecoop provides a rare observation—recorded in the 1880s, and published in 1985—concerning the preparation of intestines for storage. In this instance, the group had killed a bear. She explained how a family worked all night to save the grease, meat, and casings:

> The skin was torn off and internal organs emptied. The carcass was slung across a pole and hung over a fire where the heat loosened the tendons so that they might be stripped off and beat flat on a stone. They were spread on slats and smoked dry. The pieces of grease were trussed on stakes driven into the ground at an angle so the drip would fall on a hollowed stone to be dipped up with a horn spoon and put into dry containers [...] Her mother sent her to look in a woven grass bag that was slung to the teepee pole over their pillows, and here she found the smooth stick that turned the intestines. It was a pipe made of a section from an elderberry stick with the pith pushed out and a bunch of sinew strings included. From the corner of the door she secured a course [sic] grass sack and went to the river where the empty skins were piled. It took time and patience to turn, wash and tie them. The tying was done by doubling and folding them at one end and then inserting the elderberry tube and blowing them to full size before making the final closing. She placed them in a sack, a rolling slimy mass that soon dried sufficiently that the one end could be untied, the air released and they were folded and stored for future use. She placed the finished work beside her mother and was rewarded with a doll made from the shoulder blade of the bear. The bone had been scraped, shaped and dressed for her because she had been first to discover the animal (1985:33).

If possible, larger animals, including black-tailed, white-tailed, mule deer, elk, pronghorn antelope, moose, black bear, grizzly bear, and bighorn sheep, were hung from a tree or from specially erected poles at the kill site, and skinned immediately. Even after a collective hunt or *animal drive (slláqm)*, the fallen prey was always skinned and the hide cleaned and fleshed as soon as possible. The logistics of distance, or an absence of women in a hunting camp, often prevented a hide from being tanned in the area of the kill. In such a situation, it was folded or rolled, if possible, with wet ferns or moist clay in preparation for later tanning upon return to the camp or village.

After a large game animal had been dispatched and hung up, the animal's *throat was slit (č'łnič'cntxʷ - "you slit its throat")* to permit bleeding, and, in the past, to demonstrate respect to the large animal by facilitating the release of its so-called life force. Before butchering, a long abdominal slit was made and the liver of the elk or deer was removed and eaten raw by the hunters—a ritual in which the men shared immediate sustenance by sharing the first part of their labor. Fresh warm liver was considered a delicacy, yet several elders said the liver was first roasted. The kidneys and heart were removed, sectioned, and eaten after being roasted. The stomach was cleaned after making an incision large enough to permit it being inverted to release any contents, and then it was scrubbed and boiled before cutting it into sections, which were eaten immediately or kept whole and sun-dried for later consumption. *Animal blood (snxʷul)* or fresh marrow, or both, could be added to the animal's stomach which often served as a cooking container. This was often done by stone-boiling and adding strips of venison. After removal, the intestines were cleaned by first pulling the entire length through one's thumb and forefinger, before washing the inside and outside of the intestines prior to boiling them. Women were more adept at skinning than most men.

Once all of the abdominal organs were carefully removed, the animal was butchered by first cutting the *meat into thin strips (sčłcqqmnéwl)*, which were either *pounded* as *air-dried meat (sp'q'ʷepltn)* until they became whitish in color, or *smoke dried (scqy'éłc'eʔ)* over low fires using hardwood. Both methods of drying reduced the weight of the butchered animal, facilitating travel to a base camp or home site. A procedure for transporting a deer—killed close to a camp or village—was to *quarter the deer (xʷcéłc'ʔem)* after being dressed out. An entire deer or elk was seldom carried to camp before being quartered, and rarely by a single hunter.

The universal method for skinning a large animal involved removing the animal's hooves and making cuts down the inside of the forelegs, after which a deep subcutaneous cut was made from the neck, ventrally down to the peritoneum. A separate incision was made down the inside of the hind quarters. A final cut was made from the middle of the neck upward and around the mouth to the forehead. Organs and intestines were removed and usually placed on a tule mat or on a bed of leaves or ferns, including the *testicles (mč'méč'p)* of larger animals, which were eaten after being removed, and have a sweet taste when eaten raw. Beaver testicles were eaten uncooked or dried and used later as a medicine. Roasted *beaver tail (sql'ew' sups)* was considered a delicacy once the tough skin was scraped or seared off.

As cited, during the butchering, a common practice was to save an animal's blood by draining it into the animal's stomach for later use as food. Some hunters would remove a hide by *closing their fist and forcibly separating (čłswálxʷis* - "s/he skinned it") the skin from the animal's body. Smaller mammals were skinned by making initial cuts, and then *pulling the hide off (čckʷélxʷis)* in one quick movement. *Skinned deer head (čckʷáyaʔqntm)*, when *cooked and edible (słoxʷqín)*, was once considered a delicacy. If a slain deer's legs were not ritually placed in the fork of a tree, the hunter would break the animal's legs lengthwise with a stone to extract the *deer's marrow (čʔulixʷ st'úsc)* as a food. After a deer's legs were removed, the forelegs were called *sc'ʔéčst*, and the rear legs *sc'uʔuín*. The tendons of the deer or elk's legs were always saved for making bowstrings. Yet some elders maintained that the tendons from an elk's back legs were preferred. With larger deer, the final major operation was severing the neck head from the body, after which the head was called *čspín*.

Ray explained the common method for transporting and dressing deer, in cases where the kill site was far from the camp:

> A deer was skinned and butchered immediately upon making the kill, or after returning to the hunting camp. A strong man was able to carry a full-grown deer for a considerable distance. (Young deer were seldom killed unless famine threatened.) The legs of the animal were tied together with the pack strap and burden carried by passing the wide band of the strap around the chest. When the snow was covered with a hard crust it was possible to drag the animal to camp. If the distance to camp were very great it was customary to skin and butcher the deer before transporting it. The pieces of flesh were placed inside the skin, the legs tied together, and the whole carried with the aid of a pack strap. The blood was usually caught in the paunch and carried along with the meat (1933:91).

Smith presented a rather detailed account of how the Kalispel would dress out a bear, and certain uses and restrictions associated with the process:

They roast the head and eat the meat and the brain. When the meat is off they gather the ribs and tie them in [a] bundle and they take the skull and hang them up from a limb so that no dogs would get them; they were not put in a crotch of a tree. The leg bones, &c. were simply thrown away. If they boil the head after roasting it, they take the eyes out. They never eat the eyes. If they just throw the ribs out and the dogs get them, the bear [?] would get them or the dog. If they fell from the tree and the dogs got them it was all right. The bones were not painted (1936-8:441).

Animals provided not only sustenance to the Spokan diet, but were important as a source of valuable by-products in the form of hide, hair, antler, bone, tallow, and certain organs that were critical for the successful survival of peoples dependent upon a foraging strategy. Years ago, some older women claimed that the most valuable part of the deer was the hide because, "The meat is eaten only once, but the hide provides many things which last longer in many ways."

Hide Preparation

The processing of hides demanded considerable effort and time, and was done entirely by women. Because of their efforts, women retained a sense of ownership over the finished rawhide or tanned product. A man's wife was responsible for processing the hides of the animals he had trapped or killed in a hunt, and by custom, the older sisters or his mother performed this task for the hunter. Older unmarried men and widowers relied upon the generosity of their female kinfolk for processing hide into clothing, moccasins, and other needed products. The value of deer hide, according to one elder, could be summed up like this: "deer hide is more lasting than the meat, like with the deer, the deer's hide now holds us together."

Both men and women would usually skin the animal by *pulling the entire hide off* (*nʔawepsc*). Prior to tanning, there were basically two methods to *clean* (*xʷkʼʷicʼeʔ*) and *scrape a hide* (*čʔáx̌ʷcʼʔis* or *sx̌ʷiwčʷywe* or *ʔáqʼi* - "to scrape a hide"). It was first hand-stretched and then pegged-out on the ground, or it was stretched and laced upon a near-vertical wooden frame. Only a few elders could recall accounts of stretching a hide on the ground with pegs, and they remarked that this method was difficult, particularly when scraping more than one large hide. However, scraping ground-pegged hides was done more frequently when processing small hides; and women always had a favorite place for *scraping hides* (*snʔaqʼmn*), usually close to where their beamers, scrapers, and other hide-tools were kept (Ross 1995f, 3:323).

After an animal was butchered, the women commenced the important and often lengthy task of removing as much fat and meat as possible with a *flat, dull edged scraper* (*sx̌ʷix̌ʷeyʼéɬcʼeʔtn*), or one that was *blunt edged* (*yʼlʼyʼílʼt*), or *blunt pointed* (*nyalqs*), or a piece of worked *shale* (*nscosleʔ*). In the ground and frame method, the hide was stretched after it was first meticulously fleshed of all fat or meat by using, as has been stated, a variety of rough quartzite bifacial lithic hand scrapers. A woman then "broke-down" the grain of the hide in a laborious process by rubbing or beaming the hide with an animal's rib while it was draped over a log. A deer rib was used for processing a deer hide, and an elk rib in working on an elk hide; to do otherwise was considered disrespectful to the animal.

The size and construction of each hide-processing frame varied with its user and the type and size of hide to be stretched. This is seen in old photographs that document hides being processed on standing *wooden frames* (*ʕax̌icʼeʔtn* - "hide stretcher"). It is reflected in the methods currently used by those few Spokan people who continue to tan hides. Most frames were near-horizontal rectangles of lashed wood, approximately 2.5 m lengthwise and nearly 2 m high. The wood typically chosen for a frame was *lodgepole pine* (*Pinus contorta* Dougl. var. *latolia* Engelm - *kʷkʷlʼíyʼt*). After the edges of the hide were pierced every 10 to 12 cm by an awl, the hide was affixed to the frame by stringing a continuous length of damp rawhide line through each hole, and looping each turn of the line over the frame until all the holes were strung. The line was then drawn tight.

Upon drying, the hide was quite taut and ready to be scraped. The fleshing or final removal of meat and fat was done with a small hand-held bifacial flat stone or with task-dulled lenticular fish knives. Beaver and

259

muskrat hides were stretched upon circular frames before being scraped and tanned. The skin of a *beaver kitten* (*scnpús*) would not be used but the skins of adult beavers and a *beaver as young as two years of age* (*scqʷič̓n'*) might be processed and tanned.

A skin could be tanned on both sides after the hair was removed, or just on the inside saving the hair or fur. If the tanner wished to remove the hair after fleshing, the hide was either anchored by stones in a stream for several days, or rubbed with a solution of ashes, sometimes mixed with crushed lime. The hide was then balled with the smashed animal's brains, or else the hide was pegged to the ground, or stretched in a four-sided frame which facilitated rubbing the mashed brain material into the hide.

If a hide had commenced to rot or was mildewed, the woman submerged the *rawhide* (*q'étt* or *q'ént*) in a solution of crushed yarrow flowers or the leaves of wormwood and simmered it in warm water for twelve to eighteen hours to restore the hide's flexibility and condition. After removing the hide from the decoction, it was carefully wrung out by first wrapping the hide lengthwise in the mid-width around a stationary vertical post, and the two so-called head and tail ends were tied together, after which a stout, rounded hardwood staff was placed inside the tied ends and twisted, much like a Spanish windlass, to extract the excess liquid.

After these procedures were completed, the hide was removed from the stretching frame or pegs, *draped over a log* (*člqʷéw's* or *č'áq'ac'ʔtn* - "scraping pole" - "a smooth debarked tree"), and beamed to break or grain the hide, rendering the rawhide more pliable. Beamers were concave tools made from elk or deer rib, grasped at both ends, and drawn back and forth for *graining the fibers of untanned hide* (*saʔáq'e*). The most common tool for beaming was a *deer rib knife* (*áq'mn*), but after the introduction of European technology, the rib was replaced by a dulled *drawknife* (*áq'mn*). As mentioned above, when beaming a deer or elk, a woman used only the rib of the same species of the animal she was processing: to do otherwise would be regarded as an affront to the animal.

Depending upon the thickness of the hide, and the duration between scraping and tanning, different methods were used sometimes to further soften the hide before tanning. One procedure was to first thoroughly dampen the hide, spread it upon the ground, and sprinkle dried, broken leaves of sticky geranium, often adding the leaves of dried *Sweet William* (*Dianthus barbatus* - *qʷiqʷiʔqn'éłp*). This sweet-smelling mixture was spread over the hide; then it was folded in half, tightly rolled up, and left overnight. The following day the still-damp hide was easier to manipulate.

Prior to tanning, a decision was made as to whether the hair should remain on the hide or be removed. To *dehair* (*spšmí*) the hide of larger animals, such as deer and elk, the hide was usually removed before tanning; bear hide being an exception. Removing an animal's hair was a lengthy procedure, and accomplished by one of several methods. One technique required mixing the hair side of the hide with an ample amount of wood ash, rolling the hide with the hair on the inside, and burying the hide for a week or more, depending upon the weather. A rarely used procedure for removing hair was to weigh the hide down with heavy rocks in a stream for several days.

There were few elders who remembered hearing of dehaired tanned bison hides being used for covering tipis, though a few Spokan had words for dehaired bison hide. Such structures replaced traditional semi-subterranean pit houses prior to the reservation period. One can only surmise that the tanned bison hide was first received in trade from the Flathead, and, later, on a more regular basis, after the Spokan acquired the horse to conduct bison-hunting with certain Plains groups. Not long after the arrival of the horse, around 1730 (Teit 1930), canvas became the favored material when constructing summer tipis, eventually replacing tule mat construction. A trade item associated with equestrian needs was a horse or *saddle blanket* (*nqpčiʔsqáxeʔtn'* or *nqpíčntn*), which made easily into a *bed* (*snč̓łʔíištn* -"bedroll") when traveling. According to Work, saddle blankets made of bison skin, often called appichimans by early trapper-traders were really "saddle blankets, made of skins" (Elliott 1925, 4:262 fn.), and commonly used by fur-traders as blankets, and were common trade items (*vide supra* 1925:261). Earlier, however, Elliott (1914, 4:264) incorrectly designated a parfleche as an appichiman. Stewart also provides a description of an appichiman as "A piece of buffalo fur generally long enough to sleep on, worn folded under the saddle" (1846 vol. 1:36).

Tanning

There were essentially three basic ways that Native Americans tanned hides, using animal brains and plants containing acid such as oak. The Spokan used primarily brain-tanning, and in a few instances with small hides they used urine. Prior to applying mashed brains to a hide, it was critical to super-saturate the hide with water to ensure the hide was supple; often done by first soaking it in a stream for several days—held under by several heavy rocks. When tanning the hide of a small animal, a woman could submerge the hide in hot water for an extended period of time, while maintaining the water temperature by replacing heated vesicular stones—usually old sweathouse stones. A field method of tanning small hides involved taking strips of bark that had been removed from the base of a mountain alder, and then rubbing them directly onto the rawhide in order to tan it.

Prior to *tanning* (*hecxʷíkʷi*) a small animal's hide was rolled into a ball and placed in a *watertight* (*snčʔel'tn*) bark or tightly woven root basket containing a hot solution consisting of water and the crushed flower heads of yarrow. Upon cooling, the water was repeatedly heated by carefully placing one or two heated stones on a larger flat stone atop the rolled hide. The size of the hide determined the duration of heating the water—usually at a low heat for 8 to 10 hours by repeatedly replacing the cooled vesicular stones with heated ones. The water would later be wrung from the hide by hand or using a Spanish windlass if working with elk hide.

A large animal's hide was treated differently; but first it was thoroughly soaked in hot water for 8 to 12 hours, then removed and wrung dry using the aforementioned Spanish windlass. This method involved securing each end of the hide to a firmly anchored vertical pole. Then, an old digging stick or stout stick of wood was held at the end of the loop farthest from the pole and rotated clockwise—or counterclockwise, forcing all the water out of the hide until it was dry. The hide was then opened and tightly stretched flat just above the ground with affixed driven pegs, or stretched on a near vertical upright wooden frame. "Deer hides were rested on the top of a pole, while elk hides, being heavier, were stacked out on the ground for this process" (Schaeffer 1934-37, I-135).

Animal brains (*sc'm'qin*) were mashed, placed in boiling water and permitted to simmer, sometimes with some of the animal's fat or a bit of fish oil until the brains were sufficiently broken up so as to facilitate their absorption by the hide. The mixture of brains and fat or fish oil was then laboriously rubbed into the stretched hide. In the past, one commonly heard the expression, "Every animal has enough brains to tan its own hide." Decomposed deer brains were preferred for tanning (Smith 1991, 8:22).

One Spokan recalled her mother explaining how in the past the elder's great grandmother would massage into the deer brains a warm solution of chopped bracket fungus or small clumps of tree lichens (goat's beard, sometimes combined with wolf lichen). Upon drying, the mass was left whole or sometimes cut into small packets and *wrapped in a bundle* (*čp'lkʷíc'eʔ*) for storage in a cool and dry area of a dwelling or within the tanning shed, a special tipi or lean-to. Elderly women remembered hearing how some women mixed deer liver (if the hunters had not eaten it) with the brains for tanning, a mixture called *ʕʷámn* ("dunk" or "dip"). Dried and powdered sage brush was sometimes mixed with liver and brain to prevent the hide from molding; liver was thought to make the hide more supple and soft.

Wilson provided a brief explanation of a variation of Spokan tanning:

> [...] immediately after the elk or deer is killed, the hair is scraped off, and the skin stretched tightly on a frame, where it is left to dry; the brains of the dead animal are now rubbed in, imparting oil to the skin. This finished, it is first steeped in warm water and then dried, two women stretching and rubbing it in their hands whilst drying, after which it is again soaked, stretched, and dried. Before use, the skin is smoked, by being placed over a smouldering fire; the fire is made in a hole in the ground, over which there is a bell-shaped framework to

carry the skin, which should be so arranged as to confine all the smoke; constant watching is required to prevent the skin from burning (1866:299).

Hide-Smoking

Tanned hides intended as clothing were smoked for several days, primarily to prevent stiffening and cracking, since the smoking made the items more pliable and durable. Otherwise, if the buckskin became wet, it would remain stiff and often crack upon drying. Hide-smoking was also done to soften the hide and give it a desired color, as well as the desirable imparted aroma of smoked buckskin. Smoking a hide that had been tanned with the hair helped prevent the hide from losing the hair. *Hide-smoking* (*hesčɫʔáxʷlp*) served to "to better withstand dampness and wetting" (Ray 1933:95). Each residence had a relatively small but sufficiently large tipi for hide-smoking, made of three or four pole construction—though the number and size of the poles varied. In the past, this structure was commonly covered with either deer or *antelope hide* (*stʕančnʔélxʷ* or *sxʷlsšnʔelxʷ*). Some women preferred to erect a tri-pole structure, being more stable. Such a smokehouse was often used to smoke meat. The apex of the structure was approximately 2.5 m.

One elderly lady, who was probably the last to tan and smoke hides throughout the year, explained how after the tanning was complete, she would open the tanning structure and *hang open* (*čɫqʷéw'sis*) one or two hides, and then close the structure after lighting a *smudge fire* (*smot*) that was allowed to *burn down* (*čseʔšús* or *čqamús* - "diminish, wane, exhausted") before opening the structure's flap a second time. A few older women remembered how the upper end of a deer hide would be closed with widely spaced stitching, and the end over the smoldering fire was kept open with dry *yellow willow* (*Salix Lucida* ssp. *lasiandra* - *sqʷlséɫp*) withes to better accommodate the smoking process in the *smokehouse* (*snpʔúmɫcʔeʔtn*).

A more detailed explanation, similar to Wilson's aforementioned technique of hide-smoking (1866:299), is given by Ray of how the Sanpoil used a similar process:

> [...] a small pit was dug in the ground over which a tripod was erected. The skin was sewed loosely together so it might be slipped over the poles of the tripod. In the pit, which was a foot in diameter and half again as deep, a slow fire of rotten pine or cedar was built. Occasionally other woods were used. Both sides of a skin were smoke treated. The time required depended entirely upon the texture of the skin, but averaged perhaps four hours. Some skins, especially those to be used for moccasins were twice smoked (1933:95).

Hide-smoking was done by slowly burning dry punk bark, bracket fungus, or *decayed wood* (*yóqʷiʔ* or *nyqʷʔéɫcʔe* - "rotten inside") in the small three or four pole tipi-like smokehouse. Women had preferences as to the type of punk wood (*c'ic'ixéy'ɫp* or *yoqʷeʔ* - "rotten wood") they used to achieve varying degrees of color, and during late fall, when picking berries at higher elevations, they gathered different types of punk wood for smoking tanned hides. Red fir was probably the preferred type of punk wood for the color it imparted. The most available woods for smoking were cedar, tamarack, alder, aspen, white pine, yellow willow, and cottonwood. Dry elderberry bushes were dampened and then lit within the hide-smoking tipi, giving the finished hide a deep tan color (Elmendorf 1935-6, 1:2). A few elderly women recalled collecting at least eight types of deciduous woods, which preferably had been tunneled by termites lessening the women's load back to their residences. Old logs that had been ravaged by bears looking for termites were readily collected. In the past, women stated that they could tell by a hide's color and aroma what type of wood had been used to smoke it. However, wood from the *heart of a completely rotted tree* (*nyiqʷéɫcʔeʔ*) was most prized for *hide smoking* (*npʔomqín* or *ʔespʔúmlxʷi* or *scpʔúmlxʷ*).

The most desirable hide was one of lighter color. To help achieve this, wood ashes were rubbed into the hide after tanning prior to the later introduction of commercial chemical products. Dry *white willow bark* (*qʷúls*), when powdered, was used solely during smoking to give a highly desired golden color. When a woman's supply of punk wood became exhausted, she would substitute goat's beard moss for smoking a hide,

262

achieving the same results, except that the hide would be noticeably darker. An often desirable deep tan color was achieved by burning punk wood made from old, dry, rotting elderberry branches (Elmendorf 1935-6, I:2).

Women were the sole owners of their tanning efforts, and could give a tanned or untanned hide to whomever they wanted. Tanned hides were frequently given at certain ceremonies, such as meeting a good friend, at naming and during death rituals. It was believed that rawhide was never given at these ceremonies—the implication being that the recipient's husband was a poor hunter, or his wife was lazy, unable to properly tan hide. Clothing and other items made from hide could be traded, but they were rarely given away except in the case of one who was needy after having lost one's belongings in a house fire. It was true that during a person's give-away ceremony, *clothing of the deceased (łu λ'lil)* could be given to members of the family. Articles of hide and buckskin clothing were never washed in water, but cleaned by rubbing the soiled item with powdered clay, which absorbed any dirt, grease, or vegetable stains. Franchère observed how tanned deer skin garments "which they care to rub with chalk [white clay], to keep them clean and white" (1854:268). If clay was not available for cleaning buckskin, a baked biscuit root was dried, then powdered and kneaded on the soiled area of buckskin. Later, dried white bread or flour served the same purpose. An elderly Spokan gentleman once said, "When you ask me about our old ways, you should first know that we were once held together by language, family, and marriage, but more by the hide of animals, as well as our own hide."

Hide obviously fulfilled many needs, even as food in famine—but primarily as an elder said, "holding together" the many components of the various technologies.

The importance of hide was apparent in the status accorded an accomplished hide-worker, and in the fact that finished buckskin was often a trade item. Some recalled how *mule deer buckskin (st'lc'ʔélxʷ)* was not only relatively easy to work, but was a preferred hide when finished. The skin of a female mule deer was called *st'lc'ʔélxʷ*. Dog hides were never used to make clothing or ornaments (Schaeffer 1934-37, I-26:5).

Horn, Antler, Bone, Marrow, and Organs

All the by-products of ungulates and other land mammals were used in a variety of ways, including the hooves of larger animals; consequently, *horn (qxmín)*, *antler (qxqxmíntn)*, *marrow (st'ús)*, and *bone (sc'óm')* were indispensable to numerous Spokan technologies, which had multiple uses as tools, and, in the case of bone, sometimes as a food. Conversion of bone to tools was done most often by men, some of whom were more adept than others. Older girls learned from their mothers and grandmothers the correct way to manufacture such compound tools as leister heads and two-pronged bone pointed fishing spear heads. These were favored by an older brother or a father who would comment favorably upon the success he had when fishing.

Given the shape and condition, antlers of large animals were saved and used in the manufacture of leister heads, projectile points, awls, digging stick handles, spoons, dippers, needles, fishing toggles and hooks, probes, and fish spreaders for drying lamprey although for this application narrow split cedar shafts were more frequently used as spreaders. A common tool used to *split wood (qxém)* was the tapered end of an elk antler that had been shaped by grinding a bifacial edge with an *abrasive stone (snxʷaq'ʷmn)*, using the rosette as a striking platform. Deer antler ends were used to make a *pointed object (xʷúxʷl'm'n' - "drill")* for general prying, opening bivalve clams, making tent pegs and fish spear points, and breaking the amniotic sack by the woman to self-abort a fetus. Every person carried in his or her tool pouch a finely tapered bone for the removal of slivers; most commonly to *remove a sliver from one's hand (nwíqm)*.

Several types of hunting arrows were tipped with the sharpened ends of deer antler. Some fishing spears had a single sharpened bear *bone point (smúl'mn)*. Because of its density, fractured bear bone was preferred to deer bone, bear bone being the most dense bone of all mammals. Curtis noted how, "The fish-spear consisted of a shaft and a detachable barb made of three-pointed bits of bone bound together and connected with a line" (1907-30, 7:71). The 2 to 3 m long *fishing spear handle* (*čwéccčtn*) was made of cured, split white pine; a 2 m length served as a bison spear or for warfare. During early spring, when a deer was *in velvet* (*hes č'up'upalqʷ* - "velvet on the horns"), and before the animal had scraped the velvet from its horns, the velvet would be cut into thin strips, boiled, and eaten. Incidentally, the benefit of eating deer horn velvet—a natural source of glucosamine, chondroitin, and collagen but unknown at the time— improves the immune system and improves general strength.

A *knife handle* (*sčn'ín'č'm'n'tn'*) could be made from a section of deer or elk antler that fitted the hand and afforded a better grip. The piece of antler was cut, and a deep groove made in the smaller end to accommodate a stone blade, which was further secured by wrapping the seated blade with a continuous strip of soaked rawhide. After drying, the junction was sealed with pine pitch and tightly wrapped with a piece of buckskin or a section of fish skin. Antler tangs were used in the manufacture of knives and projectile points, by grinding with an abrasive stone to shape it properly.

The horns of mountain goat and the larger bighorn sheep were obtained primarily through trade with northern groups, though the animals once inhabited the Sullivan Lake area (STHC). Such a horn could be modified into a *horn spoon* (*la'la'mnqn tum'n'*) by making a longitudinal cut and then soaked for a day in animal or human *urine* (*xʷax*) until it became pliable. The large end of the horn was then easily opened by inserting a rounded stone held in place by rawhide to form a concave shape. Widening the horn was accomplished by forcing a stone of appropriate size between the splayed opening, and burying it for several hours in warm sand or at a small depth in the earth underneath a low fire. *Spoons* (*tú'mn*) were fashioned from small turtle shells, mussel shells, or from a duck's sternum.

Wood-splitting wedges were made from elk and deer antler, sometimes flattened by rubbing both sides of the antlers with sandstone to form what was essentially a bifacial edge; thus, making a more efficient wedge. Larger sections of green wood were split with an elk wedge after the main section had been cut off approximately 20 cm from the basal end, including the rosette that served as a striking platform. The large ends of elk horn were used as hammers and mallets for accomplishing small chores, such as breaking nuts and seeds, or driving small wooden tent pegs. Smith (1936-8:552) described how the Spokan would take deer horn to make needles or flat spatulas for removing cambium and pitch. The horn was first deeply grooved with sharpened obsidian to form the rough outlines of the intended tools; the porous center was filled with salmon oil until it was absorbed, rendering the horn less brittle, which prevented the horn from shattering when struck with a stone. Such tools were ground to shape with abrasive stones, ideally sandstone.

Awls and *large needles* (*ntxʷule'xʷ*) of bone or hardwood were used in making burden baskets, utility bags, eating mats, and specialized containers from *birch bark* (*pccŧin'*), cedar bark (the inside of the bark), cedar and spruce root, and other types of barks. Many baskets had geometrical imbricated designs, often created with bear-grass. The bone and marrow of all large mammals was saved. *Deer marrow* (*c''ulixʷ st'úsc*) was preferred, particularly from the lower leg bones of deer, which were cracked open with a stone for this purpose—a procedure called *spŧmá*. Adults and children enjoyed eating marrow, but preferred to eat the warm marrow that was taken from bones after being slightly heated first. Elderly men preferred the taste of uncooked or unheated marrow. Bear marrow was considered to have too strong taste—even an unpleasant flavor, and was not eaten. The long bones of most wading birds provided marrow, which was simply sucked out after breaking off one end of the bone. Marrow, as will be mentioned later, was an important addition to the Spokan pharmacopoeia.

The marrow of any large mammal's spine and long bones was eaten; if not raw, it was slightly warmed to prevent the marrow from disintegrating as happens when heating animal fats. *Fat around a deer's kidney* (*hulikʷŧ* or *'ulíkʷŧ*) was a delicacy, and, like portions of marrow, was added to stews along with small pieces of *mashed bones* (*spáŧ 'espŧamá*) for flavor and sustenance. Marrow could not be stored unless during winter hunts when it could be frozen and later thawed as needed.

Bones were cooked in a variety of methods, but the most expedient procedure for making a soup was not to clean the bones of blood, marrow, or hairs before first *breaking the bones into small sections* (*spáɫ* - "crushed bone"). The bone pieces were boiled so that the hairs and grease came to the top (which was skimmed away with a horn spoon or with a folded grass filter, and often eaten with cooked camas and black tree epiphytes). Such a soup was called *sx̣sétkʷ* (Smith 1936-8:439) or *y'e pn' kʷ sp'at'qán* ("tree moss with cakes") (Carlson and Flett 1989:288). Actually, the general name for any type of broth, stew or soup was *sx̣sétkʷ*. Another method of cooking bones was to place the lower leg bones of deer under an earth layer of 4 to 6 cm that supported an ember fire. Upon cooling, the mashed or fractured bones were pounded with a maul until *powdered* (*p'oq'ʷ* - "powder") and made into a soup, and was sometimes flavored with plant foods, *left over foods* (*miʔštsʔiɫn* or *sccmaʔwaqs* or *čmaʔw'aʔqsc*), or available minimal *food scraps* (*čʔiʔɫntis*).

Smith provides an on-site explanation of the dangers that confronted women intent upon breaking bones for cooking, as explained to him by a Kalispel informant:

> It is dangerous work to mash these until it is once cracked, so to hold [the bone] they take a piece of rawhide rope and double it around the piece of bone once: Sometimes it slips out and flies and many an old woman had got hit in the eyes and head with a flying piece. The fuzzy part is all mashed up fine. The harder parts of the outside they just crack into one inch pieces. This is done by an old woman [...] They pound both the knobs from the lower and the upper ends of the upper leg (1936-8:439).

Smith also provided an important and probably the only known description of how deer bones were prepared, stored, and often fermented:

> Then they [the Kalispel] dry the bones a little bit; this is mixed with deer hair and tied up and put away in a rawhide sack. This is put away for a long time and kept for hard times. It turns rancid and gets strong, but the stronger it gets the better they like it. The sack is generally buried; some will lay it away in the storehouse and this gets far more rancid and strong than the other which is buried [...] This is about the last thing to be moved when they shift camp (1936-8:438-39).

Bear and elk paunch was eaten after being stone-boiled. Most elders said that fish eyes were a delicacy, consumed raw before the rest of the fish was cooked. Yet others claim they never ate the eyes of any fish or mammal. Some contemporary authorities have noted how, during starvation situations, the consumption of animal eyes would unknowingly help to maintain a person's electrolytic balance.

In a similar manner, the entire deer head, after skinning and removing the eyes was boiled. The brains of the deer were removed for tanning and the nose, which did not have a pleasant taste, was never eaten. An additional source of food from the deer was the four protrusions located under the bottom of the four upper legs, which articulate with the lower legs. Once removed, these protrusions were mashed with mortar and pestle and immediately boiled, and the Spokan would skim off the fat, which was contained and saved in a deer paunch. After the paunch was empty of tallow, it too was cooked and eaten. Dried camas or *camas cakes* (*st't'ɫúleʔxʷ*) were frequently broken up and added to the soup, as were thinly sliced sections of fish or dried deer meat.

The preparation and cooking of fish intestines was discussed earlier, but the Spokan ate deer intestines, in particular that section which is whiter than the rest, and was considered to have greater flavor. These sections were carefully separated from the rest of the intestines prior to cooking, for if cooked together, the entire mass would be *spoiled* (*č'stw'il'š*) and considered inedible.

Some elders claimed that they never ate any mature *animal brain* (*sc'mqín*) because of its value for tanning, though some recalled—without any details—a type of porcupine head cheese, made and eaten in October. There was, however, agreement that a preferred dish was the brain of a yearling fawn, after the entire head had been sufficiently boiled to soften the small antlers, which were also eaten; only the eyes were not consumed. *Heart* (*spʔús*), *kidney* (*mt'és*), *liver* (*pn'ínč*), and *tongue* (*tíxʷcč*) being considered delicacies, were eaten raw or *roasted* (*q'ʷlim* - "to roast meat"). Bear stomach and *bear paw* (*speʔšín*) were boiled and eaten, but bear lungs and blood were never eaten. Nor is there recollection of eating the thymus of any mammal. Blood was considered tasty, and it is a nutritious food when collected and mixed with other cooked foods. It was not known if the Spokan prepared blocks of dried blood, to be used as food when hunting or traveling long distances.

Chapter VII: Environmental and Resource Stewardship

One of the earliest descriptions of the Spokan environment and natural resources was by Cox, a fur-trader, who in 1814 joined the Northwest Fur Company and spent six years in the Plateau. He wrote several books that described the environment, indigenous peoples, and how, "From the falls [Spokane Falls] to the lands of the Spokans the climate is remarkably healthy; in summer, excessively hot; in winter intensely cold; but subject during these seasons to little variation" (1831, 2:139). And yet, despite the claims of early Euro-Americans describing the healthy weather, the peoples of the Plateau were always confronted with two major logistical problems: One was their ultimate survival—knowledge and stewardship of maintaining annually predictable resources. Another was their ability to transport exploited riverine and upland resources to permanent riverine villages for winter storage. Consequently, a constant concern for the Spokan was always the distance from a gained resource to its eventual winter storage site. As one elder commented, "Which is easier, bringing an elk to the camp or the camp to the elk?" (Ross 1995).

Until recently, there were a few elderly Spokan women who could view any wooded area in climax vegetation, or any uncultivated and ungrazed grassland, and say without hesitation what plants could be in either environment. But more importantly, they could announce, with the confidence of accrued knowledge and long experience, what plants would not be present. Their ability and success was to feed themselves, which were predicated on their intimate knowledge of resource areas, and, as already acknowledged, their interpretation of the so-called carrying capacity of an area.

The strategies, abilities, and the ultimate success of these people were dependent upon their skills in tracking, reading signs, decoying, and understanding the often predictable migration and habits of larger land mammals, in addition to the availability and condition of their needed food resources. Pre-hunt and post-hunt religious rituals and behavioral prohibitions reinforced these skills. Any discussion of the Spokan annual subsistence round—and the associated predation technologies, strategies, and times of utilization—is best illustrated by a brief explanation of how the Spokan so effectively managed resources within those areas that provided their different foods. Because of their recognition and interpretation of biological diversity, including food-chains and food-webs of their natural environment, the Spokan understood the symbiotic dependencies as well as how the biotic potential of a particular biome was dependent upon and influenced by human intervention. Controlled burning, a critical activity for maintaining sustainable grassland and forested areas, and their yields of plant and meat products, was, consequently, followed carefully, and there developed the annual practice of *selective burning* (*p'ʕapúleʔxʷ*).

Selective Burning

Naturally occurring *fire* (*sur'šict*), or the cultural practice of selective burning, was recognized as an effective environmental tool in bringing about desired short- and long-term environmental conditions that favorably affected the condition and, in some instances, the quantity of plant and animal resources (Ross 1999). There are some early references (Cox 1831; Cooper 1860; Mullan 1861; Bancroft 1875; Elrod 1906; Day 1953) that specifically describe this indigenous incendiary technology. The explanations only partially increase our knowledge of how Plateau groups perceived the anthropogenic effects of ignitions upon indigenous foraging and predation techniques that they pursued during the prehistoric time, and, to some extent, the early historical period. Fortunately, the practices of prescribed burning during the late historical period have been studied for various Plateau groups (Schaeffer 1940; Stewart 1951, 1954, 1963; Weaver 1957, 1967; French 1965; Daubenmire and Daubenmire 1968; Chittenden *et al.* 1905; Arno 1976; Lewis 1977; Barrett 1980, 1980a, 1981; Hough 1890; Shinn 1980; Hunn and French 1981; Ross 1981a, 1994a, 1999; Pyne 1983; Grant 1994; Barrett and Arno 1999; and Boyd 1999). Concerning Amerindian controlled burning, Stewart stated that, "over 100 tribes in North America used fire for at least 15 different purposes including hunting, native plant production, improvement of horse-grazing, and communication" (1956:7).

Even today there is considerable misunderstanding of aboriginal Amerindian people's management of their environment, who, prior to European influence, were seen, "as natural elements of the ecosphere" (Shetler 1982:226), living in a "totally pristine, natural, wilderness world with ancient forests covering landscapes" (Williams 2005:1). However, Botkin disclaims these notions of indigenous peoples having no effect on their ecosystem:

> But Native Americans had three powerful technologies: fire, the ability to work wood into useful objects, and the bow and arrow. To claim that people with these technologies did not or could not create major changes in natural ecosystems can be taken as Western civilization's ignorance, chauvinism, and old prejudice against primitivism—the noble but dumb savage. There is ample evidence that Native Americans greatly changed the character of the landscape with fire, and that they had major effects on the abundances of some wildlife species through their hunting (1995:169).

The author is unaware of any known oral or written accounts indicating that the Spokan ignited the woods maliciously—either for entertainment or signaling—as has been recorded with some other groups (Ferris 1940:106-7; DeVoto 1953:83). It is known, however, from the historical literature and oral history, that carelessness and malicious intent did occur among some southeastern groups in the Plateau, who on occasion were responsible for summer fires that were "high-intensity, stand-replacing ignitions" (Barrett 1980:10). In this context it was not unusual for Spokan elders to adamantly claim that selective burning was always carefully accomplished for the express purpose of maintaining "healthy forest environments, "prior to established Euro-American settlement in their territory. The research susceptible to insect and disease infestations. They are also vulnerable to severe damage by wildfires because of heavy accumulations of dead fuels." (Ross 1990:201).

According to oral history, a *forest fire* (*hecp'ʕapmí* or *ʔesp'apmi*) was an unusual occurrence and, when one did happen, it was common practice to construct a back-fire by clearing or burning a U-shaped area to the windward side (Smith 1936-8:301). Yet, the occurrence of *heat lightning* (*sixʷélmxʷ*) has always been associated with forest fires, which in many instances were permitted to burn-out without any intervention, simply because there was little wind-fall or dead-fall present. But an *angry thunderbolt and almost simultaneous lightning* (*sʔuw'éčn't*) near a settlement was a matter of immediate concern, and considered even more potentially dangerous when there was *lightning with no accompanying thunder* (*st'rt'réʔm*). In the case of a lightning-started conflagration, the Spokan, if possible, set back-fires on each side of the fire—and on the upwind side—leaving the downwind side unfired.

The practice of utilizing incendiarism probably continued to a limited extent until being prohibited in the late 1920s by the Bureau of Indian Affairs on the Colville and Spokane Indian Reservations, when Bureau field agents began to jail any apprehended offenders (Ross 1981a). The environmental effects of this decree are only too apparent in Spokan oral history accounts and early photographic records, which graphically attest that there were increasing amounts of accumulated windfall, *deadfall* (*sxl'mqín* - "dead understory brush") that needed to be "*cleared away*" (*xeʔc'm'*) on the reservation as late as the 1940s.

It was said that without prescribed burning, tree growth rates and certain plant successions and locations were being drastically altered (Ross 1981a; Grant 1994), and not for the better. Prior to 1914, elders claimed there were fewer, if any, crown fires and certainly fewer flying and ground insects, particularly *hymenoptera* and *lepidoptera*. Elderly Spokan men commented upon how, with the reduction of selective burning, there was an apparent increase of deer ticks, *spruce budworm* (*Choristoneura fumiferana* [Clemens] - *č'č'c'el'šcn'*), a moth (*Depressaria heracliana* [L.]) that attacks wild carrot, and *Lepidoptera larvae* (*Phyllocnisiis populiella* Chambers), which attacks aspens, poplar, and cottonwood trees.

During the more recent reservation period, there were dramatic changes in the rights of exploitation of both restricted or dwindling traditional plant and animal resource areas, often the result of men being engaged in off-reservation wage labor. This situation required women to assume greater responsibility for the stewardship of on-reservation resource areas, namely root fields and berrying areas (Ross 1993a). A few elders claimed that as early as in 1914, the first Spokane Indian Reservation manager developed a strict policy that any Spokan who practiced controlled burning would be jailed if apprehended. Even during the 1920s and 1930s, on both the Colville and Spokane Indian Reservations, the Bureau of Indian Affairs jailed individuals, including several women, who attempted to maintain those few traditional on-reservation berry-picking patches and roots fields by prescribed burning. The last time a Spokan woman was arrested was in 1931 by the then-Spokane Tribal Forester who had a vehicle and by chance happened to be in the vicinity of logging roads that facilitated his apprehending the older woman who was afoot.

Numerous Flathead, Spokan and Colville women informants have explained that in order to evade apprehension and arrest, they devised simple but effective *delayed incendiary devices* (*cʔlúsn't*) that would ignite a wooded area many hours after the individual Indian or group had departed from the area. The most common and simple igniting device was placing a *lit candle* (*čʔul'seyʔútyeʔ*) under an overturned empty fruit or discarded (empty!) dynamite wooden box, using duff, lichens, shredded dry bark, or abandoned ground-dwelling animal nests as tinder (Ross 1999:287-88).

Because of fluctuating variables, the exact time of anthropogenic burning was not always predictable; moreover, there were memories by elders of multiple annual burnings of the same resource site, particularly wooded areas adjacent to winter riverine villages, but some areas were not burned for four to five years. Burning was usually practiced in the spring at lower elevations, and in the autumn at higher elevations. The time of burning varied from year to year, depending upon a number of regional conditions: topography, elevation, soil moisture content, force and direction of wind, and the group's occupancy of a particular resource area. The Spokan obviously knew that the greater the amount of dry litter, the hotter and more devastating a fire. According to popular wisdom, the more significant the resource, and the vaster the area, then the greater the importance of coordinating the prescribed burning of contiguous grassland and woodland areas.

An additional concern for not burning at lower elevations in the spring was the potential damage to ground-nesting and tree-nesting birds during hatching season. Several elders in the late 1960s were cognizant that the damage to nest areas was minimal with cool fires as opposed to intense fires, and that gallinaceous birds, such as the ring-necked pheasant and wild turkey, did not survive intense fires because their nests and food were often destroyed by fire (Kozlowski 1974; Lewis 1982:16). An elder described the deleterious effects upon ground-nesting birds by cattle and feral cats, "Wildlife during the past was very plentiful. There were thousands of prairie chickens during May. Now they're gone in our area. Over-grazing by cattle and the growth of brush has destroyed their nesting areas. There's too many cats, mostly wild ones that kill our birds" (Ross 1968-2008).

Another major reason for anthropogenic ignitions was to rid or reduce an area of vermin, weeds, and insects during the summer and autumn, particularly yellow jackets and hornets which became attracted when dried salmon was returned to permanent riverine villages for winter storage. Most dried salmon was cached on platforms located above 10 m in ponderosa trees, for it was believed that this height was of sufficient elevation to be above flying insects, particularly yellow jackets and hornets. Shell middens near living areas often had hornet, wasp, and yellow jacket infestations that were attracted by the deposits of fresh mollusk shells. However, the middens were not fired (which would have been difficult) to control these pests, albeit vegetation around these sites were sometimes burned. If possible, big sagebrush was carefully burned when smoke was necessary to rid middens of insects and vermin.

A few elders recalled the oral accounts of their *great-grandparents* (*ner''uye*) (likely during the 1830s to 1850s) who explained how most forested areas below 1000 m MLS (Mean Sea Level) were open, and that prior to reservation confinement, annual prescribed burning served to facilitate ease of travel, communication, and stalking of game. Ethnographers, such as Stewart (1951, 1954, 1963), studying the incendiarism

269

strategies of other hunting and gathering groups, have noted there was a near-universal use of fire to improve visibility and facilitate travel—both conditions being a prerequisite for successful hunting.

Many now deceased Spokan-speaking elders, when reflecting upon former forestry practices, have lamented the present condition of many on-reservation areas, and that as a result of modern mismanagement, travel was and is not only difficult, but often dangerous because of the preponderance of wind-fall, dead-fall, and dense understory. For example, one elder in 1966 could recall when and where various types of noxious weeds—notably deep-rooted *Russian knapweed* (*Acroptilon repens*)—had been introduced onto the reservation in the early 1940s, which he felt was the result of enforced government restrictions against on-reservation selective burning (Ross 1989a:66). The now ubiquitous plant remains but with no known Spokan designation.

In 1972, the author and a 96-year old Spokan man were laboriously traversing a densely wooded terrace along Big Tschimakain Creek looking for a particular plant and the location of the spring that feeds this creek, one called *č'mqín*. At one point the old gentleman stooped, paused in silence, and actually wept as he explained how as a teenager (circa 1895) he had hunted the terrace and could vividly recall the vegetation of the area as once being open with grasses, but which unfortunately had attracted sheep herders in the 1920s who grazed their animals in the area; but he neglected to discuss the then known deleterious effects sheep-grazing had upon root crops used as food by the Spokan. He did recall hearing of the unusually severe winters of 1861-62 and 1880-81, and how the, "Killing weather was experienced everywhere" (Olphant 1932, 1:16 fn).

The general stewardship and subsequent condition of wooded areas, where many of the aforementioned plants were gathered, was of great importance to the Spokan people. To this end, the traditional practice of controlled burning was used to increase the productivity of particular flora (Daubenmire 1968). It was done most frequently in the fall after a killing frost when the men were returning from deer hunting, or to a limited extent during deer hunting. Such modification of an area was known to increase the occurrence of certain grasses for browsing ungulates, and most elders could recall their fathers and grandfathers saying, immediately prior to burning an area to encourage the growth of grass, "I'm giving you food now so later you're my food." In the early 1960s, several Spokan elders could recall vividly when they were apprenticed to older men, who would formally teach them as to the time of the year as well as the proper conditions and areas when fires could be lit. Once the sheep herders were removed, Ponderosa pine and other vegetation became re-established.

And yet, despite the policies and actions of the Bureau of Indian Affairs, elderly Spokan were adamant in their claims that fire-treated forest areas were more resistant to fires, particularly lightning-induced and crown fires. It is quite likely that they were well aware of the beneficial effect of fire-created temperatures, particularly for releasing the seeds of the lodge pole serotinous cones. Also, *pine nuts* (*q'p'xʷʔeʔ*) from the ponderosa (Ray 1933:104) could be more easily collected after surface burning by opening the cones. The Spokan practiced the principles of continuous forest silviculture and fire-management, which they realized was critical to sustaining a healthy state for the trees they depended upon, such as Douglas fir, lodge pole pine, Ponderosa pine, and western white pine.

In 1854, Gibbs collected linguistic and ethnographic data while conducting a survey to route the Northern Pacific Railroad, along with I. I. Stevens, the first territorial governor of Washington (1853-1857. Even at this early date, Gibbs was concerned about the consequences wrought by white settlements, the encroachment and devastating effects of domesticated animals upon traditional resource sites, noting, "A drove of hogs belonging to one white man will consume the winter provision of a tribe of Indians" (1855, 1:29).

Understandably, the paramount reason given for incendiary technology was the management of forest and grass ecosystems that were, as a result, known to be beneficial to sustaining their foraging techniques and hunting strategies. As such, the Spokan realized that in order to maintain open, healthy, "park-like conditions" conducive to maintaining feed for ungulata, fire-removal of wind-fall and dead-fall was necessary. During his journey to Fort Colville, Pickering noted how after crossing the Spokane River, "I found [scattered pines] more abundant, and not confined to the immediate banks; presenting, with the absence of undergrowth, natural parks, and some unexpected analogy to the Australian woods" (Barry 1929:58).

The early Spokan were aware that soil permeability could actually be improved by the removal of accumulated pine needles since fire was important because pine needles contain poisonous hydrocarbons (Moore 1974). Though Indians did not understand that pine needles contain this chemical, they did realize they were detrimental to the growth of young seedlings. Also, the greater the amount of dry litter, the hotter and more devastating the fire would be. Naturally, this fact influenced the timing when the Spokan chose to burn an area. Elders insisted that prescribed burning was not always preferred during autumn hunting because with dry vegetation fires were less able to be controlled as a result of atmospheric conditions and certain topographical features that could cause an unpredictable shifting of high winds.

Though there existed a sexual division of labor for controlled burning, it was not always apparent since many male and female adults practiced selective burning in isolated areas. All adults were knowledgeable of the carrying capacity of the different landscapes, which annually varied with elevation, rainfall, and directional exposure. Prescribed burning should not be construed as having been random or casual, or done simply according to an individual's volition. The importance for prescribed burning was reflected in the fact that several individuals within each village or major camp possessed a *suméš* to perform these annual tasks, and were subsequently held responsible for their stewardship.

Normally a person was able to receive this power by either having recurring dreams of dwelling in the woods with certain animals, or more commonly by having a close association with an older consanguineally related male (his sponsor), one who already possessed this unique *suméš*. An example of a desired animal power for selective burning was the black bear, a tutelary spirit who could give to the neophyte the multiple powers for locating huckleberries and curing burns, a power that either a man or woman could have. The tutelary animal spirit possessing this religious power for controlled burning assumed various forms. For example, apart from the black bear, one may have either *blue grouse* (Dendragagapus obscurus - *qáɫqɫc'e?* or *qaɫqɫci?*) or chipmunk as guardian spirits, in which case the recipient would always renew his *suméš* at the power pole during the Mid-Winter Ceremony, in a ritual procedure termed *snc?unc?tis* ("to call upon one's *suméš* for guidance or immediate assistance").

Several Entiat, Lakes, and Spokan elders identified certain birds that assisted individuals who were charged with prescribed burning—specifically the *downy woodpecker* (Dendrocopos pubescens - *st'l'xʷúme?*), western meadowlark, red-headed woodpecker, and yellow-shafted flicker. One elder related how anyone knowledgeable of nature would understand why certain birds were once associated with grassland areas, such as the red-headed woodpecker and yellow-shafted flicker, who were "patron birds" of the wooded areas, because of their dependence upon standing dead trees for food and nesting; these open areas were often maintained by selective burning.

People who acted as burners were afforded complete control over decisions of frequency and strategies for burning resource areas of economic significance, and were responsible for directing the manual clearing of *Indian trails* (snqlixʷál'q) clogged by unmanageable debris or trees blown down, as well as the clearing of debris from important springs and water seeps within the group's territory. A few elders explained how their fathers and grandfathers kept naturally occurring game *salt-licks* (snčxlémtn) open from windblown vegetation. A *sxʷp'ʕápm* ("one responsible for setting a forest fire") (Egesdal, pers. comm.) would set fire to underbrush for managing a forest, and to drive deer in a "deer surround."

Spokan elders stated how beneficial forest and grassland ignition was in reducing the understory vegetation known to compete with grasses that supported deer, elk, and later horse grazing. Thus, their use of fire improved not only game pasturage, but visibility when hunting. Selective burning was frequently used to

271

move deer into prearranged areas of predation, especially where the region's topography and vegetation were more conducive to this method of entrapment. These areas were mostly open grasslands with semi-arid vegetation that recovered quickly after burning.

The Spokan were aware that selective burning encouraged serial shrubs that tended to replace conifers, and the quantity of forage increased rather dramatically; thereby encouraging utilization by browsing animals. For example, *red-stemmed ceanothus* (*Ceanothus sanguineus* Pursh. - *k'ʷlič'tyeʔłp* or *k'ʷelitč'iyeʔłp*) is an important browse for deer, a shrub that requires the heat of fire to crack its seed and prepare it for germination (Moore 1974); hence, burning was essential.

As late as the 1960s, elderly Spokan women recognized the value of late spring burning of huckleberry areas, since at that time normal soil moisture was higher and heat penetration would be shallower than in autumn. They were aware that ground and vegetation duff at this time of year invariably had a higher moisture content, and was less combustible; hence, there was less likelihood of over-burning or creating an uncontrollable conflagration. Some have pointed out that all rhizomes were dormant and protected by the wet ground, and not harmed by spring burning. However, some elders maintained that late spring snow, or an abnormally high incidence of spring rain, would necessarily postpone any intentional burning until late summer or early fall, which was true with understory or broadcast burning.

In summary, controlled burning was used primarily to reduce wind-fall, dead-fall, and generally to alter the understory to encourage the growth of huckleberries, and grazing by deer and elk. This practice aided in preventing crown fires and reducing insects, and assisted in certain tree seed release and propagation. As a result of the recent devastating fires in national forests—ones in which the understory of dead branches and other inflammables became dangerously built-up, many whites are now learning the wisdom of allowing natural and human-caused fire to burn out the deadfall, thus minimizing the greater damage of fire.

Chapter VIII: Annual Subsistence Round

The annual subsistence round reflected a major rhythm of collective social orientation and practices that gave special significance to Spokan life; a rite of intensification that was predicated upon the annual quest for food, one that was reinforced by numerous collective and even certain individual religious rites of intensification of propitiation and thanksgiving just prior to gathering, hunting, or fishing. This strategy of exploiting predictive resource sites was based upon intimate knowledge of terrain as well as the availability of plant communities and their successions and familiarity with animal population cycles and migration patterns.

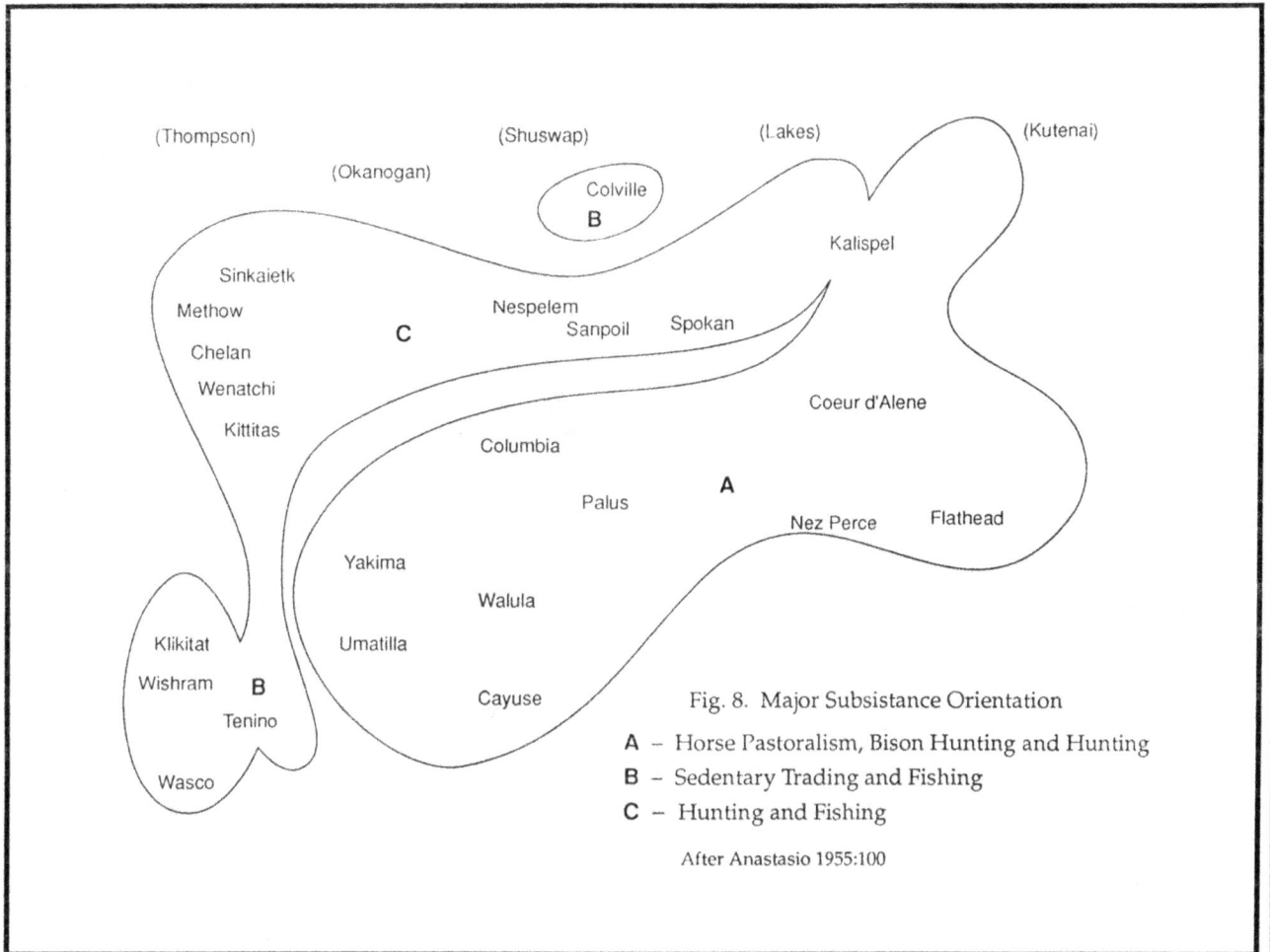

Fig. 8. Major Subsistence Orientation

A – Horse Pastoralism, Bison Hunting and Hunting
B – Sedentary Trading and Fishing
C – Hunting and Fishing

After Anastasio 1955:100

Figure 21. Major subsistence orientation

In addition to conducting food-getting activities, these often collective activities were occasions for socializing, gambling, courting, and trading, when children and adults indulged in numerous games of hand-eye coordination and dexterity, strength, and other competitive activities such as wrestling, foot-racing, shinny, stone-lifting, and ball games (Elmendorf 1935-6; Ross 1988:29-33). Adults participated in *gambling* (xcxcíʔm) and telling *traditional stories* (sqʷllúmt), both activities going often until *dawn* (ct̓x̌ ʼx̌ ʼʔéč). In

1876, according to Cowley, gambling was a "great vice among the Spokans" (McBeth 1908:77). A pre-gathering ritual was the principal ritual that actually commenced the annual subsistence round, when families departed from winter villages to join other groups in large congregations to collectively exploit sites of plant resources and certain animals.

ANNUAL SUBSISTENCE ROUND

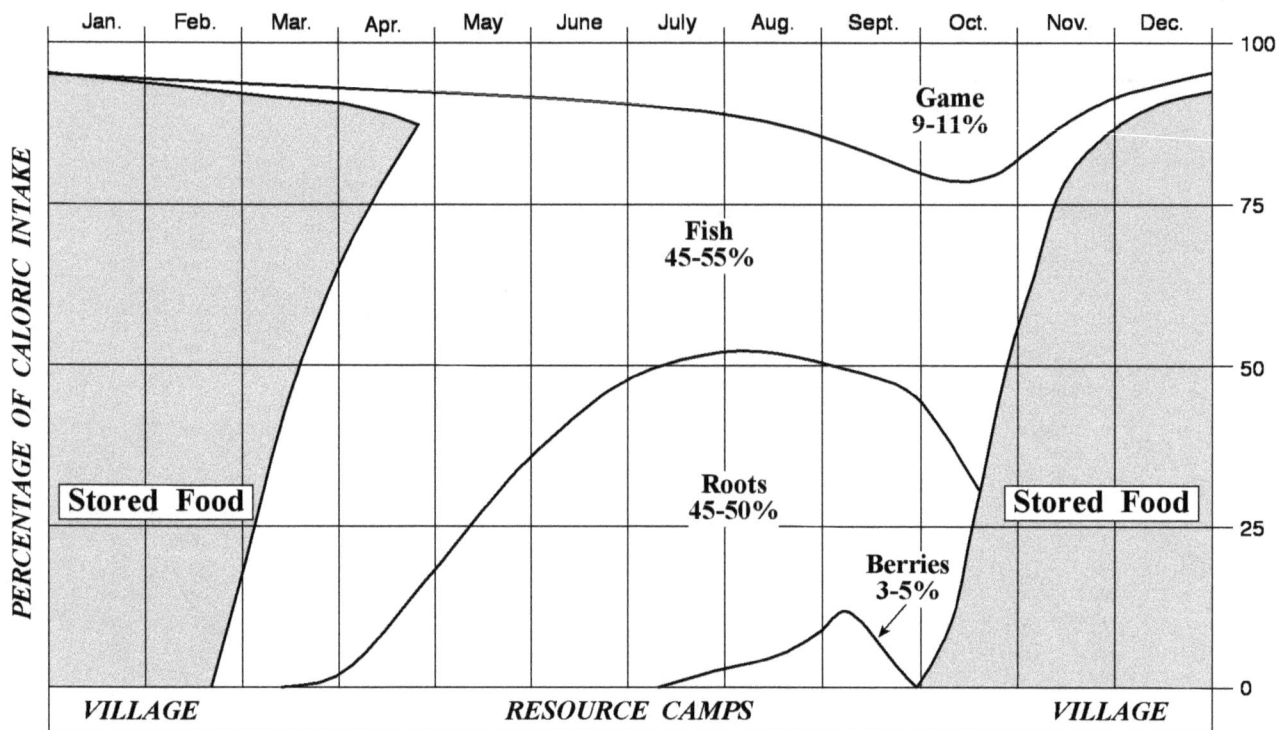

Figure 22. Annual subsistence round (by Pam McKenney)

The main annual subsistence round commenced with the arrival of warmer weather, when people would leave their winter lodges to gather and hunt available foods, individually or in small groups. It was not unusual for there to be severe shortages of stored foods by late winter, due to a prolonged winter or the partial loss of stored foods due to animal contamination, which could result in some people starving. Also, repeated freezing and thawing of even *dried meat* (*yetékʷ*) caused spoilage. Elders recalled their grandparents telling of food platform caches, strategically located on riverine basalt boulders, being swept away by early flooding and ice floes.

Alexander Ross, who lived with the Spokan from 1810 to 1813, observed the storage of winter food by the Okanogan, which was similar to that of the Spokan. His account emphasizes the great time and effort required for their survival strategies:

> We must now relate the manner in which these people pass the summer season, and provide food for the winter. As soon as the snow begins to disappear in the spring, the winter camps break up, and the whole tribe disperse here and there into small parties or families; and in this unsettled manner they wander about till the middle of June, when they assemble again in large bands on the banks of the different rivers, for the purpose of fishing during the summer season. Here, then, their fish barriers are constructed, by the united labour of the whole

village or camp assembled in one place. The salmon being then in the utmost abundance, no sooner are the barriers finished than one or more of the principal men are appointed, by general consent to superintend each. The person thus chosen divide the fish every morning, and settle all matters respecting the barrier and fish for the current year. Their authority is law in all those matters till the end of the fishing season, camp is divided into four parties, for the various purposes of daily life, and of laying in a stock of food for the approaching winter. The men are divided into two parties; one for hunting and the other for fishing: and the women also, one party cure [sic] roots and berries. All these different productions are dried and seasoned in the sun, and require much attention and labour. The fish when properly cured is packed up into large bundles or bales; the roots and berries into bags made of rushes. The stock for the winter, thus daily and weekly produced, is then, during the nights, conveyed in secret, and put in caches; that is, hidden under ground among the rocks; each family having its share apart, secure from wild beasts and the eye of thieves. During the continuances of the fishing season, the Indian camp is all life. Gambling, dancing, horseracing, and frolicking, in all varied forms, are continued without intermission; and few there are, phlegmatic, who do not feel, after enjoying so much hilarity, a deep regret on leaving the piscatory camp on these occasions. As soon as the fish season is over, the Indians again all withdraw into the interior or mountains, as in the spring and divide into little bands for the purpose of hunting the various animals of chase. In their mode of ensnaring the deer and other animals, they are generally very successful. Exclusive of hunting these animals with their guns, bows and arrows, and running them down with their horses, which latter practice is a favourite amusement, they frequently select a valley or favourable spot of ground between two mountains, having a narrow outlet or pass at one end; and the better to decoy the unwary game into it; bushes are planted on each side (1849:315-16, 1904:296-7).

Numerous historical accounts of Spokan subsistence activities were recorded in the nineteenth century, but only a few of these observations are cited here. For example, Cox in 1811 noted the Spokan subsisting on plant foods, beaver, deer, wild fowl from the area, and an abundance of salmon from the Spokane River (1957 [1832]:261). From Pickering's writings (1895:27), Barry (1929:60) commented upon the devastating effects of market-trapping upon the beaver population, as did Work (1829), who earlier had commented on the decline of beaver in the area, who also remarked upon the dependence of the Spokan upon hunting and the large quantities of salmon caught in the Spokane River. Later, in 1838, Parker observed the Spokan subsisting primarily upon fish and various animals, supplemented by plant foods, despite the introduction of agriculture.

On several occasions, Hale was fortunate to have carefully observed the Spokan annual subsistence round, and provided a relatively detailed account of their ethnobotany, and illustrated his active involvement:

At the opening of the spring, in March and April, or as soon as the snow disappears, they begin to search for a root resembling the cammass [sic], which they call pox-pox [p'$úx^wp$'ux^w - a white camas]. This lasts them till the beginning of May, when it gives place to a bitter root, termed *spatylon* [sic] [sp'$éλ$'m - bitterroot]. This is a slender and white root, not unlike vermicelli in appearance, and when boiled it dissolves into a white jelly, like arrow-root. It has a bitter but not disagreeable flavour, and is remarkable for growing in gravely soils, where nothing else will thrive. In June, the *itzwa* [$?itx^we?$], or cammass [sic], comes in season [...] This root thought by many of us to have the taste of boiled chestnuts. Before this fails, the salmon make their appearance, and during the summer months the Indians enjoy a very plentiful supply of food. While the men are employed fishing, the women are very busy digging the cammass [sic], which may be termed the principal occupations of the two sexes. They devote a portion of their time to the collection of berries, a work which is principally the duty of the younger part of the tribe. In September and October, the salmon still claim their attention: although they are, after having deposited their roes, until exhausted and about to perish, yet these are dried for their winter consumption; and unless they had recourse to these, much want would ensue, which is always the case if the salmon should be scarce. In October, they dig an inferior root, somewhat of the shape of a parsnep [sic], that is called by the Indians *mesani* [sic] [$msáwi?$]: it has a peculiar taste, and when baked is of a black colour. After this has happened, they depend upon their stores of dried food, and game, including bears, deer, badgers, squirrels, and wild-fowl; which they sometimes take in great quantities. This, however, fail them at times, and it then generally happens that their salmon [supply] becomes exhausted also, when they are obliged to have recourse to the [tree] moss [...] (Hale 1846, 4:446).

The following is a lengthy but significant account from a letter Walker wrote to *The Christian Mirror* in March 1847, describing the Spokan annual subsistence round, and various food-getting strategies, based on six years of observations. This account, made during the early historical period, is of particular anthropological value in attempting to understand what was occurring ecologically to the environment as a result of Euro-American activities, especially sustained trapping and increased hunting:

> Perhaps it might be interesting to those who know but little or nothing about Indians in this rude state of nature to know what their food is. Before the arrival of the whites in the country, they knew nothing about any kind of vegetables except what was spontaneously growth of the country. No kinds of fruits or vegetables were cultivated. The depended wholly on the wild game, the fish, fruits and roots for living. When all these failed, they had & do have to this day, recourse to the moss of the pine trees. At this moment it [famine] constitutes more than two thirds of their daily food.
>
> They have a great variety of roots and berries. Every kind of root and every kind of berry they use for food. An Indian would live and do well where a white man would starve to death. It is interesting to study the working of providence in arranging the roots of this country for there is no season of the year when there are not roots that are good for food. As soon as the snow is off, they find roots already for digging and as soon as these are gone, another comes in and so on through the whole season. Sometimes they clear away the snow & dig in the winter season. Their game is mostly gone. There are some few deer left. Some years they did get a great many. One band about sixty miles from this place drove in one day four hundred into a lake and all were taken. It is only when the snow is deep and the deer are compelled to leave the mountains and come down in the plains and the woods that they get many. The way they take so many is they make what is called a surround. Some few will take a bag of some pieces of burnt [deer] skin, make a long circle in every few [... and] stick a piece on a stick. When all is done they will began to drive. The deer will start and run till they smell the skin when they turn about and run in another direction. The people all the time coming nearer and nearer together. In this manner they huddle them together near some precipice a hundred feet or more. When the snow is deep and a little hard so as to bear the people with snowshoes and will not bear the deer, they move quickly and overtake them in the chase. The next dependence of this people for animal food is fish and especially salmon. It is astonishing what numbers ascend the Columbia and its tributaries every year. Though some years they are more numerous than at others. Of all that ascends, no one reaches the sea alive. The Indians take them at rapids by means of wares [weirs]. Sometimes they have been known to take a thousand a day. I have seen them at some rapids actually to fill the air in making attempts to pass up. The sight reminds me of a flock of [passenger] pigeons around a pigeon bed [...] It is not uncommon for many to pass the wares [weirs] and these are taken if they have laid their eggs for which they then begin to die and by the end of October all are dead. They begin to turn white at the tail and [...] towards the head so that they lose all red color [...] Some few of these bands go annual[ly] to the Buffalo. Some go in the summer and return in the fall. Others go late in the fall and spend the winter. These trips are attended with such danger and often with the loss of life and horses owing to the depredation habits of the Blackfeet. Notwithstanding the great danger they run in going to Buffalo, it seems to have no influence to keep them home. They appear to have no apprehension of danger or manifest any fear or anxiety for tomorrow [...] If all is well today, they do not trouble themselves what will be on the morrow (Drury 1976:526-7).

In early April, a greater variety of plant foods were available to **w**omen, whose work throughout the morning was intensive though much of the *afternoon (sny'ak*ʷ*qín)*was devoted to socializing as the women cleaned and prepared their harvest for transport back to the village or early summer camp. Approximately eighty percent of the harvest was not eaten immediately—or shared with the old or incapacitated residents—but carefully prepared for winter storage. Older people who remained in the village throughout the summer would be engaged in performing numerous sedentary economic tasks, mostly making mats from the previous year's harvest of tules and cattails. On occasion men would assist women during this time with the sometimes difficult task of transporting the large amounts of gathered roots to storage areas for winter.

The gathering of plant foods was done almost exclusively by women, usually from early April until late November, or until the ground froze. Basically, the principal roots gathered were camas, bitterroot, and numerous species of Lomatium, plants that constituted approximately eighty percent of the total yield of vegetable foods. In addition, numerous other types of roots were gathered during a relatively brief period, from late April or early May—until emphasis was directed toward the procurement of migratory fish resources. The termination of spring gathering was evidenced by men, women, and even older children laboriously transporting the prepared, sun-dried roots from root fields to winter quarters.

Given the importance of summer fishing activities, and the sometimes comparatively cyclical low yields of root fields, older women would—depending upon the condition—remain in these areas gathering and sun-drying their daily harvest, often until late July, when the second phase of gathering began with the collecting of berries and medicinal plants in the higher elevations. However, certain camas root fields were exploited well into August, and some women continued to return and exploit productive root areas until the first killing frost, which concluded the annual gathering of certain plant foods and utilitarian plant by-products were stored for winter consumption. There apparently was no terminal ceremony or rite that acknowledged the final departure from root areas, nor any indication that the Spokan appreciably traded roots to other groups, as did the *Kalispel* (*nqlispelišcn*) and *Flathead* (*séliš*) peoples (Egesdal, pers. comm.).

First Fruit Ceremony

Each village or early resource camp held a *First Fruit Ceremony* (*hecnaq'ʷpáʔɬqiʔ* or *sčp'um'm'*), a strict ritual of praying just prior to digging the first camas or other roots. Women would first inform their chief that it was time to dig camas and other roots. The ripened food being prayed to was called *sčp'úm'm'*, and a chief for each group would in turn designate an elderly woman, or acknowledge one who may have held the leadership role for some years—often a widow—to coordinate plant-gathering activities for the rest of the year. All the women would gather to hear the chief make a prayer of thanksgiving to their *creator* (*k'ʷl'ncútn*) (Smith 1936-8:1328) for the coming root harvest, after which the leader designated the root field to be exploited. Always, before digging, the lead woman would make another prayer of thanksgiving, a blessing for a *bountiful harvest* (*xʷaʔtaɬq*). They would remain digging camas for two to three days, and then they would reopen a formerly used pit and bake their harvest. Upon opening the pit, an equal distribution of all the baked camas was made by the head woman who would lead a procession to the chief's dwelling, and some of the harvest was gifted to the chief. He then called all the men together, leading the group in a prayer of thanksgiving for a bountiful harvest (Smith 1936-8:1317). After this ceremony and distribution of camas, the men and women would eat the cooked camas before each woman returned to dig more camas, and the men continued hunting deer. Hale, who observed the annual seasonal round of the Spokane, likened the taste of camas to "boiled chestnuts" (Wilkes 1845, 4:446).

Whipping Ceremony

Just prior to leaving the winter village to commence the annual subsistence round, one of the elderly medicine men would have a dream, one that told him it was time to hold a special annual whipping ceremony—referred to as *snqíxʷɬc'ʔem* ("driving out the inside of something"). It was conducted by several elderly shamans who would run about the village, beating upon the dwellings' interior and exterior walls with a bound spray of rosehip switches, called *xʷxʷy'épeʔɬp*, intended to drive away any old year malevolent spirits. The whippers lightly touched each child and baby, but not adults, with their switches to emphasize the community's transition from a period of cold weather, hunger, and sorrow for those who had died, to a joyous period of warm weather, renewed friendships, games, gambling, courting, trading, and replenishing their stores with available food. One of the oldest shamans would follow the whippers, explaining to young and old alike the reason for this collective cathartic ritual (Elmendorf, pers. comm.).

Pre-Gathering Ritual

Elmendorf (1935-6, 1:6-7) recorded how this once important pre-gathering ritual was staged every spring immediately when the sap commenced to run, a ceremony that was primarily an opportunity for women to collectively pray for a bountiful season. The ceremony was initiated by the women gathering early morning in the surrounding woods, and each woman commenced dancing and singing separately before gathering at a central court in the village. Eventually the women converged and sat with their laps and extended legs covered with fir boughs, waiting for the men to serve them their *mid-day meal* (*ntx^{w}ox^w qintn*). Since each woman sang her own song, one can only assume it was her *sumés̆* song. After an early meal, the women *neither ate nor drank until the sun went down* (*ta-m'is sust hu iɬn hu č'lux^w*), when the men prepared a supper they served to the women who sat outside on fir boughs. The wood for cooking the women's meals had been previously collected by the men who made the fires and cooked the women's food. Since women most often collected firewood, and were responsible for cooking throughout the year, this was a ceremony to demonstrate a man's dependence upon a woman's labors and skills. After the meal, the dancing and singing resumed and lasted until sundown when the men collected every remnant of firewood and *uneaten food* (*čma?waqs*), and burned all of it, for it was believed that if any of the first plant harvest were left, none of the food plants would bear. However, prior to this burning, some of the *remaining food* (*scq'it's*) was taken by young boys to the woods and left on *bark plates* (*c'ilelpeɬc'e*) for animals.

Over the centuries the ceremony varied according to Reverend Walker's diaries, and his observations may have been more specific for the Lower Spokan, particularly where he describes a ritual he called Tohua:

Tohua [...] the name of another ceremony only performed early in the spring, for the purpose of insuring [an] abundance of deer, fish, berries, and roots. This consists of taking up heated stones [...] It is only performed when they have eaten nothing for a day, or are, according to their acceptance of the term, 'clean' [abstaining from sexual relations]. If they have violated this rule, they believe the stones will burn their fingers. This ceremony is said to last several days, and includes singing and dancing, walking barefoot and nearly naked about the village (Wilkes 1845, 4:448-9; Drury 1976:515).

Chapter IX: Hunting

Technology

The various means of acquiring game, either through direct hunting or using delayed predation devices such as traps, snares, and deadfalls, required a variety of technologies, strategies, and rituals. And despite the similarity of predation weapons, the various techniques, tools, and weapons associated with hunting varied according to the type of animal being sought, and less upon a person's individual skills. Projectile-type weapons were most common when an individual or small group hunted, whereas thrusting and percussion implements were often better suited to larger, collective animal drives, or enclosures. Combining technologies often led to more successful results. As a once accomplished *hunter* (*sxʷčtíp*) remarked, "One man can get one *deer* (*spéw'puʔ*), two men perhaps two deer, but four men [often] eight deer." Men made their hunting and warfare weapons, as well as the various necessary accoutrements.

Bows

Projectile-type and cutting *weapons* (*in'č*), tactics, and tracking skills of warfare were essential elements in hunting. In particular, the *bow* (*čkʷín'č*) and *arrow* (*t'apmín* or *tsq'éln*) were the principal weapons for hunting game and in warfare. Woods most frequently used for bow construction were mock orange (*Philadelphia Lewisii* Pursh., var. *Lewisii* - *wáxiʔłp*), the dense and strong *oceanspray* (*Holodiscus discolor* [Maximm] - *mets'metsíʔlhp* or *mc'mec'ey'łp*), and *Western yew* (*Taxis brevifolia* - *ckʷen'čalqʷ* or *ckʷn'čálqʷ* - "bow tree"). The outer side of debarked yew wood has a honey-colored springy sapwood, and the blood-red-colored heartwood resisted compression, making it the source of a bow's recovery after being pulled and released.

Bows were also made from syringa bush that was best gathered in the winter and prepared by first bruising the wood with a stone knife to facilitate bark removal. From central Oregon, both the much-sought iron wood or curlleaf mountain mahogany (*Cercocarpus ledifolius* Nutt. ex T.&G., var. *Ledifolius*), and the extremely dense and hard white mountain mahogany (*C. intercedens* Schneid.) were acquired as blanks or finished bows through trade mainly from the Nez Perce, and they were usually shorter in length than those made of other woods, but had considerable strength. "The skin is used to cover the sinew part of the Bows which are strengthened with sinews, each bow requires two skins, as only the wide part can be made use of" (Thompson: 1916:525). Work also mentioned (1828:52) how the bows "are of yew wood overlaid on the back with the sinew of animals which are generally covered with the skins of snakes."

Once the bow was shaped, the empty moist skin of the bullsnake (*Pituophis caternifer sayi* - *sx̣ʷyúps*), sometimes called a bow snake, was pulled over the entire length of the bow, serving as a waterproof covering, a process that required the bow-maker to first:

> [...] slip [the rattlesnake skin] over the entire bow while green and allowed to dry on - [then it was] wrapped with sinew at [the] notches and for some distance down the bow - and around [the] handle - most hunting bows [were] like this - sinew string [was] *twisted* (*qastín'č*) fairly thick (Elmendorf 1935-6, 1:79e).

An early account of Salish bow-making (circa 1814) was recorded by Alexander Henry, who mentioned the manufacture of bows using wood and ram's horn:

> The outside is left undressed, but over-laid with several successive layers of sinew glued to the thickness of one-third of an inch, and then covered with rattlesnake skin. The inside is smoothly polished and displays several ridges of the horn. These neat bows are about three feet long, and throw an arrow amazing distant. The red cedar bow is made of a slip of the wood overlaid with sinew and glue like the horn bow and also well polished inside; it is nearly four feet long [...] (1901, 2:713).

279

The bow most commonly used for both hunting and warfare was a sinew-backed *long bow* (*spn'inč*), made most commonly from ocean spray. Smith (1936-8:636) described how a sinew-backed bow of Osage orange would warp and even shatter if the bow string was under pressure. A bow could be strengthened by sinew collected from the hind legs of deer in the winter, when their fat content was diminished, and which adhered better to the wood and the successive layers of sinew. Smith also described how they worked on elk sinew; even though his example is for the recurved bow, it is also applicable to any sinew-backed bow:

> Before the long sinew were applied and after the combings were removed each was placed on a flat piece of wood and pressed with a stone until it was perfectly flat and thin and about 3/4 inch wide. The ends were wrapped to hold the sinew on. They cut salmon skin into thin little pieces, put them into the water and boil them until the following day [...] On the following morning they mash it all up or some take it out and chew it up and then replace it. Then they boil it until it is all melted down [...] When they get the sinew on, it takes 3 or 4 days to dry (1936-8:637-8).

Many important observations of Salish life were made by Lord who collected a number of traditional and non-traditional Spokan weapons for the British Museum, including a bow. He noted the importance of glue for the bow's quality:

> The Indian bow is a masterpiece of skilful manufacture; its elasticity does not in any way depend on the wood used in its construction, but on the elastic ligament, procured from the fore leg of the elk; this is affixed to the wooden framework of the bow by a kind of glue made from the skin of the 'white' salmon, a glue when hardened resisting the influence of wet to dissolve it. This elastic back to the wood acts as would an India-rubber band; the bow when bent takes an arrow about a yard in length, which it propels with a force equal for a short range to that of a rifle bullet. When an Indian shoots, five or six arrows are held in the left hand, and as the string, which is made of tendons, is hauled back, the right hand brings with it an arrow; this one fired, another is seized, and as rapidly as one could reasonably count, the six arrows held in the left hand are discharged [...] Spare arrows are carried in a quiver made from the skin of their medicine animal, 'Tamanowash' (1867, 2:252-3).

Only one elder could recall his grandfather making glue from 'white' salmon skin, which was accomplished after first removing the head and tail, and about one-quarter of the body-skin was removed and then sliced into sections the 'size of aspen leaves'. A container of water was brought to a boil and the sections of skin were dropped in, and the container was placed on a low fire and occasionally stirred until the solution thickened. After use, the glue-solution was never used again, but always made fresh when needed; claiming that the smell of the simmering salmon-skin glue was "invigorating."

The aforementioned Spokan method to make a sinew-backed bow was also described by Wilson, Lord's colleague, during his on-site observation of Spokan weaponry:

> The bows are from 3 ft. 2 in. to 3 ft. 5 in. long, about 1¼ in. broad, and 1/2 in. thick, they seem to be made of no particular wood, but are backed with sinew, covered with snake skin. This skin is fastened to the back of the bow with the best cement I ever met with, as it is not the least bit affected by heat, cold, or damp; it is made from the skin of white salmon. The tips and grasp of the bow are bound round with sinew. The string is of sinew laid on loose so as to be twisted at pleasure according to temperature. The arrows are from 2 ft. 5 in. to 2 ft. 6 in. long, with a 10 in. feather, the point being generally of iron bound on with sinew (1866:297).

The highly prized sinew-backed bow was probably first acquired through trade with Plains peoples for hunting bison, and later acquired from the Nez Pierce, Flathead, or from the Kalispel who made such a bow:

> [...] bows were made by applying numerous layers of thinly-sliced deer leg *sinew* (*tínš*), glued to the back of the bow in successive layers by means of an adhesive made from boiling *deer hooves* [*sc'u?c'u?šinssn'*] or long strips of salmon skin approximately 2 cm wide, for a day or so until the mixture was soft (Smith 1936-8:635).

Spokan bows were often given personal names and apparently never loaned to other hunters. Teit noted, "The Spokan and many men of all tribes covered their bows with bull-snake skin" (1930:344), which was used to prevent the bow from being scratched and thus from absorbing moisture. There are accounts of such bows being wrapped with the skin of bull snakes and Western diamond-backed rattlers. Wilson (1866:297) and others (Teit 1928:344; Smith 1936-8:636) observed how some Spokan covered their bows with bull-snake skin, which they procured by *removing the skin* (*nʕwép*), cutting it lengthwise, and *slipping it off* (*nʕawép*) the snake. An already *shed snake skin* (*snʔawcʼʔencut*), being too thin, was never used to cover a bow; it was always collected only from a recently killed snake. There were several accounts of eel skin being used to cover bows, though the Spokan reputedly made only a glue for sinew-backed bows by boiling eel skin taken from the neck area.

Another type of bow was the *short bow* (*ckʷinʼč*), made from an elk rib—one with a relatively short range—used by the Spokan in winter when hunting a hibernating or caved black bear, or when hunting deer in thick brush areas (Elmendorf, pers. comm.). The effectiveness of the short bow was more dependent upon the hunter's stalking skills than his marksmanship. However, if an accomplished hunter armed with such a bow was able to get within shooting range, to *miss* (*xʷmeƛʼm*) was virtually impossible. Ray (1933:88) contends that the Sanpoil did once make elk rib bows, although we have no known examples of such bows, but Ray adds that deer ribs were never used, being too short.

The Spokan did not make the *horn bow* (*słumƛsčníʔnč*) of mountain horn sheep, but probably acquired some from the Nez Perce or the *Crow* (*stémči*) through trade. However, it is possible to conjecture that the Spokan made a *cedar bow* too (*cʼkʷʔčá*) for hunting since the first type of bow made for young boys was of cedar. The Spokan are not known to have made a composite, double-curved (recurved) bow, which the Nez Perce and Flathead manufactured and from whom the Spokan must have acquired it through trade. When describing the Flathead laminated bow, Turney-High (1937:114) explained how applying strips of boiled mountain sheep horn reinforced this particular composite bow, making it one of the finest bows in North America. According to Smith, the Kalispel made a type of horn-laminated bow:

> When cutting horn into strips, they cut grooves lengthwise, pour salmon oil into the porous center and let it soak up for a few days to soften the center so that it will not be brittle and break. And then they hit it with a rock. They have to cut the grooves almost thru the hard part (1936-8:552).

In densely wooded or bush areas, a hunter would kneel with the bow held horizontally to the ground with an arrow laying atop the bow—what is now called the Mediterranean stance. This position was often assumed when using a bow while riding a horse in warfare, whereas while hunting in open country, a hunter most often held the bow vertically if not engaged in close stalking.

The upper end of the bow was notched by cutting out a 4 to 5 mm flat-backed section on either side, starting approximately one cm from the end of the bow, to which a primary feather or a small secondary *wing feather* (*sqpúslʼ*) of a predator bird was attached by a fine piece of *twisted* (*mrʼkʷ*) hemp to gauge wind direction to improve one's aim. It was common for the upper reach of a bow to be decorated with a few twists of fur if one's tutelary spirit was a fur bearing animal.

A young boy was first introduced to the use of the bow and arrow when presented with a *small bow* (*cckʷinʼč*) made by his father or his *father's brother* (*smʼeʔł*), either of whom taught the boy how to shoot and care for the gift.

Bowstrings

Bowstrings, being critical to the efficiency of the bow, were manufactured from twisting and plaiting the long tendons from deer or elk legs, or Indian hemp. Teit wrote how the Coeur d'Alene "Bowstrings were twisted from the shredded sinews of deer's legs" (1930:98). The Spokan are reputed never to have made bow strings from twisted thinly split deer intestines or fascia. Sinew was preferred as it seldom broke and was more flexible than hemp, and yet a major and obvious disadvantage to sinew bow strings was that they could not hold their tension when wet.

Making a *bowstring* (*čʕacínʼčtnʼ*) was a lengthy process. The elk or deer leg tendons were first serrated lengthwise, stripped, soaked, and hung with each tendon individually weighted with a rock, and frequently turned to wring out any moisture. Once the material was damp, two equal length strips were then plaited in the customary fashion of rolling the strands together on the man's thigh or between his palms. The final stage was to stretch the entire string between two well-anchored vertical posts and permit it to dry. A finished bowstring of sinew was approximately 4 - 5 mm in width, varying in length according to the particular bow.

Before *fitting the bow string to the bow* (*čɫaccín'čm* - "middle"), only one end was spliced to make a loop that remained permanently attached to the bottom end of the bow; the other end was wound just below the top end without tension in the bowstring. A bow was strung only just before use to prevent warping the bow or unduly stretching the bowstring, and when not in use the upper end of the bow string was slipped off and wrapped about the bow.

On long hunts, each man carried an extra bow string in case of loss or breakage. In extreme situations a reserve bow string could be fashioned from a two-strand string of Indian hemp that was always carried for multiple purposes. Some elderly men recounted stories of how after eating in camp, a man might string his bow and tap it with an arrow to produce music to accompany his song. It was not recalled if the lower end was used as a resonating chamber by placing in within the player's mouth.

Arrows and Projectile Points

The Spokan had basically five types of *arrows* (*ta'ta'pmín*)—one type for warfare, and four for different types of game. An arrow intended for fighting had a foreshaft and projectile point designed to remain embedded in the victim. Similar to large game arrows, it had a projectile point of stone or bone, and only the projectile point of the war arrow was barbed. Barbed projectile points, and later metal projectile points, were used only in warfare since they were difficult for an enemy to remove without creating further tissue damage and bleeding. Lithic projectile points were always *lashed* (*snɫč'pel'*) to the arrow with thin strips of wet rawhide, and when dry they shrunk sufficiently to retain the arrow's projectile point.

The first type of hunting arrow had a relatively small so-called 'bird point' that was capable of killing a deer or elk, given the ability of the arrow to achieve deep penetration. Because of an unacceptably high risk of breaking or losing a projectile point when hunting small game in grassy or talus areas, a third type of projectile point was used, consisting of a sharpened piece of fire-hardened mock orange or other available hard-wood attached to the shaft. The fourth type of arrow had a fire-hardened sharpened end, but without a projectile point; it was commonly used for birds and when shooting suckers in shallow stream edges and backwaters, which were then *thrown to the bank* (*sk'ʷɫt'íč'm*). The remaining type of arrow, used primary for birds and small game, was a bone projectile arrow or *bone arrow* (*sčm'ál'stnʔλ*) made of any small deer tang that was further shaped and stone-sharpened on the pointed end whereas the slightly larger diameter was center-bored, partially packed with pitch before the arrow shaft was inserted during manufacture.

When available, the erect stalks of *ninebark* (*Physocarpus malvaceus* [Greene] Kuntze - *txéy'ɫp*) were collected for manufacturing arrow shafts. An elderly Spokan recalled his father saying how certain men were more skilled in making bows by possessing a unique power (*suméš*), but apparently not associated with arrow-making. Arrows made of ryegrass never had a projectile point—being effective with only a sharpened point, or a blunt end, depending upon the type of small game being sought. This type of arrow was used only with the small bow of a male child for hunting small animals or in play when rolling willow hoops used as targets to test his marksmanship.

Though different woods were used, the favored materials for making arrow shafts were *blue elder* (*Sambucus cerulea* Nutt. ex T.&G. - *c'kʷkʷálqʷ*), *blue bush* (*Sambucus cerulea* Raf. - *c'k'ʷíkʷ*), blackberry elder (*S. melanocarpa* Gray), and *red osier dogwood* (*Cornus stolonifera* Michx. var. *occidentlis* [T.&G.] - *stéčxʷ* or *Stolonifera nuttallii* Michx. var. *Stolonifera*). It is probable that the Spokan word *stčxʷnálqʷ* included all of the foliage of the dogwood bush, though the berry was called *stéčxʷ*. Stalks of the serviceberry bush provided a strong, strait-grained wood that produced a straight-shafted arrow.

Regardless of source, the wood was permitted to thoroughly dry, often heated in a thick layer of warm sand, and further manipulated until the shafts were completely straight. In some instances, slight irregularities in the shaft were removed by repeatedly drawing the concave edge of a beaver's tooth over the bent area, much like the later acquired spokeshave. In lieu of a beaver's tooth, large flakes of flint (a microcrystalline form of silica) or obsidian were retouched to produce a 6 to 9 mm crescent-shaped indentation, which was then drawn over the intended arrow until the desired straightness had been achieved. A fine-grained metamorphic rock was easily worked as an *arrow straightener* (*xwáq'l'stn* - "scraper") by shaping two small identical rectangular blocks, and then making a half round longitudinal groove on the face of each one. The arrow shaft was rotated with the right hand when placed between the two blocks as they were pressed together by the other hand. A final sanding was often done with horsetail, an abrasive plant used to give a fine finish to slate, bone, and soapstone. Certain slight indentations and other markings on an arrow identified its owner, which proved useful during archery contests and collective hunting to prevent any disputes of skill or ownership. Before shooting a large animal, the hunter would recite a series of special phrases that would gain the attention, and hopefully the assistance, from his power that would guide the arrow to its mark.

When an older boy killed his first deer, he could claim only the meat where the arrow entered, and only as much as his opened hand could cover. The young *hunter* (*sxʷčťíp*) would butcher and *dress out* (*nxʷk'ʷełc'e?is* - "to clean out the insides") the deer himself. After his family cooked the deer, he never ate any of the meat—only the small hand-size portion pierced by the arrow. The remaining meat was always given to an elder or infirm person to demonstrate the young hunter's kindness. The young hunter's first deer *hide* (*q'étt'*) was given away to a non-kin elderly woman to show his generosity and concern. If the recipient were an elderly lady, she might reciprocate by making a garment or gloves for the hunter. If the first deer was eaten by the boy, he would never have *good luck* (*xsstél'* - "good happens to someone without his control") as a hunter.

There was always an elderly man who offered a prayer—called *nč'ʕʷłc'?encútn* ("means to pray for game")—for the adolescent, which was to assist the youth to be a good hunter and provider. Similarly, an elderly woman presented such a prayer when a young girl dug her first roots (Egesdal, pers. comm.). The first root dug by a young girl was saved, cleaned, dried, and ritually placed in a small *buckskin bag* (*č'łt'k'ʷc'?ép* - "little hip bag") by her mother, who then permanently sealed the bag by sewing the opening shut. Thereafter, and regardless of age, the woman always wore her first root bag when root-digging to ensure a good harvest, a ritual called *k'ʷpúmtnm*—an expression of benevolent imitative magic.

Most arrows were *fletched* (*čk'ʷúl'l'stn* - "guide feather") except for those made of ryegrass. The best feathers for fletching were made from the tail feathers of a *red-tailed hawk* (*Buteo jamaicensis* - *skʷlkʷłʕátʕt* or *spyá?*) or the tail feathers of a bald eagle. The *wing feathers* (*sčwaxn*) of the blue crane were used on common arrows. An owl's *tail feathers* (*sqpusl'ps*) were used in fletching arrows, and, adhering to the Doctrine of Signatures, mallard wing feathers were used to fletch water arrows. A feather's shaft was first carefully split lengthwise, usually with obsidian, into two sections, thus, creating two half-feathers, each with a vane of feather barbs on one side. The outer edges of the quills were cut or singed with a hot coal to provide a slanting but even edge. For each vane, both ends were trimmed and the remaining feathered mid-section was approximately 8 to 9 cm in length. These sections were cleaned and attached to an arrow at both ends of a section by tying them with thin strips of rawhide, placed on *warm pitch* (*t'ełłtn*) and spaced "equal distant and parallel to each other" (Ray 1933:88). The area of attaching the feathers was less than the arrow's diameter to better accommodate the vanes. Elmendorf described how "arrows tipped with flint - or scraped to [a] point - three feathers [were] gummed on with pine pitch and lashed with a sinew which extends in back up to [the] nock - [the] nock [is] slightly enlarged - [and is the] primary grip" (1935-6, 1;79e).

When attaching the feather section, pitch was sometimes applied to the aft end, close to the archer's drawing hand. The use of pitch was not common, as it could become detached due to warmth when exposed to the sun in any quiver that did not have a top cover. Each of the three feather sections were purposely bowed or "humped" by moving the attached ends closer to one another, which created more pressure upon each vane, thereby stabilizing the arrow's trajectory and preventing the arrow from rotating in flight. The only exception to this practice was in the case of arrows used for fishing in shallow streams when the fish were near the surface. In such instances, the feather shaft was flat against the arrow. The rear end of an arrow was notched for placement on the bowstring. A finished arrow was approximately one meter in length. Cox described how the Salish "natives can tell by examining arrows to what tribe they belong" (1831, 2:167).

As cited, the Spokan had and used various types of poisons in sorcery and for killing dogs. At one time poison was used on projectile heads in warfare, and one of the poisons was made from the snake grease of the *Western diamondback rattler* (*Crotalus atrox* - χaχaʔúlaxʷ or χeʔul'eʔxʷ).

Teit (1930:344) recorded how "Long ago rattlesnake poison was sometimes used on arrowheads." But the most complete description of making arrow poison was given by Smith:

> They [the Kalispel] get snake grease and rub it on the points. They cut the snake in two [...] and hang it over a cup-shaped rock [...] When the snake gets warm, the grease will drip out. They stick a stick right through the snake [...] and stick it is the ground at a low angle [...] With the cut part up. They build a fire a little distance from the snake [...] Then they put a cup-shaped rock under the opening to catch the dripping grease. If one gets just a little scratch from an arrow thus treated, it will puff up and the person will die in a little while [...] They put the grease on the arrow points while it is hot or after it gets cold; it never hardens even when cold. They put it on with a stick; they cover about 4 inches of the point with the poison. When they were going to war they would go right out and get a snake; they never kept some of this poison on hand, but as soon as they had prepared the arrows they would throw the remainder away.

> Except for a poisonous arrow, war and hunting arrows were just the same. The war arrows were painted with red ochre to distinguish them from hunting arrows. They just painted about 6 inches on the point end; the paint was put right over the poison. Not every one used snake poison, but only one to whom the snake would tell, "Take me, [sic] Do this to me and put me on your arrow. I will help you lots." The man would have to be a bad one. One who would use any snake that talked to one [...] This snake that talked to one wouldn't become a guardian spirit" (1936-8:672-3).

All the components of these weapons were often acquired or made by the hunter—with a few exceptions, such as projectile points sometimes acquired by trade, particularly obsidian points. Obsidian blanks and some finished *projectile points* (*snc'l'él'stn* - "arrowhead") were bought from central Oregon and some traded up the Columbia River. Galm, when discussing the importance of obsidian to Plateau groups, stated how "Obsidian sources in the Pacific Northwest are concentrated in three main areas: British Columbia, Oregon/northern California, and Idaho" (1994:275-6).

Quivers

A *quiver* (*snq'ʷɬéʔl'st* or *snq'ʷɬél?st*) was never made from bent or steamed bark, but from animal hide, such as an untanned or partially tanned deer or coyote hide. All other animal hides, except bison and elk, destined for quivers, were tanned with the hair remaining on the inside to protect the arrows. A man always made his own quiver, and preferred the "skin of [his] medicine animal" (Lord 1866, 2:253), such as an otter, coyote, weasel, marten, beaver, muskrat, or *badger* (*Taxidea taxus* - sχʷiχʷyútšn). The owner of a quiver made from a wolverine was greatly respected, even though this formidable animal was usually killed by a deadfall. There were no memories, examples, or accounts of skunk or marmot hide serving such a purpose.

A quiver made from an animal representing a person's animal tutelary spirit was almost always completed by using the particular animal's head, tail, and legs. Dressed deer or coyote hide quivers, however, were decorated with an individual's preference for a combination of various red and yellow linear type designs, and was often further complemented by attaching feathers, small animal bones, and tails. Quivers almost always were embellished with *long buckskin fringe* (*wisš t sip'i scso*), attachments that facilitated dissipating rainwater. Decoration and any accoutrements—which indicated the owner's hunting abilities and success—were often further enhanced by a man attaching to his quiver certain power objects symbolic of a hunter's or warrior's sense of well-being and *sumčš*, and were believed to influence his success. It was unknown if scalps or any part of a slain enemy's body were ever attached to a warrior's quiver.

Since there are only a few known museum examples of the Spokan quiver (Cheney-Cowles Museum), comparative ethnographies (Ray 1933:89; Smith 1936-8:264-7; Post and Commons 1938:54) of contiguous groups to the Spokan provide an understanding of the manufacture and use of the quiver. In terms of size, quivers ranged from 50 to 60 cm in length; the bottoms were 6 to 7 cm in diameter, and the tops were approximately 7 cm in diameter. An additional wide strip of buckskin was sewn around the top on the inside to afford some rigidity, and a quiver was sewn up the side. Because arrows were always inserted point first to protect the projectile point and the exposed feathers, the base of the quiver had either a thick piece of rawhide with the edges turned up and sewn to the quiver, or a circular section of hard-wood, held in place by pressure. If willow was used as a quiver base, it was first soaked and then stitched into a flat mat. The fletched ends of the arrows projected approximately 7 to 16 cm from the top opening and usually had a soft protective flap. Prior to sewing the two edges of the quiver together to form the desired shape, some men stitched a rectangular piece of tanned deer hide along the side, approximately 12 to 14 cm wide. This rectangular piece was cut to make fringes. Some quivers were fringed around the top, and even down one side. Elmendorf wrote how "bows were unstrung when not in use - bows [were] carried in [a] quiver (*snsq'élntn*) made of rawhide down [the] side - tubular with round bottom sewed in - [and with a] flap to fasten over [the] top" (1935-6, 1:79e).

When traveling, the quiver was carried diagonally across a man's back by means of an attached buckskin strap, the quiver opening being just over the person's left shoulder. Smith (1936-8:264) described how the Kalispel carried a quiver under the left arm, with the arrow fletching facing forward. Another manner of use when hunting or traveling in a potential game area was not to carry a bow in an arrow quiver, but in its own buckskin sleeve container independent of the quiver. In winter or inclement weather, the quiver was carried under the axilla of the left arm by a strap. Upon the death of a hunter, if his quiver had power, or represented a specific zoomorphic tutelary spirit, then it was not inherited, but usually interred with him upon his death. There is no recorded evidence to prove that the Spokan buried a warrior's quiver at his death; but skeletal material has been found with series of adjacent projectile points in neat rows.

Wrist Guards

The universally used *wrist guard* (*č'łč'np'cnéčstn* - "band around the wrist instrument") (Smith 1936-8:652) was made of one piece of heavy buckskin from the neck of a deer or elk, without any decorations. A wrist guard was cut so a 9 to 10 cm half-moon shaped section would cover the archer's wrist and the base of the thumb, being held in place by wrapping and tying together the ends of the two strands of raw hide attached to the pad. A wrist guard was always worn in battle, during active deer hunts, and when participating in archery contests.

Spears

Spears were used primarily for hunting bear and for fishing, but there were a few accounts regarding the use of the spear in warfare (Teit:1928:359), or as a thrusting or trajectory weapon for small animals. The Spokan used the *lance* (*smú?ƛmn*) too, which might have been first acquired from the Plains, and probably used only for thrusting at an enemy during close range combat, but never for throwing. As stated, the favored weapon for hunting a hibernating bear was the *lance or spear* (*smúl'mn*), and was undoubtedly used for hunting a treed bear after the animal was brought wounded to the ground by bow and arrow. Such a weapon was reputed to have been used during deer drives that forced deer through relatively narrow runways where they were dispatched with hand-held spears. Deer driven into lake or stream water were often killed by spear. One elder recalled that such a spear would have a shaft made from western hemlock or *maple* (*Acer glabrum*

Torr., var. *Douglasii* [Hook.] Dippel. - sx̌ʷƛ̓'olálqʷ), usually two or more meters in length and of stout diameter. Unfortunately, no representative samples are known to exist, so it is not certain if such a bear-hunting weapon was hafted with a bone point, or simply pointed and fire-hardened.

Atlatls

Unfortunately, there are no ethnographic and few archaeological references to the atlatl within the Interior Plateau (Kreiger 1928; Cressman *et al.* 1940; Butler and Osborne 1959; Butler 1961). Krieger's work on the Snake River documents the first atlatl found in the Upper Plateau, providing the first known description of a partial spear (sometimes called a dart):

> The blade point is of chipped jasper, the shaft is a stem of charred wood eight and one-half inches long which tapers from a diameter of three-fourths inch at the nocked base to less than one-half inch at the bottom nock end. A groove one-eighth of an inch deep and of equal width extends the length of the shaft (1928:138).

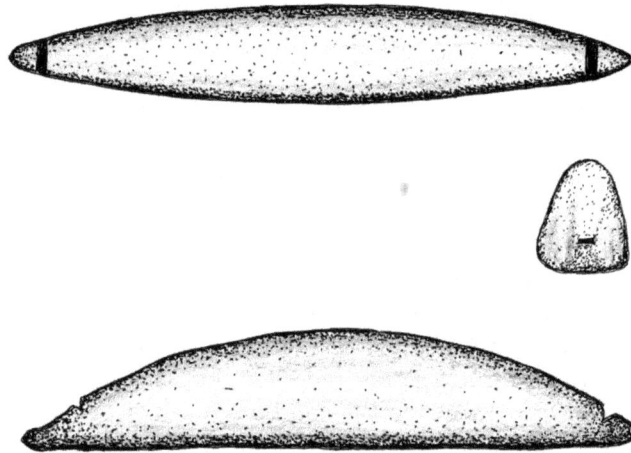

Figure 23. Atlatl stone

The Archaeological and Historical Services of Eastern Washington University—at site 45SP266, on aboriginal Spokan territory at Latah Creek—discovered an intact stone atlatl, estimated to be 9000 years old (Gough, pers. comm.). It is shown above, and is about 15 cm in length.

Universally, the technology (a spring-mass system) of using atlatls required four components: a fletched but flexible dart, a semi-rigid throwing board or platform, a projectile point, and the atlatl weight made of stone attached by lashings set in narrow "V" on each end of the underside flexible throwing board to be more aerodynamic. Atlatl weights—sometimes called banner stones—were commonly attached at mid-section of the throwing board or slightly toward the notched end (Elpel 2005). When reviewing known examples of throwing boards used by some Amerindian peoples, the throwing platform is found to be fashioned from wood approximately 40 to 50 cm in length, scraped or split to give the platform a top and bottom surfaces. The width varied from 3 to 5 cm, depending upon the maker; the thickness was one to 1.5 cm. The rear end of the board supported an attached cone-shaped protrusion secured into a cone-shaped recess or notch in the end of the dart (spear) to stabilize the missile when throwing. The other end of the platform was sometimes indented on opposite sides to accommodate the hunter's thumb and forefinger though there are other examples of how the platform was held. Unfortunately, wooden throwing boards are easily perishable. The type of large projective point varied in stone type and general shape according to the intended task.

Atlatl stones were of different design and weight, but usually loaf-shaped and highly polished. Some have inscribed designs, as with the Spokan example. Simulated studies of atlatl weights—by Peets (1960:110) and Perkins (1993, 1996)—indicate that the "distance and force of a thrown dart will be 2½ times greater than without it" (Perkins 1996 and 2005). The "weight increases the amount of energy of an atlatl" (Perkins 1996) because when the dart is accelerated by the atlatl, it flexes and stores energy like a spring, and "At some point during the swing, after the atlatl is no longer accelerating sufficiently to cause further compression of the dart, the dart uses its stored energy to push itself away from the atlatl" (Perkins 1993:n.p.).

Slings

Little could be recalled regarding the use of a *sling* (*čłqʷésšʔntʔn* - "put something string-like around a rock") (Smith 1936-8:680), a weapon once commonly used by children for hunting small animals and birds. There is no certainty if men used the sling for hunting. However, one elderly man could recall the deadly accuracy of the sling when demonstrated by his aging grandfather against various types of ground rodents. Elders have also said that to be proficient, the hunter must "sleep with his sling," which means he must practice frequently.

Slings were simple but effective devices made from a single narrow length of rawhide 40 to 50 cm long with a wide section in the wide middle pad for holding the stone missile. The release end was held tightly between thumb and forefinger, the other more-lengthy end was wound round the second finger. Aside from using a *miniature bow and arrow* (*t't'aʔpm'ín'*), young boys were taught and encouraged to use slings. The strategy was to encourage the boy to learn the proper methods of stalking game that required getting as close as possible to the animal, and not necessarily the actual kill, but rather for the youthful hunter to acquire the patience and stealth required with other more complex weapons of hunting when approaching an animal. Boys competed more for distance than accuracy when they were let loose with a fairly rounded stone or sun-hardened, rounded clay projectile; they rarely aimed at anything. Some archaeologists have said how small round stones and hard balls of clay are occasionally found in protected sites (Gough, pers. comm.). Several years ago, a boy would occasionally be seen playing with a *slingshot* (*nqʔéyuʔs*) made from a "Y" shaped *branch* (*čl'šmečst*) of thornberry or ocean spray with a rubber sling fashioned from a tire inner tube, usually made by his father or grandmother, presumably for hunting small animals or practicing his skills on tin cans.

Throwing Sticks

Informants vaguely recollected few details of the throwing stick or rabbit stick, which was a simple yet effective tool in the hands of an *experienced hunter* (*suxʷ čłip*) for killing rabbits, marmots, and smaller animals that tend to inhabit sparsely-treed areas. This implement varied in length and circumference, but ideally the throwing stick was made of a section of hardwood approximately 50 cm in length and usually with the diameter of one's thumb knuckle. The stick was steam/water-bent almost in the middle, and had no flat side surfaces that would have created an unstable flight. Holding it at the feeble end, the person would throw the stick in a side half-swing fairly low to the ground so that it spun in a relatively flat, horizontal maneuver—not unlike a propeller.

It is not known if one end was ever weighted with a small affected stone or hide-wrapped damp clay—as occurs in some cultures—which in effect caused the rabbit stick to rotate in alternately wider cycles with each revolution because the heavier end tended to double the width of killing range (R. Smith, pers. comm.), making the rabbit stick very effective to break one or more of the animal's legs.

One elderly gentleman said how as a boy he occasionally became frustrated or irritated with social matters quite beyond his control, and when he demonstrated his anger his father would loan him a throwing stick, instructing him to go outside and throw the weapon, being careful not to hit anyone. Each time after the boy returned, his father asked if he had hit anything, to which the boy replied "No." When the father asked if he had lost anything, the boy would always say "No." Finally, after several years, the now older boy returned one day after being sent out with his father's now coveted throwing stick, which he had become fairly skilled with, and when asked if he had hit anything, the boy proudly replied "A rabbit." When asked if he had lost anything, the boy finally replied, "Yes, my temper's gone forever." The father told him that the throwing stick was now his, and warned him: "To lose your temper is a way of starving; a piece of wood in your hand is more useful than anger in your heart."

Knives

Probably the greatest variation of form among all hunting or warfare implements was in an individual's knife, one acquired through trade or self-made, particularly later when one could acquire a vastly more efficient and durable steel knife, which held an edge longer than stone, for even an obsidian knife was easily dulled or broken by certain tasks or misuse. A man always carried one or more knives.

A scalping knife was an integral part of a warrior's armamentarium of weapons, as was witnessed by Alexander Ross who commented upon a man's use of weapons, "indeed, one must actually see a warrior to believe with what dexterity and ease he can use each weapon, and how nimbly he can change one for another as occasion may require" (1855, 1:306-7).

Rifles

When the *rifle* (*ululmín'č* - "iron bow") was adopted by the Spokan (circa 1830), it quickly led to major changes in collective hunting strategies. Moreover, the introduction of the rifle, gradually diminished the need for tracking and decoying skills required when using traditional bow and arrow or traps and snares for smaller animals, particularly after the introduction of steel traps. The non-traditional technology of firearms and steel traps proved to be so effective that the events of over-hunting nearly brought about the demise of the beaver, at least in some areas.

However, prior to the introduction of the rifle, a man's ability of being an accomplished *tracker* (*sxʷnʔucšnéłc'ʔem*) was even more apparent, as was the strategy of persistent hunting. At one time, some men had *suméš* to track a specific animal, certainly those of economic significance.

An early account of the vastly disproportionate value for which guns were traded to the Spokan in exchange for beaver pelts was given by Cox, who entered Spokan territory as a clerk for the early Astorians, and wrote of the more obvious material inequities:

> The great object of every Indian was to obtain a gun. Now a good gun could not be had under twenty beaver skins; a few short ones we gave for fifteen: and some idea of the profit may be formed, when I state that the wholesale price of the gun is about one pound seven shillings, while the average value of twenty beaver skins is about twenty-five pounds! Two yards of cloth, which originally cost twelve shillings, would generally bring six or eight beavers, value eight or ten pounds! and so on in proportion for other articles; - but they were satisfied, and we had no cause to complain (1831, I:199).

The first firearms acquired by the Spokan were smooth bore muskets, and much later the more prized and effective percussion rifles were also acquired through trade with trappers and traders. Once acquired, any type of rifle would be "lavishly decorated with brass tacks and vermilion, and provided with a fringed *gun cover* [*nʔep'łc'ʔín'č*], occasionally of buckskin, ornamented here and there with a feather" (Cox 1832:56).

The introduction of American and European multiple-shot firearms, such as the 1890 semi-automatic pump Winchester rim-fire (WRF) .22 rifle and different types and calibers of larger center-fire cartridges were quickly adopted by hunters who became extremely proficient in marksmanship. A definite advantage of the larger calibers of center-fire cartridges was their comparatively long range when hunting large game—sometimes the prey being unaware of the hunter's presence. There were, however, several recognized disadvantages to large bore rifles: the noise of the initial shot could panic other game, and the hide was

288

usually mutilated upon the bullet's exit, on occasion making the hide useless for clothing. Consequently, the small bore rifle and .22 WRF rimfire *ammunition* (*snč'ʔin'č'*) had numerous significant advantages over larger calibers: less costly, lighter weight, used relatively inexpensive ammunition, not as likely to damage a hide, and the noise being not so loud as from larger center-fired cartridges. A further logistical advantage of the ubiquitous .22 WRF cartridge was that most animals and some birds were not so frightened when hunted with the .22 caliber rifle. Once acquired, this smaller caliber rifle became a favorite caliber—even today a few such rifles exist. Many elders have commented upon a hunter's skill in bringing down deer with a head-shot using this highly versatile and lightweight .22 caliber rifle.

With the introduction of firearms, pistols were rarely owned by the Spokan, because they were considered to be ineffective for hunting; only a few men in later years possessed shotguns.

Traps, Snares, and Deadfalls

In the Spokan territory, extensive semi-arid riverine terraces, lowland woodland areas, and transitional vegetation zones supported a complex but well understood food web of land mammals that facilitated year-round trapping and snaring. The Spokan used the *trap* (*ʕacm'in'*), the *snare* (*nʕ'aʕ'acústn'* - "tie around the neck" or *či qsaʔcúsiʔ* - "I will snare"), and the deadfall (*č'ney'n*) year-round. Linguistically and technically, they distinguished between the *small snare* (*snacús*) and the *large snare* (*snq'aqcús*).

Nearly all types of snares employed various restrictive devices that encircled the neck of an animal, often suffocating or breaking the neck of the prey. Even for such large animals as deer, the noose was suspended from a fixed and stable tree at an appropriate height over a natural or deliberately restricted section of an animal trail. An effective method for snaring was to bend a fairly stout pine tree over the trail with the attached noose so that the triggering device, part of which was securely anchored in the ground, was released and sprung upwards when the animal placed its head in the noose. This type of snare was particularly effective, for deer usually follow a trail with their heads down, if not alarmed, thereby facilitating the snaring of the animal when it unknowingly places its head into the suspended noose. In some instances the advantage of a spring or tension trap would suspend smaller animals up and off the trail, preventing their being eaten by other creatures. A noose was made from different flexible materials, classified as *p'enép*, which included fiber, hair, strand, and rope for netting and traps. Smith described how in winter a deer was snared by a noose suspended over a narrow opening between two restrictive wing walls (1951:192). A hanging circular braided deer noose could be held in place by coating the noose with the sticky glue made from boiling deer hooves. Apparently deer were attracted by the scent of the glue (Schaeffer 1934-37, I-178:2).

Trapping (*nʔk'ʷk'ʷalk'ʷlc'qn'*) of animals was done by men throughout the year, but the most intense efforts were during winter when there was greater stress on food supplies, and when the *animal's pelt* (*spúm*) was of prime quality. In winter trappers were mainly occupied in processing the valuable beaver pelts. Land mammal traps and snares had no *special powers* (*k'ʷƛ'cinm*), though a hunter might sing over a device to encourage its success (Ross 1998:273). The trap was a larger device that effectively incapacitated or contained the animal within a structure, whereas a snare simply snared an animal's head or leg, and any trapper could provide sad and even poignant accounts of an animal chewing off a restrained leg to gain release.

A critical period of training for young, potential hunters commenced at an age when boys were taught and encouraged to develop their skills in trapping. A successful youth was accorded praise by his peers and family. Often the quest of boys learning to trap and snare was provided by small game, such as quail and rabbits being caught in unbaited snares set at the entrance of small man-made nest-like structures of grass and bush. A variety of plants were used for snaring small animals, such as Indian hemp, *braided grass* (*q'eyc'ɬsupulexʷ*), and strips of cedar-root. A boy often first used fiber rendered from stinging nettle stalks for making snares. The green stalk was first gently crushed and split open and the pith removed before rolling the stalk between one's palms to make the material more pliable. Several sections or more, depending upon the type of animal being sought, were *plaited* (*q'ic*) to a desired length.

Not only did young boys learn the techniques of trapping, they were also taught the value of pre-hunt ritual, patience, and respect for their quarry, very little of which is done today since there is little need. An example of this radical change was personally observed in 1974, and may illustrate the general loss of tracking and hunting skills since the early 1950s. When a young man wished to capture some coyotes, which at the time were being bought by itinerant furriers, he asked to borrow his great grandfather's still well-cared traps that had not been used for almost 60 years, and the old man gave his permission. Soon after that the great grandson, attired in his camouflage pants from the Vietnam War, left the house with the traps. The elder, obviously exasperated, sighed, shook his head full of white hair, explaining why he *worried* (*xʷahist*) more about the return of his traps than the fate of the coyotes, knowing the coyotes were quite safe. When asked why, the gentleman explained, somewhat incredulously, that coyotes would never approach traps set by someone who had not followed the correct propitiation protocol, and as a consequence, no coyotes would give up their lives for such a trapper, regardless of his modern technology. In fact, not only would the young man fail to catch any coyotes, but the hopeful trapper's elder would be lulled to sleep by the coyotes' laughter and ceaseless yapping. And further, his great grandson, due to his lack of respect for the coyotes, would suffer a tormented sleep from their laughter. The old gentleman went on to explain how the *fur pelt of a coyote* (*spl'yehél'xʷ*) killed in winter was more valuable because of the length and thickness of the pelt, which would have a sheen to it—one the grandson would not see.

There is no evidence or memory of the Spokan ever using long, tapering funnel traps for catching quail as was once done in California. Yet, short funnel structures were used to restrict an animal from turning once it had entered the funnel. Young boys were encouraged to catch rabbits by shoving a forked stick into a rabbit hole, and once engaged, the boy slowly twisted the stick to further entrap the animal by its hair before gently pulling the animal from the hole. A trapper's success reflected an accumulation of skill and intimate knowledge of the environment and habits of the region's fauna.

Delayed predation devices often required less intensive labor in construction and maintenance, and were effective for snaring small animals and birds, located in areas known to support relatively stable populations of small game. However, passive traps and snares were not always an efficient means of taking larger mammals, given the expenditure of energy for construction, and because it often required an inordinate amount of inspection time by the hunter once the predation device was set. Occasionally, the time, effort, and even the trapped game might be wasted if a predator animal happened to consume the unprotected quarry, sometimes even destroying the predation device.

Small game were taken with trap and snare—animals such as the *marten* (*ʔor'áɬqʷlt*) mink, marmot, *otter* (*Lutrea canadensis - ltkʷúkʷ*), wolverine, *fisher* (*Martes pennanti - cišpsis*), badger, muskrat, and porcupine. Fish bait was used to attract mink, whereas, "Pine squirrel was used as bait for lynx" (Schaeffer 1934-37, I-51:30). Wilson mentioned how otter and beaver were caught, but unfortunately neglected to describe in detail how the marten was taken, only that it was trapped "with an ingenious native contrivance something like the figure-of-four trap, so as not to damage the fur" (1866:297). Lord described how the figure-four configuration was fashioned:

Now we make the figure of 4, which rests upon the horizontal bar, and at the same time bears up the tree or 'fall.' The figure of '4' is easily made; the vertical piece has two notches cut in to it, one in the center for the horizontal piece to rest and fit in, and a second at the top to receive the end of the oblique piece, which is cut to a wedge shape at both ends. The horizontal piece has one notch to take the end of the oblique; on the other rests the fall (1867:314).

During the summer, both the fur and the meat of the marmot were highly prized, for as Lord explained:

[The Indian] never tires of hunting and trapping the little animal, delighting to use his jacket in the fabrication of rugs. The hair being thick, the marmot-robe keeps out both wet and cold, and stands an immens

[sic] even better. When skinned a long peeled stick is thrust through the body, from tail to head; thus place slantwise, one end being fast in the ground, the treasured morsel is slowly roasted over a gentle fire (1866, 2:195).

Pitfalls and deadfalls were used for *grey wolf (Canis lupus - nc'i?cn)*, cougar, *red fox (Vulpes vulpes - sẋʷoẋʷó)*, bobcat *(Lynx rufus fasciatus - p'ič'n')*, and black bear, though some have claimed that the cougar was seldom intentionally trapped, being such a dangerous and even feared animal. When trapping such animals, a hunter used a type of meat as bait that the sought animal was known to prefer. For example, a cougar deadfall would be baited with a fresh deer hoof, and "those for lynx, usually with portions of rabbits or pheasants; likewise necessarily fresh" (Smith 1951:272). It has been stated that "Neither cougars nor lynxes ate the bait—they ate nothing which they did not kill themselves, but they were, nevertheless, attracted to the trap by these materials" (Smith 1951:80). Some claim they never intentionally hunted the cougar, but cougars were sometimes caught and killed by a deadfall, when, "baited with a fresh hoof, neither cougars or lynx ate the bait, ate only what they had killed; but still would investigate castor" (Smith 1951:80). When trapping a cougar, careful consideration was always given when baiting a trap.

If single or twined strips of hemp or some comparable material was not available for setting snares for small animals, the man "made snares out of the [multiple stands of] hair of his head, with which he caught some small fish; and he also occasionally succeeded in killing a bird" (Cox 1832:100).

Despite several accounts, there is no evidence that indicates the Spokan ever attempted to catch deer and elk with pitfalls or deadfalls, presumably due to several reasons. Constructing and maintaining these types of traps consumed a great amount of time and energy, and gave no guarantee of success. Also, the chances of large confined animals being scavenged by other animals was ever present—leading to contamination of the meat or complete destruction of the animal; but even worse, the loss of its hide. Hunters were quite aware that open hunting of ungulata, though not always predictable, was considered more productive with bow and arrow and afforded the benefits of socialization and shared knowledge that always accompanied collective hunting.

Despite the recordings of Teit (1930) and Ray (1933) that hunters used seeps, springs, and salt licks for setting traps, the Spokan claimed they *never* set traps, snares, or deadfalls at a spring or *naturally occurring deer licks (snc?iłnqs-tn or sn?oyilémn)* for fear of contaminating these sites, which animals might later avoid. This notion of trapping or hunting with any method at a spring was considered disrespectful to both the mammals and water spirits, and, if violated, it was believed to be the main reason for game to leave an area. Smith (1936-8:252) claimed the Kalispel never hunted at watering places, but did so at deer licks—usually at night, early morning or early evening. As a consequence, the Spokan contend that all traps and snares were normally located along known game trails, ones situated at the end of diverging lines of vertically placed sticks, or bordered by strategically placed bushes, rock cairns, or stone walls which tended to direct the course of animals' trails and even along Indian *pathways (snqlixʷáqs)* to a set trap or snare.

During the historical period, whether as a result of the availability of salt, or of deer and elk hunters who, dismissing the consequences of spirit and resource violation, commenced to salt an area by either pouring commercial salt (or later salt blocks) on the ground or boiling salted water, decanting the thickened liquid off into a container, and repeating the process three times. This saturated solution of salt would be poured on the ground as a saltlick to entice deer and elk for purposes of hunting. Man-made saltlicks were usually maintained by a family and located near brush blinds within bow and arrow, or, later, within rifle range. In addition to *man-made salt licks (st'm'ol'e?xʷ)*, hunters were well aware of the location of all natural deer licks.

Setting the trap (hecq'q'c'm'i') required skill and considerable care to avoid contaminating the device with human odor. Open areas that bordered woodlands, and the edges of streams, were considered more productive when *trapping for fur bearing animals (ʕaʕcm'i -"to trap")*. The acceptance and use of metal traps presented the same major problem of human scent with both delayed predation and active hunting. Prior to hunting and the handling of traps and snares, conscious efforts were made to remove, or at best mask, human scents. For the trapper, this involved prior participation in a sweathouse, and after applying counter scents on traps, snares, and any cordage, which was accomplished primarily by rubbing traps, snares, and cordage with different plants to conceal human odors, particularly when working with deer traps.

One of the most effective plants used to mask human scent was *yarrow* (*Achillia millefolium L.* - *nk'ʷk'ʷálk'ʷlč'qn* - or *q'ʷcq'ʷcwiʔhúpaʔs* "chipmunk's tail"). *Coyote mint* (*Monardella adoratissima* Benth. var., *Odoratissima*, forma *odoratissima* - *x̣ax̣ałníw'et* - "menthol smell"), that was "rich in an aromatic oil with a penetrating odor" (St. John 1963:386), was effective for not only removing human scent from predation tools, but purifying weapons that had killed game, and purifying contaminated meat that was unknowingly shared with a menstruating woman (Ray 1933:135; Turner *et al.* 1980:110). Even an *old trap* (*č'n'eyn*), prior to being reused, would be similarly treated. However, when camping, items with *human scent* (*čłén'eʔ*) were purposely left near food caches to frighten away animals from trespassing.

There were problems if any trapper failed to observe certain sacred rituals to ensure some degree of success for trapping. The elders who had trapped were quick to agree that the most difficult animal to trap was the red fox, which was introduced from the eastern United States. Elderly trappers have related how this wily creature will on occasion run with the coyote, and will circle a trap "for half a night and half a day" before making a close approach. Few trappers could claim success—hence the expression "To run with the foxes and hunt with the hounds."

Even after the introduction of steel traps, Lord readily acknowledged the innovative skills of the indigenous trappers who showed the Euro-Americans how to make and use the deadfall, or what he calls the fall-trap, for the elusive martin:

> Two or three different kinds of fall-traps are employed to catch pine martens [...] To commence, we must build a half-circle, with large stones, to the height of about three feet; this done, we next procure a tolerably heavy tree, drag it to the stone building we have constructed, and lay it across the entrance. The heavy end should be the furthest away, the lighter end we poise carefully upon an arrangement of peeled sticks [...] This contrivance and one end of the tree or 'fall' are together supported on a smooth stick, which is built in amongst the stones composing the half-circle. This support stick must project horizontally from the centre of the hollow of the wall, at a height of about three feet from the ground; it needs to be firmly fixed, and must be tapered to a point, and polished as smooth as an ebony ruler. The length of this support has to be regulated by the depth of the side walls; its pointed end ought to be just six inches with the entrance walls, against the ends of which the tree or 'fall' traverses. A tempting bit of rabbit or grouse carefully skinned, for the marten is most fastidious in its tastes—if the meat is at all tainted or dirtied in the preparation it is useless as a lure—is securely fastened to a loop of cord made from the inner bark of the *cedar tree* (*Thuja gigantea*); this loop is slid upon the supporting stick, and pushed on until it reaches the hinder most part of the wall (1867:313-4).

The established etiquette of trapping and snaring necessitated a man to run his trapline almost daily, simply because any trapped animal was easy prey to predators that would consume an animal secured by these devices. As a consequence, if a passerby discovered and removed any trapped or snared animal, he would invariably give it to the known owner. After new traps had been set, the owner might *watch his traps all night* (*č'em'tw'íl'iʔ*), sometimes for several days.

Prior to Euro-American commercial trapping, winter trapping was an important and often a critical activity to supplement depleted food stores. And yet on occasion, more important than the gain of meat was the acquisition of pelts—most notably that of the ermine and the long-tailed weasel, which were in great demand during the fall and winter, when the fur was white, for the manufacture of medicine or pipe bags and articles of clothing. In summer also the then dark pelted short-tailed weasel was caught by trapping.

Trapping commenced in late fall, continuing through the winter or until the snow *became too deep* (*qʷúytn* - "high snow drift"). The most difficult condition for trappers was when their traps were covered by high drifts of loose, *dry snow* (*hi qʷqʷil'*), or when *frozen rain* (*šetiš*) sealed empty steel traps motionless, or the bait scent was obliterated by accumulated snow or ice. Most successful trappers would intermittently work their traplines for one to two months—depending upon weather and snow depth, completing their vigilance when it was apparent that they were near to over-trapping.

Though the construction of predation devices varied with each trapper, the mechanics of each device were similar for each particular type of trap. A *pole trap* (*č'néyn*)—sometimes called a squirrel pole—was constructed by leaning a lodge pole at a 45° angle against a tree and carefully securing the upper end to the supporting tree. A *pole trapper* (*sxʷč'néynm*) then secured a series of closely spaced semi-rigid slipknots made of twisted rawhide loops along a pole to catch any *Western grey squirrel* (*Sciurus griseus* - *ʔis'č'*) or *red squirrel* (*Tamiasciurus hudsonicus* - *ʔiistč'* or *lʔisc'č*) attempting to climb through the loops, that were only so narrow as to accommodate the animal's head.

The first type of trap young boys were introduced to was the pole trap, which used tightening nooses to catch squirrels and other rodents, which do not attempt to reverse direction once their heads are in a noose, but rather continue to push forward and become further ensnared. Often a number of squirrels were caught on a single pole, because each one hung suspended away from the pole, permitting continued traffic to unoccupied loops along the pole after others had been snared. With the introduction of metal wire, the pole trap became even more effective with the use of looped wire nooses instead of rawhide loops. Yet this type of trap was later abandoned.

A second type of *snare trap* (*snʔaʔacúsm'*) used for small animals was a structurally simple yet effective *tension trap* (*q'm'éy'eʔ*) that consisted of a frame-like structure held in place by two side vertical stakes on a game trail. The entire device was always situated under a tree and *concealed* (*scwukʷwékʷs* - "his hidden things") with a covering of carefully placed brush and grasses, and had only two openings: one to the game trail and one leading from a restricted trail, essentially creating a tunnel. The trapping mechanism of the tension trap consisted of one of two different types of triggering mechanism. The most common device consisted of two "V"-notched sticks. One was driven firmly into the ground and accommodated the notched "V" of the second stick, which held the reversed top V-toggle in place by tension created by a length of fiber rope made from *sp'óq'ʷiʔ* secured to a bent limb of a covering tree. When an inquiring animal sprang the noose, by taking the bait, it was lifted high enough to be safe from animal predators. There were conflicting oral accounts as to whether the Spokan ever caught deer with foot snares or with tension pole snares. Presumably, the neighboring Coeur d'Alene did not employ these methods (Teit 1930:103).

Another method of trapping learned by young boys was a suspended spring snare, consisting of a tension-held single line with a baited hook, which was sprung when the bait was taken, thereby hoisting the engaged animal well above the ground. This was often created by simply securing a flexible willow stake in the ground, bending the temporarily held baited hook over the game trail until it was sprung.

A twitch-up snare was an effective method to catch small mammals and ground-walking birds in an often artificially restricted pathway, and was easily made by attaching a noose to a bent sapling held by a simple pressure triggering device, but with no bait being used. The noose was large enough for the head of the animal to go through, but not enough for the shoulders or rest of its body to escape. The advantage of this type of snare was that the released sapling kept the carcass high above the ground and out of reach from most predators.

The same principle was used for trapping much larger game. For instance, a spring-pole snare was used in catching deer. In this case a young tree was bent until held firmly to the ground, that was held in tension with an attached notched toggle hook, or it "was bent over and tied to another small tree with a strip of bark which was easily broken. When the deer becomes caught in the [slip] noose and jerked the tree, the lashing broke, allowing the pole to snap upward and raise the animal suddenly from the ground" (Smith 1951:193).

Deadfall traps (*č'néyn*) were designed for securing large game, employing the simple but effective method of a heavy log falling on and usually killing the prey when a tripping device was activated by the animal's intrusion. Typically, the smaller end of the log was set on the ground and the heavier end was supported on a four-sided crib of loosely but carefully stacked loose sticks. As with most ground traps and snares, the prey was encouraged to enter the narrow course way by funneling the path with obstructions, as well as by the scent of the bait. The most successful lure was a beaver's scent gland, which would attract any animal, or a tethered live bird while the entrails of fish or animal further encouraged a creature's investigation. As soon as the bait was disturbed, the trigger mechanism released and dropped the heavy end of the log on the animal. The so-called figure-four was used commonly for deadfalls. There is no evidence that the Spokan used poisoned bait in traps and snares, even though they had knowledge of at least six types of plant poisons. Rather, meat tainted with *poison* (*nčn'cíntn*) was used only for killing *wild* (*ʔuw'áqʷuʔqʷti* or *sqʷqʷáw'qʷuʔt* - "undomesticated") dogs that became bothersome to a camp or village.

An early observation of how the Spokan used a type of baited deadfall to catch wolves was noted by Cox, who, in discussing the ravaging effects of an increased wolf population upon horses:

> The Indians catch numbers of them in traps, which they set in the vicinity of those places where their tame horses are sent to graze. The traps are merely excavations covered with slight switches and hay, and baited with meat, &c., into which the wolves fall, and being unable to extricate themselves, they perish by famine, or the knife of the Indian. These destructive animals annually destroy numbers of horses; particularly during the winter season, when the latter get entangled in the snow; in which situation they become an easy prey to their light-footed pursuers, ten or fifteen of which will often fasten on one animal, and with their long fangs in a few minutes separate the head from the body (1832:211).

Continuing to discuss the effects of the wolf's aggressive predation upon other large animals, Cox's inquiries and astute observations lead him to describe how effective their social organization was in meeting their individual and collective needs. But first he described the means of communication necessary for the wolf pack when maneuvering to kill grazing Indian horses, "The first announcement of their approach was a few shrill currish barks at intervals [...] These were were answered by similar barking from an opposite direction, until the sounds gradually approximated, and at length ceased on the junction of the different parties" (1832:212).

The missionary Reverend Elkanah Walker, when describing the location of adequate winter grazing range for the mission's horses, acknowledged the problem of wolves, which he poisoned with some success:

> They say there are places on the Spokane River within eight or ten miles where there is but little snow. Should we remove then there, we should be compelled to go & stay with them or the wolves would destroy them. They are so thick & desperate that we dare not leave our horses out during the night. Quite a number of horses have been bitten & some actually killed. A horse within four rods [66 feet] of the house was bitten by a wolf (Drury 1976:114)

An effective method for trapping small mammals was an unbaited *flat snare* (*nʔʔacústn'*), strategically placed and pegged at the entrance of the animal's burrow. Another technique of killing burrowing animals was to precariously balance one end of a large flat rock atop another *flat rock* (*sƛ'šn'esšn'*). The raised end was precariously held up by a *forked stick* (*nq'éyuʔs*) that had bait tied to the support, and easily collapsed when moved. Young boys usually set this type of deadfall for gophers and badgers, which were not eaten nor were their hides taken; the sole purpose of the exercise was simply for young boys to perfect their hunting and trapping skills.

Strings made of Indian hemp were used for both secular and supernatural reasons, even when attempting to gather and hunt deer. An elderly and experienced hunter would select two young boys, and after giving each boy a great length of hemp string, he would instruct each boy to walk in opposite directions, essentially forming a great circle. As each boy walked, he would tie pieces of the hemp to low branches and the tops of bushes; the purpose was to entice any deer of the area to enter the circle, not being able to escape because of the hemp ties. The hunters would easily dispatch the 'paralyzed' deer.

It was not long after the eventual introduction of *steel traps* (*ʔacpéyn*) that many fur-bearing animals were traded to professional White trappers and entrepreneurs on a commercial basis. As a result, beaver population was drastically depleted, leading to the beaver nearly becoming extinct within the Spokan territory. The demand for *winter game* (*čnk'ʷéłc'eʔ*) required the trappers to spend sometimes several weeks working their traplines and skinning their kill. As noted earlier, commercial Indian trappers would sometimes spend one or more winter months living in relative isolation in simple brush, log or canvas shelters. The logistics of time and distance in running a large string of traps sometimes necessitated the maintenance of several dwellings, which, if a *trapper* (*sxʷʔaʔcim'*) was successful, afforded a main base facility for cleaning, processing, and storing pelts. Unfortunately, a commercial trapper's time and effort more often contributed only marginally, if at all, to his family's subsistence base. Even before the reduction in the number of many commercially sought fur-bearing animals, trappers were getting only meager profit from the goods they traded with fur-buyers.

Moreover, many commodities and foodstuffs acquired through trading were invariably less nutritious than indigenous foods, frequently containing deleterious preservatives to which the Spokan people were unaccustomed. Later, the introduction of refined foods and the increasing use of sugar, began a widespread and unfortunate decline in the overall health of the Native American people, including the Spokan.

The introduction of a non-traditional predation technology and cash-cropping created a demonstrable effect upon subsistence strategies, intergroup trade relations, and in some instances the decline of certain fur-bearing animal populations. It was believed that steel traps and metal components used in snares had no special powers, as did traditional fish and animal traps—those involving communal participation to gather large numbers of fish in a relatively brief period of time. Yet elders maintained that they had often sung over the traps, regardless of size or type, thereby announcing their dependency and humility to encourage success with both the traditional traps and the introduced steel traps.

Pit-Snaring Eagles

Prior to acquiring firearms, raptors like bald eagles and *osprey* (*Pandion haliaetus* - *c'íx̌ʷc'x̌ʷ* or *c'íx̌ʷc'úx̌ʷ*) known as a fish hawk were captured using a method of decoying that attracted the bird to a concealed hunter, who then ensnared the bird by pit-snaring, which was a dangerous and tedious endeavor, and not always successful. The best sites for hunting eagles were in close proximity to the Spokane River and the mouth of both Little and Big Tschimakain, Blue, and Sand Creeks where special hunting pits had been constructed for snaring eagles during the spring and throughout much of the year when eagles and ospreys used these waterways for fishing. Some believed eagle snaring was best done late in the morning, when the birds used the rising thermals and/or orographic lift from sun-warmed steep basalt or granite walls, to soar aloft looking for rabbits and rodents.

The area of the Chewelah-Spokan Group bordering the Colville River and *Chewelah Creek* (*čłčamé*) supported numerous rock-based aeries where pit snaring was done. One type of *hunting pit* (*sn'ʔemtéw'stn x̌ʷl' nmlqnúps*), was always located in a southwest facing talus (loose granite or basalt) close to a river, and initially used large, *loose rocks* (*sn'scosls*) for construction. Smaller stones were first removed to form a circular depression at a depth of approximately one meter, and carefully stacked to form a low, circular wall with interleaving flat stones, atop of which dead branches were laid on a single stout section of pole to support the covering of fir boughs. Some pit covers were made with numerous horizontal poles that were similarly covered with fir boughs. A piece of salmon or deer meat was placed atop the main bearing pole, near a relatively small opening in the fir bough roof of the *blind* (*x̌lémmn*). Several elders recall hearing of a wood frame covered with *canvas* (*č'n'eyn*) being used as a concealment cover.

Another type of pit, using the same principle of decoying, was made by excavating the earth to a depth of one meter with top diameter of a meter and a half—large enough to accommodate a crouching adult—which was covered with a conical frame of small lengths of ocean spray or Osage orange branches. The frame was matted with several newly-made tule mats and covered with earth. As with the first type of pit, at the apex was an opening large enough for a man to reach an eagle when it landed to take the *bait* (*m'él'w'ey'n'* or *m'l'w'éy'n'* - "any bait") that was affixed to a pole that slanted in line just above the roof (STHC).

Another method for hunting raptor birds was to build an upwind smoke fire from green antelope brush or grease wood that sometimes attracted accipiters, buteos, and other predator birds—primarily eagles—to the vicinity of a hunter's lair as it searched for rodents escaping the fire.

Prior to hunting, a man always sweated to reduce human odors and to better ensure success by solitary propitiation. Once in position, the hunter waited patiently as he observed the *bird circling* (*syenwl'ši*) lower and lower until it alighted on the structure, one large enough to support an eagle for perching. The hunter would grab a leg as the eagle landed on the secured live decoy. The bait was usually a live rabbit, pheasant, or rodent. There was debate among Spokan elders if live bait was ever used, for an eagle will always attempt to ascend immediately upon grabbing a live bait—animal or fish–whereas a different bird would roost after gathering a piece of meat—eating some or all of the bait before flying (Turney-High 1937:113). The use of live bait was critical for snaring raptors—primarily meat-eating birds—since they have relatively large talons and beaks, and use only their talons, instead of their beaks, to capture prey.

The bow and arrow was not considered an appropriate means when pit-hunting, because of the obvious difficulty in manipulative skill required while under a restricted covering. But perhaps a better explanation is that a hunter's respect for so magnificent an animal was accorded a more personal encounter or challenge by fettering the eagle with his bare hands. Furthermore, there was always the danger of the hunter sustaining a wound to a companion hunter with a mishandled arrow in such a confined and covered space. The only known early depiction of pit-snaring, in this instance of the Coeur d'Alene, is a primitive but descriptive schematic and polychrome painting by Father Nicolas Point (1842:146 and 1967:149), of a deer pit measuring approximately 2 m in depth and 3 m in width and length.

An example of the Spokan hunter's ability, appreciation, and ingenuity of his surroundings in pit-snaring is illustrated by the methodology required for capturing the common *sparrowhawk* (*Falco sparvertus* Lind. - *ʔiy'éc'ic*) and common *night hawk* (*Chordeiles minor* - *sp'ʕás* or *sp'as* or *ʔiy'éc'ic*). When a night hawk dives in pursuit of rodents, the long leading primary feathers produce a booming sound when diving. A hunter, concealed in a pit near the egg-laden nest of a nighthawk, imitates this sound by tying to the fletched end of an arrow a 20 to 25 cm length of thin, narrow buckskin, to which was attached a nighthawk tail feather. The arrow, when shot into the air, and upon the missile's descent, would make the desired booming sound on account of the attached feather. As was explained, the nighthawk interprets this sound as that of an intruder and consequently is dispatched upon the bird's return. Though the nighthawk was not eaten by the Spokan, it was much sought for its feathers, particularly the long outermost primary feather on the end of each wing for later decoying. In the past, the bird's tail feathers were said to have been used as a simple head dress with feathers placed vertically in a tight headband.

Many years ago, an elderly man told the author of an eagle hunter his grandfather knew as a boy, a hunter whose right hand was severely scarred from being shredded while catching an adult bald eagle from a concealed pit. Young boys were told not to speak of the man's apparently frightening scars, nor to ever speak of his proof of ordeal; only to respect the man for his pain and bravery.

Game Enclosures

Any type of game funnel enclosure—permanent or temporary—was strategically laid out according to the topography of the selected area—one that recognized an established *deer trail* (*nutsšis* or *č'ʔulix^w sx^wuytis*) that frequently traversed along the bottoms of draws. There has been no evidence to show if the Spokan used a *permanent stone game enclosure* (*č'łpaq'mn* - "arranged circle of men"), but it was known they used a *temporary deer fence* (*sč'cš*) for deer hunting, as there is limited archaeological evidence of cairns or trenches that suggest game enclosures (Ross 1993). Only through limited recorded oral history (Elmendorf

1935-6) and comparative ethnography (Ray 1930a:80-81; Teit 1930:102) can this method of predation strategy and technology be reconstructed.

However, recently discovered in two near-adjacent canyon areas, are two unique examples of previously unrecorded series of staggered waist-high deer barrier walls, constructed using on-site flat granite slab rocks (Ross 1993). These are cultural features once used in herding deer. Each canyon site has a series of these staggered stone walls, each separate, sloping downhill, and facing a depression eroded by spring rain. The basically funnel-shaped configuration of walls narrows as the topography slopes down the surface of each narrow canyon. When hunting and herding deer into this structure, it is assumed that approximately ten to twenty or more hunters could effectively herd deer into the upper end of the canyon, and into the parallel walls of *loose talis* (*ntmpénč*). The loose rock forced the fleeing deer to follow an erratic and narrow course through a series of these alternating *staggered stone walls* (*člém*ʔ - "enclosures"), which served to conceal previously waiting hunters, and forced the fleeing deer to follow a converging and constricted route that eventually opened into a corral-like enclosure at the base of the canyon, where the few surviving deer were dispatched. These remarkable and intact examples of simple but efficient dry-wall deer barriers are situated in two relatively remote areas on the present Spokane Indian Reservation, ones that have not been vandalized and remain as they were first built. These still intact features are quite evident, and yet until recently there was no recollection that they ever existed.

When available, the strategically placed long branches of trailing blackberry branches served effectively to direct animals into traps and snares. Interestingly, the only recorded example of transplanting by the Spokan may be the blackberry, which, according to an elderly Spokan man, was done not for the location or availability of food, but to entice and then confine deer to a designated killing area. Of interest, regarding the debate of transplanting, women would carefully remove the root system with digging sticks, wrap the roots in moist buckskin, and transport them to an intended site for *replanting* (*heł q'ʷ olłq*).

Ideally, a semi-circle game enclosure or deer fence of piled brush was located at the end of a downhill draw that had talus slopes which essentially forced the game into the down-slope enclosure. The only visible egress was through a one to one and a half meter opening, further restricted by placing several stout sticks of wood horizontally near the bottom, with the top pole or stick approximately 40 to 50 cm from the ground, forcing a deer to reduce speed before attempting to jump the obstacle. Various methods were used to suspend a loop of sinew as a garrote braided nose was wrapped with mountain ash bark and covered with fresh tamarack pitch to facilitate its closing about the neck or horns of an entrapped deer.

In the case of any type of deer enclosure, whenever a sufficient number of deer had been killed, the leader or an attending chief would terminate the killing and make a decision to release those deer that had not been dispatched, knowing that to kill a large number of animals would eventually result in fewer deer. This understanding of stewardship applied whenever collective hunting took place, except with deer-jumps because the stampeded animals were impossible to be stopped.

Funnel Enclosures

Another simple but effective technology for killing large numbers of deer was the construction of large funnel-type enclosures strategically located on relatively flat ground, often along the riverine terraces of the Spokane River. More commonly, straight but converging wing-like stone and brush fences, approximately 20 to 25 m long, which were constructed so that deer being driven would be forced toward the narrow end of the enclosure where the end of the funnel enclosure was constricted by a narrow brush wall lower than the converging wing walls. At the lower end of the enclosure, two stout lodge poles were secured vertically by burying the butt ends on either side of the low brush or stone walls, to which a *noose* (*shúł*) of deer sinew cord was attached at an appropriate height to encircle a deer's head as it attempted to jump the wall. Elders claim that fawns captured during a collective hunt were not always killed, unless the spotted hide was sought, which was often the case. On occasion, fawns, young coyotes, wolves, bear cubs, and immature geese, crows, and magpies were kept as pets until they wandered or flew away (Gidley 1979:52).

To assist hunters in controlling the behavior and direction of deer, anthropomorphic-like scarecrow figures were sometimes used in controlling the behavior and intended direction of deer. Linguistically, the word *scarecrow* (*čnʔékʷmn*) applies to the specific use of small *stick figures* (*t'cɬáq'mn*) that were placed in rows, one on either side of the entrance of funnel traps, to force the path of an animal to the trap. To make the stick figures more humanoid in appearance, women wrapped lengths of narrow buckskin on the extremities. Burnt moccasins and smoldering yarrow or sage were placed atop stick figures that formed a large circle with a long-funneled opening into an enclosed area, which hunters would force the running and frightened deer into. The malodorous scent of the burnt hide, and the symbolic humanoid figures, presumably confused and even panicked the deer into following what seemed like their only avenue of escape.

From all accounts describing the various methods of collective deer hunting, the use of unburnt or burnt moccasins was often a critical strategy, particularly when hunting large numbers of deer. Curtis has described two methods of group hunting, one of which used burnt moccasins which have a very strong and offensive odor that apparently contained the deer within a given area:

> The method of driving game by hanging burnt moccasins, was learned, according to the Spokan, in a dream. The originator collected all the old moccasins available, and hung them on trees around a fairly extensive basin. Then he sent four men in to drive the deer out to the edge. Of course the animals would not pass the man-smelling moccasins, and were shot whenever they came into view and stopped in fright. A Spokan informant says that he himself saw a hundred and ninety-nine deer killed in the first drive of this kind used by his people (1907-30, 7:70).

Circle Drive or Surround

One can only speculate that certain methods of animal predation by humans, such as decoying, stalking, and encircling, and even driving game over cliffs by humans, was learned from early observation of other animals when hunting. The most successful and productive method of collective deer hunting was the *circle drive* (*stɬáq'm* - "deer drive"), when twenty to forty or more men would encircle a large area to drive the deer to a central point where they were dispatched. Prior to any collective hunt, an *individual hunter* (*šiec'*) or designated *leader* (*sxʷšʔít* - "their leader") who possessed deer power, and had dreamed of a successful hunt, would *announce* (*mey'eʔ*) this epiphany or *dream* (*qey'smn* - "I dreamt about it") to his hunting partners. This pre-hunt ceremony was known as *sk'eʔyím*.

Collective mid-winter deer-hunting was always preceded by a ceremony conducted by a leader, who, despite his known social and political skills, would publicly demonstrate his *suméš* by giving a special sweat and a prolonged fast, and provided an opportunity for other men to call upon their *suméš*:

> A leader said he was going to lead a chant - [they] were going to take a sweat bath that evening [and they] danced all night after the sweat & at dawn [they] took another bath - [they] ate nothing all the while - when they have the hot rocks ready [the] leader appoints one to summon the other men - he calls in a high voice to them - only 3 go into the sweathouse at a time - [the] leader & 2 others [go the] first time - [the] leader calls for [the] rocks [and they set 2 hot rocks on [the] floor of the sw[eat] house - [the] leader sticks out [his] head after a while - [there are] lots of people around - [the] leader calls to a boy 15 to 20 appointed by him to shuffle a certain distance and come back (this is called *čtrépm*) - he [the boy] imitates a dog-barks - [he] picks up the red hot rocks - [and] brings them to the leader still shuffling - then after a while the second man calls to a girl in the crowd to do the same & come back with 3 [hot] rocks - she imitates [a] deer - [the] third man appoints [a] boy 8 - 10 to do the same while imitating bluejay & bring[s] 4 rocks - each shuffles back and forth as many times as he has rocks to bring - if any of the men inside do not have enough power the rocks will burn the carrier's hands - the [the] leader again sticks [his] head out & tells [the] people - any of them can bring rocks if they want to by shuffling in this manner - it's the leader's power that lets them do this - [the] leader tells them to imitate one of his *suméš* - [the leader takes a] basket full of water (*yámxʷa*) - [he] pour[s] the water on the rocks and the steam wells up -

they later go out and chant and sing all the way back to their house - [and] just at dawn - then they can eat - only 3 *sisyús* [hunt leaders] do this together at one time - this is done in the morning before the night on which they give the chant - then in [the] afternoon they chant in a certain tent set aside for the purpose - [one with a] long hole [in the] top to let smoke out - then they eat - [and] sleep during [the] night - [they] get up just before morning - and [the] leader announces [a] coyote is going to come into this house they are holding the chant in - then a man from outside is appointed by [the] leader to go after the coyote - [the] leader gives him direction [while] he keeps making [a] yoohoo noise till he reaches the place where he was he keeps on making this noise and the coyote just looks at him and the man ties him and leads him back - this coyote is the leader's *suméš* & he appoints this man to go & get it - everybody sees it and are excited as he brings it back - everybody follows him back into the chant house out of curiosity & the coyote looks around as nothing was happening - [the] leader tells them to chant & all the people they chant until[the] coyote falls in a spell - [the leader] commands all go out but two men (not the 2 with the leader) stay in and skin the coyote - [the] leader changes [the] chant & chants alone before the coyote falls - he has a stick and lowers it as he chants & when he sticks it in the ground the coyote falls). They skin it - cut it up - [he] summons [the] people back in [and] gives every family a piece - & when they get home they roast it and eat it. This is the way the leader shows his power - this leader is *tλ'eʔkʷíls* - a medicine man - this whole performance is called *st'áxʷeʔ* - [it] might be other animals he'd do it too - they do this in Mid-Winter - it's just a custom to do it at that time - can also be done to get deer in winter when [they are] hoped to get if the leader has that for his *suméš* (Elmendorf 1935-6, 1:44-6).

There were different procedures prior to a late fall or winter deer hunt, a time when the animal's hide was in prime condition. These pre-hunt rituals most commonly involved individual or group sweating and the cleansing of weapons by smoking, praying over them, and even blowing a fine *spray (sŧilt)* of rosehip water on arrow tips. The following quote illustrates some of the aforementioned methods and rituals:

[After sweating] the leader, or one of the leaders might dream, or have a vision that someone's *suméš* was somewhere out-of-doors, in the woods, etc. This man would then go out to find and kill it—"capture his *suméš*, claim his *suméš*." The rule here was that no one could eat until he brought "it" back. If "it" was a deer, it was cut up into small pieces—the leaders would sing their song while everyone helped themselves to the meat which was on the ground. Just the men and women were allowed in this ritual and they were not allowed to touch it with anything but their mouths! (STHC).

At wolf-light or first *dawn (xxl'púl'eʔxʷ* - "the first light of day") of the hunt day, the hunters assisted the leader by strategically tying *old burnt moccasins (slóqʷšn* or *slqʷcín*), certain bird feathers, and strips of red cloth—the latter obtained through trade—to low branches around the periphery of the designated hunting area; "the [Spokan] Indians make a large semi-circle of burnt *appichemos* [moccasins], or skins, into which the deer driven and fall easy prey, their timidity preventing them from attempting to break the slight barrier in front" (Wilson 1866:297).

However, if the surrounded deer were able to evade the hunters, or break through the barrier, the deer hunt leader immediately removed himself as leader, since it was known his *suméš*,, for whatever reason, was not powerful enough, or his *suméš* had temporarily left him (Elmendorf 1935-6, 1:23). A more detailed description of the circle drive was provided by Father Diomedi S.J., known for his extensive linguistic, ethnographic, and ethnological research among the Coeur d'Alene, Colville, Flathead, Kalispel, and Spokan:

The great event of the winter with them [Flathead Group], is a hunt, in which the entire tribe is engaged, the general direction of which belongs to the chief who designates the time for starting. They catch their horse and bring them to a few days beforehand, and on the day preceding their departure takes place the solemn ceremony of the burning of the moccasins. All the old moccasins are collected and placed in a heap, which is then set on fire, while all standing around it say a prayer together, that God may be propitious to them during the chase. When the moccasins are about half destroyed, they are taken still burning out of the fire and distributed among the hunters, each one of whom secures a good supply of them, and then starts off according to the directions he has received from the chief.

The meaning of this custom is illustrative of Indian sagacity and keenness of perception. The object of the hunt is to drive the deer in from their fastnesses to the valley or open prairie, but the number of men not being sufficient to accomplish this purpose the burned moccasins are made to serve instead. The Indians dispersed

299

along a piece of country of seven to eight miles in diameter, carefully observe all the deer trails, and then hang their moccasins upon trees or sticks along the hunting ground, particularly on the trails. These moccasins from long usage have become so impregnated with the Indian smell, that they will be readily scented by the deer, which, being such timid creatures and shy of man's presence, will be sure either to go back or at least to keep at a distance from the moccasins. After having, in this way, forced all the deer trails on one side of a diameter, they will drive the creatures in from the opposite directions, and they, with their animal instinct, will avoid deep snow and follow the trails towards the deer enclosure. Driving them slowly, in this manner, the hunters will finally form quickly in a circle and, rushing in from all sides at once, with their dogs will give general chase (1878:31-2).

This account of Spokan deer hunting during the late historic period explains the effects of the horse upon hunting strategies, including the deer surround:

In several parts of the Spokan country where there were extensive prairies the Indians surrounded game every fall. Elk, deer, and antelope were killed in this way. A large body of people, including many women and children, made a huge circle, and moved day by day toward a common center. At night they camped in the circle. Thus they moved toward one point a few miles every day. As the circle shortened there became less chance of game getting out and the camps came to be closer together. Any game seen near the edge of the circle was, if possible, scared in by riders. Many mounted men rode to and fro between the camping parties in the circle, while others, chiefly women, advanced on horseback and on foot, carrying the baggage. In weak parts of the ring fires were lighted, especially at night, and sticks with burnt skin attached were erected here and there. At last, after a few days, or a week or two, according to the size of the ground surrounded, a large number of game animals congregated in the center. Places where game was most liable to break through were then guarded by women and children to scare them back, or sometimes by men in ambush to shoot. Then all the most active mounted men attacked the animals and killed many with arrows and spears. Those that broke away were chased and shot as they fled. This method of hunting was practiced both before and after the introduction of horses, and it fell into disuse after only the introduction of firearms, when there came to be danger of shooting one another (Teit 1930:348).

During any large hunt, and after leaving the hunting camp, the hunt leader first had a large fire built at the base of a hill prior to the hunters forming a large circle by spacing themselves, depending upon the topography and the total number of hunters, approximately seven or so meters apart. The hunters gradually gained elevation and closed their distance between adjacent hunters, all the while shouting and waving their arms as they slowly reduced the circle, pushing the deer to a high point. The leader who remains at the fire picks up a piece of wood and commences to pound on a tree trunk until a fawn comes out of the woods, looks around, and then returns with the *herd of deer* (*nq'ʷ asqsus č'ʔulixʷ*) (Elmendorf 1935-6, 1:48), that were dispatched with *bow and arrow* (*čt'apmín*).

In the past, before men used horses to conduct a *deer drive* (*tstłałáq'm* or *ixém*), the people would holler and wave hides; and later, used trade blankets to drive the deer before them into designated areas where the hunters lay in wait. On certain occasions, depending on the topographical features of the area, several hunters would conceal themselves in shallow trenches at the top, covering themselves with long grass or behind low bushes. It was assumed that deer would not escape this method of entrapment if the hunt leader had properly followed pre-hunt rituals, observed moral prohibitions, and participated in ceremonies associated with this type of hunting (STHC). If any deer broke out of the closing circle of hunters, it was assumed that the leader's *suméš* had failed him.

As cited earlier, it was a common practice for the hunters to purposely permit some deer to *escape* (*łxop*) if enough game had been taken to ensure the deer population. This was accomplished when the leader pulled out all the sticks or stakes enclosing the area.

Circle drives were a popular hunting strategy when the bow and arrow was the main predation weapon. However, with the introduction of firearms, which became universally popular, circle drives became, as already noted, unpopular. Consequently, for reasons of safety, this method of hunting gave way to a safer method of predation, namely, driving deer before the hunters in a *straight line* (*słł'áq'm*). Even Diomedi commented how successful the Spokan were on one occasion in killing a large herd of eighty-four deer using a circle drive, and how, "This mode of shooting is somewhat dangerous, and not infrequently considerable damage is done by friendly bullets" (1878:32). An example of such a tragedy was cited by Work in 1826, "It is reported among the Indians that a woman is [sic] killed at a small river on the opposite side of the Columbia, it seems she was gathering nuts, and an Indian who was hunting took her for a bear crawling among the bushes, and shot her" (Elliott 1915, 1:49). Years ago, a similar situation occurred when an elderly woman dramatically explained how her grandmother was nearly killed by a hunter who thought she was a bear as she was collecting huckleberries in deep brush.

Tree-stands

Unfortunately, there is no data or oral tradition to even suggest how often the Spokan used tree-stands for deer hunting prior to their acquiring rifles, probably since the efficiency of a rifle's range greatly surpassed that of traditional projectile weapons, despite the concomitant loud and frightening noise. Once the rifle was acquired, tree-stands were used. A *tree-stand* (*scc̓p'nálqʷ* - "deer blind in tree") was often located in higher elevations and wooded river terraces, favorably located on deer runs, near known salt-licks (*sncił̓nqstn*), and near deer-bedding areas, but *never adjacent* to springs. A hunter would use a *two-pole ladder* (*sčʼíwƛštn*) or a *notched single-pole ladder* (*snčʼíwƛštn* or *čʼiw'lštn*), even a pole *with limbs on* (*ɬʔaxntín* - "stepping place to go") (Elmendorf 1935-6, 1:28, 2:22a), to take position on a wooden platform that had been nailed or secured by hemp that extended some six or more meters up against a live ponderosa tree. They used open branches for partial concealment—but more for better surveillance of the immediate area. Normally the family that built the tree-stand was considered to have proprietary rights to its use and any game taken from it. However, a friend could ask and be given permission to hunt from the stand. In the past, and if successful, the guest hunter would share in his success by *giving the backbone and maybe a scapula* (*snqʷɬtáqs*) to the stand's owner.

A late historical type of *deer blind* (*sn'čʔemtéw'stn*), when hunting deer with rifles, was one situated on the ground in wooded areas, invariably in close proximity to any one of numerous established deer trails; generally used by only a single hunter. Most blinds consisted of a simple, low, two or three pole tipi frame, with one or two sides covered with draped pine or fir boughs. Given the feeding and watering habits of deer, a hunter would occupy the blind in early morning and again, if necessary, in late afternoon or early evening. The ideal location for a ground blind was near a deer-bedding site, which was almost always close to a wooded area, and commonly on the verge of a grass field. If possible, the blind was constructed just inside the wooded area.

Some families had several tree-stands, but only a few remain in use today—ones presumably in families for four and five generations. However, it should be noted that one rarely reckoned beyond the *fifth generation* (*ner'uye*) for usury rights or privileges of property, in most matters requiring validation by memory. Several elders, when asked why this method of deer hunting is now rarely used, have commented that, "Young men today are too impatient to spend a night up in a tree."

Snow and Water Drives

Though meat and hide were not prime during mid or late winter, the Spokan took advantage of deep snow conditions since deer, antelope, and elk were relatively easy prey, particularly to hunters wearing snowshoes. As will be discussed, a lone hunter had greater success in deer hunting if he had a good hunting dog, which was true in snowless conditions when persistent hunting by scent was the main strategy. Reverend Walker commented how the role and power of a shaman in creating snow before deer hunting was believed to be so great as "to make the snow fall so deep that the Indians could overtake the deer" (Drury 1940:130). In certain snow conditions, dogs were not used, because they are unable to negotiate deep powder snow. When pursuing ungulata over crusted snow, the use of snowshoes gave the hunter a definite advantage as the animal's retreat was impeded when *breaking through the often thin surface* (*ql'qél'w'éʔtšis*) of snow. In the past, hunters would pray for deep snow, sometimes, "venturing from winter village——knee deep in snow" (Elmendorf 1935-6, 2:15). After trapping the deer in snow, the hunter would break the deer's neck by placing his left hand over the muzzle and quickly twisting the animal's head with the other hand. Tracking a wounded deer was not difficult in minimal snow cover, particularly when *using a trained dog to track a wounded deer* (*hessččel'm'* - "catch scent"). Drury, presumably quoting Walker, used the exact wording (1940:193).

In winter hunting, men and dogs would chase deer onto frozen bodies of water where the animals encountered difficult footing and were more easily dispatched. When conducting water drives, dogs were commonly used to assist hunters in driving deer into the water where they were easily killed by hunters waiting in canoes with hand-held spears (Glover 1962:341). Though not a proper game enclosure, water was used to impede the mobility of deer. It was not difficult to weaken a swimming deer by repeatedly thrusting a spear or *knife* (*n'in'č'm'n'*) into the dorsal area of the neck muscles near the cape. A man could also kill a swimming deer by holding the animal's head under water to drown the animal. When in water, attempts were made to direct a weakened deer as close to land as possible, reducing expenditure of energy the hunter would have to bear if he had to pull his prey to shore. Deer falling through thin ice were sometimes recovered by securing the animal's head with a noose attached to the end of a long, thin, flexible pole. Nooses were made from deer sinew or long strands of twisted mountain goat hair (Elmendorf 1935-6, 1:2). This technique of lassoing, or using a pole-extended noose, was effective for securing a deer that was swimming in deep water away from pursuing hunters in a canoe or a dugout. It was easier to hunt deer as they traversed any frozen body of water with difficulty, than on frozen land. Weather conditions and the time of the year were of significance when killing deer. For example, in spring and early summer, a deer may sink in water whereas in the fall, with warmer water and deer having thicker hair and more fat, they will not always sink after being wounded or killed. It was well known that after being killed in water, land mammals tend to float, whereas aquatic animals, such as beaver, muskrat, marten, and otter tend to sink. Interestingly, Drury, again quoting Walker, described the effectiveness of the water drive, "One band [?] about sixty miles from this place drove in one day four hundred [deer] into a lake & and all were taken" (1940:193).

Fire Drives

Prior to the introduction of firearms, the Spokan and Coeur d'Alene, as first reported by Cox (1831:46-7, 1957 [1832]:214), DeSmet (1843), Mullan (1861), and Bancroft (1883, 1:263), used incendiaries as a means of successfully driving or surrounding deer, forcing game into pre-selected open grassland areas that often bordered wooded areas. Fire-driving was sometimes done several times a year, depending on the need, growth rates of vegetation, wind direction, moisture conditions, topography, and the size of the hunting party. Often a large number of deer were killed and later dressed by the hunters. As noted, this method of predation was, however, sometimes wrought with dangers, particularly to those hunters who were downwind from the fire, concealed by partially burying themselves in earth slit trenches covered with dry grasses. In 1814, Cox noted how in late summer dried grass was fired to direct antelope toward awaiting hunters concealed in ravines (1957:214). Drury, using an anonymous source, noted:

> In hunting these deer the Indians had a method of their own. After a herd had been located, some members of the hunting party, by making a long detour, obtained a position in front of it, while in the rear fired the dry bunch grass. Running before the flaming wind, the deer were intercepted by the hunters, and great numbers were killed (1976:41).

Fire, as mentioned, was effective in driving deer to sites having deer jumps. Thus, driving game with fire was a use of incendiarism in addition to the strategy of selective burning practiced in order to maintain desired ecological conditions in grassland and wooded areas. Cox wrote how in late summer Indians used fires to drive herds of antelope in the direction of concealed hunters (1957:214).

On the reservation there are several relatively long, narrow, and steep sloping canyons, which until the late 1800s served to restrict the backward retreat of fire-driven deer that were pushed to the lower ends where hunters were stationed. Brush and fallen timber provided sufficient fuel for the necessary smoke.

Prior to any fire drive, an individual possessing deer power might dream—while a visitant to the spiritual world—of having a successful hunt and announce his intentions to his hunting partners, who, at dawn, would assist him in strategically placing burnt moccasins and certain bird feathers around the designated area to be fired. The pre-set singed feathers aided the hunters when the deer attempted to avoid the frightening odor, and believed to further aid the hunter's arrows to their mark as well as indicate the direction of the prevailing wind and fire direction. Depending on the topography and the vegetation of a southwest facing hill, a fire was usually started at the base after all the hunters of usually thirty to forty men were *encircled in place* (*cła?q'mi*). The *grass was ignited* (*čulusntm supulexʷ*) early in the morning, and light orographic winds would effectively push the fire and drive the deer to a high point where the hunters, waving their arms and shouting, would dispatch the game (Ross 1999).

There are several large open areas on the northern terraces of the Spokane River that gradually rise to fairly steep south-west facing granite walls, which formed effective barriers to deer being driven by fire close to the river. In several areas there still remain many rock-rimmed excavated foxholes (Ross 1991) that were used to conceal deer hunters who had—during the previous night—further camouflaged their location by covering themselves with quantities of dried grass and low sage bushes. Unfortunately, on occasion this concealment strategy created a potentially dangerous situation, for as other hunters drove the deer before the fired area, it was not unusual for one or more concealed hunters to be burned, sometimes severely (A. Smith, pers. comm.). The earliest known recorded observation of the Spokan hunting deer by fire-driving is Cox's description:

> On ascertaining the direction the deer have chosen, part of their hunters take a circuit in order to arrive in front of the herd, while those behind set fire to the long grass, the flames of which spread with great rapidity. In their flight from the devouring element they are intercepted by the hunters, and, while they hesitate between these dangers, great numbers fall by the arrows of the Indians (1832:19).

Another method of hunting in the fall was to encircle a grazing deer herd with a sufficient number of men who lit small intermittent fires that formed a circle with only one opening at the downwind edge, or one with no apparent exit. During a fire surround, the unfired center area was occupied by older men who would dispatch deer as the fire circle was reduced, forcing the entrapped deer into the center. Encircling deer with fire could be dangerous, even a fatal experience for hunters, if winds created an uncontrollable conflagration. Any hunter who had dug a slit-trench would attempt to cover himself as best as possible with the excavated earth to prevent being burned. However, during an exceptionally large and uncontrollably hot fire, it was possible for a hunter to die from suffocation (Smith, pers. comm.). Prior to a collective fall hunt, hunters would remove as much dry plant material as possible from the center, and, as mentioned, excavate a series of trenches for protection in the event of an uncontrollable fire. In the case of an unpredicted shift of wind, hunters would dig one or more pits if the ground was soft and, if possible, bury the carcasses of any slain deer to preserve the meat and hide.

DeSmet, in 1843, witnessed the neighboring Coeur d'Alene using a fire surround method to drive deer into Lake Coeur d'Alene, where the animals were easily dispatched by Indians with spears in skillfully maneuvered bark canoes.

Deer Jumps

Ethnoarchaeological, ethnographic (Diomedi 1878), and linguistic data, as well as oral history (Ross 1993; Egesdal, pers. comm.), provide evidence that deer jumps were used in the Plateau. Teit described how the Flathead Group used the deer jump (*sntw'aq'éłč'e?tn'* or *snto?qʷmncutn* or *snto?qʷm'ełc'e?tn'* - "place where game fall"):

Sometimes, instead of a surround, driving was arranged on a great scale, the animals being driven over cliffs, where they were killed by the fall, or into coulées and defiles, where men lay in wait to shoot them. Sometimes drives were made in coulées with steep sides, the animals being driven from one end to the other, where they were met by hunters waiting for them, and between the two parties were nearly all killed (1930:348).

The Spokan were not an exception, having three such precipice jumps located on the present reservation—one several kilometers upriver from Little Falls. A second jump was approximately 800 m downstream from Little Falls, and the third deer jump was located approximately 5 km downstream from Little Falls, an area of the Lower Spokan called *scqesciłni*, the inhabitants of which in older times called themselves *spoˁqen'iˀ* (Elmendorf 1935-6, 4:11b). The site of each deer jump was approached by crossing a wide sloping terrace that essentially paralleled the Spokane River before sharply dropping off.

A major deer drive was staged at least once every winter after the Mid-Winter Ceremony, and involved many people under the direction of a shaman possessing deer power who had dreamed of a successful collective hunt. Prior to the actual hunt, men and women constructed a long brush fence that directed and eventually constricted the path of the deer to the deer jump. When possible, fires were ignited to assist the drivers in negotiating the deer toward the brush fence, and the entrapped deer were herded toward the *fence* (*č'ɬˁál'm'itn*), through an opening and over the edge of the *cliff* (*hec šn'esšn'*), by men and women who followed while shouting and waving their arms.

Unfortunately, the approach to each deer jump has since been greatly modified by years of plowing and harrowing, thereby destroying any evidence indicating if stone cairns existed to help channel the deer to the actual precipice, though several Spokan said cairns were used. However, few if any cairns remain, nor is there any physical evidence whether piled brush served the same purpose, though several elders recall accounts of how people other than hunters assisted by waving and shouting in the efforts to channel the deer. As could best be remembered, dogs were never used for driving deer toward jumps or a *river bank* (*sx̣cin*) since their owners knew that the dogs, in their excitement and haste, might follow the deer right over the edge, killing or injuring them.

Just as with a circle drive (*č'ɬˀaq'mn*) or fire drive, a man who dreamed of a successful deer drive would arrange the drive (*sɬ'ałá q'm'*), and served as the leader who coordinated the drive of thirty or more hunters. In the late afternoon, when deer were approaching the river from the foothills and upper terraces, hunters, using a fan method, pushed and herded the deer through ever-narrowing stake runways toward the restricted small end opened at the slope's end *close to the edge overlooking the river* (*čleˀmus*).

Another deer jump was at the end of a small narrow valley that emptied approximately 8 m above the Spokane River, and once the deer were driven into the higher end of the valley, they were further confined by what was essentially an enclosure or *circle of sticks* (*słatn* or *łáq'mn* or *čnék'ʷm'ˀn*) placed by hunters atop the rim of the valley several days prior to the hunt. (These figures represented stick Indians [scarecrows].) The younger hunters would simply chase the confined deer over the edge of the precipice to the older hunters who waited below to dispatch any surviving deer, which was the most dangerous aspect of any deer jump for fear that a wounded deer could kill an unwary hunter with sharp hooves. This risk was inherent in any method of hunting deer, including deer jumps. A hunter had to make certain that the animal was dead before getting close, because a hunter not exercising caution could have his stomach ripped open by the sharp *deer hoofs* (*sc'uˀc'uˀšínsšn'*).

A decoy figure once used by the Spokan, and not unlike a padded manikin, which was more representative of a human than the aforementioned stick figure, was noted by Stevens:

> I have heard of an ingenious method of hunting deer [...] they form a large circle, and upon the trees around its circumference attach pieces of cloth made to resemble the human figure as much as possible. Then the hunters enter the area and start up the deer. Each cloth having the effect of a man, the deer being afraid to pass them are kept within the circle and easily killed (1855, 12, Part 2:134).

Prior to dam construction, one deer jump—some distance down from Little Falls—was approximately 1.5 m in height, and the other wall was approximately 1.7 m in height. With both jumps, surviving or wounded deer fell onto accumulated river-exposed boulders where hunters, concealed below the bank dispatched any crippled deer, usually with a thrusting spear or bow and arrow. A few elders indicated during an extensive two year ethnoarchaeological survey of the Spokane Indian Reservation (Ross 1993), how in others areas of the river, deer were herded and then forced to follow a narrow downhill course due to extensive bordering by sloping talus slopes where they were killed by hunters concealed in the intrusive glacially-deposited large granite boulders.

Though not considered as *deer cliff jumps* (*čx̌ʷcx̌ʷícmn*), numerous sections of the northern edge of the Spokan River had deep ravines, some with boulders used by hunters for concealment, when in early evening, deer seeking water were dispatched by hunters as the deer negotiated the narrow ravines. *Yearling deer* (*nt't'qáw'sqn* - "small deer") were killed, but only because it was thought by the Indians that they would not survive on their own with no mothers.

Hunting Methods

In addition to a hunter's prehunt dreaming and rituals, successful hunting for an individual hunting deer was contingent upon the person's accumulative knowledge and ability to maintain persistent tracking prior to stalking his prey. Consequently, the assurance of bringing game within closer range was based upon a hunter's knowledge of the animal, and, quite often, his skill of decoying. One can only conclude that prior to firearms, and regardless of the efficiency of a hunter's predation technology and ability to track, stalk, and decoy, a man's greatest skill and assurance of success was patience.

Elders recalled how an adolescent was taken by his uncle or grandfather to a distant and remote wooded area to develop patience and discipline, and told to remain in one place, making no sounds, only *whispering* (*su'sw'ilš*), with no food until the older man returned—sometimes remaining until the next morning when the sponsor returned.

An example of this was narrated by a 97-year-old man, who told the author of a lesson learned from his grandfather, when he was probably five or six:

> One summer, once or twice a week he'd take me early in the morning just before dawn, and we'd sit on the ground facing north to an area near Big Tschimakain Creek—now overgrown—all day. No food, only water from the creek. He'd always whisper very softly and say the same thing every time we went. "Look out there and check what you see before we go. I want to ask you what you saw, what you heard, and if you ever felt anything." Before dusk, and just before we'd leave, he'd whisper and ask what I'd seen or heard—but not felt. He'd listen very carefully when I'd quietly tell him—very slowly and carefully, everything I'd seen or heard, but never felt. He'd often tell me, "It's when you see and also hear a thing, is when you will feel it." Even at that age I knew he was teaching me to carefully and quietly observe things like animals, birds, and even how the wind affected the trees. He always said, "You must hear what you see, and see what you hear - then you'll feel it" (Ross 1968-2008).

Tracking

Of all indigenous male hunting skills, tracking was the most important and the most difficult to acquire. Boys devoted considerable time learning the important skills of *tracking* (*n'q̌ʷč'šne'óxe'*) that included learning the habits, diets, and characteristics of game animals and their prey-predator relationships. They learned to identify an animal by its *track* (*sxúitn*—bit of fur, feather, or sound, even odor. Even at an early age a boy could identify the feces of any animal, which often revealed the general or specific diet of the animal. A young boy could distinguish the *horse tracks* (*snq'ʷq'ʷúλ'e'štn*) of his father's unshod horses. It was said *every man could recognize the hoof prints of his horse* (*mipnúłc*), known as *mipnúłts*. It was also said every man even *knew their horse's whiney*, (*nsó?xʷqists*) (STHC). Most apparent was the attention and instruction of parents and elders to encourage very young girls and boys to observe their surroundings, to understand the changes and "moods" brought by the daily and annual fluctuations of the floral and faunal environment. One elder described how his grandfather instructed his father by near-concealing a small item, or making a seemingly insignificant change in a plant which his father should note. "Parents teach their children to remark such things, and these in turn sometimes add new discoveries to those of their fathers" (DeSmet 1843:155).

Until recently, elders acknowledged that the range of tracking abilities—according to their grandfathers—varied considerably. Even if one were capable of identifying the evidence of various animals, what was most important was knowing an animal's behavior and the interrelationship and provenience of certain species at different seasons, including available food supplies and breeding seasons that would determine the strategy of a hunter. Consequently, tracking, decoying, and stalking were dominant concerns of every hunter.

The skills required for tracking undoubtedly commenced informally for young boys as soon as they were able to walk and spend time in essentially an extensive natural environment, acquiring knowledge of the various sounds and tracks that identified both birds and animals. Like most later adult subsistence activities, young boys were introduced initially to wet-tracking and later to dry-tracking (even the words are forgotten) by their fathers or other adult male kinspersons. A young apprenticing hunter considered tracking a game as an enjoyable pastime that was often competitive as to who would first identify a particular animal's track, particularly in winter when snow forced ungulata to lower elevations (Glover 1962:336). As their skills developed, so did their success at hunting young animals with bow and arrow. Opportunities for tracking larger and economically more significant game were often provided by boys spending more time with older hunters. It was known that any proficiency in tracking was an accumulative process, a specialized area of knowledge acquired only by spending considerable time and effort living in the woods, often and preferably alone.

Although a young boy's initial training was not formalized, it was encouraged by periodic acclaim and the knowledge that success in tracking was economically significant, which could later mean even survival. Every boy—and many girls—by about age ten, could identify any animal by its tracks or spoor, as well being able to determine the diet of any mammal by careful examination of the *animal's excrement* (*mnéč*), a practice known as *n?ucšnełc'e?*. The first years of training young boys in the art of tracking were not unlike a game, where success warranted recognition and claim from one's kin group and, in some instances, villagers or camp elders. Even the spoor of animals informed the identity of the animal to the hunter and the creature's diet, and when wounded, the tracks told him if the wound was of the *intestines* (*stx̣enč*), lungs, or limbs through evidence of characteristic patterns of sprayed or clotted blood on bushes or the ground.

A tracker could distinguish the species of deer as well as the gender when following fresh *deer tracks* (*k'ᵂłwičšnm* - "see tracks of any animal or person"). One winter, many years ago, the author was at a scene where a cottontail rabbit had been killed earlier by three coyotes. A Spokan elder explained, even dramatized, how two of the coyotes took turns as the desperate rabbit was forced into a tighter and tighter ever decreasing circle, until a resting third coyote pounced and made the kill.

One elderly woman, once a renowned deer hunter, explained how right after a rain, there is a distinct odor a deer gives off, one that often can be detected by humans. The same individual explained how, when tracking a frightened deer, there were occasions when, in its attempt to hide, the deer would prostrate its body with all four legs out straight parallel to the ground while concealed in ground cover.

Tracking abilities had value for one's own navigation when hunting and when in enemy territory. There are few accounts of Spokan people ever being lost, even in winter. One important reason was that a person, if possible, never travelled at night unless it was absolutely necessary. From a young age children were taught to always look back before making a turn in treeless areas and note features that would appear different upon

306

their return route. Children were instructed to try never to deviate from a pathway, but instead to travel, as much as possible, in as near a straight course as possible, recognizing and utilizing established game trails that were essentially Indian pathways. A major factor for determining one's sense of direction was wind, knowing that during night travel the wind flows downhill and reverses direction during the day. Traveling in fog was extremely difficult, but even deceptive echoes might help to determine more abrupt land features. Knowledge of the terrain was a major factor in orientation. If lost, a person could purposely lose elevation by following a drainage to the confluence of a larger stream, eventually coming to a recognized major waterway.

Children were instructed to be wary of the chirping or crying of chipmunks and squirrels, for it was believed that animals could purposely disorient a human, even causing him to become lost. This type of occasional behavior of small animals was called *co[?]tálix^wncót* (STHC). Egesdal's ethnographic and linguistic fieldwork within the Spokan-Flathead dialect continuum, revealed that the loud shriek of the red squirrel was greatly feared, and that it was the most feared of all small animals, so that upon seeing the animal or even hearing its distinctive chirp, a person would immediately burn a small piece of buckskin as a prophylactic ritual against any harm and to avoid being disoriented and wandering helplessly, always gaining elevation until reaching the snow line where he would die. It was noted that if a pine squirrel made the sound *náɫ náɫ náɫ náɫ*, a person could become 'bewitched' (Egesdal, pers. comm.).

Decoying

Successful tracking might reveal an animal's presence, but often circumstances prevented the hunter's approach within a range of at least 20 m for effectively using a projectile weapon, such as a throwing stick for small animals or a bow and arrow for larger game. At an early age, boys commenced acquiring the necessary skills of *decoying* (*míla[?]ntx^w* - "you decoyed it"), intended to bring an animal as close to the hunter as possible. Training was accomplished under the close tutelage of an elderly man—not always a relative—who taught the various skills and devices necessary to influence the behavior of birds and animals, particularly large mammals. Franchère (1854:283) and Ross (1904, 7:283), speaking of the Spokan hunter's ability to decoy, contended, "There is no bird nor beast of which they cannot imitate the voice so as to decoy it within their reach."

In the early *evening* (*sč'lúx^w*), nearly all decoying of deer was done by sound, such as rubbing and banging *deer antlers* (*qxmin*) together during rutting season, and imitating their voiced bedding sounds. Elders contend that the hunt leader would pound deer antlers against trees and groan to hypnotize the deer, and a few elders recall stories of the potential danger of attracting the elusive but dangerous cougar when using a bark *deer caller* (*sn'áʕ'*) or making sounds with deer antlers. All hunters could tell fateful stories of the extreme danger and folly of attracting cougars if they wore deer heads, hides, or horns (Smith 1936-8:285). However, there is no memory of Spokan hunters ever using deer skins or stuffed deer heads for decoying deer, as reported for the Sanpoil (Ray 1933:82) for the simple reason that such attire could endanger the hunter if attacked by a cougar. Lewis, however, wrote, "When hunting with bows and arrows, decoys or disguises of deer wolf skin were frequently used, so to enable the hunter to approach more closely without being discovered" (1906, 2:182).

Animal scent was often a successful means of decoying and attracting the attention of most land mammals; wolves and coyotes were quick to investigate the scent of any animal that was wounded and had been bleeding, particularly deer. Both of these predators were known for their extreme caution of most types of traps and attempts at decoying, and were seldom caught. A scent that was refuted to attract white-tailed deer at night during a summer hunt was freshly crushed deer vetch, which hunters released by crushing the tops of the plant—a favorite food of the white-tailed deer. It was common to use one or more previously captured fawns during collective deer hunting to entice adult deer into a clearing by hunters.

For both the black-tailed and mule deer, the Spokan had specific names for the size and specific locations of preorbital or lacrimal glands near each eye, the four metatarsal scent glands between the two parts of the hoof on all four feet, and those on the outside of each hind leg at the hock. The mule deer scent glands are slightly larger (Wallmo 1981). During rutting seasons, the glands secrete a white waxy pheromone, which attracts potential mate as well as identifies a territory when rubbed on bushes or trees. Though the Spokan were knowledgeable with all animal scent glands, it was not recalled if deer scent glands were collected and used to attract deer, as they were and are used commercially by some non-Indian deer hunters.

A *bull elk* (*Cervus elaphus nelsoni* - *tšec'*) spreads a scent from the metatarsal glands on the inside of its legs to attract a *cow elk* (*pwelščn*), which hunters collected and used in a similar fashion to attract a cow elk by hanging the detached glands in a wooded area. Whistles made from dry wild rhubarb were occasionally used to call elk. The general term for elk was *snéčlc'e ʔ*.

Boys learned at a young age to *imitate* (*nk'ʷek'ʷúl'sm*) bird calls and those of many animals. For example, from late May to mid-July, when deer have their fawns, a boy would practice enticing an unsuspecting adult doe to within bow range by imitating the *bleating sound of a distressed fawn* (*hecn'áʕ'iʔ* or *n'áʔey*), by blowing over the end of a rolled funnel-shaped bark instrument, or blowing on a cottonwood leaf held tightly between the two forefingers and the inside edges of the thumbs. Another method of decoying deer was to flatten two hardwood sticks, each approximately 2 cm wide and 8 to 10 cm long; the ends were left flat and adjoined with only a center section of the two facing sides being hollowed out. This created a partially open resonating chamber that produced a fawn's distress call when blown. Or, to *imitate a distressed fawn* (*ncucuweč*), the hunter would blow over either open edge of a fresh cottonwood leaf placed between the two pieces of flattened hardwood sticks tightly bound together by Indian hemp. Elders said how in the past some older boys were better than others in *mocking* (*m'iʔpn'úy'ʔs*) the calls of different animals. Acquiring the abilities of decoying and bringing an animal closer to a hunter was necessary, and considerable time was devoted in developing these skills. Any decoying device that imitated a distressed fawn was termed *sn'áʔ*.

Some hunters were accomplished at blowing upon a willow leaf or a broad leaf held tightly between the thumbs and heels of the hand. This same technique was successful with the use of other types of grasses, preferably cut-grass or panicled or small *fruited bulrush* (*Scirpus microcarpus* J. Presl. & C. Presl. var *longispicatus* M. Peck - *saʔyóleʔxʷ*) found near ponds and wet areas. Cupping both hands together and *blowing in short bursts between the bent knuckles* (*sxʷaw'cán'* - "whistle through cupped hands") produced a similar effect of decoying, or by using a *wooden deer whistle* (*náʕ'mn*) (Elmendorf, pers. comm.). Similarly, a man would whistle with *folded wet hands* (*snpxʷčné'ečstn*) to decoy a deer. Of interest was the Flathead practice of using a wild rhubarb whistle to call elk. "He whistles once and the elk answers, he whistles once more and the elk will come to the spot" (Schaeffer 1934-37, I-140).

To coordinate the movements of other hunters, a man could place his two index fingers in his mouth to *call someone* (*síkʷm*). A type of whistle used when hunting was made by whittling flat two matched sticks approximately 6 to 8 cm long, with a total width of some 3 cm, and 5 mm thick. Another method was blowing over a tight strand of rawhide that vibrated within a 3 cm long cutout piece of flat wood (STHC). A universal device to attract a *doe* (*smeʔm'elc'eʔ*) was with a whistle made from a hollowed deer horn to produce a sound resembling a *deer snorting* (*xoxoncút*), or that of a distressed *fawn* (*ƛ'k'ʷƛ'úk'ʷ* or *sq'ʷq'ʷltéw's* - "first born"), or its *bleating* (*náʕ'* or *sn'áʔ*) when in danger. A hunter could *imitate* (*nk'ʷek'ʷúl'sm*) a distressed fawn by holding his nose and snorting. Another method of decoying deer was for a hunter to blow as he stretched his lips with two fingers as a *whistle* (*sn'áʕ'*). Smith described how deer sounds were used by both the Spokan and Kalispel, "The hunter produced the sound while seizing his nose. Since here were some men who were unable to reproduce the call in this manner [...] When they first started [each summer to hunt in this way], hunters produced a coarser sound and increased its coarseness as the fawn grew older" (1936-8:1021).

Critical to the strategy of collective hunting was the hunters' ability to coordinate their movements in stalking and timing during open *deer drives* (*st'łałq'em'*), and not to reveal their presence. Hunters sometimes coordinated their movements by imitating certain birds by using prearranged calls. Bird calls were used to give mammals a sense of security, and it was claimed that a few hunters had the ability to entice a female deer within range by imitating the *call of a woodpecker* (*kʷlkʷléčeʔ* - "flicker bird"), which sounds similar to the cry of a distressed fawn, thereby attracting a mother doe. When in sight of one another, *arm signals* (*stur'r'si* - "motions for direction") were given. Shouting was always prohibited, which only served to frighten game. Rather, a sort of *hand whistle* (*snpxʷčnéčst*) was used, such that a man would wet his hands, cup them together, blow on his raised knuckles held parallel, and rapidly flutter the outside fingers of his right hand to achieve a range of desired sounds.

There is no memory of the Spokan—or any contiguous tribes—using duck decoys for hunting, a practice that commenced with a few off-reservation duck hunters during the 1930s and 40s. Rare was the occasion for a Spokan man to hunt duck for food using a shotgun; the time and effort required, and the cost of shells, prohibited such an activity, and unfortunately, many of the wetlands no longer exist. When available, duck eggs were always collected.

Stalking

Universally, one of the first games for children were their early attempts at stalking, when a young boy would attempt to demonstrate his stealth by surprising an older sibling or a neighbor's *pet animal* (*č'em'utn'* or *xʷec'n'*) such as a tamed raccoon or a tamed beaver that made a rather docile pet (Burnett 1904, 5:153). In time, a young hunter's ability to *stalk* (*nʔúčšn* or *ʔew'étm* - "to stalk an animal") often meant success or failure in acquiring game, particularly animals already wounded and forewarned. The same skills and abilities in stalking game were required when engaged in warfare, most notably by scouts who would attempt to ascertain the location and deployment of an enemy. Whether stalking game or an enemy, success was invariably dependent upon a person's physical stealth, patience, and the ability to communicate his observations to a main group of hunters or warriors. When using a sinew-backed bow, stealth was often more important than long-range marksmanship, for as an elderly man once explained that, "a hunter who could move like the wind before his sound, stepping when only a leaf falls, so that his arrow will always come long before *his shadow* (*sm'el'k'ʷéy'eʔ*) is detected." The Spokan used a sign language to communicate (Jorgensen 1969), as did hunters when one man could communicate with *hand signals* (*čłsuxʷmeam* - "to make a sign or signal") to one or more other hunters the number of sighted game, and, direct the other hunters' best approach to their quarry.

Boys were instructed to learn the skills of stalking by observing the behavior of certain animals. When learning to stalk game birds, a boy was told he must first see the bird before hearing it flying away—presumably having first seen the hunter. It was not unusual for an exceptionally accomplished non-kinsman to teach young boys the skills of tracking, decoying, and stalking. Such a person would be referred to as *sxʷmeʔmeʔy'éʔim'*.

Among the Spokan, *hunting* (*člip*) was the major economic subsistence pursuit during winter months, which was necessary to supplement depleted stored foods and for acquiring needed animal by-products—particularly hides, bone, and bone marrow. Deer were generally pursued individually or by small parties of men from late September until March; the main hunting of deer occurred from early summer until late fall. The importance of deer hunting can be understood from a special *deer hunting ceremony* (*snqaqʕá*) that inaugurated these predation activities. Curtis described this ritual for the Kalispel, which was essentially the same for the Spokan:

> Before inaugurating a hunt, the Kalispel held a dance called *snkaká*, in which at night the men gathered
> around a stiff rawhide, spread upon the ground, and beat on it with sticks, their bodies swaying and their voices

309

raised in song, while three or four women stood behind and aided in the singing. This was in supplication to the spirits for aid in the hunt. In the intervals between the songs some would tell what they were going to accomplish on the hunt, and others what the spirits of the animals and birds had told them in the mountains on their journeys of fasting. Each man sang his own medicine-song, being aided by the others, and then he narrated his visions, the others repeating his words after him (1911, 7:88).

As one would suspect, there were different versions of the danger if a hunter disguised himself as a deer, particularly from a cougar. However, when stalking, hunters used different visual and audible techniques to get as close as possible to the animal:

> While on hunting excursions, they [Indians] also wear caps made of the skins of the wolf or bear, with the ears erect; their heads being metamorphosed in to wolves' or bears' heads, they are enabled to approach the game with greater facility: I have seen a fellow get into a deer-skin, stripped for the purpose, with the skin of the head and horns complete, walk off on all fours, and get actually among a herd of deer without their taking notice of this deception. But the wolf is the animal they seem to imitate the best. An Indian concealed in a wolf's hide, pulls the skin of the wolf's head, with the face, eyes, and nose entire, over his own head, the ears erect, and tail in its proper place, will walk, run, and frisk about on his hands and feet, so that he can scarcely be distinguished from the real animal itself (Ross 1904, 7:282).

Hunting

As cited earlier, of the different subsistence-getting strategies, hunting of non-migratory land animals provided the smallest amount of food, approximately ten to twelve percent of the Spokan people's annual caloric intake (Ross 1995g:601). This was due to unpredictable location and fluctuation of game populations, variable weather, and the required greater expenditure of energy. Periodically, severe winter storms and the resulting deep snow would sometimes disrupt hunting—despite *packed snow* (*ché*) and the limited use of snowshoes by hunters during snowstorms. Yet deep snow often facilitated hunting as it impeded the movements of deer and elk, and there were oral accounts of Spokan men actually conducting a snow dance for fresh snow to bring snow. A severe and prolonged winter occasionally reduced various mammal populations, and often deteriorated the environment for those surviving animals through over-browsing due to the extended absence of other food sources, necessitating the over consumption of available spring's buds and other vegetation.

Individual hunting was most effective in winter by using snowshoes, dogs, and tracking to facilitate stalking with the bow and arrow. The frequency of predation was largely influenced by weather conditions, need, or simply desire. The most important game animals were the mule deer, white-tailed deer, and black-tailed deer—in that order—which provided meat, hide, bone by-products, antler, and marrow. Cooper (1830-1902), a Canada-US border railroad surveyor and biologist, noted how "The black-tail, though much larger than the red deer, is inferior for the table, the meat being generally dry and of indifferent flavor" (1860, 2:135).

The type of game, topography, structure of the hunting party, and general weather conditions, all influenced the method of animal procurement. Though hunting was male-oriented, it was not unusual for women to accompany a large hunting party on distant collective hunting expeditions to assist the men with cooking, shelter construction, *skinning* (*čłckʷélxʷi* - "to pull hide off"), and to help when transporting animal by-products—most often hides—back to resident areas.

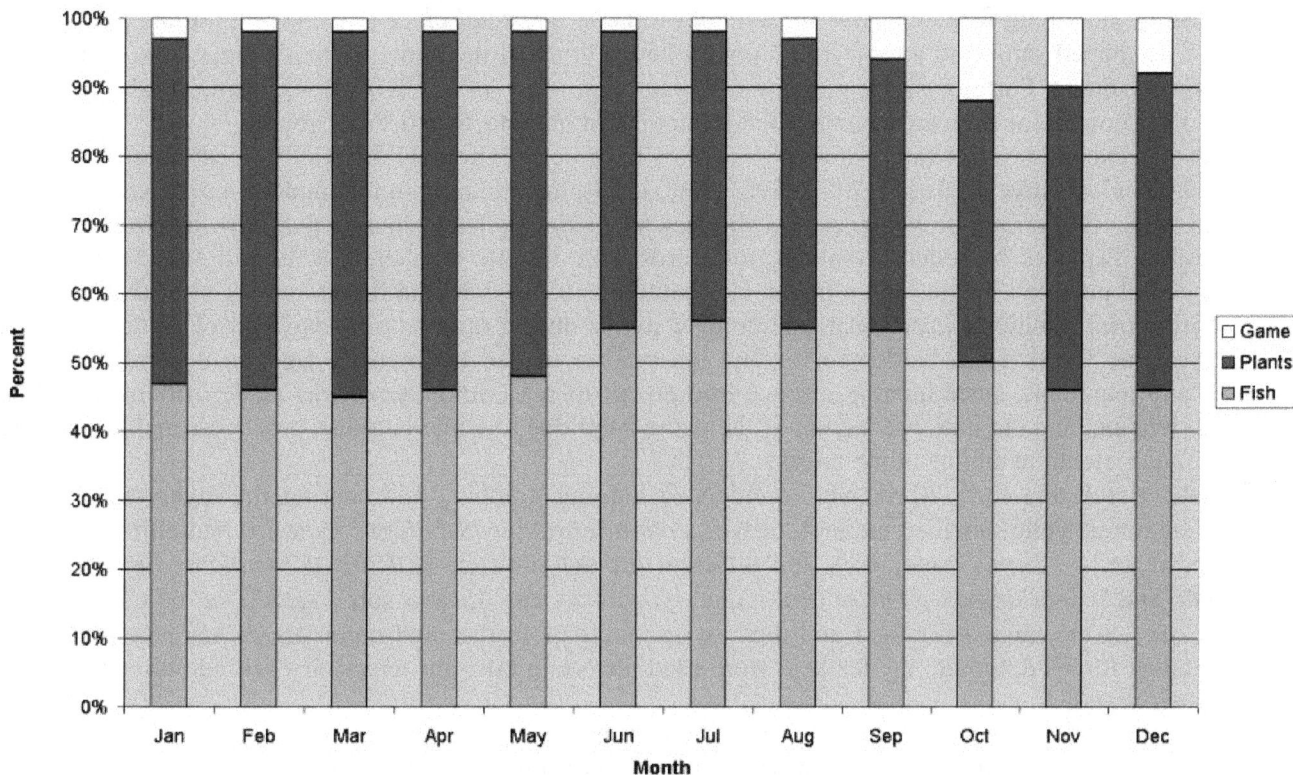

Figure 24. Caloric intake of fresh and stored foods (by Michael J. Ross)

Methods of hunting were numerous and largely determined by the particular animals sought, the size of the hunting party, the area and the distance to be traversed, and other logistical considerations. As noted, these predation methods included animal drives, surrounds, jumps, dead falls, traps and snares, and *stone confinement walls* (*č'łqal'mín*), and in winter, running down deer with snowshoes. The use of traps and dead falls, as delayed predation, extended an individual's ability and success in hunting large animals. Snares were effective only for small fur-bearing animals. Beaver casters were commonly used as bait since all animals were attracted by the scent. There were both advantages and disadvantages to using delayed predation, and the obvious advantage, was that there was no need for the hunter to be present to catch an animal, whereas the major disadvantage was the fear that animal predators could destroy the dead or immobilized game. Also, traps, snares, and deadfalls were used in areas not too distant from camps or villages, and so it required less effort and time for the hunter to daily check these devices.

As noted in Curtis's comparative accounts (1911, 7:88), the Flathead Group—including the Spokan— staged a ritual dance to inaugurate a major hunt or warfare. The night before a hunt, the men would gather around a stiff deer rawhide, which they beat upon with sticks as they swayed back and forth, each singing his medicine song. The songs were "in supplication to the spirit for aid in the hunt" (Smith 1936-8:989). Between sessions of singing, the hunt leader would explain where and how they would conduct the hunt, and others may describe their vision of the coming hunt, often revealing the area where the game would be, and even of success or failure. Later, it was called the "canvas dance" (*snqʕqʕáqsm*), and later truncated by the Flathead and Kalispel to *snqʕqʕá* (Egesdal, pers. comm.). In more recent times, it was done on the last night of

311

medicine events, and people would pitch in money to help out those traveling home to distant parts (Egesdal, pers. comm.).

A custom, now long forgotten, was for a hunter to carry a *special black stone* (*sčenš*) in his power bag, thought to be shaped similar to a projectile point, believed to assist the hunter's *suméš* regardless of the type of game being sought. Fortuitously coming upon a *group of fawns* (*ʔuɫ ƛʼkʷƛʼukʷ*) was demonstrable proof of the man's deer power, for even an accomplished hunter could only decoy a deer by sound.

With few exceptions, Spokan winter hunting sites have been extremely difficult to locate during various ethnoarchaeological surveys (Ross 1980, 1989a, 1991, 1993), due not only to the random movement of winter game and their often erratic provenience, but the lack of *in situ* skeletal remains that have deteriorated with age and often displaced by rodents. Animals and birds were usually butchered at the kill site. Some elders recalled several notable kill sites and topographic features once used as traditional hunting sites that partially remain in the oral traditions—particularly three deer jumps on the reservation—two east of Little Falls and one in the Blue Creek area. Settlement on the reservation tended to intensify Spokan dependence upon regional land mammals, since hunting in once traditional off-reservation areas was made difficult by white prejudice, fencing, and the initial reduction of the game itself due to white land-use practices, such as logging and intensive agriculture among other reasons.

In late March and early April men commenced hunting, trapping and snaring the numerous ground-dwelling creatures: yellow-bellied marmot, beaver, *cottontail rabbit* (*Sylvilagus nuttallii*, Nuttallii - *sxʷlʼótqs* - "notched nose," or *Lepus townsendi*), and different ground squirrels (*Citellus columbianu, Spermophilus townsendii*, and *S. Washingtoni*). *Ducks* (*Anas* spp, *Aythya* spp, and *Mergus* spp. - *sésƛʼxʷmʼ* or *xʷátxʷt*), and *geese* (*kʼʷsíxʷ*) were hunted for food and their by-products of feather and bone. *Small birds* (*xʷiʔxʷeyʼúɫ*) were not taken for food, though the feathers were used by young boys for temporary self adornment, usually stuck in their hair.

Once-traditional economic patterns were altered with the introduction of the horse into the Plateau, which permitted the Spokan more frequent opportunities to conduct bison hunting, trading, and even war and horse-stealing forays on the Plains. They often departed their winter villages or early spring camps in early April "for the bulls from which they return in June and July: and another, after a month's recruit, to kill cows, which have by that time become fat" (Gibbs 1855, 1:415; 1967:21). The Spokan had similar bison hunting seasonal patterns as the Nez Perce, who "hunted buffalo in the late fall and winter, returning in time for spring root digging and for the fish runs of the summer (Garth 1964, 20:52). However, some Spokan commenced bison hunting in late July and early August—with some groups returning in November, whereas some hunters would remain on the Plains until early spring. The economic significance of the horse was to lessen the Spokan reliance upon local hunting, but not on gathering roots or salmon fishing, which continued to provide the greatest amount of a predictable subsistence, and for exchange with certain groups of the western Plains (Teit 1930:346).

When planning a collective hunt, numerous pre-hunt and post-hunt activities were frequently influenced by ritual observance of sweating, specific pre-hunt prohibitions of certain foods and taboos, cleansing weapons, procedures of hunt strategy, and, if successful, the logistics of immediate or delayed transportation of meat. Pre-hunt preparations were influenced by a mutually agreed upon hunt leader, an individual possessing a tutelary spirit for the animal being sought—usually the recipient of the dream that instigated the hunt. Though all large animals were treated with respect and warranted certain pre-hunt rituals, the bear was considered the most dangerous to hunt, even in winter. Hale described how the fauna:

> [...] are now comparatively few, when compared with their former numbers. They consist of wolves, large and small, who prowl around the dwellings; lynxes, bears of the gray, brown, black, and yellow colours, the former of which were the most numerous. Beavers and otters are now both scarce. Rats, both water and musk, are seen in numbers (1846, 4:466).

Animals Hunted

Bear

A man who dreamed of killing a bear would, prior to hunting, always carefully observe certain restrictions of diet, abstain from sexual relations, and usually have solitary sweats when he would sing his power song to enlist the assistance of his guardian spirit. When ready to depart with other hunters, a man judiciously cared for his hunting gear and performed physical and spiritual rituals of cleansing any implements previously used to kill deer or other animal, by singing over the hunting paraphernalia. During the hunter's absence, none of his family would eat bear meat, lest the hunter be bitten or killed by a bear.

The concern and danger of bear hunting was further expressed by using a "weapon" consisting of special rounded maple stick, approximately 120 cm in length, on which eight black deer claws were tied to the front end; sometimes more were tied on with a strip of buckskin. The hunter would be told by his guardian spirit how many *claws (q'ʷoxʷqín'čst)* to affix to the stick:

> Any guardian spirit can help a man kill anything. If this man wanted to kill anything, even us, from far away, he could do it by using the stick and using the same noise. He could kill anything by using the stick. A man even with a tipi guardian spirit could kill anything—even bears and people. The man with the deer spirit couldn't kill bear—and only the bear—with his stick: he couldn't kill grizzlies. He could kill the rest of the animals. No guardian spirit could kill the bear, not even the bear guardian spirit; the bear could only be killed with a gun or bow and arrow because he is too strong and tough. When the bear "talked" to a man (i.e. as a guardian spirit), he told him that he just couldn't be killed by the guardian spirits (Smith 1936-8:1337).

Despite the black bear's poor eyesight, bear hunting was always a dangerous activity because the "senses of smell and hearing are very keen" (Ingles 1965:354), sometimes permitting the animal to circle and approach behind the unsuspecting hunter undetected. This animal was the largest carnivore hunted by the Spokan, and killed using various techniques depending upon the time of the year. Bear meat and hide were considered prime in July and August when bears ate great quantities of numerous types of ripened berries, a time when most bears were taken. Cox explained how, "Their flesh is excellent, particularly in the summer and autumnal months, when roots and wild fruit are had in abundance" (1957 [1832]:212). Both the grizzly bear and *black bear (Ursus americanus - nɫámqeʔ)* were active fishers, preferably for salmon, and, when available, gorged themselves on *dead salmon (hi seč'enč)*.

According to numerous oral accounts, most bears were killed in the winter while hibernating, or about two weeks prior to *hibernation (scʔíʔtcs)*, being more docile. When snow was still on the ground, a bear would emerge from its den to end its hibernation, and hunters using snowshoes would track its location, killing it with bow and arrow. Yet bears—usually in good condition—were less frequently hunted when they commenced to emerge from winter hibernation, for by then they would have lost much of their stored fat. Their diet then would be primarily early spring grasses and small rodents. During this brief period, a group of men seeing bear scat or tracks, would attempt to run down, encircle, or tree the bear using dogs, though the bear was known to be in poor condition. Later, in early spring, hunters would look for bears that tended to concentrate in dispersed areas where grasses were first commencing to grow.

When the needles of larch trees commenced to turn yellow it was an indication that bears would soon begin hibernating. Generally a week prior to its hibernating, a bear will often make a *bedding area of trampled grass (ɫqilštist č'ʔulixʷ)*, always at a distance from the intended winter den so as not to reveal the site of hibernation. During this pre-hibernation ritual, the bear completely cleansed its gastrointestinal tract and stomach of any contents by eating mushrooms. After the bear had completed physicking itself, it would eat a quantity of rotten wood, and then thoroughly masticate a small section of heavily pitched black pine bark, which together effectively plugged the large intestine. The bear's stomach "becomes shrunken and half rigid" (Ingles 1965:352) after this annual diet. Once the bear has entered its winter den, it rarely leaves except to *urinate* (*tčéy'i*), usually two or three times during its seclusion, or when awakened by hunters. If a bear had not accumulated enough body fat, the animal remained active throughout the winter—a situation that made hunting more difficult, for a non-hibernating bear was then unpredictable and more aggressive. After bears left their dens in early spring, they typically went to north-facing slopes for two to three weeks where they ate the *young catkins* (*sxʷółqn*) of willow, which served as a physic to purge the gastrointestinal tract of the impacted rectal plug.

During this brief period, hunters would visit the north-facing slopes as bears were then relatively easy to chase and kill, being weak and short of breath until resuming a more adequate diet at lower elevations. If the snow was deep and powdery, the hunters seldom brought dogs as the animals would have great difficulty running in the powder, and the hunters had to use snowshoes. However, dogs were used if the snow was crusted as a result of the snow thawing before freezing in the spring weather.

The preferred strategy was for a group of hunters to spread out in a wide front while the men looked for the characteristic large, five-toed tracks. Upon seeing tracks, the hunters would give chase. If they had dogs, they were released, and they would chase and encircle the bear—nipping and even biting the bear–until the hunters arrived. An exhausted bear frequently sat down if too weak to *climb a tree* (*hec č'íwlši*) or when wounded. If the bear attempted to climb a tree, one of the dogs could possibly be successful in biting an ear or the lips of the bear. The hunters naturally hoped that none of their dogs would be killed, which occasionally happened. Once the men had caught up with their dogs, the bear was dispatched with bow and arrow, whereas a treed bear was often brought down by continually shooting arrows to either kill the bear or to ground the gravely wounded creature. If this failed, the tree—usually a fir tree with ample foliage—would be ignited in hopes of forcing the bear to the ground (STHC).

A bear's inhabitation area was easily identified by claw marks on the bark of surrounding trees, or by a hunter who had previously identified a den with a bark-slash high enough on a tree that was above winter snow depth. The den's location was made more apparent by the bear's malodorous scent. Hunters once said that in all of nature, the breath of a bear is the worst because of its opportunistic diet. Given the geology of the Spokan area, there were few caves for denning, and dens were more often under low-lying horizontal granite outcrops, or in partially excavated earth depressions enlarged by the removal of earth and stone from under an *up-rooted* (*t'ipašalqʷ*) wind-blown older pine or fir tree. These sites were nearly always located at higher elevations on *south-facing mountain* (*čkʷkʷličn*) slopes. It was said that an adult bear could actually move large stones, if necessary, to enlarge a den or improve a hibernation site. Prior to commercial logging, and the provenience of large timber, a bear would sometimes hibernate in a large fallen hollow log or in an already partially hollow large *dead tree* (*č'éyeʔ*) that was still standing.

A planned bear hunt was always preceded by considerable ritual to ensure the success of the hunt and the welfare of the hunter and his dogs. After killing a bear, the successful hunter sang the bear's death song and observed three days of strict behavioral and dietary taboos to avoid dreaming of the bear or being burned later by fire or struck by lightning. The hunter abstained from having sexual relations during this time of observance, just as he would have done for three days prior to the bear hunt. Foods that were likely to be eaten by a bear, such as berries, were avoided during the grieving hunter's vigil. Such a dietary prohibition was strictly observed by a hunter's wife during her husband's absence. Smith (1936-8:140) noted that a Kalispel woman refrained from any food whatsoever while her husband was away on a bear hunting expedition, to ensure his success and safety.

In the past (*sq'sip*) hunters were familiar with the general bear population in certain areas, and did not engage in over-killing this animal, knowing that the female bear breeds only on alternate years, and delivers only two or three cubs during hibernation. Cubs born in the winter den remain with the mother for "about three months before they follow the mother during her food-seeking. The following autumn, the cubs will den with the mother until spring, after which she forces them to shift for themselves" (Ingles 1965:354). If possible, a bear in an opening with cubs was avoided, and it was said that only a brave hunter ever attempted to attract a sow by imitating the distress sounds of a cub.

In deep snow a hunter might use one of his snowshoes as a shovel to enlarge or excavate a clearing to the entry of a known den. Once the entry had been exposed, the hunter would, ideally, attempt to engage the bear outside of the den where it was easier to kill with bow and arrow—such arrows were always stone-tipped. If a bear refused to emerge, several methods were used to force the bear outside. The hunter could use a long pole to prod the creature, or force the pole against the bear and turn it so that it would twist the animal's heavy coat to enrage the bear.

Another method to force a secluded bear from its den was to smoke it out by building a smudge fire of green fir or pine boughs in front of the bear's den. If the den was sufficiently deep, it often forced the bear to emerge or be suffocated. Fires built near large rock areas tend to blow toward the often sun-warmed rocks. Since bears often plugged the entrance to a winter den with fir boughs, leaves, and grass, the hunter would ignite the material. If the technique of fire had suffocated the bear, after a sufficient length of time the hunter would cautiously crawl into the den with a long length of thick rawhide. He then quickly but carefully tied one end section around the bear's paws, encircling the other end around the animal's muzzle, and finally around the neck. The bear was then pulled out by the hunters, and if still alive, dispatched with bow and arrow or a heavy thrusting spear.

The opinion of Lewis and Clark—who never traversed Spokan country—was that the bear hunter "looked upon the grizzly as a foe deeply to be dreaded, and no greater distinction could come to a warrior than that won by killing one of these monsters of the forest, a feat which entitled the hunter ever after to wear a necklace of the claws of the vanquished bear" (Durham 1912, 1:54).

Another procedure was to throw snow into the *cave* (*nɬxʷénč*) or den. As soon as the aroused bear looked out of the enclosure, the hunters killed the animal with bow and arrow, after which the men would rush in and capture any small bears.

Smith (1936-8:134) has noted that some hunters could successfully create the cry of a distressed *bear cub* (*sc'qálsqn*) by partially pinching their nostrils together and blowing. In was not unusual for a hunter to take the cub or cubs home if the mother bear was killed, and after a week or two of socializing the captive cubs with the hunter's family, they adopted the behavior and habits of the household dogs (Elmendorf, pers. comm.; Smith 1936-8:45). *Black bears* (*nɬámqeʔ*) displayed aspects of human behavior (Smith 1936-8:45) in various ways, in movement when upright and ambulatory. When *skinned out* (*sčqelxʷ*), a bear anatomically resembles a human, and when nurturing and socializing their cubs. Not being able to keep an adult bear, the *yearling cubs* (*snéʔmlt*) were usually killed and butchered, though some live cubs were sold to the whites in the early 1900s (Smith 1936-8:124).

There is no reason to believe traditional trapping devices—including deadfalls—endangered the bear population, because they were often too strong and large to trap with traditional snares or traps—particularly grizzly bears. The steel trap, invented in 15th century Europe, was expensive and in short supply until 1823 when Sewell Newhouse invented the first American commercial metal trap, which has changed very little in over one hundred and eighty years. However, with the introduction of rifles, unrestricted hunting by non-Indians, and the widespread use of an introduced technology using large single and double short- and long-spring steel traps—notably the Oneida Newhouse long-spring 1855 Grizzly Bear No. 6 with a 43-inch iron trap—the black and grizzly bear population was reduced considerably. Some trappers preferred a Newhouse #15. Undoubtedly, the effectiveness of both the commercial traps, firearms, and the demands of the fur market greatly reduced fur-bearing animal populations.

Prior to the introduction of the rifle, a man's ability of being an accomplished *tracker* (*sxʷnʔucšnéɬc'ʔem*) was even more apparent, as was the strategy of persistent hunting; given the required close proximity when using a bow. At one time some men had power to track a specific animal, certainly those of economic significance. Yearlings and two-year-old bears were taken in summer and early fall with a

315

type of deadfall. In this particular variation, the deadfall was a log-walled, hut-like structure having one side open and just wide enough for a bear to partially enter. Traditionally, it had two large logs spaced apart and immediately before and parallel to the entrance. This type of setup forced the bear to straddle the two logs while entering the structure to get the bait within, thereby forcing the animal to extend its head and upper body into the structure. Once the bear tried to seize the bait, a triggering device released a large log down onto the animal. This predation device would not always trap or kill an adult bear, who would almost always demolish such a deadfall.

A different type of deadfall was more effective for killing adult bears, one made by erecting a four-legged platform, with each pair of vertical legs reinforced by two logs laid on the ground outside against each set of legs. The heavy horizontal killing log was set at the top of the platform and held in place by two smaller poles that ran horizontally to the triggering device, which was released when the bear took the bait after being forced to enter the restricted causeway (Smith 1951:1542). Using any animal's blood was an effective bait when spread over the triggering device.

When a bear was killed at an appreciable distance from a camp or village, the hunter was always confronted with the logistical decision of whether or not to transport the heavy hide—along with the meat—back to camp. Any newly butchered bear meat had to be cooked without delay, to prevent it from spoiling and rotting. To save time and effort, the bear was opened, dressed-out, and the hide placed over a fire to burn off the hair, thereby reducing the weight and cooking the meat. Dehairing a bear was not done if the hide was intended as a robe or blanket. This was best accomplished by separately tying both the front legs and the back legs together through which a long, stout green lodge pole was run through, and the bear was then suspended over a long fire with each edge of the pole supported by two erect cross-pole frames. Only after cooking was the meat removed from the bear, cut into manageable sections, and baked on hot rocks covered with subalpine fir branches. Bear meat was not cached or stored (Smith 1936-8:130-31). After skinning out the bear, the meat would always be placed atop fir or pine boughs so it had no contact with the snow or the ground. The meat was then equally distributed between the hunters, which later made excellent jerky or pemmican. Some, including the author, have claimed that bear jerky is most desirable.

As mentioned in the section on tanning, bear hide was soaked for three days by stone *immersion (nqʷel' *- "immersion of material") in still water, or anchored in a running stream with large rocks. The hide was then wrung dry using the Spanish windlass technique, and then stretched on a slanted heavy double- or triple-poled rack elevated approximately one or more meters at the support end, and the hide fleshed with sharp stones. After removing all the flesh, the hide was again placed skin-side down on the rack and beamed with an old bear rib. During hide preparation, the animal's brains were typically buried in a basket to encourage rotting, and later mixed with wood ashes and rubbed into the entire skin area. Bear hides were highly prized, and the fat was valuable as a *burn medicine (n-sɬmaq hu mer'yemisyn)* and for a variety of soaps and utensil lubricants.

Depending upon elevation, black bears were seldom hunted in late May when the meat was deemed unpalatable since they often eat skunk cabbage, nor in late July when they ravaged *red ant (Pogonomyrmex occidentalis - sxʷúxʷy'eʔ)* nests. Many years ago several elders could recall—with apparent relish—how the best pemmican was made in the fall from bear meat, using deer fat mixed with berries, and it was considered a fortifying food when traveling in winter. A bear's *intestines (stx̣énč)* were removed and cleaned by washing as soon as possible—later to be boiled for food as was done with the bear's stomach after washing, which was eaten after boiling, usually by the hunters. The head meat was always eaten after being either roasted or boiled. Bear blood was apparently never eaten, even as a survival food.

Given the ferocity of the *grizzly bear (Ursus arctos horribilis - smx̣éy'čn)*, only a person possessing specific power would attempt to hunt and kill this large and dangerous animal. As was true when hunting black bear, a man hunted the grizzly bear only after dreaming of success and observing a three day period of intense sweating, sexual abstinence, and strict adherence to numerous food taboos, ones which acknowledged the diet of the bear. An additional reason not to hunt the grizzly was that the meat is rather strong in flavor and tough in texture, and the fur was considered too thick and stiff for garments or sleeping robes. On account of the size and strength of a grizzly bear, none of the traditional delayed predation devices were effective in killing or capturing such a bear, which served only to enrage the animal.

When encountering a grizzly bear, the hunter knew it was best to stand motionless, since it was known that a grizzly rarely attacked a person who remained so. In fact, there are a few accounts of a grizzly rushing up close to a human who stood absolutely still, staring at the person for ten minutes or so, and then finally turning and walking away (Smith 1936-8:143). However, if a person panicked and turned to *run away* (*nx̣eł hu x̌ʷt'ip* - "become frightened and run away"), the bear was likely to kill him—usually by tearing the person's head off with one swipe, or by biting. Consequently, a grizzly was often avoided.

Grizzly bears were hunted during hibernation, usually in known caves or dens. The strategy of hunting was similar to that used for black bears—forcing the grizzly from its *den* or *cave* (*nloxʷolexʷtis* or *noamqe*) with smoke, and dispatching it with bow and arrow or with a heavy maple wood thrusting spear. A *spear that was bloodied* (*kʷlkʷlsmúlmn*) with the bear's blood was considered a proof of ordeal as well as demonstrating the hunter's bravery (STHC). The spear was used when bear hunting, because it was said a man had only one chance to kill such a large animal, and then at a dangerously close distance. Smith, when describing the Chewelah-Spokan Group, noted:

> Chewelah [Spokan] hunters went out late in the fall or early in the spring to get grizzlies before they had left their dens. Since they went out on purpose to get the bears, they made more preparations than the Kalispel and their method was consequently a trifle more complicated.
>
> A Chewelah hunter [stationed himself] on each side [of the entrance of the den]. Each had a pole about 4 inches in diameter and sharpened at the bottom end. These they threw right into the mouth of the den with sufficient force to stick into the ground so firmly that the bear could not pull them out. Being thrown from each side of the entrance, the sticks crossed each other [and tended to support one another to some extent]. If it were possible, they tied the tops of the poles fast to a tree [or some other immovable object] after they had thrown them [in this way strengthening the structure]. However, to do this they had to work fast. Because of the poles, the grizzly could not get out of his den while the hunters could easily shoot in through the opening (1951:147).

The behavior of these large mammals was never predictable—certainly when hunted; consequently, Spokan bear hunters were knowledgeable and respectful of a bear's strength, spirit, and physical and behavioral characteristics—even anthropomorphic ones. It is not known if the Spokan ever had any special cult-like rites associated with the bear—ones common to many bear-hunting societies. However, it is known that if a man publicly mentioned too frequently or loudly that he had slain a bear, the face of this creature would appear to him in a dream and agonize him by screaming and hugging him, even taking his breath away. As mentioned, in the past, after killing a bear, a hunter observed a week or more of special sweats when he sang a special mourning song to the spirit of the deceased bear to thank the bear for presenting himself so that the hunter's family had food and a warm bear hide blanket or robe. One elderly lady explained how throughout the winter, every time her grandfather would spread a rather decrepit black bear skin robe over her and her sisters at night, the old man would always give thanks to the bear's spirit for the use of his hide, one that would provide warmth for his granddaughters.

Moose and Bison

A *moose* (*Alces alces* - *sx̣áslqs*) with a yearling offspring was never intentionally killed, and being a relatively solitary animal it was hunted by winter tracking or in summer and late fall when eating hydrophytes in small ponds or shallow lakes. Moose hide is thick and difficult to tan and later *sew* (*t'aʔqʷúm'* - "to sew"). As today, the main reason for hunting moose—always with a rifle—is for the meat

The moose and *bison* (*Bison bison* - *qʷíqʷáy st'm'áti* - "black cows") did not frequent traditional Spokan hunting areas during the historical period, as they had earlier (Osborne 1953:266). On an occasion when he was with the Flathead, DeSmet referred to "what a glorious hunt of buffaloes!" (1966, 27:349). This missionary foresaw the eventual extinction of the bison (DeSmet 1905, 3:995). Earlier he spoke of different parts of bison which were of course preferred:

> Though some prefer the tongue, others thought hump, or some other favorite piece, all the parts are excellent food. To preserve the meat it is cut in slices, thin enough to be dried in the sun; sometimes a kind of hash is made of it, and this is mixed with the marrow taken from the largest bones (1843:120).

Haines, quoting from Twaite's later edited journals of Lewis and Clark, wrote thus of the abundant grass and lower mountains in Montana: "All these features combined to allow easy passage for the buffalo to the west slopes and the headwaters of the Snake, the Salmon, and the Clark's Fork of the Columbia" (1940:394). Haines, however, noted sightings of bison by Ross, Mackenzie, Cox, McDonald, and Kane, all of whom spent appreciable time in the Upper Columbia region (1940:390). Spokan hunting parties in late summer or early fall travelled to the region around Helena or to the Flathead country near the Bitterroot Mountains in search of bison (Elmendorf 1935-6, 1:21). Anastasio's research led him to conclude that "the Spokan, because of a poor hunting base, probably depended to some extent on trading and hunting bison" (1974, 4:170). This was a partial explanation as to why some Spokan ventured onto the Plains to expressly hunt bison. There is little evidence to suggest that the Spokan ventured onto the Great Plains for bison in the early nineteenth century (Chance *et al.* 1981), and in all probability the Spokan and the Colville formed bison hunting parties in the mid-1800s (McDonald 1927), leaving for the Great Plains in fall and returning in early spring for fishing.

According to Cox, however, "The Indians allege that buffaloes were formerly numerous about the plains, and assert that remains of these animals are still found" (1824:228). "While there is abundant testimony that buffalo had formerly roamed over the great plains between the Rocky mountains and the Cascades, they had become extinct here prior to the advent of the first white men" (Durham 1912, 1:16). Dr. Suckley (1830-69), a physician on the 49th Parallel Survey in 1853-55, recorded seeing a number of bison skulls when descending the Pend d'Oreille:

> Buffalo were formerly in great numbers in this valley [Lower Bitterroot Valley ...] For a number of years past none had been seen west of the (Rocky) mountains; but, singular to relate, a buffalo was killed at the mouth of the Pend d'Oreille river on the day I passed it. The Indians were in great joy at this, supposing that the buffalo were coming back among them (Durham 1912, 1:16 fn).

Pickering, while visiting the Chewelah-Spokan, stated, "This place, however, is not with the range of the buffalo, although apparently well adapted for them; and but a single instance was on record of a stray animal having been seen in the vicinity of Colville" (1895:27). Burnett, who observed numerous bison hunts by Indians, described the necessity of hunting by horseback:

> The American buffalo is [a] peculiar animal, remarkably hardy, and much fleeter of foot than anyone would suppose from his round, short figure. It requires a fleet horse to overtake him. His sense of smell is remarkably acute, while those of sight and hearing are very dull. If the wind blows from the hunter to the buffalo, it is impossible to approach him (1904, (1):72).

Gibbs, much earlier, remarked upon the reduction, even scarcity of bison within the eastern Plateau:

> The buffalo, it would seem, in former times, penetrated at least occasionally thus far to the westward, though now they never come through the northern passes. We were informed by an old Iroquois hunter at Fort Colville, who has been some forty-eight years in the company's services, that the last bull was killed some twenty-five years ago [circa 1828] in the Grand Coulee (1855, 1:415).

Spokan and Colville groups would take dried salmon and *pit-baked camas* (*ʔítxʷeʔ*) they traded for bison hides and meat (Chance and Hudson 1981). In the protohistoric time, when most of the bison had gone from the Spokan area, hides and robes were acquired by trade with the Flathead, Nez Perce, and Plains groups. DeSmet expressed how both the Indian and non-Indian had a preference for "the tongue, others the hump, or some other favorite piece, all the parts are excellent food" (1843;120).

Cox spoke of the absence and low-populations of certain ungulate and bison:

The Indians allege that buffaloes were formerly numerous about the plains, and assert that the remains of these animals are still found. Between Lewis River and Spokan House we see many bleached antlers of elk, together with the large curved horns of the sheep which are now found in the vicinity of the Rocky Mountains. These animals have long since fled from the plains. None of the present race of Indians have seen any of them, and are unable to account for their disappearance. We were equally at a loss to divine the cause; and whether the annual burning of the grass by the natives in hunting the deer had any influence in driving them away. I shall leave to the curious in animal emigration to determine (1957:258).

Referring to early bison populations, in the abstract of a well-researched and brilliant paper, M. Scott Taylor provides an innovative explanation for the near-extinction of bison, which quickly brought dire effects upon Plains people who were so dependent upon this animal for food and numerous by-products, and also as a trading commodity with eastern Plateau groups:

> In the 16th century, North American contained 25-30 million buffalo; by the late 19th century less than 100 remained. While removing the buffalo east of the Mississippi took settlers 100 years, the remaining 10 to 15 million buffalo on the Great Plains were killed in a punctuated slaughter in a little more than 10 years. I employ theory, data from international trade statistics by a foreign-made innovation and fueled by a foreign demand for industrial leather. Ironically, the ultimate cause for this sad chapter in American environmental history was of European, and not American, origin (Taylor 2007, n.p.).

It should be noted that President Andrew Jackson encouraged Plains market hunters, and others, to kill as many bison as possible in order to deny the Plains Indians their main food source, as well as an animal that provided many essential utilitarian by-products, such as horn, bone, and skin. As early as 1814, after the Battle of Horseshoe Bend, Jackson expressed his feelings of Indian land use in a proclamation (1:494), saying, "The weapons of warfare will be exchanged for the utensils of husbandry; and the wilderness which now thrives in sterility and seems to mourn the desolation which overspreads it, will blossom as the rose, and become the nursery of the arts" (Prucha 1969, 3:534).

Deer, Elk, Antelope, and Mountain Sheep and Goats

In the early historical period, the Spokan area had no bison, caribou, or moose, but had large herds of deer, elk, and antelope (Teit 1930:346), and fewer mountain sheep in the area of the Chewelah-Spokan Group, mainly within areas of *Pinus ponderosa* association (Kendeigh 1964:302). There were no mountain goats in the Spokan area, but their horns and fur were always acquired through trade with more northerly groups, most notably the Okanogan. At one time there were more elk in the area than now, and one of Smith's Chewelah-Spokan Group informants "remarked parenthetically that elk are said to have been numerous 'around here' long ago" (1951:222). Several elderly Spokan women recalled how, when a son or husband went off to hunt deer, they hoped he would not kill an elk, because the thick hide was difficult to work while tanning, particularly by an elderly woman.

The Spokan hunted three types of deer: *Black-tailed deer* (*Odocoileus hemionus columbianus* Richardson - *pwelščn*), a subspecies of the *mule deer* (*O. hemionus hemionus - st'úlc'eʔ*), and *white-tailed deer* (*O. Virginianus - c'ʔúlixʷ*). The best time for hunting any ungulata was in midsummer until fall, while gathering huckleberries, when entire families gained elevation to exploit edible and medicinal plants, a time when deer hides and meat were prime. Deer were also hunted in winter mainly in wooded areas as they gorged on low hanging tree moss or dug in the snow for kinnikinnick leaves and exposed shrubs. During the last half of August and throughout September, hunters would go early in the morning on day hunts to known areas where mule deer ate mountain ash berries. On several day hunts, some hunters were accompanied by their wives. The protocol of hunting required that after the deer had been killed "the leaders would sing their song while everyone helped themselves to the meat which was on the ground. Just the men and women were allowed in this ritual and they were not allowed to pick up the meat with their hands or to touch it with anything but their mouths" (STHC, Anon., n.d.).

Prior to any large deer hunt, the man who had a previous dream of success would announce his intention of a hunt to his fellow hunters who then joined him in the sweathouse and discussed where and when to conduct the hunt. This discussion was always a traditional courtesy since members of a hunting group were intimately knowledgeable of everyone's ability. It was common for a man to have a vision of a successful deer hunt during a sweating session, when a man's *suméš* could be outside in a deer area, communicating his presence and encouraging the person to venture out to listen to his *suméš*, who would guide him to the game. During winter hunts, men often chased deer on snowshoes, whereas a common way to kill an exhausted deer was with a hand-held spear. Smith recorded how during the fall hunt the Chewelah-Spokan Group" ran deer into lakes. Especially at this time of the year when the bucks were fat, they would [start] from far away before they went to the water to get away from the dogs. [In order to secure the animal] they had one canoe, made in exactly the same way as the Kalispel canoes, in each lake" (1951:167). It should be noted that the Spokan occasionally hunted with the Coeur d'Alene and Nez Perce in the Kalispel territory (Steves 1855, 1:367, 12:134).

Group hunting of *elk* (*Cervus canadensis - tšec'* for male, *snéč̓c'e?* for female), antelope (*Antilocapra americana - stˤán*), and deer using *deer drives* (*č̓ɫá?q'm*), surrounds and jumps required considerable coordination of the participants, as well as preparation of the area prior to hunting. Their efforts were worthwhile, since deer meat provided the greatest share of land mammal protein to the Spokan diet. An individual *leader* (*ši?tús*)—usually a shaman possessing deer power—might dream of a successful hunt and announce his intentions to hunting partners. At dawn, on the hunt day, they would assist him in strategically placing burnt moccasins and certain bird feathers around the designated area in a funnel-shaped fashion. These devices aided the hunters when the deer attempted to avoid the burnt scent. Symbolically, the feathers aided the arrows to their mark. The most productive method was the surround, when thirty to forty men *encircled* (*?a?acic* - "encircled or trapped deer or fish) an area, slowly reducing their enclosure, all the while shouting and waving their arms, thereby pushing the deer to a high point where they would be dispatched. To ensure that the deer would group when surrounded, the hunters often encircled a large area with empowered *little sticks* (*čnq'ʷúlmn* or *nék'ʷmn*) to contain the deer (Elmendorf 1935-6, 1:48). The practice of using the game surround was employed when hunters had only the bow and arrow, but upon the introduction of the rifle, this practice quickly declined in popularity and was replaced by straight *deer drives* (*č̓ɫá?q'm*). As mentioned earlier, cross-shooting with rifles was a potentially deadly practice for participating hunters.

Deer runs were made with strategically placed basalt rock cairns, and low stone walls that served to effectively channel fleeing deer to *talus slopes* (*n'sšén'š*) where awaiting hunters would rise from hunting pits to dispatch the animals with bow and arrow. And yet deer hunting was more difficult during the summer as deer tended to leave the concealment of brush in favor of open areas where the breeze tended to keep away flies and insects. Deer were normally more cautious when grazing in open areas; consequently, a hunter had a more likely opportunity for a kill when the deer was in cover. Since deer, most notably the white-tailed, are crepuscular, that is feeding mainly from pre-dawn and from late afternoon until dusk, that was the time when they were usually hunted. The larger-antlered mule deer tended to graze in open terrain, whereas the smaller antlered white and black-tailed deer usually inhabited brushy habitats. Deer runs were not always as distinct as elk trails.

After a successful hunt, the *leader* (*č'emáqs*) conducted a special ritual to acknowledge the assistance of his *suméš*, and to thank the deer for offering to be killed. And when a deer, for example, was killed, its *lower leg* (*scč'maqstšn*) bones would be wrapped and carefully placed in a tree crotch, after removal of the leg tendons, so that the dead deer bones would not run off and warn other deer. Deer provided not only meat but by-products such as hide, brain, dewclaws, and antler. Hunters would *remove the skin from the deer head* (*cckʷáya?qni*) before the *entire deer head* (*sɫaxʷqín*) was cooked, being considered a delicacy. Dewclaws were knocked off, boiled, and eaten by the hunters.

On the day after butchering, deer meat was cut into thin strips and hung from large *rectangular frames* (*sncqy'éłc'e?tn*) to dry for winter storage. A smoke drying rack was commonly used to *dry meat* (*scqy'éłc'e?*). Often clumps of prickly pear were secured near the base of each pole supporting meat drying or smoking racks to prevent the incursion of various types of rodents and larger animals. However, most meat drying racks did not depend upon low fires, but rather the sun for drying. Scott mentioned how, "Clam shells beneath caught the oil" (1941:217).

If butchered meat could not be hung high enough for protection against nocturnal animals in a hunting camp, hunters protected the cache *by piling brush atop the meat or leaving their personal effects near the cache* (*čłp'łq'én'e?*). During a winter hunt, when following a wounded deer, the hunters buried any killed deer in deep snow to *freeze it* (*?úxʷłc'e?is*) until the carcasses were later recovered, cleaned, quartered, and taken to the winter village. Temporary tree storage was also an effective way for hunters to cache a slain deer or elk, and protect it from other animals. Given the time of day and the circumstances of a hunt, a dressed animal could be protected by throwing a line that had been first secured to the animal's rear legs over a high limb and then hoisted well above the ground. Packs and food containers used by travelers were similarly protected from destruction or contamination by porcupines and other nocturnal animals.

The same technologies of deer hunting were employed for other large animals. However, antelope was the only large land mammal that was decoyed or enticed within bow and arrow range, often by smoke or by moving a hide or *feather wands* (*xancutn*). The flesh of "the antelope is wholesome and easily digested" (DeSmet 1843:119). Antelope, sometimes called pronghorn, were once common in the middle reach of the Spokane (Thoms 1991:3,23).

> Antelopes were very abundant until about 1820 in the Spokane country, especially on the Spokane Prairie; but they inhabited only a small fringe of the Coeur d'Alene country on the west, especially around Latahs [sic] Creek, which was their eastern limit. The last of them were killed off in this section about 1820, but they continued to be plentiful farther west, in the counties of the Spokane and Columbia (Teit 1930:96).

Osborne's archaeological finds (45-LN-3 and 45LN-1) of bison and antelope osteological material in and near a rock shelter near Spokan inhabited *Crab Creek* (*nc'oy'xʷetn*) attest to the presence of these animals (1953:266). The *mountain goat (Oreamnos americanus* - *sxʷλ'éy'* or *sxʷłé?*) and *mountain sheep (Ovis canadensis canadensis* - *łu?mné?* or *łu?mné?lščn* - "male," *xʷłxʷáł* - "female")* did not inhabit the traditional areas of the Spokan, save for the Chewelah-Spokan peoples. Mountain goats and mountain sheep products were, otherwise obtained, through trade with the Kalispel or the Lakes, who hunted them in the fall and summer in a treeless rocky area located just east of Priest lake (Smith 1936-8:238). The hide and horn were the main reasons for hunting the mountain goat. Some have said that the meat has too strong a flavor—though over time a person can acquire a taste for it.

Wolves, Wolverines, Cougars, Foxes, and Coyotes

The timber wolf was hunted, but often with difficulty, and was more likely to be killed with bow and arrow by hunters in the winter using snowshoes when the snow was soft and deep. Both the wolf and the *coyote (Canis latrans* - *snč'l'ép*) were renowned for their cleverness, fine sense of smell, and acute eyesight; consequently, they were seldom taken by a deadfall, even when dewclaw hooves were used to bait traps. A hunter always tried to avoid hunting a group of coyotes or a pack of wolves with dogs, which could prove disastrous for the hunter's dogs. Wolf meat was eaten, as was the meat of red fox. Despite the fox's reputation of cunning and caution, it was more often caught with a deadfall, and the pelts of both these animals were tanned with the fur and used in making ceremonial wear and winter hats. A winter hat made from wolf fur will not collect ice or freeze from a person's breath.

Prairie wolves travelled in relatively large packs, but in size were smaller than the more solitary woodland variety. Cox, who hunted and trapped both types, claimed:

Their skins are of no value, and we do not waste much powder and ball in shooting them. The Indians who are obliged to pay dear for their ammunition, are equally careful not to throw it away on objects that bring no remunerating value. The natural consequence is, that the wolves are allowed to multiple; and some parts of the country are completely overrun by them (1832:211).

Either by circumstance or interest, the social organization and group and individual hunting practices of wolves are noted by Cox:

The wolves almost rival the Indians in their manner of attacking the deer. When impelled by hunger, they proceed in a band to the plains in quest of food. Having traced the direction which a herd have taken, they form themselves into a horseshoe line, the extreme points of which they keep open on the gradual ravine. After some cautious manoeuvering they succeed in turning the progress of the deer in that direction. This object effected, they begin to concentrate their ranks, and ultimately to hem in their victims in such a manner, as to leave them no choice but that of being dashed to pieces down the steep and rocky sides of the ravine, or falling prey to the fangs of their merciless pursuers (1957 [1832]:214-5).

Miller explained how "Wolves had formerly been a danger, but they were extinct, along with the red and black foxes taken by the fur trade" (1990:47). And yet today, the recently much larger Canadian Gray wolf (*Canus lupis columianus*) is being introduced into Idaho and Montana, much to the detriment of dwindling elk herds, which are being drastically reduced by the Canadian wolf. Some Spokan hunters feel this will create a serious problem, since the Canadian wolf is presently protected by recently established game laws (ESA) from being hunted. Unfortunately, these carnivores carry an extremely contagious and debilitating disease, *Aleolar hudatid*, which can be spread to other warm-blooded animals who have contact with wolf feces or upon eating this animal.

The *wolverine* (*Gulo gulo - sxʷéyn*) was not purposely hunted, but occasionally taken by accident—usually in a bear deadfall, and were not remembered as being eaten by the Spokan. A trapped wolverine, if it did not destroy a trap or deadfall, could sometimes eat the bait without being caught. There are stories of the tenacious fury and strength of wolverine when confronted or cornered, and was renowned for destroying a trapper's log trap-line cabin. An elderly man once commented how, many years ago, one would acknowledge a tenacious, even mean person as a wolverine, but would only say this to him if he were a close friend with whom he had a joking relationship—but never to a woman or stranger.

A dangerous and even feared animal, one that was never intentionally stalked or hunted, was the mountain lion or *cougar* (*Felis concolor - skʷtismyéw*), an animal seldom seen. It was always said that "it was like a shadow in the woods." But if necessary, there was a method of hunting a cougar, which involved tracking the animal:

[...] in the winter when the snow is without crust and they run on a track they follow it alone or with dogs if they happen to have them and shoot it with bow and arrow [...] Chase it and it will climb a tree.

[the people] tan the hide for a blanket; the hair is short and not too valuable. They use the skin for a quiver [...] They also ate them; they like the meat much, but they never went out on purpose to get them for they might hunt long without running across one, for they are very cunning and sly as well as not numerous (Smith 1936-8:237).

Cougars were considered the most clever of all land mammals, but could become fatigued over a long distance when being chased by hunters on snowshoes when "they turned back and back-tracked on the man's trail, where it was easier going" (Smith 1951:214) because the snow trail had been packed by the earlier pursuit. Cougars were recognized as extremely intelligent and wary creatures. One Chewelah elder told of how one early fall, when he was a small boy, his mother had taken him for berry picking, leaving him just off the road south of Springdale. A mountain lion (cougar) came close to him and just laid down and stared at him until his mother approached, and the mountain lion bounded away. Elders contended that cougars were never known to attack a human, and rarely did a cougar ever attack and kill a dog.

The red fox was seldom purposely hunted or trapped, though the fur—when available, was used for hats and winter leggings and their tails for dance costumes. Nor were the skins later deemed valuable by trapper-traders; the cost of ammunition and time required to making and setting traps was not commensurate with the payment they would eventually get. It was noted how, "Red foxes and wolves are also in great numbers about the plains; but their skins are not now purchased by the [Hudson Bay] Company, as the price given for them would not defray the expense of their carriage" (Cox 1832:211). There are, however, stories of kit foxes and wolves being kept as pets in the past by young boys (STHC). Lord wrote: "A pack of prick-eared curs, simply tamed prairie-wolves, are always in attendance" (1866, 1:71).

Despite the coyote's mythical importance to the Spokan, it was hunted with bow and arrow, but was sometimes "caught accidentally in the deadfalls set for fisher and wolverine. No deadfalls were set on purpose [for coyotes] and they were caught when they were exceedingly hungry. They were eaten and the fur was used also" (Smith 1936-8:272). Some Spokan have contended that the coyote was rarely eaten; only in starvation situations—not for religious reasons, but because the meat has a terrible smell though it has a pleasant taste.

Small Game

Because of natural conditions, most smaller animals were hunted in winter, being prized for their fur for making blankets and robes, and for their meat to supplement stored food. This is particularly true of the *muskrat* (*Ondatra zibethicus* - *ččl'éxʷ*), which was killed in the summer, though reasonably safe in the winter, by men using clubs, after digging open the animal's den:

> The Spokan used to hunt hundreds of muskrat. It is said that they could catch hundreds in a day. They find a house, cut the top off & fold it back. They would plug all the outlets but one. They would sit with a sharpened arrow (not headed) a few inches from where it would have to come up to get air. When it sticks its nose up, they would let fly & shoot it right in the mouth. They would pull the arrow out and kill it with a stick (Smith 1936-8:289).

Smith (1936-8:273) described how the Upper Spokan hunted and trapped the badger, which was said to have once inhabited the area of Latah Creek drainage in great numbers. When aroused, the badger attempts to escape by frantically digging a hole, but before disappearing it would be grabbed by one or both hind legs and then killed by *hitting it on the head* (*ntaʔqíys* - "he hit it on the head") with a club or banging its head against a tree or rock. Remarkably, the badger would stop running or digging if the hunter shouted, causing the animal to become agitated (Smith 1951:209). This animal, however, was considered to be extremely ferocious when trapped or cornered, and despite the badger's slowness, dogs were mostly afraid to attack badgers because of their reputation for vicious biting and sharp claws. Because of this behavior, they were frequently driven from their burrows with water and killed with bow and arrow. Badger meat was eaten, but more valuable was the fur when fashioned into winter hats that were considered as the warmest headgear. When necessary, a folded badger hat served as a comfortable pillow.

During the late summer and early fall, the pelt of the *yellow-bellied marmot* (*Marmota flavivntrids* - *pséw's*) was sought for fabrication of robes or rugs, and as Lord described, "The hair being thick, the marmot-robe keeps out both wet and cold, and stands an immense amount of wear and rough usage" (1866, I:195). Lord's personal experience with eating and giving "testimony to the delicacy of roasted marmot" continued when he wrote how much the Spokan savored the marmot, and provides an explanation of how the Spokan prepared the animal when after being skinned by taking "a long peeled stick which was thrust through the body, from tail to head; then placed slantwise, one end being fast in the ground, the treasured morsel is slowly roasted over a gentle fire" (1866, I:195).

Deadfalls were probably more successful for killing the often unpredictable marten, mink, and otter, but they were taken by snare, rather than with bow and arrow. These animals were more important for their pelts or for making clothing than for their meat. The insatiable curiosity and appetite of the marten almost led to its demise. Both otter and beaver were considered a delicacy (Spinden 1908:206) throughout the Plateau.

323

Dogs were never involved when trapping beaver or otters, "Their terrible teeth are most formidable weapons [...] one otter will vanquish a number of large brave dogs. Every bite of the otter leaves a large gash, like that made by the tusks of the wild boar" (Burnett 1904, 5:154).

The *porcupine* (*Erethizon dorsatum* - *sk'ʷíl'*), being a relatively slow-moving nocturnal animal, was easily treed during daylight hours and dispatched with bow and arrow. But a person attempting to approach a porcupine with a club was likely to be sprayed occasionally with needles once the animal turned and lifted its tail. Porcupines were most prized for the quills and its rather sweet-tasting meat. A discontinued practice was to make a so-called head cheese from the animal's brain, once considered a delicacy. *Porcupine quills* (*k'ʷíl'mn*) were highly valued and were removed en masse from a dead porcupine by throwing a blanket over the remains, and then quickly pulling the blanket away from the carcass with the quills attached. Until recently many Spokan always carried an old blanket in their vehicle on the chance they would see a dead porcupine on the road, and wrap the animal in a blanket to remove the quills.

There was a demand for the pelts of the bobcat, *ermine* (*Mustela erminea* - *pápqɫc'e?*), red fox, and *lynx* (*Lynx canadensis* - *snqcúl*), used in adorning dress clothing and ceremonial pipe bags. The white meat of the lynx was said to taste similar to chicken. Elders claimed these animals became scarce, most notably with the introduction of commercial trapping and steel traps used by Indian and non-Indian trappers. As a consequence of Euro-American technology and greed, the ermine population was greatly reduced. Prior to commercial trapping, both the weasel and ermine were caught in deadfalls, and not shot with bow and arrows to avoid holing the *pelt* (*čnk'ʷéɫc'e?*). When trapping the *weasel* (*Mustela frenata* - *ɫɫč'ím*), in either *winter coat* (*pápqɫc'e?* - "little white animal") or its dark *summer coat* (*q'ʷsúmn*), the main purpose was to use the highly sought and valuable pelt for adorning pipe bags and special ceremonial clothing. Both the short-tailed and long-tailed weasel was trapped.

Throughout the year a favorite pastime for young boys was to track and hunt rabbits. This was done more often during the winter when the *snowshoe hare* (*Lepus americanus* - *sqʷáqʷci?*)—sometimes called a jack rabbit—was in white fur, and more desirable than in the summer when the animal was called *w'ananíče*, and was better camouflaged with its brown pelt. In open areas with no brush, a rabbit, being of poor wind, could be run down by a persistent boy who would then dispatch the animal with bow and arrow, or club it on the head. Rabbits were eaten, but little was done with the pelts, being too thin for clothing. As cited, in the past rabbit pelts were used for various types of clothing. With respect to Spokan terminology, the jack rabbit (*Lepus flavigulans*), like the snowshoe hare, in winter pelage, was called *sqʷáqʷci?*, and *ʕʷananíče?* when in summer pelage (Egesdal, pers. comm.).

The *red pine squirrel* (*Tamiasciurus hudsonicus* - *?ísc'č'*) and the *ground squirrel* (*Spermophilus washingtoni* and *S. columbianus* - *sísč'*) were favorite animals for young boys to stalk and hunt with bows and arrows, or by setting up the more productive squirrel pole to catch tree squirrels. The flying squirrel was taken by bow and arrow, more by chance unless the animal was stationary. All squirrel meat was eaten.

Both the *mole* (*Solex vagrans* - *púl'ye?*) and the *shrew* (*Neurotrichus gibbsii* - *k'ʷék'ʷt'ne?* = mouse) were often hunted by young boys developing their hunting skills, usually with ground snares set near the animals' dens. It was said their meat was never eaten.

Another small animal often killed, usually by boys with a long pole or a club, was the *striped skunk* (*Mephitis mephitis* - *xaxstéy'e?*). Skunks commonly take up residence in a hole, which, when located, facilitated their being hunted by boys and men who build a fire just outside the one entrance. Once the smoke drives the near-suffocated animal from the borrow, it was killed by clubbing, and then skinned out, and the scent gland carefully removed before the meat was roasted and eaten. The major concern when approaching a skunk was the fear of being sprayed by the animal turning and lifting its tail to the hunter, which some elders say could be prevented if one was quick and agile enough to hold the tail down. Smith provided a detailed description of the hunting of skunks and the tanning of their hides:

They get most of the skunk[s] in the fall when they hole up just like a bear. They find a hole, build a fire and suffocate him [...] They listen until they hear no noise, then they dig them out. In this way they do not get a chance to shoot the scent. Then they tan their hides with the hair on and they make robes of them by sewing them together (not in strips). They eat the meat but before they do they carefully cut out the scent gland. They left a row of tails hanging in the middle of the robe so that they hang just below the shoulders in the back. The scent gland was cut out as soon as they catch it, before they skin it and carry it home lest they squeeze it in carrying and lest they break it in cutting it up (1936-8:258).

In the late spring and early summer, while digging in the mornings and afternoons in the large white camas root fields west of Davenport, women often observed holes being used by the ground-dwelling animals. In the afternoon the women would commence to hunt for marmot and both species of *northern pocket gopher* or *mole* (*Thomomys monticola* and *T. taloides* - *púl'y'e?* or *pl'yahál'qs* - a mythic name), which abounded in camas environments. A method of hunting ground-borrowing mammals was to locate all the entrances of the inhabited maze of tunnels and then light smudge fires of sage at all but one known entrance. As the marmot exited, it would be hit with a stout stick or even a digging stick. The animals were skinned, cleaned, and roasted on sticks over a sage wood fire.

Beaver

The beaver (*sqléw'*), North America's largest rodent, which may weigh 90 pounds or more, was an important animal, not only for the skins for clothing and trade, but for making different medicines, and as a food. Beaver teeth proved very effective in making scrapers when working with wood—not unlike a spoke-shave or a dull drawknife. Teeth were used in personal adornment on clothing and strung as necklaces. "The flesh of the beaver is fat and savory" (DeSmet 1843:116), and therefore the flesh was considered a delicacy. "Beaver was both boiled, roasted, and dried" (Schaeffer 1934-37, I-109:33). Commercially, beaver was prized above all furs since the under-fur was a durable waterproof felt with a silky sheen, being in demand by European and American hat-makers.

Beaver, a strictly monogamous mammal, was hunted year round for both the meat and the pelt; the tanned hide made an excellent winter blanket. During late spring and throughout the summer, hunters would go to one of the many known beaver ponds, destroy the dam to drain the pond, and might even tear down the *beaver house* (*sqléw'stqép*), killing the cubs with clubs. In winter, a hunter would wait patiently at one of many breathing holes in the ice until a beaver surfaced to breathe, then dispatched the animal with bow and arrow. The success of hunting was increased if there were several hunters who could observe several breathing holes. Pickering mentioned how the Spokan used a type of basket to capture beaver, but unfortunately he provided no details of the device's construction, saying only how on the upper part of the Spokane River "beaver were formerly common in all these streams, [...] but, owing to the introduction of beaver-traps, they had become almost extinct" (1895:27-8). The preferred beaver trap was a #3 or #4 Newhouse, which, when possible, was baited with a secretion of oil from a beaver's castor gland. A trapped beaver may chew off its leg, and will, if able, treat the wound with musk from his castor.

Canadian mountain man, fur trader and explorer Peter Skeene Ogden (1794-1854) was chief trapper of the HBC, and led five trapping expeditions to the "Snake Country" (1824-1830). During the Snake River Expedition of 1825-1826, Cox recorded how, "Otters are sometimes seen, but the great stable animal, the beaver, is a stranger to this district" (1832:228). Wilson, an accomplished watercolor artist and botanist, acclaimed by Tolmi as an accomplished ornithologist (1963:36), often made profoundly accurate observations of traditional Spokan trapping technology, as well as its effects upon the beaver. For example:

Beavers, otters, etc, are taken with the common beaver trap, and the marten with an ingenious native contrivance something like the figure-of-four trap, so as not to damage the fur. Squirrels and the smaller animals are only eaten in time of scarcity, when they are eagerly sought after; at Colville they were nearly exterminated during a severe winter (Wilson 1866:297).

Yet as early as 1824-25, George Simpson registered an astute and considerable concern for the fluctuating, even declining, beaver population:

> There are few or no Beaver on the Banks of the Columbia owing to the rapidity of the Current and great rise and fall of the Water sweeping away their Young and not enabling them to form Lodges or Dams; they are however numerous on some of the small Lakes and Creeks in the back country and if the Natives would but apply themselves to Hunting during the Winter Months the Trade would be greatly increased (1968:95).

Concerning the Spokan, it should be noted what Fahey said: "for a time, the Indians along the Spokane River apparently trapped enthusiastically, thus depleting their own resources, but as they acquired trade goods their interest slackened" (1988:9).

The seldom-seen and misnamed *mountain beaver* (*Aplodonatia rufa - st'óx̌ʷłš*) had more mythical significance than economic. A mostly nocturnal, stout, short-limbed herbivorous fossorial animal, it is really not a beaver. It leads a subterranean existence in extensive labyrinthine burrow systems, and rarely lives in mountains. The mythical significance was probably derived from the animal's means of communicating by different types of whistling and its ability to make booming noises. Nothing significant could be recalled except one account suggesting that mountain and land beavers were both present before humans, and were considered humanoid because of the booming sounds they made by slapping their tails on water, and building so-called haystacks of plant material the animal stored inside the burrow entrance. Bagley's collection of Northwest creation myths cites how the Spokan associated an enormous beaver with the creation of Palouse Falls as well as numerous side-channels (1930:132). The Jesuit missionary DeSmet (1801-1873) recorded this about the Flathead group:

> Some of the Indian tribes believe that the beavers are a degraded race of human beings, whose vices and crimes have induced the Great Spirit to punish them by changing them into their present form; and they think, after the lapse of a number of years, their punishment will cease, and they will be restored to their original shape. They even believe that these animals use a kind of language to communicate their thoughts to each other, to consult, deliberate, pass sentence on delinquents, &c. (1843:116).

Years later, Dr. Suckley paraphrased and published a report (1855), presumably by Elkanah and Mary Walker, one similar to DeSmet's aforementioned early conclusion of eastern Salish mythical relationship to the beaver and afterlife. However, Suckley unfortunately cited the unsubstantiated conclusions by the Walkers concerning eastern Salish, when speaking elsewhere about the mortuary beliefs and mortuary practices of the Spokan:

> They [Walkers] came among these Indians [Spokan] about nine years ago, and found them to be a poor, miserable, half-starved race, with an insufficiency of food and nearly naked, living upon fish, camas and other roots, and, at the last extremity, upon the pine-tree moss. Unlike the Indians east of the mountains, they had no idea of a future state or a Great Spirit: neither had they any idea of a soul. They considered themselves to be animals, nearly allied to the beaver, but greater than the beaver—and why? Because, they said, 'the beaver builds houses like us, and he is very cunning too; but we can catch the beaver, and he cannot catch us—therefore we are greater than he. Of the soul they had no conception (Durham 1912, 1:119-120).

Beavers use their tails for steering and propulsion, not for building dams and houses, though dam construction was critical to the beaver's environment and survival, for as Burnett wrote:

> The object in damming the stream is to deepen the water, so that it will not freeze to the bottom but leave plenty of room below the ice for the storage of the winter's supply of food. In the summer the beaver cuts down the green willows and divides them into logs of proper length, so that they can be readily moved. These logs are deposited at the bottom of the pond, and kept down by mud placed upon them. The willow in its green state is almost as heavy as water, and these logs are easily sunk and confined to the bottom. On one portion of his dam the beaver constructs his house, above the water, with an entrance from beneath (1904, 5:153).

This obvious dependence upon willow is significant, since the beaver never eats fish or otter. Hence, "The beaver lives entirely upon vegetable food, and for this reason its flesh is esteemed a great delicacy" (Burnett 1904, 5:152). In fact, "The flesh of the beaver is fat and savory. The feet are deemed the most dainty parts. The tail affords a substitute for butter" (DeSmet 1843:116). And yet Parker, who had eaten beaver on

326

several occasions, claimed, "I discovered no evidence of the truth of the assertion often made, that while the flesh of the fore parts is the quality of land animals, its hind parts are in smell and taste like fish" (1840:203).

Large Birds

Birds of prey were never gathered as food, though both the *bald eagle* (*Haliaeetus leucocephalus* - *spql'qín* - "white head") and *golden eagle* (*Aquila chrysaetos* - *mlqnúps* - "black tipped tail feathers") were hunted for their feathers as well as their skins, which usually a mother or grandmother would tan with the feathers to make a son's power bundle. Usually a man made his own power bundle. It was not uncommon for a man who possessed this bird's *suméš*, to dry or desiccate the entire eagle after removing the innards to form part or all of his power bundle. This eagle was called the Nun's eagle by non-Indians "on account of the color of its head, which is white, whilst the other parts of the body are black" (DeSmet 1843, 27:334).

During July, before young eagles could fledge, and when the parents were away securing food, a man gained entrance to a low eagle's nest using a two-poled rung ladder or a *single-pole notched ladder* (*snč'íwlštn*), or, if possible, by climbing the base structure, and once inside he would remove the tail feathers of the young birds for costume ornamentation. The Chewelah-Spokan group would, in certain situations, lower a man over a *cliff* (*hecšn'éššn*) to secure an unfledged eagle (Smith 1936-8:151). However, any method was not without risk:

> The hunter was also confronted with the [dangerous] possibility that the old birds might return [before he had secured the feathers and had retired to safety]. If they returned to find the hunter in their nest, they "pulled in their head" and struck him with their body [with sufficient force to] knock him out of the nest. The hunter was killed [from the fall] (Smith 1951:102).

When securing the tail feathers from young and near-flightless eagles, a man would often throw the unfledged bird to a partner who was stationed below on the ground, since a parent eagle could easily attack the trespasser, who had no protection from the claws of the attacking eagle. Traditionally, there were four named eagle aeries near the Spokane River, each located in a high-standing granite *monolith* (*št'éššn'*). Regardless of age, a captured eagle was never kept as a pet (Smith 1936-8:240).

The *blue heron* (*Ardea herodias* - *smóq'ʷeʔ* or *skʷer'šin*)—sometimes called the blue crane—was sought for its leg bones that were used as flageolets, sucking tubes in curing ceremonies, or as drinking tubes by a woman to prevent hand contamination during her monthly confinement. The greater sandhill crane and heron were reputed to have been difficult birds to stalk and kill with bow and arrow because of the bird's keen eyesight and height (Smith 1951:92); they were always sentinel birds. The Spokan hunted the dry-land nesting greater sandhill crane, primarily below Spokane Falls in once extensive wetland areas where flocks of the large birds would congregate just prior to their fall mass migrations south, and where the cranes collected the small Indian wapato [potatoes] by wading into the water and removing the wapato with their long beaks, and then embedding hundreds of the small wapato in their breast feathers (Smith 1936-8:268) to be eaten later.

The eggs of all wading birds were gathered from water-encircled raised nests, or those nests close to water where the large eggs were deposited by the occasional summer-dwelling swans. There is no data that suggests any cultural use of their tail-feathers or flight-feathers. Eggs were also commonly collected from summer residing swans during the annual molt. Most geese and ducks were killed in spring during their molting period.

The Spokan killed birds with bow and arrow to obtain wapato bulbs held in the breast feathers, as did the Kalispel (Smith 1936-8:279). It was remembered that the greater sandhill crane never provided meat, but the feathers were used for making common arrows. Several types of larger birds were not eaten, one being the *turkey vulture* (*Cathartes aura* - *cáqʷuyeʔ*) since the meat was considered to be strong and stringy. Some claimed that the meat of any so-called scavenger birds would make a person sick if ingested. Red-tailed hawks were killed for their plumage, but never hunted for food—even if found dead, nor was the *peregrine falcon* (*Falco peregrinus* - ʕátat) ever hunted. "It seems likely that certain bird feathers were widely exchanged" (Hayden and Schulting 1997:58).

Upland Birds

The *ring-necked pheasant* (*Phasianus colchicus* - sussnúps - "long tail feathers") and *wild turkey* (*Meleagris gallopavo* - n'wxʷwxʷnáqs - "things hang from nose") (Egesdal, pers. comm.), were hunted and eaten whenever found—most commonly taken by bow and arrow, not by snares. Throughout the year, blue grouse, *sage hen* (*Centrocercus urophasianus* - kʷ'ʷtíq'ʷl'q'ʷé), *prairie chicken* or *sharp-tailed grouse* (*Pedioecetes phasianellus* - sq'ʷóqʷl'q'ʷé or s'ʷiq'ʷl'qʷ), *California quail* (*Lophortyx californicus* - sq'ʷáq'ʷl'qʷ or hesc'lqin sesikʷ), *spruce grouse* (*Canachites canadensis* - sq'xʷlúw' or sq'ʷuʔxʷl'uʔ or čskʷlkʷílps), *ruffed grouse* (*Bonasa umbellus* - skʷiskʷ or ʕuww'aq'ʷuʔt skʷiskʷs), and a sub-species of spruce grouse, *Franklin's grouse* (*Dendragapus canadensis franklinii* Doug. - qáɬqɬc'eʔ), were hunted, as was the ruffed grouse, sometimes called a drummer or brush pheasant. After the grey or *Hungarian partridge* (*Perdix perdix* - skʷík'ʷl'l'qʷ) was introduced it became a favorite pastime for boys, hunting with .22 rifles to kill the birds for their meat, and to gather any available eggs; the colorful feathers were used for dancing costumes. Some have said the plumage was not used for decoration or as brooms.

Waterfowl

A wide variety of *migrating waterfowl* (čɬq'ʷlq'ʷluʔtétkʷ) were hunted for meat, eggs and sometimes the feathers. Whistling swan and both the *Canadian goose* (*Branta canadensis occidentalis* - skʷ'ʷsíxʷ) and the *snow goose* (*Chen hyperborea hyperborea* - w'uʔw'ú or w'uʔu'ʔ) were stalked in the fall with bow and arrow. All ducks, including the *Brant duck* (*Branta bernicla* - tptpósxn) and *redhead duck* (*Nyroca americana* - skʷlaʔqín) were hunted when possible—usually in the fall during their southward migration. Coots (*Fulica americana* - stráqšn) known as mud hens and *fool hens* (*Canachites canadensis* - sq'ʷxʷlú) were often taken with snares by women in the late spring when gathering the eggs of other ground-nesting birds. It was said that a person with quick hands could catch a fool hen *by grabbing its feet* (čq'ʷm'q'ʷúm'šntm). One elderly lady contended they never removed all of the eggs of any ground-nesting bird, knowing there would be fewer birds the next season if they over-harvested.

Ducks, geese, swans, and brants appeared seasonally in great numbers, but were often difficult to hunt. Stalking birds in wetland sites required considerable time, effort, and patience; thus, they made no significant contribution to the Spokan diet. Swans were the easiest of all birds to hunt:

> In the fall most swans went south. The few which remained all winter stayed at certain springs which never froze over [...] When there was a dry snow, hunters sneaked up on them. Since swans do not fly fast, they scared them out into the snow before they could raise off the water. Then they flopped around in the dry snow, which "balled up" on their wings, until soon they could not fly. The hunter then came up to them and clubbed them to death (Smith 1936-8:267;1951:96).

Both the shy and wary native *whistling swan* (*Cygnus columbianus* - spqamíš) and *trumpeter swan* (*C. buccinator* - spqimíš) were hunted in spring when migrating to breeding grounds of west, north, central Alaska and the eastern coastal stretch of Canada, and again during their late fall return from migration. Some Spokan remember swans over-wintering within open areas of the Spokane River. Both species are noted for their grace and ease of water travel, and though not fast fliers they were difficult to stalk and kill when on water, and certainly once they had successfully become airborne. Large migratory birds that over-wintered were taken, as described by Smith in a summary of the aforementioned quote (1951:96).

Some recall older boys of the Spokan and Chewelah-Spokan group who hunted loons and turkey vultures, which were difficult to hit with bow and arrow. Any *loon* (*Gavia immer* - w'súʔɬ) with a small brood on the mother's back or swimming close by was never killed, nor was loon or vulture meat ever eaten, being too strong in flavor; this was true of osprey meat as well.

Owls

All species of owls had considerable importance for spiritual reasons to the Spokan. Owls were feared but respected for their prophetic powers and ability to communicate with humans and other animal species during daylight, but more often at night. When communicating, a human was always first alerted by an *owl call* (*húhu*), and eventually the message was given to the intended person. When speaking to a human, the owl seldom spoke of inconsequential matters, but more of serious pending issues that may announce a person's death or a pending death, or a prophetic warning. It was acknowledged that "owls hooting out of season is a bad omen [and] if an owl lights near one & 'talks' [and] makes noises is an indication that something terrible is going to happen" (Elmendorf 1935-6, 3:26). One very elderly gentleman related an experience he once had many years before with an owl's linguistic abilities and suggested powers:

> Once two small owls came into my barn in January—our time of power—and they spoke to me in Chinook, which of course I understand. After a while I got mad and tried to get the two owls out so I could milk the cow. The owls got very mad and screeched at me in Chinook, saying: "What are you doing?" Well, I stopped waving my arms because they said if I wasn't good, they would dry up my milk cow (Ross 1968-2008).

Some Spokan elders once considered the owl's prophetic abilities as more significant than that of the Bluejay, which only during the Mid-Winter Ceremony had such powers—ones important to a person's physical survival, regardless of the man's or woman's *suméš*. In the past, it was not unusual to hear elders describe different experiences they had, when a person was warned by an owl of a pending predicament, often a person's death, as we find in this account:

> The owl was the most important bird for telling us about the future, usually to warn us. It doesn't matter if it's during the day or [at] night, the owl will come and give a message. Always the owl speaks in Indian, or any Indian language [*snqélix^wcn*]. Many times I had both the burrowing owl and *snine?* [great horned owl], and could speak to them in Chinook since they could also speak Chinook [and Spokan and English]. When the owl first comes and wants to tell you a message, it will say "whet, whet, whet" and then you should know [and] listen carefully. If you're rude or disrespectful, the owl will give you the wrong message. I once was fooled when [the] owl told him his mother had just died. Well, it was a very cruel joke because my mother had died the year before, so I did grieve again. One time I was in the woods alone, and it was getting real dark, and I was far from [my] camp. [The] owl came to me and said I should return to my camp, and I did. The next morning I went back where I was before, and sure enough, there in the dust [of] the trail, almost where I'd have gone the night before, were the tracks of a huge cougar, probably waiting for a deer to come by. Many times [the] owl has come to men and warned [them] of something to happen; not only about animals, but also about white men and machines [cars and threshing equipment] (Ross 1968-2008).

Other types of owls classified by the Spokan were the *screech owl* (*Otus asia - nččx^waqs* or *nččx^wels*), long-eared owl (*Asia otus*), *great horned owl* (*Bobo virginianus - snine?*), short-eared owl (*Asia flammeus*), great grey owl (*Strix nebulosa*), saw-whet owl (*Aegolius acadicus*), burrowing owl (*Speotyto cuniculoria - nččw'č?*), pygmy owl (*Glaucidium gnoma - sq'q'áx^w*), and the large light-colored nocturnal *barn owl* (*Tyto alba - wewq'ičs*), which was more uncommon than other types because of habitat type and because few burrowing owls often used open man-made structures for nesting.

Small Birds

Numerous types of birds were hunted primarily for food by men using projectiles and snares. But meadowlark, red-headed woodpecker, raven, crow, downy woodpecker, *bobwhite* (*Colinus virginianus - sesík^w*), and many others were not known to have been hunted as prey. Magpies and crows were shot with arrows by boys for fun. They were birds considered as a nuisance to people and detrimental to ground-nesting aviary, particularly in the late spring when they ate the eggs. Both the *robin* (*Turdus migratorius* - *sxáxn'č'*), the *black-capped chickadee* (*Parus atricapillus* - *čsqáqn'eʔ*), and the easily *flushed rail* or *sora bird* (*Porzana carolina* - *hewetkʷeʔ*) were hunted and eaten by boys using bows and arrows of sharpened wood. The birds were *cooked whole with the feathers* (*sul'ám*) because the feathers protected the meat from burning; after roasting, the innards would be removed. Th*e bank swallow* (*Riparia riparia* - *m'úm'qʼʷcn* or *t'mt'mq'ey'*) was hunted in late fall, after they had commenced to build mud-nesting holes in stream banks prior to hibernating. The *cliff swallow* (*Petrochelidon pyrrhonota* - *ʔiy' écʔic*) was also hunted by boys, again using bow and arrow. Boys also stalked and kill the red-winged blackbird and the yellow-headed blackbird that were easily found in summer inhabiting tule and cattail clumps. Young men were known to snare birds from nests or tree limbs with a noose made of twisted sinew from the back of a deer, and placed on the end of a long pole. Adults never killed small birds, particularly the *rail bird* (*Rollus limmicola* - *nhew'étkʷeʔ*) or the black-capped chickadee, which, because of their song, would bring bad luck to the hunter. One elder related how the *belted kingfisher* (*Megaceryle alcyan* - *c'rís c'alís*) was once sought as a powerful *sumés* for fishing.

When located, *rock pigeons* (*Columba livia* - *xʷc'xʷuc'm'*) were hunted by young boys with limited success using bow and arrow, though some boys were said to have had some success throwing rabbit sticks into large flocks. Of the six types of swallows in the area, the so-called rough-winged swallow (*Stellgidopteryx ruficollis* - *m'om'qʷcn'*), were most utilized, particularly for fletching arrows with their tail feathers. The long tail feathers of the *catbird* (*Mimus polyglottos* - *caʔwáʔi*) were used by boys as decoration when stuck in their hair—indicators of a successful hunt.

Some birds, regardless of size, were never killed, such as the ubiquitous *black-billed magpie* (*Pica pica* - *ʔan'n'*); the meat being tough and having too strong a flavor. Species of small birds were rarely killed, since boys were taught at an early age never to kill songbirds, nor disturb their *nests* (*ʔihemèʔ*) even when hunting for eggs in the spring and early summer. For reasons now forgotten, children from an early age were warned never to harm or hunt the calliope *hummingbird* (*Stellula calliope* - *xʷnímxʷnim*); perhaps from sympathy since the *mourning dove* (*Zenaidura macroura* - *hémíshem'is*) is reputed to make a *mourning call* (*hayó t isl'ʷúy*) for its mother because *spilye*, "decreed on the last day of the animal kingdom that *hém'ishem'* would never find his mother again" (STHC). Some claimed that the *killdeer* (*Charadrius vociferus* - *sttʔítšn'*) was never hunted, and was respected for its apparent loyalty in decoying humans and other animals away from its nest by giving a mournful call, and dropping to the ground and dragging a wing as it leads the predator away from the ground nest.

Methods of bird hunting were determined by the type of bird and by the hunter's skill, and there is no recall of any type of tree or ground snare being used for small birds. However, for some larger birds, the principal predation methods were either the ground snare or a slightly raised spring-pole snare, often situated in known areas inhabited by ground-dwelling birds—usually in the spring during the breeding season. Because of breeding behaviors, particularly with grouse, the male was often snared as it ran about demonstrating its courting intentions. Some ground-dwelling birds were frequently funneled to a snare located at the end of a parallel, ever-decreasing pathway of round boulders, approximately 20 to 24 cm in diameter. A man would check his traps daily to recover the birds before other predators got them. Both the Spokan and Kalispel used a type of ground snare for grouse of which Smith provides the most detailed description:

A pliable stick was bent into a U-shape and one end was stuck into the ground at each side of the opening. The top of the twig was about six inches above the ground. The bark was left on the sticks at two places on the top of the loop, it was roughened up with the fingernail [...] Over these raised bits of bark was suspended a noose, made from Indian hemp rolled tightly. The noose was not wound with bird-cherry [bitter cherry] bark [*Prunus emarginata* Douglas ex. Hook. - *pčłiʔn*] [to make it slip more easily] nor was it greased with pitch. The snare had a single knot, not a double [knot], because once the cord got beneath the feathers it would never come off. The other end of the noose cord was fastened to something solid, such as a small tree or a rock or anything that the grouse would not snag (1951:85).

330

As previously mentioned, boys used bow and arrow to stalk and kill the *red-winged blackbird* (*Agelalius phoeniceus* - *ƛ'čƛ'ač*), the *yellow-headed blackbird* (*Xanthocephalus xanthocephalus* - *sp'rq'aqew'*), and the "camp robber" *grey jay* (*Perisoreus canadensis* - *sn'er'k*ʷ)—birds that were easily found in summer inhabiting tule and cattail clumps. After a successful hunt, bird and duck feathers were never removed with boiling water, rather by individually plucking the wing and tail feathers, whereas breast and body feathers were plucked by the handful. After dressing-out large birds and waterfowl, the meat was prepared by boiling or roasting if there was no cooking container.

Bird Eggs

The *eggs* (*ʔuʔuʔúse* or *uusé*ʔ - "bird egg") of all species of waterfowl—including such birds as swan and mud hen—were gathered in late spring and early summer from tule and cattail water bird-built nests whereas the eggs of more elusive ground-nesting birds, and those of upland game birds, were collected by chance rather than by any planned and concerted effort. However, at times an entire family would purposely gather blue grouse, ruffed grouse, and Hungarian partridge eggs. Heron and loon eggs were not collected; these two larger birds being of religious significance. Smaller song birds were hunted by small boys, but not their eggs. Swan eggs were also collected for food (DeSmet 1966:359), as were pigeon eggs.

In spring and early summer, groups of children made considerable economic contributions with their egg-gathering efforts. The greatest danger, however, to land-nesting birds were "Predators such as coyotes, red-tailed hawks, bobcats, red and grey foxes, raccoons and domesticated dogs" (Forsberg 2005:29).

Eggs were eaten raw or boiled in the shell, and eggs about to hatch were consumed with relish, and considered rather 'fortifying'. When found in great quantities, eggs were steamed by themselves in a shallow earthen pit that was prepared by first placing pre-heated stones in the bottom, atop of which was laid a thick layer of fresh grass or mullein leaves prior to placing several layers of eggs upon the covered layered material, which was then covered with a second layer of fresh grass or mullein leaves. A final layer of hot rocks was laid on top and covered with 15 to 20 cm of loose earth. A stick previously placed in the center of the pit was then withdrawn to accommodate water that was poured in the opening to create steam that was retained by quickly closing the water hole with earth.

There was no evidence the Spokan ever smoked an active hornet's nest to flush out the hornets or collected a deserted hornet nest for the storage of bird or turtle eggs, as occurred in the Southwest (McLaughlin 2003), though such nests were placed in a corner of a living area to dissuade malevolent spirits from taking up residence.

Reptiles

All reptiles were named, some being more significant than others, particularly various species of the *short-horned lizard* (*Phrynosoma douglasii* and *P. hernandesi* - *člčlšéw's*), *Western* or *blue-tailed skink* (*Eumeces skiltonianus* - *qʷiʔtóps*), *snake* (*titišúleʔxʷ* or *snpƛ'ac'eʔ* - "blue racer"), *frog* (*Ascaphus truei* - * łam'áy'eʔ*), and *toad* (*Bufo bufo* - *snakʷkʷáneʔ*), all of which had mythical and economic significance to the Spokan for food and poison.

Though frogs, toads, and some types of lizard were generally avoided, the western blue-tailed skink was considered a good luck charm. The use of frogs in making poison, and the utilitarian use of both the poisonous and non-poisonous snakeskin is later discussed. The meat of the *garter snake* (*Thamnophis elegans vagrans* (*snšixʷíl'eʔ*), after being skinned and stick-roasted, was eaten only in dire situations of famine. From personal experience, it may be stated that Western diamond-back meat was eaten, and that it has no odor, and tastes better than cottontail rabbit. To eat rattlesnake, one first removes the head and then slips the skin off before splitting "the belly and removing the 'innards,' which is one long intestine" (Lewis 1928:212).

331

A fairly complete but unfortunately brief description of snakes in the area as far north as Kettle Falls is provided by Cox (1832:228):

> No rattlesnakes are seen below the falls. A short distance above them these reptiles make their first appearance, and are numerous as far as the Chaudière falls, a couple of day's march above which they totally disappear. There is in some places a small black snake, the bite of which causes death much quicker than that of the rattlesnake [...] There are numbers of dark-brown, green, and garter snakes, but they are perfectly innocuous.

Turtles

Though the frog, toad, and lizard were generally avoided—turtles were collected whenever found, particularly before burning unharvested tules when women collected any available *turtles* (*Clemmys marmorate*, *Crysemyus marganita* Belli, and *C. Picta* - *sp'rq'ʷáqs*) in a pond or shallow lake area; being cognizant of *places where turtles were to be found* (*nʔer'síkʷm'*). Turtles were usually prepared for food on the site by either boiling the entire animal within its shell, or leaning the turtles against burning logs until their heated shells roasted the meat. Another method of cooking was to wrap shelled turtles in wet mullein leaves before roasting them in an earthen pit covered with hot rocks. A woman may prefer to prepare and cook the turtle after arriving home, having carried several live turtles with her.

Several weeks prior to gathering tule and cattails, a common practice was for one or more elderly women to take their young grandchildren to pond areas to expressly catch adult turtles for their meat–always considered good eating despite the meat being striped like that of a snake. Small turtles were never harmed or collected, even by children—"one should never kill or play with small turtles we will one day need."

The shells of larger turtles were stored for later conversion into ceremonial rattles to be used by men during the winter ceremonies. Using a turtle shell for the *shaman's rattle* (*scósl'eʔ*) may have been an influence from the Plains, since most Spokan rattles were made from the hooves of deer. A turtle shell was often used as a *serving dish* (*snʔeščénmn*). A few older Spokan were able to explain how deer search for *turtle eggs* (*nƛ'eʔɬimew't*), a food that gives them a fine, sheen-like coat. Deer are able to readily locate turtle eggs because of the urine scent deposited by the birthing turtle after delivering the eggs—a phenomenon termed *nƛ'eʔɬnéw't*. Turtle eggs were considered a delicacy when eaten raw. The present on-reservation *Turtle Lake* (*ʔer'síkʷm* - "place of turtles") was so designated for once being bountiful in turtles.

332

Chapter X: Gathering Technology

Technology

The subsistence-getting activities of gathering, fishing, and hunting were integral to the Spokan way of life, as were the by-products of hunting (hide, bone, etc.)—sometimes more so than the meat itself. Salmon was a major staple food and a valuable item of trade. But highly variable environmental factors resulted in fluctuations in the availability of land mammals and (to a lesser extent) fish. Thus, plant gathering and digging provided the most reliable source of food, involving the least complex technology and expenditure of energy. Hunting, always a year-round activity, was not always predictable, and, therefore had fewer associated rituals and taboos. Plant gathering required less intricate skills and relatively simple technology, and required less coordination for communal efforts. With occasional spring fluctuations in annual salmon runs, and the relatively complex and even specialized technology required, there was, concomitantly, extensive ritual to ensure successful salmon runs.

Of the three major food-getting activities, *root-digging* (*sx̣éct*) was the most predictable source of food, providing approximately forty to forty-five percent of the total annual caloric intake, depending upon an annual salmon run. Plant gathering required the simplest of exploitative technologies and expenditure of energy that was spaced over the annual subsistence round. Also, plants, and some of their by-products, were the most easily processed, required less effort to prepare for winter storage, and were the most diverse of all food stuffs available. Fishing was acknowledged as being the most labor-intensive subsistence activity, which in a relatively brief period of time would yield, depending upon annual fish runs, from forty-five to fifty-five percent of the annual food supply. Fishing involved the most specialized predation technology, accompanied by shamans who conducted rituals or rites of intensification.

Digging Sticks

When gathering roots and certain medicines, a woman's principal multipurpose tool was the *digging stick* (*péces?*), used in root fields or other areas during late spring, through the summer, and even into late autumn until the ground froze. There were accounts of how in the past, during times of inadequate food supply, women would dig for camas roots in known areas even after the ground had frozen and covered with snow.

The digging stick was a woman's most important and primary root-getting, and plant-digging implement—always a good companion. Years ago, it was not unusual to see a solitary elderly woman quietly speaking to her digging stick as she worked. Once it was common for a woman to give her digging stick a diminutive name—one that personalized her digger and served as a mnemonic device when relating stories to her children or grandchildren while root-digging. For example, in the late 1960s, the author accompanied two elderly Spokan women who, when holding and sometimes caressing a favorite digging stick, would vividly and fondly recall certain remarkably productive harvests, as well as exceptionally unusual roots the digging stick had exposed. Humor was never denied even to a male listener, and the always prim behavior of an elderly woman was, on occasion, altered when the smiling and reflective elder would 'lose her age' and timidly, but happily, make morphological analogies of the digging stick's harvest with a certain anatomical feature of her husband. It was reported that the topic of discussion in the women's sweathouse could dwell on the exaggerated comparison of a spouse's genitalia and a particularly large or otherwise unusually shaped root dug during that day's harvest—invariably a carrot root, particularly when a double-rooted carrot was exposed (Egesdal, pers. comm.).

The digging stick was usually manufactured by the woman herself or occasionally by a male relative—usually a husband if she was married—or an older brother if she was single. Then a section of ocean spray (noted for its strength and hardness), mock orange, red osier dogwood, red and black thornberry, black hawthorn, ironwood, or juniper was carefully chosen. A particularly durable and valued digging stick—one that would "last many generations"—was one made from mountain mahogany, a highly-sought wood traded from the Nez Perce. A digging stick could be made from the base section of the serviceberry plant that had an adequate diameter.

Upon selecting the wood, the bark was first removed with a piece of broken quartzite or a flat-edged stone, and each woman had a preferred method of shaping her digger. After being shaped to length and adequately scraped, the wood was thoroughly soaked in water for several days, after which several long strips of twisted rawhide was tied to both ends. Every day the stick was carefully bent slightly more by tightening the *twisted* (*mr'k^w* or *sartaticˇcˇ*) strands of rawhide between both ends to achieve the desired curvature of the wood as it dried. Or when shaping a digger of less dense wood, the procedure was to submerge the pre-scraped section in water overnight and then wrap it in a piece of thoroughly-soaked rawhide with an attached rock at the desired mid-section for bending. Later, after removing the rock, the digger was permitted to dry during the day in the shade, or buried for several hours in fire-warmed *sand* (*sq'épen'e?x^w*). Another method of shaping was to place the smaller tapered end on a flat stone, so that the main shaft was approximately 10 to 15 cm off the ground—depending upon the type of wood—then several stones were carefully situated across the middle of the shaft, causing the wood to bend to a desired curve at the digging end. Once the shaft had dried, the end with the smallest diameter was shaped by scraping to form a pointed but somewhat blunt end. The digging end was then carefully fire-hardened by placing it 8 to 10 cm under *hot coals* (*c'áx̣^{w}c'x^{w}t*) for several hours, always turning the shaft every few minutes to prevent burning. The length of a digging stick varied according to the woman. In the past, every woman had a rawhide *quiver* (*ƛ'aqn'e?*) or case for her digging stick (Schaeffer 1935-36, I-37:16).

Not all digging sticks were made of wood. Numerous examples of either plain or incised geometrical designs on deer antler digging sticks were excavated (Collier *et al.* 1942:84-86), some with only one prong, but many with two or more bifurcated antlers. Some examples indicate that there had been handles of elk horn, center-bored and hafted to digging sticks. There are several existing examples of digging stick handles with one end carved to represent a type of long-billed bird, probably most effective when digging bitterroot. Digging sticks for gathering bitterroot were invariably lighter and smaller in length and diameter. Some archaeologists state that certain deer horn digging sticks were considered to be crafted prestige items (Hayden and Schulting 1997:63) when highly decorated by incision, ones that probably required more labor intensive designs that indicated the special status of the owner (Cressman 1960:70).

After long use, the digging end of a digging stick would be sharpened as needed by rubbing the point on basalt or granite boulders found sometimes near root fields, which after years of use developed deep linear troughs (Lyons, pers. comm.). A few could recall older women telling of sharpening the end of a digging stick with a sandstone arrow-shaft straightener. In the early historical period, and with the advent of agriculture, iron tines from harvesting machines sometimes replaced traditional wooden shafts. Some elderly women claimed how roots dug with iron tines would possibly rot during winter storage. Traditionally, all wooden digging sticks had a *cross-handle* (*cˇq'^{w}a?q'^{w}a?léčst*) made of a section of either deer or elk antler or ocean-spray that was cut to approximately 30 to 35 cm in length. Elders recalled how a section of dogwood was preferred by some as being the most durable material for handles, whereas several elderly women said the best wood handles were made from mountain Juneberry. All women had at least one digging stick made from a section of deer or elk horn that had been fashioned by retaining the protruding and pointed spikes, which facilitated digging bitterroot. In the past, wooden digging sticks were housed in a *quiver* (*pecé? snq'$^{'w}$łté* - (Schaeffer 1935-36, I-37:16). Of the few women who continue to gather roots today, all have steel or iron digging sticks once made by local off-reservation blacksmiths, and nearly all of the few contemporary metal digging sticks have oak cross-handles, salvaged from discarded oak or hickory axe or adz handles or wooden wagon spokes. Some digging sticks had less comfortable cross-handles of steel.

There were basically two types of digging sticks: a light wooden digging stick of approximately 60-65 cm in length used for shallow root plants, most notably bitterroot; the second more common type was a heavier and longer fire-hardened wooden shaft of approximately 70 cm. Regardless of its source, the digging stick handle was always shaped, sometimes with sharp inside edge of a beaver tooth, which acted as a spoke shave. The handle was then *center-bored* (*č⁴ẋʷéple?*) with a sharpened stone to fit tightly over the larger but tapered end of the digger's shaft. The shorter digger had a deer horn handle fashioned with a taper-bore to fit tightly on the upper end of the wooden digger. The handle was the pressure-set onto the end and carefully pounded downwards on either side of the digging shaft. The author frequently dug bitterroot with an elderly woman who preferred to use an unhafted digger made from a bifurcated white-tailed deer antler, one she has used for many years.

A girl's first small digging stick, called *sp'áp'n'x̣*, was made by her mother from a section of green mock orange that had been bent to shape until dry. A rite of passage always recognized an older girl when she received her first digger. When a girl dug her first root, usually a sun-flower bulb, the occasion was referred to as *ci?cqcn'*. After digging, a girl presented her first root to an elderly person, and the recipient offered a prayer for the young girl for her continued success—a ritual known as *nč'ołc'?encútn* (STHC). Some once believed that if the girl's first root was not given away, particularly a camas, the girl's later root-digging would be tedious and not bountiful. Therefore, her mother carefully placed the bulb in a small buckskin bag that was then sewn shut and attached to a long-looped buckskin neck strap that the girl would wear thereafter when root-digging. The occasion for receiving a proper length digging stick was when the woman left the menstrual hut after her menarche, and there is no memory of how the girl's first digger was disposed, or if it was gifted to a much younger sister.

After extensive digging, cleaning, and minimal drying of large amounts of roots, the main logistical concern was transporting the harvest to the village or camp, particularly from distant root fields. Prior to the introduction of horses, all roots were carried in large split cedar root baskets supported from shoulder or head tumplines, and women were sometimes assisted by men in transporting these heavy loads as groups of people travelled in a single line to a winter storage area, seldom talking, but never hindering another person with a heavy load when attempting to pass. When men travelled with women, a young man might step out of line and run to the lead position, giving the impression that carrying such a heavy load did not bother him. Grandmothers would rather audibly tell their grandchildren, "there goes a capable young man" (Elmendorf 1935-6, 2:12).

The value and dependence a woman had upon her digging stick was often reflected when, upon the woman's death, her digging stick marked her grave. If a woman had more than one digger, one was placed at the head of her grave and the other at the foot.

Pick and Hoe

In addition to the digging stick, the pick and steel *hoe* (*utč'él'le?xʷtn*) became an important horticultural implement with the introduction of certain Euro-American crops—in particular, when planting deep-seeded plants, hoeing, or mulching crops such as corn. Iron tools proved efficient and probably conveyed greater status (Elmendorf, pers. comm.), but were never as efficient as the digging stick for digging edible and medicinal roots.

Some women used a type of pick that is best described as a metal tool that also came into use with the introduction of Euro-American crops, one with a double-ended head for digging and prying up roots. Traditional picks had a wooden handle that was inserted into a convenient length of bored antler, affixed with rawhide to a length of hardwood used more by men and older boys when enlarging entrances of ground-dwelling animals.

335

Gathering

Gathering technologies and associated activities were primarily oriented towards obtaining plant foods. All of the Spokan gathering technologies involved relatively simple but efficient tools, ones which were relatively easy to manufacture and repair. This effectiveness in food-gathering was based not only upon implements—many being multipurpose—but involved a fairly strict defined division of labor as well as the individual gatherer's knowledge of the environment, and a woman's ability to gather, prepare, and store food for winter. A person's knowledge of resources and the necessary skills complemented the simplest of tools. As discussed, the digging stick was a woman's primary gathering tool that fulfilled a wide variety of food gathering tasks. In fact, the use of the digging stick probably provided approximately forty to fifty percent of the Spokan's plant food and many medicinal plants. Various types of carrying baskets were necessary items for all gathering activities needed for food-getting, transportation, preparation, cooking, and eventual storage. As discussed earlier, baskets varied in shape and in the types of materials used in their construction. But for such a seemingly simple item, the basket was frequently an excellent example of multi-purpose technology.

To appreciate the vagrancy of site location, one must consider the numerous movements of the Spokan during the annual subsistence round, which was the most outstanding aspect of the Interior Plateau cultures. By necessity, the aboriginal inhabitants focused their economic and ritual attention upon three distinct subsistence patterns: hunting, fishing, and gathering. These particular activities delineated the subsistence cycle into these three distinct phases (Keeler 1973)—activities that tended to overlap with one another and formed a complete annual cycle of resource exploitation (Liljeblad 1972). Teit provided a succinct summation:

> In the springtime, digging certain roots, hunting and fishing on the nearer grounds; in early summer, fishing for trout and salmon, hunting and root-digging; in midsummer, root-digging and berrying, only a little hunting; in late summer, salmon fishing and berrying, very little hunting or root-digging; in early fall (about September), the same occupation as in late summer; in the late fall (October and November), root-digging and hunting in the early part, and finally only hunting. In December they went into their winter camps and left them in March. Buffalo hunting parties also left in August. Some came back in the fall about November, and some did not return until spring (1930:342-3).

In partial explanation, food stored for winter consumption was always subject to some degree of contamination, but rarely to theft, purposeful destruction or confiscation by antagonistic groups. And yet, contamination by animals was a major problem, and loss through rapid changes of weather, even unexpected thawing in late winter or early spring, often brought great sections of free-flowing ice, that on occasion quickly swept away great quantities of food that river villages cached in rock and log structures atop midstream basalt islands and raised boulders. Early spring flood waters were occasionally responsible for the loss of some *food storage cache* (*snxʷméneʔ* or *snkʷúmcntn*) located on low-lying stream terraces.

Throughout the winter months it was necessary to supplement food stores by hunting forays and ice-fishing parties venturing to selected areas of high game probability. Nonetheless, there was often great periods of leisure, when men "were left with much unoccupied time which they spent playing games, telling stories or sleeping or gambling" (Ray 1933:28). Though male activities were frequently intense, they "alternated with periods of leisure which were devoted to games and sports" (Schaeffer 1937, 3:238). During winter, trading and communication of social events were conducted on a regular basis between villages. Many elderly Spokan have related accounts of their great-grandparents, if single, often courting during the long winters, and frequently hearing at night the melodious sounds of a young suitor's flageolet.

Roots

Women gathered an estimated 250 different species of edible, medicinal, and utility plants in spring, summer, and fall during the pre-horse period. It was not unusual for the able occupants of a winter village to

336

travel several days' distance south of the Spokane River to different productive root fields south-south-west of the Spokane River. After selecting a suitable *camp site* (*k'ʷl'leʔxʷeʔlpm*), the women would *dig all day* (*ta ʔpɬnʕatnʕáttn*) for roots while the men hunted primarily for deer. While older girls assisted their mothers, boys would, usually gathered in small groups of comparable age to hunt small animals. In spring and summer most foods gathered were not consumed by the foragers, but transported back to the remaining occupants of the winter village who helped in the final preparation of roots for winter storage. While en route to a settlement, any available firewood was kept in a tipi-like lodge-pole structure covered with tule mats, or with a distant camp, where the structure may have been covered with a more lightweight hide cover.

In early spring root gathering, hunting was frequently pursued despite varying weather conditions, mostly intermittent spring rains and occasional late snow showers with bouts of cold weather. Hunters seldom drank water when hunting, believing that it would weaken them, and a hunter prided himself on his ability to cover great distances without drinking water. But when reaching a water source, they would "hold their wrists, hands up, under the cold falling water until the wrists are completely numb, and then they can drink all they want without feeling faint" (Smith 1936-8:447).

Women had extensive and intimate knowledge of their territory and the occurrences during a particular time of often predictable resources which determined their patterns of resource exploitation. Before leaving the root fields, roots and other plant products were dried, and upon returning to camps or winter village, women would store their harvest in dwellings or in platform caches erected approximately 10 m from the ground in ponderosa trees or within depleted storage pits. On occasion, platforms of poles were temporarily erected for food stored in grass sacks.

Women from three or four families, under the direction of the eldest woman, repeatedly visited different root fields, and after exploiting the resources of a particular area, they would move to another potential site and repeat the process of exploitation and eventual storage of those roots first available at lower elevations. After a week or so of gathering roots, they again returned in stages to the winter village. During the return trip each woman, and often her children, collected firewood which they would pile in a stack that belonged to that family. The prairies and meadows south of the Spokane River were traditionally exploited at this time, where the largest and most *productive root fields* (*snx̣éetn*) were located, most notably various species of Lomatium.

Distant camas root fields—ones requiring several days walking—were used annually by the same women, particularly root fields in the Palouse country, or in an area beyond Medical Lake called *čɬmuʕlšm*. Although these fields were smaller ones, they were important for supplementing roots gathered earlier than from larger and more productive root fields previously mentioned. In July, women dug two types of *white camas* (*Lomatium canbyi - p' čúxʷp'ux* or *p'uxʷp'uxʷ* and *L. cous* [Wats.] Coult. & Rose - *pewteʔ*); rather bland if not tasteless roots, eaten often with other foods. Women remained digging for several days, depending upon the available amount of firewood for heating the stones to cook their harvest. They would typically *dig roots* (*sx̣éct*) during the morning, stopping mid-day to clean their harvest while they would eat, and sew while telling stories, "stories so exciting, sometimes, no one was sewing." The rest of the day was spent in comparative leisure, *relating news* (*sm'em'íʔ*) and generally socializing. If they did not return to a base camp, they continued to dig roots.

Yellow avalanche lily or *yellow dog-tooth violet* (*Erythronium grandiflorum* Pursh, var. *grandiflorum - máx̣eʔ* or *sxʷíx̣ʷ*) were considered only flowers by adults, but children would dig and eat the young spring bulbs. Elmendorf (1935-6, 1:26a) claimed that the Spokan did not have tiger lily, but numerous elderly women described how in July and August the yellow bulbs of wild tiger lily were gathered, washed, and dried in a similar manner as camas; one with a slight bitter taste (Elmendorf 1935-6, I:26) was dug, usually from April until early July—depending upon the elevation. The large, round, clear, white tuber-like roots were boiled and then eaten fresh or washed and dried for several weeks for winter (Elmendorf 1935-6, 1:26; Turner *et al.*1980:46).

A mature bulb of *chocolate lily* (*Fritillaria lanceolata* Pursh - *č'éyč'i* or *sméta'* - "tooth") was considered poisonous by some, but as an edible root by others. Indian corn (*Perideridi gairdneri*), wild onion, bitterroot, balsamroot, and numerous species of Lomatium were collected. Balsamroot, though readily available, was a difficult rhizome to dig, requiring time and considerable energy. The white tap root and succulent young shoots of thistle root and the introduced *watermelon* (*Citrullus vulgaris* Schrad. - *čqʷq̓ʷáy'c'e?*) were used as a purge, and eaten after being crushed and steamed. Bull or *Scotch thistle* (*Cirsium vulgare* [Savi] Airy-Shawn.), now considered a noxious weed, produced an oil once considered an analgesic and placed on wounds to prevent infection. In the past, roots of this plant were cooked and eaten.

There remains some uncertainty with later Indian classification (Turner *et al.* 1980:70) of *wild celery* (*Lomatium triternatum* [Pursh] Coult. & Rose - *k'ʷexʷk'ʷáx̣ʷ* - "Indian celery" or *k'ʷaxt* - pungent odor"), and may refer to *Indian celery* (*L. nudicaule* [Pursh] Coult. & Rose - *x̣ʷx̣ʷtéɬp*), and *swale desert parsley* (*L. ambiguum* [Nutt.] Coult. & Rose - *qʷoxʷq̓ʷx̣ʷ*) often found in dry, sparsely open areas associated with *Ponderosa pine* (*Pinus ponderosa* Dougl. ex Loud. - *?astkʷ*), but harvested from more moist areas prior to its blooming in the spring, when the green stalks are about 50 cm tall. Once the top and outside leaves were cut off, the stalks were eaten. There is, however, some confusion with the Spokan term *x̣ʷx̣ʷtéɬp*, which now may include wild rhubarb and cow parsnip.

In 1837, Archibald McDonald (1790-1853), Chief Factor of HBC at Ft. Colville, wrote how successful the upper Columbia was for growing introduced wheat, corn, *common oats* (*Arena sativa* L. - *l'ew'en*), and other grains as well as raising cattle (Kingston 1923, 3:171). After Euro-American contact, the grains of *soft white wheat* (*Triticum aestivum* L. - *šisp'qin'*) were boiled and then eaten as a mush—sometimes with berries.

Some plants, such as tobacco root, were collected throughout the summer and until the ground became frozen. Three species of *onion* (*Allium douglasii* Hook., A. *Macrum* Wats, and *A. Acummatum* Hook. - *sehč*) were gathered in late spring to early summer, sometimes while digging camas. "Wild onions grow in considerable quantities along the banks of the river above the falls. They are small, and from March to May their flavor is excellent; but after the latter month they lose their relish, and become dry and hard" (Cox 1832:228). It is further explained:

> They collect large quantities of a kind resembling onions, which, in the first instance, they dry on hot stones. They are then pulverized, and, being worked into a paste, are formed into loaves from five to six pounds weight, which they lay by for seasons of scarcity. This bread has a taste resembling liquorice (1832:224).

Prior to storage, the most common method for drying large quantities of roots was to spread them on tule mats on the ground, or on tule mats raised upon drying racks near the woman's home. Dried roots intended for winter storage would often be kept for three years. Certain roots, such as white camas, which turn hard and black after baking, would be first peeled, *strung* (*sɬk'ʷéltn*), air-dried, and usually kept within the dwelling. Women collected the bulb of the white camas, but the white camas stem (*sc'hélps*) was sometimes cooked along with the bulb. *Raw camas* (*sx̣ʷel'-?itx̣ʷe?*) (*Lomatium* spp. - *čx̣íw'sšn'*), including *p'úx̣ʷp'uxʷ*) was gathered in quantity. Hale described "Poh-poh" [sic] as being a "bulbous root shaped somewhat like a small onion, and of a peculiarly dry and spicy taste" (1846, 4:206), which was dug in March and April, as were other species of Lomatium. It was common to peel and string white camas (*sɬk'ʷéltn*), which could be stored well for many years. Whenever any type of camas was to be stored, the dried roots would be placed in round baskets, flat bags, or later in burlap sacks to facilitate the removal of their husks. *Raw, unpeeled camas* (*čn'ek'ʷéssn'*) was never stored, due to spoilage and possible contamination of other winter provisions.

The farinaceous *biscuit-root stock* (*Lomantium macrocarpum* [H. & A.] C. & R., var. *macrocarpum* - *sp'x̣ʷénč*) was washed, boiled, dried, mashed, and thoroughly dried on tule mats before storage. Camas and tree moss were sometimes cooked together in an earth oven so that a jelly-like mass was formed, which was then spread on hides to dry before storing for winter in soft hide bags, a mixture often used to make broth

338

(Scheiffer 1935-36, I-35:14). Turner noted the so-called Indian consumption plant (*L. nudicaule* [Pursh] Coult. & Rose), identified as a species related to wild carrot or desert parsley (*L. macrocarpum* [Nutt.] Coult. & Rose - Turner *et al.* 1980:69).

Other roots were important to the Spokan diet, such as a type of white camas *canbyi*, which was often peeled and eaten raw, but was stored in great quantity by stringing or after being baked in an earth oven. Alvord's experience with cooked camas was that "when boiled it is often made into a kind of molasses" (1857:22). Spokan terms for different states of camas include *ʔítxʷeʔ* (cooked) and *sxʷeʔlítxʷeʔ* (raw). The so-called Indian sweet potato or biscuit root was dug in the spring and, if properly dried, would store well through the winter. Indian potatoes and the starchy, small corms (*sékʼʷnʼ*) were never stored, but instead peeled and eaten raw or boiled. The yellow corms of *Easter lily* (*Erythronium grandiflorum* Pursh, var. *Grandiflorum* - *máxeʔ*), a herbaceous perennial called lamb's tongue (*Stomatium agninum*) or yellow avalanche lily (*Erythronium grandiflorum*, also called glacier lily) (Turner 1978:26), were often the first flowers to appear after buttercups, and its roots were dug in early spring, and eaten raw while blooming, or was either stone-boiled or roasted in a small pit by placing the roots over hot stones that were first covered with mullein leaves to prevent scorching. But it was never stored, as it would rot (May, pers. comm.).

Lake Coeur d'Alene (*nčʼqínkʷeʔ*) was the major source of wapato bulbs—a hydrophyte—when in early summer women would *wade* (*nxʷésttetkʷ*) in waist-deep water and dislodge with their toes the four to six tubers of each plant, and after floating to the surface they were placed in a wide-mouth conical-shaped basket suspended onto the woman's back by a shoulder thump line (Scott 1941:211). Earlier, Barry observed how women gathered wapato by loosening the mud around the bulb with their toes. When it floated to the surface, it was "broken off and thrown over the head into" (Barry 1929, 1:46) a back basket supported by a head strap. Elders recalled their grandparents collecting these bulbs from Little Tschimakain Creek, saying how the most productive and reliable source of wapato along this creek was at the small *headspring* (*čʼčʼmʼqínʼ*). Wapato bulbs were stored well as a winter food when placed in deep excavated storage pits of vesicular basalt rock storage lined with grass and covered with tule mats weighted with rocks for protection against scavenging animals.

The nutritional importance—and for some the aesthetic value—of camas were realized by the people. It was the major *root* (*sʕʷxʷép* = common name for any plant, people, etc.) (Egesdal, pers. comm.) in the Interior Plateau, and appreciated by a visitor to the area in the mid-1890s, who left a common impression which is now an extremely rare view and contains the appreciation of the once-major food plant of the Spokan:

> Taking everything into account, abundance, size, taste and nutritious, the best of all native bulbs is doubtless that of the Camas [...] A showy plant ranging from the Rocky Mountains to California and British Columbia, sometimes so abundant on rich meadows as to tint them a uniform blue color, suggesting, as expressed by an early explorer, " [...] a lake of blue water" (Harvard 1895:112-3).

Camas and some of its many varieties—such as *Camassia quamash* (Pursh) Greene, *C. Teapeae*, *C. Cusiki* (Wats), *C. Leichtlinii* (Baker), and *C. Howelii* (Wats)—were intensively exploited by indigenous populations (Reagan 1917; Teit 1930; Schalk 1981; Thoms 1983) throughout the Plateau. During the 1804-1806 Lewis and Clark Expedition, Clark made the earliest recorded observation of the importance of this geophyte in the Rocky Mountain area, but the report also brought out the comparable significance of roots within the southern Plateau, as recorded by Twaites (1853-1913), a remarkable and prodigious scholar and critical editor:

> [...] I shall here give a more particular description of that plant and the mode of prepareing [sic] it for food as practiced by the Chopinnish and others in the vicinity of the Rocky Mountains with whome [sic] it forms much the greatest portion of their Subsistence. we have never met with this plant but in or adjacent to a piney or fir timbered country, and there always in the open grounds and glades; in the Columbian Valley and near the coast it is to be found in small quantities and inferior in size to that found in this neighbourhood or on those high rich

339

flatts [sic] and vallies [sic] within the Rocky Mountains. it delights in a black rich moist soil, and even grows most luxuriently [sic] where the lands remain from 6 to 9 inches under water untill [sic] the seed[s] are nearly perfect, which in this neighbourhood or on those flatts [sic] is about the last of this month [June]. near the river where I had an opportunity of observing it, the Seed[s] were beginning to ripen on the 9th inst. And the soil was nearly dry. it seems devoted to its particular soil and situation, and you will Seldom find [it] more than a fiew [sic] feet from an inundated soil tho' within its limits it grows very closely. in short almost as much so as the bulbs will permit. the radix [sic] is a tumicated [sic] bulb, much the consistence [sic] shape and appearance of the Onion, glutinous or somewhat slymey [sic] when chewed and almost tasteless and without smell in its unprepared state; it is white except the thin or outer tumicated [sic] scales which are fiew [sic] black and not suculent [sic]; this bulb is from the Size of a nutmeg to that of a hen egg and most commonly of an intermediate size or about as large as a common onion of one years growth from the seed [...]

Soon after the seed[s] are mature the peduncle and foliage of this plant perishes, the ground becom[e]s dry or nearly so and the root increases in size and shortly becom[e]s fit for use; this happens about the middle of July when the nativ[e]s begin to collect it for use which they continue untill [sic] the leaves of the plant obtain some size in the Spring of the year when they have collected a considerable quantity of these roots or 20 or 30 bushels which they readily do by means of Sticks Sharpened at one end, they dig away the surface of the earth forming a cercular [sic] concavity of 2 1/2 feet in the center and 10 feet in diameter; they next collect a parcel of dry split wood with which they cover this bason [sic] from the bottom perhaps a foot thick, they next collect a parcel of Stones from 4 to 6 lb. Weight which are placed on the dry wood; fire is then set to the wood which burning heats the Stones; when the fire has subsided and the Stones are sufficiently heated which are nearly a red heat, they are adjusted in such manner in the hole as to form as leavel [sic] a surface as possible, a small quantity of earth is sprinkled over the Stones, and a layer of grass an inch thick is laid over the stone; the roots which have been previously divested of the black or outer coat and radicles which rub off easily with the fingers, are now laid on in a circular pile, are then covered with a layer of grass about 2 or 3 inches thick; water is then thrown on the Summit of the pile and passes through the roots and to the hot Stones at the bottom; Some water is also pored [sic] around the edges of the hole, and also find[s] it's way to the hot Stones. they cover the roots and grass over with earth to the debth [sic] of four inches and then build a fire of dry wood all over the connical [sic] mound which they continue to renew through the course of the night or for 10 or 12 hours, after which it is suffered to cool, 2 or three hours, when the earth and grass are removed and the roots thus Sweated are cooled with steam are taken out, and most commonly exposed to the Sun on Scaffolds untill [sic] they become dry. when they are black and of a sweet agreeable flavor. these roots are fit for use when first taken from the pit, are Soft of a Sweetish taste and much the consistency of a roasted onion; but if they are Suffered to remain in bulk 24 hours after being cooked they Spoil (Thwaites 1904, 7:128-31).

Charles (Karl) Augustus Geyer (1809-1853), a noted German field artist and botanist, wrote about and assiduously collected plant specimens for the famous botanist Hooker, and spent time among the Coeur d'Alene in 1843, and with the Spokan in the spring of 1844. He observed that camas fields:

[...] are traversed by rivulets of secondary size in every direction, [...] Overflowing, during the spring, the vast rich prairies, and leaving behind pools and ponds, drying up about July [...] Stripes, or tonges [sic] of pine forest on sandy elevated lands give these wide flat Gamass [sic] prairies a pleasing interpretation. A deep blue covers these extensive plains when the Gamassis [sic] is in full bloom, agreeably vari[e]gated with sundry species of *Ranunculus* [...] Of the many species of plants that here and there exist among the dense Gamass [sic], but few come to perfection (Geyer 1846:298-301).

There are numerous accounts of the quantity and importance of camas to the diet of the Interior Salish (Point 1967; Coues 1897; Curtis 1907-30, 7:70; Teit 1930; Turney-High 1937; Malouf 1974; Thoms 1989; Turner 1978, and Turner *et al.* 1979), but it was Geyer who provided the first and most descriptive account of camas. However, Thoms (1989:209) rightly feels that Geyer's account may be too idealistic; yet his descriptions remain as a notable credit to Geyer's powers of observation, and, though lengthy, they provide an excellent ethnographic account of the digging of camas and related activities among the Coeur d'Alene, and by the Spokan as well:

The digging of the Gamass [sic] bulb is a feast for the old and young amongst the Indians; a sort of picnic which is spoken of throughout the whole year. The different neighbouring tribes meet on the same plain and mostly at the same spot where their forefathers met. Here the old men talk over their long tales of olden times, the young relate hunting adventures of the last winter, and pass most of their time in play and gambling; while on the women alone, young and old, rests the whole labour of gathering that indispensable food. They, especially the young women, vie with each other in collecting the greatest quantity and best quality of Gamass [sic], because their fame for future wives will depend much on the activity and industry they show here; the young men will not overlook these merits, and many a marriage is closed after the Gamass [sic] are brought home. I saw a young woman at the Skitsoe [Coeur d'Alene] village, who had collected and prepared sixty sacks of good Gamass, each sack containing 1-1/5 bushel; she was spoken of in the best terms throughout the village.

As soon as the Indians have returned from gathering the "Biscuit root," of which we shall speak afterwards, they begin to prepare for the Gamass [sic] grounds. The whole village is active in collecting the horses, getting sacks ready, which are mostly of Thuja and Helonias roots; and at last family after family leave the village, chattering merrily, and the group after group arrive at the plains, where there is all bustle and activity. After dismounting, they strike their camp in the groups of tall pines; the boys take care of the horses, while the older people pay their visits from lodge to lodge. Hunters return with game, or some young men bring the first salmon from the distant river, to have something to feast the visitors. All is merriment and joy, when the numerous large pine-wood fires [heating stones] illuminate the wide classic plain in the evening. The digging of the Gamass [sic] takes place as soon as the lower half of the flowers on the raceme begin to fade, or better, when the time of flowering is entirely passed. For that purpose, the Indian women use a stick about two feet long, curved like a saber, of hawthorn, which is provided with a cross piece of elk-horn on the top, serving as a handle. This instrument they use with astonishing dexterity, so that they seldom strike the point twice after the same bulb. Four or five [women] baking and drying. With the first dawn of day the industrious women and mothers start from the camp, which is frequently a little distance from the Gamass [sic] plains, on account of wood and water. They are generally accompanied by a little girl or boy to take care of the horses, and they return every evening loaded to the lodge. As soon as they gathered a sufficient quantity of bulbs, they prepare for baking. For that purpose, they dig or scrape a hole in the ground of three or four feet in depth, make a fire and throw in a good layer of red hot stones, then a layer of clean grass over those, and now a layer of Gamass [sic], the latter having before been cleaned from the adhering soil. This is repeated until the hole is level with the ground above. The fire is now moved on the top of the pit, and kept burning for about twenty-four hours or longer.

The raw Gamass [sic] bulb resembles in its substance, the common Squill. By baking, it acquires a sweet taste, and when boiled the taste is not unlike the syrup of Squills, but not so sweet. Those accustomed to that food, like the Indians, remain strong and fleshy; but a European falls off very soon if he had nothing else. Eating a great quantity produces flatulence, as has been observed by travellers before (Geyer 1846:299-301).

A young girl, accompanying her mother to the root fields for the first time, would be instructed not to eat the first roots she dug, but to clean and give them away so that she might later become a good digger and provider. Both a girl's mother and grandmother taught the young girl various songs, one unique to each plant or berry species, and that was sung before digging or collecting the specific food or medicines. Presumably, the Colville, Lakes, and Sinkaietk women sang their thanksgiving song after collecting.

After the *flowering stage (sm'l'l'ác')*, bitterroot (*Lewisia rediviva* Pursh. - *sp'éƛ'n*) has a relatively shallow root system and a thin skin, which is easily removed by pinching the skin between two fingers almost immediately after digging. One elderly woman remarked on the *sound made when removing the skin (t'ak^w t'ak^w)* of bitterroot. It was usually prepared for eating by boiling, sometimes mixed with camas or powdered and mixed in soups and stews to give a bitter flavor (Elmendorf 1935-6, 1:30). The non-Indian term "bitterroot" was because of the taste, but the Spokan word (T. Wynecoop, pers. comm.) comes from a small, *red, heart-like growth (ml'íl* - "shed blood" - "menses")* that is found in the top center of the root mass just below the surface, which is easier to remove when separating the roots from the rest of the plant. Some elders leave the heart to later fall out once the root has dried. In the past, elders ate the heart—relishing its bitter flavor (STHC). If kept dry, bitterroot can be stored for several years. Bitterroot was said to have a woody taste if dug while in flower.

Bitterroot, when first eaten by earlier Euro-Americans, was sometimes called *racine amére*, "a bitter root, which grows on dry ground, is fusiform, and though not pleasant to the taste, is very conducive to health" (Parker 1840:221). Unfortunately, Parker provided no specifics of its medicinal use.

Some of the early plants gathered—particularly in ecozones influenced by certain soil types, elevation, exposure, and sufficient precipitation—were *Ranunculacea (sčn'írmn)*, *prickly pear (Opuntia polyacantha - sxʷyéneʔ* or *sxʷiy'en'eʔ)*, and *yellowbell (Fritillaria pudica - q'áw'exeʔ)*. Yellowbell roots (*swiy'eʔ*) appeared in early spring and were once very prolific in open wooded areas, and taste like sweet potato when eaten raw or boiled with meat (Elmendorf 1935-6, 1:31). Various species of Lomatium were dug in dryer areas, whereas in wetter regions one had four species of *onion (séhč)*, which were not stored as they sprout easily. *Wild carrot (Perideridia gairdneri [H. & A.] Math. - sƛ'úk'ʷm)*, after being dug with a digging stick in early August, would be stored after the brown-gray skin had been removed and the white root mashed, dried and placed in baskets. Wild carrots were winter-stored in grass-lined pits covered with earth, and remained fresh until removed and eaten in late winter or early spring. Yet some elders explained how dried, stored carrot root did not keep well, since the larger more mature roots did not taste good. Small wild carrots were eaten raw by both children and adults or made into a soup and mixed with black moss (Elmendorf 1935-6, 1:30). Great amounts of dry *camas (Camssia quamash - ʔitxʷeʔ)* were stored in grass bags for winter use. It should be noted that in the past, elderly women would never dig any camas in flower, contending that the product would not store well, and because the taste was different.

Some elderly women were once able to discern by the *taste of the camas sxʷeʔlitxʷeʔ* if it had come from the Flathead area, a long-time source of bitterroot that was traded to even the Spokan who often remarked upon its superior flavor.

Nuts and Seeds

The laborious but necessary annual task of collecting nuts and seeds was accomplished by small family groups of related women who supervised young girls while cutting tules in the fall or digging summer roots, or gathering summer berries and fruits. With most group gathering activities, the women would gather nuts and seeds throughout the morning and in the early afternoon. After eating, they would socialize by singing songs, joking about men and generally relaxing as they processed their harvest. Though unwed women could participate, they had less to say of their experiences or anticipated relationships with men.

From mid-summer until after the last salmon fishing in the autumn, a wide variety and quantity of nuts and seeds were collected by women while picking berries. If the nuts and seeds were not processed and mixed with fish or deer meat for immediate consumption, they were later processed and stored as an "iron ration" (one that stored well) in flat spruce root or cedar bark baskets hung from the beams of dwellings.

It was believed that collected foods could be offended by the presence of a different food in the same collecting containers, so women would not necessarily pick berries the same day as collecting nuts. Also, prior to a foray of gathering nuts, the women would fastidiously cleanse their berry collecting and burden baskets, not by washing, but rather wiping with ferns or bear-grass, and were 'spoken to' during the process. Another example of caution against product contamination was that when utilizing a digging stick or a stick to knock cones or nuts from a tree, a woman would run her hand over the tool if a different type of tree was to be harvested. There was no recollection of what was said, if anything, by the harvester.

All types of seed-bearing plants were gathered. During the fall the Spokan gathered *sunflower seeds (smečtuʔ)* from spring sunflower or *balsamroot (Balsamorhiza sagittata [Pursh] Nutt. - smúkʷeʔšn'* or *semúkʷešen* or *smúk'ʷaɫxn)* and the tall *sunflower plant (Helianthus annus L. - snčnčtqin)*—both important plants that provided seeds and tubers. The *dried seeds (méčtuʔ)* of balsamroot were ground with a stone mortar and pestle, mixed with any animal fat, and eaten immediately as a type of nutritious mix called *mečtuʔ* or mixed with soups. After being roasted, sunflower seeds were eaten as an in-between-meal snack. Women gathered sunflower seeds after the flower was gone, and stored them only briefly because of rodents. No reason was given by several elderly ladies who claimed that the Spokan avoided eating sunflower seeds, yet Elmendorf (1935-6 1:32) noted that seeds were removed from the husks, crushed, and boiled into a soup.

The greatest yields of nuts were provided by both species of the short, burly *hazelnut trees* (*Corylus cornuta* Marsh, var., *Californica* [D. C.] Sharp - *q'p'x^{w}ʔálq^w*, and *C. californicum californicum* - *q'ép'x^{w}eʔ*), which ripened in August or September, depending upon the elevation, and were collected by women. Prior to eating hazelnuts, the prickly husks were first removed by either men or women—using buckskin mittens—before putting the nuts in boiling water, and after the nuts were broken open with a stone, or placed in *grass sacks* (*nƛ'aqn'eʔ*) (later burlap or canvas sacks) that were thrown into an excavated pit and pounded with a blunt-ended pole. After sorting the nuts from the shells, the nuts were again mashed into a pulp between two boards or flat rocks (Elmendorf 1935-6, 1:30). The pulp or broken nuts was often mixed with bear *grease* (*sq'^{w}úct* - "any animal grease") or rendered bear oil and made into a butter, always considered a delicacy and a valuable trade food.

A few elders recalled accounts of how in the past men hunted both deer and California quail that had been attracted to hazelnut groves located on terraces along the Spokane River. Stored hazelnuts did not store well and were placed uncracked in cedar-root containers, and the outer shells were cracked open with a stone (Smith 1936-8:458) prior to eating. However, some Spokan said that the unshelled nut would not lose moisture if properly stored. Hazelnuts were eaten raw, but never with meals. Some elders recall great quantities of prepared hazelnuts being winter stored in baskets in near-constant temperature root cellars. In times of famine, the Spokan would take ready-husked hazelnuts from known pine squirrel nests, but leave enough for the animal's survival—a ritual which Smith (1936-8:201) says the Kalispel never practiced.

The main season for collecting the much sought *white pine nuts* (*q'epp'x^{w}eʔ*) was from late August until late September; an activity called *q'ép'x^{w}eʔ*, and was done when the men were hunting deer while women often picked huckleberries at higher elevations. Since the white pine was rarely found in Spokan territory, men and women had to travel east to find stands of *white pine* (*P. monticola* Dougl. ex Loud.), and the nearest major source for white pine nuts was *Kalispel Peak* (*č'aʔsálqn* - "two peaks"), some distance from Spokan territory. Often the younger hunters were persuaded to climb the trees to better enable them to pick the *pine cones* (*sč'ic'eʔ*). Or, they would reach the lower cones with long, lightweight lodge poles, ones that had been carefully stored the previous year by stacking them upright as a tied bundle against one of the trees. Women presumably did not climb trees, rather they spread hides on the ground around the bottom of the tree to catch the cones and any loose nuts from mature cones. The long, green cones were harvested, piled in great heaps, and then covered with dry brush to make a fire to loosen the seeds. When the cones had cooled, they would be shaken, and the seeds would fall onto tule mats or hides. To reduce the volume of the harvest, and eliminate the burden of the cones, seeds not quite ripe would be released onto a hide by rubbing the cones together. On the other hand, the seeds of immature cones were obtained by placing in warm ash fires to burn off any pitch. Nutritious white pine nuts taste similar to *ponderosa nuts* (*ʔitč*).

Gathered seeds were eaten raw as a treat during the encampment, not as a meal, whereas pine nuts were stored in untanned deer hide bags for later consumption and were often mixed with deer meat or other types of animal grease to prevent spoilage (Smith 1936-8:459-460). Pine nuts were considered a delicacy, and always eaten raw. It has been claimed that pine nuts from any type of pine tree could be eaten, whereas several contemporary Spokan elders claimed pine nuts were *never* eaten.

The only edible part of *brown-eyed Susan* or *blanket flower* (*Gaillardia aristata* Pursh. - *čm'm'łčús* or *sčmłčus*) were the seeds, which were roasted for immediate consumption, as a travel food or it was winter-stored. Besides camas and certain Lomatium that were found in more semi-arid and open areas, most other seed-bearing plants in the Spokan diet were the species of *Lidiuym*, *Descurasinia*, and *Brassica*. These particular plants presented difficulties during prescribed burning, since the plants frequently grew close together in large and open areas, and were often wet, making it difficult to effectively ignite the plants. Therefore, during the early reservation period, women would torch individual plants with kerosene-soaked rags fixed to green shafts of pine.

As could be best reconstructed from oral history, elevated food storage platforms in ponderosa trees were used for nut and seed storage, as well as for other foods, and were of vertical or slanted wall construction, roofed with long, hemp-secured, tamarack shakes.

In addition to berries, several types of seeds were stored in salmon skins for winter food, as were *stored salmon eggs* (*xʷel'ʔékʷl*). If bear fat was available, it was cut into thin strips, boiled, and then placed on top of the camas before the sack was closed. The fat would be released slowly and soaked into the camas, providing a desired taste when later eaten.

Berries and Fruits

Berry-picking (*q'ʷléwi*) was an ongoing activity that commenced in June with one-day excursions, becoming lengthier and covering a greater area in July and August, depending upon elevation. Approximately thirty-four different types of berries were collected by the Spokan, and at the peak of activity, women spent sometimes a week or more, harvesting along water courses or at higher elevations where berry areas were more productive. These activities continued until after the *first hard frost* (*šit syixʷmusm*), one that *frosted the ground* (*sxʷékʷleʔxʷ*), usually in early October, and no types of frozen berries were ever picked. It was common for several women to make an *early pre-gathering harvest* (*ʔečp'uʔm*) to determine the condition and availability of certain berry crops—often gathering strawberries, which was the first available fruit to appear around the end of May. Strawberries were gathered daily for two to three weeks. Berries too high or too few for collection were readily consumed by birds.

Regardless of the season, the women and older children often returned late to their *fall camp* (*č'ʔeym'i*) after berrying and would spread their harvest on tule mats or a large section of rawhide laid on the ground to dry the harvest. In later years *they would spread tarps or blankets on the ground* (*xʷpxʷéʔpleʔxʷm*), or on large frame-supported racks of tule mats. Sometimes a low ember-fire would be maintained until the fruit was thoroughly dry. At the height of a harvest, and after several days of picking, the berries were spread on mats to sun-dry, then placed in tule or cedar bask bags and carried—sometimes assisted by men—to the winter village for storage. When drying berries, children were recruited to keep birds away from the fruit.

Red and black *chokecherry* (*Prunus virginia* L. var. *Melanocarpa* [A. Nels.] Sarg. - *łxʷłóxʷ*), Valley serviceberry, and huckleberry were major berry crops prepared for winter storage. Their importance was demonstrated by the time devoted to the labor-intensive picking, and by the variety of ways of processing the harvest. Upon returning to camp in late afternoon, the women and children would spread and sun-dry their harvest on tule mats laid upon the ground or spread upon raised, frame-supported racks. After several days the fruit was ready to be placed in tule bags for winter storage, but before consuming, the fruit was often first boiled to a glutinous-like mass, cooled, and cut into semi-rigid pieces to be consumed with meat or fish. The *seed* (*snλ'č'téssn*) was not removed. A preferred method of preparation was to *mash* (*łóci*) with a stone or hardwood pestle the collected fruit in a mortar, including the seed. Each time the mass was removed from the mortar, the worker would work deer tallow into what became basically flat, rounded disks. The grease, if permitted to harden, turned into tallow, and was not stored as the cakes would become rancid. The disks were sun-dried by repeatedly turning the congealed mass for several days in the sun. When eaten like that, each disc had a tasty *jelly-like center* (*sxʷeʔnéč*) (STHC).

A major *fruit* (*sp'iʔqáłq*) that contributed to the berry diet was chokecherry, of which there were two varieties: red and black. Depending upon elevation, both red and black chokecherries were harvested in great quantity by women from mid-June until late August. Chokecherries were first mashed with a stone pestle on of rawhide before being sun-dried on large flat rocks or on a large section of rawhide. A preferred way of eating this fruit was to mix the mashed berries with water or warm grease, or to *dip* (*múl*) small flat, oval cakes, which never became hard, into a meat broth. It should be noted that chokecherries were a desired food by voracious squirrels and various species of birds. If a meat broth was too greasy, dried camas cake or service berry cakes were dipped into the broth before eating. Most people preferred to eat mixed berries or cakes by dipping them in warm deer grease; which, if permitted to harden, turned into tallow, but were not stored as the cakes would become rancid. Every household would store great quantities of mashed chokecherries which were preferably stored in several large grass sacks or skin bags, or in other types of containers (Smith 1936-8:192). Some elders maintained that loosely flat woven grass was the best way to winter-store berries. Another method to ensure winter storage was to *pound* (*te?mintn'*) and smash the berries into small hand-size cakes, which were sun-dried until leather dry. When the purple-specked berries of both false Solomon's seal (*Smillacina racemosa* [L.] Desf.) and *S. stella* ([L.] Desf.) turned a clear red, they were gathered and eaten. To ensure winter storage, the procedure was to pound and smash the berries into manageable *small hand-size cakes* (*st'łt'łéltn*), which were sun-dried until leather dry.

Seeds in berries—most notably chokecherries—were typically not a problem for elderly people, who would spit out the seeds, whereas children were cautioned to never *swallow* (*q'e''m'im*) them for fear of choking. It was said that a grandmother would carefully remove the pits before giving the berry to a small child. Chokecherry berries, including the crushed pit, were mixed and served with other things or served alone, either cold or hot. The juice from *crushed berries* (*scnp''?etk*ʷ - "crushed") was "heated with [a] hot rock in [a] cooking basket [and] kept from day to day & heated up before use" (Elmendorf 1935-6, 1:34). Prior to immediate consumption or storage, berries were pounded into a mash with a stone or hardwood pestle in a shallow mortar, or upon a smooth flat stone, and the result was then boiled to a *glutinous-like mass* (*sxʷe?néč*), cooled, spread out in thin sheets before cutting into pieces to dry or eaten immediately. Women often worked deer tallow into the semi-rigid sections, producing flat, rounded discs or cakes, which were again sun-dried for several days, and repeatedly turned until the congealed mass hardened.

Valley service berry, chokecherry, and huckleberry were the most important Spokan fruit crops. Valley serviceberries vary in color and flavor, which grow in dry rocky places and typically ripen in mid-July, being gathered until late August by women making mainly one-day trips to known berry areas. Some women, however, would spend a week or more collecting serviceberries, placing them whole—after drying—in cedar bark containers, tightly woven baskets, or rawhide baskets as the berries are firm and not likely to be crushed. Large quantities of serviceberries were mainly prepared for winter storage by one of two methods: one procedure was to *spread* (*xʷep* or *č'łxwepm* - "to spread out on a mat") the harvest on tule mats and dry them individually; a second and more involved procedure was to dry them on rack-supported tule mats over low-standing ember fires of juniper wood that imparted a favored flavor; smoke-dried serviceberries were preferred to the fresh berries. Relatively large quantities of service berries, chokecherries, black chokecherries, and Oregon grapes were made into cakes prior to being dried and smoked as winter-stored food.

The *mountain serviceberry* (*Amelanchier alnifolia Cusickii* - a.k.a. Juneberry - *sy'éy'e?*) and the *valley serviceberry* (*Amelanchier alnifolia alnifoilia* Nutt. - *słáq*) were the most extensively used berries by the Spokan (Elmendorf 1935-6, 1:31). When berries were spread on ground mats to dry—particularly serviceberries, the ever present danger was of squirrels eating one's harvest. Children and elders often exchanged news and learned different versions of cat's cradle while acting as sentinels for bear and cougar. Serviceberry is often found referred to like this: "a delicious fruit, [was] called by travellers the mountain pear, though it bears no resemblance" (DeSmet 1843:112).

Serviceberries were considered by some as too sweet upon harvesting. A commonly favored method of preparing the berries for eating was to take the dried berries, boil them, and either mix them with tallow or simply make them into small, flat cakes, which were sun-dried to a leather-like consistency, making them an excellent storage food. The dried serviceberry cakes were later reconstituted by soaking and then stone-boiling them in a mixture of *fresh salmon roe* (*ʔék'ʷʷl*), deer meat, bitterroot, or with less palatable berries. An additional method of preparing serviceberries was to slowly immerse the fruit in stone-boiled water combined with the suet from around the *deer's paunch* (*sčt'kʷéw's*), which gave a flavor preferred by some people. Serviceberries were occasionally served with the small, blue-gray and slightly bitter red osier dogwood berries after they were mixed and mashed. Some children complained of the bitterness, but were told the mixture would make them strong.

Blackberries, both types of huckleberry, *black mountain blackberry* (*Vaccinium membranaceum* Dougl. ex Hook. - *st'šáłq* or *st'ešłqełp*; the berry is termed *štéšałq*), and the lowbush or *dwarf bilberry* (*V. Caespitosum - ssípt*), stored well. Sun-dried, stored huckleberries and black mountain berries had first to be soaked overnight and then boiled before eating. Some early whites referred to huckleberries as whortleberries, a Middle English designation for blueberries, and a name used in eastern North America. The juice from blueberries was commercially used in World War I to dye uniforms. Later, the domesticated *blueberry* (*V. myrtilloides* Michx. - *čkʷnkʷnús*) and *oval-leaf blueberry* (*V. ovalalifolium* Smith - *c'kʷíkʷ*) were best stored when canning was adopted. Once introduced, the *Himalayan blackberry* (*Rubus discolor* Weithe. & Nees. - *tełtbł*) was also gathered.

Another highly regarded berry crop was the huckleberry, both the *dwarf huckleberry* (*V. caespitosum* Michx. - *spłełp*) and the big or *taller huckleberry* (*V. membranaceum* Dougl. ex Torr. - *st'šáłq*), which were collected in great quantities throughout July and until September, depending upon the elevation where harvested. While gathering this fruit, thimble berry leaves lined the women's baskets and cushioned the berries, as well as being used to shade the huckleberries in warm weather when spread on top of the basket's contents. What was not eaten at the end of each harvest day was carefully sun-dried on large tule mats atop low willow frames for winter consumption. However, some women said they were always eaten fresh—never dried for storage. Huckleberries were often "eaten with meat or partly dried & crushed into *sts'tá'ʔ* cakes" (Elmendorf 1935-6, 1:31).

If not eaten fresh the huckleberries were later sun-dried and stored in rawhide bags suspended from interior *roof beams* (*čłxeličn'*). The inexperienced picker would be warned never to eat any of the harvest since only a greedy and selfish person would do so, one who would never fill her baskets. Pickers often carefully pruned off the ends of selected branches of a *huckleberry bush* (*st'šłqéłp*), knowing this practice would increase the plant's production the following year. Fresh or dried huckleberries were traditionally never mixed with other foods.

Elders have noted how disrespectful some people are today when they carry home large branches they have hacked or broken off the main bush, or by actually removing the entire plant by cutting or shoveling for easier picking, which are usually loaded in the back of a pick-up truck.

During the women's berry collecting, men were participating in collective deer drives. When individually deer hunting, men returned to huckleberry camps in the late afternoon and occasionally assisted, if possible, in collecting huckleberries. The importance of this berry crop was apparent in various *sacred rituals* (*hesč'áwm*) and *associated taboos* (*sčxeʔnéple?*) concerning consumption. The first berries collected were *blessed* (*hecnč'áwpá?łqi* - "blessing fruit") with a prayer of thanksgiving. Before departing the harvest area, each woman would *give some of the berries back to nature* (*xáq'l'eʔxʷi*); not to do so was considered gluttonous and disrespectful, a *rude affront* (*čsłcut*) to the plant, which may not produce again.

It should be noted that with the government prohibition against traditional selective burning, there was a definite reduction in huckleberry bushes, and as a result, the gatherers were fastidious and attentive to prayers of thanksgiving when locating productive berry patches.

A sick person was forbidden to *eat huckleberries off the bush* (*q'ʷluʔscíni* or *snsp'iqałqtn*), i.e., fresh berries—a practice with implications that recognize specific religious beliefs. Huckleberries were rarely eaten with any other foods, save for eel and sometimes sturgeon, since the berries naturally helped to compensate for the greasy fish taste. Fresh huckleberries were mixed with meat dishes or partially dried and crushed in cakes for storage. Bunches of huckleberries were often stored by placing them "in stiff [birch-bark containers] (*lúp'i*) [and] hung up on limbs or frames and [when] dried - taken off when ½ dry [and the] green ones would have been eaten" (Elmendorf 1935-6, I:31).

In the heather family, but related to the huckleberry, is the *dwarf grouseberry* (*Vaccinium scoparium* Leiberg. - *t't'áq*), a low-growing huckleberry found at higher elevations. It has red berries, not unlike those of the yew tree, and may have been an introduced plant (Turner 1978:209). *Common grouseberry* (*V. myrtillus* L.) is also remembered as *t't'áq*.

The Spokan gathered two types of *blue elderberry* (*Sambucus cerulea* Raf. - *c'kʷkʷálqʷ*) id. tree or *c'kʷíkʷ* id. berry and *Sambucus glauca* Nutt. ex T. & G.] - *c'kʷíkʷ*) from mid-August to early September. Small amounts were eaten fresh after spitting out the seed, but most of a harvest was either sun-dried or smoke-dried, always leaving the seed in the berry. Stored berries were never pitted, nor were they ever made into cakes, unless, like the chokecherry, they were stone-mashed. In winter the berries were stone-boiled and generally eaten solely as a dish.

Kinnikinnick (*Arctostaphylos uva-ursi* L. Spreng. - *sčkʷlkʷlús* and *skʷelís* for berry, and *skʷlséłp* for plant), sometimes called redberry or bearberry, was more important as a medicine, and the dried leaves provided tobacco. Mature kinnikinnick berries were the last berries to be harvested just before snowfall in late fall or early winter, and stored in tule baskets, to permit air circulation and prevent the berry from drying out so that the white pulp would not spoil or ferment during the winter. A few elders claim they continued to gather kinnikinnick berries after the first snowfall (STHC), and that they were harvested throughout the winter. But by spring—with warmer weather—nearly all would have spoiled from fermentation. The purplish red-skinned berries are relatively dry, and were commonly mixed with other types of berries when eating, to presumably soften the kinnikinnick berry. These berries were winter-stored solely in tule bags and used in winter cooking; the dried berries were reconstituted and preferably added to soups and stews.

Both *black thornberry* (*Crataegus douglasii* Lindl., var. *Douglasii*, forma *Douglasii* - *sxʷaʔnčálqʷ* id. "plant" and *sxʷeʔn'éč* id. "berry") and *red thornberry* (*C. Columbiana* Howell, var. *columbiana* - *stm'qʷálqʷ* or *xʷeʔnéč* - "berry" id. "plant" and *stm'óqʷ* id. "berry")—sometimes called hawthorn berries—were harvested from mid-August until a killing frost. After drying they are not edible. Spokan children might have felt they were inedible even before a killing frost, as both types have an astringent flavor. Smith (1936-8:189) was told that the Kalispel recognized three varieties of *black thornberry* (*sxʷeʔenéč*, and *nłq'éλp*, and *c'msxʷeʔenéč* - "small round objects"). Both the black thornberry and red thornberry were eaten in different ways: the fresh berries were eaten raw, and after mashing the fruit only a handful were eaten while spitting out the fairly large seed. The mash could be mixed with a small amount of cold grease before eating, or the berries and the seeds were thoroughly mixed by the women with a mortar and pestle, and pressed into small cakes, which were eaten immediately or stored. Both black and red thornberry cakes were made in this fashion, and when thoroughly dried over a smoke rack, they were stored as a winter food—never with any grease, for the cakes could become rancid.

The Spokan dried red chokecherries by placing them on slabs of hemlock or cedar in front of a fire to dry out before storing them in *woven baskets* (*sy'áy'qs*) for winter use. Black thornberry cakes were remembered as being quite sweet; they were served, if possible, with meats or fish. Berries of another species of *hawthorn* (*C. Brevispina* [Dougl.] Heller - *sxʷáníq'*) were collected at higher elevations. Chokecherries were important to non-Indian diet and medicine as well, as Drury records from Mary Richardson Walker's 1847 diary, "Baked & partly pressed out the juice from the thorn berries boiled the night before [...] Obtained about four gallons of thorn berry syrup for vinegar" (1976:413 fn). Thornberries were mixed together, pounded and dried (Schaeffer 1934-37, I-28:53).

Red chokecherries were collected from mid-September until mid-October. It is a fruit that usually grows near water and is reputed to be an exceptionally *sweet berry* (*st'xáłq*) as against the black thornberry, and it has a more diverse habitat. As with nearly all types of berries, both the red and black thornberry were gathered and prepared for eating or storage in much the same way. The preferred method of preparation for winter storage was to grind the fresh berries with a mortar and pestle, then to mix with appropriate amounts of tallow or fat. This mix was shaped into small patties, then air-dried until the outside was hard. However, if red chokecherries were broken open, and stored in grass bags for too long, they could become wormy. Some said they were seldom made into cakes for winter storage, as the mixture would be too hard to eat unless first soaked in warm water. Wood of the deciduous black thornberry bush—when shaped—made durable digging-sticks and pegs for tipis and for stretching hides on the ground. With the advent of agriculture, several large black thornberry bushes, having long thorns, were tied together by a long rope and secured to a saddle horn, and then dragged over a newly plowed *field* (*čłčéwm*) as a harrow (STHC). The longer thorns of red thornberry were exceptionally fine, and so made strong needles for sewing, piercing hide, withdrawing splinters, piercing ears, and for tattooing, and served as toothpicks.

All three varieties of the *wild strawberry* (*Fragaria vesca* L., var. *Bracteata* [Heller] David, *F. Virginiana Duchesne*, and *F. Californica* - *q'it'q'm*) were gathered from the *strawberry bush* (*q'et'm'm'péłp*) by small groups of women who ventured to known areas in early May. The time of collecting was an opportunity to socialize, gossip, and generally enjoy one another's company. The *strawberry* (*q'it'q'm*) was collected in *stiff* (*c'uk'ʷ*) bark containers to prevent squashing the fruit, and was never stored for winter, nor eaten with meals, but rather eaten as a snack during the harvest season. Another type of wild strawberry, identified as *Rubus idaeus* L. (*nw'ew'ew'isšelš*), was gathered whenever they were found.

Thompson was the first to note there were at least "three sorts of currants, one sweet and red, the other yellow, acid; red light acid" (Elliott 1914a, 2:122). Five types of *currants* (*ste?mtús*), sometimes called *gooseberry* (*nt'ét'm'l'ps* - "little stemmed berry"), were collected, and though difficult to winter store, were partially dried and pressed into cakes that women often mixed with serviceberries:

> In the month of August it [gooseberry] produces abundance of fruit of a small oblong fruit, which grows in thick clusters. This fruit has an insipid taste, but is looked on as healthy, and great quantities of it may be eaten without injury. It is much esteemed by the native, who preserve it for their winter's use, by making it into small cakes, which are gradually dried before a slow fire (Cox 1932:224).

The *golden currant* (*Ribes aureum* Pursh, var. *Aureum* - *sc'irus* or *p'tsp'tsxnékuł*) the *white currant* (*R. glandulosum* - *yérčn'* or *nt'ét'm'l'ps* - "gripping something by the neck") (Smith 1936-8:194), the *wax (squaw) currant* (*R. Cereum* Dougl. - *sqʷúy'u?*), and the undesignated inland black gooseberry were collected by women from the middle to the end of July—sometimes until early October at lower elevations. The small *yellow-red currant berry* (*Ribes* sp. - *yátqn*) was collected upon ripening in July, and was reputed to be poisonous, as Ray (1933:103) claimed, if collected from the north of the Columbia River, but harmless if mixed with other food or gathered from south of the river.

The small yellow-red currant was picked upon ripening in July, whereas both the golden currant and the white currant were gathered in June in moist areas, and usually eaten fresh. Wild gooseberry was not highly regarded, but was often mixed with other berries for flavor. Logistics of timing was another problem when picking these berries, for as Turner noted, "They have to be picked just as they are turning black; when green they are too sour, and after ripening they soon fall off the branches" (1978:165). Currants and *gooseberries* (*R. irriguum* Dougl. - *nt'et'melps*) were picked when gathering other types of fruit, and not sought purposely. White and golden currants were eaten fresh, and never stored, for once the currant turns brown it usually has worms, which was why gooseberries were never stored. A general term for currants was *sc'íp'u?s* ("pinched in the middle"), and sometimes called *ste?mtús*. At higher elevations, and in damp regions, the *swamp gooseberry* (*R. lacustre* [Pers.] Poir) was collected, but never stored.

So-called white currants—actually the *snowy gooseberry* (*R. Niveum* Lindl., forma *niveum - pqál'xeʔ*)—were collected, but seldom stored because they are difficult to dry, and were eaten green. However, some women recalled their grandmothers mixing gooseberries with other types of berries, especially service berries, and made into small palm-size cakes (Elmendorf 1935-6, 1:34), and stored as a winter food.

The Spokan gathered three varieties of soapberry or foamberry in May; one variety was a yellow berry and the other a red berry, and some say they once picked a third type of foamberry with a light yellow-red color. This type of yellow-red berry was until recently collected by only a few elders who designated it as a *foamberry*, *buffalo berry*, or *soapberry* (*Shepherdia canadensis* [L.] Nutt. - *sxʷúsm* for berry, and *sxʷsmétp* for plant), which were eaten raw or could be stored in bark baskets after being thoroughly air-dried. The best time to eat foamberries was when they turned pink, and were eaten fresh or sun-dried for winter eating. Fresh leaves of green, red, or yellow foamberry were eaten, but never stored.

The English term for foamberry indicates the favored use when fresh, being made into a type of ice cream. Before making Indian ice cream, a *birch bark container* (*lúp'i*) was carefully washed with *foamberry juice* (*sxʷusmnétkʷ*) (any type of grease will prevent the berry from foaming), and then a handful of fresh berries were broken open to displace the excess seeds while placing the mass into the basket, which was gently whipped continuously with a *beater* (*lúxʷtn'* or *naxlečtmn*) made from a bundle of waxberry or *snowberry* (*Symphoricarpos albus* [L.] Blake - *stmtmniʔátq*) twigs, or a flat stick for approximately ten minutes. The *foam* (*hi xʷus*) was eaten immediately; otherwise in would return to a liquid. Today, *Indian ice cream* (*sxʷúsm*) is made with an egg-beater, always sweetened with sugar, and served as a snack to children, or to adults as a late night adult snack.

Traditionally, the shallow, very soft, cup-shaped *thimbleberry* (*Rubus parviflorus* Nutt., forma *Nuttallii* [T. & G.] Fassett - *pólplqn* or *pelpelknílhmix*) was almost always eaten when picked in July to mid-August, and usually found at higher elevations in rather dense vegetation. Being sparse in distribution, it was more difficult to pick an appreciable amount. If the berries were to be transported to a camp, women would line their bark baskets with thimbleberry leaves to prevent the soft, fleshy berries from staining their containers. The large leaves of the plant were used to cover the gathering basket to keep the harvest cool and fresh, and any new growth broad maple-like leaf was large enough to serve as a temporary container when one came upon a cluster of thimbleberry bushes. Though considerable time was required to gather any substantial quantity of the delicate thimbleberry, some women would collect and sun-dry the berries for winter use, and when needed the dehydrated berries were boiled and typically added to meat dishes. Most thimbleberries were eaten raw during their collection.

The sweet-tasting dark brown raspberry-like *dewberry* (*Rubus ursinus* Cham. & Schlecht. - *tétt*) was not an important crop since considerable time and effort was required—as with the thimbleberry—since the berry-bearing vine grew on the ground. When collected, the berries were eaten either fresh or sun-dried after being collected in early August. Only a small amount of sun-dried berries were put away for winter. They were particularly juicy and full of small seeds.

Two varieties of *black raspberry* or *blackcap* (*Rubus leucodermis* Dougl. ex T. & G. - *sqʼʷiqʼʷáyqn*) and *trailing blackberry* (*R. discolor* and *R. ursinus* Cham. & Schlecht. - *mecukʷ*) were eaten fresh or dried as small flat cakes for winter consumption. The juice of these different berries made suitable dyes. Blackcap leaves, when boiled and steeped, were used to produce a medicinal tea for fatigue. *Black raspberry* (*R. macropetalus* Dougl. ex Hook. - *mcúkʷ*) known as *sqʼʷiqʼʷáyqn* (*R. leucodermis*), was collected in August, and always eaten fresh as they did not store well. However, some recall their elders sun-drying the berries and storing them in bark baskets for winter use, when they were boiled and mixed with meat dishes. Yet others said how the blackberry was always eaten fresh and never dried or stored because it was said how this berry was too juicy.

Two species of *red raspberries* (*R. Idaeus peramoenus* - *l'l'ác*, and *R. Idaeus* var. *Praermoenus* [Greene] Fern. - *nw'ewíssĺ̌s̆*) were gathered by women from late July until mid-August. If not eaten fresh, both types of red raspberries were made into small cakes, sun-dried until firm, and stored in stiff bark baskets for winter storage. During the 1900s, the juice from this fruit was used to stain white trade cotton twine and used as imbrication when making cornhusk bags. Raspberries were occasionally mixed with thimbleberries (Turner 1978:204) to add taste and consistency, even though thimbleberries were considered by some to have been superior in flavor to raspberries and wild strawberries.

Both the *black twinberry* and *twinflower honeysuckle* (*Lonicera involucrata* [Rich.] Banks ex Spreng. - *čiriálq^w* or *čilyalálq^w*) or *red twinberry* (*Lonicera utahensis* Wats., forma *utahensis* - *sc'íp'u?s*) have small, shiny berries that were picked whenever found by passing hunters from July until early September. Red twinberries, leaves and shredded bark were steeped in boiling water to make a mild laxative. Elmendorf (1935-26) called black twinberry "bearberry," whose shredded bark was steeped in boiling water and used as a physic. The time and effort to gather a large quantity was apparently not worth a concerted effort until the Spokan commenced canning fruit and making jams after first crushing the berries with the seeds, then placing the results in wax-covered or screw-top pint size *jar* (*xxál'*), which were pressure-sealed by heating. When making jams or jellies, only *rosehip seeds* (*sx^way'ápa?ɫq*) were removed before boiling the fruit prior to canning.

From mid-July to the end of August, *loganberries* (*Rubus loganabaccus* L. H. bailey [Dougl.] S. & W. Brown - *téɫtɫ*) were picked, and those not eaten as a dessert were stored for winter consumption after sun-drying. Since loganberries are a fleshy and juicy fruit, the sun-drying was a long process required to properly dehydrate the berries, and before being eaten the berries were reconstituted by stone-boiling. These fruits, depending upon species, were best located in smaller shaded watersheds and in sparsely wooded areas. California or Pacific yewberries (*Rubus ursinus*), when available, were collected but not stored.

The *red willow* (*stčcx^wéɫp id*), also known as Western dogwood or red osier dogwood, was found along water courses or moist areas. The plant has small edible white to blue-gray berries—each with a smooth *pit* (*snλ'č'téss̆n'*)—which were harvested from late August to October. These *red willow berries* (*stčcx^wnálq^w*) were usually eaten fresh or mixed with other types of berries after mashing the fruit using a mortar and pestle. Opinions regarding preferred taste varied with each speaker, but there was consensus that the berries, when white, are less bitter than later, when the berry is dark. The fruit was eaten after being picked and not known to have been stored. Individuals were cautious not to overindulge, for fear of diarrhea, a condition which could be severe and even debilitating to anyone any distance from his or her camp. Willow leaves were dried and mixed with sweet grass, and sometimes with other types of leaves as a tobacco (as discussed in Chapter XV).

James Teit (1930:343) provides the only known reference that the Spokan gathered and consumed a variety of the *dogwood berry* (*Californica* A. Mey., var. *Pubescens* [Nutt.] Jepson - *stečx^w*), which, in addition to being used as a food, found use more often as a cough syrup when the fresh berries were mashed, heated and drunk as needed. The white to lead-colored, or blue berries were sun-dried and stored for winter. As with all stored berries, they had to be kept dry to prevent rotting and possibly spoiling other adjacent foods. It was said that the thin, flexible but strong branches were once used extensively in constructing weirs.

Rocky Mountain juniper (*Juniperus virginiana* L. var. *scopulorum* [Sarg.] Lemmon - *púnɫp*) had a wide variety of uses, but mostly as a medicinal plant. It was claimed that a person could eat only few berries because of the strong flavor and pitchy quality; sometimes drunk as a tea before entering the sweathouse. The branches, bark, and berries were used primarily as a multipurpose medicament. Until recently, most traditional elders always kept a can of water and mashed juniper needles over a low fire upon their *wood stove* (*snur'šict*) as a general purifier, as well as to keep malevolent spirits from a dwelling. Another, but more specific, reason for heating juniper or subalpine needles on a hot stove was to *prevent fearful singing or*

350

crying noises from emanating (*nc'll'ósmɬlt*), or sounds that mocked a *dead person's voice* (*čk'ʷssč'e?cínmis* - "he was ghosted by a dead person's voice")—believed to predict another person's death (Egesdal, pers. comm.).

Snow bush (*Ceanothus velutinus* Dougl. ex Hook. - *k'ʷlíč'tye?ɬp* or *wíwanɬp* or *w'atén'eɬp*) was used to fumigate a dwelling by placing small pieces of bark, crushed leaves, or washed berries on a hot stove, and used as an insect repellent when in a summer camp by placing several branches on a fire (Turner *et al.* 1980:119 and 1979:276,). But the dried berries—being edible when mixed with other berries—were bunched together and served with other types of berries. The dried stalks of the snowberry bush could be cut near the base and bundled together as a broom. As noted, snow bush is sometimes called greasewood, buckbrush, or sticky-laurel.

Squashberry or *high-bush cranberry* (*Viburnum pauciflorum* Raf. - *qʷlís*) is commonly located in damp wooded areas, and the sour fruit was picked in the fall as the berry commenced to turn red, and was eaten raw after discarding the large flat seed. Unfortunately, because of deforestation, many traditional harvest areas no longer exist.

Oregon grape (*Berberis aquifolium* Pursh - *sqʷúyu?* or *B. nervosa* Pursh - *sc'érs*) berries do not ripen until September, and were harvested into early October by women making short day excursions as the plant was widely distributed. But the fruit was never eaten in great quantities, largely because of the tart taste, and were first smoke-dried which imparts it a tangy flavor. Oregon grape berries have a sour taste if not first smoke-dried, which some say imparted a tangy flavor, and the berries were often eaten fresh after being first boiled—never eaten raw. Prior to being stored for winter, the dried berries were carefully boiled, and after draining the resulting mash was formed into small fist-size orbs, sometimes mixed with a handful of serviceberries to add flavor. The prepared fruit was occasionally mixed into meat dishes.

A plant extensively used by the Spokan was *Wood's Rose* (*Rosa woodsii.* - *xʷxʷy'épe?ɬp*). The fruit, if not eaten during harvesting, was boiled and formed into cakes for winter consumption. However, some elders could not recall the rosehip ever being stored, whereas several said it was stored in the past. Not only were *rosehip berries* (*sxʷay'ápa?ɬq*) gathered for food and medicine, but various parts of this important and ubiquitous plant served as a prophylactic device for protecting one's home, sweeping graves to rid any lingering malevolent spirits, and to prevent the return of ghosts, and used to carefully sweep the interior of a sweathouse prior to sweating. The boiled root of this plant produced an intense purple dye used for staining hemp and the imbrication of baskets. Rosehip berries, collected during October, were edible until early winter, when the fruit froze and became dehydrated, turning a dark color. As a food, it was collected by people wanting to supplement a restricted food supply when traveling. However, some elders, being currently made aware of the high vitamin C content, occasionally nibble on this fruit. In some areas, where extraordinarily large hip roses grew, women gathered them after a killing frost and removed the skin of the fruit, before the unseeded berry was cooked and served with deer meat. In early autumn, deer meat "was pronounced sweet and delicate" (Durham 1912, 1:41).

There is debate as to how extensively the fruit of the *mountain ash* (*Sorbus sitchensis* M. Roem. ssp. *grayi* [wenzig] C. L. Hitchc. - *čkʷlkʷlsálqʷ* or *ékʷkʷelesal'qʷ* - "tree with red berries") was eaten, being a bitter fruit, which was claimed to contain hydrogen cyanide. The berries were collected in August and September, and was a food favored by both deer and bear, and for migrating *cedar waxwings* (*Bombycilla garrulu* - *λlth ta alqw*) during mid-winter migration. However, elders recall the berries being first boiled and mixed with other types of *mountain ash berries* (*čkʷlkʷlús* - "red berries") (Egesdal, per. comm.) as a dish, or added to meat broths or stews. There is no recollection that this berry was traditionally stored for winter, but once canning was introduced, most women stopped using traditional methods of drying fruit for storage. Few elders now bother to make preserves of mountain ash berries. Sadly, the knowledge of preserving berries and

351

other fruits has been either discontinued or simply lost due to disuse—having been replaced by the ease of acquiring commercial and often less nutritional foods.

As early as the mid-19th century—just prior to the reservation period—the Spokan quickly adopted and maintained large gardens and orchards of many non-indigenous berry bushes, fruit trees, and rhizome food plants. These non-indigenous foods included *plum* (*Prunus domestica* - *čqʷiqʷáys*), *blackthorn plumb* (*Prunus spinosa* L. - *čt'et'eʔúseʔ*), *apple* (*Malus pumila* - *ʔarelesalqʷ*; *fruit* is *ʔapl*), *apricot* (*Prunus armeniaca* - *čkʷr'kʷr'iʔs*), *beans* (*Phaseolus vulgaris* L. - *pín* or *ɫm't'm't'ós*), *beets* (*Beta* sp. - *ƛ'm'ƛ'úm'*), *cauliflower* (*Brassica oleraceea capitata* - *picčt*), *corn* (*Zea mays* - *liplí*), *melons* (*Cucumis melo* L.), *peach* (*Prunus persica* - *čwepúseʔ*), *potato* (*Solanum tuberosum* L. - *patáq*), *cantaloupe* (*Cucumis melo* var. *cantalupensis* - *čʕaʕáxc'eʔ*), and *rhubarb* (*Rheum hybridum* Murr. - *xʷxʷtéɫp*), often associated with *cow parsnip* (*Heracleum lanatum* Michx. - *xʷxʷtéɫp*). An example of adaptation, utilization, and linguistic designation is the *domesticated blueberry* (*Vaccinium myrtilloides* Michx. - *čkʷnkʷnús*).

There was consensus that indigenous berries played a crucial role in the Spokan diet for most of their pre-history and history, and despite the apparent high-division of labor by gender, all children enjoyed berry-gathering excursions, and assisted their mothers and grandmothers in harvesting. It was not unusual, however, for a male berdache to accompany and assist women in this labor, most notably during huckleberry harvest, for a male berdache usually had huckleberry power.

In strictly adhering to the *ritual of praying* (*ʔesč'áwm*) before gathering any plant foods, a woman prayed as she moved from one berry bush to another. Praying was done by the person always facing east (Elmendorf 1935-6, 1:4). A personal experience of the importance in giving thanksgiving was apparent when the author gave a quantity of huckleberries to an elderly Spokan couple, who, after some deliberation, asked if the berries had been prayed over, but they were accepted, since a non-Indian person would not know this. As Schulz cites (pers. comm.), the major concern—even fear—of women while picking or camping in high yield berrying grounds, was the presence of bear.

When picking berries or digging roots, the women seldom engaged in conversation. The main reason given was that a person would feel restrained and not free to efficiently exploit a plant or move away to a more productive site if one was distracted by having to raise her voice or shout to a distant partner, which was considered as being disrespectful to the plants in an area. The social courtesy of continuing a conversation would be denied when a person attempted to increase her range of harvesting. Thus, only group *singing* (*snkʷnkʷney'i* - "they are singing") reinforced a sense of consciousness of kind and did not require a distracting dialogue. Singing was more frequent if younger children or grandchildren were part of the entourage.

Most of the Spokan major *berrying areas* (*snqʷʷlew'mn*) were north and northeast of the reservation, and were annually maintained by women who practiced controlled burning. As was recalled, traditional huckleberry patches were acknowledged to have been more cared for by a family, but the principles of usufruct applied among the Spokan, thus, precluding any notion that a family had ownership of large berrying areas. Mutual sharing of resource areas, except in areas of certain medicinal plants, thus, reduced conflict and maintained a basis for socialization. During longer berry excursions, accommodating non-family elders would take care of the smallest children. One elderly woman remembered her fictive berry grandmother. Unfortunately, most traditional kin terms that applied to these previously traditional fictive relationships have since been forgotten. Suffice to say, the so-called berry grandmother had no granddaughters, but was fortunate to adopt a fictive granddaughter whom she favored with her attention and knowledge.

As with all other aspects of Spokan life, behavioral protocols existed with regard to berry gathering. For example, a recent widow was forbidden to pick any berries, for it was believed that breaking this taboo could ruin the entire crop, and, "The belief was that the ghost might follow the widow to the berry patches and harm other pickers, and blast the crop" (Teit 1930:175), which was not a concern since animal and plant foods were

352

always shared with elder widows and widowers. There was an account of a named woman being ghosted while picking berries:

> Many years ago, just north of here [Wellpinit], a young woman had married a widower who had not observed the prescribed time of his mourning period after his wife died. One day his new wife went out by herself to pick huckleberries, and they say that the ghost of her husband's deceased wife was walking ahead of the new wife, also picking huckleberries, but she was in human form. After a while, the young woman called out to the unknown figure ahead of her, and the woman turned at looked at the new wife, and she suddenly realized the woman was dead—she was the ghost of her husband's first wife. The young new wife collapsed in a coma, and was found the next afternoon by her husband and some of his friends. The young wife was treated by a curing shaman, and later, upon her recovery, she told them what had happened (Ross 1968-2008).

Apart from established dietary needs, berry bush branches served numerous utilitarian functions. Snowberry branches were preferred for making brooms by gathering the branches together and binding them with Indian hemp. Several types of fan-shaped combs, a labor intensive item—a prestige item—for harvesting huckleberries, were made by taking eight to ten split sections of mock orange, approximately 20 cm in length, bundling them together, then tying them at one end and soaking them until supple. The loose ends were separated and inserted in earth or clay until dry. A similar but larger comb, often thirty-five cm in length, and with wider spaced teeth, served to harvest huckleberries by racking the fruit into baskets. These berries are small and difficult to harvest efficiently with just one's fingers. Consequently, a third type of berry-harvesting comb was made, one with wooden combs and elongated teeth to rake the berries.

A variety of stems twisted singularly or in bundles were used for making tools, musical instruments, kindling, animal traps, fishing weirs, medicines, brooms, and containers, and also as combs. Another method used by women when harvesting heavily laden huckleberry bushes was to beat the bush with a *stout wooden staff* (*sp'im*) or a *bundle of dried snowberry bush branches* (*l'xʷtn'ey'ɬp*), causing the berries to fall onto tule mats spread beneath the bush. The introduction of canvas and woolen blankets increased the efficiency in collecting huckleberry from the bushes by using a method called *snčɫc'im*, whereby two women each held a corner of the blanket approximately one meter off the ground, the two opposite ends were secured around the base of the bush, and a third woman beat the bush. The blanket served two purposes and it acted as a trough for funneling the harvested berries into a waiting receptacle; the coarseness of the blanket effectively retained all the leaves and twigs that were dislodged while beating the bush.

There was no memory of collecting berries of *dwarf dogwood* or *bunchberry* (*Cornus canadensis* L.) or eating them by the Spokan, though Turner noted how they were eaten by Coastal Indians (1978:208).

The Interior Salish sustained themselves by gathering roots, stems, fruits, bark, nuts, seeds, greens, gums, and certain lichens. Although varying form year to year, vegetative food constituted less than forty to sixty percent of the total food base. These plant foods formed a critical supplement to the seasonal salmon harvest, and fish shortages, often due to loss through cache damage or contamination, theft, or insufficiency of season gathering. If winter reserves, along with the stored salmon, were exhausted, starvation became imminent and forays were made into wooded areas to gather traditional starvation or famine foods. For example, Indian celery was commonly gathered as a famine food in late winter, after brushing the snow away from rocky areas of known production (Wynecoop 1985:82). During the summer, wild celery was dug and eaten before it bloomed, and its green stalks were eaten raw; it was never cooked. In late spring and early summer, the stalk was pulled off near the ground and found to be sweet.

Famine Foods

There were no recent memories of the Spokan experiencing the need to consume starvation (*šéy't*) foods, despite the occasionally prolonged winter or an exceptionally early winter (see Appendix J). There was, however, consensus among elders that the main reasons for famine were a lack of deer in the winter, or when a family had an insufficient amount of food saved; storage facilities on normally high Spokane River rock caches being destroyed by rafting ice; stored foods being partially or completely destroyed by animal contamination of storage pits or repeated freezing and thawing from water seepage; dried salmon and deer meat stored in high tree platform caches being hit by destructive and dispersing high winds—more susceptible were those tree caches in ponderosa *copses* (*nčomalqʷ*) on the north side of the Spokane River. Ray cited how among the Sanpoil, "Carelessness was probably responsible for more acute food shortages of food than natural conditions. But shortages of this sort usually found compensations in the industriousness of others" (1933:107). DeSmet stated that, "The Indian when he has nothing to eat does not complain, but in the midst of abundance he knows no moderation" (1843:204). Parker, described how the "the Indian mode of living is very precarious, and yet they are seldom anxious about the future. When they have a plenty, they are not sparing; and when they have little to depend upon but moss. They have for some time past got a good many trout from the Barrier [weir] but last night it was broken by the height of the water" (Elliott 1914, 4:281). At a later date, Work again described that, "The Indians have had no provisions and the people were starving when they got a little" (Elliott 1925, 4:269).

On occasion, during a shortened winter, the Spokan would commence food-gathering activities in late February. But usually in late March, when the snow had appreciably *melted* (*hecʕ'ámtí* - "when black soil shows through"), women would commence traveling daily in small groups to higher riverine terraces to collect the first plant foods. Elmendorf (pers. comm.) states that people would sometimes venture from winter villages even when the snow was knee-deep, so that they could exploit different areas made warmer by the winter sun. In particular, women would dig camas in open, well-drained, south-facing slopes while the men with bows and arrows would also hunt singly or in small groups for the first ground-dwelling animals that occupied warmer, south-facing talus slopes.

Ray (1932) and others have noted the dire conditions that sometimes existed in the northeastern Plateau, when people resorted to traditional starvation foods. Cox cites a pronouncement of a Spokan or Colville village leader regarding the condition of starvation:

He inweighted [sic] principally against gambling, and their improvident thoughtlessness in neglecting to provide during the summer and autumnal months, sufficient quantity of dried salmon for spring, which is the season of scarcity; by which neglect they have been frequently reduced to starvation (1832:170).

One of the first accounts of lichens as an important famine food was noted in 1814 by Gabriel Franchère who spent a spring near Kettle Falls with the Astor party, and was able to observe what he called a springtime famine:

[...] we met a family of Indians who had had nothing to eat for several days. They were in a sad state, thin and gaunt, scarcely able to move. This happens fairly frequently among these Indians, their main food during the winter season when hunting is not good consisting of a sort of paste made from pine moss cooked and reduced to a thick consistency to form black loaves. I was sufficiently curious to try it and found that it tasted like soap. Nevertheless those who have eaten it tell me that when moss prepared this way is fresh, it tastes quite good with meat (1969:155).

Elsewhere in Franchère's Journal, this early explorer and critical observer offered a variation of the aforementioned quote:

We found at this place some Indians who had been fasting, they assured us, for several days. They appeared, in fact, reduced to the most pitiable state, having nothing left but skin and bones, and scarcely able to drag themselves along, so that not without difficulty could they even reach the margin of the river, to get a little water to wet their parched lips. It is a thing that often happens to these poor people, when their chase has not been productive; their principal nourishment, in that case, of the or pine moss, which they boil till it is reduced to a sort of glue black paste, of a sufficient consistence to take the form of biscit [sic] (Franchère 1854:279 and 1904, 6:346).

Durham quotes DeSmet, who described the use of pine moss during periods of famine:

It is a parasite of the pine, a tree common in these latitudes, and hangs from the boughs in great quantities. It appears more suitable for mattresses, than for the sustenance of human life. When they have procured a great

354

quantity, they pick out all heterogeneous substance, and prepare it as they do the camash [sic] it becomes compact, and is, in my opinion, a most miserable food, which, in a brief space, reduces those who live on it to a pitiable state of emaciation (1912, 1:128).

The method of preparation of tree moss was reported by Wilkes who visited the Sinkaietk. This preparation was similar to that of the Spokan. After the moss was collected in large quantities it was placed in a pit dug in the ground. Fire-heated stones were added and the pits are all covered up closely with earth. When the pits were opened after twenty-four hours the moss was soft and could be molded into cakes and dried (1845, 4:449).

Recognizing the need and advantages of famine foods, the Euro-Americans failed to understand the nutritional value, relative ease of procurement, processing, and storage of the Spokan's diverse animal, fish, and plant food supply. Even though times of famine were frequent some of the Pacific Fur Company, long before government *farm agent* (*suxʷk'ʼʷółłqm*) programs, offered to assist the Spokan in growing potatoes, "but to this they replied, that it would interfere with their hunting and fishing, and prevent their women from collecting their own country fruits and roots in autumn, and thereby render them lazy" (Cox 1832:190).

There is no evidence that DeSmet ever witnessed famine among Plateau Indians, but it is likely he heard of such conditions, for he expressed a criticism, if not condemnation, of the Indians not possessing a so-called Protestant work Ethic:

> Indians linger on the Columbia as long as a salmon can be caught. Careless of the approaching winter, they do not lay in sufficient stock of provisions, and till late in the fall they may be seen picking up the dead and dying fishes which float in great numbers on the surface. In the immediate neighborhood of a camp the air is infected with the scent of salmon in a state of putrefaction [...] (1905, 2:558).

In times of *starvation* (*míš t sʔíłn* - "nothing to eat" or *hesčsqʼméltni* - "he is hungry") (Egesdal, pers. comm.), stored foods within a winter village were first shared along kin lines. When stored foods were depleted, due to resource contamination or prolonged winters, the Spokan pursued secondary harvesting by extracting limited amounts of gathered seeds and nuts from the known dens of squirrels. "Squirrels and the smaller animals are only eaten in time of scarcity, and then they are eagerly sought after; at Colville they [squirrels] were nearly exterminated during a severe winter" (Wilson 1866:297). This was a noted exception since Indians killed various rodents as famine foods, yet rarely completely exploited a squirrel's food cache of nuts to prevent a decline in the squirrel population. Several oral accounts relate how women would break the ice of ponds, and wade in the icy waters to collect stored bulbs of *wapato* (*Sagittaria latifolia* Willd., var. *Latifolia* - *sqáquʔcnʼ* or *sqaqwen*) that muskrats had laid up for the winter (Kirk 1975:157). The first account of famine was provided by Cox, who succinctly described the primary famine food for the Spokan, "Yet not withstanding these advantages, such is their improvidence, that they are often reduced to starvation. In times of scarcity they collect a quantity of pine-moss, which they boil and form into a kind of black cake about half an inch thick. It is a horrible preparation, and has a bitter saponaceous taste" (1831, I:197).

Cox continued his appraisal of various types of foods, and even when not confronted with such dire conditions, the value of the horse as food was appreciated by both the Spokan and Euro-American trapper-traders, and how occasionally they killed a fat horse in lieu of beef. Caywood, who conducted extensive archaeological excavations at Spokane House, noted how non-Indians were at times dependent upon horse meat "from the number of horse bones found, horse meat must have been part of the diet [...] Many a good horse probably appeared at the dinner table when hunting was bad and meat supplies were low" (1956:46). Durham wrote how, "Horseflesh, in fact, was to become the staple diet at the posts on the Spokane and the Okanogan, and it is recorded that eighty cayuses were consumed in a single winter at Spokane" (1912, 1:13). Elliott quoted Work's 1825 diary of how Work's men were "obliged to kill a Mare for food (1917, 4:263). Boiled horse and deer hooves were considered a delicacy. Cox, when identifying Spokan foods, claimed, "They have no repugnance to horse-flesh, but never kill horses for food" (1831, 1:201). And yet Cox, at another occasion, observed how:

355

We lived principally on deer, trout and carp, and occasionally killed a fat horse as a substitute for beef [...] Foals or colts are not good, although a few of our men preferred them. A horse for the table should not be under three years of age or above seven. The flesh of those which are tame, well-fed, and occasionally worked, is tender and firm, and he fat hard and white: it is far superior to the wild horse, the flesh of which is loose and stringy, and the fat yellow and rather oily (1831, I:197).

The cambium of any fir or pine tree, most notably Ponderosa, white fir, Douglas fir, and subalpine fir, was collected in late winter to supplement depleted food larders, and was collected in the spring, being considered a delicacy. The *cambium layer* (*c'éxʷiʔ*) of lodge pole pine was collected in late spring. During a winter or early spring famine, women would venture to laboriously dig camas from the frozen ground. This expended needed energy as the bulbs were found at a depth of 20 to 30 cm. Frozen camas in the ground retained its flavor until the shoots commenced to *sprout* (*ƛ'éč'č'sm'* - "a sprout") in the mid-spring. Camas roots were sometimes mixed with balsamroot, a root that was dug in winter as a famine food, and has a fresh celery-like taste. Whole camas roots or mashed cakes were often mixed and cooked with a *moss* (*šáwtmqn* - "tree lichen"), and when raw, the roots were called *sqʷl'ápqn*; often used to make soup. Rose *hips* (*sxʷay'apałq*) were eaten as a winter survival food (Ray 1932:108).

An exceptional hunter's *suméš*, in times of famine, may appear to him in a dream or in the sweathouse, telling him that there was a deer nearby that would 'give' himself as needed food to the people. One elder explained how in his grandfather's time:

> One man was sent up to a high ridge to get a deer. Once he got there he looked around and could see only a coyote looking north. He went to another ridge and saw several deer looking east, so he carefully circled the deer three times. He shot all three deer for his people. Nothing of the deer was wasted; all the organs and blood were eaten. Later, the skins and entrails were buried near the night fire. In the morning they were dug up and boiled. They were buried three times and boiled, and after the fourth boiling the soup was a white color and ready to eat (Ross 1968-2008).

Hydrophytes (*nkʷrʔétkʷ* - "water plants"), most notably *watercress* (*Rorippa nasturtium-aquaticum* [L.] Schinz & Thell. - and *Nasturtium officinale* R. Br. - *nx̣estétkʷeʔ*), a European introduced plant, were eaten throughout the summer, but also in winter when *food was scarce. nx̣estétkʷeʔ* was the geonomic designation for the present day town of Springdale where many hydrophytes flourished. Cattail rhizomes were assiduously collected throughout the winter to supplement other foods, particularly when *they are starving* (*ʔesčsq'méltni* or *čiʔmscúʔt* or *hecšešíʔti*).

The extreme condition and demands of hunger always meant that certain discarded animal bones and organs were gathered and prepared in different ways as food. For example, after the arrival of the horse, and during times of starvation, the soft parts of a horse's hooves, including the frog, were eaten as food after the horse had been killed. A survival soup was made by crushing animal bones, or using the bones of a recently killed deer by slowly cooking them—included the marrow—under a low ash fire. The Spokan had a word for *gnawing on bones - snšpéw'sm* or *šepim'* (STHC). Only the long leg bones of deer contained marrow, which was preferred when eaten raw.

Ray, when writing of the Sanpoil and conditions of food shortages, was told famine was a rare occurrence, save for the earthquake that created an unusually heavy fall of volcanic ash. Inadequate stored foods were usually the result of personal carelessness in protecting stored food or collecting insufficient amounts. However, in situations of extreme food shortage, as with the Spokan:

> [...] game and salmon bones which had been previously deposited for ceremonial reasons in the branches of trees, were removed and used as soup bones. Usually a bit of flesh had adhered which could be boiled off. Afterwards the bones were carefully replaced in the trees [...] Pieces of hide, cut from *old clothing* [*q'spewlxʷ*] or robes, could be rendered (Ray 19332b:107-8).

Though there was no recollection of the Spokan designating mussels as a starvation food, research verifies mussels were an important food whenever available. Therefore, Post's data concerning starvation foods among the Sinkaietk is interesting, describing how "Mussels [*skokóina*] were of first importance [...]

Starving people would camp by these beds [Okanogan River] and gather them with a fork stick through holes in the ice if wading was impossible. They were easily opened and were then boiled" (1938:29).

Hunters and gatherers were "rarely exposed to relative dietary deficiencies leading to malnutrition; they may, exceptionally be faced with *gross* deficits" (Dunn 1978:111). Since *starvation* (*miš t s?íłn* - "no food" or *hescsq'méltni* - "hunger") was an unusual occurrence, it is not known if insects were sought and eaten [entomophagy], though it did not happen at other times. Small ground-dwelling animals, though easily accessible during winter, particularly with deep or drifted snow, were considered a food source despite the effort to locate and dig the animal from its burrow, as happened in such areas as the Great Basin (Lockwood 2004:116-7, 177-178).

Any mention of severe famine must recognize the practice of anthropophagy or cannibalism, of which there are no such accounts for the Spokan. However, Cox mentions an unfortunate situation that occurred after a group of seven Canadian white trappers and an English tailor, which left the Rocky Mountains by canoe and entered the Upper Dalles, where they got caught in a strong whirlpool, causing them to lose their canoes and most supplies including blankets. As a result of their mishap, only two of the men (Dubois and La Pierre) were in any condition to work. After three days of difficult footing in flooded river terraces, over-land snow, and drinking only water, the first man died, only to be followed by four others. Finally, only one survived (La Pierre), who was found on the Upper Lake of the Columbia River by two Indians who brought La Pierre to Kettle Falls, and then on to Spokane House. An inquiry was conducted for La Pierre's proclaimed self-defense (?) in killing Du Bois, and for cannibalism of the fifth man. La Pierre admitted knifing Dubois in self-defense to prevent being killed and eaten. La Pierre was not returned to Canada, but released for lack of evidence (Cox 1957:278-9).

Farming and Animal Husbandry

Within this monograph there are numerous references to the Euro-American surveys, but the problem of reconstructing the location of some aboriginal root-digging areas is sometimes difficult, particularly with certain root crops. The resource areas were destroyed by cattle, sheep grazing, or more devastated by plowing. Work's journal of 1826 (5:284) recorded how "They brought three pigs and three young cows from Fort Colville" (Kingston 1923, 3:170). Also, the practice of the HBC to provide *domesticated goats* (*Capra hegagrus hircus - sxʷƛ'ey'*) to outstations proved to be detrimental and devastating to traditional roots fields. Goats caused damage to indigenous plants, and were apparently introduced relatively early, for Cox mentioned his pleasure when, "We get a little milk from our goat which is a great luxury as we have neither sugar or molasses for our coffee" (Cox 1832:50; Kingston 1923, 3:170).

Hale incidentally reported a bull and two cows arriving at Fort Colville from Vancouver in 1825, "and from these have sprung one hundred and ninety-six head of fine cattle. They have likewise thirty mares with foal, and sixty grown horses (1846, 4:445). Cattle were introduced to the Spokan area as early as 1841, and were immediately destructive to many traditional root fields. Fahey (pers. comm.) stated that cattle were probably introduced to this area by the HBC at an even earlier date. And some elders could recall how the introduction of sheep was devastating to traditional huckleberry areas.

Often the best indication of camas fields is the fire-cracked rock from earth ovens, unless they have been plowed under or removed by farmers. Several older Spokan recalled using horses to plow large camas fields at the turn of the century, particularly when camas became a cash crop for other Indians unable to *dig roots* (*sxéct*) because of time or simply for not having access to traditional root fields. When the deleterious effects of mechanical harvesting became apparent, usually after two to three seasons of plowing—traditional methods of root-gathering were, in some instances, reinstated.

Difficulties of farming by the Spokan were reported in 1874 by Harvey, Farmer-in-Charge at the Colville Indian Agency during a survey of the Spokan settlements: "I visited the villages of the upper and lower

Spokans consisting of about fifty lodges; they cultivate small patches of ground, but do not farm to any extent" (1874:n.p).

Naturally a major factor affecting root production was annual precipitation. Testimony to this was given by a noted regional ichthyologist, who, in conducting extensive field and stream research for many years within the area, stated:

I think that periodic droughts also affected camas. One field I observed at Turnbull National Wildlife Refuge that blossomed from 1980-1986—failed to bloom in draught years of 1987 and 1988. Its [further] demise was devastating in the 1990s when the refuge allowed cattle to graze the vegetation. Camas was gone within about 2 years after grazing commenced (Scholz, pers. comm.).

As a result of the comprehensive 1855 railroad surveys by Stevens, who heralded the many benefits a railroad would be to settlers, cattlemen, and farmers, it was found that "The whole valley of the Coeur d'Alene and Spokane is well adapted to settlement, abounding in timber for building and for fires, exceedingly well water, and the greater portion of the land arable" (Stevens 1855 1:254).

Chapter XI: Fishing

The Spokan had developed an essentially riverine-oriented culture: a successful lifestyle in which approximately fifty percent, sometimes more, sometimes less, of a predictable annual caloric intake was obtained from fishing—mainly *anadromous fish* (*sw'ew'ł*). Spokan strategies were not unlike those of other Plateau peoples situated along the Columbia and Spokane Rivers, since their culture was shaped and controlled by their abilities and technologies to exploit this riverine environment. Both fishing and gathering provided the greatest portion—over ninety percent—of the total animal caloric intake; the rest was derived from hunting, which was more unpredictable and consumed more time and energy. Walker has noted the importance of salmon to the Plateau diet by comparing this resource to the bison of the Plains, and posits that "most Plateau ethnic groups relied on salmon for at least 50 percent of their diet" (1967:9). Scholz's comprehensive study of fish yields for the Spokan is noteworthy:

> Multiplying the population of 1400 by the adjusted per capita consumption (976 pounds) yields 1,366,400 pounds of salmon consumed annually by the Spokane Tribe. Assuming that the bulk of the fish were Chinook salmon and the average weight of Chinook salmon is 18.5 pounds (Beiningen 1976), the total number of salmon harvested annually was 73,800 [...] This represents a minimum estimate of the catch. If Walker's (1985) estimate of 2500 for the population is used, 2,440,000 pounds or 131,900 fish were harvested annually by the Spokane Tribe (1985:37).

The importance of salmon to the Spokan diet was illustrated by their being recognized "as salmon eaters" (Johnson 1969:60). But unfortunately for the Coeur d'Alene tribe, the passage of anadromous fish was prevented by Spokane Falls. It was only natural that an explanation for why salmon could not negotiate the extreme height of Spokane Falls was formulated—an oral history of how the Coeur d'Alene refused to recognize a request by *spiiye?* (coyote) for marriage of a Coeur d'Alene wife.

The importance of salmon was reported as late as 1846 by Howison, who, despite his unfortunate term 'simple-minded', actually understood and appreciated the importance of salmon to Plateau diet, one that was reinforced by belief and ritual, particularly during the first phase of spring fishing:

> No reward of money, or clothes, will induce an Indian to sell salmon the first three weeks after his arrival; and throughout the whole season, upon catching a fish they immediately take out the heart and conceal it until they have an opportunity to burn it, their great fear being that this sacred portion of the fish may be eaten by dogs, which they shudder to think would prevent them from coming again to the river. When it is remembered that the many thousand Indians living upon this river, throughout its course of more than twelve hundred miles, are almost entirely dependent upon salmon for their subsistence, it would lessen our surprise that these simple-minded people should devise some propitiatory means of retaining this inappreciable blessing (1846:47-8).

Reverend Eells (1843-1907), of the American Missionary Association, spent nearly fifty years in the Plateau, primarily among the Nez Perce in the 1840s, but later he also worked among the Spokan and observed their annual subsistence round—particularly their dependence upon fishing—and made this observation:

> In April a large number met in one plain to dig a root called popo [white camas - *p'uxʷp'uxʷ*]. In May they returned to this place [Tschimakain Mission], and after remaining a few weeks moved to a large camass [sic] plain, ten miles from us. The camass [sic] is their most substantial root. It remains good from May till the next March. In June salmon begin to go up the Spokane River, which passes within six miles of our house. At first a barrier was constructed near some falls, ten miles from this place and perhaps fifteen miles from the camass [sic] grounds. At that place salmon were taken only during high water, and then not in large quantities, as the barrier extended only a part of the way across the river. While men and boys were employed at the salmon, the women were digging and preparing camass, and daily horses passed between the two places, loaded both ways, so that all could share both kinds of food. As the water fell another barrier was built farther down, extending across the entire river; and when completed men, women and children made a general move to the place. If I judged correctly, I saw there at one time near one thousand persons, and the number was rapidly increasing. From four to

eight hundred salmon were taken in a day, weighing variously from ten to forty pounds apiece. When they ceased to take salmon, about the first of August, they returned to the camass ground, where they remained till October, and then began to make preparations for taking the poor salmon as they went down the river. During this month they were very much scattered, though not very remote from each other. In November they went to their wintering places (Eells 1894:94-5; Edwards 1900:21).

Work noted in 1825 how occasionally during spring salmon fishing, "owing to the [great] height of the water they are not getting any salmon" (Elliott 1915, 1:29). Interestingly, John Dease also remarked how in 1827 the salmon were very scarce, "which is attributed to the [low] height of the Waters" (Lewis 1925, 2:105).

Aboriginally, the people's aquatic and terrestrial subsistence resources were subject to fluctuations that were not only unpredictable, but occasionally imposed severe limitations upon the inhabitants' total caloric intake. Of the three aforementioned subsistence patterns, those of fishing and gathering were more dependable than hunting. In the early 1840s, Hale described the quality of the Spokane River and the dependence of the Spokan upon salmon: "The river itself is pretty: its waters are transparent and it is joined in its course by many bubbling brooks. To judge from the number of sheds for drying salmon, it must abound with that fish. The average width of the stream was about two hundred feet" (1846, 4:438).

Though figures vary, fish resources accounted for approximately fifty percent of Spokan diet (Knudson 1982:32). It is quite apparent, from numerous sources (Bryant and Parkhurst 1950; Walker 1967; Hewes 1973 and 1998; Bailey and Saltes 1982; Schalk and Cleveland 1983; Schalk 1977, 1986), that even the fisheries would vary in production from year to year—a resource that later became even less available because of Euro-American incursion, dams, and commercial fishing. At a point just above Fort Spokane, Nine Mile Dam was constructed in 1909 (Caywood 1950), and after 1910, when Washington Water Power commenced to construct several hydroelectric dams at principal fishing sites—the mouth of the Little Spokane River and at Little Falls—there was a general decline in the numbers of anadromous fish. In fact, the power company destroyed both of the major weirs (Fahey, pers. comm.), barriers that stopped all migratory fishing above Little Falls (Ross 1993). There were no fish ladders built for the Spokan in either dam Grand Coulee and Little Falls dams as had been promised, and, as noted by Walker (1967), there was the gradual failure of the salmon fisheries, which they relied upon as an important and a predictable source of food, creating an even greater dependency upon game and plant foods.

Prior to the construction of Little Falls Dam, the Spokan were promised that fish ladders would be constructed. However, "A 'ladder' was built at Little Falls. It was constructed as a wooden chute without any baffles to provide resting spots. Inspections by Washington Department of Fish and Game personnel indicated that it was totally ineffective in passing salmon" (Scholz, pers. comm.).

Even prior to dam construction, the differential availability of migratory fish, because of topographical features—such as Kettle Falls, Little Falls, and Spokane Falls—required aboriginal groups to annually exploit these once traditional major fishing sites. Numerous anthropologists and historians (Cox 1831; Gibbs 1855; Hunt 1936; Ray 1939, Anastasio 1955; Walker 1967; Hewes 1973, 1998, and Osterman 1995) have emphasized the importance of cross-utilization of economic resources, particularly migratory anadromous salmon. Walker noted the importance of salmon to Plateau diet by comparing this resource to the bison of the Plains. The same author posits that "most Plateau ethnic groups relied on salmon for at least 50 percent of their diet" (Walker 1967:9). Such reliance was particularly important to the Spokan as a major source of food even though other types of stream and lake fish were abundant.

The uncertainty of hunting, but less so with fishing, appears to have been the basis for many of the specialized rituals and strict behavioral taboos that men strictly adhered to when propitiating the supernatural for success in fish and animal predation. In contrast, root gathering required fewer religious observances and behavioral prohibitions when women were gathering plant foods (in areas of what are now termed zones of predictable resource occurrence).

The Spokan's dependence upon salmon for sustenance and trading was reflected in their extensive and specialized fishing technology, a dependency that was further substantiated by numerous rituals as well as behavioral and dietary prohibitions while fishing. Their reliance upon salmon in particular was apparent in the naming of villages: several of the months indicate different major salmon runs they fished, and the designation of the Spokan tribe have three sub-bands, named after a specific fishery, a condition of water, or a species of salmon. This dependence was embodied even in the naming of the Spokan people, as noted by Teit (1930:145) in his cross-cultural comparison of certain tribal names in sign language:

Spokan.—First the sign of "salmon" or "fish" was made, then the fingers were raised to the mouth and a motion of swallowing made. The sign means "Salmon eaters," or "People who eat salmon." The Spokan were so named because they were the only tribe of the Flathead Group having salmon in their country, and they were the most eastern tribe of the region using salmon extensively as food.

Depending upon weather, collective fishing commenced at the end of April or beginning of May and continued, according to species, location, and stream conditions, until early autumn. People converged at various fisheries situated along the Spokane River to mutually exploit the various species of anadromous fish—sturgeon, trout, various other fish species—which were present in considerable number, particularly at Kettle Falls, Little Falls, and Spokane Falls. It is estimated that Little Falls attracted over one thousand Indians, producing as many as 800 salmon a day (Scholz 1985:14). Beach, an early observer in 1862, noted how the Indians at Little Falls fishery "put up at least 250 tons of dried fish during the fishing season" (1869, 78:238).

The methods of procurement were largely by *spear* (*łuʔmin*), *weir-trapping* (*ʔoléwltn*), *dip-netting* (*múl'mn*), *drag-netting* (*sqʷʸóx̣ʷ*), *line-fishing* (*čqʼqʼéyʼeʔtn'*), and by lassoing and spearing salmon from a horse during the historical period. There are several excellent ethnographic descriptions (Elmendorf 1935-6; Walker 1967; Bouchard and Kennedy 1975) of Plateau fish procurement technology, processing, and storage methods as well as associated economic and ritual behavior. Individual fishing methods were essentially passive or delayed predation with set nets, weirs, line-fishing, and traps; and active fishing with spears, leisters, harpoons, gaffs, dip nets, and even by hand.

The first major activity in spring was the construction and laborious repair of platforms as well as wicker and rock weirs, which had been damaged or completely destroyed by ice-rafting (Ross 1991:5.38), and high water-borne debris in late winter and early spring. Collective effort was required to install or repair existing fishing structures before the arrival of salmon, particularly any dislodged massive stone *anchor weights* (*čptápleʔtn*) that had to be laboriously reset at the base of the many stanchion poles and supporting pylons, and the manufacturing, reinstallment and securing of vertical and horizontal willows, which was accomplished by young men.

The peoples of the eastern Interior Plateau were highly dependent upon a wide variety of fish, particularly the four species of *salmon* (*Oncorthynchus* spp. - *smłíc*), which ascended the Columbia River and Spokane River in great number (Glover 1985; Walker 1967; Hewes 1998), that eventually spawned in the numerous tributaries within the Columbia watershed—as far upstream as Spokane Falls. The four species of anadromous fish important to the Spokan diet were the *coho* (*Oncorhynchus kisutch* - *čsuʔ*); *Chinook salmon* (*O. tshawytscha* - *smłič* or - [*mił*] - "many [*ič*] backs" or *čsuʔ*) (summer and a fall run); the *chum* or *dog salmon* (*O. keta* - *sčʼlw's*), the *sockeye* or *humpback salmon* (*O. nerka* - *nmáqícn*); and the *salmonid steelhead* (*O. mykiss* - *x̣ʷménʼeʔ* or *čsuʔ*) or *rainbow* (*x̣ʷx̣ʷmeneʔ* or *qʼʷosqʼʷos*). Other migratory and non-migratory fish were economically important to the peoples of the middle Columbia River. Various species of trout: *Dolly Varden* (*Salvelinus malma* - *łqʼíqʼcčst*), *bull trout* (*S. confluentus* - *łʔay* or *ʔupucin*), the introduced *brook trout* (*S. fontinalis*), and *cutthroat* (*O. clarki lewisi* Girard - *hičqʼʷʷays*) were taken in stream and lake environments. Many other forms of aquatic life were collected on a regular basis, such as brown trout, a *small trout* (*čciwʼeʔ* or *pipsł*), and Pacific lamprey—commonly called eels. Other fish species taken were *mountain whitefish* - (*Prosopium williamsoni* - *x̣ʷx̣ʷyʼucn'*), pygmy whitefish, *lake chub* (*Couesius*

361

plumbeus), *white sturgeon* (*Acipenser transmontanus* - *c'mtús* or *c'em'tus*), and *Northern pike-minnow* (*Ptychocheilus oregonensis* - *q'ʷeʔeč*). Introduced species of economic importance were *yellow perch* (*Perca flavescens* - *c'qc'iq*), *large-mouth bass* (*Micropterus salmoides* - *łq'łáq't*), bullhead (*Ictaluridae*) (see Appendix K), and several other species of small fish, such as a *small black sucker* (*twéck* - of the genus *Catostomus*) (Osterman 1995:31, 37), which is now extinct.

Despite the aboriginal success and reliability of the annual subsistence round, Euro-American incursion began to drastically deplete the once traditional food resources of the Spokan. Eventually, even the *fisheries* (*snq'iq'ʔem'e'y'eʔtn* or *snq'q'm'éy'eʔtn'*) began to vary in production from one year to the next, a condition that became exacerbated by the agribusiness activities of whites. It was noted by Simms that "the gradual failure of the salmon fisheries, upon which they rely so much for support, the greater scarcity of game, the low price of furs and peltries, the setting up of the country by white, are the uncertain tenure by which they return to their homes" (1876:129).

Though all men and women collectively assumed different responsibilities when at fishing stations, there were always three critical roles performed by specialized individuals, ones with *suméš* who were always stationed at the major fishing weirs:

- The fish leader (Si?tUs or sa?na?nq'L or C'em'tw'Ile?), sometimes called a fish chief (?ilmIxWm), was one who assumed overall responsibility in coordinating a group's fishing efforts and delegating responsibilities when necessary. His role was much more secular and traditional, often serving year after year. While fishing for salmon, the fish leader would be referred to as the (C'em'tw'l'i? or CixWpI).

- The fish shaman (sxWm'e?tsEw'L or em'tw'Il'i?C - "the distributor") was a special shaman who conducted all of the rituals and ceremonies to encourage, even entice, the salmons' further migration to the traps—called niXEm ("to drive fish into trap"). In addition, this person also had complete authority and responsibility for equally distributing the day's catch to every man, woman, and child. His role was religious—even esoteric—and was further reinforced having been given final approval by the group's chief. However, if his sumES proved not powerful enough to bring an adequate number of salmon to the weir, he was relieved of his position and replaced by another shaman with salmon power.

- The fish trap keeper (C'em'w'il'i? - "man who watches the traps") was always older and was the most experienced fisherman, who not only supervised the construction of the traps and weirs, but was responsible for their daily maintenance throughout the fishing season. Such a man might even live year round at a major fishing station, particularly at Little and Spokane Falls and at the mouth of the Little Spokane River. His primary role was to watch over the trap during the day, returning early the next morning (Elmendorf 1935-6, 1:54).

It was remembered how a fish trap keeper would often spend the entire evening carefully observing and monitoring the facility, most notably in the spring and summer, looking for downstream floating logs, which, if left unattended, could possibly destroy a weir.

The importance of salmon was reflected by special religious ceremonies requiring—at designated times—the abstinence or consumption of certain foods, when the fish shaman reiterated behavioral taboos:

> This man had complete control of the communal aspects of salmon fishing, setting the time for constructing weirs and traps, over-seeing the work on them, conducting the First Salmon Ceremony, supervising the distribution of the catch, seeing that women did not come too close to fishing sites, and the like. If the fish were few, it was necessary that he communicate with his guardian spirit, determine why the salmon had not come, and pray for forgiveness should, for example, some individuals have offended the salmon by breaking a taboo (Newcomb 1974:184).

When the repairing of the fishing weirs was completed, the fish shaman would have a dream of salmon arriving upstream, an occasion for him to wear a feather headdress and decorate his body with red ochre before conducting a propitiatory ceremony to further attract the migrating salmon. Such a person worked closely with the fish leader, who directed all thanksgiving rituals. The fish shaman was naturally accorded considerable respect for his abilities and power for attracting salmon to the area. Though the ceremony was repeated with little variation from time immemorial, everyone shared in their attention to detail, and their apprehension as to whether the salmon would appear.

The following is explanation description of the procedures used by a certain young man with salmon power, one who replaced the first fish shaman because no salmon had arrived at the weir:

[He went] down to the river [where he] got pine needles & started a fire and put sunflower leaves on [it] & made a smoke doing the way his *suméš* had told him—[he] did this 3 times in different places—each time smothering the fire with sunflower leaves & raising a smoke—he sat down on the bank by the river and soon saw a little salmon jump out of the water & go across the surface of the water—flitting—and dove out of sight again—[the] water [was] about 5 ft. [long]. Deep in [the] trap & fish starting filling [it] up above the surface and threatened to upset the weir so he went back to tell the people [and he] told the chief to send down 6 men to get a salmon for the meal—3 poles to stick the fish on *sxʷwʹéʔm* to tell the people to come down and get [the] salmon for the trap was almost falling over—the men brought their poles back full & they took the rest out and laid them on the rocks by the river—[and they] passed them around among all the people—everybody got some—they kept bringing them up until dark when everybody roasted them on sticks [...] (Elmendorf 1935-6, 1:55-6).

If their efforts were successful, as in the above account, and some salmon were caught, the salmon chief would direct the ritual of eating the *first salmon* (*saxeʔwʹiʔili*) of the season at the *First Salmon Ceremony* (*snxeʔwiƚ* - "they are eating the first salmon"), and served as a sacred rite of intensification, which was essentially a first fruit ritual, conducted when the salmon commenced to arrive en masse in May. It was reported that the last traditional First Salmon Ceremony was held in the late 1880s (Elmendorf 1935-6, 1:23).

After the *first large salmon* (*smƚič*) entered a trap, it was removed and the head cut off and set aside. The salmon was then carefully eviscerated before the fish leader, who reverently lifted the salmon in an offering as the congregation prayed in thanksgiving, with hopes that the ceremonial salmon would communicate with the other salmon regarding the kindness and respect accorded by humans, which hopefully would entice other salmon to the fishery. The salmon was then stone-boiled and eaten by only the attending *fishermen* (*xeʔwʹiʔíli* - "men are eating the first salmon of the season") (STHC), a group often called *nxeʔwʹiʔiliʔ* ("assembled fishermen"). During the same day, when the weir traps were being filled, salmon were removed and distributed to all those attending, even visitors from afar.

Given these conflicting oral accounts, Elmendorf provided a presumably more credible account of who shared in eating the first salmon: "The first salmon taken was always eaten only by the chief and his minor leaders—and after stone-boiling the salmon before the *assembled fishermen* (*nxeʔwʹiʔlʹʔ*), among the elders of the Spokan" (1935-6, 1:23). During this occasion, elders would give lengthy and dramatic accounts of previous fishing episodes that had taken place at that particular fishing station—mentioning unusually large salmon previously caught, the efforts required to carry the fish ashore, and how many people the fish fed. Oral history records that some elders could vividly recall names given to such "grandfather fish," as well as the respect they felt for the salmon who permitted itself to be taken, and the unique abilities of a particular salmon chief who was believed responsible for their *bountiful harvest* (*xʷeʔsiƚn* or *xʷeʔsqʹoƚq*).

Some elders claimed that the first salmon was never killed and eaten, but ceremoniously released after being caught, after the salmon leader held the fish above his head while praying for a bountiful fishing season as the group sang their thanksgiving. Before releasing the fish back into the water, the fish leader would implore the salmon to swim back to the other fish and tell them of the people's kindness and respect—even reverence—for salmon which the humans depended upon for subsistence and life. A few elderly women said how the bones of the first salmon were carefully removed, fleshed, and thrown back into the river to ensure a constant migration of fish.

The people believed that if the thanksgiving ceremony was conducted incorrectly, or not done at all, then other salmon would not enter the fish traps, or their number would be greatly reduced. If this occurred, then it was concluded that the salmon chief did not have sufficient power to entice salmon into the traps. Another reason for salmon avoiding a weir trap was that the salmon chief had violated some taboo. In any case, as previously cited, the Salmon Chief would be immediately replaced by another salmon chief—one who in the past had been successful, or by a shaman who had earlier dreamt of his success.

Thereafter, an appointed fish trap keeper was responsible for maintaining a general stewardship over the fish site while ensuring that river debris did not damage or block the valuable weirs. Consequently, the main concern was not theft, but one of a more serious nature—the constant danger of a water-borne log or a tree hitting and destroying a trap or blocking the weir. Older boys often shared the responsibilities of the men because, being younger, they were often abler to clear any floating debris from the weirs. The fish leader's vigilant watch over the weir and the traps was throughout the night without eating or going home, but remaining until sunrise when he was relieved (STHC, Anon., n.d.). Such collective cooperation and concern reflected the people's dependence upon salmon, and the strict obligation for following any decision of the salmon chief. It was believed that he who waits at a fish trap and has *suméš*, could *entice fish* (*ƛ'eʔkʷílš* - "one who does the enticement") (STHC) to the trap. It was believed that if there was no fish shaman, the fish would simply not come (Elmendorf 1935-6, 1:23). In addition to the power associated with one who was an *expert fisherman* (*nekʷenkʷeʔ*), it was believed that fish with *suméš* could return a brief distance to *attract other fish into the awaiting traps* (*č'em'tw'íl'iʔ*), but only if the First Salmon Ceremony had been properly conducted.

The salmon chief and his helpers oversaw the strict division of labor for such onerous tasks as collecting firewood for drying and cooking fires, catching and processing fish, their redistributing, and eventually transporting their catch to winter village caches for storage. This *distribution of salmon by leader* (*sxʷmlswéł*) was strenuous, demanding considerable cooperation and a well-defined division of labor. The fish leader had authority to equally distribute and give the entire day's catch away (Elmendorf 1935-6, 1:23), and, "The huge catches of salmon taken each summer at the great fish weirs were divided equally among all present [...] Participation in the fishing activities was not a prerequisite to receiving a share" (Ray 1977:24). Earlier, Father Diomedi noted how "people unable to fish, for reasons of age or circumstance are provided" (1878:27). Walker and Lahren commented upon the overall high level of ritual and activity:

> Since sturgeon, trout, and salmon moved up-river as the season progressed, the mouths of the Sanpoil and Spokane rivers, and Kettle Falls were the areas of the greatest fishing activities, and the largest traps were located there. The beginning of the salmon season was celebrated by the ceremony of the first salmon rite. A five-day period ensued during which the handling, eating and distribution of salmon was ritualized. Visiting was common and gambling was widespread. Women cooked and dried the salmon and gathered berries if time permitted (1977:78).

Fishing commenced early morning, continuing until approximately 10:00 a.m. or noon when activities stopped, but resumed in the late afternoon. During the autumn fishing, *dog salmon* (*Oncorhynchus keta - sc'lewes*) entrails were sometimes collected after a day's fishing, dried, and slowly cooked by stone-boiling into a stew to *be eaten* (*qepeʔsʔílni*) by the fishermen after the day's efforts. Whenever salmon were caught, the intestines were boiled to make a dish called *sp'iẋénč*. The *freshly laid eggs* (*pkʷełtm* - "it laid eggs") of salmon were often gathered and eaten raw. Once the fishing became productive, the males of other visiting tribes would join in the fishing, often assisted by their wives in the processing and drying of the salmon.

During the months of June and July, food gathering activities continued with considerable intensity, with women harvesting plant foods in traditional *root fields* (*qʷom* or *snẋectn*) while men remained fishing. The groups commenced to disband until the close of the summer salmon season in August. However, some men would travel to fall fishing sites for dog salmon and *silver salmon* (*O. kisutch - nxʷméneʔ*). Also, in summer, some families would travel to and camp at *Liberty Lake* (*słq'etkʷ* - "wide body of water"), where they caught a type of small trout, a fish with a sucker-like body and mouth like that of a whitefish (or kokanee) (STHC), as well as great numbers of bass, most probably introduced about 1890 (Scholz, pers. comm.). Evermann (1896a) and Scholz (pers. comm.) state that coho salmon, also called dog salmon, were mostly spent by their arrival at Latah Creek.

Well into the historical period, the Spokan diet was largely dependent upon salmon, as Cowley observed:

Several families of Indians had combined their tepees near Pine Street and Sixth Avenue into one community lodge about 80 feet long, and after religious exercise partook of a feast of venison, fish, circular cakes of wheat flour based in a skillet, coffee, sugar, and the sweet dried camas root [...] The Spokane River, with its two principal falls, furnished the salmon, the spring salmon being taken at the falls below the Lapray Bridge and the fall salmon just above the mouth of Latah Creek and another lesser fishery on the Little Spokane (1916:6).

Cowley's daughter, Mrs. J. L. Paine, spent her childhood at Spokane Falls, and commented to Drury—having spent nine years with the Spokan—about the importance of fish and local game to the Spokan: "While father never did any hunting in the early days [...] we did not lack for game. The Indians would bring us venison and other game and often salmon from the River. In those days the salmon in great numbers came up the river and formed an important part of the Indians' diet" (1949:6). Mrs. Paine recalled this familiar scene:

Indians made themselves at home in our little log house. Some of my earliest recollections are of one or more old Indians warming themselves by our fireplace. They would come in without a word frequently, sit down by the fire and remain there for an hour or more; then go out as silently as they came (Gaston 1914:75).

Even prior to the extensive construction of dams on the Columbia and Spokane Rivers, there were a number of white-introduced agribusiness activities which proved deleterious to the fish populations of these rivers. Hewes presents several cogent arguments for this decline, such as mining, particularly placer mining, and the resulting increase of silt held in suspension "which reduces the penetration of light to aquatic photosynthetic micro-organisms, thus reducing the total amount of nutrients available to a given area" (1973:146). The lumber industry also wrought major changes to the quality of watercourses and caused the deterioration of aquatic resources, particularly fish. Hewes succinctly summarizes these effects:

The lumber industry, a characteristic activity of much of the area, has had a well-known destructive effect on the fishing resources of streams and lakes. Removal of the forest cover bordering small streams exposes the shallow water to direct sunlight, raising the temperatures above the toleration of cold-water fauna. The toleration is based on the amount of dissolved oxygen in the water, which is greater at lower temperatures. On a larger scale, lumbering promotes erosion and flash floods, which, with the debris left from trimming, etc., physically obstruct the migrations of fish to their spawning grounds. The effects of agriculture and pastoral occupancy of the land adjacent to streams are similar to those of the lumbering industry. Increased run-off follows plowing or grazing, leading to the cycle of floods, silting, and choking of streams with impassable blocks of debris. Direct blockage of fish migration is more often due to the construction of dams, diversion ditches, railway embankments, and highway embankments with culverts which fish cannot enter from below. Grand Coulee Dam, 350 feet high, has eliminated at one stroke some 1100 miles of salmon streams in the upper Columbia Basin (1973:146-7).

The only advantage of white settlement to the fish population may have been the excessive trapping of beaver (see Appendix L) which probably removed hundreds of thousands of beaver dams, considered disadvantageous to salmon as well as indigenous trout. Scholz (pers. comm.), however, feels that "overfishing in the lower Columbia River caused decline [of fish] at Kettle Falls and in the Spokane River," and disagrees with Cook, contending that "beaver dams were not a factor in reducing salmon and trout populations." The main threats to Columbia River fisheries and other aquatic resources were summarized by Ellis:

1. Agriculture: erosion silt and blockage of streams by irrigation and drainage canals.
2. Livestock raising: erosion silt from over-grazing, organic wastes from dairies, and wool washings.
3. Mining: erosion silt from open pits and quarries, blockage or diversion of streams by dams and flumes, tailings and dredge wastes, chemical pollutants from smelting.
4. Lumber industry: erosion silt from cleared areas, logging debris, flush-dams and mill dams, sawdust and paper-mill wastes.

5. Transportation: stream blockage by culverts in highway and railway embankments, silt from erosion of cuts and fills, silt from harbor and channel dredging, fuel oil and bilge wastes.
6. Miscellaneous: organic, mineral, and chemical wastes from various manufacturing plants; municipal sewage; stream blockage by water supply and power dams; hot water discharged from chain-reaction piles (1937:147).

October was a period of intensive collective labor in preparation for the coming winter. After the onset of *cold weather* (*s?ísstči?* - "it is winter"), women devoted considerable time to collecting prime tules, used during the winter to manufacture housing and sleeping mats, various types of containers, and hats. Men spent time at the fisheries exploiting the last fish runs that would supplement much needed winter stores, particularly the runs at Latah Creek for dog and *white salmon* (*sč'lwes*). This flat peninsula living site was called *n'xʷanxʷom* or *n'xʷa?nxʷm*, where remnants of a series of stones across the Spokane River are still visible, and served as anchors for a platform trap of vertical poles—2 m high, woven together at an opening in an apex of V-shaped rock enclosure (Ross 1984b).

November was devoted to collecting great amounts of firewood, *finishing of winter homes* (*čn?uy'uy'éɫxʷtn*), and making the last preparations for the three or four month period of relatively sedentary living—when the Spokan lived largely off the products of their pre-winter subsistence activities. Winter confinement was particularly enjoyable for children who spent much of their time listening intently to elders relating in detail their previous experiences of traveling to far away places, as yet unvisited by the young but attentive audience.

Apparently, no particular ceremony marked the end of the salmon run, though the Salmon chief would—from time to time—offered thanks to the salmon that had provided the Spokan this food. People camped at these sites during the main activities, and occasionally returned to winter villages for the purpose of transporting the dried salmon to family winter storage caches.

Subsistence-getting activities continued until older individuals eventually returned to their *riverine winter villages* (*čnuyéɫxʷtn* - "building houses") to prepare for winter, whereas others remained at fisheries for the last fishing. The few remaining families, and families from afar, after fulfilling their needs, would leave the fishery with no further commitment to their hosts, often not seeing them until the following year. Some Spokan families and people from other tribes would gain elevation and enter the wooded areas and high meadows to hunt animals and gather autumn berries, roots, punk wood for smoking hides, and necessary medicinal plants. One elder remarked how in the past, it was generally recognized that by late October, and even early November, the fishing season was over when the eagle population commenced to depart.

One may conclude that salmon was the mainstay of the Spokan economy, being a highly nutritious food that stored well and was important as an out-trading commodity. Cross-utilization of resources was facilitated by established polyadic relationships based on intergroup marriage, polyglotism and, to some degree, the ethnocentric concept based rights of usury and even regionalism. Though not delineated here, the peoples of the Interior Plateau had a sophisticated and extremely detailed taxonomy for all fish, their anatomical structure as well as certain associated behavior. The principal basis of classification was the covert category between migratory and non-migratory fish (Osterman 2005:39).

There was consensus among Spokan that the most unfavorable impact on their diet was the tragic loss of salmon; even non-Indians have remarked upon the unfortunate consequences of salmon loss. Periodic fluctuations in salmon during pre-dam construction was exacerbated with the indirect and direct physical and chemical effects of Euro-American lumber, livestock, agriculture, and mining.

Aquatic Animals

Salmon

For taking individual salmon, the favorite thrusting implement was the leister or harpoon (discussed in detail later). Once caught, any fish deemed to be sick was thrown back into the water. This critical decision was made by carefully observing the color of the skin, which apparently was usually diagnostic.

Regardless of the type of procurement method, once the fish was on shore (except the first single salmon), women would immediately begin to *gut the fish* (*ntlénči* - "to gut a fish"). The first step was to cut off the tail, unless it were to be used as a storage pouch for *dried fish eggs* (*xʷel'ék'ʷl'*) or to be hung vertically on a drying rack. Butchering a fish was called *xʷcím or ntele' nčm'*, when they would open the salmon by cutting down either side of the backbone with a sharp stone fish knife (shown below, and about 8 cm long), and remove the entrails, roe, *tail* (*sups*), and the head. Salmon heart and gills were eaten. Kane described the Spokan procedure for preparing and storing roe, "The mode in which they cure them is by splitting them down the back, after which each half is again split, making sufficiently thin to dry with facility, a process occupying in general from four to five days" (1859:314).

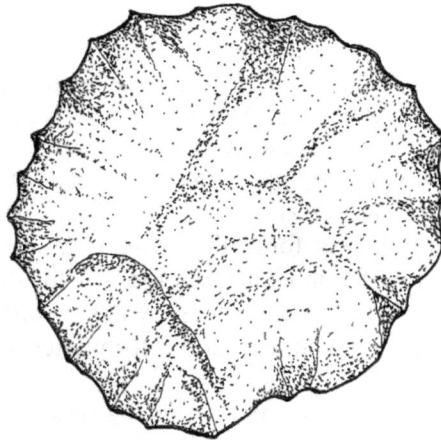

Figure 25. Serrated flint fish knife

Another method of storing salmon was observed by Lt. Robert E. Johnson, a member of Wilkes Expedition), who described how the Okanogan did it: "they are at once roasted, and then exposed to the sun to dry on a shed, of which the meat is pounded and made into balls, which are stored for winter food [...] and constitutes almost their only food" (Wilkes 1845, 4:431-432). Most often, the salmon was then sliced down both sides of the *fins* (*sq'q'ʷen'e*), the side cheeks were removed, and the meat was removed from the ribs before pulling back on the head to remove the *back bone* (*ʔasxm'*) and the attached ribs and innards—being careful not to dislodge the air sacs, which were always carefully removed and cleaned. The intestines were saved to make an evening stew after a day's fishing. The stomach was not saved, but the roe was always carefully gathered to be eaten fresh or stored for future use by boiling or sun-drying. Women would then string salmon meat and place it in running water to wash away the oil which, otherwise, would cause the meat to become rancid. Salmon skins were held near the fire until softened and then eaten.

Elders said how after cleaning salmon, the innards and other offal were *never*—out of respect for the salmon—thrown back into the river, yet it is interesting that Nancy Perkins stated how, prior to Coulee Dam, at Kettle Falls, "The huge fires were ready and waiting the landing of the trap's catch and the slaughter of the fish. They were cleaned and dressed, the remains being thrown back into the water for food for the living fish" (Ward and Maveety 1995:22). Again, it must be stressed that the concern and fear of *human scent* (*spuxʷpálqš* or *melexʷ* - "the smell when someone passes by") on the parts of fish being thrown back into even moving water, that would turn the fish away from waiting tarps/weirs, was the reason for such a prohibition (Scholz, pers. comm.).

Despite the numerous changes wrought by diffusion and the direct introduction of Euro-American technology, methods of processing and drying salmon never changed; the only thing that did change appreciably was the means of transporting heavy loads to winter villages, which was later done by horses:

> When salmon are caught, they are laid on the rocks, the heat from which and the direct rays of the sun serve to loosen the skin; they are sometimes slit and dried whole, but the more favorite way of curing, especially with those Indians who have to carry their salmon a long distance, is to strip the flesh from the bones, mash and pound it as fine as possible, and then spread it out on mats to fry in the sun; three or four days usually accomplish this, and it is then put up in log baskets holding from seventy to eighty pounds, a convenient weight for packing on horseback (Wilson 1866:298).

The 1824-25 travels of fur-trader George Simpson provided him with numerous opportunities to observe how the Spokan and other Columbia River groups prepared salmon for winter storage (winter stock):

> The Indian method of preserving salmon was to split the fish into four strips and hang the quarters to dry on scaffolds along the river bank. Sometimes the process was carried further, the dried salmon being pounded between two stones to a flaky pulp after the manner of pemmican. In this readily preferable form it was packed into large baskets (2 ft. x 1 ft.) made of grass matting, lined with cured salmon skins and closed with a covering of the same material [...] Salmon cured this way could be kept sound and sweet for several years (cf. 1968:40-1).

In 1854, geologist and ornithologist George Gibbs (1815-1873) visited the Spokan and noted the dependence of the Spokan upon their fisheries and the general lack of game in the area: "The high plains, which extend from the Spokane River to Lewis' fork of the Columbia, and which belongs to them and the Nez Perce, though bleak and exposed to violent winds, affords grazing for their stock and an abundance of roots used by themselves for food, while their river supplies them with salmon" (1855a:415).

The methods of preparation and storing salmon and roe for winter by the Sanpoil and Nespelem were, of course, the same as with the Spokan:

> Salmon was stored as soon as it was taken from the drying racks. The heads and flanks were placed in separate storage bags, usually made of tule [...] . Sometimes the bags were lined, and layers of fish separated, with Dragon Sagewort, to keep maggots away. When filled the bags were closed by sewing. The average weight of a well filled bag was approximately a hundred pounds. Salmon roe was wrapped in salmon skins which were then sewed up, and stored on elevated platforms. The roe decayed somewhat with time but in such a state it was considered a more desirable food. Salmon oil was not stored in skins (Ray 1933:76).

DeSmet observed how other fish came up with salmon: "Great quantities of trout and carp follow them, and regale themselves on spawn deposited by the salmon in holes and still water" (Twaite 1904, 4:191). Kane, always an astute observer, remarked how "The young fish return to the sea in the spring strange to say, yet succeeded in tempting them to take any description of fly or bait" (1859:219). Suckley described how "The salmon of these waters, unlike those of other parts of the world, do not take the hook; and, strange as it seems, they are said never to stop searching after the source of the stream they are in" (1855, 1:299). Marine biologist Gile noted how salmon "do not feed after they enter the river [Columbia]" (1955:141).

Though salmon was the primary source of protein, there were times, according to several early traders, when the salmon they got were not good: "We are getting a few bad salmon in the barrier [weir], but the most of them are so bad that they can scarcely be eaten" (Elliott 1914, 3:164).

After moving to Spokane in 1876, Reverend Cowley concluded, "In after years, when the white people commenced putting traps in the Columbia river, the salmon stopped coming up this far, until now you never hear of one of them up here, after" (Durham 1912, 1:105).

Trout

Cutthroat trout (Oncorhynchus clarki - hi čq'ʷiqʷʷáys or tw'éckʷ), when dried and smoked, stored well and were always a favored food, particularly during winter. *Steelhead trout (rainbow trout - n-xʷemen'eʔ)* may have winter-runs (November to April) or summer-runs (May to October) in the Columbia, and reported traveling 1,600 km to the lower Spokane River, and were widely distributed in the Columbia Basin, "similar to that of spring Chinook salmon" (Gilbert and Evermann 1895:3-4).

McDonald recorded large trout, weighing two to four pounds, being caught by both Indians and whites in the Spokane River between Little Falls and an area now called the Bowl and Pitcher. McDonald further acclaimed, "The Spokane River was known worldwide, as one of the finest trout rivers in the world [...] In the 1890's a group of four sport fisherman from Spokane, fishing at the Joseph LaPray Bridge [a wooden trestle bridge built by James Monaghan in 1865] near the present day Long Lake Dam], returned to the city with 250 fine trout" (1894:208).

The brown trout (*Salmo trutta*) was introduced from England between 1940 and 1950. It was more successful in Kalispel waters, and rarely found in Spokan streams (Scholz, pers. comm.).

Sturgeon

The Columbia sturgeon was an important food fish and "was first described by Lewis and Clark. They attain a length of from ten to fifteen feet" (Franchère 1854:281 fn), "and a weight of 400 pounds" (Douglas 1904, 5, 1:269). *Sturgeon (Acipenser transmontanus - čm'tús)* was the first fish taken in the early spring (Osterman 1995:34), with either a type of articulated *two-pronged harpoon head (wécč)*, which the fisherman would use while atop exposed rock islands or outcrops near deep water. The other method was using a baited hook-line. Both techniques were used during the months of August and September when there was "a plentiful supply of prime sturgeon. The fish attains a great size. Some of those we took were eleven feet in length; and, with the entrails out, weighed from three to four hundred pounds" (Cox 1832:224). Once blacksmithing was available, a *giant hook (šnq'ítmn)* was used to facilitate hooking sturgeon and removing them from the water.

An early description of the Columbia River sturgeon was provided by Franchère, who noted that the months of August and September provided excellent sturgeon, "This fish varies exceedingly in size, I have seen some eleven feet long; and we took one that weighed, after the removal of the eggs and intestines, three hundred and ninety pounds. We took out nine gallons of roe" (Twaites 1904, 6:322). Franchère commented upon how extremely fat and oily the fish is and of the dangers of over indulgence, "thus several of our people were attacked with diarrhea [...] but they found a remedy in the raspberries of the country which have an astringent property" (1904, 6:322).

Alexander Ross (1849:108), speaking of the lower Columbia, described "how sturgeon are also very abundant, and of uncommon size, yet tender and well flavoured; many of them weighing upwards of 700 pounds, and one caught and brought to us, measured 13 feet 9 inches in length and weighted 1,130 pounds."

Years earlier, David Douglas, when presented a sturgeon by his Indian companion, wrote thus: "I requested him to select the part which he considered the best, and cook it for me. This request he took as a great compliment, and I must do him the justice to say that he afforded me the most comfortable meal I had enjoyed for a considerable time, out of the head and spine of this fish" (1904, 5, 1:269).

As was his way, and after quoting Pliny of the sturgeon's great repute and culinary attributes among the Greeks and Romans, Lord (1866, 2:179) acknowledged the presence of the sturgeon in the Columbia and

Snake Rivers, as well as the unusual physical and behavioral characteristics that make it such a difficult fish to capture:

> Sturgeon arrive in the Columbia early in February. One would never imagine a fish clad in stiff unyielding armour could ascend rapid torrents and leap falls that puzzle even the lissome salmon; but the strength of the sturgeon is immense, and the power it can exert with the tail would be incredible to those, who have never seen the rapid twists, plunges, and other performances this fish goes through, when it has a barbed hook in the jaws, or a spear between the joints of its mail.

Though a difficult fish to land, and one that often requires assistance to bring ashore, sturgeon were valuable for meat as well as the fat deposits in the neck. Sturgeon fat was used for mixing with red or yellow ochre, primarily for making pictographs, because this was the best and most enduring media for rock art. Lord, when describing "Madam sturgeon's family," noted how bushels of roe were collected: "Sturgeon can produce a great many thousand, which the Indians dry these eggs in the sun and devour them with oil, as we eat currents and cream" (1866 1:177).

Catfish

The *catfish* (*Ictalurus punctatus* - *ʔupupcin*), introduced in about the 1890s, was not a difficult fish to catch, and where found, it was eaten fresh or dried—even smoked as winter food. Scholz (pers. comm.) maintains that the other type of catfish, *Tadpole Madtom* (*Noturus gyrinus*), the smallest of the Madtom catfish, was also an introduced species in the Snake River during the 1890s, and was not found in the Columbia River.

Whitefish

Both species of *Mountain whitefish* (*Prosepium williamsoni* - *x̣ʷx̣ʷy'ucn'* - "sharp-pointed mouth") and *P. coulteri*, were taken usually by spear throughout the Spokane drainage system, most frequently during February, as attested by Bean, a member of the U.S. Fish Commission Survey: "Whitefish were very abundant in the Spokane and Little Spokane Rivers and large numbers were observed. In the Spokane River at the city of Spokane Falls [Spokane] large numbers could be seen from the city bridges. They would lie close to the bottom keeping in the shade of the bridges" (1895:55-6).

Sucker

Within the *Catostomidae* family, three types of suckers (*qʷeʔč*) were taken: *bridgelip sucker* (*Catostomus columbianus* - *čléneʔ* - "[čl] - it [face] hangs down, [eneʔ] face"), *longnose sucker* (*C. catostomus* - *sxʷimineʔ*), and *largescale sucker* (*C. macrochellus*) (Scholz and McLellan 2009:87). Some gave the general term of *chelána* for suckerfish, which occasionally were substituted for salmon if the salmon runs were late, and served as a temporary food (Scholz, pers. comm.). Work stated how "The Indians are getting a few trout and sucker in their barrier [weir], a part of which they give us (Elliott 1914, 4:280).

The confluence of the Columbia and Spokane River—called *sch'map* or *hi λ'λ'im'* - "it comes to a point"—was a favored site for fishing camps while catching large suckerfish (*Catostomus* spp.), particularly during early spring in the shallow waters, by using articulated crossed-bone gorge hooks. While standing in the water, men and older boys caught slow moving suckers with a double leister. In late afternoon, the women opened and cleaned the day's catch, and placed the fish on racks to sun-dry. What fish was not eaten while camped was dried and the dried fish was carried to root fields as food when digging roots.

Bullhead

Within the family (*Ictaluridae*) of bullhead, the three introduced species of bullhead were: brown *bullhead* (*Ameiurus nebulosus*), *black bullhead* (*A. melas*), and *yellow bullhead* (*A. natalis*), presently referred to collectively as *ʔupupcin* ("hairy mouth" or *ncocƛ*ʷ*ane* - "fringed head") (Scholz, pers. comm.; Osterman, pers. comm.).

Bullhead were sometimes caught by both men and women from the shore with a long-handled pole that supported a framed net. One elderly lady claimed that women, because of their patience, were the best bullhead fishers, and often enjoyed taking several younger grandchildren to teach them patience.

Minnows

The first four types of minnows—*long-nose dace* (*Rhinichthys cataractae*), *leopard dace* (*R. falcatus*), *R. osculus*, and *redside shiner* (*Richardsonious balteatus* [Richardson] (* łq'éneʔč* or *łaq'* - "wide" or *sx*ʷ*imíneʔ*)—were called *łqiene* or *sx*ʷ*imine*. *Northern pike minnow* (*Ptychocheilus oregonensis* - *q'*ʷ*éʔč*), which "is an onomatopoeic term referring to the sound that the fish makes when it is caught" (Buchard and Kennedy 1975:10; Osterman 1995:36). The northern pike minnow is native to the Columbia River. *Carp* (*Cyprinus carpio* - *nłcíc'eʔ* or *łq'łaq*ʷ*t*) was an introduced species in the late 1890s. Carp, like sucker, when necessary, supplemented salmon shortage. Elliott cited the trading with the Indians for carp and recalled receiving "ab[ou]t 40 small *black carp* [*Mylopharyngodon piceus*]" (1917, 8:186).

Lt. Johnson claimed that when salmon were scare, the Spokan ate "a 'kind of carp'" (Wilkes 1845, 4:438). Several elders recalled how carp were gotten at the aforementioned confluence of the Columbia and Spokane Rivers while fishing for suckerfish. Thompson cites how "we got a few carp from the Spokane" (Elliott 1917, 3:186).

Lamprey

"Three species of lamprey are found in the Columbia Basin" (Neuman 2007:12), usually called *eel* (*k*ʷ*útul* or *k*ʷ*utwen*) by the Spokan. The Pacific species *Lampetra tridentata* Richardson were easily captured in late spring until late summer when this anadromous, polyphagus, parasitic fish migrated to an *upstream area* (*nc'ʔilš*) to spawn, being semelparousus spawners. The boneless lamprey migrated only at night, and having a round, down-turned mouth for sucking or clinging, was well adapted for ascending any encountered solid or most rigid physical barrier. During July through October, lamprey metamorphose from larval to juvenile forms (Richards and Beamish 1981). "Lamprey could be harvested from May to September, depending on the year and their progression upstream" (Neuman 2007:8), and, "Darkness was required for successful eel harvesting" (Neuman 2007:8; Bayer *et al.* 2001:14).

An interesting mid-summer observation of the amount of lamprey was made at Kettle Falls in 1932, when it was recorded how "The salmon came close behind a run of eels which turned the surface of the dam black as they made their way over the barrier (Anon. 1932:n.p.).

The importance of lamprey "can be recognized through myths, oral history, language and terminology, trade beyond the Columbia Plateau, and required a specialized fishing technology separate from that of salmon" (Neuman 2007:1). Lamprey was an important food that could be eaten immediately or stored for many years if properly prepared by smoking or drying. Once dried, eel never decayed; before eating it was heated by roasting. One elderly man had several samples of dried lamprey he had caught in the early 1930s and 1940s, and explained how dried lamprey were once an important trade item onto the Plains.

Numerous elders recalled capturing great numbers of lamprey ascending the slanting face of Little Falls Dam, but once Grand Coulee Dam was constructed, lamprey were no longer captured by the Spokan, only through trade was this meat acquired. Prior to commercial damming, eels were captured by holding an open burlap sack below the eel, and upon slapping the cement of the dam above the eel's head, it would release its hold and fall into the sack (STHC). The recognized strategy for capturing lampreys was for several men to commence at the bottom of the dam face, using long-forked or hooked poles to force the lamprey to release its hold, until all the available lamprey were taken (Downet 1996:23). One elderly woman said how she helped support her now deceased husband's double-poled ladder, which he would place precariously against the sloping dam to capture lampreys with a long hooked stick. A major concern was to avoid cutting an eel because the smallest amount of blood would cause any lower eels to release and drop into the dam pools.

Eels were captured in a number of ways depending upon their location, but in the late 1920s and early 1930s they used treble hooks. Eels were also taken by fisherman at Little Falls using pole-held nets while standing on platform scaffolds. When out of reach, dog or deer blood was dropped on the head of an eel, causing it to release its hold. As an elderly Spokan woman explained:

> I can recall when we'd catch eels here at Little Falls. Once they were very plentiful and caught usually by men and older boys during the late spring. The main attraction of eel meat, being very greasy, was it mixed well with the very unusual taste a person gets when eating large numbers of huckleberries. The eel's head was thrown away as it was too oily, though old people would eat the head, but they'd never eat the mouth. The *back round tail* (*stustušin*) she didn't use (Ross 1968-2008).

A more detailed account was given by a 97-year-old Spokan, who kindly offered some desiccated eel to the author in 1968, which he had collected at Little Falls prior to the construction of Grand Coulee Dam. After being stored in a woodshed for almost sixty years, it was dusty but still slightly greasy:

> I remember Little Falls during the 1920s and 1930s as [the] best area for catching eels, usually right now—in late June and early July, and by both men and women. Before the dam [Little Falls Dam] was built, we could gather eels all night long as they hung by their mouths on to the many huge boulders, getting each of us a half large sack. Usually we'd throw small stones or sticks at or ahead of [the] eels so they'd fall into our sacks. Many years ago, after day-fishing, many different groups would join us in eeling—sometimes as many six different tribal peoples. To open and clean, eels were cut up the back and the skin was removed before making numerous long cuts, and then spread open with small notched cedar sticks (*t'łáqmn* or *hecxp'ím*) after removing the guts. Any non-pitch wood made good drying sticks to hold the cuts open. It takes a long time for eels to dry 'cause of all the grease, most of the grease was near the head. If air-dried properly, the eel could last for two to three years with no spoilage. Sometimes eel was smoked, but was good to eat when fired. Eels, after skinning were baked to get rid of some of the oil, and were baked or roasted slowly over a fire. Most [prepared] eels were stored for winter use, and the skin was not eaten (Ross 1968-2008).

The same elder explained how in early summer, prior to the construction of Little Falls Dam, his father captured migrating eels that were stored for brief periods of time—at least for several days—in several large partially submerged rock-anchored willow-woven covered pens that were situated in one of the larger water-eroded rock depressions. This method of live storage was effective until the water level receded. No reason or name was given for eel-penning, except that with other fishing, there was not sufficient time to clean all the eels caught; hence the holding pen. Yet Smith claimed that the Spokan never corralled fish (1936-8:377), and Hewes (1998:622) says that eel pens were not known on the Northwest Coast, nor in the northeastern Plateau. However, according to oral history and recalled accounts, the Nez Perce built holding pools [pens] for lamprey (Landeen and Pickham 1999:141).

A valuable by-product of lamprey was the grease/oil, used for curing by massaging or rubbing on areas of muscle soreness, often just prior to entering the sweathouse. One elderly lady recalled how as a child her grandmother massaged an ache she received while playing. The oil was often heated with an immersed hot rock in a small rawhide container. Any oil or grease was later removed with the rough upper side of a yarrow leaf.

As a food, eel were often cut into cylindrical sections before cooking over a fire (Close *et al*, 2004:153). Mock orange or other sturdy hardwood peeled sticks were used to cook sections of eel (Hunn 1990:160).

Spier and Sapir explained the method used by the Wishram for preparing and cooking eel, which was the same for the Spokan:

> These [eel] were split and cleaned, but the head, tail, and backbone left in place. They were cut into four or five segments, about five inches long. To roast them, a stick was thrust through from the inside, and then stuck into the ground so as to lean obliquely over the fire. To cook eels over an open fire. They were roasted until brown" (1930, 3:179).

Mussels

The existence and use of freshwater bivalve *mollusks* (*Anodonta*, *Gonidea*, and *Margaritifera margaritifera falcata*) within the southern Plateau area was pointed out by Lyman (1980:127, 1984;97). Remains of a number of shell middens exist today along the Spokane River, despite severe damage by road and house construction. But more devastating to middens has been the erosion caused over many years by seasonally fluctuating water levels—covering and uncovering the middens—as attested by the many large middens on the Columbia and Spokane Rivers (Smith 1936-8:206). In fact, along the southern edge of the Spokane Reservation—bordering the Spokane River—remains the scattered remnants of five known major middens (Ross 1993), located on once-stable sections of the river terrace. Each of the five major mussel beds was named.

Prior to utility dam construction, all prehistoric riverine villages could be located by large middens of mollusk shells. Even today one may see a once large *baking site* (*snp'i?qeltn*) located approximately 300 m above Little Falls Dam, at a site once known as *sntmpenč*. The largest midden, known as *snp'i?qéltn* ("caved in cliff") (Ray 1977:46; Ross 1991:5.7, 5.3), was destroyed in the mid-1960s by house construction. Recently, an extensive and previously unknown Spokan midden was excavated where Latah Creek flows into the Spokane River (Lyons, pers. comm.).

Another large midden site was destroyed by a landslide in an area called *sntmpenč*, where numerous food storage pits were destroyed; in oral history was a battle, and a chief named Salmon was killed and rolled down the terrace, thereby causing the landslide. Directly across from the slide is a feature called *rattlesnake cave* (*čłqʷax̣n*), where coyote stored material for his summer lodge.

When diving for mussels—such as *western pearlshell* (*Margaritifera margaritifera falcata -sk'ʷk'ʷr'én'e?* or *s?ax̣ʷu?s*) and *winged floater* (*Anodonta nuttalliana - kʷk'ʷl'án'e?* or *kʷla?tqné*)—each man gathered his harvest in a special *cedar* (*Thuja plicata - mšéłp* or *?astqʷ*) or willow basket; both of open-weave construction that allowed the water to quickly drain when lifted out of the water. If available, cedar was the preferred wood, which tended to last longer, whereas the less durable but more available willow material was good for only one season. Upon surfacing, the man deposited the mussels in a basket situated on a stone-anchored raft platform or tule bundle boat, also anchored by one or more pedestal anchors, or else he waded to a close shore with his basket of mussels. Regardless of the material used for construction, any open-work basket was called *snqc'aqs*. The raft anchor shown here would usually be about 34 cm in length.

Figure 26. Clam-gathering raft anchor

After being gathered and shucked, *dried clams that were strung* (*sʔax̣ʷus*) served as a tasty supplement to winter foods, even as a starvation food. Lyman's extensive primary and secondary research led him to conclude that "the instance of faunal turnover in the prehistoric record would suggest changes in human exploitation practices, and would be expected if; in fact, river mussels were an important food resource for staving off starvation: such resources were probably exploited optimally" (1984:98).

Mussels were, according to taste and preference, eaten raw or cooked by boiling until the shells opened, and the meat was removed and cooked again. Several elders recall hearing of large quantities of mussels being steam-cooked in piles of dry-wall constructed ovens; no indication of any linguistic designation being given (Ross 1968-2008). Mussels were prepared by boiling after being removed from the shells (Smith 1936-8:206). More specifically, fresh water mussels were baked, broiled (Post 1938), or steamed in a small pit (Spinden 1908). Great quantities of mussels were dried over open low-burning embers, which served to smoke-dry the meat as well as maintain some control against insects, which rid any low-lying vegetation near drying racks. The word for a type of large dry-wall, slab-stone oven for steaming large quantities of mussels has been forgotten, though several elders recall it being used. Before steaming, the interstices were packed with moist clay to hold the boiling water.

After cooking and smoking, the mussels were *stored for future use* (*č'ɫwiʔscúʔtmis*) after being *strung together* (*q'l'*) on twisted hemp lines and hung as *dried strung mussels* (*sʔáx̣ʷuʔ*) within winter dwellings as an important winter food, often eaten whole or reconstituted with soups and stews—or eaten with pit-cooked tree moss. Another method of preparing mussels for *winter storage* (*snelq'ʷ cintn*) was to sun-dry them.

Several elders could recall their fathers explaining how they and other children were required after a large mussel feed, to collect the empty *shells* (*sččmíeʔ*) and deposit them on already existing *shell middens* (*maheckʷ*) comprised of only mussel shells. Middens were situated sufficiently away and downwind from the riverine village since the smell of rotting meat would create offensive odors and other sanitation problems, in addition to attracting unwanted animals. A major problem in summer was how freshly discarded calcareous shells attracted insects, which were a menace, and frequented residual water caught in open shells, particularly the bothersome *fungus gnats* (*Bradysia coprophilia* - *p'p'č'im'*) and the seemingly ubiquitous mosquito. To help alleviate these situations, women would resort to making up-wind smudge fires by placing yarrow plants on the coals, thereby creating a repugnant odor and smoke to repel bothersome insects. Collected and dried wild strawberry plants, including the roots—a mixture called *nq'ʷq'ʷal'c'q'ʷl'qn'*—were put in a hot pan or spread on the hot ashes to rid an area of bothersome mosquitoes and other insects (May n.d., p. 1).

374

In the past, some anthropologists claimed that gathered fresh water mussels within the Plateau was relegated as either a late winter/early spring starvation food, but not as an important source of protein by some ethnographers, even though mussels were collected in great quantity and winter-stored (Teit 1928:118; Hunn 1990:166). Yet Lyman, who questions the importance of this food to the diet, despite numerous large middens, feels that, "River mussels were apparently never more than a dietary adjunct for prehistoric peoples. It seems unlikely that human selection would play a major role in exploitation of a minor food source" (1980a, 2:127). However, Stevens's more recent and significant research (2000a:74-86) challenges this notion, citing how *Margaritifera falcata* were, unknowingly, an important source of protein, iron, and calcium, particularly for pregnant and lactating mothers. Post cited how the Sinkaietk gathered mussels in the winter "with a forked stick through holes in the ice if wading was impossible" (1938:29). As cited, there is further evidence of how, "Starving people would camp by these beds and gather them with forked sticks through holes in the ice if wading was impossible. They were easily opened and then baked. Some people liked them so much that they gathered and baked them in times of plenty, though never in warm weather" (Collier *et al.* 1942:95).

When referring to fresh water mussels, many Indians called them *oysters* (*sk'ʷk'ʷr'én'e?* or *sk'ʷal'áne?*) (STHC), as we find in the following account related by a Lakes woman:

> [...] as a 7 or 8 yr. old girl her grandmother made her stay all night on a [willow withe suspension] bridge with [the] slats removed between her & the land—in [the] morning [she] said the oysters told her that if she fell in after that to come to the bottom and to walk out on it—"we never swim" they said "but we never drown although we are on the bottom" (Elmendorf 1935-6, 1:42).

Crayfish

A favorite place for women to harvest freshwater *crayfish* (*Orconectes virilis* - *c'óy'x̣e?*) was at Big Tschimakain Creek. When *fishing for crayfish* (*mšeli*) they would bait small thorn hooks with meat, and then slowly drag in their catch. Another and more productive strategy was to fill a *flour sack* (*swipłλ'aqne*) or *burlap sack* (*k'ʷúp'e? - gunny sack - λ'aqne?*) with freshly chopped meat and blood, that was submerged in a stream to attract crayfish that would hang onto the meat and the blood-soaked sack as it was pulled ashore.

The most productive procedure for catching crayfish was to kill a small animal, such as a badger or raccoon, and after removing the major organs, the carcass was spread partially opened along the abdominal incision with several notched cedar or hardwood sticks, which the crayfish would enter. Another method to retain the opening was by inserting varying lengths of willow within the abdominal cavity to maintain a partial opening. The carcass was then weighted with enough stones to sink it to a stream's bottom, and periodically the fisherman would recover the carcass, which often contained crayfish eating the remaining meat. After *gathering a catch of crayfish* (*hecnšélli* - "to gather crayfish") a gut-wrapped stick was inserted in the carcass, and after a period of waiting it was withdrawn with the crayfish clinging to the encased gut-stick, a procedure called *nšélm*. Only the large ones were kept, while the smaller crayfish were thrown back.

DeSmet observed how possums caught crayfish in marshes and ponds:

> To catch them he places himself on the bank, and lets his long hairless tail hang down in the water. The crayfish are allured by the bait, and as soon as they put their claws to it, the opossum [sic] throws them up, seizes them sideways between his teeth, and carries them to some distance from the water, where he greedily but cautiously devours his prey (1843:117).

Crayfishing with a baited spear (*šel*) was practiced from an early age by both boys and girls who were encouraged to contribute to the family larder by *crayfishing* (*šéli*). If successful, the children would afterwards evenly distribute the crayfish among themselves, regardless of age or success. Children were warned to be careful of being bitten by crayfish, but were always praised after a successful gathering of crayfish. Crayfish were caught by a process called *šel*; using a baited spear. Crayfish were used as bait for both line-fishing and pole-fishing, or else were eaten after cooking in hot water, and were taken in all the major streams. A particularly productive area for catching crayfish was Latah Creek, along a stretch called *nc'iʔc'óy'x̣ʔem* (STHC). In the spring the *snxʷey'min'eʔm* would travel south to *Crab Creek* (*nc'iʔc'oʔy'x̣m'* - "small crayfish") (Elmendorf 1935-6, 2:12), to gather large amounts of crayfish. The crayfish was sometimes eaten raw, but it was usually prepared by first skewing five to six at a time on a bark-stripped length of red willow and roasting over the fire until the crayfish was very crisp.

Fishing Technology

Though every possible form of fishing technology existed among groups on the Upper Columbia and Spokane Rivers, there was little difference in the principles and materials in constructing the many types of collective and individual methods for catching fish. Variation was predicated more by the size and location of a fishing station, bed and bank configuration, water depth, anadromous or resident fish, and the presence or absence of waterfalls. Larger predation devices, such as weirs and some types of traps and netting, required collective cooperation, and individual fishing depended upon the fish and the method of procurement. Walker and Lahren, citing Scholz's extensive research on Spokan fishing techniques, aptly noted:

> The Spokane were a people deeply dependent on fish resources. It has been estimated that they caught some 1200 lbs of fish per capita year and that 90% of it was anadromous in origin [...] Their fishing gear was designed for complete exploitation of the various anadromous species as well as other several resident species. They employed traps, weirs, and set nets [passive techniques] as well as active techniques including dip nets, spears, leisters, hooks, and gaffs (1977:3).

Weirs and Traps

As with all Plateau groups, the fishing technology of the Spokan was composed primarily of *weirs* (*spáʔλuʔséčt* or *sqʷyóx̣ʷ*), *traps* (*q'ʷyox̣ʷ*), *corrals* (*sčłt'ič'm*), and various supplementary fishing implements. But the most apparent differences of their fishing technology, in comparison with those of other salmon-fishing groups down-river, were in linguistic nomenclature and fish classification; not necessarily the selection of materials or the type of structures used. Successful techniques and knowledge required for the various construction methods have evolved over time, probably from contact with different contiguous groups.

Fishing weirs were quite effective for trapping large quantities of anadromous fish dependent upon *traditional spawning grounds* (*sncpúmntn* - "place where salmon spawn") in the Spokane River, which connected with the Columbia River. *Building a weir* (*q'ʷyóx̣ʷm*) or *fish weir* (*sq'ʷyéy'x̣ʷ*) required long fences of upright, rock-anchored poles in the water—poles that supported attached willow mats that often stretched from shore to shore, thereby restricting and directing the passage of fish into the attached traps. The heights and lengths of fishing weirs were determined largely by the configuration of the stream's bed and banks, and by water depth. However, all weirs had similar construction: a series of upright *lodge pole pine in a row* (*sq'ʷyóx̣ʷ*) connected by two to three horizontal rows of poles lashed to them to support the willow barricades. Given the smaller creeks and no major river system, the Chewelah-Spokan Group (see Appendix M) had no large or extensive weirs, rather they "only built wood weir across creeks. There were no weirs across sloughs since they had an insufficient number of good boughs for this they built no brush weirs at all" (Smith 1936-8:38).

It was important that the timing and the entire weir construction was first organized and directed by a man who had the proper *sumés̆* for such a venture; otherwise it could prove disastrous if the weir collapsed when struck with large floating river debris, or if a great number of congregated *salmon* (*smłič*) pushed against the structure causing damage. The most responsible and experienced headman was always a powerful shaman, one who further enhanced his power by carefully covering his upper body, arms, and face with oil-based red hematite the night before the weir or trap construction, fasting for three day before, and after a solitary sweat praying over his religious paraphernalia while asking his *sumés̆* for help by providing guidance when directing the next day's labors. Given the powers of propitiation, and the uncertainty of anadromous fish, this traditional and specific ritual was never taken for granted.

Women were forbidden from attending or watching the initial collective cutting and gathering of lodge poles, willow, and balsam boughs. The larger pylon platform poles were rafted together and floated to a downstream area or the proposed site, which had always been a previously used location. Hereafter, women played an important role in assisting with making the fir barriers before the boughs commenced to wilt, lose their needles, and become less pliable.

Though there are various accounts of Spokan weirs, the following description by Curtis of a tripod-weir is important since he explained how the tule woven panels or fencing were made, and the methods of securing them, as well as certain essential structural configurations:

> The construction of a weir was begun by erecting a tripod of stout poles in the water at each bank, and similar tripods at intervals across the stream. These were used to support two lines of six-inch poles, one at the surface, the other on the bottom of the water. The space between the two lines of poles was protected by interwoven tules, and on the downstream side a single panel of similar fencing was constructed at an oblique angle from the shore to one of the tripods in the stream. This contained two openings large enough to admit the passage of salmon, which, entering the quiet water thus enclosed, were speared from the shore or the top of the weir. In the fall, when the salmon-trout were reversing downstream, the top was built on the upper side of the weir (1907-30, 7:71).

Large weirs were anchored by a *row of pylons* (*sq'ʷyóx̣ʷ*), three or four in number, depending upon the weir's length, and each pylon was constructed of three large lodge poles secured together at the top, with the butt ends properly spread apart and anchored on the stream bottom by piles of large anchor stones. Smith was informed that "(The Spokane sharpened them to a blunt point. [Whereas] they were practically not sharpened at all on the Columbia where they use stones around the bases of the poles.) The poles are rammed into the bottom and not pounded with a rock; it is done from a canoe" (1936-8:326). Two of the pylon poles formed basically a vertical triangle, secured flush against the side of the weir. Each pylon was known as *sq'éy'mntr*. The base of the third pole jutted out at a 45° angle supporting the other two poles, similar to erected *tipi poles* (*c'lx̣ʷnté?s* or *sq'ey'm't*), and the longer up-stream pole's angle from the ground was greater. Each pylon was further stabilized by numerous large stone weir weights affixed horizontally across members of lodge pole near the base of the poles (Elmendorf 1935-6, 1:54, 2:13-14; Smith 1936-8:326). Sometimes, as reported by Smith (1936-8:326-30)—whether from observation or informants' accounts—around the base of each pole, large sections of clay were deposited and held in place under inverted blanket-like layers of stone-weighed fir boughs. Each pylon was further securely attached with strips of willow bark to the upstream side of the weir, against which the fish would accumulate as they attempted to make their annual upstream migration. In full migration, fish exerted considerable force against the weir; thus, the great need for stabilizing the pylons. In areas of fast water, the pylons were further reinforced by twinning *woven saplings* (*λ'x̣á*) of maple with willow bark, with "a hole left in the bottom of one on the side upstream 8-10 inches in diameter" (Elmendorf 1935-6, 2:28), to permit excess salmon a passage through the *woven weir* (*sq'ʷyox̣ʷ* - "willow fish trap").

The *peeled bark from lodge poles* (*čsr'r'a?lqʷis*) was sometimes stripped and woven to secure sections of the poles above water (STHC). Initially, a primary consideration in weir construction was location, given the configuration of the stream's bed and banks. Though weir locations remained the same 'for all memory,' the sites were originally selected in areas of less stream flow pressure so as to reduce potential damage by any large concentrations of salmon. Consequently, weirs were best situated in wide and relatively shallow sections of water, and all known weirs were situated where the respective stream widened, for ease of construction and the apparent advantages of slower water, and a maximum increased span of the weir.

At some fishing stations, the Spokan used several large weirs, essentially wing dams, which were stabilized at both ends by large stone abutments extending out into the stream—often 3 to 4 m in length.

377

Several weirs took advantage of large mid-river accumulations of water-deposited *gravel bars* (*sm'q'ʷl'ičn'* - "humped up in the middle"), which in effect reduced the needed width of the weir and provided sufficient anchoring for the two mid-stream weir ends. In all probability, for a weir that was divided by a gravel bar, each of the two *sections of water* (*n'x̣ʷq'ʷpu?setkʷ*) would have an attached trap (STHC).

Most weirs had triangular fishing platforms at each pylon. Larger and more productive weirs had walkways on the upstream side that ran the length of the structure, providing fishermen with an easier access when *spearing fish in the water* (*?esnɫuɫw'étkʷi*), or when repairing a damaged section. The walkway—made of willow—was supported at each pylon or brace by a section of lodge pole that jutted out and above the water at a 45° angle. Walkways were also reinforced by a second piece of lodge pole set horizontally, extending approximately 60 cm from the main brace. When weirs had triangular fishing platforms at each pylon, the two upstream poles of each tri-pole were slanted vertically and held tightly against the long stretch of willow staves. For further stability, the third or downstream pole of the pylon was lashed at a slanting angle to the two attached near-vertical poles. Fishermen would use *double pronged spears* (*sx̣ʷƛ'ulá* - "maple shaft" or *wécč*) and leisters for spearing, or hand-held rigid looped nets when catching or migrating salmon from the fishing platforms.

Depending upon the width of a weir, a barrier may require hundreds of red willow withes that were then attached to the top, middle, and bottom of each row of *long, strait horizontal lodge poles* (*sq'éɫp*) that ran the entire length of the weir, forming an impassable palisade for large fish; permitting smaller fish to pass through. In sections of fast moving water, the bottoms of the willow withes were further secured with closely placed poles anchored with stones. Some weirs had *woven tule mats* (*sy'ay'qs*) or ones fashioned from small balsam fir, kept in place and *supported by poles* (*sq'ʷiix̣ʷálqʷ*) secured to the upright poles. Damage to a weir was not unusual, considering the thousands of salmon frantically attempting to simultaneously continue their migration against obstacles constructed of woven natural materials.

The figure below (Walker 1967), prepared by Stephen Allured and Frank Leonhardy, illustrates what is termed a "double weir."

Figure 27. Fish weir

As noted, all fisheries were treated with the utmost respect, since there was always the fear that any inappropriate behavior or violation of a taboo could lessen or even prevent the occurrence of salmon. There were occasions when the Spokan *restricted* (*hec lic'*) the number of salmon entering a weir for fear of its destruction by the sheer number of migrating fish. Elders claimed that the blood of a male dog poured into the water kept the salmon from pressing against a damaged section for a time usually sufficient to make any necessary repairs.

All weirs had different types of traps attached to one or more openings on the up side flow of the river—such as barrel, wedge, platform, cone, and basket traps. Again, the configuration of the bed and banks, and the resulting hydrodynamics of a particular section of the stream determined the types of trap chosen for a particular location. The decisions as to where weirs and traps were best located had been determined over many years of use, and were geonomically designated—names which indicated the type of enclosure and on occasion the surrounding features of its location.

A type of brush weir was made in the fall and situated in smaller streams with lower water levels. This simple but effective type of weir was communally built under the direction of a headman who assigned various tasks that were necessary to block a wide stream section with *sub-alpine fir boughs* (*mr'inłp*) or *grand fir* (*Abies grandis* [Dougl. ex D. Don] Lindl. - (*qʷélenƛsn* or *qʷelcen* or *st'qʼʷelqʷ*) brought in by floating from higher elevations in eastern Idaho, which were supported and held in place with intermittent vertical lodge poles driven into the stream bed. The tightly bound fir boughs permitted free stream flow but restricted the passage of any large fish.

Willow was an invaluable material to the Spokan, fulfilling a number of needs and a wide range of purposes. Both men and women gathered willow in the late spring when the plant was most pliable, and before a wooden area adjacent to a stream was selectively burned. When working with willow there was no strict division of labor. A main use of willow was the labor intensive manufacture of large, open, woven sections for fishing weirs and traps, certain traps and snares used in the delayed predation of land mammals, frames used for skinning and sweathouse frames, and structures for living and food storage. Women also made various types of large, wide-mouth burden baskets from willow, including open-weave baskets for gathering freshwater mussels. Willow was indispensable for framing tule mats, as well as in the construction of cradleboards, toys and musical instruments, as discussed elsewhere.

Despite the aforementioned methods of constructing and anchoring weirs, it was not unusual for a weir being swept away by rain-swollen waters, as cited in the early spring of 1841 by Elkanah Walker, "The water had risen & carried off the weir so that they could not supply us with any fish" (Drury 1976:151). Weirs were completely dismantled after the last major salmon run except for the large pylon anchor stones which were kept in place. Pylon and weir poles were kept on site and stored through the winter in tied bundles stacked near-vertically against large ponderosa trees.

Barrel Traps

As the name implies, this type of trap was essentially an elongated barrel approximately 5 to 6 m in length, nearly 2 m wide at its midsection, and shaped by a series of hardwood poles 4 to 5 cm in diameter and approximately 2 m in length, which were covered by willow withes attached to a number of spaced hoops that decreased in diameter as they neared each gathered end. A barrel trap was attached to an opening of approximately 80 cm to a meter in the weir. The rim of the open end was wrapped with successive lengths of stripped willow bark. When completed the unattached end was secured by a stone crib that securely held the ends of the poles that passed at right angles through the openings of the trap. The larger fish were trapped when entering the downstream end of the barrel trap, and only the smaller ones were able to exit through the other end. Larger barrel traps had a hinged rectangular opening of woven latticed willow on the top to empty the trap of fish at necessary intervals, which was done hourly or daily, depending upon the run.

Because of the basic cylindrical shape, and woven construction, barrel traps were sometimes referred to as basket traps, as expressed by Hewes (1998:629), "Where the Little Spokane River joins the main Spokane River was another important fishery, with a wing-dam or weir, in which basketry traps were set, where the fish were speared." The versatility of this type of conical barrel trap or basket trap was described by Curtis, "A conical basket-trap with a funnel-shaped opening at the larger end was made of cattails and used at the bottom of smaller streams for taking trout and salmon-trout. It was sometimes used in connection with the weir, being placed above the opening in mid-stream" (1911, 7:71).

During his now-celebrated visit to Kettle Falls, Kane observed and made several sketches of a chief's basket trap, which apparently was set out one month before anyone else was permitted to fish: "This basket is constructed of stout willow wands woven up the falls strike against a stick placed at the top, and are thrown back into the confined space at the bottom of the trap, which is too narrow to allow them to attempt another jump" (1859:217-8).

Wedge Traps

A wedge trap was attached to the downstream opening of a cross-stream weir, forcing the migrating salmon to be channeled by two walls of woven willow held in place by vertically driven lodge poles, and the walls eventually forced the salmon to enter a gradually narrowing passage, where the salmon were taken with a leister or spear, or clubbed with a stout piece of wood. A wedge trap usually emptied into a large round corral trap to contain fish not caught at the weir. Fishermen working inside the corral would pass dead or captured salmon to other men outside, who in turn carried the fish to shore to be processed by attending women.

Corral Traps

Viewed from above, a *fish corral trap* (*sq'ʷóx̣ʷ*) appeared as a rather bulbous structure, and yet a type of weir having palisade-like wings of willow mats (*sq'ʷyox̣ʷ* - "netting") that channeled fish into one or more openings. In that sense, it was similar in construction to a wedge trap. The upstream opening had a large funnel of willow mats that forced salmon into a large near-circular enclosed palisade. Enclosures were made of numerous vertical pine lodge poles driven into the bed of the stream, and the length of each pole was determined by the water's depth; the top of each pole would be at least one meter above water level. Enclosures were completed with willow withes secured to a series of at least two rows of horizontal sapling poles that connected and were secured to each upright pole. A problem with most fully-enclosing traps, for *corralling fish* (*sk'ʷɫt'íč'm*) was that a large run of salmon could possibly destroy the structure; consequently, it was not unusual, during a high run, for a weir to be opened after an unusually successful day of fishing. However, a corral trap, being an integral part of a weir, was less subject to such damage by overcrowding fish.

Several early historical accounts attest to the abundance of salmon, mentioning certain details of catching salmon. But a particularly noteworthy observation was made in 1826 by David Douglas, who surveyed the Spokane House shortly after it had been abandoned, in which he described a fishing site—a type of square fish corral with numerous funnels—that was productive until the construction of Little Falls Dam, and located several kilometers downstream from the mouth of the Little Spokane River:

> At nine o'clock in the morning [I] crossed the Spokane River to the old establishment [Spokane House] on the south side, where we found old Mr. Finlay, who gave us an abundance of the fresh salmon from his barrier, places in the small branch [Little Spokane River] of the main river. After breakfast, and having the horses crossed, left that place at noon for the Columbia. An hour's ride from that place passed the Indian camp on the north side of the river, where they were employed fishing. Their barrier, which is made of willows and placed across the whole channel in an oblique direction, in order that the current which is rapid will have less effect on it, has a small square 35 yards enclosed on all sides with funnels of basket-work (just made the same manner as all traps in England), and placed on the underside, through which the salmon passes and finds himself secure in the barrier. When the spearing commences, the funnels are closed with a little brushwood. Seventeen hundred were taken this day, now two o'clock; how many may be in the snare I know not, but not once out of twelve will they miss bringing a fish to the surface on the barb. The spear is pointed with bone and laced tight to a pointed piece of wood a foot long and at pleasure locks on the staff and comes out of the socket when the fish is struck; it is fastened to the staff by a cord. Fifteen hundred and sometimes two thousand are taken in the course of the day (Lavender 1972, 2:116).

After the abandonment of Spokane House, Jaco Finlay and his extended family were permitted to continue their residence at the structure he helped locate and build. In the spring and summer of 1826, "David Douglas, the famous English botanist, visited him [...] and found the family subsisting upon a vegetable diet of camass [sic] and moss cakes, cooked *a la Indiene* " (Elliott 1930, 1:7).

In the early 1920s, an elderly Spokan woman wrote in pencil on ledger paper the following unpublished account of salmon corral traps that were annually rebuilt near the confluence of Latah Creek and the Spokane River:

> In good salmon season one night's catch would almost burst these correls [sic]. When the traps were full, the *Eel-me-whem* [chief] would tell his anoncer [sic] to call the people down to the traps, which was good news to the encampment, it meant salmon distribution. Everybody in camp went down to the traps happily, no one was backwards. Visiting people from other tribes included, good salmon years these corrals (traps) caught enough Salmon to last them all winter, cured [dried] in a way it [they] lasted a long time [...] Building salmon traps was real work, try now to build and stay in the cold water and hold a 1000 strong salmon without nails, spikes, wire

netting or cement. My grandfather tells of his father would walk down river or Broadway, get to [the] river in low water time, if you look real close and know what you are looking for, you will notice some rows of rock in the river bed, this was the sight [site] of one of their salmon corrals [traps]. These rows of rocks were what held logs down [...] Even while the Salmon was filling the traps, the many different camps dotted on the prairies [were] digging and harvesting their vegetables (Anon. n.d.).

T. Becher, in his early history of Spokane, quoted an early resident, a Mr. Bently, who arrived in Spokane in 1882, and witnessed the Spokan and Coeur d'Alene using both the basket trap and the corral trap, and explained the methods of heat-curing their catch at Spokane Falls as late as 1882:

> When we came to Spokane, we lived right at the falls. The Indians passed right by our door, sometimes 100 times a day, on their way to the fishing grounds below the falls and near the mouth of Latah Creek. Their fishing season lasted about a month. One method they used was the dip net. The fish rested in the holes and eddies below and along the side of the falls and the Indians were very skillful in catching them with the nets. Another method was the 'corral'. It was made of switches. It was cone-shaped, with the small part on the bottom. It was placed on top of the falls and, as the fish jumped, they often landed in the wide part of the corral. They jerked and dried the salmon right there at the falls. The driers were 50 to 100 feet long. The pieces of salmon were hung on the ridge pole and then covered with skins. A fire was made at one end and the smoke was fanned into and through the driers (Becher 1974:243).

Although Smith (1936-8:319 and 377) wrote how the Spokan never corralled fish, unfortunately he does not specify if he is referring to the Kalispel-related Chewelah-Spokan Group or the Spokan proper.

Raised Terraced Stone-Fishing Platform

A *stone-fishing platform trap* (*snč'wéstn*) was often attached to a weir—often near the pylons to provide further stability—and was found at the mouths of main feeder streams, such as Little and Big Tschimakain, Latah, Blue, and Sand Creeks. This type of trap was an elevated open platform made of narrowly spaced sections of lodge poles set at right angles to the weir, and supported by a raised stone crib. The platform floor was on a level just higher than the stream. By careful spacing of the lodge poles, smaller fish were permitted to continue their passage *upstream* (*nc'?íłš* - or *čqéltč* - "he went upstream") or *downstream* (*nʕaxʷt* - "go downstream"), whereas most of the larger fish, once they were upon the enclosed raised platform (a crib), were prevented from returning to the water. When fish flopped onto the platform, a fisherman would kill them with a *wooden club* (*ssp'qíntn* or *sp'í* - or *sp'intn* - "salmon club") before the fish escaped off into the water (Elmendorf 1935-6, 2:13)–a simple method which was most expedient for killing salmon. Fish were equally distributed after each day of fishing, either by a salmon chief, or if one was not there, by the person who was the ranking clubber (STHC). It has been further recorded that small platform traps had no salmon chief. A stone-platform trap was also used in the main stream, and was attached at the downstream apex of a weir that formed a 'V', which essentially channeled the fish into the trap. Elmendorf (1935-1936) and Ray (1936:122) visited a strategically located year-round site at the mouth of Latah Creek *peninsula* (*sntu?t?ulim* or *n'xʷa?nxʷm* - "flat peninsula" or *n'čʕacu?snwexʷtn* - "a place where people were hung," or *ntu?t?ulmétkʷ* or *ntu?tu?úλimétkʷ* - "jumping creek") and the Spokane River. The people of this area were called *sntut?uli* or *sntu?t?ulixʷi*, and the site was a major fishing station with a large permanent winter village called *n'xʷa?nxʷm* or *ntu?t?ulm* or *n'xʷanxʷom*, and the inhabitants were known as *sntu?t?úlxʷi*. On the west side of Latah Creek was a dog salmon camp, remembered as *snč'luʕ isełxʷtn*. The *Upper Spokan inhabitants* (*snt?úlixʷi*) took advantage of a *long, flat sandy peninsula* (*nánxʷm*) formed by converging waters that deposited gravel carried in the spring and early summer. Over time, this annual condition made an ideal location for a once-large 'V'-shaped rounded granite boulder *platform trap* (*snč'wéstn*). The base of the platform trap was made by placing large, rounded river granite boulders across the stream, some of which may be seen today at low water as it crosses the Spokane River on the west side of the creek. *Latah Creek* (*sntu?t?ulim*) was an important source for a small fish called *tw'éck*. It should be noted that the people inhabiting the area of Latah Creek were both Spokan and Coeur d'Alene.

The mouth of Latah Creek was also an important site for procuring dog salmon; it was so productive that the Coeur d'Alene, Kalispel, Flathead, and Nez Perce came annually to mutually exploit this resource. While in residence, families would periodically gain elevation to better enable men to hunt deer, and for women to gather various species of berries and other plant foods and available medicines.

A type of platform trap was constructed by weaving a sufficient number of 2 m long slender poles, which were then situated between a weir opening and stabilized by anchoring with rocks in such a way that the upstream edge was raised above the stone foundation (STHC).

Hunt (1966), in editing John Mullan's field notes on the Spokan, mentioned how conducive the environment of the fishery at Latah Creek was for the inhabitants, and described how productive this fishing site was for the Spokan who shared it with the Coeur d'Alene. Hunt's account was attested by Mullan:

> This is a great fishing point for the Indians, as shown by the number of barriers in the bed of the river for catching salmon. The hills and plains around afford fine grazing for their large bands of stock. Fuel from the large pine forests is had in abundance; while nature furnishes them the shoals of the fattest salmon. The salmon ascend this stream [Spokane River] to the upper falls [Spokane Falls], that are two and half miles above the Lahtoo [Latah or Latah Creek] to the very mountains (1861:119).

Unfortunately, the pressures of encroaching white settlements, most notably the *City of Spokane* (*sλ'xetk* - "place where swift waters flow"), forced the people to leave the site: "The people from this area, the Upper Spokanes, upon being forced from this area, chose to settle in the Coeur d'Alene Indian territory and the Kalispel Indian Reservation at Usk, Wa[shington]. Their intermarriages, their religious preference was also a deciding factor" (STHC).

Actually, all Spokan fishing weirs had purposely built slots in the tule or willow mat barriers that were large enough to permit the easy passage of smaller trout, yet restricted the migration of larger and more economically important salmon.

Single or Multiple Stone Fishing Platform

Another similar salmon fishing technology used during the fall was to reconstruct, if necessary, any of the several damaged "V" shaped low stone-platform dams that extended completely across the shallower upper reaches of both Little and Big Tschimakain Creek. The height and width of each fish dam was sufficient to cause the fish to be stranded when they attempted to jump the obstacle, and relatively easy to catch. Sometimes women would camp with the men and help in the cleaning and drying of their catch over low fires built under existing fish-drying racks. After spending five to six days fishing, and before leaving the fishing camp, their catch was equally divided among the fishermen who would then carry the fish to their respective winter villages (STHC). The largest permanent stone fish barrier—not far from the base of Little Falls—stretched almost across the Spokane River, and in low water many of the original foundation stones may still be seen.

Smith described how effective fish dams were for catching large quantities of smaller fish, claiming that the Spokan did not use this method, while the Chewelah-Spokan did. Some of these structures were still visible in 1936 (1936-8:360).

Men would fish for salmon in the late summer on the upper reaches of both Big and Little Tschimakain Creeks, first erecting a south-west-facing ramada or sunshade made of poles that supported a cover of tule mats along the stream's edge, which were approximately 4 to 5 m long. The bed of the shaded section of the stream was covered with small pieces of crushed granite to enable the fishermen to better see the salmon, which were presumably temporarily blinded as they swam from an area of bright sun into the *shade* (*čsč'áylq*k* - "shade tree" or *sk'*er'łx*).

Another method for catching salmon was when several *salmon spawning* (*hescpumi*) streams that fed the Spokane River were modified by excavating a *trench to divert* (*słíču?us*) the fish into a confined space, where they were taken with a minimal expenditure of energy.

Funnel and Cone Traps

The *cone trap* (*ʕʷoléwltn*, or *funnel-shaped basket trap - múlmn*) was effective when situated in such a way "that a waterfall or riffle fell into the trap" (Elmendorf 1935-6, 2:45):

The trap was made of two cones, the *smaller inside cone* (*qʷse?éƛs*) was set inside the *larger outside cone* (*xʷƛíčn?*), closely resembling a windsock or an elongated, straight-sided tapered funnel. The outer cone was made with saplings of 5 to 6 cm in diameter and 4 to 5 m in length, were secured to a series of willow withe hoops that diminished in diameter with the course of the stream; the larger butt ends of the poles were always at the opened end—facing downstream. The longitudinal poles were spaced approximately 5 to 7 cm apart to permit smaller fish an escape, and a hoop of twined serviceberry stems formed the open rim of the trap, to which the open butt end of the cone was secured. The open rim of the large and smaller cone was successively wrapped with stripped willowbark, which supported several spaced, loop handles that came just above the stream level, and were used by several men on either side of the opening to raise or lower the opening given fluctuating water levels. The front or entrance of the trap faced *downstream* (*nʕáxʷt* - "he went upstream"), whereas the constricted *upstream* (*čqéltč* or *nc'?íłš*) was closed, containing several large stones that weighted and thereby stabilized the widest facing downstream, which was bound temporarily to the larger opening of the outer cone, sometimes called a *shell* (*xʷli čn'*). The smaller opening emptied into the larger cone, thereby preventing the fish from escaping (Elmendorf 1935-6, 2:22 and 4:27).

In relatively fast-moving water, the large or downstream end of the cone trap was elevated well out of the water by stacked stones or by cradling the end in a stout wooden "H" crib of two stout vertical up-right poles driven into the stream bed, and connected with a horizontal pole. The lower upstream was similarly secured, only in a lower "H" crib at the lower restricted end. The larger and open end was raised, allowing the fishermen to verify that the trap was undamaged, and to facilitate the removal of fish. The open end of the outer cone was further supported by ropes, which permitted greater ease when the trap was filled with salmon, and could be pulled to shore and emptied. Attached ropes facilitated relocating the trap.

Some large stationary single or double funnel traps had a top-frame trap door that facilitated the removal of salmon. The high productivity of this type of trap required that it be frequently emptied, because during the day when heavy runs of fish were being caught, it was imperative to periodically empty the trap as too many fish could possibly destroy the trap by sheer number and weight. Immediately before emptying a trap, the blood of a gaffed salmon or dead dog was often released into the water to discourage fish from further entrapment. Any blood was later dissipated by the swift-running water. Elders maintained that if dog blood was used, it had to be from a male dog. Some weir-attached funnel traps could be temporarily closed off with bush closures during the night or prior to emptying during day runs.

Work commented upon the Spokan catching "7 or 800 salmon per day" (Elliott 1914, 2:99) at a weir near the confluence of the Spokane and Columbia Rivers. The ever-observant Douglas, who was with Work when he described a funnel fishing trap used by the Spokan on the Columbia River, probably near the mouth of the Spokane River, remarked about the Indians

[...] who were busily engaged in snaring salmon, in traps made of basket work and shaped like funnels. Here they had already caught one thousand seven hundred fish in the morning, having speared and thrown on shore that number, while many more remain within the snare awaiting their fate. The spear is pointed with bone, laced tight to a pointed piece of wood, which is frequently fastened to a long staff with a cord. During the best part of the fishing season, from one thousand five hundred to two thousand salmon are caught on an average day (1904, 5, 1:361).

Scholz *et al.* (1976:52) discuss the catch *v.* escapement in the Upper Columbia River Indian fisheries, and how the "tribes actively and routinely practiced fish management" (1985:94). Scholz *et al.* cited Koch who noted the practice of Indians "allowing upstream escapement of salmon during the early portion of the run at the time they held their First Salmon Ceremony."

Suspended Basket Traps

The various forms of basket traps were determined by the natural bed and bank configurations, and other physical features of each individual *fishing site (snq'q'm'éy'eʔtn')*. Work's 1826 journal entry provides a brief but excellent account of the basket traps at Kettle Falls, one which described the number of fish taken by the different Indian groups, and provided a description of using basket technology:

> Visited the, falls [Kettle], today, where the Indians are fishing. They are now taking about 1000 salmon daily. They have a kind of [oblong] basket about 10 ft long [and] 3 [feet] wide and 4 [feet] deep of a square form suspended at a cascade in the fall where the water rushes over a rock. The salmon in attempting to ascend the fall leap into the basket, they appear to leap 10 or 12 feet high, when the basket is full the fish are taken out. A few are also taken with scoop net and speared (Elliott 1915, 1:37).

Having visited Kettle Falls on numerous occasions, Cox recorded the "vast quantities of salmon which they dry and preserve for use during the winter and spring months" (1957 [1832]:189). Another early observation and recording of basket traps on the Columbia at Kettle Falls was by Thompson:

> The number of fish caught there was enormous and the manner of catching was peculiar. Spears were also used, of course, but the main catch was by means of baskets hung from the end of poles across and close to the falls, into which the fish dropped after a vain attempt to swim up through the water running over the ledge or reef forming the falls. These baskets were constructed of hazel or birch osiers woven together with withes and roots (Elliott 1918, 1:11).

Much later, both Wilson and Lord were each able to provide fairly comprehensive and singularly important accounts of the Spokan and other groups using fishing baskets at the three mentioned falls-fisheries. Wilson, who, despite his unfortunate use of the pre-Enlightenment terms 'savage' and 'squaw,' provided ethnographic data describing the importance and quantity of salmon in the Columbia and Spokane Rivers, as well as details of the predation technology and division of labor associated with the processing and the eventual distribution of salmon:

> At the Kettle Falls of the Columbia and great Falls of the Spokan, salmon are caught in a large wicker basket, suspended from the rocks at one end of the falls, and projecting slightly into the water. At the foot of the rock there is an eddy, and the water coming down with less force at this point, the salmon here make their chief effort to leap the falls, the greater number, however, fail to clear the rock, many leap right into the basket, whilst others strike their noses against the rock and fall back helplessly into the trap below. Emptying the basket is a most exciting scene, two savages, with nothing but a loose wrapper round the loins, and armed with stout wooden bludgeons, jump into the frail structure, which quivers with the struggling fish and falling water, and the work of slaughter commences. One blow on the head from the practiced hands settles the account of each fish, which is then thrown out on the rocks and carried to the general heap, from which they are portioned out to the different families every evening by a man known as the 'salmon chief,' when the squaws take them in hand for splitting and drying. From 400 to 500 salmon are taken in this manner; the number of fish ascending the river is perfectly extraordinary, the water seems perfectly alive with them, and as many as a dozen have been counted in the air at one time. Some are seen to clear the falls at a single bound, whilst others fall back into the eddies to recruit their strength for another trial [...] . When the salmon are caught, they are laid on the rocks, the heat from which and the direct rays of the sun serve to loosen the skin; they are sometimes split and dried whole, but the more favourite way of curing, especially with those Indians who have to carry their salmon a long distance, is to strip the flesh from the bones, mash it and pound as fine as possible, and then spread it out on mats to dry in the sun; three or four days usually accomplish this and it is then put up in long baskets holding from seventy to eighty pounds, a convenient weight for packing on horseback. During the fishing season the Indians live on the heads, hearts, and offal, which they string on sticks and roast over the fire, keeping the dried fish for winter use (Wilson 1866:297-9).

Wilson further observed the aforementioned site, and made an additional description of the fishing techniques at Kettle Falls:

The salmon arrived at the foot of the fall in great numbers & proceed to leap them; all day long you see one continual stream of fish in the air, many of them clear the whole at a single leap [...] The Indian way of catching them is very ingenious. They hang a basket made of willow or crab apple, over the rock at the side of the falls, the salmon in jumping strike their noses against the top part & fall into the basket below; they catch from 700 to 1000 salmon a day in this manner which are equally divided amongst them in the evening by one of the chiefs. The most curious sight is to see them empty the basket, two men strip & jump into it armed with wooden bludgeons with which they knock the salmon on the head & then pass them on to others on shore; it is rather an awkward situation in this same basket as part of the fall, though not the full force of it, runs right over their heads nearly drowning them whilst what with the weight of the fish & the rush of the water the frail baskets rocks about in anything but a pleasant manner (Stanley1970:114).

Lord, at the same location and time described procedures used to catch, process and, cure the spring run of salmon; but unfortunately he provides no detail of the actual baskets and their construction, in some cases large baskets that required two fishermen per basket. The English, incidentally, used the term 'pannier' to describe any large *wicker fish basket* (čʔolʔolqín):

As soon as the water has risen sufficiently for the fish to leap the falls, at it they go, and in leaping often fall back into the baskets. I have seen 250 to 300 salmon taken from out one basket two or three times a day. I have likewise seen over a hundred salmon in the air at one time, and often six or eight tumble into a basket together. Two Indians go naked into this huge pannier, each carrying in his hand a heavy wooden club, and, utterly reckless of the water dashing over them, and scrambling about amongst the struggling fish, they seize one after another by the gills, give each salmon a crack on the head with the club, then fling it out upon the rocks, whereon the squaws are waiting; the women pounce upon the stunned fish, lug them away, cut off their heads, split them open, take out the backbones and hang them upon long poles to dry, keeping a small fire always smoldering underneath the poles to partially smoke the drying fish. Salmon cured in this way I have known to keep two years perfectly sound (Lord 1867:260).

Lord witnessed and commented upon the gathering of different tribes at Kettle Falls prior to the late spring salmon-run, and provides an invaluable and fairly comprehensive explanation of salmon harvesting with what he called wicker hampers:

About three weeks preceding the arrival of the salmon, Indians begin to assemble from all directions. Cavalcades may be seen, day after day, winding their way down the plain [...] - [...] wives, children, dogs, horses, lodges, weapons, and skins [...] The smaller children are packed with the baggage on the backs of horses, which are driven by the squaws, who always ride astride like the men. The elder girls and boys, three or four a horse, ride with their mothers, whilst the men and stouter youths drive the bands of horses that run loose ahead of the procession. A pack of prick-eared curs, simply tamed prairie-wolves, are always in attendance.

[...] The men, who are all, when at the fishery, under one chief, whom they designate the 'Salmon Chief,' at once commence work—some in repairing the drying-sheds, which are placed on the rocks (as are also numbers of lodges) at the foot of the zigzag [path down a near-vertical cliff]; others are busy making or mending immense wicker hampers, about thirty feet in circumference, and twelve feet in depth. Little groups are dragging down huge trees lopped clear of their branches—rolling, twisting, and tumbling them over the rocks, to be fixed at last by massive boulders, the ends hanging over the foaming water not unlike so many gibbets [wooden fasteners]. These trees being secure and in their right places, the next work is to hang the wicker baskets to them, which is a risky and most difficult job: but many willing hands and long experience work wonders; with the strong ropes of twisted bark, the baskets are at last securely suspended. By this time the river begins to flood rapidly, and soon washes over the rocks where the trees are fastened, and in to the baskets, which is soon in the midst of the waterfall, being so contrived as to be easily accessible from the rocks not overwashed by the flood.

Whilst awaiting the coming salmon, the scene is one great revel: horse-racing, gambling, love-making, dancing, and diversions of all sort, occupy the singular assembly; for at these annual gatherings, when all jointly labour in catching the winter supply of salmon, feuds and dislikes are for the time laid by, or, as they figuratively express it, 'The hatchet is buried.' [...] The medicine-men (doctors and conjurors) of the different tribes busily work their charms and incantations to insure an abundant run of fish [...] (Lord 1866, 1:71-3).

386

Lord interrupted his account to explain how at first he was unfortunately not permitted to photograph the fishing activity of the Spokan and other groups, because his large camera had been declared "a box of bad 'medicine' that would surely drive every salmon away; and not until an Romanish priest [...] explained it to them, did they permit a photograph to be taken" (1867:73). In an earlier publication, Lord had provided an early, detailed account of the dependence of these people upon the migrating salmon, and described the processing and distribution of salmon as well as the rarely mentioned curing-houses—smoke houses:

The watchers announce the welcome tidings of the salmon arrival, and the business begins. The baskets are hung in places where past experience has taught the Indians salmon generally leap, in their attempt to clear the falls. The first few that arrive are frequently speared from the rocks. They are in such vast numbers during the height of the 'run,' that one could not well throw a stone into the water at the base of the falls without hitting a fish: fifty and more may be seen in the air at a time, leaping over the wicker traps, but, failing to clear the 'salmon-leap,' fall back, and are caged. In each basket two naked Indians are stationed all day long; and as they are under a heavy fall of water, frequent relays are necessary. Salmon three or four at a time, in rapid succession, tumble into the basket. The Indians trust their fingers under the gills, strike the fish on the head with a heavy club, and then fling them on the rocks. I have known three hundred salmon landed from one basket betwixt sunrise and sunset, varying in weight from twenty to seventy-five pounds.

From the heaps of fish piled on the rocks, boys and girls carry and drag them back to the squaws seated around the curing-houses; with sharp knives they rip the salmon open, twist off the head, and cleverly remove the backbone; then hang them on poles, close under the roofs of sheds the sides of which are open, they dry them slowly, small fires being kept constantly smouldering on the floors. The smoke serves to keep away the flies, and perhaps also aids in the preservation of the fish. The only portions eaten by the Indians during the catching are the heads, backbones, roes, and livers, which are roasted, skewered on sticks.

When thoroughly dried the fish are packed in bales made of rush-mates [tule], each bale weighing about fifty pounds, the bales being tightly lashed with bark-ropes. Packing in bales of equal weight facilitates an equitable division of the take. Horses are purposely brought to carry the fish back to winter-quarters, and the two bales are easily packed on each horse. The fishing season lasts for about two months: then the spoils are divided, and the place abandoned to its wonted quietude until the following summer brings it another harvest (Lord 1866,1:73-5).

Another early and more detailed description by the same author mentioned how similar the Spokan fish-basket trap was to the English method of trapping eels:

It is made of split vine-maple, lashed together with strips of cedar bark. These baskets vary in size; some of them are fifteen feet long, and six in circumference [... they] place their wicker traps in the centre of the stream; a dam of latticework on each side reaches to the bank, so that no fish can get up-stream unless through the trap. Another plan [...] where the water is shallow, is to build a little wall of boulders, rising about a foot above water, slanting the wall obliquely until the ends meet in the centre of the stream at an acute angle; at this point they place the basket. By this plan all the water is forced through the basket, increasing the depth and strength of the current. In happy ignorance of their danger, the fish ply steadily up-current, until they suddenly find themselves caged.

When a sufficient number of fish are in the basket, an empty one is carried out and set, the other brought ashore; its contents are turned out upon the grass. [Women], old and young, knife in hand, squat round, looking eagerly on; and as the captives lie flapping on the ground, in the [women] rush, seize a trout, rip him up, remove the inside, and then skewer him open upon two sticks. Poles having a fork at the end, are placed firmly in the ground, about fifteen feet apart. Other sticks, barked and rubbed very smooth, are placed in these forked ends, on which the split trout are strung. small fires are kept smouldering below the strung-up fish. When thoroughly dry, they are packed in small bales, and lashed with the bark of the cedar tree (Lord 1866, I:86-7).

A variation on the use of the fish basket was noted by Curtis, who described how, "At waterfalls a stout pole was thrust horizontally into the bank, and from it was suspended a very large tule basket in such a position that fish trying to ascend the falls would strike a framework above the basket and drop back into it" 1907-30, 7:71).

A Colville elder, who often fished for salmon at Little Falls as a young man, described a rather simple but effective method of how the Spokan used a type of basket trap that was attached to a long log over one of the many water-eroded deep granite basins. The log was secured by wedging both ends between large rocks:

> Several men would cut a long log and we'd heave both the cut [tapered] ends in a natural slot in the rocks on the shore line where the salmon came to rest before making their jump up the falls. Then we'd let the other end swing free, and it'd bump up against one of the many large [protruding] rocks out in the water. The men would then walk [along] the log to the rock. All along the log willow baskets were [partially] set into the water to catch the salmon. Before Coulee Dam, we'd sometimes make the baskets with chicken fencing—not willow—as they used to do years before. Some men would use a[n] iron gaff on the end of a long pole to empty the baskets because too many fish would make the basket too heavy to pull out of the water; even bust up the basket. After the salmon were caught, they'd be piled in a dish-like rock. When the hollow rock was filled, the salmon were distributed among the tribe present in the area, whether they'd helped or not. Even small children were given a share of the fish, usually the smaller fish (Ross 1968-2008).

An elderly Spokan woman explained how, in addition to using basket traps at Little Falls, the men:

> [...] also speared the salmon by standing on rocks just below the falls. They'd build new wooden platforms each fishing season, and [would] spear the salmon moving up stream. The spear head had a line attached to it which the device used in retrieving the caught salmon. The spear [harpoon] head was made from bone that was hollowed out so a sharpened wooden staff was pushed into. The head was carved with one or two sharp ears to withstand the fighting [salmon] without [being] pulled out. The point would go into the salmon's body and then turn like a fish hook to stay in the fish itself. Later, these heads were made of iron by a blacksmith in Reardon, he also made our iron digging-sticks (Ross 1968-2008).

Kane described a type of large fishing basket used at Kettle Falls, one that was "constructed of stout willow wands woven together, and supported by stout sticks of timber, and is so placed that the salmon, in leaping up the falls strike against a stick placed at the top, and are thrown back into the confined space at the bottom of the trap, which is too narrow to allow them to attempt another jump" (1859:217-8).

It should be noted that in later years, with the acquisition of chicken wire and hard wire, the Indians at Kettle Falls fashioned light-weight fishing baskets (Scholz, pers. comm.)

Fish Nets

There were basically seven types of *fish nets* (*xyép*): a *vertical dip net* (*múλ'mn*), a *span net* (*ltkʷúkʷ*-"otter"), a *stretched net* (*ʕʷoléwltn*), a *drag net* (*sqʼʷyóxʷ*), a stationary or *set fish trap net* (*xʷlíčn'*) called a fish basket net, a *net span weir* (*nqʷléw's*), and *basket* or *dip net* (*múlmn*). The kind of net used was decided by the type of fish sought, the configuration of the bed and bank, the stream flow, water depth, and in some instances net ownership.

Durham, not citing his primary source, described the use of two nets being used at the mouth of the Little Spokane, the up-stream net being woven more tightly, permitting only the smaller salmon to continue their migration:

> They would make two nets, one considerably higher than the other, and stretch these across the river, the higher net above the lower. The fish which they were after, known as the *s'chiluize* [salmon] in Indian, never went backwards; they were caught in the space between the two nets, and at the end of the season were dried and preserved for food during the winter (1976:146).

All netting material was made from Indian hemp that was first twisted into cordage and wound on a straight spindle. According to Smith:

> [...] this approach was also used by the Spokan in fashioning nets. He further noted the size and method of making a net: The meshes, which were very small, about 1/3 inch in diameter, were made of uniform size by knotting the cord around a stick. The net was from 1½ to 3 feet in depth and was rather more round at the bottom than funnel-shaped. To it a hoop, about 14 inches in diameter, was affixed. It was made of willow or service berry wood, not of cedar which would have been too light. The ends were lapped and tied (1950:339).

Becher wrote how A. J. Miner, who, in 1857, passed through Spokane en route to the mine fields of British Columbia, observed women being more active than men in using dip nets at Spokane Falls (Hunt 1966):

> I saw 300 Indians drying fish in the sun in the woods where the city hall now stands at Howard and Front. This was a great fishing place for the Indians in those days. The [women] took the fish in dip nets and after they cleaned them, the [men] would dry them in the sun (Becher 1974:244).

Despite the aforementioned account, Teit's claimed that "Dip nets were seldom or never used [...] The Nez Percé and Walla Walla used them for catching salmon, but the Spokan did not use them" (1930:349). Yet while visiting Kettle Falls, Kane (1859:219) described and illustrated how smaller hand-held nets were used at the end of the declining fishing season when the salmon were crowded together near the surface:

> These nets are somewhat like our common landing-nets, but ingeniously contrived, so that when a fish is in them, his own struggles loosen a little stick which keeps the mouth of the net open while empty; the weight of the salmon then draws the mouth close like a purse, and effectively secures the prey.

When describing the manufacture of certain materials used in making fishing nets, rarely is there any recognition of flax, as reported for the distant Wishram (Spier and Sapir 1930, 3:176). And yet, DeSmet, when describing fishing nets of this region, observed how "The Indians use it [flax] for making fishing nets" (1847:89). It was reputed that Whitman "raised a little flax, though not much, for want of seed" (Durham 1912, 1:77).

Scaffold Platforms

Several scaffold *platforms* were strategically located at Spokan Falls, ones that permitted the Spokan and other groups to *fish* (*q'q'm'éy'e?i?*), primarily for salmon, with nets sometimes called scoop nets that were hafted to a hand-held pole with hemp or pliable green serviceberry bark.

A 1900-1909 photograph (PO5.1.1) documents the use and construction of several *platforms* (*p'náp*) located immediately below Little Falls that were similar to the platforms used at Spokane Falls. Each of the two photographed platform poles was constructed of three parallel poles, approximately 18 to 24 cm in diameter, and 3 to 3.5 m in length. The larger ends of each horizontal *platform pole* (*sq'ʷix̌ʷálqʷ*) appear to have been wedged between appropriate horizontal crevices in the granite walls of the exposed stream channel. Each horizontal platform was stabilized with four single narrow secured planks spaced and secured every meter at right angles to the larger wedged support poles. The photograph shows a fisherman using a dip net with handles of approximately 3.5 to 4 m length. The outward end of the platform is located approximately 3 m from the cliff-supported base, permitting the fisherman to stand directly over a relatively large backwater.

When fishing from a scaffold, or standing atop rock boulders in midstream, the fisherman would always keep the spear handle as vertical as possible once a fish was speared, and then bring the spear handle up vertically hand over hand, trying not to swing the fish away from his body, since the weight of the catch could break the spear and would cause an unnecessary expenditure of energy. In these cases, leister heads had to be permanently hafted to the handles. After spearing a salmon with a leister, and bringing the fish to arm's length, the fisherman would, if possible, turn to a companion and then spread the outer two prongs to release the fish into his partner's grasp. If a fisherman using a leister was encumbered by his spear, he would kill the fish by biting it just behind the head to break the *backbone* (*snx̌ʷrmtáqs*), or else another fisherman would release the salmon and kill it using a club. "When a fish was caught, it belonged to the man fishing from the platform at that time" (Smith 1979:8).

Scaffolds were used to spear or gaff-hook dead or exhausted salmon after spawning. The latter method used an attached compound gaff made from a naturally occurring branched section of hard-wood, by bending and sharpening the end of the attached branch. The main hard-wood section was then reversed and the end was hollowed and secured to the tapered end of the pole handle. One end of a lanyard of plaited hemp was secured to the gaff, and the other end to the shaft in case the gaff became detached. While passing the gaff

389

below the surface of the water, the fisherman, upon feeling the gaff touching a salmon, would quickly jerk the gaffed pole upwards—usually with a fish. Gaffs were also made from sharpened deer horn, but were replaced by the 1850s with the more durable and efficient iron gaff (STHC; Hewes 1998:629). Sucker fish were commonly taken by gaffing. *Gaffs* (*snqit'mn*) were unknown until iron hooks were introduced by Europeans.

As noted, with the use of large logs for constructing fishing platforms, there is no indication that the Spokan ever used logs or any type of fish deadfalls, reported for the Flathead (Turney-High 1937:123).

Dip Nets

The manufacturing of dip nets required considerable skill, time, and patience, and the size of the net and the mesh was determined by the type of fish to be caught. According to size and length, dip nets were basically of four types, and all types were used mainly at Spokane Falls, Little Falls, and Kettle Falls. Smaller pole nets were approximately 3 to 3.5 m in length, made by starting at the feeble end, and splitting the dressed pole in half for about one meter. Smaller dip nets were racquet-shaped. The extreme end of the split was tied off to prevent further separation. These two parallel strips of wood were then formed into a hoop by using steam or soaking in hot water to make the two strips more flexible before attaching the two ends of those strips together by overlapping and securing them with Indian hemp. The process of bending and permanently reshaping the strips was made easier by first wrapping them around a circular stone, or inserting appropriate and varying lengths of wood inside the circumference of the circle. The resulting hoop became the frame that held and spread the net in an approximate circle. A small dip net was owned by an individual fisherman, usually the one who had made the net.

A second type of small single-handle dip net was fashioned from a dressed hard-wood pole, one that varied in length according to the net size. The net hoop was made from a section of carefully selected and split cedar, to an estimated thickness of approximately 3 to 4 cm, with a width of roughly 5 to 7 cm; large enough to later accommodate a bored hole of sufficient size to accept the tapered end of the net's long handle. Prior to affixing the pole to the net loop, it was necessary to shape the net hoop by first thoroughly soaking the length of cedar prior to steam-bending the section into a loop. Once the hoop was dry, a hole large enough to accept the tapered end of the long pole handle was bored and further secured by wrapping the pole end to the hoop with Indian hemp. This configuration made the frame stronger, and was, thus, preferred when netting larger fish, such as salmon. Apparently the supporting cross segment of the pole extending through the center of the net hoop seldom interfered with catching large salmon.

Larger dip nets were of two types, according to the type of pole used to support the net. One form had the net attached to a naturally occurring forked end of a section of hard-wood in which the two projecting limbs were overlapped as a splice and secured by wrapping with pitch-covered hemp. The opening of the net varied in size according to the maker, being approximately 60 to 80 cm in diameter and also depth, sometimes longer. Nearly all nets had a slightly curved bottom approximately one half the diameter of the opening. The attached pole varied from 3 to 5 m in length.

Another type of large, long-handled dip net was fashioned from a single shaft of elderberry, approximately 3 m in length. One end was end-split roughly for 1 to 1.5 m before being securely wrapped to prevent further splitting. Both wands were spread and held in place with several strategically placed secured cross sections of wood that maintained the appropriate shape of the net-loop. A variation on this was made by splicing and thereby securing two sections of Douglas fir to the net end of the pole. The ends of each extension were brought together, over-lapped with pitch-covered hemp to form an oblong net loop roughly 60 cm wide and 80 cm or more in length.

The dip net, or what some called a scoop net for taking salmon, was described by Lord (1867, 1:259):

> The salmon keep close to shore, to avoid the more rapid current, and to take advantage of the eddies to rest during their upward run. The Indian builds, or rather hangs, a kind of stage over the water, and lies upon it, around with a net like a shrimping net, about four feet diameter, fastened to the end of a log pole. He passes this

net down the current and allows it to be swept on as far as his arms can reach, then he hauls it out and plunges it in again, upstream as far as possible. In this way I have seen a savage take thirty-five to forty salmon an hour.

David Douglas observed and described a common method of dip-netting salmon from platforms along many streams of the Columbia River:

Before the water rises, small channels are made among the rocks and stones, dividing the stream into branches, over which is erected a platform or stage on which a person can stand. These are made to be raised, or let down, as the water falls or rises. A scoop net, which is fastened round a hoop held by a pole twelve or fifteen feet long, is then dropped into the channel, which it exactly fits, and the current of the water carrying it down, the poor salmon swims into it [...] when the individual who watches the net instantly draws it and flings the fish on shore. The handle of the net is secured by a rope to the platform, lest the force of the water should drive it out of the fisher's hand. The hoop is made of *Acer circinatum* [maple], the net of the bark of an *Apocynum* [Indian hemp], which is very durable and tough, and the pole of pine wood. The salmon is of good quality, generally weighing from fifteen to twenty-five pounds, sometimes more. I measured two—the first was three feet four inches in length, nine inches broad [...] (1904, 5, 1:267-268).

Teit commented on whether the Spokan used the dip net: "The Nez Perce and Wallwalla used them for catching salmon, but the Spokan did not use them" (1930:349). Yet in the same paragraph, Teit stated, "Dip nets were *seldom* [italics added] or never used" (1930:349), when referring to the Spokan. However, Teit acknowledges the use of dip-netting along the Columbia River, noting that among the Spokan "large nets were used a great deal at the mouth of the Little Spokan for catching various kinds of fish" (1930:349).

Double-Handled Dip Net

A double handle dip net was made by taking two lengths of dressed green Rocky Mountain maple (*Acer glabrum* var. Torr.); one length, approximately 60 cm long, was bent to make the forward edge of the frame, and spliced with the forward end of the other section. The handle lengths of the frame were then brought together and held by intermittently wrapping the mated lengths with pitch-covered hemp. The looped end, from which the net would be suspended, was broader at the forward end since an attached cross section (used as an auxiliary handle) separated the handles just back of the net some 40 to 50 cm. The basket-shaped dip net varied in measurement from 1 to 2.5 m in depth, and a meter and a half in width.

Dip nets were used most often in deep water at the base of water falls; some larger, double-handled with two supporting shafts to better sustain the weight of the captured salmon. Dip nets were used less frequently during torch-fishing when catching smaller fish, or when one man speared a large fish and his partner would net the fish (Elmendorf, pers. comm.). Dip-netting was often done during the day from canoes.

Curtis was fortunate to observe when the Spokan commenced to reconstruct weirs and use their dip nets: "as soon as the water fell below the highest stage, they began to construct weirs across the smaller streams and to fish with dip-nets at the rapids of the Columbia" (1907-30, 7:71), where the Spokane and Columbia Rivers converged.

Drag-Nets

A drag-net was essentially a long net roughly one meter to one and a half meter in height, without any type of frame except a thick vertical bundle of willow withes secured to each end of the net. It was stretched across a stream by one or more men at either end. Additional fishermen assisted—near mid-stream—by holding the topmost edge of the net above the water. A drag-net was most effective in water that was relatively shallow and not fast running, permitting fish to be speared as men walked downstream after the net. When speared or hand-caught, the larger salmon were passed or thrown from the net to be placed on tule mats or clubbed by men wading in the water, a process called *sq'ʷɬt'íč'm* or *snšéλč'm*.

Stretch-Nets

A stretch net was basically a seine net the Spokan, Sanpoil, and the Nespelem used during the fall when the river level was low. The large stretch nets were "used a great deal at the mouth of the Little Spokane for catching various kinds of fish. They were stretched completely across the river, one net being set some distance upstream above the other" (Teit 1930:349). Hewes, quoting Teit (1930:107), described how the Spokan "stretched large nets across the stream to intercept the fish, instead of building weirs of stakes and brush" (1998:629). Stretch-nets, as used by the Sanpoil, are described by Ray:

> The average seine was thirty or forty feet long and about six feet wide, made of cord spun from Indian hemp. The size of the mesh was usually about six inches. Ropes about twenty feet long were attached to each end of the seine on the upper side. At the loose end of one rope was tied a large block of cedar which was charred so that it might more easily be seen at night [...] The water surrounding it would reflect the light, but the black block would not. Along the upper edge floats were placed at intervals of about twenty inches, and directly opposite each float, on the lower edge, were placed sinkers. The floats were usually of cedar, oblong in shape, and about eight or ten inches across. The sinkers were round flat stones secured with a hoop of willow. The hoop or ring was shaped and then cord tied across it at right angles. Upon this cradle was placed the stone and over it other cords were passed and fastened to the ring. An efficient sinker which could easily be fastened to the net was formed thus without working the stone.
>
> Seines were used only at night. A place where the river was uniform in depth and the bottom smooth was always selected so that the seine would not catch on rocks on the river bed and overturn the canoe. Two men were necessary to manage the seine. They paddled to the point where the fishing was to be done, dropped the seine, then spread it by pulling the rope attached to the end. The seine was hauled ashore before it was emptied. A successful night's seining netted from forty to a hundred salmon (1933:69).

In 1854, Lt. Grover, a member of Governor I. I. Stevens's railroad surveying expedition, wrote of a gravel bar that divided the river channel just below Spokane Falls, a site that accommodated a stretch-net where the Spokan "Indians had constructed wing-walls of loose rock across one arm, leaving a raceway between their extremities, in which, by means of nets, they caught salmon in passing. A long trestle-work was built on the bank, upon which their captives were laid to dry" (1855, 1:312). A drag net often varied in length in accordance with the width of the stream.

Gill-Nets

Though there are only a few recollections of gill-nets being used by the Spokan, they had terms for this technology for catching early spring salmon during the historical period. Hewes, however, is undoubtedly correct when he states: "The gill net was also probably not used in aboriginal times, nor the ordinary gaff" (1998:622). Most commonly a gill-net was made from Indian hemp, but a type of woven *tule net* (*siʔy'áqs*) was used in relatively narrow and shallow water courses—one that restricted the upstream movement of salmon, whereas hemp gill nets were favored for deeper and wider sections of water. The hemp-net was held stationary with poles at either end, and the length was held upright by several fishermen who would *spear fish* (*łuʔmi t sw'éw'ł*) near the net or caught in the net, which was called *ʕʷoléw's*. Some gill-nets were anchored to the stream bed with rocks.

There are only a few accounts of how a gill net—being stronger than a tule net—was constructed primarily to catch large salmon, and preferred when fishing in often swifter and deeper water. The following account of gill-netting was gathered in the early 1950s from an elderly Spokan fisherman:

> Long ropes of hemp were woven together into a net-like fashion, making 3" - 4" squares, 2, 4, 6 feet wide, depending upon the depth of the river. These were tied to rocks on the bottom for anchoring. Some of these nets were long enough to stretch and tie down on each bank of the river. Some spanned the deepest part of the river, where [only] the largest fish travelled. These "nets" were made so that when a fish tried to go through the net, it would get caught by the gills (STHC).

392

After the construction of Grand Coulee dam, and the subsequent restriction of annual salmon migrations, there was no reason to use gill nets. Unfortunately, no examples of this type of net exist. Many years ago, a young Spokan man found a balled-up hemp fishing net in a deserted allotment house, but unfortunately never saved it. There is no record that the Spokan ever used fish-wheels—an introduced technique by Euro-Americans—as did some groups further downstream of the Columbia River.

Leisters, Spears, Harpoons, Gaffs, and Clubs

The Spokan used primarily three kinds of *fishing spears* (*nɫw'étkʷtn*). The first type was a leister—actually a trident or *three-pronged spear* or *pronged barbed fishing spear* (*sxʔƛʔqn* or *scc'ʔƛʔqn*) with the head attached to a long handle which varied in length from 3 to 7 m, commonly used for catching salmon. The head of the leister was a composite of deer horn or bone affixed to the main center shaft constructed of sharpened maple or elderberry wood or a select piece of deer antler. Each of the two slightly flared side shafts were similarly of maple or elderberry wood; each hafted with a short section of sharpened bone and secured with pitch-covered waterproof hemp.

This entire three-prong unit was called *čeλp'óqane*. Thrusting the leister down onto the dorsal area of a *fish* (*sw'ew'ɫ* or *č'em'tw'íl'iʔ*) caused the two outer prongs to secure both sides of the fish as the middle prong pierced the backbone. Once a fish was caught, the harpoon was then quickly run vertically up through the man's hands, and the outer prongs were spread to release the catch. Sometimes an attending man or woman assisted in releasing the fish. These multi-pronged leister heads were not detachable, being socketed onto the spear handle, which could float if the leister was lost from a person's grip. Or, if a leister head did become detached, it would still retain the fish since the barbed head was usually fashioned from cedar. The leister head was generally attached to a long lanyard of hemp held by the fisherman or someone else, and could be retrieved when detached. A harpoon head was removed at the end of the fishing season and carried home, and the cedar shaft was left vertically secured to a medium size lodgepole pine.

Burnett provided a delightful story of comparative technology and skills of spearing between white and Indian when spearing salmon. A white immigrant had carefully brought with him a steel gig (leister) he used for years when fishing catfish in the Mississippi River:

> [...] again and again he tried his skill, but always failed. The fact was that the salmon, one of the most muscular of fishes, with keen sight and quick motion, had seen the thrown gig in time, and had effectively dodged it. Our immigrant came back greatly mortified because the Indians could beat him in catching Salmon. He understood, after this trial, the difference between the agility of the salmon of the Columbia and that of the sluggish catfish of the Mississippi (1904, 5:79).

A second type thrusting fishing implement was a two-pronged spear, called *sxʷƛ'ulá*, one with two single shafts of sharpened, fire-hardened maple wood, each shaft having a double-pronged detachable head of wood or bone (Wilson 1866:298). The two shafts of horn-hardened maple or elderberry wood were attached to the shaft as two non-detachable prongs. Each barbed probe or spear head was completely wrapped six or seven times with Indian hemp, and were further secured and water-proofed by several layers of *warm conifer pitch* (*t'éɫtn*) applied successively until a thickness of 4 to 6 mm was attained. Securely attached to the spear shaft was a twisted hemp line, with the free end looped around the fisherman's ankle; thus, serving as a lanyard.

There were several other types of fishing spears, and if possible, they always had handles of cedar because they were lighter and floated if accidentally dropped when using. According to Smith (1936-8:677-678), the *two-pronged spear* (*wécč*), which varied from 4 to 7 m in length, was smoothed by repeatedly passing it between two smoothing stones made of grooved sandstone—similar to an arrow straightener. The two prongs were made from ocean spray with sharpened deer horn tips, and were securely attached to each prong at an acute angle with the tips facing inwards toward the shaft, and tightly wrapped with strips of wet *pitch bark* (*pčłín'*), which did not soak up water and become loose. The stout base ends of each prong were shaped parallel to the spear so that they came together in a flush manner, as seen in the example below (circa 1860). The head of the harpoon would be about 13 cm long. The shaft is wrought iron, with hardwood barbs atop balled pitch over the wood shaft.

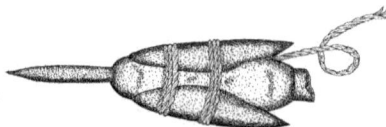

Figure 28. Fish spear head

The two prongs of a spear used for catching salmon were approximately 40 to 55 cm long, and for smaller fish approximately 20 to 30 cm, with the larger bottom ends being attached to the spear shaft, while the protruding sharpened prong ends were spread. This unit was then inserted into the hollowed end of the shaft that contained heated pitch, and finally stabilized by carefully wrapping both the shaft and the bottom of the prongs with strips of damp mountain ash bark. Often the two flat barbed prongs were made of split, shaped, and sharpened deer femur, covered with pitch and held in place by three separate wraps of triple-stranded Indian hemp.

A third type of fishing spear was actually a harpoon, one with a detachable head—single-pronged barbed wooden head—which remained embedded in a salmon if driven in with adequate force. A harpoon was never thrown, only thrusted, and was used more in the spring to catch sockeye and spring salmon. This type of harpoon required a different method fishing, as explained by an elderly Spokan, who said how his grandfather would slowly and cautiously move the butt end of the harpoon through the water until he "felt" a fish, when he quickly reversed the harpoon and thrusted it through the side of the fish. Burnett observed the skillful and patient use of this kind of harpoon:

> With this spear the Indian fisherman lies down or sits close to one of these narrow channels with the point of his spear resting near where the fish must pass. In this position he remains motionless until he sees a fish immediately opposite the point of the spear, as the fish slowly ascends the rapid current; when, with a quick motion of a juggler, he pushes the spear clear through the salmon before the powerful fish can dodge it. The buckhorn at once slips off the end of the pole on the other side of the fish the first flounce he makes; but he is securely held by the thong attached to the pole. No spear could be more skillfully designed or more effectively used than this (1904, 1:79).

When not in use, a harpoon head was removed, and the Douglas fir harpoon shaft was stone-weighted and hung from a tree to prevent warping, as described by one elderly man, who remembered how the lower free-end was sometimes secured with a fairly heavy 'pendulum-rock' to keep the harpoon from swinging if there was any strong wind. Every day, before use, the shaft was darkened with pitch. It was claimed that this implement was more successful for *torch-light fishing* (*npawaʔŋ'eč*) at night when wading in *shallow water* (*xxm'ul'eʔxʷ*) or from a canoe. Gaffs, however, were most effective when fishing from a platform when fish were stopped by a weir or for recovering exhausted salmon from shallow water. The gaff-hook was pressure socked to the pole and attached with a lanyard of Indian hemp or *bitter cherry* (*Prunus emarginata* [Dougl.] Walpers - *peklhán'*) bark twine. Commonly, the gaff was moved slowly through the water until a fish was "felt," and then the gaff was quickly jerked up to properly impale the fish. Gaff-hooks were blackened as needed. The gaff-hook was most effective in retrieving exhausted or dead salmon after spawning, and easily pulled onto a bank, and every family had at least one such tool.

Another type of fishing spear was simply a shaft of horn-dressed maple or elderberry with a bone spear point:

394

[...] the Indians were employed in spearing the salmon, which is almost the only mode used for taking them during the first of the season. In this they are very expert; and to see an Indian thus engaged, is an interesting sight. He stands on the edge of the foaming pool, with his spear poised and pointed, his body in constant and graceful motion, and the eye intent upon his object. When he discovers a fish with[in] reach, he instantly darts the spear with unerring aim, and secures his prize (Hale 1846, 4:455).

Wooden fish clubs varied in form and effort of construction, and commonly made quickly from appropriate lengths of driftwood found at the site. Both men and women used clubs to stun or kill a fish caught by other means. An excellent illustration of a harpooned salmon being clubbed by a naked fisherman is an expressive and detailed sepia wash sketch by Kane, as shown by Nisbet (2005:100). Clubs were most effective when large numbers of salmon were being caught at collective weirs, and being thrown to women who would then club or spear the catch. One elderly lady happily recalled how her mother and her friends had endearing names for "old and trusted" fish clubs, as they named their digging sticks; but never the same name. She also explained how when clubbing exhausted fish in shallow water, a woman would chant the name of her club to attract the fish; even the dead fish were presumably so attracted by the women's singing/chanting. Diomedi observed the balance between strategies of individual and collective fishing: "The technologies of individual spearing [was] forbidden if it interrupts collective method, particularly [near] traps" (1878:26).

Line-fishing, Hooks and Bait

Prior to the arrival of the horse and trading with Euro-Americans, all fishing line was made from braiding two long tightly rolled lengths of Indian hemp or flax, thoroughly waxed with hard tallow or rubbed with pine pitch to prevent the line from snarling or twisting too freely, which would weaken the line if it became kinked. The section of fishing line that would be in the water was usually made less visible by rubbing the line with green leaves just prior to fishing.

Men and women, as well as young boys, would hook-and-line fish throughout the year—including ice-fishing—primarily for small non-migratory fish such as minnow and Northern pike minnow. Though hook-and-line produced fewer fish than the seasonal weirs and nets, the number of fish caught by this method warranted the expended time and effort and—in some instances, given the rights of usufruct—promoted social interaction with non-Spokan who came to fish the Spokane River.

The strategy and use of line-fishing involved one of three methods: The first and most common procedure was more successful in smaller streams, deep pools, and back eddies using a line of braided Indian hemp or flax with only a single baited *bone hook* (*čq'q'm'éy'e?m'*), and often a *fish pole* (*čt'úpple?tn* - "line" and *čq'q'm'éy'e?tn'* - "pole") fashioned from dried fir approximately one meter in length. Traditionally, fishing line was made by braiding 2 long, thin sections of Indian hemp or flax of unequal length, which was lengthened by adding the additional single section of hemp over one uninterrupted line so the ends of line were never adjacent. After acquiring horses, fishing line was often made by braiding either three or four strands of horsetail together, a material that did not rot so readily as hemp and was impervious to destruction by gnawing rodents. Smith (1936-8:339) noted how the Kalispel would wrap the fishing line from the tip of the pole to the hand-hold to ensure control of the line if the pole happened to break.

The Spokan used a variety of different types of fish hooks and bait, depending upon the type of fish sought. Multiple hooks were typically used for *smaller fish* (*sxʷimíne?*), being less likely to break the *fish line* (*čt'úpple?tn*). For the same reason, a *single set hook* (*ča?cqín'tn'* or *ča?acqé*) made from either ocean spray or mock orange proved more advantageous for use on larger fish. The use of the set-hook exemplified delayed predation, and usually involved a single set-hook attached to a pole or a series of set-hooks attached to an anchor line so that the baited hooks were approximately 30 to 40 cm above the stream bed. A set-hook arrangement often involved using four to six set-hooks that were properly spaced and suspended 30 to 40 cm off the stream bed by a line. A float was attached to the line and suspended in the water midway between an anchor point and the shore. After twilight, set hooks were positioned and baited by passing the hook of the barb through a small piece of whitefish or chub. The barb was 3 to 5 cm long and was fastened to a larger shank by means of drilling holes to accommodate several strands of horse hair. Upon becoming wet, the wood swells and; thus, affords a tight grip or closure. The shank of the compound hook was made of either serviceberry or a skillfully worked piece of bone of about 3 to 5 cm long. At the bottom of the line was another piece of serviceberry or bone, hafted at a 45° angle, and to the end was attached a sharp tapered barb; both the hafted pieces and the barb were attached together with tightly wound Indian hemp or stripped willow bark.

Single-hook set-line fishing often required a hemp line being secured to the upper end of the hook's shank with the other end of the line being tied to a tamarack or pine pole that had been stripped of bark before being thoroughly dried and fashioned. At water level, a line ran from the vertical pole to a rock on the bottom of the stream. Another line was tied to the top of the pole, and then run out to the stream to either a *cedar bark float* (*snpéwmn* - "fish float." Fish floats were fashioned from inflated fish bladders, serving also as child's toy (*pepéw'e?*) (Egesdal, pers. comm.). Nor was it uncommon for a man to quickly fashion a float from a small bound-bundle of dry tules, which served to prevent the set-hook from settling on the *stream bottom* (*ništétk*ʷ). Fishing with hooks was one method of *hand-fishing* (*?ecnčlšétk*ʷ), one with no apparatus—simply a sinker and a hand-line baited with bits of crayfish gathered by partially submerging a long stick with fresh meat tied to it.

A method of set-line-fishing required a long set-line that was attached at both ends—one to a stationary stake driven into the river's bank, and the other end anchored to a large stone in the water well away from the stream bank. The set-line could accommodate multiple hooks, sometimes as many as twelve hooks, baited as already mentioned. This method of fishing required periodic attention, given the potential size and number of fish, which, if caught and not harvested, could possibly destroy the fisherman's rig. Methods and success of set-line-fishing were the responsibilities of an individual. As with trapping, another person might—upon seeing a full set-line—empty the line and kill the fish before delivering the catch to the known owner.

A fishhook was often made from a secondary branch of hazelnut, and then baited, except for catching salmon, because salmon did not eat once they had left salt water. According to Johnson (1972:449), a Canadian biographer, who quoted Lord:

> The Indians all say that salmon never eat when in the rivers; and I could never discover that they had any recorded instance, or even tradition, of a salmon being taken with bait [...] I have opened a very large number of salmon at various Indian fishing-stations, on their first arrival, and during every stage of their wasting vitality, and after death ended their sufferings; and not in a solitary instance did I discover the trace of food in the stomach or intestinal canal (1866, I:45).

When relating his observations of fishing a year later, Lord explains that migrating salmon, once in fresh water, would never eat, and thus would never take bait:

> It is curious the Columbia salmon never take a bait after they leave the salt water. I have tried every expedient I could think of to tempt them, but always without success; and from careful inquires made of the different tribes of Indians on both sides of the cascades, and from the officers of the Hudson's Bay Company at the various trading posts, I am quite sure salmon are never taken with bait after they leave the sea (1867:260-1).

Years earlier, Kane (1859:219 and 1971:124) made a similar observation of the anadromous salmon and their not eating once entering the Columbia River:

> The young fish return to the sea in the spring. Strange to say, nothing has ever been found in the stomachs of the salmon caught in the Columbia River; and no angler, although frequent trials have been made by the most expert in the art, has yet succeeded in tempting them to take any description of fly or other bait.

Obviously, there was some variation in the material and shape of the hook, depending upon the materials used and the type of fish being sought. Most hooks—prior to the introduction of iron and steel hooks—were fashioned from sharpened ocean spray, yew wood, or splinters from a deer's lower front leg. For large fish, a simple but effective articulated double hook (a type of cross-hook or toggle hook) was fashioned from two pieces of ocean spray, elderberry or serviceberry, each approximately 6 to 9 cm in length, that had four tapering sharpened ends. The two pieces of wood were first laid parallel to each other and affixed together by wrapping a short length of Indian hemp around the center of the two shafts. While angling, and when the *fish are biting* (*k'ʷʔéyi*)—most notably *jumping for insects* (*ʔecč'ɬk'ʷk'ʷeʔcín'iʔ*)—these X-shaped gorges are swallowed by the fish, and each sharpened shaft spreads and secures the catch. Quite simply, "The fish-hook consisted of two sharp bones crossing each other at right angles" (Curtis 1907-30, 7:71). Elmendorf documented the use of "two pieces of thornberry baited with grass hoppers or worms" (1935-36, 2:670).

Figure 29. Articulated fishhook

A common hook was made from where the base of an Osage orange or ocean spray forked from a larger branch, which was then whittled with a hole or butt that could accommodate the attached *fishing line* (*čt'úppleʔtn*). Some hooks had one or more barbs to hold the *bait* (*m'l'w'éy'n'* or *t'k'ʷqnéyeʔtn*) as well as the fish.

Though the Spokan had various types of hooks, they preferred using a hook made from the thorn of a blue-black thornberry bush, and the *blackberry thorn* (*sxeʔnéč*) was then baited with *grub worms* (*Cordyceps* sp. - *sxʷyálqʷ*), *night-crawlers* (*Lumbricus terrestris* - *q'l'éylmxʷ*), *grasshopper* (*Aeropedellus clavatus* - *t't'ác'eʔ*), *caterpillar* (*Malacosoma californicum* [tent caterpillar] - *čy'l'y'l'k'ʷtéɬp* or *čyilyilq'ʷteɬp*), *salmon eggs* (*ʔék'ʷl id.* fresh or *xʷel'ék'ʷl' id.* dried), *doddle bugs* (*Myrmeleon formicarius Myrmeonidac.* - *ppátiʔqs*), *crickets* (*Acheta assimilis* - *sy'el'w'én'eʔč* or *sérsr*), *sage grasshopper* (*Melanoplus rugglesi* Gurny - *l'ʔuw'eʔlewe*), sectioned lizard tail, other types of meat, and trout gizzard (Smith 1951:310). An unknown species of a poisonous cricket was used for baiting hooks (STHC), and was used until the 1920s by the Spokan.

Oliphant recorded how, in 1877, Lt. William R. Abercrombie observed the Spokan using grasshoppers to bait hooks: "As fast as we dropped in a hook baited with a grasshopper we would catch a big trout" (1927:166). In fact, "The greatest part of the work was the catching grass-hoppers," as Lt. Abercrombie related to Herbert Gaston (1927:166).

Lord, always an astute observer of fishing activities, wrote of using a fish eye [salmon?] to *bait a hook* (*m'el'w'ey'n'ʔem*), but "Grasshoppers they took readily, and I have often caught a trout, [...] when only one leg of the insect remained on the hook; the white meat from the tail of the river crayfish is a very favourite diet" (1866, I:83). Bait varied according to the fish being sought, type of hook, and what was available as bait. Lord made the following observation of how the Spokan baited hooks:

> The hook (made of bone or hard-wood) is baited with salmon-roe. The Indians never use the roe fresh; dried in the sun it becomes extremely tough and acquires a very rank oily smell. The fish take it greedily, and in this manner large numbers are captured. Another bait equally fatal is made by cutting a small strip from the belly of a trout, and keeping the shiny part outermost—winding it tightly round the hook, from the barb, to about an inch up the line, securing it by twisting white horsehair closely around it (1886, I:85).

The *fishing pole* (*čq'q'm'éy'eʔtn'*), though not a later introduction, was used solely for resident species, particularly after the depletion of anadromous fish following the construction of Grand Coulee Dam. In the historical period, even prior to the dam's construction, sinkers for fishing lines were first made from pounding and folding the lead of spent *bullets* (*m'l'm'íl'qʷ*) (.45-70 and .45-90 caliber) salvaged from the Army military firing range backstop at Fort Spokane.

397

Traditionally, the most commonly used *sinker* (*čp't'áple?tn*) was an elongated grooved or holed stone, tied approximately 20 cm above the baited hook. The size and weight of the particular sinker chosen was determined by the stream flow, bed and banks configuration, and the estimated strength the line required.

According to Hewes (1998:622), fish poisons were presumably not used by the Spokan, even though the Spokan had a variety of poisons for other purposes. Yet Turner (1978:103) recalls chocolate tip roots being used by the Okanogan and Kalispel as a fish poison. Bouchard and Kennedy (1984a:30) documented how the Colville similarly poisoned fish with an infusion of this root. When young, the tubers of this plant are safe to eat. There are no known oral or written accounts of the Spokan using wormwood as a fish poison.

Bow and Arrow Fishing

Arrows used for fishing were never hafted, rather simply *sharpened* (*nxʷƛ'aqsn* - "to sharpen a point") to catch mainly the slow moving suckers and carps that were found by fishermen wading in relatively shallow water and back waters from early spring until late autumn. Even when line-fishing, a sucker fish seldom took a bait, so the arrow was the most effective means for catching this particular fish. An ordinary bow was used, but the arrow was never attached to a line, as little skill was required to retrieve a wounded sucker. Some elders, however, said they used to catch sucker and carp by hand in shallow pools in late summer by hanging over their arms over areas of shaded water, and children attempted to catch this fish using forked sticks. It was claimed that carp often became easily tired when chased by children in shallow water, and, thus, became easy prey.

Torch-Fishing

After the major salmon runs, usually for one to two weeks in late fall when streams were low, men engaged in *torch-fishing* (*hecur'úsi* or *urúšm*) for whitefish and salmon in smaller streams, and for sucker in early spring. The most notable sites were Little Tschimakain and *Big Tschimakain Creek* (*sč'm'qín'* or *snkʷtnétkʷ* - "big creek"), the Little Spokane River, Blue Creek, and *Sand Creek* (*?ełčíw'e?m'n'* - "place of small fish") where whitefish and a small fish called *čč'iw'e?*, and salmon would congregate at *spawning beds* (*sncpúmntn* - "the milk") made milky and cloudy from salmon *spawning* (*ntu?t?úli* - "cloudy" or *cpúmni*). Another major site for torch-fishing was at the confluence of the Columbia and Spokane Rivers where the Sanpoil and Lower Spokan had constructed a weir of nearly 30 m across the Spokane River, and attracted salmon into the traps using pitch torches at night (Bohm and Holstine 1983:2).

Men would torch-fish from either the banks of streams with narrow constrictions, or astride logs or larger log rafts that were joined together by hemp and floated into the river, or from anchored rafts in wider areas of water using a two-pronged leister or a sharpened bone-set gaff. Since the water surface should ideally be smooth, they fished at wider, slow-moving stream sections. Smith noted that "There could be no moonlight, for it prevented the fish from being blinded on the one hand and the spearers from seeing the fish on the other" (1950:326). Some men would use this method of fishing in smaller streams until early winter or when ice formed, and again in early spring when thawing commenced. Walker too observed the Spokan torch-fishing (Drury:1976:114).

Sometimes certain long sections of stream beds were covered with crushed granite to enable the spearmen to better see the salmon, which were presumably blinded as they swam from an area of bright sun into *shade* (*čsč'áylqʷkʷ* - "shade tree" or *sk'ʷer'łxʷ*). Many years ago there still existed several areas of naturally exposed hard clay beds that served the same purpose. Sunshades or extended ramadas were erected on narrow streams at traditional fishing sites to prevent the sun's glare from obscuring the fishermen's view of the fish. Where a side trench were excavated, "The bottom of the trench was lined with quartz and other light-colored stones to provide greater visibility" (O'Neill 1962:7).

When attempting to *fish with pine pitch torches* (*hecʔurʼusi*), leisters or spears were the common predation technology used. It was reported how single-handled dip nets were used for catching smaller fish by scooping (Elmendorf, pers. comm.). Night fishing from a raft required that an earth-filled basket be attached to the end of a meter-length pole for extinguishing any embers that may fall onto the beaten cedar bark or tule mats from a pitch-wood pine torch embedded in another earth container, or by one of the fishermen who held a torch of one of the fishermen. The hand held *pitch torch* (*cʼékʼʷsšnʼ* or *λʼʔústn*) was made by splitting several sections of pitch pine branch or stump into narrow, thin strips that were bound together at the smaller end to make a torch approximately one meter in length.

When using a dugout canoe, one man was responsible for maintaining and guiding the craft and sat aft while poling or paddling. The other man situated himself forward—in front of the torch—in order to be less visible while waiting to spear a fish. These roles were periodically reversed due to the intense eye strain and fatigue upon the man fishing. Once a fish had been speared, or *hooked onto* (*čqʼlʼxʷntém* - "it was gaffed") by a *gaff* (*snqʼítʼmn* - "big hook"), the commotion would often frighten the other fish away, but they would quickly return once the commotion had ended. After catching the fish, the spear man would remove the fish, kill it with a *wooden cudgel* (*sspʼqíntn*), and then throw it up onto the bank or in the craft. On occasion, several families would spend days in a camp by a stream while the women gathered roots and the men deer hunted. At night the men fished and the women often assisted the men in cleaning and later drying the fish on racks.

Ice-Fishing

It was not unusual for the shallower sections of the Spokane River, and many of the feeder streams, to ice-over to a depth that would support ice-fishing. Cox recalls what a Spokan man said about how his people had been betrayed by the whites. The eloquent speech belies the severity and near-dire consequences of a previous winter, and the consequences of ethnocentrically perceived cultural relativism to both man and beast:

> Three snows have passed away since the white man came from their own country to live among the Spokans. When the Evil Spirit thought proper to distress the white people by covering the waters of the rivers with ice, so that they could not catch any fish, and sent snow all over the mountains and the plains, by means whereof their horses were nearly destroyed by the wolves, when their own hunters in fact could not find an animal, did not the Spokans take advantage of their afflictions? Did they rob them of their horses like Sinapoil dogs [sic]? Did they say, the white men are now poor and starving; they are a great distance from their own country and from any assistance, and we can easily take all their goods from them, and send them away naked and hungry? No! (Cox 1957 [1832]:210).

Elders claimed no fishing shelters or windbreaks were built when ice-fishing; but some insulation was afforded each man who would sit on several cattail mats placed close to his fishing hole. As soon as he caught a fish by a leister or baited line, the fish was quickly removed. Though it is not known if the Spokan ever employed jigging for smaller fish, they probably did with dry bait. Trout and suckers were most often taken, usually when they were swimming upstream, a time when fish were concentrating more on eating, and, consequently, said to be less cautious. The three-pronged leister was used for ice-fishing (Teit 1930:349).

Schaeffer described how the Flathead preferred a method of winter fishing by jigging through an opening in the ice, using a "piece of thorn bush with a thorn attached, with a line of twisted horse-hair [...] attached to a line with sinew. A piece of meat or a grub worm served as bait" (1934-37, I-102:29).

At various times in late winter, often after a warm Chinook wind, fish were occasionally trapped above frozen ice in the melted surface, a condition known as *čɬʔoc cqeʔíčnʼ*, when fish could be easily taken; such a wind was called a foehn wind (or *Föhn* in German), or a Chinook wind, i.e., a rapid, descending, warm, dry wind, generally known as a "cleaning-up" wind (Elliott 1932, 3:249); a wind with orographic lift. It was said that the "white man brings climate him" (Elliott 1932, 3:248).

Fish-Lassoing

Though not a traditional method of fishing, and one used only under certain circumstances in the fall when the Spokane River was at low ebb, men on horses used lassos to catch salmon returning downstream during spawning season. The procedure was for a man to ride his horse into a wide and relative shallow section of the river that had a school of salmon; keeping his mount still, he gradually lower his lasso into the water among the slow-moving salmon, waiting until a fish entered the vertical loop, at which time the fisherman quickly pulled the rope up with the fish he wanted. Some claim salmon were caught in shallow waters with a noose of Indian hemp at the end of a long pole, before the use of the horse.

One elder recalled using this procedure of fish-lassoing from a horse, carefully explaining that one never practiced fish-lassoing near any type of fish entrapment, for if a horse urinated or defecated in the water, salmon within the immediate area would temporarily leave. There were several photographs (circa 1920s) of several Spokan men in mid-stream lassoing salmon from their horses just below Spokane Falls.

Major Spokan Fisheries

The Spokan utilized at last ten anadromous fisheries, but the major fisheries the Spokan depended upon were Kettle Falls, Little Falls, Little Spokane River, and Spokane Falls. The Spokan were not only dependent upon annual anadromous fish migrations, but also on various species of resident fish, such as sturgeon, suckers, trout, and whitefish, often taken with weirs and other methods during the spring and winter months. Other important fishing sites were Sand Creek, Blue Creek, Latah Creek, and Little and Big Tschimakain Creeks (Scholz 1985:39). Just downstream between Blue and Sand Creek was a *sacred mount* (*čɫʔem'tu*) that overlooks the Spokane River where a young boy would conduct his vigilance to hopefully gain fishing power.

Kettle Falls Fishery

Just south of the confluence of the Columbia and Kettle Rivers is Kettle Falls, reputed as "having been the second largest salmon fishery on the Columbia River and an important trading center, at least since some time in the eighteenth century" (Chance *et al.* 1977:16; Scholz *et al.* 1985:26-33). In 1811, Thompson was the first white person to visit Kettle Falls, describing how the mutual exploitation and sharing of a common resource served to socio-economically facilitate multi-task grouping, and "At this village were natives from several neighboring tribes, at a kind of rendezvous for news, trade, and settling disputes, in which these villagers act as arbitrators as they never join in a war party" (Glover 1962:336). It was estimated that as many as 1,000 Indians participated (Eells 1894:95).

When Parker wrote that Kettle Falls "is occupied by some half dozen men with Indian families" (1838:293), the men who must have been Europeans, for later he wrote of the "Kettle Indians, who numbered five hundred and sixty" (1840:307). Parker in 1836-7 estimated the number of Kettle Falls Indians as five hundred and sixty (1840:307). Hale, when speaking of the resident population, contended that "The number of Indians actually residing about the falls, is about one hundred and fifty; but during the height of the fishing season, there are often a thousand, consisting of all the Spokane tribe who are generally included under the name of the Flatheads" (1846, 4:455-6).

On 22 June 1811, Thompson was informed that Kettle Falls was called *lith-kpy-ap* by the inhabitants of the area; meaning "basket net" (Elliott 1918, 1:11-12). The word was pronounced with a deep guttural sound and a slight accent on the middle syllable; a Salish name derived from *ilth kape*, meaning 'kettle' and *hoy ape*, meaning 'net' (Thompson 1950:275). The name was undoubtedly a description of several deep water-formed depressions in the stream beds where fish were caught by a net or basket kettle; hence the present name, Kettle Falls (1950:275). Yet, according to Hale, the people at Kettle Falls "are called "*Quiiarlpi*," (Basket People) from the circumstances of their using baskets to catch fish" (1846, 4:444). Suckley claimed the

400

Colville (whom he called *Squeer-yer-pe*) name for Kettle Falls "is *Schwan ate-koo*, or deep-sounding water" (1855, 1:299). Kane, however, claimed, "The Indians have no particular for them, giving them the general name of Tum-tum, which is applied to all falls of water" (1971:123).

The term "Basket People" was appropriate, since a lithograph of Kettle Falls by John Mix Stanley (1862, 12(1):158-159, Plate XLVII) shows two Indians, a man with a net on the end of a 4-meter pole, and a woman with a head-tumpline basket (Bushnell 1924).

Figure 30. "Kettle Falls, Columbia River"

In 1829, Work visited Kettle Falls, where approximately 1000 salmon were taken daily, using what he called a fishing basket:

They have a kind of basket about 10 ft long 3 wide and about 4 deep of a square form suspended at a cascade in the fall where the water rushes over a rock, the [sic] salmon in attempting to ascend the fall leap into the basket. to leap 10 or 12 feet high. when [sic] the basket is full the fish are taken out—A few are also taken with [a] scoop net and speared (Ellis 1915a, 6, 1:37).

Meyers (1919, 3:197), in a description of the falls and the different downstream currents that determined where the salmon "are thrown to the surface and in sight by the boils, not whirlpools, when speared. The Indian name for the falls is *Swah-niquet* (pronounced as unique)."

Kane provided a brief description of the technology, yield, and weight of salmon yield: "1700 salmon have been taken from this basket in one day. I weighed three. One was 35, the other 32 each. One man has the whole of control of this fishery. There is one spot where if a basket was placed they might catch 3 or 4000 a day" (1971:314). Some, "Salmon as heavy as one hundred pounds have been caught in the falls") (Howay *et*

401

al. 1917, 3:188-9). These baskets "were constructed of hazel or birch osiers woven together with withes and roots" (Elliott 1918, 1:11). Work, when visiting Kettle Falls on 6 August 1826, again described how the basket was used:

> The baskets are of an oblong form of different sizes according to the situation where they are to be used. Sometimes ten feet long, four or five feet wide and are as deep; they are suspended in a favourable situation in the falls, where salmon in attempting to leap the cascade jump into the basket (Elliott 1915, 1:37).

The well travelled and observant DeSmet (1801-1873) witnessed how a basket was emptied of approximately 250 salmon seven or eight times a day (Chittenden and Richardson 1905:482). Simpson, Governor-in-Chief of the HBC territories in North America, remarked how at Fort Colville, about 4 km from Kettle Falls, "salmon are so abundant, that as many as a thousand, some of them weighing upwards of forty pounds, have been caught in one day with a single basket" (1847:150).

While visiting Kettle Falls, DeSmet, in an ethnocentric and critical fashion, described the methods and results of drying salmon for winter consumption: "In the immediate neighborhood of a camp the air is infected with the scent of salmon in a state of purification; they are suspended on trees or on scaffolds, and to this unwholesome and detestable food has the improvident Indian resource, when the days of his long lent commence" (1905, 2:558). Earlier, Kane, speaking of scaffolds, noted how "the salmon are afterwards sewed up in rush [tule] mats containing about ninety or one hundred pounds, and put up on scaffolds to keep the dogs from them" (1859:314).

Fortunately, DeSmet (1843:418) provided another brief but accurate and probably the most detailed description of the fishing technology, and the prodigious production of salmon at Kettle Falls, information seldom provided by a painting regardless of the artist's skill, given problems of depicting relative numerical scale:

> The basket is made of willow, from fifteen to twenty feet long, five or six wide, and about four feet deep, with a high back upon one side, which is designed to rise above the surface of the water. A stick of timber is firmly anchored in the rocks below the falls, extending out over the stream twenty to thirty feet. To this the basket is suspended, and so far submerged as to leave the back just above the water upstream, while the opposite side is several inches below the surface of the water, and downstream. The ascending salmon rise up the side of the basket and spring into it, where they are held, their passage up being arrested by the high back; and as they never turn their heads downstream the current they are retained securely. After the basket in this manner is well filled, a man descends into it and hands out the fish. Two hundred salmon, weighting from six to forty pounds each, have been caught in this manner in a few hours. They are also speared in great numbers. It was a common occurrence [...] to take three thousand salmon in a day, since there was no limit to their numbers, and a whole band of Indians were engaged in the work. The fish were divided equally among the women each day, the number of females in each family forming the basis of distribution.

Gibbs described how the *Squeer-yer-pe* (Colville) Indians would "kill hundreds of thousands of these fish [salmon] by spearing them [...] In many places the water appears to be alive with them, and the shores are thickly lined with the dead and dying fish" (1855, 1:299). Earlier, in 1843, DeSmet had given the same quote (Durham 1912, 1:121).

According to Curtis (1911, 7:56-60), the major fishery on the Columbia River was at Kettle Falls (Johnson 1969:60) where different autonomous groups annually camped and mutually exploited migrating salmon, using different methods of fishing. The main groups that fished at Little Falls were the Columbia, Palouse, Lower Spokan, and Sanpoil. *Kettle Falls* (*sx̌ʷnétkʷ*), being the major fishing station in the eastern Plateau, was also mutually exploited by *numerous groups* (*xʷʔúleʔxʷ* - "many lands"), namely the Coeur d'Alene, Colville, Flathead, Lakes, Nez Perce, Okanogan, and Sanpoil (Wilkes 1845, 4:474). Ray presents a more inclusive list of groups who exercised usury privileges for fishing at Kettle Falls: "Each fishing season saw many persons from of the Kalispel, Coeur d'Alene, Spokane, *snkált*, *sqasílt*, Sanpoil, Nespelem, *snqʼaiétkʷ*, Methow, Chelan and Okanogan groups congregated at Kettle Falls" (1933:116). Father DeSmet observed collective utilization, noting how, "From eight to nine hundred savages were there assembled for the

402

salmon fishing" (Chittenden and Richardson 1905, 2:480), and, between episodes of baptizing babies, he declared an unqualified appreciation of the Columbia River salmon, describing how they were caught by the Indians:

> An enormous baskett [sic] was fastened to a projecting rock, and the finest fish of the Columbia, as if by fascination, cast themselves by dozens into the snare, Seven or eight times during the day these baskets were examined, and each time were found to contain about 250 salmon. The Indians, meanwhile, were seen on every projecting rock, piercing the fish [with spears] with the greatest dexterity (Chittenden and Richardson 1905, 2:481).

The importance of Kettle Falls as a major fishing station to so many people was fortunately realized by:

> [...] an aged chief, with a name far too guttural to be unwritten, who in the year 1842, had made me a formal cession of the neighbouring soil. On that occasion, he had given the Company [Hudson's Bay] the land and the woods, because the whites would make a better use of them than himself; but he reserved the Caudiere Falls as necessary to his own people, remarking that the strangers, being able to get food out of stones and sand, could manage to live very well without fish (Simpson 1847:152).

An early description of the settlement at Kettle Falls was made by Thompson, who described the main village and the unusually large multipurpose drying racks and raised living structures, which verified not only the yield of salmon, but certainly the adequate facilities for properly drying their large catches. It should be stressed that it was essential to air-dry salmon in such large structures, for it was critical to prevent prolonged exposure by direct sun, which would quickly separate the skin from the flesh, resulting in spoilage of the meat by ever-present fly larvae. Also, direct sun would force oil to the surface, thereby making the fish rancid. The relative size and structural complexity of these living and drying sheds were noted by Thompson, indicating their importance:

> Here for the Country, was a considerable Village of the Natives who have given their name to these Falls; which are about ten feet of descent in a steep slope, in places broken: This village is built of long sheds of about twenty feet in breadth by from thirty to sixty feet in length, they were built of boards which somehow they had contrived to split from large cedars drifted down the River, partly covered with the same and with Mats, so as to withstand the Rain; each shed had many cross poles for smoke drying the Salmon (Glover 1962:335).

Years later, in the summer of 1847, Paul Kane, an early and astute observer, explorer and artist, painted various aspects of the fishing activities, lodges, and *smoking salmon* - (*sncqqiy'eɫceʔtn*) at Kettle Fall, describing how "Salmon is almost the only food used by the Indians [...] the two months fishing affording a sufficient supply to last them the whole year round" (1859:219). Kane, when illustrating and describing the lodges at Kettle Falls [Pl. XXXI; Fig. 124; CRIV-308 to 312, 315], explained how "The lodges are formed of mats of rushes [tules] stretched on poles. A flooring is made of sticks, raised three or four feet from the ground, leaving the space beneath it entirely open, and forming a cool, airy, and shady place in which to hang their salmon to dry" (1859:216).

A further major contribution of Kane's critical observation of fishing technology is an informative watercolor of a suspended fishing trap and platform at Kettle Falls. The three-sided enclosed caged platform appears to be a rectangular poled structure approximately 2 m at each end with only a slightly longer open front to accommodate salmon entry, and the platform floor was constructed of a series of hafted parallel poles that support the three, which were made of hardwood lattices to permit easy draining. The entire platform was suspended at an angle with the open and highest side to the river to prevent salmon from escaping. This painting illustrates how the platform was attached to a series of (seven?) slanting large timbers that apparently were secured at their upper ends with piles of stone. The later paintings and description made in 1847 by Kane of the Kettle Falls fishing, and the cultural landscape with dwellings and fish-drying racks, are invaluable and illustrate the multi-floored structures and use of large moveable tule mats to control wind flow and the amount of exposure of sun to drying salmon. This artist described the importance of Kettle Falls, and its summer yield of salmon:

403

Fishing [...] is under the exclusive control of Sepays, the "Chief of the Waters," The salmon commence their ascent about the 15th of July, and continue to arrive in almost incredible numbers for nearly two months; in fact, there is one continuous body of them, more resembling a flock of birds than anything else in their extraordinary leap up the falls beginning at sunrise and ceasing at the approach of night. The chief [xaʔtús] told me that he had taken as many as 1700 salmon, weighing on an average 30 lbs each, in the course of one day. Probably the daily average taken in the chief's basket is 400. The chief distributes the fish thus taken during the season amongst his people, everyone, even to the smallest child, getting an equal share. By the time the salmon reach the Kettle Falls, after surmounting the numerous rapids impeding their journey from the sea, a distance of between 700 and 800 miles, they become so exhausted that their efforts to leap these falls, their strength often proves unequal to the task, and striking against the projecting rocks they batter their noses so severely, that they fall back stunned and often dead, and float down the river, where they are picked up some six miles below by another camp of Indians [...] None of these salmon coming up from the sea [700 to 800 miles] ever return, but remain in the river and die by the thousands; in fact, in such numbers that in our passage down the river in the fall, when ever we came to still water, we found them floating dead or cast up along the shore in such vast numbers as literally to poison the atmosphere (1859:217-8 and 1971:124).

Thompson's close and perceptive observations further dispelled certain notions of what he called early superstitions, which he may have harbored regarding the violation of any procedural practices while fishing, and perhaps certain ill-based notions of some of his readers as regards Indians:

[...] experience has taught them the delicate perceptions of this fish, even a dog going to the edge of the water, the salmon dash down the current, and any part of one of them being thrown into the water, they do not return until the next day, especially if blood has been washed; in spearing of them, if the fish is loose on the Spear and gets away, the fishing is done for that day [...] I looked upon a part of the precautions of the Natives as so much superstition, yet I found they were not so; one of my men, after picking the bone of a Horse about 10 AM carelessly threw it into the River, instantly the salmon near us dashed down the current and did not return until the afternoon; an Indian chief dived, and in a few minutes brought it up, but the fishery was over for several hours.

It is a firm belief of the natives of this river, that of the myriads of salmon that annually leave the salt water ocean and enter fresh water rivers, not one ever returns alive to the sea; they all proceed to their respective spawning places, accomplish this, and soon after (a few weeks) die of exhaustion. That is the case of those who come, and beyond these falls there can be no doubt, as after the spawning season the shores are covered with them, besides all that are carried away by the stream. It does not appear that they take any nourishment after they leave the sea as their stomachs are always empty. Whatever the history and the habits of the salmon may be, they form the principal support of all the natives of the river. The dogs that with impunity eat all other fish die when they eat raw salmon but when cooked the dogs eat it with safety (Glover 1962:335-7).

Reverend Elkanah Walker wrote in his diary of the fishing technology, yields, and storage he observed while visiting Kettle Falls. Interestingly, he compared the yield of energy from fishing to that of planting crops:

It is astonishing the number of salmon which ascend the Columbia yearly and the quantity taken by the Indians. They are one of their greatest means of subsistence. It is not uncommon for them to take a thousand a day. Some of them, I should think, would weigh 20 pounds. It is an interesting sight to see them pass a rapid. The number was so great that there were hundreds constantly out of the water. They will leap quite a distance out of the water and pass rapids where it would seem impossible for anything else to pass. It is not uncommon to see them strike against a projecting rock and roll back again. The Indians are quite expert in taking them. They have different modes according to the nature of the rapids. Their mode in the Spokane [River] is to make a wear [weir] and then spear them. In other places they take them in what is called a basket which is suspended to a projecting rock where the salmon pass and in leaping the top and fall back where they soon die from the pressure of others on them. In many places they spear in the night by a fire light. Their mode of preserving them is to cut them into thin pieces, taking out all the bones, when they are hung up until they are perfectly dry. Then they are cached in a pile of stones where they remain until needed for food. The Indians are not so improvident as one might suppose. During the season for obtaining their provision they are actively engaged. It costs them more labor to obtain the spontaneous production of the earth than it would to raise the same amount by cultivating the soil (Drury 1976:113-4).

The significance of fishing at Kettle Falls was observed earlier by Hale (1846, 4:445-6), who noted that the resident population of approximately one hundred and fifty Indians, during the height of the fishing season, often exceeded a thousand "consisting of all the Spokane tribe, who are generally included under the name of the Flatheads." Wilkes (1845, 4:444) and Hale (1846, 4:472) provided a further description of a type of fishing basket used at the Falls, and the eventual distribution of fish:

[...] the number of Indians actually resident at the falls is 150, but during the height of the fishing season there are often nearly a thousand. The fishing apparatus consists of a large wicker basket, supported by long poles inserted into it and fixed in the rocks, [sic] which the fish, in attempting to jump the falls, strike, and are thrown back into the basket. This basket, during the fishing season is raised three times a day, and at each haul, not infrequently, contain 300 fine fish. A division of these takes place at sunset each day, under the direction of the Chief man of the village, and to each family is allotted the number it may be entitled to: not only the resident Indians, but all who may be there fishing, or by accident, are equally included in the distribution. In September and October the salmon still claim their attention: although they are after having deposited their roe emaciated and about to perish, yet they are dried for their winter consumption.

Lt. Johnson (4:455-6), of the same expedition, recounted the technology, procedure, and approximate yield of fish baskets:

The lower part, which is of the basket form, is joined to a broad frame, spreading above, against which the fish, in attempting to jump the falls, strike and are thrown back into the basket. This basket, during the fishing season, is raised three times in the day (twenty-four hours) and at each haul, not infrequently, contains three hundred fine fish (Wilkes 1845, 4:444).

A later observation of basket fishing technology and salmon yields was given by Angus Bahn McDonald (1816-1859), who was "six feet, four inches tall, with long red hair and bushy whiskers. When excited, his language was a mixture of Gaelic, English, French and various Indian dialects (Fuller 1931:81), as well as German, Greek, Italian, some Hebrew" (Howay *et al.* 1907, 3:223), and was principal agent at Fort Colville trading post at Kettle Falls from 1852 to 1872. McDonald wrote of the numerous inherent dangers and extreme efforts required while fishing:

Salmon are taken at these falls by basket and spear, The spear in rest in the hand of a naked Indian standing on the foam-drenched cliff. As the eager fish glances to the surface of the whirlpool, looking to his leap, he is pierced and dragged quivering ashore. Now and then, however, the spear man loses his life. I have known two athletic Indians seal their fate in this way [...] The basket is a vessel made of stout hazel or birchen osiers hung to the lower edge of the Falls by a rope of the same boughs. The fish that fall in their leap are cast back and fall by scores into the ever open basket. When it is full, two strong, hardy men strip and club in hand go down through the drenching cold foam into the basket to knock the yet living in the head and heave them up or hand them up with the already dead. One basket has caught a thousand salmon a day in this way. About fifteen minutes of that shivering spray is all they can stand and then a new relay of fresh men take their places. These splendid fish are so thickly crowded in the billows at the foot of the falls that I often thought they could be shot. This, however, the Indians would not allow. Probably the salmon is the cleanest and shyist [sic] of all fish. (Howay *et al*, 1907, 3:198-199)

James Bernard, a former chief of the Colville and Lakes tribes, provided a detailed personal account of the fishing technology and yield of salmon at Kettle Falls in 1885, which illustrates the dependence upon salmon:

There would be over a thousand families of Indians there then. Each family got its share of fish from the baskets, besides what they caught for themselves with spear and gaff hook [...] some families got as high as 15 fish a day. Each family would put up for [the] years food [...] 250 to 500 dried fish per family. The Indians then traded salmon to the white settlers and Hudson's Bay people for tobacco, flour and powder.

I compute the value of the surplus salmon from our fisheries used in trade or barter at about one thousand pounds of dried fish a year per family. About two thousand pounds of dried salmon were kept by each family for its own food—the average weight of a dried salmon was about ten pounds [...] four pieces each weighing about 2.5 to 3 pounds. The fish varied in size, the average of the big salmon was about 50 pounds [...] some freshly caught fish weighed 60 to 70 pounds or more.

Comparatively few salmon come up the Columbia River to Kettle Falls now [1930] sometimes we get five or six fish a day in the baskets for all the Indians of all the tribes [...] one day we got 30 fish [...] some days we get none. Before the whites destroyed the salmon fishing, 300 to 400 fish a day were caught in the baskets at Kettle Falls, besides the hundreds caught with spears and gaff hooks. Some Indians used to catch 20 to 30 salmon a day by themselves that way. Now a person may fish all day and never get a fish (1930: n.p.).

Gibbs commented how "The fishery at Kettle falls is one of the most important on the river" (1967:19). Although he noted the importance of stone houses, he unfortunately never described them. A long-time resident of Kettle Falls, Harry Crofoot, recalled certain non-traditional innovations in the fishing apparatus, as well as varied fishing technologies:

The Indians shared a trap [...] It was probably six feet high or maybe more; it came down to a "U" shape at one end. There were three men at the front of the basket and another man at the front of the basket and another at the bottom end. Then they fastened hog wire from the top clear down to the bottom. The fish would jump up and hit the hog wire and fall into that "U" shape at one end. After they got several in there, they would take a gaff and get 'em in the gills and drag 'em out and back up onto the rocks and kill 'em (Bohm and Holstine 1983:2).

The most useful summary of fish production at the main fishing station at Kettle Falls is provided by Scholz and his colleagues:

The average catch per day at Kettle Falls for the communal fisheries was about 1000 fish. This figure does not include the numerous auxiliary fisheries located near Kettle Falls nor the fish caught by individual spearsmen so, conceivably, it could be doubled to about 2000 fish. Most of the reports above suggest that the peak of the run lasted for approximately 60 days. Multiplied by the average daily catch the annual harvest would be 60,000 fish if the 1000 figure is used or 120,000 fish if the 2000 figure is used. To be conservative in providing for a minimal estimate of the catch an average of these two values, or 90,000 fish will be used. This number seems reasonable, if low, considering that Suckley (1855) reported that the Kettle Falls Fishery produced "hundreds of thousands" of fish annually. This figure also does not include a late winter/early spring fishery for steelhead that was utilized principally by members of the Colville tribe (1985:32).

According to Bogn and Holstine (1998:2), Glen Ford, an elderly Spokan man, remembered how there were actually two falls prior to any dams:

[...] an upper and lower falls. There were also large 'kettles' that were ground right out the rocks [by the river]. Some were three or four feet across and maybe five to seven feet deep—that's where in the fall. The salmon would go upstream to spawn [...] you could see 'em jumping. The river was just full of fish, absolutely full of fish. The Indians speared some with spears. Then had a basket they hung below the falls. When the salmon didn't jump far enough they'd fall back.

Kennedy and Bouchard noted how "In the 1980s, despite the greatly reduced number of migrating salmon, a First salmon Ceremony was reintroduced at Kettle Falls" (1998:242). This revitalization ceremony—long after the end of the successful salmon runs—was an admirable public demonstration of faith and respect for the past when salmon was a major food for thousands of people who annually fished at Kettle Falls.

Little Falls Fishery

Before Grand Coulee Dam was constructed, the last major fishing stations for salmon on the Spokane River was at Little Falls, *Spokane Falls* (*sƛ'x̌ʷétkʷ* - "fast water" or *stɬuputqu* - "swift water") (Meany 1922, 13:213). Little Falls fishery commenced in early spring, and was also an important fishery, annually attracting many different groups—mainly Columbia, Palouse, Lower Spokan, and Sanpoil (Ross 1870, I:489) who fished, traded and socialized. Steelhead, eels, and suckers were taken until the main salmon season commenced late June or early July.

The importance of stored salmon from Little Falls fishery, was noted in 1862 by L. P. Beach while conducting a cadastral survey of the north terraces of the Spokane River contiguous with Spokan occupation site, and noted, "The Indians put up at least 250 tons of dried fish during the fishing season" (1869, 17:238).

The importance of Little Falls fishery as reported by Winans to Simms, was that this fishery was used by eight different ethnic groups: the Calispells [sic], Coeur d'Alenes, Colvilles, Lakes, Meshons [Metows], Okanogans, and Spokanes (Simms 1875:361).

Behind Little Falls, to the north, are the remains of numerous house and storage pits, an area called *snt'k'ʷene?tn?* where a large permanent village was once located. Several kilometers above the Falls is an important rock that resembled a turtle, known as *sp'r'k'ʷa*, and a burial ground that was destroyed and covered with earth during road construction (Ross 1993). This area was where a battle between the Spokan and Columbia Indians took place. Oral history emphasizes the importance of the Little Falls fishery by noting how even during winter months there were at least ten permanent houses at this site (Elmendorf 1935-6, 2:15b).

Little Spokane River Fishery

The importance of multiple weirs and basket traps at Spokane and Little Spokane Rivers is noted by Work, who stated how as many as 700 to 800 salmon were taken daily (Elliott 1914, 2:99), and by Scholz and his colleagues:

> The Little Spokane was known for steelhead and the main river for salmon. This was a permanent fishing spot used in summer and fall for salmon and late winter and spring for steelhead. It produced as many as 140 to 200 salmon a day at the height of the fishing season (1985:14-5).

An early observation of a large weir and the people at the mouth of the Little Spokane River, known as *snxʷmene?ey* or *snxʷmeme?* or *snxúmé* or *snxʷnénm*, was made by Alexander Kennedy of HBC, which is important since he provided valuable descriptions of the types and numbers of fish taken as well as trading with other groups who collectively utilized this important fishing station:

> The methods they pursue in catching these Fish is by barring up the River with Stakes, which are ingeniously fixed to resist the force of the current between these stakes which extend right across the River: a few openings are left at one end for the Salmon, which are always going up the River to get through. At the end when these openings are left, a square Place is enclosed with Stakes which arrest the salmon in a kind of pond, where they are speared and taken out, but previous to the Indians spearing the Fish they hut up all the little openings that are left for them to come in at (Kennedy 1823:23).

George Heron, a government interpreter, whose father Francis (Frank) Heron was an early fur trader with the HBC, spent his entire life living with Salish-speaking people, and married a Spokan woman (Lewis 1920, 1:32). Being a polyglot who spoke English and French and numerous Salish dialects, he became acculturated to Indian life, and eventually "was acknowledged to be one of the best Indian [government] *interpreters (súxʷnmicinmsxʷ* or *nmicínm* = pl.) in the entire Northwest" (Lewis *vide supra*) for many years. From age ten until age fifty, he spent time every year (*?axlspéntč*) observing the fishing activities at the mouth of the *Little Spokane River (snxʷméne?* or *snxʷménm*), and when en route to and from Montana (Lewis 1920, 1:31). In 1863, George Heron observed how at Little Falls the various Indian groups gathered to exploit the seasonal run of salmon, and the methods of constructing their weir:

> The flat between the two rivers (Spokane and Little Spokane Rivers) was a meeting place for Indians— Colville, Spokane, Pend d'Oreille, Coeur D'Alene, Moses' and Nez Perce tribes. They met and camped here in the greatest friendship. They were not on good terms with the Kootenay and Yakima tribes, and had no intercourse with them. During the summer season there were from a hundred to a thousand Indians camped on the flats by the River catching and drying fish. The principal trap was maintained in the Little Spokane a short distance above the mouth. It was made by setting up piers across the river formed of poles erected in the form of a teepee. Horizontal poles were lashed to these piers and a basket work of willows bound on them. There were two lines of these fences across the River. The upper one was tight; but the lower one had frequent small gates made by lashing sticks to the upper horizontal pole and leaving them loose at the bottom, so the fish could push into the enclosure going up stream; but the current would close the gate after them. The fish came into the trap in countless

thousands and were speared by the Indians [...] The trap was [later] torn out by the whites while Mr. Waters was agent (Lewis 1920, 1:33-34).

During late summer (August or September) in 1826, David Douglas observed the construction and subsequent fishing activities at Little Spokane: "the natives constructed a barrier across the Little Spokane, placing it at an oblique angle so that the current would not wash it away. After the traps filled with salmon, the Indians would spear them" (1914:364).

Reverend Peter Burnett, an Episcopalian minister, recorded the salmon runs of both the Spokane and Little Spokane Rivers, and the conflict of government agents who were attempting to move the Spokan onto the Spokane Indian Reservation. He also described the conflict between Indians and settlers, and the ensuing destruction of Spokan weirs in the Little Spokane and main Spokane River at the junction of the Little Spokane, which, if successful, would presumably have forced the Spokan to leave a traditional village and relocate to a designated but restricted area to become farmers. Lewis, quoting Reverend P. Burnett (1904), stated how:

In the early [18]80s the salmon ran thick in both the Little Spokane and Spokane Rivers. During the salmon season, although the Spokane Indian Reservation had been created and an effort was being made to force the Indians onto the reservation, the Indians still maintained fish traps across the Little Spokane River and main Spokane River. There were 25 to 35 teepees during the salmon season. Major Simms and Major O'Neal of the Colville Indian Agency made constant efforts to get the Indians to move onto the [Spokane] reservation and the Indian teepees and salmon traps were destroyed in an effort to force the Indians to leave the spot.

I recall some trouble over the Indian[']s fish traps [...] the Indian[s] had a number of these traps [...] The early settlers, including the people at Spokane Falls, demanded that the Indians close their fish traps at least once a week to permit some of the fish to go upstream, as their traps caught virtually every fish that came along. When the Indians refused to close their traps one day a week, a party of settlers interested in fishing [...] came to the traps and tore out three or four of them.

Later the Indian agent tore out the remaining traps in an effort to force the Indians to quit the spot and move onto the Spokane Indian Reservation. There were so many fish in the stream during the fishing season that no one, except some of the oldtimers who actually saw the fish, would believe me if I attempted to tell you about it. The fish were so numerous that it was no sport whatever to catch them. The Indians caught and smoked them by the ton (Lewis 1925:17).

Further description of Spokan fishing technology at Little Spokane River was provided by Wilson, who was attentive in observing the variations of fishing technology along the course of the Spokane River:

At the junction of the Great [main] and Little Spokan Rivers, an elaborate contrivance is made for catching the salmon on their way both up and down the stream; on their way up they are caught in a similar manner and by the same arrangement as that described as in use amongst the *Okinagans* and *Shimilkameens*; but in addition to this, runs are made, with stones, through which the salmon have to pass on their way down, and at the end of these, which gradually contract, a small stage, slanting slightly upwards from the mouth of the run, is erected. The salmon coming down with the current carried on to the stage, where he is speedily dispatched by the attendant Indians. In the erection of these runs, much ingenuity is shewn [sic] and considerable time and labour expended. Trout, suckers, etc., are taken with hook and line, or by a weir and basket trap; the latter was employed very successfully in a small stream at *Sinyakatan* on the Pend' Oreille river. Two barriers of willow wands were made across the stream, about five feet from each other, in both of which a hole was left for the fish to pass through, and the one in the upper barrier was made to lead into a large wicker basket somewhat of the mousetrap pattern, the fish having to squeeze its way through a small hole which closed immediately behind it. The spear used has a detached head fastened to the pole by a piece of string, similar to that in use amongst the 'Cowitchians' (1866:298).

More specifically, the Spokan understood the life cycle of the salmon and often constructed gaps in their weirs that allowed salmon smolts and small fish to pass freely downstream to the ocean (Scholz, pers. comm.). Hewes (1998:629) mentioned this important fishery at the confluence of the Little Spokane and Spokane River, where a weir or wing-dam with basket traps were set. And as late as 1915—prior to the construction of Little Falls Dam—it was reported at Latah Creek that the white salmon, or dog fish, used to come up the river in great numbers. I have seen them so thick in the river (Cowley 1916:104).

As late as 1925, Lewis remarked about what he called a Great Fishing Place at the mouth of the Little Spokane River:

> The place [*čxʷyep* - "mouth of Little Spokane River"] was also a great fishing place. The Indians had to [sic] fish traps [weirs] across both the main Spokane river and the [mouth] of the] Little Spokane river, and there were fish for every one. When I first settled there the fish were so plentiful that it was no sport to catch them. I have the salmon, big ones weighing many pounds, lying together one above the another, so closely were they packed on their efforts to reach the spawning grounds (1925b:104).

Spokane Falls Fishery

It is fortunate that during the 1853-5 government sponsored Mississippi to the Pacific Railroad Survey, John Mix Stanley made a detailed painting (see Figure 5, "Falls of the Spokane," in Chapter I) of Spokan Falls, one that clearly illustrates the stratigraphy of the parent rock where Indians positioned themselves with spears, gaffs, and netting to catch migrating salmon as they attempted to work their way up the two major channels of water.

In the late 1880s to 1890, it continued to be an important fishery for different Indian groups, as well as non-Indians, particularly in early spring:

> In days prior to the coming of the white man to the Northwest, one of the most travelled Indian trails was the one leading from a point near old Fort Walla Walla to the Columbia Valley. This trail crossed the Spokane River near Spokane Falls. In the spring, when the salmon were running up stream, the fish were congregated by the thousands below the falls. This campground was a favorite rendezvous of members of many tribes that inhabited the region of the Inland Empire. The salmon could be easily speared and smoked for future use, and the native tribes took full advantage of that fact to secure an abundant supply (Scott 1968:6).

Given the physical features and water course of Spokane Falls, various fishing methods were used, as cited by Stimson:

> The whole Spokane Tribe, and often members from other tribes, would gather in June by the river to fish for salmon. Spawning salmon once swam all the way to the Spokane Falls, and catching them there were spears and nets, then cleaning and drying them for storage, was a major industry that employed hundreds, all taking orders from a Salmon Chief (1985:160).

Several fish biologists for this area, Scholz *et al.*, best summarized the importance of both Little Falls and Spokane Falls, the two major Spokan Indian salmon fishing sites:

> Despite the fact that there they were forcefully and illegally evicted from some of their favorite sites after the establishment of the Spokane Reservation, a large number of Indians continued to fish for salmon and steelhead in the Spokane until 1911 when Little Falls Dam blocked migratory fishes from the upper portions of the river. Even after this period fishing continued on the lower portions of the Spokane River until Grand Coulee Dam, constructed on the mainstream Columbia below the confluence of the Spokane, permanently blocked salmon from the upper Columbia, including the Spokane Basin, in 1939; although the Indian fisherman could be counted in the few hundred instead of thousands (1985:20).

Lt. Grover, in a letter to Stevens, emphasized the importance of this fishery, to other groups, saying how "the Spokan camp was surrounded with its thousand horses, [...] and just below the falls, where the bar divided the channel, the Indians constructed wing-walls of loose rocks across one arm, leaving a race between their extremities, in which by means of nets, they caught salmon in passing" (1855, 1:512).

Despite the later reduction of salmon in the Columbia River due to commercial fishing and different pollutants, great numbers of salmon continued to reach the Spokane Falls fishery, where as late as 1896 Spokan and other groups annually continued to gather for the express purpose of mutually exploiting this critical food—as well as trading:

Spokane Falls was famed far and near among all the Indian tribes as the best place for a *stamoos* [italics added] [salmon trap ...] The salmon were caught and shared by all in common, including visitors who worked on the traps and assisted at the catch [...] an *ill-ah-mih-hum* [salmon chief] was appointed who distributed the communal catch to all those present at the fishery [...] The salmon season generally lasted six weeks to two months, and in that time immense quantities of fish were caught, and the surplus was dried in the sun and packed for future use [...] In the fall *scale-a-wis* [italics added] - the white salmon season, when the white salmon run [most likely either coho or fall Chinook (Scholz, pers. comm.)] usually in numbers less than the red salmon, but the Indian got his chance for another supply of fresh fish and also an opportunity to add something to his store of dried food (Chase 1896:15).

This renowned fishery at Spokane Falls was visited annually by the Spokan, one of whom was a young girl, who later described her memories:

When I was five years old [1860] I was at Kettle Falls with my grandmother and watched the Indians spear salmon. There seemed to be a sort of shelf of rock on which the Indians stood. I could see the salmon leaping, but the spearsmen struck only at the ones that fell back. I asked my grandmother why that was, and she said, "Those salmon are the weak ones—they have no strength left to fight. If they speared the strong ones they might be pulled from the rocks into the foaming water below. Several men stood on the rocks and the salmon were taken from the hooks and passed along up the banks to the women, old men and children, who carried them away to be prepared for salting and drying (Wynecoop 1985:66).

Scholz (1985) and his colleagues have carefully researched the studies of McDonald (1894), Gilbert and Evermann (1895), Stone (1883:476, and 1885), Craig and Hacker (1940:216), Fulton (1968:24, 1970:16 and 22, and 1994), and many others in explaining the devastating effects upon upriver salmon and steelhead production that were wrought by fish wheels, hydroelectric dams, commercial fishing, and pollution from different industries, particularly logging. The aforementioned authors "felt that the commercial fisheries located from the mouth [of the Columbia River] to Celilo Falls intercepted the upriver runs and point to these fisheries as the principal culprit in causing declines in the upriver runs" (Scholz *et al.* 1985:103). The following quote summarizes the disastrous effects upon anadromous fish populations, ones that ultimately proved disastrous for the diet and economy of indigenous groups in the eastern Plateau:

There is no reason to doubt [...] indeed, the fact is beyond question [...] that the number of (chinook) salmon now reaching the headwaters of the Columbia Basin is insignificant in comparison with the numbers which some years ago annually visited and spawned in these waters. It is further apparent that this decrease is not to be attributed to either the contraction of the area accessible to them or to changed conditions in the water which would deter the salmon from entering them. We must look to the great commercial fisheries prosecuted in the lower river for an explanation of this decrease, which portends inevitable disaster to these fisheries if permitted to continue. The relations of the decreased number of salmon in the headwaters to development of the commercial fisheries is brought about in a very instructive way by an analysis of the salmon canning industry from 1866 to 1893. After 1866 each succeeding year operations were extended until reaching their culmination in 1884 [when 40.3 million pounds of salmon were harvested]. From this time on the catch declined, reaching its lowest point in 1889 [20.6 million pounds]. Up to 1888, practically the entire pack consisted of king or chinook salmon and the fishing season did not extend beyond the first of August. In 1889 the packers began canning bluebacks and steelheads to make up the deficiency in the supply and extended their operations to the first of September (McDonald 1894:18).

Latah Creek Fishery

Latah Creek (Hangman Creek) was a major fishing site for numerous groups besides the Middle and Upper Spokan. The inhabitants of the Latah Creek area were known as *sntuʔtʔulixʷi*. The fish trap at Hangman's Creek was called *nxanxʷm* (Elmendorf 1935-36, 2:12).

A detailed description of salmon and Spokan fishing technology at the mouth of Latah Creek was recorded by Clair Hunt, who surveyed the area—including both the Colville and Spokane Indian Reservations—during the late nineteenth and early twentieth centuries:

The trap consisted of two barriers across the stream about 100 yards apart. Each barrier was made in panels, at ends of which were supported by large tripods set in the water and resting on the river bed. The panels were made of two parallel and horizontal poles about thirty inches apart. Woven willow mats attached to the poles on the downstream side made a continuous fence across the river. The mats extended down to the bed of the river. They were woven in a open pattern to permit the flow of water and yet closely enough to prevent the Salmon passing through. The lower barrier had a large opening in the center to allow the salmon to enter. This opening was closed with a mat when it was desired to prevent the escape of salmon. The upper barrier had no opening. Frequently, the lower barrier was jarred when a big fish ran head on against it before he had found the opening. When the fish were to be taken out, the opening in the lower barrier was closed. Men went into the cold water naked except for loin coverings. With their hands they caught the fish and threw them out rapidly on to the grassy bank (Hunt 1936:12).

James Glover, who lived near Latah Creek, was one of the early pioneers of Spokane who developed fur trade with the Coeur d'Alene, and he wrote in 1873:

[...] Spokane was the great rendezvous for all the Indians in this part of the country. They would come here each autumn from miles around to lay in their winter's supply of dried fish [...] The white salmon, or dog fish, used to come up the river in great numbers. I have seen them so thick in the river that the rocks on the bottom would not be visible [...] The Indians took the fish out at a shoal near the flat at the mouth of Latah Creek. They had traps set there and besides they spear the fish and hook them out in all sorts of ways. They would build high scaffolds of willow limbs and dry the fish without salt (1985:35, 38).

Chapter XII: Firewood, Cooking, and Food Preservation

A major factor in the preparation, cooking, and preservation of food was fire-making, a near-daily task requiring the acquisition of firewood, which was a major energy source sought and gathered constantly. There is no recorded or remembered explanation for the origin of fire, though usually an elder could recall an indiscriminate act by the mythical *spilyeʔ* who first provided fire to man through an error of the creature's judgment.

Firewood

The two main sources of firewood were *driftwood* (*stxʷúxʷ*) and dead timber, either *fallen* (*kʷcíč*) or standing, particularly an old dead tree without bark, one that has been *bleached white by the sun* (*paʕlalqʷ*) (STHC). Such trees were relatively easy to splinter into *kindling* (*sƛ'ƛ'uʔk'ʷeʔ* or *swr'šictn* or *c'qʔtáɬq* - "wood stick"). Elders referred to a dead lightning-struck tree as being *thunderstruck* (*scc'áqʼ*). After storms, driftwood was occasionally available, and collected by women and young boys venturing along the river's edge gathering and then rafting the wood up or down stream to the village or *campsite* (*ƛ'ʔelpm* - "to look for a campsite"). Women often simply secured a bundle of firewood with a *rope* (*pséščn'tn* - "wood gathering pack instrument") (Egesdal, pers. comm.). The following quote illustrates the constant concern for firewood, the importance of which cannot be overemphasized:

> The news had been given the day before that a fine dry tree had blown down and this meant wood for all. The high wind was a friend of women for it crushed the trees into small pieces. The women took their straps and started before the dawn cast its gleam upon the eastern sky. They had filled up the hill where snow and mud lay frozen. The crumbled tree was about halfway up that long hill. Moveable parts of the tree were soon carried down to the campground. By ten o'clock, according to our time, the carriers had gone back to gather the last bits of wood (Wynecoop 1985:5).

A major and continuous task was to *gather firewood* (*psešm*), which was accomplished almost daily by women. Upon finding any wind-fall after a storm or high wind, collectors stacked the wood as evidence of ownership, which later would be collected and carried back to camp by the man's wife. Before transporting *firewood* (*sč'čp'n'ús*) any distance, large pieces were reduced in size by splitting with stone mauls using elk antler wedges. Long sections of dead trees were shortened by holding the butt end of a long section against one of two aligned standing trees, with the second tree serving as a fulcrum (about one-third the length of the section), and then applying pressure by pulling until the section broke.

Standing dead trees and trees struck by lightning were felled by first pounding and shredding to facilitate burning away above the base, where the diameter was smaller, and the bark, particularly with Douglas fir, is considerably thinner than at the base. When a long-standing dead tamarack, one that had turned a *weathered silver color* (*pqlálqʷ*), was dropped, much of the timber was fractured by the impact when falling (Arnold Wynecoop, pers. comm.).

Many years ago, an elder related how his great grandson had commented on how noisy and even loud the split pine kindling was that the old man had used to make the evening fire. To this, the elderly man replied, "It's making a noise—as you call it—because an owl once sat on the small limb now being used as tinder, and if you listen very carefully—instead of talking, you would hear what the owl was saying."

There are few recorded accounts of what must seem today to be a rather mundane activity. But securing adequate amounts of firewood, for both immediate use and for long term storage, was a constant concern for any hunting and gathering people. When returning home, men and older boys were responsible for bringing firewood, which they would deposit just outside the village, to be brought in from there by the women.

In addition, it was a daily practice for elderly women to collect and transport firewood using a long and continuous strip of rawhide thong to secure the load to their backs. One half of the wood-carrying strap was looped through the other end; this free portion was supported as a thump-line from the woman's head or passed over her shoulders and *carried on her back* (*hecpséši* or *q'ʷéłtm* - "to pack on the back"). Traditionally, when assembling the load, the woman would place *one last loose stick atop her load* (*č'c'ápqnm* - "long object lies") (Egesdal, pers. comm.) before returning to the village or camp. The reason for this last stick is unknown today, except to perhaps better secure the load. Elderly women might spend an entire day collecting any available wood—including small twigs—to bring back to her village. Smith noted how "Old people, restless and wandered around in the woods near the camp and piled wood against a stump or tree to dry [...] They just want something to do" (1936-1938:520). The importance of firewood was further emphasized in an oral history by a Spokan woman:

> The weather was very wet and the women were driven to the hills in search of wood because the river (Columbia) had risen and soaked the drift piles in the backwater of the Kettle (famous fishing station). This wood had always supplied the winter fires. The women paddled upstream, loaded their canoes, and drifted back to a point nearest their tepee. Then carrying it on their backs it was stored in great piles near the doors. This was a daily task for the surplus accumulated against the heavy and hard days of the winter that often brought sickness. The task of gathering fuel was a sacred duty granted women, since the true approach to harmony was through service well done [...] She must race miles to gather broken pieces of wood, trusting to chance for provision. If a log was easy to split she used the horn wedge and stone maul to fashion it into thin slabs (Wynecoop 1985:2).

The same author reiterated the significance of collecting firewood and maintaining heat in the dwellings during the cold winters, "The tepees were extended and made warmer, and getting wood was an endless task. Piles of fuel were brought and covered with old grass mats. Long trips were made to gather pitchy knots and pieces of wood for torches" (Wynecoop 1985:36).

There had been an unspoken protocol regarding the giving of wood and the acceptance of wood from a non-kinsperson. To give or accept firewood could imply that the recipient was not able to gather his or her own wood, because they were either incapable or lazy. But when firewood was collected by a small group of men—as it usually was—every participant received a portion relatively equal to his domestic needs and responsibilities. In addition, any man or woman who was infirm and without family assistance, was given firewood by the community; this applied to other types of resources too, such as food. An elder who was experiencing difficulty in starting a fire of gifted but wet wood from a much younger man, remarked that such a fire was called *čqʷitn'usm'*. Firewood gifted by a friend was said to burn warmer, seldom smoked, and the "flame images" danced more lively than from one's own collecting.

Open firepits in wood and grass dwellings had two constant worries: the danger of *fire* (*sur'šict* or *sʔulíp*) to the structure, and the possibility of a baby crawling into an unwatched fire. To prevent grass and floor mats from igniting, two parallel green logs were placed on each long side of a fireplace pit. Ray's experience with the Sanpoil and Nespelem affords creditable ethnographic data on house fires:

> Houses occasionally burned by ignition from sparks, or as a result of children playing with fire. There was little danger of a fire spreading throughout a village for the houses were too separated. Roof fires were extinguished if possible by dipping brush tied to the end of a long pole in water and applying it to the mats that were burning. If it appeared hopeless to save the building all efforts were concentrated upon removing the lower mats of the wall (1933:44).

Even in modern times, firewood remains an important concern for some elders. This was illustrated by the following experience the author had in the mid-1960s, while conducting some research on traditional fishing methods for the Spokan tribe. This involved interviewing the few remaining elders, one of whom was a 97-year-old gentleman who lived on the edge of Wellpinit by himself. The author had never met him, but after knocking on his screen door and introducing myself, I explained the purpose of my visit, to which he quickly replied, "I remember nothing about those times." Thanking him, I turned, walked off his stoop, stopped before his wood pile located next to his stoop, and truthfully remarked out loud, "Never have I seen wood ricked so neatly. Did your grandson do this?" The elderly gentleman immediately swung open the screen door, and said, "No, only my old hands. But any man who knows how firewood should be stacked, is someone I'll talk to." We spent most of the day doing just that.

Tree Felling

The primary reason for felling a tree was for firewood or making a raft. Depending upon a person's needs and location, there were no restrictions as to which tree he should fall—preferably one nearest the man's dwelling or the place of eventual utilization. Tree fallers generally exercised experience and caution when dropping a tree. For example, when on a steep slope, the tree was under-cut so that the tree did not roll down the slope, nor fall away if the trail was higher uphill, which would have led to greater effort to recover the wood. Given the existing technology and the effort required in dropping a firewood tree, the choice was always one that was dead and reasonably dry. There was no memory of a tree being felled by chopping and removing wood with stone tools. However, fire was used to *drop a tree* (*stékʷp'i*) whenever a *catface* (*sčtmw'álqʷ* - "hole in the tree") was located within reach. In this procedure, a fire was lit within the hole, and with repeated burning and scraping, the hole was greatly enlarged until the tree fell. The danger was to keep the fire from getting out of control and setting the entire tree or surrounding vegetation ablaze.

An old *dry tree without any bark* (*pʕala'lqʷ*) might be cut down with a technique similar, according to elders, to a beaver's efforts: sections of the dry wood were gradually chipped away with sharpened wedges of elk or deer horn that were pounded with stone hammers. Horn wedges were sometimes driven with stone hammers or a type of hammer made from the low trunk of a large *thornbush* (*sxʷeʔxʷʔenčeɫp*) or the root of a white birch. Thornbush was preferred, since it could be whittled to a shape similar to a small *stone sledge hammer* (*ntaʔqíntn*). The large root of white birch has wood grain that goes in many different directions, and will seldom break. A *root maul* (*nsp'qíntn*) was fire-hardened by placing the tool in a hole roughly 15 to 20 cm deep, which was filled with hot coals. It was imperative to keep turning the root hammer to keep it from igniting, being withdrawn when judged to be properly fire-hardened. A definite advantage of using a wood maul in lieu of a stone maul was that wood mauls seldom damaged horn wedges. Always a laborious process, the hammering and repositioning of the wedges was continued until both the *stump* (*nxʷxʷc'úseʔ*) and the balanced base of the supported tree were at a precarious point; then the tree was tipped over.

Tinder

The Spokan used a number of plant materials for tinder (*qʷúp* - "crumbly"), which, like firewood, were collected along with dried grass whenever found, and usually kept in a buckskin pouch tied to their belt (Elmendorf 1935-6, 2:64). The best tinder was gathered from the inside bark of a dead *dried, shredded cottonwood* (*snqópeƛ* - "anything rubbed until fuzzy"). Other desirable tinder materials were shredded sage bark, crushed grasses, crushed rodent nest material, antelope brush, dried shredded cottonwood down, *punk wood* (*yóqʼʷiʔ* - *rotten wood* or *c'ic'ixéy'ɫp*), shredded aspen or paper birch *fungus* (*Mycelial* sp. - *yóqʼʷiʔ*, a general term for fungus) mold, and dried grass, particularly *bunch grass* (*Agropyron spicatum*, var. *Inereme* [Scribn. & Smith] Heller. - *supúleʔxʷ*). Cheatgrass was softened by rubbing the material until it was pliable and combustible, and was called *y'uʔtis* (STHC). Crushed *puff-ball* (*Bovista pila* - *sʔitš* or *B. plumbea*) was also an excellent tinder. A few elders recalled bunchgrass being used for tinder. If necessary, a pulverized dry bird nest or *cattail duff* (*sqʼʷastqín*) or shredded dry mullein leaves served as tinder. The aptly named fireweed, a sagebrush-like plant about one meter in height, could be pulled completely from the ground and used without further preparation for making fire.

If any of the aforementioned tinder materials were damp, they were then crushed with hardened pine pitch and sprinkled upon the sticks or splintered wood for a more immediate and intense combustion upon being lit. *Dried pine needles* (*č'émeʔ*) were effective in fire-starting, after pounding and adding *powdered* pitch (*čp'q'ʷičeis*). The placement of tinder, when constructing a fire, commonly required *placing kindling under larger pieces of wood to permit air circulation* (*č'łcáqʷpc'eʔtn*).

Lord, known for always speaking of the necessity of woodsman skills, wrote of what he called "gumwood," remarking that Indians considered this tinder so effective that they traded it to trapper traders for tobacco:

> The light so obtained was almost as bright as the magnesium light, and rendered the minutest objects perfectly conspicuous. Gum-stick is obtained from dead, not decayed, pine-trees; it is a most singular looking material in appearance, not unlike a piece of deal [i.e., fir or pine wood] that has been soaking for a long time in oil; it is immensely heavy, and quite translucent at the edges (1867:202).

The safest way to transport tinder–usually shredded cedar or cottonwood bark—during inclement weather was under one's shirt, in a small pouch held securely in the person's axilla by a buckskin strap over one's shoulder, which contained a small fire drill. Such a container was approximately 15 to 20 cm in length. When hunting or trading on the Plains, the Spokan would start fires by breaking dried or even *old desiccated bison chips* (*smnčsqáxeʔtn* - "large deposit of animal feces"), which were quite combustible after shredding. When large amounts of dried bison feces were available, it was not uncommon—even preferred—to use this fuel for cooking, as the material provided an intense and fairly smokeless fire. Another excellent tinder was shredded antelope brush or *greasewood* (*Sarcobatus vermiculatus* [Hook.] Torr., var. *Vermiculatus* - *sxʷmásq'lt*), a wood that burns quickly with an intense heat. Seed-hairs of fireweed made an excellent tinder.

There is little detail regarding the practice of burning greasewood to communicate to persons beyond audible range by voice or drum, nor could any elders recall how the signaling system was coded. Burning greasewood gives off a black smoke which is visible from a great distance.

Fires within villages or camps were seldom permitted to burn out. As noted earlier, this practice necessitated a seemingly continuous gathering of firewood. Even small sticks gathered by children were a valuable contribution, since dwelling fires for warmth and cooking created daily demands of fuel. A woman leaving a camp was often met by a friend's inquiry, "*going after wood?*" (*hesčłúk'ʷ*). Any young person would be favorably commented upon for bringing home an armful or bundle of firewood, particularly pieces of pitch wood. *Women carrying wood on their backs* (*hecpseʔši*) was a common sight. Two or more women—usually sweathouse partners—would make a wood-collecting expedition if they intended to travel any distance from a camp, or certainly if they were going to a new area. Women were also responsible for starting and *maintaining fires* (*sčp'nús* - "wood placed on fire"). During the winter, a woman visitor might compliment her hostess by commenting upon how warm and pleasant the dwelling was.

Slow-Torch

During winter and inclement weather, an important skill was the ability to carry fire from one camp to another by placing a burning wood coal in the center of *bracket fungus* (*Fomes pinicola* [Swartz] Cooke) or in dry, rotten cottonwood, or in a big section of poplar. This would serve as a *slow match* or *slow torch* (*sƛč'ét'p'* - "slow motion") (Smith 1936-8:418), which could be reignited when blown upon. The shredded inner bark of big sagebrush could be twisted and used as a slow match. A similar process for making a slow match or slow torch was to take a sheet of buckskin-like parasitic growth from a large fallen tamarack tree, or a long section of cedar bark, and working the material by continually stretching, rubbing, and kneading it into a large ball, which then could hold a glowing wood ember. This type of slow match was carried in a small but damp section of cottonwood bark until needed. The person carrying such fire was called *skʷénpm* ("the person carrying the fire"). An unclassified *sage-like brush* (*qʷl'qʷl'mnełp*), which was pulled from loosened soil, could smolder all night, and in the morning commence burning when fanned or blown upon (STHC). Apparently, slow torches were made from long, split sections of dry pitchy pinewood, which would smolder but not ignite until it was swung in the air, fanned or blown upon.

When traveling from one site to another, the so-called torch bearer was usually an old woman who occasionally swung the approximately one meter-long stick to maintain the smoldering embers. Smith (1936-8:418) reported how the Kalispel would carry a slow match during inclement weather in one's axilla, by first placing a large lit ember rolled in damp moss. When large migrations were made, each family would designate elderly woman to be responsible for carrying and maintaining their slow match. After the group reached their winter or summer camp, a pine stump or an old log would be located, and a communal slow-fire would be made so as to save the time and effort of restarting a fire. Pine stumps were invariably chosen because of the high concentration of pitch, and the only danger and concern in overnight camps was if a root fire accidentally got started. If this happened, it would not always be apparent, even upon abandoning the camp. But under certain conditions, such a fire could commence and spread underground, following the often pitchy roots that often surface, causing further damage.

Percussion Method

Depending upon an individual's skills and the materials at hand, the Spokan used two methods for starting a fire—either percussion or friction. The most efficient and frequently employed way for starting a fire was the former approach known as *strike-a-light* (*t'sítctn* or *pa?xis*). Two stones of different density would be struck to *create a spark* (*tíw*). One stone would be an orange-yellow *iron pyrite* or *flint* (*st't'ʕiʷan'e?* or *st't'w'an'e?* or *st't'ʕ'w'án'e?* - "flint strike-a-light"). Naturally, the advent of steel quickly replaced iron pyrite. In either case, the spark was directed toward tinder that was held in the palm of the left hand.

The percussion method, as described by Elmendorf, was discontinued later:

> Long ago the people made fire by rolling dry grass together in a bunch & struck a rock of kind known as *st't'ʕ'ʷán'e?* [flint] on any other kind of rock—struck these together over the grass many times until the spark caught in the grass & then fanned it by blowing—the rock was orange yellow—(? iron pyrites)—plain dry grass used for tinder—rub it together till it is broken up fine (1935-6, 2:64).

A comprehensive Smithsonian monograph on the universal use of fire as an agent in human culture was by Walter Hough, who very early commented on the difficulty in collecting information on fire-making from ethnographic sources(1890:58-82).

Fire Drills

Despite the wide variation in fire-making methods using friction, there is little evidence that the Spokan ever used the fire plow for fire-starting; a method whereby the person would, with a relatively short section of rounded hardwood, held at a 45° angle, would rapidly push the shaft to and fro on an already grooved base of cedar or other soft wood until a spark ignited the tinder. However, some claim they never used a bow-drill. But there is linguistic evidence that the Spokan probably had knowledge of a bow-drill, whereby a loose bow string was looped around the ignition shaft, allowing the individual to quickly alternate rotating the vertical-socketed ignition shaft by passing the bow back and forth in a horizontal motion. More commonly, a type of fire drill was used, one made with a center-board piece of split softwood—preferably cedar—while the other individual would quickly rotate the ignition shaft between both palms into a slight depression on a stabilized horizontal base.

Starting a fire by *friction* (*sxúlk'ʷptn* or *c'íčtn*) was a tedious and time-consuming process—one that involved using a type of *palm drill* or *twirl stick* (*sxʷúlk'ʷptn*) made from a *pitch top* (*nc'ay'ím'tqn*) of a *small Ponderosa pine tree* (*ssá?tkʷłp*). This type of *fire drill* (*xʷúlk'ʷptn* - "between the hands") required a *dry and pitchy tip* (*snč'ámqn*), measuring 25 to 30 cm in length and from 10 to 15 mm in diameter (Smith 1936-8:415). Smith (1936-8:37) stated that the Upper and Lower Spokan preferred to use the top of the pine tree for their twirl sticks, and according to Smith (1936-8:417), poplar was never used as a fire platform, nor

416

was cedar used as a fire-drill. Fire-making was less tedious after steel had been introduced, permitting the use of what was primarily a strike-a-light, called *t'sí tctn*. A person held a piece of flint between his right thumb and *index finger* (*c'oq'ʷmn*) as he struck the flint to make a spark into a small amount of folded hemp or any type of tinder. Smith (1936-8:421) described how a fire was ignited when the end of the flint was carefully struck with a piece of iron.

A traditional dwelling had one or more fire-hearths approximately 8 cm wide and 20 cm in length made from a dry piece of cottonwood, tamarack, yellow pine or cedar. The hearth-board was modified in one of two ways: one type had only a conical depression in the top, whereas the other form had a top and bottom conical depression connected by a small opening. With the first type, the fire-maker inserted the rounded but larger end of the twirl stick into the depression. Holding it firmly between both palms, it was rotated rapidly as his hands worked down the shaft. The person repeated the process until *falling sparks* (*tíkʷt*) from the wood dust, created by friction, ignited the tinder, which was managed by an *assistant* (*ʔepłčn'šítmn* - "he has a helper") who continually poked the dust into the depression with a stick.

The other type of hearth-board—preferably using a dry section of yellow pine—had a hole that opened to the ground, which was fashioned by an awl or a knife tip, thereby connecting both the top and bottom conical-shaped hole to one another by a slight opening that permitted a spark to ignite the tinder below the hearth-board. The same process was duplicated, except that the tinder was placed in the upper conical depression, which upon igniting would ignite additional tinder in a small depression under the hole of the hearth-board. Both types of hearth-board were held in place by the fire-maker kneeling on either end. Being a tedious process, it was common for a fire-maker to be replaced by another man or woman, in quick succession. One of Elmendorf's informants demonstrated this procedure:

> [...] *šsát'qʷłp*, yellow pine while still a young [yellow pine] tree the top is cut off & rubbed with a stick of hard wood—the sparks or what dust caught in dry grass—whittle the *šsát'qʷłp* while still a young tree—the sparks down flat and make a hole in one edge not quite through—end of long stick (rounded) [was] put in the hole & and revolved rapidly between the palms—[the] hearth [was] held between the feet—[and] put the grass on the ground under the hearth—when it smolders they pick it up & blow on it until it bursts into fire (1935-6, 2:64).

When speaking of the advantages of the lucifer match, Lord was apparently humbled when observing the Salish method of fire-starting, by using:

> [...] a round piece of wood and a flat piece; the former he tapers to a conical sharpened point, in the latter he scoops out a hollow place a trifle larger than the cone; laying the flat piece on the ground, and, placing his feet firmly upon it, with his hand he rapidly rotates the end of the stick in the hollow place, by rubbing it between his palms, and at the same time pressing it firmly down. Very soon the dust thus rubbed off begins to smoulder, and at last ignites. This burning dust is next placed in dry bark or moss, and blown upon by the fire-starter into a flame. Cedar bark is best, but it must be very dry, sound, and free from knots (1867:271).

From an early age, both boys and girls were taught how to build a fire, and young boys would have contests demonstrating this necessary skill. Boys were taught how to *start a fire from wet wood* (*čqʷitn'usm'*), by pounding a section of damp wood into shredded strips, and then blowing or waving the strips until they were relatively dry. An unusual way to start a fire was observed and recorded by an early Spokane resident who observed a Spokan Indian making a fire, using a dry rotten log:

> Then the Indian would roll a small stick between his hands, one end pressed into the log. The Indian kept doing this until smoke came and [the] fire started. I have seen fire started this way. Then the Indians kept [the] fire burning as long as they were in camp (Lewis 1927:10).

Long after the introduction of *friction matches* (*sur'šictn*) in 1827, and the patented phosphorous match in 1836, the aforementioned procedures for starting fire continued to be used by the Spokan for many years because of the ever present and debilitating concern of moisture.

Unfortunately, the incidence of house and tent fires increased with the introduction of kerosene, because although it was intended primarily for lamps, it was also soaked into cans of wood chips, to more easily light iron stoves; with the introduction of (wood) houses, accumulated soot lead to devastating *chimney* (*t'péptn* - "stovepipe") fires.

Night Fires

Banking a night fire while in a hunting or resource extraction camp or winter village was accomplished by erecting either a rock or wood windscreen (never a granite or large river pebble, which could explode), or by placing the fire in an excavated earthen depression to reduce the effect of circulating drafts. The word for placing the last piece of wood—preferably poplar—to bank a night fire was *sččopqín*, indicating the significance of banking a night fire. Even within a dwelling, a fire was often banked by covering the end sections of firewood with earth. If available, *pitch wood* (*sƛ'ƛ'úk'ʷeʔ*) from a section of *downed pitch-top tree* (*sn'cay'ím'tqn*), rotten wood, or *root wood* (*soxʷép* - "root")—often a certain supply of pitch—was burned to maintain a fire at minimal combustion until needed again. Before sleeping, a night fire was completely covered with ashes, often using a *deer scapula* (*č'ʔulixw snc'mɬq'ey'*) as a hand shovel.

In multiple family winter dwellings, with two or three night fires, there was seldom need to add firewood before morning, but Elmendorf (pers. comm.) was told by older informants how the very elder occupants would, when necessary during the night, stoke and add wood if necessary. Since older persons were required to get up periodically during the night to urinate, they were the ones who often woke before anyone, and would stoke the pre-dawn fires.

Cooking

With few exceptions only women cooked food. Exceptions to this strict division of labor were when men were away from an established camp or village, which necessitated men to cook their food, or when running traplines or hunting, occasions when with several hunters, the youngest man cooked for the group. However, on brief expeditions—even for several days, a man invariably relied on pemmican or jerky that was always carried, or if on a long trap-run, the trapper cooked one of his catch.

Cooking and Eating Utensils

Prior to the introduction of Euro-American metal utensils, all solid foods were eaten with the fingers; only wood, bone, and horn implements were used for non-solid foods. None of these once traditional Spokan implements still exist as artifacts or in current use for ceremonial cooking. Regardless of the type or size of *cooking container* (*y'ámxʷeʔ*), soups and stews were cooked in one single large container and stirred with long-handled wooden spoons, which were then used as ladles when serving to individual bowls or cups. A *food ladle* (*snč'ɬmúlmn*) was made by longitudinally cutting the base of a mountain sheep horn or a bison horn, then steaming open the base flange to a desired shape. Liquids were ladled and drunk by using large mussel shells. Spoons were carved from wood or from mountain sheep that had been steam-bent (Collier *et al.* 1942:87). Some spoons were carved from deciduous wood or made by boiling and manipulating the breast bone of larger ducks to a desired shape. Spoons were sometimes fashioned from small deer craniums, often retaining one horn as a handle. The earliest utensils had protocols: "even prior to the acquisition of metal eating utensils, men and women were always careful to never exchange or use the other's knives, which were kept separate to avoid offending the animals hunted or the fish caught" (Miller 1990:62).

All families possessed both pinewood and hardwood bowls made by alternately burning and scraping out pine or hardwood burls, which served effectively as individual soup and stew containers. Once the soft under-shell of a turtle was removed, the more rigid top shell served as a dish for solid foods and even stews. Drinks, soups, and broths were served in containers made from deer skulls that had been boiled and shaped by placing a hot round stone in the now-supple skull to attain the desired shape and size. The blood of a deer was placed in a deer's stomach, and mixed with camas and moss before cooking as a broth. Some wooden containers had a single handle made by modifying and attaching a deer antler with rawhide stitching. *Small cups (łppósen)* were also fashioned by boiling the cranium of an immature deer until it was soft, and when cooled the edges of the cranium could be gently turned out to reinforce the rim.

After acquiring metal pots and cauldrons for cooking, the cooling iron pot, once cooled, was placed on the ground so people eating with sharpened sticks could spear bite-size pieces of meat and other solid foods. Meat that could not be torn apart was cut to shape with a stone knife and eaten by hand. Dry foods were served on small tule mats or dishes made from sections of bark; in temporary camps, mullein leaves were often used as plates. A functional and durable *dish (snn'eščémn)* or *plate (qpéłc'e?)* was quickly fashioned from a section of black cottonwood bark, and even used as a communal food tray.

With the acquisition of metal cooking utensils, changes in certain protocols were observed when cooking food by *boiling (nt'púsntx^w - "you boiled it")* in metal pots and cauldrons, regardless of the kind of food being cooked. For example, it was first believed that anyone who ate foods cooked in metal, particularly camas, could become sick and could lose their *suméš*. Years ago, some elders recalled hearing of a taboo against cooking ceremonial designated foods in metal pots.

Another strictly observed precaution when cooking with non-trade utensils, or using iron or copper cauldrons, was that only non-menstruating women would stir the boiling contents with their bare hands and arms, never using metal utensils. The same prohibition existed when stone-boiling in root baskets; a person could use only her bare hands to mix or remove cooked food. Initially, this belief pertained to many traditional foods prepared in metal cooking containers, such as trade iron and copper cauldrons. However, such trade utensils became popular after introduction, and eventually were accepted for cooking almost all foods. Cauldrons proved more efficient when cooking for large groups and when greater quantities of meat were needed. As fragments of stored *meat aged (č'éw'lši)*, they would fall off and be placed in a boiling cauldron for making soup or stew. This process was called *snt'a?qetk^w (STHC)*, or *(snaʕłełk^wm)*, when sometimes over-boiling the meat to strings.

Despite the availability of metal utensils, some elderly women reported how, when cooking a sacred meal, their mothers and grandmothers were capable of stirring a large pot *(snt'pústis - "her boiling pot")* or an iron cauldron of *soup* or *stew (sxsétk^w or sp'ixénč)* with their bare hands, yet never receiving burns. Some have said that a sleeveless dress was worn for such special occasions, or when cooking for a large number of people attending certain ceremonies. Even after acquiring metal pots and cauldrons, it was common to stone-boil deer meat that had been cut up and placed in a *tightly woven basket (ƛ'ic'ƛ'c't or yámx^we?) (STHC)*, which one elderly woman said always tasted better. This type of cooking basket was water-tight when sufficiently soaked.

Complying with the belief that certain types of non-traditional technology would negate the power or sacredness of a food or ritual, it is understandable that with the introduction of metal tools, such as shovels and pitchforks, there developed certain taboos against their being used to transfer heated rocks used in sweathouses and earth ovens. Though this custom is no longer adhered to, it was once believed that metal implements would 'contaminate' the foods and those who ate them. Yet the practicality and efficiency of steel knives was quickly recognized as more efficient and less time consuming when butchering, and steel axes were used when splitting wood for heating sweathouse stones or for cooking when iron stoves were adopted.

In the past, when women were preparing and cooking food—particularly meat—they carefully observed specific rituals and behavioral taboos to acknowledge the food was really a fortuitous gift—a practice which apparently varied within the Plateau. An example of this is illustrated when a Lakes woman, Mourning Dove, commented upon those practices:

> [...] old Spokan woman did not follow our beliefs. Once Mother was shocked to see the old [Spokan] woman skinning deer head opposite our fireplace. She gouged out the eyes and threw them at the door, where the dogs eagerly gobbled them up. Such things were forbidden to women until after menopause. When our family

had moved higher up into the mountains, the Spokan couple had been invited to share the tipi, so the breach of taboo made by the woman occurred inside our home. Mother did her best to make amends by cleaning up the area where the eyes fell and offered a prayer in apology (Miller 1990:117).

Fortunately, some types of foods were eaten raw, most notably berries, greens, nuts, certain fish, and most animal organs—unknowingly providing a greater range of vitamins and enzymes. Nonetheless, cooking made available a wider range of plant foods as well as improving the digestibility of fibrous foods and absorption of nutritional content that was vital for survival, especially in situations of environmental stress. Also, the various methods of cooking food, either by hot-rock steaming/baking in pits or mounds or by roasting, were determined by the type of food being prepared. While baking food (namely roots) often required several days, steam cooking in closed pits with sufficient water generally required less time (Thoms 2005:2). Open-roasting of meat required minimal time.

It should be noted that almost invariably, most missionaries and some Euro-Americans were largely dependent upon the labors, generosity, and ever-present hospitality of the Indians for their housing and food. However, in the following description of housing construction, food storage, cooking, and cooking utensils, DeSmet not only abused his obligations as a guest, but failed to be cognizant of the effects of missionary and settler-induced acculturation, which he so ethnocentrically—sometimes totally inaccurately—described for future readers:

> Imagine their dwellings, a few poor huts, constructed of rush, bark, bushes, or of pine branches, sometimes covered with skins or rags—around these miserable habitations lie scattered in profusion the bones of animals, and the offal of fishes of every tribe, amidst accumulated filth of every description. In the interior, you find roots piled up in a corner, skins hanging from cross-poles, and fish smoking over the fire, a few dying embers; an axe to cut food being seldom found among them. The whole stock of kitchen utensils, drinking vessels, dishes, etc., are comprised in something like a fish-kettle, made of osier, and besmeared with gum—to boil this kettle stones are heated red hot and thrown into it. But the mess cooked in this way, can you guess what it is? (1905, 2:558).

Stone-boiling

The techniques and strategies for cooking involved stone-boiling or *roasting on sticks stuck in the ground around a fire* (*nc'l'c'lús*), or earth ovens, depending upon the amount of food and the type of food to be cooked. Meat was sometimes roasted by being impaled on a sharpened forked green stick with the forte end stuck at an angle in the ground—a process called *n'c'k^wusis*. Roasting meat primarily outside of the dwelling was termed *čwulwulpíce?*. During winter village occupancy, food was always cooked inside, but cooked out-of-doors when residing in resource camps from April to late October. Exceptions were those occasions when men cooked outside while occupying temporary winter hunting camps. After butchering game, men used a *roasting stick* (*čq'ʷlmín*)—one always made from a green deciduous branch, and never pine or fir, which would impart an unpleasant taste to the food.

There were three methods of *stone-boiling* (*nur'é?łc'e?is* - "she stone boiled it" or *čƛ'q'ƛ'áq'mis* - "she heated it"): by basket, in a small, open skin-lined earthen pit, or in an earth oven or *closed pit oven* (*ne? p'i?qnté?s*). To boil water in a tightly woven basket, the container was sometimes first lined with rawhide, and a small trivet of hard-wood (usually freshly cut red willow) was placed inside the container to prevent the basket from being *scorched* (*hi x^ʷíx^w or k'ʷi?* - "smell of burnt hair"). Lewis paraphrased Alexander Ross (1956:297) on how "Food was usually boiled in baskets with hot stones, or, especially in the case of roots, baked over hot stones" (1906:183).

Another type of stone-boiling container was a strong, oval-shaped and tightly woven basket of cedar roots that was vitreous, and approximately 30 cm in diameter and height. A *bark boiling basket* (*słq'aq'*), preferably one of stripped birch bark, was relatively easy to make when stone-boiling in resource camps. Two long sections of bark were carefully bent in a U-shape, overlapped at the base and edges, and the entire shape was wrapped with long lengths of split red willow before caulking the base and outside edges with pitch.

Sliced pieces of deer meat were placed in the bark basket and cooked by replacing heated stones as needed. As a matter of taste, *boiled strips of dried meat* (*snʔaɫétkʷ* - "reconstituted") were considered a delicacy when eaten with vegetable foods. A similar dish was made with *boiled fish* (*lukʼʷéstiʔs*).

An expedient method of cooking by a successful hunter, who was some distance from his home, was to cut the deer meat into short, thin strips, which were then stone-boiled in the deer's paunch placed in an excavated earthen depression. The outer edges of the container were spread and held in an *upright position* (*toxʷ*) by a series of vertical stakes placed under the outside of the paunch to maintain a maximum shape and capacity. When in place, two or three medium fist-size stones were placed on a trivet made from woven green, deciduous red willow branches. Once the deer meat had been properly cooked, so was the paunch, which was eaten with the deer meat.

A more stable method of stone-boiling was in an earthen depression, commonly done when people were traveling and, thus, restricted in what utensils they could carry. A depression was first excavated in the ground and then lined with either clay or a piece of rawhide large enough to line the depression, and yet large enough to have material remaining to form a wide enough surrounding lip; held in place by weighting with stones. Wooden pegs could also be used to secure the ground flaps. But once the material had such holes, its use was restricted. This method required the use of a woven red willow trivet to protect the rawhide basin from scorching or being holed. Trivets were not used if an earthen depression had been lined with clay. Unfortunately, there is little information as to whether the Spokan used this method of stone-boiling. However, it was used by the Sanpoil and Nespelem (Ray 1933:39-40), and, due to spatial proximity, sharing of knowledge, and through intermarriage, it can be reasonably assumed that this cooking method was used by the Spokan.

Stone-boiling was an efficient method for boiling water and elders recalled how a container of approximately two liters of water could be brought to a boil within three to four minutes with a hot, fist-size vesicular basalt or small but smooth granite stones. Though not cited in the literature, every woman had three small vesicular stones for stone-boiling, and each stone was given a diminutive name. In preparation for stone-boiling, a fire was first made to heat the *small stones* (*ššnʼšenʼš*), and when sufficiently heated, each stone was removed from the burning *embers* (*stʔíkʷ* or *cʼíxʷcʼxʷt* - "charcoal coals") and carefully placed with tongs into the water-filled container.

Depending upon availability or choice, the placement and removal of heating stones was accomplished in various ways. The simplest procedure was to use two separate flat pieces of deciduous wood or a freshly cut willow stick with the thin end being looped and secured to its handle just above the hand-hold with a stripe of bark. A third method employed a webbed ladle-like implement made from forked green wood, with the two forks being interlaced with rawhide. A fourth type of implement involved splitting a section of green deciduous wood, after securely encircling a long, thin strip of bark one third from the lesser end. A small stone was placed at the base of the fork, spreading the ends, which were then interlaced to accommodate the cooking stones.

Stone-boiling was done daily, and, unlike the pit or earth oven, involved cooking only enough food for one or two meals. As mentioned, stone-boiling was quickly replaced with the introduction of the more durable iron *cooking pot* (*čλʼqʼnλʼaqʼmn*), *pan* (*sncʼéwʼʼmn*), and particularly the *large kettle* (*sntʼpústn*). And as a result, a *copper kettle* (*ntʼpúsmn* - "thing to boil in" or *sntʼústn* - "a large copper kettle") or an *iron cauldron* (*snʼšnʼšáqs* - "rock basket") was considered a valuable addition to a family's cooking implements. One may also argue that the use of iron pots and pans were unknowingly beneficial in providing hemoglobin to one's diet. The large meal was frequently in the evening after the adults had returned from various activities.

Earth Ovens

Earthen ovens were essentially steam ovens built in an area of excavated earth, varying in size according to the amount of food to be steamed. Although no longer used, they were a most efficient method of cooking large amounts of food with a minimum amount of wood, primarily because of the efficient retention of heat when covered with earth and various flat plant leaves using steam generated by pouring water on the contained hot stones. The *earth oven* (*snłqʷmíntn*), sometimes referred to as *pit-cooking* (*sq'ʷlim*), usually accommodated the cooking of a particular harvest by several families. As many as three or four families would construct, maintain and use the same earth oven, often for many years. An oven's preparation was a lengthy process that involved a collective effort to initially excavate a new pit, or remove the *heating stones* (*ur'šict* or *čƛ'aq'ntxʷ* - "you heat it") from one that been used previously. The *pit* (*słqasq'e'* - "open or uncovered pit") was normally excavated by a woman using digging sticks to a depth of approximately 1 m, with a width close to 2 m, and a length of 2 to 3 m. Some pits were smaller, and some were larger, depending upon the occasion or amount of food to be cooked.

Beside the prepared excavation, a large fire was built with four o̲r five layers of wood that had been cross-layered. If available, all groups preferred to use cottonwood bark and limbs since they burn longer and with greater heat than conifers (Turney-High 1933a:263). The *deep pit* (*ništúlexʷ*) was then filled with rounded vesicular basalt stones that had earlier been heated to a reddish-yellow color. After the fire burned down, the hot rocks were removed using large tongs made from two pieces of green red osier dogwood with flattened ends, or, if available, fire-hardened sections of debarked maple limbs. The bottom of the pit was then lined with approximately one half of the heated rocks, and then covered with a thin layer of earth. Two or more pre-soaked debarked deciduous poles of small diameter were stood vertically in the earth that covered the stones—the poles being held in place with numerous layers of bags of food made of tules or grass—all of which was next covered with a thick layer of gathered grasses and leaves.

The more common types of grasses used for earth ovens were bear-grass, bromegrass, and sweet grass. Also used to cover the food and hold the steam were leaves from mullein, *skunk cabbage* (*Lysichiton americanum* Hultén & St. John - *t'ímuʔ* or *hinexʷ* or *stámuʔkʷn*), and sticky geranium. Ryegrass and lady fern were used. The leaves of *ryegrass* (*Elymus cinereus* Scribn. & Merrill. - *néwłtn* or *pspsnéwłtn*) were collected for late summer pit ovens, whereas some other types of grass were gathered during the spring and stored by stacking them in a cool, dry place within the dwellings. The leaves of brown-eyed Susan were also used in lining pit ovens. Any surviving seeds that were not too burnt were later eaten. Most root steaming was often from late April to early October. When covering food bundles, if possible, dry leaves were rejected in favor of green leaves or grass. Bunchgrass was used to line and top cooking pits (Elmendorf, pers. comm.).

Atop the final layer of vegetation cover, the remaining hot stones were spread evenly with a long forked pole and covered with a final layer of earth. After the vertical steam hole poles were removed from the pit, water was poured into the openings and then plugged with earth (Elmendorf 1935-6, 1:28) to contain the steam that was readily generated. At this juncture, a *harvest prayer* (*sčp'um'm'* or *p'um* - "ripened" - "turn orange") was given by the oldest woman present—solemn words that recognized the gift of food and expressed their hopes that none of the contents would be scorched. The entire process of pit-cooking was called *čƛ'q'ƛ'áq'mn*. Cooking pit sites would be used year after year and were common features upon the cultural landscape in all camps, village sites, and certain resource sites. Some of these once used pits are features of the cultural landscape (Ross 1993).

Depending upon the size and contents of an earth oven, the time to adequately cook the contents could be two nights and three days. Throughout the entire process there were always certain women who had been designated as *keepers* (*sxʷčšt'ím*) who were responsible to ensure that the stone-heating fires were maintained. These women were further distinguished by the distinct fashion of their hair; gathered and tied behind their heads with a vermilion-colored length of buckskin (Elmendorf 1935-6, 1:28). During the two or three days of cooking, men were never permitted to come near the pits, for fear their presence would cause the food to burn. If necessary, the attending women may replace the topmost layer of stones with a new layer of heated rocks. However, depending upon the size of an earth oven, once properly-laid, it was not often necessary to replace the top layer of heated rocks.

Large quantities of camas was pit-baked, and the time required for cooking depended upon the types and amount of camas to be cooked. For example, *black camas* (*Camassia quamash* [Pursh] Greene var. *quamash* - *sxʷeʔlítxʷeʔ* - *uncooked* or *ʔítxʷeʔ*) was cooked for *two days and nights* (*ʔaslásqʼt*). DeSmet described a slight variation of the construction and layering of a camas earth oven:

> [...] they make an excavation [...] from twelve to fifteen inches deep, and of proportional diameter, to contain the roots. They cover the bottom with closely-cemented pavement [rounded vesicular basalt], which they make red hot by means of a fire. After having carefully withdrawn all the coals, they cover the stones with grass or wet hay; then place a layer of camash [sic] , another of wet hay, then a layer of camash [sic], another of wet hay, a third of bark overlaid with mould, whereon is kept a glowing fire for fifty, sixty, and sometimes seventy hours (1847:117).

The celery-flavored roots of a small *white camas* (*Lomatium farinosum* [Geyer] C. & R. - *tʼúxʷeʔ*) were boiled, mashed, and molded into palm-size cakes and sun-dried on mats, later used in soups or as a porridge when mixed with water—but seldom eaten raw (Elmendorf 1935-6, 1:32). Two other types of *white camas* (*L. Cous* [Wats.] C. & R. - *péwyeʔ*) and (*L. canbyi* [Wats.] Coult. & Rose - *pʼúxʷpʼuxʷ*) were always husked when dug, and sometimes small amounts were baked overnight and eaten by women the next day if they remained in the root field for several days—as occasionally happened.

In such a field situation, the procedure was to *dig a pit* (*nɫxʷúleʔxʷm*) approximately one meter long and 30 cm deep, and the depression was then filled halfway with wood, at which time the women set the wood on fire to heat the grapefruit-size vesicular basalt stones placed on top of the wood. After the fire burned down, 6 to 10 cm of earth was used to cover the embers. If available, skunk cabbage or mullein leaves were spread over the earth, and several layers of roots were then spread evenly and covered with two or three layers of leaves of skunk cabbage, or mullein—whatever was available. The roasting pit was then covered and sealed with loose earth, half a hand's length, and a fire was built atop the entire oven, and left to bake overnight. On the day the *pit was uncovered* (*sƛʼqásqʼlʼ*), the food containers and loose roots were carefully removed after a small but significant thanksgiving ceremony held by the oldest woman—a ritual to recognize the efforts of those who had participated in making possible such a bountiful harvest.

There were other types of plant foods cooked in an earth oven and never stored: chocolate lily, yellow bell, cow parsnip, wild thistle, four species of *onion* (*Allium Geyeri* Wats., *A. Douglasii* Hook. - *qʷléwi, A. Macrun* Watts., and *A. Acuminatum* Hook. - *séhč*), *Indian potato* (*Claytonia lanceolata* Doug. ex Hook. - *kʷnʼkʷínʼmʼ*) (a starchy corn), *spring beauty* (*C. Lanceolata* Pursh, var. *Multiscapa* [Rydb.] Hitch - *sqʷasqʷuʔenʼ* or *skʷenʼkʷínʼem*), skunk cabbage, valerian (sometimes called tobacco root), and numerous species of Lomatium.

Tree moss was cleaned, bagged, and later cooked by layering it with bagged camas and often an indigenous sweet *edible tuber* (*Carum Gairdneri* [H. & A.] Mathias) (Hitchcock and Cronquist 1981:336), and *yampah* (*Perideridia gairdnerii* [H. & A.] Mathias - *tlʼekʼʷpám*)—sometimes called false-caraway or Bigseed Biscuit Root, or Indian carrot (Turner *et al.* 1980:71), which is a type of parsnip, similar in taste to wild carrot. However, the more exact designation for the *Indian carrot* (*Daucus carota* L. [H. & A.] Gray) is cited by St. John (1963:309), who claims that this plant was the source of the cultivated carrot (*vide supra* 1963:311). In recent years, these two different plants—wild carrot and cultivated carrot—have been given the same linguistic designation: *sƛʼúkʼʷm*.

423

Cooking tree moss usually took three days of baking until it was properly cooked, requiring the fire to be rebuilt every morning, and recharged with water that was poured through a *hole* (*nɫxʷúleʔxʷ*) dug in the middle of the pit, or several holes, depending upon the size of the oven.

Other foods such as chokecherries and two types of serviceberries were prepared by steaming. A pit approximately twice the capacity required to accommodate the amount of carried or gathered roots for a meal was dug. Heated rocks were then placed and spread evenly at the bottom of the pit, which supported two upright green deciduous sticks to properly *vent* (*snmotqnéɫxʷ*) the oven's smoke. Roots were then placed on top a *layer of mud* (*sƛ'očʼólʼeʔxʷ*) or clay, which sealed in the heat. After the roots were covered with a layer of earth, clay, or mud, and then layers of grass, the vent stakes were removed and the resulting vertical space filled with water and plugged to contain the steam. Cooking with the earth oven was an effective method for the dehydration of large quantities of plant foods that had been previously *prepared and stored for future use* (*člwiʔscuʔtmis*). Steaming always reduced the cooked tubers in both size and weight.

There was always a strict division of labor when preparing an earth oven. Women were solely responsible for the cooking, for as mentioned, it was believed that if a man helped, the food might become overcooked and, thus, would not be edible (Elmendorf 1935-6, 1:24, 1:29). Also, game would always evade any man who helped to prepare an earth oven. In the past, men and boys were never permitted within the area of an earth oven, nor were they permitted to assist in any way—not even for collecting the needed wood, which was entirely the responsibility of the women. More succinctly, the word *hecnčʼcʼépni* denotes "a man's penis should not be near the pit" because "it's like the penis is blocking the cooking" (Egesdal, pers. comm.).

An example of a man's unwelcomed and once forbidden presence while constructing and firing an earth oven was in the late 1960s, when the author assisted an elderly couple in gathering a large quantity of black tree lichen and camas. After considerable discussion and vague recall of procedures for making an earth oven, the elderly gentleman magnanimously decided that he would assist his wife, despite her stern objections that the harvest would be burned if any man was involved in preparing the oven, or even approach the fire-pit while cooking. The following day, with considerable anticipation by the woman, and apparent trepidation of the husband, the oven was uncovered, only to discover that all of the laboriously collected and prepared lichen and camas had been burned beyond use.

Ember and Ash-cooking

In the past, both ember and ash-cooking were used to cook small amounts of food—usually in temporary camps when only a few people were traveling overland. Ash-cooking was a more contained procedure, and involved placing the fish or thin strips of meat packed in mud or clay, and covering with hot ashes until the embers had cooled. This method was basically a miniature surface oven, a procedure that produced no steam. Ember-cooking, not unlike roasting, produced a more intense heat for cooking meat, while embers were moved as needed with green sticks. Small birds were placed on hot embers to *singe* (*nƛ'óɫsis*) them—to essentially remove the feathers as well as cook the meat, which was easily removed from any bones. Singing the hair from an animal was termed *ʕ'ʔantes* or *čqʼʷlíčeʔ*. Birds were first gutted and then packed in clay before cooking in coals or hot ashes. After cooking, the now-hard clay capsule was broken open and most of the feathers were left adhering to the clay sections.

Of interest is how traditional cooking methods were quickly adapted to newly acquired foods and cooking materials, such as flour and tin baking utensils. The latter was used to make pans or containers for baking *camp-fire bread* (*snqʼʷlʼúʔ*). A container of mixed biscuit dough was placed in a loosely covered tin or an iron Dutch oven, then completely buried in a pre-heated excavation, and covered with hot coals and ashes. The same cooking implements and food stuffs were readily moved into households, often using only traditional Indian foods. Furthermore, as will be discussed, ember or ash-cooking was frequently used when cooking the bones of different animals.

Open Cooking

This method of cooking was reserved for roasting meat that had been cut into small pieces, or for broiling fish that had been beheaded, cleaned, longitudinally sectioned, and held open with wooden skewers of either cedar or yew wood, and finally baked over hot coals. Meat cooking, using this method, was done more commonly in hunting camps, occasions when the meat from the hunt was most likely the only food available, and each man cooked his portion of the meat according to his individual preferences. After a sweat an evening cooking fire was made, and later its banked embers often became the center for socialization and the recounting of significant details and fortunes of the hunt. A fire that cooked meat, one that popped with droplets of fat, was said to have been "the warmest of fires"—one that recalled memories for older hunters, and was said to soothe their aches and pains from previous unsuccessful hunts.

When asked about hunting and trapping activities, a few male elders could recall their fondest memories when they caught, cleaned, and *roasted* (*sq'ʷlím* - "to roast") their first small mammal caught by snare, throwing stick, or bow and arrow. *Roasted meat* (*sq'ʷlpéɫc'eʔ*) and selected organs often constituted the only food in a winter deer camp. Roasting was the favored method of cooking salmon, particularly over a *hardwood* (*m'c'm'c'ey'ɫp*) fire that always ensured a unique flavor and retained the moisture (Hewes 1998).

Some animals were prepared only by roasting, such as skunk, chipmunk, tree squirrel, and owl, whereas blue grouse, sage hen, prairie chicken, duck, ground squirrel, rabbit, and ground-hog were boiled (Schaeffer 1934-37, I-106:33).

Roasted fish (*lk'ʷésnt*) was considered a delicacy, but there is no evidence that the Spokan ever roasted smaller fish caught using line-fishing. Rather, these were often encased in clay and baked after removing the innards, since the skin remained attached to the clay when the now-hardened shell-like container was broken open. With the introduction of corn, one method of cooking trout was to clean the fish, insert a section of peeled and diced Indian celery for flavor, wrap the fish in corn husks, and roast it in either a small *roasting pit* (*sq'ʷl'épm* or *snq'ʷl'éptn*) or upon open coals. White fish were prepared and cooked in this manner. Any baked or roasted food was known as *sátsqʷ*. Franchère commented how he "found the white-fish more delicious in flavor, even than salmon" (1904, 6:369).

During large gatherings, salmon was a preferred dish, cooked over open fires by both men and women. With few exceptions, a salmon would be opened with a cut down the back, permitting easy removal of the entrails, spine, and most of its ribs. The salmon was then held opened with *cedar skewers with whittled points* (*nxʷƛ'xʷƛ'áqsm*), which helped to affix the fish to an upright *split cedar shaft* (*nšt'úsis*) or leaning slightly toward a pile or long line of tended embers, with the skin side away from the heat. The secured *salmon filet* (*sl'l'm'en'č* or *hec t'el* or *hec laq'*) was, after a time, *turned around* (*p'lč'mstés*), and designated people would periodically investigate the stage of broiling. A person who expressly made filets was called *sxʷt'elm* during the time of her activities (STHC).

Food Preservation

All plant, animal, and fish products intended for storage were dried by exposure to the sun, fire, or smoke, or a combination involving several of these techniques, depending upon the time of the year and the type of resource. Plant foods were nearly always sun-dried either using horizontal mat platforms or on ground-bearing tule mats. Fish and meat were dried upon large double-slanted racks, latticed to facilitate air-drying, which served to keep the fish or meat above *smoke-drying* (*cqy'éʔɫc'eʔm*) fires. Such foods were also processed by placing them on horizontally raised or suspended, flat, open, wooden racks above smoking or low-drying fires. Regardless of their construction, large food-drying racks, particularly fish racks, were communal property; only the smaller plant-drying apparatuses were built, maintained, and controlled by an individual family. After the last large deer hunt or major fish run, all drying racks were disassembled, carefully scraped of any remaining flesh, washed, bundled, and stored—if possible—on trees on the site.

Smoking and Drying Sheds

With land allotment (29 May 1908), and the eventual availability of lumber, each family constructed a permanent *smoking shed* (*snp'umłc'e?tn*) and *drying shed* (*sncqy'ełc'e?tn*), which, given the time of year, was used for drying either fish or deer meat. The smoking shed was frequently a tipi-form with two *tilted* (*wel'*) parallel side walls that met at the top. One end was completely enclosed as was the entrance end which had a hinged door to permit entry. Along each *parallel long wall* (*nxlenč*) were horizontal poles from which meat or fish were suspended over low ember hard-wood fires.

A drying shed was either a rectangle or square box-shape with vertical walls, or a version of the smoke shed, except that each wall had openings large enough to permit sufficient air to *dry* (*scqiy'ełc'e?*) either the suspended fish or meat.

Meat-Drying Racks

Drying racks for deer or elk meat varied in shape and size. Those located in riverine villages—near deer jumps, or in traditional upland communal hunting camps—were larger and often *rectangular in shape* (*scqy'ełc'e?*), whereas with smaller amounts of game acquired by an individual hunter or a small hunting group, they were first transported to a home base where women helped to cut and slice the meat, and then prepared for storage by using smaller racks for drying the processed meat. In temporary hunting and gathering camps, when a few deer were killed, a small round tipi-like tripod drying rack, approximately 2 m high, or a square-based four pole tipi-like structure was erected. Both types of drying racks featured a square, open lattice platform situated approximately half the distance (1 to 1.5 m) between the ground and the apex of the structure, upon which either fish or meat could be suspended above a small smoke-fire of willow wood (Elmendorf 1935-6, 1:7).

A large salmon, elk, or deer *meat-drying rack* (*scqy'ełc'e?* - "dried meat" or *sncqy'ełc'e?tn* - "place to dry meat on") was one of three types which were determined by the amount of fish or game to be dried. The longest and largest drying rack was constructed with a lodge pole tripod at either end of the structure that served as the principal support of the actual drying rack. This type of large rack could be lengthened by strategically placing one or more supports, made by tying the feeble or upper ends of two lodge poles together in an inverted "V", and each pole base was spread several meters and anchored with stones or by excavated earthen depressions. Lashed to the outer edges of the slanting poles were a series of horizontally connected thumb-size branches—of smaller diameter—made from willow, red osier dogwood, ocean spray, or Osage orange. Each overlapping horizontal pole was secured with strips of the inner bark of cedar to the larger slanted pole. Small, thin sections of the elk or deer were held in place by pinning the meat with narrow, sharpened, short-jointed pieces of hard-wood having naturally formed "L" shapes, when cut and fashioned from the smaller branch shoot of a larger support branch. Any wood used in making drying racks was always debarked to prevent tainting the meat. Because of differential distances of the meat above the drying or smoking fires, it was necessary to re-set the horizontal bars several times a day to ensure uniform and adequate drying. Dried willow and alder were preferred as smoking and drying woods.

A second type of large communal meat-drying rack was made by securing each double corner of a long, flat, horizontal, open-lattice covered lodge pole frame from a tripod structure. The drying area could be 3 to 4 m in length, and approximately one meter wide. A variation was to have each end of the flat drying rack supported atop a stout horizontal timber that ran between two tripod supports.

A third method of drying fish or game was to take two debarked feeble ends of serviceberry stakes, which were over-lapped, and then tied together with thin pliable water-soaked cedar strips. When erected, the

426

section formed an arch, after the two stout, sharpened ends were spread and secured vertically into the ground. Each arch was approximately 2 m from the next, and the base of each arch-pole was sunk in the ground at a depth adequate to ensure stability, which was repeated with a varying number of arches until the rack was the desired length—creating a half-dome form not unlike a Quonset hut. The structure was further stabilized by attaching a series of horizontal, small-diameter, debarked deciduous branches. From these sections, meat or fish were hung approximately one meter or more above a series of smoke fires. Similar to the first type of drying rack, it was also necessary—during the course of several days drying—for the horizontal rows of fish to be interchanged by raising or lowering them as needed.

When possible, wood from the *red osier dogwood bush* (*stčxʷnálqʷ*) was preferred for drying fish, since it never blackened either fish or meat. For taste, *smoke-dried meat* (*scqy'éɫc'e?*) was preferred to sun-dried. For obvious reasons of taste and duration of storage, sun-drying was used for preserving smaller amounts and types of foods, such as mussels, or thinly-sliced animal meat and fish. In addition, berries could be spread on a *drying mat* (*q'c'ús*). Depending upon the type of drying rack, one or more smudge fires were built, and children were sent daily to gather driftwood and smaller dry fallen tree limbs to fuel the fires. Wood for smudge fires was always a hardwood—not pine or fir, which imparted an unpleasant flavor to the meat. If possible, a smudge fire was built to hasten the drying and to protect the meat and workers from insects— particularly to keep *flies* (*hamáɫtn*) and other insects away from the exposed meat during summer months. When fishing near areas of standing water, a further defense against mosquitoes was to make a smudge fire by placing yarrow leaves or *pineapple weed* (*Matricariam matricarioides* [Less.] Porter - *nc'lc'l'xʷqin*) on hot coals, thereby creating a foul-smelling odor. Placing dried wormwood leaves on a smudge fire had the same effect. Another method for combating flies and insects used by the Upper Spokan at the Latah settlement was when, "The Spokanes would place their fish inside bark strips they peeled from the pine trees early in the spring when the sap had just begun to run, and swing the dried [fish] flesh high up among the pine trees, where the flies wouldn't bother it" (Cowley 1916:104).

While drying deer or elk meat, it was common for successful hunters to *roast* (*q'ʷlim*) small cuts of meat for immediate consumption over an open fire with roasting sticks, and it was said to have been the preferred way to *cook* (*nt'pus*) deer meat. And regardless of the amount of fresh or *s*moke dried meat a family had, they always shared with those without, "Meat was for anyone who wanted it–if a man said 'what became of the meat I bought in'–it would be shameful" (Elmendorf 1935-6, 1:8).

Fish-Drying Racks

Though a *large fish-drying rack* (*suxʷéltn*) at a fishing station was constructed by both resident men and women, anyone—including visitors and unrelated individuals from other groups—could use the structure (STHC). Examples are those once found at Spokane Falls, Little Falls, Kettle Falls, and at the mouth of any creek flowing into the Spokane River. Fish-drying racks were often similar in material and design as meat-drying racks, but usually greater in length. They were located at fishing stations where nearly all *drying of salmon* (*he?ct'eli*) took place, not at the more distant villages and camps. If possible, a *rack* (*q'ʷuƛ'š*) would be located within a *shady area* (*hesč'éyle?xʷ*) to facilitate a slower, more gradual and thorough drying. Smoke *dried fish* (*scqésɫ* or *lk'ʷés*), stored well if kept dry, and produced a preferred taste, more so than even *air-dried salmon* (*č'exʷsmɫič* or *he?t'éli*), and was still edible after two years. A preferred wood for smoking salmon was damp willow, preferably red willow. Under good conditions, it took approximately one month to adequately dry fish for storage (Ruby and Brown 1982:16).

Large quantities of fish—primarily salmon—were dried on one of two types of drying racks. The smallest structure was almost identical to the so-called previously mentioned arched Quonset-type meat-drying rack, whereas the larger fish-drying rack is best illustrated by Paul Kane's fortuitous water color sketch of a multi-purpose structure he made at Kettle Falls in 1847, while exploring the Hudson Bay Company

427

territory between 1846-48 (Garvin 1927:217). Extrapolating from the scale of several human figures in this painting, it appears that the average fish-drying rack—slanting or "A" frame—was approximately 24 m in length, 7 to 8 m in height, and roughly 14 to 16 m in width. These large communal structures were essentially a large "A" frame of lodge pole construction—partially roofed by numerous tule mats, which were periodically moved to provide shade for the salmon drying on a large tule-covered pole floor, being approximately 2 m above the ground. Draping fish filets over horizontal fishing rack poles was called *sluk*ʷ*lést*.

All fish to be dried were opened, cleaned, and placed on the horizontal cross-pieces secured to each side of the upright slanting inverted "V" braces. Fish were basically secured for drying by one of several methods: looping an opened salmon over a horizontal cross-piece, or pinning the tails of two filleted fish, and hanging each on either side of a horizontal pole. With smaller salmon, a woman passed a long length of a sharpened stick through the tail before hanging it to dry or to be smoked. Opened and cleaned smaller fish were suspended for drying by passing a long horizontal dressed hardwood stick through one of the gills and out the mouth before hanging over a low fire. The same type of rack accommodated fish that were split-opened, halved, and held in place by running a sharpened, narrow, hardwood piece of wood through the tails. Any fish so large that it had to be first scaled or skinned was called *p't'áy'oseʔ*.

As previously noted, when metal tools were first introduced, they were not always used in lieu of lithic tools, except in instances of prolonged or difficult labor saving chores. "The use of new metallic tools and other manufacture goods probably did not have much serious effect on total fishing efficiency, aside from increasing the number of fish that could be properly cleaned and prepared by a skilled worker" (Hewes 1998:622).

A three or four pole tipi was erected for smoke-drying small quantities of fish, suspended above a smouldering smoke fire from a series of debarked hardwood horizontal poles placed through the gill and mouth of each open and dressed fish. The fish-ladened drying poles were situated on the larger slanting poles. Salmon that had died after spawning—called *púmnɬc'eʔ*—were collected, gutted, and placed on racks until sufficiently dry. Fish preserved as winter food in this manner produced a distinct bitter taste, one that was preferred by men (STHC).

Several methods of drying fish—as well as roasting fish—required first removing the *salmon backbone* (*sx*ʷ*líkn*) after opening the dorsal area (and not opening the underside of the fish, as is commonly done by non-Indian fishermen). The flanks were then splayed open with sharpened split cedar stakes that held the fish to a main but slightly slanted upright support. When asked, only a few elders remembered hearing of a method used many years ago for drying large fish—one in which a woman would take a gutted salmon, and using a sharp knife she would make a series of tongue-like "V" cuts in the flesh before placing it on a drying rack. Summer smoking took approximately two to three days. But it was worth the time and fuel, for Spokan men and women enjoyed *bed time snacks of dried fish* (*qepesʔiɬni*) as a delicacy and presumably to induce sleep (STHC), usually of *air-dried dog salmon* (*seč'énč*).

To preserve the notably oily sturgeon, the lower section was first cleaned, and then the upper part, which contains most of the oil, was spread flat on a tule mat to facilitate making an alternating pattern of 10 to 14 cm long cuts into the meat—similar to the method just cited. The sturgeon was then spread and kept open with short, sharpened cedar or red osier skewers, and affixed to an upright shaft of cedar placed in the shade until the fish was stiff enough to remain open. The author observed some examples of drying sturgeon with various configurations of skewers, which at the time appeared as an art form. In this manner, sturgeon meat will store well for many years if kept dry.

Elderly Spokan claimed that because of the amount of oil in raw eel or smoked sturgeon, a person, if possible, always ate fresh huckleberries along with it. Both eel and sturgeon were once considered delicacies. All fatty meats and *fatty fish* (*čq*ʷ*im'lstn*), particularly the *fatty meat* (*čq'*ʷ*im'lsc* or *čq'wim'lstn*) of eel was, more palatable with huckleberries; eel by itself was considered only 'half a dish' unless served with

428

huckleberries. The preparation of eels required greater time and effort than sturgeon. Prior to being smoked or sun-dried, the sides of the eel, after being opened lengthwise and cleaned, had to be permanently spread by making alternate and staggered lengthwise cuts that were kept open with a series of cedar skewers. Suckley mentioned how, when cleaning salmon for drying and storage, they were "scarified in various directions, and then hung for a short time in the smoke of a fire. They are then hung on poles or the branches of trees, where they are freely exposed to the wind. In a month they become perfectly dry" (1855, 1:300). DeSmet observed how, when salmon was once dry, it was pulverized and "mixed with oil [of] a sufficient quantity for the rest of the year" (1847:109).

Salmon, after being *cleaned* (*nʔaw'ic'eʔ*), were either pegged open with short sections of willow with *sharp, pointed ends* (*nxʷx̌'x̌ʷ laqsm*) or hung over one of the horizontal poles as a pair of fish, after tying the tails of two fish together. The fish *trimmings* (*sqʷʷoʔn'asc'óm'*) were saved and made into a *late afternoon fish stew* (*sp'ix̌ʔenč* - "cooked fish intestines") by the women, to be eaten by the fishermen after completing a day's fishing. *Fish scales* (*snlšim'c'eʔ*) were not removed but remained with the butchered fish which was hung from a green stick, and held over an ember fire until crisp and curled, and was considered a delicacy. It has been noted that the only portions eaten by the Spokan Indians while fishing were the head, *backbone* (*ʔásx̌m'*), roe, heart, gills, and *liver* (*pn'ínč*), which were roasted and *filleted with small pointed sticks to cook or dry more quickly* (*hecx̌p'im*) and roasted on sticks (Elmendorf, pers. comm.). Some recalled how after thoroughly cleaning a salmon's stomach, it was then boiled for immediate consumption.

If not eaten immediately, salmon roe was stored after either fermenting by sun-drying, or by a method involving spreading the eggs on tule mats to dry, or by removing the egg-laden pouches intact and then hanging the sacs to air and sun-dry. Roe prepared in this manner was later often eaten with berries or reconstituted in soups. Thoroughly cleaned spring salmon stomach was a preferred dish after being boiled for immediate consumption. Fish eggs were fermented in various ways by placing the clustered roe in small skin-covered baskets, or stored in air-tight birch bark baskets before burying in a cool place, more often in the floor of the main dwelling. After a month or so, the container was opened and the fermented eggs eaten after being boiled with any type of soft berry. Some recalled hearing how the fermentation of roe went until late April or early June when they were boiled and eaten with any available stored dry berries. Eating only fermented fish eggs was considered a delicacy.

Fish skewers, preferably fashioned from lengths of narrow-split cedar, were used to hold open the fish when broiling or smoke-drying. Another *method of preparing salmon* (*čsúʔ*) was to bury the discarded bones and skin in *sand* (*sq'epén'eʔxʷ*) for five days, and then mix these parts with crushed washed nettles. A few elders remembered accounts of *pounded dry fish bones* (*sntaʔx̌axʷqn*) being cooked as a soup. Spring salmon bones caught in late autumn were saved and sun-dried on raised cattail mats before being pulverized. The powder was carefully stored and used to make winter soup.

Cooked tripe (*m'al'án'čiʔ*) from deer was also a favorite dish. One elder recalled how, prior to WW I, fish heads filled with stored roe or different types of dried berries were made into a soup during the winter, "and us children really liked to drink the soup." After cleaning any species of fish, the women always put aside the bones, which, after being spread on mats to sun-dry, were pulverized to a *coarse* (*c'ič*) powder by using a stone mortar and pestle, or a rawhide basket with a flat stone in the bottom which served as an anvil. The *bone powder* (*sntaʔx̌axqn*) (Smith 1936-8:441) was then eaten dry or mixed with other ingredients as a soup. If not eaten immediately in soups or stews, *powdered fish bones* (*sntaʔx̌áxʷ*) stored well when kept dry in a spruce root basket sealed with pitch, or in a dry, untanned deer intestine container.

A major concern when drying meat or fish was for the racks to be high enough to prevent camp dogs from reaching the drying meat or fish, and yet low enough for thorough drying. Consequently, older children, serving as sentinels, were responsible for frightening and keeping scavenging dogs and other animals away from drying racks, which was necessary at large fishing stations when fish intestines were hung on racks to dry. Elders recalled hearing stories of large wind-articulated, humanoid-looking scarecrows made of bound tules and grass, erected in the immediate vicinity of drying racks to *scare* (*člaxmíst* or *kʷuss*) and to *chase away* (*qixʷntm*) any dogs, crows, and other scavenging animals. Some elders claimed a *wooden face mask* (*l'el'uq'ʷs*)—one used year after year—completed the figure. Anthropomorphic figures had no special power, rather their purpose was to provide frightening theriomorphic appearances to scare any scavenging birds or animals.

Jerky and Pemmican

An efficient way of drying and preserving different types of meat, namely venison, bear, and salmon, was to reduce the weight and volume of a protein-rich *ready-to-eat food* (*sciⱡn*) as jerky or pemmican. Either type of dried meat or fish was utilized by persons on extended forays, the value of which was quickly recognized and adopted by Euro-American explorers and trapper-traders, as attested by Lord's early and astute observations of how the Spokan prepared jerky. Interestingly, as a naturalist who expounded on the plight of certain biting insects, Lord emphasized the necessity of smoke fires during the process of making jerky which involved "cutting it into *thin strips* (*qqeʔt c-t'el*) and drying it in the sun; small fires should be kept smouldering under the drying flesh, to keep away the flies. All the fat and bone should be removed" (Lord 1867:255). He further observed methods of meat preservation, explaining how "strips of meat simply sun-dried or dried over a slow fire can easily be carried long distances without undergoing decomposition" (1867:249).

Unfortunately, the definitions of jerky and pemmican are not consistent with many of the early accounts by some historians when referring to the finished dried meat product as pemmican, when actually it was jerky, the critical difference being that pemmican always contained berries and animal fat. Teit was correct when stating how pemmican can be of two types, with berries or kept moist:

> [...] made into proper pemmican by mixing it with hot grease (fat or marrow) and kneading it into balls or cakes. ones were crushed on flat stones with hand hammers and mauls in order to extract the marrow. Sacks containing pemmican were often sealed if intended to be kept for a long time. Tree gum was sometimes used for this purpose. No berries were used in pemmican, as they were thought to make the meat too sweet. Nearly all the bags used for storing and carrying meat and fat were made of rawhide. Ordinary dried meat was sometimes wrapped in mats (1930:94).

By definition, and without the benefit of added berries, dried meat—even when mixed with marrow, fat, or tallow—was not pemmican, nor was it as fortifying or as nutritious as pemmican. There was consensus that the best jerky was made in late summer or early fall deer camp, when the deer were in prime condition for winter. It has been suggested that women were responsible for processing a greater portion of both jerky and pemmican. Properly dried pemmican was eaten throughout the winter, provided that it had not been exposed to moisture. Making bear jerky or pemmican was a rather laborious process, as it was once done. But if properly prepared, it is a delicious food, though some say it was only just palatable (Merk 1931:347). Smith has recorded how the Kalispel stored bear meat:

> Black bear meat will not get rancid after it is smoke-cooked (i.e. dried) unless it is in the hot sun for a long time. It is stored on top of the plain camas; the camas draws the grease out of it; it keeps the camas soft and it makes it taste better. The camas is eaten without being cooked any more and sometimes they soaked them up in cold water to soften the camas and they eat this. Or they soak them up in meat broth. They store both bear's fat and meat on top of the camas, or both together [...] . If they want to store bear meat in a parfleche, they put a layer of meat and then one of fat, and so forth (1936-8:443)

Prior to Euro-American incursion, *meat* (*sqéltč*), notably deer and bear meat, was often *stored* (*scqy'éⱡc'eʔ*) for long periods of time as *pemmican* (*spxʷpxʷqʷé*) in the form of cakes or stuffed into deer intestines. When deer, elk or fish was half dry, it was processed as *hammered food* (*sctéʔ*) by pulverizing with stone mauls, all the while adding grease together with berries—preferably huckleberries, or serviceberries, pounded dry camas, or crushed hazelnuts—and sometimes with bear oil and grease (Elmendorf 1935-6, 1:3). Between families there was little variation in the procedure for making pemmican, albeit the ingredients often varied according to preference, as did the ratio of dried meat, fat, and berries (notably serviceberries) vary. Another account of adding fruit to pemmican was given by Franchère during his travels of 1811-1814:

> About fifty pounds of this meat is placed in a [wooden] trough (*un grand vaisseau fait d'un tronc d'arbre*), and about an equal quantity of tallow is melted and poured over it; it is thoroughly mixed with one mass, and when cold, is put up in bags made of undressed buffalo hide, with the hair outside and sewed up tightly as possible. The meat thus impregnated with tallow hardens, and will keep for years. It is eaten without any preparation; but sometimes wild pears or dried berries are added, which render the flavor more agreeable (cf. 1904, 6:380).

Lord provided several early explanations of how the Spokan made pemmican:

> Dried meat was frequently made into pemmican by being pounded with pestles, mauls, and the stone hammers in mortars, on flat stones, and on rawhides—usually on a flat stone with a maul. A large mat or skin was spread on the ground and the flat stone placed in the middle. The jerked meat was stored in sacks, and was generally eaten without further preparations [...] pemmican for those who can [...] is a very capital material to carry, on a long march; indeed, it often constitutes the only diet of the trapper and fur-trader. It may be made as follows:—Cut either deer or buffalo flesh into thin shreds, and dry it well in the sun; next pound it into a pulp between two stones, and as you pound it throw it into a bag made of hide previously prepared. When the bag is nearly filled pour in melted grease nearly boiling hot, until the bag is filled, then sew it up firmly. Many prefer to eat it as it is cut off in thin slices (1867:249).

Pemmican was a food that hunters often carried throughout the year, particularly during the winter because (unknowingly) it had a concentrated nutritional value in relation to its weight, and could be eaten without further preparation; not being quick to spoil when being carried and kept dry. In time, fur-trading companies of North America learned the practice of making pemmican from the different indigenous cultures that inhabited the more northern clines. Each company used slightly different ratios in their respective recipes. The following was that of the North West Company:

> Lean dried bison meat was in common use along that part of the river. The meat was smoked and pounded fine into "beat meat." Fifty pounds of this was mixed with 20 pounds of "soft" fat (taken from around the spine and ribs) and 20 pounds of "hard" fat (from other parts of the carcass). These were slowly melted together and tightly packed in skin bags, 30 inches by 20 inches by four inches. A bag of those dimensions provided the standard 90-pound carrying weight. Dried service (June) berries often were added to the mixture (Bond 1971:98-99).

DeSmet described a way the Flathead used to preserve bison meat, which was to cut it into slices "thin enough to be dried in the sun; sometimes a kind of hash is made of it, and this is mixed with the marrow taken from the largest bones" (1843:120). George Simpson's early journals (1847) cite how pemmican was often eaten raw during the mid-day meal, but sometimes cooked in the evening and eaten with flour or boiled with potatoes, if available, or with *roast potatoes* (*s$^{?}$acq^w*). Apparently, from personal experience, he noted, "Carefully made pemmican, flavored with berries and sugar, is nearly good; but of most persons new to the diet it may be said that, in two senses, a little of it goes a long way" (Merk 1931:347).

Not all *pounded dry meat* (*st$^{?}$éltn*) was made into pemmican, but occasionally stirred into soups and stews to add flavor and to thicken the dish. In particular, old dry deer meat will take on a *whitish color* (*sqsaqn'e$^{?}$m'*), and was boiled and usually mixed with roots as a stew (STHC). A constant concern with the winter storage of meat was the occurrence of *spoilage by worms* (*yuƛ'mstm* or *sx^{w}yálq^w*), caused by larvae-laying flies, most notably blow flies. The area of spoiled meat was called *hi yux*.

The Spokan preferred sun-dried serviceberries for making pemmican. Elders were also adamant that an important step in making good pemmican was to place the thinly sliced pieces of meat on a *smoke-drying rack* (*sncqáy'eƚc'e$^{?}$tn*), over low-smoldering hardwood fires to keep off any flies and to assure a deep smoking and thorough drying of the meat. Smoked meat was less likely to become moldy, and the preferred smoking wood for meat was mountain alder. In some instances, red willow, cottonwood, or even lodge pole pine was used for smoking meat.

When making pemmican, stone pestles were used in lieu of wooden pestles when pounding berries in order to thoroughly crush the small hard stones in the fruit. Rendered fat was brought almost to a boil to increase the permeation when poured into a large rawhide container of mashed berries and dried meat. The container was sealed until the mass of meat and deer marrow had congealed, and later removed for use by manipulating and kneading the skin container. These containers were stored suspended from the rafters of a dwelling.

All families made a fish pemmican by placing "unseeded berries in a mortar, then mixing them with pulverized dried salmon" (Ray 1933:101). An interesting observation made by Reimers (1973:15) is how the Spokan may have added *pine seeds* (*sʕátkʷⁱɫp*) to the mixture when making pemmican. Fish, notably trout and salmon, was *stored for winter* (*sqʷomen*) consumption by first pounding the dried meat into powder, and boiling before serving.

It is interesting, and certainly true, that "Pemmican made possible the development of the interior communication system of the Northwest Company, and it was on this foundation that Simpson built the remarkable transportation system of the Hudson's Bay Company" (Merk 1931:346). Simpson cited the HBC standard recipe for making pemmican, saying it was ordinarily made from bison meat:

> The lean of the flesh was cut into thin broad slices which were hung up to dry in the sun or before a fire. Drying took about two days. The strips were then reduced to a pulp by pounding with a wooden flail on a sheet of rawhide spread out on the *prairie* [*čⁱčewm*] and the containers made from buffalo hide were packed about half full with the pulp, after which an almost equal weight of melted buffalo fat was stirred in to a total of ninety pounds. Meat and fat hardened together after which the bag was securely sewed up (Merk 1931:346).

Root and Berry Drying

A common method for drying large quantities of roots or berries was to spread them on tule mats laid on a sunny section of ground, or on raised horizontal tule mats placed atop drying racks near the woman's home. Roots, intended for winter storage, would often keep for three years if kept dry. Certain roots that had been baked could be stored, such as white camas, which turns hard and black after being baked, peeled, strung, and finally air-dried. Raw white camas was gathered in quantity; after cooking it was called *p'úxʷp'uxʷ*, and often stored as were other species of Lomatium. It was common to peel and string white camas, which stored quite well in baskets hung in dwellings or stored in flexible containers of cedar bark or spruce bark. Biscuit root was stored when thoroughly washed, boiled, dried, mashed, and made into small palm-size, flat, oval cakes. After drying, the cakes were put away for winter in large, flexible tule bags or covered baskets, and some families used stitched deer hide *containers* (*čq'oxʷé*) for storing bitterroot. Meat of course was never stored in skin bags.

Because of the availability and desire for huckleberries, great quantities were harvested, and if possible, dried on large berry racks, often within the berry camp to reduce weight and volume prior to carrying the harvest to a camp or village for storage. Large raised berry-drying platforms were 4 to 5 m long and approximately one meter wide. These racks were simple in design with "H"-shaped supports every 2 m, connected by long, intermittent cross pieces that supported the tule mats dressed lodge poles. Larger drying racks had each of the four corners supported by a tripod. All participants would collectively spread their day's harvest on the mats, atop the waist-high drying racks to facilitate sorting. Racks were ideally located in shaded areas to discourage fermenting and spoilage. Flies were presumably kept away by the camp's children, and adults who maintained smoke fires from slow-burning rotten logs. Before leaving the camp, the women would roll the mats to be carried back to lowland villages, disassemble the drying racks, and tie the cribbing material into linear stacks, which were carefully stacked on end and tied against trees until the following year.

Food and Wood Storage Facilities

A paramount concern for any foraging people was the proper storage of their plant, fish, and animal foods and the Spokan were no exception. Approximately seventy to eighty percent of total caloric sources were obtained over a period of approximately seven to eight months, and by the end of October, the food gathered was usually adequate until spring. Stored foods were supplemented by winter hunting, which unfortunately was not always sufficient to prevent starvation, as has been recorded (Cox 1831). Consequently, food storage was a critical issue, and the Spokan had developed various methods for safe food storage to survive the winter months.

The most daunting problems they faced were loss of stored foods, restricted hunting due to extreme weather, diminished deer populations, and on occasion unpredictably prolonged winters. Without exact figures, anthropologists are in general agreement that foragers, with good harvests in temperate areas, would gather, process, and store—if possible—approximately two to three times what a normal winter would demand for their survival. However, for whatever reason, if food supplies were diminished in late winter, it was an accepted practice for families to *exchange food* (*ʔeymscín* - "food swap"), but only under certain conditions of scarcity. Only *food that was stored* (*sčʼɫwiʔscúʔc*), could be given on demand to anyone (Elmendorf 1935-6, 1:8), particularly during periods of starvation. There is little likelihood that a *previous fall's food provisions* (*čʼeʔyéyeʔ*) was ever considered adequate. Younger members sometimes sought residence elsewhere, but this did not always alleviate conditions wrought by an inadequate food supply. There is no memory or written accounts to imply that the Spokan, during periods of extreme starvation, reduced their population by suicide, infanticide, or senicide.

Despite an earlier account (Ross 1904:297), theft of stored food was not a common problem. The two major reasons for food loss were the devastating results of natural causes, such as contamination by animals eating and urinating upon stored food while scavenging, or by ice from spring thaws destroying cached food storage structures atop river basalt outcrops. Work observed, "parts of the Spokane River frozen over" (Elliott 1914, 4:273). As a consequence, storage facilities situated on large mid-stream erratic basalt monoliths could be damaged by an early spring or by warm Chinook winds that created a build-up of large erratic chunks of ice, which could raft over the storage structures and remove them entirely. Unfortunately, though it occurred only very rarely, a constant concern regarding food stored in late autumn was fire from lightening or a wind-swept fire burning off low brush near a village. Walker's wife, Mary, noted how a raised storage platform was accidentally destroyed, burning several bags of dried camas in a drying fire (Drury 1976:360).

Many dried roots were stored within the living structure in shelved-pantries or in suspended grass bags or cedar bark bags hung from overhead supports, and even in stacked bent *cedar boxes* (*mʼimʼš*). Camas, being the major root food during the winter, was stored inside on either sides of each dwelling's entrance or *threshold* (*čłnčʼmep*). Though other types of roots—along with dried fish and meat—were stored within winter dwellings, the principal storage facilities were often located away from the dwelling. Until the reservation period, the Spokan used at least ten different types of *storage places for food* (*snkʷúmentn* - "food storage cache"), some of which were determined, not so much by the amount and type of food to be stored, but rather the presence or absence of certain topographical features within an area. Though it is difficult to ascertain due to variation in terrain and differences in types of food storage facilities, probably fifty to seventy per cent of winter food was stored in circular pits within well-drained talus slopes.

Prior to the acquisition of the horse, the problems of variable seasonal food availability and storage, which were dependent upon prehistoric adaptive logistics of procurement, are addressed by Galm and Nials:

> Suggestions of long-distance movements into and out of the Columbia Plateau on an annual basis are considered highly improbable. Not only are models of long-distance seasonal movements suspect from an energy exchange perspective, they are also inconsistent with much of what is known of predator-prey relationships, particularly with regard to the seasonal movements of herbivores. Equally important, the notion of annual movements into and out of the Upper Columbia region during early prehistory is difficult to reconcile with the

433

need for critical social interaction between related bands maintained through regular macroband gatherings. Food caches, placed near central base settlements and used to supplement overwintering supplies, are one possible form of storage during these early-dating occupations (1994:4.15).

Woodsheds

As cited earlier, the year-round importance of collecting firewood required considerable time and effort. And, until recently, on-reservation residents were dependent upon wood for heating their dwellings, and even now—during winter—some supplement commercial sources of heat with firewood. Traditionally, every dwelling, regardless of type or time of the year, had one or more structures for storing wood; even today over half of the Spokan homes have woodsheds. The size and form varied by the individual builder's effort and needs. Even now, a woodshed also serves for the dry storage of leather gear and metal equipment.

The principal function of a *woodshed* (*snlúk'ʷtn* - "place for wood" or *št'péslk'ʷp* - "place to stand up single firewood" or *nluq'ʷtn*) was to protect stored wood from moisture. Therefore, the material and construction of the roof was paramount, as were the sides of the structure—even for so simple a woodshed as a lean-to, which was always roofed. To save material and effort in retrieving firewood, one wall of the woodshed was frequently the wall of the larger dwelling, particularly of a long-house, never of a pit house, due to its *slanted roof* (*nč'mqnelxʷ*). The principal covering materials, apart from the structural lodge pole frame, were dry, flattened, pine bark or cedar; black cotton bark was avoided. With the paucity of cedar within the Spokan territory, long, split sections of tamarack were often used for shakes. Given availability, and the effort to split shakes, the walls were sometimes made of over-lapping bark sections, secured vertically to supporting lodge poles, with the lowest layer being overlapped by the next higher layer successively from bottom to top (Smith 1936-8:520). The slanting roof was fashioned from secured over-lapping sections of bark or split tamarack.

A large woodshed was a major feature upon the cultural landscape, and one that was built and often shared by an in-residence extended family. Some woodsheds had a simple A-frame, constructed of two pairs of slanting lodge poles secured at the apex, approximately 2 to 3 m in height, and supported a series of poles that sloped away from the frame to the ground. A ridge pole was attached to the apex of each upright but slanted A-frame. The entire structure was roofed with over-lapping sections of bark or split tamarack, and each section was held to a series of cross-poles with lengths of cedar or spruce root. An open entry was framed. There are accounts of a woodshed being built as a tipi, using three poles to form a tripod:

> In front and to one side of the door of the tipi they build a round wood shed like a tipi but not as carefully built. It has about the same number of poles [...] There was no excavation but it was on top of the ground. There was only about one ring to a mat. There were 2 rows of mats and they left it open at the top from where the upper edge of the mats is. It is about as big as a tipi: about 10 to 20 feet [in height] depending on the number of families in the dwelling. There were 2 layers of mat; there was no cedar bark at the bottom. One side of the woodshed was left open, about 4 to 5 feet wide; it was never covered; the opening reached the peak and was never covered by a door. The door was on a side not facing the tipi door (Smith 1936-8:519).

Storage Pits

The most common and conspicuous extant features in any long-term inhabitation site are the (sometimes numerous) food storage pits for each dwelling. Nearly all *food storage pits* (*snt'k'ʷéneʔtn* - "place to store food," or *snłqʷmíntn* or *snkʷúmcntn*), were located in excavated, loose talus slopes to facilitate bottom drainage of rain and melt water. Despite the known ethnographic descriptions, and our knowledge of all the materials used in constructing food storage pits, there is only the following recorded observation of how the structure was roofed to prevent water damage:

> After filling a subterranean food cache with sacks and baskets of food, the pit was first overlaid with unpeeled poles [probably lodge poles], which were then covered with wide, flattened sections of cedar bark that

434

supported thick layers of grass or pine needles, atop of which 20 to 30 cm of earth was placed (Smith 1936-8:530-1).

Food storage pits were first lined with a thickness of thorn berry branches, and then a layer of dead pine needles were spread over the thorn berries, or dead leaves served as a top layer over the thornberry branches. Women would also line storage pits with copious amounts of grass to prevent the stored food from freezing. Sometimes leaves of pineapple weed were carefully placed in alternate layers in meat or berry storage areas to prevent flies and bugs (Turner 1979:272). At one time deer bones were stored in food storage pits, which later were used to make soap or bone soup. A few elderly women recalled their grandmothers hearing how after storage pits were covered with layers of earth and stones, lumps of pitch, to ward off animals, were spread upon the roof.

The entrance to a food pit was usually through a framed slanted door on the lowest down-edge of the pit, where one could more easily gain access to the stored food. Several long cedar bark slabs were probably secured to a frame that served as a door, which would be completely removed upon use; and, after being replaced, secured with several wedging logs. The edges of the doorway were plugged with grass, and if the family was going to be away for some time, the entrance was covered with dirt (Smith 1936-8:533). The entrance was further protected from snow and rain by several long, permanent roofing poles, extended beyond the doorway which supported several split tamarack or cedar shingles for further rain protection.

An excavated pit might be lined on all sides, as well as covering the floor with slabs of cottonwood bark. Dry, dead pine needles were packed against the walls and on the floor before filling the storage pit with dried foods. The stored contents—always in grass, tule, hide, or bark bags—were covered with more dry pine needles prior to sealing the pit with adequately sized sections of black cottonwood bark to keep the contents free of rodents and from freezing.

The main damage to stored food was caused by different types of rodents, most notably the omnivorous and destructive *brown rat* (*Rattus norvegicus*), *pack rat* (*Neotom* sp. - *héw't*) and numerous *short-haired* (*čłssáxl'x̣ʷ*) rodents, and even the small and innocuous *deer mouse* (*Peromyscus maniculatus* - *sx̣ʷlx̣ʷl sč'ém'ey'eʔ*). Two other types of mice were responsible for eating and damaging stored food: notably the ubiquitous house or field mouse, and the *Western harvest mouse* (*Reithrodontomys megalotis*), both now called *k'ʷék'ʷtn'eʔ*. All rodents, particularly the northern pocket gopher, presented constant problems to the long-term storage of various dried grass seed crops.

There were always two major concerns when storing food in such a pit: to prevent contamination or destruction of food by animals, such as rodents and bears, and to prevent moisture. Once a stored food became wet, it quickly spoiled. The small size of the ubiquitous rodents allowed them to enter a storage pit through the interstices in the talus. Animals were sometimes deterred by a ring of prickly-pear cactus that encircled a storage pit, but this was useless once it had snowed. Moreover, a storage pit that had not been properly sealed off could be contaminated by animals urinating within the structure, since rodents, such as the common house mouse and other burrowing creatures, were known to have destroyed stored food by urinating on inadequately sealed food containers, whereas a bear was capable of removing any human-laid stone covering, log structure or storage pit with considerable ease, and then destroying the food contents. As a consequence, winter food was sometimes cached in trees and raised platform storage facilities. Only thoroughly dried plant foods and fish—basically non-odorous foods—were stored in food pits, given the danger of bears. Because of this concern, fish tended to be stored in tree storage facilities or raised platform storage houses—since large animals usually had more difficulty gaining access to such structures.

As previously emphasized, the second potential problem when storing food in pits was moisture and the resulting mildew. Since food storage pits were often impervious to rain, and pit construction permitted air-flow, the only occasion for the occurrence of mildew would have been if the entrance to the storage pit had not been properly sealed, or if damaged by a scavenging bear or wolverine. It is known that Plains peoples used charcoal in food storage pits to absorb moisture in semi-subterranean pits, but there is no data regarding this practice for the Spokan. Though difficult to conclude from the archaeological record, food storage pits have been found with appreciable amounts of charcoal, which of course will last longer than unburned wood. Many tuber crops were traditionally stored in a fire-hollowed log lined with grass to prevent freezing (Smith 1936-8:533). One elderly lady explained how a standing or downed fire-hollowed log was ideal for food storage when lined with bear-grass, because the charcoal, being endohydric, absorbed moisture, and the grass prevented the food from freezing. Smith cited this type of food cache being used by the Kalispel (1936-8:533). Throughout the winter, food pits were occasionally opened in dry weather to air stored foods (Teit 1930:342).

Food storage pits were generally in the immediate area of the winter village, or a major fishing station if inhabited year round. An extended family in residence might have 3 to 12 such pits that varied in size according to the size of a family. Some food storage pits had a diameter from 2 to 7 m, and were often 2 to 3 m in depth, essentially cone-shaped with stabilized broken basalt rock walls with a slope of about forty-five degrees. Over ninety percent of all known Spokan pit houses and storage pits are located on terraces or slopes with a predominantly south-west exposure (Ross 1993).

Winter food was stored in loosely *woven fabric bags* (*čt't'qʷíc'eʔ*) and placed in food storage pits or other types of storage facilities; dried roots were effectively stored in a *grass sack* (*ƛ'áqn'eʔ*) to keep the food from freezing. Often any type of storage bag would be further protected from rodents and vermin by stacking fresh wormwood leaves between each layer of dried salmon. Flexible storage bags were made from tule, cattail, silverberry bark, *clematis bark* (*qe'tesnineʔ*), willow bark, and Indian hemp. In the case of a multiple family storage facility, particularly with camas sacks, each family could easily identify their storage container.

Prior to a winter hunt to supplement stored food, men would carry lozenges made from bits of dried meat and hard-dried camas that had previously been pressed into small hard cakes called *maʔƛ'q'ʷá*. These lozenges were used not only to relieve and avoid dryness of throat, but to provide sustenance. Even in summer and late fall, when fishing or hunting, men would remove from a storage facility adequate amounts of *hard smoke-dried camas cakes* (*m'am'áɫq'ʷl't'n'*) to supplement their diet while traveling. *Powdered camas cake* (*stkʷɫiʔi*) was used in winter stews and soups, and was stored in a number of ways. One method of storage was to thread freshly-made cakes on grass fiber strings, and suspend them within a dwelling on cross-poles in order to keep them dry in wet weather (Elmendorf 1935-6, 1:38).

Wilson observed how various types of berries and roots were processed for winter storage:

> There are several kinds of roots eaten, of which the Cammass [sic], made into cakes of a not unpleasant flavour, is the best and most used. Of berries, that known as the 'service berry' is the most common, and is gathered in August and September, when it is dried in the sun and put up in mats for winter use. The wild cherry, and a small white berry of a very bitter taste, called by the Spokan *stee xchux*, and growing on a bush something like the elder, are found in great quantities in some districts. Hips and haws, angelica, the seeds on the Oregon sunflower pounded into meal, and the berries of the kinnikinik [sic], or *uva ursi*, fried in grease, are also eaten. In times of great scarcity, a dark brown kind of moss, like horse-hair, is eaten. It is boiled for two or three days and nights until reduced to a white tasteless pulp, but does not seem to be very nutritious (1866:296).

Underground Caches

Recognizing the risk of late winter starvation, or situations of food contamination, various types of storage structures—such as platform storage, tree storage, and pit storage—were universally used. In addition to stored foods, families would have *caches of hidden food* (*st'ekʷn'ʔéy'eʔ* or *scwkʷwékʷs*) in *personal storage places* (*snkʷmlscutn*) whose locations were known to all, but were apparently accessible to only that family. During winter each extended family was near-dependent upon summer- and fall-gathered foods stored in different types of facilities—some of which were *underground caches* (*snɫqomín*) that differed from the aforementioned more larger and circular storage pits. The Spokan frequently used an underground cache to store dried winter salmon (Bancroft 1875, 1:285 fn).

The principal reason for using an underground cache was to protect food from marauding animals (Smith 1991:8,58), and there are several detailed references to this type of underground food storage facility in the eastern Plateau (Teit 1930:63, 229; Smith 1936-8:530). The most detailed description of an underground cache was recorded by Smith when working with the Kalispel, and presents a detailed description which represents a comparative ethnographic model:

> They dug a hole about 3 feet deep and from 3 or 4 to 8 feet in diameter depending on the number of families [...] They were built by the women generally [...] They wall it up inside with a single layer of tule mats, held in place by the stuff inside. Then they lay 4 logs around the top of the hole in a square near the edge of the hole. Then they lay poles across the top, right close together; any kind of poles are used which will hold [...] The 4 poles are about 12 inches in diameter and the bigger the better. There was just one layer of poles, which were unpeeled. These were covered with one layer of cedar bark. And then they cover it over with dirt over the top and down the sides to a depth of one or more feet [...] Where cedar bark is scarce, they pile a lot of grass (any kind) on or dry pine needles [...] The grass layer is a couple of feet thick; but it does not take a very thick layer of pine needles to turn the water: they mat down better than the grass.

> They cover it with bark and the dirt is piled on so that it looks like a mound. The door is closed with 2 or 3 layers of cedar bark and they put grass on top of it with no dirt piled on. The door was cut in one wall of the cellar [...] It is sloped and just enough to get under the roof and the log around the edge, by crawling in on the hands and knees or on the belly. These caches were put right close together in one place for the whole encampment. They are dug where it is easy digging. Dryness is not much of a factor for the chances are that the food is all used up by the next thaw. Food was never left in these over the summer [...] Women dug the hole with their digging -sticks; they did not use special paddles.

> They use the same hole year after year. When empty, they close it over, probably so the skunks will not get in and ruin it. Next year they clean it out and use it again [...] They use the same poles and bark year after year [...] (Smith 1936-8:530-531).

Work also recognized the problems of storing perishables—including lead ball and gun powder—underground in dry ground, "property hidden [... and] ought to have wood all round it on very side so that the earth could not touch it, otherwise it will in a very short time be rotten and spoiled" (Elliott 1914, 3:183)

As noted earlier, it was common for a family to have a private underground cache site for concealing property often meant for later redistribution to kinspeople, or when being absent with no elder kinsperson present. But to avoid conflict, it was apparently not unusual for a Spokan family to temporarily bury private property. Elmendorf (pers. comm.) thought private caches may have become more popular with families owning smaller, more valuable and durable trade items, and when leaving on extended tours (bison hunting?) buried certain items. The junction of the Little Spokane and Spokane Rivers, once referred to as the Forks (Elliott 1914, 3:277 fn.), was where Lewis often searched for hidden caches, and he points out how there was still evidence of these excavations above Little Falls:

> A hole was dug in a suitable dry place, lined with barks, grass and sticks and property one wanted to leave behind was carefully stored away in a hole which was then covered with cloth, hide or bark and filled up with dirt. The hole was then tramped over, and the dirt packed and leveled, and the surplus dirt thrown so as to leave no trace to show the existence of the cache. So hidden property was often left for months, even for several years (1925:102-3).

It is worth mentioning Kane's observation of food caches in the region of Tschimakain Mission: "There are numerous Indian caches of dried salmon in the vicinity, which are very seldom robbed, although left in isolated spots for months without any person in charge" (1859:214-5, 1971:122). Four years later (1849), Stanley painted the same scene depicting the abandoned mission, still with Spokan dwellings and the large storage platform as depicted earlier by Kane. An earlier and more detailed drawing of Tschimakain Mission (1846) was executed by Charles A. Geyer in December 1843. Yet, after living with the Walkers for six months, Geyer was asked to "leave after Elkanah found it necessary to tell him to leave that they could no longer entertain him" (Drury 1940:183; 1976:265). However, before leaving, Geyer graciously wrote a note of appreciation in Mary's autograph album which included the following, "Through the whole dreary winter, you entertained the stranger under the hospitable roof of your inhabitation in the wilderness—not like a stranger, but as a friend" (Drury 1976:289 fn). Three years later, Paul Kane, who spent time from 1846 to 1848 in the Columbia Basin, visited the Walkers and executed a pen and ink sketch of the Walker's cabin, barn, and storehouse (Clarke 1994, 1:11).

Geyer later supported and encouraged Spaulding in collecting plant specimens, as did Asa Gray, who wrote to Spaulding on the proper procedure for collecting and thinning roots and bulbs as well as how to wrap and press them for shipment. Gray particularly appreciated the dedication and efforts of Spaulding who sent packages of seeds and specimens of bulbs and roots he collected to the National Institute in Washington and to the Botanical Gardens in London (Oliphant 1934, 2:99-101).

Root Cellars

With the reservation system, a number of cultural and logistical factors led to the adoption of the *root cellar* (*snpatáqtn* - "potato cellar" or *nq'ymáqs*), which differed in structure from the underground cache. It was constructed by first excavating a flat rectangular depression, then lining it with stones large enough to hold in place vertical boards that were further stabilized by placing earth behind the boards. Horizontal pit-sawn planks were placed at a right angle on top of each opposite vertical upright to form the roof. The final and most critical stage of construction was adding a ventilation shaft, which tended to moderate temperatures and circulate the air, thus ensuring better preservation of the food by preventing any moisture collecting within the structure. Access was provided via a small door at one of the ends, usually facing south or southwest to provide better visibility when in the structure. The entire structure was covered with earth, up to 70 to 90 cm. Until recently, a number of these cellars that still had roofs were in comparatively fair condition, though no longer used.

During the allotment system, walled root cellars gained popularity and became a necessity with the advent of carpenter-built lumber houses. Consequently, there was an increased dependence upon non-seasonal commercial agricultural foods requiring less mobility and greatly reduced the necessity to exploit traditional migratory game, even resident animals. Root cellars accommodated canned foods, thereby changing and facilitating many new methods for the preservation and storage of food. For example, the storage of meat in burlap bags had several important advantages to storing meat in traditional rawhide containers, such as the parfleche, because flexible burlap bags were porous, thereby permitting better air circulation, and yet preventing contamination by insects and spoilage. Elders remember when every home had one or more such storage structures.

Later, non-indigenous root and tuber plants, such as carrots, potatoes, parsnips and other root crops were stored in beds of sand under the lower wall shelves of root cellars. Prior to the introduction of root cellars, a family in early fall would dig wild carrot that topped and placed outside in loam pits at least 40 cm deep to prevent freezing, remaining fresh and tasty until the late winter or early spring when excavated.

The floors of nearly all root cellars consisted of flattened clay, often applied in layers up the side walls for 25 to 30 cm to prevent the presence of burrowing animals and to help maintain a more constant temperature—clay being endothermic. Winter food storage pits, logs, caches, and later cellars required great quantities of *fallen, brown, ponderosa pine needles* (*č'eme?*) for further insulation, and stuffed under and in between food containers. The capacity of storage areas was greatly increased by the use of *shelves along the wall* (*nx̣lenč*) of a root cellar, and some cellars had an end *cupboard* (*snčsléw'stn*) as well.

The mean temperature was more constant in a partially subterranean root cellar. With the advent of lumber houses that had chimneys, and the use of dry-food cellars, the principles of air circulation became a critical concern. Stored foods were naturally better protected and stored longer with the introduction of canning—*canning fruit* (*k'ʷlk'ʷálč'qn* - "canned food"), meat, and even fish. As testimony to the success of these particular storage structures, not too many years ago there were several examples of deserted root cellars that had both canned and dry-stored roots that were, even after 60 or more years, probably still edible.

Bank Caches

There were only a few brief oral accounts of the Spokan using *bank* or *sidehill* (*nč'ʔelłniʔw't*) caches (Smith 1991:8.60), or of their rudimentary construction. There was, however, recall by two elderly women of several such caches that once existed just below Little Falls Dam. These caches were located in the banks above high-water levels—sites that had already been excavated near-horizontally into the upper terraces of the Spokane River, and said to have once been productive hematite mines, but once exhausted the excavated sites were modified into salmon caches. One advantage of such structures was that they were more stable than the surrounding matrix of deposited sand and river gravel.

There was no recall as to whether the bank caches were internally supported in any fashion, probably because those observed were relatively small and naturally walled and roofed with intact compacted clay or cobbled stones. It was claimed that each cache entrance was approximately 2 m below the once-eroded surface of the existing stream terrace; nor was it known if a bank cache had any type of back-vent for air circulation, since the constant stream breezes were probably sufficient. It would have been extremely difficult, even dangerous, for an elderly person to negotiate the unstable *steep bank* (*ʔustcin*) if a person attempted to gain access by rafting in a point below the entrance, and then climbing up the bank. It seems reasonable that a person gained access more readily through a vertical door when assisted by one or more people, who probably lay just slightly over the edge of the terrace to assist an individual while being lowered to the entrance. As once explained, it was remembered how the same procedure had been employed when digging hematite.

The bank cache was similar to what Smith (1936-8:534; 1991:8.60) identified as a "side-hill cache," once used by the Chewelah-Spokan Group, who had apparently excavated several such storage sites in an area of hard-packed clay—one with a roof supported by several horizontal lodge poles that may have supported a sloping, framed, layered cottonwood bark slab roof.

Rock Platform Caches

Prior to the building of the Grand Coulee Dam, some families who resided near Spokane Falls and Little Falls stored part of their fish reserves on large, relatively flat granite boulders located midstream in the Spokane River. These storage areas were made with river-borne logs, not unlike a log cabin, having a flat but slanting or hipped roof, with the low side facing south-west. No one could recall the dimensions, but may be inferred from the size of existing boulders, at least those that have not been destroyed by dam-building, or the ones that have been identified as once being used for this purpose. One elderly woman recalled her grandmother saying that two of these large flat rocks were of mythical significance, and they are still visible (Ross 1993).

Storage Houses

The traditional Spokan *food storage house* (*snłqmín*)—being larger and more substantial than a wood storage shed—was available to a large group of families (Elmendorf, pers. comm.). In contrast, a smaller storage *shed* (*st'qéłxʷ* - "temporary brush shelter") belonged to a single or extended family's winter dwelling. Though the shape of the typical food storage structure has been recorded (Elmendorf 1935-6, 1:8), the actual dimensions and the nature of the covering materials are conjectural, and can be only tentatively reconstructed on the basis of the scanty details of the structures available. From the few details available it may be construed that such a food storage house was of pole construction, probably with an outward slanted shake roof with sides of woven willow.

439

The storage house was seldom used in the summer since the people had access to fresh food, and were often away on the annual subsistence round. All winter storage facilities were scrupulously cleaned prior to departing the winter village. In a large dwelling, winter foods were sometimes stored within an *inside storehouse* (*xléneʔ*), located at one end or the other of the structure. After acquiring saws and broad axes, many winter dwellings had a *small log-constructed storage structure* (*sqʼecʼéłcʔxʷ*) located adjacent to the main dwelling. To protect dried fish from dogs and wolves, storage platforms were raised "about eight to ten feet above the ground [...] bark and matting are placed over them to secure them from rain" (Suckley 1855, 1:300).

Stone Over-Hang Caches

Though never common, there are several magnificent surviving examples of prehistoric stone storage structures on the Spokane Indian Reservation, near Little Falls (Ross 1993)—structures most likely used for the winter storage of fish. In one rather spectacular instance, the rock storage house is roofed by a huge, horizontal, over-hanging slab of granite that was clearly positioned by earlier glacial movement—a large rectangular slab that juts approximately 2 m out from its raised base; the outer edge is 90 cm above ground level. The remaining once-open three sides are still dry-walled with pieces of heavy, flat granite that provided a complete enclosure for any stored food stuffs. When the structure was examined, only the top section of one wall had been partially removed; the remaining two walls were in perfect condition (Ross 1993).

A second type of *rock house* (*sšnʼšéłxʷ*) or storage structure was found in the same area near a once-important fishery, but differed in that an anchor or support wall was a large granite monolith, and the remaining 3 walls were made by stacking and interleaving flat sections of fractured granite to a height of 1 m, the length of each of the two parallel side walls being approximately 1 m. The stone roof, still intact, is a simple but effectively constructed feature of 4 nearly-parallel, long sections of granite slabs, and fortunately remains as an outstanding and ingenious example of using a naturally occurring stone ledge, culturally modified with existing dry-walled talus slabs (Ross 1993).

Platform Storage

Nearly all *raised storehouses* (*čqʼʷmáqs*) were made of wood; basically a roofed and close-sided platform supported usually more than 2 m above the ground by 4 long vertically pre-set stout lodge poles, each approximately 3 m in length. A lower rectangular roof frame was formed by securing four horizontal lodge poles to the outside tops of the four vertical support poles. Given the size of an extended family, and the amount of food intended for winter use, the actual dimensions of the storage platform were approximately 2.5 m in width and 4 m in length. Four horizontal lodge poles formed the edges of the *floor* (*xlélptn*), and were secured outside by vertical support poles. The platform, or floor, was a successive series of undressed lodge poles laid side by side; alternating one butt end with the top end of the adjoining pole, and secured to the floor frame with strips of bark from red or black thornberry or from serviceberry. For summer inhabitation, the floor poles were covered often with pounded sections of cedar bark—the underside being placed up with a final cover of buckskins.

The platform house was an excellent example of a multi-purpose structure, for in the summer, prior to it being used for food storage, people sometimes slept in the empty but enclosed and roofed platform. This was especially true for older children, who certainly enjoyed the privacy away from their parents and younger siblings.

The walls of a storage house were made by affixing horizontal lodge poles to the outside of the four main vertical support poles, and these were further secured at the top to the lower rectangular roof frame. Two vertical poles, and a short horizontal pole, attached to the floor frame and roof frame, formed the doorway. There were no windows, only an east-facing door. The closure of each wall was made in a variety of fashions:

either overlapped tule mats were affixed to a series of parallel lodge poles of small diameter, or a framed shingled wall of overlapping flattened tamarack or cottonwood bark was attached to the slightly tilted lodge poles—tamarack being more available than cedar for both the Kalispel and Chewelah-Spokan Group (Smith 1936-8:140). The outside bark layer was held in place by pressure from a series of horizontal poles secured at each end to a vertical support post. With the introduction of the steel axe, bark was replaced by long shakes of split tamarack.

For the storage of food and personal property, the most common type of storage platform was the *raised platform* (*sxláqs* - "ledge, platform"), and often a family had one or more such structures. Raised platforms were multipurpose, and as mentioned, were often used as summer sleeping dwellings and, with some minor structural modifications, for drying food after harvest. Because storage platforms were temporary, they were relatively simple in construction, using only limited types of building materials. Consequently, the best source of information about *platform storage* (*čxléw'stn* - "shelf" or "ledge") facilities is the old photographs of rural Spokan settings. Smith fortunately provided rather detailed comparative data on storage structures used by the Kalispel, and Teit described how the Coeur d'Alene used such structures:

> Scaffolds of poles were erected near all the more permanent lodges for the storing of saddles, skins, and other goods, to keep them out of the way of dogs. Anything of value was covered with mats, which were often fastened down as protection against the wind. Spare baskets, mats, poles, and frames for stretching skins were also often placed on these scaffolds (1930:63).

A common type of food storage house, reported for both the Lakes and Spokan (Elmendorf 1935-1936, 1:26a), was an early historical structure built on four corner stilts made of lodge pole pine. The limb stubs were kept intact, thus, forming a ladder. Lower platform caches were reached by temporarily leaning a notched log ladder against the tree. The storage structure, usually 2 by 2 m square, was roofed with long-split tamarack shakes, and walled with vertical willow withes that provided some ventilation. The building's platform was approximately 2 to 3 m from the ground, and had an east-facing door. Such structures were used primarily for winter storage of salmon.

Similar to this was the *framed wood storage shed* (*št'péslk'ʷp*), one that was not on stilts, but built outside each major dwelling, and enclosed and roofed with large sections of bark or sewn fiber mats. A more rudimentary but effective type of winter food storage house was the one built atop four poles three or more meters above the ground, and roofed with layered fir boughs, called a *sxláqs*.

After any raised and enclosed food storage structure had been filled with winter food, the owner would erect one or two small deadfalls inside to catch rodents, baited with grease. Rodents could eventually *gnaw* (*čxepím'*) through the siding of the structure, and in one night might contaminate at least some of the food with urine, or worse, gnaw easily into the grass or cattail storage sacks (Smith 1951:78). A common procedure of preventing rodents and other animals, particularly large adult raccoons, from gaining access to platform caches was to surround the base of each vertical lodge pole with a thick ring or collar of overlaid prickly pear cacti.

It is not believed that every family used tree or platform storage facilities for protecting winter food (Smith 1936-8:533; Elmendorf, pers. comm.), given the restrictions or lack of needed natural features, and the expenditure of energy in manufacturing and maintaining the structures that were more exposed to the elements and marauding animals. Also, above-ground storage facilities required poles or trees to support walled platforms, which were structurally less capable of housing large amounts of food. Therefore, the storage pit was the most enduring and efficient floor storage facility, given the required surface area of an above-ground facility, the expenditure of energy in manufacturing, stability, access, and storage capacity.

John Mix Stanley, one of eleven artists, who from 1853-54 accompanied Isaac I. Stevens, during the Northwestern Pacific Railroad survey, produced a series of magnificent sketches and paintings—some later made into lithographs illustrating food storage structures. The paintings were commissioned by the U.S. Pacific Railroad Expedition and Surveys (Stevens, 1860). One of them shows what is now referred to as

441

Tschimakain Mission (Stanley 1862, 12(1):146-147, Plate XXXIX), and includes a partial but excellent illustration of a very large and unusual rectangular flat food storage platform, held approximately 3 to 3.5 m above the ground. From the angle of the representation, it is difficult to arrive at any exact dimensions of the flat platform—perhaps one meter to 120 cm wide, and more than 2.5 m in length. Each of the platforms two short ends were supported by two long lodge poles, crossed and secured at the upper ends just below the apex of each pole. The butt ends were spread to form an inverted "V". There were no walls or fixed roof, but apparently the stored food was ridged along the length of the platform, and protected by what appears to be earth atop of probably tule or cattail mats. A detailed pencil sketch of Tschimakain Mission was made by Charles Guyer in the spring of 1844 showing the buildings and gardens (Bamonte and Bamonte 1999:19).

Figure 31. "Chemakane Mission"

Prior to acquiring horses, the last collective fall deer hunt required several days or more of arranging food for the old and infirm who would remain in the village. Men commonly left first to reconstruct known platform and tree caches, which were storage sites used several times a year to temporarily store deer meat as the entire village hunted and gathered roots for several weeks. While the men hunted deer, the women devoted their time to digging roots, returning each mid-day to the nearest cache for processing their harvest and *drying* (*scqiy'etc'e?*) the roots, which were placed in grass sacks before temporarily storing them in storage platforms, or by burying them in rock piles. During these activities, women were sometimes able to supplement the winter stores by berrying (STHC). As the men hunted in small groups, any deer killed were dressed and either hung or temporarily placed atop storage platforms. Older boys would remain to protect these sites, while the men continued to hunt deer until a sufficient number had been taken, and after the last

442

hunt, the men would retrace their way back, always stopping at the previous cache to secure the stored meat. This logistical practice saved time and energy by not returning to the village with a load of meat after each major kill (STHC; Elmendorf 1935-6, 2:41).

The most apparent feature of the winter *storehouse* (*sxláqs* or *qʷeqʷcen'eʔ*) and summer dwelling was the universal use of a peaked roof. With such a roof, the top and leading edge of one southwest roof partition overlapped the opposing roof partition at a 45° angle, and the peak of the roof was approximately 2 m from the floor. The only published reference to constructing a storehouse roof is from Smith (1936-8:526), who provided a definitive description of Kalispel construction, which fortunately included the Chewelah-Spokan Group "who never numbered more than one hundred" (Smith 1936-8:140). Smith reported that they did not use a continuous ridge pole for stabilizing the rafters and roofing. However, the lack of a continuous horizontal ridge pole does not suggest architectural deficiency, since the closeness of the inverted "V" rafters was sufficient to support the roofing material of double-layered split hemlock shakes (Smith 1936-8:527). More importantly, the additional winter snow load must have required a series of inverted "V" ridges.

As previously cited, if they occupied a village that was near or on a favorable fishing site, it was not unusual for a family to sleep in the emptied storehouse throughout the previous warm months. In summer it was not necessary to sleep on robes; often large sections of buckskin sufficed, since tule mats were placed atop the single layer of cedar bark. Being off the ground, occupants were free from ground-dwelling vermin and had the advantages of *cooling breezes* (*hi xáʕ*). Entrance to the platform storage structure was by ladder, and each family built their own storage house, after the women collected all the necessary materials, and then erected the structure, a type of construction that typically lasted for six to eight years. Because of its large size, such a structure served as a temporary dwelling and storage house. If necessary, the fishermen and their families slept in such a structure during high winds and blowing sand.

Tree Storage

It would be difficult to even roughly approximate the percentage of dried salmon that was stored in any roofed tree *platform cache* (*čxlew'stn*), which was essentially a high, built larder. However, given the crucial role played by salmon in the Spokan diet, the importance of these structures is certainly appreciated. As noted earlier, tree storage platform caches were erected solely on Ponderosa pine trees, and when empty they frequently provided cool sleeping areas for adults and children in the heat of summer, prior to being filled with stored food.

All of the known tree storage areas on the present reservation were located within several hundred meters of the Spokane River. These storage areas once existed as groves, and were given specific geonomic designations acknowledged by informants as once existing, but now largely forgotten. The last Ponderosa salmon *storage area* (*snʔelk'ʷmn*) could be seen until the late 1960s, when it was sadly clear-cut to make pasturage in an area near Little Falls Flats, once called (*cqescí* or *hec m'm'q'ʷmaq'ʷ* - "tiny mounds"). One elder, discussing his grandfather and others, was told:

> [...] how after a large fish harvest at *cqescí* [Little Falls] the men would collect from the women the hundreds and hundreds of huge salmon they had cleaned and sun-dried on racks between the storage trees and the falls. A man would stand on each of the [protruding] branch stub[s], and the women made several long lines so they could pass one fish to the next person, which I suppose was easier than packing them. Men would take turns on the steps, 'cause it was busy and hard work passing the dried stiff salmon from one man to the next using only one hand. Some men, I suppose, would lean against the trunk of the tree. Each fish was somehow tied to the one below; each layer of fish was crisscrossed with the next one. The first couple of layers were tied to the platforms that were supported by several limbs. I knew, even as a young boy, that the fish were tree-stored so animals would not spoil [them with urine] or eat the cached fish. Also, the platforms were too high for hornets and wasps (Ross 1968-2008).

The most distinguishing feature of storage trees was that *none* of the lower *tree branches* (*sčlčl'šmečst*) were cut away, since they were used as ladders to reach the food *storage house or platforms* (*snłqmín*), which were reputedly always above 10 m to prevent the invasion and destruction of stored food by hornets and yellow jackets. Considerable effort was expended when making or refurbishing an *elevated fish storage platform* (*stxaláks*), making certain there would be adequate air circulation, but secure enough to stand river valley winds. The roughly square platform was made of lodge poles, secured by each of three or four poles being angled from the edge of the platform to the base of a lower branch. Each side of the storage structure was made of long pieces of wedge-split larch, secured by a now-forgotten method of lashings to a rigid frame of poles with approximately square walls and floor. The two-sided sloped roof of latticed poles was covered with split, overlapping larch shakes. The upper end of each shake had two bored holes through which both ends of twisted hemp were passed and secured by tying to spaces under right-angle roof poles. A small crawl entrance was through several tightly wedged slabs of straight cedar.

Such platform structures were used for storing sections of butchered deer meat, which was quite heavy, and used on occasionally for winter storage, which indicates how well they were constructed (Elmendorf 1935-6, 2:41). It was probable that each tree cache stored one or two family's winter salmon.

Hide and Intestine Food Containers

Though not a major storage facility, the *parfleche* (or *nc?a?úlxtn* or *snc'?ú* or *snk'ína* - "pillow") was a useful *storage container* (*sčq'e?yic''e?*) for food and for packing items when traveling, sometimes called *pn'pn'aqs* ("folded ends"). When dry food was stored in a parfleche, the bundle was called *snt'k'ʷene?tn*. The parfleche was probably introduced from the Plains via the Flathead and Nez Perce to the Spokan in the late prehistoric period. Those of the Flathead and Nez Perce were usually decorated with geometric polychromatic designs, and the Spokan did the same for parfleche storage containers. One can only assume that the *painted parfleche* (*čq'ey'íc'e?*) was an introduced art form to the Spokan from the Plains. Fur traders adopted the semi-tanned parfleche bag for storing salted bison tongues, and as saddle bags (Elliott 1914, 3:189). The word parfleche was derived from the French *pare une flèche*, because the hide was strong enough to deflect or parry and arrow.

To ensure durability, and to maintain a somewhat flat shape, the parfleche was made from either bison or horse hide. This rather unique yet ubiquitous container, was also made of elk or bison rawhide taken from the animal's nape, and was shaped much like a large envelope. During construction, rawhide was first soaked and then bent over poles to give a general shape, then the hide was folded shut, and the leading edges were secured with ties of rawhide. Parfleche bags were used primarily for the winter storage of food, and as a carrying container that was slung on either side of a pack horse, thus permitting the transport of weighty and sizable loads by horse or by a person. The only description of the Spokan parfleche is by Elmendorf:

> [The] whole skin of [the] animal [was] stripped off—tanned [and] often turned inside out—leg parts [were] stuffed with duck, goose, or pheasant feathers—parfleches often tied to [a] rafter pole in back of [the] sleeping place [...] Designs [were] painted on with vermilion in bear or beaver fat oil—also with blue lay—showy ones usually [were] tied up on rafters because the paint came off easily—no incised designs [...] No mice got into a parfleche because they always made such a noise that the owner was warned [... Parfleches] were dried & folded over poles along the edges—usually rectangular in shape when closed [... the] thickness [was] determined by [the] diameter of the poles [it was] dried over—[a] head-line for carrying—*lčíčn'*— [with a] leather pad to fit the forehead [of] 4 or 5 inches wide—*nłqʷaúskn*—leather lines were attached to each end—sometimes carried across the chest—with women the only method of carrying loads (1935-6, 1:66-7).

Skin and intestine storage and carrying containers were waterproof, made from the untanned skins and intestines of salmon and sturgeon. The shape of the salmon or sturgeon determined the form of the container, which were used principally for the storage of roe and fish oils. One existing salmon container demonstrates how the tail was kept intact, and only the head and gill sections of the body were removed, and the area of the detached head was replaced with a flat oval wooden disc. The circumference of the disc edge was grooved to accommodate a tightly wrapped piece of rawhide to secure the contents, which often consisted of *dried roe* (*x*ʷ*el'ék'*ʷ*e*ʔ). Such bags were suspended from the rafters of the winter dwellings. Deer and elk intestines made effective storage containers for the fat and marrow that was collected when butchering animals.

Elmendorf described a type of *leather storage container* (*smt'íkltn*) used by the Lakes, made "from the neck leather of deer or buffalo hide [...] used for carrying food on [a] journey or day's hunting—men & women both carried these—Spokanes didn't seem to have these" (1935-6, I:68), and when finished it was not unlike a parfleche, except that the rawhide box was square. The rawhide was first cut in an outline pattern that resembled a broad cross. After a thorough soaking, the cross section was divided into thirds; the outer thirds, and the two opposite arms were bent at right angles to the main length of the pattern, one forming a side while the attached section became the top. The bottom and remaining side was made from bending the long length of the cross at the juncture of the cross arms. The outside edge of the top of the box was perforated to accommodate a length of buckskin, which was then tied to a length of buckskin attached to the opposite side of the *box* (*snt'íkltn* or *šn'šn'éne*ʔ). The sides, where the edges contacted another side, were held in place by corner-stitching with lengths of rawhide. Once the hide had completely dried, it was fairly rigid, save for the hinged top section. One side of the box had two parallel cuts that were vertical with the top and bottom, which accommodated a belt to permit the person to carry food while on a journey (Elmendorf 1935-6, 1:68, 1:80).

Dried cooked onion was pressed into flat cakes and stored in flat, stitched *rawhide deerhide* (*čq'ox*ʷ*é*) containers, whereas deer intestine was used as containers "for grease [...] meat or fish [that had been] dried & pulverized [sometimes adding crushed] hazel nuts [...] berries or camas might be crushed & added [and] bear oil or pieces of bear grease worked into this and stored in intestine [as] hammered food" (Elmendorf 1935-6, 1:3). Any intestine container was called *p't'mán*, whereas a skin sack was known as *čk'ux*ʷ*é*.

Though no untanned elk or deer skin bags are known to presently exist, there were descriptions indicating that each animal skin bag was closed by tightening the top portion and wrapping a rawhide wrap around it, which facilitated storage of this type of container by suspension. Historians Ruby and Brown (1982:16) have written that the Spokan stored dried salmon underground in large containers; this information is probably from Teit (1930:333), who noted this practice by the Coeur d'Alene, but specifically not for the Spokan. There are no written—and were few oral—accounts of the Spokan using *fishtail* (*súps*) as a storage container for dried roe, though one elder recalled hearing of such a practice.

Bark, Root, and Hemp Baskets and Bags

In making baskets, weaving was not a known technology for the Spokan, who practiced twining and coiling. "The third major method—plaiting—is scarcely represented, and true weaving has not been found in the region" (Conn and Schlick 1998:600). Both the more flexible coiled grass and coiled cedar or spruce root and bark baskets were used for storing winter foods, since wooden containers were not used for storage. Hide was often an adequate substitute for wood. Though there is a paucity of descriptive information concerning the actual construction of the cedar *storage box* (*m'im'š* or *šn'šn'éne*ʔ), except that they were fashioned with the inside of cedar bark for the purpose of storing dried meat and fish for winter consumption. The contents of a rectangular box were apparently protected by a flat lid attached with twisted hemp to the top of one long side of a support frame of Osage orange, which formed the four-sided rim. No examples are known to exist.

Teit (1930:329) claimed that because the Flathead and Spokan lived in either an arid or *prairie* (*čłčewm*) environment, they seldom made bark baskets, though numerous examples exist today in private collections, museums, and with some Spokan. As cited previously, the Spokan made various types of baskets, and from different materials, including a type of durable *bark basket* (*snq'*ʷʔ*étk*ʷ*tn*). The best description was from Ray's research with the Sanpoil:

Baskets of cottonwood or pine bark [*sloq'k'én*] were utilized extensively for the storage of berries and roots. Cottonwood was preferable. Since bark of the quality desired was usually far up the tree the latter was ordinarily felled as the first step of manufacture. In some young trees the lower bark was sufficiently clear to be used, in which case it was not necessary to cut the tree, but the baskets were correspondingly small. A tree from one to two feet in diameter was commonly selected. After felling, one end of the log was raised from the ground and blocked in that position, so that the underside would be free. A section reasonably free of defects and knots was cut from the trunk. The length and manner of cutting depended upon the type of container that was desired. For a basket with one vertical seam and a flat bottom, a section about four feet long was removed by making two cuts at either end and one cut lengthwise. Two round pieces of bark, equal in size to the diameter of the trunk were cut separately. These parts were then assembled. The body of the basket was sewed together along the side opening. Then hoops of willow were fitted and sewed to either end, and sometimes to the middle for added strength. Finally, one of the bark discs was sewed to one end of the cylinder to form the bottom. Later, after the basket was filled, the other disc was sewed to the top. Willow bark thread was used for all stitching (1933:37-8).

Ray also described a second type of bark storage basket commonly used by the Sanpoil, one that was similar to the Spokan storage basket:

[A] type of bark storage basket had two longitudinal seams and a U-shaped bottom. For its manufacture it was necessary to remove from the log a section of bark twice as long as the proposed height of the basket (usually about four feet) but extending only half way around. Usually both halves were removed to provide material for two baskets. The long piece of bark was heated at the midpoint to permit bending without breaking, then doubled (with the weather side of the bark outside) and sewed up each side with willow cord. Willow hoops were added [...] holes as were present were patched with pieces of bark to adhere on the inside with pine pitch. These bark storage baskets were superior to woven ones for food subject to attack by vermin or too great a loss of moisture (1933:38).

Flat grass storage sacks were flexible and breathable, and were approximately 80 cm to 1 m in length and commonly 30 cm across the top when flat. They were used for winter storage of raw small white camas, dry camas, and dried meat after the tops had been closed by stringing twined lengths of hemp through holes. Grass sacks were usually stored flat, one atop the other on each side of a dwelling entrance (Smith 1936-8:427). The Spokan used storage sacks of woven cattail leaves for storing dried roots and meat. Crushed or whole chokecherries were stored in *grass baskets* (*sy'áy'qs*) that were stacked in a platform storage structure for winter use. Cylindrical birch bark tubes with pitch-sealed sewn bottom and top plate were used for storing dried foods within dwellings and platform storage facilities. Dried camas was stored in a similar fashion, but in *cedar bark boxes* (*mim'š*), and, if kept dry, remained serviceable for many years.

Traditional methods of storing food were not completely abandoned with the introduction of canning. Even today, those few families who continue to dig roots, preserve certain roots by sun-drying; and yet no one uses an earth oven for cooking roots, only occasionally for school instructional purposes. Preservation of many once traditional foods made meaningful gifts and contributions to social gatherings, most notably at funerals. It was always apparent at funeral ceremonies that the root foods collected, processed, and stored by a family, *belonged to them* (*sč'ɬwiʔscuʔe*), but could be redistributed to others.

Baskets and other containers served numerous important functions for collecting, carrying, and storing roots, berries, and other fruits. They were used for carrying butchered meat, dried fish, and water, as well as for stone-boiling water. Moreover, various types of plant fibers, grasses, bark, roots and strips of both tanned and rawhide were used extensively in the manufacture of these storage receptacles, just as they were used for making hats, bags, housing and clothing mats, lashings, bow strings, traps and snares, tumplines, basket twining, and many other articles of use.

Women spent time in late spring and late autumn—assisted sometimes by older unwed daughters—gathering the various materials used for twining, twilling, sewing, and hafting. They stored great quantities of thinly split lengths of spruce, cedar, tamarack, and willow roots, which were scraped and coiled before use and carefully stored in cool locations within each winter village dwelling. When stored properly these materials would last, if necessary, for many years or until needed. A woman took as much pride in the proper storage of these materials as she did with her larder.

When a woman received visitors or visited others, her work ethic and domestic responsibilities required that she always carried on her person a *sewing* (*t'q^{w}um'*) pouch and necessary materials so that she could remain productive even while socializing. A common expression, "An industrious woman's hands are always working," was once commonly heard among elderly women, particularly in the presence of young girls and young unmarried women.

The Spokan made at least seven types of rigid and flexible bags and baskets, many in different shapes: coiled, rectangular, and round baskets, flat-twined bags, *woven cedar baskets* (*nq'c'áqs* or *yámx^{w}e?* - "woven cedar basket"), and bark baskets from pine, birch, cottonwood, and cedar. These served many functions, but were used primarily for food collection and as winter food storage containers. Both *inner cedar bark* (*q^{w}étx^{w}łp*) and *outer cedar bark* (*č'i?lélx^w*) made light but strong baskets, and the pliable bark of a young cedar tree was easily made into a basket if needed. A large *bark vessel* (*słq'qí*) for cooking meat was made from a deciduous tree—often black cottonwood—in which a large encircling section was removed after incising a top and bottom horizontal cut. The vertical and parallel ends were overlapped and stitched before folding in the bottom, which was overlain and secured.

The materials, techniques, and decorations of coiled baskets were cited by Conn and Schlick:

> The most important single material used throughout the Plateau for coiled basketry was red cedar-root, used both for foundation splints and for sewing elements. Strips were also cut from cedar sapwood [...] Various other plant materials were used for decoration. Some were selected for their attractive natural colors, such as pale ivory bear-grass and garnet-red wild cherry. Other native plants such as Oregon grape and dogwood, as well as alkaline mud, supplied dyes with which bear-grass and Phragmites reeds were dyed yellow and black respectively (1998:606).

Ray's description of how the Sanpoil used and manufactured a birch bark basket was applicable to the Spokan:

> Birch bark baskets [*p'ína'?*] served as emergency cooking vessels and receptacles for berries while picking. They were made in a variety of shapes, mostly round in section but some were elliptical. Depth and diameter were approximately equal. A willow hoop was bound to the top of each type with parallel stitches of willow bark string. The seams were sewed with a zigzag stitch using the same string. Loop of hemp cord or buckskin were often attached, to which a tumpline might be fastened. These baskets were never decorated or provided with covers (1933:38).

A *pack* (*scqíčn'*) was "built on a multiple rod foundation of finely split cedar or spruce-roots" (Ray 1933:35), and was coiled and elliptical in shape, increasing in diameter from bottom to top, and functioned essentially as a burden basket. Teit cites how the Coeur d'Alene burden basket had two flatter sides to prevent rolling on the person's back (1928:54), and was also identical in construction to the Spokan burden basket. A much sought material for basketry was stripped tamarack root, which was durable and easy to work with, being so pliable, and was collected primarily by women who would commence digging approximately 2 m from the main tree, and follow a root near to the end. It was then cut off, stripped, coiled, and permitted to dry. Prior to use, the root was soaked again, and separated into *narrow strips* (*qqe?t mux^{w}mix^w*), commencing at the large end and peeled lengthwise. Packs were carried by a head or shoulder tumpline.

Flat, flexible bags varied in size, and were made of cattail, tule, and various grasses. Baskets were manufactured from the narrow sections of white pine root that was dug approximately 2 to 3 m from the tree's base. Immediately upon collecting, the roots were peeled. Later, after soaking until soft, the roots were hand-split lengthwise and stored until needed. When collecting and preparing roots for weaving baskets, this procedure was similar to that employed when collecting spruce and cedar-roots for manufacturing baskets; similarly, white pine roots were used for making baskets. The best were roots approximately 2 m in length, and split lengthwise in strips 2 to 4 cm in width, coiled, and permitted to dry. Before use, the strips were soaked until pliable and split into desirable widths. Such bags were typically not long—a bag 1 m long was unusual.

The introduction of wool—most commonly in the form of trade blankets—was another non-traditional influence upon the manufacture of utilitarian soft bags and the imbrication of selected traditional baskets. Teit explained how old or worn blankets were unraveled, and the wool strands used for imbrication—yellow being favored for designs, along with red, blue and other colors (1930:49). "Imbrication seems to have been adopted by the Spokan and Kalispel about 1800, but it never spread to the Pend d'Oreilles and Flathead" (Teit 1930:329).

The shapes and size of utilitarian containers were determined largely by their intended use, though most containers were multipurpose. Eventually, traditional fiber and *bark baskets* (*čłq'ʷálqʷ* - "peeled bark" or *scčłq'ʷálqʷ* or *nq'c'áqs* - "woven") began to be replaced by metal containers, via trade. Trading of particularly fine baskets continued within the Plateau (Turney-High 1941:76). However, only a few Spokan continued to use traditional baskets; and those who still have a few baskets now treasure them and rarely use them. The last Spokan artisan who worked with plant materials and cornhusk was the late Nancy Flett, a knowledgeable ethnobotanist.

Also, until the early 1900s, an open, flexible, straight-sided, round, flat-bottomed traditional Spokan *basket* (*yámxʷeʔ*) was made by the *coil* (*q'ʷumčsncút* - "to coil up") method using a continuous series of bound Ponderous pine needles. Though the size of the basket varied, it was always made from freshly-picked *green pine needles* (*čc'c'w'éčst*), never with *fallen pine needles* (*č'émeʔ*), which were no longer pliable. This skill was taught to Spokan school children boarding at Fort Spokane by older women, who eventually made them for sale to whites. The outside of this type of basket was impregnated with and used for stone-boiling when fitted with a green-wood trivet (McCarty, pers. comm.).

A bark basket with a rawhide liner, was made when the bark was green, and; thus, easier to remove, or later when the bark had been soaked and made pliable. Gathering the rough bark involved first scraping away some of the outer surface, which facilitated making circling cuts around the tree at intervals at the length of the intended *container* (*łccín*). The removal of pine bark was often aided with a type of slick, a long, thinly-tapered length of hard-wood tool that was gradually and progressively slipped under the bark. Food containers made of *pine bark* (*céxʷiʔ*) were lined with buckskin, to prevent the bark from imparting an unfavorable taste to the foods.

Peoples of the eastern Plateau made a *temporary bark basket* (*słq'qín*). Smith described its manufacture and use by the Kalispel:

> [It] was made of yellow pine bark generally. About two-thirds of the way [up the] tree was a place about 3 feet long where no branches come off; they climb small tree, peel this bark off, dig a hole and put the bark in it to boil food. They put hot rocks in [picking them up] between two sticks, keeping the rocks as clean as possible. They cooked meat, bitterroot and eggs in this way [...] It is done only in summer before the bark sets (1936-8:442).

Cottonwood and birch bark can be peeled off more easily than pine, and required less effort for gathering enough material for manufacturing a basket, particularly if one were needed to be made on the site for gathering or carrying food. A *paper birch basket* (*lúp'iʔ*) was easily made by cutting a rectangular piece of bark, and removing a square portion from the lower *right side* (*sčhečt*). The final shape was much like an inverted "L". The bark was then pulled away, soaked until pliable, and formed into a long tube by bringing together the two vertical edges. The long edges were then perforated to accommodate the stitching. The bottom was made by folding the long side and stitching it to the opposite short side. This type of basket varied in size and was used when picking berries and for winter-storing dried roots.

When making a bark basket, the bark was first peeled off in long strips and soaked for several days to facilitate being bent up in the middle, to be shaped by pinning pieces of bone or wood in pre-bored holes, usually made by an awl before soaking. The bottom of a bark basket could be either flat, with flaps sewn up the sides, or pushed up after stitching, and then soaked again, thereby creating two legs. The protruding legs prevented rotting of the basket if placed on the ground for an extensive period, and allowed the basket to fit over a person's thigh while they processed its contents when sitting. Stitching a basket's sides, bottom flaps, and the reinforced rim was invariably done with hemp or thin lengths of soaked willow bark. The few remaining elderly Spokan women, without exception, claimed that green willow was best for stitching the rim to the circular reinforcing willow rod.

A type of water-carrying container was made from a *deer paunch* (*sx̣x̣ép*), which served as a waterproof liner for a grass or root basket of appropriate size. However, the most common type of basket for carrying water was a *cedar-root basket* (*łčcíʔn*) that had handle loops to facilitate carrying. Smith (1936-8:602) provided a more detailed comparative account of how the Kalispel made water-carrying containers by weaving with the small cedar-roots found growing into fallen rotten logs. These containers were called *sqʷéwm łčcíʔn* and served for stone-boiling small amounts of water. The top of the container was doubled or rolled for strength to attach a carrying strap. A temporary yellow pine *basket* (*słqʼqi*) could be made quickly for stone-boiling simply by folding the bark in such a manner that the container had four distinct corners.

Baskets intended for cooking could be made *water-tight* (*snčłelʼtnʼ*) in several ways: one method was to line a woven basket with fish skin or an animal's inverted stomach. Another method was to manufacture a tightly woven basket of split cedar-root, which became vitreous when soaked before stone-boiling. In both cases, a green freshly cut red willow trivet was first inserted to prevent scorching the container while stone-boiling (STHC).

When a *woman was weaving a basket* (*ʔesqʼcʼmí* - "she is weaving a basket"), she may modify the construction to facilitate it for specific tasks, usually by attaching a short length of *lacing* (*xpʼmín*) as a handle or for securing it to a saddle. The head or shoulder tumpline was undoubtedly the most effective method when it was necessary to *carry* (*ʔukʷučénʼ*) numerous loads between resource areas and their final destination. A carrying handle on, say, a *berry-picking basket* (*snqʷʼlʼéwʼmn*), even a child's *little berry basket* (*yʼáyʼmʼxʷeʔ* or *snqʷʼqʷʼlewʼmn*), permitted uneven motion of walking or collecting without berries being spilled. Some children had *small bark baskets* (*čššrʼep*) for picking berries.

Despite there being no recorded linguistic designation for the Spokan annual subsistence round per say, the importance of these seasonally determined movements were reflected by naming the specific lunar months according to when major foods were acquired by hunting, trapping, fishing, and gathering. Quite characteristic to the Plateau, the Spokan had developed a comprehensive and accurate understanding of animal-plant relationships that required an intimate knowledge of so-called food chains and food webs upon which they were dependent. Their classification of animals, fish, and plants, as near as can be discerned (Osterman 1995), were complete and suggest a classification based essentially upon form and function, as well as color and observable behavior.

Chapter XIII: Transportation Technology

Being foragers, the Spokan had a logistical concern for the often difficult expenditure of time and energy in transporting gathered animal and plant foods as well as utilitarian resources from areas of exploitation to summer camps or villages for utilization as well as for winter storage. Prior to acquiring the horse, they were solely dependent upon human portage for carrying food and other resources overland, and the use of various types of watercraft when crossing the wide and deeper sections of the Spokan and Columbia Rivers. For traveling overland, horses could be used for transporting heavy loads in lieu of human portage (Elmendorf, pers. comm.; Hudson *et al.* 1981:125). Because of terrain, dogs were never utilized as beasts of burden (Elmendorf, pers. comm.).

Log Rafts

The most rudimentary form of watercraft was the *raft* (*sclč'éwł* or *sƛč'éuł*), which was seldom used for distant water travel, but more for transporting heavy loads on both the Columbia and the Spokane Rivers for short distances. This relatively simple raft was undoubtedly used more than any other type of watercraft because of the restricted sources of cedar and other canoe-building material, and of course the time and energy required to construct a bark or dugout canoe. The importance of log rafts was cited by Teit, who felt the Spokan and Flathead proper "are said to have had no canoes long ago, only rafts of poles" (1930:350). Boating poles were called *c'k'ʷéwłtn*, and a pole boat was termed *c'k'ʷéwł* (Egesdal, pers. comm.).

Log rafts were essentially a double or a multiple *log raft of lashed poles* (*slč'éwł*) that formed a rigid platform that accommodated considerable weight and numerous occupants, and was durable and relatively simple to construct. There were two types of rectangular log rafts, both of the same design that involved essentially similar building techniques. One type was relatively shorter in length and not so wide, requiring only one person for poling. The second type of log raft was of greater length and required two polers—a bow-poler and a stern-poler.

Rafts were not used for going any great distance because of direction control and the difficulty in poling, either up or down stream, and were used primarily to transport their winter *edible root* (*skʷn'kʷi?n'm*) supply from highly productive areas, located south of the Spokane River, to the more inhabited shore across the river from the north to the south shore. Until recently, several elderly women recalled hearing the elders describe how—prior to returning home from southern root fields—women would temporarily store large amounts of harvested roots in grass sacks in trees on high platforms before ferrying their harvest across the Spokane River on large rafts. Poling was the sole means of propelling such a raft, except when heavy loads were pushed or line-dragged by men on shore or when in areas of manageable water depth.

Because of buoyancy and durability, the preferable wood for this type of larger, rigid watercraft was cedar acquired as driftwood since there was not an abundance of this wood within the immediate Spokan area. As a consequence, log crafts were generally made of any type of available wood, including large but manageable sections of delimbed pine, fir, or cottonwood driftwood.

When constructing a multiple log raft, the alternated butt-to-top longitudinal sections were held in place by either wrapping each adjoining log to the next or securing the logs with several debarked lodge poles of smaller diameter, lashed with heavy hemp cord covered with pitch and secured at right angles to the main platform. Though two or more men made a log raft; upon completion, any adult of the village could use it without gaining permission. After use the raft was returned to where it had been originally found.

Bundle Boats and Tule Rafts

There are few descriptions and no known photographs of Spokan bundle boats or tule rafts, apart from Teit's comment about their occasional use by the Spokan. Concerning the Sanpoil tule rafts, "It seems that tule rafts were used to a slight extent by the Spokan, and possibly used by others" (1930:350). Teit's work with the Coeur d'Alene described tule raft construction: "tule rafts were pointed at both ends. They were made of lodge mats rolled into bundles, or tules tied in long bundles which were tightly lashed together. A well-made raft resembled a canoe, and was almost as good as one" (Teit 1930:108).

Fortunately, many years ago, one elderly Spokan man remembered early accounts of how, before 1881, tules were used in the construction of two types of craft: one described as a flexible bundle boat and the other as a pole-rigid rectangular tule-bundle raft. Both types of ingenious bundle boats were made from two large pontoon-like bundles, each constructed from 50 to 80 dead tules. The fore and aft ends of both bundles were interleaved and then tied tightly with hemp, thereby creating somewhat elliptical pontoons of 3 to 3.5 m in length. Additional stability and rigidity were provided by two poles, each of which ran the length of a pontoon and was secured with hemp. Both parallel pontoons were kept separate—approximately 50 to 60 cm apart— by fastening each end of two shorter poles at 90° to each longitudinal pontoon pole—one forward and one aft. The shorter poles supported an attached open willow withe mat, which formed a platform that could accommodate one or more large open-weave collection baskets. These boats were extremely light and buoyant, and lasted from spring until late fall. New ones were always built in the late spring from flexible willow and stored tules.

The other type of raft or float was a smaller, flat, *rectangular tule raft* (*scλč'éwł* or *snlc'ewł*), primarily for collecting mussels from deeper sections of the Spokane River, and in both Little and Big Tschimakain Creeks. Bundle boats served primarily as floating platforms on which to place the collected mussels—more recently called oysters by some Spokan.

When necessary, both types of floats retained their position against the current by a heavy hemp rope attached to a large stone anchor located on the stream bed. The anchor line was detached after use, and the anchor remained at the site until next needed. In summer and fall, the Spokane River was seldom deeper than up to a man's shoulders, so the larger, more rigid watercraft were mainly used as temporary storage platforms while the men gathered mussels. The so-called "bundle boat" was less tiring to negotiate than rigid pole rafts because of its greater buoyancy, and when being used in relatively shallow water. Occasionally a person would wade in shallow water and pull the boat with an attached lanyard while gathering mussels.

There is no evidence that the Spokan ever constructed or used any craft similar to coracle, a craft which, when covered, would have been similar to a small inverted sweathouse.

Dugouts

There is no way to determine when the Spokan adopted dugouts, though Teit (1930:350) wrote that only after the Spokan acquired iron tools (adzes) did they manufacture dugout canoes. It is presumed they used only rafts of poles and tules for water travel if they did not acquire dugouts by trade. But once they had adequate iron tools, the *dugout* (*stiłm*) was the most common form of water travel, commonly made from ponderosa pine, poplar or black cottonwood logs—rarely cedar. Thompson, looking to build boats of cedar, recorded the lack of cedar in Spokan country (Elliott 1919, 1:17). More specifically, Gunther maintained, "The canoes of eastern Washington were often made of pine. They were shovel-nosed and poled along the river" (1950:197). Teit acknowledged the effect of iron tools on the construction of dugouts:

> Spokan [...] are said to have had no canoes long ago, only rafts of poles. It seems that tule rafts were used to a slight extent by the Spokan [...] In later times, probably with the introduction of the first iron, the Spokan began

451

to make dugout canoes of poplar and other logs, while the Flathead adopted the bull boat of the plains area (1930:350).

Dugout canoes (*stím* or *sšléwł*) were made from various woods; the favored tree was *Western white pine* (*Pinus monticola* Dougl. ex Lamb - *cč'éy'łp* or *k'ʷxʷtn'ey'łp* or *λ'i'yálqʷ* - "canoe tree"). When finished, a canoe was called a *λ'yé'*. Elmendorf provided a brief description of how the Spokan "would chop a log hollow inside [...] with a *sharp stone* (*nšł'séwłtn* or *snšl'céwtn* - "sharp rock") and paddle across [the] river" (1935-6, 2:40). A dugout canoe made with fire and a stone adz was referred to as *scnšłéłc'e'* ("product of having axed a cavity"), and the process of burning inside the cavity was referred to as *éłc'e'* (Egesdal, pers. comm.). In the absence of suitable driftwood, a tree was dropped. Cox described how the Spokan would fall a tree:

> Their only instruments consisted of a chisel generally formed out of an old file, a kind of oblong stone, which they used as a hammer, and a mallet made of spruce knot, well oiled and hardened by the action of fire. With these wretched tools they cut down trees from thirty to forty feet in circumference; and with unparalleled patience and perseverance continued their tedious and labourious undertaking until their domicile was roofed or their canoe fit to encounter the turbulent waves of the Columbia (1957:177).

A much later description of Spokan dugouts was recorded by Curtis, but apparently he made no known photographs of this watercraft:

> Among the Spokan and the westerly Salishan tribes dugouts, fifteen to twenty-five feet long carried three to eight men, were made, the Spokan using pine logs, and others cedar. The tree was felled by means of elk-horn chisel and stone maul, hollowed out by burning with hot stones, and finished with a horn-pointed adze. All tribes used the single-bladed paddle, shifting from one side to the other after two or three strokes (1907-30, 7:71).

Even after acquiring metal tools, Wilson remarked how, "There are few wooden canoes, and those very badly made, having none of the elegance so noticeable in the construction of those seen on the coast" (1866:302). A later explanation of how the Spokan constructed a dugout is provided by Elmendorf's field notes:

> [The Spokan] cut down a big tree & hollowed it out by burning & chopping—watched carefully while burning to avoid getting [the] sides too thin—[then they would] dig it out with stone adzes [with a] handle about 2 ½ ft. Long [and with a] slit in the end & [then the] rock [was] bound in [the handle], [the] rock is blunt, not sharpened, but had sort of an edge[;] this was held against [the] burnt part & hit with another rock—[dugout] canoes (*stím*) [were] about 25 x 2 ½ or 3 ft.—made of *s'étkʷłp*—"yellow pine"—not pointed on [the] end [but] left flat & sloped back to meet [the] water—no thwarts - *sk'ʷáwltn*; [the] paddles were also made of *s'átkʷłp* - "ponderosa" (1935-6, 2:67).

There were basically two types of dugout canoes: a large one for transporting heavy loads (Elmendorf 1935-6, 1:8a), and a lighter and more carefully crafted dugout for extensive water travel. Because of distance and requirements, the need for watercraft was more frequent with the availability of horses and increase in trade (Chance and Hudson 1981:125). However, Elmendorf (1935-6, 2:8a) was told that dugout canoes were never used for traveling, rather for carrying loads short distances, and that the shape of the tree, prior to falling, determined which type of canoe would be hewed and fashioned.

Gibbs (1855, 1:403) noted how the Spokan supplied dugout canoes to Walla Walla, where the people resided in an environment essentially devoid of trees large enough for constructing canoes. The only two other references to dugout canoes were made by several elders, who recalled their elders recalling accounts of how dugout canoes were once acquired from the Sinkaietk (southern Okanogan), as an elder described when her Sinkaietk grandmother had married into the Spokan and brought her father's dugout canoe with her as the bride-price.

Unfortunately, the only remaining example of a Spokan dugout canoe, called *sn sstm'sqaxe'tn*, is located on a roadside just south of Wellpinit, and was last used as a horse watering trough in the 1930s (Ross 1993). This unique feature is currently without cover and has deteriorated beyond restoration. The site of this dugout canoe is adjacent to a once free-flowing spring known as *Coyote Springs* (*snčšr'éw'stis* or *č'ɬm'l'm'el'mn - spílyeʔ* - "slobbers"), which, according to *legend (sqʷel'um't*), is the place where water first sprung. It was believed that after one of Coyote's antics, he was hung by his heels and his saliva accumulated to form the spring (STHC). Elders say that this once important spring *never froze (swéʔitn'* or *sw'ey'itn'* or *nsulkʷ* - "cold water" - "never freeze"). However, after road construction it ceased to flow.

Bark and Wooden Canoes

Prior to acquiring the horse, the principal method of transportation was walking, and to a lesser extent by watercraft such as the *ram-ended or sturgeon-nose bark canoe (snčmini*). One can only speculate as to when the Spokan commenced to manufacture bark canoes, which were probably first acquired through trade with the Kutenai, or trading and intermarriage with the Coeur d'Alene and Flathead (Mason and Hill 1901:523-537; Ray 1939:143). When speaking of the Nez Perce, Gibbs acknowledged the paucity of "wood in their country, and they depend upon the drift wood brought down by the stream for their fuel. Their canoes are purchased from the Spokanes" (1967:9). It was not known if the Spokan constructed canoes or acquired them by trade. Gibbs maintained the eastern Salish—including the Flathead—had no canoes at all (Gibbs 1855,1:415).

Some bark sturgeon-nosed canoes were acquired from the Lakes people (Elmendorf, pers. comm.), which Teit (1930:350) posited as the oldest type of canoe in this area, preceding the sharp-nosed dugout canoe. The earliest mention of the manufacture, use, and even repair and comparative aesthetics of the Spokan bark canoe was recorded by Wilson who fortunately could not refrain from suggesting certain limitations of potential technological innovation:

> There are few wooden canoes, and those very badly made, having none of the elegance of design so noticeable on the construction of those seen on the coast. The canoe in general is made from the bark of the white pine, and is so light it can with ease be carried on the head from one stream to another, yet is capable of holding three persons with a considerable quantity of baggage. These canoes are very fragile, and it is usual to carry a supply of gum to mend the cracks or holes that may be made during the journey. The paddler sits in the centre of the canoe, and uses the common paddle; as this requires shifting from side to side, it is somewhat curious that the double bladed paddle has never been thought of by the Indians (1866:302-3).

The unique sturgeon-nosed canoe was pointed under the waterline, both fore and aft, and was constructed of pre-soaked bark carefully stripped from spruce, birch, balsam or white pine trees. This unstable canoe design had no fore or aft stem-pieces and the bark sides were stitched in a sloping cut-water pattern, with both stem sections being formed with closed sectional hoop ribs. "Most examples had a bottom that was straight or slightly hogged" (Adney and Chapelle 1964:168), with batten ribs that were U-shaped and bent with steam or heated water, which held and formed the covering sections of bark. A *bark canoe (ƛ'yéʔ*) had at least one mid-sectional thwart—some had two or three thwarts evenly spaced according to the length of the craft. Sections of pre-cut bark for the gunwales and bottom were slightly overlapped and stitched with peeled and split lengths of cedar or spruce root, and sealed with pitch that had been first boiled until black and applied while warm. As with other types of bark for canoe construction, willow bark was gathered in the spring, once the sap commenced to flow. The interior bottom of any type of canoe was lined with *loose grass mats (sy'ay'qs*) or *woven willow withes (nx̣lélx̣ʷtn*) to sit on and to prevent a person from stepping through the bottom of the craft (Elmendorf 1935-6, 1:8). The birch-bark canoe was called *sxoiéɬp'*.

The early mention of iron kettles may indicate a time when the Spokan modified the design and manufacture of watercraft, for as Work recorded, "The men were employed the whole day gumming the canoes & had not the Indians favored us with the lend of their kettles to boil pitch it would have taken another day to finish this business" (Elliott 1914, 2:109). It should be noted that Work's journals provide ample evidence that trappers and fur traders spent considerable time splitting or hewing wood for housing and making plank boats, and as Work noted, how "gumming [was done] several times a day" (Elliott 1914, 1:193) and "The men employed gumming & repairing canoes. We had no gum till the Indians were employed to gather it" (Elliott 1914, 4:261). Further information was cited by Work, who recognized the need for a division of labor in bark canoe construction and repair, and wrote how "the women were sent off to gather gum to repair the canoes" (Elliott 1914, 4:264). Work further described that "We had no gum till the Indians were employed to gather it" (Elliott 1914, 4:261).

In the past, most maritime and riverine peoples universally conducted often elaborate rituals prior to commencing the construction of a wooden boat; the Spokan were no exception. Rituals were primarily to keep the craft from sinking or being swamped in bad weather (if over-balanced with too heavy a load):

> Men joined in [a] ceremony at building of [a[canoe [when they would] dance, fast, sweat—[the] sweathouse made [a] man more peaceable and agreeable—[and] focused all [his] faculties on canoe-building—[and] if [a] canoe went wrong after [being] built—[it was] supposed to indicate incest or impurity [by one of the workers] (Elmendorf 1935-36, 1:19).

The canoe was the most efficient water craft for fur traders, many of which were lost or severely damaged with the bark or skin coverings torn by swamping, capsizing, rapid fluctuation, and rising of spring runoff, or striking stream boulders, rapids or strong currents. Sometimes the streams were too low or even near-dry, with ice floes, or hitting drifting partially submerged logs while dragging canoes when portaging, or when badly laid up in the Spring (Elliott 1915, 1:19). Work further wrote that in one instance the "water [level] has fallen at least 16 feet" (Elliott 1915, 1:18). DeSmet described how in early May, "The mountain torrents had overflowed, and the small rivers had suddenly left their beds and assumed the appearance of large rivers and lakes, completely flooding all the lowlands (1843, 27:368).

Elmendorf provided a detailed description of Spokan bark canoe construction:

> [...] birch bark [was] got [ten] in spring & fastened on canoe frame lengthwise in strips–[the] outline [was] staked out on [the] ground–[the] top gunwale poles [were] fastened to stakes—and willow ribs [were] sewed to [the] poles with [strips of] willow bark–[the] bark [was] sewed to [the] ribs on [the] outside with willow bark– then another layer of bark on [the] outside was securely & evenly fastened–[and] pitched in & out with warm pine pitch into [the] seams–[the] outside bark [was] removed before putting [it on the] frame–[the] stern [was] square or bow-like with [a] cross pole–[the] bow [was] folded up & pointed with rings of willow inside & [with] extra layers of bark–[the] point curved up some—paddles [were] made of any good splitting tree—split by men with horn wedges and mauls–(stone) held in split stick with rawhide) into slabs scraped [with] sharp edged rocks into shape and finished off with stone scrapers–[the] shape [was of] no particular difference (1935-6, 1:8-9).

Plank Boats

The only indication of the Spokan making plank boats was offered by Work in 1825, who earlier had mentioned the use of pit saws, "Had four of the men off seeking timber to saw for boats, they felled nine trees none of which would serve, they are a good distance up along the River seeking it. Wood of the dimensions required, 40 feet long & 14 inches square, is difficult to find" (Elliott 1914, 3:170). Presumably, "Good cedar timber suitable for boats is said to have grown above the mouth of Deep Creek four or five miles above the Fort [Spokane]" (Elliott 1914, 3:170 fn).

Given the private and commercial use of contemporary watercraft, *every boat* (*stim̓*) used by the Spokan is commercially made of metal and plastic, rarely of wood.

Poles and Paddles

The use of poles or paddles for propelling a watercraft was determined by whether the vehicle was a raft or a canoe, since, as mentioned, poles were used for rafts, and paddles for canoes. For a bundle boat, either a paddle or a *pole* (*c'k'ʷéwłtn* - "to pole") was used, depending upon the water depth. (Or, the bundle boat would be controlled by a person wading next to it when collecting mussels.) In general, the raft and dugout canoe would be poled in shallow, slow-moving waters. Poles were simple and quick to make from small-diameter lodge pole pine that had been debarked, and repeatedly rubbed over with the concave curve of a mule deer horn—the large end of the pole end may be pounded and trimmed for better purchase in mud or sand.

It was a more formidable task to make a *canoe paddle* (*ʔax̌ʷlméčstmn* - "to brush the water" or *ʔáx̌ʷmn* or *ʔax̌ʷméčst*), which were usually fashioned from dried, split deciduous wood—preferably alder, hemlock, or sometimes yew, and after splitting the wood with a stone-wedge, the paddle's desired shape was attained by laborious scraping with hand-held, sharp-edged stones, one that varied slightly from those made by other paddle-makers, but not intentionally. The main difference was due to an individual's skill that could be recognized by another paddle-maker, and upon completion it had a broader blade than that of contemporary paddles. A locally-made *cedar paddle* (*ƛ'mótn*) was always considered a gracious gift, being easier to handle and less tiring than one made from hemlock or alder, and of course lighter but yet more durable. Paddles were an example of multi-purpose technology, being used as snow shovels or, in the case of discarded paddles, for carefully removing household fire-pit ashes.

Paddlers normally knelt in a fore aft single row with each alternate person paddling to either a starboard or larboard position to maintain a desired course, whereas a single paddler always sat in the stern and would periodically alternate his strokes from larboard to starboard as needed. In dugout canoes, a single paddler ideally sat in the stern, or stood more mid-ship when propelling the craft in shallow water by poling. Though it is not recorded, it may be assumed that a lone paddler would use the so-called "J" stroke when maneuvering the lighter, more maneuverable bark canoe. Curtis observed how a man "used the single-bladed paddle, shifting one side to the other after two or three strokes" (1907-30, 7:71). At one point in his travels, DeSmet "was making his way up the Columbia in an Indian canoe with two blankets unfurled by way of sails" (O'Hara 1909, 3:250).

Snowshoes

Snowshoes, first developed by the French Canadians, and known as *raquette de neige*, were basically of three types: the smaller ovoid-shaped frame, flat *bear-paw* (*ax̌omé*), and the elongated Canadian-type *trail snowshoe* (*sc'wétšn*) with slightly *upraised tips* (*cuwwússn*) or *toe pieces* (*euwússn*), permitting a man, if necessary, to run, and which were preferable for traveling in open country and on relatively flat *trails* (*šušwé*). However, the shorter flat bear-paw snowshoe proved more effective when climbing steep hills and in densely wooded areas with underbrush. Because of the width of bear-paws, the person was required to *shuffle* (*kʷekʷixʷšn'* - "shuffling feet") when traveling by alternately slipping the inside edge of one snowshoe over the inside edge of the other. Men apparently never used paired snowshoe poles, but rather a long *snowshoe pole* (*t'kístn*) to facilitate traveling on snow, or for regaining their balance or footing when traversing difficult or steep terrain, or while *putting on snowshoes* (*č'ew'e?č'šn'm*) before *tracking large water-oriented mammals* (*sntéc'étkʷ*), such as moose.

Transporting heavy loads in the winter—over snow, ice, or ice floes—was facilitated by using *snowshoes* (*ʔax̌ʷm*), which helped maintain balance and conserve energy when traveling over deep, loose snow, and were also useful when water courses were frozen solid, thereby rendering watercraft impassable. When not wearing snowshoes, the Spokan would, as Diomedi observed for the Coeur d'Alene, carry them strapped on their backs or in a type of parfleche, "a kind of impervious wrapper, made of greased deerskin" (1878:30), to protect the rawhide bindings and web-work from moisture.

Design and certain construction methods varied, depending upon the type of snowshoe being made. The manufacturing was always done by men in early spring when the preferred whitish, dense green *hard-wood* (*m'c'm'c'ey'ɬp*) of preferably green Rocky Mountain maple, was more pliable and easier to work than many other hardwoods. *Bearpaws* (*sx̌ʷƛ'oláqʷ*) were often constructed from stout lengths of elderberry. A pair of trail shoes required either two or four long parallel knot-free sections of maple limb or elderberry, approximately 1 m to 110 cm lengths. These sections were first thoroughly pre-soaked and then carefully steam-bent to shape over a frame-jig until each end overlapped, which were then tightly secured together with interlaced lengths of hemp or strips of rawhide. It was explained how a few men preferred to shape the lengths of soaked frames by placing each in a jig of upright stakes that were then covered with earth to prevent scorching from hot coals and embers and were covered with a final layer of earth. The earthen form was perforated with a series of vents to permit water to enter and create steam after closure.

Another procedure for making trail shoes without a jig was to hang the pre-soaked shafts over a low, smoldering smoke fire of lodge, prior to bending the shaft into shape. These were then held in a desired shape by twisted sinew. Or, a person may completely submerge the two or four frame lengths in a stream, secured by heavy stones, usually overnight or longer. Each piece was then bent to a teardrop shape by temporarily tying each bend at both ends with wrapped rawhide, while the near-center was pushed apart to a desired distance by several stout wedge-shaped sticks. Both types of frames were treated with either hot water or steaming, until each shoe could be adequately spread without breaking. Afterwards, temporary wraps were made at several points to hold the wood in what would be its final form before spreading the frames with flat sections of hardwood.

After overlapping each pair of spliced ends together, and while the wood was still supple, the forward or wider end of the snowshoe was carefully bent upwards to a desired position by temporarily weighting each shoe with a heavy object—such as a heavy log—at the base of the toe-slope, and tying several lengths of rawhide from the tip to under the weighted object, with the free ends secured to the frame until dry. After six to eight hours the frame lengths were removed and fashioned into either an ovoid-shape, bear-paw or trail shoe.

The final stage of construction required taking two or more strips of rawhide that were twisted before wrapping them at right angles to the form. A series of single-strand rawhide was then interwoven at roughly 45° to the doubly-twisted rawhide. The entire perimeter of the shoe was next wrapped with double-strand hide for strength as well as for providing a surface edge for better traction. Webbed foot-platforms were made by securing both ends of two parallel pieces of hard-wood to either side of the frame; one near the toe and one near the heel. *Weaving* (*nʔλ̓čam'ú*) the supporting webbing was completed by placing finely woven greased rawhide mesh over the foot platform, and attaching a *foot strap* or *stirrup* (*ncʔλ̓č'm'ú* or *sn'λ̓čšnti*). A person's foot was further secured by a *heel strap* (*c̓ném'*) made of twisted hemp or tightly braided buckskin that was attached to the foot platform.

As cited, snowshoes fulfilled multi-purpose tasks, such as the bear-paw being a more effective shovel than the up-turned trail shoe if a stranded trapper or hunter had to excavate an emergency snow-bank or tree-well overnight or storm shelter. Though the Spokan had the term *froze to death* (*č'ɫiʔxʷxʷmúss*), there were no accounts of such an occurrence. However, an elder recalled his grandfather, a *trapper* (*suxʷʕaʔcim'*), tell of how a trapper who had been caught in a severe snowstorm for several days, marooned without sufficient food, survived by eating the rawhide webbing of his snowshoes, which the grandson said would have been impossible with modern plastic snowshoes. The apparent advantage of being able to eat, if necessary, the rawhide webbing in a survival situation was a disadvantage since rodents and other animals could also devour the rawhide webbing, particularly if freshly greased. When required to winter travel during extremely cold weather, it was not uncommon for a person to wrap wool blanket rags about his legs for warmth, a practice called *čy'il'y'l'xʷqasčšn*.

A hunter caught without snowshoes in an unforeseen snow storm, or a steep rise in elevation, could improvise with bundle fir boughs *tied* (*lič'*) to his feet, always with the cut stem ends leading, and the upper side of the bough facing up. Emergency snowshoes could be made by first digging through the snow to get sections of cottonwood bark near the tree base, which were shortened to length and secured to one's feet with lengths of rawhide. It was known that women tended to use a smaller type of bear paw snowshoes for snow traveling and as shovels for clearing snow at dwelling entrances, or when sitting on snow.

Sleighs, Toboggans, Improvised Sleds, and Tumplines

Other forms of traveling or transporting loads were toboggans, frozen animal hides, or sleds. In deep snow, on sloped or flat land, the most efficient method for transporting large game was to improvise a simple type of runnerless *sled* (*p'p'np'úle?xʷ*) using only fir boughs secured together at the butt ends, and pulled by hemp or buckskin thongs attached to the thickest end of the boughs. For transporting heavy loads for long distances over snow, a man could place a slain deer or trapped hides atop the upturned side of one or more fir branches. A reason for using this method was if a hunter had to stop while going up a hill, the reverse-facing fir needles served to help arrest the load from sliding downhill—much like skins on cross-country skis. Another method a winter deer hunting party or individual could use to transport large amounts of dressed deer meat in open country was for each successful hunter to attach the loose ends of a chest tumpline to an open but frozen hide—as a sled, which was then pulled. One elder recalled his brother once using the intestines of a slain deer for a tumpline to pull the carcass over the snow.

Some elders remembered their parents giving them commercially built toboggans in the late 1800s, and though used primarily by children, toboggans were occasionally shared with a mother or grandmother when several or more children would go to collect firewood. Prior to mechanized transportation, there were accounts of ranchers using toboggans to transport hay to stranded cattle. When on flat ground or going up a rise, such a vehicle was always pulled, probably with a type of shoulder tumpline harness. One elder remembered how as a boy he attached a *wooden box* (*n'sn'én'e?*) onto his *toboggan* (*nčcqmíntis*), but forgot how he had secured the box onto the toboggan. A few elders recalled the ownership and use of horse-drawn, iron-runner sleighs in the late 1800s and early 1900s. Sleighs pulled only by one horse were used for attending church or visiting when there was adequate snow. Sleigh and buggy *harnesses* (*čʕʷoxʷc'a?sqaxe?tn*) were often decorated with metal bell ornaments called *dogbells* (*čpaséw's*). A one-horse buggy was called *np'n'p'n'łn'iw't*.

In 1864 the HBC post used bobsleds, which on occasion were pulled by two horses (Durham 1912, 1, I:52); but there is no evidence the Spokan ever used what is being called a bobsled, since a proper bobsled had two separate trucks, each with two attached parallel runners, and sometimes with a *passenger box* (*nčcqmintis*). The front runner was always articulated by a foot-bar or rope loop to facilitate intended steering.

Though there is no known photographic evidence, it is most likely that when the Spokan adapted to agriculture, they used horse-pulled stone boats for clearing rocks from fields intended for plowing. Walker's diary for 9 August 1841 mentions the first wheeled vehicle at Tschimakain Mission, "No doubt this was one of the high-wheeled, one-horse carts which the artist Paul Kane called the 'Red River cart' and which was in common use at Fort Colville" (Drury 1976:163 fn). Drury also cites a 12 August 1842 diary entry of Walker regarding a sled being pulled by two horses for hauling hay (1976:201).

By necessity, both men and women were required to occasionally transport heavy loads of food and other material over long distances. Both genders used single or double extended hand-loading, which was common for transporting objects over short distances. Bulky and loose loads—such as firewood—were carried by women using a chest or head thump-line that suspended the load on one's back. So-called rigid burden baskets of food (roots and berries) were sometimes transported with a head or shoulder thump-line. There is no account of a man or woman using a balance pole as a carrying device, a method requiring a person to place the mid-point of a pole behind his neck with his shoulders supporting the pole and the balanced loads suspended on either end. A common way of carrying any large game animal was to use a double-manned suspension pole with a man at each end, the animal being suspended by passing the pole through the front and rear feet which were tied together, the pole ends being placed on the shoulder of each man.

Various types of open *back packs* (*sq'ʷéɫt*) were used to *pack* (*q'ʷéɫti*) and transport large bundles of materials stacked and tied as open loads, such as dressed meat, firewood, *dried fish* (*lk'ʷést*), tules and cattails. An open back pack used by both men and women to carry a heavy load invariably required either a head or shoulder *tumpline* (*lč'éčn'*); women preferring the *head tumpline* (*čɫqʷéssn'* - "forehead strap"), thereby leaving her hands free for better balance, carrying smaller items, or for other activities. All tumplines were basically a flat, *wide* (*ɫaq't*) strap of doubled buckskin or one made from two or three lengths of braided hemp, measuring from 1.5 to 2.5 m in length, varying in width by preference. To evenly distribute the weight, the head tumpline had a center section, approximately 8 cm wide. The load was suspended by a tumpline from the forehead, passing over the shoulders, and rested against the person's back. Likewise, the shoulder tumpline had a greater width where it passed over the front of the chest and around each shoulder before narrowing and partially resting the weight against one's back. Exceptionally heavy loads—or lighter loads for a considerable distance—were cushioned with shoulder or forehead pads made of matted layers of moss, or multiple folded layers of mullein leaves, or sections of bear hide. Tumplines were usually made of tanned deer hide or woven hemp. However, *rawhide* (*mulxʷ*) from bison was more durable than deer hide, and thus preferred.

Before the horse, closed bundles or rigid basket packs were nearly always carried by women. When traveling with household items, or items that could not be secured by stacking, it was necessary to have closed bundles which were basically of three types of enclosed or contained packs. The most common bundle pack was created by placing a load in the center of a buckskin hide, then tying the corners together to accommodate either a head or shoulder tumpline load. A second type of closed carrier was a rolled tule pack in which items were rolled up tightly in a tule mat with the ends tied off and carried with a *pack strap* (*lč'éčn*) made from hide or *braided rope* (*nq'acéʔus*). A third method for a woman to carry a load, usually gathered fruit or roots, was a rigid wide-mouth basket that was often suspended over the back from the woman's head by a tumpline. Smaller and less heavy gathering baskets were supported from the waist or by a belt, the top being closed by tying a braided buckskin or *hemp line* (*ƛč'éčn*).

Using a tumpline had the advantage of leaving a person's hands free for carrying other items, such as a *walking staff* (*c'k'ʷéčstn*) or lighter hand loads. The tumpline permitted a person who was tired to *rest* (*meɫm*) the weight on a large stone or log, or against an embankment without completely removing the load. A person carrying a burden supported from the head by a burden device (*nʕeščcneʔw'štmn*) could carry additional items, or easily release the load in rough terrain if the person began to fall, freeing his/her arms. The head tumpline was called *čɫqʷéssn'*. Shoulder tumplines or straps were probably preferred to head straps when carrying exceptionally heavy loads (Pickering 1895:101). To lift a heavy load, the woman stepped over the shoulder tumpline, squatted, and after positioning the strap she simply stood, sometimes assisted by a another woman who helped to initially lift the load into position.

Horses

The most dramatic change in transportation occurred when the Spokan acquired the *horse* (*snčɫ''aʔsqáxeʔ* - "cow elk dog" or *sntɫc'aʔsqáxeʔ* - "riding animal") from the Shoshone of southern Idaho (Haines 1938a:436) in the late 1700s or early 1800s. The Flathead "placed [...] the date of acquisition of the horse at about 1600, it was probably about 1710-1720" (Haines 1938a:436. cited by Thompson 1916:330-334). Roe maintained, "Spanish horses, handed up through Apache raiders to Shoshone traders, reached the Interior before 1725" (1955:78). Franchère, commenting upon his earlier southern travels to the south, and seeing a thousand or more Spanish horses in a troop, wrote how, horses came "from New Mexico, and are of Spanish race. We even saw some which had been marked with a hot iron by Spaniards" (1854:270). Clark Wissler (1870-1947) also felt that the Coronado and DeSoto expeditions (1742 and 1751) were an early source of lost or abandoned horses (1914, 1:1-25), as later reiterated by Haines (1938, 40, 1:112). Pickering wrote that, "Horses were found by Lewis and Clark among the tribes of Interior Oregon, having been derived from the Spaniards of New Mexico" (1895:319). Lord agreed with the same origin, but noted there is little certainty about when horses were acquired by the Spokan, who claimed it is difficult "to say when horses were introduced into Indian country west of the Rocky Mountains. But most probably about the commencement of this century [18th]. They are clearly descended from Spanish stock—stout, compact, enduring animals, seldom exceeding 15 hands" (1866, 2:87-8).

Ewers recorded how, "The Flathead are believed to have obtained their first horses from Shoshonean tribes to the south during the first quarter of the eighteenth century" (Ewers 1955:435; Fahey 1974:16). Earlier, Schaeffer (1901-1969) cited how the Flathead "as a result of the introduction of the horse, were afforded access to a more dependable and abundant source of food, the plains bison" (1937, 3:228). Galm noted:

> Knowledge of the care and handling of horses spread from the southeast and reached the vicinity of the Columbia Plateau around 1750, probably via Shoshone Indians to the south. In this case, the instrument of change was largely beneficial. The addition of the horse provided these cultures with a better means of hunting game and a new measure of wealth and status. Above all, horses expanded the limited range of these hunter-gatherer societies, granting them the mobility to hunt and trade further afield (1994:6.2).

Curtis maintained the Spokan initially acquired horses "in the first decade of the eighteenth century, and guns were acquired a few years later, for the traders were in their country at an earlier date" (1907-30, 7:56). Much earlier, in 1813, Cox (Stewart and Stewart 1957:190-191) concluded that the Chewelah-Spokan Group were well supplied with horses in the fall of 1814 when he was visiting this group, and how the Spokan considered wealth primarily in terms of horses, which they acquired during an annual trade with the Nez Perce (Steward and Steward 1957:115-116). Even approximate date of initial diffusion, or when a trade item was physically introduced, is sometimes speculative. Contrary to the aforementioned time span, establishing the date of the horse's introduction to the Spokan, Elmendorf 1935-6, 2:42) reiterated his principal informant's (Sam Boyd) statement that his great grandfather claimed the horse was introduced to the Spokan in approximately 1850. And yet the effects of the horse upon Spokan culture were well documented as early as 1811 by Franchère, who, despite a sometimes ethnocentric attitude of cultural differences, nevertheless, made significant observations of riding as well as the techniques of making necessary tack:

> The women rode as well as the men. For bridle they used a cord of horsehair, which they attached around the animal's mouth. With that he was easily checked, and by laying a hand on his neck, was made to wheel to this side or that. The saddle was a cushion of stuffed deerskin, very suitable for the purpose for which it was designed, rarely hurting the horse and not fatiguing the rider so much as our European saddles. The stirrups are pieces of hard-wood, ingeniously wrought, and of the same shape as those which are used in civilized countries. They are covered with a piece of deerskin, which is sewed on wet, and in drying stiffens and becomes hard and firm. The saddles for women were furnished with the antlers of a deer, and resembled the high pommeled saddles of the Mexican women (Twaites 1904, 6:270).

Franchère further observed how the Spokan "Indians are passionately fond of horse races: by the bets they make on these occasion they sometimes lose all they possess" (1854:269), and as was also noted earlier by Cox who wrote of what he felt were the unfortunate economic consequences of betting:

> Their chief riches are their horses, which they generally obtain in barter from the Nez Percés, in return for the goods they obtain from us [trapper-traders] for their furs. Each man is therefore the founder of his own fortune, and their riches or poverty are generally proportioned to their activity or indolence. The vice of gambling, however, is prevalent among them, and some are such slaves to it, that they frequently lose all their horses (1832:105).

Franchère further described the procedure for breaking a horse:

> The Indian who wishes to capture some horses, mounts one of his fleetest coursers, being armed with a long cord of horsehair, one end of which is attached to his saddle, and the other a running noose. Arrived at the herd, he dashes into the midst of it, and flinging his cord, or lasso, passes it dexterously over the head of the animal he selects; then wheeling his courser, draws the cord after him; the wild horse, finding itself strangling, makes little

459

resistance; the Indian then approaches, ties his fore and hind legs together, and leaves him till he has taken in this manner as many as he can. He then drives them home before him, and breaks them in at leisure (Twaites 1904, 6:342).

When the Spokan acquired the horse it was already *domesticated* (*tx̌ʷóx̌ʷ* or *t'k'ʷíls* - "become straightened"), and was used both for *riding* (*snčłc'aʔsqáx̌eʔ* - "riding animal"), as a *saddle horse* (*snč'mtéw'stn*), and pack horse. However, after two years of age, some stallions were castrated, whereas geldings were used nearly always for riding. Commonly, a *mare* (*sx̌ʷq'ʷéłt*) was kept for use as a *pack horse* (*sx̌ʷq'ʷéłt*), and usually owned by a man's wife. Every herd of horses had a mare lead horse, "and they would follow her" (Schaeffer 1935-36, I:35). A woman's saddle was called *nt'slx̌tcísqáx̌a* or *nc'l'x̌ʷčiʔsqax̌eʔ*, and often a *beaded hide robe* (*tctpusiúti* or *člp'uʔseyʔuty'eʔ*) was spread over it (Elmendorf 1935-6, 4:21).

The earliest recorded observation of the Spokan pride and achieved status in owning and outfitting a horse with accruements was cited by Cox:

> His horse, the noble minister to the pride, pleasure and profit of the mountaineer is selected for his speed and sprit and prancing gait, and holds a place in his estimation second only to himself. He is caparisoned [sic] in the most dashing and fantastic style; the bridle and crupper are weightily embossed with beads and cockades; and head, mane and tail are interwoven with an abundance of eagle plumes which flutter in the wind. To complete this grotesque equipment, the proud animal is bestreaked and bespotted with vermilion, or with white clay, whichever presents the most glaring contrast to his real color (Durham 1912, I:56).

The arrival of the horse permitted an increase in frequency and range of mobility onto the Plains by the Spokan for conducting warfare, food-getting activities (Haines 1955:17-21), and transporting heavy loads when trading. The horse, both the *Appaloosa* (*Equus caballus* - *mámn*) and the more *common pinto* (*E. cabullus* - *sq'ey'yelx̌ʷ* or *q'íy'elx̌ʷ*), accommodated the aforementioned activities with other interior Plateau groups in task-grouping (Anastasio 1955).

Any spotted horse was extremely desirous, and always considered a favorite among the Spokan (Hale 1846, 4:458). Roe, in discussing the care and attention with which the Plains bison-hunting groups traded their horses, which they were dependent upon, "for procuring food and for the preservation of life itself" (1974:259), acknowledged the skill they had developed:

> The castrating operation, like Indian therapeutic or ceremonial surgery at large, was apparently very much of a ritual in most tribes, though were some exceptions. The Flatheads followed the Spanish technique, as possibly other tribes also may have done, through the influence of dispersion (Roe 1974:258).

In 1806, Meriwether Lewis, after observing several surgical procedures of gelding, concluded that the Flathead method was far superior to those practiced by the English and American (Coues 1893, 3:1012). Schaeffer's account of the Flathead gelding of horses is the most complete, and discusses how the potential of a horse for competitive racing was judged by looking at its penis. This is an example of the Doctrine of Signatures, since the antelope possesses the speed and maneuverability that would be invaluable in a horse for hunting and warfare.

> [...] if it was long and large, the horse was not a fast horse: if the penis was not large, it would be a fast runner. Those horses would be the ones which were castrated and the blood vessels of the scrotum would be tied with sinew from the antelope (1934-37, I-86:13).

Pack horses had no appreciable role in expanding the range of gathering plant food, but did reduce the time and labor by enabling the Spokan to increase the weight of loads that could be carried greater distances in less time to winter residence and *storage* (*snt'k'ʷeʔ*) facilities. The impact and importance of the horse was reflected in the Spokan classification by age: a two year-old was called a *ʔeslspéntč*, three year-old was *čeʔłés*, and a five year-old was called *clčspéntč*. More specific designations were based upon type of horse, gender, and breed (STHC).

All Spokan men and women were excellent equestrians, having commenced to ride—often solo as soon as they were ambulatory. In fact, an example of an Indian's great dependence, familiarity, and trust was observed by the author in the early 1970s, when visiting a family who owned numerous horses. The rancher' son was approximately two-years of age, just managing to walk, and was playing in a horse-breaking corral while walking unattended among eight horses, occasionally swinging on the tail of a nearby horse. On alerting the father—who had ridden Brahma bulls in rodeos—of the child's danger, the man replied: "Oh, the boy's fine, he's learning to ride, and he'll soon have his own horse, indicating *he already has his own colt (q'q''ʔič)*." Wilson observed how a young boy "becomes cunning on horseflesh, and, when he can scarcely walk, may be seen galloping about on bare-back horses" (1866:295).

The stamina and ability of both horse and rider—both Indian and non-Indian—is reflected in a comment by Reverend Spaulding: "Once rode seventy-four miles in one day. Often he made sixty" (Drury 1949:107). Alexander Ross wrote of a woman's ability and dexterity in managing a horse, "a woman with one child on her back and another in her arms will course the fleetest steed over the most rugged and perilous country" (1849, 7:330).

Equestrian accoutrements first acquired by the Spokan were of Plains design and manufacture. Over the years, Spokan technology, materials, and design remained essentially similar to Plains methods and decoration. A lead rope for riding and leading pack horses was replaced by a *leather halter (lʕ''ʷóstn)*, permitting better control by the rider or packer. Prior to the introduction of bridles, *reins (ʕacʕocsqaχeʔtn)*, and halters assisted the rider to indicate direction by pulling the free end of a hemp or horse-hair rope tied around the *lower jaw (k'''yépeʔst)* of the horse in the direction that he wanted the horse to go. The old style bit was called *snč'c'átq'''*. Franchère described how, "For a bridle they [Spokan] use a cord of horse-hair, which they attach round the horse's mouth; with that he is easily checked, and by laying the hand on his neck, is made to wheel this side or that" (1854, 6:269). Years later, Meany's secondary research of Work's journals led him to describe how, "the bridle is simply a piece of rope fastened under [the] jaw which seems sufficient for the management of the most refractory horses" (1925, 2:141). However, the eventual introduction of the *metal bit (k'''ɬacpaʔsqáχeʔtn)* quickly replaced the former mouth rope loop, and *commercial sissle rope (ʕacsq'áχeʔtn - "thing to tie the horse with - horse implement")* replaced horsehair ropes. Most riders and stockmen now use neck-raining. An early and more detailed account of the Indian bridle claimed it was:

> [...] nothing more than a rope of horse or buffalo hair fastened to the lower jaw by a clove hitch; this makes a very severe and effective bit, and the rope is very convenient for tethering the horse when out hunting or wishing to dismount; the same rope is also fastened round the horse's neck when turned out for the night, the whole length being allowed to trail on the ground behind him, a plan which permits the horse to choose his own grass, and enables the rider to catch him with ease when required (Wilson 1866:302).

It should be noted that the strongest, and yet flexible, organic material available to the Spokan was horsehair—preferably horsetail—which was less affected by dampness than hemp, rawhide, and certainly buckskin and bark/cambium lines. When properly braided as a closed or solid braid, horsehair is essentially more impervious to wear than other cited materials, for as an elder stated, "Horsehair can be braided into an open sheath."

Metal horse bits were not used until being introduced by Euro-Americans, which was true for the *chest strap (k'''ɬq''n'čsqáχeʔtn')*, the *martingale (noxʷétc'eʔtn)*, and the tail *crupper (č'ɬq''élstn)*. Horses ridden by women often had highly ornamented beaded collars (Teit 1930:354). *Braided horse's tail (čsq'c'úps)* was commonly used to manufacture lightweight but strong martingales, and ceremonial martingales were made by *braiding (q'c'ím)* bundles of differently colored horsetail hair. In full regalia, an owner's horse had a plaited band placed above a decorative knot in the tail, called *čsč'np'ups*. A *tailstrap (čɬq''úps)* was almost always made of a section of flat leather or braided buckskin. Horses were caught with a *horse-hair rope lariat (ʕacsqaχeʔtn)*, and though rarely necessary when traveling, at least two legs of a horse were commonly *tethered (ʕacsqaχeʔ)* or hobbled with a horse-hair rope.

It is not known when the saddle with front and back cantle was introduced because men commonly rode *bareback (kʷnʔem'tícn')*, as did children learning to ride. The first saddles are believed to have been fashioned from a composite of several modified elk or deer horns, making what was called a *ʔaym'ʔósqu* ("deer horn saddle")—a design that was later replaced by wooden frames (STHC). Eventually, three types of saddles were used: the *pack saddle* (*ʔa'yʔaym'áw'sqn'* or *amʔamʔatáqs*), the woman's saddle, and a man's *riding saddle* (*snmq'ʷičn'* or *q'lq'álqs*). The last type was a composite wooden frame of dry, near-rotten aspen wood, covered with stretched rawhide. The front and back of the wooden frame had a high front and back cantle respectively. Durham, citing Franchère (1854), stated how the Spokan adopted, "The form of the saddles used by the females proves that they have taken their pattern from the Spanish ones destined for the same use" (1912, 1:42). Wilson commented upon how "the Indian women here all ride like men & very graceful & good riders some of them are" (Stanley 1970:115).

A pack saddle was made by connecting a pair of simple X-frames, each one created from two straight and sturdy wood sticks, crossed over each other and secured with wet rawhide. The device had one X-frame at each end, connected to each other on either side of the horse. Because the upper portions of the frames protruded up above the horse's back, loads could be easily secured along the top of the horse, in addition to each side of the *animal* (*xʷixʷey'úł*). This type is probably what was observed by Wilson (1866:302), who described how both men and women used:

> [...] either a saddle of the common Mexican pattern, a leather pad, or a piece of buffalo skin thrown over the horse's back; the women ride after the manner of men, and use an exaggerated form of Mexican saddle, having a very high pommel and cantle [...] A piece of buffalo skin is placed underneath the saddle to protect the horse's back, but they are dreadfully galled notwithstanding this precaution.

The introduction of the horse required hide and hemp-working to produce different tack for horses. In time, however, by-products of the horse were used, such as *horsehair* (*t'úxʷn* - "horsetail") which was braided in varying diameter to make rope, *saddle cinch strap* (*č'łqʷnčsqáxeʔtn*), and a *hobble* (*heclč'lč'ést* or *lč'lč'šisqá* or *sč'ƚʔa'cʔaʔccin'šn*)—products all required in a horse-human relationship. A long lead for tying a horse or pack train to a stationary object was called a *ʕacsqaxeʔtn*, whether it was of hemp or rawhide. (1866:302). White horsetail was twisted into cords for making a *cinch strap* or a *bridle* (*č'łqʷnčaqáxeʔth*). Until recently elderly Spokan men told of how a person sleeping on the ground would protect himself from rattlesnakes by encircling his bedding of fir *tree boughs* (*t'qélpntm*) with a rope made of horsetail hair, whose rough texture was believed to irritate the snake's abdomen; presumably preventing it from crawling over and biting the sleeper. If an individual was in a dry area, then prickly pear could be used to encircle the bedding. The Spokan and Colville used mashed roots and leaves of valerian to repel rattlesnakes (Turner *et al.*, 1980:142). In 1989, an elderly man adamantly stated:

> The use of a horse hair rope used to prevent snake bite was true. We always used such a rope when we slept on the ground. We circled our bag or blanket with such a rope, and no one was ever bitten. The old T.S. couple who lived just east of here [1904] made many ropes from horsetail, hobbles, martingales, and pegging ropes, all made from braided horse hair. They'd work on making them throughout the year, not only in the winter, and sell or trade them to other Indians or Whites at rodeos and sometimes in town [Spokane] (Ross 1968-2008).

An elderly Spokan recounted how before World War I, his father supplemented his income by manufacturing on a mule-ear saddle bench such items as the *Indian hemp rope lariat* (*łxʷpústn*) or, later, *modern hemp rope* (*spoq'iłp*), hobbles, martingales, and pegging ropes from braided horsetail. At one point the elder smiled and looked away while he said:

> I recall many years ago when we'd been running Cayuses (wild horses) up north near the town of Chewelah, and seeing hundreds, just hundreds of them damn swarming, sunning rattlesnakes, who'd stand right up on their tails, weaving and swaying back and forth like buck grass in the wind, just scaring hell out of them horses. The snakes in the way would move quick-like so they wouldn't be trampled. After passing through, I'd always wave back with my hat so they'd better see me, cause you'd never know if your horse would be tripped or break a leg in one of them damn gopher holes. And if you fell, those snakes wouldn't bother you if they'd remember you'd waved (Ross 1968-2008).

Undoubtedly the *stirrup* (*snčql'ql'utéw'stm'* or *snčłqlqlwétmn*) was introduced with the saddle, and the *first type of stirrups* (*snčłql'ql'w'etmn*) were made "of wood, which is more pleasant and comfortable to the foot than metal, especially in cold weather" (Wilson 1866:302). *Stirrup covers* (*čxʷépšntn*), when used, were fashioned from a single section of water-molded rawhide that was attached to the stirrup (STHC).

It is not known when the wool *horse blanket* (*nqpčiʔsqáxeʔtn*) was first adopted by the Spokan, an item that served as a bed and a sleeping robe when persons were horse-camping. A much sought saddle blanket was one of bison hide tanned with the hair, called *nqpčiská*. Any deer or bison hide saddle blanket was always placed with the hair to the horse's back.

The short *riding quirt* (*qíxʷmn*) was made of braided rawhide with a wrist strap that varied in length according to the maker and the buyer or trader's preference. The first *rein* (*č'łqacpaʔsqáxeʔtn*) or lead rope was made from Indian hemp; and was later replaced by those manufactured from leather or braided horsetail, and eventually sisal *ropes* (*ʕacsqáxeʔtn* - "horse tie"). Some elders felt that the use of horseshoes (*q'aʔšiʔsqáxeʔtn* or *q'aʔšísqáxeʔ*) became popular for draft and riding horses when blacksmithing was probably learned from either the soldiers at Fort Spokane or government farm agents.

Cox, when speaking of equestrian accoutrements, the maintenance of horses, and the condition of Spokan horses, noted how during his stay:

> The Indian horses are never shod; and, as we were equally with them deprived of smith, farrier, and iron, we were unable to introduce that valuable practice into the country. Owing to this circumstance, their hoofs, particularly of such are in constant work, are nearly worn away before they are ten or eleven years old, after which they are unfit for any labor except carrying children [...] They are hard taskmasters; and the hair rope bridals, with the padded deer-skin saddles which they use, lacerate the mouths and backs of the unfortunate animals in such a manner as to render them at times objects of commiseration [...] . (1832:215-6).

Approximately thirty years after the war of 1857-58, another more detailed account of the care and use of horses by the Spokan came out, but it unfortunately fails to acknowledge the dire results that the revengeful and wanton slaughter by Colonel Wright had upon the number and quality of later breeding stock, taken presumably for tactical reasons by Wright's soldiers: "eight hundred beautiful animals were shot, in addition to a number of horned stock [...] together with burning a number of dwellings and barns of grain" (Hunt 1966:71). Rev. Walker sadly wrote how "it took the major part of two days for two companies of soldiers to complete the task of shooting all the horses. A heap of bones long remained to mark the place of slaughter" (Drury 1940:242).

A rather critical explanation of how the Spokan presumably treated their horses was made by Wilson:

> No selection seems to be made to improve the breed, and many are wretched specimens of horse-flesh; they have great endurance, are sure-footed, and very hardy, requiring little care at the end of a day's journey, when they are simply turned out to graze, and in the morning caught up and saddled. The Indian treats his horse very cruelly; most of them have large open sores on the back, and the numerous scars on the head and the unwillingness of the horse to let anyone touch that part, show the effect and cruelty with which the rider uses the butt of his whip. The Indian mounts clumsily and slowly from either side of his horse [...] The horses are trained to dash up at full galop [sic], and come to a sudden stop at a motion of the rider's wrist, a practice which causes much injury to the feet [...] No care is taken of the horses during the winter; they are turned loose to pick up their living as they best can by scraping away the snow and eating the dry unnutritious grass below, in consequence of which they are a long time recovering flesh in the spring, and, being ridden long before they are strong enough, soon get broken down (1866:301-302).

But one of the most detailed and revealing accounts of the horse, its care, training, and even disposition, was provided by Gibbs, an early explorer and surveyor who conducted linguistic and ethnographic observations of the Spokan during 1877. His comments elicit the seldom described smells, sights, and sounds of horses in an Indian encampment, but again with the deprecating and unfortunate term of squaw for women:

> The Indians ride with a hair-rope knotted around the lower jaw for a bridle. The men use a stuffed pad, with wooden stirrups. The women sit astride, in a saddle made with a very high pommel and cantle, and in travelling carry their infants either dangling by the cradle-strap to the former, or slung in a blanket over their shoulders; while children of a little large growth sit perched upon the pack-animals, and hold on as best they can.

The horses are trained to stand for hours with merely a lariat thrown loosely around their necks, the ends trailing upon the ground. With the whites they are at first as shy as are American horses or mules with the Indians; but they suffer handling from the squaws and children with perfect contentment, and hang around the huts like dogs. When camping near them we often found the horses an intolerable nuisance, from their incessant whinnying during the night. Whenever the mosquitoes were abundant they posted themselves in the smoke of the fires. It is the business of the squaws in travelling to pack the animals, the men contenting themselves with catching them up; and they pile on the most heterogeneous assortment of luggage with a skill that would immortalize a professional packer. In breaking horses the Indians usually blind them before mounting, often tying down their ears in addition. A strap or cord is then passed around the body of the animal, loose enough to admit the knees of the rider. Much time is spent in soothing and quieting the beast, as the Indian has plenty of it upon his hands. When everything is ready he vaults to his back, always from the off-side, slips his knees under the girth and tightens it, withdraws the muffle, and sits prepared for a series of stiff-legged plunges, ending in a charge. If the horse throws himself—for the rider he cannot—the quick straightening of the leg releases the knee, and he is prepared for the emergency (Gibbs 1855, 1:405).

Needless to say, the acquisition of the horse was the major reason for extending the range and frequency of trade and the movement of seasonally gathered foods to winter repositories, acquiring personal status, and conducting warfare with certain Plains groups. However, an unfortunate consequence of the horse and introduction of agriculture was the rapid destruction of many traditional root fields on and near the reservation when the *plow* (*t'l'úleʔxʷtn* - "farm implement") was used to *plow* (*t'l'úleʔxʷ* - "to plow") to facilitate harvesting camas. Once the Spokan adopted agriculture, *draft horses* (*t'qt'qcnéčsgt* or *swipsqáxeʔ* or - "white man's horse") had *straw-stuffed collars* (*q'l'psqáxeʔtn* - "horse collars") and other types of appropriate harnesses and tack for pulling stone-boats, weeders, one-bottom plows, seed drills, harrows, *wagons* (*x̣ʷólq'ʷ*), and in some instances for operating stationary threshers.

In many situations, after the logging and general clearing of proposed agricultural land, it was necessary to scrape and level moguls and glacially deposited mima mounds. This was best accomplished by using the more practical single horse drawn tumblebug, which quickly replaced the longer and deeper two horse-drawn patented Fresno model (Sprague, pers. comm.). The simplest of mechanical farm implements, the tumblebug, had no wheels, but instead only a skid on either end of a heavy metal sheet scoop one to two meters long. When full, the scoop was emptied by tipping upright a long extended metal handle.

Prior to having metal implements for harrowing, a man would harrow newly plowed ground by tying several long sections of cut black thornberry branches together, suspending them from his saddle horn, and dragging them over the plot (STHC). Not long after acquiring the horse, the aforementioned agricultural technology was introduced, and it became necessary for the Spokan to plant and harvest *hay* (*supul'eʔxʷ*) as winter feed for an increasing number of cattle and horses.

Before acquiring wagons, the most efficient means of transporting heavy loads over open areas and relatively flat areas was by horse using the *travois*, (*lq'ʷóstn* or *ʔay'ʔay'm'áw'sqn'* - "sticks on either side of the horse"). There are no references in the literature that such a carrying device was used by the Spokan to transport heavy loads, though Elmendorf (1935-6, 1-73) described how sick persons were carried on a *horse-pulled travois* (*ʔesckʷáqsts* - "it [horse] pulled the travois" *id. hesckʷaqsts ɬu lq'ʷóstn*). It was probably similar to the Plains Indian travois, which was a simple horse-drawn drag made of two long poles approximately 3 to 4 m in length (often using the dog poles for the wind flaps of a tipi). The two poles were stabilized by crossing the *narrow* (*qqeeʔt*) end of each pole over the other, which was tied together at that point, and further secured above the horse's back, and kept in place with a chest strap made out of one or more long strips of rawhide. The larger ground ends were spread apart and held in place by attaching two smaller poles at right angles to the main poles, and the lowest cross-member was approximately one meter from the bottom ends. This configuration supported a woven lattice of rawhide or stout willow branches that formed a web platform to accommodate a tipi, household goods, and other implements. Historical accounts (STHC) stated that an earlier form of *pack saddle* (*amʔamʔatáqs*), suited for pulling a travois over relatively level

464

ground, was made by attaching deer antlers to a double-crossed wooden frame, which accommodated the attachment of the travois poles.

Of interest are the frequent references in Walker's diary of the danger for cattle and horses to eat rushes [tules] when there was a shortage of feed due to deep snow (Drury 1976:179, 221, 230, 292, and 375), but unfortunately he never cites the exact effects, although it had been a major problem during the severe winter of 1847. Drury further recorded Walker's diaries, stating that, "The natives with over forty head of cattle and perhaps up to 200 head of horses had made no provisions for feeding them in severe weather. Hence their losses were almost total" (1976:380). The grievous effects of these losses led to the murder of several shamans, who had earlier presumably been warned, as cited by Walker (7 January 1847): "their medicine men had not brought a favorable change in the weather, [and] they deserved to be killed" (Drury 1976:389 fn). According to Walker (27 March 1847), an elderly Spokan related how "their medicine men had been the cause of their horses dying" (Drury 1976:391).

Dogs

There is uncertainty as to whether the Spokan, prior to acquiring the horse, used the dog (*Canis familiari - ssqáqxe?* or *xxƛ'cín'*) as a *beast of burden* (*nqʷqʼʷsm'íčn?šn?*); but the dog did serve numerous functions: tracking, scavenging, hunting, companionship, security, acting as camp sentinels or as a *protector* (*qe' č'ɬwhencútn* - "dog as a protector"). Lord observed how dogs were kept "solely for the chase and protection of their camps" (1867, 2:215). With regard to using dogs for transportation, and based on early interviews, Ruby and Brown concluded, "the Spokanes little used their dogs for packing as they trudged to and from the root grounds; starvation and inbreeding had deprived Spokane dogs of much size or strength" (1982:21).

There are few references of the Flathead Group using dogs for transporting goods with either side-panards or a travois, which could have occurred prior to the coming of the horse. In fact, Franchère wrote in 1845 that, before the horse, Spokan families moved their possessions with the help of dogs, dogs bearing little packs or dogs dragging the A-shaped frames of trailing sticks across which baggage was lashed. It was possible that some dogs transported goods in the winter using sleds, for Thompson recorded on 8 January, one of his men, "beat a dog useless and the sled we made got broke and was with the dog thrown aside." (Sperlin 1913, 1:5). Thompson, during the same severe winter, claimed that his "Dogs could no longer haul their loads owing to depth and softness of the snow" (Elliott 1911, 3:200). Thompson, during the same time, claimed, "the dogs were unable to move their loads, a cache was made" (Elliott 1911, 3:200).

There were several types of game dogs, the most common ones being specifically for tracking and treeing or cornering bears, and for locating (but not killing) beaver (Smith 1936-38:402). Some dogs were "trained to kill ducklings before they fly [...] killing one and go on to the next one" (Smith 1936-8:403-404). Consequently, dogs were never purposely fed, but instead kept lean for purposes of hunting—particularly when tracking or chasing deer over crusted snow or ground. Dogs "were only half-fed by their owners, to train them to look after their own welfare and continue the much admired craft of hunting" (Miller 1990:23). Ogden remarked that there was always a universal precaution—though rarely cited in the literature—that when trapping beaver and muskrat, all Indian and non-Indian trappers were careful never to bring a dog because, upon the sight or scent, a dog would immediately kill any beaver (Elliott 1904, 10:344).

Dogs were used for tracking wounded animals and trained to locate an *animal's spoor* (*mneč*). The most definitive description of the dog's behavior is afforded by Gibbs, whose time with the Spokan, and his linguistic abilities and his writings, helped him provide a credible description of how dogs participated in village life:

> In describing the household goods of the Indian, his dogs are not to be forgotten. They vary considerably in form with different tribes, but always preserve the same general character. Quarrelsome and cowardly [*nxel'éw's* - 'coward"], inveterate thieves, suspicious and inquisitive, they are constantly engaged in fights among themselves, or in prowling around the lodges for food. The approach of a stranger is heralded by short, sharp

yelps, succeeded by a general scamper. They all bear the same mysterious resemblance to the cayote [sic]—the sharp muzzle, erect ears, and stiffly curling tail. Notwithstanding their worthlessness, they seem to have a strong attachment to their owners, and an Indian camp would be a novelty without its pack of curs (1855, 1:405).

Perhaps the best physical description of the typical Plateau dog comes from Smith's Kalispel and Chewelah-Spokan ethnography:

They look something like Eskimo dogs, with their ears pointed and they stand straight up [*čłtxʷtxʷéneʔ* - "straight ears"]. Their tails were moderate in length. They barked even a long time ago. And they also were in all mixed colors; no colors were considered better than others [...] (1936-8:401). They did not breed [dogs] with wolves or foxes (1936-8:406).

An early observation and description of the indigenous dog of the eastern Plateau is afforded by Lord, one that suggests the dog's origin owed paternity to the coyote:

The true Indian dog, as I have seen it in the Kootanie [sic] country, among the Spokans, and other tribes that have had no opportunity to cross the breed with any imported dog, is beyond all question nothing more than a tamed cayote [sic] or prairie wolf; a most apt and appropriate name, for a greater thief does not exist. Although partially domesticated—by that I mean taught to hunt, come when called, and forsake their wild brethren—still they retain every type and character of an untamed animal (1866, I:218).

Prior to hunting it was common to *train a dog for tracking* (*sxʷččél'm'*) either bear or deer, and incidental hunting of upland game birds. Either a male or female dog could become a *trained tracking dog* (*sxʷččel'm's*) and was considered as not only an indispensable hunting companion to its trainer, but an extremely considerate and *valuable gift given to a close friend* (*snkʷłxʷcʼštwéxʷ* or *lmmštwéʔxʷ* - "they exchanged gifts"). Such a recipient would later reciprocate with perhaps a horse, or occasionally a portion of choice meat from a successful hunt. It was not unusual for an exceptional tracking dog to be loaned to a good friend or to an acquaintance. The person borrowing the dog, if successful, acknowledged the favor by reciprocating with a share of the kill.

In training, hunters agreed that a good tracking dog had to possess several qualities: a strong sense of smell of game, a meanness to people, and never to be distracted while tracking—even by another animal. As regards the training given to a dog to be mean, there was consensus in the early observations by non-Indians that dogs were frequently beaten by their owners. There was recall of past dog trainers rubbing live *hornets* (*Vespula maculata* - *sqʷúʔł*), *fire or piss-ants* (*Solenopsis geminata* - *sxʷúxʷyʼeʔ*), red ants (*Formica* spp. - *sxʷúxʷiyʼeʔ*), or any type of *hymenoptera* (insects) into the chest of young dogs to make them mean. According to Smith:

They [the Kalispel and Chewelah-Spokan Group] never tried to make a dog good and friendly. They only try to make it behave itself by beating it up [...] Dogs are beaten by men and women. Dogs belong to a family or to a person if he is single. A person could not beat another's dog. If a dog got into a cache, he chased him away but he would not beat him up. He left this for the owner to do. He would do it as soon as he found it out for if he did not the dog would do it again and the other party would kill it tho[ugh] he could not beat it before. He did not have to pay him for killing the dog (1936-8:405).

Each owner followed a different regime when dog-training, often employing unique methods, depending on the trainer's experience and the dog's temperament. But regardless of training methods, all dogs were excellent swimmers—particularly dogs for hunting deer and beaver. Every day a man would swim with his dogs to bathe them and increase their endurance for swimming. Given the topography and the number of hunters, a cadre of deer hunters and their dogs may commence a day's hunt along a river drainage, often starting in higher elevations, forming a long, spaced, crescent-shaped drive, with hunters on either end going ahead of the others. As they lost elevation, the dogs pushed the deer before them, and eventually into the water. Deer, but not elk, will, if at all possible, go to water to escape pursuing dogs, only to be dispatched by waiting hunters. As cited, there was variation of training between dog owners when training a hunting or tracking dog:

Dogs were taught to mind the [owner's] voice [...] Not very often did they make a pup a deer hunter by putting its nose in the mouth of a freshly killed deer. Then they press the deer's sides so it expels puffs of air as tho[ugh] it were breathing [...] This suffocates almost [sic] the dog, who inhales the scent. Also they rub the *musk* ([*sčéč'pλ̣ʔšn*] from the deer's hind leg on pups to make them good deer dogs (Smith 1936-8:408).

Schaeffer's account of how a young puppy was trained by the Flathead to be a good bear or deer hunter, involved opening the stomach of the dead deer or bear, and placing "the pup in, until he nearly smothers and this will make a good hunter of him" (1934-37, I-157:28).

There were essentially two types of tracking dogs: ones that followed only the scent of game, and others trained to follow the scent of blood from a wounded animal. In training for the blood scent, a young pup was wrapped in a fresh hide from either a deer or bear, and forced to struggle until it was released; a procedure that was repeated until the dog demonstrated an ability to distinguish bear blood scent from that of a wounded deer.

Training a beaver-hunting dog never entailed rubbing the dog with *beaver testicles* (*st'lnt'n*). Rather, following the Doctrine of Signatures, the heart of a diving duck was rubbed on the dog's nose to train the dog to dive just below the surface and then burrow into the entrance of the beaver house; surfacing beavers were then killed by the men with clubs. There was disagreement as to whether beaver houses were typically destroyed by hunters after first draining the beaver pond. One elderly man said, "A beaver house or dam was never destroyed. If so, some of the Indian people would die, because the beaver are intelligent people; [they] were here before Indians and helped the early Indians" to build their dwellings." Yet several older men recall the destruction of beaver houses to facilitate killing the beavers. In winter, dogs were used to locate beaver breathing holes in frozen ponds.

Another method of training dogs to *follow deer tracks* (*nʔucšnétc'ʔey*) was to have them wear the bloodied hooves of the animal, which had been cut off and rubbed in the dog's nose and sometimes on its chest. This technique; however, was not always used during collective hunting of bear or deer; furthermore, a trainer might tie a patch of blood-soaked deer or bear hide to the shoulder area, in order to familiarize the dog to a particular species. As previously mentioned, a man training a young deer-tracking dog might place the puppy's face in the mouth of a slain deer to improve the dog's ability to track.

Presumably, the same procedure was used to train dogs for hunting and retrieving birds (STHC). This is likely because the Spokan concluded that the low meat (protein) yield of any winged game, in comparison to the high cost and expenditure of energy using bow and arrow, or later with shotguns, was simply not worth it. For example, prior to firearms, ducks and geese were hunted on land and in shallow river bays or trapped by early morning ice that had formed on ponds. A hunter would simply follow his dog as it ran from one bird to another, breaking the neck of each bird, which was later picked up by the hunter.

Every hunter owned several dogs—some as many as five, each with a specific hunting skill; some were invaluable for hunting bear, being notably brave and never intimidated, regardless of circumstances. But only a few had dogs that were trained for beaver hunting, which was done mainly only throughout the winter. During winter hunting, and with a slight warming thaw, the snow would become hard again with freezing, causing a dog to cut the pads of his feet. Such injuries were treated by covering the afflicted *paws* (*sn'qʷq'ʷsm'ičn'šn'*) with a thick layer of warmed pitch before covering them with either matted grass or tarweed. Interestingly, there were no recalled accounts of hunters protecting a dog's feet with rawhide or buckskin boots when traveling or hunting in winter, though it was probable they did. Both leather and later canvas were cut and tied to a dog's sore feet.

An important hunting technique for a solitary deer hunter was the strategy of persistent hunting, when the dog followed the scent of the unseen animal, presumably never giving up the chase until the deer was dispatched by the hunter. A *dog capable of tracking game* (*sčt́íp*) was considered valuable. But if the dog attacked a deer during a hunt, or simply ran an animal for sport, it was deemed worthless and killed immediately by the owner.

A man and his dog were constant companions, yet some claimed that a dog was never allowed inside a dwelling, while others, as already noted, contradicted these claims (Schaeffer 1935-36). This may have been dependent upon the time that the particular person recorded his comments and the individual observer's attitudes regarding dogs. Historically, the Spokan were known to be much more strict with dogs than presently. In severely cold weather, some owners would dig a hole near the dwelling to provide a cover for the dog (STHC). However, Elmendorf (1935-6, 1:4) recorded how the Spokan would permit some dogs to sleep in the vestibule of a long-house during winter months. Yet in describing the use of dogs, Lord, a man from a country where a dog is man's best friend, suggests that they were permitted in an owner's dwelling without devitalizing their abilities as sentinels:

> The Indians use them only for driving game. Putting a pack of the wolfish scrubby curs into a pine forest is like loosing so many wolves; away they tear, rushing up everything that comes in their way [...] Bears are generally either tree'd or driven to the rocks; surrounded by these snapping pests they take no heed of the hunters, who, stealing close up, kill them, without risk of attack [...] Entering an Indian camp on foot, be it night or day, is really a ris[k]y thing to do. The prick-eared guards swarm out from every lodge, like wasps from a shaken nest (1866, 2:223-24).

Only the dog's owner could feed his dogs, and then he was careful not to overfeed them, knowing that this would lead to their becoming overweight and lazy. In fact, dogs were never fed during the summer, but expected to scavenge for themselves. Nor were dogs ever groomed or clipped. To house, feed, or make a *pet* (*č'em'útn'*) of one's dog was believed to impair the animal's acute sense of awareness, and, thus, reduce their great value as sentinels and for hunting. If a dog lost its interest or abilities in hunting, or began to howl incessantly throughout the night, it would be killed by the owner. What must have been a common practice during the fishing season, and seldom cited, is Lord's observation that, "Dogs are fed in great measure on fish; the salmon that die" (1866, 2:224).

Dogs and horses were never named after humans; rather a dog received a *pet name* (*yeye?*), for example (*kʷekʷil'e?* - "little red"), from its owner, one that usually represented a physical feature, color, or unusual marking, or a unique behavioral characteristic of the animal. Within the Plateau, it was said if an unusually good hunting dog died, the owner, out of respect, would *dig a grave* (*?ecmq'móq'ʷ*) for the animal (Collier *et al.* 1942:4). After an appropriate time, a hunting partner would replace his friend's loss with another but untrained dog.

Men felt that if children were permitted to play, feed, or direct the activities of a dog, the animal would lose its ability and even desire to hunt effectively, because then it would no longer be a bit *wild* (*ʕwuw'aq'ʷu?t*). This did not mean that children old enough to talk were not permitted to communicate with dogs, or, for that matter, dogs with children. Typical of any animal-human relationship, it was believed there existed some degree of mutual intelligibility. An observing *adult* (*kʷtnálqʷ*) would never ask the child to divulge the content of a conversation he had with a dog, knowing that later in the child's approach to puberty, this child-dog relationship might be a significant aspect of the guardian spirit relationship (Smith 1936-8:409). One elderly person claimed that only small boys—not girls—were able to communicate with dogs. Many years ago, the author was told by an elderly Spokan how his younger brother had certain problems socializing as an adult, because he had as a child endured a prolonged and high fever; later, as a young man, he could communicate with any dog—often sitting across from one another, shaking their heads in unison while "talking".

A man never hit or disciplined another person's dog—at least not publicly, because it was believed such an action would make a hunting dog lose interest in hunting, or become disruptive, lazy, or stubborn to his owner's commands. A dog's erratic behavior was often explained as being due to sorcery or gradual poisoning by a person who had fed the dog powdered bones—usually human. A dog that constantly fought with other dogs, or bit another person, was killed by the owner. A howling dog was often surreptitiously poisoned by an irate neighbor. DeSmet complained about the number of free-roaming dogs when traveling through Spokan

468

country, claiming that "each Indian family had six or seven dogs and that, since they were not fed, they became very cunning in raiding his supplies" (1905:115). DeSmet further complained how bothersome dogs were to the missionaries, raiding their food supplies, claiming the missionaries told the Indians, "We told them they might make their own hearts about killing the dogs & we would make our hearts about staying with them. If they had not killed the dogs, we were determined to move off" (Drury 1976:109). Walker lamented upon the frequency with which domesticated dogs killed many of their chickens (Drury 1976:399, 366 fn), and destroyed a leather horse halter (Drury 1976:332), and how, "The ravenous dogs would eat leather when nothing else was available" (Drury 1976:275 fn).

Dogs were too valuable to have been killed and eaten for no reason. However, a dog after death may have its hide tanned with the hair on to make a robe, particularly if it had an unusually *variegated* (*hi q'ey'* - "different colors") colored hide. Dogs were never castrated, nor did the Spokan ever eat them (Wilkes 1845, 4:438). However, an account by Chief Louis Wildshoe claimed that horse and dog meat were eaten at Fort Spokane (Lewis 1927:9).

Trails

Prior to horse drawn wagons there were no roads—only *trails* (*snqlix*ʷ*álq*). Nearly all present day paved and dirt roads on the reservation were once a *trail* (*šúšuw'eł* - "any trail"), and were once undoubtedly well-defined game trails. Both animal and human trails were naturally more defined at shallow water crossings and places providing ease of traversing steep hill slope gradients. It was understood that a passerby would always clear any debris or wind-blown branches from a trail or even a major pathway. Elders told of how on seldom-used trails, one could find a hawk feather tied from an overhanging limb to protect the traveler from ghosts when traveling at dusk. In such situations, a single traveler always sang, but never whistled.

Though there are few existing memories of specific trail names, there was agreement that all major trails were given a geonomic designation; frequently involving the location of a resource or recognizing an ideographic event or human encounter with an animal or supernatural familial. A well known example is Ghost Road, a dirt road near Wellpinit, so named because ghosts once were known to inhabit this dirt road. In the past, all major and some minor trails were named for orientation or a certain significant ideographic event.

Bridges and Stone Causeways

There are several reports of suspension bridges having been constructed by the Spokan, but they provide no details. Elmendorf (1935-1936, 2:4) provides a cryptic explanation of the Spokan making such structures to facilitate transportation over riverine and *canyon* (*henc'?íłš*) water courses. Bridge construction could have been possibly done three or four generations before Elmendorf's fieldwork:

> [...] suspension bridges [were] made of willow or red willow bark—willow withes braided three or four strands as [the] floor of [the] bridge suspended to [the] tree one either side of [the] stream or canyon—*nxalíus* ("with path across")—2 or three of the withe slats [were] side by side across [the] stream—slat[s] laid across them were woven through the interstices (1935-6, 1:41).

There were locations where the Spokan made bridges by up-ending a near-fallen tree—one of appropriate length to make a *log bridge* (*nxléw's*) to span a fairly narrow water course. There were several remembered oral accounts of how a common and simple method of making a single-walk bridge was to chop down a *tall tree* (*wʕossnálqʷ*), so that upon falling it spanned an often deep but narrow land feature.

At one time on the Little Spokane River, near its confluence with the main Spokane River, there was a major stone fishing platform which was reputed to have served for many years as a causeway or *bridge* (*henp'néw's* or *nxalíws* - "path across"); but unfortunately the structure has since been destroyed, and scattered, though some features are still visible, and on close observation still suggests its once multipurpose use. In the Spokane River, near the mouth of Latah Creek, large anchor stones for weirs are still to be seen, and served as a causeway. Similarly, up-river from Tum Tum, and near the site of Spokane House, is a causeway made of large exposed boulders that once supported a fishing weir.

The matter of building bridges may never be resolved, for Sam Boyd (Elmendorf's primary informant), when speaking of using roughly-made dugout canoes for transporting heavy loads across streams, contended that the Spokan made no type of suspension bridge (1935-6, 2:40). However, Eells described in his diary for 22 April 1848 (Chap. XIV) how he and his party, "Crossed a small stream, very deep, so that [we] were obliged to unpack our mules and carry our baggage across the stream on an Indian bridge" (Drury 1970:71). Eells also made reference to "an Indian bridge strong enough to support a horse" (Drury 1976:fn71), and later relates, "In crossing an ill constructed bridge, nearly afloat, the animal upon which the Indian rode went down, but fortunately the loading went over the head of the poor creature & fell upon the ground" (Drury 1976:468).

Chapter XIV: Clothing and Adornment

Fortunately there are numerous existing representative examples of traditional Spokan clothing, including war accoutrements and forms of personal adornment, in museums, photographs, and in personal collections of the Spokan. Because of the interest in material culture by early historians, travelers, and anthropologists, there are also detailed illustrations and descriptions of how such items were manufactured and decorated.

With few exceptions, clothing generally indicated not only a person's gender, but often during certain rites of passage and collective rites of intensification, one's tutelary spirit, by the type of hide and accoutrements or applied design. The very clothing worn for certain rituals was believed to have an inextricable relationship with one's *suméš*, as was true for some types of hair style, facial painting, and personal adornment. Tailored clothing could reveal the sewer's identity and ability for creating a garment that served multipurpose tasks.

Clothing and Accoutrements

Until the 1840s, nearly all *clothing (slnacłq'áyt* or *xcnúm'tn*) was made of brain-tanned female black-tailed and white-tailed deer (Elmendorf 1935-6, 2:28; Schaeffer 1934-37, I-34:5), or occasionally from elk hides which were far less plentiful. Also, thick elk hide was more difficult to work and sew, particularly by an elderly woman who often had not the strength to *work a hide (xʷikʷi*) from elk. A woman who had difficulty processing elk hide was called "grandmother" even if she had no children or grandchildren. People wore a minimum of clothing; going barefoot during the spring and summer, but wearing moccasins when traveling overland and during winter. In summer, men wore only a *breechcloth (nłqʷépuʔstšn* or *nłqʷe*), or, to be more exact, a *G-string (sk'ʷłišút* - "an underbelt"). While stationed at Spokane House, Work noted (1823) that some children in warm weather went about naked, whereas others wore tailored clothing, as did adults.

The clothing of men and women differed in pattern, and oral history makes several references to how many Spokan had barely ample clothing prior to the 1850s. Only people of status and wealth had *ceremonial clothing (sqlixʷlscút*) as well as certain utilitarian garments, whereas "Only exceptional hunters had full costumes" (STHC), which were called *stc'atsatsqéncn* (Elmendorf 1935-6, 1:28).

Schaeffer's (1934-37, I-134) extensive field work with the Flathead and other eastern Plateau groups describes how female white-tailed and black-tailed buck hides, obtained during summer, were traditionally used for clothing.

However, the changes from traditional clothing to non-hide apparel was rather dramatic, even sartorial. Washington Irving (1783-1859) always expressed great sympathy for Native Americans, and had access to Bonneville's extensive notes, which he transcribed. The material reveals what was fashionable for both the Spokan and the voyageur, and how Indian trappers were influenced by indigenous accoutrements and clothing. Bonneville described white trappers as wilderness vagrants:

> The wandering whites who mingle for any length of time with the savages have invariably a proneness to adopt savage habitudes; but none more so than the free trappers. It is a matter of vanity and ambition with them to discard everything that may bear the stamp of civilized life, and to adopt the manner, habits, dress, gestures, and even the walk of the Indian. You cannot pay a free trapper a greater compliment than to persuade him you have mistaken him for an Indian brave; and in truth, the counterfeit is complete. His hair, suffered to attain a great length, is carefully combed out, and either left to fall carelessly over his shoulder, or plaited neatly and tied up in otterskins or partly colored ribbons. A hunting-shirt of ruffled calico of bright dyes, or of ornamented leather falls to his knee; below which curiously fashioned leggings, ornaments with strings, fringes and a profusion of hawkbells, reach to a costly pair of moccasins of the finest Indian fabric, richly embroidered with beads. A blanket of scarlet or some other bright color, hangs from his shoulder, and is girt round his waist with a red sash,

in which he bestows his pistols, knife, and the stem of his Indian pipe; preparations for peace or war. His gun is lavishly decorated with brass tacks and vermilion, and protected with a fringed cover, occasionally of buckskin, ornamented here and there with a feather (Durham 1912, 1:55-6).

A later description of the effects of trade material and clothing upon traditional attire was afforded by Wilson, who described how different types of acquired and modified clothing denoted certain statuses and accomplishments by the wearer, either man or woman:

> The common dress of a man is a cotton shirt, a blanket or buffalo robe, reaching from head to foot, and fastened by a sash tied round the waist so the upper half can be wrapped round the body in wet or cold, and in fine weather be allowed to fall over the legs like a long kilt, disclosing the finery of a striped cotton shirt, breech clouts of blanketing, nicely ornamented leggings and elk skin moccasins. Caps, coats, and trousers, of European manufacture, are often worn by the chiefs and dandies, as also leathern hunting shirts and trousers. The women, when not able to obtain European clothing, wear leather dresses with long fringes, leggings, and moccasins (1866:299).

Yet, by the late 1890s, the perceptions of and the function of certain non-traditional dress and accoutrements by some Indians had sadly changed:

> At a later period the growing scarcity of furs and similar peltries, commenced to be supplied by the white man's blanket and by his ginghams and calicoes, to no small detriment of both the comfort and health of the natives. To-day, the Indian arrayed gorgeously and picturesquely in the triumphs of the chase and his natural ingenuity, is a thing of the past. He can only be seen at Washington, D.C., where occasionally and to serve a purpose, the Indian Department is wont to manufacture him to order (Palladino 1894:5).

Given the available indigenous material and traditional technology for manufacturing clothing, at first glance there were few perceived differences in the finished products of unadorned clothing. Distinctions, however, were more apparent in hide finishing and stitching, as certain women were noted for their abilities in processing, tanning, and sewing garments. Until recently, the finest compliment a Spokan woman could receive was about how carefully a garment or pair of gloves had been stitched, with even spaces, and, depending upon the method of hide-smoking, how light in color the item was. Also, when viewing a *tanned* (*síp'i?*) but uncut buckskin, a person was careful to view the woman's work always with the sun behind the hide, so the observer could comment favorably upon how smoothly the skin had been scraped, or that the woman's husband was an excellent shot if there were no holes in the hide. When rifles were adopted, men invariably shot deer in the head with the more popular, lightweight, and economical .22 Winchester rim-fire WRF bullet, thereby reducing the damage to the animal's hide.

Any type of garment or item of worked hide displayed a worker's ability. Further distinctions of clothing, particularly ceremonial garments, were achieved by ornamentation with various types of beads, feathers, shells, and even porcupine quills. Flat geometric designs on garments were achieved with dyes, more often with red and yellow clay. Teit recorded that beaded clothing designs replaced geometric patterns, though most designs remained geometric "except perhaps among the Spokan" (1930:337). The figure here shows some characteristic designs on the sides of men's leggings (Teit 1930:339).

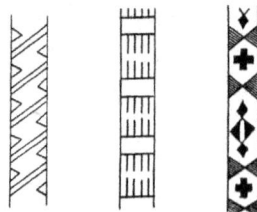

Figure 32. Designs on men's leggings

Carla Dove, the nation's only full-time forensic ornithologist, examined the feathered materials collected by the Lewis and Clark expedition (McLaughlin 2003:220), and described the use of flattened feather shafts used by certain groups for quilling. But there is no indication that the Spokan employed round or flattened feather shafts alone or in conjunction with porcupine quills for decorating garments.

Designs and adornments were most often created by the woman who made the item, and often made symbolic expressions of design or personal achievement in warfare, even displaying a person's tutelary spirit. Major changes in ceremonial clothing design and adornment were facilitated by the introduction of such items and materials as ribbons, silk, cotton, wool, thread, needles, and scissors. The introduction of cotton and wool garments created new concerns during the storage of such clothes, namely, moths and mildew odor. Various scented plant materials were used to combat both problems. In particular, cedar chips, crushed fresh yarrow leaves, and the aromatic black seeds of orange honeysuckle were sprinkled among the folded fabrics. The seeds of *wild tiger lily* (*Lilium columbianum* Hanson ex Baker - *poxʷcútn* or *stxcín* or *maxeʔ*) were mashed and sprinkled in storage containers with clothing. Fresh leaves of *blue lupine* (*Lupinus wyethii* Wats. - *qʼʷiqʼʷiqenełp*) or Sweet William were used to scent stored clothing and bedding, and if there was tule mat flooring in the sweathouse (Turner *et al.* 1980:105). Various pleasant scents from plant flowers and leaves were used as perfume by both men and women, as were the dried testicles of beaver, which were used as a *moth repellent and a perfume* (*qmépeʔ*) (STHC).

Sewing Needles and Thread

Considerable time and skill was required when cutting tanned deer hides into patterns using obsidian knives; and before sewing the buckskin into different types of tailored clothing and for other utilitarian needs. Tanned hides traditionally had to be pierced with an assortment of bone needles and awls; preferably made from the splinters of a bear's femur bone, which produced durable needles that tended to hold a point better than other type of bone, since it is the densest of all mammal bones.

Needles made of hardwood had to be further shaped with a sharpened beaver incisor or using obsidian, and then shaped and smoothed by rubbing carefully against deer antler to "break down" the cells in order to further harden the wood. A final finish was given by rubbing both the wood or bone needle with scouring rush, a plant whose epidermis is impregnated with silicon, which formed a smooth and well-defined needle (Turner 1979:62). Needles were also made from the *sharp thorns* (*xʷiy*) of red thornberry, and were preferred for sewing clothing and articles from tanned deer hide. However, for making gloves or mittens of coyote or rabbit skin, the smallest holes were achieved with splintered long bones of deer, bear, or elk, *being pointed* (*xʷúl'mn* - "pointed object") by rubbing the sharp end on a section of sandstone. Although needles made of hardwood and certain thorns were preferred for sewing tule and cattail mats, they were seldom used for sewing hides. After sucking the marrow from the long bones of an animal whose hide was to be worked, some women, after tanning the hide, made needles from the now-dried crushed long bones of deer, elk, or bear penis bone.

Not all needles came from an animal's leg bones, as attested by The Upper Columbia Archaeology Survey (Collier *et al.* 1942:92) that uncovered five bear penis bones from burial sites as well as earlier comparative evidence found at Kamloops of bear penis bones with incised designs and drilled eyes (Smith 1900:430). Some claimed the bones may have been used as needles or for their magical significance. Cline's work with the Southern Okanogan (1938:60) agrees with Collier *et al.* (1942:92) that bear bone, often the penis bone, was used as an awl because of its durability.

Piercing deer and elk hide with awls and burins was done primarily to facilitate the use of a threaded needle, or to facilitate the use of stitching materials when threading by hand without a needle. Given the type of hide, and the intended product, a woman might choose not to sew a *seam* (*st'aq*) together with a needle, but rather *to pierce* (*łuweła'eʔ*) the hide with a sharp-pointed awl to accommodate fine sinew cord stitching.

The techniques of sewing were first taught to girls when they demonstrated an interest. On such an occasion, a grandmother would make and present to the young novice her own *sewing bundle (čɫxʷeʔpleʔ)* complete with various needles, coils of plant thread and sinew along with instructions regarding their proper care. As the girl grew older, a person's comments on how well she sewed were considered pleasant; but to be told that her skills would one day compare with those of her grandmother, were the most gratifying and undoubtedly inspirational. The young girl's efforts always brought encouragement from her family, and often the women of the camp or village would, with carefully phrased admiring remarks, pass among themselves an example of her skill. An exceptional recognition was when a male or female kinsperson requested that the young girl make an item of clothing or a bag. Moreover, steel needles were an appreciated gift to an elderly woman.

Dresses

All of the known existing examples of Spokan women's dresses were apparently examples of garments made after Euro-American contact, which naturally reflect the influence of having access to traditional material, and the ability to use beads as ornamentation. Prior to that contact, women always wore near-ankle length *buckskin sleeveless dresses (sp'y'álqs)*, which Elmendorf described as "wide open under [the] arms [with] no sleeves—the parts [from an] arm or leg of deer for sleeves [which] hang down loose over [the] shoulder [and are] tied together on [the] shoulder" (1935-6, 1:11). Translations from the STHC corroborate Elmendorf's description and give a more detailed description of the *traditional sleeved dress (snʕacɫq'éy'tn* or *spy'alqs* - "hide dress or shirt"):

> They were sewed up the sides, [left] open under the arms, [and the] arm [sic] or leg[s] of a deer [were used] for sleeves [that] hung down loose over the shoulders. The dress was tied together on the shoulders, near the neckline, sometimes tied down the side, but not on the sleeves. [The] sleeves always hung loose, cape-like [...] Leggings came up to the

According to Elmendorf (1935-6, 1:11), the general term for any type of woman's dress was *snacɫq'áyt*, whereas a wing dress (*snq'xʷámin*) was one with covered arms, such as a ceremonial garment decorated with elk wisdom teeth and *secured with a special belt of buckskin (ʕacápl'qs)*. A loose, unbelted dress was called *nl'al'óq'ʷeʔ*. As a result of Euro-American trading, a much preferred *garment (sqʷiqʷy'ac'eʔ)* was made of dark blue serge wool, which always enhanced the appearance of attached elk wisdom teeth, and considerably heavier with the number of attached elk teeth, and was always an item of praise. In the summer, women wore a comfortable *ankle-length loose fitting dress (nl'al'áq'ʷeʔ)*. Some women chose animal claws and shaped mussel shell to decorate a special dress; or a woman might decorate a dress by using six to ten colored porcupine quills, tied together at one end with the loose ends slightly flared out (Elmendorf 1935-6, 1:3).

Women frequently took tanned hides, and would fold over the rough edges, and with an awl make matching holes for accommodating short strips of mountain goat hair or sinew (Elmendorf 1935-6, I:7). Some women decorated a new dress with a series of vertical *straight lines (čq'xiʔšnm'elqs)* using red ochre. One fabric dress was photographed of a Spokan woman, "with square cut sleeves bordered by a contrasting color" (Paterek 1994:212).

After acquiring trade goods, velvet was a choice material for making *beaded dresses (čk'ʷun'ɫnčst)*, often with a *beaded yoke (ɫp'ɫip)*; both were worn on special occasions. The introduction of solid colors and patterned fabrics led to fashioning *women's dresses (snʕacɫq'ey'tn)* and men's shirts that were artistically decorated with strips of colored cloth. Some had tightly-bound short hangings of horsetail hair, beads, small trade bells, and perforated clam shell discs and dentalium. Other clothing decorations were "brass hawks bells, obtained via trade" (Caywood 1954:30). A heavily-beaded yoke would further enhance a particularly fine woman's costume, and fortunate was the woman who had sewn *tiny, gold bells upon her dance dress* (*čpasáw'e?*). Women made a *decorative war dress* (*čk'ʷun'ɨn'čst*) that was worn during certain dances, decorated with bells, elk's teeth, and thimble bells.

Shirts

With the acquisition of trade materials, outstanding hunters had *full costumes* (*?e čʕacʕacqin'šn'* or *sx̱x̱éƛ'i?šn'*) with *red wool leggings* (*?iy'sl'x̌ʷ* or *stc''atsatsqéncn* or *sc?acacqin'šn'*) and a *belt* (*snlč'éw'stn* or *scʕacʕacqin'šn'*). They also "wore a *buckskin shirt* (*sp'iy'ál'qs*), one that came down around the hips with a vertical slit in front to admit [the] head" (Elmendorf 1935-6, 2:28). Pre-pubescent girls traditionally wore aprons made of woven tree bark, and on occasion were decorated with quail feathers or strips of fur. A particularly well made *man's shirt* (*sp'yálqs* or *sqal'tm'x̌ʷál'qs* or *snʕacɬq'éy't*), and a woman's *dress of buckskin* (*slnatsɬq'a'it*), decorated with dyed *porcupine quills* (*k'ʷil'mn*), was worn only for special occasions. Often, both men and women's leggings had designs (Teit 1930:339,340).

It was not unusual for men and women to indicate an achieved but temporary status by applying red ochre mixed with sturgeon oil—usually with *horizontal stripes on women's dresses* (*čq'x̱i?šnm'alqs*), and vertical stripes on the back and front of men's shirts. Men and women enhanced certain selected articles of clothing for special occasions by appending strips of *fur* (*spúm*), ermine tails, beads, and feathers—such as a single feather from a golden eagle. The sleeves of men's shirts and buckskin yokes, as well as the two vertical side-seams and bottoms of women's dresses and leggings, had *fringe* (*x̱ste?yé* or *scocóʕʷ* or *cuw'áƛqstn* - "something hanging in strips") to facilitate the shedding of rain water. Fringes varied in length, and were often 15 to 20 cm long.

Breechcloths

Men and older boys wore a breechclout or breechcloth (*nɬqʷépu?stšn* or *nɬqʷepu?sčšn* or *nɨkʷé* or *nɬqʷé*) made from buckskin, and was worn only in the front, not the back, since the material was doubled and held by hanging over a belt of twisted buckskin (*ʕacápl'qs* or *sy'ep'wn*) made from several sections of twisted rawhide. The length varied, but the width was approximately 14 to 16 cm. There is no evidence that the breechcloth was ever decorated. During ceremonies, a wider breechcloth of approximately 30 cm was worn in the front and back, both ends being passed through and over the man's belt. In cooler weather, and for warmth, men wore a breechcloth with a section of animal fur sewn to the buckskin over the area of the genitals (Elmendorf, pers. comm.).

Undergarments

Men were not known to wear *undergarments* (*č'x̌ʷátax̌ʷn* or *č'ɬištál'qs*), yet linguistically there was a designation. In winter the women wore a type of *under-skirt* (*sx̌ʷátax̌ʷn*), or a more complete garment best called *underwear* (*č'ɬyštálqs*) made of buckskin. Women could elect to wear a patterned *buckskin garment* (*nlqʷlqʷow'a?ɬc'e?*), one worn under a dress next to the skin (Elmendorf, pers. comm.). All under-dress garments were called *č'ɬ?i?štepɬ* (STHC). It is not known if a woman's undergarment had *sleeves* (*sp'čstáx̱n*).

Blankets

The most highly sought curly-fur blanket was a well-tanned *bison robe* (*qʷspélx̌ʷ* - "bison hide") or *bison blanket* (*spapsí?n*), which was warmer than a *bear blanket* (*mx̱ey'čni* or *sčlx̌ʷélx̌ʷ* - "grizzly bear blanket"). Both were tanned on one side with the hair intact, and used in the winter as a sleeping cover or wrapped about one's body for warmth, particularly after emerging from early morning winter swimming (Elmendorf 1935-6, 2:31). Bearskin robes and blankets were lined with marten skin (Elmendorf 1935-6, 1:62). "Buffalo robes were generally used for bedding, being spread upon a rough mattress of pine boughs and moss, or of tall *rye grass* [*Elymus cinereus* - *psps-néwłtn*] and rushes from the swamps" (Durham 1912, 1:109).

Every adult and older child possessed a *blanket* (*sic'm* or *smlk'ʷic'eʔ* - "whole hide with fur") for warmth when sleeping, made from the hides of bear, beaver, or skunk. Skunk hides intended for a blanket were never tanned or smoked, but prepared by carefully scraping the inside of the skin with an edged scraper, and then working the hide by rubbing folded sections against each other with both hands. *Bison horn scrapers* (*pšmin*) often were hafted with a sharpened metal plane blade, and were used for removing fat from hides once they acquired metal.

Skunk hides were always sewn together with fine sinew when making a blanket in the fall, as were fur hats made from tanned skunk hides. The most complete description of preparing a needle and fashioning a skunk blanket was by Smith:

> They get lots of skunk skins and tan them by scraping them until soft, but not smoking them. They made a blanket out of these by sewing them together. They don't weave them in strips as a muskrat blanket is done, but they are sewed together with sinew cord and a bone needle made of the bone of the lower part of the deer's leg bone. After boiling the bone they break it in two with a stone. They extract the marrow [*s't'us*] with a stick and eat it. And then they crack the bone into splinters. They find a splinter that is straight and sharp. They put a hole through it [...] , in the middle and thread it with sinew cord. Or sometimes they don't use a needle to sew these skins but only a bone awl with no hole in it. They make a hole in the skins by turning the awl round and round and then, when the hole is made, push the sinew cord through the hole after rolling the sinew cord into a point on the thigh (1936-8:714).

Rabbit skin and skins from muskrat and squirrel were seldom used to make any type of clothing, except the scarf, since the skins were too thin and difficult to work or stitch. Some made winter caps from several squirrel skins, often after the meat was eaten. Yet, several young adult sources maintained incorrectly that squirrel meat was never eaten, nor was the hide ever used in making any type of clothing, as these were unworthy animals to hunt, and hunted only by young boys.

Some blankets and robes were made from muskrat, deer, coyote, and rabbit—the last being twisted and braided for additional thickness and strength. A few elders remembered blanket robes made from tanned muskrat hides, and were said to have been quite warm and durable, yet laborious to make. Smith described the Spokan method of making a *muskrat fur* (*sn'teíc'eʔ*) blanket, and how "the Kalispel used to make a *muskrat blanket* [*syéym*], which was similar with the Spokan" (1936-8:713), and goes on to state how "they cut the skin into thin strips & twined them into a blanket. Then they beat the blanket with a stick so the hair will completely cover the stitches [...] they were much warmer than a bearskin cloak, because the hair of the latter is stiff" (1936-8:713).

With the advent of Euro-American trade, certain clothing materials and styles of *Indian clothing* (*sqlixʷscút*) changed, but most notably when the Spokan acquired the *Hudson's Bay Company blankets* (*sʔupcníčeʔ* or *stáqéy'* or *stáqaʔi*), and a type of *dark blue blanket with a black border* (*sqʷisqʷy'ac'eʔ*) made of heavy wool, which were worn by men during formal occasions, regardless of weather. A blanket was folded length-wise and carried over the man's right shoulder, across his body and pinned at the waist with the right arm uncovered, a fashion called *ny'ik'ʷx̌nic'eʔ*. These dark blue blankets were sometimes refashioned into dresses, hooded capotes, or *men's leggings for war dancing* (*qʷiqʷiʕt*). A man was sartorially attired for a ceremony if he was fortunate enough to have *dark blue beaded leggings* (*čłk'ʷl'k'ʷl'cín'šn'*), which were highly prized and worn only for a *ceremonial dance* (*sq'weymn cúti*). Some leggings fashioned from a *red trade blanket* (*skʷilc'eʔ*) were highly prized, and were presumably preferred to blue, since Work contended, "Blue cloth does not take well with them" (Elliott 1915, 1:34).

The thick navy-blue trade blanket, called a *nq'lqséw's* ("to hang together"), was worn by men when war dancing or medicine-dancing, and was so called because of three circular beaded designs—the center circle being larger than the two side circles. Later, the much-sought *Pendleton blanket* (*st'uxʷlm'ic'eʔ*) was frequently made into clothing of choice. Of all trade cloths, wool flannel was the most highly prized material, and any cove, such as a blanket was called *čłxʷupneencutn* (STHC).

Capotes

The *voyageur-hooded capote* (*stqay'ál'qs* - "long hooded coat") was first introduced by French sailors to Canadian trappers and the Métis in Acadia in the 17th century. Because of style and warmth, the Spokan adopted this garment as a trade item. Later, an HBC blanket might, like the capote, be fashioned into a *hooded long coat* (*čsnlqʷoʔqnm'ist*). The capote was commonly made of a single melton (molton cloth) blanket with no seam up the back, and secured as a waist length garment in front with a wrap-around waist sash—possibly not secured by buttons, rather by loops and doubled-ended wooden togs.

These warm and often water-proof garments were highly desired by Indians, trappers, and fur-traders for winter travel. The capote served in an emergency as a cagoule if one had to winter bivouac, since the garment was water repellent and provided excellent protection against wind and as an effective night shelter by stuffing the garment with dry leaves or, if available, dry grass to provide further insulation when used as a sleeping garment. Capotes with an attached shoulder cape, one that encircled the wearer's shoulders, afforded further protection. A shorter version of the cagoule was a *parka* (*stqay'á*), having a long shoulder cape that hung over one's back between the waist and the knees. This type of heavy winter garment was first called a blanket coat by Alexander Mackenzie (1801:244). Francis Back (1991:6), when quoting Louis-Armand de Lom d'Arce (1666-1715), a French army officer who explored and first mapped the territory along the Mississippi Rivers (1688-89), claimed the capote was "the most proper merchandise needed for the beaver trade" (1702, 2:64). Capotes were not known to have been worn by the Indian wives of trapper-traders (Gottfred 1991:10), only blankets or fur robes. Men never sewed any other type of garment, only the capote (Schaeffer 1935-36, I:20).

With the introduction of wool, a type of head cagoule that was peaked or slightly domed and tapered on either side over the ears to provide neck protection as well as for securing both ends under the chin was worn by men hunting or when running traplines in cold weather. Such headwear probably diffused from Canada, or after direct contact with French and Scottish trappers who first introduced the long-body cagoule.

Robes

Hides from bison were highly sought, having been obtained from trading expeditions onto the Plains. A tanned *bison hide robe* (*scq'iʔtálqs*), with the hair on the inside, was the warmest type of robe and was preferred as *bedding* (*mlk'ʷelxʷ*) during winter. Elk hide robes were rough and more bristly than the preferred bison hide robe (Schaeffer 1935-36, I:20). But more often a family had robes made from beaver or yellow-bellied marmot, and prior to acquiring the HBC hooded capote, women fashioned a type of *hooded robe* (*stáqaʔi*) from either beaver or marmot skins, being similar to the later trade capote. Both the front and back side of the robe *tapered to a point* (*hi λ'λ'im'* - "it comes to a point") at the bottom, often hanging nearly to one's knees, and was worn for hunting or during winter travel. A hood, when not being worn on the head for warmth, served effectively for carrying small possessions. Lord observed how, "Marmot fur [was] used in making rugs [robes]" (1886, 2:195), which were thick and water-repellent, and "The meat was a delicacy when roasted over a low fire" (1866, 2:195).

Marmot and beaver skins were first prepared by cutting off the leg skin and head before tanning, after which the skins were laid out in a rough rectangle and sewn together. Smith (1936-8:733) described how the Kalispel, after dressing the wet, green skins, cut them into strips, that were then laid alternately by overlapping each strip partially onto the edge of another one, and twisting them so that the fur was on all sides in a long and continuous length. The robe was completed by weaving the length of hides to a desired size and shape. Schaeffer cites that for the Flathead, "Sometimes the hides of both male and female elk were used for body robes" (1934-37, I-134).

A *lap robe* (*čy'il'xʷépstšn*) was a loose garment used by both men and women when occupying inadequately heated dwellings during cold weather, and wrapped about the body, and later, when traveling in a buckboard in cold weather. Another type of lap robe, called a *č'łq'ʷumq'ʷmn'cútn*, was a thick, heavy, tanned bison skin that was wrapped about one's body when traveling in an open horse drawn sleigh.

All garments for winter wear were fashioned with the fur on the inside, and before cold weather commenced, they were smoked by spreading them outside on racks over small smudge fires to rid them of any vermin and to impart a pleasant aroma. During winter the men wore bear skin robes lined with marten fur (Elmendorf 1935-6, 1:62). Like the capote, robes served when over-sleeping outside in winter, and were similar to the modern "elephant's foot" bag, and served as an emergency sleeping bag when dried leaves, moss, lichens, or any existing grasses were stuffed in the robe around the sleeping person's legs and mid-riff for better insulation.

Capes and Shawls

There were few memories or descriptions of a *cape* (*ʕepsłxʷpús* or *q'ʷóspqn*) once worn by Spokan women, but there is mention (STHC) of a *beaded cape* (*słuxʷpus*) that slipped over the head. Understandably, there is confusion now between what is the difference between a cape and a shawl. In several old photographs, an *elderly woman* (*sy'o?psčín't* - "powerful person") might be wearing what appears to be a cape, a favored garment called a *xxp'el'čst*, typically ragged and apparently faded from long wear. Teit stated how "Some skin ponchos were in vogue among the Spokan and Kalispel" (1930:334).

For additional warmth, women wore a type of cape that was wrapped about the shoulders and draped down over one's bare arms, called *pčpčsta?xn*. Prior to trade cloth, the item was fashioned from a depilated tanned pelt made soft by repeated beaming and kneading.

With the introduction of trade cloth, older women frequently wrapped an old but *favorite shawl* (*xxp'él'čst'* or *č'łcʕʷw'ic'e?* - "one with short fringe"), which was *pinned* (*?utč'él'n*) together with a kilt-like pin or a large *safety pin* (*sčč'?éple?*). A fringe shawl was called *t'łscowic'e?*. It seems likely that the historically ubiquitous *woman's shawl* (*?am?amtl'ečstn'* or *sq'l'eps*) was quickly adopted with the introduction of bolts of wool and cotton material, which were easily fashioned into shawls to provide further protection against the cold and rain. Prior to this, outer garments of tanned hide were not always impervious to moisture, nor were garments greased for this purpose because of the problem caused by rodents who would eat any so-called grease spots, and there was the resultant problem of creating cold spots if greased.

As stated, the most common method of carrying a baby was the cradleboard, but with the introduction of the shawl it was not uncommon for a mother—visiting short distances within a camp or village—to *carry her baby on her back* (*?ecq'ʷélt*) in a shawl that was secured in the front by a *cord of twisted hemp* (*nqq'éw'ptn* - "attached fiber") or a single line of buckskin. Such a shawl for carrying a baby in safety and comfort was called *č'łcʕíc'e?* or *nq'ewptn*. A woman's shawl was another example of a multi-purpose garment, as a sleeping rug or a temporary shelter, and for carrying things. When bathing naked, women tied the ends of several shawls to an adequate number of vertical sticks so as to create a visual barrier from unwanted male observers.

Leggings

Spokan men and women traditionally wore *leggings* (*sxéλ'i?šn* or *sxiλ'łxʷm* - "tied onto something at the top") during the winter. Leggings were usually made "from the hides of the white and black-tail does" (1934-37, I-135:6). Each leg had a separate undecorated cover without fringe, the bottom end being stuffed

478

into the wearer's moccasins, or tied about the wearer's ankles, and each leg section was sewn on the outside to prevent the seam from chafing against one's legs. In making such garments, the buckskin was first carefully scraped clean of hair before tanning to prevent snow from catching in the hair, which could present a problem of adhering ice-balls. During the winter women wore *knee-high leggings* (*sx̣ƛ'x̣éƛ'i?šn* or *snq'ʷuƛ'šn'*) made from tanned buckskin or otter with the fur on the inside, but later they were fashioned from bolt wool or blankets acquired through trade.

Each individual legging was supported by a suspended belt made from plaited mountain goat hair, or a *buckskin tie string* (*čacqé*) about 5 cm in width with one end sewn to the legging, and the other end wrapped about the wearer's G-string. Both men and women's leggings were made with a gradual tapering toward the bottom of each legging, and some leggings had *long leg ties* (*člč'pew'sčšn*) that were tied to a belt. When traveling in extremely cold weather, men would further protect themselves by wrapping their legs with *leggings tied to a belt* (*scʕacʕ?acʕin'šn'*), often made from bearskin with the fur on the inside. Cox (1849, 13:219) noted that some men's buckskin leggings were decorated with porcupine quills, as were some bison robes.

One man in his late nineties showed the author a pair of bearskin leggings, with the fur on the outside, and explained that this fashion was adopted as a substitute for chaps worn by many Indian cowboys as protection against bushes and in densely wooded areas in cold weather. Replication of Euro-American styles was considered fashionable, but not always practical when using traditional clothing materials. For instance, wearing bearskin leggings with the fur, either inside or outside, was extremely fatiguing, particularly if the leggings became wet and the person was afoot.

For additional protection during winter travel, men and women might use wrapped buckskin, not unlike puttees, which tended to keep snow from their feet and ankles. Men secured the buckskin tops above their knees with circular wrappings of buckskin thongs or directly to a belt. Alternatively, a man might wear large closed sections, essentially tubes of tanned buckskin he would step into with the perforated ends or *lacing* (*čqʷxʷcín'šn'tn'*) on the outside of each legging for adjusting the diameter of the leggings. In emergencies, *rags* [were] *wound around the legs* (*čy'il'y'l'xʷqasčšn*).

Red and dark blue trade flannel quickly became a favored material by women, being considered quite fashionable for manufacturing certain items of clothing for both sexes. Especially valued was *red flannel* (*?íy'sl'xʷ* or *?íy'sl'xʷ*) from which women made dresses and *ladies leggings* (*x̣ƛ'x̣eƛ'i?šn*) for special occasions and for ceremonial dancing. Men wore around their feet, ankles, and legs a style of leggings called *č'k'ʷl'k'ʷčinšn* that were decorated with dark blue beads when dancing (STHC). Some men further enhanced their dancing regalia by wearing small bells tied around their knees, known as *čʕcʕacín'šn*. The figure here illustrates designs commonly found on the front of women's leggings (Teit 1930:339).

Figure 33. Designs on women's leggings

When necessary, an additional type of ankle-to-knee puttee was made from sections of black cottonwood bark that encased each leg when traveling in wet snow and held in place with lengths of buckskin or any available and pliable material. As previously cited, men wore black cottonwood puttees when commercially logging in wooded areas as protection against being bitten by Western diamond-back rattlers.

Socks and Stockings

Socks (*nq'ʷλ'q'ʷúλ'šn*) were often made of mountain goat hair that was first "ratted out and wrapped around the foots before put[ting the foot into [a] moccasin—[and] only used in coldest weather –in wet weather bunch grass was laid in [the] bottom of [the] shoe called *nsíuxn*" (Elmendorf 1935-6, 1:65). In winter, men and women wore tanned *deerskin socks* (*cq'oxʷé*) stitched up the back as a tube with an attached shoe piece, always wearing the fur next to the skin. Women further enhanced their ceremonial dress by wearing thick trade-item *red-striped stockings* (*snq'ʷúλ'šn* - "sock-liner"), and though not always seen, they were known to be worn often with a *red dress* (*kʷill'qs*). With the introduction and widespread occurrence of European cheatgrass, women made men's *stockings* (*snq'ʷmšín*) of tanned deer hide, which were stuffed with pounded dry cheatgrass or other types of grass. The soft material was stuffed into stockings that were worn inside men's fur-lined boots during winter hunting (STHC).

Moccasins

Throughout the Plateau "the hides of the white-tail and black-tail buck were used for moccasins; also the hides of the buck, doe, and fawn elk" (Schaeffer 1934-37, I-134). Spokan *moccasins* (*síp'i?šn* or *q'axán* or *sp'síp'i?šn* - "Indian footwear" or *sqelixʷšn* or *q'e?ešín*) were of two basic shapes: low moccasins worn by men and a *high type* (*čqʷxʷcín'šn'tn*) worn by women *through all seasons* (*?oqʷcín'šn'tn* or *óʷoxʷcin'čn'* - "tip top moccasins"). Women's moccasins had *long lacing* (*qʷxʷcín'šn*), which was pulled together above the ankle and further secured with *buckskin strips* (*acclné*). The figure shows some typical Spokan moccasins (Teit 1930:335).

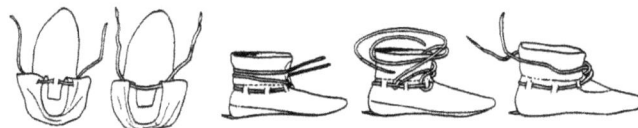

Figure 34. Spokan moccasins

In warm weather, and when it was raining, a person went barefoot. Children would go barefoot throughout the summer, as did all men. In cold weather both sexes wore loose moccasins stuffed with the untanned hides of small animals, moss, deer hair, or various types of dried grass. For special ritual occasions *dress moccasins* (*łe?me?mútmšn* - "sitting down moccasins") were used when sitting down, but never worn for walking. Before the introduction of trade beads, dress moccasins were decorated with dyed and flattened porcupine quills. The *moccasin tongue* (*čłtk'ʷí čnšn*) of ceremonial moccasins was decorated with flat-pressed colored quills, and later with beads, and in some cases with small hawk's bells, which always gave a pleasing sound when dancing or walking. (Teit 1930:338). There are no existing examples, nor is it known if the Spokan even quilled or beaded the soles of a dead person's moccasins—once a practice with some Plains groups. "A moccasin with short tongue and seam down the front of the foot was in vogue among the Spokan" (Teit 1930:334).

Winter moccasins differed from those worn in warmer and drier weather. Different ground mosses and rock mosses were preferred for stuffing moccasins, as were mullein leaves and dried bear-grass. If available, bunchgrass was the preferred material for stuffing moccasins in the winter (Elmendorf, pers. comm.). Moccasins were stuffed with the soft pieces of buckskin tamarack, as discussed in the section on cradleboards and bundling. During long travels, the soles of moccasins could be patched with scraps of leather held in place by soft pine tree pitch. For emergency footwear during the summer, a person could wrap and bind his feet in successive layers of green leaves from the sunflower, thimbleberry, or even the mullein plant; the leaves were held in place by pitch or buckskin wrappings. Moccasins were cleaned by immersion in a *boiled* (*slk'ʷest*) solution made from shredded alder bark; after wringing the moccasins dry, they had a new, red appearance.

The Spokan methods of *lacing* (*ʔoxʷcínšn'tn* - "moccasin string") are illustrated by Teit (1928:335). The moccasin string was called *ʔoxʷcínšn'tn* or *čʕʷoxʷcinsntn*). The most detailed descriptions of Spokan moccasin construction are from personal examination of museum examples and by Elmendorf:

[Moccasins were made with [a] pointed toe–[the] tongue comes up [the] instep and [around the] ankle & is sewed with sinew to [the] puckered front at [the] round end–[and] cut square at [the] other–[the] heel is sewed up [the] back in [a] simple seam [...] & pointed and cut off & sewed across [the] bottom]—straight strips (5 or six inches wide [and] 3 to 10" long] are sewed all around to where [the] tongue leaves [the] front [and] folded over in front of [the] ankle—leather thongs [are] fastened each side of [the] ankle–[the] leather thongs[are] fastened over in front of [the] ankle]–[the] leather thongs [are] fastened [on] each side of [the] foot just in front of [the] ankle where [the] tongue leaves [the] side [and] passes through [a] hole in [the] tongue & bottom–the string is *stxtsaninxn* (1935-6, 1:61-2).

There are several sources of information regarding the patterns of moccasin trailer pieces (the portion of the sole that extends out the back) used by the Spokan. One fairly representative collection of Spokan moccasins in the Museum of Arts and Culture in Spokane show that moccasins had any number of tails, from one to five, which probably were similar to those reported for other groups (Teit 1930:73; Ray 1933:46). According to Teit (1930), after the arrival of the horse, and with increased trade, changes in the shapes of footwear became apparent, usually with more individual sections being used in their manufacture. In the figure here, the top row illustrates seven types of moccasin trailers, and the next two rows illustrate six moccasin toe designs (Teit 1930:338).

Figure 35. Spokan moccasin trailers and toes

481

Hats, Headdresses, and Headbands

Various styles of headgear were worn by all adults and children during the winter and by women throughout the year, if only a headscarf or a manufactured *decorative cotton handkerchief*, (*č' łyalčíntn*) which replaced the coiled hat (Conn and Schlick 1998:609). Prior to women wearing trade cloth, and the recently ubiquitous colored *bandana* (*čyál'x*ʷ*qn*), the most common head cover was a *dome-shaped basket hat* (*hecnk'*ʷ*álč'qn* or *snqxqayámuxqn*) made from coiled woven Indian hemp, which was later replaced with the introduction of cornhusks. Men wore a type of skull cap called *sna?xána?qn*, made from a section of elk rawhide, thick enough to be waterproof, with a visor and side-flaps for further protection when needed (Smith 1936-8:746) in winter.

If a man wanted a bill or visor on his cap, his wife or mother would double a section of hide, leaving the fur on the outside, and stiffen it with a piece of rawhide before attaching it to the hat. Smith (1936-8:748) described how certain Kalispel and Lower Spokan curing shamans wore a headpiece made from the skinned and tanned hide of an entire animal, sometimes one as large as a bear or wolf. With smaller animals, the nose of the animal became the visor.

Any winter headwear made from animal fur, such as beaver, fisher, otter, coyote, deer fawn, fox, muskrat, rabbit, wolf, and lynx, was called *spomqn*. Women always made their hats and the men's. A *fur cap* (*spomqm*) was made and worn with the fur on the outside, and was always tanned. On occasion, a fur cap was made from a *raccoon* (*Procyon lotor* - *hmhúwye?*) or fisher with the animal's tail hanging from the back.

During the winter, children and adults wore *fur hats* (*sq*ʷ*ácqn*) made from the pelts of the animals listed above. Women wore *deer rawhide hats* (*sna?xána?q?n*) that had a high-shaped dome with the fur always on the outside. Hats of tanned hide with hair were often reversible, affording greater warmth during the winter when wearing the fur side next to one's head. Men's hats were peaked both at the front and back to provide better vision and provide protection from sleet and snow. It was said how men's hats were fitted with muffs for a person's ears; probably protected with a long pelt wrapped around the head and secured below the chin. A special type of *fur cap* (*k*ʷ*átskn*) was made from coyote fur, but unlined (Elmendorf 1935-6, 1:62).

The basic construction of a winter fur cap required sewing together the two long ends of a hide, making a circle to fit the diameter of the person's head, and then stitching an additional piece of hide on top that defined the hat's circumference. Since the fur was on the outside of the hat during construction, it was inverted after sewing so the fur was on the inside and the stitching on the outside.

A woman's *twined basketry hat* (*snqyqy'ám'x*ʷ*qn* or *snqxqámuxq?n*) was worn during ceremonial dancing, and made from twining stripped and split spruce or cedar-roots, a style that gave way to cornhusk caps in the early historical period with the introduction of *corn* (*Zea mays* - *liplí*). Women wore their *cornhusk hats* (*snqqy'ám'x*ʷ*qn'* or *q*ʷ*ácqn*) for ceremonies and for special public occasions. Cornhusk and basketry hats displayed geometric imbricated designs using differently colored plant materials. Some designs were fashioned from dyed fiber, and Spinden felt the Nez Perce women had attained the highest quality of workmanship and design in making so-called basket hats (1908:193).

It is not always possible to extrapolate details of material or construction data from early photographs. But fortunately, Ray's description of subconical hats worn by Sanpoil women (1933:49) is valuable, as well as Teit's observation that the Spokan women made a type of hat from dressed skin, and a woven cap similar to that of the Nez Perce (1930:336-7). Woven caps were made and used by both the Kalispel and Spokan (Teit 1930:336). There is no evidence that Spokan women made hats of tule, grass, or willow bark, as reported for other Interior Plateau groups (Teit 1930:235).

As previously mentioned, the introduction of the horse encouraged not only polyadic task-grouping (Anastasio 1955) for trading, bison hunting, and an increase in warfare by eastern Plateau groups with certain peoples of the western Plains, but influenced the style of dancing regalia and costumes worn by the Spokan. For example, one of the most dramatic influences upon apparel was the introduction of the full or Plains type

482

war bonnet (*c'lqintsút* or *t'silqéntn*), most notably the *feathered war bonnet* (*c'lqintn*), worn at pre-war ceremonies, but never during combat, "and adds nothing to it to acknowledge outstanding deeds or victories" (Elmendorf, 1935-6, 4:18). Some have said that a warrior could wear his war bonnet only while traveling to an engagement. A man always made his own war bonnet, and feathers never designated any particular deed of bravery or ethnic identity.

The *wheel-shaped eagle-feather headdress* (*č'łcqopqn*), *porcupine headdress* (*ncl'aw'sqn* or *snaw'sqn'i*), and deer-hair headdress were probably not worn traditionally by the Spokan, but were a later imitation of the Osage (Teit 1930:341). Prior to acquiring the aforementioned Plains-type feather headdress, the traditional Spokan headdress was typically of eagle tail or red-tail hawk feathers that stood near vertically, being held by a *headband* (*łqʷessn* - "dancer's headband"), and continued to be worn by a few men until the late 1920s, as shown by some existing photographs (Wynecoop 1969:38; A. Sherwood, pers. comm.).

Presently, only the more larger and ornate Plains-type headdresses are worn at festive ceremonies and powwows, often made from non-traditional materials, such as a scalp-piece and other accoutrements that serve as expressions of artistry, effort, and imported materials. The most dramatic contemporary feathered head dress is one of eagle feathers fashioned in a fan or wheel shape that sits cup-like, tied upon the dancer's head. Many dramatic changes of clothing are still apparent with dancing costumes and accompanying regalia, all of which are individualized by a dancer's imagination and fashioned by the choreographer's ability.

Decorations on hats, besides fur attachments, became possible when the straw and felt cowboy type of hat was quickly adopted, giving rise to a fashion that accommodated flat, braided, or twisted hatbands, which were frequently beaded or served to support inserted side feathers; hatbands were of varying width and material. Eventually, the introduced practice of silversmithing brought even more innovations and artistic expressions with hatbands. A *hatband* (*łqʷéw'stn*) was individually fashioned from flat or braided buckskin, even twisted calico cloth. Traditionally, one never saw a hatband made from rattlesnake skin—a sign of disrespect. However, different animal pelts and fur were used as hatbands.

The *headband* (*łqʷqíntn*), beaded or otherwise, was worn by both men and women, but originally it was used primarily by men. A hat band was made by simply folding a piece of flat or twisted buckskin for purposes of absorbing perspiration during physical exertion, such as hunting or cutting wood, and served to keep one's hair away from one's face, and were not made of rawhide, since that material would expand with perspiration, and would be less sanitary when later it shrank upon drying. The *mink* (*Mustella vison* - *c'xlécn* or *c'axaλé*), an animal often taken with a deadfall because of the difficulty in trapping such a wary animal with a baited trap, provided a functional and decorative headband, particularly after tanning the hide with the fur intact. With the availability of needles and beads, both men's and women's head bands, once plain, became beaded with both curvilinear and geometric designs. But normally a cloth headband was solid or with a simple design. With the introduction of a brimmed western-style hat, the owner may fashion a hatband made from *rattlesnake skin* (*xáxáʔułáx̣w* - "the untouchable ground").

Head Scarves

Men and women wore a fur neck piece, a type of scarf when winter traveling, and it differed only by the animal pelt and the maker's design. Men and children, being outside more often than women in the winter, wore a *scarf* (*qʼʷłqʼʷécn*) to protect the neck and close the top opening of a shirt. Thus, scarves were not worn with robes or hooded coats. The skin from either an owl or a rabbit was long enough to make such a head cover; the feathers of the owl were left in place, as was the rabbit's fur. After wrapping the scarf around one's neck, the ends were tied together with buckskin, leaving the ends loose in the front.

With the introduction of cotton and wool, the *kerchief* or *headscarf* (*čyál'x̣ʷqn*) became popular since these materials were more flexible, colorful, and easier to cut and sew than tanned hide. Because of these practical and aesthetic considerations, headscarves soon replaced woven hats, and, without exception, adult women wore scarves from their first public appearance in the morning until their evening retirement. Even today, for the few remaining traditional elderly women, the scarf fulfills numerous multipurpose functions: carrying small loose items, or as a kerchief for binding a grandchild's wound, as a *handkerchief* (*č²ep'²ép'stn*), or as a small towel or for other numerous perceived requirements. In the past, the kerchief completely covered the person's hair, the ends of the material being pulled together and tied at the back.

Until recently, at a solemn ceremony, such as a funeral service, without knowing the participants, one could readily identify the elderly, and therefore invariably the traditional, women, who, with a characteristic style of dress, tended to be seated together. Without exception, each woman's scarf was made of silk or cotton, and usually with varied designs having a range of colors, which initially may strike the casual observer as being at variance with the sorrow and pain in the woman's face.

Vests

The *vest* (*č'ɫč'n'č'n'p'aχn'* or *snč'napχn*) was not a traditional item of clothing, but was introduced from the Plains and worn only by men. The earlier string-tied ceremonial garment provided opportunities for artistic expression by creating geometric designs by using dyed porcupine quills. Later, after acquiring steel needles and trade beads, the now-buttoned vest provided greater opportunity to create colorful floral and faunal designs—the rose and eagle being predominantly displayed. Eventually, many tanned deer hide vests were lined with patterned silk or cotton materials after the application of beaded designs. Vests are seldom seen being worn casually by men or women, but very finely decorated vests are occasionally worn by men at dances and other festive events.

Gloves and Mittens

In cold weather, and to reduce the hands' surface area exposed to the cold, everyone wore *mittens* (*sčml'k'ʷéčst* or *sčm'el'k'ʷéčst*) or *gloves* (*spčpečst*), depending upon the task they were involved in. Mittens had separate coverings for the forefinger and the thumb, thereby affording better dexterity for lifting or manipulating during a task such as hunting. Gloves and mittens were usually made from coyote, with the fur outside. Gloves for hunting were made from buckskin, permitting better tactile perception for manipulating a bow and arrow or later for loading rifle ammunition. In extremely cold and blowing weather, when winter hunting, snowshoeing, or running a *trapline* (*²a²acéptn'*), a man often wore mitten-sleeves that went as high as his shoulders, or supplement regular mittens by wrapping sections of animal fur about his forearms, much like gauntlets (Elmendorf, pers. comm.).

During the late historical period and for sometime afterwards too, buckskin gloves were worn for special ceremonies and as trade items to both Indians and non-Indians. With the introduction of glass and metal beads and steel needles, there developed a flourishing exhibition of talent in making curvilinear designs on gloves and other articles of clothing, particularly vests, mostly with colorful patterns of animals, flags, and other imagery. Many ceremonial *beaded gloves* (*pčpečt*) have relatively large semi-rigid cuffs that accommodate almost complete scenes of animals or floral patterns. Later buckskin or commercial canvas working gloves were not decorated.

Dancer's Apron

A *dancer's apron* (*snɫqʷepúsčšn*) was worn by most contemporary male dancers and some women. It is difficult to establish if the Spokan adopted its use from the Flathead or Nez Perce, or directly from their contact with Plains groups. The apron was worn on the front and back, and often made from a section of wool blanket (*supcnic'e²*) that provided a foundation for curvilinear beaded designs that some claimed signified the wearer's accomplishments in warfare (Elmendorf, pers. comm.). Sections of tanned leather or complete pelts of small animal fur were attached to the apron, as were feathers, which were kept in place by a single or braided strip of buckskin tied behind the person's waist. Contemporary aprons are very finely fashioned, often with different colors of material and decorated with silverwork, bells, small mounted mirrors, and traditional items, such as bone and shell. Most contemporary dance aprons have chainette fringe and ribbon work of variegated colors.

Belts and Suspenders

Belts were used by both men and women for securing clothing and supporting various types of gathering and utility bags, most commonly a flapped pouch for carrying fire-making items and personal effects. Nearly all men's and women's *belts* (*atsap'alqs* or *snⱡč'é*) were manufactured from buckskin; but after the arrival of the horse, belts were made with plaited horsetail or *mane* (*sčc'iwlps*), and eventually were replaced by commercial *suspenders* (*snkʷ'ⁿⱡtsnʔoⱡupstn*) upon the introduction of agriculture and logging, occupations that accommodated tailored farm clothing.

A *belt of buckskin* (*qacⱡ'qs*) was manufactured by either plaiting or twisting sinew or strips of tanned or untanned hide, and was approximately 5 cm wide. In time, the edges of a single flat piece of buckskin would curl into a roll, which facilitated tying the ends together. This narrow rolled underbelt was worn by all men next to the skin, and it functioned as a sort of G-string that supported the loincloth (Smith 1936-8:734).

Three or four long strands of mountain goat hair were twined or rolled on a woman's thigh. This was — always done in private, because a woman's thigh was never exposed, even to her husband. It was used in edging buckskin belts so that they would be more resistant to wear and last longer. Goat hair was used for the same purpose on the edges of clothing, to prevent wear (Elmendorf 1935-6, 1:2). Some women would dye a goat's hair belt with vegetable dyes, but no surviving examples exist to show the colors or designs.

All men and women had a *support belt* (*snλč'éʔus* - "over belt") that was worn over a man's shirt or a woman's dress, primarily to keep the garment gathered, and often served to support a belt *purse* (*snululímtn*). The *woman's belt* (*snp'lč'alqs* or *qacápl'qs*), made of braided or twisted tanned buckskin or from plaited buckskin, was sometimes decorated with small animal fur. When wearing her ceremonial wing dress, a woman wore a special type of belt called a *ʕacapl'qs*.

With only one reference, and no mention within any Spokan ethnographies, it is still plausible that Theodore Winthrop (1828-1861), during his rather extensive travels along the Lower and Middle Columbia, did observe a Spokan named Oh-hai, a volunteer among the Klickatats who was wearing, "A broad-beaded band acrossed [sic] his breast, like the ribbon of an order of nobility" (Mullan 1863:56). One may more convincingly speculate that the chest band was a personal affectation. The major reasons for changes in style and material of *traditional clothing* (*sqlixʷscút* - "Indian clothing") occurred not only through contact with Plains peoples, but certainly with Euro-American contact and sustained trade for non-traditional materials. For example, the introduction of cloth permitted easier manufacture of the *sash* (*snlčéw'stn*), which replaced sinew belts. Such changes in ceremonial clothing continue to take place even today.

Bags and Pouches

Very important to one's physical health and spiritual well-being was a small draw-string buckskin bag that contained objects of personal religious significance—usually items representing certain powers given over a period of time by one's guardian spirit. Both men and women wore such a neck bag, and its size varied according to the owner/maker, often 7 to 10 cm in length. These sacred objects were obtained in many different ways: presented during the Mid-winter Ceremony, found in one's sweathouse after surviving treatment for a serious illness or having been sorcerized, and presented directly by a specific animal, told by a certain bird or animal where the intended recipient should look for the object, instructed in a dream where the object may be found, or the person may simply find an inorganic anomaly during his or her travels, such as unusual crystals, sand concretions, geological anomaly or fossils. One such bag the author examined contained three uniquely unusual if not rare items: a near absolutely round iron concretion, a cruciform garnite crystal habit, and a prysmatic staurolite cubric schist (Doughty, pers. comm.). It was believed that a sacred item was presented by one's *suméš*, and thereby enabled or identified an individual with a certain power.

A woman commonly wore a *small waist bag* (*sp'áp'x*ʷ) on her hip, usually for special occasions (STHC), and was invariably artistically beaded with floral designs of personal choice, or with porcupine quills before trade beads. Young boys and girls wore a small bag when traveling or away from a camp or village. A man's *waist pouch* (*hesčk*ʷúl*) was of tanned hide, whereas a woman's larger, rather flat, square shaped pouch was sometimes manufactured from cornhusk, flat-woven cedar-root, or soaked interwoven cedar bark. Flexible cylindrical and flat utilitarian and ceremonial women's bags were made by twining the fiber from greasewood, sagebrush, or the bark of Scouler's willow and chokecherry. But on occasion these pouches were made from other vegetable fibers (Elmendorf, pers. comm.).

A woman, when attending ceremonies, had a special waist bag or *hip bag* (*iče?ep*) when wearing a wing dress. With the introduction of beads, traditional imbrication materials were gradually replaced by the production of beaded bags, particularly the *beaded hand bag* (*čšr'ečst*).

The *tanned hide with the hair* (*ču?pú*) of an unborn fawn might be made into an attractive ceremonial bag that was sewn up the center and decorated. The tanned hide of a *newly born fawn* (*ƛ'k'*ʷƛ'uk'*ʷ), *one with white spots* (*spapiča?qn*), was highly prized by its owner, and was called *snʕaw'pel'x*ʷ. The skin from either a recent *elk* or *deer miscarriage* (*xn'tsqaxe?*) was similarly used to make a bag. An exceptionally fine, rare and highly prized bundle was fashioned by taking a *pelt from a coyote that had been killed by lightning* (*spe'y'h él'x*ʷ), and the bag had a drawstring to secure any sacred contents. A man frequently made his *power bag* (*s?elk'*ʷlscut* - medicine man's small *suméš* bag) from tanned deer hide, or the entire untanned hide of an animal that represented his particular power, for example, using the hide of a particular bird, marten, otter, or other small animal. Some shamans' power (medicine) bundles were made from the skins of water-dwelling animals, such as *river otter* (*Lutra canadensis* - *lttk*ʷúk*ʷ) or beaver. It was understood, even feared, that a medicine man's or shaman's bundle was never to be handled by anyone but the owner, nor was it ever placed on the ground, but always hung when not being carried or in use during a ritual. A medicine bundle was typically folded or rolled several times upon itself, and wrapped securely with a long strip of rawhide. Douglas described an Indian bag "of curious workmanship, made of Indian hemp, a species of *Apocynum, Helonias tenax*, and eagle's quills, used for carrying roots and other such articles (1904, 5, 1:362).

While a medicine or curing shaman sang over his bundle, and when his power song came over him, his hands commenced to *tremble* (*cacálqepm*), often uncontrollably, and the bundle would unwrap by itself, first throwing off the encircling ties. Nor was it unusual for a power bundle to contain several significant natural anomalies, such as unusual forms of sun-dried clay concretions, fossils, and frequently yellow or red lumps of ochre. Swatches of color or designs using plant colors of black, blue, green, gray, red, and yellow were most common, apart from certain hues of blue obtained from duck excrement (Anon. 1974:5).

During the historical period, imbrication was accomplished with yarn and strips of tightly rolled cloth. Some examples of a finished bag had "the warp strands [...] turned in at the top and bound down by weaving with the weft [i.e., filling]. Often buckskin or cloth is bound onto the rim of the bag and sometimes a drawstring of rope or thong is run through this buckskin or cloth edge" (Anon. 1974:7).

(For information on bags made of cornhusks, see the section in Chapter VI on grasses and cornhusks.)

Bustles and Roaches

Bustles were first introduced from the Plains, most commonly made of eagle feathers that *stand out from the tail* (*č̓'c̓'l'čn'úps*), and varied in shape and material, depending on each male dancer, and the imagination, skill, and the resources of the maker. A large bustle required the feathers of two bald eagles, and was worn commonly at a war dance. *War dancers* (*suxʷwenšm*) further enhanced their appearance by wearing *under the chin beads* (*č̓ʔem'cin*), long beads made from bone, whereas the smaller round pony beads were glass. Often the *long beads* (*čususšnús*) were separated by small sections of drilled latigo leather.

The *roach* (*nc'láw'sqn* - "head ornament") was most commonly fashioned by taking a relatively narrow back strip of tanned porcupine pelt that was then sewn to a buckskin *roach headdress* (*snc'láw'sqn*) made from the back section of a porcupine after being tanned and then fashioned to a shape desired by the dancer, who could control the movement as he wanted while dancing. This head ornament was secured to a dancer's head by first gathering six or eight opposing tuffs of crown hair, which were then tightly braided before passing the left set of braids through, and over the base of the roach to the braids on the right side. The opposite braids were then tied together to secure the roach to the dancer's head (G. Flett, pers. comm.).

Chokers

The influence of Plains culture, as well as trade in the pre-historical and protohistoric period with the Flathead and Nez Perce, was most apparent with the Spokan adoption of men's ceremonial garments and certain accouterments. Unfortunately, it is difficult to say when the Spokan adopted the use of the *choker* (*č̓ʔem'cíntn* or *č̓ʔem'cín*). Chokers were, and continue to be, a popular neck ornamentation, being distinguished by the individual's choice of its size, materials, and the configuration of ceramic or metal beads, shell, and long bone beads. Some contemporary chokers have *metal bells* (*č̓'ʔałqʷ'l't* - "they have bells on their throats"), preferably silver bells. The foundation material was a selection of rawhide, tanned hide, colored cloth, or open, i.e., with no foundation at all, but with ornaments being strung according to the owner's sense of design.

As with most adopted complex ceremonial items, there is no discernible Spokan style of construction or design motif for chokers, which are worn mostly at ceremonial dances.

Breastplates

Through increasing social and economic intercourse and influence from the Plains, Spokan men adopted a *ceremonial breastplate* (*sxʷλačen'i*) made from a series of long, vertical, relatively narrow, hollowed bones attached in numerous double horizontal rows to the front of the garment. "Later these bone 'hair pipes' were made of cow bone and traded commercially to the dealers for the Indian trade by Armour and Company" (Sprague, pers. comm.).

The only few existing examples of the *long bone breast plate* (*č̓ʔélstn*), and those depicted in photographs, indicate how traditional ones were quite similar to those now worn by men at ceremonial dances. Present examples vary primarily in the plastic materials now used to manufacture the imitation bones, whereas they were originally from bone, which actually afforded chest protection from missiles and thrusting weapons. The concept and early examples of the *breast plate* (*słʕałqʷ'l'ts*) undoubtedly diffused from the Plains.

Consequently, considering the aforementioned types of clothing and various accouterments, the ceremonial costumes of both contemporary male and female dancers are quite different from traditional attire. For example, most men now wear bells and other ornaments that are *tied at the dancer's knees* (*sn'łqʷépuʔsčšn*) to accentuate the sound and movements of each step. In lieu of eagle feathers, some contemporary bustles are made from goose or turkey feathers, or rooster hackles, sometimes dyed and tufted differently. These costumes are often very complex in their colors, designs, and configuration of different materials. Anyone watching something like the Prairie Chicken Dance cannot help but be moved by the tempo of repetitive drumming, flute blowing, and the extremely dexterous motions and the choreography that serves to accentuate the sound of hawk bells and other acoustic accouterments on their magnificently individual costumes.

War Accouterments

The above discussion of how the Spokan acquired many different dances and costume accouterments explains a similar process of adaptation of war accouterments by the Spokan—mostly through trade and stimulus diffusion with the Nez Perce and Plains groups in a relatively brief period of time. Warfare and ceremonial clothing and accouterments, primarily dancing and costumes, underwent the most conspicuous changes.

Regardless of the conflict of cultures and misunderstanding of Amerindian ritual and symbolism, many of the Amerindian changes of costume and regalia must have been a most dramatic, even stirring, sight for the chronicler Lieutenant Adjutant Lawrence Kipp, a member of a punitive expedition of 700 soldiers under the command of Col. George Wright, who, on 1 September 1858, fought and defeated approximately 500 Coeur d'Alene, Palouse, Spokan, and Yakima Indians at the Battle of Four Lakes. When describing the battle and the entrance of the Indians, Kip began with the following admirable description:

> Most of them were armed with Hudson Bay muskets, while other had bow and arrow and long lances. They were in all the bravery of their war array, gaudily painted and decorated with their wild trappings. Their plumes fluttered above them while below, skins and trinkets and all kinds of fantastic embellishments flaunted in the sunshine. Their horses, too, were arrayed in the most glaring finery. Some were even painted, and with colors to form the greatest contrast–the white being smeared with crimson in fantastic figures, and the dark-colored streaked with white clay. Beads and fringes of gaudy colors were hanging from their bridles while their plumes of eagle feathers interwoven with the mane and tail, fluttered as the breeze swept over them and completed their wild and fantastic appearance. 'By heavens! it was a glorious sight to see. The gay array of their wild chivalry' (Manring 1912:199; Hunt 1966:199).

War Spears

There is no known existing example of a Spokan war *spear* (*łuʔmin*). The most complete description of war spears is by Teit, based on his comparative work with the Coeur d'Alene and other interior Plateau groups:

> War spears were usually about 2 meters long, with a point of flaked stone either leaf or knife shaped, rather long and narrow. All were sharp pointed and double edged. After iron came into use, some of them were serrated near the base on both sides. In later days, when buffalo were chased on horseback, a longer spear with a narrow point was sometimes used for stabbing game (1930:115).

Shields

The Spokan and Kalispel used a *shield* (*šλʾe* or *sšλʾéλčst* - "something to protect the body") (Smith 1936-8:681) made of rawhide, preferably from the thick neck hide of an elk. The shield, approximately 35 to 40 cm in diameter, was not flat but slightly dome-shaped to help deflect arrows. A round frame was first made by soaking ocean spray or serviceberry until it could be bent into an oval. After lashing the two hides together with Indian hemp, the entire perimeter of the hide was pierced with an awl and sewn together over the frame with Indian hemp.

There were different methods of holding a shield: one way involved bringing together two narrow long flaps from opposite edges of the outermost hide behind the shield and sewn as a handle or forearm wrist strap. A second way of gripping involved two parallel wooden slats being secured to both ends of the frame, onto which were attached one or two wrist straps, which would be grasped when in use, or slipped over the wrist when a *warrior* (*x̣ix̣ilšúƚ* or *sux̌ʷyílš*) used his bow and arrow. A man normally painted a representation of his guardian spirit on his shield, for protection. Spears, shields, and certain garments were decorated with eagle feathers, which usually were an indication of status or unique deeds. Smith, when describing the Kalispel use of a war shield, stated:

> During a war, only 1 or 2 warriors would hold such a shield. Generally the ones who held the shield are two who are braver than the rest; they have no bow and arrow, but a thrusting (never throwing) lance and a club. They would go up to where the foe had entrenched themselves in the rocks, &c., and kick the entrenchments down and put the enemy to rout so that the ones behind with the bows and arrows could shoot them. They say that once a person turns and runs he never turns back (1936-8:681).

There is no evidence that the Spokan ever made wicker, bark, or split wooden shields, nor are there any known existing examples of rawhide shields. Furthermore, Teit was informed that:

> No long hide shields and no wooden shields were employed. Their only shield was circular, made of two thicknesses of skin from the neck of buffalo, moose, or elk bulls. In later days many shields were exactly like those of the Crow and other eastern tribes, but the old-style shield was retained by many men and was considered as effective. Shield covers were used, but possibly not with all shields. Shields and shield covers had painted designs, and many were ornamented with eagle feathers and scalp locks (1930:359).

Clubs

Unfortunately, there are no known examples of Spokan war clubs or any good descriptions, only references to a type of *club* (*sp'í*) used for killing salmon. The comparative material of Teit, however, described how wooden war clubs were "wrapped or ornamented with ermine skins, otter skins, and charms" (1930:359). One can only presume that war clubs had a two-sided or circular grooved stone head to offer defense against an opponent's shield or for direct bodily contact.

War Shirts and Cuirasses

Though Elmendorf (pers. comm.) could provide no details of war shirts and cuirasses by the Spokan, he acknowledged their use, and was told how men adored their ceremonial and war shirts, often with ermine tails and sections of horsetail hair, ribbons, beads, and strips of trade cloth.

Fortunately, there exists an example of a Spokan *war shirt* (*snč'ƛapx̣n*) that was recently returned to the Spokane Tribe by the Burke Museum, one that had been purchased from a Spokan in 1928 by Ray (Record 2346), who provides the following description of this now unique acquisition:

> [The] pattern of the shirt is representative of the type worn by men at the time of the coming of the Whites. The neighboring Sanpoil and Nespelem Indians wore the same type of garment. At some previous date, however, these people wore a less completely tailored garment and we may infer that the Spokane did the same. This particular specimen retains the slit type neck of opening common to the earlier types, but adds beaded "V" shaped flaps of flannel, both front and back, hanging from the neck. In the later style the throat was probably more often left open, but cut in the same "V" shape. The pendants of yarn and ribbon on this shirt presumably indicate a similar use of fur in earlier times; this was certainly the custom with the Sanpoil (Ray 1933:233, Plate 1, Fig. A).

The only previous known mention of war shirts being used by the Flathead Group is Teit's cryptic description of weapons of offense and defense, in which he cites how "Cuirasses of rods of wood and slats of wood were in use among the Okanogan and Sanpoil, and some of heavy hide were employed. Some of the latter were low, and only encircled the waist. Tunics of thick elk hide were worn by a few men" (1930:256).

Later, in his comprehensive Flathead Group ethnography, Teit provides further information regarding the types of cuirasses, but qualifies his earlier statement of materials used in making such a protection chest garment: "Long ago cuirasses of heavy elk skin and rawhide were in use; but they were discarded after the introduction of the horse as cumbersome and inconvenient in mounting and riding. Cuirasses of slats and rods of wood were probably not used" (1930:359). (please verify)

Hide perforations were used as a mode of decoration, and, according to Ray (1933:49), the Sanpoil say that they, in common with the Spokane, borrowed the custom from their more war-like neighbors (the Nez Perce?), where the warriors alone used such decoration. After adoption its use was confined to those persons having particularly strong guardian spirits, such as a grizzly bear, and here only when a specific grant of the privilege had been made by the spirit, always accompanied by a promise of immunity to arrow and bullet wounds (Ray 1933:49).

Smith's unpublished Kalispel field notes provide certain details of construction:

[The] vest [was] made of thick skin; the neck skin of elk or buffalo was used mostly. It was made of a single layer [...] it comes down to the waist and fits under the arm holes. They make it in two pieces. There is one string on each side of the two pieces, which are brought together and tied. There are about 3 strings down each side. A man can tie his own vest. The hair is removed; it is stiff and it protects one [... it probably was not painted]. If the enemy saw them wearing it, they would shoot at the legs (1936-8:684).

One may reasonably assume that given the close proximity, economic exchange, and social intercourse between the Sanpoil and Lower Spokan, the Spokan adopted similar means of chest protection, as did the Chewelah-Spokan Group. This type of *body armor* (*sulullmálqs*) or vest effectively protected a man's thoracic region and back. It would have been made from two sections of rawhide, held in place by attaching the front and back section together with strips of sinew.

There is no known oral history or established ethnographic accounts of the Spokan ever using breast plates of rawhide encasements, woven saplings, or wood slats as protection in war against arrows. Gibby and Ball maintain how in 1939, during the construction of Grand Coulee Dam, a 104-year-old Colville (?) elder identified and demonstrated the use of a recently-excavated breast plate (1997:54).

Helmets

In combat involving hand-to-hand fighting with percussion weapons (clubs and tomahawks) and missiles projected with often high accuracy and force, the use of shields and protective head gear were of great concern to any warrior. In addition to having a shield, a *helmet* (*xaƛ'qéʔntaʔn* - "something put around the head") afforded a warrior the best protection from blows to the head.

Again, one must rely upon Smith's comprehensive and extensive ethnographic fieldwork with the Kalispel, who is the only ethnographer known to discuss head protection in the Plateau:

To protect themselves from the long bone [arrow] points, they take the broad ribs of the elk, scraped thin [...] They were woven together probably with sinew and not with Indian hemp for this would be too big and would leave too big a gap between them. Or they may have had holes punched in them and were then laced together with sinew, but this is just guessing. Each piece was 4 or 5 inches long and the pieces would be plenty long enough, for it was made to stand up around the head (like a feather-bonnet) (1936-8:684).

There is no evidence that the Spokan used a similar helmet, though they had a name for such an item. Turney-High (1941:86-87) cited how the Lower Kutenai did make a sophisticated type of cuirass from dog-bane or ocean spray; but it apparently was not used by the Upper Kutenai, which may be questionable.

Coup Stick

The Spokan and other tribes from the Flathead Group used coup sticks (Teit 1930:390) in warfare, a practice probably adopted from the Plains where warfare and bravery dominated war ethos. Most commonly, a *fur-wrapped coup stick* (*čxʷálqʷ* or *čxʷlalqʷ*) was made of wood or bone of any length, but usually it was approximately 30 cm long. Many coup sticks were personalized with incised painted designs, and often with a loop of twisted hair attached to the handle end, and went about the owner's wrist when on horseback. The purpose of the coup stick was to touch an enemy on a pre-designated part of his body, which was announced beforehand to his comrades. A person gained greater kudos and recognition if he were the first to touch the enemy, and if the owner of the stick were not wounded and able to defend himself. Yet, a seldom-understood, secondary function of the coup stick is explained by Teit:

> The coup stick was also used in friendly greetings [...] A long coup stick was used for striking or touching friends in a meeting ceremony. If a party of people were approaching on a friendly visit, even though they were known to be coming and were out to meet them. When within sight they advanced toward them in a line abreast, singing. When within a few hundred yards they broke into a gallop and charged on the visitors as if in war. When within striking distance they all reined up their horses short, and one of them tapped the leader of the visitors on the shoulder with the stick. This is said to have meant that he chose him as a friend (1930:390).

Personal Adornment

Fashions of clothing, color, beading, and attachments of fur and feathers, shell, animal teeth and bone, and paints, permitted both men and women with ample opportunity for individual expression, which publicly reflected the wearer's status, manipulative abilities, and other individual social, economic, and even certain personal accomplishments. There was less opportunity, however, for refined adornment of the body; no cheek labrets were worn, and scarification was not done, though tattooing was done for both men and women. Only women had their nasal septum pierced to accommodate a small bone plug or a perforated ground shell ornament that hung slightly below the septum. Teit noted that the ornaments or nose pins used by the Flathead and Pend d'Oreilles "were rare among the Kalispel and Spokan" (1930:340). Earlier, Curtis described, "Until about 1845 the custom of wearing a small bone spike or a dentalium shell in the nasal septum was in vogue" (1907-30, 7:72). Most women had multiple ear lobe holes that were drilled by another woman using a bone drill to facilitate inserting a narrow twisted fiber for holding objects, such as shells, beads, and feathers. The dentalium shells shown here would be about 8 cm in length.

Figure 36. Dentalium shells

Facial Painting and Tattooing

Facial painting and tattooing among some men and women were common means to indicate status and achievement, and were often displayed during specific religious rituals including funerary rites as well as during curing activities, when, on occasion, a patient's face was painted with red ochre. Crushed and powdered insect gall was used by shamans when curing, and for tattooing. Large quantities of galled branches were allowed to thoroughly dry while stored in a cleaned and stretched dry deer stomach, because once the gall has dried, it gives off a fine russet colored dust, which can only be stored in a smooth closed container. During certain ceremonies, a participant may cover his or her face with different colors such as red, yellow, or blue designs made from finely ground clays.

Facial painting and tattooing were art forms executed singularly or with a combination of red and black pigments (black was made from different types of charcoal), used exclusively when tattooing the face with a series of straight lines. Red was the predominant choice of color for facial designs. Mineral paints were usually kept and carried in a small buckskin *clay bag* (*yúcmn*), that was closed with an attached buckskin drawstring. After depilating each *eyebrow* (*cpɫn'éy'* or *cpcpɫn'ey'*), the site was painted with red paint in a straight line (Anon. 1978:9). It was not known if there were tattoo specialists, but, as with all manipulative skills, there probably were such individuals.

Temporary facial and *body painting* (*sisčúpeʔ*) was used by both sexes for either utilitarian or ceremonial purposes, though presumably fewer men were tattooed. Late winter and early spring travel over sun-reflecting snow demanded the application of grease-based powdered charcoal, which was applied to the cheekbones and eye-orbits to prevent *snow-blindness* (*kʷim's*). The same procedure of applying charcoal was common when traveling by canoe if there was intense sun reflection off the water.

Ceremonial facial-painting was predominantly practiced by men and, as with tattooing, the major colors were red and black—the latter color being used by Bluejays during the Mid-Winter Ceremony. Individual designs of red ochre were used by principal participants during curing ceremonies, Mid-Winter Ceremonies, warfare, woman's Sun Dance, and by a novice during the Vision Quest. It was said that the principal woman who directed the opening of large, communal pit ovens always had black facial designs, presumably to ensure that there would be no food burned. During the early time of mourning, a widow would indicate her grief and *agony* (*hecmíxʷti*) by covering her forehead with charcoal. The vocal and often dramatic choreographic performances of a noted story-teller were often further enhanced with red hematite facial designs, or covering the face entirely with hematite.

After a day's work and bathing, or taking an early morning sweat, some women would on rare occasions put "a little vermilion on her forehead. Men and women both painted, but women more so [and] the designs were at the fancy of the individual" (Elmendorf 1935-6, 1:74). It was thought that during the Mid-Winter Ceremony, all the principal adult participants painted their faces in different designs with powdered-grease red ochre, which heightened the atmosphere and assisted an individual to have a dream by facilitating him to better communicate with his or her *suméš* (Elmendorf, pers. comm.). Of value are Ray's (1933:81-2) extensive descriptions of Sanpoil facial paintings, though he makes no reference to the contiguous Lower Spokan.

Teit provides a lengthy and detailed description of various individual designs when describing body adornment by the neighboring Coeur d'Alene: "It seems that tattooing was common long ago, and practiced by both sexes [...] They consisted of both geometric and realistic figures" (1930:87). Teit's observations further reinforce the close socioeconomic relationship between the Spokan and Kalispel:

> Tattoo marks were also in large measure symbolic. Like painting [facial] tattooing was done by both sexes. However, it was not common. Wrists and forearms were the chief parts tattooed, but some men had tattoo marks on the legs and body as well. The Kalispel and Spokan are said to have tattooed much more than the Pend d'Oreilles and Flathead (1930:341).

Teit commented that line facial tattooing was rarely done by the Spokan (1930:341), but the Coeur d'Alene apparently used "Pictures and symbols of guardian spirits [which] were painted or tattooed on the body" (Teit 1930:193). However, the Pend d'Oreille and Flathead never used facial *tattoos* (*sƛ'ƛ'áqist*). And yet Wilson noted, when speaking of the Spokan, of how, "The women often tattoo the upper lips with thin blue lines" (1866:293). Teit, much later, claimed, "It seems there was no face tattooing, or that it was exceedingly rare" (1930-341).

492

Tattooing was a relatively painful process, one that required the desired coloring agents, mineral dyes, and soot being implanted via repeated application of dyed porcupine quills to the sub-epidermal skin (Ross 1995e:769). Another method of tattooing was to place earth pigments or charcoal in a desired design upon wet skin, perforate the skin with a sharp bone needle, and then rub the overlying material into the wound, using a selected colored clay (red or yellow) or soot. Black designs were initially achieved with finely ground black earth, charcoal, or soot.

Beginning with the historical period (1804-1866), the introduction of *gunpowder* (*snp'q*ʷ*mín*) replaced traditional means of producing an unusual but distinctive blue-black tattoo (STHC). Some people chose to tattoo their wrists and forearms in what were essentially symbolic designs, and a tattoo mark on a man's arm was called a *sq'éiy'áxn*. Men tattooed their legs and presumably the thoracic area. It was said how either a man or a woman with arthritis of the elbow or knee might seek relief by tattooing the afflicted site, presumably to release the pain. Though both Coeur d'Alene men and women tattooed their wrists and forearms (Teit 1930:87), there is no agreement that the Spokan did not.

Mutilation and Scarification

There are very few descriptions of skin mutilation by the Spokan. For instance, Ray claimed, "Scarification [...] was known among the Spokane" (1932:198). Teit is again referenced, particularly when he reveals the significance of scarification by the Coeur d'Alene to condition young boys for later *demanding* (*k*ʷ*ulst*) tasks:

> Scarification practiced by all young men during their training at puberty. Cuts were generally made on the arms and legs, and sometimes on the insteps, and backs of the hands and fingers. Some men training to be shamans or warriors cut their bodies as well. Sometimes a long slash followed each rib; or, again many short horizontal cuts, occasionally close together, one above the other, were made on the upper arms or elsewhere. Some youths rubbed charcoal, or white and red ochre into the wounds, which, when they healed, were similar to tattoo marks [...] Burning with live coals taken from the fire was also practiced, as well as burning with dry stalks of tule, which were lighted and allowed to burn out on the skin. Cutting is said to have been intended to let out bad blood, to make the person healthy, light-footed, active, and prevent illness. Burning was for the purpose of enabling him to stand severe pain without flinching (1930:169-70).

The Spokan neither used lip labrets, nor did they color their teeth for any reason, though some Lakes women pierced the nasal septum (Elmendorf 1935-6, 1:73). Traditionally, women would have an older woman pierce a hole through the nasal septum with a sharply pointed bone to later accommodate a small oval-shaped piece of colorful shell, but never feathers or strung beads. Nose ornaments "were rare among the Kalispel and Spokan" (Teit 1930:340). Ear-piercing was done by a village specialist who had considerable experience and, more importantly, a reputation for not inducing infection. Girls had the operation when quite young—at two to three years of age (Elmendorf, pers. comm.). Both ear lobes were pierced with a fresh hawthorn needle, and replaced by a small greased peg that was turned several times a day. Both men and women had pierced ear lobes, women with only one hole in each lobe, whereas men had one hole in the lobe and sometimes several more located in the thin scapha between the anti-helix and outer helix on the edge of the ear. After piercing an ear lobe with a cactus spine, the hole was kept open by inserting a bunchgrass straw. Smith presents a more detailed description of ear-piercing by the Kalispel:

> They drill [a] hole in [the] ear, sometimes one and sometimes two. The holes were always in the lobe. If there were two holes, one was close to the cheek and the other on the outside: If there was only one, it was in the center of the lobe. Most men had only one in each lobe. Both ears were always the same. There were never more than 2 holes. Women have only one hole in each ear. Not many women have holes, most have none. They drilled the holes with bones (1935-6:759).

As cited, all young girls had their *ears pierced* (*nⁱx*ʷⁱ*x*ʷ*én'e*ʔ*nct*) to accommodate personal ornaments, including shell *ear pendants* (*sn*ʕ*ac*ʕ*acéne*ʔ - "earrings") made from different species of the genera *Haliotis* and *Glycymeris* (mussels) (Erickson 1990:98). Oblong, top-drilled pendants were made from ground black slate, and occasionally large relatively flat sections of abalone were stone-drilled as pendants (Collier *et al.* 1942:154). Women's ear pendants were also manufactured from torus-shaped ground shell beads, traded from the Northwest Coast. *Cowry shells* (*Cypraea spadicea* - *t'm'ayóye?*) traded from the coast were highly prized for decorating women's ceremonial garments and as ear pendants. The value of traded abalone beads, manufactured from *California red abalone shell* (*Haliotis rufescens* Swainson - *x̣ey'qs* - "abalone beads"), depended upon the finished shell's size and color. The brilliant iridescent gradations of pink to brick-red on both the concave and the convex side of abalone, were critically judged when trading. Indigenous beads were manufactured from Olivetti-shells (*Olivella biplicata*, *O. Boetica*, and *O. Pedroana*), which were cut and ground to shape (Erickson 1990:94).

Both men and women wore earrings (Elmendorf 1935-6, 1:73), which most likely were ear drops made of thin twisted sinew, strung with sections of stone or shell beads. These were later replaced by ceramic and glass beads. The decision to do piercing, and the number of piercings, apparently never reflected any particular gender status.

Beading and Porcupine Decoration

Prior to the diffusion of Euro-American trade goods, some ceremonial garments were decorated with beads made from marine mollusks and stones traded from the Northwest Coast, and occasionally shell beads from local freshwater mussel shell, now considered *old time beads* (*čpápas*). Freshwater and terrestrial mollusks were thought thinner and deemed inferior to the shell traded from the coast. Local and traded shell beads were particularly valued for their size, shape, and color—red and orange were most favored because of the variegated colored nacre, or the iridescent inner layer of the shell.

As noted, ceremonial garments were decorated with porcupine quills after being thoroughly soaked for two or three hours and then flattened between the artist's fingernails or with a deer rib. Only the largest quills were plucked from the unskinned porcupine (Schaeffer 1934-37, I-65:44), which were stored in a bark container until needed. Quills that were too large were split into two sections before soaking for two or three hours. The quills were then stained with plant dyes, and tied to the garment with thin strips of sinew, usually from the tendons of a deer's hind legs. After finishing a quill pattern, the piece was placed on a flat rock near a fire and sprinkled with water. "Another flat rock was then heated slightly and drawn over the quillwork, to further flatten it" (Schaeffer 1934-37, I-67:46).

Another type of bead was made from the ripened berries of *silverberry* (*Elaeagnus communtata* Bernh. ex Rydb. - *p'úk'ʷi?* or *sp'óqʷi*) and *mountain ash berries* (*čkʷlkʷlús*) that were strung with needle and a strand of hemp by a grandmother for a grandchild. One elderly lady remarked that though the fragile berry necklace did not last very long, their memories she would always have. Women collected the hard, white seeds of hoary puccoon, which were strung as water necklace for young girls, and were also crushed to make a red paint. Women's ceremonial dresses were decorated with *elk tooth beads* (*snqʷ'ʷx̣mín* - "elk wisdom tooth") which, throughout the Plains and Plateau, "are perforated at the root biconically through the labial and lingual aspects of the tooth with a tapered drill" (Wood 1957:382). These paired permanent canines were attached more commonly on women's ceremonial apparel.

Since tooth enamel is the densest of all biological materials, and the most durable natural material for beads, drilling enamel with stone tools was a rather laborious procedure. Considering that a large and mature elk has only two cuspid teeth in the maxilla, it was astonishing that an old dress once observed by the author weighed approximately 6 to 7 kilograms, having been heavily ornamented with as many as eighty to a hundred elk's teeth. Consequently, an elk tooth ornamented dress was extremely valuable, considered an *heirloom* (*s?elk'ʷmn*), passed from mother to daughter, and often gifted at memorial feasts to a younger woman of the owner's family, or bequeathed to a granddaughter at a name-giving ceremony, or to a favored daughter-in-law upon the owner's death. A deceased *woman* (*sm'en'*) was, however, on occasion buried in her elk tooth beaded dress. A Nez Perce burial (45-AS-9) once revealed a one-year-old girl with a dress almost completely covered with 230 elk teeth, which required the teeth of 115 elk (Sprague 1959:21). Elk teeth adorned dresses were prestigious items used sometimes as gifts.

A much-valued *bead* (*čcm'úse'*) was the incised and non-incised *tooth-shaped dentalium* (*Dentalium pretiosum* Sow. - *lqʷalew'aqs* or *st'ałq'ʷl't* or *sxʷƛ'čén* - "small on one end"), collected on the southern coast of *Vancouver Island* (*čsúnkʷ*) by the Nootka, and acquired by the Spokan through trade (Erickson 1990:94). Dentalium shells were valued according to their individual nuances of shape and color, considered as family heirlooms, and on occasion served as a means of exchange for other items. The rim of select large dentalium were stone-drilled to accommodate tufts of fur to further enhance their appearance and value.

Spinden wrote (1908:220) that dentalium were not commonly used as *money* (*sqléw'*) in the Plateau, as they were in Northern California and throughout the Northwest Coast, but used rather as ornamentation. Traded beads from marine mussel shell were indigenous to the Northeast Woodlands Iroquois and Algonquian tribes. Some Eastern Woodlands groups "used the woven colored strips of colored shell beads as mnemonic devices to record important events, as message devices during recitation of a ritual or ceremony, and as symbols of treaties and agreements" (Spencer, Jennings, *et al.* 1965:396). Galm noted the importance of marine shell in the Plateau, and how, "Marine shell constitutes a second, significant trade commodity in Plateau pre-history. Shells were used primarily as items of adornment or ornamentation, typically occurring as beads and pendants" (1994:288).

Despite archaeological and historical evidence, and the present Spokan term *lʕʷolew'aqs* for wampum (STHC), there never was in either form or function any so-called wampum within the interior Plateau (Sprague, pers. comm.). Pickering used the term "'wampum' for describing strung dentalium shells, which were used as 'money' by the Chinook" (1895:14); a designation that became common along the Columbia River for dentalium. The notion of wampum beads as money is a recent construct, and yet, as mentioned earlier, Pickering undoubtedly acquired the term wampum beads for such art forms during his earlier coastal studies, and of course the Spokan had tubular barrel-shaped beads made from bird bones (Collier *et al.* 1942:88), and Pickering later observed how the Chewelah-Spokan Group made what he called wampum beads "made of bird bones" (1895:26; Barry 1920, 1:59).

The most common type of bead was a flat disc bead made from marine mussel shells, most notably the plentiful *Margaritifera falcata* that were traded from the Northwest Coast, already cut from the parent shell. These beads were ground to a circular shape, varying in diameter from 3 to 5 mm, then center-drilled with a small hole about 2 to 3 mm in diameter, with a thickness of 2 to 3 mm. The finished products were strung into varying lengths and numbers of strands as necklaces, but were not affixed to garments.

Stone, bone, and a few shell beads were made by the Spokan and worn by both men and women in single- and double-strand necklaces. Smaller beads were made from shell or stone, shaped by repeated abrasion and then center-drilled for stringing or as ear-pendants. Some of these beads were acquired as finished products and exist in the archaeological record (Sprague 1967), but there are few surviving examples of clay beads apparently made by the Spokan. Similar to shell beads, stone beads were always strung and worn about the neck in either single or double strands or as ear pendants with gradations of pink to brick-red.

The laborious manufacturing of stone and shell beads was largely replaced by the introduction of European-made metal, ceramic (Prosser), and glass beads. All of these found immediate utilization and expression in the form of numerous *bead articles* (*'ečk'ʷl'k'ʷul'*), eliminating the laborious preparation and application of porcupine quills. Copper beads were made by cutting and rolling sections of copper sheets into varying lengths, and were used for decorating clothing and for making men's and women's necklaces. To attain and renew a luster, both copper and brass beads were shined by rubbing with wood ashes. With European-made beads, all types of *shiny beads* (*čp'č'íč's*) were considered attractive and most desirable. Venetian beads were of excellent quality and texture and were much in demand. (Peltier 1990:6).

Even today, many Indian bead workers use a size classification of beads, based on a bead's diameter, and so seed beads are under 2 mm in diameter. Pony beads were 2 - 4 mm, and crow beads 4 -10 mm in diameter. Imported glass beads from different countries were made my various techniques.

Brass beads (*lolʕwáqs* or *člepleptnús* or *čckʷcíkʷs*) were acquired as finished products, but some long brass beads were made by the Spokan from spent .45-70 rifle shells discarded by the soldiers who regularly practiced firing at the U.S. Army rifle range at Fort Spokane (near the confluence of the Columbia and Spokane Rivers) (Combs 1962); some were acquired directly through trade with the soldiers. Elders claim that it was not difficult to collect expended brass and lead that had not been recovered by the military for reloading. Spokan men resourcefully saved their expended brass .22 caliber Winchester rim-fire cartridges, and larger center-fire calibers, by first removing the spent base, and expanding and reshaping the casings by auguring the inside with an appropriate size metal nail. Used .45-70 and .45-90 brass cartridges were re-used and flattened by hammer and rolled over nails or straightened barbed wire to make tubular beads. Some metal trade beads were faceted.

A wide variety of glass, ceramic, and metal trade beads were obtained by the Spokan who highly valued the bead's "structure, color, and ornamentation" (Sprague 1985:91). Certain beads were of *clear glass* (*člepleptnús* or *čc'k'ʷc'ík'ʷs* or *člq'lq'ús*) that came in various sizes, such as the very small *seed beads* (*čcm'úseʔ*). "Larger varieties of drawn beads for beadwork are often called pony beads or pound heads" (Sprague 1991:91). The greatest demand was for polychrome glass and ceramic beads—most notably the Bohemian (Czechoslovakian) and Venetian molded beads. For six hundred years, the Venetians dominated the world's glass bead industry, with beads that most notably included magnificent and highly sought multi-layered and corrugated Paternoster beads, ones with a star pattern on the ends which often resulted in stripes on the outside. The Dutch produced the dogan bead, and the French produced many brass beads; even the HBC produced a bead called "Cornaline d'Aleppo". The Japanese never made molded beads, and their seed beads are post-WW II (Sprague, pers. comm.). The Chinese produced mainly a light blue glass padre bead.

The *long, glass beads* (*čwswsšnús*), both polychrome tubular (drawn bead) and cane beads, were preferred for decorating men's vests and the long gauntlets of men's ceremonial gloves, particularly with the Venetian drawn bead—a "winding bead." Among the Spokan, European-made clear glass beads, or what the Spokan sometimes called *crystal beads* (*čxʷiyxʷiynctús* or *w'ɫw'ɫ*) (Sprague 1985), seldom replaced dentalia beads. Likewise, European and Oriental trade beads never replaced the highly-prized attached pendants of elk's teeth, which commonly adorned a woman's top dress shawl or yoke, sometimes on both the front and back of the garment.

Glass beads (*sčk'ʷul'*) were opaque, translucent, or transparent, and of varying size and appearance, which were classified by the Spokan: *clear* (*člepleputenús*), *cut* and *faceted* (*čp'č'p'íč's*), monochrome (solid blue being initially preferred), or fancy wound polychrome beads (eventually the most highly sought) (Sprague 1991). Long, polychrome, and *monochrome glass beads* (*čwswsšnus*) were popular. As cited, some beads were made of brass, which became popular early in Euro-American contact, replacing many indigenous shell beads and some trade beads.

Trade beads initiated a flourishing in the general forms of geometric, floral, and curvilinear decorative beaded designs that became possible with the introduction of smaller beads, thereby permitting more solid designs and often more detailed designs. On occasion, truly magnificent and intricate patterns covered the entire facing of a woman's *utilitarian belt bag* (*syep'wn*), sewing bag, and hand bags carried later during ceremonial occasions. A once common bead pattern was a small whirlwind. Sometimes a husband or older son would sketch in charcoal the initial design, which in the hands of a talented and patient sewer produced floral patterns that were artistically shaded by a gradation of different colors, giving an impression of depth to the subject. Exceptionally fine beadwork was a signature to the artist's imagination and skill, and an admiring person might say, "*She's a talented bead-worker*" (*ʔec k'ʷl'l'scút*).

An important and much sought after item—associated with beading—was the *steel trade needle* (*čłxʷépleʔ*), which came in various sizes. The thickness of the particular base material, most commonly cloth, influenced the size and diameter of the needle. Both girls and women made necklaces of calico china (ceramic) beads that had transfer-print designs. Trade buttons were widely adopted for securing clothing, and for complementing beaded designs on flat surfaces of clothing. The black, white, and calico Chinese buttons (the latter made from transferring print designs) were highly prized on ceremonial clothing. Also, there existed hundreds of different styles, such as the large, corner-less, blue facetted bead, which found a ready market within the Plateau. Young girls were encouraged to sketch on paper their own beading patterns, usually of floral designs. No one ever had propriety rights over their designs. Requests by the non-Indian population for Indian-made beadwork and cornhusk products became an incentive, as well as a means of income for many elderly women until the late 1950s.

Non-Indian strung glass beads became popular for making rosary beads, at least by those Spokan who had converted to Catholicism as a result of proselytizing by early missionaries. The author observed an old and finely crafted rosary that belonged to a woman in her nineties, who said the item was made by her mother, probably in the 1870s. After many years of constant use and rubbing, the rosary's *faceted beads* (*čp'č'p'íč's* or *w''iłw'ł* - "cut beads") had become worn smooth and black. In addition, it had what appeared to be the original silver crucifix.

It is not known if the manufacture and use of bracelets developed when trade beads were adopted by the Spokan. Many smaller beads and discs were used for pendants and ear-pendants and for *braid wrap decorations* (*snʕacacen'eʔ*). Dresses, cradleboards, tobacco pouches, moccasins, and dancing gloves were adorned with glass beads. A granddaughter would highly prize a *small beaded bag* (*čk'ʷk'ʷl'íʔs* or *hesčk'ʷúl'*) made and gifted by her grandmother. It is not known if Spokan men traditionally ever did *beadwork* (*sčk'ʷúl'* or *čpeʔkʷúm'* or *sčk'ʷúl'*), but some contemporary Colville, Nez Perce, and Spokan men do beadwork now, and are considered better at it than some women. Trade beadwork commenced at least as early as 1870 (Sprague, pers. comm.).

Despite the universal availability of beading materials, "Crow and Blackfoot beadwork were more alike but that the Salish beadwork resembled more the Shoshone, Bannock and Ute in appearance" (Schaeffer 1934-37, I-138).

Necklaces and Pendants

Nearly all archaeologically recovered aboriginal pendants were manufactured from clam shell, both fresh water and salt water varieties. Fewer examples were of abalone (*Haliotis*); the more common shapes were oval, rectangular, triangular, and trapezoidal (Collier *et al.* 1942:95). Of several oval flat green stone pendants found archaeologically one type had been center-bored and the other top-bored; these were probably neck, not ear, pendants because of their large size and also because they were unmatched. As mentioned, necklaces were made from dried corn, glass, brass, and ceramic beads, reworked brass cartridges, and shell and stone beads. Necklaces, ear and neck pendants, and wide bracelets made of copper were manufactured from copper of European origin (Collier *et al.* 1942:158); a copper bracelet was called *kʷkʷi'k'ʷil'p* or *kʷkʷl'k'ʷil'ssn*. Later, copper buttons and bells became highly desired trade items. Men and women wore, during certain dances, necklaces made from deer dewclaws, beaver claws, or upper canines and incisors from elk. Deer claw ornaments made a louder and more preferred sound. After acquiring corn, a *necklace* (*sɫaɫq'ʷl't* or *sq'l'éps* - "string of beads") was made by stringing kernels of corn; naturally colored corn was preferred.

It is not certain as to whether the various bone pendants found archaeologically (Collier *et al.* 1942:88) were worn by both men and women, but it is possible that both genders did, since it is known that men and women wore various types of neck buckskin bags. Elmendorf noted the importance of small buckskin bags for carrying love charms and prophylactic objects, such as:

[...] certain weeds & roots stuffed into little buckskin bags & carried these in another bag around their necks, in their belts or around their persons somewhere—prevented burning, protection from fire, house won't burn down—or charm for retaining affection of husband or gaining that of a loved one (1935-6, 1:74).

The beaks of the Western pileated woodpecker were used as necklaces or pendants by stringing through the nasal openings (Collier *et al.* 1942:92). What may be interpreted as a necklace or pendant quite likely served as an amulet that certainly had some religious significance. Several surveys and graves exposed by erosion have revealed elk and beaver teeth necklaces (Elmendorf 1935-6, 1:3; Collier *et al.* 1942:89; Ross 1993). Some bone pendants were crafted to imitate elk teeth. One can only surmise that eagle head and claw necklaces were worn to represent a tutelary spirit, as would a necklace of bear claws. The extensive Columbia Basin Archaeological Survey (July 1939 - September 1940) in eastern Washington revealed several examples of bird beaks from the relatively large *Western pileated woodpecker* (*Dryocopus pileatus - st'l'x*ʷ*úmeʔ* or *spwálqn*) that had been drilled, apparently for use as part of necklaces; but none was decorated by engraving (Collier *et al.* 1942:92). There is no evidence the Spokan used either the bones or feathers of the Lewis's woodpecker as decoration, and no ethnographic significance could be remembered of the rarely seen *black-backed woodpecker* (*Picoides arcticus - tčółtsíyutsum*), except for the belief that, like other woodpeckers, it would nest in the hair of a recalcitrant child.

Rings and Bracelets

Prior to the introduction of various types of metal finger rings, women's rings were made primarily from shell, predominantly "made from the purple-hinged or *rock scallop* (*Hinnites giganteus*) which is found along the Pacific Coast from Alaska to Mexico" (Collier *et al.* 1942:94). A *finger ring* (*čn'pqin'čst*) made of cross-sectioned bone has been found (Ross 1993), as well as ones of cross-sections of mountain goat horn (Collier *et al.* 1942:88). The *bracelet* (*cč'łyrk*ʷ*cnéčst*) became more fashionable, particularly with the introduction of beads and brass, which was easily pounded and manipulated to shape. Sprague (pers. comm.) saw few metal trade rings among the Spokan, but said they were apparently more appealing to the Palouse.

As recent as mid-1960, elderly women displayed considerable pride and pleasure upon recalling how as young girls they would make "spring bracelets and necklaces" by intertwining or twisting flowers attached to their stems.

Mineral and Plant Dyes

Most dyes used for staining or painting were usually extracted by boiling various mosses, lichens, and other plants, or the direct application of numerous powdered minerals. The main difference between organic dyes and mineral substrates was that a plant dye was derived from boiling a particular type of vegetation, whereas a specific subtracted mineral dye was invariably mixed with various types of oil, most notably oils extracted from the neck of the Pacific sea lamprey or sturgeon. Fish oil-based pigments were used to paint petroglyphs, and have proven to be more durable, rather than bear grease as some younger Spokan have claimed. One elderly Spokan man recalled being told by his grandfather how bear grease once served as a medium for paints and dyes used for painting on wood and *hide* (*q'étt ełx*ʷ), but not on stone. When *bear fat* (*scocóq*ʷ) was to be used as a paint medium, it was first cut into thin strips, dried, and then *rendered* (*sčt'eʔk'*ʷ*ew's*); it remained as a heavy liquid and never became hard or flaked.

When *weaving a basket* (*y'éy'm'*), sometimes a *grass basket* (*x*ʷ*ax*ʷ*aʔƛé* or *syáy'qs*) was decorated with imbrications of geometric design patterns by fashioning artistic expressions with dye-stained grass. An intense purple color was acquired by soaking the peeled roots of Oregon grape in boiled water with its *berry* (*sc'áls*), producing varying colors from yellow to deep purple, according to the length of time the grass was soaked in pigmented water. Boiled chokecherry bark produced a dark red dye which was used to stain porcupine quills and basketry. Green was obtained from boiled roots of Indian carrot and the leaves of snowberry. A light pink or violet color was produced from boiling the leaves of *Richardson's penstemon* (*Penstemon richardsonii* Dougl. ex Lindl., var. *richardsonii* - *sqey'séłp*), found on dry basalt ledges. Black dye came from wild carrot root, tree moss, *charcoal* (*c'íxʷc'uxʷt* or *sc'i?xʷatkʷp* or *c'áxʷc'xʷc*), and black loam. Wolf lichen, sunflower root, alder bark, yellow ochre, the *lichen* (*Bryoria capillaris*), *yellow moss* (*Cladina mitis* - *skʷalyó*), and *Oregon grape roots* (*s?oxʷéps*) produced varying hues of yellow. Red and brown colors were acquired from different grades of red ochre, huckleberries, and chokecherries. Gray pigment was produced by burning animal bones. Some mineral dyes for making black, orange, and yellow were, however, obtained by the Spokan through trade. Mineral dyes, according to color, were carefully stored in a *buckskin bag* (*p'ukʷl?e?tm*), whereas plant dyes were gathered fresh each year. Mineral dyes were used to achieve yellow, blue, brown, and red colors, and for producing curvilinear designs on flatwork, particular hidework (Ross 1995f, 2:323).

Dyes, paints, and, in some instances, soot and *ground charcoal* (*c'áxʷc'xʷt*) were used to decorate hide, stone, wood, or even a person's face on ceremonial occasions. An unusual and pleasing cherry-red color was made by boiling chokecherry bark, and then concentrating the solution for coloring porcupine quills and coloring hemp for imbrication of baskets. Blue was attained from blue clay, and a light blue color was made from "a type of dried duck dung" (Peltier 1975:27).

The most predominant mineral dye color was *red hematite* (*sčt'e?k'ʷew's*), and was "made from pulverized iron oxide minerals and sometimes from clay containing iron oxides" (Boreson 1998:618). Boreson's (1987) earlier analysis of iron oxide minerals in the Spokan area revealed the use of quartz, hematite, and maghemite. Yellow colors were derived from the minerals limonite and goethite (iron hydroxide—$HFeO_2$, occurring in yellow or brown earthy masses and in crystals), whereas, "White paint was made from burned bone, kaolin (a clay), gypsum, or diatomaceous earth, green was made from copper carbonates, and black was obtained from charcoal or graphite" (Boreson 1998:618).

From the findings of Erwin (1930:38), it can be assumed that the Spokan used "water, saliva, *grease* (*sqʷʷúct*), tallow, fish eggs, glue, and resin as vehicles for the pigment." Leechman (1932:38) cited saliva being used in making pigments. After mixing the color pigment or plant stain with grease, it was then applied with brushes (made by chewing and shredding the ends of red willow or dogwood), or directly with the artist's fingers. Feathers may have been used as brushes. Raw pigments were stored in small sewn buckskin bags, approximately the size of an adult's fist, and secured with a *drawstring* (*nqʷʷúsp* - "drawstring bag"). Local pigments were of such a high quality and abundance that Spokan women would trade them for camas and deer hides with other groups, such as the Colville (Post and Commons 1938:69). Elders recalled that some quarried lumps of hematite were so large that they had to be broken up to permit their removal from the quarries, and for ease of transportation.

Hair Styles

Apart from facial painting and perforating noses and ears, all adults devoted time to fashioning their hair in styles that differed between men and women, since both men and women tended to wear a full length of *long hair* (*čwissnqn*). Wilson (1866:293-4) summarized his observations of Spokan hair style and characteristics:

> The hair is black or dark brown, course, strait, and grows to an extra length; there are various modes of dressing it; sometimes it is allowed to fall down to its full length; at others, a lock on each side of the head is confined in a brass keeper, whilst the remainder is put in one or two long queues, bound around with beads or ribbon, and otherwise ornamented; other modes are to have the hair braided and falling down in long plaits, or cut short in front, leaving a row of stiff bristles, which, standing up from the forehead, give a peculiarly wild and savage appearance to the face. From exposure to the weather, the hair often turns to a russet brown colour; but the absence of grey hair, even amongst the very old men, is especially remarkable, very few instances of greyness having come to notice.

Men were careful, if not fastidious, in styling their hair for special events, such as warfare, ceremonial dancing, or when required to dress in their regalia. For example, both men and women, especially prior to attending a Medicine Dance, would, after rubbing tallow in their hair, apply powdered white clay or powdered orange-yellow or red hematite. A special *man's hair arrangement* (*nqʼcʼuʔsus*) was to fashion a small braid of forehead hair gathered at the hairline, which if long enough, could be ornamented with a colorful cloth or strips of fur; occasionally the braid of hair was tied back into a loop (STHC). Narrow strips of marten fur were wrapped around a man's braids for special occasions (Elmendorf 1935-6, 1:62). The men's hair fashion was generally called *čʼnʼčʼnʼpʼus*, and, as mentioned, was often decorated (STHC). Another unique occasion was when a warrior intended to commit suicide. He would *let his hair fall straight back* (*ntʼhehxʷcʼuʔsus*), keeping it from his face as he galloped toward an enemy in an *heroic ride* (*nqclšenč*).

If a man had carefully saved the brushings of his or some other person's loose hair, he could make a *queue* (*sčtʼłtʼá*) for special occasions by binding these hairs together and tying them to his braid. Such braids were single, double, or triple; a man's single braid was called *kʼʷłqcʼápqn* ("braided back of head"). Both men and women tied the ends of their queues together so they did not come over or past their shoulders. Smith recorded how men's and women's queues could reach the person's knees (1936-8:750). It is not known if deer or horse hair was ever braided into a person's coiffure. Both men and women's braids were always tied off at the bottom with strips of buckskin.

Attentive to the clothing and appearance of the indigenous people and the change of hair styles, Curtis not only photographed several Spokan women's hair arrangement (Cardozo 2005, Plates 47 and 67), but wrote how much attention adults gave to their hair:

> The men doubled it up behind and tied it in a knot, cut the forelock square at the level of the nose and curled it upward by first rolling it on a heated stick. This was done every morning after the bath [swim]. About 1850 they began to leave the forelock uncut and to throw it back above the forehead, while at the sides the hair hung in two braids in front of the shoulders, and at the back fell loosely. As a rule the women made a braid at each side, doubled it up, and wrapped it with strips of bone beads. They now allow the braids to hang in front of the shoulders, and at the back fell loosely (Curtis 1907-30, 7:72).

Men and women commonly parted their hair in the center and bound each parting in place with a short length of buckskin just below the ear. Each of the two gatherings of hair was then braided, one on either side, with each end tied off with a bit of buckskin. For special occasions, the women affixed different types of center-drilled or double-holed shell, usually flat or slightly cupped, round sections of abalone, olivella, or mussels. Once copper was introduced, some people favored this material, which was fashioned into flat round or ovoid-shaped discs by both men and women. Prior to wearing these copper ornaments, a bright finish was attained by rubbing the object with wood ash.

A particularly attractive hair style for a young woman was to wear two wide, *flattened braids* (*čtłtłpéneʔ*). Younger women carefully *fluffed* (*ntłtłpénʼeʔ*) their hair before making loosely tied braids in order to make them appear wider. Braids were further enhanced by braiding each section of hair with varying widths of narrow fur strips, such as tanned ermine, weasel skins, or feathers that hung from the end of each braid. Women who chose to temporarily leave their *hair unbraided* (*čmixʷqn* or *mixʷu*), added shell *discs* (*slmixʷuʔ*) to gain more appeal. Occasionally, women bound their braids, placing *bone hair pipes* (*ččʼnʼčʼnʼpʼéneʔtn*) near the ears. In historical times, thin modified pieces of neatly rolled pieces of tin cans served this purpose (STHC). A young pre-menarche girl might wear her braids over her ears like *puppy-dog tails* (*nčʼnʼłtʼenʼeʔ*). It is not known if men, like women, wore ear discs on *unbraided hair* (*slmixʷuʔ*).

For a woman of any age, the easiest hair style and hair management was to fashion her hair into a *single braid* (*čqʼcʼpeneʔ*) or a *ponytail* (*sčtʼłtʼá*) that hung down her back. In the past, a bone hair-pipe was used as a *clamp-like device* (*čʼčʼnpʼmintn*) for holding small braids, but was replaced often with artistic designs fashioned from tin containers, which were cut open and rolled into tubes of varying length, with the shining side exposed around the braid. Given a woman's hair style and the occasion, she might have, before braiding her hair, applied *hair grease* (*pʔƛ'qn*) made from mixing tallow with, preferably, the fine dry powder obtained by crushing green subalpine fir needles, thereby giving a pleasant aroma and pleasing appearance.

Both men and women could fashion their hair into a *single forehead braid* (*nq'c'aw'sqn'*) that hung freely to either side of the head. A variety of this arrangement by men was when all the hair was gathered at the top into a single braid, and then divided into two conventional braids. Some men would create a type of pompadour by pulling their front hair down over their forehead, placing a heated green wood stick parallel to their forehead, and octagonally against the hair (about halfway down), then bending the hair forward at a right angle and holding the stick there for several minutes. As a result, the hair lock would stand straight up with the upper half bent back at a right angle (Smith 1936-8:750).

Plaited and twisted hide and fur strips, feathers, single shells, elk teeth, and strung beads, traditionally used as pendants and hair ornaments, were replaced by different colors of cloth and silk ribbons acquired through trade. Men and women usually attached pendants and other forms of adornment to the hair on both sides of the head near the ears. Plain and embroidered trade silk and ribbons became popular on dresses and men's shirts and vests, and were adapted as *braid wraps* (*č'č'lč'pen'eʔ*). Sometimes a young woman *purposely left her hair unbraided* (*nwixʷneʔ*) when in public, and, when possible without her chaperone's attention, looked demurely at a young man, hoping to attract his attention.

However, standards of appearance and cleanliness discouraged the display of *disarrayed hair* (*yéc*), especially in public or when attending a ceremony when a man *would grease* (*čłalqn*) or used hair oil (*č'p'óƛ'qntn*) on his hair before adopting a particular hair style. Children, however, let their hair remain loose until just prior to puberty, but never *uncombed* (*čyaqn*) or unwashed. Older girls and boys adopted different hair styles, such as *parting* (*snq'xʔáw'sqn* - "part in hair") their hair in the center and then plaiting it into *two braids down each side* (*čq'c'q'c'péneʔ* - "hair braids"), or into *one strand down the back* (*č'łq'c'ópqn*). Until some Spokan men started serving in the armed forces in WW I, all men (and women) *parted their hair in the middle* (*nčłuʔsus*). The practice of *parting one's hair* (*nc'łanaʔqn*) on the side was a much later style.

When a girl experienced her menarche and succeeding menses, she was instructed to carefully gather her *hair* (*q'ʷómqn*) into two *tight* (*c'ʕan*) braids—tying each into a knot *over each ear* (*čtłtłpn*). Sometimes a mother or grandmother was present to *braid the hair* (*čq'c'q'c'péneʔm*) of a young woman prior to her seclusion. As previously cited, a young girl was always careful to collect any fallen or loose hair, which she balled up and gave to her mother during her daily visit, which the mother would later carefully dispose outside of the menstrual hut by burning—never by burying—to prevent sorcery, and any person who had cut his or her hair was extremely careful to dispose of the cut hair by burning, again to prevent it being used by a sorcerer.

Elderly Spokan who had attended either a mission or government school recalled the severe humiliation they experienced when forced to have their *hair cut short* (*čxʷicqn*), with the *back cut straight across* (*č'łxʷet'cn*) and in the front. One elder, who had this done to him as a boy of twelve, felt embarrassed and guilty in that he was misrepresenting his tribe by his drastically altered appearance; so at night he would gently pull on his hair so it would again grow. He explained that he could shed his white clothes off, but he could not restore his Indian identity. For both boys and girls, *short hair* (*čxʷixʷacqn'*), or to have one's hair *bobbed* (*č'łxʷet'cn*), was considered demeaning and disfiguring, and a personal loss of identity. Every fall, upon their return to school, girls would have their *long hair* (*čwisšnqn*) shortened.

Collins's article on Indian schools shows a rather pathetic photograph of "New Recruits—Spokane Indian" (1880-1885), taken at Forest Grove Indian School, just south of Portland, showing Indian boys and girls with their long hair just prior to a second photograph (1881) showing the new students, four young Spokan boys and seven girls in uniform, staring unhappily at a camera

Off-reservation schools often used photographic propaganda to generate financial support and convince a sometimes skeptical public that Indians could be civilized. Shorn hair, military uniforms, erect postures, and self-confidence comprised part of the idealized American image that officials hoped to convey. Wilkinson [Head-master] envisioned his students returning to their reservations, assuming positions of leadership, and guiding their people through an ongoing process of acculturation (2000:471).

The etiquette of hair combing was confined to the immediate extended family. Grandmothers were particularly devoted to combing the hair of their young grandchildren. One would *comb one's hair* (*qʷošqin*), but traditionally a wife would first comb her husband's hair before he retired, always before combing her own hair. It was said that in the morning a man's wife would comb his hair before tending to her own grooming—which some elders remembered not so much as protocol, but for the woman to add her husband's hair grease to her own hair while grooming. A once common expression of love was to *stroke the hair of a loved one* (*cšiw'ntxʷ* or *čixʷntm* - "to pet or stroke") (STHC).

It was remembered how a girl would always comb her brother's hair; but never did a boy comb a girl's hair, nor did a man ever comb a woman's hair, regardless of their relationship. Both small boys and girls had their hair braided by a mother or grandmother, once the hair was somewhat manageable. Usually a boy had either one braid in the back or one to each side. Before a girl's hair was long enough to make two side braids, the mother or grandmother would make four or five braids.

Combs

The Spokan had three types of combs, any one of which could be used by both men and women. The most common type differed only in length; the shorter comb was 10 to 12 cm in length, whereas the longer *comb* (*sušmín* or *čošlšsqáx̣eʔ* or *sip't'*) varied from 12 to 15 cm in length. The shorter comb was usually made of carefully worked bone (Collier *et al.* 1942:87). Most combs were fan-shaped by gathering numerous slender, pre-sharpened pieces of hardwood, preferably bow wood, at the broad base of the comb's handle. The ends of the teeth were spread to give a flat and open-ended appearance and held in place by weaving a long, thin strip of wet rawhide or hemp in and around each of the teeth in mid-section. Some combs were double-set by alternating a longer and finer tooth, and were held apart by shorter but wider teeth.

Women often combed their hair with a *berrying comb* (*ssípt*), made by first bundling together twenty to thirty dried sharpened elderberry staves, which were then secured together at one end with numerous turns of hemp. The comb was made from equally spaced shafts of split hardwood, kept in a fan-shape by securing one or two parallel strands of hemp at right angles to the combing staves—one immediately at the bundled end, and a second binding about a third of the way up the teeth. The combing or open ends were sharpened, and the ends rounded as needed. Each stave was spaced by a long intertwining length of hemp at mid-length of each stave. A similar type of head comb was made from the thornless wood of ocean spray or from mock orange. The former type was favored for hair grooming as well as for berrying combs, particularly for huckleberries. Reference has been made to a wooden comb (Wynecoop 1985:75) having been used in 1815, but with no details of construction.

A more elaborate but durable comb was made from either ocean spray or buckbrush, and served for both grooming and for stripping huckleberries from heavily laden bushes. Women were claimed to have been more adept in making this type of comb as a gift, and it was received with considerable pride by a young daughter or granddaughter. The author observed such a comb that was made in the 1870s by an elder's great grandmother. The chosen five to six sections of wood, approximately 20 to 25 cm in length, were debarked, soaked until supple, and then flattened with a stone pounder. Upon drying, the five or six prepared sections or staves were smoothed with an abrasive stone, and split lengthwise before bending the staves over in the middle. The bent midsections were bundled together and secured with a length of wet rawhide approximately 10 to 12 cm from the top of the bundle. To keep the staves or teeth of the comb separated, the women would interweave a long narrow piece of buckskin, approximately 2 to 3 cm long, between each stave. A second row

502

of intertwining buckskin strip was repeated approximately 1 cm below the first woven course, leaving teeth of approximately 6 to 8 cm long. The end product was from 18 to 20 cm long, and was never decorated.

The use and variety of accouterments has obviously changed owing to the many years of diffusion, direct trade, and means of catalogue purchasing. There is only incomplete recall of what may have once been traditional Spokan accouterments that were worn on dance costumes and clothing for special events. Several renowned Spokan silversmiths and makers of traditional dance costumes have successfully demonstrated the importance of incorporating the sometimes extreme variations in design and even material into contemporary costumes. One young Spokan artist explained that, "Our survival as a people is predicated upon our ability to change, to adapt and recognize the functional and aesthetic values of other people."

Chapter XV: Tobacco and Pipe Complex

Smoking Ceremony

Regardless of the reasons that brought men together, all occasions had definite customs of etiquette that invariably required smoking. Smoking as a group was more meaningful than what a casual observer might have concluded—ceremonies that acknowledged the pipe owner or *leader* (*ʔeskʷisnmé* - "he holds the pipe") as well as certain protocols and courtesies. Sitting in a circle, the pipe-owner first filled the pipe with tobacco and passed it to another person seated to his left, who would light the pipe, and was, by custom, the first to smoke before passing it to the man to his left. The pipe was always passed in a clock-wise direction, each person taking as many puffs as he wanted while the others talked, awaiting their turn to smoke. Some participants never fully inhaled, but simply held the smoke before exhaling. The pipe was passed around several times, or until the tobacco was burned out, and the pipe was allowed to cool before being refilled by the pipe-owner who would hand it to the person who had finished the pipe to light, and the passing ritual was resumed. Tobacco ceremonies could last for a day or more, or until the visitors decided to leave. Each man had two pipes: a large one for hosting, and a smaller one when away from his home. Special pipes were sometimes used by curing shamans when treating a patient to acquire a *trance* (*smóyyx̣eʔ*) (Egesdal, pers. comm.), or by an individual when propitiating his *suméš*.

Tobacco

The various species of ruderal, soporific *tobacco* (*Nicotiana* ssp. - *smén'xʷ* or *sméʔenx̣ʷ* or *slíqʷl'aʔxʷ*) plants, such as *Nicotiana bigelovii*, *N. rustica* L., *N. Trignophylla*, and *N. attenuata* Torr. ex Wats.) were once native to the Central Andes. With plant diffusion and trade, certain species eventually reached southern Native Americans, who in turn traded them to more northerly groups. Turner *et al.* (1980:140) acknowledged Lerman's earlier findings (1952-54) that wild tobacco was grown but not cultivated in various areas of the Okanogan-Colville territories, stating that "Wild Tobacco (*Nicotiana attenuata* Torr. ex Wats.), sometimes called Coyote tobacco, was cultivated and smoked aboriginally" (Turner 1978:218) by the Coeur d'Alene and Flathead. Medicinally, "Coyote tobacco was used to soothe itchy scalps, cuts and sores, eczema and hives, mixed with bear fat, it made a balm for burns. Chewed leaves relieved toothaches" (Nesbit 2007:143).

Though there is little evidence of the Spokan growing tobacco, various contiguous groups did and traded cultivated tobacco to the Spokan (Turner 1978:218). The shredded root of licorice root was used as a stimulant when smoked or chewed, being held in the mouth between the lower teeth and lip; the menthol taste was particularly relaxing when chewed.

Given the providence of tobacco, Teit (1928:112) noted how the Spokan traded tobacco to the Coeur d'Alene. The Spokan continued, in some instances, to use the leaves from various local non-tobacco plants for smoking, which were dried before crushing. As noted, smoking was an integral part of both socialization and sacred rituals—most often for purification.

Prior to an excursion onto the Plains to hunt bison, or a commitment to war, a man smoked his pipe, and, by hyperventilating, was often able to see if he would have success or failure, thereby encouraging or discouraging his intentions. Elmendorf (1935-6, 1:33) cites how only men *smoked* (*sl'iqʷl'eʔxʷ*) kinnikinnick, but several elderly women recalled their mothers and grandmothers smoking kinnikinnick mixed with bear's ear (*Plantigo major* L.) in short, small, stone elbow pipes.

Probably the most extensively used plant that provided tobacco was kinnikinnick bush from which the leaves were harvested almost year-round. After a harvest, the leaves were first dried on flat stones (Elmendorf 1935-6, 1:6) and then stuffed into buckskin bags and beaten with a stick to break up the rather tough leaves.

Even the dried pounded *kinnikinnick berries* (*sk*ʷ*lís*) were frequently mixed with dried sweet grass and smoked, as was a combination of *dried kinnikinnick berries, leaves* and *tobacco* (*sk*ʷ*l's*éɬ*p* or *sq*ʷ*ƛis l* or *kq*ʷ*liis* - "kinnikinnick leaves"). Various species of *grasses were pulled up* (*sliql'e*ʔ*x*ʷ), gathered together and allowed to ferment before drying (sometimes by burying), and then crumbled and mixed with kinnikinnick for tobacco (STCH). Kinnikinnick leaves remained green all year and were always available as tobacco, either unadulterated or mixed with other plants. After the introduction of tobacco by fur traders, Indians preferred commercial tobacco (*N. Tabacum* L.) to indigenous tobacco, except during sacred rituals. Collected sweet grass was plaited into three strands, essentially *braided as a rope* (*nč'isémn'tn*), and occasionally mixed with shredded, dry wild licorice root or Canbyi's Loveage (hereafter called *x̌ásax̌*) which was smoked on ritual occasions, a plant that is similar to Western sweet cicely, which in mythical times were considered "brothers" (Turner *et al.* 1980:64).

In a later account, Lord, though he was not knowledgeable of Amerindian culture, explained how he felt it was necessary—if he wanted to smoke—to accept the traditional practices of procuring tobacco, even from bushes and trees:

> The inner bark of the willow is by no means despicable substitute for tobacco, when scraped from a twig and dried; it is best dried by being scraped up in frills round the stick and held before the fire, then crumbled off and placed in the pipe-bowl. The leaves of the *Uva ursa* are also dried and smoked in great quantities by the savages west of the Rocky Mountains, who call it *kini-kin-ick*. I cannot say that I like either the one or the other, but if we cannot get what we like we must have what we can (1867:250).

Any plant used as tobacco was sacred, particularly when smoked in a pipe during ritual occasions. *Tobacco smoke* (*mén'x*ʷ) was considered capable of ridding an area of malevolent spirits, and clarifying a person's thoughts in addition to gaining the attention of one's tutelary spirit prior to propitiation. Traditionally, a common tobacco was sometimes made from a grass called *c'qe*ʔ*taɬq* (species unknown), which was picked when green. After being wrapped, it was put away or buried until it commenced to rot—actually fermented, after which it was opened, permitted to dry, and mixed with a small quantity of kinnikinnick before smoking. *Tobacco mixtures* (*hi snč'isémn*) of any the following plants were smoked: mullein, hemp, sweet grass, wild licorice root, kinnikinnick, dry inner shredded red willow bark, dried *valerian* (*Valeriana edulis* Nutt. ex T. & G., forma *edulis.* - *msáwi*ʔ), wild rose, dried huckleberry, and red osier dogwood bark. Given the smoker's preference, tobacco could be made from the inner bark of red willow, which was greatly improved when "the inner bark was scraped from a twig and dried; it is best dried by being scraped up in frills around the stick and held before the fire, then crumbled off and placed in the pipe bowl" (Lord 1867:250). Both the leaves and seeds of *Balsamorhiza* were pounded and mixed as a substitute for tobacco. Edible valerian was sometimes called "Stick-root".

One elderly Spokan, who had spent his youth logging with the Flathead, recalled discussions about earlier forms of tobacco and how one man described using the fresh needles from both the *white fir* (*Abies grandis* [Dougl. ex G. Don in Lamb.] Lindl. - *q*ʷ*élcn*) and subalpine fir, which were gathered and carefully heated on a pre-heated double bit axe until browned. The resulting dried product could be stored in a can to prevent it from becoming moist, and when smoked the tobacco had a strong or even a very strong taste.

Cannabis was combined with other plants as a tobacco, but given its availability, some men preferred to smoke it in an unadulterated state. Smoking unadulterated cannabis naturally assisted in soul-flight, enhancing one's visions and temporarily bestowing prophetic abilities, thereby facilitating and expediting a smoker's wishes and words to his tutelary spirit. For these reasons, tobacco or cannabis was used sometimes when curing and prior to but not during warfare or ventures requiring hand-eye skills. It was known that tolerances and behavior differed when under the influence of this drug.

Tobacco was always considered sacred, regardless of when it was smoked or with whom, and was smoked with every ritual as a means of purification (of self and immediate area) and propitiating one's *suméš*. The pipe was never used in the sweathouse, though tobacco was sprinkled on sweathouse stones for specific reasons during the last sweat session. Stone ground tobacco leaf was used sometimes in the sweathouse as an emetic when a person swallowed a sufficient amount to stimulate regurgitation, thereby *cleansing himself* (*yecxʷkʼʷúm*) in a ritual before death, usually by suicide in the sweathouse, as previously described. It was common practice for a married woman to gather plants used as tobacco for her husband; however, a male shaman gathered his own tobacco. Several elders recalled how a gift of tobacco established or reinforced a relationship between two men. For ritual use, women gathered their own tobacco.

Tobacco and the etiquette of the smoking ceremony were associated with certain protocol that functioned to emphasize an inextricable aspect of both profane and sacred rituals. Pipes were significant during certain ritual ceremonies and important to a man's social interaction and status. As previously cited, when an individual's pipe was shared with company, *it was always passed ceremoniously around the circle* (*nšlčmteʔs*) by the owner with great respect, and in accordance with a specific protocol prescribed for the particular occasion. The pipe was inhaled only two or three times by each man who held the smoke for approximately ten seconds. With the loss of the language, traditional customs, and religion, the obligations and *hospitality* (*cwélm*) to an absolute stranger were also lost—practices which had been noted in nearly all early contacts with the Spokan by Euro-Americans. The most apparent manifestation of this was either a formal or informal pipe ceremony.

In evaluating the importance of tobacco, Cox interpreted its use in fur trading as a confusing ritual, but his judgment was fraught with erroneous notions of character and responsibility:

> The Spokanes, like all other Indians of the interior, were inordinately fond of tobacco, and to gratify their appetite would resort to industry when all other motives were powerless to lure them from their habits of indolence. No business, however trifling in importance, could be transacted until the negotiants had been indulged in an extended preliminary smoke. A party would arrive at the fort with the produce of their traps, deposit it in the floor and gravely squat around the heap in a circle. Thereupon the trader would light his long peace pipe and go through a ceremonial performance directing his face to the east, giving a solemn puff in that quarter, and then repeating the performance with his face towards the cardinal points of the compass. After a few quick puffs, he would then pass the pipe to the chief, who would go through the same ritual, after which the calumet would be handed to the Indian next on his right, who would give a few whiffs and then pass it along. In this way the pipe would pass from hand to hand until the tobacco burned out, then the trader would present the party with a quantity of tobacco for individual smoking, which they would generally finish before taking up the business of barter, remarking that they had been "a long time very hungry for a smoke." The smoking over, each man divided his skins into different lots, and made it known to the trader that he was ready for business, indicating his wants and that he was ready to trade each little pile for some particular article or articles. The business transacted, another smoking match followed a preliminary to their departure for their village or encampment. The traders at Spokane House found them shrewd, hard dealers, not a whit inferior to any native of Yorkshire, Scotland or Connaught in driving a bargain (Durham 1912, 1:56).

DeSmet, in a similar passage (1843, 27:362), noted that the pipe was passed counter-clockwise, and adds: "Here, as everywhere else in the Indian country, the everlasting calumet was first produced, which went round two or three times in the most profound silence."

Men and some women smoked tobacco that had been gathered and processed by others, and many Spokan said how their grandparents and great-grandparents were extremely careful when gathering their own smoking ingredients for fear of being poisoned by a malcontent or a sorcerer who wanted to harm or kill them:

> They tell how my great grandfather, who couldn't speak English, was a very powerful person [shaman]. One day [ca. 1860?] a woman came to his home for a visit. No one knows, but for some reason he went outside and after a while came in again, but the woman was gone. After a while, he must've mixed his pipe tobacco, but as soon as he started to smoke he knew something was wrong, 'cause the tobacco tasted and smelled kinda [sic] strange. He asked his daughter who had been out back if the woman visitor had fooled with his tobacco, but she only knew the visitor had been near his place. He died within three weeks. No one really knew how it happened,

506

but they suspected the visitor had put some small shavings of *m'sm'sáwiʔ* root ("little" *m'sáwiʔ*) into his tobacco bag (Ross 1968-2008).

With the arrival and residence of trapper-traders, many eastern Plateau Indians developed a taste for commercially made plug *chewing tobacco* (*q'ʷeʔq'ʷeʔsmen'xʷ*), which was frequently used as full or partial payment to Indians for their services.

Stone, Clay, Wooden, and Copper Pipes

A *tube* or *straight pipe* (*sntxmélc'eʔ*) and the *elbow pipe* (*snmén'xʷtn*) were made by the Spokan from steatite; whereas the preferred red, green, and black soapstone elbow pipes were acquired through trade with eastern groups, such as the Flathead and Coeur d'Alene; often originating from trade with Plains groups:

> Pipes were of soapstone of various colors, red and black being the most common. Catlinite was procured from Plains tribes and also from the Shoshoni. A red soapstone, duller in color than catlinite, was obtained near Pend Oreille Lake; a brown kind from the Coeur d'Alene country and occasionally green, yellow, white, gray, and mottled from western tribes. Black soapstone was common in the Flathead country (Teit 1930:380).

Some elbow and straight *smoking pipes* (*mmám'xʷt*) were of catlinite, and some were of "talc schist with some mixture of actinolite. Talc schist is similar to steatite but more schistose" (Collier *et al.* 1942:72). Catlinite platform pipes (named after George Catlin who first observed such a Plains quarry) were commonly procured as a finished product in trade with Plains groups, and were considered quite valuable by their new owners. Blanks of both black and red catlinite were traded onto the Plateau from Plains groups for completion. The archaeological record suggests that the tubular pipe was not only the most frequently found type among the Spokan, but that "the tubular pipe was the only form in the Plateau in prehistoric times, and that it was supplanted in recent times by bowl [platform] and elbow forms from the east" (Collier *et al.* 1942:72-4).

Metal pipes were acquired in trade from trapper-traders, but were apparently few in number—probably in the form of a dual pipe-hatchet, as Wilson noted when describing an example of a trade tomahawk, which was "a small hatchet with a pipe head at the back; they seem to be mostly made at Birmingham or in the eastern states of America" (1866:297).

The most definitive but unpublished study of the making of Plateau Salish stone pipes is by Schaeffer (1934-37, I-131-133). The general shape of any pipe was first made by working the stone to a rough form, followed by constant and laborious repeated rubbing with an abrasive flat hand-piece of granite or sand stone, and then brought to its final shape by abrading with wet sandstone. Some archaeologically recovered elbow pipes (Collier *et al.* 1942) were crafted with a narrow, rectangular footing below and to the rear of the bowl, and there are several examples of platform pipes with expressive relief modifications of the sections supporting the bowl.

A finished stone pipe was smeared with salmon, eel oil or slime, rubbed into the stone and allowed to dry, and then rubbed with *horsetail* (*Equisetum laevigatum* L. - *tkʷtin'* or *t'uxʷen'* or *t'úxʷn'* - "jointed grass growing in water")—a scouring weed that has an epidermis impregnated with silicon—thereby giving the pipe a *smooth finish* (*t'ec'*). Pipes were periodically treated by carefully rubbing with either animal fat or fish oil.

A straight wooden round pipe was made by drilling a 15 to 20 cm length from any of the later mentioned stem woods, with a stone-hafted bow drill, or by rotating a stone-tipped shaft of hard-wood between one's palms while holding the stout stem in a secured vertical position—often held between one's knees while sitting. Once the narrow inside stem passage had been drilled, a larger cavity for tobacco was made on the larger end, packed tightly with near-wet clay, and then permitted to adequately dry. Then it was bored with a much larger stone-headed drill, so that the bowl became large enough to accommodate tobacco, and thick enough to prevent it from being burned or scorched. Though not known, it is conceivable that before

507

smoking, a man would first remove the often cracked broken clay bowl liner before carefully re-lining the inside with moist clay, which was permitted to dry before smoking.

As noted, the forms of stone and clay tubular pipes varied in length and diameter, ranging in length from 5 to nearly 15 cm. The tobacco chamber or bowl seldom had parallel sides, but was rather "bell-shaped" (Collier *et al.* 1942:161), which was not a common shape since a straight sandstone pipe required less effort to manufacture than a stone elbow or platform pipe—despite it being more fragile than other types of stone, but more stable than a clay pipe. There is no evidence that pipe bowls were fashioned from horn or bone. Pipes were probably not made from clay, primarily because of their fragility, though the Sinkaietk apparently were known to use clay for making pipes (Post and Cummons 1938:65; Teit 1930:278).

Nothing is recorded or remembered as to what age a young man commenced to smoke, or a young woman. As near as can be determined, a woman seldom smoked a pipe (Teit 1930:165) until she was an elder, and then most likely in solitude, "When there was less noise and she had more time for her thoughts and reflections." There are, however, accounts of a group of close but unrelated elderly women who, after a *late afternoon* (*čwoss*) sweat, shared a pipe, "after closing and putting the sweathouse to sleep." One elderly lady remembered how, as a young woman, she had been given a small black stone elbow pipe by her Sinkaietk grandmother—a pipe that was smoked with a very short extended wooden mouthpiece.

Pipes were frequently given names by their owners; all pipes used in curing were named. Pipes used in curing rituals received differential care as they were cleansed to maintain their appearance and appease their spiritual power; even sung to, oiled, and rubbed after use. A curing shaman would put his pipe to "bed" by carefully wrapping it in a small tanned animal hide, then feeding the bowl small bits of tobacco that were mixed with special plants to demonstrate and reinforce the shaman's established relationship with the pipe. A shaman's pipe—being sacred—had the power to transmit and receive communiqués from one's guardian spirit regarding the nature of another's illness and the required treatment. Elmendorf was told, with no further recorded information of its ritual use, of a *courier pipe* (*snmán'x*ᵂ*tn*) (1935-6, 2:43).

Schaeffer's work regarding pipe making amongst the Plateau-speaking Salish, led him to conclude that "The skill to make good pipes was obtained through experience and was not obtained from any supernatural" (1934-37, I-131:2).

Pipes recovered archaeologically from two major sites at *Fort Spokane* (*č'łiyáq'i*) (Caywood 1952 and 1954; Combes 1962, 1964; Pfeiffer 1981:222) include some pipes of wood, sometimes "in exact reproduction of a clay pipe" (Caywood 1952:11), used along with a trade pipe made of copper. It is not clear if these and other artifacts were actually used or intended exclusively for the Spokan or for resident soldiers at Fort Spokane, or if "the collection of pipes reflected the poverty and ingenuity of the owner" (Caywood 1954:23). The most complete study of trade clay pipes is by Pfeiffer, one that "provides a continuum in a single artifact category which spans the pacific Northwest Fur Trade from 1810 to 1871" (1981:221).

Pipe Stems

Prior to the frequency of trade and influence with Plains groups, stone elbow and tube pipes seldom had wooden or bone stems. But it is not known if the Spokan traditionally incised or painted any *wooden pipe stem* (*snt'péptn* or *snmenx*ᵂ*tn* or *t'píptm*), though incised stone pipe bowls have been found (STHC), and Ray concluded that "All [pipes] were small in size; stems were seldom longer than three inches" (1933:168). There is no evidence that the Spokan did silver inlay work on pipes, or acquired such pipes through trade. The most common wood for making pipe stems was generally rosehip bush (Elmendorf 1935-6, 1:6), whereas Schaeffer (1934-37, I-133) noted how the Flathead used a select branch of Rocky Mountain ash.

As noted, the first wooden and sectional stone mouthpiece extensions were probably a later introduction from the Plains, being round, oval, or flat (rectangular) in shape. Upon acquisition, wooden pipe extensions were decorated with strips of untanned animal hide, and sometimes with attached feathers hanging from the bowl end of the stem. Elbow pipes were usually smoked with an attached wooden mouthpiece; preferably made from hollowed sections of snowberry bush, rosehip bush, thimbleberry, or willow, or by removing the pithy center of a small section of mock orange which was first allowed to dry before attaching to the pipe. The pith was easily removed after the section of wood dried, for the pith shrank, permitting easy removal by carefully twisting it out. Most pipe stems were rectangular (in cross-section) and approximately 30 cm in length, with the mouth end was tapered flat on each of the four sides. The end inserted into the pipe had a gradual rounded end, being held in place by pressure. One elder recalled seeing a pipe stem fashioned from the long bone of a heron.

Pipe, Tobacco, and Utility Pouches

A Spokan man always carried with him a *pipe bag* (*snč'iséh*), varying in length and width, depending upon the size of the pipe, and was most commonly made from a long rectangular section of buckskin with both long edges sewn together and the bottom stitched closed. Dried grass was sometimes bunched together and stuffed into the bottom of the pipe container to protect the pipe from damage in case the bag was accidentally dropped. A pipe bag was closed by bunching the open top together with an attached buckskin string. The longest pipe bag was a Plain's type, measuring 35 to 40 cm in length, and from 12 to 15 cm in circumference.

A pipe bag made from the hide of weasel or badger was highly prized, particularly one made from *otter fur* (*ltkʷélxʷ*) with the tail attached. It is not certain if Spokan pipe bags were ever decorated by painting; but it was recalled that some had beaded designs, and some men's pipe bags were decorated with flattened and dyed porcupine quills much earlier.

Medicine bundles frequently contained tobacco, but seldom a pipe, which usually had its own special hide container. A known exception was an elderly Sinkaietk woman, married to a Spokan, and a reputed sorcerer, who carried a small stone elbow pipe and tobacco in her tanned deer hide medicine bundle, along with several small crystals and nodules of ochre (Ross 1964-1967). It was reported that in the past a shaman may have a *bag made from unborn fawn* (*snʔaw'pel'xʷ*), preferably a *spotted fawn* (*sɫpaʔpí* or *spapíčaʔqn* - "with white spots"), or even a *yearly fawn* (*sqʷqʷɫyew's* or *ʕukʷmukʷ*), in which he carried his medicines, often along with a small tube pipe and tobacco. Given a shaman's abilities and particular power, the tube pipe was favored often for removing an intruded object or malevolent spirit by sucking with the tube pipe.

When traveling, a man wore a *tobacco pouch* (*snčísemntn* or *snč'ísemn*) that contained a strike-a-light for lighting his pipe. For security and protection of the contents, the pouch was a *long, drawstring bag* (*čk'ʷxʷew's*), which often was secured by his belt, and usually decorated with symbolic art that often represented the owner's tutelary spirit. Another type of tobacco pouch was essentially a *small drawstring bag* (*nqʷusp*) to safeguard against the loss of tobacco, or one with a flap on top that could be secured with a top wrap-around strip of buckskin to safely contain the tobacco, which was suspended by a buckskin loop around the man's neck. Some pipe bags had two compartments: one for the dried tobacco and the other for a pipe. Prior to the influx of the longer Plains Indian sectional pipe, the short Spokan pipe did not require a special pipe bag. But once adopted, the longer Plains pipe was carried and protected in such a container. All tobacco pouches were made using one of two methods: the simplest was to cut a section of buckskin with two lobes, fold it over, and sew from the center of the bottom up the two adjoining sides, leaving an opening at the neck of the bag, which was closed by a strip of attached buckskin. The second method required two separate sections of patterned buckskin being joined by stitching the entire circumference, except for the intended opening. Weasel skin made an attractive tobacco pouch.

Tobacco pouch designs were achieved primarily by applying moistened mineral dyes, ones not as durable as plant dyes when working on buckskin. Relief designs were made by the application of flattened and colored porcupine quills. Utility and ceremonial pouches were frequently decorated with typically significant animal bones or bird claws, often representing a particular tutelary spirit. Examples with painted designs—from the early historical period—still exist among a very few Spokan. Such a tobacco pouch, which belonged to an elderly lady, was seen and admired by the author some years ago. With the pouch was a small, black stone elbow pipe that had been her father's, and still used by the elder daughter.

In addition to the tobacco pouch, every man carried within a utilitarian pouch a *knife* (*n'ín'č'm'n'*) and a tool kit containing a *thorn* (*k'ʷalaʔiɬm'l'š*) for removing splinters and for *pinning* (*kʷaʔlá*) clothing, a strike-a-light, some tinder, and a ball of hemp. Women carried a small tool bag containing thumb scrapers, awls, needles, and thread; these were used when visiting or traveling. Elderly Spokan women continued to wear a worn cardigan sweater with two pockets, one with tissues or a handkerchief for the noses of her grandchildren. The other pocket invariably contained several fishing hooks and line, in the hope of persuading any visiting anthropologist to take her fishing, while they surveyed sections of the Spokane River.

Chapter XVI: Games, Dances, and Music

Maintaining a successful adaptation as foragers demanded that any highly-mobile foraging people achieve and maintain abilities in strength, endurance, and manipulative skills. However, living as hunters and gatherers afforded the Spokan considerable leisure time—certainly for the men. Free time was often devoted to games, dancing, music, and other forms of entertainment. None of these social activities was irrelevant or without additional benefits, particularly for developing cooperation skills, individual expression, and maintaining hand-eye coordination necessary in hunting, fishing, and warfare—even entertaining grandchildren.

Leisure activities as well as compulsory physical and intellectual activities assisted all young boys and girls in their physical and social development. Many of these activities served as enculturative devices between generations, stressing individualism as well as encouraging collective cooperation. Participating and supervising gave elders status, respect, responsibility, and worth, often regardless of an elder's age. When making reference to an older person's strength and athletic ability, it was often said, "Only when a man was a grandfather would he speak of his past [athletic achievements]." Gambling games facilitated the redistribution of property (on occasion asymmetrically), always through the implementation of power, and of course was a way of even acquiring status, if only temporarily. Forms of entertainment provided welcome leisure and respite from required tasks, and served many social and physical health functions that promoted a person's integration within a community and between groups.

Spokan children spent less time with their parents and more time with their aunts, uncles, and grandparents who taught them how to *play* (*memscút*) games, ones who often made toys required by various games and activities. But now, the few remaining elders complain how children's free time is dominated by television and computer games, which being passive promotes inactivity, obesity, poor health, and invariably fewer social skills. Another unfortunate and unhealthy dimension to staying indoors is that fewer children play outside or explore their surroundings, thereby not acquiring the experience and knowledge of an environment that was once essential to their physical and spiritual survival.

Games

Games (*c'iʕana* or *x̣ʷláɫq*), such as gambling, and contests testing strength, endurance, certain spiritual power and hand-eye coordination, were favorite pastimes for the Spokan. Numerous gambling games played by men and women indicated just how dedicated they were; some gaming could last for several days, and frequently saw the gain or loss of sizable quantities of traditional forms of wealth. Undoubtedly, the most important gambling game was the stick-game, which often involved several villages. Success in nearly all games was based largely on hand-eye skill, memory, and often individual religious power. Many games were typically accompanied by singing, drumming, and, on occasion, dancing. A gambling song was called *sélálqʷm*.

Children were expected to be very circumspect in their behavior when in the presence of adults, tending to speaking only when spoken to, and seldom engaging in certain types of games, unless encouraged to do so by an adult. Most male and female elders recall how quickly they were admonished if they became foolish and behaved like a *clown* (*swxpoʔsmscot*), *acted silly* (*w'el'm'scut*), or even *spoke silly* (*tékʷn'cnm'ist*) in the presence of an adult. The worst thing anyone could do was "running one's mouth" or "talk of something you know nothing about" (*x̣ʷt'pawʔsqn*). This situation would happen, claimed one elderly man, "but only my grandmother would *wink* [*nčip'sm*] and warn me when no one else would."

Elders often related pleasant memories of when, as children, they experienced many enjoyable times away from the camp or village, hunting or checking their traps. Unfortunately, the nature and knowledge of leisure activities, games, and athletic contests have changed dramatically during the late historical and contemporary period, largely because of the effects that white culture has wrought upon Amerindian cultures. Perhaps the most devastating aspect of this cultural change—one that drastically altered attitudes toward leisure—was the introduction and social enforcement of the so-called Protestant Ethic and its concept of regulated and apportioned time. These notions were the antithesis of the Spokan *Weltanschauung*, who, as hunters and gatherers, possessed a lifestyle that afforded considerable leisure time, particularly for the extended family. Increments of hours and named days did not exist. Missionaries and certain government agencies believed that the Indians' enlightenment and ultimate conversion to a *world* (*st'úlixʷ*) of agriculture and industry, required strict adherence to a regulated time and work schedule and ethic. The games that allowed and encouraged interaction, affirmation, and cohesion among these people, sadly gave way to white cultural activities and perception of leisure time. Even the Christian tenet of the Protestant Ethic stipulated the dire consequences for one if he deviated from missionized paradigms of industry, threatening in their *devil's talk* (*č'ɬʔaxʷʔaxʷkʷniʔ* - "he is coaxing")

Elderly women would excel—as well as instruct grandchildren—in the use of various mnemonic devices as aides in the telling of lengthy stories and myths. One such popular device was the *sucker fish skull* (*sčánaʔqn*), which is composed of numerous bones whose shapes are representative of different land mammals. A storyteller would hold individual bones while relating long accounts of the particular animal represented, and stories of the origin and physical development of the animal. For example, one particular bone would represent an ungulate horn or antler (STHC).

Children spent considerable time emulating adult behavior by playing with dolls and other toys that represented adult activities and responsibilities. Both children and adults participated in games of endurance that involved stone-lifting, stone-putting, tug-of-war, jumping, swimming, and even holding one's breath competitively for long periods of time while under water. Games of dexterity—such as ring-and-pin, hop-and-stick, and cat's cradle—were popular and, during the winter storytelling by elders, cat's cradle was a favorite for both young and old.

Women often participated in and competed with men in games and contests, and men frequently requested women with exceptional skill participate with them in certain games. Endurance sports contributed to men's skills required for success in fishing, hunting, and warfare. Consequently, older children were encouraged to participate in games and sporting events if they hoped to develop the physical skills necessary for adult activities (Ross 1988). Boys would be favored with *small bows* (*cckʷín'č*) and *arrows* (*t't'aʔpm'in'*) used in peer competition. Girls presumably never played with boys' toys, nor did boys play with girls' toys. Furthermore, older girls and boys seldom played together, though a father might fashion a *toy* (*m'l'm'el'čst*) for his daughter—less so a mother for her son. It was believed that it was only proper that a strict division of labor of the adult world should commence with the use of children's toys. With boys, an active avuncular role by one's mother's or father's brother was apparent. Uncles—given circumstances and residence patterns—sometimes spent more of their leisure time with nephews than did a boy's father.

Several types of children's toys were revealed by the government-sponsored and extensive 1939-40 pre-dam archaeological excavations (Collier 1942 *et al.*). There were several well-preserved examples of wooden watercraft found in the grave of a small boy; each craft had a pointed bow and stern. Several miniature bows and arrows were found, which may not have been toys. "Possibly they had some religious or magical significance" (Collier *et al.* 1942:101).

As cited, adult games and associated skills were based primarily upon hand-eye coordination and physical conditioning, and were often prototypes of skills required for subsistence activities and warfare. For instance, when men gathered at spring and early summer fishing sites to rebuild, repair, and secure fishing weirs. Sometimes repositioning large anchor stones against fast-moving water, they engaged in weight-lifting, stone-throwing, and wrestling matches. Consequently, abilities of strength and coordination were necessary,

512

and men who displayed prowess in any of these physical abilities, could acquire nicknames among their peers—names that recognized their abilities to lift heavy stones or perform other related physical tasks.

Wrestling

A common competitive activity among men was wrestling, including free wrestling, Greco-Roman wrestling, and a form of standing-leg wrestling that prohibited *kicking* (*tr'qsqélix*ʷ*m*), where only leg sweeps and hip throws were permitted. Though the rules varied according to participants, a winner was declared when an opponent was thrown free or forced to his knees (Ray 1933). Ray described that among the Sanpoil, a victor, in addition to winning his bets, "was privileged to turn upon his opponent and cuff or kick him without the latter offering any resistance" (1933:166). Younger women would competitively and publicly *wrestle* (*q'mnwéx*ʷ or *sq'mnwé* - "holding each other"), and were often the subject of betting by both sexes. Women never did leg wrestling or threw another to the ground; rather one won the contest by pushing and shoving or holding onto to each other's dress sleeves to immobilize her opponent. Men and older boys competed in arm-wrestling.

In all competitive physical activities involving contact with an opponent, particularly wrestling, a concern was that a competitor never lost his temper, which could have dire consequences, warranting either verbal humiliation or physical reprisal. Children from an early age were taught *never* to "lose his or her strength and reasoning" when angry, for they would become disoriented and unpredictable, and thereby not trustworthy by others in later stressful situations.

Kicking Game

Only men engaged in what was called a *kicking game* (*stʔlqaʔnuw'* or *stlqnwéx*ʷ), when two men—using only their feet—would kick each other in what was basically a free-for-all, until one verbally announced his withdrawal. On occasion, several visiting teams would compete, as reported by Teit (1930:135):

> Often 30 or more men played on a side. They formed two rows, facing each other, and after taunting each other, at a given signal by the "chief" of the game they rushed forward in close formation and kicked each other until one line fell back. Sometimes the two opposing rows were drawn up close together or within striking distance and lines made on the ground close behind each. At a signal they began kicking, and which ever side pushed the other back over the line won. When a man was forced back over his own line by an adversary he was out of the game.

Prior to a contest, participants were warned never to kick an opponent in the genital area, otherwise the guilty person or team lost the match. It was understood that a person should never severely kick a *rival* (*ʔewtús*) above the waist, since the kicking game could be quite dangerous if an opponent inflicted a traumatic injury to a person's liver or kidneys, or broke an opponent's ribs.

Despite the agreed upon rules, one can only wonder how restrictive this would be during the heat of "battle," particularly when during a contest men and women were audibly betting on the outcome, thereby intensifying and extending the duration of the combatants, who in turn probably responded to the vocal support by the crowd. It was claimed that observers often declared the winner by cheering more loudly for the man whom they judged to have won.

Stone-Throwing and Lifting

Stone-throwing was done with relatively round stones of varying size and weight, involving one of two methods of throwing the stone for a measured distance. The first method was not unlike the present day procedure of putting the shot-put with one hand, whereas the second method required a contestant to lift the stone with both hands in one motion as he attempted to press the stone above his head. Once in position, the contestant simultaneously jumped straight up and pushed the stone away as far as possible. An observer marked the distance, and an opponent used the same stone and attempted to surpass the distance in a different or the same direction.

Another contest of strength involved lifting an unusually heavy stone, much like doing a dead-lift, that required the contestant to lift the stone by wrapping both arms about the stone as much as possible, standing erect, if possible, with the stone. At low water, there remain on an exposed bed of the Spokane River, several large weir pylon stones that are reputed to have been used in this game (Ross 1993). There was no recollection as to whether games of strength were in any way dependent upon a certain contestant's *suméš*.

Pulling

Many contestant games involved pulling or tugging an opponent, providing exercise as well as entertainment. Such games included neck pulling, whereby two contestants looped a circular section of plaited rawhide rope over their heads, attempting to dislodge one another, or pull their opponent over a line marked on the ground. As noted, individual and collective pulling contests were invariably subject to intense betting by non-participants who supported their chosen team by loudly shouting encouragement and praise for the slightest advance.

On a much larger scale, tug-of-war involved two teams of ten or more men and women—opposite one another—pulling a long plaited rawhide rope. A team was declared the winner when it pulled the other team across a designated line.

A variation on the above tugging contests was a sport called *finger-pulling* (*sq'álx^wn'wx^w* - "hooking one another"), or sometimes called finger-hooking, in which two older boys or men would pair off; each person hooked his middle finger with his opponent's, and then pulled until the winner straightened the other's finger. The game could be won prematurely without straightening the other's finger if one opponent succeeded in pulling his opponent across a line drawn in the earth, or by dislodging the other from his footing. Women were not known to play this game because the obvious danger of *dislocation* (*mawłł scom* - "bone dislocation") of fingers.

Older Spokan informants related how their elders recounted to them, in what would probably have been the late protohistoric period, how teams would have their own songs, always profane, used primarily to coordinate the collective physical efforts and psychological intensity during a large team contest. As with nearly all adult games, participants and spectators placed wagers on their favorite person or team.

Hopping

There are only a few ethnographic references of any significance regarding hopping; one is by Smith (1936-8:966) who described an endurance game that several Spokan could recall, but with little or no detail. He explained how the so-called *hopping game* (*esq'q'^{'w}a?ƛƛ'q'^{'w}é?i* - "imitating the prairie chicken dance") was staged by both young and old males and females, often with one gender challenging the other—a contest which was invariably won by women. A variation of this was a summer game that required men to squat on their heels with their hands on their parted knees, whereas the women playing the game squatted, but with their hands clasped to hold their knees tightly together. The object of the game, for both men and women, was to see who could hop the greatest distance in one leap, or over a set distance in a given time, or to win by hopping to a designated object or line in the ground before the others.

That women often won at hopping is interesting, since boys training to receive their *suméš* were known to have been instructed to do this strenuous exercise almost daily by their mentors (Elmendorf 1935-6, 2:61). An elderly lady said men would never win because they laughed so much at the women's performance. There was a different version of this athletic event:

> They have 2 lines and the players face each other and bounce back and forth from one line to the other *íy'á?há?hí?*, *'á?há?hí?* is what the men say. The girls are humming a high *m'm'm'm'*, *m'm'm'm'*. They have got

to learn to sit up like that; they fall over the first time. There is either one or two on each side; there is never more than 2 on each side. It is a test of endurance [...] They take a little, short, quick jump. It makes no difference how fast they go from one line to the other; one keeps right up with the other. When one looses [sic] time he has got to stop and usually falls over from fatigue. There is no gambling on this game: it was just a pastime. The lines are about 4 or 5 feet apart (Smith 1936-8:966).

Body-Spinning

Throughout the year only children played a non-competitive game of body-spinning that involved a boy or girl spinning until *dizzy* (*snsnlmtu*) and falling to the ground or upon the snow. Some recall how when spinning, and before falling down, they would attempt to walk a certain distance, or walk up a hill, or through an obstacle course. There was no point to the game, only to act and feel foolish, as one old lady recalled. This was a particularly difficult activity when in snow, an effort called *šrrótmqn* (Carlson and Flett 1989:271).

Spinning Tops

Both Chewelah-Spokan and Kalispel girls and boys played a game of *spinning tops* (*seʔsíʔƛyeʔe* or *sʔsíʔƛiyʔ* - "something thin and spinning around") throughout the year, but mostly during winter evenings when confined by inclement weather and outside darkness. But some people played the game in late winter to encourage the coming of spring (Smith 1936-8:969). Tops were made from a fashioned circular section of thick bark, or occasionally from an appropriate piece of thin driftwood that was further shaped. Through the middle would be a center-hole, fashioned to accommodate a hardwood stick that was thick enough to fill the center-hole, but long enough for children to take between their palms to spin. The diameter of the disc varied from 8 to12 cm, and the spinning post was approximately 12 to 14 cm in length. Balance was best achieved by an exact centering of the post, and making the lower part have the same length as the upper section. Some tops were decorated on the upper side with charcoal or hematite dots that appeared as connecting patterns when spun, further delighting the children.

The object of the game was to see who could spin their top the longest, which meant everyone had to release their tops simultaneously. This was done by tightly holding the upper end of the shaft between a contestant's two palms, and on the release signal he put the top in motion by quickly pulling the right hand backwards while pushing the left hand forward. A snow-swept section of a frozen pond provided the best surface for top-spinning. At the end of winter, both the Spokan and Kalispel would throw their tops in the fire, and new ones made again with winter confinement (Smith 1936-8:969). The use of string- or hemp-spun tops was a concept introduced by Euro-Americans.

Stick-game

At large gatherings, the most important and often intense physically competitive adult game was the *stick-game* (*xaʔxeʔwils* or *scʼlalqʷi*), sometimes called the *bone stick-game* (*kʼʷunʼkʼʷí*), and remains today a popular form of entertainment and a contest when people can *gamble* (*xcxcím*). Depending upon the time of year and the weather, the game was played either inside or outside on a site that could accommodate numerous players and observers.

The primary objective of the stick-game was to see which of the two teams could acquire—mainly by guessing, legerdemain, and use of individual *suméš*, even sorcery—the most sticks from their opponents.

The game called for two teams facing one another, often sitting on robes or blankets. The members of each team were seated in a row side by side facing their opponents who sat in a row directly in front of them, separated by a distance of approximately 1.5 to 2 m. The leaders (team captains) always sat in the middle of their respective teams. Teams were also further separated by two long parallel rows of poles or logs laid end-to-end, called the *pounding boards* or *poles* (*sčlalqʷ*), behind which each team sat and which served for pounding in rhythm upon with their sticks.

There was no limit to the size of a team. Games have been played with as many as twenty or thirty players to a side, and there have been games with only one, two, or three players to a side. A stick-game could last for a day and even throughout the night, when several fires were lit for visibility. And some have said how in the past, a powerful game could last for several nights and days. When the phrase *they are going to play a stick-game* (*qsc'lálqʷi* or *čsp'álqʷm*) was heard, everyone was indeed happy.

Both men and women could be players in a stick-game, not being segregated by gender. *Stick-game bones* (*kʷn'k'ʷin'* or *huy'ussn*) (Culin 1907:308) used by women were smaller in diameter and slightly shorter than those used by men. Men played with bones that were approximately 6.5 to 7.4 cm in length, and from 1.5 to 2.0 cm in diameter. The bones were always in sets of four and near-identical in length and diameter. "Some bones were made from deer horn or a section of a deer's tibia just above the ankle. One of each pair of bones was a 'chief', one with no markings, and a second bone was always marked with two or three [black] lines in the center that circle the bone" (Anon. 1967a:n.p.).

More specifically, each set of four bones consisted of two pairs, and for each pair one bone would be marked with a black strip around the middle, and the other would be plain white. Only rarely would a *player* (*sxʷc'lálqʷm*) mark a bone by encircling it with a single, blackened strip of twice-wrapped and thinly shaven rawhide, usually 2 to 3 mm in width. The leather band would be secured in the middle of the bone by first removing a circumference of bone so that the top of the band was flush with the surface of the bone. Gaming bones appeared as ivory in color, and completely smooth in texture having been rubbed during many years of use (Culin 1975:308).

In his extensive survey of Plateau stick gaming, Brunton described how some gaming bones were manufactured from human bones, whereby providing the player with greater powers of deduction when guessing:

> Using gambling bones manufactured from the bones of a famous gambler made one practically unbeatable, but at a certain amount of risk. For example, a story was related in which a person made such a pair of bones from a deceased woman. He enjoyed a fantastic run of luck. However, at night a ghost of the woman appeared to him and insisted on sleeping with him. He finally was forced to get rid of the bones, after which the ghost never again appeared (1994:587).

Elders said how they would protect their bones—when not is use—by wrapping them in a fur hide that represented their tutelary spirit, and then carefully put them away so that no one could get to them, presumably to inhibit the bones' loss of power. One elder said his grandfather had a set of special bones that had power, because the deer from which they had been made had purposely presented himself to be killed, so that his grandfather could use the bones from the deer's legs.

Prior to a stick-game, participants often took a sweat and propitiated their guardian spirit (*sumés̆*) for success. A player usually attempted to enhance his or her odds of winning by secreting on their person or in their clothes "bits of rosehip leaves, [the] stem and flowers to keep evil spirits away" (Anon. 1967:n.p.). Or a person might receive *gambling power* (*xcxcmí*) or *good luck in gambling* (*xsstél'*) by catching a juvenile western blue-tailed lizard; if it released its tail off in the individual's hand, then the person would have good luck (STHC).

Traditionally, the game used twenty-one sticks, each with a sharp point at one end. But over time, nearly all Indian groups reduced the number of sticks—usually by mutual consent of the participants–to eleven or fifteen, so that the games take less time. Counter sticks for the game were sometimes made of ocean spray, but preferably from freshly cut serviceberry wood which hardens after being peeled, shaped, and dried in the sun. Dried, whitened serviceberry looks just like bleached bone, and some individuals would finish their counter sticks by burying the bones in moist wood ashes for several or more days, thereby bleaching them so that they had an almost white appearance. Elders recalled how in the past a young man was cautioned "to never reveal where he harvested the wood" (Anon. 1967:n.p.) that he had gathered for making the counting sticks.

In recent times—after two teams had agreed to play one another—a collection of individual cash wagers would be made, which in the past consisted of horses, saddles, blankets, shawls, and other personal articles that were waged on the outcome of the game. Some have said how even weapons were waged. Also, in the past, scores were tallied by a person using his own method of tallying the score, whereas today one member on each side carries a notebook or blank paper on which each individual wager is recorded. The cumulative wagers were totaled, and after a reasonable period of time, the wagers would be matched and the money placed in a large handkerchief or scarf placed on the ground midway between the two teams. However, before Indians learned to write, the team leaders committed the individual wagers to memory, and when the game was won the winnings were distributed to the participants without any error being made (Anon. 1967:n.p.).

At the outset, the counter sticks were distributed ten to a side, and *one stick* (*nk'ʷalqʷ*)—the kick stick—was embedded by its point in the ground midway between the two teams. Each team leader then embedded in the ground each of the ten sticks that had been distributed to his team. These sticks were arranged in a neat row in front of the pounding board.

In most of the games, each team leader usually had a set of four bones, which he hoped would be selected for use in conducting the guessing contests that would determine the game. Initially, to determine which leader could choose which four bones would be used, and which side would take possession of the kick stick, each leader would take a pair of his team's bones (one of them plain white, the other with a black stripe) and conceal them under a hat, scarf, blanket, shirttail, or an adjacent woman's long dress. A player then moved the bones back and forth under cover to deceive the opposing team leader. Next he would bring them out of cover, but held out of view in each closed hand as he crossed his arms over his chest. The leader then guessed which hand of the opposing leader held the plain white bone, indicating his choice by pointing. Participants preferred the term "pointer" to "guesser" since there was much more to the challenge than random guessing. Naturally, since the *stick-game bones were shaken and hidden by an opponent* (*ʔu miʔnɬtm*), there was no assurance that the pointer would be correct. If one leader did choose correctly, and the other did not, then the winning leader took both pairs of his team's bones, acquiring the kick stick for his side. He had the choice of deciding which set of four bones were to be put into play for the duration of the game. During these machinations of juggling and concealing the bones, each leader would make false motions so as to gauge the other leader's facial reaction (Ray 19332b:156).

One technique—often a power-based skill—was for a bone-hider to surreptitiously *switch bones* (*c'aq'm' ín'eʔ*) after he was pointed at. This legerdemain was of course a form of *cheating* (*ʔenc'oq'm'ín'ʔey'* or *nc'q'm'ín'm'*). Some of the phrases one might have heard during a game were: "matching bones for the *kick stick*" (*mal'l'qʷew'éy'*) (STHC); "he won the kick stick and a few sticks right off, but lost the bones when he pointed the game without winning back the bones"; or "*I am going to point you*" (*kʷ ʔiqsc'óq'ʷm*) (STHC).

The winning team's leader won the right to be the first to start their chant, always accompanied by the pounding of sticks in unison on their respective pounding board. However, "old timers never used [a] pole to pound [their] sticks, rather they swung their hands, palms up from side to side in time with their song; never bet money, bet shawls" (STHC). *Stick-game songs* (*st'slálaqm*) were numerous and each person had *their own song* (*sne'lalqʷm* or *sc'llálqʷm*), though rarely were there words to any of the chants; rather they were characterized more by a particular tune. After the chanting had commenced, and the players began pounding with their sticks, the team leader handed out the bones, usually one pair to a player to the left of him, and the other pair to the player to his right. However, this was not mandatory since he could select any player of his choice to shake the bones. An important part of the game was what has been called "sudden death."

After all of the upright sticks have been expended by wrong guesses, the sticks that have changed sides during the course of the game and are now behind the pounding board are then surrendered for each wrong guess.

It is "sudden death" from then on and the game ends when one side runs out of sticks. In some games, one player may have a long run of good luck and his opponents miss on every guess until they have lost all of their sticks. Such a player is then said to have made a "home run." This is also a very recent vernacular expression [sic] in games that run longer than usual, players may leave the game and are replaced by other players who also have wagers placed on the outcome of the game. Many side bets are made between individuals after the pot has been closed to further betting. There are no bookmakers and one must promote his own bet by financing some one [sic] to call or match his bet. The stakes are placed in the open area between the two teams (Anon. 1967:n.p.).

The object of the game was for an opposing member to guess which hand held the plain bone—the one without the marking. For guessing wrong, the guesser's side was penalized one stick for each miss on each pair of bones. If the guesser was unable to guess correctly on both pairs, he had to surrender *two sticks* (*ʔaslálqʷ*) to his opponents. The opposing leader then attempted to guess the hands holding the plain white bones by the two players on the other team. When both pairs of bones were in possession of one team, the guesser could indicate his guess by any of four hand signs. A person might point with his hand or index finger either to his right or left. That meant he was guessing that each opposing player was holding the plain white bone in the left or right hand, depending on the direction the finger was pointing to. Or he could point with his index finger straight down, which meant that he was guessing that the opposing players were holding the plain white bones in their inside hands (i.e., that the player on the right facing the guesser had the white bone in his right hand, and the player to the left facing the guesser held the plain bone in his left hand). This was known as the inside guess. The other sign was when the guesser extended his arm straight away from him with the palm up and the fingers closed, with only the *thumb* (*stúm'čst*) and the *index finger* (*sc'oqʷʼⁿm'n*) extended to make a sign of victory. This was the *outside guess* (*p'arqíc'eʔ*), and the guesser won if the white bones were held in the outside hands. If he succeeded in guessing one pair, he was said to have scored a single, and he scored a double if he guessed correctly on both pairs of bones. When the pointer was faking points to conceal which hand holds the plain bone, this was known as *ʔec kʷskʷusʔey'* (STHC).

Each team had various agreed upon hand signals, and even head signals to denote a decision as to whether the right or left hand had the all-important white bone. The guessing motions were as follows (let U denote the unmarked bone, and M denote the marked bone):

- the thumb and forefinger separated in front of the guesser, the other fingers flexed—"UM—UM"
- the index finger is pointed downward and the other fingers are flexed—"MU—UM"
- the left index finger points to the left—"UM—UM"
- the index finger points to the right—"MU—MU" (Ray 1933:157).

The guesser paid a penalty of one stick for every miss, and his side could not take up their chant until they had successfully won both pairs of bones. Then the other team's leader started to guess. The game's outcome was in doubt sometimes for long periods of time, particularly when the sticks changed sides and the lead was frequently won or lost by either side. The game ended when one side gained possession of all their opponents' sticks. If a team won the kick stick, but went on to eventually lose the game, they were called *šiʔtálqʷm* (STHC).

By this arrangement, it would seem that a game could be finished very quickly if a side were unusually fortunate in winning the kick stick at the outset, and then going ahead and causing a series of misses and rapidly gaining possession of the ten sticks on their opponent's side. The rules were such that when a team lost its initial ten sticks, then the side having possession of the bones must 'knock down' a stick for every miss of its opponent from the row of sticks embedded in the ground in front of the pounding board.

Elmendorf (pers. comm.) was told how sorcery was often part of the game, and, consequently, a player might have enough power to break the hand bones of an opponent. When an opponent was overpowered, the *sticks break, fall apart* (*síq't*), or when a person with power wins the last stick, "the bones in your hand break or shatter, thus breaking the victim's power so that he could not win another stick"(STHC). Another demonstration of sorcery was to make an opponent's hands close so tightly, that when winning the last stick, the person's hands had to be pried open to recover the bones. After this experience, the person may become quite ill. A malicious power could hit a person while he was hiding the bones, and the pointer would be unable to guess which hand was holding which bone. Yet, a person's power could "hit" them unexpectedly, so the other leader could not guess in which hand the opponent held the white bone, called *χaʔχaʔw'íl'š* (STHC).

Rolling Dice

Throughout the Plateau, the popular *game of rolling dice* (*sxʷxʷl'qʷúleʔxʷm'* - "he played a rolling dice game") was a gambling contest played by both women and men. It was a game with many variations of rules, and of different types of dice made from muskrat or beaver teeth, or deer bone. Examples of beaver teeth used as dice, some whole and others with numerous drilled holes, have been located by archaeologists (Collier *et al.* 1942:153). The four dice or *bones* (*míčʼmčʼeʔ*) were fashioned from beaver teeth, or from a long 16 to 20 cm section of *deer rib* (*cčʼełp*), shaped in such a way that the bones were relatively flat, but cambered lengthwise from the center to the edges. Each deer bone had almost identical dimensions and an oblong outline some 20 mm at the mid-section. The four bones were bleached white with wood ashes, yet the top or front of the bones were never decorated or marked to indicate distinction. Two of the four bones were marked with a single row of small, shallow holes, and the undersides of the remaining two bones were marked or inscribed with diagonal grooved incisions. Red or yellow hematite would be moistened and rubbed into the holes and groves to better delineate the designs. Scoring was based on the principle of guessing the value of what an opponent held, and one with the most points was determined by the *dice count* (*wáłčʼn* or *xʷícu* or *sλʼícn*).

The Kalispel, Spokan, and Kutenai usually played this game indoors throughout the year upon a *blanket* (*sicʼm*) or hide with the hair to the underside (Smith 1936-8:960). Two or four people played at a time, with a person playing until he lost. The object of the game was to play for sticks, a number that varied according to the configuration of the four thrown dice. Smith provided an explanation of the scoring system:

> If all the backs come up, the thrower wins 4 sticks from his opponent. If all the fronts come up, the thrower wins 4 sticks from his opponent. If a pair of fronts come up, the thrower wins 2 sticks regardless of what the other 2 are. If a pair of backs come up, the thrower wins nothing. There is nothing given for anything else [...] A player does not lose sticks if he looses [sic] the throw; he just looses [sic] the dice. One man does not loose [sic] his sticks until his opponent wins (1936-8:960-961).

The dice game had several other variations in the design configuration of the dice and point valuation in the scoring system, but all traditional dice games used count sticks to keep score and for concluding the final value of the winning individual or winning team. As was true with the stick-game, or any gambling game, the use of personal power was believed to have consequences.

Shinny

Similar to lacrosse, *shinny* (*spʼkʷlʼém* or *spqʷλeʔé* or *spʼukʼʷlʼem*) was a favorite game that used a *stuffed buckskin ball* (*qeʔsčʼčʼxʷum'* or *sčʼčʼúmʼeʔ* or *skʼʷkʼʷxʷúm'*), or one made of dried rawhide tightly *stuffed with hair cut from a deer hide* (*čxʷxʷicpm'*) and stitched with deer sinew. Some balls were stuffed with wet grass that were then rounded and packed before encasing. Such a ball would be propelled with a *shinny stick* (*nqʷtxʷqín* - "bent on the end," or *spqʷλeʔéti* or *p'kʼʷlʼʔetín*) made from a long, curved section of deciduous wood with the end carved to a spoon-like depression on a naturally occurring *stick with a hooked end* (*pʼókʼʷlʼe*). Twelve or more contestants made up each team and the game was usually played on a designated *shinny field* (*snpʼkʷlʼéʔtn* or *npʼkʼʷkʼʷʔeʔmíntn* or *npʼukʼʷlʼeʔmíntn*), commonly a level grass or earthen area. Shinny was restricted to men since the tactics were aggressive and quite physical, and often resulted in some serious injuries as each team, when trying to score, would attempt to propel the small ball through two upright field poles fiercely defended by the opposing team. If successful, a *goal* (*máhoʔ*) was counted if the ball passed through the opponent's upright sticks at opposite ends of the field. The length of playing fields varied from 200 to 300 m, but they had no side lines—being somewhat restricted only by the observers.

As expected, both observers and participants would wager on the game, bringing an intensity to the game that was often physically shared by spectators. A favorite and less violent form of shinny was played by both men and women. But even this mixed-gender variation was remembered to have caused injures when participants clubbed, hooked, or even kicked an opponent. A male player was forbidden to touch the ball with his hands. Fortunately, the ball was too large to conceal in one's mouth, as was possible with the Woodlands Indian game of lacrosse. During mixed games, women were reputed to be as competitive as men, but more vicious because they could use their hands and execute body blocks. It was said that field judges were present during the men's game. Fouls were part of a team's strategy, though there was no recall as to the consequences of a foul. Games played between villages sometimes expressed old hostilities, particularly when players themselves had cause to place wagers on their performance. All adult games were imitated by children who learned, honed, and tested their skills to the loud pronouncements and encouragement by parents and elders.

The strategy of both forms of shinny was for the team possessing the ball to play the ball from one side to the other as they approached the opponent's goal. If and when they reached that goal, the ball would be hit to an exceptionally fast player, who would try to break away from the group and hit the ball between the uprights. Shinny was not a game played to condition men for warfare, as occurred in the Northeast Woodlands, when games would last for many days, with entire villages following and supporting their village or clan, often traveling for many miles.

Ring Game

Numerous games were played to encourage and competitively test the skills required for successful hunting , such as the ring game. Not only did adult men enjoy playing the competitive *ring game* (*xʷlqʼʷúlʼeʔxʷtn* - "something to roll on the ground" or *x̣ʷqʼʷú* or *x̣ʷllqʼʷalʼéʔxʷtn* - "ring for game"), but older children were encouraged by parents to play this game among themselves in order to develop dexterity and hand-eye coordination needed for later adult activities. The ring game would be played on a stretch of cleared and level ground 1 m in width and approximately 6 m in length. Two low backstops—each consisting of stacked and parallel poles laid on the ground, were set up at each end of the playing area.

Each *ring* or *hoop* (*xʷlqʼʷúlʼeʔxʷtn*) was made from a section of previously water-soaked *rounded twig ring* (*qécqʼcʼƛéʔe*) of willow, and into the end of each stick one of the "two long semi-circular teeth from the center of the top jaw of the beaver" (Smith 1936-8:953) was inserted to hold the ring in a circle so it could serve as a *rolling ring* (*sqécqʼcƛeʔé*). A ring was about 12 to 15 cm in diameter, and carefully wrapped with a minimal amount of buckskin, to which were attached fifteen to twenty differently *colored beads* (*sčloʔcut*), secured around the inside perimeter of the ring. Each colored bead was assigned so many *hoop game sticks* (*ilmíntn*). Prior to acquiring trade beads, flattened sections of variously colored porcupine quills were used. Every player had a *stick* (*iƛméƛstn* or *ƛʼaq*), made from a straight piece of ocean spray about 5 cm in diameter and a meter or more in length. Beneath the mounted horn or tip was a piece of buckskin with a similar wrapping about the middle of the pole where it was gripped. Later an *iron-tipped pike* (*ilʼmʼiʕelʼ*) replaced the more traditional wooden stick.

The game was played by either two contestants or between two teams made up of an equal number of players. Certain men had reputations for their considerable skill and coordination in this activity. It was actually a form of gambling, since the score would be kept by the number of sticks each person accumulated from an initial pile of 20 sticks. The winner was the first person or team to acquire all twenty sticks. Prior to the game, each contestant selected a certain color of bead and wagered any number of sticks on that particular color. It happened that the game could become noticeably competitive, particularly with betting by observers, and hopefully quarrels were avoided:

> Elderly men known to be honest and disinterested were appealed to or asked to act as referees or arbitrators to settle all disputes in the game. These referees used slender sticks or pointers, with which they righted ring and stick, thus ascertaining accurately the position of the beads. Their decision was final (Teit 1930:131).

The game commenced with two contestants standing near one backstop, and one would roll the ring toward the opposite backstop while the other would run with the ring. When the ring hit the backstop, it would bounce into the air, and the contestant nearby would try to score by throwing his stick in such a manner as to have the ring fall on his stick—one side of the ring, and preferably the opposite side as well. They would then count the number of colored beads touching his stick. Each bead counted a different number of possible points, and a player would receive that many stick counters, based on his earlier wager. The person who ultimately had the most stick counters "when they are all gone from the pile wins" (STHC). A player would make two consecutive attempts to score before the next man tried his skill.

Paul Kane observed the same game being played at Kettle Falls by different Salish groups, including the Spokan, and provided a rather succinct description of the aforementioned game. Except for the use of trade beads, this was the more traditional version of the ring game:

> The principal game played here is called Al-kol-lock, and requires considerable skill. A smooth level piece of ground is chosen, and a slight barrier of a couple of sticks placed lengthwise, is laid at each end of the chosen spot, being forty to fifty feet apart and only a few inches high. The two players, stripped naked, are armed each with a very slight spear about three feet long, and finely pointed with bone; one of them takes a ring made of bone, or some heavy wood, and wound round with cord; this ring is about three inches in diameter, on the inner circumference of which are fastened six beads of different colours at equal distances, to each of which a separate numerical value is attached. The ring is then rolled along the ground to one of the barriers, and is followed at the distance of two or three yards by the players, and as the ring strikes the barrier and is falling on its side, the spears are thrown, so that the ring may fall on them. If only one of the spears should be covered by the ring, the owner of it counts according to the coloured bead over it. But it generally happens, from the dexterity of the players, that the ring covers both spears, and each counts according to the colour of the beads above his spear; they then play towards the other barrier, and so on until one party has attained the number agreed upon for the game (1859:217 and 1925, 7:310-11).

Spectators often danced and shouted encouragement while waging on their favorite participant. A variation of this game was to have one team compete first, followed by the other team. For a man to win, he did not need any special power, or even *sumés̆* for that matter; but certain *traditional songs (sc'llálqʷm)* were sung to presumably encourage the participants (STHC).

Ball and Pin

Games of dexterity were practiced by all Interior Plateau peoples, meriting public acclaim and certain temporary statuses for any notable accomplishments. Ball and pin games were popular for all ages, and usually played even indoors during the winter. Participants required varying degrees of hand-eye coordination, which was naturally affected by the size of the ball hole and the pin in use. A common method of making an egg-size ball was by repeatedly folding and bending a moist tule, though some say a long cattail leaf was adequate. One last loose end "was looped around to form a ring, and sinew was used to wrap the point between the ball and the ring and the end of the ball" (Ray 1933:161).

A long fire-dried hawthorn pin was attached to the ball with sinew or hemp line, approximately 45 cm long. The player would hold the ball in his mouth, drop the ball, and as it fell attempt to skewer it with the hand-held pin. Scoring was on the basis of where the pin stuck into the ball–in the nose, the ring, or any other part of the ball. Ray provided a description of how the Sanpoil played the game, which has not been played for many generations by the Spokan:

In play the ball was first placed in the mouth; this served to steady it, and to keep it damp so that the pin would not crack the tule. The ball was dropped from the mouth while the pin was held in the right hand, and an attempt was made to catch it with the pin. Each time the ball was dropped the player exclaimed *stslaqóp* "stick." Each time that he was successful he called the name of the month, in sequence. This custom was termed "shortening the year" (1933:161).

The Spokan played a variation of ball and pin using a larger fist-size ball made of tule or cattail. In this case, the ball had one hole drilled through its center, created by using an angled-tipped piece of hardwood. A second piece of hardwood, only several millimeters shorter than the first had a sharp end attached to the ball by a long length of sinew or hemp. The objective of this game was more difficult, for the player had to toss the ball into the air and attempt to insert the attached pointed stick into the hole in the ball. A player won by having the largest number of successive placements of the pin in the ball. This game is commonly played today by non-Indians.

Spear-Ring Game

The arrow-ring game was a variation of the ring game, played by boys and sometimes men, which improved a person's skills with a bow and arrow for hunting and warfare. The *ring* (*sqcqλʔé* - "rolling a ring") was made by wrapping stripped willow bark around a series of equal but overlapping willow branch ends, usually 10 to 20 cm in diameter. Two men or boys played the game on a fairly level and brush-cleared section of ground, with each opponent or team standing approximately 7 to 12 m from where a man would roll the ring. A score was counted only when an arrow hit the ring. In team shooting, two men might shoot their arrows when one of them felt that it was most advantageous, or both could shoot simultaneously, and for safety reasons, multiple shooters always shot from the same side. The game was won by who ended up with the greatest number of his opponent's arrows, which were kept after each round as a prize; or they may have agreed earlier to return each player's arrows. Smith (1936-8:956) described how the Kalispel would count a point only when the arrow stuck in the ring, thereby carrying the ring away; simply knocking it over did not count.

Several individuals or teams might play a variation of this game, if only to better demonstrate their individual proficiency with spear or bow and arrow. They would send the particular projectile through a ring that was larger—approximately 30 cm in diameter, but interlaced with a series of interconnected thin strips of rawhide that supported a smaller rigid ring of 3 to 4 cm in diameter. The object was to send one's arrow or spear through the small aperture, without having the projectile engage the webbing. Not unlike darts, the nearer to the center ring scored the higher points. And yet, if a contestant hit the mesh twice, he would be disqualified (Teit 1930:131-132).

The following early account of this once popular gambling game described the commitment and potential losses or gains of the contestants:

> [...] the favorite games is one played with two pins or arrows, and a small ring, and in which only two can join at the same time. A small piece of ground tolerably level is chosen, on which two wooden butts are laid about fifteen feet apart and parallel to each other; each player is provided with one of the arrows, which are of wood and pointed with thick iron wire, which is evenly balanced by lead wrapped round the opposite end. One of the men takes the ring, in the inner circumference of which six beads are fixed, and rolls it along the ground, and the game is to run after the ring and throw the arrow, so that when stopped by the wooden butt the ring may fall upon it; both players throw their arrow at the same time, and, to enable a man to count two beads of the same colour, he must rest above his arrow. Two of the beads are red, two blue, and two white, arranged so that those of the same colour are opposite to each other; white counts three, red two, and blue one, and the score is generally ten, but this, as well as the value of the beads, is arbitrary. Very heavy stakes are lost and won at this game, which seems to have great fascination for every Indian, and frequent are the cases of men losing horses, blankets, guns, and all they possess, during a run of bad luck (Wilson 1866:300).

522

Ice and Snow Snakes

Only several older men could recall hearing of the winter game of ice and snow snakes being played on a snow-covered field over a prepared course, or on a fairly straight and level section of a frozen stream. In the latter case, it was mostly played by men; rarely by boys since it was feared that a younger person might break through the ice and drown. On land, snow snakes was played after a narrow and level course was first prepared by the participants who stamped a straight line in the *snow* (*smék'ʷt* or *mék'ʷ*). The objective was for each participant to take his turn in throwing a spear underhand as hard as possible along the prepared ditch without the spear jumping from the course, thereby being eliminated. The winner was the man who slid his spear the farthest. The so-called spear was not actually a hunting or fighting spear, but one fashioned from a roughly 2 m length of dressed ocean spray. It was never fletched or decorated, because such modifications would surely increase friction and thus reduce the distance it travels. A man would smooth the spear by rubbing a deer antler over the entire surface, thus breaking and sealing the wood cells. This smoothing process "hardened" the entire surface, and helped to seal it from moisture.

Ice snakes differed only with the playing surface, which on ice required a flat section of frozen water cleared of any snow, but not being physically confined to a prepared channel. A more open course caused the participants' spears to vary in its direction. However, this was of little significance because the winner was simply the person who slid his spear the farthest. There is no recall as to whether teams ever played this game or if only individual participants played it. Men would bet on whomever was thought to have the greatest strength and skill.

Snow Games

During the long winter season, children spent considerable time indoors during the dark hours listening to older people tell and sometimes act out an episode in oral history. But during the day, children played outside at different snow games. The first accumulated snow also brought the first bruised egos, resulting from throwing well-aimed snowballs or maneuvering an unsuspecting younger sibling into a *snowdrift* (*sqʷúy'tn*).

Children—mostly boys—played burrowing games during the winter when the snow was of the right consistency and depth to make snow tunnels that were excavated with a mother's borrowed snow shovel, or, after wood roofing, simply dug with split cedar or a discarded hemlock shingle; using a father's snowshoe as a shovel was strictly forbidden. Accumulated snow was removed by pulling or passing a loaded section of hide, which was dumped outside by a playmate. Some of the tunnels were not only rather long, but complex and often connected to others via adjoining passages.

Under the proper snow conditions, children of all ages would make what are currently called "snow figures." They would stamp out figures in the snow and ask others to identify their creations. Children in winter made standing snow figures that could represent an enemy for snowball fights. They also created raised figures of humans and animals sculptured from mounds of packed snow that often depicted certain characters from well known stories. Along the terraces of the Spokane River, children made animal and human figures as well, imitating adults fishing by excavating channels in the snow, which presumably directed "water" through *small stick weirs* (*sqʷyxi*). Pine cones were often used to represent fish.

Sledding

Both boys and girls enjoyed a winter activity which can best be called *sledding* (*qʷaweéle*) or coasting on frozen deer hides. One or two riders maintained stability and some direction, with the lead child pulling up the front end of the hide, and the other child doing likewise with both sides of the deer hide. By directing the nap of the hide downhill, the hairs of the deer hide would naturally be facing backwards, thereby not creating any resistance. On steep slopes, children sometimes used fir boughs for sledding by holding up the stout end of the branch with the upper side of the branch facing the snow, and with the ends of the needles facing an uphill direction. The best sledding took place when the snow was crusted with a recent thin layer of powder snow.

By the early 1900s, some children had access to home-made and some commercially produced sleds. There were a few flat-bottom long-sleds and a few articulated toboggans or what some have erroneously called bob-sled. Many years ago, toboggans were used on occasion for several utilitarian chores: bringing in firewood and even deer when a hunter killed an animal near the winter village.

Rolling Objects on Ice

The only description of a more recent winter game of *rolling stones* (*qamʔtú*) is by Smith (1936-8:959) who explained how the Kalispel modified the game once glass beads had been acquired. More than likely, it was played by the Spokan, certainly the *Chewelah-Spokan Group* (*sloʕʷtéw'si* or *lotew'si*). On a smooth section of river or pond ice, four men would sit on tule or cattail mats in a circle about 2 m apart from one another. One man would roll a smooth round stone toward the stone of an opponent next to him. If his stone hit the other man's stone, then he won the man's beads; but if he missed, he had to surrender his beads to the opponent. The beads might represent other items that were given a value of so many beads—often clothing or a blanket. Once a player lost all his beads, another man would take his place. The game continued in a clockwise direction until only one had all the beads, and no new players joined the game. Stones apparently were never thumb-snapped as it done later with glass or steel marbles.

Another winter competitive game was played on a long section of smooth ice by all genders and ages. The contestants took turns rolling a ball or ring at a small square or circle. A contestant would be eliminated if his or her object missed the mark (Teit 1930:133). Some elders recall children playing a similar game on level ground—a version of hoop-and-stick, in which each one of several children attempted with his or her stick to roll his hoop farther than the others.

Archery

Competition with the bow and arrow was conducted by only boys and men—always separately. Prior to competing, the participants agreed upon the distance to the *target area* (*snt'at'aʔpéʔčstis*), the type of *target* (*snt'at'apéčstn*), the number of arrows one could use, and what the prize would be for the winner. Other people might also bet upon their chosen archer, particularly if the contestant was considered an *excellent shot* (*ʔiw'ačst*). Competition involved seeing who could project the arrow the farthest. But the archer with the greatest skill was determined by an individual's accuracy in hitting a pre-arranged *target* (*t'apmín*). The stance most frequently assumed—certainly in competition—was one with the extended bow being held vertical to the ground. The choice of arrow and bow type was never prescribed, but as a rule hafted arrows were used. Though competitive spear-throwing was done by men, there are no known accounts of the Spokan staging spear-throwing contests for either distance or accuracy, spears being primarily only for thrusting, or, as mentioned, with arrow-ring contests.

524

Knife and Axe-Throwing

We can only assume that the Spokan competed in throwing knives and axes when these tools and weapons were first fashioned from different metals. Folding and straight knives and axes were thrown at standing trees or into the flat-sawn ends of fallen trees in an over-arm motion. With the arrival of trapper-traders, the favorite axe for all Indians was the single-blade HBC cruising axe, favored for throwing and as a general all-purpose survival tool. In fact, this type of axe was acknowledged—and still is—as the most valuable survival tool. It is probable that axe-throwing was taught to the Spokan by trapper-traders.

Knife-throwing involved considerable force, and knives were thrown by holding the end of the handle—never by holding the point of the knife. Holding the knife by the point is essentially ineffective after one and a half revolutions (Bulmer, pers. comm.). Unfortunately, there appear to be no such references in Work's journals regarding axe or knife throwing.

Horse Racing

Probably one of the earliest accounts of *horse racing* (*sq'ᵂq'ᵂuλ'e?š* or *q'ᵂq'ᵂuλ'e?šm'* - "to race") among the Spokan, the Flathead, and Coeur d'Alene was by Cox, who in the summer of 1815 described how intense was the *gambling* (*xcxcí?m*) and competition between thirty-some Spokan, Flathead, Coeur d'Alene, and Chaudière (Kettle Falls) riders over an 8-km course that was a level plain "with a light gravelly bottom and some rearward jockeys were occasionally severely peppered in the face from small *pebbles* (*sčxᵂaq'ᵂsšn*) thrown up by the hoofs of the racers in front" (1957 [1832]:215).

Years later, Wilson also claimed this sport was "a very favorite pastime in summer, and the stakes are sometimes large" (1866:299). In fact, Wilkes had described earlier how for the "Spokanes, one of their great amusements is horse-racing" (1845, 4:487). Horse racing could be staged anytime, anywhere, and to any distance; but during the reservation period it was customary for men to race their horses on a circular or oblong *race track* (*snq'ᵂq'ᵂúλ'?ščn'* or *snq'ᵂq'ᵂúλ'e?štn*) at the reservation *fairgrounds* (*sny'aʕ'qíntn'*), which often served as the *old powwow grounds* (*čšlčenč*). Many years ago, prior to the *old race track* (*snq'ᵂq'ᵂuλ'e?še'n'* or *sny'aʕ'pqin'tn'*), the distance or course of competitive racing was determined by the participants. Some races were relay races between two or more teams. Competitive racing was called *čsepšl'šew'si*.

Betting on horses was a common pastime, and the consequences were thought to be influenced by a person using his personal *suméš* to determine—at least influence—the outcome of a race. Franchère recorded: "These Indians [Spokan] are passionately fond of horse-races: by the bets they make on occasions they sometimes lose all that they possess. The women ride, as well as the men" (1904, 6:340). He further described how "Horse-racing was then the royal sport on the Spokane gravel plains, before baseball had been invented" (Durham 1912, 1:42).

One elder, who once lived near Wellpinit where the Catholic Church is now located, explained how when he was a young man (1882), just after the establishment of the Spokane Indian Reservation (1881), a person's power could help or even kill a competitor's horse. He related how one day he was riding his small pinto, he met an old man astride a large buckskin-colored horse: "I said to the old man that, 'My small horse is much faster than your big horse.' The old man pointed his right *c'q'ᵂmin* [index finger] at my horse, and my pinto dropped dead."

The above incident demonstrated that a shaman could kill a horse. If so, then he could just as likely improve its ability in racing. Yet such influence was not limited to shamans. Men could receive in a dream or receive from a shaman an object that would improve a horse's ability for racing, warfare, or protection from becoming sick (or sorcerized). The nature of the device or markings on a horse at a particular time—often reflecting the Doctrine of Signatures—was always symbolic of strength, speed, endurance, surefootedness, or whatever was thought to best serve the owner for a designated task. Prior to the horse commencing an activity, its owner might sing one of his power songs for the horse's pleasure and hoped success.

Powwows

A major source of contemporary entertainment, games, and dancing is the annual *powwow* (*sy'a?pqinm*) held just south of Wellpinit on what has—over the years—become the traditional *powwow ground* (*sny'aʕpqín'tn*). The site currently has several large open shelters, which house the many exhibits that are brought for display and sale by Indians from numerous reservations—some quite distant. Many of the participants camp in trailers, tents, or tipis erected on or immediately adjacent to the powwow ground. The three-day event commences with a flag opening ceremony and closes with another similar ceremony, and always under the direction of military veterans. It should be noted that all Amerindian groups have for many years and in several overseas wars demonstrated their strong sense of citizenship and patriotism, evidenced by such ceremonies, as well as headstones in various cemeteries.

Years ago, ribbons and other prizes were awarded for competitive displays of agricultural products, farm animals, canned and dried goods, hide clothing, beading, and feather work. Meats, vegetable dishes, and baked goods were judged for their excellence. One remarkable elderly woman remembered how her bitterroot pies were always acclaimed.

Rodeos

Once the rodeo had been introduced into the eastern Plateau—from both the Plains and the Southwest—this colorful, dramatic, and always dangerous activity became an important aspect of Spokan entertainment and rural economics with the trading and purchasing of cattle and horses, and of course betting. The major events were calf-wrestling, Brahma bull-riding, saddle broncs, and of course roping calves from horse, and contemporary spectator events and roping techniques differ little from the early rodeos. Rodeos now, however, have more spectacular costumes, new events (such as barrel racing), and modern concessions, all of which are perhaps more appealing to a larger and more diverse audience than they were a hundred years ago. Some rodeos were, and are still, held in conjunction with powwows.

Years ago an elderly Spokan, a former Brahma bull and experienced rodeo circuit rider, explained how participating in rodeos—most notably intertribal contests—was, to him as well as to some other Indians, a type of latter-day warfare in which he could compete against those whose past relations had been based on traditional conflict. He explained how the actual physical exertion and pain afforded him the elation of victory that his distant forebears must have once felt when winning against an enemy while riding a horse.

The *rodeo* (*snpn'pn'ʔúscut* - "bucking") and its various functional and artistic accouterments offered many Spokan opportunities in silversmithing, leather-working, braiding, and art work using various mediums, including paintings, as well as stone and cast bronze sculpturing (G. Flett, pers. comm.).

Stock Whips, Quirts, and Lassoing

Prior to Euro-American contact, the Spokan had whips, but mostly short ones—actually a *quirt* (*qíxʷmn*)–which was used only with horses, never in any competitive game. Once *cattle* (*st'm'áʔ*) were acquired, the Spokan adopted the long stock whips and lassos of the Euro-American cattlemen for working cattle and horses, and eventually displaying considerable skill in various competitive games associated with rodeos. The main objective of competitive stock whipping was the rapidity of cracking the whip in a given time or the skill to dislodge or simply hit a distant object. Apart from stock lassoing, the main demonstration of this skill was largely stationary when a person using different maneuvers would step through the whirling lasso (*ɫuxʷpustn*) in various ways. By the mid-1860s, the Spokan made lassos of split rawhide, "always three or four stand" and 10 m in length (Lord 1867:207). A working quirt invariably had a single or plaited buckskin or rawhide wrist strap. Owhi, a Spokan Indian and a presumed horse-thief, was the father of Laquoit by a Spokan woman, who was a half brother to Qualchan (Lynn Pankonin, pers. comm.). In 1853, Winthrop wrote how "Owhhigh [sic] presented me, as a parting gift, his whip [...] a neat baton with a long hide lash and loop of otter fur for the wrist" (1863:74).

Any type of *whip* (*qíxʷmn*) or *short hand quirt* (*ɫqíqxʷm'n'*), used in ranching or during a rodeo, was never used in whipping people brought before a council for punishment. The whip once used for disciplinary reasons was quite different in style, weight, and design. Actually, communal whipping had been discontinued by the time of rodeos.

Baseball

After being introduced in the early 1900s, *baseball* (*č'ɫsep'ecin'* or *č'ɫsep'am'i* or *kɫsáptsín*) quickly became a popular and competitive game, played as a summer sport by young and old men, often at fairs and family outdoor gatherings. The rules and equipment were nearly the same as those of the present game.

Before that the Spokan played a similar game called *kɫsáptsín*, which used four bases, each with a batter and a catcher. A ball (a stitched leather sphere stuffed with deer hair) was thrown from one position to the next in rotation as each *batter* (*suxk'ɫsáptsín*) attempted to *hit the ball* (*pókʷla*). If the hitter missed, the catcher threw it to the next position. When the batter hit the ball, all hitters would run to the next base—exchanging positions—unless the ball was caught, or the ball *rolled on the ground* (*xʷál'q'ólax*). This would score, unless the catcher tagged the runner (Elmendorf 1935-6, 3:25).

A traditional non-competitive game played by young boys was to hit stones or fir cones with a large enough stick to propel the object some distance. Apparently the aim was to first toss the projectile in the air with the left hand, and then hit it with the "bat" held in both hands. As best remembered, rarely did another person act as a pitcher because of the danger, particularly when hitting stones.

Years ago, the City of Spokane adopted the name "Spokan Indians" for their baseball team, and only recently, "the Tribe allowed use of the name Spokane Indians for the city's semi-professional team. Recently tribal members designed the team's logo" (Scholz, pers. comm.).

Agility and Balancing

Children and adults tested their agility and balancing abilities with a game similar to the Euro-American game of skinning the cat, by jumping forward and backward over a stout stick held on each end by the jumper's hands (Ray 1933). An individual's agility could be demonstrated in other ways as well. For instance, children were adept at walking considerable distances on their hands. During the early reservation period, and after the construction of allotment houses, it was not unusual for an elderly man to entertain his grandchildren or great grandchildren by walking down the porch stairs on his hands, which was said to be more difficult than walking up the stairs in such a manner. This was once personally observed by the author when one man, well into his late seventies, needed little encouragement to perform this feat on what were obviously unstable porch stairs; much to the delight of his grandchildren and great grandchildren, but also to the obvious consternation of his wife.

The balancing of light weight lodge poles or smaller lengths of wood on one's forehead, or the end of a finger, was frequently followed by tossing the balanced pole into the air so that it landed on the opposite end of the man's hand where it would stay erect only momentarily. It was further explained that the most difficult object to balance on a finger was a raven's wing feather. One elderly lady recalled balancing on one finger her mother's digging stick by its point, and her mother's quick admonishment for playing with tools. Running or hopping across a relatively shallow stream, using only the protruding stones, was apparently never considered competitive, but it always elicited great cheers from other children.

Foot-Racing

Running was almost a daily scheduled event or spontaneous occurrence—even after acquiring the horse—and was recognized as an important aspect of physical conditioning for children, men, and women. Consequently, a child's greatest ambition was to become a great foot-racer, to be *čqéclšmntm* ("one who likes to run"). A few remaining elderly men's warmest memories were of the reputation they had acquired among their people, and with other groups, as once being acclaimed speed or distance runners. Foot-racing was a favored activity among boys and girls who were encouraged by older siblings, adults, and grandparents, who in turn took considerable pride in these accomplishments by their children. The Spokan were aware that in the "old days" all good runners had a more pronounced *pigeon-toed* (*pnpnšín*) stance than walking with their feet straight and parallel. Wilson made a similar observation, "The toes turn inwards, and from constantly being on horseback, the legs are usually bowed" (1866:293).

The following brief account was by an early Chewelah pioneer of an extraordinary Chewelah-Spokan man who worked as a local laborer on a white-owned ranch:

> I believe he was the nearest approach to a wild Indian that I ever met. He never seemed to get tired. I have seen him in the foot races during a Sunday afternoon when he would take on any one that wanted to run, at any distance from 100 yards to three miles, winning at all distances. He finally offered to run the entire distance of three miles, while allowing the opponents to run the relay, each running a short distance. Even then he was always the winner. When completing any task he would give voice to a most blood curdling war whoop that could be heard for miles (Graham 1929:4-5).

The importance of a man being a good runner was sometimes first indicated when a baby boy was observed to take his first step, "whoever sees him should pick up a moccasin and throw it between his feet—this will make the child a good foot racer, or a good hunter, strong on his feet" (Elmendorf 1935-6, 3:58-9).

Teams of men participated in marathons, usually 15 to 40 km or greater in distance. Runners were encouraged by family and friends, who placed large wagers on a team or an individual, and it was recalled how some supporters would run as far as possible next to their chosen team or individual to give advice and encouragement. Nor was it unusual for runners to bet on themselves, particularly if a man possessed a power bundle or a specially acquired sacred item that was believed to assist him in his efforts (Elmendorf, pers. comm.). Acknowledging the Doctrine of Signatures, such a bundle might have contained a bird's feather or a swatch of fur from an animal that was believed to be particularly swift, more likely an item from one of his guardian spirit animal or a bird who represented great speed.

On occasions of large gatherings—when mutually exploiting a resource, such as fishing at any of the large falls—a camp or village would often pit their best runner against runners of other camps, villages, or groups. Later, in the evening, or years later, they would recall specific victories, and again regale themselves with often long and detailed accounts of a runner's stamina and ability, who brought acclaim to their group. During the early 20th century, some renowned Spokan foot-racers toured county and city fairs, competing against non-Indians for prize monies, and invariably acquitting themselves in speed and endurance. Wilson wrote how the Spokan men "are well-made, active, and capable of great endurance" (1866:293).

In 1811, prior to the effects of acculturation and altered diet, Thompson cited the physical achievement of Spokan runners:

> [...] an old white headed man with the handle of a tea-kettle for an ornament about his head. He showed no signs of age except his hair and a few wrinkles in his face, he was quite naked and ran nearly as fast as the horses. We could not help but admire him. I invited the horsemen to invite all their people to smoke, which they set off to do in a round gallop, and the old man on foot ran after them and did not lose much ground (Elliott 1914a, 1:55).

Until recently, elders entertained their grandchildren and others with stories of their running abilities. And on one memorable occasion, the author observed a Spokan woman in her mid-70s as she told a van filled with teenagers en route to a root field, how when she was young no one could catch her. Her granddaughter must have recalled her grandfather's favorite expression of challenge, "like dragging meat across the nose of an old coyote," because the young girl proceeded to politely challenge her grandmother to a foot race. The van was stopped off the highway, and the two contestants—young and old—got out of the van and took off running. The contest was won by the grandmother, since the girl fell down laughing at her wobbling but game grandmother.

Of all the early games and types of contests, foot-racing and some of the now famous runners were recalled with greater detail and pride than the others. Elderly men described, often with considerable emotion, some of the rather lengthy and arduous courses taken by the competing athletes. Nor was it unusual for such an account to conclude with a reflection upon when, during the "time of chiefs, before cars, how better the people were in health and spirit." A documented event of the Indians' ability to run long distances was reported by Hale:

> The officers at Wallawalla mentioned that some of the Indians had remarkable powers of undergoing fatigue, and instanced the case of one who performed the journey from Dr. Whitman's mission-house to the forks of the Clearwater, a distance of one hundred miles, between morning and sunset. This man is in the habit of performing this treatment on himself annually (1846, 4:465).

Swimming

All Spokan were excellent swimmers, due in part to the provenience of the Spokane River, numerous creeks, and many small lakes. Also, given their dependence upon fishing and the gathering of fresh water mussels, this was often a daily activity. Both men and women could *swim* (*nčaλíp*) and *dive* (*ʔúst*) from early youth, and parents made swimming a daily activity when a child could walk. Children and adults normally propelled themselves using either a side stroke, back stroke, or more commonly the dog-paddle. Everyone knew how to *float* (*pl'íp*) on one's back or stomach with equal skill. And yet, there were accounts of young children who, despite their parents' warnings, drowned when playing on thin spring ice—a tragedy associated more with the effects of hypothermia and the difficulty in getting solid footing than their inability to swim.

Breath-holding contests for men and boys were staged in order to improve the skills needed when diving in relatively *deep water* (*nqʷést*), primarily for fixing weirs, installing weir anchors, and gathering fresh water mussels. Elders recount that, for conditioning, men—after leaving the sweathouse—would swim across either the Spokane or Columbia Rivers in the winter, when the ice permitted it (Ross 1988). Throughout the year, men, after leaving the sweathouse, would plunge into a stream regardless of the weather, often after making an opening in the ice. Since adults always swam naked, men and women had their own swimming areas, nor did members of the opposite sex ever bathe together (Ray 1933). Young and old engaged separately in swimming contests based on distance and speed.

Smith (1936-8:968a) and others have mentioned how the Kalispel and Spokan would meet at Little Falls, and compete to see who could stay under water the longest, sometimes wrestling one another while submerged. The same author noted how:

> At Little Falls on the Spokane River there is a rock in the middle of the stream in the swift water which makes a little falls with a whirlpool below. Men float down and then relax and get carried over the falls into the whirlpool and get twisted all up in all kinds of shapes (Smith 1936-8:968).

In the late spring and early summer, several large rocks are still visible at a particular site, where men would dive off into an area of swift back-water, powerful enough that it forced a swimmer back in under the pounding water. Two men would compete by simultaneously diving into these falls to see who could first recover a purposely placed relatively *heavy stone net sinker* (*čp't'ápl'eʔtn'*). Some men competed to see who could swim the greatest distance under water, which was always a favorite betting sport when visitors from other groups gathered during fishing season.

Dolls

A *little girl* (*šešuʔtn'*) typically would take great pride in being gifted with a doll whose head was sometimes made from an inflated *fish bladder* (*pepéw'eʔ* - "child's toy"), and a section of the salmon's intestines had been split lengthwise and then rubbed with tallow until soft before stuffing with deer hair or fresh green mullein leaves, and then sewn closed. A doll's head, arms, and legs were fashioned from buckskin and usually stuffed with deer hair. Dolls were dressed with buckskin garments made by the girl's mother or grandmother. The introduction of canvas and cloth replaced traditional materials for making the clothing of a *doll* (*ʔoxʷtel'éy'eʔ*). In fact, a rather pathetic example of a *toy doll* (*c'am'oseʔ*) was once on display some years ago in a local museum; it was about 30 cm in height. The stuffed cloth *rag doll* (*c'aʔmóstʔ*) figure was of a young girl made from a white flour sack, and attired in a buckskin dress; but on the exposed face and hands were many small red dots, approximately 2-3 mm in diameter, and meticulously drawn with red ink, apparently to represent an anonymous child who had survived smallpox. One can only wonder if the faceless figure had been given to a child as a prophylactic device to prevent her contracting this once-often-fatal endemic disease, or as an opportunity for the doll-maker—perhaps a grandmother—to care for an infected grandchild.

Dolls were always faceless, and regardless of the type of hide or skin used to make a child's doll head. A mother or grandmother never drew or painted a face on any type of doll, even though the figure usually had hair, detailed clothing, and footwear. To replicate or represent an actual or fictive living or deceased person would constitute a danger to the doll's owner as well as the person it represented, for whatever happened by accident or intent to the doll would afflict the person so represented. An anthropomastic review and ethnography (Elmendorf, pers. comm.) indicates dolls were never given personal names of living or dead persons; and there was no recall if a girl's doll was interred with a deceased child, nor is there any evidence in the archaeological record of such a practice.

For both small boys and girls, a *child's toy* (*xʷʔλxúʔλiy'éʔe*) was always named and attended by various miniature paraphernalia that represented a domestic environment or certain behaviors, even such as warfare. A young girl's dolls undoubtedly served to inculcate later duties and responsibilities for when the child became an adult, certainly a mother. To *play with a toy* (*m'l'm'él'čst*) was, for both girls and boys, always symbolic of adult responsibilities. Until recently, several elderly women could vividly recall the names of favorite dolls they had in their nursery. Unfortunately, few examples of dolls have survived. However, several elderly women could recall how their mother or grandmother would quickly make a doll from corn husks, some with a head made from a small gourd with facial features in either charcoal or red hematite.

Clay Projectiles

Not surprisingly, Spokan boys had a type of war game in which they threw blobs of damp clay at one another. They normally used long sticks and pellets of either white or *blue clay* (*sč'iɬt*) found in the Spokane River or its various tributaries. Such pellets were easily made by rolling the clay between one's palms until it was the size of a robin's egg or larger, and served as missiles by sticking a pellet to the end of a stout section of willow approximately 2 m in length. The aim was to propel the ball of clay at an opponent of the opposite team, though often the entire group would be engaged with their weapons in a free-for-all. After a battle, all of the children would go for a swim to clean off the splattered clay. Older boys played the same game, only not with clay missiles, but with buckskin balls stuffed with deer hair. There was apparently some agreement that stones were too dangerous to use as missiles.

Stone-Skipping

Whenever children were near calm water, they played a rather spontaneous game of seeing who could skip a flat stone the most times over the water before it sank from sight. The boy or girl or grandmother attaining the most grazes was the undisputed winner—until the next day's game. Frequently rematches were staged to settle a doubtful count.

Slings

All boys were given a toy sling at an early age, which in time and with practice they learned to use as a fairly efficient weapon for hunting rodents and birds, but not large animals. The material and design of a *sling* (*čłaqʷsšntʔn*) was fairly universal, each being made from a long strip of buckskin with a patch or pocket at mid-length that held a round stone or dried ball of clay. One end of the strip of buckskin was wound around the boy's right thumb, while the free end would be pressed against his hands with the fingertips. After whirling the loaded sling horizontally over his head, or somewhat vertically at his side, the boy would release the free end, thereby projecting the missile to the *target* (*snt'at'apéčstn*). It was remembered that in the overhead position, the sling would be spun counterclockwise (viewed from above), whereas in the side vertical position the sling would usually be spun clockwise, because the stone could then be released higher than if done counter clockwise—to avoid obstacles on the ground, such as brush. Smith (1936-8:680) wrote how the purpose of the sling was not accuracy, but rather to see who could throw his missile the greatest distance.

There were no forked wooden slingshots until the arrival of pneumatic automobile tires and inner tubes, which provided the needed elastic material for children and young adult males to project small stones at trespassing dogs or unsuspecting birds and small animals.

Echo Games

A favorite pastime for all children was to play an *echo game* (*snm'ƛma?k'ʷá*), one that involved any number of children shouting sometimes for hours at a large monolith, such as a large piece of granite that jutted out from the parent rock, or in a small but high stone-walled canyon, thereby producing resounding echoes. The child producing the most unusual and clear *echo* (*p'uw* or *sp'wíncn*) achieved status until the next contest. Boys would stage contests that involved imitating the different sounds of animals and birds—ones that might indicate distress, mating, or agitation. These skills were often later used in stalking and decoying various game.

Several kilometers upriver, on the north shore of the Spokane River, is a special sacred area with numerous large monolithic sections of glacially-deposited granite slabs and round boulders. Several have pictographs. Upon visiting the site, some elders recalled playing the echo game near the many large imposing boulders, but always when some distance from their parents, who objected to the loud noises as being harmful or disruptive to nature, or simply disrespectful. There are two other echo areas on the reservation just above the south-facing Spokane River terraces, which have a series of relatively tall vertical granite cliffs with numerous recorded pictographs (Ross 1993).

The only recalled precaution associated with this activity was the warning by elders that children were never to imitate the sounds of large wild animals or monsters, because those sounds could attract such creatures who might take the offender away—a form of social control for sacred art forms.

Related to echo games was another child's game, once referred to as *houpée*, in which contestants would attempt to judge "how far a shout would carry" (Linklater 2002:17). There is no recall as to how one was declared a winner, or if adults ever participated. In many circumstances of congenial social grouping, to speak inordinately loud or to shout was once considered inappropriate—even rude—for, as was explained, in such situations, this meant that a person had lost control of his or her feelings, and only bad things would be said—things the offender would regret later. As someone once claimed, "boisterous speaking or shouting does not come from one's heart." To speak softly meant that a person was sincere—telling the truth—whereas one's voice and even face 'contorted' with one's loud words or shouting. A Flathead elder once explained to Steve Egesdal that, "the word ʔeswnéxʷisti meant, "What he says, thinks, and does all walk the same narrow path together. " More literally, this means "he is being/holding true" (Egesdal, pers. comm.).

Cloud Interpretations

While not a formal type of individual or group competition, the interpretation of cloud shapes was an enjoyable way for children to occasionally pass the time during late spring until late fall, when they would lie on their backs and attempt to interpret and associate the various shapes with an animal. Many an elderly man recalled with pleasure how, when as a *small boy* (*ttw'ít*), he would join his friends in interpreting the shape of a *cloud* (*sctm'íp*), one that often suggested to an imaginative youth a certain animal or anthropomorphic creature. Several boys would compare their interpretations, and perhaps later tell their grandmothers stories based upon their interpretations; but there were no remembered accounts of a boy having his future *suméš* appearing to him as a cloud in animal form. As an elder once explained, "Everyone has the right and ability to see things of Nature differently."

Whistling

Boys commenced to learn how to whistle at an early age, and became proficient by puberty. The resonance of voiced speech-sound and the quality of timbre of an individual's whistle, were often so distinct as to identify the person before he was seen (Meyer, pers. comm.). Loud or shrill *whistling* (*sikʷ*) was accomplished in various ways—usually by stretching each side of the mouth with the two index fingers, or by placing the forefinger and thumb at each side of the mouth and drawing the lips tightly across the lower teeth.

By an early age, all children could produce a high, shrill whistle by blowing forcibly upon a broad blade of grass made taut with the top of grass held between the knuckles of both extended thumbs and the bottom portion held tightly by the base of both hand. This technique created an often loud and sharp sound because the grass—as a tympanic membrane—vibrated, and the sound was further amplified by the partially enclosed space between the *clasped hands* (*c'np'ečt*), which served as a resonating chamber. This procedure was typically perfected by the boy as a 'squirrel call' or for imitating certain deer calls.

Another once-popular procedure for making a whistle-like sound—similar to a flute sound—was to clasp both cupped hands together with the thumbs parallel and the four fingers of the left hand placed over the extended right forefinger and immediately in front of both thumbs. The sound was made by blowing directly upon both thumb knuckles, and the melody was regulated by opening and closing one's right hand fingers, but always keeping the right forefinger in place. There was no significance to this method of whistling except to gain a distant child's attention or by amusing a crying baby to stop. The author recalls making such a sound using this method once before going to the back door of an elder's home, and how, within minutes, the elder, who was doing chores in an out-building, responded in kind, only louder.

One must reason that girls practiced and became proficient in certain male activities: whistling was one of many such activities. It was always thought by the men of that time that young girls and women never whistled, based upon the assumption that a woman had not the ability to learn it and considered it improper. However, many years ago, several elderly ladies often went for gathering medicinal plants and took some of their young grandchildren with them, who eventually wandered away and went out of sight, which caused some concern when they noticed it. Before setting out to *search* (*hec λ'éʔmi*) for them, an elderly woman might let out a series of high and piercing whistles. After returning from the root field, one of the ladies said to the author, "It must have shaken all the [aspen] leaves for miles around."

Whistling at night was strictly forbidden, since it was believed such a sharp noise would draw the attention of a ghost or an owl, and it was displeasing and upsetting to them. It was claimed that night-whistling could create ominous and even severe winds destructive winds to structures.

Some people were first recognized when whistling a certain *tune* (*síkʷcaʔn*) or because of a unique style of whistling. Several elders mentioned how sad it is that young people today seem rarely to whistle during the day, even for their own pleasure.

Cat's Cradle

Every Spokan adult—most notably every woman—was skilled in playing the universal game of *cat's cradle* (*l'eʔčíw'čstn'* or *scqʷ'aqʷíxʷ* or *qʷaqʷíxʷ* or *syanéčstm*) called the "string game." Women, however, were reputed to have excelled at this game of dexterity, often in conjunction with storytelling. Until recently, grandmothers invariably carried a long loop of thin buckskin or a rolled sinew cord for deftly constructing a wide selection of configurations that represented various objects. Years ago, older Spokan children carried a long narrow section of buckskin or twine for many purposes, but mostly to make string figures. It took only a minute for an elderly lady to perform some of her favorite patterns when simply asked if she had her string with her. She would readily bring it out to *teach* (*m'imeyeʔm*) and entertain grandchildren and like-minded visiting anthropologists.

Traditionally, the *string* (*scqʷ'aqʷíxʷ*) used for constructing *different configurations* (*ƛ'čƛ'čéčstn'*) was made from a long, thin thong of buckskin, with the ends tied together. When the loop was stretched out, it measured from 50 to 65 cm in length. In the late 1960s, the author visited an elderly lady, who upon hearing a car approach her home, quickly took from her cardigan sweater pocket a long loop of buckskin she always carried, and placed it around her neck, saying, by way of explanation, "Ah, you know how the grandchildren always enjoy a story about *spilyeʔ*." Some elders excelled in their repertoire and were sought by both the young and the old. Particularly valued were those elders who were skilled in imitating the voices or sounds of the many characters depicted in their stories.

When making single representations of certain animals or features within the natural environment, the child who was first able to properly identify a particular string configuration was rewarded with praise and even predictions of his or her later success in storytelling upon becoming an elder. Most animals, birds, certain fish, a few constellations, major human anatomical features, and even cultural structures were represented. All adults exhibited varying degrees of skill in cat's cradle, enjoying a reputation for their extensive repertoire of characters—some adults could execute nearly a hundred configurations. An elderly woman, who, owing to rheumatoid arthritis in her hands, could not bead or sew as before, explained how fortunate she was that she could still play cat's cradle with her grandchildren, because only then could her fingers "fly like a pair of birds building a nest."

String figures were sometimes composites and vital to illustrating a long story or explaining how a certain animal had been created. They were often made for certain rituals during the winter months, and most frequently in the evening, in the hope of "shortening the moon so better weather would come" (Elmendorf, pers. comm.).

A few of the most elderly women commented sadly upon how younger women and children were no longer capable of making string figures. This was a lamentable explanation for not only the loss of storytelling and winter entertainment, but the inability of young women to master and maintain the various arts of basketry and sewing—skills once based upon hand-eye coordination and finger dexterity.

Bullroarers

During the summer boys enjoyed playing with bullroarers, which could never be really competitive, given the variations in the construction of each bullroarer; nor is there any memory of what it was called. A boy's first bullroarer was often made by his father, uncle, or an older brother by first splitting a section of hardwood to get a 1.5 to 2 cm thick section, usually 15 to 30 cm long. However, Smith said how the Kalispel used cedar (1936-8:971), which might have been too light a wood, and was perhaps weighted. The bullroarer was then tapered from the center lengthwise to each end, and from the long center line to the edges by using a sharp piece of obsidian. In form, the bullroarer was an elliptical airfoil, not unlike a boomerang, only attached to a long length of two strands of twined buckskin. When spun, it created a 'roaring' or shrill sound as a result of the relatively flat object rotating and vibrating when traveling through the air. Different sounds were obviously created by the size and position of the holes. A hole was first drilled on the thinner and smaller end to accommodate an attached length of spiral-split buckskin or twice twined hemp—rawhide was too heavy. The relative simplicity of construction never proved to be an obstacle for the beginner. Rather, learning to get the bullroarer played out and kept aloft was the challenge.

The bullroarer was always launched by holding the carefully looped end of the line in one's right hand and holding the bullroarer in the left hand above the head—with about 10 cm of line played clockwise above his head, as he gradually let out on the length of the line. It was always spun in clockwise circles. To keep a bullroarer airborne, it was necessary to always keep it above the ground at a height equivalent to the boy's head. Any effort to bring it higher would immediately stall the bullroarer. Noises made by a bullroarer varied according to the thickness, the surface, and the number of holes in the elliptical shaped instrument; but it is not known if they were ever drilled or perforated in any fashion, as some cultures have learned to do in order to produce different types of sounds. The Spokan bullroarer made only a whirring sound (*I, I, I, I*) (Elmendorf, pers. comm.). Bullroarers were never decorated, or believed to imitate the voices of spirits, ancestors, or animals—as in some other cultures. Since few elders could remember bullroarers, it is not understood what, if any, deleterious effects were created upon weather or nature when they were used. Smith offers a concern the Kalispel had:

> They [children] had to play with it away [from village and people] where because if the older people saw them, they would stop them, saying that it would make the wind blow. They did not want the wind to blow because of the canoes; there was always someone out in a canoe and he will have to work hard also because they were afraid of fire, because they had the fire outside of the lodge and if a grass fire gets started in dry summer it would burn the village out (1936-8:971).

The only observable damage a bullroarer could cause was if the line broke, and momentum propelled the missile at a person or into a drying rack. Children were forbidden to play with bullroarers—as stated earlier by Smith—near people and settlements. In addition, following the Doctrine of Signatures, it was believed that the small wind from a bullroarer could attract an even greater wind from Nature—one that would cause serious destruction. For the same reason, a bullroarer was never used at night, because some elders believed might attract a ghost (*sk'úsk'a*).

Storytelling

Some types of storytelling were not simply relaxing for an audience; but often were serious and instructive, even sacred. Nearly all storytelling was done during the winter months when the evenings were long and not interrupted by absent adults returning from doing outside or distant chores. Moreover, children were not permitted to play or even go outside when it was dark. There was no specified seating arrangement or structure of time or sequence for telling a story. Some oral accounts were known to require several evenings to complete. *Old people* (*nt'č'mi?sc*) were once extremely skilled in their often long and dramatic accounts of the creation of the world, its plants, animals, and unique land forms. It was not unusual for a gifted storyteller to act out with dexterous movements and imitate the recognized individual behaviors and voices of as many as ten characters in one story. Adults would cease their work if a noted storyteller was visiting, and communally join with the children in expressing their acclaim and appropriate reaction to a feat or incident of some notable character. As with all preliterate peoples, stories of the mythical charter were critical for the proper enculturation of the children's mores and folkways, ones that prescribed the proper behavior for children as well as reiteration for adults. A wide variety of themes were universal, but those of physical transformation seemed to dominate, particularly those of creation which were most instructive and dramatic.

Storytelling and situation-acting was a major form of family entertainment and *relaxation* (*m'etxʷn'cút*), at least until the advent of the radio and, more recently and unfortunately, that of the television. Interesting is an astute comment made several years ago (1967) by an elder who recalled the dynamics and pleasure of winter storytelling, and how this was disrupted with the installation of electricity and the purchasing of radios and later television sets. The elder explained that when his family first installed a radio, the eldest male in the family, his grandfather, said, "Now you have brought in the Devil." However, the teller of this story then lowered his voice, and said, almost imperceptibly (so his deceased grandfather could not hear), that actually his grandfather was wrong, since "The real Devil was the television we brought into our home." Even many years ago, the major distinction between elders and younger people was one between those who enjoyed telling stories and those who preferred not to listen to these "old-fashioned" stories, which elders feared would not be taught to *their descendants* (*snt'er'mep* or *al 'i s ntr''emcp* - "they are my descendants").

Repetitious storytelling, often accompanied by situation-acting, adhered closely to local and often regional motifs that reinforced and increased a young listener's knowledge of the significance of past and often distant events. Nonetheless, it was truly an individual skill, and one's ability was based upon a number of variables, such as age and the possession of a particular power. Usually women were known to be the best storytellers, and a laudatory compliment of a woman would be that *she has many good stories* (*nxsxsáplqs*) (STHC). However, some *blind* (*čyesčnmpqíni*) people apparently had the greatest repertoires of stories, and were the most gifted in imitating the various theriomorphic creatures who inhabited the region, particularly giants, dwarfs, and weird beings that were dramatically represented in the stories. Among the Spokan was an elderly curing blind shaman and *storyteller* (*wit'sn'múlaxʷ* or *sxʷm'e'm'éy''em* or *sxʷmáʕam* - "teacher") who lived at Little Falls, and whose oratory skills and storytelling abilities are still recounted by several elders (Ross 1991).

Certain individuals who were recognized as being exceptionally gifted storytellers were known to have a special *suméš* (Elmendorf 1935-6, 3:5). As with the previous description of an exceptionally sound and presumably inanimate flute that had the power to demonstrate its power to play by itself, it also happened that the wind would sometimes express its pleasure when an exceptionally gifted storyteller recited a past but dramatic event. Elders claimed how, in the past, smoke from a fireplace or chimney never came into the room when a gifted storyteller recited an account of unusual bravery, strength, or friendship; and how the wind would blow against the dwelling making unusual "noises" at appropriate times during the oral account, noises that were not unlike humans speaking, humming, or singing softly, sounds only understood by certain shamans. Such noises were never made by ghosts.

As noted, an elderly individual, often a *tricky person* (*qʷqʷílqʷlt*) was an exceptional storyteller, and on occasion would recite a *tricky story* (*tsptsáptík'ʷal*), which was often a cycle of stories, parts of which he selected to tell separately to fool or *trick* (*qʷíl*) an audience (Elmendorf 1935-63, 3:6).

Stories served not only to explain the origins of all things in the natural and supernatural worlds, but were a means of reiterating axiomatic values and morals; thus, implementing social control by depicting what would happen to a person guilty of a specific moral transgression. This enunciation of their mythical charter and the artful use of analogy and metaphor were frequently employed during storytelling sessions. Some accomplished storytellers were ventriloquists (word meaning literally "belly speaker") and quite skillful at performing legerdemain and what some have claimed as achieving individual and even group hypnosis—at least mesmerizing the listeners, if not putting them to sleep.

Apart from pre-ritual training for certain rites of passage, the only formal enculturation of children was provided during storytelling sessions, as some elders pointed out. Yet the ethical teaching was confined to the time of the story, not after. An adult never asked a child about the significance or moral of a story after it had been told; "to embarrass [c'e?š] or humiliate a child was to close his ears, and he'll see but never hear things carried by the wind [Nature] or by our [elders] words." Or, an inquiring child might have been told by a grandmother that the child's granddaughter or grandson would later share their own dreams with those characters in oral accounts. It was said that the young listener, after hearing the same story recited for many years, was better able to explain to his children or grandchildren the important aspects of the spiritual and dream worlds, which were inextricably related to understanding different natural phenomena.

The last traditional storyteller was still living in 1982—an elderly woman who possessed a remarkable and respected ability for eloquently describing the many characters of her stories, as well as dramatically replicating the various expressions and relevant actions of the animals. A listener's age was not a requirement for delight, but sometimes it was a problem in the situations she physically and verbally projected so well to both the appreciative youth, adults, and even an attending anthropologist. Her ability was such that a person who did not speak Spokan had at least a general grasp of the unfolding plot, and could often identify the various types of animals which were being artistically recreated by the woman's remarkable ability to enact each animal's physical characteristics and movements with accompanying sounds.

She enjoyed a reputation as a gifted storyteller—and several of her friends—once explained the difference between Indian storytelling and what they understood to be the method of their non-Indian friends and acquaintances. They explained how, in the past, the many songs and stories describing the supernatural powers and abilities of animals were believed to be true by children and many adults. Children were never told later that any mythological account was not true. She went on to say:

> You white people tell your children stories of Santa Claus, the tooth fairy, and other unusual people, and animals, and, how if your kids behave nicely, they'll be given presents and nice things; just as we do. But later you tell your kids the stories are not real or true; just make believe. But then, how can your kids believe what you say about other things when they get older. You then can't control your older kids with only words, you have to use [physical] force (Ross 1968-2008).

Stare-Downs

A competitive game played during the confining winter season by both young boys and girls—and sometimes with a parent—was called a *stare-down* (*słenúsm* or *sxʷúxy'e?* or *xxaxapu* or *čxaxápus* - "to stare"), a name which is apparently a misnomer, for according to Smith, it really meant a "sullen face" (1936-8:754). However, that too is misleading since an individual could win the contest by getting an opponent to *laugh* (*xʷe?*), or by presenting a distorted face. The first person to *blink* (*čcapsm*) or *wink* (*nc'ip'sm*) lost the game.

Some contended that this game was played only within a family or with a person whom one trusted, for in the past it was considered rude, even dangerous, to stare at a person, particularly a stranger since an older and more powerful individual could gain control of another—usually of a younger person—by intense staring (hypnotism); a form of *mal ojo* ('evil eye'). The only opportunity children and adults had to practice stare-downs, apart from actually playing the game, was when children practiced within the immediate extended family. Otherwise, when an adult stared at another adult, it was considered rude, inhospitable, and even dangerous, since only a sorcerer or a person who had a "head disease" would embarrass or frighten another by staring. An uninvited stare could have implied sinister ulterior motives, particularly because it was believed that one was brought under another's power by *intense staring with eyes bugged out* (*čxc'xíc's*). An exception was when a curing shaman, in a darkened room or dwelling, would presumably hypnotize a patient, and on occasion many of those present. Yet even then it was thought that when a practitioner hypnotized his patient, he did not achieve this with his eyes, but rather with his voice, which tended to relax or soothe the patient.

This game was played by several elderly Spokan women until their deaths in the early 1970s. One elderly woman, who seemed always to win, once explained: Only an old person—one with jowls, wrinkles, and few teeth—could shock her younger opponent into laughter. The game was played at night and in low light, with the woman pulling an unbuttoned cardigan over her head, which facilitated a certain amount of legerdemain as she deftly inserted into her mouth a pre-rolled bit of buckskin or several stones. She then removed the cover and began making strange vocal sounds, thereby presenting a truly distorted face, much to everyone's delight—or perhaps in a few cases fear. Her quite elderly and proud husband said that he had never seen the same face twice when she told stories.

Shadow Figures

The ability to entertain children by making an assortment of shadow figures was a cherished and well-recognized skill. Sadly, it has become a lost art among the Spokan, particularly with the introduction of electric lights and diffused lighting within dwellings. The best figures—mostly of fully represented animal bodies and heads—were once done with only a low fire or the light of a kerosene lamp. Shadow figures tended to move and dance because of the shimmering light from the fire or kerosene lamp. The display of shadow figures on a flat piece of canvas (from an old tipi?) became even more animated if the storyteller, or an elderly assistant who knew the routine, would provide sounds and even give some figures speech. It was not unusual for two or more people to provide a humorous or frightening story by creating two or more interacting characters.

It was said that although the storyteller's repertoire might be limited, the children's enthusiasm seemed never to diminish—though perhaps this was to avoid having to go to bed. Only a person's hands were used to make a *shadow* (*sm'el'k'ʷéy'eʔ*)—never with any additional props or rigid silhouettes. When asking one elderly lady why there are no more shadow figure games, her paraphrased reply was, "The coming of electric light, but more because of television and my old arthritis; besides, all of our grandchildren and great grandchildren prefer television, I can't do figures in color."

Card Games

Traditionally, cards for gaming were made from the stiff hide of young deer, birch bark, or thinly split cedar (Thompson 1916:276). In a traditional card game called *welúkʷs*, two cards would be drawn by the dealer and placed face down by the dealer, and one of the players would bet on the card's value. The dealer would then go with one or the other of the cards (Carlson and Flett 1989:155). More cards would be dealt until the same card in another suit came up. Another popular card game was *spásm*. *Playing cards* (*m'em'scútn'*) is not what one would now describe as a favorite pastime for many Spokan—because of TV, which sadly has brought the most apparent change in entertainment, even familial social interaction.

Poker was introduced with playing cards, but never became so popular as to replace traditional forms of gambling. Many elders have said they learned to play *poker* (*č'k'ʷul'slk'ʷptn*) while in the military during WW II, but seldom played it upon return.

Guessing Games

A popular guessing game played by both men and women was for a person to hold in his closed hand an array of sticks of different lengths with the exposed ends level with one another. After each person had drawn a stick, the person drawing the shortest stick lost and had to sit out, while the sticks were again collected and held as before—a process that was repeated until only one person remained and he was declared the winner. The game was simplified when a person held only two different length sticks in one closed hand, and the person who pulled the shortest stick lost the game.

Another guessing game played was for an adult to conceal in his or her cupped hands a stone or some other small object. After shaking their cupped hands, the object would be transferred to either of the hands before asking the opponent to guess which hand held the object. Some adults were noted for their skill at performing different legerdemain (sleight-of-hand or artful deception) maneuvers in a display of skill and dexterity, sometimes associated with a person's *sumés̆*. It became a guessing game when the adult first showed a child an object, and after chanting and performing various hands movements, the adult would open his now-empty hands, asking the child to locate the secreted object. After an appropriate time of mounting suspense and often incorrect guessing, the object was dramatically revealed to the child, having been in the adult's clothing or pulled from behind the youth's ear with legerdemain. A universal game was for an adult to hold out both hands with an object in one hand, and ask a child to *guess (esč'ɬʕawʕáwi)* which hand held the prize.

Unfortunately, with the advent and intrusion of television, as well as on- and off-reservation tribally-owned gambling casinos, an increasing number of Indian and non-Indian patrons have come to be more dependent upon these modern facilities for entertainment. Some individuals find that non-traditional diversions are proving to be a source of social and economic conflict, more than as a cost-free and instructive entertainment.

Dances

Dancing was performed during numerous socioeconomic and religious functions for all ages and genders; but the most apparent ceremonial function of large group dancing was bringing people together in a major rite of social and cultural event. In fact, it was noted: "there are old women [who] seemed to dance much better than the others" (Elliott 1914a, 1:49)

Even secular-type dances were important events for enculturation, socialization, communication, exercise, and exchanging news. As such, these events were eagerly anticipated and well attended, even by the most elderly. In fact, the Spokan practiced numerous dances; some were not always scheduled, but many were performed at certain times and for specific reasons. Most dances were of religious significance, designed to accomplish a specific need that confronted the Spokan. For instance, the Mid-Winter Ceremonies and the accompanying Medicine and Bluejay Dances focused on world renewal of resources, and for reiterating collective and individual mores and norms and in some instances to renew or acquire a *sumés̆*. For some people, a dance was an event that publicly recognized an individual's successful rite of passage.

The following listed dances allowed a participant to be assured of renewing her sense of identity within her natural, spiritual, and social world. However, the known history of Spokan dances demonstrated the many effects that diffusion and contact with Plains culture had upon Spokan culture; particularly after acquiring the horse in the early 1720s, and the resulting intensification of warfare and trade. Teit, when describing what he called the Turkey and other animal dances, noted that:

> Dances were performed in which the dancers imitated the actions of birds and quadrupeds, but it is not clear whether the dancers were members of any societies or dancing organizations. In later days the turkey dance was introduced, the dancers wearing feather bustles, and imitating the walking and actions of the wild turkey. The dancers stooped forward, walked stiff legged, held one hand up to the forehead and the other back at the backside. Most of the animal dances were named after the animals imitated, such as deer, bear, dog, raven, [and] chicken. Some of the leaders of these dances wore regalia appropriate to each dance (1930:387-8).

As a result of these many ongoing events, and the effects of missionization, deculturation, and the eventual acculturation, an apparent evolution of dances occurred in the form of more introduced dances, changes in costume, choreography, and meanings—thus serving totally different functions than they did aboriginally. The Spokan have, for example, adopted other dances, such as the *Snake Dance* (*sčewíleʔ swénš* or *ʔinʔinnp'm'n'cót*), *Blanket Dance* (*čɫsp'amiʔ*), *Cup Dance* (*lpót swéns*), *Happy Dance* (*snpyéls swéns*), *Wolf Dance* (*nc'íʔcn swénš*), *Eagle Dance* (*mlqnúps swénš*), *Snake Dance* (*sč'ewíleʔ swéns*), *Winter White Rabbit Dance* (*sqʷáqʷciʔ swén*), *Prairie Chicken Dance*, and several other dances acquired through contact from Plains cultures.

Music and various sound instruments—such as flutes, whistles, drums, and rattles, along with songs—were integral to the coordination of the group and also emphasized various aspects of the dance ritual. These dances became less frequent at social events, though there is presently a revitalization of certain traditional ceremonies that involve dancing, even team dancing and competitive dancing. *Modern dancing* (*q'ʷiʔmncút*) is done with no apparent scheduling at the Wellpinit Community Hall, or when young people are having a party; no special costumes are worn, and the music is provided by popular recordings. Every adult knew all the songs and dances, which, on appropriate occasion, they actively participated in. From an early age, children learned to appreciate adult dances and songs, which, when possible, they imitated.

Not only did the dances change, but so did the costumes and the music. The so-called War Dance is a notable example, for in the past there was only one drum, whereas now one may hear as many as five drums; even the choreography has been greatly altered. "All these dances are now practically pastimes and very little of their old meanings remains" (Teit 1930:391). There has been a revival of many once traditional dances, which are well-attended by both young and old.

War Dance

After the Mid-Winter Ceremony, some of the Spokan men would commence to make preparations prior to venturing forth to the western Plains for bison-hunting, trade, and stealing horses, which often involved warfare. Prior to leaving, men and women would gather in a *War Dance lodge* (*snwénštn* or *sntl'qmin*) to perform the *War Dance* (*swénš* or *xyílši*), an occasion for the warriors to discuss their proposed military tactics while *war dancing* (*hecwéʔnši*); and their concerns for those participating, including the selection of older boys who may assist with picketing, watering, and assuming general care of the horses; and selection and preparation of their equipment and weapons. However, if the war party was too large, the ceremony would be held outside to accommodate what could be an entire village.

The night's festivities commenced with the first beating of a *war drum* (*pumíntn*) with the *drum stick* (*sp'ɫčép* or *sp'min*), or when the ceremonial leader, carrying a fur-wrapped pole bedecked with eagle feathers, dramatically led his entourage during the ceremony. While the first song was being sung, a *shaman* (*sxʷqíxʷm*) would run among the participants waving a bundle of rose hips in one hand, and often a whip in the other hand, to rid the ceremony of any malevolent spirits. The medicine man always *hollered and waved* (*mkʷént ntáqsis*) at the gathering as he ran among the participants, and when satisfied with his performance, he would signal the other dances to follow him; thus, commencing the dance (STHC).

During intervals, the *War Dance drummers* (*sxʷɫsp'ɫčép*) would increase their playing in volume and intensity as the dancing warriors—sometimes in concert—worked themselves up as they became possessed by their guardian spirits (Elmendorf, pers. comm.). This vigorous pantomime became even more intensified by the women's weeping, wailing, and sometimes keening in painful remembrance of past times when some men did not return, and in anticipation of those who would not return after the pending warfare. Those men who left in the *pre-dawn* (*šels x̣lpulexʷ*)—sometimes called wolf-dawn—never stopped dancing throughout the entire ceremony; but those not participating in the war party were permitted to rest as needed.

During the War Dance, each man wore some part of the animal which represented his guardian spirit: commonly a section of fur if the animal were large, or the entire hide with fur if the animal was small. The pelt was displayed by wrapping one or more times around his wrist, elbow, or ankle, or even as a headband if it were a narrow, folded, or twisted pelt. A head—including the pelt—of an amphibious animal might be worn throughout the dance. All through the dance, each man usually had his *war dancing stick* (*sy'aq'pqínm*), which enhanced his appearance and intensified any altered identity and association with his guardian spirit by painting his face with red hematite. A man never wore these power representations over clothing, only when wearing a breech clout. If a participant was naked, he would paint some of his body with red or yellow hematite, and some would work moist clay into their hair. Usually it was only the men going to war who removed all their clothes. It has been reported (Smith 1936-8:1265) that for the Kalispel there was a *medicine hat* (*ƛ'ʔkʷíƛš*), but one that was not associated with curing *per se*, but with the war dance.

When war dancing, leadership was only temporary, but always led by a man who had had a dream or a message from his tutelary spirit to fulfill this role, one who had already demonstrated his abilities in leadership, astuteness, bravery, and outwitting the enemy (STHC). The strength and commitment of the leader's guardian spirit was apparent to all present by the man's struggle to come out from under the spell while he received a message from his *suméš*. Or, the power-appointed leader might sing a new power song, or say how—while unconscious—he could already see their enemy. He might be instructed to tell all his followers that they should conduct a special sweat before leaving for war, as would he. This was an occasion when all the warriors called upon their *sumés* for guidance and protection during the venture. The leader of the dance was always the leader of the war party (Elmendorf 1935-6, 1:25).

Understandably, the War Dance was a Medicine Dance, an occasion when the warriors would sing and call upon their guardian spirits for guidance and protection. Certain warriors made vows to extract revenge for a friend who had been killed during a previous engagement, promising the surviving kin of success in respecting their grief. War dances commenced slowly, but by the second half of the ceremony, the singing and dancing increased in tempo as participants would dance and sing throughout the night. Teit has described how "all bore weapons and the dancers advanced making motions as if looking for the enemy, looking for tracks, scanning the horizon, attacking an enemy, stabbing with spears and striking with tomahawks" (1930:392), and *war-whooping* (*t'qʷcíni*).

As men prepared for war, they sang their power songs and discussed their plans; women would line up on each side to help each man sing his power song. The women never danced, but mostly cried as their fathers, brothers, and husbands sang—knowing that some of them would not return. The term *čłsp'im* referred to the entire ritual of singing, going from camp to camp, singing farewell songs, receiving articles of clothing; and, in later years, money being thrown onto the canvas and being later distributed by the leader to the other warriors (STHC).

The following is a brief, but older account of the war dance:

> In the beginning, the women did not dance at all. They formed two lines on each side of the dancing warriors, watching. Wailing and crying as they did not know if they would see their men alive again or not. The drummers sang and the men danced for hours. All of a sudden one signaled a yell, [and] all would emit their war cries, dash for their horses and be off in time to arrive at their destination at day break (STHC).

When a large war party was being formed, "persons would go from camp to camp singing a farewell song" (STHC), a custom called *snqʕqʕáqsm* ("narrow nose or road") (Egesdal, pers. comm.). This song or *hymn* (*qʷélm'*) was sung after a War Dance, as it was after a Medicine Dance or even a stick-game. Just before the men left for war, this *farewell song* (*nqqʔáqsm*) was sung by all members of the village or camp. Then—just before daylight—people would donate various objects including clothing, which were equally distributed to the warriors according to their need. Members of a war party limited the amount and type of clothing they took—usually only a breechcloth and an eagle feather tied in the hair as their only adornment.

Prior to the start of the ceremony and dancing, a *man with special powers* (*sxʷqíxʷm*) was responsible for ridding the dance area of any evil spirits, and he would dance and sweep away evil forces with a bundle of rosehip branches; spirits that may have been indiscriminately released by a sorcerer, or that were designed to harm a specific dancer. Such a man had special power to discern where an evil force was located; when found, it would be gathered up by the bundle of rose hips to be later burned outside by the shaman. It was apparent which, if any, branches had captured an evil spirit because the spirit-ladened branches moved and trembled. If there was no drum to accompany the ceremony, a canvas, called *snč̓łsp'min*, would be beaten upon in lieu of a drum.

There is some question as to how recent is the War Dance among the Spokan and Lakes (Elmendorf, pers. comm.). Smith was told by the Kalispel that, "They never had a war dance until short time ago" (1936-8:1009), and the father of one of his informants remembers the arrival of the War Dance (1936-8:1013). Elmendorf (pers. comm.) asked if it diffused from the Plains with the horse, which in turn increased the conflict between the Spokan and certain Plains tribes as a result of the increasing economic need for stealing horses, and for the often concomitant status.

Victory Dance

Given the success or failure of a war expedition, the weather, and other logistical variables, it was never predictable as to when a war party would return. Typically, the war party would announce the day of their arrival by sending ahead an older boy, one of the attendants, to bring news of who had died so that the widow and relatives of the *deceased* (*łu λ̓'lil*) could prepare themselves. Often a war party would not return until early spring, hopefully with stolen horses and sometimes articles—such as bison meat and robes—gained through trade with different peaceful tribes. When there had been a successful raid, the Spokan staged a second dance, a *Victory Dance* (*syúλi swénš*), to celebrate and to hear the different individual and usually dramatic accounts of bravery. Part of the Victory Dance was held in a War Dance hall, suitable for the distribution of meat to kinspeople, and eventually for the redistribution to the elders and the infirm.

After a warrior gave his account of the battle, he made a sacrifice of a present, sometimes to a deceased warrior's surviving kinspeople—a ritual called *čq̓ʷq̓ʷl'úm'tn*. In the instance of an individual's outstanding performance of bravery, everyone—even children—danced around him as they *honored his exploits of bravery* (*čwénšmntm*); all the while his fellow warriors gave their personal accounts of his bravery, and often even reenacted his special deed.

If a man had been killed in battle, every effort was made by his fellow warriors to recover the body. If successful, they would take the body a safe distance away from the enemy where he was interred in a *war burial* (*sk'ʷplstwéxʷ*). Afterwards, the men would conceal the grave by riding their horses back and forth over the surface to conceal the burial site. It was said that if a warrior dug up an enemy's grave, then he would be killed in the next armed engagement.

When an elderly group of warriors gathered at a funeral—especially if the deceased had been one of their friends—it would be an occasion for *telling war stories* (*hecq̓ʷq̓ʷl'úmti*). Those who had died in combat were recipients of accolades that honored their individual performances and any personal sacrifices the deceased had made for a *comrade* (*sil'áxt*). In such a manner, respect was accorded to the memories of the surviving kin and friends. During the Victory Dance, a *warrior* (*x̓ix̓ilšn'ł*) on occasion might make a sacrifice or present a *gift* (*sčq'ʷll'um'tis*) to a member of a grieving family, usually to an older boy who would thereby have a better memory of his father's brave death. Often after gifting, one or more friends of the deceased warrior gave a dramatic yet humble *account of a harrowing experience in warfare* (*čq̓ʷq̓ʷl'úm'tn*) (STHC). The speakers always recognized the brave and unselfish efforts of the warrior who had died. However, such acclaim invariably described the deeds of others, and not of oneself, for it was said that a warrior's public arrogance would sooner kill him than an enemy, or take his strength (*suméš*).

Sun Dance

The only known published reference to the Spokan having a Sun Dance was made by Teit, who unfortunately never witnessed the ritual, but wrote that "A sun dance something like that of the Coeur d'Alene was kept up by the Spokan as a distant dance, often performed by itself" (1930:386). The only account of the Spokan Sun Dance given to the author was provided by a 92-year-old Spokan woman who explained what her grandmother told her about how in each winter village—during the time of 'people before whites and horses'—an old woman would stage a Sun Dance to propitiate the *sunrise* (*sk'ᵂk'ᵂƛ'íp*). This ceremony would ensure an abundant root crop in the coming late spring and summer.

The best example for reclamation would be when, after mid-winter, an elderly single woman or an elderly widow of each village would be chosen to spend the rest of the winter by herself in a *small ceremonial tipi* (*hecq'áq'n'ɫxʷ*), which was approximately half the height and circumference of a normal structure. During the woman's relative seclusion, all her needs were tended to by the village by older children who carried water, food, and messages, and ran errands; older boys gathered and delivered wood for her fire. This special tipi's entrance faced east, to catch the first rays of the sun.

An elderly woman gave the following account of this once annual rite of intensification, which was believed to bring a mild winter, no sickness, and an early spring, and an abundance of roots, game, and fish:

> The old woman had a very special power for the sun, but only for one year. Right after this annual ceremony another widow or elderly lady was chosen for the next year's ceremony. When the woman needed things, like food, water, or firewood, the kids would bring these things from their parents. The old lady would sing much of the day, but more in the early morning just before dawn, and again when the sun would go down. In the late winter and early spring, the old lady covered her right hand, half her face [right side], and neck with red paint [ochre], which she'd also put in her braided hair. The right side of her buckskin dress was also matted with this red paint. When the early morning sun was just halfway above the horizon, she'd put only her one painted hand and her half-painted head out [of] the tipi, and she'd look at the sun through her spread fingers [right hand]. She'd sing a power song. We'd creep near her tipi to listen, but the words didn't mean anything to us, maybe 'cause we were too young. When the sun was full, she'd pull her paint-covered face and hand into the tipi, but keep singing. All during the ceremony the first rays of sun would make beautiful colors on all the plants and the new leaves [spring time]. This was important because once the leaves turn color [in the late fall] there is always more evil in the world. The old woman would ask, not often or loudly, for food, fire-wood, and basic things for all her people. During the day, never at night, the old woman's request was fulfilled when other folks brought to her those things she needed. The old woman had [a] very special power in her relationship to the sun. I can still remember, as a child, seeing red paint [ochre] in her braids (Ross 1968-2008).

Cup Dance

Presumably, the *Cup Dance* (*l'pót swénš* or *člmšqíntn*) was performed at all dances, including the major Mid-Winter Dances. Some elders said that it was another example of a dance that evolved during the early 1900s, and was in some ways similar to the Friendship Dance and the Circle Dance (which were often performed together). The name of the dance is significant because a cup would be located in an obvious place in front of the speaker's dais or in the middle of the structure. This is of further significance because a *cup song* (*člmšqíntn* - "love song") was a rather *lonesome sounding song* (*čnáqs* - "alone" or *č'upéls* - "sad" or "homesick"), and was considered a supper dance song since it was a prayer sung just before midnight, when people stopped to eat supper at most of the dances. Singing at the Winter Dance was generally known as *snkʷnkʷnám*. A flute was played at intervals during the dance, and:

> An equal number of men and boy dancers, three or four to each side lined up six to ten paces back of the cup. As the drummers beat the drum softly and sang, the dancers would dance slowly and approach the cup in

reverence, as one or two [would] rise and dance backwards to the starting point again. They do this three times and break for midnight supper (STHC).

This apparently revitalized dance was incorporated into the Roman Catholic Church just prior to Holy Communion services. The priest was attended by some men and older boys, bedecked in sacred garments and wearing bells. Currently, certain Catholic Church ceremonies are referred to as Indian Services, probably because there is currently a Jesuit priest who speaks Spokan, and in his entourage are both men and women singers who accompany him as a drum is played, while the laity sing as the priest leads the procession into the church. "The priest or priests, the acolytes, the scripture reader, all [the laity] follow the drum to the altar" (STHC).

Friendship Dance

During the late 1800s and early 1900s, a number of dances were established, mainly diffusing from Plains culture, including the *Friendship Dance* (*čn'áxnwi* or *čn'axnwexʷ*), probably based upon earlier dances that inaugurated war, horse-stealing, and foraging expeditions (STHC). These social dances had several similarities, such as forming a large circle which always moved in a counterclockwise fashion with each dancer, shoulder-to-shoulder, gracefully sliding their feet sideways in keeping with the singing. Two large circles were formed, one within the other. The inner circle, composed of new friends, moved clockwise. The outer circle, composed of their hosts, moved counterclockwise. During the dance:

[...] one may choose someone out of the audience or from the circle, either man or woman, girl or boy, take his arm and enter the circle so as to be face to face with the outside circle and dance in the opposite direction, counter clockwise, as they shake hands with everyone they meet face to face for the duration of the dance, no matter how many times they may meet (STHC).

The dance would be held in the evening, and commenced by the lighting of a large outside bon-fire. Drummers commenced drumming as the participants later worked their way inside the lodge or hall:

The men were never elaborately dressed, only a single breech-cloth, a feather tied in their hair. One feather if he was single, two feathers if he was a family man. Their torsos, [and] upper bodies were heavily greased, their faces and bodies [were] red. Each man had his own color of paint and style of painting for himself and his horse (STHC).

An important ritual at the end of the Friendship Dance was to inform the Master of Ceremonies of any new or renewed relationships, which he would publicly announce to all the audience. There was always an *announcer* (*sxʷw'ew'é?m'*), a person who would enliven the occasion and entertain the participants with his humor and repartee. Also attending was a repeater who repeated—at proper intervals—the leader's words, and an interpreter, whose function was to *interpret* (*čmyépl?em*) the words being addressed to the participants. As previously stated, an interpreter may perform this function by explaining the words of a man speaking in glossolalia when possessed by his *suméš*.

Social dances were important occasions for meeting new acquaintances, renewing existing friendships, and reinstating disrupted relationships, all of which would be signified at the end of the dance by an exchange of small gifts between partners.

Circle Dance

The Spokan had a *Circle Dance* (*šl'šl'čm'n'cút*) when the dancers would *go around circle-wise* (*šlič*) as they did a shuffling, almost a gliding sidestep. Each *dancer* (*sxʷénšm*) would stand should-to-shoulder, men and women standing alternately. At one time, dancers would form two circles with both the inner and outer circle facing one another as they shuffled sideways, a maneuver called *sqʷʷéplwis*. Dancing commenced once they began singing the song. What was unique about this dance was that as soon as the singing started, a man or woman, upon seeing someone with whom they would like to dance, would first wave a handkerchief to gain the attention of the other as an *invitation* (*qs čnx̣nwex^wi*). If successful, one would grab the person by the arm (*sčn'áx̣nʔ*), known as *grabbing of the arms* (*čn'áx̣nwex^wi*) (STHC). As with all social dances, there was an announcer, an interpreter, and a repeater. After dancing with a new or old friend, a person would give that person a small gift, a keepsake called *x^wc'štwex^w*. This dance was clearly quite similar to the Friendship Dance.

Prairie Chicken Dance

In recent years there has been a dramatic revitalization of the *Prairie Chicken Dance* (*snx^wrmncútn* or *sx^wl'mncút swénš*) among the Spokan, which culminates once a year in the fall when Prairie Chicken dancers from much of North America gather on the Spokane Indian Reservation. The dancer *who does the Prairie Dance* (*ʔesq'^wóq'^wl'q'wey'*) is judged by his costume, regalia, and of course his ability to transform into a prairie chicken; which even to a novice is not only dramatic but obvious by the dancer's athletic ability to swoop low over the dance floor, all the while maintaining a dance step that is unique to his particular tribe (G. Flett, pers. comm.). In the past, those with greater *suméš* could bend their body closer to the ground. Many of the dance steps and regalia have been unchanged for many generations, and each tribe can be recognized by different dance steps and ways of responding to the drum beats. But universally, when a dancer was transformed by the beat of the drums and singing, he would commence to shake like a Prairie Chicken rooster. Some dancers were able to dance as they crossed one leg across the other while precariously maintaining their balance.

A man has Prairie Chicken *suméš*, which some believe is contained in his dance bustle, and when not in use the bundle is carefully wrapped and cared for. In the past, it was not unusual for a man to be so imbued with his *suméš* that any observer could note the strength of his power by how the dancer protruded his lips almost straight throughout the dancing; imitating the beak of the prairie chicken. Transformation was made complete by the melodic drumming and tempo, which at times encouraged the dancer to sing his unique Prairie Chicken song. Some have said that a young man's prairie chicken *suméš* came from his father.

There are various accounts explaining how this dance commenced in the Eastern Plains. Briefly, many years ago, some young boys were pretending to be warriors, and upon coming over a rise in the tall grass they saw hundreds of prairie chicken hens dancing and whirling about. Eventually, a white rooster prairie chicken approached the boys and asked what they were doing. One boy replied, for all of the group, that they wanted to be warriors. So the rooster instructed them to replicate the dance they were watching and they would become strong and brave warriors (G. Flett, pers. comm.). Another account is that on the Plains, a group of young boys were hunting gophers when a white prairie chicken appeared and instructed the boys to take his dance to their people.

An actual prairie chicken dance was observed by the naturalist Lord, whose description explained why the Indians copied the birds' behavior, and which he believed ultimately gave rise to the traditional ceremonial Prairie Chick Dance. And for anyone, even now, seeing the contemporary dance, can appreciate the dancers' choreography, costume, and facial expressions in emulating the birds' behavior:

> There were about eighteen or twenty birds present on this occasion, and it was almost impossible to distinguish the males from the females, the plumage being so much alike; but I imagined the females were the passive ones. The four birds nearest to me were head to head, like gamecocks in fighting attitude—the neck-feathers ruffed up, the little sharp tail elevated straight on end, the wings dropped close to the ground, but keeping up by a rapid vibration a continued throbbing or drumming sound.
>
> They circled round and round each other in slow waltzing-time, but never striking at or grappling with each other; then the pace increased, and one hotly pursued the other until he faced about, and *tête-à-tête* went whirling round again; then they did a sort of 'Cure' performance, jumping about two feet in the air until they were winded; and then strutted about and 'struck an attitude,' like an acrobat after a successful tumble. There were others marching about, with their tails and heads as high as they could stick them up, eventually doing the 'heavy swell;'

others, again, did not to have any well-defined ideas what they ought to do, and kept flying up and pitching down again, and manifestly restless and excited—perhaps rejected suitors contemplating something desperate. The music to this eccentric dance was the loud 'chuch-chuck' continuously repeated, and the strange throbbing sound produced by the vibrating wings (Lord 1886, 2:309-10).

Grass Dance

The interpretation and choreography of the grass dance, not really a Spokan dance, is thought to have come from the Plains Indians, namely the Crow who presumably acquired it from the Sioux and passed it on to the Salish in 1887 (Schaeffer 1935-38, I-55:34-43). The dance was held as entertainment any time of the year, mostly during the winter months, but not during the Mid-Winter ceremonies.

When dancing, the belief was that they could attract and acquire their individual *suméš* by repeatedly swaying back and forth like long clumps of grass in the wind. This dance was distinctive since there was little or no shuffling or movement of the feet; only the swaying of one's legs, hips and up-thrust arms. It was explained how once there was some semblance of coordination between the dancers, who always formed a moving circle so that they could see the others, and they became possessed by their individual *suméš*. The rhythm was maintained by usually three drummers, who may or may not sing. Once a dancer could see and feel his tutelary spirit, he would repeatedly sing one or more of his or her power songs.

Only a few contemporary Spokan participate in the Grass Dance, and that too only when on the Western Plains while visiting friends during rodeos or during Prairie Chicken dancing (G. Flett, pers. comm.).

Dream Dance

The millennium *Dream Dance* (*ʔestín'i*) was probably adopted by the Spokan, which was an integral part of a religious revitalization movement in the Plateau (circa 1878-1885) (DuBois 1938) in opposition to Christian missionaries, and as a means to revitalize older and more traditional sacred beliefs of origins and man's relation to the supernatural. People, sometimes called Dreamers, had visions—prophesies of cataclysmic events—such as pandemics and earthquakes. Simms wrote, "The Sanpoels [sic] and Nespeelums [sic] [...] are wholly under the control of their preachers or prophets, who are called dreamers, and are distinct from the drummers [Sanpoil], who live lower down on the Columbia" (1875:361).

Owl Dance

In the past, the Owl Dance was held for young men going to war, not knowing if they would return. The men stood in a circle around a large bonfire, and each wore a deer tail on his head, sometimes with an eagle *feather tied in his hair* (*snʕacáw'sqn*). Their families and friends stood behind them in a circle, singing and often crying. This dance was similar to the War Dance, as the war party left immediately after the dance while it was dark, traveling over known terrain until reaching their enemy at day break, or continuing through the next day, making their first camp that evening after going into Montana. Some expeditions took three or four days to reach the enemy's camp or village.

The contemporary Owl Dance (*hecnín'ey swenš*), known as the *Happy Dance* (*snpyéls swenš*), is another social dance that is actually a variation of the Circle Dance, which is presumably a dance of Spokan origin (STHC), the major difference being that midway through the dance:

> [...] the song beat and the drum beat decidedly changes to short, loud and sharply-measured beats and the two [long sides] of the circle stomp their feet in time with the drum as they rush toward the center, the men raising and waving their fans or what ever they are carrying in their hands and the ladies waving their hands or a kerchief, all the while shouting to the person who is opposite to them, they just as quickly raced back to the original line and continue dancing. At a dance where there are many drums, each drum may be held to "5 starts"

so the shouting and rushing toward the center is done only five times. Where there are only 2-4 drums, this may be repeated as many as eight or more times (STHC).

Either a man or a woman could take the initiative in asking for a dance. If one refused to accept, it was agreed that the person who refused would pay the other (Eli, pers. comm.; STHC).

Horse-Tail Dance

Though there are reasonable questions regarding the origin and validity of this dance, it can only be assumed that this dance came onto the Plateau with the arrival of the horse, and was conducted by the Spokan until approximately 1956, after which it was no longer staged. Fortunately, under the encouragement, support, and efforts of George Flett, the dance was revitalized in 2007, including singing traditional verses, drumming, use of traditional customs, and spirit-inspired choreography. Former horse-tail dancers came from several Canadian reserves and some Salish and Sahaptain reservations.

It is claimed that this rarely mentioned dance was sacred, since every dancer possessed horse *suméš*, and it is so-named because each male participant wore a horse-tail suspended from the back of his waist, which sometimes was attached to a feathered bustle. One man was always the leader of the Horse-Tail Dance—a whip-man, who, after singing the first verse, gave permission to the dancers to commence. As with most Spokan dances, the participants danced clockwise in a large circle to the accompaniment of four or five drummers. Each dancer had either a stick or wand; the dancer with the stick was considered a 'stud' horse who would, with this stick, control the direction of the 'mare' dancers.

As each dancer sang his individual *sumés* song, he had the feeling that his feet were not touching the ground, but rather floating. The older and more powerful dancer was capable of positioning their bodies in a lower and more difficult and strange stances because of their wisdom, experience, and more intense *suméš*. Other dancers always assumed a more upright stance while dancing; not having the experience, skill, or adequate power that came when acquiring new verses to one's power song.

The main function of the dance was for each man to honor his war horse, so that the owner's dancing enabled the animal to gain endurance and speed to better enable the owner to survive in battle (G. Flett, pers. comm.).

Gift Dance

The Gift Dance is probably a fairly recent (1920s) outgrowth of the Circle Dance and the War Dance. In this event, a married or single male would ask another single or married female to dance; the person asking was required to give a present to the other man or woman. A married person could ask a single person to dance, and vice versa. It was understood that the recipient was obliged to immediately reciprocate with a present, but never the same type of gift. The value of a person's gift usually reflected his feelings and concern for the recipient.

But like gift-giving in the present day, there were protocols and pitfalls in giving and receiving gifts at this dance. Many years ago it was said, probably facetiously, that "Whips make dogs, and gifts make slaves," and manners prevented a person from ever bringing or giving away a gift he had received at a previous Gift Dance. But there was typically no danger of that happening, since the recipient invariably treasured a beaded item, such as a necklace or some other gift that they had received many years earlier, and would say how it always reminded them of the gift-giver.

Winter Dance or Song Dance

The *Winter Dance* (*st'áx̌ʷa* or *str'qem*) or *Song Dance* (*snk'ʷnkʔnaí*) (Elmendorf 1935-6, 1:19) was a collective propitiation for good weather, plentiful game, health, and happiness in the new year to come. It was

546

always held during the Mid-Winter Ceremonies when the two principal dances were the Medicine Dance and the Jump Dance, as will be discussed later in more detail.

Important were the profound actions and rituals of an *appointed man* (*sxʷqíxʷm*) who would first rid the area of all malevolent spirits and forces by certain rituals and ceremonies that had specific functions. However, the general intent of the ceremony was to propitiate helpful forces that would not only protect the village, but benevolently assist in the occurrence of resources for the coming annual subsistence round, particularly fish. During the winter confinement, the advent of warmer weather, and the availability of fresh food resources, were greatly anticipated.

The way a shaman renewed his power at the Winter Dance was observed by Norman Lerman, a noted Plateau ethnographer, when in 1954 he witnessed the Okanogan dancing, a ceremony near-identical to the Spokan:

> Before performing, a shaman will begin humming a song softly while he sits or stands in some part of the room. As he sings louder he approaches the [power] pole (set up in the center of the room). He may walk around the pole singing to it or hold out his arms to the pole as he sings. When he grasps the pole in both hands he has become one with his guardian spirit. As long as he is holding the pole his words are not his own but those of his guardian spirit. Guardian spirits speak unintelligently and in a low voice, and, therefore, the guardian spirit's words must be transmitted to the audience by another person. For this purpose an interpreter stands by the shaman and repeats the guardian spirit's speech in a loud voice. The interpreter may be anyone in the audience and is sometimes another shaman. This pipeline from the guardian spirit via the shaman and the interpreter continues for as long as the guardian spirit has something to say to the audience. As a rule the guardian spirit makes prognostications of the future, gives free advice, and makes comments on present events (1954:35-6).

Jump Dance

In the past, a special structure was erected for the *Jump Dance* (*hestrqmí* or *str'qém*), always held in conjunction with the Medicine Dance during the Mid-Winter Ceremonies. The Jump Dance would be done only by adults capable of jumping high off the ground with both feet being brought together. The dancers circled the floor in a counterclockwise direction, always with their bodies slightly bent, thereby making it more difficult to perform the dance. In the center was the singer who sang his unique power song. Near him, and not dancing, was another man, a *repeater* (*suxʷč'ɬpetm*) who would repeat each of the singer's words—always quite loudly so that all the dancers could hear every word.

During the Mid-Winter ceremonies, parallel tipi poles were placed lengthwise on the floor, several feet apart. The giver of the dance would jump dance within these two poles until everything he owned was given away, even blankets and clothes, except his loincloth (STHC). He cried if something was omitted until it was found and given away. The *chaser* (*sxʷqixʷm*), a man with several bundles of rosehip branches, would sweep about the dance floor to rid the area of malevolent spirits.

Frey recently described a revitalized Coeur d'Alene Jump Dance, which is comparable to that of the Spokan. He noted how after each night's ritual of dancing and singing, there is a morning meal:

> The Jump Dance is ended with a "certain song," signaling that participants are "free to go outside." Following the song, a morning meal is shared by all in attendance. This might include camas, along with sandwiches, cakes, pies, and coffee. It is not unusual for some participants to fast from food and water during the entire two- or three-day event. The fasting helps to focus the dancer's prayers and, as an act of sacrifice, acts as an offering for that which is being sought in prayer. After the morning feast, all the participants return to their homes to rest until evening, when they reassemble to continue the Jump Dance (2001:238).

Medicine Dance

The *Medicine Dance* (*nʔixʷmi* or *str'qém* or *staxʷeʔ* or *hestrqmɪ*) and the Jump Dance were traditionally held during the last week of December or in January, during the Mid-Winter Ceremony in the song house. The *first announcement for this dance* (nˤa aˀc'e'ˀx̣ey) was by a man who had a dream and his tutelary spirit had told him to make the announcement, or by a young man who was instructed by his future guardian spirit that he may be *acquiring a certain power* (nƛ'eˀkʷlšcutm) during the ceremony. Normally, a Medicine Dance lasted for seven or eight days. However, if a man received his Bluejay power, then the dance lasted only three or four days (Elmendorf, pers. comm.). After such a *two- to three-night Medicine Dance* (ˀes nˀixʷmi), there was a *large feast* (siy'aq'yiqaqs). When a medicine man, *one possessing medicine* (pɬéw't?), has his Medicine Dance, he is finished for the year and he may attend another Medicine Man's Dance, but not participate in it. The Medicine Dance was always staged in the *song house* (snkʷenm'eɬxʷt'n) or what some called a medicine dance structure. Prior to entering this ceremonial lodge, four shamans would participate in a special sweathouse session:

> [...] one a leader & he would call out & tell some men to take up a red hot stone & carry it in [with] bare hands & he would do it—some one of the men in there would take the whole bucket & pour it on the rocks—then they would go back to the tipi & dance awhile (Elmendorf 1935-6, 1:24).

The *medicine dance structure* (st'áxwa) for a Medicine Dance always had three fireplaces. After the all-night dance, and at first light, a special sweathouse would be built by designated men. Elmendorf explained how:

> Only four men went into [the] sweathouse—one [was] a leader & he would call out & tell some man to take up a red hot stone & carry it in [his] bare hands & he would do it—someone of the men in there would take the whole bucket & pour it on the rocks—then they would go back to the tipi & and dance a while (1935-61:24).

All of the participants would enter the lodge in a clockwise direction, to show respect for the Bluejays. After this grand entrance, all of the food brought in would be collected and placed outside for the midnight dinner, a meal that traditionally consisted of small strips of deer meat. There was invariably a large amount of food, since every family brought some late in the afternoon every day during the ceremonial period.

During the night's ceremonial activities, no one could eat the traditional midnight meal, even small children, no matter what their age or degree of hunger, until the medicine dance leader had a dream in which he left the lodge and then returned with his *suméš*. However, at midnight, just before eating commenced, one man was sent to collect one or two buckets of water, which the lead singer distributed to the participants to drink. After eating, and if the Medicine Dance leader possessed deer power, he might foresee where the next day a small herd of deer would be congregated as an offering to the people. In that case, the leader would simply say, "Tomorrow there will be meat for [the] evening meal." After seven or eight days and nights of dancing and singing the ceremony was terminated:

> [...] with [a] big feed on the last morning [when] everybody cook[ed]—then they would go and put out *tcinéq'umn*—the little sticks to keep the deer from coming through when [the] deer [were] surrounded—*ci'itús*—wound pound on [the] tree[s] & [the] deer would come out of the brush where they had hidden and [would] come down toward the crowd so they could shoot them—[the] leader made [a] groan like [a] deer to bring them out. Next year a different *ci'itús*—[but] might be the same one [... the] leader for the war dance—then he [would] lead the war party out to find the enemy (Elmendorf 1935-6,1:25).

A person who ate any food at a non-designated time during the Medicine Dance would become ill or even die, unless treated by a curing shaman. The first bit of food eaten would stick in the person's *trachea* (sx̣ʷóp'ɬq'ʷlt), and eventually *choke* (q'eˤeps) him unless it was sucked out by the head medicine man, usually a sucking shaman.

This solemn Medicine Dance ceremony was under the strict direction of a leader, always a medicine man, albeit there were other *gathered medicine men* (uɬƛ'eˀkʷilš). Everyone's attention was on the *power pole* (n'št'eus or n'ípuˀstn or nšt'ew's or nyípuˀstn - "something that stands among"), sometimes called a *ceremonial* or *power cane* (ck'ʷečst or čxʷlal'qʷ or sq'etscht'); located in the middle of the floor. Some referred to the cane or pole as *t'kíkst* ("family tree") (Elmendorf 1935-6, 3:54, which was wrapped with fur and decorated with deer hooves, various types of animal claws, deer and elk teeth, and deer hoops, which rattled when the power pole was shaken by the leader when he commenced the dance, and the *ši?tus* would first:

[...] untie the deer-hoof *scosl'e?* off the *ck'ʷečst*, the center pole and beat against those who are in trance, just hard enough to move the *scosl'e?* rattle, he would beat upon their bodies from head to foot [as he sang] *?e sc'aq'emin?em t ɬu t suméšc* "You are being thrown down under the spell of your *suméš*" *he? sčc'osqntm*: the leader is beating the one gently about the head. Meantime the leader is singing his medicine song, he has never stopped. Then the one he is "working on," may regain consciousness, [he] may raise himself up. If he is unable to stand alone, he is told to hang onto the cane awhile, regaining some of his strength. The revived one will begin [his] own song [this song is an introduction, usually sung very slow]. Then he changes his song - [changes the tempo and gets into the real song, he starts to sing louder]. This is the invitation for the rest of the people to get up and join him in the song and dance! Meanwhile this revived person remains standing by the cane, singing. When he regains all of his faculties, he tells them all his story - what he experienced while in his trance - what the power is - what it will do for him - how he is to use it, etc (STHC).

A curing rattle was sometimes used by the dance leader to revive an unconscious participant by gently shaking, and "barely touching the unconscious patient with his medicine rattle" (STHC) near the person's head—a maneuver or ritual termed *he?s čc'osqnm*. One elder mentioned how the leader may offer his cane to assist a person who was unable to stand after being revived from a *power-induced trance* (*astsq'amínm ɬu tsúnécs* - "thrown down by his *suméš*") or has *fainted* (*ƛ'l'íl*). Once the person regains his faculties, he would describe what he experienced while in a trance, what he saw, where he went, but most importantly, what type of power he now possesses.

The ceremony would continue as another person commenced to shake while gripping the pole, and would sing one or more of his power songs, being joined by all the participants who would sing a power song if they had one. Once a traditional curing shaman said how in the past, only the patient could hear and understand the medicine man's curing song being sung, which later he would forget when he became well— regained consciousness. A curing shaman, particularly during the Medicine Dance, was capable and often demonstrated his power to 'see' what was causing a person's illness, what others could not see. Whenever an individual refuses to sing or dance after receiving his *suméš*, it was likely he was very ill, but a curing shaman could remove the sickness for a season (STHC).

After a time the leader would order that all of the fires be extinguished before he temporarily left the lodge to search the area for enemies or lingering sickness, and often he became aware of accidents or other misfortunes that may happen to one of the villages. Upon reentering the lodge, he always ordered that all the fires to be rekindled, after which he would proceed to make several announcements to demonstrate his prophetic abilities and skills as a curing shaman. He would, as an example, predict that a certain known person was soon to arrive, or a stranger riding a particular type of horse was going to give to a man or woman whom he named; these things invariably happened.

It was not unusual for several people to be seen in a trance when the leader returned, and he would untie a string of deer hooves off the *ck'ʷečst*, and, with one hand beat those in a trance from head to foot, all the time shaking his special rattle and explaining to others that they were under the spell of their *suméš*. More often, the l*eader would gently beat the unconscious person about the head* (*he? sčcosqntm*) as he sang his power song. Eventually, the person whom he was beating upon would *regain consciousness* (*nče??spu?us*) and attempt to rise, sometimes requiring assistance, which was given by the leader who might tell him to grab the cane as he regained his strength (STHC). Once on his feet, the person commenced to sing rather slowly his power song, increasing both the tempo and volume until all those present stood and joined him in his song, as they commenced to dance (STHC). More dramatically, and according to Elmendorf (1935-6, 2:23-24), the leader would address a man:

"I saw you dying and you'd have been dead now if I hadn't stopped you—I'm sure." He takes and redo[s] red woodpecker feathers [*nixʷúm*] & puts them in the person's hair & says "I mark you"—[he] tells the person then to go home & what to eat & do—then he tells them the reason they were near passing [on]—for instance, they had

549

offended someone or made an enemy—the person confesses what they had done then he *nixʷú* ("rescues") them: [he] puts the tail feathers of a woodpecker in their hair [... they] go on dancing—on [the] last night the leader calls the people whom he has fixed up with the feathers—toward [the] end of the dance—(*uyʼúscn* = end of dance)— [he] removes the feather (*ntʼsqúʔsqn* = "take[s] the feather from their head") [and] takes the feathers out & stores them away—[the] young man has been appointed by the *ciʔitús* to put the cane away in a certain designated place—off away from the village—the people whom he had fixed up with feathers and saved wouldn't die, that year at least, on account of having offended someone—after the leader had come back he would/might announce some event that would happen & it would usually come to pass [...] The leader would tell those he'd saved that they'd be there at the *nixʷmí* next winter, but if they weren't alive then it would be because he had failed to save them.

Just prior to grasping the power pole, some men would carefully and respectfully affix one or more of their guardian spirit relics to the pole in the hopes of intensifying his or her spiritual relationship with their *suméš*. When a man or woman grasped the power pole with both hands, their power would be renewed as the supplicant sang his or her power song, and the participant was totally possessed by his power, causing him to shake and tremble as the power came to him, all the while describing events that would be likely to occur in the near future, or warn him of things to avoid. This sacred ritual was often an occasion when a young person received a tutelary spirit, or in some instances, an additional guardian spirit. It happened that a person could be possessed year after year by his or her *suméš* when singing or dancing during the Mid-Winter Dances. Such a reoccurrence often intensified a shaman's power.

All people attending the medicine dance renewed their power and relationship with their tutelary spirit, all the while holding onto the cane as they sang their power song. It was not unusual for a person to first receive his power when in a *trance* (*čpspas*), and upon regaining consciousness, "he tells them all his story— what he had experienced while in his trance—what the power is—what it will do for him—how he is to use it, etc." (STHC).

With the *end of the medicine dance* (*uyʼuʔsšinʼ*) on the last night of the Mid-Winter ceremonies, which was announced when the medicine man removed the feathers from the hair of the person he was working with. After their use, the mat and feathers were collected and carefully stored away until the following year by a curing shaman. The ceremonial leader appointed a young man to carry the cane or pole out far away from the village to a designated location, where the sacred paraphernalia was carefully concealed and protected until the next Mid-Winter Ceremony.

Conversely, this ritual was a time when a person could have his power taken by a participant, usually a sorcerer, which was a dangerous time for a shaman when he was at the power pole to renew his power and sing his power songs, because one or more of his guardian spirits could be stolen by a more powerful shaman. If this happened, the participant revealed and sung only the songs of his minor or less powerful tutelary spirits, for once a shaman had his power(s) taken from him, he was powerless, and the sorcerer might even kill the defenseless shaman. Though an individual's principal guardian spirit would not be stolen with the others, it was weakened. Conversely, if a man lost his most powerful guardian spirit, "all the rest are lost too" (Smith 1936-8:1299).

The following is a brief account of how, during the Mid-Winter Ceremony, a woman acquired her *suméš*. It was one that many considered given by a non-traditional animal, but a *curing power (lemlmt slaqʼist)* that gave her status as a bone-worker who could do reductions, set broken bones, and remove illness from bones:

After receiving my power, I was careful to renew my gift by always going to the Medicine Dance. Years later, in 1938 when I was 39 years old, I was at a power ceremony and someone near the power pole accidentally blew on me and I started to sing, and at the same time my curly hair straightened out, and it has been straight ever since. I then felt forced to go to the power pole, and my right hand started to shake. Even the pole started to shake, and it even started to dance and move all about. At the same time, my brother, who was always jealous of my power, came to the pole and put his hands on the pole to stop it dancing. I'll never forget this 'cause he

550

couldn't pull his hands off, and he remained stuck; his hands I mean, to the power pole. I sang and danced for nine nights. Finally, my song came to me and I knew I should doctor sick people; any people, no matter what tribe they were. The last night of the ceremony, I left the longhouse with my uncle and others in a pick-up truck. As we drove through the fields, all the cattle cried and ran after the truck until we got to the fence, then they had to stop. I knew then that cattle were my guardian spirit—my *suméš*.

A few years ago, an old friend was very ill—going to die [...] I bought cattle ribs and bread at the store and took these to her, and asked her daughter to make supper, telling her that after we all ate, her mother would be well after she ate the meat off the cattle ribs. We went to the living room, and I sang my song as I moved my hands over her chest—never touching her, but I could still feel pressure [power] from my helper. All the time I sang my song, and finally took from her chest a feather her ex-husband had gotten a man to put there. Before it was light [dawn], my friend was well (Ross 1968-2008).

A principal purpose of the Medicine Dance was to entice deer into the area, so that they could be hunted after a ceremonial breakfast on the day of the ceremony:

[...] then they would go and put out *čníq'ʷmn*, the little sticks to keep the deer from coming through [...] When [the] deer [were] surrounded, the *ci'itús* [leader] would pound on [a] tree & [the] deer would come out of the brush where they had hidden and come down toward the crowd so they could shoot them—[the] leader made [a] groan like deer to bring them out (Elmendorf 1935-6, 1:25).

Though there is a quasi revitalization of certain dances, it is unfortunate, according to many elders now gone, how few of the once popular and traditional games are performed today. After extensive inquiry, it has become clear that the conservators of traditional Spokan entertainment and other activities, particularly storytelling, tended to be grandmothers who related to their grandchildren stories and situation-acting. But the gradual loss of the language, and the advent of government and mission schools, led to radical cultural changes and economic and social displacement of many traditional attitudes and activities when all *Native Americans* (*sqélixʷ*) were discouraged, even forbidden, to participate in their traditional leisure activities and games. Devereux spent many years in studying the demoralizing effects of early off-reservation schools, saying how "It must be stressed that acculturating agencies are often far more anxious to destroy native beliefs than to replace them with new beliefs" (1956:73).

Moreover, the traditional and functional division of labor, once based upon age and gender, was now totally distorted, being replaced by the demands of Christianity, which were often related to agribusiness. These changes meant a rather strict segregation of children, often in *absentia* from their immediate families, through distance missionary and government formalized schooling, and discouraged extended kin group activities. As noted above, the introduction of *electricity* (*sʔuw'éčn't*) effectively changed the atmosphere of evening and winter storytelling—replaced by the now ubiquitous television set. As a consequence, during the periods of missionization, tribalization, and enforced confinement to a reservation system, the characters of stories, geonomic designations of landforms, and many of the characters of oral accounts began to be altered and even forgotten.

The former relative ease of the lengthy periods of socialization of extended family and kin groups was lost through drastic socioeconomic changes—forcing these once successful hunters and gatherers to adapt to a subsistence system based on monocropping and animal husbandry of non-indigenous animals. Not only were some of the indigenous animals and plants replaced by ones central to the Spokan religion and subsistence quest, but also were the associated skills, physical endurance, hand-eye coordination, and cooperative collective behaviors were to a great extent irretrievably lost.

Musical Instruments and Songs

Songs

Olsen has aptly noted how song was the prayer of the Plateau (1998:546), a means of individual and group expression when propitiating supernatural powers for certain needs, whereby coordinating a peoples' sacred and personal transformation with nature and all of its elements. It is worth mentioning that most rites of passage—save for the girl's menarche—was accompanied by music, song, and dance. Again, as Olsen (1998:546), an ethnomusicologist, wrote:

> Song and rhythmic movements functioned in a central role with respect to personal power, protection, communication with natural forces, healing prophecy, and prayer. They solidified the supplications for renewal of resources, clarified roles specific to men and women, and manifested property in the natural scheme of things. Songs and dances supplied a pride in group and tribal heritage.

Perhaps a more inclusive understanding and appreciation of song was informally offered by Salish ethnolinguist Steve Egesdal, who worked with the Spokan, and wrote how "Songs [were] on virtually everything and for everything: riding, warring, berry-picking, dancing, curing, cradle, hunting, after killing bear, and so on. Song was incredibly important for traditional life" (Egesdal, pers. comm.).

Guardian-spirit songs were examples of collective singing of individual power songs, and were performed during the Mid-Winter Ceremony—most notably the *Winter season song* (*nʔistčéɫxʷtn*) (Egesdal, pers. comm.). During this ceremony, a young man would, for the first time, publicly sing his guardian-spirit song, which proclaimed his unique *suméš* and acceptance of responsibilities as a young adult. This was first cited by Curtis (1911, 7:87):

> [...] a January medicine song was announced by a man singing his medicine songs. This host and other assembled for four nights in the longhouse, each performing a complete repertoire of spirit songs while grasping a central pole. Each dancer tied an offering to the pole, which at the ceremony's end was secreted high in the wilderness (Olsen 1998:555).

Apart from Allan Merriam's extensive and innovative work in ethnomusicology with the Flathead (1951; 1967), there are some translations of traditional Spokan *songs* (*sqʷélm*), but unfortunately few recordings were made (STHC). Fortunately, in 1976, Larry Parker recorded a number of Spokan songs (Olsen 1998:562) for KSPS-TV, Spokane, Washington, such as Circle of Song, Season of Grandmothers, and People of Rivers. A large number of cassette tapes with nearly one hundred different Spokan songs and chants have recently been found, and are being translated by the Spokane Tribe.

Musical instruments employed by the Spokan were based primarily upon the principles of percussion and wind, and were used collectively or by individuals for recreational and ritual occasions. The casual strumming of a drawn bowstring with one's fingers, or thumping on it with a loose arrow, was not considered as a musical instrument per say, even though "children used small musical bows; one end in the mouth against the teeth [held by either the] left or right hand [as the other hand] used an arrow to tap the string" (Smith 1936-8:1023). Flutes and whistles were instruments with the greatest range of sound, shape and use—more so than the drum or *rattle* (*cósal'eʔ*). The more sophisticated multi-holed flute was recognized for producing notes and a wide variety of melodies, many of which were traditional tunes, or ones composed by the player.

Two close *reciprocal sweathouse friends* (*slʔáx̣t*) can sing one another's *suméš* song without any harm to either. However, "power can never be borrowed in this way—might react against an individual who had not legitimate control of it" (Elmendorf 1935-6, 1:39-40).

An example of non-traditional musical instruments being introduced by missionaries was noted at St. Mary's among the Flathead, which included the "clarinet, flute, tambourine, piccolo, cymbals, two accordions, and a bass drum" (Lothrop 1977:101).

Flutes

The only Spokan musical instruments of aboriginal manufacture, in any number, were the flute and the drum (Merriam 1951, 3:368). In the past there was always more than one man among the Spokan who had the power and skill to manufacture flutes. In most cases a performer composed secular songs, whereas power or curing songs were composed by shamans and sorcerers, words and melodies given them or assisted by their guardian spirit. Flutes were made from a wading bird's leg bone or a bird's wing bone (eagle or osprey), even hollowed grass stalks, or deciduous woods that were split lengthwise and hollowed out with stone and the two halves secured together with wet strips of rawhide. Regardless of material, they were drilled with holes for producing various notes. Unlike Euro-American flutes, Spokan flutes were held vertically, and the musician blew into the end holding the reed, or blew at an angle over the open end if it was a reedless flute.

Flutes, however, differed in their construction and use, the critical difference being that one-holed flutes in both the Plateau and Plains were blown as warriors went into battle. McLaughlin reiterates Catlin's observations for the Plains Indians, of how: "Single hole bone whistles were not musical instruments but were sounded during battle and on ceremonial occasions" (2003:138).

A shaman with certain song power could compose love songs for a flute owner, or while hidden play his own flute while his male client claimed the affections of his intended love. At every opportunity the *suitor* (*sntxʷsmcút*) would play his *bone flageolet* (*x̌awístn*) or *flute* (*člmšqíntn*) when near the young woman whom he was *courting* (*čłq'em'n'énʔey'*), an instrument believed to have been capable of composing an *Indian love call* (*čłx̌ʷal'qʷm*) with no assistance from its owner. It was believed that some love flutes had their own power and would prove favorable in their purpose if the owner demonstrated his respect by caressing, singing to, and even 'feeding' the flute. It was not unusual for the flute's owner to oil the instrument and wrap it with martin or weasel fur after every musical session. Flutes were used by men when praying, as the music was believed to facilitate the dissemination of his thoughts and hopefully please the power being propitiated.

A *short bone flute* (*x̌wístn*) was made from a wing or leg bone of a wading bird (e.g., a crane) or a bald eagle's ulna bone after the bone had been first sucked to remove the marrow and permitted to dry before fashioning the holes. Each bone flute was approximately 10 to 12 cm long, with three holes on top, one near the back end (which was never closed), and a slit near the mouth end with gum or tallow inserted in it and secured with narrow wrapped sinew straps. Such a flute was used only by a medicine man (Smith 1936-8:1018), and during a curing session it was often hung from the practitioner's neck by a buckskin cord tied around the mouth end.

Some elders said how the open bone flute was used for sucking illness from a patient, rather similar in shape to the musical flute, only shorter with no holes, save on either end for sucking. Or, after playing a song to receive his tutelary spirit, the shaman covered the holes of his flute with his fingers, placing the flute to the intruded site, and then sucked out the cause of illness. Either the practitioner removed blood in this manner or the patient would regurgitate blood, which might contain the intruded object (Elmendorf, pers. comm.). However, some claimed that the short flute was never used in curing, only ceremonies (Smith 1936-8:1018). But there was no agreement as to whether curing flutes were decorated, or if the instrument was played intermittently during the group medical inquest or between curing sessions.

A curing shaman might receive his curing flute from his guardian spirit who would 'gift' the shaman with one or more curing songs. These songs were never passed on to anyone. After a successful but difficult curing session, the song could, however, be adopted by another shaman into his repertoire of curing songs. In that case, it would never be played again by the original shaman, nor could a person ever play a tune that had not been properly transferred, for fear that he would choke to death while playing.

Another type of flute, called a *čłx̌ʷálqʷ*, was 45 to 50 cm in length and 7 to 10 mm in diameter with six finger holes, each equally spaced approximately 2.5 to 3 cm apart. This particular flute was made by either hollowing a straight section of elderberry (after removing the heartwood), or by splitting longitudinally a straight section of hardwood, such as maple, and furrowing a long, smooth half-channel in each section before mating the halves together and securing intermittently with wet strips of rawhide. Upon properly drying, the two halves were secured and tightly closed by temporarily wrapping with hemp. A blowing hole, located at one end roughly 12 to 16 cm from the blowing end, would be a lengthwise slit approximately 3 cm long. Inside a small round ball of pitch or tallow was placed, one that vibrated when air was forced over the restricted space (Smith 1936-8:1017). There was no mouthpiece.

Wooden flutes were often painted red and usually had geometrical or curvilinear designs (circles or diamond shapes) cut into the flute, which the maker would further enhance by covering the instrument with damp ochre and rubbing off the excess, leaving paint in the precut recesses. Only men and older boys played such an instrument, and could be played before women and children, but never by them, and was played for music only, not for curing or courting. Smith (1936-8:1025) described how the Kalispel, and most likely the Upper Spokan as well, after acquiring rifles, would take a disused gun barrel and make it into a flute by drilling several finger holes. Such a flute could be carried into battle, tied to one's wrist, for use as a weapon (club) when in close quarters.

An older boy's prized toy was a *willow flute* (*člmšqíntn* - "love song instrument"), often made by his grandfather or uncle, who would then proceed to instruct the boy in the proper use, storage, and etiquette of the instrument. Inconclusive debate and lack of recall surround the question whether a man's flute was interred with the owner upon his death. One elderly man, who was the last Spokan practitioner, claimed he had been told many years ago that such a powerful flute, if blown by another, would kill the man.

A love flute, eagle bone whistle, a shaman's rattle, a sacred stone pipe, a shaman's sucking tube, or power bundle, were accorded great care and respect by an owner. As mentioned, an individual oiled, rubbed, and of course prayed and sang over the instrument of power before and after its use; an indication that presumably inanimate but sacred tools or instruments had animate power.

Whistles

The most practical use of whistles was for communicating with fellow hunters when tracking deer or other game. It also provided entertainment for children and one's own pleasure, and as was mentioned earlier, boys were taught at an early age to whistle using only their fingers and perhaps a blade of grass. They also learned to make whistles out of bone, wood and other materials at hand. Though the ulna of a wading bird was preferred, one elder recalled and displayed a whistle made from a bald eagle ulna, which he felt may have been used by a man with bald eagle *suméš*. The whistle such as the one in the figure below might be approximately 8 cm in length (Collier *et al.*, 1942:87).

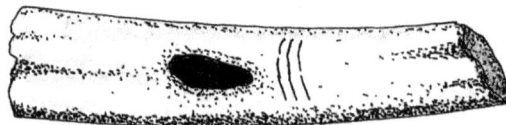

Figure 37. Bald eagle ulna whistle

A simple and secular *whistle* (*npúx̣łcʔetn*), often made as a gift for a young boy or by a man to entertain himself while relaxing or traveling, was quickly fashioned from a section of the edible cow parsnip stalk or from different types of dry *creek weeds* (*nłxʷłxʷé* - "something with a big hole in it"), as long as the stalk has a hollow stem (Smith 1936-8:1021). These field whistles had only one hole at the blowing end, which was made by cutting a section of dry reed, with the top cut at a 45° angle, and then removing a wedge-shaped piece just below the top cut on the higher (longest) side. Such a whistle could be used by a boy as a blowgun with small stones or balls of clay as projectiles. The favorite, and of course safest, type of pellet for blow guns were quickly made by rolling fresh, wet grass into an appropriate diameter.

A more durable whistle was made from willow or elder wood, when gathered in the spring when the sap was running. After cutting a section approximately 10 cm long, the maker then gently tapped the entire surface with a smooth stone or a stout stick to loosen the *bark* (*č'i?lelxʷ*), permitting the sleeve of bark to be temporarily removed to facilitate cutting a proper hole in the bark, to fashion the section of willow. The bark was then slipped back onto the length of wood. Perhaps the first prized gift by a boy's father or grandfather, even before receiving a small bow and some arrows, was a willow whistle, made in the spring when the sap commenced to run in red willow or red osier:

> I remember my excitement and the satisfaction of my grandfather when he made my first wood whistle, and I blew it all the time; after a while I'd think he [grandfather] wished he'd never made it for me [...] A friend of mine got his first whistle from his widow grandmother, who'd made it, and could make it whistle like a bird (?). When I got older, we used to think she always had her own bird whistle. After we helped her [with] chores, she'd make it sing. She was good; better than any of us (Ross 1968-2008).

In addition to flutes, medicine men often carried a medicine whistle that was— given the situation—part of the curing ritual. As with the flute, a shaman or sorcerer always made his own whistles (Elmendorf, pers. comm.), and there are a few known surviving examples among the Spokan. One is an old shaman's whistle crafted from eagle bone, given many years ago to the author by an elderly woman who explained that it had once been used during certain curing ceremonies by her mother's father. Three Spokan bone whistles made from the ulnas of a whistling swan were found by Collier and his colleagues, each was approximately 16 cm in length, and the apertures were about 2.5 cm "from the proximal end, and the whistle notch is about 1 inch from the resulting open end" (Collier *et al.*, 1942:87).

Figure 38. Blue heron (?) ulna bone whistle

Though no other known examples exist, the received wisdom was that the Spokan fashioned a type of *horn-tip whistle* (*x̣x̣w'istn*) from a deer horn prong that was hollowed after removing the very tip, a whistle that presumably could blow by itself after a hole was bored through one side of the horn near the large open end. There was no type of reed, so apparently the player simply blew across the large open end while "fingering" the diameter of the small side hole.

Drums

The Spokan made a variety of drums, all of which have since evolved in size and decoration, primarily due to Plains influence. The *drum* (*pumíntn*) was associated with group ritual, and always proved effective in heightening the atmosphere of the activities by varying the intensity or frequency of the rhythm when appropriate. In some rites of intensification, such as pre-warfare rituals and certain types of curing, the drum was instrumental in creating an anticipated conclusion or to dramatize a certain phase of the ritual. A few elders said a drum was blessed before use and spoken to by one or more drummers when drumming. Yet there was no consensus if the drum—by itself—was sacred, or required any attending ritual; but there was agreement how a drum's owner was fastidious in the care of the thin, rawhide drum head. However, a few elders explained how a curing shaman may have a small drum, one he beat upon prior to a group medical inquest to intensify and heighten the group's expectation as well as the patient's. Numerous Amerindian groups did assign sacred status to drums. Among the Spokan, men were recognized as the sole drummers. A drummer always used only one drum stick, never two.

Depending upon the size of the desired percussion instrument, drums were made by men from a block of dry black cottonwood or cedar. Prior to the introduction of steel tools, the wood block was first partially hollowed out using carefully watched fire, working the top to a desired depth, and then upturning the block and repeating the process. A more precise hollowing and inside shaping was accomplished with stone tools, as was the smoothing of the outside. The process was not a lengthy one, usually taking several days to fashion a drum of approximately 10 to 12 cm thick, with a diameter of roughly 40 cm. A second and more difficult and time-consuming method of making a drum was to first roughly shape a rectangular length of dry cedar by repeatedly splitting away long sections of wood until the block was a relatively thin, long, flat rectangular section of wood, which was then thoroughly soaked and steamed to form a circle with both ends overlapping. The wood was formed using a circular jig of pegs driven into the ground, which held the wood in place as it dried. When ready, each end of the drum was bored with two large holes parallel to each of the butt ends, which were then brought together so the pairs of holes overlapped, and then secured together with strips of rawhide. The thickness of the drum wall varied from 15 mm to 2 cm.

After the drum form had thoroughly dried, a drum head was made from a single, roughly circular dehaired elk or deer hide of appropriate size, and was soaked until supple. The intended drum hide would be large enough to form the head as well as cover the sides of the drum with enough hide to partially cover the underside. The perimeter of the hide, when dried, was perforated to form a series of holes with an awl or by inserting the sharp end of a deer antler tang every 4 to 5 cm, and the prepared drum head was again soaked and stretched loosely over one opening of the drum, and down over the sides with the ends rolled and tied to opposite rolled sections. A completely wet hide drum head, if stretched too tightly, would, upon drying and contracting, collapse the drum. Therefore, when finally situating the drum head in place, it had to be only slightly damp. All the rolled ends were then brought together and tied as one large knot, thereby permitting the *drumme*r (*suxʷsp''ɬčepm*) to hold the drum in one hand when drumming.

Prior to using a drum, the drummer carefully placed the drum near heated coals to sufficiently shrink the head and thereby create a tight tympanic membrane. Larger drum heads were often painted with designs, typically using red hematite. Not unlike today, some large drums had strung deer dewclaws suspended from the sides of the drum. This type of small drum accompanied a war party for their pre-battle and post-battle ceremonies.

In later years the Spokan made a much larger drum, often referred to as a *war dance drum* (*sp'ɬčép*), and it was held off the ground in various ways, but mostly by at least four stout vertical sticks strategically secured to the drum sides, and was played by two or more men who sat squat-legged to *drum* (*spp'im*). *Drumming* (*sp'ɬčepi*) was always done by men, and usually there was a *head drummer* (*sxʷsp'ɬčep* or *sxʷsp'ɬčep*) who was the leader of the group and responsible for the drum's care and storage. A drum stick (*sp'min*) was made of hard-wood; shaped by the owner's inclinations. The drumming end was always covered with several layers of otter or martin skin with the fur on the outside to protect the drumhead prior to commencing to *drum* (*sp'ɬčep* - "to beat with a stick, to drum"). Some drummers attached strips of weasel or otter fur to the handle ends; eagle feathers were also a fashion. Apart from heightening the audience's anticipation, the main function of drumming at the War Dance was coordinate the dancers and to maintain or vary the tempo of the dancing.

Within the Services Building on the reservation is an enlarged photograph of Spokan elder John Stevens sitting and playing a drum that is held approximately 15 cm off the ground on four upright stakes affixed to the sides of the drum.

Rattles

Depending upon the intent of the user, there were several types of rattles. A *pebble rattle* (*č'léčstn'*) made from a section of thoroughly soaked rawhide was sized appropriately by being stretched over a round stone or tightly stuffed and forcibly packed with grass or deer hair. After the hide had dried, the stone or the stuffing was removed. Then three or four pebbles, and the end of a rounded piece of wood, were inserted and the gathered loose ends of hide were soaked again and tightly sewn to the partially inserted handle. A variation was made by soaking the hide, piercing the center, and projecting the handle through the hole before wrapping a length of wet rawhide around the loose exterior pierced flanges. Some men attached eagle feathers onto the end of the handle and onto the projecting top of the handle, if the latter style had been made. Pebble rattles produced a unique sound, and were used during dancing and by shaman during certain curing rituals by the Spokan; being monotonous, the sound was said to be somewhat hypnotic, or at least suggestive.

A similar type of rattle, called *c'aʔaλá*, was used by a leader during warfare to presumably summon the will and determination of his men. Such rattles were never decorated or hung with ornaments. It has been said that this type of rattle was never used in ceremonies, only in warfare (Smith 1936-8:1020). Some Spokan claimed that the rawhide rattle was used during the group medical inquest by some shamans prior to curing a patient. A medicine man's rattle was called *scosl'eʔ*, and he would shake it as he danced and sang one of his power songs.

Other by-products provided by deer were dewclaws, which were made into *dewclaw rattles* (*čt'ewá*) after being boiled off from the deer's hooves; some men simply heated the dewclaws and removed them by hitting the leg with a stick. Since every hoof has two dewclaws, each deer produced eight *dewclaws* (*clápʔšn*), and once the dewclaws had dried, a *hole was bored* (*łxʷntem*) through the tips of approximately twenty to fifty hooves with a stone awl. Each was then tied to a piece of narrow buckskin—1 to 1.5 m in length, and secured by tying a knot larger than the small hole. A finished dewclaw string was from 10 to 15 cm in length, and the final attached lengths were approximately 1.5 to 2 m in length before being looped several times and attached to a dancer's cane. The dewclaw tips pointed upwards, making an appropriate *sound* (*cos*) whenever a medicine man thumped the end of his cane on the ground or shook it above his head during the Medicine Dance. The most complete description of the dewclaw rattle staff is from an elderly Kalispel man, recorded by Smith in his field notes:

> They used a rattle made of deer hoofs hung on a stick. They boil the hoofs, and then pull them off the leg so that they are hollow. Then they bore a hole in the tip of each hoof & put a buckskin string through it [...] Lots of these strings were tied to the end of one stick; 20, or 30, or 40 strings. Each string is about 5 feet long; the pole was longer than the strings so that they would be over one's head. These were used in the war dance (1936-8:1031).

Strings of deer dewclaws were attached by wrapping one or more lengths to the ankles of dancers; but not the knees, as seen in some contemporary Indian dancing. Similar noise-producing anklets were made by putting small stones inside stiff rawhide balls, each a bit smaller than a lemon. These would be strung together and wrapped around a dancer's ankles. Sometimes an individual dancer might use several such anklets at the same time. Only male dancers used this type of rattle at dances and ceremonies.

Other rattles were crafted from the dried shells of painted turtles, by stretching a wide strip of wet rawhide over the head and tail opening, in order to retain three or four stone pebbles inside the shell. The affixed rawhide served to secure the fully inserted wooden handle. It is not known if rattles had personal names—as flutes often did.

Chapter XVII: Medicine and Health

During the prehistoric period (11000 BCE to circa 1804), the Spokan had an adequate medical system for successfully treating existing illnesses and diseases and maintaining health. This knowledge was comprised of an extensive corpus of time-tested explanations and therapeutic procedures that were inextricably related to the notion of supernatural and natural causes. It was common knowledge that the, "ideas and practices relating to illness, are for the most part inseparable from the domain of religious beliefs and practice" (Glick 1967:32). Such an inextricable but causal relationship was recognized by the Spokan, who, being foragers and gatherers, were in some respects, more concerned with prolonged illness than immediate death because of their need to maintain a high degree of mobility in order to successfully exploit animal and plant foods as well as their by-products, since a sometimes serious consequence, illness, could debilitate an individual's food-getting activities as well as necessitating the time and attentive need of familial care-givers.

Given the traumatic effects of deculturation, resulting in a concomitant loss in many areas of medical knowledge among the Spokan, and the unfortunate introduction of non-indigenous diseases, the general term "medicine" is frequently misleading, particularly since it once had different meanings and applications for traditional Spokan. Ethnomedically, a person often sought to possess a certain curing *sumeš*, a unique ability to manipulate one's health, at least influence supernatural forces that had been temporarily given to a man or woman during a power-seeking ritual. Medicine and its application was synonymous with "power" in that sense, but, as applied here, medicine invariably denoted a person's ability to cure or maintain health, regardless of malady or procedure. This individual power was either malevolent or beneficial, for a practitioner could be a sorcerer or a curing shaman. A sorcerer practiced malevolent procedures, but could, on occasion cure.

Prior to white-introduced diseases, often in the form of pandemics (Boyd 1985, 1999), and the incursion and often the decultural effects of Christian missionization, and the eventual confinement of Indians to reservations, it was a complex system of therapeutic procedures based on a holistic paradigm that made a distinction between natural and supernatural causes of what we now term illness (psychological) and disease (physical). Lévi-Strauss always maintained that the, "shamanistic cure is the exact counterpart of the psychoanalytical, but with 'the inversion of all the elements'" (1963:199).

Disease, being a physical-chemical phenomenon, "seems to be defined independent of illness" (Fabrega 1978:15). Yet during the prehistoric period, there was presumably not always a clear phenomenological distinction between the contemporary medical terms *illness* (*cex^w* or *sil'sl't* - "psychological") and *disease* (*swéyt* - "pathological"). There existed, as was best remembered, only a classification of maladies that had a definite physical and traumatic origin, *physical injury* (*lx^wup*), or those of supernatural or spiritual etiology. It should be noted that physical injury could be caused supernaturally (Turner, pers. comm.). Spencer, Jennings, *et al.* (1965:224), when writing about the Sanpoil who presented a broad interpretation of so-called natural and unnatural afflictions, which is applicable for the Spokan, stated that, "Shamans cured 'unnatural' diseases, those which arose through acts of men or inhabitants of the spirit world - 'Natural' illnesses, injuries, headaches, or colds, did not call for shamanistic treatments." Brown *et al.* 1996:195), in defining ethnomedicine, cite how "Cultural adaptations to diseases [and illnesses] include behaviors and beliefs that function to limit morbidity and mortality [and ...] there are beliefs and behaviors about appropriate therapy for diseases [and illnesses]."

The general perceived success of a curing shaman, given his or her diagnosis and treatment—the so-called clinical reality—was the practitioner's therapeutic and social relationship with the patient and attending kinspeople and others. It was incumbent upon the practitioner to evaluate and distinguish between what is presently called the "curing" of disease and "healing" of illness (Kleinman 1978, 2:75). Consequently, the

Spokan believed there existed essentially two principal explanations for any natural and personal malady. Naturalistic or somatic etiologies were often related to external misfortunes such as fractures, dislocations of extremities, burns, wounds, bruises, certain skin irritations, or snake and insect bites. Given the circumstances, even occupationally incurred injuries or episodes of negative emotion or paranoid hallucinations were considered to be caused by natural causes, since maladies and misfortunes often had predictable explanations—cause and effect being more apparent and immediate than supernatural causes, and usually required only self- or familial treatment. Spokan explanations for naturalistic injuries were always clear, realizing that an injured person had not violated a *tabu* (*xaʔxéʔt* = anything sacred) (Egesdal, pers. comm.), either in diet, behavior, or failure to properly acknowledge a prescribed ritual.

On the other hand, personal etiologies were invariably psychogenic, ones interpreted as resulting from the patient's improper behavior which required the assistance of a medical practitioner who, in attempting to cure the patient, would analyze the patient's previous or ongoing behavior prior to making a diagnosis. A curing shaman—never the patient—may have a dream that revealed the reason for the patient's condition, and, as will be discussed, there were numerous procedures for attempting to identify how the patient had violated established moral prohibitions or norms of behavior. In the case of suspected or even known sorcery, it was sometimes difficult to immediately identify the individual responsible for the illness, or how the patient's behavior was responsible for his or her illness. Traditionally, a Spokan curing shaman might dream of a remedy, one that was not necessarily given by his guardian spirit, but by a different tutelary bird or animal, or even by an *unknown person* (*stmél'is*) at a time other than during the Mid-Winter Ceremony.

Concepts of Illness and Disease

The Spokan classification of maladies, excepting the specialized terms of illness and disease, were based upon the occurrence of either natural or supernatural explanations. However, in reconstructing certain Spokan explanations for the causes of many illnesses, and even certain diseases, it was difficult, as mentioned above, to establish clear divisions between pathogenic (disease) and psychogenic (illness) origins. Only recently, even in contemporary non-Indian or allopathic medical systems, some pathogens were considered an accepted explanation for disease, whereas *malevolent medicine* (*kʼʷlkʼʷlečʼeʔ*), i.e., illness caused by sorcerer, was rarely viewed as psychosomatic. As a consequence, the Spokan believed that the principal causes for malevolent illnesses were, in most cases, sorcerers using various mechanisms and rituals, such as spirit-induced illness or possession, spirit loss or spirit control intrusion of a pathogenic object or spirit power, possession of one's tutelary spirit, or poisoning through sorcery, particularly when a *healthy person became suddenly seriously ill* (*čskʷiséyst*) for no apparent reason. "Throughout native North America [...] sickness was understood to be the result of the intrusion into the body of some sort of malevolent influence. The central metaphor of curing was removal of some 'thing,' visible or; otherwise from the body" (Moerman 1979:60).

The principal reasons for sorcery were *revenge* (*sʔeyčst*) or jealousy toward the victim, or a previous incidence of humiliation caused by the patient against the sorcerer, or someone who had enlisted the skills of the sorcerer. Soul loss was not always the cause for physical illness; but rather for different degrees of temporary or permanent *mental illness* (*qʷaʔqʷuʔoʔ* or *n-sil'qin*), in which prolonged cases could result in death (see Appendix N). Yet there are recorded instances of a person willing his soul to leave so he would die, often when experiencing extreme and unrepentant grief, such as the loss of a long-time spouse. Ray wrote:

> Soul loss is the remaining major disease concept of the Plateau. That is the belief that the animating human soul may become temporarily detached from the physical body without death occurring immediately. The accompanying illness is invariably serious—usually the most serious of any ailment—and death comes very soon if the soul is not recovered.

Care should be taken not to confuse this concept with guardian spirit loss [...] The loose usage of the two terms, spirit and soul leads to confusion, with serious theoretical consequences. Clements falls into this error in his paper on disease concepts (Clements 1932:190-201, 225-240), when he attributes soul loss to the entire Plateau, which is far from the truth. To repeat, the soul is the human animating force; the spirit is the non-human extrinsic tutelary (1939:100-101).

Prior to contemporary explanations of disease and illness by physicians (though still with some indecision), there was consensus that most illnesses were—with some exceptions—contracted when a person was outside at night, or due to sorcery. On the other hand, physical maladies were most common during the winter, and for good reason, given the occasion for stress and depression induced by winter and unpredictability and stress of supplementing a sometimes inadequate diet. As already mentioned there was the notion that sickness floated about during the night, a continual pronouncement by adults that reinforced a child's or an adult's fear of being outside after dark. Even being out during twilight was considered a cautionary time when not only ghosts, but a pantheon of malevolent spirits and forces were believed to have bounded in human areas. Consequently, it was believed that the period of twilight transition was most dangerous, a time when malevolent spirits, if encountered, could commit malevolent activities. Though there was no recall of the word for this natural and spiritual transition, it was universally recognized that it was a time and dramatic demonstration of nature's power and its effect upon animals and birds.

According to Rogers (1944:560-61), who paraphrased Clements's concepts of disease (1932), the Spokan, as did most Amerindian peoples, believed there were six primary causes for diseases: 1) sorcery, 2) breach of tabu, 3) disease object intrusion, 4) spirit intrusion, 5) soul loss, and 6) poison. It should be noted that Clements's paradigm is not universally accepted (Hallowell 1935:365), for as Ray maintained, the principal cause of spiritual *illness and even death* (*q'ʷʔéwi*) was soul loss, the belief that, "the animating human soul may be temporarily detached from the physical body without death occurring immediately [...] Death comes very soon if the soul is not recovered" (1939:100). Ray's study of the distribution of cultural traits in the Plateau, stated, "the soul is the human animating force; the spirit is the non-human extrinsic tutelary" (1939:102). Yet a Spokan could become unconscious or experience death by losing his breath spirit (a vital force or power). The Spokan concept of a breath spirit was not the same as a Christian soul, as taught by missionaries.

The forté of the Spokan medical system was treating the patient in a holistic manner, one that acknowledged the inextricable relationship of physiological and psychological clinical signs of illness, and with only few exceptions they separated the somatic from the psychic. Unfortunately, with the introduction of Western medical science, given its empirical tenets, it became increasingly difficult to accommodate traditional medical episodes, corresponding beliefs, and medical procedures. In fact, much of indigenous prophylaxis, diagnosis, and therapy tend to be rejected by physicians as well as by most contemporary younger Spokan (Ross 1980c). Fortunately, there were those few in the medical community who recognized the value of traditional medicine (Abrahamson 1989; Ross 1982a), and in some instances have succinctly identified the significance of indigenous beliefs and medical practices:

People maintain their medical traditions because they affect undesirable biological states in expected ways, and because they are effective ways for dealing with disruptive events that cannot be allowed to persist. (2) A consequence of these meanings is that some kinds of sickness episodes also perform an ontological role—communicating and confirming important ideas about the real world—analogous to the one [...] others have attributed to religious belief and ritual (Young 1976:5).

Given the individual techniques used by Spokan practitioners during psychodramatic treatment, and the variation of etiologies that reflected personal thought and behavior, and an extensive *materia medica* (*k'ʷul'ɬmer'yémistmstm*), all adults had an explicit understanding of how their personal behavior influenced and even controlled their sense and state of well-being. In most instances, the dispensing of nostrums must have proved effective treatments for sorcery-induced conditions since the anticipation of a known desired effect was, and is, critical for psychological recovery.

Medicaments

The Spokan medical system was predicated upon an impressive pharmacopoeia of probably more than 350 local floral, faunal, and natural medicaments, of which approximately 70 to 80 percent were probably chemically active (soluble) when taken internally and absorbed, primarily in the stomach (Davies 2006, pers. comm.), and constituted the basis of a conservative and relatively successful medical system. Some chemically active medicaments were also applied externally. Ray (1933:215), however, concluded that approximately 50 percent of plants gathered were medicinal; realizing of course that certain foods possessed medicinal properties. Clune, in summarizing Ackerknecht (1942), who was one of the earliest and an outstanding ethnomedical historian, "estimates that the medicine men [...] throughout the world had a pharmacopoeia that consisted of 25 to 50 percent active drugs!" (1976:6). Unfortunately he does not speak of placebos, which were critical to the Spokan pharmacopoeia.

Though a great deal has been forgotten about the once traditional Spokan ethnopharmacology, it may be said that many flora, fauna, and medicaments were based on the Doctrine of Signatures; physical characteristics that included one or a variety of features, namely texture, color, shape, taste, and smell. Selection was based upon observed physiological effects.

Acknowledging the primary cause and explanation of illness among Amerindian societies was often self-induced through guilt or realized as sorcery-induced. It must be further emphasized that the significance of the indigenous pharmacopoeia—when administered by curing shamans during highly dramatized and intense rituals—was often what is now called faith-healing (psychosomatic). Clune (1976:6) further noted, "American Indians treated the person and not the symptoms [...] medicine men of the New World were much more worried about the mental attitude of the patient and not the symptoms. Here faith-healing was practiced." Ultimately, and according to Moerman (1979:61), physiological symptoms are based on a wide range of sociological and physiological phenomena, and, "The underlying theory of psychosomatic medical treatment is that the therapist can influence this pathological pathway and can, in fact, reverse the signs, the valances, the external forces causing the harm, and therefore heal."

The Spokan classification of flora recognized, as previously described to some extent, a particular plant's shape, color, taste, and certain geonomic designations of medicaments that indicated the place where a certain plant was found, or one that cured certain maladies. Unfortunately, the identities of many floral, faunal, and geo-medicaments are now mostly forgotten, along with knowledge of their preparation, application, and associated ritual. The importance of floral medicaments was apparent from the solemn propitiating ritual that a person observed by praying or chanting a song of thanksgiving when collecting any medicinal plant, or part such as bark, roots, leaves, sap, pitch, or fruit.

Male and female sorcerers were solely responsible for collecting plants used surreptitiously in their malevolent intent, always in secret and even to the exclusion of their immediate family, who in some instances may not have been cognizant of the person's true vocation. It was claimed that sorcerers never traded or gave away their potions or medicaments, which of course could likely be used against them.

Women were the principal gatherers of all plants, being extremely knowledgeable of where and when to gather any type of plant for food, medicine or other uses. The locations of plants for poisons, love potions (aphrodisiacs), or for treating specific maladies or a broad spectrum of afflictions were closely guarded secrets. In the past, women acknowledged there were sometimes slight differences in a plant's taste, potency, depending on the elevation, soil type, sunlight exposure, plant and animal association, time of collection, and the power released by her 'gathering song.' Consequently, many Spokan medicinal plants were gathered only before dawn. Also, the medical formulae and the composition of medical compounds were not universally known, often being esoteric and the property of a single woman, whose unique knowledge and associated rituals were invariably passed on only to a daughter or a granddaughter who indicated an interest in curing, or a "calling" or "gifting" by a later endowed *suméš*. Women seldom revealed to non-family members where they gathered certain medicinal plants, or recited to others the words of their personal collecting songs, the belief being that once revealed, some plants diminished in their effectiveness for curing. The designated medicinal plant received, because of certain ritual and a pronounced incantation, the, "power to cure disease and alleviate suffering" (Saigerist 1944:132).

Several elders have explained how since the 1950s, with the rapidly increasing loss of knowledge of traditional medicaments, their preparation and associated ritual of application, it became necessary for a knowledgeable person to locate and properly gather and administer medicines from plants for less knowledgeable persons. Eventually, only a few older women were likely to share their knowledge with elderly non-kin sweathouse partners, ones whom they had for years confided with regarding personal problems, domestic crises, and other serious personal concerns. However, the practice of this knowledge is now gone.

The prescribed sources and use of medicaments was not always based upon the Doctrine of Signatures, but rather on the actual observed cause and effect of a medicine's immediate or long-term effectiveness, or, in sorcery, of their deleterious physiological or psychological effects. Even in *contemporary allopathic medicine* (*maλiyé* or *mryemistn*) it can be difficult to evaluate or quantify the psychogenic benefits of pharmacologically active or inert placebos that were administered to achieve a desired effect. The desired placebo effect is not constant (Moerman 1983:13). Therefore, with Spokan ritual, a patient was rarely able to discern the physiological process of his or her treatment, but rather was more concerned with the ritual aspects of treatment. Consequently, the effectiveness of traditional holistic and salutogenic medical systems was inextricably dependent upon contextual religious ritual, and the known abilities and dedication of the curing practitioner—an individual who enhanced his or her skills by virtue of religious power and prophetic abilities (Ross 1980a).

Negative belief can kill while positive belief can heal, and according to Hahn and Kleinman, "The beliefs held by persons [...] play a significant part in both disease causation and its remedy" (1983a, 4:3+13-16). It is also understood that all medical systems utilize placebos, as did the Spokan, which were often therapeutically effective in curing as were the so-called placebos used in sorcery; beliefs and expectations can cure or kill. In fact, "Placebo response parallels that of 'pharmacologically active' drugs" (Hahn and Kleinman 1983:17). It has been personally observed, when elderly Spokan were treated in modern medical facilities, that the power of suggestion and use of placebos by both curing practitioners and sorcerers may be effective. Further, extensive research maintains, "a placebo is between 30% and 60% as effective as the active medication [...] regardless of the power of the medication" (Frank 1975a:197).

Inextricable to curing ritual was the ritual observed prior to gathering medicinal or food plants. A gatherer would always first attend the sweathouse and communicate his or her intentions, promising to *pray over food* (*ʔečp'uʔm*), usually announcing the specific medicinal plant or utilitarian plants being sought. Sometimes a person—while in the sweathouse—would ask directions or assistance from his or her tutelary spirit, or of the quested plant's spirit. In addition, the gathering of certain medicinal plants was always preceded by strict observations of specific dietary and behavioral prohibitions. Revelation of a needed plant, or the type of medicinal plant to use, might come to the curing shaman in a dream or through powers other than the patient's *sumés*. As noted earlier, when collecting medicinal plants, or even utilitarian and food plants, the person *sang a medicine song to herself* (*moxʷmóxʷqnm*), one of thanksgiving. While singing over the intended source of *medicine* (*mryémistn* or *maλiyéh* or *sʔelk'ʷlscút* - "medicine bundle") to soothe and placate the plant, the person prayed that the plant would retain its curative powers. As already noted, while gathering, an individual would explain (sometimes out loud) how the plant—as a medicine—would cure the intended patient. This initial phase of curing involvement by the shaman-collector was considered vital to his or her commitment and success in curing. It was said how women, being the near-sole gatherers of medicinal plants, passed on their personal sacred gathering songs only to her daughters and granddaughters.

562

The most powerful and therefore sacred plant in the Spokan pharmacopoeia was wild Canby's Lovage (*Ligusticum canbyi - xasxa*), also called "licorice root" which was used for treating numerous maladies and for ritual purification in all individual and group ceremonies. It was believed that *spilye* gave this root to the Spokan, and taught them how to recognize its power and how to use it properly for purifying and treating sick people. Canby's Lovage was recognized and widely used by non-Indians from the time of their first contact with the early trapper-traders, as illustrated by this remark by Elliott: "Here in the spring of 1813 certain rivals in the fur trade were encamped awaiting a supply of the fragrant weed [Canby's Lovage] from Spokan House" (1918, 3:170). Early users of this root were unaware that this plant contains several active phytomedicinals, including the saponin-like triterpene glycosides, including glycyrrhizic acid, which, when mashed and taken as a tea, can increase circulation.

Canby's root still has a rather wide distribution, and until recently people rarely told others where they dug the plant, even though all adults were quite cognizant of the plant's wide and profuse habitation. Many years ago this plant was widely gathered in the late spring until early summer and traded among the Spokan and to other groups. The root was dried and then usually cut into sections about 4 cm in length and stored in a buckskin bag or else strung and hung in one's home. Adults always carried pieces of Canby's root for protection whenever they were away from their homes for health reasons, and for the plant's pleasurable and distinct taste. Some elders continue to use this root as a general broad spectrum prophylactic medicament by grinding or shredding the root to a fine dust, which is then steeped in hot water and drunk daily. It should be noted the close relationship of Canby's root to *L. porteri* for peoples further south, and also to *L. verticillation* (Turner, pers. comm.).

Until recently, when collecting or using Canby's root, a person always sang a special song acknowledging the dependence that humans had upon this gift for its curative and protective powers. While preparing the root for use, one was always assiduously careful in demonstrating one's respect by singing over the plant, offering thanks by referring to the many times the plant's power had cured or saved a friend or relative. In the past, a common practice was for elders to cut small pieces of the root with a stone knife (steel was never used as it, would negate the plant's power), placing a small piece under the tongue, never swallowing it until only the fibers remained. Bits of this plant were chewed, sometimes daily, to 'clean one out' and provide a general feeling of well being. Accounts of the plant's use vary. Not too long ago some people would administer licorice root by placing small bits in an atomizer and breathe in the scented fumes, which was often done by placing bits on a hot stone in their home or while in the sweathouse. One elderly man recalled:

> My father, and others of his generation [ca.1940], would chop *xasxa* into small pieces and mix [it] with their cigarette and pipe tobacco. The inhaled smoke was thought to be good for their lungs. A few older people [both men and women] still place *xasxa* in a metal pot on the stove and let the fumes spread through the house to keep evil things away. Some also use balsam needles if they are short of *xasxa*. Of course *xasxa* is used, as I said, in the sweathouse, and again it was chopped up fine and placed in a bucket of water. The mixture was then sprayed on the hot stones by a man spewing out a fine spray from his mouth. Some people will put small bits of *xasxa* directly on the hot stones to make a sacred smoke [...] to purify people's thoughts by driving away all evil. It was also done to purify the sweathouse and to help a person have a vision of his guardian spirit (Ross 1968-2008).

Another important medicinal plant for the Spokan was wild rose, used for treating a wide spectrum of maladies—everything from ghost illness to common colds. When visiting a patient in an off-reservation hospital, a curing shaman would conduct a purifying ritual, now rarely done. The curing shaman first made an infusion by steeping the shredded bark from wild rose stems in boiling water, and after the infusion had cooled, the practitioner would fill his mouth with it and then *spray* (*tilntx^w* - "to spray with water") over the patient and the bed in a *fine atomized-like mist* (*čpux^welpm*). This was done three times to purify the area and the patient's bed, clothes, and bedding so that the curing shaman could work without fear of being contaminated by hospital germs or non-traditional medications given the patient, and to protect the patient from any lasting sources of malevolent power if the patient was thought of being still sorcerized. This ritual of cleansing was critical to protect the curer from ingested patent medicines.

The leaves from an extensive armamentarium of plants were collected, again invariably by women who prepared and used them primarily for producing beverages and medicines. Noted favorites were Canadian mint (*Mentha arvensis* L. var. *glabrata* [Benth] Fern - *x̣aʕx̣ʕáy̓łp* or *x̣ax̣aiłp*, syn. *Mentha arvensis* L. *canadensis* L.), Claspleaf twisted stalk (*Streptopus amplexifolius* [L.] D.C.), and both species of trillium (*Trillium ovatum* Pursh. and *T. petiolatum* Pursh.). *Bracken fern* (*Pteridium aquilinum* Kuhn. - *txétxitkšt* and *P. pubescens* Underw.) and buttercup (*Rannuculus*) were collected, and many types of greens—too many to be listed here—were collected as foods and medicines.

There is no evidence that a person or family had exclusive rights over a medicinal plant area; rather, one simply did not discuss his or her source for these important medicines.

The blue elderberry plant provided another popular multipurpose medicine, serving as a poultice when mashed, heated, and placed upon open wounds to prevent infection and tetanus. A febrifuge decoction of dried flowers of blue elderberry was applied externally for fevers. Elderberry juice (*stsnp'ítk^w* - "crushed berry juice" - *stsnp'e'ítk^w*) would be, "then heated with hot rock[s] in [a] cooking basket - [and] kept from day to day & [it was] heated up before use" (Elmendorf 1935-6, 1:34), and was drunk as such or diluted as a tea to reduce fever. Hollow main stems of the elderberry tree served as an *inflator* (*npiúmn*) of animal intestines and large animal bladders for storing certain foods (relocate).

Once medicinal plants were collected, they were carefully kept separate during storage because certain species could never be permitted contact, as they might contaminate other plants, which could result in a reduction or loss of the plant's potency, or even disable the curing shaman due to lack of respect. In the past, women were quite cognizant of all the medicinal plants within the Spokan pharmacopoeia; but one was never certain of ratios or amounts used by another person when making compounds, simply because one rarely spoke of these matters, and it was once considered rude to make such an inquiry. Long ago, the more compelling reason for secrecy was the belief that if one disclosed the ingredients, one's medicines could possibly cease to cure.

A woman might be instructed by her *sumeš* to camp for one night at a certain place where the plant grew, and before digging or collecting the plant she would pray and give thanks to the animal or bird that was instructing and guiding her. This inextricable relationship between the supernatural, medicines, curing rituals, and individualized remedies was once apparent, especially during the introduction of non-indigenous diseases, and the ensuing dilemma of how to treat unknown maladies. A curing shaman would only treat a patient if s/he knew the remedy and associated ritual, and unfortunately the indigenous healing methods were only rarely successful in treating non-traditional illnesses.

Dream Medicines

A topic seldom discussed was the use of dream medicines in the past, which were considered special if not unique because a man or woman acquired the identity and specific location of a particular plant, as well as the identity of the patient to whom it should be administered, through dreaming. Knowledge was not always from a guardian spirit, but, "by some unknown person or by some animal or bird" (Smith 1936-8:1066), one that was familiar with the plant's location. Such an epiphany may occur only once in a person's life; it could possibly be repeated when other types of plants were similarly revealed. The plant's efficacy and curing power was dependent upon how carefully the curing shaman adhered to the ritual revealed during his dream. A curing shaman's success in restoring a patient's health with a dream medicine was never compensated or rewarded, since this esoteric knowledge was a unique gift from a greater power, not to be sold or traded.

The uniqueness of any dream medicine was that it could be any type of plant, even a weed, which received power only when collected by the person who dreamed of its use. The recipient of such a dream always conducted a special ritual of intense sweating several times a day, usually early in the morning and again in the evening. To properly cleanse himself prior to gathering the plant, and during the time of preparation, the seeker abstained from any sexual relations. Smith described how the person, after locating the plant, would face a certain direction, insert the digging stick in a prescribed manner, and, "while digging sing a song of thanksgiving given during the dream" (1936-8:1066). Also, one invariably fasted throughout the day after gathering the plant. It was once explained that even an ordinary plant—such as a weed—can have curing power if the collector believes in its intended efficacy, and the collecting-shaman has faith in his or her ability and *suméš* relationship.

A person's ability to find and use such a plant lasted only as long as the person refrained from revealing his or her dream, or the nature of the medicinal plant, or the ritual when administering the medicine, to anyone. However, the knowledge and ritual of curing with a gift-medicine remained within a family, passing from father to son, or mother to daughter; but only when the curing shaman was too old or not ambulatory. A few have said how, "A son was sometimes sent out to get the root and bring it home to the old father who would prepare it, though the son knew how to do the latter also" (Smith 1936-8:1067). Prior to the bequeathment of a plant's identity and location, the younger son or daughter was instructed in the specific prayer associated with collecting the dream medicine, a prayer that was always sung over the plant prior to gathering. If this ritual was not done properly, the medicine would not cure, and might even kill the patient. The knowledge and use of a dream medicine could never be given, even to a family member. There was also the strict practice of surreptitiously burying or burning any part of the gathered plant not used as a medicine, or administered.

Shamans

A *shaman* (*suxʷλ̓ʼeʔkʷílšm* or *λ̓ʼeʔkʷ̓ilš* or *nλ̓ʼéʔklšsútn*) was the principal individual involved in sacred matters, one who acted as a liaison between the sacred and profane worlds. Shamans could be male or female, or in some instances a berdache who sometimes possessed a curing power acquired by a variety of ritualized procedures; but more often through a vision quest, dreaming, receiving a sign, inheritance from a kinsperson, survival of a severe illness, and, less frequently, resurrection after experiencing a *long death-like coma* (*qʷm̓íp*). The ritual of preventing a patient's death was known as *nʔixʷmi*. A shaman's curing knowledge and skills for such things were acquired through serving as an apprentice to a known practitioner, or to a sponsor and guide during the often long and arduous apprenticeship (Jilek 1982). Therefore, the primary task of the curing shaman, if possible, was to administer to chronic, non-incapacitating physical and psychological problems, situations that were often drawn-out periods of suffering, sometimes reoccurring or cyclical in character, often not fatal and usually only partially debilitating, thereby enabling the sufferer to maintain a semblance of his or her daily routine (Jilek 1982).

Either a male or female shaman (a Turic word [*šamán*] meaning hysterical state or severe trembling) could have more than one type of power, and the power most sought was for *curing* (*λ̓ʼeʔkʷ̓ilš*), which at times must have presented a dilemma since a practitioner, as will be discussed, could be accused of sorcery if the patient died, which occasionally happened. As often happened, it was necessary for a sorcerer to adapt the apparently contradictory indigenous roles of healer and sorcerer while preserving healer and control agent (1978, *vide supra*). In other words, "The healer frequently functions in a dual role as sorcerer and must be capable of the kind of cognitive adjustment that will smoothly incorporate both roles" (Landy 1977:472). Landy also made a critical assessment of the effect of Euro-Americans upon traditional shamanistic medical systems and a curing shaman's role and status:

> Prior to contact, in addition to ameliorating the effects of illness and disease, the curer's activities were oriented toward enhancing and/or reinforcing his social position. Although role prescriptions were traditional, he would still have to rationalize nonsuccess, and ordinarily he would have to compete with the curers in the number and profundity of his achievements (Landy 1974:106).

As cited earlier, curing shamans never accepted any form of traditional payment, though he could occasionally accept a gift of clothing, food, or, until recently, gas-money. Many years ago, while travelling to Montana with an elderly curing shaman, he explained how, "I never receive or accept any payment; but [I] may accept a little money for gas, but not for my services." It was believed that to profit from a supernaturally given *suméš* would bring harm, even cause a curing shaman's death, indicating an arrogance and total disrespect for supernatural power. Accepting a material gift in exchange for a supernatural use of power would diminish his or her power, and might cause one's children—if any—to *become ill* (*qʷu čnilntm*), their guardian spirit to *fly* (*t'uxʷt*) or hover over the shaman while dropping stones or animal feces upon the greedy individual's head, or even cause one's *suméš* to fail and quickly scamper away. Not receiving payment was recognized by a shaman as a positive aspect of the healing treatment, that his curing was supernaturally inspired and not for any material gain. An elderly man, who had been a curing shaman, further explained to the author the matter of no remuneration and also explained how and why he gave up (released) his *suméš* as a result of his humiliation in an urban medical center:

> I never took money because I knew I was chosen to do this kind of work—helping and curing sick folks. What's in your heart should never be in your pocket. My sincerity was a sort of test; a sign of my dedication. I've a calling to doctor and help people who need me. I knew I could help if the patient [and his family] believed in me. The pain I went through also showed them my power, but also how I'd take theirs [away from them]. The worse thing was when I first came here [an emergency room as a patient] and they made me take all my clothes off in front of everyone, even the nurses—all strangers (Ross 1968-2008).

Until recently, the few knowledgeable Indians who maintained their traditional religious beliefs (wholly or in part), typically sought explanation and cure from more traditional and conservative practitioners, especially in times of exacerbated stress and unrecognized traditional causes of illness. Unfortunately, this often entailed travelling to less acculturated reservations. With this traumatic loss of medical knowledge, patients often sought care in urban hospitals, usually under pressure from younger non-speaking Spokan members of their family. Consequently, and unfortunately, patients often suffered from the cross-cultural misunderstanding and even overt ridicule by some physicians and medical personnel (Ross 1980c). This was exacerbated when they found themselves in unfamiliar physical and social environments, such as a hospital or clinic. A principal responsibility of a curing shaman was to recognize and make public any signs of improvement, or indicate whenever the patient was *feeling better* (*mʔéɬ*) during the curing ritual, which would seldom be tolerated by a physician, and may even be a reason for ridicule, as has been personally witnessed on numerous occasions when visiting elders whom the author knew for many years.

Until recently, the more traditional Spokan practitioner was often able to treat patients who believed they were afflicted with self-induced maladies or even by sorcery, and would seek care from known practitioners, seldom from physicians. The ability and status of a curing shaman was reduced, which was certainly questioned by younger, less traditional patients who invariably sought treatment from hospital or clinic-based physicians. Given the increasing technological complexity of equipment, inaccessibility of pharmaceuticals, and remoteness of facilities, there was no way curing shamans could treat diagnosed traditional maladies. This dilemma of care, understanding, and diagnosis of the acknowledged Indian patient was further exacerbated by, "The routinized impersonality now so intrinsically a component of the modern professional role" (Gould 1965:208).

From the late 1940s to the early 1990s, one of the last Spokan curing shamans was a well-respected and acculturated elder who was fluent in Spokan (STHC) and knowledgeable of different systems of philosophical and religious beliefs and the practice of indigenous rituals and some medical procedures (Ross 1984c). He often worked closely with a Jesuit priest who resided on a close reservation, one who knew and sang all of the traditional *curing shaman's songs* (*sc'ey'keʔ*) and often assisted the priest who believed in the efficacy of *administering medicine* (*sxumyán*) to Indian patients who sought help.

It was believed possible for a curing shaman to experience failure when treating a patient, or worse, lose his curing power for any one of several reasons. For example, if a patient failed to respond to treatment, the practitioner would remain near the patient or in the immediate area, sometimes for several days, all the while trusting that he would dream of his curing spirit. If successful, his *suméš* would appear and instruct him as to the correct etiological explanation and the proper course of treatment, since some curing shamans had more than one type of *suméš*. A curing shaman could lose his power if, when treating a patient, he was excessive or remiss with medication or substituting a different medicament, or doing more than his tutelary spirit instructed him to do, or even more serious, if the shaman in any way acted arrogantly or disrespectfully to the patient or family, or ignored the fact that any violation of an imposed restriction might bring death to the practitioner. In fact, "the [offended] animal [tutelary spirit] will kill him [the shaman] himself" (Smith 1936-8:1285).

Some shamans could enhance their power for curing by owning a special *power whistle* (*x̣x̣w'ístn'* or *npx̌ʷéłc'ceʔtn* - "blew by itself"), one made from a bird leg that could "blow by itself at times" (Elmendorf, pers. comm.), often making the proper bird call or song. It was said that such a whistle was never inherited, like a flute, but rather made by the whistle's owner from a dried elderberry stem or a large bird femur. Prior to making a special power whistle or flute, any tools, like borers and scrapers, were carefully purified by the manufacturer three times during a special ritual in a sweathouse. Upon completion of the instrument, the new owner gave the whistle a secret name, decorating it with feathers and fur from animals that served as representatives of his tutelary helpers; not all shamans' whistles or flutes were decorated. During a curing ceremony the shaman might use this instrument for curing a patient after sucking and removing an intrusive object, such as a feather, large clots of blood, or a small pebble inserted by a sorcerer. Upon the shaman's death, the whistle was buried with him.

When medicine men treated illnesses that were not considered serious or life-threatening, they seldom used extensive rituals or administered medicaments, but rather became 'listeners' who engaged the patient to discuss his concerns, which often treated the presumed malady. As one elder stated, "Listening is sometimes better than chewing medicines." One may say—how on occasion—the most helpful aspect of a curing practitioner's ritual and attention, was not the use of medicaments, but what may be called symbolic healing, "that does not rely on any physical or pharmacological treatments for its efficacy, but rather on language, ritual and the manipulations of powerful cultural symbols" (Helman 2000:191). Several elders mentioned when grandmothers were in residence, they were "listeners" who probably best understood the stresses and concerns of a younger family member, or of an age-mate. Familial medicine was often based on what is termed "somatization". "The cultural patterning of psychological and social discards into a language of distress and mainly physical symptoms and signs" (Helman 200:182). Apparently, talk-therapy was sometimes successful for treating patients who were in a coma through sorcery or had complete or partial loss of ability to speak, and were usually incubated with warm blankets as older family members sang and spoke to the distressed person. In was said that fright could render a younger person temporarily speechless, whereas the same condition in an older person could be due to a slight stroke or because he was ghosted.

A shaman who dispensed medicaments was known as a *sxumryám*; actually a curing specialist, one who on occasion worked with another practitioner. Individuals with serious illnesses were invariably those who had violated a serious moral prohibition, or had been sorcerized and could be treated only by a powerful curing shaman. However, when administering to a seriously ill patient, a major concern of all curing shamans was if one's healing *suméš* would be maliciously taken by a sorcerer, one who had a more powerful *suméš*, a situation called *čłwentm*. If such a concern confronted the practitioner, before attending the patient, the concerned shaman would always first sweat while carefully washing himself in the sweathouse with a solution made from steeped mashed plants found near his *suméš* spring, which served not only to purify his body and mind, but to protect him against any malevolent forces. The specific term for such a spring could not be recalled by informants—only that it was quite small and never froze in the winter, as was true with all sacred springs or seeps. Such a spring was thought to have been an *artesian well* (*y'l'y'al'qn'* or *p'úp'stn'*), one that formed a *round top of bubbling water* (*sp'ost* - "where water bubbles up"), and was considered to be sacred water since the shaman's *suméš* also drank this water. Persons without *suméš* avoided designated sacred springs (STHC). Because the sources of most artesian wells were located in granite sub-surfaces, the water was often not only dark, but with a fairly bitter taste due to iron particles, and the taste was believed to be beneficial to pregnant women, which of course it was—a notion of revulsive medicine.

After sustained Euro-American contact, a major problem with the introduction of non-traditional communicable diseases, such as measles, small pox, and typhoid, was that Indian practitioners were faced with an undaunting and critical dilemma of seeking an effective treatment, and, "While some curers adapted their roles successfully to the demands of acculturation and others have become so battered as to be attenuated and in danger of extinction" (Landy 1978:230). Given the very nature and obvious results of virile and dangerous pathogens, if is impossible to speculate on the cognitive processes that may have led a shaman to modify what were hopefully adaptive medical procedures and rituals.

Practitioners

In every medical system, there have been numerous types of practitioners who specialize in treating particular physical medical maladies or syndromes. Both Spokan male and female shamans represented different types of specialization; not all of which are recalled—probably since the late 1940s. The importance of curing shamans is evidenced by the names of various specialized roles. For example, for different maladies requiring some degree of specialization based on one or more different *suméš*; one may have been known as a *λ'e?kʷłλš*, *tłkʷílš*, a *sxʷłopm*, a *sxʷmryem*, *suxʷmr'yen?*, a *sxʷmryemis*, a *λ'e?kʷílš* or *t'ła?ákʷílc*, a *nλ'e?kʷlšscutn*, a *xumrám*, a *λ'e?kʷílš* or a *nλ'e?kʷlšscút* - "one who doctors"), a.k.a. medical practitioner. But presumably, a particularly powerful practitioner had the power and ability to cure any malady. The actual importance and role of self-treatment and family treatment were all but forgotten by the late 1950s, and even prior to that, many traditional and established rituals and medicaments were becoming obscured, often by the more acknowledged and dramatic notions and interpretations of traditional shamans as they attempted to cure a sorcerized person. If a person was a shaman, it was not axiomatic that he could treat illness; he should rather possess a capability that required the skills of a curing shaman referred to as a medical practitioner. Such people usually had one or more guardian spirits (tutelary spirits) from whom they received their specific power(s) to make a diagnosis and a prognosis, and eventually to cure the patient. It was believed that prior to deculturation, there were practitioners who specialized in specific medical conditions, such as birthing, poisoning, burns, bone-setting, and other debilitating afflictions (Ross 1995a).

Alexander Ross, when among the Sinkaietk, acknowledged the skill and what he called supernatural gifts possessed by all curing practitioners, whom he called *tla-quill-aughs*:

> In all Indian tribes there are three or four characters of this description [...] . men generally past the meridian of life; in their habits grave and sedate, with a shyness and cunning about them. Like all Indians, they possess a good knowledge of herbs and roots, and their virtues. All classes stand in awe of the *tla-quill-aughs'* power or ill will, and their opinions have much influence in most matters. They are consulted in all cases of sickness. All classes avoid, as much as possible, giving them offence, from a belief that they have the power of throwing, as they express it, their bad medicine at them, whether far or near, present or absent. The people believe they can converse with the good and the bad spirits [...] (1849, 7:286-7).

After spending time with the Spokan, Wilkes witnessed a curing ceremony using the bones of spirits of dead kinspeople, all the while conducting a curing ritual throughout the night. This is the first recording of such a ceremony:

> Towards morning, they retire into a separate lodge which is closed up & made perfectly dark, when a small hole is made in the top, and the spirits descend through it in the shape of small bits of bone; these are received on a mat, a fire is made, and the spirits belonging to a number of their friends already dead, are picked out. The

medicine man then selects the particular spirit of each individual present, makes all sit down, takes the bones representing the spirit and lays it on the head of the individual, among his hair, with many invocations and grimaces, till it is supposed to descend into the heart of the individual and resumes its former place (1845:449).

Though difficult to say, perhaps ten to twenty percent of men and women shamans were curing shamans (STHC). With increasing loss of traditional culture, the skills of curing were eventually lost, and as a result there were fewer people who could interpret traditional illness due to sorcery. As a result, a sick person believed to have been sorcerized would often seek medical attention from curing shamans on less deculturated reservations. On the Spokane Indian Reservation, the Indian Health Service has gradually replaced medical treatments. Compounding the role of the curing shaman was the problem that most illnesses and diseases were seen as 'white diseases,' and could only be treated by non-traditional physicians (Eli 1974:n.p.).

One uncertain dilemma in the traditional Spokan medical system was that all sorcerers were shamans, but not all shamans were sorcerers. Thus, there was always some trepidation that a supposed curing shaman could be a sorcerer. That happened because it was invariably dark when a curing shaman conducted his ritual, thereby providing an environment and opportunity to kill the patient, or recover an object or a malevolent force which he had earlier surreptitiously inserted, or manipulate a malevolent force from afar without detection, maintaining his presumed status as a practitioner. Consequently, a patient was not always certain if an attending shaman was a curing practitioner or a sorcerer, for, as Lieban noted:

> The contrastive roles of sorcerer and healer may be assimilated by scheduling each for the appropriate situation, whether that he strive for health or service for "justice" [the rationalization underlying vengeance sorcery—when X, the healer, treats someone whose illness the same X, as sorcerer, was responsible for—the apparent discrepancy in behavior can be explained by resorting in turn to relevant values of the roles involved (1960:132).

Medicine Bundles

No two medicine bundles were the same. All shamans had one or more medicine bundles to carry and protect different sacred objects given to them by any one of their tutelary spirits: objects that represented a unique *suméš* which enabled an individual to perform a particular task or fulfill a wish. As a result, the now rather general term *medicine bundle* (*sʔelkʼʷlscút*) did not mean that the owner was a curing shaman; it meant simply a type of power bundle. Regardless of one's *suméš*, there were two types of medicine bags. The first was a small buckskin sack—approximately fist-size—completely enclosed when tied off with a buckskin drawstring: an item carried by all shamans. The second type of a curing shaman's medicine bundle was a larger and more elongated rawhide bundle to contain all needed medical paraphernalia, often made by the individual from the hide of a complete desiccated animal, one that often represented a curing shaman's tutelary spirit, sometimes with the animal's scalp and attached limbs. This bundle was essentially a folded side-stitched case with an end flap of worked rawhide that was secured with a long, narrow tie of buckskin, being large enough to accommodate a small stone pipe and other paraphernalia. When transported, the bundle was carefully secured under the owner's left arm by a strap, and a medicine bundle was always made by the owner—never anyone else, regardless of kin or marital relationship. Teit, however, wrote how the Flathead Group made a rawhide cylindrical medical bag, but that, "their use is probably not very ancient, at least among the Spokan" (1930:327).

Before adding any new item to the bag or bundle, or renewing a medicine, the curing shaman would take the newly "given" or acquired items individually with him into the sweathouse for purification; but the entire bag or bundle was presumably never taken into the sweathouse. However, one old man remembered a grandmother seeing her *husband* (*sx̣elwʼiʔ*) taking his medicine bundle to the sweathouse. After each new item was separately purified, a practitioner would, if necessary, take an entire bundle of medicines and paraphernalia when attending a patient. When not being carried or in use, one's medicine bundle was vigilantly wrapped in a larger skin; sometimes it was of another animal, often one of his larger tutelary animals, or a "relative" of his primary animal guardian spirit (*suméš*).

Such a rawhide or buckskin bag or bundle was usually decorated with a choice of designs using hematite, with *fringe* (*xste?yé* or *scoleóʕʷ* or *cwʾáλqstn*), feathers, shell beads, bones, or other objects of significance. The leaves of certain medicinal plants, such as wild rose, rabbit brush, or wild licorice root (*x̣ásax̣*) were always carried within both a medicine bundle and auxiliary bag. When needed, these special leaves were often pulverized by grinding before sprinkling on the stones of a curing fire while administering to a patient when in a sweathouse. Every day a curing shaman would sing to his medicine bundle, always expressing his gratitude for all it had done for him and the people whom he had successfully treated. It was said that such a recitation was a solitary form of liturgical prayer for all the people whom he had cured, and hopefully for those whom he would cure. When speaking to the medicine bundle, and before leaving one's dwelling to attend a patient who the *practitioner had dreamed was ill* (*snwučsuméštis* - "shaman" - who sees or dreams of another's illness"), a small fire was made and shredded *x̣ásax̣* was sprinkled on the hot stones to produce a pleasant smelling smoke, and to purify the medicine bundle and its contents—all the while the man sang one or more of his medicine sings. To protect the contents from being maliciously tampered with, wild rose were always placed in the medicine bundle and renewed by its owner when needed, but not daily.

A shaman's medicine bundle contained the practitioner's *curing paraphernalia* (*k'ʾʷuʔłm'ʾs*), such as different types of sucking tubes as well as power objects including various bones, special roots, unusual clay concretions or a *crystal* (*hi x̣alssn* or *čx̣alssn*), shells, bits of red or yellow hematite, special feathers, teeth, a small tube or elbow pipe, tobacco, and dried animal organs and scalps. These items were invariably carried in his medicine bundle, or on his person, depending upon the required ritual and treatment of a particular malady. Consequently, a person, through time and experience, would add or take away items from his assemblage of curing paraphernalia. Upon his death, the medicines and the bundle were destroyed by burning, since a major concern was whether one's medicine bag would be stolen during or after the curing shaman's life by a sorcerer and used maliciously against the family of the deceased practitioner. One elder claimed that the medicines, paraphernalia, and bag—all of which would be dangerous to anyone else—were buried along with the deceased practitioner.

Curing Procedures and Techniques

Procedures for curing a sick person varied according to the patient's particular self-proclaimed malady, or the diagnosis of the curing shaman. When considering the many variations of curing techniques and ritual procedures such as transformation or soul flight (Winkelman 1989:22) legerdemain, hypnotism (Winkelman 1986), spirit language, guardian spirits, songs, rituals, medicines, and the paraphernalia of a curing shaman, the choice of treatment was usually determined by the shaman's diagnosis. One must realize how receptive a patient and his family were to the practitioner's impressive power, knowledge, and assurance for success of treatment which were critical to a treatment.

Soul loss occurred on being sorcerized, because of a person's violation of a tabu, or for no apparent reason. During this condition it often happened that an individual was unaware of this danger. Rev. Walker, in a 1842 letter to Reverend Jonathan Green, American Board missionary in the Hawaiian Islands, described a soul recovery ceremony of a Spokan man observed by Johnson and Hale of the Wilkes Expedition while visiting Tschimakain for three months in the spring of 1841. Hale's explanation is more detailed than Walker's earlier letter to Green, and showed the universal belief of misfortune, sickness, and even death of another being first apparent in a curing shaman's dream:

> Their ceremonies were connected with their superstitions, and one of the most remarkable of them was called 'huwash' [*suméš*]. This results from the belief that the spirit within a person may be separated from the body for a short time, without the person being aware of it, or its causing death, provided it be quickly restored to

him. This account of losing the spirit is supposed to become first known to the medicine man in a dream, who communicates it to the unhappy individual and who in return, immediately employs him to recover it. During a whole night, the medicine man will be engaged in hunting it up passing from one lodge to another, singing & dancing (Hale 1846, 4:448-9; Drury 1976:515).

Treatment of a self-proclaimed malady was, if possible, sought by the patient who might verbally implore his tutelary spirit to *restore his or her health* (*heł x̣ssemil'š*), and in a case of psychogenic disease, this sometimes proved beneficial. It was believed that one's tutelary spirit could assist the patient in recalling an event or reason for his or her condition by explaining an appropriate procedure and course of treatment to the sick person. If possible, it was important for the patient to attempt to reconstruct what he had done to cause his malady: had he perhaps spoken or even thought ill of someone, possibly dreamt poorly of a person, or stolen from another, or had he been uncharitable and not shared with someone in need. A guardian spirit might appear in the patient's dream, or while in the sweathouse, or he may hear a bird or animal speak to him, telling him what he must do to regain his health. The patient may not always be unable to recall such incidents; but might be helped by the practitioner to recall such an event.

Often a sick person was attended by his family and others of the camp or village who would sing and pray to demonstrate their support, and, if able, the sick person had to sing as well, thereby publicly acknowledging his condition and sometimes declaring what he believed to be the cause of his malady. Afterwards, it was not unusual for the sick man to give gifts to those attending him. Sometimes he, or his family, would give away all of his personal possessions, which later may be returned to him by the recipients, or later through gambling, as his recovered powers sometimes were greater if he had followed the advice of his guardian spirit.

The Spokan shared with all Plateau peoples certain universal *curing procedures* (*nλ'e?kʷlšcútn* - "the way a medicine man practices"): *sucking* (*sxʷłóp'm* - "sucking shaman" - "sucking to cure" - *łóp'm*), *blowing* (*sxʷpúxʷm* - "blowing shaman" - "blowing to cure" - *púxm*), acupressure and manipulation, incubation, sweating, shaman's dreaming or analysis of the patient's dreams, psychic projection or transformation, eliciting confession, hydrotherapy, spasmophilia (chronic or acute hyperventilation), poultices, medicaments, inducing vomiting in the patient, and shock. In addition, the Spokan were experts in the procedures of bone-setting and reductions for dislocations. The most complex and dramatic procedure, however, was sucking, blowing, or using both tactile and non-tactile (more symbolic) manipulation with one or both hands (acupressure) when curing. Most of these procedures— often in the case of sorcery-caused illness—were conducted for the sole purpose of removing from the patient a physically or spiritually intrusive object, or intrusion of a malignant power, loss or possession of a guardian spirit, or illness due to the patient violating a moral prohibition, even to recover his displaced *suméš*. In some instances of *poison* (*čnílmn* or *nčn'c'in'tn* - "Indian poison") or disease-object intrusion (Rogers 1944:559), it was presumed that a sorcerer or one of his familiars was responsible by having *physical contact* (*čn'xʷ*) with the victim. Even though all adults were familiar with poisons, if one had been poisoned it was generally assumed that a sorcerer had been the poisoner (*sxʷnčn'cinm* or *sxʷčnílm*).

In the past, some curing shamans were specialized and became renowned for their ability in one or more of the aforementioned procedures. One may assume that a specific procedure was often preferred when treating a particular malady, and the decision as to who would treat was sometimes determined by the *way a medicine man practiced* (*nλ'e?kʷlšscútn*). But, as will be discussed, invariably the *curing shaman who ultimately treated a patient was determined by the shaman who first dreamed of the patient's identity and condition* (*λ'e?kʷílš*). Traditionally, it was not unusual for a *group of medicine men* (*utλ'e?kʷílš*)—through mutual knowledge and consent—to decide which of their number would treat a patient, nor was it uncommon for several (being different in age and experience) to cooperate in assisting another shaman when treating a patient.

Prior to a medicine man's dreaming of a person being *sorcerized* (*wičeʔ* or *q'ewntm* - "to place a spell") by either disease object intrusion or spirit intrusion, a person was likely to suspect that he was a victim when experiencing recurring dreams of being sorcerized. Initially, such dreams were only psychosocial, but gradually there developed a combination of such physiological—even clinical—signs such as unsteady gait, *dizziness* (*silsilpqin*), impaired vision, ringing in the ears, severe headaches, *trembling hands* (*xʷir'ečt*), and loss of appetite, and eventually losing interest in performing required responsibilities. These conditions were further reinforced—even exacerbated—when observed and commented upon by the person's family and close friends, one of whom may have earlier dreamed of the person's present condition.

An example of the importance of a shaman's dreaming to discern a patient's malady and the cure, was the rare occasion when a curing practitioner experienced dream magic. Such a phenomenon usually occurred only once, and, as previously noted, often revealed to the dreamer a certain plant and necessary ritual for curing. After having this dream, the practitioner always gave this knowledge to another practitioner as a gift; never receiving any material compensation, for otherwise his guardian spirit would forsake him. It might, however, happen that the practitioner would give this knowledge to a younger member of his family, who was then sent out to gather a certain plant, and upon return be instructed in its proper preparation, application, and any esoteric knowledge and ritual necessary for its effective use.

A shaman who became ill would attempt to cure himself, which was possible only if his guardian spirit came to him in a dream and explained what he should do to *restore his health* (*heł xssemil'š*). Self-treatment was preferred to asking assistance from another shaman, for fear that the other shaman might take his power or even kill him during the course of treatment. More powerful shamans feared one another, and the greater the other's power, the greater the fear. And yet, a curing shaman requiring treatment by sucking was more likely to seek such assistance, but *not* for any malady requiring blowing. This was because the consequences of blowing were sometimes less predictable since the identity of the patient's guardian spirit would be revealed, particularly if the participating shaman wanted the other man's guardian spirit, or intended to kill his patient.

Most curing procedures of a medicine man were well known, the successes of which were based on various factors: the personality of the curing shaman, his often demonstrated physical transformation, his medical entourage and medical chorus, the physical setting and psychological atmosphere of the ritual, the shaman's eventual physical display of the cause of illness which served as proof of the malady or ordeal, and the ability of the curing shaman to overcome the power of the sorcerer.

As noted earlier, there were shamans who could kill just as they could heal. A shaman might be *an evil person* (*nʔaxʷʔaxʷkʷisqélixʷtn id.* sorcerer) or a *bad person* (*ty'a*), one capable of *killing a person* (*snplsqélixʷtn*) regardless of motive or means. A person who was not a medicine man, but who unsuccessfully attempted to cure himself, was called a *nƛ'eʔkʷlšscútn*, while a person who pretended to have the powers of a medicine man, but did not, was known as a *ƛ'eʔkʷlšscut*.

In addition to the aforementioned, the more obvious curing procedures used by medical practitioners were: *legerdemain* (*tqtaqt* or *ƛ'ekʷšms* - "to remove from" - "slight-of-hand"), patient and group hypnotism, manipulation or acupressure, deep massage, sucking by mouth or with a sucking tube at the site of illness, blowing or using smoke, atomizing water over the patient, administering *medicaments* (*mryémistn*), the practitioner communicating to his spirit helpers using glossolalia or a *spirit language* (*sč'ey'eʔ*), and ritual dancing or singing—often supplemented with an extensive *herbal materia medica* collected by plant *specialists* (*sčeʔheʔheʔčcs*) or by a shaman who was a specialist. There was essentially no detailed information regarding medical specialists, though several elders agreed there were such practitioners, some of whom would occasionally work together when treating certain illnesses. As noted, "traditional medical knowledge is rarely uniform [...] traditional practitioners are [were] considered in one of the two aspects of healing: divining or diagnosing the ultimate causes of an illness, and identifying the nature of an illness and treating it" (Sargent and Johnson 1996:389).

Since curing ceremonies were never conducted during the day, curing shamans could attend a patient only *after it was dark* (X̣'e č'mip). Some elders explained how the room would be in *near-complete darkness* (č'ey) while the curing practitioner conducted the curing ritual, and some stated that a blanket or tule mat was held between the patient and the fire while the shaman conducted his ritual, allowing only minimal light to see what he was doing. Others claimed that often a *low burning fire* (ttekʷ) was maintained during the ceremony to create a desired psychological effect upon the patient and those attending by creating very suggestive shadows. Whenever a curing shaman was successful in removing the cause of illness, and despite the room being relatively dark, those near the shaman could see a *shimmering light* (cikʷkʷ or c'ek'ʷ) given off by the malevolent object—a proof of the strength and vitality of the object, which the shaman then proceeded to neutralize.

It was often difficult for the shaman to maintain the psychological heightening of the patient and the audience, as well as his near-continual singing prior to the actual treatment. As a result, a shaman's performances were quite demanding, even tiring when working even for only several hours, during which a shaman never sang while actually working on a patient, though some claim they did. This was a time when no one else could sing, and despite presumed restrictions, some onlookers have stated how they felt compelled to sing.

With the advent of commercial electricity, until recently, when a curing shaman was curing a patient, every electrical appliance in the dwelling had to be disconnected and carefully draped with a blanket or hidden to prevent the intrusion by any non-traditional power, such as electromagnetic power that was believed to negate the shaman's power. The Spokan universally believed in the so-called Image or Doctrine of Limited Good (Redfield 1953:30; Foster 1965:296), which stated there is only a limited amount of power in the world, regardless of form, and a human can never increase or decrease this power; it simply moves and is manifested where needed. As a result, any electrical device would diminish the practitioner's power, and if his power is diminished, several conditions could cause the malady to leave the patient and enter the practitioner's body. The main reason given was that the patient had ingested non-Indian medicines which could poison the practitioner, certainly if he had been using sucking as a treatment. This was always a paramount fear when treating a patient in a hospital. Or, as previously mentioned, if all of the electrical devices had not been unplugged and properly covered, the shaman's power would not attend him or help the patient. In the past a non-Indian would never be permitted to attend or observe a traditional curing ceremony, since it was firmly believed that the shaman's familial powers would not help him, but might even work against him for such a violation, and thereby give the same illness to the shaman.

A curing ceremony rarely lasted more than three nights, usually only one night if the patient was cured. Since the patient was nearly always in a darkened environment, the evil force or object in the patient's body would be visible as a dim and sometimes shimmering light, varying in intensity and motion. A constant danger was that when the curing shaman placed his hand on the site of intrusion, the object or force might break into several pieces and migrate elsewhere, even deeper into the person's body, or simply evade the shaman's hands as he blew on the site in an attempt to force the malevolent intrusion to where it could be more easily extracted. An intrusive spirit or object was manipulated, forced, or drawn—depending upon the location of the object or spirit—to a joint in the leg, arm, or neck, but more commonly to the patient's head, more specifically the *fontanelle* (sntoqʷm'ow'e?sqn) where it was withdrawn. Some claimed that success was frequently achieved by removing the suspected cause of the malady from any of the extremities.

After being removed, the inserted spirit—once a forceful but ethereal evil—appeared as a white amorphous object that was usually no larger than 3 or 4 cm at it greatest length or width. It was an object that could be pulled or kneaded, but after release it always returned to its original form, "sorta like a willow catkin." Once removed, the object was held tightly by the curing shaman in his closed cross-cupped palms, and depending upon the shaman and the nature of the force, there were different rituals to neutralize the extracted force or abject. This was accomplished by either blowing over one's clasped hands until the object was no longer warm, or by submerging one's hands in either a *container of cold water* (*čłept nsulqʷ*) or in a moving stream, after which the mass simply disappeared (disintegrated?). Another procedure for neutralizing a withdrawn malevolent force was to smoke the force or object by holding one's hands for some time over a low open smudge fire. The Spokan are not known to have buried or inserted a retrieved spirit in a piece of wood.

Using a sucking tube, blowing, or by passing his hands, the shaman would carefully remove a sorcery-intruded physical object, such as a feather, a knot of hair or sinew (often from the sorcerer's animal spirit), a tooth, a piece of wood, a horn, or bone, or any diminutive organic or inorganic object. During the ceremony of removing a malevolent force, the intruded object would be ritually disposed of by the practitioner. It was commonly believed that when a person has been cured, his *sumés̆* would be even more powerful. The intruded object was often displayed to the patient and sometimes even to an attending group as a proof of ordeal and success.

When a curing shaman was possessed by one of his spirits, and speaking in spirit language, one of his attendants would serve as an *interpreter* (*sxʷnmicínm* or *sxʷnmíci*). But a person who *spoke foolishly* (*hi nqʷawcn*) was not considered to be speaking a spirit language, rather in glossolalia. However, a man or woman who garbled their words or *spoke backwards* (*tekʷn'cn'm'ist*) was known to be under the power of Blue Jay sorcery (Ray 1937:596-597).

Not every medicine man was capable of curing. Few had the power and ability to cure, despite having a guardian spirit. It is not generally recalled as to whether a curing shaman possessed a unique power for treating a specific malady, regardless of their tutelary spirit. For example, a special person who drove away evil spirits was known as a *sxʷqíxʷm*; whereas some shamans had only the power and ability to administer medicines, and were known as a *suxʷmryén*. Many years ago, one curing shaman claimed to have four types of curing power, each power being dependent upon one of the four separate tutelary spirits he possessed. One of his powers was for treating traditional illness and the other three were for curing non-traditional maladies. If for some reason a curing shaman died after successfully treating a patient, the affliction could return to the former patient.

Regardless of the type of malady, ritual, or medication used by a curing shaman, the main objective was to restore a physical and psychological balance within the patient, which was accomplished, as mentioned, by removing or displacing a physical object or a malevolent force or spirit. Most physical and psychological maladies were heat illnesses, though many types of mental illness, shock, and excessive grief were seen as instances of a cold illness. This concept of complementary opposition (as cited elsewhere in Chapter XVIII) is the belief that a *cold treatment* (*ns?aho? mir'yemistn*) is best for a hot illness, and vice versa, for both internal and external illnesses and injuries. A sick person may feel that his illness is hot, though he may be cold to the touch; that means to restore a balance, the illness was removed or dissipated within the patient's body or treated with a 'cold' medicine, just as a cold illness was best treated with a hot medicine.

The most common and frequently used procedure for self-curing was the daily sweathouse ritual, when a person would rejuvenate himself physically and mentally; restore his balance by communicating with his guardian spirit, to whom he could express his fears and concerns; and thank his tutelary for all it had done for him. A man never lied to his guardian spirit, for if he did so, the all-knowing spirit would *abandon him* (*čsúxʷxʷmntm*). Everyone believed that wellness was the guardian spirit and one's body being in concert, while illness was an imbalance—a disruption caused by moral transgression, a malevolent thought, or by sorcery.

Diagnosis

Though a curing shaman might dream of a person and his illness, it was not always possible for the shaman to cure the patient, since it was not unusual that the person responsible for the patient's malady happened to be more powerful than the practitioner. In such a case, the shaman might enlist the *assistance* (*čn'šiš*) of another practitioner, one who had greater powers than he to help during the curing ritual. However, their powers were never combined; only the more powerful shaman directed the curing ritual, and made the final decision of treatment and ritual. Or, if the practitioner was unable to discern the cause of the *sickness* (*swéyt* or *sq'ilt*), he would most likely be unable to affect a cure. In the case of sorcery, the afflicted practitioner would have to be more powerful than the sorcerer if he were to cure himself; and it was remembered how a sick shaman could cure himself without seeking the help of another curing shaman, but only if the afflicted practitioner had greater power than the sorcerer. When a curing shaman dreamed of someone with a malady, and yet failed to help that person—only suggesting there was a sickness and that he should seek help—the sick person might cure himself and then kill the shaman who had the dream.

It is presumed that during the period of deculturation, alienation and demoralization were factors in various types of psychological maladies, "characterized by the inability to cope with a life situation, leading to [...] preoccupation with threat, depression, self-blame, guilt, and shame" (Csordas and Kleinman 1996:18). Though not always associated with mental illness, or psychologically perceived sorcery, there was, and still is, sometimes relative deprivation when, "a negative discrepancy between legitimate expectation and actuality, or between legitimate expectation and anticipated actuality, or both" (Aberle 1966:322). More germane to the Spokan was that, "contacts between groups of radically different culture often involve deprivation for some or many members of one of these groups (Aberle 1966:326), primarily the Spokan. Several elderly men cited how when they were much younger, and working off-reservation without traditional support (sweathouse, "native" language, and even certain foods), they often experienced depression (relative deprivation), and they could not properly communicate with their tutelary spirit. Jilek believed that any group experiencing relative deprivation and cultural confusion [develop], "Anomic depression [...] a chronic dysphoric state characterized by feelings of existential frustration, discouragement, defeat, lowered self-esteem and sometimes moral disorientation" (1982:52).

A curing shaman was made aware of a person's medical situation by his dreaming of the condition, or being informed by his guardian spirit, or even by an animal who was not one of his so-called entourage of tutelary spirits. The first step in making an accurate diagnosis depended upon the practitioner's ability to elicit a confession from the patient, or, if the patient was *unconscious* (*λ'lil'*), from the group members who invariably provided an adequate explanation for the patient's condition. There was once consensus that a curing shaman needed only to place his right hand on the crown of the patient's head (Elmendorf 1935-6, 2:32) while the patient made his confession, and this would reveal to the shaman the cause, diagnosis, and prognosis. Once the confession began, the shaman's hand would *shake* (*xʷr'*)—sometimes uncontrollably, and all the while restraining the patient from raising himself against the shaman's efforts. The curing shaman, or one or more of his assistants, always attempted to restrain the patient from unnecessary movement in order to keep the intruded object or concentrated malevolent force in place and not allow it to become relocated somewhere else in the body through violent or strenuous motions.

When the patient was unconscious, or *in a coma* (*qʷm'íp*), or became *deathly ill* (*míxʷt*), or *unexpectedly ill* (*čskʷisey'st*), or was experiencing a *severe relapse* (*xpelxʷeʔ*), the curing shaman would encourage the patient's kin group and friends to recount certain events which may have led to the condition; a procedure which later will be discussed in the section describing group medical inquest. The patient's kinspeople and friends naturally had the same concerns of acquiring the patient's recent history of behavior and diet before any *minor relapse* (*xpéʷlxʷʔentm*) had occurred. A person's initial awareness of illness was when he first physically experienced a disability, or when he became aware of a pending malady by his dreaming, or it was revealed by someone else's dream, or even by an animal that was not his *suméš*. Often the revealing shaman would attend the patient in his dream.

A *medicine man* (λ̓ʾʔekʷíłš) (Elmendorf 1935-6, 2:22) who was capable of meditating and formulating a diagnosis based on another's dream, and not always the patient's, was called a *ʔec čʾłƛ̓ʾuʔƛ̓ʾuʔ* (STHC). Prior to a person becoming ill, someone in the community might have experienced a *prophetic dream* (*snwečm̓tus*) that foretold—often in detail—what misfortune or malady would befall a certain member of their group. In the past there was consensus that the person who had such a dream would inform the person concerned. If he failed to do so, then he too would suffer the consequences of his dream. This belief existed until recently among only a few living traditional elders.

It was not unusual for a person to be warned of a pending illness, tragedy, or even death by one's tutelary spirit—usually during a session in the sweathouse, or in a dream. As mentioned, it has happened that an animal not associated with a person's guardian spirit might tell him or her of a pending illness. Elders recalled that it was more common for a person to sometimes receive an inconclusive physical sign, such as a unique sound made by an *ominous wind* (*čʾłxaʕlstn*), a rock breaking open for no apparent reason, or the unusual and even aberrant behavior of an animal, which indicated that the listener or observer was going to *become ill* (*ésʕayʾx̣ʷteyn*). A person might be warned of a pending illness or tragedy when observing only a single tree in a copse swaying in the wind, or experiencing a strong gust of cold air on a warm day. Warnings—really omens—were usually only that; they seldom indicated the specific type or time of a person's pending illness. Because of the inconclusiveness of a portent, a person would seek the assistance of a shaman—one who could interpret the significance of the so-called omen. Nor was it unusual for a person to be forewarned by his or her guardian spirit of an impending illness, or even the person's death, or one in his family. Quite often a bird—usually an owl—or another nocturnal animal, would announce a pending malady to a person *during a dream* (*łu qeyʾs*), or when one was alone in the woods, "sometimes he only cried or sounded like he was sobbing or *blowing his nose* (*heʔc łottʾi* or *ndax̣ʷsax̣ʷpaqs*), or *loudly inhaling nasal mucus* (*łtʾłotʾlš*)" (STHC).

When making a diagnosis, the major concern and effort of the curing shaman was to analyze the patient's dreams—particularly *bad dreams* (*scł-qeyʾs*), bad-vision dreams, or *nightmares* (*čʾsčʾsqeyʾs*). The attending practitioner would *interpret the patient's dreams* (*ʔeccčʾłxʷuʔsmisti*) or dire *premonitions* (*ʔec moyʾyʾx̣eʔey*) in an attempt to identify the reason for the patient's predicament. It often happened that after the dream analysis was completed, the patient displayed *signs of improvement* (*msslsułm*) and would commence to *regain health* (*xstwilši*), and to *heal* (*pʾʕax* or *pʾaʔáx*).

The dreams of a curing shaman, as to the cause and treatment, were typically accurate; but there were several accounts of a curing shaman being misled by a sorcerer's *suméš*:

> I remember one once very powerful shaman who had a dream of a boy who was going to be badly hurt in a rodeo. Well, the man never warned or told anyone of his dream, and sure enough, the boy was hurt bad. Right after the dreamer heard of this, he went high on a side hill and started to shout out loud his dream so everyone could hear him. Finally, one old woman climbed the side hill and told him his *suméš* had lied (*yʾoʔyóqʷm* - "to tell a lie"), [which presumably it never does]; the shaman should of told or somehow warned the boy. The man never hurt the old woman for saying as we all thought he would. The shaman died right before the lady. We thought maybe the man had been told the wrong thing by a sorcerer who was jealous (Ross 1968-2008).

The patient always agreed with a shaman's diagnosis since it was understood that any lack of faith or doubt in one's practitioner's pronouncements or ritual, could mean *continued illness* (*ni-op weyt*) or even death. Significantly, only the shaman would make a prognosis unless the patient wanted to die for whatever reason, usually the belief that he was being sorcerized by too powerful a sorcerer. After hearing the patient's confession, as well as any pertinent reasons for the malady by others, the shaman went into a trance while singing his song to gain his guardian spirit's assistance prior to concluding and announcing the diagnosis. At this juncture in the ceremony, it was important for the patient to accept his status and condition as a patient, one who needs help, and the ability of the shaman to cure him. These procedures, and others, were frequently and dramatically manifested in what anthropologists call the group medical inquest (Ross 1983:139), or what some contemporary physicians call the medical inquest.

576

A most important and dramatic aspect of diagnosing, treating, and administering a patient with any malady, particularly supernatural illness—one with a psychiatric etiology, i.e., a culture-bound malady—was the *group medical inquest* (*yáq'q'm'i?*); which, "no doubt was highly effective in the treatment of certain neurotic or psychosomatic disturbances" (Lewis 1971:53). This therapeutic interview was essentially a group therapy, that provided, "support, protection, acceptance, and stimulation" (Frank and Powdermaker 1959; Jilek 1982:88; Ross 1989), a collective ceremony when the patient and shaman were joined by family and friends, and on occasion the entire village who publicly demonstrated their moral support of the patient, and provided physical assistance and moral support for the family during treatment (Turner 1964). Moreno (1955) defined the group medical inquest, "as a therapeutic, controlled acting-out taking place under the guidance of therapists [curing shamans] in a safe treatment setting." The process of curing practitioners, in many instances, particularly with the patient who has violated a cultural tabu, receives—during the group medical inquest—collective support from the group (Dressler 1996:260).

This unique collective ritual of intensification was actually a psychodrama—one heightened by a medical chorus of several women who sometimes chanted or sang medical songs, as a person played a flute. All of this biopsychosocial ritual treatment and "collaborative care, theoretically provided greater opportunities for enhanced self-concept, management of emotional disturbance, or emotional support" (Mehl-Madrona 2010, 14:9). It was believed to facilitate a shaman's power flight when seeking a vision or recovering a lost or captured soul. If soul-loss was considered the cause of a person's illness, then a single flute, sometimes played intermittently by an assistant, served to sustain or recreate an emotional high among all those present, including the patient, if conscious. The flute was believed to be a way to communicate with the soul, calling it back. Some elders claimed that drumming by the laity was never part of the group medical inquest or curing ritual, but a single flute played intermittently by an assistant served to sustain or recreate an emotional intensity among all those present, including the expectant patient. However, if the patient was unconscious, any one of the participants having intimate knowledge of the patient could offer an explanation to the assembled group. Some have said—and this has been personally experienced during curing ceremonies—how a repetitious chant often achieved a desired near-hypnotic state; for combining the chanting in a darkened room along with certain individual expectations and the belief in the presence of power, were all conducive to further enhance any heightened psychological state. Yet a few elders said they never recalled any drumming or flute playing during the curing session.

Lewis provided an excellent, even perceptive description of this collective medical rite of healing and the different functions of group therapy; most of which was done by the Spokan:

> The rhythmic music and singing [*modulis et cantilena*], and later the dancing of the shaman, gradually involve every participant more and more in a collective action. When the audience begins to repeat the refrains together with the assistants, only those who are defective fail to join the chorus. The tempo of the action increases, the shaman with a spirit is no more an ordinary man or relative, but is a 'placing' (i.e. incarnation) of the spirit; the spirit acts together with the audience, and this is felt by everyone. The state of many participants is now near to that of the shaman himself, and only a strong belief that when the shaman is there the spirit may only enter him, restrains the participants from being possessed in mass by the spirit. This is a very important condition of shamanizing which does not however reduce mass susceptibility to the suggestion, hallucinations, and unconscious acts produced in a state of mass ecstasy. When the shaman feels that the audience is with him and follows him he becomes even more active and this effect is transmitted to his audience. After shamanizing, the audience recollects various moments of the performance, their great psychophysiological emotion and the hallucinations of sight and hearing which they have experienced (Lewis 1971:53).

The intent and effect of drumming by the curing shaman's assistant was to focus and coordinate the attention of the patient, and those attending upon the shaman and his performance, and was described—often

577

rather critically by Alexander Ross, who initially questions certain aspects of the ritual, but acknowledged the benefit in treating a severe wound, of which there was no question:

> [...] the drummer's beating and singing, the noise may be heard a quarter of a mile away. With all this absurdity, many extraordinary cures are performed by these people. They have a profound knowledge of all simples, and if the complaint be manifest, as in cases of cuts and wounds [...] their skill is really astonishing. I once saw an Indian who had been nearly devoured by a grizzly bear, and had his skull split open in several places, and several pieces of the bone taken out just above the brain, and measuring three-fourths of an inch in length, cured so effectively by one of these jugglers, that in less than two months after he was riding on his horse again at the chase (1849, 7:290).

The social dynamics and mutual interest demonstrated during a group medical inquest toward a patient were apparent when kinspeople and attending friends actively participated in attempting to elicit the cause of illness when being questioned by the shaman. A curing shaman once explained how important it was for his success if the patient—early in the curing ritual—publicly acknowledged what he thought was causing his debility (Ross 1981c), and why "even though the shaman grants little validity to patient self-diagnosis, the curer directs the patient's search for a diagnosis in directions required by community knowledge of the patient's social condition, thus leaving little leeway for patient choice" (Press 1978:78).

When discussing the attitude of impersonality, Press further noted that a critical aspect in curing is when practitioners, "take their cues from patients, accept their stated symptoms at face value and, thus, offer a guarantee that the patient's peculiar *anxieties* (*nyem'l's*) and sick role preferences will be validated" (1978:75).

Though the designation 'sick role' serves different functions, and, "In biomedical terms, a successful outcome is elimination of a disease or disorder, in sociological terms it is termination of what Parson (1958) called the 'sick role'" (Csordas and Kleinman 1996:9).

Therefore, the Spokan group psychotherapeutic medical inquest served additional functions when acknowledging the sick role: it gave the patient a brief but often significant managerial role; to ameliorate further patient *anxiety* (*nše??l'smist*) by validating the patient's status, to allow the patient to expiate his guilt thorough confession (Sigerist 1970:390), and to collectively facilitate group confessions of any perceived *sins* (*nč'xʷum*) or bad habits by the patient, thereby preventing illness to the participants. Once the patient confesses his guilt, the medicine will work (Hallowell 1977:136). This collective psychodrama generally allowed the displacement of responsibility and self-imposed guilt for failure from the patient to others (Madsen 1964). The group medial inquest also functioned to integrate the group, restored moral order, served as an effective therapeutic psychosomatic session, and publicly permitted the shaman to demonstrate his power and ability. During such a collective curing session, it was not unusual for a member of the attending group to assist a patient to *try to recall* (*še??lsmíst*) a forgotten but probable cause of his affliction. This would often be critical for *rehabilitation* (*heł x̣stwil'š*), particularly if the patient was slightly comatose or temporarily unconscious.

When a shaman worked on a patient, depending upon the sickness, he often had another person who was an assistant or a member of the patient's family, sitting near the patient's head. If the patient was lying on his back, the shaman might instruct the person to cradle the patient's head, particularly when a patient with mental illness or who was experiencing soul-loss required physical contact and reassurance. Sometimes an assistant was required to restrain a patient.

During the group medical inquest, the curing shaman would always ask if the patient had angered someone or inadvertently humiliated a shaman, particularly one who was possibly a sorcerer. Naturally, if the patient was unconscious, the curing shaman would ask this question to the group. The practitioner would:

> [...] not talk to his guardian spirit or invoke it; it is supposed to be right with him. Nor would he tell how he got his curing power; he told about this when he first made his medicine dance [...] If the medicine man has dreamed of the cause of the man's sickness he proceeds with the curing right away. If he has not, then he has to

find out what is wrong with him before he can cure; if he can not find out then he tells him that he can not and that he can not do anything for him and he quits (Smith 1936-8:1278).

The group medical inquest ritual took place only at night, lasting from several hours up to several evenings, because the sessions continued until the patient died or was completely rehabilitated. This in turn required the curing shaman and his entourage to often reside temporarily with the patient's family, thereby affording the opportunity to learn reasons for the patient's illness and anxiety—reasons that had not been enunciated during the group medical inquest. Individual or collective sociosomatic decisions as to treatment were almost always determined during the group medical inquest. Consequently, the progress:

> [...] or course of an illness episode, [was] defined by a sequence of decisions leading to diagnosis and treatment. This work broadens the notion of process to include not only the patient and therapist but the network of people who may be engaged with varying degrees of responsibility in the decision-making process, termed the *therapy management group* (Scordas and Kleinman 1996:10).

This collective ritual thus recognized that the principal elements in successfully treating most spirit illnesses—apart from physical rehabilitation—were the techniques of engaging the patient in conversation and confession. This sort of verbal interaction between patient and practitioner helped not only in making a diagnosis, but tended to relieve a patient's anxiety or fear—nearly always the basis of *psychosomatic malady* (sx^{w}mr'yem). An additional function of the group medical inquest was to establish the prognosis—one which might publicly absolve the shaman, "of any obligation to cure" (Kennedy 1984:24), but established what might be recognizable stages of recovery, particularly with long-term illness, and *he cures* (n$^?$ix^{w}usis - "rescues") the patient.

The medical historian Sigerist noted an important function of disease, for the malady may be seen to serve as punishment and atonement for sin, and:

> As a consequence of this view of disease as punishment, the sick man was marked with a certain stigma. He was not a guiltless victim. To be sure he suffers, but he has deserved his suffering because he has sinned. Through his sickness his sins become a matter of public knowledge. The diseased man is branded with his sinfulness. Thus sickness isolates him in an especially harsh manner (1970:390).

There was consensus that social isolation of a patient was recognized as being even more detrimental to the recovery of a sick person; therefore, the patient's role was publicly validated before the cause, usually behavioral, could be expiated, or often before a shaman would attend a person's malady. A major aspect in curing a patient was not to physically or socially isolate or further stigmatize the patient for the cause of his affliction. Once the cause of the malady had been established, and when the patient made restitution (critical to his treatment), then it was not brought up again by anyone, for he had been cured. Prior to examination, sickness was not always thought of as malicious punishment resulting from sorcery, but sometimes—as suggested earlier—as an atonement that served to expiate a wrongdoing, often necessitating a purification ritual. But if it was determined that the cause of one's illness was sorcery, it would be the sorcerer—if identified—who might be killed or excommunicated, depending upon the severity of the affliction. Because of the recognized severity of killing a suspected sorcerer, one cannot assume that killing such a convicted person meant his or her death, nor was there any such recall.

Considering the functions and success of the aforementioned Spokan group medical inquest, one may say there was always a linear process from the initial awareness of sickness to eventual wellness, in which the critical aspects of disease etiology, medical diagnosis, and of course resulting familial care and treatment occurred. Therefore, the principal function of the Group Medical Inquest was a notion predicated on the assumption that there were significant homeopathic relationships between rituals and a person's desired change of behavior and condition. However, it was often extremely difficult to distinguish the differences between the compatible personalistic and naturalistic etiological systems, or to determine which was more successful. In naturalistic systems, the patient and his family initially assumed a more apparent managerial and medical role, which if not successful within the informal familial setting, progresses or evolves to a personalistic system, whereby the shaman makes the diagnosis and invariably administers directly to the patient's needs, but which continued to involve certain aspects of the naturalistic system. And, as has been noted:

> In personalistic systems people also know the kinds of behavior—sins of commission and omission—that may lead to retaliation by a deity, spirit, or witch. To the extent they can lead blameless lives they should avoid sickness. But personalistic causality is far more complex than naturalistic causality, since there are no absolute rules to avoid arousing the envy of others, for doing just the right amount of ritual to satisfy an ancestor, fore knowing how far one can shade a taboo without actually breaching it. Consequently, in such systems one has less control over the conditions that lead to illness than in the other, where rules are clearly stated (Foster and Anderson 1978:780).

Medical Paraphernalia

A curing shaman used a minimum of curing devices, relying more upon his reputation, knowledge, curing abilities, and *suméš*. Elders were emphatic as to how—in the past—the mere presence of a practitioner was psychologically as well as physically therapeutic, and those who had been patients explained how, when a curing shaman entered the room, it was as though a heavy weight had been lifted from their body (Cline 1938:163). They became more alert, yet confident in the knowledge that this man or woman was going to cure them. Perhaps even more important, and therapeutic to a patient, was the knowledge that the sole intent and concerted effort of the practitioner, along with his *suméš* and knowledge of medicine, was to reincorporate the person back into a balanced and healthy social and spiritual world.

There is debate and uncertainty as to how often a practitioner would use a curing pipe during his curing ministrations. Some Spokan elders have explained that a pipe was important to the curing shaman's medical paraphernalia, and that it was a special pipe, nearly always a tube pipe, one used only when sucking. Before the practitioner ever commenced his diagnosis, he always judiciously washed his hands in a decoction of wild rose, sometimes mixed with mashed yarrow root and leaves. Also, before attending a patient, the curing shaman would devote considerable time to smoking his pipe, no matter how sick the patient was. This was sometimes a lengthy procedure, the purpose being to better hear and understand any messages from his tutelary power as well as from those attending. It was explained how:

> [...] the practice of smoking before curing someone was so the curing doctor could better "see" what was really wrong, and maybe who the [sorcerer] was and how he'd used his *suméš* to make the person sick. When you used to watch them [curing shaman], I'd always thought they were relaxing, letting their *suméš* get loose, sorta fly around, go other places and hear other things about the sick man. To me, when the shaman was smoking, thinking—maybe dreaming—that he'd gone away. Maybe his smoke went up to other things [powers] who'd tell him ways to help the sick man. He [the curing shaman] even looked not so heavy 'cause he'd never move, like his *suméš* lifted him, no matter how long he sat cross-legged next to the patient. Maybe his body was there, but *suméš* took him [possessed] for a while (Ross 1968-2008)

Different types of sucking tubes were of aid in certain treatments, but again, the demonstrated skill and power in treating was often too personal, immediate, and direct to be separated by paraphernalia. The importance of establishing a particular thought or breathing rhythm in the patient was best accomplished by suggestion, hypnotism, or the shaman's low *humming (nkʷn'icin' or nkʷenm'ey'eʔ)*—not with drumming, which would negate any real sense of final anticipation of recovery by the patient. The last known Spokan curing shaman once said, "Drums are to keep people awake, to keep 'em moving or jumping; but together."

Feathers were occasionally used therapeutically in several ways: for stroking an unconscious patient or a distraught young child, or helping an agitated person to relax. As will be discussed, feathers—important items in a shaman's armamentarium—were also used by curing shamans as prophetic devices in making a medical diagnosis or prognosis. As cited earlier, each curing shaman had a medicine bundle or bag that held sacred items he used to enhance his power and related ability, but which seldom had contact with a patient, except when he used a small nodule or bit of red hematite powder that would be applied to the patient's face. A

580

person who was wounded or severely cut would—following the so-called Doctrine of Signatures—paint his face with red hematite, which a man always carried to ameliorate the *bleeding* (*mlál'*) by self-treatment, and for other purposes.

Prophetic Medical Procedures

Prophetic *medical* (*mry'e*) oracular devices and vaticinatory procedures used to make diagnoses and prognoses varied in form and application. But each one was applicable to one of two areas: physical manifestations that were publicly demonstrated, or verbally induced psychological imagery that was interpreted by the medical practitioner by dreaming or experiencing a vision. More specifically, physical manifestations were culturally understood devices manipulated by the shaman, or unique interpretations or signs given by animals. For example, a still, *deep pool* (*čɫq'q'l'i?*) of water could possibly reveal to a curing shaman the image of a person who would eventually become ill or die, or of someone who knew the potential patient. Certain animals and theriomorphic forms could communicate the identity of a potential patient to a shaman; some species were believed to have more power than others with this ability—most notably owls. Commonly, even *sweathouse stones* (*ssoʔɫessn'*) would on occasion audibly *speak* (*qʷel*), thereby being prophetic to a person with the ability to *hear* (*sewn?*) and interpret such pronouncements, always to a curing shaman. A sick person might be informed by a bird of an imminent illness. But that same bird could prevent or treat the malady if the person gave all of his possessions away—a proof of generosity to the community, and commitment to faith in the spiritual world.

Among curing shamans there were various rituals prior to making a patient's prognosis—rituals that required the active involvement of the shaman's tutelary spirit, which may reveal a sign that was an affirmation of a patient's condition. Woodpecker feathers were used in medicine by both sorcerers and curing shamans, as explained by a Spokan elder:

> When a curing shaman came to a sick person, he'd take a woodpecker feather, and before he danced and sang his *suméš* song, he'd lay the feather flat in the sick man's open [supine] hand. If, when the doctor finished his song and dance, everyone knew the patient would get well if the feather stood up, but he'd die if the feather stayed flat in his hand (Ross 1968-2008).

The type of shaman or medicine man who had unusual prophetic powers was called *níxʷmi?*, one who was able to predict what was going to happen to a healthy person, such as sickness or some serious physical danger. When the *níxʷmi?* asked a person if he thought something was going to happen to him, and the person said yes, then the *níxʷmi?* would make every effort to protect the person from the pending illness or danger. In the course of events, if the threatened person lost his *suméš*, or if stolen, then the *níxʷmi?* continued his efforts to support and protect the afflicted person (Elmendorf 1935-6, 4:10), who may have felt obligated to affect a cure.

The author personally observed a case illustrating prophetic illness when an elderly Spokan woman had recurring dreams that she was alone in her woodshed, and could hear the walls making popping sounds and exuding a liquid that was not blood or water, but a substance similar to pine pitch. During these dreams, the inside walls of the structure were always completely covered with cockroaches (*Periplaneta americana - č'el''xʷičn*), garden spiders (*Argiope aurantia - tupl'*), and yellow jackets, which crawled over the woman and stung her exposed arms and legs when she attempted to remove them from the walls, which continued to produce popping sounds and exude the pitch-like liquid. Two weeks later, the woman—for the first time—experienced painful skin eruptions that were confined to her arms and legs, and eventually commenced to suppurate. At last, her family prevailed upon the woman to consult the Indian Health Service *physician* (*sxʷmr'yern?* or *maliémn*), who quickly concluded that the woman's condition was an allergic reaction to a newly-acquired soap she used when bathing. The *doctor* (*sux'ʷmrycm* - "one who administers medicine") prescribed a medicament that proved ineffective. In *frustration* (*m'eʔeʔels*) with the physician's explanatory model, the woman travelled to a different reservation where she enlisted the assistance of a curing shaman who concluded the patient was a victim of sorcery, and should submit to traditional ritual and natural medicines, which proved successful, as did the shaman's measures to negate any of the psychosocial effects created by any of the sorcerer's future machinations. The woman recalled a dream she had prior to her dermal afflictions, of being in what she felt was a woodshed. She had chosen to ignore her dream, or, more specifically, she neglected to enlist the assistance of a shaman who could have interpreted the symbolic significance of the woodshed's *prophecy* (*ʔe nʔíxʷmi* - "shaman who will make a prophecy"), and would have understood the meaning of the popping noises (warnings) and pitch-like liquids that proved prophetic of her dermal eruptions. In retrospect, the woman knew the dermal eruptions were caused by sorcery-induced yellow jacket bites in her dream, and the liquid pitch from the walls, as mentioned, was actually suppuration. The woman finally realized that her condition was due to an accusation she had made by identifying another woman as being a sorcerer.

In the past, the importance of dreams predicting misfortunes or illnesses was demonstrated by the once daily ritual of an elderly woman within the household, who carefully listened in the early morning to each adolescent relating their dreams, some of which were frequently interpreted as prophetic. During early enculturation, children became aware of the significance and meaning of symbolism they remembered in their dreams, often repetitive past or present events. Usually by puberty they were able to understand events and situations that they or someone else should possibly avoid to prevent illness or misfortune. It was understood that if a person had a dream of pending malevolence, or if there was an accident to anyone in the camp or village, the intended victim should be warned. The recipient of this knowledge might— in appreciation— provide a small gift to the dreamer. A sick person may have a dream in which he was told how to cure another sick person. If the dreamer obeyed his dream and cured the other person, then he too would be cured, and at the same time acquire the song of his *suméš*. Egesdal informally wrote (pers. comm.) how:

> The shaman begins the song by saying how he will do his worst (be ineffectual), which means he will do his best. Sort of an opposite thing, or at least self-effacing. Then he talks about the soul going over to the other side, and he has to go over there to retrieve the soul.

During the curing session, a practitioner would commence to sing the patient's *suméš* song, at first very softly—barely audible, even *pianissimote*, the patient or those attending, but gradually increasing the song to a crescendo until the patient, albeit unconscious, could presumably hear the song. Once the patient joined the curing shaman in singing, it was apparent the person was cured; if the patient did not sing, it meant his health would continue to be bad and he would eventually die (STHC).

The Spokan possessed numerous spiritually-based rituals, devices, interpretive signs within nature, animal communication, and dreams, which, when interpreted, were prophetic of pending cultural events as well as unique occurrences in the natural world. Though such an experience could occur to anyone, regardless of age or gender, certain people were more likely to be sought by a particular animal or power source to symbolically reveal or directly disclose a future occurrence. People possessing unique power could identify, propitiate, and often communicate with designated animals which were capable, if they desired, to achieve the wishes of their so-called human host.

A physical example of a prophetic device used during the Medicine Dance was the *Feather Curing Ceremony* (*sníxúm*) in which five unattached *primary red-headed woodpecker feathers* (*nʔixʷuʔmʼ*) were placed on a small 25 by 30 cm flat *woven tule mat* (*Schoenoplectus acutus* - *cčlúrʼmʼenʼtn*). The feathers, when on the mat, were called *stʼuʔmʼú* (Smith 1936-8:1282), and they would be arranged loosely with the untied shafts toward the shaman. Some elders said that the feathers were not loose, but rather the ends were attached with thin strips of buckskin or Indian hemp, and there were only four such feathers. In any case, during the feather curing ceremony, the curing shaman would hold the mat firmly and level with both hands, all the while singing his power song until the mat would commence to move and eventually shake violently as the unattached feathers assumed an upright position:

The four men who carry the mat can not breathe toward the mat when carrying it to [the] wall else they would blow the souls away, tho[ugh] they can watch it out of the corner of their eye. But coming back it makes no difference about breathing on it for the souls are all settled (Smith 1936-8:1283).

The feathers would *vibrate* (*yityátilš*) until standing still and straining against the mat, indicating that the circle of power was complete, and would reveal an image in the mat that identified the cause of the patient's malady. The circle of power was completed when the souls of four of the participants came to the shaman separately, each making a buzzing sound as it returns to the mat, "and he can tell which [soul] belongs to which person" (Smith 1936-8:1283). The head curing shaman then placed one soul in each feather. After the ceremony, each soul returned to its respective person.

The final diagnosis was made when the shaman interpreted the image in the mat. If the image was indistinct or even split, it may indicate that the patient, or someone in attendance, doubted the shaman's ability and power, or that the illness was caused by a sorcerer who was present. It was not recalled if the patient or others in attendance could view the image; probably not. But it was known that the erect *feathers were later often placed in the hair* (*npatkʷaʔwsnqntm*) of the patient to make her forget what caused their depression or sorrow. In the case of a serious illness, the mat revealed the identity of the sorcerer or the type of affliction, and the feathers would fall to the mat, indicating the curing shaman's success in identifying the sorcerer or cause of malady. The shaman then *removes the feathers* (*nc'qaw'sqn*) from the attendants' heads. This displayed information would then be revealed to the attendants, and often followed immediately by a curing ceremony, which lasted until dawn, at which point they put out the fire and left the lodge. Women always made these small mats, and thereafter only the particular owner-shaman and his four assistants could touch them. It is not known if the mats were later ritually burned or buried after use.

According to Smith, the Chewelah-Spokan Group had a variation of the mat ritual, which differed in the way the principal curing shaman dealt with the four men who brought the mat into the room, and how it was brought in (a man at each corner), and the use of the feathers during and after the ritual. The following is how the head curing shaman publicly and impressionably demonstrated his powers:

Before he [practitioner] puts the one feather in the hair of each of these persons, he tells each all about themselves. He tells each what they have been thinking about, perhaps of suicide, or a woman leaving her husband or a man of leaving his wife or leaving their children. They say that it is always true. Then he tells them just how they have got to act until the summer is gone; the way to live; what kind of clothes to wear, etc. If they follow his orders until summer is past they will be cured. If they do not live up to his orders, then the medicine man tells them what will happen to them and it does happen if they do not. They will die, their "breath" leaves them for good. He tells them how they will die (Smith 1936-8:1282).

The second and most common form of prophetic occurrence was a psychological image which was manifested in a shaman's dream, and previously unbeknownst to the patient, though it was generally assumed that most prophetic abilities were inextricably within the realm of a curing shaman's power. There were occasions when children had prophetic dreams of impending medical problems, and other instances of disaster affecting family members or close friends. It was considered dangerous to a child, or an adult for that matter, if the person who had a recurring dream that predicted a specific patient-condition, failed to reveal the particulars of the dream to an adult. An adult could be informed of an impending malady to himself or another when receiving a *dream of a guardian spirit* (*sqéʔis*), one that could reveal a future situation.

Dreams involving prophetic pronouncements by certain animals were not always understood, and in such instances a shaman would be consulted for interpretation. However, one of the animals in a dream may be a sorcerer in disguise, attempting to capture the dreamer's power—particularly when one animal is biting or fighting a different type of animal, or if a bird appears in the dream with a message.

Patient Individuality

The aforementioned case of the moth illustrates the Spokan's acknowledgement of a person's often power-based medical skills. The primary theme or core of their successful medical system was greater recognition of the value in accepting an individual's prophetic powers—a far cry from the disdain expressed or believed by some modern physicians, who knowingly or unknowingly treat their patients as biological systems to be fixed only by those with the appropriate certification. Consequently, the Spokan's consideration of an individual's self-knowledge was a key to their successful physical, psychological, social, and more importantly, spiritual adaptation.

An individual's transgressions, however, from what were universally recognized and accepted as the proper moral order, were not tolerated, and were considered often the very reason for illness and disease. Individuality was, therefore, a major reason for the existence of different types of curing shamans. "Every disease is a punishment [...] Nevertheless, sickness is not only punishment. It serves to expiate sin. If a man becomes ill, he can thereby atone for his wrongdoings and find purification" (Sigerist 1970:390).

A major forté of any curing shaman was his ability to adopt an individual and personal approach with a patient; always believed to be a major consideration for effective curing when the patient was convinced of the healer's possession of power (*sumés̆*).

Practitioners used different techniques, medicaments and rituals, all of which accommodated the various causes of maladies, as well as the perceived sick personality of a patient. A shaman might elect to treat a patient by combining sucking with blowing and hypnotism, or only treating with acupressure. The Spokan fortunately had a broad armamentarium of both simple and compound medicines from which to choose, forming an often complex paradigm that could be used by a curing shaman in order to treat spiritual illnesses. But, with familial medicine, there was less diversity in the ritual—if any—when administering what were undoubtedly fewer selections of medicines as well as the ritual and personality of the individual attending the family member.

An additional aspect of many traditional medical procedures—important for rehabilitating a patient, but often totally absent in allopathic medicine, was a practitioner's physical and often spiritual contact with the patient, particularly with sucking, acupressure, and many other procedures. The most dramatic and assuring indication of his curing power and commitment, was when a shaman appeared to adopt the form and sounds of one of his familials.

Sucking

One of several universal curing procedures for removing a malevolent spirit or intruded object from a patient was by sucking. The practitioner would locate the site of the malevolent spirit or intruded object by first placing his hand on the forehead of the patient. Then, after making a diagnosis, he would place his mouth on the area adjacent to where he was to *suck* (*qʔem* or *qeʔé* or *ɬqʼílš̆mis* or *ɬopʼm qeʔé* - "sucking to cure" or *sisiúsú* or *sxʷɬópʼm* - "curing by sucking"). For example, if the intruded object or malignancy (evil spirit) was in the patient's neck, the practitioner would lay his face over the site and remove by sucking. If the cause of illness was due to intrusion, the shaman would, after removing the object, display the object to the patient and to those in attendance. Depending upon the type of sickness, a sucking shaman was careful to never put his lips at the site of intrusion; he would do that only near the intrusion or at a *body joint* (*sčʼmosx̱n*). Many sucking shamans would also first blow over the site of pain or illness before sucking to remove any attending malevolent forces. If available, he would use a bison horn with a perforated tip to withdraw an ailing substance or malevolent force. Acknowledging the Doctrine of Signatures, a sucking shaman may have the tutelary power of a mosquito.

Prior to the actual removal by sucking, and after making a diagnosis and locating the site of intrusion, many curing shamans would spend considerable time relocating the malignancy through manual manipulation (acupressure) to a site more favorable for extraction by sucking. Some claimed that the curing practitioner could actually see the malignancy without feeling, and manipulated only to relocate the malignancy, whereas some have said they were able to locate the site of intrusion by passing their hands over the patient until they sensed an area of intense heat. The cause of illness did not always appear as a lump, even though the patient may have been suffering from an *internal tumor* (*súkʷt*), one which may be a grayish fatty substance generated in a *dead body* (*tmney'*) that had been subjected to moisture for several days. Certain curing shamans who removed intruded objects were called a *sxʷƛ'ékʷm* or *ałáʔaqʷílc* ("sucking practitioner"). A *sucking practitioner* was referred to as *sisyús* or *sxʷłóp'm*.

In some instances, depending upon the diagnosis, and regardless of where the malignancy was located, a shaman might commence at the patient's feet, progressing the manipulation until the malignancy was at the top of the patient's head or relocated in one of his hands or feet. It was said that with certain illnesses, it was easier to remove the intrusion if moved to an extremity or joint; the object was then removed by sucking directly on the site. However, when healing specific afflictions, shamans would suck an intruded object from a patient's body using different types of tube devices, such as a hollow long bone, a section of elderberry, bone whistle, or a tube pipe. When not is use, these items were carried and protected, as mentioned earlier, in a hide container similar in shape and construction to a pipe bag.

After sucking to remove a sorcerer-induced object, it was important for the shaman to dramatically display the object, a feather, piece of hair, piece of bone, ball of hair, small piece of animal hide with the fur, lizard, human tooth, or *maggot fly* (*Lucilia sericata* - *č'eč'łuʔ*) to the patient and those attending the curing ceremony, as a means of proving the patient's rehabilitation. However, not every practitioner had the ability to cure by sucking, nor could all shamans treat a patient by blowing to remove intruded objects, which was usually a small feather, piece of bone, small stone, tooth, or a malevolent spirit that resembled a small white object that was usually 2 to 3 cm in length, and upon removal appeared stretched not unlike a section of tendon. The mass was immediately disposed by being placed in a fire by the curing shaman.

The object or malevolent spirit was always slowly and carefully taken away by the practitioner and dramatically burned in the presence of the patient and on-lookers, or disposed of in water. However, what must have been even more dramatic was when the curing shaman chose to retain the malignancy, and depending upon what type it was, carefully placed the physical malignancy in a special stiff rawhide container, or an opened fresh bivalve shell that was immediately closed, and wrapped with Indian hemp before nesting it in a cushion of mullein leaves, often wrapped with wild rose stems.

When sucking to remove spirit intrusion or possession, the shaman, if successful, would displace or neutralize the withdrawn power by placing it in both his hands, rubbing them together as he sang his song while placing both his hands in water or passing them over a low smudge fire on the floor near the patient. It was not uncommon for a sucking shaman to *throw into the fire* (*ncq'mnuusis*) whatever he had extricated from the patient. On the other hand, one of the last curing shamans claimed, "When I take out a sickness or evil from the body, I don't find it necessary to put it in water or fire, I simply keep it in my own body—nothing bad ever happened to me.

With few exceptions, the shaman did his curing behind a hanging tule mat or, later behind a suspended blanket. Near the final stages of removing an intruding physical or spiritual object, the sucking practitioner could, despite the group's singing, be heard to groan during his often seemingly desperate physical efforts to extricate the object or spirit from the patient's body. It was said that when the shaman had the power in his hands, he would be thrown about on the floor or behind a *curtain* (*nil'xʷsélxʷtn*) or mat partition; going through apparently uncontrollable and violent contortions as he wrestled, sometimes even desperately struggling (*ʔel'ist* or *p'is*) to hold the malevolent power after its removal. A practitioner often had to *struggle so hard he ran out of breath* (*xʷcp'esč'iʔt*) (STHC).

Several elders recalled how—as a further proof of ordeal—when the practitioner removed an intruded organic object it was burned, producing a crackling sound as it emitted what was best described as a shower of sparks. Those near the fire could sometimes detect an ozone-like smell. There was never any visible ash after the object was burned, since it was completely neutralized. A sucking shaman often had as a tutelary spirit a bird whose skin he always carried in his power bundle. While curing, the bird, as a guardian spirit, would converse with the shaman the whole time, advising, or simply giving him the power to cure. When a person without curing power became ill, he might call upon his tutelary spirit to come and help him *get well* (*xstw'il's*), or "restoration to health" (*restitution ad integrum*). It was explained that his *sumés* might not be a bird, but instead might be thunder or a type of fish.

The earliest recorded account of sucking by a Sinkaietk practitioner was by Alexander Ross, who in wonderment described the various machinations of removing a malignant spirit by a curing shaman:

> The moment the bad spirit is gone out of the sick person, the *tla-quill-augh* [italics added] sucks the part affected with his mouth to extract the bad blood through the pores of the skin, which, to all appearance, he does effectively. How he manages to do it I know not; but I have watched him, and seen him throw out whole mouthfuls of blood, and yet not the least mark would appear on the skin. By the colour and quantity of the blood he announces the character of the disease, He goes through the same ceremony with various parts of the body till he expels the evil spirit altogether; or if he fails to do so, and the patient dies, he fixes the death on some rival in the profession (1849, 7:289).

Several of Elmendorf's Spokan informants had intimate knowledge and experience with the procedures required for removing a malady by sucking. They explained how a shaman would be first approached by the family or friends of the patient, who sometimes would:

> [...] offer him a certain sum to come & doctor the sick man – [the] medicine man would touch the patient on the crown of his head & find out what was ailing him – [the] doctor would find out where the pain was – if [he] was stabbed he would suck [some] blood out and by putting his mouth [*snč'máłq'ʷ* - "inside his mouth"] to [the] wound [and] spit it into [the] fire – & tell him he'd be all right – if he had a pain the med[icine] man would suck out a little blood – just enough to spit out & he'd be cured right away – over night & he'd be up – blood was the only thing he'd take out of his body – med[icine] man can take *sumés* away if he wants it awful bad but hardly ever did that because it was very wicked and the victim died – as soon as the *sumés* [was] taken away he was good as dead – died almost at once & could not be saved (1935-6, 2:9).

The medical practice of removing an accidental wood or stone splinter—sometimes a sorcerer's intruded object—or a malevolent spirit, was, undertaken by a curing practitioner whose guardian spirit was the mosquito, and was most successful in treating dermal maladies associated with hematomas caused by intrusion. It was thought that most shamans with mosquito power were women:

> I never knew my husband's grandmother 'cause it was a long trip away, and anyway, I don't think his family liked me until my children came. After the old lady died, my husband told me when his grandmother was young, his mother said how his grandmother got a huge hump on her back. It came overnight, and no one knew what to do. After supper, a woman [shaman] came to the house, and after a while she worked on the girl, but she made no cut, but sucked, and sucked until all the bad blood was out. She spit it all in a basin she took when she left before morning (Ross 1968-2008).

Sometimes the curing shaman would actually *suck blood out of a patient* (*hec puxʷ* or *łq'ilšmis*), spitting the blood onto a low nearby fire, which served to publicly verify that the malevolent spirit or intruded object had been removed and neutralized. Such a performance gave credence to elders who said how an unusually powerful medicine man could suck blood from an injury or hematoma by *laying his mouth* (*sxʷłopm*) over the injury without leaving a mark, or breaking the *skin* (*ełxʷ*), or causing any *swelling* (*sik'ʷsik'ʷsik'ʷ*). In the case of an *infected* (*čníl*) stab or arrow wound—more frequent with the introduction of iron—the medicine man sucked the blood out of his patient and spit it into a fire; such a practitioner was called *sxʷłopm*. It was also possible for a powerful practitioner to suck the blood from an injury and *leave no hematoma* (*sxʷłopm*) when removing an intruded object (STHC). A sore or inflamed area was never sucked upon or manipulated, but rather was treated externally with a topical medicine. One elderly woman said she felt a curing shaman

586

would, before a final sucking, place a small fish bladder with blood into his mouth, and break it with his teeth to achieve the desired effect.

A curing practitioner might also remove small, white maggot-like worms by manipulating the afflicted area with his hands, never by sucking. Smith gives the only account of this special worm-induced illness, which among the Kalispel and Chewelah-Spokan Group caused, "sores quite often on the neck, occasionally on the hands, feet, body; it swells up in places and breaks and turns into running sores; similar to scrofula and syphilis; it leaves scars. To cure this they extracted the worm that caused it" (1936-8:300).

In the past there was consensus that any form of manifested evil could actually never be destroyed; such forms of malevolent power could only be removed and displaced or temporarily neutralized. Elmendorf (pers. comm.) was of the same opinion, saying that power can only be displaced, but never destroyed or diminished. In other words, a primary premise contended that a person was incapable of creating an evil force, only manipulating and directing it through ritual, and only by sorcery. Conversely, only a person with power could ameliorate or cure a patient who had been *dusted* (*łil* - "sprayed") with a special powder by a sorcerer, a practice called *płaxntm*. Such cases were often difficult to treat once the Indian patient had been hospitalized and attended by a physician who had invariably administered syncretic medicines, and for reasons already cited. In fact, it was firmly believed that a person seeking medical treatment in an urban hospital was more likely to die (Ross 1980b, 1981d, 1983b). One case cites such logistical difficulties, when the curing shaman was unprepared:

Once [in 1967] I was called to the hospital to see a [Spokan] Indian person who was in ICU. All the doctors and nurses said his gut was blocked because he'd really bad cramps. The man asked if I'd work on him in the traditional way 'cause the hospital was not much helping him. I'd come from a friend's house, and left all my medicines there, so I'd no medicine "pipe" [sucking tube]. What could I do. I said I'd help. He had a private room, so I closed all the curtains, making the room pretty dark. The only thing I could do, after singing my song, was to suck on his belly, and after a while out came a large, soft bloody mass I flushed in the toilet. The next day he was better, and they sent him home (Ross 1968-2008).

Curing shamans were not always told in their dreams what exactly the nature of the sorcerer-inserted object was, though they often knew the identity of the sorcerer. Prior to sucking, the practitioner slowly manipulated by massaging with his hands the inserted object to a site conducive to its removal. If the patient's face was the area of intrusion, then the sucking shaman would *place his mouth over the illness near the patient's face* (*łq'ilšmis*), or, after manipulation, would suck near the neck to remove the cause of affliction. However, in most cases an object or spirit would be withdrawn from the major joints of the extremities, the ends of the toes or fingers, the neck, even the top of the head. A curing shaman, after locating the intruded object or malignancy, may elect to remove the intrusion by sucking on an opposite area of the patient's body, particularly if he had first experienced difficulty in relocating the object to a more desirable site of extraction.

When not using a bone sucking tube, a shaman first placed both his slightly cupped hands over the site of extraction, and then proceeded to suck with his lips directly on the site or on top of his cupped or interlocked fingers. The actual sucking procedure may last only a few minutes and, depending on the nature of the inserted malignancy, the procedure was repeated several times. It was reported how sometimes the patient would suddenly sit upright, scream, and regurgitate while the curing shaman was sucking, and then the patient's vomit would reveal the sorcery-intruded object, a demonstrable proof of ordeal, and proof of curing (Eli 1974).

As was personally observed on numerous occasions, when shamans were conducting a curing ritual in a hospital, and if there was no oxygen apparatus present, the traditional practitioner would, after making a diagnosis, exercise extreme caution by first covering all electrical apparatus before smoking the room with smoldering sweet grass. Such a bundle was also waved directly over the patient before he touched the patient to rid the area of any malevolent force(s), all the while singing one of his *suméš* songs. Only then would he commence to tend the patient by either sucking or laying his hands while the room was in partial darkness.

587

A further and unsettling conflict for the patient was the often different diagnoses given by the shaman and the physicians, particularly since the latter often has no knowledge or concern for alternative explanations of illness, ones that could not be scientifically demonstrated and even showed disdain for the patient's traditional beliefs. Another problem was treating a hospitalized Indian. A sucking shaman had when treating an Indian patient who had undoubtedly received synthetic medicines, the fear—even *a fortiori*—that he might ingest administered synthetic medicaments which were likely to destroy his curing powers. The concern grew if an Indian patient had an intravenous solution or had been administered any patent medicines. Another fear for both the patient and the shaman was the unfamiliar sight and sounds of mechanical and electrical medical equipment and monitoring screens. Only a traditional elder could have understood and appreciated the tenuous and threatening atmosphere created by other patients and medical personnel.

Adhering, again, to the principles of the Doctrine of Signatures, a curer might rub the patient's face with red hematite dust to encourage him and better enable him to face the sucking of the blood and object from the site of intrusion. It is noteworthy that during the Mid-winter Ceremony, a Stellar's Blue Jay, "who specialized in sucking illness from patients [would] paint their faces red" (Turney-High 1937:29). It is known that Spokan curing shamans often painted their faces prior to treating a patient by sucking. Once this was accomplished, the patient's health and condition would be completely *restored* (*xstwil'šil* or *xstw'il'š* - "regain one's health"), or at least the patient was ambulatory by the next morning.

Until a person was completely cured, regardless of his malady, he could not eat huckleberries as that would surely kill the patient. Until recently, one never brought huckleberries to a person who was hospitalized, for it was believed that such a food would kill him since it was too sweet; whereas the patient was encouraged to eat bitter red willow berries, thought to assist in the curing when sucking was the main procedure. The patient made every attempt to comply with the practitioner's strict instructions, particularly regarding the patient's recuperating diet. Once the patient recovered, he often gave his gloves, moccasins, camas bulbs, and a robe as a *gift* (*nč'oʔc'ʔencútn*) to the curing practitioner, but never gave money.

A brief account has been available about a personally observed incident involving a 94-year-old Spokan man, who many years ago was in a post-operative ward with several non-Indian men. The main concerns of the old man were if any of his organs had been removed during surgery, if he had received a blood transfusion during surgery, and what type of person—man or woman, good or bad—had he received blood from. A great fear, as he explained early one morning, was how the man next to him had died during the night, and the elder Spokan stayed awake all night in fear that the soul of the deceased would entice his soul to accompany the deceased man's soul to some unknown place. The elder explained how the now wandering soul could make him ill; therefore weakening his resolve to live, leaving him dead so his soul would leave him—to go away with the dead person's soul.

An elderly Spokan woman related an account her grandmother gave many years ago of an elderly curing shaman, who had smallpox scars all over his face and neck, who:

[...] worked on my young brother [in 1912] who'd really bad pain arthritis [perhaps rheumatism], in both his knees and ankles, which swelled twice as much again. The [curing shaman] came to our house and stayed two days while he treated my brother, who now had awful pain. After supper, it was dark when the [curing shaman] rubbed my brother's legs—all over, pushing and rubbing from the top to his ankles. I can't recall if he used a medicine, maybe, but it was mostly dark [in the house]. After midnight the doctor sucked two times on the inside of each ankle and each knee, and the blood he'd sucked out, he'd spit right on the [board] floor. But we couldn't see any holes in my brother's knees or ankles, and yet he filled his mouth with blood each time he sucked. The next day [the curing shaman] left and said to my father and mother that my brother would get up and walk. And he did, and never had any scars (Ross 1968-2008).

An example of *bad medicine* (*q'ʷuʔq'ʷuʔɬ*) used by a sorcerer was his taking a *power feather* (*kʷlkʷléčeʔ*) from a Pleated woodpecker (*Melanerpes erythrocephalus* - *kʷlkʷléčeʔ*), a Downy Woodpecker, or a *Hairy Woodpecker* (*Picoides villosus* - *spwal'qn*), and inserting the feather in his victim. This was a common procedure for killing a person. To locate an inserted feather, or have one dropped by such a bird on a person, the sorcerer would sing for a *woodpecker's feather* (*nʔixʷuʔmʼ*), a ritual known as *kʼʷsntes*. A feather from any species of woodpecker was sometimes used by a sorcerer as a warning to an intended victim, usually left in an obvious place near the dwelling of the intended victim. Once a curing shaman located and removed the feather, and conducted the proper ritual to neutralize the spell, the patient's health would be restored. After a curing shaman *saved a patient from death* (*nʔixʷuʔsis* - "he rescued them") through ritual, the patient often immediately regained his previous healthy state.

In some curing sessions, the practitioner's *suméš* entered the patient's body and would attempt to overpower the sorcerer's *suméš* that had control of the patient's *suméš*, which was impossible if the malevolent force was too powerful. When this happened, another curing shaman was called to remove the inserted item or malevolent force that was sometimes sent back to the sorcerer, who would not be harmed if he saw it being returned, or would die if he failed to make this observation.

A patient could die if the shaman failed in his efforts, which were always acknowledged as exhausting ordeals. There was no assurance the curing shaman would be successful. When a patient *dies by sorcery* (*čsʔululqnʼcut*), it was always indicated by the *patient's eyes* (*čkʷƛkʷƛʼustnʼ*) quickly rolling back (STHC). A major concern of those attending the curing ceremony, including the curing shaman, was the fear that the malevolent spirit might get loose and avenge itself upon one or more of those present.

It must be reiterated that the curing shaman might actually be the sorcerer who was responsible for the death of his patient, which may become apparent during the treatment or when the sorcerer had withdrawn the patient's *suméš*—a person now to be feared. Another paramount concern of a sorcerer who posed as a curing practitioner was the fear that the malevolent spirit might get loose during the curing ritual, and it could avenge itself against the sorcerer, because the patient's power might be greater than the sorcerer's *suméš*.

The author personally observed a curing ceremony involving a 14-year-old girl with extensive suppurating dermal eruptions on her forearm, ones that apparently had been neglected and concealed from her grandmother for nearly a week with a bandana she had used to wrap the wound. Once they were discovered, a shaman was called to treat the girl's wounds, which required the practitioner to *lick with the tongue* (*tʼmʼam*) the infected area and suck away the accumulated *suppuration* (*mcʼołt* - "pus"), which he then *spat* (*ptax̣ʷm*) into a small container he had brought. After carefully cleaning the wound, the shaman covered it with an unidentified tallow-base brown medicine before wrapping mullein leaves over the entire area; held in place by some unidentified soaked leaves (the room was essentially dark during the entire procedure). The rest of the procedure was later explained three nights later, when the curing shaman sent one of his cohorts, Coyote, only to find the family had pulled all the shades and locked the doors. Coyote therefore entered surreptitiously, only to find the girl's still suppurating arm completely enclosed with plastic wrap. The next day the shaman arrived and said that his *helper* (*čštʼncútn*), Coyote had come to a locked house when everyone was asleep, but still he (the shaman) was able to gain entry. But because the shaman feared losing his curing power, he did not remove the plastic. Later, when the shaman returned, he told the grandmother to remove the plastic wrap so he could repeat his treatment. She did, so then the shaman again licked the wounds before wrapping the girl's arm with fresh mullein leaves, and instructed the grandmother to replace them twice a day. Within a week, the girl's arm was cured with only a slight reddening of the area, which eventually disappeared.

A similar instance occurred many years earlier when an elderly woman's great granddaughter, who had multiple open sores on both of her forearms, attempted to treat her chronic skin inflammation with a salve given by the Indian Health Service (Abrahamson 1989), which proved ineffective. In frustration, the old woman took the girl to a shaman she knew on the nearby Colville Indian Reservation. In her account she describes how the sucking shaman "first put on what I think was dry clay, what we call *sčʼiłt*, mixed with ground redstone [hematite], but nothing happened. After two days of this, he finally cured her by licking the wounds, and in two days she was well, and never had [any] scars."

It was not unusual for an older boy, who thought that he might later receive the power of curing, to commence his training by treating injured domesticated animals and certain small wild animals, creatures who would talk to him. The boy might have a dream that he would, as an adult, have an opportunity to practice his skills on a person. He might passively attend a curing ritual, if invited by a practicing medicine man. The young person was warned, however, that once he received his *sumés̆* he should never be arrogant or speak of his accomplishments, for his power would leave him, or worse, could kill him.

A shaman never startled a patient while administering treatment; rather he would often kneel on one side or the other of the patient throughout the entire healing process. This was true for any type of healing procedure, laying on of hands, acupressure, sucking, or blowing in which case the patient would be lying on the ground.

Blowing

A now seldom-used practice of healing was for a shaman to *blow* (*pux^wm*) over a patient who had assumed a *pronograde position on his back* (*ccql'ˀecutiy'eˀ*) or *lying on his stomach* (*ttɬis̆útiy'eˀ*), usually in the patient's dwelling. According to Smith (1936-8:1304), the ceremony of curing by *blowing* (*spúx^wi* or *ˀec pux^wm* - "he blows away the evil spirit"), usually with his *breath* (*scpewls̆* or *stspaúle*) over the patient, was called *skaip*. When blowing, usually the shaman assumed a kneeling position on either side of the patient, but never straddled over the person.

As with most curing rituals, the shaman, only if he had tobacco power, commenced his blowing ritual by first smoking a small stone pipe, sometimes hyperventilating, which was believed to enhance his abilities to enlist the curing powers of his *sumés̆*, and also helping the practitioner to concentrate on locating the cause of illness. Prior to curing, the shaman always sang one of his curing songs—ones without words—but never told the patient the particular curing power he was going to use, if he possessed more than one power. Sometimes, throughout the entire curing ritual, the attendants—if any—would sing their songs. A curing shaman usually informed the patient of his dream just prior to attending the patient; this was important for the malady to be validated, and for the patient to accept the judgment and the given procedure of the practitioner. Presumably, the patient was always fastidious in adhering to the conditions of the attending shaman's dream.

A curing shaman may interrupt his treatment and cease singing in between so that he could provide the patient an explanation of how and why he was sick, and all the while the assembled attendants continued to sing. This knowledge of blowing had been given to the shaman in a dream by his tutelary spirit, often a bird. However, if the shaman had not dreamed of the person's condition, but was asked to come and administer treatment, it was incumbent for him to make a diagnosis, but it was not always possible. If after examining the patient, he was not able to make a diagnosis, the shaman would simply leave.

Tobacco smoke was believed to help purify the site of curing as well as the patient and any attending people. Prior to blowing smoke over the patient, the curing shaman would manipulate and prod the patient's body, which might reveal a suspicious mass causing the malady. Following this examination, the shaman attempted to 'see' the illness by blowing over the patient's entire body, first by blowing over the legs from the feet to the chest, and then doing the same ritual with both arms to concentrate on the cause. All the while, the curing shaman held his mouth approximately 15 cm over the patient when blowing—sometimes blowing tobacco or sweet grass smoke over the patient as he worked. Once the practitioner found the area or site of illness, he would not touch the patient again, but would *blow with his mouth* (*pux^wm*), forcing the illness to leave. After the shaman had successfully removed the cause of illness by blowing, and the patient no longer experienced a sense of heaviness caused by the affliction, he knew he had been cured. When curing by blowing, the only time a shaman actually placed his mouth on the patient was if the patient had been severely cut, stabbed, or shot.

A concern of being treated by a practitioner who administered his cure by blowing over the patient was whether the practitioner was a sorcerer using a curing procedure that could intentionally kill the patient by taking his life breath away from him. Some have said that a sorcerer could only capture a patient's breath, causing a coma, but not kill the patient.

After observing a Flathead curing ceremony by a traditional practitioner, DeSmet used the pejorative term "conjurer" when describing the end of certain procedures and the singing of the attending group:

At the end of each stanza the doctor joins his hands, applies them to the patient's lip, and blows with all his strength. This operation is repeated till at last the doctor takes from the patient's mouth, either a little white stone, or the claw of some bird or animal, which he exhibits to the bystanders, protesting that he has removed the cause of the disease, and that the patient will soon recover (1843:151-2).

Blowing was also used in cases caused by object or spirit intrusion, and upon removing the intruded object or spirit, it would often hover just over the site of removal, giving off a low light. The practitioner would deftly catch the object or spirit in his cupped hands, and *blow* (*sxʷhúp'm*) forcefully but carefully on his closed hands before further neutralizing the subject of evil by placing it in water or carefully throwing it into a fire; simply blowing the evil force away did not kill the guilty sorcerer. All the while, another shaman might sit at the head of the patient, holding a section of fur or an entire hide from his familial guardian spirit upon which the neutralized *evil spirit (n'e m čxʷt'pmitts*—"an animal or projected evil power"—will jump and it would be carefully brushed onto it by the practitioner. After folding the fur several times, a trusted person would take the bundle to a stream, where it was immersed for a time considered sufficient to rid the force of the spirit. Doing this could also identify the sorcerer, who would possibly drown during this procedure. Some informants claimed that ridding the evil object or spirit in fire did not necessarily kill the perpetrator. If the sorcerer was not killed, then at least his power would leave him. Similarly, if a curing shaman attempted to exceed his abilities or was arrogant his guardian spirit would leave him.

Furthermore, the malevolent spirit was capable of making a person quite ill by speaking to his intended victim while he slept, causing him to slowly waste away. The attending shamans, one by one, would take turns dancing on a large *hewn log (šlq'ʷalqʷ*), while one shaman sang *his medicine song (čn'ekʷn')*. A group of shamans was called a *λ'eʔλ'eʔkʷílš* or a *uł λeʔkʷílš*. Curtis (1911) was fortunate to have recorded the Spokan version of the rite of curing by blowing, which was presumed to have diffused from the Northwest Coast people:

A woman who is still living fell sick in the winter. She was very ill until spring, and then her body began to waste away. She was very thin, but she could still walk. A medicine-man, HolaIakn [*xʷláyaʔqn*], and a Spokan medicine-man named *Schicheltsaln*, came to cure her. One of them blew his breath over her, from the feet to the head; then the other did the same, and when they had finished, she was dead [in a faint]. In a little while the medicine-man returned and made her alive again. When she was better, she sang a song, which said: "I was going to die, by the name of Skaip [*sq'áyp* - her *sumés*]; but now Skaip is going to leave me, and Skaip wants to take the black horse. If we give him the black race-horse, we will receive a little bay horse in two days, and in two days more I will receive a little bay mare, each with a name." Her husband owned a very fast race-horse. "It is well; we will give away that horse." They began to dance in their lodge, and continued throughout the day and night, and in the morning they gave away the horse and everything else they had, until nothing was left in their lodge.

About two days after this woman was well, and they moved to the Kalispel river [Clark Fork], where the other Indians were camped, gambling. Her husband began to play, and won a couple of blankets. A man came to him and said: "Give me one of those blankets, and I will give you a pony. Yonder it is, a little bay horse. His name is Billy." So they traded, and the man swam the pony across the river and asked his wife if he had got the right bay horse, the one of which *škaip* had told her, and she answered: "That is the one. I will receive my little bay horse in two days more." Two days later some Spokan were there, and one of the men, *šhkaiúshi*, was preparing to return to his tribe. Said he to the woman's husband: "I am getting ready to go home, but I have no blanket. If you have one, give it to me, and I will give you this pony." "Go and ask my wife," said the man. The

Spokan tied his pony outside the lodge, went in, and said: "If you have a blanket, give it to me and I will give you a pony, a little bay mare by the name of Lower Front." So the exchange was made (Curtis 1907-30, 7:89-90).

Some blowing and sucking shamans occasionally interrupted their curing ritual by dipping their fingers in water (Smith 1936-8:1234) and then alternately sucking on them between sessions of blowing over the patient, after which they shook the water off on the ground away from the patient. One elder thought that dipping his fingers was done to "cool" or neutralize his breath to better counteract the area of affliction. Another method used just before commencing to treat a patient was for the blowing shaman to fill his mouth with water, and then expel the water in a fine mist-like spray over the entire length of the unclothed patient to purify the area as well as help him to concentrate his powers for the task at hand. Apparently, cooling a patient in such a manner could indicate the remaining severity of his affliction, which often gave off discernable heat. Spraying water also protected the curing shaman if it had been determined the patient had been sorcerized. It has been observed that the practitioner will have a staff of wood with deer claws affixed to the upper end, which rattle as the curer strikes the ground while spraying his patient.

A very dramatic curing ceremony was observed by the author many years ago in a large Spokane hospital, when a curing shaman, prior to treating an elderly unconscious Spokan man, purified the room with sweet grass (he opened the old style window so as not to alert the staff or set off a fire alarm). Having "smudged" the room and the patient, the shaman circled the bed three times while he pounded the end of a *staff* (*nšt'ew'stn*) decorated with eagle feathers, fur, and a badger mandible, all the while chanting his *medicine song* (*snλ'e?kʷlščútn*). The latter two were of his family, particularly the badger. The effect of his performance was even more dramatic when viewing the various stations of complex medical equipment and monitors that were slowly becoming more obvious as the sweet grass smoke slowly drifted out the window.

Acupressure

A practitioner, who cured essentially by manipulation, *massage* (*yilkʷ*), or acupressure, would frequently sing one of his songs during the entire curing ritual. This practice was known to gain the assistance of his *suméš,* relax the patient, and create a certain atmosphere conducive to the treatment. At some point in his singing, the practitioner's spirit would reveal to him the cause and cure for the malady, an occasion for him to stop singing and announce to those present his diagnosis and success. However, any curing ceremony could take two or three nights to make a diagnosis, but most sessions lasted for several hours. Once the practitioner located the area of the object or spirit intrusion, he slowly massaged the limbs of the patient, commencing with the legs and then working the arms directing the acupressure toward the person's *thoracic area* (*sčč'maxʷcč*), thereby to concentrate and localize the malady if the patient had complained of chest pain. Some would manipulate the malady to the top of the patient's head. The shaman would use a particular curing technique that favored manipulation and massage so that the intruded-object or malevolent force could be removed from either the top of the head or from one of the feet. Supposedly malignant masses, such as neoplasms, were usually withdrawn from where they were first located by systematic *probing* (*welukʷs*), and seldom moved to another site for fear of dispersing the agent of cause. Removing a large malignancy required considerable power and physical effort by the curing shaman, who might become fatigued with a difficult case; moreover, there was always the risk that his helping power would leave him.

With the knowledge of medicine and anatomy, there was, to some degree—given the location of the heart and spleen—an established physiological dichotomy: the *left side* (*čc'iqʷe?*) in mammals and humans was more important in certain aspects of curing. For example, it was said that curing shamans always did their acupressure/massage or laying of hands on the left side of the body, even when the objector spirit was eventually removed from the patient's right side. It was significant that only Blue Jay shamans were not restricted from working both sides of a patient when curing during the Mid-Winter ceremonies.

592

Massage and manipulation were often facilitated by using tallow or grease, in addition to certain roots, that were pounded and rubbed on the afflicted area. Sunflower roots was a common choice. The young green stalks of mountain alder were mashed and rubbed into sore muscles. Shamans might vary the procedure by removing the object or spirit from the feet or even the head, depending upon which would be the easiest and safest part of the body. A physical sign of success was if the patient experienced a *bitter, burning sensation* (*q'ʷxqax*), particularly *in his chest* (*č'ɬʕʷaʔxelsi*) or over the heart (*sčč'maxʷcč*). A patient always knew when he was cured, and the practitioner rarely told the patient explicitly that he had been cured.

Sometimes certain maladies caused by object or spirit intrusion that could have been treated by suction were not, for fear of contamination. For instance, sorcery-induced maggot-like worms were instead manipulated to a central location and then removed by the practitioner *squeezing (p'ʔl)* with his hands on the site. Prior to this ritual, the curing shaman would cover his hands with red ochre, and then pass them back and forth three times over smoldering sweet grass.

Laying of Hands

Even with the known benefits of acupressure, it was universally understood that certain shamans could cure some maladies simply by touching or passing his hands over the patient, sometimes in a manner that was dictated by his diagnosis. Persons who were not shamans knew from experience that touching, feeling, stroking or holding could relieve another's tension or anxiety. For example, physical contact between familial members was sometimes purposely reinforced by humor, singing, and skits that distracted and redirected another's concern. It was said that long ago there was always time to *listen (sunúmt)* to what one was saying by a person who needed to tell another, even a stranger—that one can only tell something if another will listen, now called the Stranger Role. The often heard expression was, "You white people look, but you can't see, and you listen, but you can't hear, you touch but don't feel." Some have said that "Indian doctors are blessed with magnetic powers in their hands" (Randolph 1957:144).

Regardless of a practitioner's technique of curing, and after purifying the site with one of several types of sacred plant smokes, the important ritual of establishing physical contact commenced when the curing shaman first placed the palm of his *right hand (chečt)* on the patient's forehead. Some explained how the curer would then remove and place his hand, almost touching the person's forehead, and then gradually lessen and increase only slightly the space, thereby giving the patient a definite sensation of fluctuating pressure as the practitioner altered the distance.

The practice of a curing medicine man or practitioner laying both hands over a patient was more frequently utilized than sucking, depending upon the diagnosed malady. The procedure always commenced with the practitioner passing his hands over the entire surface of the patient's body, all the while singing one of his power songs; sometimes he was accompanied by the attending family and friends. The main objective of the curing ritual was to find the location of the injury or intrusion, by sensing an area of the body that was unusually warm. Prior to passing his hands over an unconscious patient, the practitioner would often try *gently shaking, barely touching the unconscious patient with his medicine rattle (heʔs čc'osqnm)* (STHC); this technique usually revived the patient so that treatment could commence.

Prior to a practitioner treating a patient by the laying of hands, the curing shaman almost always smoked his hands by passing them slowly over a low fire of one or more different powdered dried grasses or special roots, such as *xásxs* that had been placed on coals situated near the patient's head. The act of sprinkling shredded subalpine fir needles on hot stones was a preferred procedure used by some shamans who repeatedly purified their hands by passing them through the smoke. During any of these smoking rituals, the patient was always lying nearby on a tule mat or a robe in his dwelling or in a longhouse, but never in the shaman's dwelling. There were various reasons for a shaman smoking his hands: one was to protect himself from the effects of any malevolent force or article while curing the patient, or he may have been instructed to do so by his guardian spirit, a procedure which in no way neutralized or lessened the efficacy of the sorcery-induced malignancy. Another reason for smoking one's hands was sensory—psychological—whereby the patient and laity became more and intense with the shaman's machinations.

Prior to healing some curing shamans dipped both hands in a thick mixture of moist hematite and clay, which would dry quickly when the moist hands were passed over the warm site of injury or intrusion; even the patient's face may also be painted with red ochre mixed with tallow. It was believed that yellow ochre and various colors of clay were never used in this manner, though some said a woman's forehead was first decorated with a yellow band before being treated, but it could not be remembered for what type of illness it was used. As a practitioner sang an appropriate song—one of his power songs—he passed his hands over the patient, and he was careful not to touch the patient's body, even after the patient became well. The only thing that the practitioner ever touched was the actual intruded object or malevolent spirit—offending sorcerer's *suméš*—as it was removed from the patient. Another method of purification was to 'smoke' one's hands in smoldering *sweet* (*t'íš*) smelling grass that was used to kill the Blue Jay (Smith 1936-8:1274). From time to time during the curing ritual, the practitioner would raise his hands, passing them three times through a low fire of wet smoldering fir boughs to purify them from any malevolent force he may have contracted during the curing ritual.

One elderly Spokan man related a curing ceremony his father had narrated to him, which his grandfather had attended, a curing ceremony that took place just prior to 1881. Both the grandfather and his brother had the same power to cure by the laying of hands. The patient had been sorcerized in such a manner that he was experiencing continual, excruciating, almost debilitating headaches. The grandfather, attended by his brother, passed his hands over the patient's head, and eventually extracted a walnut-size tumor from the area of the man's fontanel. He described it as a bright, shimmering object with hues of green, red, and yellow, making what he described as a whirring sound. Only after the practitioner had placed both of his hands in a copper *bucket of water* (*yámxʷa*) did the mass become still. The grandfather explained how the removed malignant force was from a powerful shaman, and would be greatly reduced in size by momentarily boiling it in water until it was neutralized, something he had never seen before. Once the intruded object or malevolent spirit had been removed, and was being held inside the curing shaman's tightly cupped hands, he would blow on his hands to negate the illness's power, unless the curing shaman took it as one of his guardian spirits. After blowing on his hands, the shaman might decide to roll the sickness in his hand into what may be described as a white tube approximately 3 to 4 cm long, which was then dramatically shown to the patient and the participants, as a proof of ordeal. This now inert mass was either burned or submerged in water to negate any further problems. Some practitioners were known to keep the removed mass in their medicine bag along with sacred paraphernalia. It was not unusual for a practitioner to simply blow the now-desiccated object away.

The following is an explanation of what a patient felt and experienced when he was successfully treated many years ago by a curing shaman:

> My sickness was near my stomach; a small hard-like ball just under the lower edge of my right rib, but not on the rib 'cause I could move the thing from side to side with my hand. My father had one on his back, but never did anything 'cause it didn't bother him. Mine only hurt real bad when I'd lay down or slept on my stomach, and I didn't want to go to the hospital 'cause I knew they'd cut me open, and I knew I'd die. We were home, and it was all dark—only a candle by my bed—and the [Indian] doctor cured me when he kept passing his hands back and forth over my lower chest. He never touched me, but I'd always felt a strong pressure, like warm air was pushing against my body. He did this for about a[n] hour before he removed with both hands, and he held a sorta yellow-white gristle-like thing he showed us before putting it in water. I'm still here and never [have] any more pain (Ross 1968-2008).

Hydrotherapy

594

The widely accepted belief was that water was the source and maintaining force of all life, and that water played a major role in curing many illnesses. Consequently, hydrotherapy in the form of *hot rock bathing* (*četmeλâ*) was commonly used for the treatment of upper respiratory maladies, sprains, arthritis, rheumatism, general muscle and joint aches and pains, and for restoring a general sense of *physical well-being* (*xssšítm*). For example, in the warm months, several men would first partially divert a stream by reconstructing a narrow *canal* (*st'l'étkʷ*) or channel to a previously excavated hole approximately one meter in diameter and a meter and a half deep. After the excavation was filled with water, one or two of the men would quickly place ten to twelve pre-heated vesicular basalt stones into the *heated pool* (*čtmλâ*). Once the water was sufficiently heated, the stones were always removed by hand, never with a forked or looped stick. Such a major pool was located below the rock walls at an area called the *Devil's Gap* (*četk'ʷlus*) just off the south-east edge of the reservation. This area was known to be inhabited by numerous types of evil spirits and theriomorphic creatures; hence the geonomic designation. Unfortunately, the exact location of several hot water springs was not provided by Cox who claimed that these, "highly sulfphric [sic]" (1832:189) were hot enough to boil a suspended container of water. Though in a different, but unknown location, Parker described how:

> The warm bath is used both by sick and healthy persons [...] They construct a steam bath in the form of an oblong oven, two or three feet high, about six feet long, made of willows, each end inserted into the ground, forming an arch, which is covered with grass and mud, or more generally with skins. In this they place a number of hot stones, upon which they pour water. The person who is to go through the process enters and is enclosed nearly air tight, and remains until a very profuse perspiration is produced, and often nearly suffocated. He then comes out and plunges at once into cold water [...] whether summer or winter (1840:237).

Within the present Spokan reservation, there were also once traditional hydrotherapy healing sites, such as mud holes and spring-fed excavated pools. The relatively simple but effective medicinal *mud bath* (*če?tmlalxʷ* or *čatml'al'xʷ*) was made by placing hot stones in a large pitch-sealed framed bark container (later metal) of *wet mud* (*sλ'oc'olexʷ*). After the stones were removed, the hot mud was used as a common treatment for numerous types of *foot problems* (*sc'rc''eršin*), but was never used when a foot was *swollen* (*pexw* or *sukʷú*). In a case of swollen feet from an *insect bite* (*k'ʷe?é*), an *infected sliver* (*č'tšm'pqín'čst*), or a painful stone bruise, the feet were immersed in a solution of air-temperature muddy water. Depending upon the individual and the logistical proximity of a specific site, the type of malady, and the prescribed course of treatment, a patient would seek out the most favorable of sites. If possible, a patient might choose to use several *sulfur springs* (*sn?aq'ete?kʷ*) once located in the aforementioned *Devil's Gap area* (*sna?q'ʷete?kʷ*)—ones known for their ability to heal a large number of dermal and osteological maladies, which one elderly lady recalled her grandmother treating as if that was probably rheumatism.

A common form of hydrotherapy was to wrap the patient in a robe, or later with a trade blanket, and submerge him into a rock-heated pool or depression of water where he remained until the water commenced to cool. The person was removed, and the procedure was repeated after a second super-heating of the water by the immersion of hot rocks, which were partially covered with a willow mat so as to protect the patient's feet from burns. This form of hydropathy was good for numerous skeletal and muscular complaints.

Ross, who spent time with the Okanogan and Spokan, provided a rather complete description of an Okanogan hydropathy or sweathouse, and the extensive logistics and labor involved in a treatment, which varied only in location from what was practiced among the Spokan:

> To construct one of these baths a good convenient place for wood and water. The hole is then covered over with a thick coat of earth, as close as possible, leaving only a small aperture or opening on one side, barely sufficient to admit a single person to creep in on all fours. This done, a pile of wood, is with a considerable number of stones laid thereon, is set on fire in the centre, and when the wood is consumed, and the stones red hot, water is thrown over them, causing dense vapor and intense heat; yet in the midst of this suffocating cloud, where one would suppose a salamander itself could hardly live, the Indians enter stark naked, and no sooner in than the aperture or hole is closed upon them. Here they keep singing and recounting their war adventures, and invoking the good spirits to aid them again, rolling and groaning all the time in this infernal cell for nearly an hour; then all

at once they bound out one by one, like so many subterranean spectors issuing from the infernal regions. Besmeared with mud, and pouring down with sweat, they dash into cold water, and there plunge and swim about for at least a quarter of an hour, when they return again to their cell, groping through this fiery trial twice – morning and evening – on all great occasions. On all occasions of peace and war; of success in their enterprises, and good luck in hunting, the bath is resorted to. In short, great virtues are supposed to arise from the regular observance of their general custom of purification (1904, 7:293-4).

During the winter, men and women *always* bathed separately in different areas of a stream: sites made accessible through a round one-meter hole that had been broken in the ice—a preparatory procedure believed to stimulate a person's body and circulation. This was done daily, seldom alone, and at no specific time. Once the opening was large enough to accommodate an individual, he would submerge enough to have the water *over the entire body* (*čmlk'ʷem'ic'eʔ*), after which—if available—he would immerse into a hot stone-heated water pool. In early morning, a man often assisted in preparing his ailing wife's hot bath by first heating the necessary vesicular stones, grinding and boiling a sufficient quantity of introduced *wild horse radish rhizome* (*Armoracia rusticana* [Lam.] Gaertn., B. Mey. & Scherb - *č'éič'i*), putting it into the bath, which after sinking to the pool's bottom a layer of oil will rise and cover the surface to indicate the pool was ready for bathing. Several elderly women claimed only the vegetation was used and that the mashed root was too irritating for some elderly people. Whenever an oily plant was used for this purpose, it was always the responsibility of an attendant to later boil the rocks separately, in order to cleanse them of any residual oil.

As mentioned, men and women never bathed together when naked, whereas one or more women, sometimes daily, enjoyed their open private wintering bathing areas. These were also made by breaking a hole in a frozen stream or river. When a woman's bathing site was in use, boys and men were forbidden to visit or observe it—even at a distance, which was believed to make a boy or man lose their visual acuity or even make them blind. Until recently, many of the elderly men attributed their longevity, near-complete recall, and their acute vision to a lifetime of bathing daily in cold water, and having never looked at naked women.

Elmendorf described a series of bathing pools used by women for bathing, relaxing, and—if needed, hydrotherapy. This type of several channel-connected pools was:

> [...] made in [the] women's quarter – [with] curtains set up between [the] main river & these pools – made of reed matting – close to [the] river – [and] dug oblong holes & lined them with rocks – fire lighted and [the] rocks heated – poles [were] oblong about 6' long lined with good sized rocks – 3 of them – ditches dug from them to the river – cold water [was] let in from river by opening ditches – 3 pools full – hot rocks and ashes for soap [were] put in first pool – [a hot] rock or two in second pool & 3rd was [a] cold dip – if they had a dress or anything they wanted to wash they carried it along with them from pool to pool – after bathing in first pool or bathed in second – [they] dipped in [the] third as [a] rinse – [then took] little switches [*t'snsúʔtmn*] of bush or twigs and switched themselves dry by [a] fire (1935-6, 1:65).

Another method of hydrotherapy was a *foot bath* (*nq l'utetkʷm*) made by placing hot ashes and embers into any water-tight receptacle. This treatment was considered excellent for a sprained foot or a persistently aching foot. Boiled ashes also served as a foot bath poultice for lessening the swellings and pressure of large hematomas. Once a section of cloth was acquired, wood ashes were placed in boiling water to bleach cloth and to clean bandages. A third treatment for hematomas was to mash the de-spined skin of *prickly pear* (*Opuntia polyacantha* Haw. - *sxʷyén'eʔ* or *ʔepłwéyt*), which was applied to the skin or onto the *hematoma* (*ncx̣ʷum*).

Revulsive Medicines

Universally, and throughout time, all cultures seem to have recognized and utilized—internally and externally—various forms of revulsive medicine in their pharmacopoeia; however, one can only speculate as to how such selections were made. Was the decision to utilize certain plants influenced by the external physical appearance of certain plants, or, by trial and error, by the perceived internal effects? Perhaps the often external abrasive feeling or internal bitterness may suggest the principles of revulsive medicine, that is, pain or discomfort will effectively treat the patient's malady, and drive the pain or affliction away.

The introduced *fiddleneck* (*Amsinckia intermedia* - *sxʷixʷít*) has minute spines that cause immediate irritation to the skin, and was a general type of external repulsive medicament. Another was fireweed, as mentioned earlier, also effective as an external revulsive medicine for reducing dermal pain and joint pain. As with most revulsive medicinal plants, the leafy stalks were carefully swept over the injured area, thereby numbing the pain. Another procedure for treating joint pain was to slap the afflicted area with the plant's stalks. For treating any deep muscular pain, the leaves of fireweed were mashed with a stone or wooden pestle, and the juices would be caught in a stone or rawhide container, and then soaked up with a section of buckskin or moss. This was essentially a poultice when placed or tied on the area of pain. Fireweed was also effective as a revulsive medicine for reducing deep dermal pain; the leaves would be pressed onto the area by another person or held in place with a section of buckskin, and occasionally renewed if there was no skin blistering.

There were other types of revulsive medicine, such as small pieces of freshly cut *poisonous water hemlock* (*Cicuta douglasii* [DC.] Coult. & Rose - *yiníxʷ* or *hi níxʷ* - "it is poisonous") stalks that were warmed before being administered externally as poultices for rheumatism. Hemlock, the poison introduced by The Europeans, containing the alkaloids conune and coniceive, is *Conuim maculatum* (Turner, pers. com.).

The use of revulsive medicaments—based on the principle of homeopathic medicine—served one of two purposes: as an irritant taken internally to induce vomiting, or as an abrasive plant applied externally to stimulate circulation, temporally dull the pain of an injury, or treat arthritis or rheumatism. For example, sprains or severe muscle soreness required different revulsive medicaments, such as stinging nettle, wavy-leaf thistle, or an unidentified biennial lacy thistle that was carefully brushed over the area of pain. The abrasive plant would be carefully brushed lightly over the skin, thereby creating a *prickly sensation* (*tstas*) that would, after repeated passes of the plant, *numb* (*čšul*) the area. One elderly woman, who followed this treatment until her death, said how the patient would think that the wing tips of many butterflies were just touching. The phototoxic fresh leaves of cow parsnip served as an effective revulsive medicine, but were used with caution since prolonged application could cause *mild burns* (*ɬmáq*).

These common external medicines were counter-irritants, or revulsive medicines, such as stinging sagebrush nettles and buttercup, and were always self-administered or given by an older family member; seldom was a shaman required to treat arthritis or rheumatism with these medicines. Counter-irritants were common familial medicines, known and used by everyone, and not requiring a shaman's services. A popular treatment for joint pain and for muscular therapy was to take the mashed roots, leaves, and flower of sagebrush and buttercup, and place them directly on the afflicted joint. Unfortunately, if left on the skin too long, the patient will suffer painful burns, especially children and older people. One very arthritic elderly man sustained first degree thermal burns to the outer epidermis of his knees after he self-administered an oily mass of crushed buttercup plants on both knees, and unfortunately fell asleep during the treatment. Apparently, the irritants are normally neutralized by cooking (Turner, pers. comm.)

Another treatment for certain dermal afflictions was using different forms of revulsive medicine, such as the readily available leaves of stinging nettle, or the young, freshly gathered leaves of *poison ivy* (*Toxicodendron rydbergii* L., var. *rydbergii* [Small] Rybd. - *sʔulʼáqeʔ*). Caution was always exercised during the treatment by holding the stems in pieces of buckskin, and the branches were carefully swept lightly back and forth over the pained area to bring relief by barely touching the skin. When a person came into direct contact with poison ivy, the result was painful and was treated with powdered clay or fine earth, or by applying a solution of ashes in water to the rash. A compound of tallow salve or grease was administered externally to treat areas of poison ivy or, if anticipated, to prevent the skin from developing irritation.

The prickly stem and leaf hairs of *narrow-leafed Phacelia* (*Phacelia linearis* [Pursh.] Holz. - *sxʷixʷáy't* - "slivers") and *scorpion weed* (*P. hastata* Dougl. ex Lehm. var. *leucophylla* [Torr.] also called *sxʷixʷáy't*) were rubbed gently on painful arthritic joints for relief.

Inhalation and Respiratory Phytotherapy

Because illness and some diseases were related to definite concepts of the supernatural, it was not unusual for spiritual *inhalation* (*púxʷm*) to be practiced by a shaman who was a *curing specialist* (*sxʷpúxʷm*). This procedure was best performed during a sweathouse session, often before a particularly onerous or dangerous undertaking, or specifically when desiring to communicate with one's tutelary spirit. Inhalation therapy—using dried leaves of certain plants placed on hot stones—was believed to be conducive for acquiring a vision, for physical and spiritual purification, and for determining a diagnosis or prognosis of a patient. During the process, the identity of the patient's sorcerer might be revealed, as well as the curing shaman's best method of treatment.

The Spokan recognized four distinct procedures associated with inhalation therapy. One procedure was conducted daily in the sweathouse during the second session designated for cleansing, and did not always involve the use of medicinal plants being placed on the hot sweathouse stones; rather controlled deep breathing—not hyperventilating—was practiced to promote a general sense of well-being. Dried leaves of brown-eyed Susan were crushed and inhaled to treat nasal congestion.

Of the remaining three procedures, two were conducted in the sweathouse for spiritual reasons during the last or third session, and were, thus, best characterized as rituals. One of these rituals required the person to hyperventilate in the hope of helping the individual to see and communicate with his guardian spirit while under physically induced hypoxemia. This ritual was also conducted in the sweathouse, being essentially a medicinal treatment for one with a physical malady or a diagnosed psychological problem, or even a temporary *mental block* (*sl'íp*), and involved situating the heated stones just inside, at the right of the entrance, thereby permitting the patient to lie in a pronograde position in the center of the sweathouse.

After the sweathouse fell out of fashion in the early 1950s, inhalation therapy using steam was conducted within a dwelling, usually in the kitchen or bedroom by simply covering the patient's head over a steaming container, depending upon the condition and the mobility of the patient. Inhalation therapy is rarely done today.

The most efficacious medicament for upper respiratory conditions, and for certain spiritual afflictions, was wild licorice root that was scraped, cut into small pieces, and then sprinkled upon the hot stones during a curing sweat. It was also administered using steam inhalation to promote expectoration because it "moistened the inspired air and helped to relieve inflammation and spasm of the upper respiratory tract" (Anon. 1966:1686). Unfortunately, some contemporary users of wild licorice root sometimes confuse it with *western sweet cicely* (*Osmorhiza occidentalis* [Nutt.] Torr. - *xʷayt*), as found in this account: "*O. occidentalis* grows in drier areas and usually at somewhat lower elevations than *L. canbyi*, although occasionally the two plants can be found growing near each other" (Turner *et al.* 1980:71).

The fragrant leaves of wormwood, tarragon, or *dragon sagewort* (*Artemisia dracunculus* L. - *c'ic'ixéy'lp*) have a pleasant menthol-like fragrance (Turner *et al.* 1980:76), and were mashed and steeped to release the volatile oils for producing vapors to treat bronchitis. In some instances of inhalation phytotherapy, medicinal plants were placed in boiling water. This fourth procedure was commonly supplemented with either pine or fir pitch, often by first crushing the pitch and needles of subalpine fir or other types of fir tree needles. After the solution went off the boil, the patient was hooded with a tanned deer hide, and he *would kneel on his hands and knees* (*q'ʷiqʷ'i?šénm*) over the fuming container, breathing deeply for approximately ten to fifteen minutes. The procedure was repeated until temporary or permanent relief resulted.

A broad-spectrum medicine for treating flu, fever, and upper respiratory congestion was obtained by *steeping* (*łuc*) the roots of purple avens or *old man's whiskers* (*Geum trifloium* Pursh - *spíleyʔ q'itqém's*), and then drinking the solution as needed. The same infusion, incidentally, was drunk by a forlorn woman in the hope of regaining the affections of her estranged husband. Another important plant in the Spokan pharmacopoeia was fireweed used as a demulcent, emollient, anti-inflammatory, and antispasmodic agent and for certain external maladies such as an astringent and a poultice. Even the young shoots and leaves of fireweed were eaten raw or cooked and used in this way.

Medicinally, the *fir sap blisters* (*čč'aʔč'alqʷ*) of any fir tree could be used for different purposes, particularly by heating the collected *balsam blisters* (*st'iqʷlqʷ*) and then inhaling the fumes during inhalation therapy when the *patient's head* (*spłqin*) was draped to retain the fumes. Pitch from either the white pine or birch was heated directly or in solution, and thought to be effective when a person with upper respiratory problems inhaled the vapors while confined under a *hide or blanket placed over the patient's head and shoulders* (*łuxʷpqín* = head, *łuxʷpaxin* = shoulder/arm). Most elders felt that *white pine syrup* (*mrinłp*) was more potent than birch syrup, which served as a sudorific agent for inducing profuse sweating, and considered very therapeutic. Also, the fresh needles of grand fir, gathered from the higher reaches near Chewelah, were mashed and then placed on hot rocks to create a scented steam that was inhaled by a person suffering from upper respiratory afflictions. Various infusions of Canada mint were used often for inhalation phytotherapy, as the mint has a strong aromatic from the volatile oils, which also contain medicinal flavonoids and carotenes. Freshly ground leaves of all mint plants were important in many aromatherapy therapies.

There was some uncertainty as to whether the leaves from *goldenweed* (*Haplopappus carthampoides* [Hook.] Gray, var. *erythropappus* [Rydb.] - *pipeʔičey'eʔ*) were dried and burned to make a medicinal smoke, which was inhaled under an enclosed head cover to treat upper respiratory congestion. Unfortunately, often the specific preparation and curing attributes of many plants have been forgotten, and in some cases, a Spokan orthographic designation may fail to explain the medicinal uses of the particular plant, unless analyzed by a competent ethnolinguist.

There was no recall of how *Long-flowered Mertensia* (*Mertensia longiflora* Greene - *st'rt'réʔms sc'ʔékʷs*) was prepared or administered as a medicine. Yet one elderly woman said a concoction was drunk to treat tuberculosis and persistent coughing. The effects of Mertensia were known to be unpredictable, it depended on the patient's age, weight, and the quantity administered. Obviously the effects were due to the plant's varying amounts of active alkaloids. There was, however, agreement that other medicaments were also frequently administered for tuberculosis.

Not all *upper respiratory* (*hec č'úxʷmi*) maladies were treated by inhalation therapy, but more commonly treated by making warm plant infusions and drinking them as a *tea* (*lití*). The flowers, leaves and stems of blossomed Coyote mint were steeped to make a medicinal tea, or for inhalation by a patient with congestion of the head or constriction of the upper respiratory tract. *Peppergrass* (*Idahoa scapigera* [Hook.] Nels. & Macbr. - *nkʷk'ʷá*) was chewed to treat colds, and was rather popular with children who enjoyed chewing the peppery pods. The treatments for a person suffering from a chronic upper respiratory affliction, and *choking on excessive phlegm* (*nłukʷłc'ʔancót*), were essentially the same as those for tubercular or *consumptive* (*sč'xʷúm*) patients, as will be discussed. When available, a general remedy for colds and flu was to drink fresh blue elderberry juice three to four times a day until cured.

Colds were treated by scraping the inside of *aspen bark* (*mλ'mλ'ts*) into a small container of boiling water and after cooling, it was drinking it as a medicinal tea. Some preferred to simply chew bits of aspen bark, and swallow the liquid. Small pieces of bark from aspen trees were chewed, and the juice was swallowed as a medicine for colds. Another method was to chew poplar bark and *swallow* (*q'mí*) the juice.

The Spokan gathered the small, bitter, *blue juniper berry* (*psnłp*) when in high country, and the larger juniper berry at lower elevations; these were boiled separately or together, and drunk to treat colds. Both types of juniper berries were named *púnłp*, after the tree. In fall and spring, a very mild infusion of the poisonous False Hellebore root was carefully steeped to make a tea for the treatment of a severe or persistent cold. Fresh leaves and the branches of *big sagebrush* (*Artemisia tridentata* Nutt. - *k'ʷel'k'ʷmnílhp*) were drunk as a tea before the patient invariably went to the sweathouse to complete his therapy for respiratory problems. Freshly gathered leaves of *common sagewort* (*A. vulgaris* L. var. *ludoviciana* [Nutt.] Jeps. - *n'ek'ʷn'k'ʷtíłha?p*) were mashed and then placed in the nostrils to treat cold or a headache.

In the fall—and at higher elevations—when most medicinal plants were harvested, women gathered the entire low-growing bitter wintergreen, sometimes called *little prince's pine* or *little pipsissewa* (*Chimaphila umbellata* [L.] Bart. - *kew'esw'esxn'íka?*), and all of the plant, roots, stems, and leaves were an effective treatment for pulmonary emphysema, bronchitis, nonspecific pneumonia, and sore throat when the plant was boiled to make a tea, which was drunk every couple of hours, though some would *nosily inhale* or *suck* (*ło?pis*) the smoke when the dried leaves are burned, also thought to be therapeutic for upper respiratory afflictions.

Warmed and diluted tamarack sap was similarly administered as a treatment for upper respiratory afflictions, and used by adults and children for treating sore throats when diluted in hot water and drunk as needed. When administered by a bone or horn *spoon* (*łú?mn*)—never metal—the different types of *dried sap* (*pkʷkʷalqʷ*) were permitted to dissolve first, thereby making it easier to swallow. Tamarack sap was used as a *medicinal syrup* (*sncémim*) after it was evaporated and the liquid had the consistency of *molasses* (*lamnás*). The *drier form of tamarack syrup* (*čpkʷpkʷxʷkʷálqʷ* or *snc'em'c'm'*) was made from the liquid inside the usually smaller balls of pitch that were glazed and hard on the outside surface of the bark. Unfortunately, this could also stick tenaciously to a person's teeth if it remained too long in the patient's mouth. As noted previously, when a person had upper respiratory problems, then pitch from either the white pine or birch was heated and the vapors inhaled under a hide or blanket head hood.

The inhaled fumes from burnt aspen bark were used for the treatment of a specific spirit illness but the name of the illness was forgotten. *Peeled aspen bark* (*čsr'alqʷntxʷ*) was also burned to create medicinal smoke that could be inhaled to treat specific spirit illnesses, notably bad dreams of past events that had afflicted the dreamer's family or self. Sometimes aspen and cottonwood barks were boiled together to make an infusion for treating certain spirit illnesses.

Young cottonwood bark was chewed and the combined saliva and juice was used for treating colds and mild upper respiratory problems. A cough remedy was prepared by scraping the sap from a tamarack tree, aspen, or willow with a deer rib or scapula, and mixed with honey as an effective cough medicine. These trees contain salicin, which decomposes into salicylic acid. The Spokan traded with the Coeur d'Alene for sap from both the higher elevation subalpine fir and the white pine, which was mixed and boiled to make a *cough medicine* (*st'iúłí*) to treat upper respiratory congestion. Coughs were also treated with a bitter solution made from the mashed inner bark of chokecherry that was steeped and drunk. The same medicine was applied to sores (Elmendorf 1935-6, 1:43).

A broad spectrum medicine for a cold, sore throat, fever, antiheumatic, and general upper respiratory maladies was the root of *long-tailed wild ginger* (*Asarum caudatum* Lindl. - *spusl'tełp* or *xʷít*), which was scraped, cleaned, chewed, and swallowed periodically as needed. Lozenges or troches made from the dried bark of the subalpine fir tree could also be administered to treat upper respiratory ailments or influenza. Wild ginger is soothing as it contains flavonoids and 6% glycyrrhizin (treitelpene), a substance that is sweeter than sugar. A medicine for a persistent *cough* (*snłxʷum't*) was prepared by steeping dried chokecherry bark to make a tea, which has a bitter taste.

The fresh needles of sub-alpine fir were mashed, boiled, and inhaled in winter to prophylactically *keep colds away* (*čp'q'ʷusm*). Until recently, most traditional homes kept a coffee can of low water and several handfuls of fir needles at low heat on the back of a wood-burning stove. Another tree medicine for treating colds was made from the bark of *Engelmann spruce* (*Picea glauca* [Moench] Voss, ssp. *engelmannii* [Parry ex Engelm.] - *c'qc'iqnɫp*), which was collected when hunting in higher regions, usually above one and a half thousand meters. This bark was cut into small narrow strips, boiled in water until an oil-like film appeared on the surface, and then allowed to cool; it was then strained and drunk as a medicinal tea for respiratory difficulties. A universal treatment for treating nasal congestion—the same as for colds—was to take a section of Engelmann bark, shred it into small strips, pound it, and place it in a receptacle of hot water. The patient would then place a blanket or cedar bark mat over his head and inhale the confined fumes.

Upper respiratory afflictions (*šey't* - "tired" or "short of breath")—tuberculosis in particular—were commonly treated by shredding the fresh bark of chokecherry, which was boiled to make a solution, strained with woven grass filters, and drunk. The cambium deposits of sap under fir tree bark were made into a *medicinal tea* (*st'iq'ʷlqʷ*) for treating whooping cough, severe colds, and tuberculosis. Unknown to the indigenous people are the now established medical benefits of consuming cambium scrapings which contain the natural pharmacological substance pycnogenol, known to be a powerful antioxidant (Harman 1992:39). A sore chest was sometimes treated by making a mixture of *rendered tallow* (*sčt'kʷew's*) and pitch, which is then heated and rubbed onto the patient's chest to bring relief.

The Spokan used a number of different types of teas for treating upper respiratory afflictions, as well as for a *deep chest cold* (*snɫxʷumt*). One such tea was *Coyote mint* (*Monardella odoratissima* Benth. var. *odoratissima*, forma *odoratissima* - *x̣ax̣aʕáy'iɫp* or *nx̣ax̣ʕáɫníw't* or *nx̣ax̣ɫníw't*). The crushed leaves of bergamot, an aromatic herbaceous perennial, sometimes called scarlet bee-balm, *wild bergamot* or *monarda* (*Monarda fistulosa* L. or *M. didyma*), was also a strong antiseptic for treating throat infections, as well a pulmonary aid for pneumonia. Fresh crushed bergamot leaves were sometimes placed on hot sweathouse stones by a curing shaman as a purifier during the second session in the sweathouse. The vapors were inhaled by the occupants while one person at a time covered his head with a deer hide while bending over the hot stones. The dried powdered leaves were important as an insect repellent when dusted over exposed meat. A treatment for pneumonia was administering an infusion of Big Sagebrush roots.

Wild sarsaparilla (*Aralia nudicaulis* L. - *čeʔčeʔɫnéɫp*) has strongly aromatic stems and cord-like aromatic roots, which were ground and strained through a balled grass filter, then *diluted* (*nxʷiskʷ* or *čɫc'áwneʔ*) and used to treat sore throats and *laryngitis* (*hecnsékʷm*), and for *flavoring* (*ʕʷim'* or *mérwiʔ*) bitter medicines. This infusion was also considered to be effective for treating nasal, *esophagus* (*sxʷopɫq'ʷl't* or *sk'it* -"windpipe") and throat ailments. The fumes are inhaled, usually when a drape of buckskin material was placed over the head of the patient sitting on the ground with the container held under his face, or on the ground between his folded legs. Wild sarsaparilla leaves were steeped, strained, and the infusion was drunk as tea for fighting influenza and general fever. Uncooked but scraped roots of biscuitroot were chewed and the juice swallowed to treat a sore throat.

The buckbean plant (*Menyanthes trifoliata* L.) contains menyanthin (bitter glycoside) and was remembered as being an effective treatment for respiratory maladies when the leaves were mashed, placed on hot rocks in the sweathouse, or inhaled while the patient's head was under draped material.

A solution of dried, powdered yarrow root was drunk to effectively treat fever, as the volatile oil contains astringent properties—flavonoids and alkaloid achilleine—that serve multiple functions, such as an antiallergenic, diuretic, diaphoretic, antispasmodic, demulcent, anti-inflammatory, and as an astringent.

In the case of severe chest pain, difficult breathing, and expectoration of copious amounts of mucus or blood, a common treatment was to boil several nettle roots in water, and after straining through a *grass strainer* (*snč'ɫsoʔmin*) it was drunk as a decoction. Some elders were able to recall how drinking nettle leaf soup would cause a person's lips, throat, and esophagus to *burn* or *sting* (*yip'x̣x̣*).

An important, universally used broad spectrum medicinal plant was *m'sm'sáwiʔ* (*Frasera montana* Mulford), known for its tonic properties, and often called elkweed, green gentian, deer tongue, or deer's ear, and it was administered for influenza, headache, and upper respiratory difficulties. The yellow root was mashed and heated to make an infusion that the patient drank after cooling. To cure upper respiratory afflictions, *m'sm'saw'i*ʔ roots were placed on hot coals, creating a small area of concentrated fumes, and the patient knelt over the embers with a hide or blanket while inhaling deeply.

Tall willowherb (*Epilobium paniculatum* Nutt. ex T. & G., forma *paniculatum* - *čmroy'áyaʔqntn*) was steeped as a tea and drunk for curing upper respiratory congestion and inflammation. The brown and highly nutritious but foul-smelling roots of tobacco could be eaten *raw* (*xiw'*) or boiled to make a tea to relieve respiratory congestion. Red willow bark contains water soluble phenolic glycosides, flavonoids and salicylate, as do aspen and black cottonwood leaves, and one elderly woman recalled her mother saying how aspen and cottonwood leaves were steeped (separately?) and drunk as a tea to cure headache. Speaking of aspen, "Some Canadians have conceived a very superstitious idea of the tree. They say that its wood was used in constructing the Cross, and its leaves have not ceased to tremble" (DeSmet 1843:113). It is something few contemporary Spokan believe.

Colds and flu were sometimes treated by gathering and mashing the small, round, whitish leaves of *false Oregon boxwood* (*Pachystima myrsinites* [Pursh] Raf. - *skʷlkʷlséłp* or *sqʷelqʷeleséłp*), which were then steeped in boiling water and drunk as an infusion when cool. The bark from young aspen was chewed, and the pressed juice was drunk to treat colds. The medicinal plant wild licorice root, an antioxidant adaptogen, was also used as a prophylaxis or for treating certain spirit illnesses as well as numerous somatic maladies, such as laryngitis. Pieces of the root were chewed as a lozenge for sore throat. For general maintenance of health, pieces of the root were eaten raw, steeped as a tea, or sprinkled on sweathouse stones. A broth was made by boiling several fish heads of any species and was drunk to medicate a cold.

A soothing tea infusion from boiling kinnikinnick leaves was favored by some when treating colds, sore throats, and mild *fever* (*sƛ'aq'*). For example, dried, crushed leaves of rabbitbrush were added to a medicine bundle, and later used to sprinkle on sweathouse stones to treat upper respiratory problems. The mashed leaves of mugwort were heated and used as a mentholatum to clear the nostrils and sinuses. The powdered roots of False Hellebore were carefully inhaled to clear the sinuses and nasal passage and for treating severe colds.

Coma

There were numerous psychological and physiological reasons for a person to experience a *coma* (*qʷm'I*), which could first have been perceived as simply a *faint* (*ƛ'eʔl'i'* - *č'ilxʷspʔus*), in which case a crushed subalpine fir bough or crushed wild licorice root would be passed under the unconscious person's nose. However, if a person's vital signs were barely detectable, it was assumed that the person was passing away, and the services of a shaman were required to find the person's breath-soul, which may have already departed, but was still *hovering* (*hi q'eʔ*) near the patient. The attending shaman would also go into a trance, sending his tutelary spirit to locate and attempt to return the patient's life force—thereby to *bring the patient back to life* (*xʷl'xʷiłt* or *xʷlxʷilstn*). After a person was *revived* (*ʕeł xʷlíl*), or brought *back from death* (*xʷl'llxʷilt* or *nč'eʔʔspuʔús*), the individual might not have any memory of the experience. This is quite different from when a shaman went into a self-induced trance when intentionally sending his guardian spirit to seek whatever was the intent for a patient losing his *suméš*, which was thought to have caused the coma. As noted earlier, a person might go into a temporary coma when maliciously or accidentally induced by fright. However, only the former cause required the attention and skills of a curing shaman. Another reason for coma might be that a power song, once belonging to a deceased shaman, had been sung without permission from the family of the deceased by the unconscious individual. A person in a coma may not necessarily have been considered *paralyzed* (*ƛ'lléłceʔ*).

602

There is debate as to the extent of a person's awareness or the degree of being in a trance, but they are 'possessed' when they believe they are (Lewis 1971:65). Stewart explained:

> It matters little whether manifestations of possession are in reality due to physical or psychical abnormalities or whether they are artificially induced by auto-suggestion. The essential factor in possession is the belief that a person has been invaded by a supernatural being and is temporarily beyond self-control, his ego being subordinated to that of the intruder (1946:325).

Just prior to treatment, the shaman or an assistant would produce from his bag *dried roots* ($x^w a\Omega it$) of an *unidentified plant* ($k^w l k^w \acute{i} l q n$), which he scraped and mixed with the shredded dry leaves of kinnikinnick before sprinkling upon several heated coals held in a small clay pot, or upon the inside of a freshly cut section of aspen bark, that was held under the nose of the unconscious person. The same concoction was useful to treat upper respiratory maladies, or when steeped as a tea for nasal congestion. Placing the smoke of this plant under the nose of an exhausted or unconscious Blue Jay dancer during the Mid-Winter Ceremonies has found to be effective for reviving the individual (Quintasket, pers. comm.).

In addition to these methods, many curing shamans would shake a rattle or blow smoke about the head of a patient to revive one who had fainted, who was temporarily unconscious or in a coma. There were no long-term therapies or preventive measures for a person known to experience *fainting spells* ($q^w unm'q^w \acute{e}m'ulp$), despite the previously mentioned explanations for these afflictions. Immediate cure was achieved by placing or blowing either finely crushed fir needles or *x̣ásax̣* in the patient's nose. Passing smudged sweet grass under the nose of a person in a coma was sometimes thought to be beneficial.

Mental Illness

Any discussion of mental illness is fraught with the problem of separating clinical psychological problems and concomitant behavior from certain religious or supernaturally-induced conditions. There are varying degrees of behavior that are commonly termed mental illnesses, either of short duration or permanent conditions that ranged from severe grief to psychosis, and as has been recognized, "organic events play a significant role in the etiology of many mental disorders, it is possible to see the role of cultural differences as particularly relevant to etiology" (Anon. 1973:399), conditions that tend to be cultural-bound—ones known to cause certain medical syndromes or conditions, that is, a medical situation believed to have been created by either a known and recognized external natural cause—including an animal—or a perceived confrontation by a sorcerer, either of which could be diagnosed as responsible for the malady.

Until recently, it was universally understood that an individual—invariably a shaman—displaying what is presentably termed abnormal, even bizarre, behavior was not what is now clinically defined as irrational or psychotic condition, but rather proof that one was possessed and being controlled by a spirit. Even a child could be the recipient, and, therefore, the conveyer of a spirit-sent message, and in such instances the person may speak in glossolalia or assume a trance-like condition. During such a situation, the individual was always carefully protected from any harm and external interference until he was released from spiritual control. It was said that some persons were known to have a propensity for being temporarily *possessed by a spirit* (*hec q'ewm*).

A common and contemporary Spokan term for one with sustained irrational behavior was *wil* ("strange, foolish") (Carlson and Flett, 1989:166) which was not definitive as to a cause. Consequently, there exists a near-universal, cross-cultural problem of defining unusual behavior, particularly behavior observed during many intense rituals when a participant was possessed. There was consensus, however, among the elders that in the past, a *shaman's dream* (*qey's*) was more explicit about a person's mental illness.

Extreme cases of temporary or permanent psychotic conditions were invariably the result of the individual being sorcerized, and in some instances the patient could be cured. Seeing or even hearing a ghost was sufficient cause for a person to be temporarily disorganized, or even with culturally defined irrational behavior. To see a ghost was reason for a person's erratic behavior; but with proper treatment by so-called social incubation, the patient eventually regained his/her senses. (See Appendix O.) The Spokan term for what might be called social incubation could not be recalled, but it was remembered that the patient's immediate family, extended kin group, and friends would congregate and be solicitous of his condition, who would always be telling stories of their collective or individual humorous experiences with the patient, who was sometimes wrapped with a robe or blanket. Massage and *luke warm* (*nm'al'*) drinks were offered, most commonly tea made from the dried stems of wild rose plants, which upon steeping in boiling water turned into a red color, which was also administered as a tea. The same treatment of social incubation was followed when a person initially lost a loved one.

When asked about the role of ghosts and mental illness, the following explanation was given:

Us humans are really dumb creatures and animals choose who they want to give power to; gambling, curing, fishing, hunting, gathering food or whatever. But, if it [*suméš*] is misused, then the animal will punish you in one way or another, and if this don't [sic] work, your spirit will take your *suméš* away; the one he gave you before. And because your *suméš* becomes one with your guardian spirit, this means you're no longer whole.

Sometimes it [mental illness] is [caused] by a person [sorcerer] who's hurting you, and you start to do many crazy things. He'd make you do strange things so people thought you're crazy. It may be a man or woman who makes you crazy so your family would maybe ask one of them to cure you, which was easy because the evil person knows what was done; how to cure you. Some did these things so they're jealous of you or your children. Or so they could get you as a [mate], even if you're already married. This happened when they seemed to be curing you, but they're really getting more control over you.

These people [sorcerers] were so powerful they could make it so a man knew he's doing what he shouldn't; not what he wants to do. This was usually the cause of mental illness, when your inner self is fighting hard, but losing control with your mind (Ross 1968-2008).

Several elders recalled their parents explaining how another cause of psychotic behavior was when a solitary person was kidnapped at night by a theriomorphic creature [usually *sc'en'éy'yi*], but was never physically harmed, always releasing before dawn the next day. Such a victim had absolutely no memory of his ordeal—only of experiencing a horrible smell, but nothing visual or auditory. Proof of the person's ordeal was the horrific odor from the patient's clothes, which were then discarded or more often burned upon his or her safe return.

In the past, there was agreement that one reason for temporary mental illness was the eclipse of the sun. "Some people who became confused, remained so after the eclipse was over." One elder explained how:

In the time of wagons, my grandfather told of a young man, a bachelor from Inchelium, who was visiting us during a solar eclipse, when all the birds and chickens went silent. The man built a huge bonfire to light things up. After the sun came out again, he'd keep piling wood on the fire to keep it going. When people told him the fire wasn't needed, he ran away, and people had to chase and bring him back. He was always crazy after that (Ross 1968-2008).

A woman once explained how making fun of people who display neurotic behavior can bring to oneself mental illness, and anyone who made fun of a cripple, a speech impediment, or any physical disability, would soon contract that physical debility. Children were always instructed to never play-act with a person's crutches or *walking stick* (*c'k'ʷéčstn* or *sck'ʷečst*), because, in time, the so-called actor will require the same type of prosthetic. One man explained how when he was younger a grandson received as a gift a used tricycle from an off-reservation yard sale, and family elders took it away saying that in time he would require a wheel chair. Temporary and permanent soul loss were ways of explaining a person's erratic behavior, mental illness, going into a coma, or death, all believed to have been the result of sorcery. People who had been ghosted were experiencing extreme grief, or had been badly frightened, could go into a coma or experience *paralysis* (*λ'llełc'e?*). Some years ago, when visiting an elderly lady, the author entered the home through the back door as was customary for known visitors, and upon entering the living room, a five-year-old great granddaughter leaped up and shouted. The old woman, who was remembered to never say a cross word, immediately *scolded* (*xeʔneltm* - "to scold") the child, saying, "You should know that scaring a person can cause his soul to leave; he could've died or become crazy from his fright."

It was said that a person could go into a coma if his breath-soul had been taken through sorcery; but more often this happened when a man—being unaware that he has another's guardian spirit—goes into a long trance [coma], "so his family will get a doctor [curing shaman] to tell them the unknown spirit helper brought him back, saved his life so the man could always be helped by his new power."

When a person was observed *making incoherent or foolish speech* (*nqʷawcn*), a shaman was called to treat the patient, often using physical incubation by confining the patient under a warm robe or attending the individual during repeated hydrotherapy. Some claimed that an incoherent person, or one with rambling speech, could be cured by blowing the smoke of sweet grass (sometimes called smudging) through a tube into the person's face. As referred to previously, what is now clinically diagnosed as mental illness was once considered to be a cold illness, one that required warm treatment.

There was a case of an individual who was comatose because he was unable to sing a *sumés* song of a deceased man, one whose ghost was unhappy and wanted to hear it sung. Another man became comatose after he attempted to sing the power song of a deceased man, which he had no right to.

Apart from other medicinal uses, and until a few years ago, both *Fraser montana* Mulford *m'sm'sáwiʔ* and Canbyi's Loveage (*xásax*) were traditional medicines administered to treat mild cases of depression and nervous disorders. They were eaten raw by nibbling small pieces of either medicament at appropriate intervals. Some elders, knowingly or unknowingly, contended that these medicines could restore a person's general mental and even physical health if they had been weakened by a diet containing too many sweet foods. Even today, a few Spokan administer *m'sm'sáwiʔ* as a cure for these reasons, claiming that *m'sm'sáwiʔ* was a mild stimulant used for tiredness, or eaten for strength when travelling long distances.

Rev. Walker mentioned in his diary (Drury 1976:305), how an Indian or non-Indian patient, suffering from depression or a mild case of malaise, was given a cup of hot tea and repeated as needed. The tea was made by mashing and steeping a fresh root of sumac, said to produce a sense of exhilaration, which was repeated as needed.

Wolfgang Jilek, who has written extensively on ethnographic and ethnopsychiatry among various Salish Amerindian groups, uses the term anomic depression to describe the universal functions of certain shamanistic rituals that have a cathartic abreaction in an appropriate group setting. More succinctly:

> Anomic depression is a chronic dysphoric state characterized by feelings of existential frustration, discouragement, defeat, lowered self esteem and sometimes moral disorientation. This state is often the basis of the specific psychic and psychophysiological symptom-formation manifested by contemporary sufferers from spirit illness who turn to spirit dancing for genuinely therapeutic reasons (Jilek 1982:52).

Osteology

The activities required by the Spokan to maintain their existence as hunters and gatherers presented numerous situations that required an explicit knowledge of animal anatomy, which, in a real comparative sense, was invaluable in treating broken and fractured bones, and joint dislocations of humans. Even older boys and girls had an exceptional and often complete comparative knowledge of animal muscular-skeletal structure, what some today may call field or survival medicine when applied to humans.

There were specialists in setting bones or immobilizing sprained extremities, but it was also remembered that a few people, were better qualified to do reductions. It can be assumed that with the introduction of horses and cattle there was an increase in the frequency and number of broken bones and fractures of the Indians. Cox noted the frequency and cause of some fractures and pointed out that "common fractures, caused by an occasional pitch off a horse, or a fall down a declivity on the ardor of hunting, are cured by tight bandages and pieces of wood like staves placed longitudinally around the pad, to which are secured by leather thongs" (1831, I:248).

The Spokan had essentially two types of casts: one of buckskin and one of rawhide. A buckskin cast was applied to the broken extremity after a *splint* (λ'*aq*) was first made by placing one or two opposing stout pieces of split, flat-surfaced hardwood on either side of the injured extremity. The two splints were wrapped with buckskin and were left in place until the bones knitted or until the cast was no longer deemed necessary, presumably after the bones had properly knitted. One lady recalled how several layers of moss or mullein leaves were first applied, then the splints were set just before the final wrapping of buckskin. This type of layered cast was easily adjusted to expand in order to accommodate blood circulation. Damp or soaked rawhide was seldom used for setting broken long bones of the arm (ulna and radius), for fear of impeding circulation once the hide had dried. An emergency cast was made when an individual was many days from home, by taking, if possible, a deer's or elk's stomach void of any contents, and wrapping the opened stomach around the break area. The limb was then placed intermittently near a fire to help desiccate and harden the improvised cast. Several sections of wood were secured to the cast to help prevent accidental articulation. The person never contracted an infection probably because of the hydrochloric acid initially present within the stomach.

In the field, under emergency conditions, a splint would have been used to treat a broken bone until a cast was available. When possible, a long bone fracture was first packed with moist clay, and held in place by wrapping the extremity with buckskin, or, in an emergency situation, holding the clay with an opened length of cottonwood bark before wrapping the improvised cast with several lengths of buckskin thong.

Any broken finger bone or sprained joint was immobilized with one or two appropriate lengths of relatively flat sticks. One or two splints were applied only if the humerus was broken. It was explained that a crutch, if necessary, was easily fashioned from an appropriate length of wood that had at the upper end a "V", which was padded with wrapped moss or layered buckskin. A hand-hold was provided by an intact but shortened limb offshoot. A person with a crippled leg who required a crutch to be ambulatory was referred to as *hec p'anšn* or *ʔec nc'k'ʷaxn* ("he is walking with the aid of a crutch").

A broken *clavicle* (*sč'máłqʷl't*) was treated by immobilizing the arm against the person's chest with a series of wide buckskin bindings. Broken ribs were similarly bound with buckskin wrappings, and a single broken *rib* (*čč"éłp*) received the same treatment. There was no recollection as to how a broken *ankle* (*čłqʔupc'inšn*) was treated; but one may assume that the *ankle* (*č'mcnéneʔšn*) was immobilized by strapping it with a rigid device to prevent articulation, or wrapped with buckskin to discourage articulation. In the case of an elbow being severely bruised, or dislocated, experience demonstrated the value of immobilizing the limb by strapping it to the patient's chest.

The common method for treating a severe *sprain* (*nt'ucšn*) was to wrap the area, if possible, with a section of buckskin. This wrap also served to hold different types of heated plant leaves to reduce pain, a process that was repeated as needed. As will be discussed, the Spokan also used various ways of treating sprains such as soaking the sprain in *tepid water* (*nmal'qʷ*), or if possible applying a plant infusion or a solution of mud or clay diluted with warm water. Minor sprains were always treated by hydrotherapy or the periodic application of heated mullein leaves, mud, or clay. Opinions differed about whether a heat or cold treatment was to be used for sprains, particularly since some elders maintained that any sprain was a hot injury requiring cold applications.

Reductions

Because of present day Indian Health Service facilities, there is little knowledge of manipulating joint reductions, which in the past was apparently a skill possessed by most adults, even an older boy. Finger and shoulder reductions were not as difficult as a hip reduction, a procedure that required several people to stabilize or even immobilize the patient while pulling (reduction) and simultaneously rotating the displaced limb. The skills required for a finger reduction were acquired by most older boys who frequently engaged in the once popular finger-pulling contests, sometimes with a finger being *dislocated* (*mawɫ scom* - "dislocated a bone") during the intensity of competition. Such a reduction was probably self-manipulated by the person in pain or by a sympathetic and experienced playmate.

One elder recalled how on several occasions his father administered his own reduction for a recurring accident-prone shoulder. He would first hold a short, stout stick in the hand of the injured arm, which he then placed in the high crotch of a tree limb before forcibly dropping his body while twisting, thereby resetting the head of the humerus. It is not known if the Spokan ever did reductions on a dislocated *hip joint* (*snʔatx̣ʷaqstšn*) by excavating a hole in the ground, packing *earth* (*hec mlk'ʷmuleʔx̣ʷ*) around the entire leg, and then pulling the patient straight up while several companions twisted the dislocated hip joint.

There was little recall of how a dislocated *elbow* (*sč'moʔsáx̣n*) was reduced, except that—given the severity—most patients always suffered post-procedural complications of pain; which later often resulted in restricted articulation and range of motion, often sustaining nerve damage. As can best be deduced from one explanation, the most painful aftermath of an elbow reduction was either the ulnar or radial collateral ligament damage acquired via the accident or ensuing treatment. Some years ago, it was said that the best "bone man" was a bronc or Brahma bull rider.

Arthritis and Rheumatism

Some of the most debilitating physical conditions of old age, apart from cataracts that affected some Spokan people were arthritis and *rheumatism* (*c'alc'alc'óm'*). It was claimed (Cox 1831:249) that rheumatism was indeed, rare among the Spokan, and yet Cox described in some detail the hydropathic treatment he received one winter from an elderly Spokan curing shaman when suffering from a severe rheumatic pain in his shoulders and knees, therapy that required him to plunge early every morning into a river—undoubtedly the Spokane River—that was, "firmly frozen, and an opening [had] to be made in the ice preparatory to each immersion" (1831:249). In 1816, Cox also observed a similar treatment required by a fellow trapper-trader suffering from severe rheumatism. A small sweathouse structure was covered with deer skins, and upon entering the practitioner poured water on the heated rocks after closing the door flap:

> [...] and the man [was] kept in for some time until he begged to be released, alleging that he was nearly suffocated. On coming out he was in a state of profuse perspiration. The Indian ordered him to be immediately enveloped in blankets and conveyed to bed. This operation was repeated several times, and although it did not effect a radical cure, the violence of the pains was so far abated as to permit the patient to follow his ordinary business, and to enjoy sleep in comparative ease (Cox 1832:126).

With the widespread availability of balsamroot, it was common in early spring for small groups of women to make half-day expeditions to where this common sunflower grew, and they would dig great quantities when the new growth was approximately 12 to 16 cm above ground. This stage of development was called *suwíya*, and when:

> [...] gathered in great quantities & crushed and roasted until warm in an open trench dug in [the] house beside a fire & hot rocks placed in [the trench and] covered with dirt & [the] crushed mass of roots [were] put in - [and the] patient rolled around into that and covered with a robe - [he] lies there until it cooled - [and then the patient was] generally cured - for rheumatism, sprains, or pains of any sort - even pneumonia - [it] was used as a poultice - [and] cooked until [it] can be crushed - for bruises [it] draws out inflammation (Elmendorf 1935-6, 1:43).

During the mid-1860s, Wilson (1866:300) also recorded a similar treatment by the Spokan for rheumatism when the patient was instructed to endure an exceptionally hot sweathouse before being released into cold water, a therapy of sudation that was repeated over a fairly long period of time before he gained any relief.

607

Human osteological material revealed by archaeologists indicates the prevalence of arthritis among the Spokan and other contiguous peoples (Bourke 1967:357; Sprague, pers. comm.). One should stress that certain types of severe joint pain were caused when a person neglected or refused to give up his or her *suméš*, and this was presumed to be responsible for their physical discomfort. However, if it were deemed that one's joint pain was the result of advanced age, or an earlier traumatic injury, or a bone break, then a number of internal and external treatments were available.

It seems evident that within the Spokan pharmacopoeia there were definitely more medicines for arthritis and rheumatism than for any other medical condition. Some curing shamans had a unique power in treating this debility; such practitioners were known as *t'łá?ák*ʷ*ílc* (Elmendorf 1935-6, 2:25). Specific specialization of medicine and curing rituals and procedures, including unique religious powers, has obviously been lost for many years.

The rhizomes of yellow pond lily were collected by women who dislodged them with their toes or by a using a *hooked stick* (*?ú p'čstn*) when wading in relatively shallow water, which were then transferred to a basket suspended from her head or by a shoulder tumpline onto her back. Four to six edible bulbs were then *baked* (*p'y'áq*), and while still warm, sliced sections of the root were applied directly to the area afflicted with arthritis or rheumatism. This process was repeated until the patient acknowledged some relief. A similar treatment was stone-baking the roots of "Indian carrots" (*Lomatium macrocarpum* [Nutt.] C.& R.) (Turner 1977, 31:468), and either placing warm slices on the joint, or administering minute pieces of this plant to the patient to eat, presumably for temporary relief from arthritis. It was said how this treatment numbed the patient's pain, thereby often reducing his *cries of intense pain* (*pr'p'ir'é?m'n'*). A person experiencing severe rheumatism could apply the macerated bulbs of death camas directly onto the site that was first covered with bear grease to prevent the skin from sustaining burns.

A more elaborate process for treating rheumatism was to excavate a 2-meter length pit in the floor of the patient's dwelling, which was first lined with old heated sweathouse rocks, then layered with balsamroot, just prior to being covered with earth. The patient was wrapped in a robe or large section of buckskin, and remained in whatever position necessary until the rocks had cooled (Elmendorf 1935-6, 1:43), and, if necessary, the procedure was repeated several times—even days—until the person was cured.

A general purpose medicine for stopping minor external bleeding, and for relief from rheumatism, was the application of what is sometimes called *female biscuitroot, desert parsley* or *chocolate tips* (*Lomatium dissectum* [Nutt. ex T. & G.] Mathias & Const. - *č'eyč'i*). The roots of chocolate tips (a.k.a. desert parsley) were cooked in ashes, mashed, and applied directly to a rheumatic joint—often held in place by a buckskin wrap. This plant smells similar to mountain valerian, and is collected in May and June while the roots are small and white. Presumably, it is edible before the plant is at its very young stock, at which point it becomes poisonous (Turner *et al.* 1980:66). The large roots were pounded and applied as a paste to the afflicted region of either man or horse, and covered by several layers of warmed mullein leaves that were held in place by several wraps of buckskin or hemp rope. The mashed leaves of yellow pond lily were mashed, heated, and applied to a sore back or smeared over an *arthritic joint* (*sčt'pipss*). Dried powdered leaves of hoary puccoon or western stoneseed were heated and placed on arthritic or rheumatic joints—being replaced as needed. The roots of warmed pounded mule-ears were applied as a poultice to relieve the pain of arthritic or rheumatic joints (Turner *et al.* 1984:85).

Smoking Indian hemp was known to relieve arthritic or rheumatoid patients of their pain when smoked several times a day. The difficulty of following this once traditional treatment today is twofold: many patches of Indian hemp have been destroyed by over-grazing and agriculture; and, some of the elders who are cognizant of the present socially-deemed problems of "pot smoking," refuse to acknowledge any medicinal benefits from smoking this plant.

Only a few elders could remember their parents gathering bluebunch wheatgrass (*Pseudoroegneria spicata* [Pursh] A. Löve ssp. *spicata*) to treat arthritis by making a decoction of bunchgrass in boiled water, in which the patient bathed his or her hands or afflicted limb until the solution cooled. The process was repeated as needed. Though not used today, an analgesic poultice of mashed, cooked bulbs of death camas was once used to treat strain and bruise pains. Also as a topical anti-rheumatic poultice for rheumatism (Moerman 2009:514).

Another type of revulsive (or hot/cold syndrome) and analgesic poultice medicine was to place and hold heated sections of balsamroot to the painful rheumatic area. The most common treatment for a patient with chronic rheumatism was to dig a large quantity of balsamroot, which were split and then roasted until warm before being spread in a shallow ground depression. The patient was first covered with a robe or hide before lying directly upon the prepared roots until they were cool. Though the process might be repeated in the same day, it was said that it was usually done only once a day. A similar treatment for joint discomfort—pneumonia and other upper respiratory afflictions—was to pound the dug roots of heated balsamroot, which were applied to the thoracic area that was first covered with a hide or section of cloth. An internal anti-rheumatic infusion or decoction for arthritis was made from the dried crushed roots of fernleaf biscuitroot, which were carefully stored for winter use.

A beneficial and herbaceous perennial plant for both internal and external maladies was *stinging nettles* (*Urtica dioica* L. ssp. *gracilis* [Alt.] Seland var. *lyalli* - *c'c'áxiłp* or *c'cáxełp* or *c'ic'ixey'łp*), when from April to June—before flowering—the fresh finely toothed green-blue leaves were used as a burn poultice and for soothing bruises, and as a treatment of rheumatism or arthritis. It is now known that rubbing or beating oneself with stinging nettles, or to have a friend whip the patient's painful area with stinging nettles—a treatment often termed urtication—caused blood to be brought to the surface, thereby removing toxins (formic acid) that may cause arthritis. Urtication was sometimes used after the patient emerged from the sweathouse or after leaving a heated pool and plunging into a stream of cold water. This process was repeated three times, or less if the afflicted site became numb. Stinging nettle leaves were administered as an astringent and as an antidote for stings. Interesting that by cooking or drying nettle leaves long the stinging effect, and could be eaten.

A general treatment for minor forms of arthritis was to collect the yellow colored tips of mountain tamarack (*Larix lyallii* Parl.), which were boiled in water and when warm the arthritic joint was bathed in the solution. An individual with a *throbbing ache* (*sik'ʷ sik'ʷ*) was advised to seek relief in a solitary sweathouse which was made just tolerably hot; and, later, after exiting, refrain from the usual cold water plunge. A more conservative treatment, but perhaps more offensive to occupants of a dwelling, was to cook the big roots of pasture wormwood in an open fire, clean and then mash them before placing the noxious mass on the patient's aching legs. Often the prepared material was wrapped and left until morning (STHC).

Medicines made from Douglas fir and pine trees were also effective for managing intense pain or throbbing aches. It has been recounted how several elderly women would gather on a regular basis for a social as well as a therapeutic session, during which they immersed their arthritic feet into a metal wash bin that was filled with an infusion made from hot water and mashed fresh cedar boughs.

Another effective treatment for sore arthritic and rheumatoid joints was to collect juniper twigs and twills which were first boiled and then stirred through a grass filter; after the decoction had cooled, it was sometimes strained a second time before drinking. In addition to drinking the solution, the mashed and heated twills were mashed with the tree's berries and applied directly to the area of discomfort by encasing the mass in a fold of buckskin. All aromatic trees, such as western red cedar and juniper, were used extensively for a variety of medicines.

Various parts of animals and their organs were an integral part of the Spokan *materia medica*—being used as zoo medicaments for different medical treatments, most notably for episodes of pain. For example, a *beaver's castor* (*qamépe?*), i.e., the *scent gland* (*st'înt'n*), contains an oil that was rubbed on the site of pain. Also, a castor could be mashed and soaked in warm water and this infusion was drunk to combat various internal pains. Skunks were killed with a long pole, and after skinning, the complete hide was boiled in water until the oils surfaced, which was collected upon a small section of buckskin and administered directly to any joint in pain.

The use of animals and insects in the Spokan pharmacopoeia was rather extensive, as was explained by an elderly man, who had at one point experienced severe pain in his right hip, one that had been broken when he was a young man breaking horses. Whenever he experienced intense pain, he would, if available, place a live spider in his right pocket, which presumably relieved his neuralgia. Certain organs of some animals were used as medicaments, but more often the spirit of the animal served a critical role in curing.

Though the Spokan used tattooing for body ornamentation, there is no written evidence or oral accounts that support the notion that they tattooed arthritic or rheumatoid joints in order to rid the person of pain, a procedure that was done by some Plateau groups (Teit 1928). Nor did the Spokan apply charcoal to a rheumatic joint. Yet, it was recalled how moist clay, worked into thick paddies, heated and held in place over an afflicted area—usually the knee–was beneficial. Arthritic hands were treated by repeated kneading of lumps of heated clay.

Paralysis

It is difficult to determine the frequency or actual etiology of past situations when one was *paralyzed* (*sƛ'lléłc'e?*), since a person could be paralyzed by sorcery, head or spinal cord injury, infection of the central nervous system, or any one of numerous cerebrovascular diseases. It is difficult, if not impossible, to reconstruct the etiology of different cases of paralysis, since some maladies were believed to be the result of sorcery or a moral transgression; whereas some conditions were considered, at least initially, to be the result of natural causes. Consensus was that anyone suffering from seizures had been sorcerized and could only be treated by a curing shaman. Similarly, a sorcerer was responsible for a person's epileptic fit, and it was also tended to by a curing shaman. During the stage of seizure, the sorcerer's projected power was always within the victim. Consequently, the situation would be dangerous for the sorcerer, who must always return—regardless of his form—to retrieve his power, particularly to recover one's projective power. A shaman who ignored or misused his power could become paralyzed or even crippled.

The general treatment of limb paralysis—most notably paralysis caused by a stroke—was to incubate the person first or the affected limb in warm wrappings, water, or, if possible, warm mud. The limb was periodically massaged by a family member, to gradually extend the limb's range of motion. Some elders could remember the use of revulsive medicines being used as therapy for muscular paralysis, but only in extreme cases. Hence, for cases of paralysis, it was recalled that physical massage, manipulation, and hydrotherapy were considered the best treatments. In summer, the tops of fresh *deervetch* (*Lotus nevadensis* [Wats.] Greene - *nt'št't'šén'č* or *nt'št'šel'š*) were crushed and placed in a warm bath to externally treat anti-spasmodic conditions in muscular paralysis; some claimed how this plant was administered as a tea to 'relax' the heart. Strokes were apparently not a common *physical affliction* (*t'uqʷt'uqʷ ulm*), and yet one elder remembered how, before modern medicine, a curing shaman might instruct a stroke patient to hold or even rub a dead magpie to the afflicted area. It was also believed that this procedure would be repeated to prevent the stroke from spreading. However, the paralyzed area sometimes spread to either a right or left extremity, which is quite common with cerebrovascular disease. Another treatment for temporary or permanent paralysis was, as described earlier, using hydrotherapy by *immersion* (*nt'ipmist* - "person immersion").

A sorcery-induced malady was the result of a person maligning another, which could cause partial paralysis, loss of voice or even death, through what people now call *throat cancer* (*sci-yumt*). Treatment for partial paralysis was to lay the patent in a pronograde position in a sweathouse, and carefully massage the afflicted area. As a warning, or as a prelude to a more debilitating condition, a sorcerer could first make *numb* (*sueł* or *čsul*) the limb or affected area of his victim. Several elders have said that this situation was not unusual, one that was successfully treated only by a curing shaman and never by a non-Indian doctor.

A person who had spoken ill of someone, or had lied, may experience a partial distortion of his face, usually on one side, an affliction known as *stčúntn*. A curing shaman called *stiy'é* could cure the individual by painting that side of the patient's face from his forehead to his *chin* (*k'ʷi?épe?st*) with red hematite (Smith 1936-8:1236). Sometimes the shaman used mashed *wild cow-parsnip* (*Heracleum maximum* - *xwxwTelʕ*) bulb externally on the area of paralysis.

Understandably, persons were generally reticent to discuss epilepsy, but did acknowledge its existence. One can perhaps conclude that this condition was rare. A person experiencing an *epileptic seizure* (*λ'l'λ'el'íl'*), one with involuntary tonic or clonic contractions of the musculature, was considered to have been the victim of a sorcerer, or to have been maliciously poisoned. It was not said if an afflicted person's tongue was immobilized with a padded gag of buckskin to prevent biting or *severing* (*č'łxʷel*) the tongue. An elder explained how a small child's seizures would be temporarily cured when wrapped in several wool blankets; but nothing could be remembered of the frequency of seizures.

There were no accounts of a male curing shaman treating a woman within a sweathouse. For example, a woman who had a minor stroke that affected her right side, experienced severe headaches, bouts of blurred vision, and frequent motor difficulties with her right leg making her simply collapse. The following account was given by the last Spokan curing shaman, one with no details of dress or decorum:

> Once we were in the sweathouse, and the heat was pretty extreme. I first had the woman press the palms of her hands against the side [temporal areas] of her head as she breathed deeply. After about five minutes I'd massage the back of her neck, sometimes pushing my knuckles real hard in her shoulders [trapezius]. After a while I pulled out an animal—like what you'd call a[n] octopus, 'cause it had many legs. The lady felt better right off, but I treated her again several days later to make sure I got all the animal out (Ross 1968-2008).

Muscular Therapy

The most common external treatment of sore muscles, *muscular cramps* (*snckʷélšn*), and strains and sprains, was to use massage or some form of hydrotherapy to bring relief. A relief for sore or aching muscles was to immerse the fresh, green stalks of mountain alder into boiling water, and decanting to make a paste which was rubbed on the afflicted area. People with *sharp pain* (*k'ʷup'p'p'i k'ʷup'p'*) in the thoracic area, or a bruised *tendon* (*tinš*) in one of the extremities, sought relief by using deep massage or applying heated poultices made from *soft, sticky, pine tree pitch* (*hi piq t'ełtn*). Sweet cicely root, similar to ginseng, was first split and then applied without heating as a poultice for a sore muscle.

During fern harvest in the early spring, and after the snow's melting revealed one of the first flowering plants, women would go forth and gather large quantities of the large and prolific Bracken Fern, Lady Fern (*Pteridinum aquilinum* [L.] Kuhn), and the small, delicate Oak Fern (*Gymnocarpium dryopteris*), from moist and shaded areas. Moist ferns were used primarily to cover food when pit-cooking. Though bracken fern could poison horses, when heated in an earth oven, it will have no deleterious effect.

As noted earlier, the *sagecup buttercup* (*Ranunculus glaberrimus* Hook. var. *glaberrimus* - *sčn'írm'n'* or *sčná?λmn* or *čenirem'en'*) was another medicinal plant collected for the management of pain in the treatment of sprains and strains. There were two ways to administer this medicine, but most often the mashed flowers of several plants were placed on a small piece of buckskin and held on the painful joint (Turner 1984:189). But one had to act cautiously, for if the flowers were left on too long, the skin would sometimes suffer from severe burns, and would frequently blister. The second procedure could also be dangerous, for after boiling the plant's petals three times, the solution was carefully decanted each time to *remove* (*λ'ekʷšms*) glycose and the poisonous and principal antibiotic substance protoanemonin (Kirk 1975:23; Turner and Szczaqwinski 1991:104). From an early age, children were cautioned not to touch the buttercup, for the petal's oil was easily transferred to the face or any other part of the body that it might touch, creating painful blisters. And yet, Turner also notes that, "Cooking, like drying, eliminates the irritating properties of protoanemonin-containing

611

plants, through apparent conversion of protoanemonin to anemonon (1984a:184). Another universal treatment of strains or pains was to take a handful of buttercup leaves and flowers, which *bloom* (*sc'ʔék'ʷt*) in late winter or early spring, and crush "into a mass–[and] put onto a piece of buckskin and tied on for blister poultice and for strains and pains" (Elmendorf 1935-6, I:43). A poultice for poison blisters was to take warmed freshly crushed buttercups, which were then wrapped in a section of buckskin and applied directly to the area. Years ago, a poison for coyotes was made by mashing the entire buttercup plant and then cut into meat as a fatal bait (Turner *et al.* 1984:119).

Another type of revulsive medicine was crushed stinging nettles, that were carefully applied to elbows or knee joints to treat rheumatism. It has been reported (Smith 1936-8:1072, 1074) how muscle pain in the back would be treated by strapping a skunk's scent sac which, despite the malodorous scent, was applied to an adequately wide section of buckskin, and then strapped over the site. This remedy apparently relieved any *back ache* (*sc'ʔλéʔus*), *leg ache* (*sc'aʔλšín*), or *arm ache* (*sč'áʔλáxn*). More commonly, fresh mule-ear leaves would be heated and mashed before being applied as a poultice to an area of muscular ache, and replaced as needed. Pineapple weed (*Matricaria matricarioides*) was considered a wide spectrum medicament, particularly for treating sore muscles by repeated applications of a warm solution made from mashing the fresh leaves of this plant. An individual experiencing *muscular spasms* or *tremors* (*xʷrxʷrílš*) might smoke *Cannabis sativa* L. (hemp or marijuana), which contains the now familiar substance tetrahydrocannabinol (THC). The castor of a male beaver could be either applied directly to an area of pain, or the patient would drink a warm mixture made after the gland had been mashed and heated. A common antidote for blistering or muscle spasm was the application of bear grease.

A very interesting example of sympathetic magic was the explanation as to why a woman would have a sore neck when she failed to acknowledge the obligations of the levirate by not marrying the brother of her deceased husband (Sapir 1916, 3:327). This was a condition termed *ʔe nc'eʔ rusi*, and it occurred when the rejected *brother-in-law* (*nq'ʷíc'tn* or *seʔstem'* - "woman's brother-in-law") felt humiliated and, thus, his "neck is out of joint" (Elmendorf, pers, comm.; STHC)—an appropriate metaphor. A woman's sister-in-law was called *ʔis čew*.

Dental and Gums

Prior to white incursion, and the inevitable introduction of non-traditional foods—particularly sugars and simple carbohydrates—the Spokan had few caries or other dental maladies. Furthermore, all Native Americans had aligned occlusion of the *mandible* (*k'ʷiʔepeʔst*) and maxilla (Class 1). Older children and adults practiced good dental hygiene, based partly upon the practice of rinsing one's mouth with water after eating and brushing one's teeth in the morning with the shredded end of willow or some other deciduous plant. Wood ashes from fireplaces were sometimes used for cleaning teeth after eating an exceptionally oily food. Frequently, peoples who ground their food with stone mortars and pestles, would gradually have their teeth abraded and worn down by the miniscule stone particles, as also by wind-blown sand.

Archaeological findings demonstrate that abscesses did occur and undoubtedly caused severe toothaches, which eventually required *tooth* (*xléxʷ*) removal. *Tooth extraction* (*nc'oʔqéysm*) was commonly accomplished by binding the tooth with a narrow section of wet rawhide, or a strand of horsetail hair, and then pulling until the tooth was removed. Semi-hard tree gum packed around an abscessed tooth also facilitated its removal. Masticating catnip leaves may help reduce the pain of a dental abscess. The use of poisonous plants as revulsive medicines was mentioned earlier when describing the treatment of a sore or abscessed tooth, that of chewing a leaf of Oregon grape to gain temporary relief. The leaf—used in small amounts—was beneficial, but when thoroughly dried, smashed, and placed in food, it could cause the victim to die slowly with no apparent explanation of cause. A few elders recalled how the entire mandible or maxilla often became entirely numb when this treatment was applied, and the patient may even fall asleep during treatment. Most commonly, the dried, poisonous roots of either yellow pond lily or *white water-lily* (*Nymphaea odorata* Ait. - *láklek*) were applied directly to the tooth (Turner *et al.* 1980:110) for relief from a severe *toothache* (*ciqíntem*) or *abscess* (*p'p't'íč'*).

The most common method for alleviating oral pain was to chew on the cleansed root of the readily available yarrow plant, which temporarily anesthetized both the upper and lower gums. Similarly, an abscessed tooth that was difficult, or thought impossible, to remove, was impacted with heated yarrow root to give temporary relief. Toothaches were often treated by packing a section of boiled thistle root (*Cirsuim* sp.) around the afflicted tooth, repeating it if necessary. A toothache could be cured by chewing on several fresh blue-green leaves of catnip leaves, or applying the mashed stems of Clematis directly on the tooth. Some claimed that in the past, a person's toothache could be cured without any medical application, but by a curing shaman placing both his hands firmly on either side of the patient's jaw, and slowly rubbing both sides in circular movements while he sang a special curing song. A nursing baby with a sore mouth was medicated with a fine powder made from wild strawberry leaves (*Fragaria* sp.) that were dried on hot, flat stones and dusted, on the suspected area of irritation.

A once common medication for severe toothache was chewing the washed root of wild ginger, which, now we know, contains chemically active glycyrrhiza, "[the] sweet tasting compound is the acid ammonium salt of nitrogenous tri-basic acid, called glycyrrhizic [and contains up to 6% glycyrrhizin]" (Sykes 2007:2). For temporary relief from tooth ache, crushed seeds of goldenrod were applied directly on the gum surrounding the tooth.

Black cottonwood catkins, once used as chewing gum, were gathered and stored for treating toothaches by simply chewing the unprocessed fuzzy growth. To temporarily reduce pain in an abscessed or broken tooth, an application of small pieces of *soft pitch* (*t'éłtn*) were applied to the tooth. The Spokan considered that the best medicine for treating a *toothache* (*henc'e?réysi* or *n'ce?reys*) was the pitch found under the partially peeled bark of a *lightning-struck tree* (*snc'q'míntn*), preferably a Douglas fir tree. Pitch would be packed around an abscessed or broken tooth; after three applications, the pain would at least subside if not *disappear* (*č'łč'luxʷ* - "from sight"). In addition, several pleasant sweet and nutty tasting roots of wild carrot were mashed and applied, as needed, directly to an aching or abscessed tooth. Toothaches were also treated by rubbing both sides of the gum where the tooth was located with washed black tree lichen.

The Spokan had numerous treatments for a *canker sore* (*he?nq'ʷmałq'ʷt* - Herpes simplex, *H. labialis*, and *H. progenitalis*) and recurring virus skin infections, which were treated by administering powdered white clay topically. In addition, powdered clay was dusted on minor wounds to stop bleeding and to encourage the formation of a scab. Oral herpes simplex (*Herpes labialis*) was also treated by making an infusion of boiled western red-cedar boughs, and upon cooling, a piece of small buckskin was saturated with the solution and periodically placed on the herpes for several days. One elder thought the leaves of *mashed thistle* (*Cirsium undulatum* [Nutt.] Spreng - *čqčíq*) were mashed and placed on a lip or oral herpes.

Probably the most effective and commonly used procedure for tooth pain was to *chew* (*kʷek'ʷe?cníłš*) several freshly mashed leaves of kinnikinnick, or the leaves of a small and ubiquitous plantain, known as *Plantago major*. Similarly, the Spokan would place the *chewed leaves inside the mouth* (*srč'małq'ʷl't*), and after a few minutes the person *spat* (*sptáxʷ*) it out. Alternatively, the broad leaf would be chewed, keeping the leaf flat, and then the bruised underside would be placed on the *sore* (*čł?oqce?* or *spoct*). Another treatment for an abscessed tooth was to mash the leaves of western sage (*Artemesia ludoviciana* Nutt.), placing the mass into the cavity to lessen the pain. Catkins from the tips of young willow were boiled to make a solution that was rubbed on the gums of children when their permanent *teeth* (*xlxléxʷ*) began to erupt. This solution was also used by anyone with a sore mouth or gums; but it was never swallowed.

Pine pitch was used routinely to reduce the pain of a toothache or abscessed tooth, by encasing the afflicted tooth with moist pitch until the pain subsided. After three different applications, the pain would subside if not disappear altogether. It was recalled that the best pitch was found under the partially peeled bark of a lightning-struck tree.

The *small female catkins* (*scc'íč'e²e*) of willow were boiled to make a solution that was rubbed on *sore gums* (*c'erɬmalqʷ alt*), a procedure used to relieve the pain of small children who were teething. Some elders claimed this procedure frequently acted as a general *anesthetic* (*ičstm* - "anesthetic"), by inducing sleep in the child. A dangerous but effective treatment for an open abscessed tooth was to cut a small bit of water hemlock root, insert it into the tooth, and hold it in place with some *tallow* (*snlóqʷ*). Given the location of the infected tooth, and the amount of hemlock, either the entire mandible or maxilla could be completely anesthetized for long periods—as long as four hours at a time. One patient claimed that as a boy he became unconscious; not waking until the next morning after an infected tooth was treated with water hemlock. One should also emphasize that, with the application of any floral *materia medica,* the practitioner had to be attentive to the plant's presumed efficacy, the relative age and body weight of the patient, and the age and amount of medicine given to the patient. Elders were aware of how over time, a dried, stored medicament will lose some of its medicinal effectiveness.

Oral problems were treated in a variety of ways, depending upon the problem and the age of the patient. Babies sometimes developed a sore mouth when first taking solid or bitter foods, and then they were treated by boiling a small amount of red willow (*Cornus sericea*) bark to make an infusion, placing it on a small piece of buckskin, and swabbing inside the mouth several times a day. This procedure was repeated sometimes for several days, or until the baby was again comfortable. For teething problems or soar gums, some mothers mashed wild black currants (*Ribes petiolare* Dougl. - *stm'tú* - "something you suck on"), and would work this around the baby's or child's gums as a *medicine* (*mr'uy'elyn*). This remedy was also used for treating a child's sore throat.

Alum root was an important broad spectrum medicament in treating babies and children, most commonly used for a sore or inflamed gum or mouth. A piece of freshly dug alum root was scraped clean and held by the mother, as the baby or child sucked until the root became tasteless, "An alternative method was to boil the root and rinse the mouth out with the solution" (Turner *et al.* 1980:138). The young stems of sumac produce a milky latex, "used as a salve on sores and on poison ivy rashes" (Turner *et al.* 1980; Spier 1938:166). Ray cites how mashed sumac leaves were chewed to treat gum sores, and, "The leaves were also used for *sore lips* (*c'erɬsplim cin*). In this case they were mashed and rubbed on the lips" (Ray 1932:219). Freshly mashed leaves from any type of mint were applied to gum sores and oral eruptions.

Dermal Therapy

Some of the most common and often debilitating external conditions are various types of dermal eruptions, carbuncles, burns, cuts, hematomas, *blisters on the hands* (*shekʷkʷéčst*), *blisters* (*st'íkʷ*), slivers, insect and snake bites, *acne* (*pukʷpukʷu sus*), *hives* (*čqʷupíc'²ey*), and general skin rashes. A mashed root of balsamroot was applied as a wet dressing or poultice to draw out blisters. The ever-dangerous rattlesnake bite was treated by a curing shaman who was a specialist (Elmendorf 1935-6, 1:22) in treating such bites, as well as insect and spider bites, presumably by placing one of his fingers or a hand on the bite. Alexander Ross observed a man who had been bitten by a rattlesnake, and was effectively treated (1849 7:290). After removing the poison of a snake bite by sucking, common plantain broad-leaf Plantago (*Plantago major*) was partially chewed and the under-side of the leaf placed on the site to suppress pain.

The fresh juice from either *huckleberries* (*Vaccinium membranaceum* Dougl. ex Hook.) or *low-bush mountain blueberry* (*V. caespitosum* Michx. - *npekʷpkʷáxen*) made an anti-inflammatory decoction for treating burns and sores. Some elders claimed any type of freshly mashed berry was effective if applied immediately after being burned.

From March until June, mashed roots of hoary puccoon (*Lithospermum ruderale*) were mixed with lard, and made into an ointment by simmering the concoction until thoroughly mixed. After cooling, the ointment was applied to burns, sores, and cuts. The leaves of this plant made an antihemorrhagic infusion for internal hemorrhaging, particularly when spitting blood (tuberculosis?).

Crushed roots from the medicinal and edible yampah plant were heated and repeatedly applied to wounds and sores to reduce pain and prevent infection.

As late as the early 1900s, there were a few curing shamans who possessed the skill for treating rattlesnake bites by sucking directly on the wound or using a bone whistle or a section of hollow elderberry stem. By the late 1920s, such wounds were treated by shamans without mosquito or rattlesnake power (Elmendorf 1935-6, 1:22). Little was known of their techniques for treating snake bites, except that wild licorice root was chewed to reduce pain. There was no memory of using a tourniquet to restrict the spread of snake-bite poison or septicemia, though a tourniquet is currently used for restricting the placement of septicemia. Poison blisters were treated with a poultice of warmed freshly crushed buttercups, wrapped in a section of buckskin and applied directly to the area. This same method was useful for treating sprains. The leaves of wild ginger were also gathered before a killing frost and stored dry, to be used as a poultice after soaking the leaves in heated water.

While on route to Spokane House, David Thompson provided the following explanation regarding treatment of snake bites, a method used initially by all Plateau groups:

> The Hunters assured me that a full grown snake biting in a fleshy part, unless instantly cut out, and well sucked, is fatal in three or four minutes. I saw a Hunter who had been slightly bitten in the calf of the leg, the part was quickly cut out and sucked, he had no other injury than a stiff leg, with very little sensation in it, he said it was like a leg of Wood, but did not prevent him from hunting (1962:373).

Though septicemia undoubtedly occurred in the past, no one remembered the prescribed treatment. Fortunately, this condition is currently treated by the Indian Health Service. Septicemia was and is currently recognized as a dangerous condition, particularly when the vein or artery is red, and the lymph glands in the groin or axilla are pronounced and tender.

Dermal eruptions were commonly treated by applying a *poultice* (*c'p'q'mín* or *nq'nq'téɬp*) to the afflicted area. There being more than one type of poultice, it depended upon the injury and its location as to what type of poultice was chosen. For example, many dermal conditions were treated with a special poultice called *maλiyé*, which was made by mashing juniper berries between one's hands, then forming the pulp into a cake before applying it to the area. An emergency or common field poultice was made from mashed wild rose leaves (*Rosa acicularis*) that were heated with enough water to make a paste-like consistency, and was repeatedly applied to the site as needed. The leaves of juniper—approximately 4 cm in length—were gathered and boiled and poured upon a folded pad made of buckskin or compressed black tree lichen, and then applied as a poultice for boils and sores.

As cited, the long, wide inedible leaves of mule-ears were used in a variety of ways, and the roots served as an effective poultice after being dug and then placed in a hole covered with earth and baked with coals. The roots were mashed and spread directly on a boil or carbuncle, covered with the plant's leaves and left overnight. If the first application did not bring the core to a head, the procedure was repeated. Dermal eruptions were also treated by applying the crushed leaves of *wild tobacco* (*Nicotiana attenuata*) to the site.

For treating dermal eruptions, the inside of fresh aspen or cottonwood bark was first scoured with a *sharp edged* (*xʷixʷít*) stone knife—or a heated knife, and the bark was tied directly to the patient's skin. Or, the inner bark of chokecherry was broken into small pieces and steeped until cool before washing any sores and eruptions. This bitter-tasting solution also served as a cough medicine. Heated and grass-wrapped serviceberry (*Amelanchier alnifolia*) bark was reputed to be an effective treatment for muscle strain or bruise, mainly of the extremities, when soaked in stone-heated water and then applied at the affected areas.

Skin ulcers were treated by first taking a dry fresh water mussel shell, which was pounded into a fine powder, mixed with any available grease in another dry mussel shell to form a *paste* (*c'p'q'mntn*), and then applied to the affected area. This mixture was often applied several times a day throughout the duration of treatment. Another treatment for skin ulcers or wounds required scraping the sapwood away, and applying the bark of buckbrush (*Ceanothus velutinus*), pulverized and mixed with any type of tallow.

There are accounts of persons having a case of *sunburn* (*sqocsši*), and before various ointments, greases or oils were applied, an individual was first treated by applying a section of buckskin or cloth *soaked* (*łutct* or *łuct*) in cold water on the afflicted area. One elder recalled how one old treatment was to first apply a solution made by boiling mashed yarrow leaves and then cooling it. She explained how some families had their own recipe for treating sunburn, which actually was not common. The point is that a woman may be correct in saying her family's recipe for treating a certain malady is unique; not so much in the general nature of a medicament, but rather in the associated ritual and the varying amounts of each ingredient utilized.

The small, bitter, white roots of *msáw'i?* (*Aleriana edulius*) were eaten raw, made into a tea, or mashed and applied to the afflicted area of a patient who had skin disorders—particularly boils. Any type of *skin itch* (*qʷupelxʷ* - "spring fever") was treated with moist mud or clay that was held against the site with buckskin or wrapped in mullein leaves. Despite the foul smell, the *msáw'i?* plant, when mashed and heated, was used to treat boils, sores, and rashes. Some have said that the reason this plant was so effective as a medicine was because its smell becomes even more intense after cooking. The heated mashed leaves of Western white clematis was a dermatological treatment when applied to sores or boils as a poultice.

Minor cuts and *skin rashes* (*čłocqe?*) were washed with a disinfectant made by steeping the *bare tips or buds of tamarack* (*ncacqʷl'šqn'*); but once the Spokan had commercial soap, they used this to wash a minor wound in lieu of a mixture of poplar ashes (lye) and water. If available, crushed allium (onion) was applied to minor cuts to prevent infection. A useful antiseptic was to mash and place the moist stalks directly to the wounds, which contained thymol. Though not realized in those days, the bulb of this plant contains the inert antibiotic allicin. Both that and thymol are powerful astringents and styptics—possessing other sulfur-containing phytochemicals which often allay pain. Dry leaves of yellow Indian paintbrush (*Castilleja thompsonii* Pennelli) were powdered and placed in hot water to make an infusion, which was poured, while warm, over an open wound as an antiseptic. Crushed catnip leaves placed on minor cuts produced a mild antibiotic effect.

Pieces of *hard pitch* (*t'aq'ʷéy'*), preferably ponderosa pine tree pitch, were collected from a variety of trees and used as medicines when mixed with animal fat, rolled in a piece of buckskin, softened by warming, and then applied as a poultice. Warmed pitch was pressed onto a *carbuncle* (*sc'óm'c'm'*) and any *furuncle* (*sc'c'y'úm't* or *sc'm'c'm'* or *sc'iy'nm't* or *siy'ey'úkʷ?*) to release the pressure, draw out the central necrosis, and prevent (unknowingly) staphylococcus infection before and after the site had erupted. Pitch from white pine was sometimes mixed with inner scrapings of aspen bark and used as a treatment for a *boil* (*p'p't'ič'* or *sc'm'c'm'*), a sore, a carbuncle, or a minor open wound.

For the treatment of minor cuts, boils, or sores, or as a poultice, the peeled stems and roots of *sweet coltsfoot* (*Petasites sagittatus* [Banks ex Pursh] - *xoxtíłp*) were cleaned, crushed, stone-boiled in a basket, and the hot root-mass was bound to the wound (Elmendorf 1935-6, 1:42).

Another effective poultice for boils and carbuncles was made by stripping the sharp spines of a section of prickly-pear cactus (*Oppuntis* sp.), heating the spongy leaf by baking, and then squashing it before it was applied to the boil—being held in place by a wrap to draw out the poison. For any infected wound, this treatment was repeated as needed until the poison was removed. The core of a carbuncle was, if possible, removed with one's fingers or using tweezers made from a small section of any partially split hard-wood. One elder recalled a curing shaman extracting a partially subcutaneous carbuncle core by sucking, because the man's tweezers, made from a fresh still-attached articulated mussel shell, invariably had proved too awkward.

616

An effective way to treat a boil was to peel the bark from blue elderberry, soak it in hot water and let it cool before placing the underside of the bark upon the boil, thereby bringing the boil to a head, which also facilitated extraction.

Most skin rashes were effectively treated by taking the root, stems, and leaves of wild rose, which were mashed before boiling and washing the afflicted area with the decoction—often requiring repeated applications. This treatment was also used for the removal of carbuncle cores. The leaves of western sage were mashed and placed directly on the area of *rash* (*čpócc'e?*) to relieve pain. Mule's ear is an inedible plant, and its long, wide leaves were used sometimes for pit-baking camas. The root of this plant was also used as a poultice, by first burying it in a firepit, and baking it until it becomes soft, and then mashing and smearing it on dermal eruptions such as furuncles and carbuncles. A furuncle or carbuncle could be brought to a head if the prepared root was smeared on the eruption and then carefully covered and secured with buckskin and left overnight. By morning, the furuncle would have erupted, as would a carbuncle, which might have one or multiple cores. It was established that any source of heat would prevent the spread of furuncles or carbuncles, which—unbeknown to people at the time—contain staphylococci.

Another effective poultice was made from fresh black cottonwood leaves, and sometimes the bark, which were thoroughly soaked in hot water. The same medicament was used to facilitate the draining of boils and for treating furuncles or septicemia. These types of maladies were also effectively treated by stripping the bark from a *blue elderberry bush* (*Sambucus caerulea - c'kʷkʷálqʷ*) and soaking in hot water before applying the bark directly onto the wound; this method invariably brought the infected core to the surface. The roots of both mule-ears and balsamroot were dug, roasted in embers, and upon cooling were mashed and applied directly onto boils, or often wrapped in place overnight until the boil erupted. A general and easily available poultice was made from wood ashes, which were placed in a container of boiled water, and once the solution was warm it was poured directly on the site.

Three rather common dermal irritant-causing plants were poison ivy, water hemlock, and stinging nettles. All were treated by applying to the afflicted area the urine of an adolescent, or a paste of mashed swamp-parsnip bulbs, which are poisonous. Another treatment for poison ivy—following the principles of homeopathic medicine—was to steep mashed poison ivy leaves in hot water to make a diluted tea. Another traditional treatment involved covering the irritated dermis with powdered white clay. One elderly lady, married to a *Sinkaietk* (*snq'?éw'si* - "different group") man, recalled how his mother applied the milky latex collected from mashing sumac stems directly to the affected areas. The sun-dried brown buds of cottonwood would be ground into a fine powder, heated, and then sprinkled on poison ivy wounds. Poison ivy rash was said to have been treated also by drinking a tea made with crushed peppergrass leaves, though some said it was best to first rinse the affected area with the warm solution and then place the saturated leaves directly upon the rash.

Frostbite was not an unusual occurrence for the Spokan, given any prolonged exposure to severe cold winter conditions. When one became aware of the condition, it was treated immediately by placing the foot or hand in snow, and with gradual melting, the cold melted water presumably would draw out the frost. In the case of frostbite on the face, usually the nose, the person would hold packed snow to the injured area. If a friend or partner were present, the victim would place his bare feet or hands against the stomach, or under each *axilla* (*sč'ɬč' maxn* or *snč'máxn* - "armpit") of his companion. Allopathic medicine, however, refuses to utilize snow, contending it would be exceedingly detrimental to circulation.

An important medicinal plant product within the Spokan pharmacopoeia was *soft pine pitch* (*piqt'éɬtn*), which was effective in treating many types of dermal infections: acting as a poultice for furuncles and carbuncles, curing bacterial skin infections, and curing what were probably staphylococcal infections (*impetigo contagiosa*) of the skin. The removal of an insect's stinger was usually accomplished with *split* (*nsq'ew'sí*) wood tweezers, a fresh bivalve shell, or with a small bit of pitch. Pitch was also warmed, sometimes mixed with white clay, and placed while warm on follicular infections and herpes simplex. A handful of *pitchy, bare tips of ponderosa pine trees* (*snssaʔtqʷłpqn'*) would be snipped off, boiled and applied to wounds in order to prevent swelling and infection. Repeated applications were used if necessary.

Cutaneous skin irritation and minor subcutaneous pain were treated by rubbing the warmed grease from a beaver's scent gland, which was rubbed on the site until the skin was dry, the grease having been absorbed.

The Spokan used *insect gall* (*sccǔpeʔ* or *siscǔpeʔ*)—the diseased tumorous growths of certain plant tissue, produced by the larvae of *female gall wasps* (*Biorrhtza pallida - sqʷuʔł*) on deciduous bushes; but some practitioners preferred gall taken from rose bushes, and from some other shrubs too. After the long nodules were collected, dried, and crushed to produce a fine red powder, this was mixed with grease or tallow, and smeared daily upon the afflicted areas for minor infections. Once the gall was ground and mixed with fish oil or rendered animal fat, a bright red color appeared. Insect gall was also believed to effectively treat vitiligo (leukoderma), a rare condition in which there is temporary or secondary *depigmentation of melanin* (*pʔáq'lʔeʔmús* or *sčʔqʔltčísc* - "white patches") in sharply demarcated areas of the skin. It was said that this treatment did restore some skin color, even after the *medicament* (*sascupeʔ* or *scupeʔ*) was removed. Elders further claimed that there once were explanations for this condition, but are now forgotten. However, they all agreed that the condition developed in the fetus during a woman's pregnancy. The same medicinal mixture was used to treat teenage acne and impetigo, an acute inflammatory skin disease. An oral account described how at one time the fine dust-like powder from plant gall would be used by a sorcerer, when in a *crowd* (*xʷeit sqelixʷ*) of people, by surreptitiously blowing a small amount in the face of an unsuspecting victim to inflict illness. Another treatment for vitiligo was to gather sap from the lumps on the rose bush, which was then dried, powdered, and mixed with boiled deer hoofs, and powdered red hematite as a medication for *loss of skin pigmentation* (*pʔaqleʔm*). Since gall contains approximately sixty-six percent tannic acid, it was understandably effective as a pigment upon human skin or for dyeing fabric.

At puberty, both pre-pubescent boys and pre-menarchial girls could be afflicted with *acne* (*čpukʷalqʷ* or *čpukʷpkʷalqʷ*), and were cured by repeated applications of red hematite powder mixed with animal fat, which after drying, leaves a red patch. Acne was also treated by powdering lumps of insect gall mixed with a small amount of fat to hold the powder on the afflicted area, and a few elderly women recalled how snowberries (*Symphoricarpos albus*) were crushed and the paste liberally applied on acne and to dermal sores.

The sap from *aspen* (*Populus tremuloides* Michx. - *mʔlʔmʔltéłp* or *mel'meletełp*) was an important internal medicament, and until recently the peeled aspen bark was used by a few elders to make an infusion that was drunk or mixed with other *materia medica* and applied externally to treat certain dermal eruptions and a variety of skin diseases. Scrapings from the inside of *aspen bark* (*mʔλmλté*) were crushed and heated in water to make a bitter, yellow-colored infusion that was drunk unadulterated, or mixed with other plant substrates and then applied externally to cure dermal rash and certain skin eruptions, such as a *scab* (*henc'aʔróslqʷpi*), boils or an *abscess* (*pʔpʔt'íč'*) and carbuncle sores, particularly *open* or *weeping sores* (*wixt*). The last Spokan practitioner claimed that administering a spoonful of boiled aspen bark tea every hour was the best, and described how this infusion was effective when poured over a severe dermal eruption. One caution was that all the aspen bark scrapings must be carefully hidden until the patient had been cured, and only then were the scrapings carefully collected and burned. People were cautioned to never purposely remove a scab, but rather have the *scab fall off naturally* (*nt'ehxʷk'ʷus*); and then ritually disposed of by burying, never burning.

But more often the fresh aspen leaves were placed with pieces of dried aspen bark, crushed in a mortar, heated with a small amount of tallow, and, upon cooling, placed on a rash or dermal infection. A mild rash could be treated by mashing snowberries, mixing with warm water to make a paste, and applying that directly to the afflicted area, and repeating as needed. Snowberries made an effective poultice when mashed and applied as a cold paste to the site. Prickly-pear cactus, after removing the spiny skin, would be heated, mashed to a paste, and applied every few hours as a poultice or for treating a rash. *Powdered pine pitch* (*čp'q'ʷíc'ʔis*) was used externally to treat babies and adults with general body rash. A medicine man was known to request a person with severe rash to bathe in a warm solution made of the crushed roots of aspen or yarrow.

A *blister on the heel* (*hekʷkʷ epšn* or *čłč'mepšn*) or a *blister on the toe* (*hekʷkʷqʷšin*) could be treated by opening the swelling with a sharp plant spine - several were always carried in a person's belt pouch. A medicine for *foot rash* (*sptakšn*) was to gather fresh thornberry leaves, which were folded and placed in moccasins and then crushed by pounding the moccasin with a wooden mallet or stout piece of edge-rounded wood. Treating a blister was never considered a serious procedure—the major concern being infection. Apart from oral history, there are unfortunately no known records to support the claim that the highly contagious disease impetigo (*contagiosa*) set in once children were sent to mission and government schools, which had environments of questionable hygiene. Without any documentation, one can only assume that crowded boarding school environments were ideal conditions for spreading various infectious diseases (Collins 2000:472). These types of lesions consist of pustules that spread easily among babies and small children, and apparently it was believed that a successful and common treatment for impetigo was to place the underside of warmed sections of alder or aspen bark directly onto the afflicted sites. However, once children returned home they resumed the daily practice of bathing.

The sour-smelling roots of mountain valerian (*Valeriana sitchensis* Bong., ssp. *sitchensis*) were boiled in water to make a paste-like solution, used primarily as an antiphlogistic treatment for skin inflammation; moreover, the dried and powdered roots had some effect as an antiseptic, when dusted on open wounds and cuts, but the best results were obtained when the dried roots were made into a paste using marrow or grease. Some claimed that the plant's sour odor was the principal reason for the effectiveness of this medicine .Thus, it was used externally as a geo-medicament for the treatment of different types of skin maladies, particularly *severe dermal eruptions* (*čpócc'eʔ* or *pucm*) and scabies from itch mites or *nits* (*Sarcoptes scabiei* - *č'č'stin'eʔ*).

In winter, the chapped lips of adults and children were treated by working deer tallow into the lips; but prior to application, the person could blow the heat from a hot coal onto another's lips or carefully inhale for self-treatment, thereby facilitating the distribution and penetration of tallow. In an emergency—when away from the village—a man might rub ear wax upon his lips to reduce his discomfort (Smith 1936-8:1070). Bone marrow, preferably that of deer, was another treatment for chapped lips and hands. When one's skin became cracked due to severely cold weather and bled, the condition was known as *sw'aw'íʔxʷ*.

Tea made from the decoctions of mashed, steeped yarrow was used extensively as a diaphoretic to increase perspiration. Warm, mashed yarrow leaves were used to reduce minor skin irritations and moderate pain, being replaced as needed.

Warts

Apparently, the most common of all dermal afflictions was the *wart* (*sy'ey'úkʷeʔ* - "to be stingy") and the Spokan sometimes attributed a person's warts to his contact with any insect or animal, or to his behavior. Warts were removed by tying a slip knot made from a horse tail hair or a thinly cut piece of rawhide or buck skin, and simply pulling the wart out by the roots. Some preferred to apply a small amount of pitch to the wart before pulling it, whereas others would simply burn the wart away with the end of a hot stick. Warts were commonly permitted to grow in size, at which point they could be cut with sharp obsidian, or later with a knife. A combination of these two approaches was to first encircle the growth with a piece of horsehair, to contain and raise the wart by gently pulling it, and then cut the wart with a sharp piece of obsidian or knife. Warts were never worn off with sandstone or incised off.

There have been various explanations of the causes and appearances of different types of contagious and benign epithelial tumors and warts. Consequently, their etiologies and treatments differed. The most *common wart* (*Verrucae vulgares*) was called *xi č'ł špcinct* ("it may grow on your neck"), thought to have been sent by a sorcerer as a sign of death, unless removed. Warm white conifer pitch, mixed with lard, was commonly applied to warts, generally after bathing or leaving the sweathouse.

The bruised leaves of common dandelion (*Taraxacum officinale*) exude a white, sticky, rubbery, milk-like substance which was applied directly to a wart. Unknown to the Spokan, the ubiquitous dandelion roots are rich in potassium, beta carotene, and beneficial endesmanolides, taraxacins, and eudesmanolides, and were also used as a strong diuretic. The leaves of mountain dandelion were steeped as tea as a diabetic medicine, and the leaf greens were eaten raw in the spring as a blood purifier.

Neoplasms

All ideas regarding neoplasms, both benign and malignant tumors, were largely speculation, since prior to contact with Euro-American introduced diseases, most Spokan knew few types of tumors. Neoplasms invariably occur internally and some can be detected only during an autopsy, which was never done. There is no evidence the Spokan diagnosed what may have been more obvious tumors, such as nasopharyngeal or oropharyngeal candidiasis (thrush) neoplasms. Lord noted that during his travels he never observed an instance of goiter, saying that "Goitre [sic] does not exist on this side of the Rocky Mountains" (1866, 1:236).

The traditional Spokan diet was high in iodine-rich foods, such as various species of fish—a diet that would not have led to exophthalmic goiter, if such a condition existed. And yet the Spokan had terms for *goiter*, *hec ʔiɫnm* or *snskʷsqʼmeltn*, claiming that there was no known effective treatment, only the application of heated *mullein leaves* (*smén'xʷ*) to the swollen area for temporary relief. Mullein was an introduced plant (Turner, pers. comm.).

However, certain benign and malignant neoplasms—as diagnosed by oncologists—were sometimes treated by sucking shamans, often when a person wanted to follow a more conservative regimen, and did not want such radical treatments as surgery, radiation, or chemotherapy. One such case of conservative treatment was related by a particularly powerful and rather successful curing shaman many years ago:

> A white woman whose husband was Indian was told she probably had cancer. Well, the doctors wanted to open her up right away; get it out. Her husband knew of me and called if I'd help, which I did. I was careful to explain to her everything I was going to do, and she said OK. After sweating and praying much of the day, I started working on her when it was dark, and I sucked on her belly [umbilicus] off and on for several hours, stopping every once and a while to dance and sing one of my songs. Before dawn I left, but first told her she had to firmly believe I had cured her. A week later her mother came and insisted she go to the hospital for the surgery. But first they x-rayed her and she had no great lump in her stomach. She was cured (Ross 1968-2008).

Maligning a person was a serious matter and, as stated earlier, often resulted in grave consequences as evidenced some years ago when an unfortunate case of throat cancer occurred involving a Plains Indian who conducted a type of year-round camp that catered to many international clientele in an area south of the Spokane Indian Reservation. After the man died, the *Times* of England had an obituary of his death, saying he died of throat cancer, and subscribing to the Doctrine of Signatures principle, various Spokan elders who knew of him were all of the same opinion that he contracted cancer of the throat because he had instructed non-Indians regarding spiritual ways, but even more grievous and sacrilegious, was how the man permitted men and women to sweat together. There was consensus among the elders that this was the reason why the man had died of throat cancer, an unfortunate but applicable example of the Doctrine of Signatures.

Another case of speech paralysis caused by throat cancer was related many years ago by a well known Spokan curing shaman who, before his death, travelled throughout the Northwest with the author to cure Indians. He explained how many years ago he treated an Indian on the Flathead Reservation in western Montana:

> An old man who had been a great tribal leader, but had to give up his tribal office because he could hardly speak. He once always used to laugh and could speak of great and wonderful things for his people. His family told me his illness stopped him from speaking, even singing because an evil man had placed an evil lump on the

man's vocal cords. I waited, as always, 'til it was all dark outside, and then my *sumé* came into my body. My hands were shaking, but I could still pass them over and around his throat, and only then did I remove the bloody lump from his throat. After several days, the man could sing, laugh, and tell his people once again of great things (Ross 1968-2008).

A treatment for throat cancer, which is still used by several elderly women, is to collect strips of hemlock bark, always before dawn or after evening darkness. In both cases, the woman gave a prayer of thanksgiving to the tree, and a prayer to her *sumé* for successful treatment. The collector always stripped away the inside of the bark strips and dried the scrapings using the heat from a wood fire, never placing the material in the sun. The dry scrapings were steeped in hot water and drunk as a tea twice a day, always just before dawn and the second dose after darkness.

Hematomas and Swellings

A common and apparently effective treatment for sprains, swellings, and trauma hematomas of ankles was to place wood or lava ashes in boiling water, and submerging the ankle or other site until the solution cooled; the solution was then reheated and the procedure repeated three times. Some contend that certain hematomas were opened, immediately if possible, with a thorn or any available sharp object. A person would always be careful not to have any contact with the withdrawn blood, and the site would always be flushed with any number of infusions.

Some swellings were more difficult to treat, depending upon what was determined to be the cause. Only soft swellings were typically treated externally with medicines, usually with cold compresses made from padded, folded buckskin that had been soaked in cool water. Some said that powdered clay would be first sprinkled on such a swelling, and that fresh meat was thought to be of some effect in reducing swelling. More difficult to cure were hard deep sub-dermal masses or tumors near the skin's surface, which were apparently never incised. As cited earlier, there were several incidents reported of hard internal tumors being removed by a curing shaman using traditional ritual procedures.

Wounds and Burn Therapy

Given the extensive use of open fire and hot stones, elders maintained that burns were rather common—certainly among unsupervised and crawling children. The initial treatment was to immediately immerse the affected part in cold water or pour cold water over the burned area. Fresh aspen leaves, if available, were bruised before soaking and the under side applied directly to the burned area for about an hour, or, until the leaves appeared to be drying, at which point they would be replaced with newly soaked leaves. Aspen leaves were also applied to boils and sores, and generally served as material for a broad spectrum poultice.

Burns could also be treated by using the leaves of a common broad-leaved plantain (*Plantago major* - *čnłmłmqeʔéneʔ* - "chipmunk's tail" or "frog leaf"). The leaves were softened by rubbing several together, so that the liquids were released onto the burn, atop of which the bruised leaves would be placed, not unlike a poultice. What is interesting about the leaves of this plant is their absorbent ability; they were used also on areas of suppuration. The leaves were changed when suppuration commenced to *soak through* (*n'lpác'*) the wrappings. Fresh leaves and stems of kinnikinnick served as a decoction for numerous antihemorrhagic dermatological problems, and also mashed or rubbed together to soften them to release their liquid, and then applied directly to any small burn.

A method for treating burns was to first cover the site with fresh, wet *black cottonwood* (*P. balsamifera* L. ssp. *trichocarpa* [T. & G.] - *mulš*); the leaves would be applied and replaced until the pain was gone. A rather questionable procedure was also described–how mature cattails were used in burn therapy by mixing the catkin fluff or down with animal grease and finely ground clay and the applying it to burned areas.

Another method for treating burns was to cover the burn with the crushed, dry sporangia of sword fern (*Polystichum munitum*).

An important source of medicinal greens was hydrophytes gathered from streams, ponds, and marshes. For example, the Spokan used fresh water stream algae (*Spirogyra* spp. - *nmtrʔétkʷ*) for treating burns that had blistered, a procedure, as described by Turner *et al.* (1990:69) for the Thompson Indians, which also gathered the slimy green algae from the stream by twisting a stick to which the algae hung. The algae was then carefully placed upon the burn blister as a poultice. This treatment was repeated as needed.

The dry seeds of *Coyote's bow and arrow* (*Pterospora andromedea* Nutt. - *spílyeʔ tʼapmí*), sometimes called giant bird-nest, or pine drops, were ground to a powder and applied directly to a burn. An old method used by both the Kalispel and Spokan for treating burns was to mash any animal's brains and mix them with soot that had been collected from the top edges of tule mats where the smoke had been emitted for some time (Smith 1936-8:1080), and applied to the burn.

Again, the value of yellow pond lily is cited, when the leaves were dried and ground into a powder, which were saved for sprinkling on open surface wounds to stop bleeding and presumably prevent infection. Upon healing, a *wound* (*sɫxʷú*) treated in this manner never produced a *scar* (*sqxtʼím* or *sqʼtím*). When in the woods, away from a camp or village, pitch and resin were often used to draw out the pus of an infected wound. Fresh or dried roots of valerian (*Valeriana sitchensis*) were pulverized and applied directly to wounds, preventing infection and helping to heal them.

Cardiovascular

There is consensus within the contemporary medical community that—prior to that unfortunate transformation of deculturation—there once had been no known cardiovascular disease among the Spokan. Cardiovascular problems accompanied and were exacerbated by a radical change in diet—from one of moderate caloric intake of fish, vegetables, fruits, and low cholesterol meats, to a diet of simple, refined carbohydrates and the unvaried products of monocropping. One can only speculate as to the full significance of how the Spokan traditional medical system attempted to adapt to the devastating consequences after being exposed to a broad spectrum of Euro-American introduced pathogens. The many physiopsychological ramifications of this pathological condition were probably never fully realized by the Spokan, nor did they recognize the accumulative adverse effects of a radically different diet and physical activities. Undoubtedly, they must have struggled to develop prophylactic procedural rituals and pharmacological treatments for dealing with certain non-traditional illnesses and diseases, such as cardiovascular problems and even diabetes. Unfortunately, traditional medicaments and procedures were ineffective for cardiovascular afflictions, and new Spokan words have been recently introduced into their lexicon, such as *heart murmur* (*nɫxʷlxʷpméls*), *tachycardia* (*ɫxʷlxʷpʼmʼelʼs* - "heart skipped a beat"), *arrhythmia* (*ɫxʷɫxʷɫels*), and *angina* (*skʼʷupʼpʼi*). No one can say how extensively were physiological cardiovascular conditions acknowledged. Yet the Spokan did recognize certain named heart "problems" caused by psychological pressures.

Prior to Euro-American contact, the only prevalent cardiac episodes were the occasional *heartburn* (*čewʼwʼenʼnʼ* or *ʼrʼpels* or *čɫʎʼlltín*), what some termed *čʔulpspʔús* ("the heart quivers") from occasional over-indulgence to rich foods, a condition that could occur when going from eating dry stored foods during the winter months to a radically different diet of fresh deer meat and fish. A common treatment for heartburn was to chew the root of fringed sage northern wormwood (*Artimisia frigida* Willd.). In the spring, heartburn was caused by eating too much salmon. McDonald said heart disease was uncommon to the Indian (Howay *et al.* 1917, 3:212).

Most Spokan elders believed that the cause of *heartache* (*čcʼeʔrʼels*), or the patient's *cause of death* (*čʼɫʎlltin*), was not always physiological, but due to emotional reasons—usually typical of younger unmarried people. Small bits of *Ligusticum verticillatum* [Geyer] Coult. & Rose, a species related to wild licorice root,

622

were mashed and steeped in hot water as a tea for treating perceived heart problems (often only indigestion). Some elders claimed that *deer vetch* (*Vicia americana*) seeds, perhaps from another species of vetch plant (*Lotus corniculatus* [S. Wats.] Greene.), were crushed and diluted with hot water to make a tea that acted as a sedative to treat tachycardia.

Prior to the services of the Indian Health Service, a person thought to have rheumatic fever was treated by a curing shaman who made an infusion from freshly peeled alder bark (which contains salicin, also found in the bark and leaves of willow trees, particularly willow). The peeled bark turns orange on the underside when exposed to air, and it was steeped in hot water and drunk as a tea to treat rheumatic fever. The same medicine was routinely given for heartburn. Until relatively recently, and prior to modern medicaments, persons with high blood pressure ate raw *green peppers* (*Capsicum annuum* - *snxʷúxʷy'e?tn*).

When a man had a heart attack, he was placed in a sitting position, and a practitioner, if available, would press forcefully with one hand against the man's *sternum* (*sqqámqm*), and with the other hand press inward against the man's back. The pressure was released and repeated if necessary.

Bleeding

Most lacerations and cuts were minor and rather common when working with lithics, particularly obsidian. If pressure failed to clot the wound, then *coagulation of the blood* (*snxʷúl*) became a concern. If available, an individual could place a wad of *cobwebs* (*sčqʷsélp*) directly on the cut, thereby creating a chemical reaction (thrombolysis) between the blood platelets and the cobweb, which contains active vasoconstrictor substances, as well as several plasma proteins. Grandmothers always carried a small wad of cobwebs for treating minor cuts of grandchildren. This in turn causes the release of phospholipids that contribute to thromboplastin generation, thereby serving as a hemostat or styptic. Physically, the mesh structure of cobwebs greatly enhances immediate release of those chemicals responsible for coagulation. The clinical effectiveness and range of general utilization of cobwebs as coagulants was evidenced by the constant practice of collecting any cobwebs they found by both men and women, and storing in a stiff, dry salmon skin.

Externally, minor skin wounds were disinfected with a solution made from boiling the scrapings from the inner bark of tamarack in water. Some elders claimed freshly ground horse radish could be applied to minor scratches; this presumably drew the ends of the wound together, prevented infection and never caused scarring. If available, chocolate tips were gathered, mashed, and placed on small cuts to stop bleeding. To coagulate a bleeding wound, the crushed roots of barren strawberry (*Drymocallis arguta* [Pursh] Rydb.) were applied to the site, sometimes placed on duck down if possible. Small pieces of Canby's lovage coagulate the blood when pressed onto a minor cut. Crushed catnip leaves were pressed into cuts or minor scrapes before bandaging.

When available, freshly mashed leaves of the perennial herb *goldenrod* (*Solidago canadensis* L. var. *scabra* Torr. & A. Gray - *nt'ekʷʷsésml'š* or *pupawl'ákʷa?* or *S. spathulata* DC. var. *neomexicana* [Gray] Crong), were placed on abrasions or minor open wounds to stop bleeding—a treatment that was an antiseptic one although they did not know it. What they did not know was that the leaves, flowering tops, and seeds contain saponins that are antifungal, serving as an antiseptic, anti-inflammatory, astringent, and a diaphoretic. A decoction of mashed leaves and seeds was drunk as an abortifacient.

A once traditional method for treating a small bleeding wound was to take the fruit of blue elderberry, when in season, crush the seeds, boil them, and upon cooling applying the result directly to the wound to stop minor *bleeding* (*mlál'*). It has been stated that the same treatment was used upon cattle or horses that had cuts from barbed wire (STHC).

The gray-green leaves of an unidentified plant were used as a bandage; after it was first rolled between one's fingers, peeled apart, dampened, and applied to small cuts. The leaves of this plant were also used to

623

treat eczema and sores (STHC). Another method for stopping external bleeding was to take red willow (*Cornus sericea*) bark and chew it before placing it directly on the wound, or it was sometimes bound to the site. Placing powdered willow (*Salix* sp.) bark directly on the wound was reputed to stop minor bleeding and was supposed to be good for abrasions.

Some recall this method of using willow bark also being used as a treatment for muscle soreness, but the decoction was first warmed before applying. A few elders recall that when a person was away from his settlement, and suffered a cut, almost any type of berry was mashed and placed directly on the *open wound* (*slxʷup*), which often stopped the bleeding. Berries have astringent properties, as most acid-bearing plants have, and they probably reduce infection. The ubiquitous yarrow served to stop superficial external bleeding; for that several leaves are mashed and applied to the wound. If the wound was painful, the plant's root was also gathered and mashed with the leaves. Some recall the use of shredded dry willow bark being sprinkled on superficial cuts.

In the case of a person cutting, but not severing a major *blood vessel* (*q'áq'łuʔ*), the accepted treatment was to apply continual pressure until the blood hopefully coagulated. The Spokan had a thorough knowledge of comparative anatomy, and understood an animal's arterial system and the inevitable consequences of excessive blood loss, and were cognizant of major pressure points for certain main surface arteries. Unfortunately, they had no method for stopping major arterial bleeding, since the aforementioned application of pressure would hardly be life-saving in the case of major arterial bleeding, even a major surface artery. In such a case, the person knew he would die.

However, some claimed abdominal internal hemorrhaging was treated by drinking an infusion of mashed roots of *Columbia puccoon* or *Western stoneseed* (*Lithospermum ruderale* Dougl. ex Lehm - *siy'áy'ts'kʷn* - "hard on top" or *čcemenálw* or *čcmnálw* or *cmcmlqíxʷ*), which may suggest the Doctrine of Signatures, since the long mashed taproots yield a red dye roots, used to make a red dye (Teit 1930:218; Turner, *et al.* 1980:91). It was believed that this plant would treat internal hemorrhaging–sometimes called bloodroot—if an infusion of this liquid was drunk. Puccoon seeds were also mashed and often mixed with crushed roots to make a concoction that was drunk for treating internal bleeding. Smith (1936-8:1220) also claimed the mashed taproots of puccoon were used as a paint and sometimes added to medicinal concoctions for a bit of flavor if the patient was a child.

The gummy exudate of black western chokecherry was mixed with an unknown plant and drunk to treat postpartum bleeding. The mashed roots of the small *fruited bulrush (Scirpus microcarpus - šetpwícyeʔ)* hydrophyte were reputed to have been used as a medicine.

Interestingly, knowledge of "bleeding and the heart" was extended to affairs of the heart. For example, it *bleeds after removal* (*t'ehʷk'ʷséltn* - "twice wounded") was an explanation for a clinical condition called cardiomyopathy, or more commonly a broken heart of a loved one, the notion being that after a scab falls off, the wound will bleed again (STHC). As mentioned, the Spokan recognized whipping as a form of punishment, but never used any physical castigation severe enough to result in deep wounds with copious bleeding. A decoction to stop intestinal bleeding, or for use whenever there was blood in the stool, was made from the mashed roots of goldenrod; first being steeped by boiling, and then strained and drunk as needed.

Mountain juniper (*Juniperus communis*) branches and berries were mashed with a wood pestle and mixed with warm water to make a thick poisonous solution, which, when brushed on projectile points would kill deer or in warfare. A medical use was to make diluted solution of scrapped juniper bark and mashed needles, which was drunk to treat internal bleeding or hemorrhaging.

Yarrow, as noted, was a broad spectrum medicine, unknowingly containing chamazulene and various chemically active properties, which include anti-inflammatory and anti-spasmodic properties, thereby making yarrow effective for the treatment of numerous maladies. These properties were made available for curing by steeping freshly mashed yarrow stems and leaves in hot—but not boiling—water, and drinking it as a treatment for any internal bleeding that may have been indicated in the patient's urine or feces. The Spokan understood that a possible cause of blood in the urine was that the person received a traumatic blow to the kidneys.

There is no indication that the Spokan ever attempted *to bleed* (*čhitemsk*ʷ or *chik*ʷ*emsk*ʷ or *m'l'il'*) a sick person by phlebotomy or venesection as therapy, nor did they resort to moxibustion as a form of mortification for skin maladies or to cauterize deep arrow or bullet wounds after extracting the missile. When relating old accounts of Euro-American phlebotomy to some elders, there was consensus that it was a cruel and unnecessary medical procedure, claiming they never used what may be termed phlebotomy to release the pressure of a large hematoma. And yet, according to Cox, the Flathead did practice a form of phlebotomy, "For contusions they generally bleed, either in the temples, arms, wrists, or ankles, with pieces of sharp flint, or heads of arrows: they however preferred being bled with the lancet, and frequently brought us patients, who were much pleased with the mode of operation" (1832:125). However, there was an account of abdominal surgery, "I have also seen them cut open the belly with a knife, extract a large quantity of fat from the inside, sew up the part again, and the patient soon after perfectly recovered" (Ross 1849, 7:290).

Following the then-still-popular European practice of phlebotomy, Whitman (1802-1847), in one of sixty letters to Walker (Whitman, December, 1843:np), described, "I think it was favorable that you were bled and that it relieved you, but I do not think it strange that you were weaker after it [...] if you are no better, you may want more bleeding to the neck if pain continues in the head" (Drury 1976:259). William H. Gray, who studied medicine for sixteen weeks in the early 1830s in New England, though never graduated, preferred to be called Doctor Gray, and recommended and assisted Walker in bleeding, "An old Indian quite sick. Was bled this evening which offered him some relief (Drury 1973, 1:426). Alexander Ross wrote generally of the Flathead group and of their "knowledge of phlebotomy, none can be more expert and successful" (1904:308).

Blood Purifiers

With no knowledge of hematology per se, the Spokan believed—as do nearly all people—after enduring a long winter of environmental stress and certain deprivations, that the body could be rejuvenated if certain rituals and procedures were followed, not unlike the obvious annual ceremonies associated with the rebirth of Nature. Different floral medicaments were taken to *cleanse* or *flush* (*ƛ'áq's*) one's system. The already cited malodorous plant *Valeriana edules* (*msáw'i*ʔ), with greenish-yellow flowers, was considered a powerful blood purifier. Many people preferred to make a blood purifier by cutting pieces of *m'sm'sáw'i*ʔ root into boiling water, and then drink the solution. Others preferred to chew the raw root, a treatment once used for skin disorders such as boils and open sores.

The pits of chokecherries were mashed in a stone mortar and pestle, and then boiled in water to make a rather strong decoction, which was strained before drinking as a blood purifier. Another technique was to gather young *Douglas-fir tips* (*nc'c'q'áłpqn'*), boil them whole in water, and drink as a tea. A well-known blood purifier was an infusion made from crushed foamberries (*Shepherdia canadensis*), which was also drunk as a tonic. Some have said that the *leaves* (*sčq'*ʷ*x̣*ʷ*nxes*) of this plant were sometimes mashed and boiled with the berries. By preference, a spring tonic was also made from steeping the leaves of *alumroot* (*Heuchera cylindrica* Dougl. ex Hook., var. *cylindrica* - *hititmn'ełp*); it was also used for treating fatigue, stress, trauma and general malaise. Alumroot, which contains antioxidants, was used extensively for internal and external maladies, particularly for children. Crushed fresh alum root leaves were used as an astringent and in the treatment for diarrhea and as an all-purpose dermal astringent.

Cinquefoil roots (*Potentilla gracilis* Dougl. ex. Hook - *npaqčn'e*) were mashed and steeped in hot water and drunk in early spring as a blood purifier. It was reported how the Okanogan-Colville also used this tea for treating diarrhea and gonorrhea (Turner *et al.*1980:127).

Menstruation and Birthing

Certain difficulties associated with birthing have been discussed earlier. One concern was nausea, most commonly treated by steeping fresh or dried red raspberry (*Rubus idaeus*) leaves in boiling water, letting it cool, and drinking it as needed, a concoction often flavored with mint (*Mentha arevnsis*) leaves. There are now only few accounts of bark from the *raspberry bush* (*snw'esšn'eɫp*) being scraped and used as an infusion. Unknown to the Spokan were the minerals contained in raspberry tea that were beneficial to a menstruating woman:

> The berries and leaves are rich in iron and they contain minerals—phosphorus, potassium, magnesium— which help build the blood by carrying iron from stores in the liver, spleen and bone marrow to needy tissues, particularly the reproductive organs in particular. [...] Its action on the uterus assists contractions and checks hemorrhage during labor and delivery. After delivery, it strengthens and cleanses the system and enriches the mother's milk supply. Raspberry leaf tea helps stimulate and promote normal menstrual function (Cook 1984:34).

One elderly woman recalled her mother scraping small bits of the inside of smooth sumac (*Rhus glabra*) bark to make a tea that aided in ameliorating her *nausea* (*smčky*ʔɫcí or čpxʷpqnéltni), and further afforded the sufferer a general sense of well-being. A mild solution of finely ground white clay was drunk to achieve the same benefits for a person with nausea, for either a male or female. Morning sickness was commonly treated by making an infusion from several small broken sections of chokecherry branches steeped into boiling water, which upon cooling was drunk as needed. Another treatment for morning sickness was to steep the young mashed tips of Douglas fir in hot water for drinking, as it was believed the pain would stick to the *pitch* (*sƛ'ƛ'úk'ʷeʔ*), and thus ameliorated.

Gynecological and Obstetrical Treatments

Given the nature of the topic, there exists little recorded information concerning traditional classifications of gynecological and obstetrical problems, as well as the treatments used by earlier and more traditional Spokan women. Men were seldom privy to such knowledge, and, until recently, there was consensus among women that such matters were discussed almost exclusively among themselves; not with men, even one's husband. With few exceptions, men were excluded from observing or discussing women's obstetrical troubles, which were not thought to be the concern of men, but only serve to make the women unduly nervous. The confinement of women to the menstrual hut, and beliefs about contamination, simply added to the lack of knowledge by men regarding such matters. A man was even excluded from his wife's delivery.

The more common gynecological problems occurred during menstruation. In the case of leukorrhea, there would be an abnormal discharge from the genital tract; and it involved only the vulva, rarely the vagina. This condition could occur in a woman or girl at any age. For the Spokan, there was only one known treatment, a mother or grandmother packed the patient's labia with mashed blackberries, which, as reported by elderly women, would eventually stem the discharge. The same treatment was apparently used to alleviate menopausal symptoms (Cook 1984:33-35). An alternate method to alleviate *menstrual cramps* (*nckʷeɫšnm* - "to have cramps") was to take the leaves of catnip, possessing medicinal properties; they were either chewed or steeped in hot water in order to release an oil that is now known as nepetalactone isomers, that acts as a mild sedative. Either skunk cabbage or the bark of *high bush cranberry* (*Viberum pauci florium* Raf. - *qʷlís*) were scraped, mashed and made into an infusion which was drunk as needed to alleviate menstrual cramps.

In the past, women experiencing dysmenorrhea (painful menstruation), or who had no pain but only nausea and some vomiting, or suffered from a sense of pelvic fullness, would often find temporary relief with hydrotherapy (Julie Ross 1963:47). The woman was often assisted by another woman who would excavate a relatively round hole approximately a meter in depth immediately adjacent to a stream. When completed, a narrow channel was dug to divert enough water to fill the hole. After damming the channel, three or more heated *visceral basalt stone* (*slaq'ist sšenš* - "porous stones") were placed in the excavation, covered with copious cedar boughs. If cedar boughs were not available, a large Douglas-*fir branch* (*sčc'q'łpéčst*) was substituted. With the stones in place, the *dam* (*stqép*) was opened briefly to fill the hole, then closed again. After the water was heated, the woman entered the pool by stepping on the boughs, some of which made contact with the hot stones and would sit until the water was cool. This hydrotherapeutic procedure was repeated at least three times, each time emptying and then replenishing the reservoir before renewing the hot rocks and fresh cedar or fir boughs. Menstruation was presumably increased (emmenagogue) by drinking an infusion of fresh catnip leaves.

Smith (1936-8:939-940) described how early in the morning the Kalispel and Chewelah-Spokan women used a variation of the aforementioned hydrotherapy procedure as a treatment when experiencing amenorrhea. A stream-filled side-hole, large enough for a woman to sit in water up to her chest, was first filled with water that was brought to a boil by submerging as many heated stones as necessary. After removing the stones, several handfuls of mashed roots of horse radish (an introduced plant) were thrown into the pit of boiling water. Being an oily plant, the roots sank to the bottom and the oil remained on the surface, where the scent and texture of the oil benefited the patient. Some believed the heated earth under the rocks was more beneficial than the heated water. When a woman experienced difficult dysmenorrhea she would sometimes drink a warm infusion of mashed strawberries or snowberries, repeating it if needed.

An infant with *colic* (*nc'er'enč*) was given a paste of finely ground white clay, and small amounts were placed by the mother in to the infant's mouth. After the Spokan commenced growing horse radish—an introduced plant—it was crushed and mixed with powdered white clay, and; similarly administered orally in small bits to an infant experiencing colic. Or, after steeping either the root or the bark of snowberry in hot water, a piece of buckskin was saturated and placed in the mouth of the afflicted baby to suck for relief of colic. Another procedure was to take a small piece of buckskin soaked in an infusion of *catnip* (*Nepeta cararia* L. - *tkʷikʷágy'kst*), which was hand-held in the infant's mouth to suck on. A significant number of elder women agreed that when the cradleboard and baby pouch was used, there were fewer incidents of colic. To support this belief, contemporary pediatricians note that many cases of colic have been successfully treated when a parent snugly swaddles the baby, particularly when traveling or walking (Czorny, pers. comm.).

Trillium was used for various postnatal problems experienced by nursing mothers. Unfortunately, few of the elderly women could recall neither the details of how this plant was prepared nor the specifics of application, or, in most cases the trillium rhizome was crushed, heated, and applied as a paste to treat the sore nipples of a nursing mother. Some claimed that trillium was also used to treat menstrual discomfort, which suggests that the rhizome or the leaves were rendered as a decoction and drunk.

Several oral accounts describe how various accomplished older mid-wives were successful in treating infrequent cases of an implanted placenta, separated prematurely from the uterus (*abrutio placentae*) and uteral prolapse. In all cases, the concern was not with the apparent pain, but rather with if there was severe hemorrhage or total placenta previa, which often meant fetal loss and even the woman's life. In order to prevent a woman from having a large baby and difficult delivery, a concoction of mashed stalks and leaves of *mountain ladyslipper* (*Cypripedium montanum* Dougl. - *c'sqáqne? qe?šíš*) was steeped in hot water and drunk as a tea.

Probably fewer difficulties of delivery existed prior to the reservation period, though it was related how on different occasions a woman required the assistance of an older midwife or female family member who was known to be experienced in helping a woman who was having difficulty in expelling the fetus after delivery. On such occasions, a rather standard procedure was for the attendant or midwife to forcibly manipulate the frontal abdominal area with repeated downward motions until delivery. It was not known if any mid-wives had a special skill for this procedure; success was usually based upon experience and

627

confidence. To induce muscle relaxation during and after labor, an infusion of Rocky Mountain juniper needles was given to the woman to drink, and the boiled stems of *lady fern* (*Athyrium filix-femina* [L.] Roth. - *kʷskʷsšen'eɬp* or *skʷskʷsšeneɬp*) was made into a tea to reduce labor pains. The root stocks of this plant were also used to make a tea to reduce general body pains.

The only recalled treatment for lack of breast milk, was to grind the crushed roots of Oregon bitterroot (*Lomatium dissectum*) and make it an infusion. The preparation, treatment, and scheduling was invariably the responsibility of the young mother's mother.

The roots of *false Solomon-seal* (*Maianthemum racemosum* and *S. racemosa* [L.] Desf. - *t'axt*) and star-flowered Solomon's-seal (*Maianthemum stellatum*) were mashed and steeped to make a tea that was drunk to regulate menses. Most homes kept a supply of dried blue elderberry bark which, after boiling and consuming as a tea, would induce vomiting; it was often used as a general *intestinal purge* (*nxʷk'ʷeɬc'e?nct*) for both men and women. If too large a quantity was taken orally it created severe peristalsis; thus, it was sometimes used for inducing an illicit abortion. The topmost leaves and several stems of yarrow were mashed and steeped to make a tea, which when drunk could cause abortion. Another abortifacient decoction was made by steeping the crushed stems and leaves of yellow yarrow (*Achillea millefolium* L. var. *occidentalis*), and drunk as a hot liquid.

Gastrointestinal

Apparently men and women viewed various gastrointestinal maladies in different ways. In the case of a young woman, sexual intercourse and the menarche were sometimes believed to be the cause of *abdominal pain* (*snc'a?aλénč* or *nc'e?renči* - "stomach hurts" or *sp'ac'* - "diarrhea" or *sp'cem'á*). Some post-menarche women felt their abdominal pains were more frequent and severe during the menstrual cycle, or eventually during menopause. As with most patients, it was often difficult to explain what type of pain one was experiencing, or the exact location. For example, if a person *felt like vomiting* (*če?če?t*), there were several explanations such as being poisoned, or simply experiencing a case of *indigestion* (*henc'e?rénči* or *snc'é?r'enč*), or that they were being sorcerized by an object placed in their food, or an object *inserted* (*ncaqʷ*) during sexual intercourse. Whatever the explanation for anorectic disorders, there was agreement that the person was constipated (*nc'opups*), and required a laxative. Depending upon the severity of the *stomach cramps* (*č'e?r'enč*), and if it was felt that the cause was not sorcery, the person might be given a warm draught of juice from prickly-pear to hopefully relieve the pain. It was said that if a man did not smoke, and was suffering from gastrointestinal difficulty, he could easily induce vomiting by inhaling deeply several times from a pipe, or chew and swallow some commercial tobacco. Only a few elders continue to treat problems of mild indigestion by eating four to six—depending upon size—raw bitterroot shoots which were thoroughly chewed before swallowing. Other foods were avoided during treatment.

When seasonally available, the milk juice from freshly mashed *mountain dandelion* (*Agoseris glauca* [Pursh.] Raf. - *snlqʷús*) leaves were administered periodically throughout the day as a laxative or general purgative. The plant was once a medicinal for a woman suffering from depression during her menopause. However, an elderly woman was not sure if the mashed composite seeds of this plant were also given in addition to the mashed leaves, or if a tea was made from a combination of the leaves and seeds. A cathartic infusion of cascara bark or Pursh's buckhorn (*Frangula purshiana*) was made by crushing the plant's bark and mixing with warm water before drinking. Another type of infusion was prepared from the roots, leaves, and stalks of Salmon-colored Collomia (*Collomia grandiflora* Dougl. ex Lindl.), which served as a laxative when constipated.

There is no reliable data regarding the incidence or frequency of peritonitis or appendicitis; On the basis of the diagnostic procedures followed in those days, it must be assumed such conditions existed, but there were known accounts of acute gastroenteritis, caused probably by excessive indulgence in alcohol (in later

628

times), acute amoebic dysentery, or excessive burns (Lyght 1966:555). When describing this condition, several elders say it could have been accidental or intentional (sorcery or murder), and induced by poisons. In usual cases of gastroenteritis, the common treatment was to take only a small quantity of *cottonwood mushroom* (*Polyporus sulphureus* [Bull.] Fr. - *hápu*)—an effective purgative—which, interestingly, was also used for cleaning buckskin. The rhizome of wild ginger was crushed to make a concoction which was drunk as a laxative and to relieve bowel or stomach spasms. There were a wide variety of carminative plants, such as wormwood, yarrow, mugwort, and wild carrot to relieve flatulence, anti-spasmodic activity, and colic, and to relieve abdominal cramps, and to allay intestinal bloating, pain, and spasm.

The glycyrrhetinic acid in tea made from crushed *xásax* affected the digestive tract, serving as an anti-inflammation and an anti-convulsion. Further, licorice root tea promotes a secretion of insulin, thereby protecting the liver from toxin although they did not know it. Fresh juice from mountain blueberries made an effective astringent and decoction remedy for treating acute and chronic stomach and gastrointestinal disorders, including dysentery, colitis, and diarrhea. The sap from aspen was steeped as a tea and also drunk for general digestive problems. A common remedy for diarrhea was to drink a tea from the flower heads of goldenrod.

The earliest known account of treating dysentery with berries was cited by Cox who apparently felt it was necessary to use an indigenous remedy, one presumably recommended by a Spokan:

> From June to the latter end of August they [Spokan] have an abundance of deliciously flavoured salmon, which, from its richness, at first produced a general dysentery among our people. We found the wild raspberries an excellent remedy for this disorder, which was effectively checked by their astringent qualities (1832:223).

A common treatment for *stomach ache* (*nc'aʔƛénč*), general nausea, and constipation, was to dig and boil a handful of yarrow roots, which were eaten for relief when cooled. Another treatment for non-specific abdominal pain was to take small amounts of freshly gathered Oregon grape roots that were boiled, mashed, and then strained through matted grass to make a tea, and drunk; however, too great a quantity could kill the patient. General gastrointestinal discomfort or stomach pain could be treated by boiling mashing juniper berries to make a *tea* (*lití*), often called Indian tea, which would be first strained through a filter of balled grass, before drinking. Juniper berry tea was also given to one *bloated by gas* (*čsuqʷpenč* - "gassed up"). An infusion made from crushed bee-balm leaves was drunk, and considered an effective treatment for upset stomach and general nausea.

According to Elmendorf (1935-6, 2:44), the Spokan collected an unidentified white root known as *xʷét*, that grew predominantly near Wellpinit, and was administered to a person with any stomach pain or disorder. The patient was first wrapped in a blanket or robe and then given a tea made by pouring hot water over the mashed root, stalk, and leaves. Fresh, crushed kinnikinnick berries were placed in a birch bark basket, and boiling water was poured over the mash to make a tea that was drunk as a physic (Elmendorf 1935-6, 1:63). The chewing of too many mashed leaves of *fireweed* (*American angustifolium* L. Scop. - *qʷaqʷaɬqnéɬp*) was known to stupefy a person, but there were no accounts of the Spokan using the plant in such a manner, even though fireweed leaves were chewed as needed for abdominal cramps.

An important plant in the pharmacopoeia was *snow buckwheat* (*Eriogonum niveum* Dougl. ex Benth. - *q'et'bnbwéxʷyneʔ* or *q'et'bnwexʷtbn*), used both externally and internally for treating diarrhea, blood poisoning, and general abdominal maladies. The stems and roots were first mashed and then boiled and drunk as a tea. The mashed leaves of snow buckwheat (Eridgonum niveum) poultice was believed to prevent or treat dermal infection. A medicament for treating abdominal pain due to difficulty of micturition was to mash and boil the entire flat-topped *spiraea plant* (*Spiraea betulifolia* Pall. - *st'št'šɬqéɬp*) to make a concoction that was drunk twice a day.

During Franchère's 1811-1814 stay in the eastern Plateau, he commented upon the exquisite flavor of salmon, an extremely fat and oily fish, and for one unaccustomed to this diet diarrhea was often the result of over indulging. Consequently, "they found a remedy in the raspberries of the country which have an astringent property" (Thwaites 1904, 4:322). A cure for diarrhea was to boil the mashed root of sulfur flower (*Eriogonum heracleoides* Nutt.) to make a tea.

A broad spectrum treatment for gastrointestinal maladies was to grind into bits a section of tamarack bark (sometimes called larch), which were placed in hot water, steeped and then drunk as a tea. Through frequent use it was observed, like so many observed indigenous treatments, how tamarack bark proved beneficial, but now we know that this bark contains the chemical arabinogalactan, now known to be not only a roughage, but apparently beneficial for the gastrointestinal tract, in addition to helping the immune system.

Some elders recalled how in cases of severe abdominal pain, or suspected cases of poisoning, the patient was given a drink of warm water with finely ground burned animal bones (*carbo animalis*), which is endohydric. The charcoal drink was administered three times a day until the pain subsided, and though no longer used, a powdered charcoal drink was also believed to be an excellent means of overall physical purification. Another cause of constipation, even *painful bladder bloating* (*nšey'yoplqsm'*), was from eating too much white camas, commonly treated by encouraging the patient to *vomit* (*nˀoccqéˀc'ínm* or *snˀoccqeˀcín*), after which any one of the various types of soothing teas was drunk.

Postnatal women experiencing abdominal pain often found relief by drinking a medicinal tea made from mashed kinnikinnick berries. Bark was harvested in the summer from chokecherry bushes, and often stored for winter use, and a person drank a medicinal tea from small pieces of dried bark placed in hot water, mainly to cleanse his digestive tract. Chokecherry tea was also administered to make a person feel as though he was capable of *becoming well* (*xstwíl'š*). To reduce the effects of stomach cramps, a warm solution of the crushed stems of snowberry steeped in hot water was applied directly by pouring over a patient's abdomen while lying on his back, or by repeatedly applying buckskin that was saturated in the solution to the abdominal region.

No one clearly remembered what type of abdominal pain was treated by having the patient drink a warm decoction made from the grease of a beaver's scent gland. The medicine was drunk several times a day by the otherwise fasting patient. Patients experiencing gastrointestinal maladies were sometimes encouraged to vomit, by physical or chemical means. A more expedient method was to insert a finger or a stick with a shredded end, into the throat and possibly touch the epiglottis. Vomiting through chemical means was by drinking an infusion of boiled nettle leaves, strained through a rough grass filter. A less drastic treatment for stomach ache was to *boil* (*nptap*) a particular unidentified *grass* (*skʷrúleˀxʷ*) and strain through a grass strainer and drink it; alternatively, it would be soaked into a section of folded buckskin and rubbed on the stomach. Another method to induce vomiting was to mash several small fresh wild cow parsnip leaves—a mild poison—and swallow them, along with copious amounts of water.

Other techniques existed for *cleansing oneself* (*cniłc mir'yemistm* - "to cure oneself") by vomiting. A person could easily induce this reaction by tickling his throat with a long feather, or inserting it into the throat and twisting the shaft. Probably the most common procedure for *gastrointestinal purging* (*nxʷk'ʷłc'ˀencut* - "bowel elimination") was to make a mild infusion from the inner green layer of cascara bark (chittam) and drink it as a mild physic. To induce vomiting, the more bitter and stronger outer bark was prepared as an infusion; in the latter use, the bark was *always* pulled from the top downward when gathering. An effective *emetic* (*nxʷk'ʷłc'eˀncút* - "cleans insides") was made by mashing and then steeping the ripe fruit of greasewood or *antelope brush* (*Purshia tridentata* [Pursch] D. C. - *tskʷ'ʷásk' cístn* or *sxʷem'asq'el* or *xʷemasq'elt*). Another expedient method to induce vomiting was to eat only two or three berries from the sticky currant, sometimes called golden currant or the sticky currant (*Ribes viscossimum* Pursh). Unfortunately, in mild and warm climate, these plants harbor large colonies of ticks.

An unclassified plant, known only as *xʷiʕit*, was used as a general remedy for stomach disorders. It has a small, round, and white root, and the root, stem, and leaves were gathered and steeped as a tea, and administered to the patient who was first wrapped in a robe or blanket to further encourage perspiring in order to rid the person's system of the malady, sweating being a universal principle in curing. The bark of this plant was scraped and also used as an adulterant with kinnikinnick to make a tobacco. For purification, shavings from the root were sometimes placed on sweathouse stones, which, when inhaled, acted as a diaphoretic by promoting sensible perspiration (diaphoretic - producing perspiration). In addition, fresh shavings could be held under an unconscious person's nose for revival. Grandmothers often carried bits of this root to place under the nose of a grandchild who was suffering from a cold (STHC).

Roots of wild carrot were mashed and made into a decoction that was drunk by adults to combat diarrhea and other digestive difficulties. Wild rose contains various vitamins including flavonoids, pectin, and organic acids, which when steeped as a tea and drunk, was a diuretic and laxative. Also, a decoction made from boiling slightly mashed leaves of kinnikinnick served as a diuretic.

The bright red berries and foliage of baneberry (*Actaea rubra* [Ait.] Willd., var. *arguta* [Nutt. ex T. & G.]) Lawson, a member of the Ranunculaceae family, were known to be poisonous if taken in large quantity. However, small amounts of baneberry, if crushed and boiled in water, served as a physic despite the almost immediate effects of nausea and, depending upon the amount, sometimes severe peristalsis—used as an abortive.

An individual suspected of being *maliciously poisoned* (*čnílmn* - "poison"), by any one of many known Indian poisons, was encouraged to immediately regurgitate, which often necessitated that the patient induce *spasms* (*sqcmín* or *sqqám'qm'* - "reflexes") by pressure on their epiglottis with a finger, or an adult's finger in the case of a small child. Often, a victim of poisoning, or even one with severe gastrointestinal problems, would *vomit dark blood clots* (*meɫkʷ meɫkʷ* or *ncxʷúm*) from the *stomach* (*sništeɫc'eʔ* or *ʔurín*) or *large intestine* (*stxenč*). Small amounts of death camas root were chewed and swallowed to induce vomiting, and was always considered a dangerous practice, particularly for very young and old people. As mentioned, some men preferred to chew and swallow small amounts of *tobacco* (*N. tabacum*) to achieve the same results. Until recently, the bark and berries of the chittam bush were an effective emetic; the outside brown bark was discarded, taking only the stem and yellow green inner bark, which was steeped in boiling water before being drunk upon cooling.

Another method to induce self-regurgitation was to take an emetic, such as powdered yellow clay or white clay, mixed with water to produce a rather thick drink. Several elders recall drinking a mild solution of clay and water as a cure for vomiting. Involuntary *belching* (*q'ʷiʔq'ʷʔimt*) was of no medical significance. For cases of gastrointestinal hemorrhaging, the roots of Oregon grape were crushed to make a thick tea, which was given to the patient as needed. To stop postpartum hemorrhaging, an infusion of the entire parsnip flower wild buckwheat (*Eriogonum hetracleoides* Nutt.) plant was administered to the patient.

An interesting interpretation by a staunch Christian non-Indian of a shaman's powers, and his ability to treat abdominal maladies, was cited by Mary Walker in her diary entry of 28 September 1844, relating how she carefully attended a young Spokan girl with a grossly distended abdomen due to an enlarged bladder, and how she attempted to release the pressure by inserting a catheter, which had no effect. "She died without having the medicine played [being attended by a traditional practitioner]. The first instance I recollect" (Drury 1976:290 fn).

There were numerous other plants used to treat gastrointestinal disorders, such as using the mashed fresh blue-green leaves of stinging nettles that were sometimes mixed with the boiled roots of young rose bushes, and drunk as an emetic.

Hiccups

The most common treatment for an adult or child experiencing *hiccups* (*sq'ʷsqʷʕmt*), was to have the person hold his/her breath for as long as possible, or rapidly drinking a large amount of water. Hiccups were never treated by scaring the person, for fear that the frightened person could possibly have his breath-soul leave, often causing immediate death or else putting the individual into a trance that only a medicine man—if he were successful—could correct by enticing the hovering soul back into the unconscious person. In a prolonged trance, a shaman might attempt to revive the person by *blowing smoke from a special herb in a pipe on him* (*čq'ʷa qíntm*), using a mixture of medicinal herbs such as the tobacco.

One elder recalled how when a child had hiccups, her grandmother would take old dry fry bread, and make her swallow it after being crumbled as a cure.

Urinary Tract

When an older man experienced difficulty with micturition, he ate raspberries (*Rubus idaeus*) which served to acidify urine and increase its flow, or dry nettle root was powdered, mixed in water and drunk to encourage micturition. Until recently, several elderly women made a diuretic from the decoction of the flowers from *red hawthorn* (*Crataegus columbiana* Howell, var. *columbiana* - *stm'óqʷálqʷ* - *xexay* = berry), claiming this was also a generally good cleansing spring tonic. Consuming large amount of fresh service berries was also an effective diuretic. Urine retention and bladder infection was treated by drinking an infusion of crushed wild carrot.

People with cystitis or *urinary tract* (*tčéy'*), *bladder* (*sntčéy'tn*), or *kidney* (*mt'ós*) infection were commonly treated by administering *bearberries* (*sčkʷlkʷl*)—often called kinnikinnick berries—which have astringent properties that contract tissue and arrest discharge and bleeding. There was consensus that all edible berries were good as a diuretic when eaten in too great a quantity, and so were eaten to correct leukorrhea in women and to treat diarrhea. Urinary tract infection was also treated by drinking mashed licorice root tea.

A child experiencing difficulties with enuresis (bed-wetting) was treated by drinking a small infusion of mashed Sitka mountain-ash branches that had been steeped in hot water. The child was awakened and given this medicine three or four times during the night, which was also a febrifuge for anyone with a high temperature. Bed-wetting was also treated by making the child drink a warm solution of nutty tasting mashed yampah leaves.

Geophagy

Clay, argillaceous earth, was used both internally and externally as a medicine, being composed essentially of hydrous aluminum silicate—kaolin—and is endohydric (Römer 1976:270), with "a large adsorptive capacity" (Lupibereza 1951:59). Pharmacologically, argillaceous earth is termed bolus, and its medicinal properties were recorded by Hippocrates as possessing curative powers. As early as 1868, Ehrenberg described how clay-eating denied the fetus some nourishment to facilitate the delivery (1868:123). Later, in 1892, Modigliani realized geophagy relieved pregnancy-related nausea (1892;123), with which Laufer agreed later (1930:109). The medicinal effects of geophagy were clinically established by Ispasescu who maintained that "geophagy is an empirical treatment of illness by virtue of the aluminum silicates which are efficacious in absorbing and neutralizing secretions of pepsin and hydrochloric acid" (1968:30).

As a medicament, clay was used for treating poisoning, constipation, diarrhea, infectious intestinal disorders involving flatulence, and even dermal abscesses and open wounds (superseding antibiotics?). Geophagy was administered primarily in treating diarrhea, a common affliction in the early spring, when there was a change in diet from stored foods to fresh roots and plant foods. Several elders noted that their ancestors probably learned of this treatment of earth-eating from closely observing deer and elk, who frequently experience diarrhea in the early spring when their diet changed from browsing shrubs to grazing grass, particularly new *spring grass* (*Andropogon* sp. - *sqʷa?yól'e?xʷ*) (Ross 1964-67 and 1981b). In early spring, the dependence upon stored food and the urgencies of hunger were relieved by gathering and eating sometimes too many balsam plant roots, which can cause diarrhea, and was treated by ingesting diluted solutions of ferruginous (rust-colored) clays.

It was reported that people eating too much salmon during the first salmon runs could develop the 'runs' themselves, a condition traditionally treated by ingesting clay. Again, unknown to them, clay was composed of powdered hygroscopic argillaceous earth containing aluminum silicon oxides, and sodium. Preferably white clay (kaolin) was used by a pregnant woman for nausea and vomiting during the first trimester of her pregnancy.

The Spokan were quite aware of the absorbing properties of powdered white clay having been dissolved in water and drunk as a medicament for 'irritable' stomach problems. Argillaceous earth was also administered orally to a person suspected of having been poisoned, thereby causing the patient to regurgitate the stomach contents. The principal gastrointestinal absorbents were kaolin, magnesium trisilicate, muscovite, chlorite, and other ingredients depending upon clay formation and location (Ross 1981B). There was no recall if the Spokan ever baked clay to impart a smoked flavor when eaten whole or in a solution. However, limonite (a ferric hydrate, often called brown hematite) was mixed with clay as a medicament.

It is impossible now to reconstruct the extent of the trading network for clays possessing obvious different properties, if only by color. For example, a type of blue clay was traded in from the area of Republic, Sanpoil River, and the large quarry at Blue Slide in the Pend Oreille watershed at the confluence of Ruby Creek and the Pend Oreille River. Blue clay was important to the Spokan corpus pharmacopoeia, as it is a "very fine unctuous material composed of seritie and kaolin" (Glover 1941:88). This material was collected in free form from several mineral springs just south of the Spokane River. As cited earlier, there are at least four existing geophagous clay pits located in the southeastern area of the Spokane Indian Reservation. Unfortunately, the evidence of most traditional Spokan quarries has been obliterated by the once intense activity of brick and tile manufacturing, and, more devastatingly, the alteration of stream systems through damming and watershed modification (Ross 1993).

There are reports that during periods of starvation, as in many parts of the world, argillaceous earth was used as a dietary supplement; but that can be a dangerous practice, since opinions are "almost unanimous in stating that the habit when indulged, causes anemia" (Laufer 1930:105). There is no memory or recorded evidence that excessive geophagy occurred among the Spokan.

It is, however, of interest and ethnomedical significance that both Spokan male and female adults once ground dried hardwood or animal bone to make a solution, which was drunk for treating poisoning, abdominal disorders, and digestive disturbances. As already mentioned, dry, powdered white clay was a common remedy when sprinkled on open or suppurating wounds.

Diarrhea

As cited, *diarrhea* (*sp'ác'* or *sp'cm'á* - "stomach boiled") was not an unusual occurrence for foraging people who periodically experienced a radical change from eating stored winter food to fresh collected plant foods, particularly during the transition to fresh fruits, or when ingesting large amounts of fat after brief winter periods of low caloric intake, or when a baby was being weaned and first introduced to solid foods. If a baby or small child had severe diarrhea, it could have been disastrous, particularly if the condition was complicated by dehydration.

For babies and small children with colic, a warm solution of water and powdered clay was administered as a drink, usually flavored with fresh mashed leaves of any one of the available mints, particularly the upper crushed stems and leaves of Canada min. The roots of common *peppermint grass* (*Lepidium densiflorum* Schrad., var. *densiflorium* - *nkk'ʷá*), and the leaves of *peppermint* (*M. piperita* L. - *xaʔxaʔyłp*), were used as broad spectrum medicine, being chewed to stop diarrhea, or steeped as a tea for treating colds and various upper respiratory ailments and for numerous gastrointestinal problems.

When travelling or hunting, a field method of treating diarrhea was to chew several kinnikinnick leaves into small bits before swallowing them. In the case of an infant or a small baby, a piece of buckskin would be rolled and soaked in a decoction of crushed kinnikinnick leaves, which the child would suck, serving to act as a mild but usually effective efferent. For treating children and adults, a more concentrated solution of clay was drunk, whereas elders and babies received a smaller *dose* (*člcnnúk'kʷ*). A child's diarrhea—always a serious concern—was treated with an infusion made from the roots of black hawthorn.

At an early age, children were warned never to eat too many elderberries when they were *thirsty* (*nx̣m'pcín*) and away from home when exploring, since overeating invariably led to diarrhea. Depending upon the amount eaten, the child could become clinically dehydrated and in a dangerous condition if not found and adequately rehydrated.

A common cure for diarrhea was to collect *foamberries* (*sx̣ʷsmélp*) from the *foamberry bush* (*Shepherdia canadensis* [L.] - *sx̣ʷúxsm*), often called soapberries. The fresh berries were mashed and steeped in hot water as a tea. In the past, *raw cattail rhizomes* (*p'štp sx̣ʷepl*) were dug, cleaned, and soaked in hot water until the solution turned red, and then drunk once or several times as needed to stop the diarrhea. Another treatment was to chew dandelion leaves or mash a handful of these leaves, which were then boiled, strained, and drunk as needed. Similarly, the roots of wild strawberry, both *Fragaria vesca* and *F. virginiana*; both now called *q'ít'q'm'*, were prepared in the same manner, only this was a treatment primarily for children.

Diarrhea was commonly treated by collecting the root of wild buckwheat or sulphur flower, and the mashed root was boiled in water and the concoction was drunk when warm. This procedure was also reported by Ray (1932:218) for the neighboring Sanpoil and Nespelem, and it was also used by the Spokan. The mashed leaves of this plant were stone-heated and applied to minor cuts and used as a poultice. In cases of chronic diarrhea, the leaves and roots of fireweed were mashed and then cooked in boiling water, and upon cooling, approximately 5 to 10 ml was given to the patient. The same treatment was often successful in treating colic. An antidiarrheal decoction from the root of arrowleaf buckwheat (*Eriogonum compositum* Dougl. ex Benth) was taken for diarrhea. Another treatment for diarrhea and dysentery was an infusion of common chokecherry bark.

The chewing of hoary puccoon roots, or drinking tea from its mashed seeds, was effective as a treatment for diarrhea. Again, the astute observations of native peoples as to the effectiveness of certain indigenous plants proved effective despite being unaware of a plant's diuretic and antimicrobial properties. Scouler's willow (*Salix scouleriana*) root served as an antidiarrheal decoction. An infusion of Canada goldenrod flower heads was also an effective antidiarrheal.

Himalayan blackberry (*Rubus armeniacus* Focke) root was an effective remedy for diarrhea, especially effective to treat *dysentery* (*henc'e?c'e?rénči*), a condition of serious concern when a patient passed blood and pus directly or in the stools. Both diarrhea and minor internal bleeding were treated by drinking, as needed, a tea made from steeping the scraped inner bark of either red or black thornberry bush. Diarrhea was also treated by making the patient chew a yarrow root or drinking a warm concoction of powder yarrow root. Another treatment was to take the bark of wild rose, which was either chewed or taken as a medicinal tea made by mashing and steeping the root.

Diarrhea was rather common in early to late spring for those who ate too great an amount of fresh salmon, and they were treated by any of the aforementioned medicaments.

Laxatives and Diuretics

Almost all known laxatives used by the Spokan came from plants, an exception being drinking great quantities of warm water with almost insignificant amounts of geomedicament clay. Another exception was to drink small amounts of warmed fish oil, or to ingest small, thin pieces of warmed animal fat that had been boiled in water, and to drink the solution. The most common and effective treatment for cases of *constipation* (*ncpú* - "bound up", *čsuq'ʷpenč* or *snsaápx̣ú*) was from the use of *cascara leaves* (*čq'ʷiq'ʷisáłqʷ* - "black berry tree" - "laxative bush") and the outside *brown chittam bark* (*Frangula purshiana* DC - *čq'ʷeyq'ʷeysá*), commonly called chittam (Chinook Jargon phrase chittam stick = "laxative") or buckbrush. The bark was first stripped from the bottom of the tree, always in an upward motion, then scraped, leaving the yellow-green inner bark which is steeped as a tea. The bark peeled from the top to bottom, on the other hand, was boiled and drunk to induce vomiting.

Chittem leaves were sometimes broken and boiled, and the decoction or liquor was drunk after cooling to treat constipation. An exposed stem could be cut into short sections of roughly 4 cm each, boiled, and upon cooling the infusion was drunk as a physic or cathartic, bringing satisfactory results to the gastrointestinal system. Chittam bark was stripped, and then dried and stored for medicinal use during winter. The berries of this bush were also used as a laxative when mashed and made a decoction. The medicinal importance of the entire plant was recognized by non-Indians also. In fact, St. John (1963:278-79) claimed that it was gathered by Indians in great quantities, prepared, placed in sacks, and sold to the drug trade as *cascara sagrada*.

Another treatment for constipation was to eat mature seeds of the small broad-leaf plantain (*Plantago major*) that were first mashed and soaked in water. A common gastrointestinal laxative was a decoction of wild ginger rhizomes, which also served as a medicament for stomach troubles. Several ground roots of spreading dogbane (*Apocynum androsaemfolium* L.) were ingested as a cathartic. Large amounts of this root were considered poisonous (Moerman 2009:69).

Another treatment for constipation was to chew the leaves of kinnikinnick, or to mash and boil a handful of leaves, and then strain with matted grass and drink as needed, or to place the plant's bark in a birch bark basket and pour boiling water over the contents, and drink when warm (Elmendorf 1935-6, 1:63). Similarly, the roots of wild strawberry were prepared in the same way, only this was a treatment mostly for children. *Chokecherry berries* (*łxʷłóxʷ*) and the bark of this tree were also rendered as a tea for curing constipation when either the fruit or the bark would be steeped in boiling water, and drunk after the infusion had cooled. Medicinal barks were collected in summer, dried, and stored for winter. Raw or cooked yampah leaves were also said to be an effective laxative.

Hemorrhoids

Of all maladies, people were most reticent to discuss internal and external *hemorrhoids* (*lapsłxʷép*), but they were acknowledged as a problem. Immersion of one's hips in cold water brought some relief by partially contracting the hemorrhoid veins. Some sources said that the freshly mashed and mildly astringent leaves of any mint plant, such as Canada mint, could be used as well as the leaves of peppermint and those of *spearmint* (*Mentha spicata* L. - *nx̣ax̣ałniw't*), also present designations for peppermint), which contains a soothing and strongly aromatic oil, providing relief when applied directly to external hemorrhoids. The volatile oils are antiseptic and antiviral, and can be quite toxic, particularly with children having laryngeal spasms. *Morning glory* (*Convolulus arvensis* L., var. *glabrata* [Benth.] - *x̣nx̣x̣mé*) was another medicinal plant (Smith 1936-8:665), reputed to be effective for internal hemorrhoids by inserting the mashed roots into the rectal vault as a shallow suppository. It was agreed that anyone with incipient constipation should drink more water, since becoming even slightly dehydrated could result in hard stools that further complicated a person's constipation, and could lead to or complicate existing hemorrhoids.

With the occurrence of bloody stools, a person would drink an infusion made of mashed goldenrod root, after being strained and boiled, several times a day. Another common procedure for the treatment of hemorrhoids was to take any type of tallow, grease, or bone marrow, and rub it around the *anus* (*snč'múps*) with one's index finger or with a small piece of buckskin containing the lubricant. If necessary, the person would insert or impact grease into the lower part of the rectal vault as needed.

635

Many years ago, an elderly man claimed he had been told by his great grandfather "that hemorrhoids came with the white people; [because] we never sat [directly] on the ground, we squatted; and we always drank lots of water."

Ear, Nose, and Throat

An *earache* (*snc'e?réne?* or *t'n't'én'e?*) was treated in one of several ways, depending upon the seriousness and the amount of pain, as could best be explained by the patient. An old remedy was to take from either a male or female beaver the two large glands in its abdomen, which open through the cloaca, and are approximately 4 cm long, "One pair secretes a yellow substance called castoreum, and the other pair secretes an oil" (Ingles 1965:244); the oil-secreting gland was placed in boiling water, removed with a stick and, when warm, twisted and placed around the patient's *ear* (*t'ene?*) as well as within the ear. With the cessation of pain, the glands were removed. These particular glands, along with the beaver's scent glands, were always saved and stored for future medicinal purposes. Over time they became desiccated, but could be easily reconstituted in warm water. A fresh beaver's castor was also squeezed so that the liquid would enter the ear canal, reportedly bringing quick relief (Smith 1936-8:1097).

Either a child or an adult with an earache could be treated by taking a hot pipe stem—immediately after smoking—and placing the detached pipe stem close to the afflicted ear, and gently blowing warm air directly into the patient's ear. A similar treatment was to first chip flakes of dried wild licorice root, smoke them in a pipe bowl, and gently blow the smoke into the patient's ear using a hollowed section of willow, thimbleberry, or snowberry. A rather unique example of multipurpose technology was when a father took a short section of elderberry plant, removed the pith, and warmed the stem over an open fire, then placed one end only several millimeters from the child's concha, and gently blow warm air into the child's ear through the open shaft. The young sprouts of thimbleberry were used as an antiscorbutic.

Heated bits of wild licorice root were also placed around a patient's sore ear to alleviate pain. Another treatment for a sore ear was to collect the warm grease taken from a beaver's loins, and then place the substance in and around the ear. The warm leaves of wild ginger were mashed and placed as a poultice for ear ache. Some preferred to treat a child's earache with a small amount of warmed lamprey oil that was dripped from the mother's finger or on a bit of rolled oil-saturated buckskin. The same treatment was effective for removing an active polyphagous *earwig* (*Forticula auricularia* L. - *k'ʷic'íe?*) from a person's ear. Some Spokan incorrectly felt they had no word for earwig, which was believed to have been introduced probably in the early 1900s (T. Wynecoop, pers. comm.).

Mothers were judicious when periodically removing *ear wax* (*sn?oq?óqʷne?* or *sn?óqʷne?*) from children's ears, using the *tip of a grouse feather* (*nxʷl'kʷpéne?*). The bulk of the barbs were first stripped away from the shaft, and the remaining tip was moistened with the *tongue* (*ticxʷcč*), slowly inserted into the ear and twirled, a process called *nxʷl'kwpéne?* (Smith 1936-8:1204). A woman also performed this process for her husband, and a grandmother for her married daughter. It was claimed that when a person said he was troubled with a plugged ear, this was sometimes an excuse for not hearing the advice of a mother-in-law or from one's wife.

Treatment for a *nosebleed* (*sn'm'l'l'áqs* or *sn'ml'l'áqs*) was simple and immediate: the forefinger was pressed tightly under the *nose* (*sp'sáqs*), or a section of buckskin soaked in cool water was placed against the back of the neck while lying down. It the case of a *profuse nosebleed* (*n't'lt'q'áqs*), the nose was impacted with a small but tight wad of buckskin or rolled mullein leaves, or a rolled *Plantago major* leaf that had been first mashed by chewing. Elders remember their grandparents explaining how a nosebleed could be stopped by taking finely ground clay, mixed sometimes with ground charcoal, and impacting the afflicted nostril. A former remedy to stop extensive nose bleeding of a child or baby was to pack the nostril with cobwebs, or insert the tail of a live turtle in the bleeding nostril.

636

Every family had a variety of treatments for treating a *sore throat* (*nc'a?ráqʷlt* or *he?*), one that commonly involved gargling or simply drinking a tea made of one or more plant infusions. Roots were also used, particularly wild licorice root, which were chewed or sucked for sore throat, and often collected during yearly pilgrimages to *Mount Spokane* (*čqʷ'ᵂulsmn* - "cottonwood"). This same root would be dried and crushed before steeping as a tea to treat *laryngitis* (*hecnsékʷm*). A thick mash is made by pounding the sweet-tasting yampah root, then gargled to treat a sore throat or to reduce swelling from infection and to treat colds. Soar throats in children were always a concern, and one treatment was to boil the leaves of Canada mint to make an infusion that was drunk to sooth the ailing child's throat. Small bits of fresh smooth sumac leaves "were chewed and permitted to remain in the mouth for some time to aid the healing of sore gums" (Ray 1933:219) and rubbed on sore lips.

An interesting and effective treatment of a sore throat was to collect the fine earth from outside a rodent's hole; the small pile of earth would be warmed by rolling a hot stone over it, and then placed in a small buckskin bag, which was tied or held at the region of the patient's upper neck. The process was repeated until the patient presumably received relief.

Sore throats were more commonly treated with different steeped plant infusions that were first used as a gargle, and sometimes swallowed. Traditionally, ground salt from animal salt licks was placed in warm water and drunk—a procedure that was later refined with the introduction of commercial salt. A common and readily available treatment for sore throats was for the patient to place several small subalpine fir pitch blisters in his mouth, and after sucking and working the closed pitch around inside, break the pitch blisters with his teeth and swallow the flavored solution.

The root of a green to white-flowered plant similar to true licorice, also called wild licorice root, was an effective cure for sore throats when the rhizome was mashed, boiled, and after straining through a grass mat filter, drunk as needed. The dried roots of *sweet grass* (*Hierochloë odorata* [L.] Beauv. - *sxsésty'e?* or *?opopqín*) were chewed for treating *laryngitis* (*cerłqᵂ' ałqᵂ' lt*). Another treatment was to use a small piece of sun-dried pitted fruit, or a section of dried meat, even a small hard camas, which the patient rolled about with his tongue and eventually dissolved in his *mouth* (*splim'cn*) thus serving as a *lozenge* (*nč'?ałqᵂ'l't* or *m'am'ałqᵂl?tn'*). This type of lozenge was sometimes carried by hunters in case they had to combat thirst until they were able to get water. Another procedure for treating laryngitis, but no longer used, was to first wash black tree lichen in a flowing stream, soak it in hot water until soft, wring out the mass, and then wrap the warm tree lichen around the patient's throat—a procedure that was repeated until relief had been achieved.

Thrush (*Canadida albicans* or *C. stomatitis* - Turner, pers. comm.), an Anglo-introduced disease, was treated by first pounding fresh roots of wild Indian carrot and then putting the mashed substance on the area of affliction. It was not uncommon for a baby to develop a sore throat when commencing to take solid foods, and in such cases the usual treatment was dabbing a bit of buckskin that was first saturated with a prepared solution of *red willow bark* (*stečcxʷ*) that had been first boiled, which the baby sucked upon. Mouth ulcers in both adults and children were treated by placing warmed freshly mashed leaves of fireweed on the afflicted area.

A serious, even dangerous predicament confronting both fish-eating children and adults was removing a partially swallowed fish bone, particularly if the person was unable to extricate the bone himself, or if the child or young person commenced to *panic* (*yipełc'e?*). Such a situation required the immediate assistance of a shaman who had the ability to feel the object, and could withdraw the bone. There are numerous accounts of this happening, and one elder described the procedure he had seen his father perform on a boy during an encampment at Little Falls prior to the dam's construction:

> People were hollering of what had just happened, and so my father went over quickly and started to sing very quietly one of his [power] songs, all the while one of his good friends held the little boy in both his arms— like a bear. The helper sat down with his legs out straight with the boy leaning back against him as my father moved both his hands very slowly in several repeated upward motions over the boy's throat, but not his mouth.

637

About the third time the bone was in the boy's mouth and my father pulled it out. He then carefully buried the salmon bone (Ross 1968-2008).

Nearly forty years ago, several elderly men could occasionally recall the difficulty when attempting to extract a fish bone caught in a *person's throat* (*sx̌ʷopʼɬqʼʷlʼt*). Opinions varied as to whether it was preferred to be removed by another person's fingers, by an articulated device, or by a curing doctor; the latter was probably a form of legerdemain (slight of hand). In the last approach, the patient would stand, lifting his chin up at a 45° angle with his mouth open. The shaman would then move both of his hands in repetitive circles around the patient's neck, while singing his song. Then he placed his opened hands with the thumbs together slowly up the patient's neck, over the mandible, and finally over the patient's mouth. As can best be recalled, the shaman would then close both hands, stand back, and open both hands, displaying the bone. A shaman went on to say to the author that, although he was told that Blue Jays were restricted in their ability to *cure* (*maƛiyém*), he did remember they would easily remove needles from children's throats, as well as fish bones, mostly sucker fish bones.

Eyes

The visual acuity of land-dependent hunting and gathering peoples was a critical aspect to their survival, as with all foraging people. Therefore, Spokan had developed an impressive armamentarium of prophylactic medicines and treatments dealing with *eye* (*čkʷƛʼustn*) health, and had a curing shaman who specialized in *doctoring eyes* (*čmalyústn*). Both adults and children took considerable pride in their ability to see better than another, sometimes demonstrated during contests or tasks. Consequently, a person with exceptional eyesight might attribute his ability to a tutelary animal, like any one of the accipiter birds, which often meant he also had abilities as a seer or one who could "see" what other people could not, similar to a Blue Jay's power.

A person who prematurely lost his visual acuity was thought to have been the victim of sorcery, or had violated a tabu, seeing something he should not have seen. Unfortunately, the clinical explanation may have been any number of reasons, such as ophthalmic herpes, glaucoma, infectious trachoma, laceration, or any traumatic injury. No matter what the individual's medical profile, the Spokan in general—like all indigenous people—may have been less afflicted by ophthalmic problems than currently found among the present population. This might have been due to several factors, including the absence of artificial lighting and the greater quantities of berries and antioxidants in the diet. However, the Spokan tended to suffer more from sore eyes during the winter, because of daily exposure to wood smoke when confined within dwellings, as well as snow glare. Some elders cite this as the primary cause of the relatively high incidence of cataracts in both older men and women, and how, "The Indian lodges had no good method of ventilation. When fires were needed in cold weather, the accumulated [sic] smoke often became disagreeable. The missionaries felt that this was one reason why so many of the natives suffered from eye trouble" (Drury 1976:179 fn). Despite this claim, it is interesting that until recently, seldom did one observe an elder wearing glasses.

Father DeSmet observed how frequently older Indians suffer from ophthalmic afflictions, and commented on what he felt were the plausible causes:

> [...] first, because they are frequently on the water and exposed from morning till night to the direct and reflected rays of the sun, and next, because living in low cabins, made of bull-rushes, the large fire they make in the centre fills it with smoke, which must gradually injure their eyes (1843:151).

Years ago, some elders believed that a man or even a horse could become permanently blind by running too strenuously for too great a time or distance. Such an incident occurred with one of Smith's Kalispel informants, which prompted him to cite the incident (1936-8:214). It was also related to Smith how a man's blindness was attributed to when as a young boy he stuck sticks in the eyes of a live bird (1936-8:1316).

Snow blindness (*skʷím's* or *st'ikʷs*)—always a serious affliction—was presumably cured by excavating a small depression in the snow, packing it down, placing a heated stone into the hole, and then having the patient kneel down while keeping his head covered with a robe or hide, and also keep his eyes open as he is bathed by the steam. Elders said that steamed water will not work, only steam from melting snow; another example of the Doctrine of Signatures or Similarity. This would be done every hour, sometimes for several days, or until the patient was cured. It could not be concluded if the application of deer bone marrow, if available, was beneficial in treating snow blindness when rubbed into the person's eyes.

Until recently, a *cataract* (*sčpáqs*) was sometimes attributed to sorcery, or it was believed that the affliction was due to a person's prolonged staring at a naked woman as she bathed. A personal instance was with an elderly gentleman who was convinced that his cataracts were due to a sorcery, and was further frustrated since there were no local shamans whom he felt could treat him, and would have had to travel to a distant reservation and stay with a known shaman. However, he feared that doing so might only worsen his condition, explaining, "The farther you're away from home, you've even less care and protection." We never made the trip, fearing he had no protection from further sorcery by going to a Sahaptian-speaking reservation.

A favored treatment for sore eyes was mixing mashed wild licorice root with the *grease found around a deer's kidneys* (*?ulíkʷ*), placing this on a small piece of buckskin or a mullein leaf, and placing the mashed leaf or mixture on each eye to reduce swelling and pain. Some preferred the mullein root, which was also mashed and used without any type of grease, and then applied directly to the eyes. Grandmothers and mid-wives commonly washed the eyes of the newborn in this fashion. An old method for washing a baby's eyes was the application of the nursing *mother's breast milk* (*qem*), and a variation of this was done to strengthen a baby's eyes, which involved mixing a small amount of the mother's lactated milk with the scrapings from the inner bark of Oregon grape, and then dripping the solution into the corner of the child's eyes by laying the cradleboard flat on the ground. A solution for treating sore eyes was made by mixing mashed snowberries in warm water and then the eyes are bathed as needed. Some elders claimed that a poultice of mashed snowberries was soothing to an injured eye.

An injured eye—due to trauma or a pointed object—was treated by intermittently dripping a concoction made from *mare's milk* (*snsšlc'asqasqems*) and the mashed buds of serviceberry (*Amelanchier alnifolia*). If no object was in the eye, a dog licking the eye may bring relief. Treatment of sore eyes or simply as an eye wash, was to administer "the inner part of the root [Oregon grape], which was shredded and soaked in cold water until the liquid turned yellow. The fluid was dashed into the eyes or the face was immersed in it" (Ray 1933:219). Ray also noted that the roots of *sticky geranium* (*Geranium visosissimum* Fisch. & Mey. - *tóqʷe?*) were first boiled to make a concoction, and when warm was used to wash sore eyes. Sore or strained eyes were treated by steeping the scraped and mashed inner bark of *wax currant* (*Ribes cereum* Dougl. - *yerec'en*) in hot water, and applied upon cooling.

Given the concern for treating one's eyes, there was once consensus that the notable acuity of some elders was due to their daily ritual of washing their eyes. There existed a variety of formulae for making eyewashes, most being time-tested family procedures. For instance, the inside of the bark from white fir would be scraped and placed in a small quantity of warm water and used as a general eyewash, usually in the morning and before retiring at night. When travelling in high country, a person could use the young branches of Rocky Mountain juniper to make a decoction for bathing his eyes by steeping the twills. Several elders cited how this procedure helped people who suffered from cataracts or general inflammation of the eyes. *Shooting star* (*Dodecatheon pauciflorum* [Durand] Greene - *xʷetxut* - *kʷiólip* or *hwíthut*) roots were mashed and steeped in hot water as an infusion for bathing sore eyes. This plant was probably named after an unidentified bird (May n.d., p. 7), which Turner feels may have been a curlew (pers. comm.).

Tips of young, budding serviceberry bushes were also mashed, mixed with mare's milk, placed on several buckskin pads, and applied to the eyes to relieve pain, or if the patient had what may have been conjunctivitis. When out hunting and away from the village or camp, a person could remove the bark from any fir tree, scrape the inside cambium next to the wood, boil the cambium, and strain the infusion through a mass of grass to filter out the remaining bits of cambium, which was then applied as a wash to treat sore eyes. Probably the most common eyewash was an infusion made from either fresh or dried rose petals, that were applied when needed, or by some elders every day, who consequently could "always thread their own needles."

Until recently, several elderly ladies would treat their grandchildren's eyes with a warm solution from an *orange honeysuckle* (*Lonicera ciliosa* [Pursh] DC - *čyilyal'ál'qʷ* or *čirirálqʷ* or *čiλiáλá* - "wrapping around a tree or a bush"). Orange honeysuckle tended to be the preferred plant for washing a person's eyes. The fresh leaves and stem of orange honeysuckle was steeped in warm water and both eyes were bathed three times, and later repeated if needed. A common eyewash was made from mashing fresh sticky geranium, and then steeping it in hot water before washing the eyes; this was often frequently done once a week by elderly women.

The roots of spider tail or rattlesnake weed (*Chaenactis douglasii* [Hook.] H. & A. var. *achilleaefolia* [H. & A.] A. Nels.) served as a prophylactic medicinal when steeped in hot water as an eyewash infusion. Ray (1932:221) makes a qualified explanation of how the roots "were boiled and some of the liquid was swallowed by the surviving members of a family after the death of one, 'to avoid contracting consumption.'"

The author knew three elderly Spokan women who often gathered for the day to sew and gossip. After a respectful length of time, the oldest woman would *joke* (*čpoʔscánm* - "to joke"), "I've never had to use eyewash, but I have plenty for you ladies." Until recently, even among the few elderly women, there was pride in their acuity, which was expressed and demonstrated in different ways. For example, when asking a woman how she felt, one might be handed a finely beaded pair of gloves, with the remark, "I still do my own beadwork." Daily care of one's eyes was not unusual, as seen by the following testimony given by the granddaughter of her 97-year-old great grandmother:

> The old woman never really learned to speak English, and she never went to a church or government school, but still she knows many things. Every day she *washes* [*cʔew's* - "to wash face"] her face and bathes her eyes with a solution made from a plant [rose petals] that grows just outside. Her eyes are clear, perfect, and she can still do beautiful beadwork with no glasses (Ross 1968-2008).

The Spokan had a number of treatments and medicinal washes for *eye* (*sčkʷλ'ústn*) infection, removing *foreign objects in the eye* (*čt'ipús*), etc. Rosewater made from steeping petals in boiling water and letting the solution cool, was used until fairly recently as an eyewash for treating cataracts, glaucoma, catarrhal conjunctivitis (pink eye), iritis, retinitis, and hypersensitive eyes, as well as for removing physical irritants, including smoke, pollen, *dust* (*sqʷʔuɫ*), or fallen *eyelashes* (*sčupupús*). On occasion a mother or wife would pull or roll back an *eyelid* (*čxʷépstn*) to remove a larger object, or even both *eyelids* (*čxʷpxʷépstn*) in the case of blown sand. Even the famous botanist David Douglas acknowledged the problem of blowing sand in his eyes, making "them so sore and inflamed that I can hardly distinguish clearly any object at twelve yards distance" (1904, 5 [1]:349).

Roots of cow parsnip were pounded and added to water to make a paste for washing sore eyes or irritated eyes. As an *eye wash* (*čmur'yustn*) for infection, an infusion made from the mashed roots of shootingstar was applied as needed. After using the sweathouse, elderly women would bathe their eyes with rosewater in order to maintain their vision for doing needle work. The inner bark of chokecherry was steeped to make an infusion that brought relief to tired or strained eyes. Some elders recalled the use of an infusion of shaggy fleabane (*Erigeron pumilus*) for washing their eyes. The ubiquitous black tree lichen was also used to treat sore eyes, and after being thoroughly washed, and permitted to sun-dry, it was folded and patted into a smooth, damp pad, which would then be placed upon the open eye. Another treatment for medicating sore eyes was to take a fresh section of horsetail, carefully collected by removing the top section, and placing one's thumb or forefinger over the opening and removing (at the internode) the bottom section from a lower section. The contained liquid would be released into a child's sore eyes by removing one's digit from the upper end, thereby temporarily breaking the vacuum, not unlike releasing liquid from a pipette. Any *eye medicine* (*čmr'y'usís* - "he healed his eye") from a plant was gathered by the mother or grandmother of each family who would determine the required medicine, strength, and duration of treatment, depending upon her diagnosis and the patient's age.

Ripe snowberries could be mashed between a woman's hands and placed as a mass upon one or both sore eyes for babies and younger children, but only the liquid would be used. This procedure would be repeated until there was relief. The inside of cottonwood bark was scraped off and steeped to make an infusion as an eyewash. Sometimes buckskin or mullein leaves were soaked in this solution and applied directly to the sore eyes; similarly, small sections of wild licorice root were shaved, steeped in hot water, and drunk when lukewarm, as a medicinal tea for colds—but more often as a medicament in treating a sore or infected eye when applied directly to the eye(s) with a saturated pad of buckskin.

An old treatment for sore eyes was to *bathe the eyes* (*sčk^wƛ'k^wƛ'ústn*) with a solution made by scraping the dirt off the root of Oregon grape, mashing the tuber, then placing the shredded root in hot water to extract the contents, which turned the water yellow. Some elders bathed their eyes with an infusion made of pitch extracted from grand fir blisters which, after drying, was powdered to facilitate its absorption when placed in hot water. This, however, was not done every day.

A common debilitating affliction of the eye was a foreign object, and given the proximity of the Spokan to the river, it was often wind-blown sand. Without mirrors, a man or woman had to rely upon another person to remove the irritant, which invariably required the use of a moist or damp soft object, such as the narrow tip of some buckskin, or the tip of a tapered, *folded leaf* (*p'ulk'ᵂ picčƚ*). If possible, a person would attempt to wash the eye(s) before other procedures with unadulterated water. With a child, the mother would hold the eyelid up and insert her tongue to hopefully retrieve the bit of sand or other type of foreign object.

As a result of their extensive work with obsidian and stone, it was not unusual for a man to get a sharp *sliver* (*ƚuʔuwečt*) in his eye. Removal of such a potentially razor-sharp object was a serious procedure. It could be removed by the person hitting the back of his head with his hand to remove the object by inducing hydrostatic pressure in the eye. A more accepted procedure was to have another person lightly touch the sliver with a narrow stick with warmed pitch on the end, or use *tweezers* (*aqpeʔcncutn*) made of split hard-wood. In addition, a warm solution made of powdered dry chittam could be applied to the afflicted eye, a procedure that was repeated until the object was removed. A similar treatment was using a steeped decoction of waterweed (*Elodea canadensis* Michx. - *snupleʔx^wétk^w*). Alternatively, an eyewash could be used, one made by scraping the inside bark of aspen to remove the sap, and then boiling the bark, and letting it cool. It is not known if the Spokan ever removed such an object from an eye by sucking. If such a procedure were successful, the sharp object would then be in the mouth of the person offering treatment, and might have become lodged in their mouth, throat, or lungs if not sucked out without extreme caution.

When removing a foreign object or an *eyelash* (*sčupús*) lodged under an eyelid, a healer or helper would first mash snowberries directly to the afflicted eye, after which the *eye lid* (*čx^w epstn*) was rolled back with a small debarked branch of any deciduous bush, to reveal and make possible the extraction of the small physical irritant. For children, a medicinal wash was made with this berry and applied directly to the eye.

Fever and Headache

Fever (*ƛ'ʔáq'*) was associated with physical illness, whereas a *headache* (*c'ʔarqin* or *sčaʔaƛqín*) was understood to be the result of tension, eye-strain, another illness, or even sorcery. If the diagnosis for a headache was related to illness, then there were numerous medicinal treatments. Probably the most universal treatment for headache was dried, shredded willow bark, valuable as a medicine because of the now known beneficial effects of salicylazosulfapyridine. The bark would be shredded before being steeped and drunk as a tea. Every home had a copious supply of this bark. Another tree medication for headache was the pitch from the shady side of a fir tree; after being heated, the pitch was placed on two pieces of buckskin, which were gently held against each temple, where they would remain until relief was achieved. Both the fresh yarrow leaves and roots were mashed, boiled, and then drunk as a tea for combating fever. Small quantities of smooth sumac bark were gathered after the leaves had turned red, then boiled as a tea and drunk to bring down fever. Sumac bark, as also that of numerous other bushes and trees, was collected during the summer, dried, and stored separately from other medicine. Mary Walker described in her daily diary how she occasionally administered Shoemake [sumac] root to her son for minor maladies (?), "which seems to exhilarate him so he was frolicsome all day" (Drury 1976:305 fn). Unfortunately she never explained if she learned of this treatment from the Spokan, which she probably did.

A general treatment for fever, headache, and colds was to administer a medicinal tea made by steeping the crushed small leaves of False Box in hot water, and drinking the solution. The raw, mashed fresh leaves of catnip could be bound to both temples of a patient's head, and after sleeping, the person would apparently awake without any further discomfort. Headaches were also treated with the spills or tips of *western red cedar* (*Thuja plicata* Donn ex D. Don Lamb - *mšéłp* or *ʔastqʷ*), being placed in hot water and then bound to the patient's temples to bring relief. Severe headaches could be treated by taking two small buckskin bags and placing several pinches of powdered wild licorice root into each bag; one on each temple was then held by a headband. Dried leaves of wild ginger were also crumbled to make a decoction or tea for treating headaches

As both a general prophylactic and cure for headaches, some elderly women wore a small cachet of yarrow leaves about their neck or carried in a *small bag* (*axéneʔ*) when away from home. A more immediate treatment for headache was to boil yarrow leaves and inhale the scent while the patient's head was under a blanket or a hide, to contain and concentrate the fumes. Some elders felt that yarrow tea was adequate for curing a minor headache. Yarrow was a major medicament in the Spokan armamentarium of medicines. Fresh *spills* (*čcc'w'é*), i.e., young flushing needles of the evergreen tree (more often fir needles) would be placed in hot water, and then applied to one or both temples to treat headaches. A severe headache could be treated by eating a small piece of wild licorice root raw, or holding the stalk on the spot of the pain with a narrow band of buckskin or cloth. This important medicinal plant (*xásax*) was collected by women during the time of the bitterroot harvest. Young girls, when digging wild licorice root, were cautioned at an early age not to bring back the older roots, as often they had worms.

While headaches can be annoying and even debilitating, of greater concern was fever. A broad spectrum medicinal febrifuge or antipyretic was western mugwort (*Artemisia ludovicana* Nutt, var. *ludoviciana*. - *snq'nq'tełp* or *nq'nq'téłp*), which grows in a damp area or *swamp* (*čłq'q'l'iʔ*). The bluish leaves were first crushed and then steeped in boiling water, and upon cooling the infusion was drunk to treat fever. An infusion of steeped mugwort was also drunk as a remedy for *cold* (*sʔahóʔ*). Elders claim that the large brown tap-root of this plant would also be brewed and drunk as a tea to reduce fever, and the root could be stored for several days if wrapped with grass and inner pine bark, which will turn red and become indigestible if exposed too long to the air (Elmendorf 1935-6, 1:42). This type of sagebush was often called "rotten bush" since mugworts are considered odoriferous. When available, an analgesic poultice of fresh mashed watercress was applied to the forehead to treat a headache.

As cited earlier, the crushed leaves of both species of the fragrant monard were broad spectrum medicinal plants when drunk as a tea, being an active diaphoretic (sweat inducing), to treat skin as well as mouth and throat infections, headaches and fever as a poultice, and as a strong antiseptic. Some claimed that crushed leaves were effective in repelling insects and occasionally placed within a burial site.

The long gray-silver leaves of rabbitbrush produced a tea for fever or a cold, and were also taken during winter as a general prophylactic tonic. Fever was also treated by steeping the small leaves of False Box in water, then drinking as needed—a treatment also valuable for flu and colds. The leaves and twigs of rabbit brush—thought by some to be poisonous—served numerous uses, including the smoking of hides. Mashed rabbitbush leaves were rubbed on horses to prevent both the large horsefly and fierce-biting *deerfly* (*Chrysops vittatus* - *č'atnłq*), and the large iridescent horsefly (*Stomoxys calcitrans* - *č'č'átn'łq*), sometimes called *blue bottlefly* (*č'č'at'nłqq'ʷq'ʷatqn*), and the small housefly (*Musca domestica* Linn. - *čk'ʷk'ʷʔen'eʔ*), and other insects. Rabbitbush leaves were also steeped to make a tea that was believed to cure fever, headaches, and colds. Another medication for patients suffering from cold or fever was to prescribe a tea made from the mashed fresh leaves of an unidentified variety of mint, which, according to Turner (pers. comm.), may be sage (possibly *Monardella odoratissima*), and proved effective if the solution was drunk as hot as was tolerable.

In early spring, the roots and young shoots of pineapple-weed were collected for treating a high fever and headaches by making an infusion that was drunk as needed. If available, the fresh leaves of the pineapple-weed were mashed and steeped in hot water and drunk to combat fever, or applied directly to the site of the headache. The highly aromatic leaves of this plant were soaked for several hours and applied directly to a *sore area* (*poc*) to relieve pain. Another method reputed as effective for ridding headaches was to *crush* (*p'est*) the entire pineapple weed, which was then rolled into cloth and sniffed. Interestingly, the bulb-like flower heads of this plant are almost identical to the tubers of white camas, and were called *w'aw'íckʷl'eʔs mč'meč'ps* ("meadowlark testicles"). Some people would treat severe headaches by applying heated pineapple-weed leaves that had been mashed and thoroughly soaked before applying directly to the forehead or back of the neck, and was said to be soothing. For heat stroke, a tea could be made of either fresh or dried pineapple-weed leaves, allowed to cool and drunk as needed.

It was said that in early spring, one took care never to drink any water made from long-standing melted snow as one could contract a fever, and possibly die within three weeks, regardless of treatment.

Colds and Influenza

A general remedy for colds, fever, and flu was a tea made from the crushed leaves of False Box, and drunk as needed. Another medicinal infusion was a tea made from the fresh leaves of rabbitbrush; and served as a broad spectrum medicine for treating fever, headaches, cold, and *chills* (*suy'*). Some believed this plant to be poisonous, certainly if sufficient amounts are ingested by grazing cattle (St. John 1963:476). Fresh yarrow leaves were also boiled to make a tea for curing flu and the introduced catnip was used to treat colds by making a steeped fusion.

A medicament used for colds, upper respiratory afflictions, upset stomach, and as an eyewash, was prepared by steeping a solution of ground wild sarsaparilla roots that was then strained through bunched grass and drunk. The most notable medicinal leaves came from the mints (*Mentha arvensis* L. and introduced *M. piperita* L.), which made refreshing teas for the treatment of colds and upper respiratory maladies, as a diaphoretic, a diuretic, and for stomach pain. This plant was also effective for treating flu when drunk as a tea, and was prepared by pouring boiling water over the entire mint plant, after it had been cut off at the roots (STHC). The leaves of *wild mint* (*M. arvensus*) were used as a febrifuge infusion for fevers and coughs (Moerman 2009:304). Another type of mint-smelling plant, *Swamp Gooseberry* (*Ribes lacustre* [Pers.] Poir.) (Turner *et al.* 1980:107), known as *nx̣ax̣ałniw't*, was drunk as a tea for upper respiratory conditions by crushing and steeping the leaves in hot water. Roots of peppermint grass were stored for winter use against colds; when needed they were scraped and eaten. Most people today consider the leaves and bark of wormwood to be poisonous, whereas in the past, both the leaves and branches of *Dragon Sagewort* (*Artemesia dracunculoides* Pursh. - *c'ic'x̣éy'łp*) were steeped to make a tea, which was drunk to treat influenza.

Severe coughs and cold associated fever were treated by making a strong tea decoction of mashed *Coyote's strawberry* (*Geum triflorum* Pursh. - *spilyeʔ q'ít'q'ms*). After cooling, the same solution was used to bathe sore eyes.

Both the leaves and branches of *short cut-leaf sagebrush* (*Artemisia tripartita* Rydb. - *k'ʷełk'ʷeleménłp* or *qʷelqʷeleménélp*) and big sagebrush were used extensively in making a variety of medicines for a wide spectrum of maladies, most commonly as a tea for tonsillitis, and sore throat, as a laxative, and presumably

643

for treating smallpox. The leaves of either plant were used to clear sinuses, nose, and throat by inhaling mashed leaves—sometimes while in the sweathouse. Freshly gathered (or dried) leaves of bristleweed, more commonly called goldenweed (*Pyrrocoma carthamoides* var. *carthamoides*) were mashed, steeped in hot water to make a tea, and drunk as needed to treat a cold or upper respiratory problems.

The stalks, leaves, and attached flowers of *purple penstemon* (*Penstemon richardsonii* Dougl. ex Lindl. - *sqey'séłp*) were collected when in bloom to make a strong infusion, which served several purposes: treating typhoid fever and colds, and as a general tonic in early spring (Ray 1932:221; Spier 1938:165; Turner *et al.* 1980:139). A variety of the perennial herb *sulphur flower* (*Eriogonum umbellatum* Torr. - *npaqčn'ełp* or *napaqčn'eč*) was used as a cold remedy after mashing and steaming the leaves and then inhaling it.

After removing the spines and bark, sections of the inner pith of *devil's club* (*Oplopanax horridus* [J. E. Smith]. Miq. - *x̣ox̣o'iłp'* or *x̌ʷux̌ʷugwáy'łp*) were split and mashed, and steeped in cold water to produce a yellow solution that was drunk as needed for colds. The roots of this deciduous shrub were also used to treat dry coughing or consumption. Though not known at the time, this plant has antiviral, antifungal, antibacterial, and antimycobacterial properties (Lantz *et al.* 2004:34). Turner *et al.*, when referring to Okanogan-Colville use of devil's-club, mentioned the intrinsically spiritual relationship between this plant and human use:

> To keep the medicine cool in the summer, it was put down by a creek; but one had to be careful not to allow the shadow of another person to pass over it, or it would lose its power as a medicine. The medicine would be 'shamed'; 'You might as well drink water' (Turner *et al.* 1980:73).

In late fall, when passing through the higher and more northerly areas between present day Gold Creek and Helena, on their way to and from the Plains, the Spokan gathered great amounts of the small blue berries and the stiff, small, acute leaves from the juniper bush. When needed, the bitter berries were mixed with bits of mashed leaves, "each with a linear indistinct gland on the back" (St. John 1963:18), which provided a pleasant aroma, which were first crushed, then boiled. Upon cooling, this concoction, known as *maλiyé*, was drunk to combat colds and general upper respiratory maladies. The more recent growth of black cottonwood bark was chewed and the juice was swallowed as a treatment for colds. A tea was made by steeping the leaves of *purple sage* (*Pamona incana* [Benth.] Dougl - *snk'nk'taqín*), and drunk as needed. An infusion of skunk currant (*Ribes glandulosuma*) leaves was drunk as a tea to treat a child with a cold.

Poisons

Given the type and amount of a poisonous plant, and the physical condition and tolerance of the patient, virtually all poisons are medicines and many medicines are poisons. However, there was only limited recall of a poisonous medicinal plant being used in sorcery by the Spokan, though as discussed, plant poisons were commonly used to kill unwanted dogs. On the other hand, some poisonous plants, in limited amounts, were used as revulsive medicines, which were administered either internally or externally, yet the majority of revulsive-type plants were used externally. An example would be poison ivy, which upon contact *always burns* (*swul'aqeʔ*) most people, but remarkably was also used for therapeutic reasons. Occasionally, to counteract the application of a revulsive or poisonous medicament, the treated area of soreness or pain was rubbed with tallow until the site had *cooled down* (*c̓éł*). Mashed leaves of *windflower* (*Anemone multifida* Poir. - *waʔs*) were rubbed on bruises as revulsive medicine.

Interestingly, the amount of medicine administered depended upon the size and age of a person. Correct estimation was critical to the patient's successful treatment, and, thus, care was taken to ensure that the so-called medicinal poisons were taken in the correct dose. There were other types of revulsive medicaments to externally treat, for example rheumatism. A small root section of European-introduced poison hemlock (*Conuim maculatum* L.), which contains the conium alkaloids coniceine and concune, was mixed with tallow, and rubbed on the afflicted joint, and was reported to temporarily anesthetize the site.

Elders could not recall if the sharp spines of devil's-club stems, petioles or leaf veins were used as a revulsive medicine, or if it was considered a sacred plant that had widespread distribution among many groups in the Northwest (Turner 1982); one with magical powers (Turner and Bell 1973:278; Turner 1982:27). Turner's seminal publication of this plant lists a wide variety of internal and external uses of devils-club, notably, "as a dermatological aid [...] in treating ailments of the respiratory and digestive systems" (Turner 1982:28; Lantz *et al.* 2004).

There is no knowledge or record of how frequently the numerous types of poisonous plants were used as medicaments, or in what strength. Unfortunately, the indigenous name of a once noted potent poisonous plant, one used to kill animals and people, could not be remembered, except that it was found in the mountains, and the stalk closely resembles that of mountain valerian, but which Turner (pers. comm.) feels could be *Indian False Hellebore* (*Veratium viride* Ait. - *sč'láq'mn*) (Turner *et al.* 1984:50). This plant was "taken with extreme caution as a medicine for innumerable ailments. But eating even a small portion can result in loss of consciousness, followed by death" (Turner 1995:139). Elders claimed the entire plant was so poisonous that just touching the plant would presumably kill a person. Thus, it was carefully dug and manipulated with several forked sticks, and after the sticks were used, they were burned, producing an unusual sparkling fire. When preparing the poison, sticks were again used to manipulate the root, which was always sliced thin with a flake of obsidian. One elderly woman claimed that it required only a small bit of root in the food of a dog or person to kill within minutes.

A person with a *leg ache* (*scáʔaƛšín*) was administered with a small decoction of False Hellebore, that was carefully prepared by mashing and steeping in hot water. After cooling, the still-warm leaves were placed or rubbed over the afflicted area to numb pain due to severe arthritis; or one would rub the entire lower or *upper leg* (*sčč'melpstn*) with the leaves or with the mashed root that had been similarly prepared. False Hellebore *plant seeds* (*ssaʔqín'* or *snλč'tessn'*)—being extremely poisonous—were rarely taken internally. Rather, they were used more as an external medicinal supplement by macerating the seeds and adding them to the concoction of crushed False Hellebore leaves. The undersides of the crushed leaves were then applied to bring relief of arthritic joints when a person was experiencing *intense pain* (*t'eʔšéłc'eʔi* or *p'ír'*). Those who have experienced this treatment were in agreement that the area of application would be completely numbed, without any sensation. The leaves of this plant somewhat resemble the leaves of the plant now commonly called *mule-ears* (*Wyethia amplexicaulis* Nutt. - *pʔíč*). This so-called compass plant was named "for Capt Nathaniel J. Wyeth, early explorer and trader in the Pacific Northwest" (St. John 1963:518). St. John also stated that this plant is not poisonous, but according to some, the *seed* (*snλ'čtéssn'* or *scpkʷúleʔxʷ* - "round things on the ground") is poisonous. A once effective treatment for arthritis was to place roots of mule-ears in a small pit and cover with dirt, then bake them by placing hot coals atop the small earthen mound. After cooling, the roots were removed and mashed before being placed on the afflicted joint, or the prepared mash was left to cool overnight before placing it on a boil or carbuncle. The root of mule-ears was warmed, split open, and *tied* (*lič*) in place on an arthritic joint. An important utilitarian and medicinal plant was *bunchgrass* (*Pseudoregneria spioata* - *st'iyíʔ*).

Years ago, one elder contended that considerable caution should be exercised when using False Hellebore, since even a small amount swallowed would prove poisonous: stating how she had placed some mashed seeds in deer meat to poison several menacing dogs. Other Spokan claim that the large grayish-green leaves of this hydrophyte were collected, soaked in hot water, *squeezed* (*p'ʔím*), and placed on the site of pain. Elders once claimed when collecting this plant, they noted that the growth of False Hellebore is comparable in growth to deer antlers.

Wilkes, when speaking generally of the Flathead group, maintained that if curing practitioners decided their patients were "hopeless cases the medicine men used a poison of the wild cucumber bryonia" (1845, 4:362). The mashed berries, used in small quantities, were applied to cleanse dermal ulcers.

To kill a person, plant poisons were prepared by first macerating the required stalk, root, or leaf, and carefully removing the desired amount, which was placed in an intended victim's food or meat so baited to kill a dog. The eggs of an unidentified poisonous ant, known as *nč'e?č'?ey'čn'*, were gathered and carefully mixed with the blood and placed in raw meat to poison bothersome dogs, or make a person sick if bitten by this ant (STHC).

The blue-flowered monkshood (*Aconitum columbianum* Nutt. ex Torrey & Gray var. *columbianum*) is an extremely poisonous plant, and was effective when a sorcerer wanted to kill a person. Several elders recalled the nature and use of the plant, but not if the leaf, berry, root, or exuded matter, or a combination, that contained the poison. White heath (*Cassiope mertensiana* var. *fragilis*) is also thought to be a highly poisonous plant.

The Spokan used different varieties of water hemlock, often growing in close proximity to water: one type is water (swamp) parsnip (*Sium suave* Walt.- *yiníx^w*), and a variety of parsnip (*Heracleum maximum* Bartr. - *smešenm*), often referred to as a woman-plant, and produced a yellow parsnip-looking root that was eaten, as were the edible stalks— the leaves cause irritation when eaten (St. John 1960:312). The root apparently tastes *sweet* (*t'íš*), not unlike the flavor of celery, particularly when eaten before the plant is flowering. The young stalks were harvested, peeled, and eaten, but never stored. When the young stems and leaf stalks are stewed, the first cooking water is decanted and replaced with fresh water, cooked again and are then similar in taste to stewed celery. Smith noted how the Kalispel had no wild cow-parsnips, and would often trade for them from the Spokan because "the Kalispel were crazy for it" (1936-8:170). It was claimed that wild parsnip could become quite poisonous if left in the ground for several years before harvesting (STHC). Turner *et al.* (1980:60) recognized a variation of parsnip called "Indian parsnip" (*Cymopteris terebinthinus* [Hook.] T. & G. var. *terebinthinus - ałapíspés*) which was used as a general tonic when the mashed roots were steeped as a tea and drunk as needed.

The other so-called variety of parsnip was *cow parsnip* or *wild rhubarb* (*Heracleum lanatum* Michx. - *x̣^w x̣^w télp*), referred to as a 'man-plant'; it is not jointed, nor does it bloom. The roots and stems of all varieties are not poisonous (Turner *et al.* 1980:62), but the leaves produce an irritation upon exposure to ultraviolet light, and were considered poisonous to animals and humans, causing death through severe bloating. An additional danger was that this plant sometimes grows near poisonous water hemlock, which is a poisonous variety presumably used to kill unwanted or troublesome dogs, and by sorcerers to kill their victims. A *true story* (*sm'e?m'í?*) was told of how the only way to kill a certain dog was with poison:

> Yes, near old Red Bones' place was a real wild dog; huge, black, and vicious. He lived in a large pile of brush and slash maybe 300 paces from the house. Whenever Red Bones went to town, the dog would claw his way into the house and eat what he wanted. One time, maybe about 1910, me and my friend were here and Red Bones said to kill the wild dog with our [WRF] .22 rifles. We went to the slash pile, and all we could see were two huge shining eyes staring out. Well, we shot at least 20 bullets into him, and still he lived, but barely. Later, Red Bones left some poison (?) near the door, and this is what finally killed him (Ross 1968-2008).

Children from an early age were warned never to collect cow parsnip, which, according to Turner (pers. comm.), is more commonly confused with water parsnip (*Sium suave*), and is extremely toxic to humans and animals. The plant has a light yellow to white flower, and the powdered root was once used as an arrow poison. Some claim there is no treatment for a person with a skin break or wound, who would die a painful death if he touched the fleshy rootstock of this plant. Once, before going out with an elderly man to collect this plant, his wife jokingly said to him, "Be sure you pick the [leafstalks of the] woman-plant." The introduced poisonous hemlock contains the "very poisonous alkaloids conine and coniceine, which can cause blindness, paralysis, and death" (St. John 1963:311).

Two bulbs from an unclassified plant (*k^w e?núnx^w*) would be split and ground up to mask their appearance before being surreptitiously placed in an intended victim's food. The person who ingested it would display a *rabies-like* (*q^w o?q^w áw'*) condition: sweating, agitation, and convulsions. In the final death throes,

646

the victim's jaw would lock, causing an inability to swallow, drooling of *saliva* (*sptax̣ʷ*), and even foaming. General paralysis would spread, always resulting in death. A *harbinger of early spring* (*sx̌ʷúpx̌ʷup*) was the appearance of yellow bell (*Fritillaria pudica* [Pursh] Spreng. - *swiy'e'* or *q'ʷów'x̣e'* or *q'aw'ex̣e'*), which grows in often wooded, shaded areas. These small, edible, starchy roots were dug just before the shoots developed. If not eaten raw, they could be steam-cooked. When large quantities were gathered, they were sun-dried and stored for winter. Once the plant matures, it becomes poisonous, and is then called *č'eyč'i'*. A sufficient quantity of such mashed roots, if taken internally, could poison a person or a marauding dog.

The bulbs and seeds of both varieties of death camas—*meadow death camas* (*Zigadenus venenosus* S. Wats.) and *grassy meadow death camas* (*Z. Gramineus* Rydb. - *w'estn'* or *hiw'esten*)—were also poisonous if taken internally. It is not known if the seeds of wild black cherry (*Runus serotina*)—an introduced small tree with edible fruit—were recognized by the Spokan as being poisonous as they contain cyanogenic glycosides (Turner, pers. comm.).

Apparently the most *violent illness caused by eating a poison* (*nčn'n'éyn*) was from certain animal products, such as rattlesnake and *toad* (*snaqukʷa*). For example, Teit noted that among the Flathead Group, "Long ago rattlesnake poison was sometimes used on arrowheads." (1930:344). Wilson, as an interested observer of the indigenous pharmacopoeia, commented upon:

> [...] the use of rattles of the rattlesnake for the same purposes that the 'secale cornutum' [ergot, diseased rye seed] is used for in England, the rattles are pounded & taken in water [...] the other is the cure for consumption by a concoction of three roots, this if really the case will be very valuable. The cases of cure (if true, which I am inclined to believe) are very remarkable. It seems to arrest almost instantaneously the decay of lungs; one woman who was stretched on her bed & given up as lost was quite cured in a fortnight & is now able to walk about & perform all the hard drudgery which falls to the portion of woman in this part of the world (Stanley 1970:116).

Various procedures to poison a person often involved the poisonous toad. This is further substantiated by Teit's inquiries concerning malicious charms, which he prefaces with an explanation as to how a woman might take a bit of skin from a rotten corpse, which, "she anointed berries or other food that the man would eat" (1930:394). Teit, when describing the Flathead Group, described other and more detailed explanations for the gathering of toad poison:

> [...] to hang a large black toad by the legs to a branch, to put a small cross stick in its mouth to keep it open, and sometimes also a skewer through its body. A cup was placed underneath to catch the poison which ran from its mouth, the toad being left hanging until dead. Some women, instead of this, put the toad on a flat rock, placed another flat stone on top, and crushed it to death. The juices of the body were then collected and put on food to be eaten by the person to be poisoned. When a person ate toad poison his stomach was spoiled, he lost his appetite, and he died as if in consumption. Women sometimes poisoned men through jealousy (1930:394-395).

But a more deadly poison was *toad poison* (*nča'ncíntn*) made by slowly cooking the skin of the *toad* (*Bufo americanus* - *snʕakʷk*ʷáne'*) to release the poison within the parotid glands, which was carefully collected. This deadly poison was also used by both the Kalispel (Smith 1936-8:1229) and the Spokan, which led Wihr to describe how bufotenine, a psychoactive substance, is a, "poisonous hallucinogenic alkaloid (5-hydroxy-N N-dimethyltryptamine), and is just one part of the toad's secretions [...] and was used by Northwest Coast shamans as a hallucinogenic aid" (Wihr 1995:51). There is, however, no evidence of shamanistic use of bufotenine by the Spokan, though this type of death was always associated with a person who had his food poisoned from the collected drippings of a suspended crushed toad (Elmendorf 1935-6, 1:41). Nor is there evidence the shaman ever chewed fresh catnip leaves for hallucinogenic effects.

A similar description of how the neighboring Kalispel collected and applied this poison was given by Smith:

> They take a toad and hang it up by the hind legs. He dies and they catch the grease which drips out of it in something put under it to catch it. The grease is what is used. It is put in the food of someone (man or woman) they hate. Then the man is poisoned and dies a lingering death; maybe he will be sick for a year. He just withers away; nothing tastes good to him; he gets this; it is something like S. B. and he

finally dies [...] They did not make this out of frogs. It is made in summer when the sun is hot and this serves to melt the grease out. It is also made of snakes in exactly the same way, i.e., with the grease warmed out by the sun and never by a fire. The garter snake is used for this, not the *bull* [*sxʷiyups*] or rattler (1936-8:131 poison were often apparent to the hapless victim, for within a day or two, he would experience a severe flaking of his skin:

> If frogs [toads?] were eaten – the eater's [skin would] crumble away like "dandruff" – [a] person could poison an enemy by crush[ing] the frog between rocks & hanging it up by one leg to catch the drippings – these were put into the enemy's food & they would be poisoned and their skins would get like dandruff & they'd crumble away (Elmendorf 1935-6, 1:41).

Children from a young age were warned to avoid contact with certain insects and *reptiles* (*titišul'e?xʷ*), particularly snakes, frogs, toads, slugs, tadpoles, *spiders* (*tpttupl'* - "spiders"), wasps, and yellow jackets, since some of these creatures were known to be poisonous. Owls and scavenger birds, such as crows and ravens were to be avoided, for it was believed that, as happened with small animals, a child's eyes could be pecked out and eaten. According to Lord, the Spokan had a "superstitious dread of doing them [ravens] an injury, noting how, "I have seen them so gorged with dead mules' flesh as to be unable to fly into a tree; flapping their wings, to aid in hopping faster, they scram into the bushes in a most undignified manner, too full to even croak" (Lord 1866, 2:149).

An example of what may be called homeopathic medicine was given by an elderly lady some years ago, as she explained:

> I knew an old lady and her sister who both had rattlesnake power. In the spring and summer they would catch many rattlesnakes [Western diamondback], but never killed them though. They used long forked sticks to hold [the] snakes behind the neck, and they would milk the venom from their fangs. This venom was used later by the women to treat people who had T. B., [and] as I remember, they rubbed the venom very lightly on the person's body. Some people were cured (Ross 1968-2008).

In the case of malicious, intentional or accidental poisoning, it was common to swallow copious amounts of salmon oil or animal fat as an antidote (Turner *et al.* 1990; Hunn, Turner, French 1998:535; Elmendorf, pers. comm.), which encouraged regurgitation.

Parasites and Insects

The Spokan had to contend with a broad spectrum of introduced virile diseases, various pathogenic infectious and parasitic illnesses, different types of fungi, respiratory and pathogenic afflictions, and skin maladies such as ringworm of the feet, *scalp* (*soq'ʷqn*), and a host of other parasitic problems. Unfortunately, all of these became more frequent as children were forced to attend government and missionary boarding schools. In turn, many children contracted and brought home with them—at the end of term in June—an array of parasites, such as stomach *pin worms* (*Enterobius vernicularis* [*Oxyuris vermicularis*] - *snxm'sénč* - "pin worms in the stomach") and *abdominal parasites* (*snxm'pm*). The most common oral treatment was to give the child afflicted with parasites a solution made from boiled tamarack sap, a vermifuge which was considered a delicacy. It was an apparently effective antithelmintic for worms, particularly tape worms. Another common method of ridding the body of tapeworms was to take small amounts of freshly gathered Pacific yew needles, crush them, and then steep them in boiling water and to drink the decoction at least three times a day until the patient was cured.

Many elders contend that tamarack sap was good for many stomach maladies, even stomach cancer, but primarily for ridding the individual of tape worm. Boiling the root of stinging nettle and straining the solution through balled grass was effective when drunk for de-worming a person. The roots of a wild rose would be dug, cleaned, and boiled to make an infusion that was drunk for ridding a person of worms. A fresh wild mashed carrot root was made into a decoction, and drunk as a tea to treat intestinal parasites. Bracken fern root (*Pteridium aquilinum*) was mashed and eaten to eliminate tapeworms.

One cannot be certain, but elders recall how when attending the Fort Spokane Boarding School or the Spokane Day School, children sometimes contracted what may have been typhoid (enteric) fever, probably due to the infection *Salmonella typhosa*, which is caused by poor institutional sanitary conditions, such as improper disposal of contaminated urine and fecal materials. A few elders vaguely recall the premonitory signs of sore throat, vomiting, diarrhea, lethargy, and other clinical symptoms. Since there are few known records or oral conclusions regarding morbidity, what was observed may have been ambulatory typhoid.

Lord commented upon the profusion of flowers, and their wonderful scents, as well as the swarms of biting sand flies at the *confluence of the Columbia and Spokane River* (č'łyaq' or č'łyekʷ or sč'mep):

> Nothing could have been more enjoyable, had not clouds of sand-flies filled the air, stirred up by the feet of the mules and horses as they trampled through the grass. They pranced upon us at once, and covered the animals so thickly that they looked black. Plunging, kicking, and rolling on the grass with their loads was of no avail. Unlike the mosquito, that left only a lump, blood trickled from their puncture of the sand-flies' lancets. They whirled round our heads like angry bees, savagely attacking every available spot. We picked large branches of twigs, to drive away our assailants (Lord 1867:284).

In the winter, the Spokan employed the practice of *placing a hide out to freeze* (łuʔscúxʷlxʷ) to rid it of any vermin. Also, items of clothing and bedding suspected of housing *head lice* (*Pediculus humanus capitis* [Linn.] - č'č'stin'éʔ), *body lice* (*P. Humanus corporis* - č'č'stín'eʔ - "little bad things") and occasionally *pubic lice* - qʷtáxʷeʔ) were placed outside the dwelling for several hours to rid the articles of any *vermin* (ƛ'oʔsqinm - "search for head lice"), which were immobilized in the *bitter cold* (c'ér'ti) and easily shaken off. Soiled woolen blankets were cleaned and fluffed by beating them against frozen snow—a practice called čłłc'íʔčiʔs. In the summer, clothing and bedding were spread on racks and smoked for the same reason. The dried flowers of sweet-scented bedstraw (*Galium trifolium* Michx.) were used as a perfume and placed in bedding.

Pubic lice were also widespread in situations of overcrowded living conditions and limited bathing facilities in boarding schools. Such conditions were also conducive to *fleas* (*Pulex irritans* [Linn.] - kʷtkʷít'ps), which were unknowingly brought home in the children's clothing. Even for those children who did not attend a government or mission school, a grandmother or mother would periodically *take care to search a small child's hair for lice* (čłtqnaʔsqélixʷ), to *delouse* (ƛ'oʔsqnm) a person, or when a child complained. Lice were understandably a constant concern, even in the winter when clothing or bedding could become infested.

The itch mite (*Sarcoptes scabiei*) causes scabies, and was also introduced to families in the same manner as were *bedbugs* (*Cimex lectularius* - kʷeʔkʷʔéłc'eʔ). There were other forms of dermatitis. But nature provided treatments, learned through trial and error by the Spokan. The narrow green leaves of *Clematic columbian*, known as c'iʔc'iʔxéy'łp, one that grows along streams, was placed in bedding to repulse bedbugs. Moreover, the unpleasant smelling leaves would also be placed with stored salmon to prevent flying insects and ʔakʷtíłš ("crawling insects") and other vectors from spoiling the storage (STHC). An indication of stored fish or meat being contaminated by insect larvae was the appearance of a maggot, most notably from the *green blowfly* (*Phaenicia sericata* - hamáłtn), and *large horsefly* or *stablefly* (*Chrysomya rufifales* - qʷqʷátqn'). Children were taught never to kill *ladybugs* (*Hippodamia convergens* - nłqʷqʷčil), but to avoid them.

Because of the often close and unsanitary conditions associated with institutional schooling, students invariably acquired a wide range of parasites by *mutual transference* (ƛ'qoʔsqnwéxiʷ), and often children returning home on vacation from school were infested with horse flies or the *larvae* (čkʷkʷʔén'eʔ) of the *house fly* (*Musca domestica* - xmáłtn). Infested children were immediately dusted with the dried and pounded leaves of dragon sagewort. Given the variety of institutional vermin, concerted efforts were made by the mother or grandmother, once these children had returned home for vacation, to rid their young charges of unwanted parasites. Mothers would *diligently search for head lice* (m'aʔm'osqin'iʔ), and once one was

649

found, it was carefully *removed by pulling it along the hair shaft* (*šašác'qn'iʔ*) with *a fine, long-toothed wooden comb* (*ƛ'qoʔsqncútn* or *ƛ'ʔósqntn* - "louse/nit comb") made from a thin but wide section of western red cedar with the spring growth removed, and the teeth fashioned with a sharp-pointed stone (STHC). Often upon locating the lice, a person would mash or pop the parasite by a practice termed *ƛ'iqʷms*, which replicates the sound produced (STHC). A mother may rid her baby or small child of lice by repeatedly biting with her incisors any vermin wherever found, a practice referred to as *k'ʷaʔk'ʷaʔqín'm'*. The sweathouse often eradicated many of the aforementioned school-contracted parasites, as did washing the child's hair with different infusions, particularly a decoction made from boiled cascara bark. Elders recalled how in the sweathouse, Dragon Sagewood leaves were placed on the hot stones to rid a person of lice, bedbugs, and fleas.

Walker, while at Tschimakain ("place of springs"), in a letter of October 1841, "suggested that another possible reason for his move [of residence during subsistence quest] was that if they [Indians] did not, 'they would be overrun with vermin'" (Drury 1976:138 fn). And in the same letter, he again reiterated how adamant he was that no one Indian family should camp near the mission for fear they would might also build their homes close by—primarily because the, "Indian camps were always infested with vermin" (Drury 1976:284 fn). Obviously, neither Walker nor the historian Drury ever actively participated in a sweathouse session, and, therefore, failed to understand that such a ritual served to rid the participants of lice. Drury cites a policy of Walker, who seldom permitted a "poor" Spokan into his home, but once happened and when:

> He [the Spokan Indian] finally laid down after a while, but was up very early & took his leave. But we soon had evidence that he had left much behind for the Indians with we found that they were swarming with lice & I have felt all day as though I was covered with them (1976:139).

An *insect bite* (*ɬuʔɬw'éɬc'eʔ*), particularly those from the *yellow jacket* (*Vespula pennsylvanica* - *sq'ʷʔɬ*), was treated primarily by chewing a fresh leaf of kinnikinnick, and placing the underside of the leaf on the wound, which often removed the *stinger* (*swer'ép*), and anesthetized the wound. Insect bites were also treated by chewing the leaves of a small *wood rose* (*Rosa gymnocarpa* Nutt. ex T. & G. - *xʷxʷy'épeʔɬp*) and spitting the solution onto the bite. If this plant was not available, a man would blow his nose in his hand, placing the *mucus* (*snós*) on the wound. Or, if salt was available, a person would treat the sting of an insect by rubbing salt in the wound until the pain subsided—a procedure that also presumably prevented swelling. The leaves of wild rose (*R. nutkana* Presl.) were chewed and placed directly on an insect bite to ease the pain and prevent inflammation. When the mashed leaves of catnip were rubbed on the skin, the oils prevented insect bites.

If available, the leaf of fresh Plantago was chewed and the under-side of the leaf placed upon a painful insect bite; relief was almost immediate, after which the leaf was buried. Another treatment of wasp or hornet sting was to take any one of three species of onion, which was peeled, cut in half, and then rubbed on the site. There was no memory of cauterizing a painful insect bite. A common treatment was to place a heated congealed mass of goldenrod leaves directly on the site of insect stings or small animal bites to relieve, or at best sooth, the pain. Probably unknowingly, this treatment also served as an antibacterial. A strong tea made from freshly crushed catnip leaves served as a mild sedative, one with antibacterial properties.

White willow bark (*Salix glauca*)—along with cambium—could be boiled until the solution became yellow-brown, and externally administered in a variety of ways for treating minor wounds, dermal eruptions, scabs, and lice, as well as ridding the body of a *nit* (*č'č'stín'eʔ*) - i.e., the egg of a *louse* (*qʷtáxʷeʔ*) or other parasitic insect, and the active ingredient was acetylsalicylic acid. Powdered or moist clay applied to an insect bite was known to reduce pain and swelling.

An aggravating insect was the ubiquitous *mosquito* (*Culex pinguis* - *c'asláqs*) that inhabited wetland areas and summer camps near water. Smudge fires were not always a practical way of preventing bites; so men, given their scant clothing and presence out-of-doors, would attempt to protect themselves by, "Rubbing in soft fat on their skin, which is also a good plan to allay the terrible ceaseless itching" (Lord 1867, I:281). It is not clear if Lord was referring to the Spokan who may have painted their bodies with vermilion to help

650

prevent insect bites, or another contiguous group he had visited. Apparently the best procedure was to use smoke or smudge fire to prevent being bitten, particularly by the female sandfly. This blood-sucking, two-winged irritant was identified by Lord as *Simulia columbaschensis*—commonly called brucot, a designation apparently used in the past by English entomologists —whereas further research indicates that this creature is the one that present-day entomologists would refer to as *Simulium nocivum*. It is interesting that Lord, a biologist, had a deep and methodical understanding of natural systems as well as the environment of the fauna and their interdependencies. Consequently, he, like the famous botanist David Douglas, had a unique perspective as a non-anthropologist, and made rather cogent observations, most of which are still considered correct. He might have had some personal experience with what he referred to as the "burning fly," for he noted that it "is a most appropriate name for this insect as the puncture it makes is as if a red-hot needle was thrust into one's flesh" (Lord 1867:286). There was no notion that the *bumble bee* (*Bombus terricola* - q'ʷiq'ʷáyaq'ʷúʔɫ) constituted any problems to humans or animals.

A wide variety of mashed roots—some not identified by ethnobotanists—were chewed or steeped as tea for fever from insect bites, or the mashed leaves of certain plants were applied directly upon the wound. Crushed yarrow leaves served as a mosquito repellent when fresh leaves were dubbed over one's body. But if the individual was already bitten, the same procedure proved an effective treatment. After playing outside, children were always carefully examined during the warmer months to see if they had a woodtick (*Dermacentor andersonii* - a.k.a. [Rocky Mountain wood tick] - or *deer tick* (*Lxodes dammini* and *Ornithodoros* spp. - sč'č'c'él'ščn'). Children were warned not to play near *greasewood bushes* (*Purshia tridentata*), as this bush often harbors wood ticks (Turner 1979:242).

There is little recollection of the mythical or even economic significance, if any, except as fish bait, of insects such as *daddy long-legs* (*Phalangium opilio Linneaus* - stam'ól'y'eʔ or sč'ey't), an unidentified beetle (m'eckʷl'íw'y'eʔ), *stink bug* (*Acrosternum hilare* [Say] - p'uʔp'uʔmúɫ), darting (striding) *water bug* (*Aquarius remigis* - ppátiʔqs), and another hydrophobic legged but unidentified type of *water bug* (nʔopl'qsétkʷ) associated with *green moss* (snmtr'étkʷ). The so-called aquatic species of the ant lion or doodle bug (*Myreleon* spp.), a voracious ant predator, was also used as bait, and an unidentified small water bug called nʔopl'qsétkʷ. A general term for ant was sxʷúxʷíy'eʔ, and all hard-shell bugs were classified as nč'l'xʷíčn'.

Bandages

The most common type of *bandage* (nlč'séltn) was made by taking strips of willow bark, and binding the wound with the inside of the bark against the wound. In cases of emergency, or when there was no available willow bark, mullein leaves were crushed and the undersides wrapped upon the wound, being held in place with any supple material. Some individuals would chew the willow bark strip before applying, or, if possible, cobwebs were balled and applied directly on the wound before bandaging.

One elder related how as a young man he had been logging one winter by himself with a cross-cut saw that was rested on an ingenious roller-jig he had made from a wooden thread spool. Unfortunately, he once severely cut a leg when the saw jumped from jig, and the only thing available as a bandage, besides his clothes, was a dressed hung deer he had killed early in the morning. He took the stomach, shook out its contents, wrapped this around his bleeding thigh, and held it in place using his belt. After returning home several days later, his wife replaced the wrapped deer's stomach with a clean cloth bandage, and they realized the wound had properly congealed, and that there was no infection, probably due to the hydrochloric acid from the stomach. He said he later had no scars.

The same man later explained how when treating a minor cut or wound, and if willow bark and mullein leaves were not accessible, a person would sprinkle—if available—dry powdered clay upon the cut or wound as an effective field method for stanching the bleeding, which also afforded some protection for the wound. In some instances, any type of deciduous leaf was mashed before applying to a bleeding wound, and held in place with a series of grass wraps. An old and desiccated cattail stalk served as an effective and very absorbent type of field bandage, once the stalk had been halved by cutting lengthwise and applying the open-celled portion directly to the wound. Fluffed moist cattail down was also applied to burns.

A grayish green, white-veined long leafs of *rattlesnake plantain* (*Goodyera oblongifolia* Raf. - *nki?íws* - "split in the middle") were first split or peeled lengthwise before briskly rubbing them together between one's fingers. The leaf was applied to the afflicted area of a minor cut or sore (STHC). Subscribing to the Doctrine of Signatures, "A woman wishing to become pregnant would split open a leaf of this plant and blow on it several times" (Turner *et al*. 1980:52).

Sewage Pharmacology

Unfortunately, the term "sewage pharmacology" is misleading even though medical anthropologists have acknowledged the benefits of using human urine and animal feces, which once were universally of benefit in many peoples' pharmacopoeia. Though the Spokan recognized the value of sewage pharmacology, there was no recall of the term for such practices. This now-adopted phrase, however, is appropriate when considering how both human urine and animal feces were once universally used as external medicaments in treating a variety of maladies, even though medical anthropologists claim that it was due to the beneficial effects of using the ammonia which is released from the alkaline properties of feces and urine (Forbes 1968:246).

Human feces was not used, but horse and cow feces were used by the Spokan as a poultice for both humans and domesticated animals. Partially dried animal feces—having the consistency that permitted it to be shaped as a thin round pad—was placed directly on the afflicted site. For example, a horse suffering from a stone impacted in the frog of its hoof was treated by packing the hoof with fresh manure, then wrapping the hoof in hide or several layers of burlap until the stone eventually emerged out through the top of the hoof within three to four days.

It was known that when away from a camp or village, and while lumbering, hunting, or herding cows or domesticated *sheep* (*lmotú*), if a person sustained a serious open wound, it was immediately covered with partially fresh sheep or cow feces for several days—a practice that prevented infection. Some claimed that after the wound had healed there was never a residual scar.

Even prior to the introduction of metal-related infections, the Spokan were concerned with what is now known as tetanus or lockjaw, which may be gotten from wood splinters, surgical wounds, postpartum uterus, and even burns that could possibly have been a predisposing factor that could carry the anaerobic, sporulating bacillus (*Clostridium tetani*) found in soil and animal feces. Of course metal increased the likelihood of mortality, given the brief period of incubation, which once established had no known cure at the time. Regarding the etiology of any disease, one could only speculate as to the relationship between cause and successful treatment. However, the Spokan knew that after extracting a wood splinter one should, if possible, urinate upon the wound to prevent infection. The same procedure was used in treating cuts from barbwire, fishhooks, and other sharp pieces of metal or wood, and only recently has it been known that the pH (hydrogen ion concentration) of human and animal urine is acid, and will, upon application, neutralize such alkaline-based pathogens as *Clostridium tetani*. The critical chemical element in urine is urea, known to kill many bacteria and fungi.

Horse and Dog Medicines

Nearly every reservation Spokan family owned one or more working horses, animals they were dependent upon for transportation to conducting trade, and warfare, and acquiring status. But before being forced to adapt to a more sedentary reservation existence, one based largely upon agriculture, the indigenous non-patent medicines required to maintain the health of their domesticated animals were often the same as their own. Until quite recently, some deserted horse barns contained, along with patent medicines, a variety of bottled home-made concoctions or hanging dried plants and animal oil-based emoluments. In treating horses with distemper or colds, an excellent *horse medicine* (*q'ʷóxʷq'xʷ*) was made from biscuitroot (*Lomatium ambiguum* [Nutt.] C. & R.)—the same Spokan word which also glosses as *q'ʷóxʷq'xʷ*. The oily yellowish-brown leaves were crushed and the large white-fleshed, yellow-skinned tap-root was easily stripped (producing a strong parsley aroma). The crushed roots and leaves were placed in an open buckskin bag pulled over the horse's nose, forcing the animal to inhale as a treatment for distemper. If needed, the leaves could be smoked and held under the horse's nose to inhale in order to open its nasal passages. This process was repeated until the horse's nose commenced to drain (STHC). A similar treatment was used for a horse diagnosed with a cold. The horse owner removed and rubbed between his hands the oval-shaped, unequal yellow-like leaf segments, and then placed the crushed leaves upon the horse's nostrils, which was repeated until the animal's nose drained. Mashed biscuitroot of the same type was warmed and used to treat a horse with a swollen knee by rubbing, and then layering and securing the root intermittently against the knee. Or, if available, several handfuls of an entire buttercup plant were mashed and held against the horse's swollen knee. Mashed leaves and branches of rabbitbush were mixed with water and rubbed on horses to protect the make a smoke which was placed under the animal's nostrils to cure distemper.

Crushed chocolate tips roots were used on horses with a cut or multiple lacerations, just as they were used to stop minor cuts and bleeding with humans. The same medicament was used if a horse had heaves or what may have been considered lung problems by heating the long roots of chocolate tips, which were then mashed and placed in a nose-bag for the horse to inhale. A similar treatment involved placing a handful of burning fresh yarrow stalks and leaves in a bucket of hot coals, which produced a smoke that permeated a burlap bag held over the smoking yarrow; the bag as then wrapped about the horse's nostrils to rid the animal of distemper or any upper respiratory malady (STHC). Another treatment in the fall was to gather the dried powdered roots of chocolate tips, which were burned, and the smoke was place under the nose of a horse. Mature roots and tops of this plant "were considered poisonous" (Turner *et al.* 1980:66).

Only one elderly rancher remembered how the crushed leaves of white clematis were rubbed on open leg wounds of a horse. Application was judiciously done since clematis bark contains strong chemical constituents like protanemonin (Turner 1984), which may irritate the skin and even mucus membranes. He could not recall if it was ever used for on human skin eruptions or wound.

In the spring, an annual concern was if a horse became diarrheic when it commenced to eat fresh grass. This situation was treated by feeding the horse a mixture of grass and chopped horsetail, the latter being a poison for *cattle* (*st'm'áʔ*) if eaten in too great a quantity. A constant concern with horses—once barbed wire had been introduced—was the fear of infection from wire cuts. If and when this happened, they were treated by mashing several handfuls of blue elderberries, boiling them, and placing the cooled mass upon the cut to stop bleeding and later infection.

Both humans and dogs suffering from cracks in their feet were treated with a variety of medicines to reduce pain and permitted the dog or person to continue going barefoot. The most frequent treatment was to thoroughly rub the injured feet with tallow or grease, which for both man and dog had to be temporarily covered with either mullein leaves or bits of twisted Indian hemp or buckskin, held in place by lacing with either of these materials. When possible, the cracks of injured feet were treated by filled with pitch that had first been cooked until black and then applied to the feet while soft. If available, both the sticky round heads and the tap roots of several *tarweed plants* (*Madia glomerata* Hook. - *t'eɫšisqá*) were mashed and applied directly to the hoof of an injured horse, a dog's pads, or a person's feet. Tarweed was also mixed with pitch, and eaten as a gastrointestinal binder. The seeds of this plant are edible, being eaten raw (St. John 1963:506).

Non-Traditional Diseases

The entire medical profile of the Spokan—and of all Native Americans—was unfortunately radically change with the introduction of contagious pandemics and epidemics into the Plateau (Boyd 1985), such as *smallpox* (xʷʔít̓ qʷmqʷmiʔp), *chickenpox* (čɫʔócqeʔ - "visible on the outside"), influenza, fevers, malaria, *dysentery* (hnc̓eʔrénči), *tuberculosis* (henɫx̌ʷúm̓ti) and other upper respiratory diseases, *measles* (sč̓ocqʔíc̓eʔ), and several *Treponema* parasites. The effect on indigenous populations was devastating, both physically and psychologically, and may have partly responsible for the development of certain religious movements within the Plateau (Du Bois 1938; Walker and Schuster 1998). Reverend Walker stated how, "The measles have gone through the country carrying off great numbers" (Drury 1976:432). Drury, after reading Walker's diaries, wrote, "The constant flow of fur traders and Indians back and forth across the mountains could easily have introduced the measles epidemic into Oregon [territory] before the arrival of the 1847 immigrants" (1976:372). According to Drury's secondary research, there was, "A virulent strain of measles [that] brought death to hundreds of natives in the Upper Columbia River country in the fall of 1847" (1976:380).

Wilson felt that venereal disease was introduced to the Spokan in 1859 when U.S. troops were first stationed at the Colville post (1866:293). *Venereal disease* (hesč̓swéyti) was extremely depilating, particularly *syphilis* (*Treponema pallidum* - tcínúk), an adopted Chinook word, which interestingly may indicate the immediate source or by trading contact (Egesdal, pers. comm.). Scott cited several of Gibbs' (1877, 1:207) observations of indigenous treatments for introduced venereal diseases, "For a tonic and venereal medicine [...] the aborigines used a decoction of the Oregon grape [...] for gonorrhea, a tea steeped from a species of fern and the smoke of certain plants and woods (1928, 2:160).

Despite the aforementioned, there were apparently no demonstrable cures for syphilis, whereas *gonorrhea* (*Neisseria gonorrhoeae* - sčcnukʷkʷ) was reputed to have been treated with several medicinal plants, but none that could be identified by any now known Spokan designation or description to establish a known Spokan designation. The roots of *ryegrass* (*Leymus unereus*) were mashed and placed in boiling water to make a medicinal decoction that was drunk several times a day to fight the gonorrhea infection. However, the Colville-Okanogan used numerous plants for treating *venereal disease* (hesč̓swéti) (Turner *et al.* 1980). Though likely, there is no information regarding amebiasis, giardiasis, or vaginitis, or other protozoan infections, which does not negate their existence. Smith (1936-8:1063,1081) mentions a treatment for gonorrhea, an unidentified white swamp root that produces a red tea, which was drunk twice a day by any woman afflicted with gonorrhea, one that was said to be successful. Another treatment of gonorrhea was to drink a tea made from steeping the red seed heads of smooth sumac. It was claimed that gonorrheal sores were treated with heated mashed flowers of wild buckwheat.

Traditional methods of curing often proved ineffective against these new illnesses and diseases. Even the sweathouse, once a tried and true treatment for so many maladies, unfortunately led in many instances to the development of pneumonia, or simply killed a person with a high fever. Parker, though not speaking of the Spokan, was witness to the devastating results of using the sweathouse and latter cold plunge upon the great mortality when Indians:

> In the burning stage of the fever, they plunged into some lake or river and continued in the water until the heat was allayed, and rarely survived the cold stage which followed. The shores were strewn with the unburied dead. Whole and large villages were depopulated; and some entire villages have disappeared (Parker 1838:191).

Needless to say, the decimation of large numbers of people was detrimental to more than the Spokan's social structure. A thorough and comprehensive study of non-traditional Plateau disease may be found in Boyd's Ph.D. 1985 dissertation and 1990 publication.

A common and often dangerous treatment for smallpox and measles (heat illnesses) during the winter was for the patient to suck—if available—a large *icicle* (*ʕʷóxʷiqs* or *st'olilá?qn*) while sitting in front of an open or stove fire heavily wrapped in blankets. The explanation given for this treatment was based on the so-called hot/cold syndrome as well as the Doctrine of Signatures, which simply implied that a person being *cold* (*?ixʷmús*) inside, and *hot* (*λ'aq'*) outside was experiencing an imbalanced physical state, which could be corrected by an administering an opposing type of plant medicine. Consequently, the Spokan subscribed to a universal notion of the hot/cold syndrome (Foster 1978), a.k.a. "complementary opposition" in which some maladies were treated by ingestion or external application of opposing medicaments. That is, a hot medicine—by color, texture or taste—treated a cold illness; whereas a warm medicine, also designated by such characteristics, treated a cold illness.

After people realized that attempts to cure smallpox and certain other infectious diseases by using the sweathouse was actually killing the patient, this once traditional ritual for curing was discontinued, and less drastic methods of treatment were relied upon. A questionable treatment for smallpox was to place several small pockets of fir pitch in the patient's mouth, who would not chew or break the casing, but rather would swallow the flavored *saliva* (*sn̓ʕawpcín* or *sptáxʷ*). A similar treatment for smallpox was to scrape the balsam blisters, boil them, and then drink the strong tasting solution. Some elders could recall being administered this solution as children during the 1898-99 epidemic. There are several interesting accounts (STHC) of the Spokan immunizing themselves by taking the dry scab of a smallpox cutaneous eruption, grinding the crust, and placing the powder into a small subcutaneous cut made in the skin. It has been stated (STHC) that this process of *immunization* or *inoculation* (*spoct*), during which they purposely scratched (*nt'ehk'ʷus* - "scab drops off") their skin, quickly became a procedure in the Spokan's *precious medications* (*nkʷtnaqsin mr'ay' e?mistis*).

Tuberculosis (*nłxʷum'ti* or *henłxʷúm'ti*), a pathogen once unknown to the indigenous population, was sometimes called *consumption* (*hec č"úxʷxʷmi* or *sč'xʷum* or *snłxú?mt*) due to a patient's wasting away. It could be either pulmonary tuberculosis (*tubercle bacilli*) or tuberculosis of the bowels. Although certain plant medicines and inhalation therapy were administered for tuberculosis, some elders said that they heard that traditional medicines had no beneficial effect against this disease. Tuberculosis was sometimes treated by boiling the mashed roots of fleabane (Erigeron), a.k.a. *gum weed* (*Grindelia nana* Nutt. - *ntítal'xús*), and boiled to make a concoction which was drunk. There is no information if the patient sweated. A decoction of common mullein leaves was also used to treat tuberculosis. Snowberry bark gathered in late summer and early fall was first pounded, placed in boiling water to make a medicinal tea, and drunk several times a day to suppress lung infection, particularly tuberculosis. Scott, quoting his father (1924, 2:98) who used data from Gibbs' observations (1877), contended, "Tuberculosis was always widely prevalent [...] and more after the advent of the whites. Exposure to cold and wet weather and the bad effects of firewater, impure air and the exotic diseases of the whites increased the mortality from tuberculosis" (Scott 1928, 2:161).

With the introduction of tuberculosis, snow bush was thought to be an effective remedy. The twisted stalk of snowberry and trillium were gathered for use as medicine; in the latter use, as a tea. Tuberculosis—as well as whooping cough—was also treated by drinking a tea infusion made with the *sap nodule* (*st'iqʷlqʷ*) under the bark of any fir tree. The *white fir blisters* (*st'iqʷlqʷ*) from both grand fir and subalpine fir, were boiled and the bitter liquid was drunk as needed to treat any type of serious cough, particularly with whooping cough or a tubercular cough, including smallpox. Tubercular and whooping cough patients drank a tea made from dried, powdered subalpine fir blisters, which by experience and reference was sometimes reinforced with freshly mashed green needles from this tree. Small pieces of Engelmann spruce were; similarly boiled, diluted in hot water, and drunk as a tea for a serious cough. Some people remember, in the past, taking the pitch from lodgepole pine, boiling it in hot water, and drinking only this decoction, rather than water, until cured. Because of the strength and taste of this decoction, a thin broth made from deer meat was drunk beforehand to prevent regurgitation. Small yellow elderberry buds could be smashed or rolled together between one's palms and steeped in hot water as a tea for treating pulmonary tuberculosis.

There is no indication as to how frequent a problem cancer was for the Spokan, since autopsies are a recent medical procedure. Yet it is acknowledged that it did exist. The most common treatment for gastrointestinal and renal cancer, was for the patient to finely chop some tips from either a tamarack tree or subalpine fir tree and steep them in steaming hot water, then strain it into another receptacle, and drunk upon cooling. The same medicinal tea was used to treat whooping cough, though a parent might also have administered a spoonful of tamarack sap to a child, a syrup that was considered a delicacy. Years ago, tamarack sap, which contains a natural sugar, galactan, was given to children with whooping cough to reduce the pain of swollen tonsils and adenoids. Tamarack sap was also an effective *medicinal* (*snc'émc'm*) for the treatment of various abdominal maladies, particularly for ridding children of tapeworms. In more recent times, it was thought to be beneficial in treating colon and stomach cancer, and was drunk in varying dilutions to treat upper respiratory afflictions. For internal use, the sap from a tamarack tree was used, because *tamarack syrup* (*snc'emc'm or sc'm'qin* or *nc'em'c'm'* or *snc'em'c'm'*) seldom had a pitch flavor. Some elders believed that a spoonful of tamarack sap, taken with a cup of warm water, was beneficial in treating stomach, colon, and rectal cancer.

One treatment for a person suspected of having a cancer, was to drink a tea made from the pulverized bark and long, curved, bright scarlet berries of devil's club. Because of the taste, it was considered a type of revulsive medicine. On the Northwest Coast, this plant has "hypoglycemic properties [and] may help the user to enter a trance state" (Wihr 1995:52).

Nowadays, the main debilitating medical condition among most Native Americans—including the Spokan—is diabetes mellitus (both Type I and Type II), due to a hereditary or developmental disorder of carbohydrate metabolism, often attributable to improper diet, one high in refined simple carbohydrates, i.e., sugars. Spokan elders were undoubtedly correct in saying that both type of *diabetes* (*t'e?šéłc'?ey*) were introduced and became established—actually becoming endemic—when the primary caloric intake shifted from traditional foods to white-introduced foods, mostly refined and simple carbohydrates. Ensuing medical complications of diabetes are many, including blindness, amputation and even death.

When treating Euro-American diseases, it was said that Spokan curing shamans rarely sang traditional curing songs, but instead composed ones that were apparently more descriptive of the patient's clinical condition and appearance. There was a linguistic variation on songs sung when treating non-traditional maladies and disease. The following is one of many individual curing songs, which were sung in when treating traditional maladies, but in English for suspected Euro-American diseases:

[In Spokan:] *lemlmtš qe?eł č'łčicntn łu? skʷe?rúle?xʷ myémistn nsc'?ar'qín n sweyt n t'ey'e? sweyt.*

[In English:] Thank you. We have reached once again the time when the grass comes up. The medicines for headaches, and all other sicknesses, for serious illnesses or anything that makes you really sick (STHC).

Most elderly men and women once had a fear of reservation Indian Health Services, even though some widowers and widows would go there several mornings a week to socialize with old friends. There was a much greater fear for an elder if s/he had to go and receive help at an urban medical center in Spokane or Seattle. As one older lady, reflecting upon her knowledge and experience, and displaying no hostility, said:

Those medical people experiment and even steal organs and parts from patients at night or when unconscious [drugged] or *anesthetized* (*ičstm*). They [doctors] don't understand when women get older, having raised their children, grandchildren, and like me, great grandchildren—some of the smallest have taken my breast—that we are prepared for death. But we don't want to suffer in those places [hospitals] where we eat strange foods, are undressed, and let them take things [feces, urine, and blood] from us - to do what? Humans, even us Indians, [are] like trees, once old [we] don't bear leaves anymore, we become hollow and stiff, and only the strong wind should knock us over, not [strange white - *suyápi*] people (Ross 1968-2008).

In cases of suspected sorcery, the elderly victim was in a stressful psychological dilemma because they feared that if that were hospitalized by a condition caused by sorcery, then the true source of their ailments would never be recognized by a physician. Furthermore, they felt that they would probably die when released from a hospital and returning to the reservation, being again exposed to the sorcerer's vengeance. It was personally known that several such sorcery victims felt that any reserve of faith or strength that they had, had been negated by the non-Indian medicines, foods, and treatments. These fears were naturally reinforced by the presence of night sounds, impersonal contact, numerous electrical devices they believed negated a shaman's traditional power. These were once accepted reasons as to why some curing shamans would not treat Indian patients in hospitals, clinics, or administrate Indian medicaments in such an alien, even perceived hostile environment. Consequently, nearly all of these sorcerized elders felt that it would be best if they went to a rest home or lived with an off-reservation relative, rather than go home. Often there appeared to be no change in intensity of the patient's sorcerized condition even when usually several hundred kilometers away from the suspected sorcerer, a patient may attempt to leave the clinic or hospital.

For some elders an alternative to urban medical facilities was to attend Indian Shaker meetings on either the Colville or Yakima Indian Reservations. A few elderly sick people have had a younger relative drive them to the Shahaptian-speaking Umatilla or Yakima Indian Reservations to attend their more traditional Indian Shaker healing ceremonies or services by a traditional practitioner. It has been said that, when seeking treatment at any of the aforementioned healing ceremonies, it is always best to seek older Indian practitioners, whom they felt were more competent and less dangerous than younger practitioners (Ross 1981).

Sanitation and Hygiene

Sanitation and hygiene were primary daily concerns, at both a personal level and also regarding communal living and the disposal of human waste. To a *visitor* (*skítstsn*), the most apparent sign of cleanliness was the area of a village or camp, which was swept daily with brooms made of various stiff vegetation, usually made of snowberry withes with one end wrapped with Indian hemp. Small household *brushes* (*xʷkʼʼʷmín*) for sweeping were fashioned from a large bird, duck or goose wing. Women were responsible for sweeping the area of their dwellings and a designated section of the public area. Young girls assisted their mothers, receiving praise from the elders for their efforts. As with today's elders, one's home was a source of pride, ideally being kept scrupulously clean and tidy, which, if not, would reflect badly upon a woman's domestic abilities, or worse, her industry and diligence. A visitor never commented upon the neatness of a host's home, which would have suggested an unusual condition of pre-visit care and attention. In the not too distant past, any dwelling occupied by an elderly couple or an incapacitated man or woman was tended to daily by older, often unrelated girls.

Refuse—as generally attested by archaeology—was not a problem for the Spokan by the mere existence of certain prohibitions against waste, and being organic they used only biodegradable things and so little refuse was generated. However, with the reservation period, each homestead had a site where metal, glass, and other inorganic garbage was dumped, currently being sought by bottle collectors. During the prehistoric and early historic periods, seldom was any food left after a meal, and what was not eaten was put aside and reheated for the next meal, or made into a soup or stew. Any bones, gristle, or an unwanted cut, would be put outside and immediately consumed by any one of many dogs. The main meal was in the early evening.

Some natural materials had multiple, if not countless uses. For instance, the inner bark of gray willow was shredded to make absorbent diapers, menstrual pads, and as a bandage when dressing a wound. Fresh Dragon Sagewort leaves were layered as diapers for babies, or applied to a baby's bottom if he had a rash. For example, the soft fluff from *mature cattail heads* (*qʼʼʷsqʼʼʷastqín, young catkins - sx̣ʷóɫqn or sqʼʼʷastqín*), and black cottonwood catkins made serviceable diapers, when stuffed inside a cradleboard near the baby's bottom. The fragrant leaves of Dragon Sagewort were also used as menstrual pads during the menses. After a woman's delivery, Dragon Sagewort leaves were layered and applied as an absorbent pad to the woman's labia until she stopped bleeding. Absorbent pads were also made from pounded cedar bark (bast) and from layered mullein leaves; all were carefully burned after use. One elderly woman heard of beaver skin once being used many years ago for this purpose. The leaves of rabbitbrush also served as a sanitary pad.

Bathing

Without providing any specific reasons, Cox concluded that, "The Spokans are far superior to the Indians of the coast in cleanliness, but by no means equal in this respect to the Flatheads" (1831:115). Understandably, bathing was an important ritual for people of any age, given their exposure to earthen floors, activities of subsistence gathering by digging and processing their harvest, and the requirements of hunting and working with blood and grease. Adult men and women, as previously discussed, adhered to a strict commitment of daily sweat-bathing, which was the principal activity for maintaining physical cleanliness by removing any accumulated grime and perspiration. To properly cleanse one's body, a deer rib or a wooden scraper was used during the second session, a time designated for physical cleansing. Women would later—after the men's sweat—take into the sweathouse a basket of ground moss to achieve the same purpose, if scraping was not deemed necessary.

A daily occurrence for all young children, immediately upon rising, and after their toilet, was to plunge and bathe in the nearest stream or the Spokane River, a practice they continued throughout the year, unless smaller streams were frozen with ice too thick to break, in which case the person rolled in the snow after each sweating session. Boys used their designated area of bathing, which was always located a distance from where the girls bathed in their designated area. Elders have said that even in the case of icing, older boys would—if possible—simply break the ice and follow their daily regime of bathing, which was known to condition and improve a person's general physical condition and to generally improve the young person's ability to withstand future adverse situations, such as pain and physical deprivation. Like the children, men and women never bathed together; the men used a more distant site, and the women had their separate area. Early morning bathing sessions ensured that all children learned to become accomplished swimmers at an early age. Men and women never swam together, but rather in separate areas since they always swam naked.

Every village and camp had several types of bathing pools similar to those used for hydrotherapy, and were frequently used for medicinal reasons as well as cleansing. Most men preferred the sweathouse for daily physical cleansing. If they are not near running water for a plunge, they used any relatively shallow pool that permitted one to lie submerged to get a thorough soak. In cool weather or winter, three preheated stones were used to *heat* ($\check{\lambda}\,'q\,'\check{\lambda}\,'\acute{a}q\,'is$) the water, which were removed prior to use. If suffering muscle stiffness, a person might use a hide or blanket to hold the heat after leaving the sweathouse, covering all but his head.

Within the extensive number of ethnobotanical specimens, one of the most important plants for physical, medicinal, and spiritual cleansing was the wild rose. There were almost daily occasions when a baby, small child, or elderly person performed ablution rituals in the dwelling, typically because of ambulatory difficulties. To cleanse and purify one's body, the entire wild rose bush, including the roots, were pounded and placed into boiled water, which was poured over all or certain parts of the person. Prior to acquiring large metal cauldrons, total immersion was impossible, unless the bather was a baby or small child.

After attending a person's funeral, the ritual of bathing and attending the sweathouse warranted considerable caution against spiritual contamination. This required the participant to take a bath with copious amounts of rosewater, believed to purify the bather, to purify anything that had been touched by the deceased (including weapons, stick-game bones, counter sticks), and to wash away his ownership (STHC).

Until the early 1900s, and as previously cited, all children and most adults would swim daily in the main river or in one of four major streams. Older children swam throughout the winter. An elderly man would supervise the boys' swimming, as did an elderly woman who assumed the responsibility of the young girls. Even in the winter, prior to breakfast, men and older boys would often swim in the river after first breaking a hole in the ice, if necessary. Girls and boys washed their hair on a daily basis—adults less frequently, and never in a river to prevent pollution of fish and other aquatic life. After performing a physically difficult task, a man would rub sand, horsetails, or the smooth edge of a bone over his body to remove dirt and perspiration, but never in naturally running water. Walker's diary of 23 March 1841 cites how for five loads of ammunition he enticed a Spokan man to swim across the near-frozen Spokane River to retrieve a boat (Drury 1976:138).

In addition to daily bathing, including ritual sweating, the Spokan were fastidious about personal hygiene, particularly washing their hands and faces before and after all meals, many foods being so-called finger foods. Cleansing was best accomplished by crushing or rubbing the leaves of western clematis (*Clematis occidentalis*) in water; thus, producing a lather that was very effective for removing any grease, dirt, and food particles. This preparation was also used to treat boils or sores, even on horses. In the past, there were two daily meals, one before sunrise and one in the early evening. When deemed necessary, such as prior to a bear hunt, the fresh leaves of balsamroot or spring sunflower were placed on the glowing coals of the sweathouse to produce a profuse spiritual and diaphoretic cleansing.

The daily commitment of sweat-bathing was the principal method for maintaining cleanliness. While steaming during the second session, the body would be scraped with a deer rib or a *wooden scraper* (*ʔáx̣ʷmn*) to remove accumulated perspiration. A confined baby's cleanliness was also a concern, particularly from insects or any vermin that might inhabit the cradleboard, even though the child's carrier would be cleaned once or even several times a day. This concern was satisfied by using long, thin switches or, more often, the long linear leaves of *wormwood grass* (*Artemisia frigida* Willd.) that were placed under bedding or in a cradleboard to keep vermin away, particularly bedbugs.

As noted, the Spokan subscribed to well-established moral prohibitions for the proper disposal of feces, urine, and catamenial blood. Doing so served to prevent problems of personal hygiene and public sanitation, and to prevent any human waste being instrumental in the delinquent person being sorcerized. There existed a strict belief that any unpleasant or offensive scent was—with few exceptions—disruptive of one's well-being, and to be avoided or attended to by a purification ritual. The (once) immediate interment of a deceased person was an effective assurance in maintaining public health and preventing personal contamination. Those bodily wastes—hair, feces, blood, and menses—thought most dangerous if available to a sorcerer, were disposed with great concern and attention.

Perfumes

The Spokan traditionally used an assortment of plants for scenting clothing and bedding, and with the acquisition of cloth and wool, scents were used on women's shawls, sweaters, and any other hide or fabric material that needed to be stored. The dried petals, leaves, and scraped bark of various plants were used to make a *sachet* (*cmcm'ɫqixʷ*), which was placed among the hide and later cotton and wool clothing. The flowers of wormwood and sagewort (*A. ludoviciana* Nutt., var. *canadicans* [Rydb] - *nq'nq'téɫp*) have an aroma that was appreciated when storing clothing, and noted for protecting cotton and woolens from the ubiquitous clothes moth (*Tinea pellionella* [Linn.]). There was consensus that the most common and effective sachet was made from the white-woolly perennial herb pearly everlasting (*Anaphalis margaritacea* [L.] Benth. ex C. B. Clarke, var. *margaritacea* - *cmcm'ɫqixʷ* or *cemémɫqixʷ*), gathered in late spring for making sachets. Pearly everlasting was always a thoughtful gift for a close friend when presenting a sachet to another woman on a visit, "Being a good provider, you must have much pemmican, so I made this for you."

Only a few elderly women could recall their mothers and grandmothers using a beaver's scent gland on both men's and women's clothing, as well as a coiffeur before certain social gatherings. The very greasy gland imparts a pleasant aroma upon any thing it had contact with.

Shampoo and Hair Tonics

The appearance and cleanliness of an adult's or child's hair was a daily concern, and it was said that a woman would comb her husband's and children's hair before they retired and again upon rising the next morning. Even the common act of endearment by a mother when "she gently, lovingly smoothes her child's hair down with the palm of her hand" was termed ʔecɫácqnm (STHC), and demonstrated her concern and attention to her family's hair and appearance. Though incompletely recorded, elders had terms for the appearance and condition of a *person's hair* (q'ʷomqn). For example, even though a man had used a hair dressing, it might still be the case that *his hair is greasy* (hi čɫolqn), or a woman's recently washed hair was a fluttering, *glittering sight* (hi ɫáll*—referring to fluttering cottonwood or aspen leaves. Often both men and women would rub mashed beaver gland oil into their hair after washing their hair (Smith 1936-8:281).

The Spokan were fastidious in their personal hygiene and appearance, apart from daily sweating and water-plunging, and throughout the winter they adhered to strict practices of hair care, possessing an array of different plants for washing their hair and for medicating several types of infrequent scalp disease. As near as can be discerned, women were solely responsible for collecting and preparing the necessary plants, as well as administering various shampoos and tonics. Crushed leaves of blue clematis (*Clematis columbiana* [Nutt.] T. & G. - k'ʷek'ʷsaʔsn'naʔ) were steeped in hot water as a hair washing solution.

Leaves from the macerated roots of four plants: *buckbrush* (*Ceanathus anguineus* - wíwanɫp or watn'é), snowbrush, sunflower, and snowberry bush (sometimes called waxberry or snakeberry)—each produced an oil, which, after boiling, made a solution used as a shampoo, hair-dresser, and medicament for treating *dandruff* (snppúɫaʔqn' or snppoɫeqn' or snpp') or itchy scalp. Adult women would gather the roots of balsamroot in the spring, and boil the roots to produce a solution for washing their hair. They believed it helped to make a woman's hair grow longer. As evidence of this belief, the procedure was followed after a widow ended her time of mourning and could permit her hair to grow long again. A multipurpose hair-dresser and solution for treating dandruff was to steep the tops of tall willowherb in cold water until an oil-like substance was formed, which is then applied to the hair.

Snowberries were often called *tmtmn'ey'ʔaɫq*. Dandruff was also treated by washing the hair with a warm solution made from *mashed strawberries* (*Fragaria* spp. - q'étq'm'). Some people preferred to use the sweet-smelling green sticky leaves, which were pounded and then boiled for a few minutes; upon cooling, the oily solution would be worked into the scalp and then rinsed with untreated water. Dandruff was cured by mashing wild tobacco leaves in hot water, and allowing it to cool before washing one's hair, and again rinsing with water. In the spring, another type of shampoo was made by mixing the green leaves of dogwood with adequate amount of water before vigorously rubbing the leaves together to produce a *foam* (xʷus). Elmendorf observed that during the construction of a mock-orange or syringa wood bow, the syringa bush "leaves were put in baskets and rubbed with water into [a] froth [and] the leaves were [then] thrown away and [the] froth [was] used for shampoo" (1935-6, 1:79d).

Shampoo was also made by mashing the fresh leaves and pink flowers of sticky geranium (*Geranium viscissimum*), and prior to stirring in hot water to produce a fragrant shampoo, the warm solution was poured over the reclining person's head. The same solution was used for dampening stored deer hide before tanning, and the round green leaves of this multipurpose plant were occasionally used for lining a pit oven. Another hair treatment used in the summer was to immerse one's hair for approximately twenty minutes in either a cold or warm infusion made from wild rose flowers, and then rinsing the hair in clear water; the process may be repeated for several days. At one time, mashed foamberries were placed in boiling water, cooled, and used to wash a person's hair that had dandruff.

Another multi-purpose shampoo, hair tonic, and *hair-dressing* (p'óʔƛ'qis) was a gelatinous mass made by placing several crushed handfuls of fresh subalpine fir needles between cloth or tanned buckskin, pulverizing the contents to a powder, then mixing with animal grease, tallow, or deer marrow (bear marrow has too strong a scent). A woman might add bits of mashed rhizome of wild licorice to this prepared mixture if her efforts were for treating a scalp itch. Nowadays, several globs of Vaseline might be used with the wild licorice. Some once preferred to supplement bits of spearmint, Canada mint, Coyote mint, or, if available, the white flower of cow parsnip. This mixture was kneaded until soft, giving a creamy appearance before being placed in hot water and stirred until the ingredient was in suspension. Girls and young women worked this mixture into their hair while massaging the scalp, sometimes before retiring. In later years, before retiring the woman wrapped her head in a section of tanned buckskin to preserve the bed clothes, and in the morning the solution was removed by a thorough rinsing (STHC). Such a mixture was used during a "guest sweat," when the host would drop small amounts onto the hot sweathouse stones that provided a pleasant aroma.

In the spring, freshly-picked leaves of Lewis's mock orange made an excellent soap or shampoo when first rubbing the leaves vigorously with water in one's hands, leaving a pleasant scent. Soap was made by adding a sufficient quantity of readily available cottonwood ashes with water that provided a mild abrasive for cleansing the skin.

Shampoo and hair tonic was easily made by adding mashed leaves and scraped cambium of willowherb in boiling water, and applied upon cooling. Until the early 1960s, several elderly women who continued to use the aforementioned plants for making shampoo, avoided *commercial soap* (*c'éw'stn*) as being too expensive and preventing them "from enjoying going to the woods to collect various plants", which gave off natural aromas. Even though a Spokan term exists for *bald head* (*n'ło?q'ʷóʔsqn'*), there is no recollection of anyone being completely bald, and only a few elderly women's hair may have been said to be thinning, even today. However, some adult men and women saved any loose hair, as discussed earlier, to prevent being used by a sorcerer.

Cottonwood ashes contain lye, and made an excellent soap after the ashes were soaked overnight in water. The upper half of the solution was then carefully ladled out and boiled. Upon cooling, it was often used to wash a person's hair or for other types of body bathing. A hair shampoo was also made from the green leaves of red osier, which formed a foam when vigorously rubbed between the hands. Men and women would rub salmon oil that had been mixed with crushed green fir needles to give their hair an acceptable sheen and a pleasant aroma. Whenever salmon was part of a meal, the people would afterwards run their hands through their hair. Ray wrote of a similar procedure for the contiguous Sanpoil and Nespelem:

> Another method of applying oil to the hair was to rub it with testes of the beaver which had been wrapped in buckskin and allowed to stand until the oil soaked through. Such bags containing testes were worn attached to the clothing to be ready for use when desired. They were rubbed on the clothing as well as the hair (1933:53).

The neighboring Spokan also used diluted urine to wash hair that was extremely greasy, and immediately afterwards they would thoroughly rinse the hair with warm water. It should be noted that only recently have a few Spokan men taken to wearing *a beard* (*supcín*).

Deodorants

All Indians were aware of how human scent was often more likely to reveal their presence to animals than the sight or sound of humans, for the acute sense of smell by animals was effective in alerting them of potential danger by hunters. When necessary all adults used deodorants; but hunters were especially conscientious, and used various means of obscuring human odors.

Upon leaving the sweathouse—and prior to hunting—a person had a choice of approximately twelve different plant deodorants that were effective in masking human odor. However, the main deodorant was made by crushing the leaves of the near-ubiquitous mullein plant and rubbing the leaves over his entire body. When a hunter was away from a sweathouse, and in an area with few scented plants, he would locate the nest of any ground-dwelling rodents, such as a pocket gopher, meadow-dwelling ground squirrel (*sisč'*), including *Spermophilu douglassi* and *S. richardsonii, Cuv.*), and the ubiquitous yellow-bellied marmot. The hunter would excavate and recover the finely ground earth, which he then applied to his axilla and genital area. As mentioned, not all beaver castors were eaten as some were saved, dried, and ground into a sweet-smelling powder, also useful as a deodorant when placed in the axilla or the area of a man's genitalia.

In addition to using finely-ground earth as a field deodorant, mashed fresh lichens were applied to obscure human odors. Most commonly dry moss would be held in the axilla until game was sighted, then the moss was discarded to permit the free movement of the hunter's arms. Elders have maintained how the use of moss as a deodorant effectively eliminated both insensible and sensible (perceptible) sweating of the axilla (Ross 1984a). Lichens, most notably dry-pounded Goat's beard, and even a combination of green pond *algae* (*nmtr ʔétkʷ*) and *fungus* (*yóq'ʷiʔ* - "decayed wood"), reduced body odors. They contain many substances and (unknown) sugars and acids that protect the plant against harmful microbes, including odor-causing bacteria. Having a high acid content, lichens were also effective as a medicine.

To further observe this cleaning ritual, a man—when taking his last plunge after the third sweat, and often prior to hunting—had a choice of approximately six different types of plant deodorants. When hunting a man always carried one or more of these deodorant plants to mask human scent. It was said, "Originally Coyote used this plant [mullein] to wipe spears, harpoons, animal snares, arrows, fishing hooks, and fishing lines, to cleanse them and remove his scent from them; modern Indian men use it for the same purpose."

Yet human scent was important for keeping other animals, particularly coyotes, from scavenging a dead deer left by hunters pursuing other deer. Consequently, hunters always placed something touched by humans on the body of the deer—a glove or kerchief, or even urinating near the hung deer, or placing ear wax or nose mucus on a stick atop the deer.

Hunters often gathered dry punk wood, which, after pounding to make a fine powder, was used as an absorbent to mask human odor, and on occasion it also served as fire tinder. Powdered charcoal and fine dry clay were also used as body deodorants and so-called antiperspirants; but at this late date, some younger Spokan claimed it was only conjectural as to whether Spokan hunters used these materials as deodorant. A few elders recalled a once common means of masking human scent was for a hunter to carry a bundle of macerated fir needles, preferably of subalpine fir, in a *buckskin pouch* (*sčwaxn*) in the axilla of his left arm—a procedure called *sits ha isch*. Mashed snowberries served as an effective deodorant when applied in both axilla.

Depilation

Though not a daily ritual, depilation of facial hair was practiced when deemed necessary, sometimes daily by younger men. Traditionally, any facial hair was considered unattractive, even repugnant. Consequently, both men and women were fastidious in removing facial hair, sometimes even one's *eyebrows* (*cpcpłnéy'*), which men preferred to have in a relatively straight line. Wilson noted how, "Both sexes pluck the hair from every part of the body, for which a pair of pincers is generally carried" (1866:293). Depilation was typically done by using a fresh-still attached bivalve of a fresh water mussel shell, or a piece of split hard-wood as tweezers. Hair removal was also accomplished by pressing the hair against a small, smooth, flat stone or smooth hard-wood with one's fingernail, and then pulling abruptly. An elderly man with failing eyesight might recruit a daughter or older granddaughter, one with more acute vision to best accomplish this task of grooming. Both the *upper lip* (*sčłč'méys*) and *lower lip* (*sč'mépeʔst*) were completely depilated. Men were careful to remove any *nose hair* (*nʔopopáqs*) using partially split hardwood tweezers. Even from old photographs, it is difficult to say if the Spokan ever straightened the hairline over the forehead. The Spokan never removed *axilla hair* (*nʕopáxn*), nor did either sex ever remove *pubic hair* (*spúm* = fur). "Pubic and other body hair was not removed" (Teit 1930:341). Older pubescent boys in boarding schools were required to use a straight razor to remove facial hair. There were no accounts of men *removing hair on their legs* (*č'opʔapaxnn*) or *hair on one's arms* (*nʔopʔapaxn* or *ʕʷopaxn*), which at best was minimal.

662

The only illustration of tweezers is provided by Ray who described how they were sometimes painted by the Sanpoil: "Three types were made of bone, one of wood. The bones selected were usually ribs of small mammals, since they were of the proper size and very flexible" (1933:55-56).

Dental Care

Apart from the archaeological record, it is sometimes difficult to determine how fastidious the Spokan were regarding dental care, but it can be assumed, apart from abrading by sand and fine ground stone in their processed and raw foods, that the general diet was conducive to healthy oral hygiene. Indians had perfect alignment (Class 1) of the mandible and maxilla, and possessed a universal genetically inherited feature.

When necessary, adults made for themselves and their children a *toothbrush* (*nxʷkʼʼʷxʷkʼʼʷ*) by chewing the thick end of any debarked section of green or red willow, so the fiber would be splayed and, thus, more effective. No substance was placed on the brush though very fine clay particles were immersed in water to make a gritty solution to clean teeth from eating eel. Brushing the teeth was not a daily ritual.

In the spring, catkins of *Salix* trees, particularly from the black cottonwood and aspen—were chewed as gum, which also served in cleaning one's teeth. Every adult carried one or several toothpicks, commonly made from a hawthorn, wood splinter, or stiff stem of grass. These were typically carried with other implements in a waist pouch that served as a personal utility bag. Fish bones were never used as a *toothpick* (*nwecʼiʔsnʼcútnʼ*) by adults because of their concern that even an adult could accidentally swallow the bone when coughing or being surprised. Many years ago, one elder said how in the past this would have been disrespectful to the salmon.

Teeth were also occluded by masticating salmon. A major reason for certain dental problems of many—certainly older Indians—was being exposed to wind-borne and ingested sand, as Lord aptly noted: "During the drying, siliceous sand is blown over the fish, and of course adheres to it. Constantly chewing this 'sanded salmon' wears the teeth as if filed down, which I at first imagined them to be, until the true cause was discovered. I have an under-jaw [mandible] in my possession whereon the teeth are quite level with the boney sockets of the jaw, worn away by the flinty sand" (1866, 1:75). Washington Irving quoted Bonneville's initial—and unfortunately rather simplistic—impressions of the different groups living along the Columbia River who depended upon salmon: " [...] they are poor and dirty, paddling about in canoes, and eat fish. Their teeth are worn out; they are always taking fish bones out of their mouths. Fish is a poor food" (1843, 1:213.).

Hygiene

Upon first awakening, and leaving the dwelling, men and women went separately to different areas to make their toilet. Upon returning each family member cleansed their hands and face with warm cottonwood ashes from the evening fire. Before eating, it was customary for every person to thoroughly rinse his or her mouth with water, and then, while *praying* (*sčownt*), spit the water in the four cardinal directions in a brief water ceremony. Some have said that long ago, as one faced each of the four directions, a brief blessing was given to the water, the earth, animals and fish, and finally to all plants and trees, all those things that they were dependent upon. As one elderly lady explained:

> In the past, the oldest woman of each family would give all her family and any over-night visitors a cup of water; best was spring or well water, but never tap water. Of course the ceremony had stopped even before there was plumbing on our reservation. I still do this, but my family no longer do because the young people feel it's foolish. Long ago, after the ceremony, each of us would make a wish for something good to happen that day (Ross 1968-2008).

Adults were fastidious in trimming their *fingernails* (*qʼxʷqʼxʷqínčst*) and *toenails* (*qʼxʷqʼxʷqínʼšn*), as they were with their children's, a task normally assumed by a grandmother for her grandchildren. The obvious concern associated with predominantly hand-manipulated chores and skills was that a broken or a partially

663

removed nail could be temporarily debilitating. A universal procedure for trimming nails was to use an abrasive sandstone arrow-sharpener, or, as was once demonstrated by an elderly woman, the flat side of an abraded hide scraper. However, if obsidian was used to trim nails, then the parings were always carefully—even ritually—disposed of in a fire or buried, since they could possibly be used by a sorcerer to cause serious illness to the careless person.

To maintain the health of a society, one that adhered to an annual and highly mobile subsistence round as the Spokan, it was necessary for the existence of a pharmacopoeia that contained a wide variety of floral, geo, and faunal medicines, as well as the technology to effectively process, store, and administer these medicaments when required. For any medical system to have been successful for nearly 11,000 years, it was also necessary to have medical practitioners, who in nearly all instances could be male or female shamans. In the past, families with their intimate knowledge of plants were often quite capable of diagnosing and effectively treating certain medical problems. Though now long forgotten, there was some evidence that the Spokan, like many cultures, had specialists, shamans who dealt with psychological illnesses.

With all hunting and gathering people, there is considerable evidence that a major reason for having a successful medical system was their intimate knowledge of comparative muscular and osteological anatomy between humans and other animals. A people's acute knowledge of how certain animals treated certain maladies was incorporated into the Spokan armamentarium of medicaments, which occasionally reflected the Doctrine of Signatures. As mentioned previously, an example was geophagy for treating diarrhea.

What is most difficult now to reconstruct was the treatment of an individual who had any form of diagnosed mental illness, either by sorcery or self-conceived. And further, it is not unreasonable to say that the Group Medical Inquest was not only a major form of therapy, but occasionally the only successful means of rehabilitating a patient. As mentioned, though not conducted anymore, one had only to attend such a session to realize why some non-Indian observers refer to this dynamic and engaging ritual as a psychodrama.

The most dramatic and unique aspects of the Spokan medical profile, and what they classified as traditional maladies of illness and certain physical disorders, changed drastically with the introduction of Euro-American epidemics, that were often devastating pandemics. Another factor that caused major disruption to the Spokan medical system was the introduction of Christianity, which inevitably led to alternative life-styles and of course newer and fundamentally different explanations of how and why one became sick or even died.

Chapter XVIII: Religion and Mythology

Religion

The aboriginal Spokan religion might be best termed supernatural animism, and thereby inextricably related to a person's ever present environmental interpretation and resounding behavior. Mythology served to effectively explain and even verify the origins of the natural and supernatural environments, and the coming of animals, plants, and later people, but perhaps, more importantly, to explain and sustain a moral order or charter that defined mores and traditional customs. More generally, but always apparent, the mythical charter also explained and delineated moral prohibitions, and why humans were required to behave in certain ways within the natural and human environment. Malinowski (1954:112) stated how belief in a truly animistic religion was an integral mechanism that accommodated personal power and expression for the collective good of a society, and how, "Religious belief consists in the traditional standardization of the positive side in the mental conflict and satisfies a definite individual need arising out of the psychological concomitants of social organization".

According to animism, every plant, animal, fish, section of water, natural phenomena, unusual land form, distinctive geological form, the wind, etc., possessed a power which could not be lessened or controlled by humans. It was believed to maintain a balanced and holistic understanding of an often unpredictable environment, and it could temporarily improve an individual or group—often through certain types of shamans—but only through humility, belief, and ritual.

Within the Spokan mythical charter, there were several comprehensive areas of belief regarding the breath/life-soul, sweathouse deity, tutelary spirit (*suméš*), ghosts, spirits, theriomorphic beings, malevolent beings (sorcery), water creatures and other forces within the spiritual world. Ray (1939:169) also grouped these areas as: the soul, ghosts, spirits, dangerous beings (evil dwarfs, monsters, demons, ogres, and giants), and *guardian spirit* (*suméš*). The main figure of Spokan animistic belief was the *sweathouse deity* (*t'úpʔyeʔ* - "great grandfather" or *k'ʷuilistʔn*), now called a supreme being (*k'ʷl'ncútn* - "he made himself") by Spokan Christians—a benevolent force who created the order of the universe, as well as humans, animals, plants, and spirits. The Spokan were once strict in acknowledging the assistance and guidance of all cultural manifestations within their perceived pantheon. Before performing a particular task, a person made a silent prayer to acknowledge a specific spirit mainly associated with that resource or endeavor for guidance and success. For example, roping a *calf* (*k'l'k'ʷl'eʔl'xʷ*), releasing a hunting arrow, or even such presumably mundane activities such as smoking a hide were usually preceded by a brief prayer.

Despite certain terminologies, and the strict training as a Jesuit priest, DeSmet expressed an unbiased, respectful, and fairly accurate explanation of the dichotomy or balance of the physical and psychological commitment and intensity required by a curing shaman to project his *suméš*. The following account is very relevant in this context:

> [What] the Indians call Power, is at times limited, say they, to the procuring of only one object, as the cure of some disease. Some other Power, again, is not so limited, it extends to many objects, as success in hunting, fishing, waging war, and avenging injuries. All this, however, varies according to the degree of confidence reposed in it by the individual, the number of his passions or the intensity of his malice. Some of the Powers are looked upon, even by the savages themselves, as wicked in the extreme, the sole object of such Powers is to do evil. Moreover it is not at all times granted, even when professing to be most powerful medicine-men, earnestly desire it (1847:267).

Unfortunately, due to the effects of missionization, the diffusion and transmutation of religious precepts and rituals concerning much of traditional religion became truncated and, with transliteration, made diachronic ethnographic interpretation difficult. As a consequence, little of traditional religion and acknowledgement of supernatural familials and *sumeš* exists today. Ray is one of the few to advise that, "Care should be taken not to confuse this concept [of the soul] with guardian spirit loss [...] The loose usage of the two terms, spirit and soul often leads to confusion, with serious theoretical consequences" (1939:101), and ethnographic interpretations. Ray further wrote how corresponding guises of mythological beings was weakly developed:

> The one amorphously defined deity of significance functioned mainly at one point of time in the distant past. This was the occasion when he decreed that mythological beings should cease to exist as such but that two new and exclusive characteristics from the corresponding guises of mythological beings would thereafter occupy the world. These were human beings and animals, each deriving their distinctive and exclusive characteristics from the corresponding guises of mythological being…

> Following this change, the character of the mythological being was partially recoverable by a man or woman through achievement of a vision in which a supernatural entity appeared and offered to become the tutelary and protector of the person. This spirit first appeared in the vision in the guise of a man but, before disappearing, took on the form of an animal.

> This guardian spirit thereafter maintained its association with the person to the latter's death and could even sometimes be inherited. All aspects of the contemporary practice of religion and all ceremonialism revolved around the guardian spirit, with the consequence that the anthropological designation is uniformly "guardian spirit religion" (1977:19-20).

Despite the difficulties associated with attempting to determine the present existence and knowledge of traditional religion, it was apparent that a few remaining Spokan-speaking elders had a duality in their religious belief: one of varying syncretic beliefs. Some identified the existence of a breath-soul, but had no belief in a soul as taught by early missionaries. With missionization, the term *qeʔ čšiy'epl'eʔ* was adopted to designate our guardian. Until recently, most traditional elders believed in ghosts, and given personal circumstances, one could remain on earth as an ephemeral ghost-form after death, but not as a soul destined to what some non-Amerindian peoples perceive as a *heaven* (*sčč'másq't* or *šc'masq'p*). Elmendorf noted the Spokan had no definite concept of a land for the dead (1935-6, 3:26).

Concerning the concept of an afterlife, Curtis too noted, "there was no definite conception of the future world" (1907-30, 7:76). However, Lord, nearly fifty years earlier, when expressing his understanding of religious beliefs held by the Plateau peoples prior to Christian missionization, questions the effects of missionization, but acknowledged traditional beliefs:

> The Indian notions of a future state are, as far as I have been able to learn, dim and indistinct, but they have notions of the kind that is evidenced by placing bundles of moccasins in the graves as if for a journey [...] The Flatheads (Salish and *Kalleespelm*), it is said, believed the Sun to be the Supreme Being, and that after death the good, i.e. the brave and generous went to the Sun, while the bad remained near the earth; others supposed that the worthless ceased to exist after death (1866, 2:239).

Lord's inquiries also led him to conclude that, "The Indians of the present day have learnt the whiteman's belief in a future state of existence beyond the grave, and the more reflecting seem to accept it with great satisfaction" (1866, 2:249).

The advent of Christian missionization introduced to some converts a different concept of the *soul* (*snxpéw's* or *snxpáu's* or *kʷulsch* or *snxpeq's*), one that prevented individual interpretation and expression. Nor, as cited, was there traditionally any concept of an *afterlife* (*sxʷélmn* or *nʔaxʷʔaxʷkʷisqʷlixʷtn*) until being introduced by missionaries, nor was there a ceremony to wash away original sin when the *baby is baptized* (*k'ʷúl'l'*). However, a profane yet major creative figure was Coyote, a trickster whose frantic and lascivious behavior modified the distribution and form of most animals and land forms. In many ways, Coyote manifested the power, strengths and even weaknesses of a culture hero in oral history, and served numerous functions of social control, enculturation, and even as entertainment for young and old alike—under certain circumstances.

The daily rituals and beliefs associated with magic constituted a paramount and pervasive major area of the Spokan religion, which influenced—sometimes determined—one's daily interpretation and interaction with personal and general sociocultural relationships, and with the natural and supernatural environments. For the Spokan, magic was a complex and even specialized aspect of religion; the term and concept of a formalized religion was not traditionally a part of the Spokan belief or syntax because such would have contradicted the function of magic. The concept of the supernatural was more inclusive since animism (*snunxʷen'n'eʔ* - "to believe in") was based upon the ability to affect change through ritual, individual tutelary power, animate spirit hierarchy, *shamanism* (*t'łáʔákʷílc*), and even sorcery.

Consequently, the nature of Plateau religion was individualized with respect to the mythological beings that imparted specific types of *suméš*, and the inimical relationship between a man and his guardian spirit—a conceptual relationship acknowledged by Teit (1930) and Ray (1939). The traditional Salish-Spokan relationship with nature was compromised, in accordance with Judeo-Christian dogma, practices, and attitudes, which dwell on the other worldly aspects of existence, and rejected the sacred-environmental relationship that was essential to the Indian people's survival. One Plateau anthropologist, when examining the changes within animism wrought by church deculturation, noted:

> [...] concepts of *suméš* are acceptable as long as they are utilized within the Christian context which declaims any negative or detrimental usage, and sanctioned only with a syncretic perspective; attributing the source of guardian spirit power to the Euro-American concept of God, not the temporal persona of spiritual nature embodied by the mythological beings of the traditional Plateau cosmology (Walcott 1986:7).

Supernatural Power or Magic

The English word magic, occasionally used here as a transliteration, almost invariably implies the use of supernatural (*skʷˈussc'eʔ* - "force that frightens you") or spirit power. There are, however, occasions when I have substituted the term magic for supernatural power to facilitate, if not accommodate, non-Indian notions of power for the reader. The use of supernatural power involved the manipulation of an area of belief and accompanying ritual to achieve malevolent or benevolent effects upon a person or thing—generally for personal gain by a shaman or for the service of others. However, supernatural power was available to anyone who, through ritual or song, incantation, manipulation of symbolic objects, power projection, or possession of a person's clothing or body part, could influence another's health, behavior, or even bring about death through sorcery or wellness. Supernatural power was used to influence certain cosmological conditions or aspects of nature that were economically significant.

Three different types of supernatural power or magic (Malinowski 1954) were practiced by the Spokan: imitative or sympathetic, contagious, and projective; used extensively in numerous magico-religious rituals to effect either malevolent or benevolent change in another person or animal. Imitative or sympathetic magic involved ritual based upon the Law of Sympathy, that is the concept of homeopathic behavior—the belief that 'like brings like.' For example, an early report by Cox (1832) of tying a primary wing or tail feather of a red-tail hawk into the *mane* (*čxʷíclps*) of a colt which will give the horse speed and endurance, or using red ocher on one's face to imitate blood during a curing ceremony. A *gifted story-teller* (*sxʷmeʔm'e'yʔem*) would imitate the sounds and body positions when relating an account of several animals, thereby creating a better visualization of the animals' behavior; the audience could, thus, assume that the story-teller had taken on the personality of one or several different animals. Also, during a funeral, participants would demonstrate their grief and *pain* (*c'ʔermís* or *cnúʔu*) by keening, even lacerating their arms to signify sympathy and grief for the deceased. Wishing or praying for a person's safe *journey* (*člkʷumptín*) was sympathetic magic. Perhaps a more dramatic example of imitative magic was during the Mid-Winter Dance and the Bluejay Ceremony when a person got transformed and became a Bluejay—so designated by his behavior and appearance after blackening his face like the bird, hopping about and making cawing noises, thereby assuming the powers and physical abilities of the Bluejay that were then physically and visually manifested to the attending participants.

It is often difficult to separate contagious magic from imitative or sympathetic magic, since contagious magic was based solely on the assumption that a shaman could affect malevolent change in a person by surreptitiously taking an article of clothing, or any possession, or physical part of a person, and doing to the object what was believed would happen to that person. An example was placing the clothing of the intended in fire so the victim would suffer burns, or holding the possession of an intended victim under water with a rock so that over time the individual would experience a wasting death. A common defense against contagious magic was for an individual to hide or destroy any of their cut or fallen hair; it was never to be kept in a person's guardian spirit bundle. Human excreta, as cited, was always carefully buried to prevent a sorcerer from recovering the feces and doing malicious harm to the person. The same concern attended the *ritual burial* (*sntmtmn'ey'tn*) of a child's deciduous teeth, usually by the mother or grandmother who judiciously buried her child's first teeth. Urine was apparently not always considered as being potentially dangerous; it was used sometimes as a medicament.

The teaching and necessary involvement of ritual and prayer to achieve success was apparent at even an early age. Any First Fruit Ceremony acknowledging human use of plants, animals, or fish, were examples of both imitative and contagious magic that demonstrated a participant's gratitude as well as the humility the recipient felt toward the source of food, and that ritual was a way of acknowledging the people's dependence upon the natural and supernatural worlds.

Projective magic implied that change could be brought by the projection of words, a song, a miniature bow and arrow, or other means. The sounds of a young man playing a love flute—carrying his amorous desires to a young woman—would influence and hopefully capture the girl's love. Projective magic was a common vehicle used by a sorcerer to bring illness or death to his intended victim. For instance, a sorcerer might send a feather from a meadowlark that was 'shot' inside the victim, or a sliver of bone; even a small pebble could prove disastrous if not removed. Upon diagnosis of such a malady, the inserted object was recovered by the attending curing shaman, using legerdemain, or *sucking with his mouth* (*t'mam t'mant*), or by blowing over the site of intrusion. If successful, the curing shaman would then show the inserted object to the patient and all those attending as a proof of ordeal.

Magic was an important aspect with all gaming encounters and athletic events, particularly ones involving betting. An example, as cited earlier, was when someone kept on his person a Western blue-tailed lizard for luck while gambling. And yet the notion of good or *bad luck* (*č'sstél'*) is a recent phenomenon for the Spokan, for in gambling luck was not traditionally applicable since it was believed that a person's good fortune or misfortune was not the result of simple chance, but rather the instigation of magic and power—one's own or that of someone else. Magic was a prevalent and necessary behavior in a Spokan person's daily life, expressed in rituals that afforded some sense of control over uncertainties, and undoubtedly ameliorated certain anxieties.

Sweathouse Rituals

The sweathouse structure represented the supernatural world, and was universally considered as always being sacred when occupied, a place where any person possessing an appropriate power and song, and with adherence to proper *sweathouse ritual* (*kʷuilistn*), would be attended by a certain supernatural force. A sweathouse was used for various sacred and profane occasions: curing, socializing, physical and spiritual cleansing, social control, enculturation, acquiring *good fortune* (*xsstél'*) such as success for gambling, prophetic predictions regarding a pending dangerous venture of warfare or horse-stealing, hope for *good fishing* (*nmsčstétk'ʷi*), and even foreseeing an *impending doom* (*č'lč'lč'n'ʔecút*). One's prophetic abilities were sometimes more acute during sweating when confined with one's power and even different powers from one's companions. When sweating with strangers, one rarely called upon his tutelary spirit for fear of it being taken if the stranger had a more powerful *sum*, if so inclined.

Each extended family built and maintained their own sweathouse, and it was common for widows to often have their own collective sweathouse, though in a large extended family all of the women would sweat together in the same sweathouse, but always after the men's session had ended. When using the same sweathouse, men would, after sweating, restack and even reheat the vesicular basalt stones, and fetch sufficient water. However, a man *never* remained in the vicinity during a woman's sweat, nor did men and women ever sweat together. Traditionally, the nine vesicular basalt stones were heated by first placing three stones in each crevice of three parallel logs, and the remaining three rocks in the crevice of two additional parallel logs atop the base logs. With repeated use, sweathouse stones became fragile and light in color, and after four to six months of continual daily heating, sweathouse stones were unable to sufficiently hold the heat, and would break and then were discarded.

The ritual of sweating was performed on a daily basis, either *early morning* (*skʷekʷst*) or late afternoon, by both men and women—never together. By preference, but not as a rule or habit, men and women often sweated in the morning during the winter, prior to first eating, and again in late afternoon. Certain activities of the day would determine the time of sweating, though a man usually sweated early in the morning before making a long journey or conducting a solitary or collective hunt. It was common for a man to sweat both early morning and late afternoon for at least three days prior to embarking upon a dangerous activity, to achieve both physical and spiritual cleanliness. An elderly Spokan man once noted, "A good winter sweat always made my bones want to move."

Prior to a participant's entrance, the water man or leader would judiciously sweep the floor and the walls of the structure with *rosehip stems* (*xʷxʷy'epɫp*) to remove any malevolent forces, snakes, *spiders* (*tup'el*), or creatures that might have taken refuge during the night because of the remaining warmth from the stone hole or any part of the sweathouse interior. Before using the sweathouse, the host might cover the earth floor with white sage, cedar or small fir boughs, or, for a curing sweat, a tule mat that was doubled and used as a bed for the patient who may have to assume an orthograde position. If necessary, the host or the water man might place certain dried, ground *medicinal or aromatic plants* (*sčɫilstn*) just inside the doorway to the right. The general term for plants was *npaqčn'ečst*. These plants were later *sprinkled upon the heated stones* (*čp'q'ʷú?sis*)—during the third sweat and final sweat—to purify the participants and further rid the structure of any lingering malevolent forces, and to facilitate and announce the people's propitiation to tutelary spirits by creating an atmosphere conducive to attracting any such spirits that may be sought by one or more of the occupants. Shavings from rosehip stems were sprinkled on the hot stones, and occasionally shredded bits of wild licorice root, a favored purifying and medicinal plant for the Spokan.

When the sweathouse was being used exclusively for curing, the heated stones were placed in an excavation immediately to the right just inside the entrance to better accommodate the patient, who nearly always assumed a prone position within the sweathouse to facilitate his treatment by a curing shaman. A curing sweat always required the use of only three stones at a time—never more. No special form of vesicular basalt stone was required for a curing sweat, but stones that had been used to *destroy* (*č'ɫxʷelm*) a sorcerer's power were always buried and never used again. The same caution was strictly observed for stones that an illness had been cast upon. One elder recalled how red-colored vesicular basalt was often preferred for a curing sweat.

Prior to sweating, stones would be heated until *red hot* (*ckʷlkʷilsšn*). For the first sweat, at least three of the preheated stones were placed in the center depression by the *water man* (*sxʷɫilm*), who was usually the sweathouse leader, and by tradition he was the first to enter. Prior to the daily non-curing sweat, individuals entered the sweathouse in a clockwise fashion until the first person—the water man or the leader—stopped

669

and sat to the right of the door (as viewed from outside). Also, given the clockwise movement within the sweathouse, he was the first to leave, whereby terminating each sweating session.

Immediately before each sweat, the heated stones were transferred from the outside firepit to the sweathouse in one of several ways: with a stout piece of willow branch bent back onto itself—the end tied to form a loop—much like a lacrosse stick; or by using a stout piece of hardwood that was tied off approximately one third from its lesser end, then split and spread to serve as tongs. Traditionally, the sweathouse leader designated a man to bring him three heated stones to the entrance of the sweathouse, which the leader took individually with his bare hands, and placed them one by one in the center hole. The few Spokan who sweat today frequently use a metal shovel or pitchfork to transfer the heated stones from the fire to the center hole; but elders once condemned this procedure, saying that metal made by *suyápi*, would negate the power and sacredness of the sweathouse.

The host of the sweat was not always the leader, nor was he the first to enter the sweathouse. In such an instance, the person closest to the entrance pulled the flap down.

Water in the sweathouse was contained in a *rawhide basket* (*aʔxénʔ*), or sometimes in an opened deer's paunch—held in place on a tri-pole frame. More often, a water-tight basket, woven from either cedar or spruce root, served as a water container. A leader might ask, as a courtesy, which man wanted to sprinkle the water on the stones. Taking water from a basket or a braced rawhide container, the leader or the designated water man commenced the *sprinkling of water* (*č'p'q'ʷúʔsis* or *hi t'upye sláq'ist* - "on the stones"). Some would use only a cupped hand, whereas another person might use a handful of looped bear-grass or a sprig of cedar or fir bough for sprinkling the water. Years ago, a water man would recite four brief but significant sweathouse songs as he sprinkled water on the hot stones. During a curing sweat the shaman usually sprayed the stones with water held in his mouth, creating a fine spray, and after applying water to the hot stones, the curing shaman—in solitude or with others—would sing his song. The person sprinkling the water, particularly a younger person, was subject to criticism by the other participants if too much water was applied, when the water man might be accused of "drowning the stones." Or, if too little water was applied, comments might be made that the stones would "die of thirst."

Whoever was first to sprinkle the water would commence to sing his *suméš* song, and, usually after he finished singing, the others would collectively sing their individual power songs, but not loudly. And if someone not associated with the daily sweat stood outside, purposely listening to the songs or the conversation, it was considered rude, even though the muffled conversations and low chanting were often difficult, if not altogether impossible, to understand. If such a listener did not leave, s/he could become very ill.

Some elders told how in the past, one or more persons' compatible *suméš* would gather at night in a vacant sweathouse, and, before the light of a winter's day, a man upon approaching the sweathouse might see a low light—a shimmering glow—and think that a friend had come early to commence the sweat. Smith described this for the Kalispel as an apparition that "would disappear. Sometimes when he got close, he would hear a song inside the sweathouse: *'nu' nu' nu'* etc., *ha' ha' ha'* in monotone. And then the voice would stop and talk a little [... This] Sweathouse Man is called *t'ópi'ya* - 'grandpa sweat' or *sláqíst*" (1936-8:547-9).

The first sweat was social; essentially a gathering that involved intense joking, exchange of gossip (particularly a person's most recent amorous conquest), and the maintenance of joking relationships among the participants who tended to sweat together each day. These joking relationships were reinforced when referring to each participant by his given sweathouse nickname, a name never used away from the sweathouse, unless in private with those whom he sweated with daily. An individual took great pride in his designated and unique sweathouse name. A man may have several such names, but always the first name was more significant since it invariably had obscene overtures; ones depicting gross exaggerations of strength or weakness of a woman's genitalia, an aberrant relationship with an animal, or of a man's unusual physical feature, or a unique behavior; not always complimentary.

The second session was primarily a cleansing sweat, when depilation was common, being accomplished with an articulated fresh bivalve or with split hard-wood tweezers. Until recently it was a common practice for older men, even outside the sweathouse, to habitually pluck *facial hairs* (*ʔecqʼʷmus* - "fur on the face"). When in the sweathouse, both men and women routinely *scraped* (*ʔáqʼm*) their bodies with a deer rib, a once-sharp stone (such as an old and dulled skinning stone), or a wooden scraper that was not unlike a cambium scraper. If asked, a participant would scrape the back of the person next to him, which was reciprocated.

Prior to special sweating—such as before warfare or bear hunting—a man would observe strict procedures to ensure absolute physical cleanliness, including a solitary sweat for securing the attention of his guardian spirit, who may tell him if he would have success or failure. A person could be told of pending failure by a variety of ways; his dreaming or someone else's dream, by his guarding spirit, or even an animal other than his tutelary spirit, most often an owl. Regardless of a pronouncement's source, the man would not pursue an individual activity, or as a leader of a group, or relegated responsibilities to another if he was told of failure.

Any ritual prior to hunting or warfare required the man to "cleanse his insides" by using a piece of red willow that had been slashed and serrated with sharp stone, typically obsidian—never with metal, for in the past it was considered spiritually dangerous to have metal in a sweathouse. The person then soaked the two prepared willow withes before entering the sweathouse for the second cleansing sweat. Once inside and settled, he would pass the feeble end of one of the prepared sticks into his right *nostril* (*snčʼmaqs* or *snɫxʷaqs* - "the hole"), pushing it to the back of his throat, where he would grasp the protruded end, pulling the willow withe out his mouth. The procedure was repeated with the left nostril, using the second serrated stick. After sweating, the sticks were disposed of, and never used again.

Another and rather physically severe emetic cleansing procedure involved taking a hardwood shaft of small diameter, and chewing the larger end until it was properly frayed, which was placed in the person's throat. During the cleansing sweat, the larger frayed end of the emetic shaft was then rotated clockwise while being swallowed, until the frayed end passed the esophagus and into the stomach, thereby permitting the removal of *bile* (*míc'mc'eʔ*) and gastric fluids, and inducing the person to *vomit* (*n'occqeʔín*) as the emetic stick was removed. Another method for removing bile was to take a narrow section of water-soaked red willow that had been folded in half so that the end was a U-curve, which was then inserted past the throat and into the esophagus. Either of these procedures was done only prior to hunting bear. Perhaps, as several elders had suggested, the bear was *humanoid* (*qlixʷméɫc'eʔ*) and, thus, warranted considerable respect.

Young men would induce vomiting by running thin willow sticks down their throat to promote cleansing. If possible, they would temporarily exit the sweathouse to a nearby excavation designated as a place for *vomiting* (*nwétč'lštn*). Canadian-born Andrew Dominique Pambrun (1821-1862), an early Catholic fur trader and explorer to the region who served as Isaac I. Stevens's secretary, guide, and interpreter, and later an Army brigadier general, and also liaison for Colonel Steptoe, reported how in the spring:

> [...] it is a common practice for an Indian to take a number of willow withes, make them [as] pliant as possible, six to eight of these are held in a row, and shoved down the throat into the stomach, of course the points must come in contact with some vital parts, while being wounded from ulcers or cause hemorrhage and death ensues. [T]his operation is performed to throw up the bile, in place of taking an emetic. There are other practices that are perhaps not so injurious, but are not healthful (1979:179).

The most detailed account of "passing the willows" is provided by Hale who observed the Nez Perce ritual of cleansing one's self for curing any type of prolonged fatigue, and once completed permitted the practitioner the ability to endure fatigue over long periods of time; a treatment which men commenced at age eighteen. The Nez Perce ritual took seven days, whereas the Spokan ritual lasted only one day. The Nez Perce man takes:

> [...] three or four willow sticks, eighteen inches long, and thrusts them down the throat, in order to cleanse the stomach by bringing up bile, blood, and coagulated matter; a hole is then prepared, of sufficient depth for a

671

man to sit upright, with his head above the ground. This is usually dug near a running brook. On the second day they fast, and collect other willow sticks, of one-eighth of an inch in diameter, the distance of the naval from the mouth being their length. These are slightly rounded and made smooth, and are passed down to the bottom of the stomach, which cause a severe irritation and vomiting, and is continued until it produces a burning sensation: this is repeated from time to time until noon, and not infrequently as often as eighteen or twenty times. The number of sticks is diminished as the throat becomes sore. When noon arrives, they plunge into cold water, and remain there till evening [...] (1846, 4:464).

Another less aggressive way to cleanse the gastrointestinal tract while in the sweathouse was to induce vomiting by inhaling a crushed freshly-dug wild licorice root, a process that was repeated each time just before the person left the sweathouse to *bathe* (*cáwlš*). As noted earlier, a less dramatic procedure to induce vomiting was simply to tickle one's throat with a feather.

The third and final sweat was for spiritual purification and, on occasion or need, communication with a person's guardian spirit. If successful, it might cause the man to *faint* (*λ'eʔłit̓*) when his guardian spirit attended him, or he may experience a *fainting trance* (*λ'eʕl'íl'* or *čpspas* or *stsqntm*) while being visited by his guardian spirit. To be more receptive, and better able to have *hallucinations* (*snw'ečm'tús*) in order to receive one's tutelary spirit, a person could 'settle' himself by hyperventilating as he prayed; focusing upon his intention, to the point where *he is hallucinating* (*ʔecnw'ečm'túsi*). It was sometimes necessary to revive a person from a trance by blowing sweet grass smoke about his head, a ritual called *čq'ʷaqíntmq'ʷaʕ*. When *regaining consciousness* (*nč'eʔʔspúʔus*) a person might find in his lap an item that represented a certain guardian spirit, such as a patch of fur, a *claw* (*q'ʷoxʷqinčstn* or *q'ʷoxʷq'ʷoxʷqin'čst*), tooth, or feather. Such a proof of acceptance indicated that he had indeed been paid a *visit* (*čxʷim'sq'élixʷ*) by his tutelary spirit. The gift was carefully saved as part of his power bundle, and after acquiring "power objects" from numerous visitations, a shaman would store them in a large power bundle, carried like a bandoleer (STHC). Just prior to leaving the sweathouse, men would *pray* (*č'aw* or *k'ʕaw*) for continued health and well-being of their family and friends.

During the third and sacred sweat, men and women were careful to never blow their noses, refrained from *flatulence* (*ip'q'ʷ* or *p'uʔú*), never spoke ill of anyone, or used any profanity. With exceptions for special types of sweating, such as curing, a daily sweathouse ritual was delineated into three definite sweats, each session lasting from ten to fifteen minutes.

Though no musical paraphernalia was permitted in the sweathouse, a man, during a solitary sweat, could—while hyperventilating—blow on an eagle wing bone whistle. If a person's tutelary spirit were an eagle, he might feel himself being rocked from side to side, with his arms pinned, as the bird engulfed him with its wings. Or, if the man were in a trance-like state, he might be taken on a journey by his guardian spirit, which might tell him of pending events, such as success in a particular hunting venture. Another example of soul flight once related to the author was how a dipper bird (*Cinclus mexicanus* - *q'ʷxʷm'in'*) assisted a man on an ascent up through a *waterfall* (*st'ipmétkʷ* or *st'pmétkʷ*), carrying him eventually to a wide section of the contributing stream, where he was enabled to *see* (*wičn*) a reflection upon the water, one that was *prophetic* (*nt'č emin* - "reading signs, significant image"). Charles Wilkes was informed "that the spirit [*suméš*] within a person may be separated from the body for a short time, without the person being aware of it, or causing death, provided it be quickly restored to him" (1845, 4:448).

While sweating, it was not unusual for a young man to first receive his tutelary spirit, or to learn the nature of his *suméš*, sometimes when he fainted or was in a trance. A potential guardian spirit might speak or brush against him, even teach him a power song, which upon regaining consciousness he would sing. Such an occurrence was encouraged as the *sláq'ist* sang his prayer-like song. The true significance of this song might be later interpreted by the novice's adult sponsor, who explained how the boy's guardian spirit would continue to add to his song with the boy's later deeds. When sweating for the third time, it was not uncommon for an older boy to take with him the bone of an animal he hoped would appear and possess him. During the third and final sweat session, the sweathouse stones might speak only to the person intended to receive communication directly from his tutelary spirit or another's person's guardian spirit. As was once explained:

> [A] sweathouse can talk. There may be more than one person in the sweathouse and yet the stones will speak to usually one person. Speaking by stones is done when the water is sprinkled on the hot stones, first the stones began to sputter before talking. Stones may be encouraged to speak if a man will sprinkle water that has pieces of *x̣ásx̣s* cut up. When the stones talk, they'll often explain to a man of a coming death or illness. The stones are able to talk because a power of the listener comes to them [the stones]. Stones are only heard by a person with power, and only by the man the power wants to hear the message (Ross 1968-2008).

During a curing sweat, the stones may speak to a curing shaman; the understanding, of course, the voice, was from his *suméš*. Tutelary spirits usually spoke only while water was being sprinkled on the stones, sounding only like sputtering except to the one intended to receive the message. If the message was not clear or complete, the so-called recipient would sprinkle some wild licorice root onto the stones to clarify the message, which was repeated or clarified. The message may *bring news* (*m'em'éy'ʔem* - "to bring news") of an impending death or illness of a family member or friend. While sweating, each person had his back against the curved wall of the sweathouse; but often only one person could feel the structure tremble, and he knew he was about to receive a message of importance concerning his welfare or one of his kinspeople or a friend; sometimes the communication would be received from the sweathouse itself, not from the stones—usually sent by a shaman's animal helper.

After each sweat, the person would *plunge* (*č'r'ipm*) into the Spokane River, or a small stream sufficiently dammed to create a sufficiently large enough depression to provide adequate water for full submersion by all participants, or into the runoff of a spring that had been dammed to provide enough water for full submersion. If the water was frozen, the participants broke through the *ice* (*sxʷúyntkʷ* or *mawɫ sx̣uynt*), or simply rolled in the snow, though there were certain exceptions. Springs were never dammed as plunging pools.

The sweathouse was an accepted method for an elder to commit suicide, by pouring all of the water onto the heated stones, thereby causing heart failure, generated by the extreme heat of the surrounding air. This particular procedure indicates the intense heat generated in a sweathouse, which may reach temperatures as high as forty to sixty degrees centigrade. A family always buried all of the *sweathouse stones* (*sčur'ésšnʔ* or *sšoʔɫescn'*) used by a person after the individual had died under such circumstances, and the sweathouse was burned.

It often took several weeks for a young novitiate to adapt to the intense heat of the sweathouse, and during this time the father or uncle would gradually increase the heat. When a young male novice first commenced a regimen of daily sweating, it was not unusual for older men to tease him by pouring excessive *water on the stones* (*hi t'upƛe sláq'ist*), often driving the young man from the sweathouse, usually accompanied by the comment, "Where are you going, to the menstrual hut?"

The sweathouse took on particular significance after mortuary rites and burial of the deceased, when all the participants who attended the body were careful to conduct special protracted sweats, usually every day for one month. For further purification, the mourners would commonly drink a decoction made from mashed rosebush petals mixed with other cleansing substances—even red ants, if available. It was critical that the name of the deceased not be mentioned in the sweathouse for fear of dreaming of the deceased later, who would consequently have difficulty during the prescribed time of spiritual reincorporation in a life hereafter.

673

Vision Quest

The most dramatic and significant spiritual and physical transformation an older boy could experience was while on a solitary *vision quest* (*xaxasq'* or *hescʔuncúti* - "he is seeking a power, a spirit" - *cwncút* - "go on vision quest" - *snw'ečm'túsm'* - "he saw a vision"). If successful, the seeker would be attended by a guardian spirit who represented a specific power who gave the novice a song, a medicine bundle, knowledge of certain moral prohibitions, and occasionally part of the tutelary's body. The vision quest was an occasion when the boy was totally dependent upon his own survival skills, physically and psychologically, since his only clothing was a breechcloth, and he was provided with no fire-making tools, and certainly no food. Some said that by the late 1800s, some boys were permitted to take fire-making equipment. To meet his needs of shelter and warmth, the solitary novice was totally dependent on the skills founded upon his attention and on the lessons of older agnatic kinsmen, and it must sometimes have been a frightening solitary vigil for most young boys.

It has always been thought there was consensus among the Spokan elders that a girl, and later a woman, could have *suméš*, which sometimes was more powerful than a man's *suméš*. Of particular interest is Elmendorf's report (1935-6, 1:4), of being told by his elderly informants that women seldom received a tutelary spirit, but elsewhere he acknowledges women receiving a *suméš* (1935-6, 2:31).

Both boys and girls sought their guardian spirit in different ways, often being instructed to follow the procedure and setting that proved successful for either the father, mother or another older consanguineal kinsman. An elder explained:

When a boy or girl, aged twelve to thirteen, had prepared for going on their vision quest, usually early summer, they were told to "follow the mountains," taking only a bow and arrow, elk knife [before having steel] and fire-starting kit. The boy had to furnish all his own food throughout the summer [...] He had to see no one, at least every effort was made to avoid any peoples. The boy stayed alone all summer, or until he got his *suméš*. He sweated every day. Not only was the boy to learn about his guardian spirit, but he had to continue to learn his survival skills from his surroundings, which would later be valuable to all his people. Before the boy left [home], he was told by an old man how he could get scared when he first heard or saw his guardian spirit, which almost always came as an animal. When the boy returned home, his father would only ask: "Did you find something?" If he didn't get no *suméš*, he'd go back next summer. During the vision quest, the boy might have a vision, generally at night when dreaming. The tutelary spirit instructed him on what he should do to have a proper life; about his song and his bundle. The guardian spirit told the boy he would come at night and speak to him, and always at the winter dances. The boy knew the spirit could also come to him in the sweathouse. In the old times a guardian spirit would teach the beginning part of his power song, maybe leave part of his body [tail, claw, fur, or some distinguishing body part]. Long ago, the animal guardian spirit could speak in the boy's tongue or in a spirit language the boy understood. Very young boys would sometimes forget their songs, but learn them again during the Mid-Winter Medicine Dance (Ross 1968-2008).

A long and informative explanation of the vision quest, and the role of the tutelary spirit, was provided by Curtis:

"At ten years of age I was with a party of six men, who were hunting mountain sheep on *stukuqaus* [the mountains at the head of Yakima river]. They left me on a large lake and [went] on to hunt, up among the high rocks. I was frightened, and was crying, when a finely dressed man suddenly appeared, and said: 'Young boy, what are you afraid of; what are you crying about? Your hair will be white before you die. You will be a very old man. If you are shot with a bullet or an arrow, or cut with a knife, that will not kill you, for you are going to die of sickness. Do not be afraid of being shot. That is why I was so foolish [reckless] when I was a young man. When the hail comes,' he said. 'it strikes my body, but it does not go through. That is the way it will be with you when the bullets fall on your body. Look at me now. Here is the way I do.' Then he showed me how, when I was wounded, to spit out blood, and turning he walked away. I saw that it was a badger. Many times Badger has come in my dreams and told me what was going to happen, and it has always happened. He promised me songs, some of which he gave me then, and others of which came to me later in dreams. He told me to wear a belt consisting of a strip cut from a badger-skin, including the nose and the tail; and a cap of badger-skin with an eagle feather attached to it" (1907-30, 7:85).

A girl might commence to receive or be made aware of her power when she first learned to speak. Recognizing the girl's interest and subtle change in behavior, one or both parents would send the girl when she was of reason to a certain place not too far from their home, where she might receive her power (Elmendorf 1935-6, 2:31). The next day the girl would be taken to a shaman who would explain to the girl what actually had happened, and how when she was older her guardian spirit would again appear and bestow upon her a certain *sumés̆*. However, when a young girl was recognized later as being the recipient of a power, it was usually not until after her menarche that she could, through further visitations or dreams, know what type of power she had received. Some have claimed that a girl, regardless of age, could always explain to her parents what had happened, and they would know the type of power and the identity of their daughter's tutelary spirit. At the girl's menarche, the true significance of all the girl's earlier dreams and encounters with her guardian spirit would be revealed. One elderly woman described how, just after her menarche, when she was leaning over a small still pool of spring-fed water to wash her face, she saw her guardian spirit in the water, who proceeded to speak to her through a small bird perched on a nearby bush.

There was an instance, when in the winter, a young girl was sent from her home at night to recover a certain rock that had been placed earlier by a parent. She was told that if she were successful, an animal representing a particular power would later, after the girl's menarche, properly bestow his power upon her. In happened that a father might take a power bundle to a proposed vision quest site which he would leave some distance from the house, directing a son or daughter to later go and retrieve the bundle. If successful, the person would receive his guardian spirit some years later during a two- to three-night Medicine Dance. Even though young children might receive their *sumés̆* through dreaming, or seeing their tutelary spirit, in other ways they rarely would exercise these abilities because older and more established shamans would be offended by such presumptuous aspirations by immature novices who had not been properly instructed. It was also said that a precocious child would be sorcerized when making premature assumptions of his or her presumed or assumed spiritual abilities.

The parents of a boy or girl would decide at what age the child should commence their vigil, and as indicated, often the child was relatively young, particularly girls, as we find in the following account:

> One winter night, when I was about six, my father told me to follow a trail that went from the back of our house, a trail which went across our horse *meadow* (*čɬčéwm*) and then down a draw where my father had our sweathouse. I was to go all alone to the sweathouse and bring back an old sweathouse stone, one I knew, because us children played with it, always calling it curled bear cub because it was still black and looked like a rolled-up cub. I was to come back with the stone and give it to my uncle [*mother's brother - ssiʔ*] who lived with us. All the time I was gone, my uncle and all the adults sang their special power songs. I knew I had to go, even though I was very scared, and always thinking something bad would happen to me in the dark. It was the first time I'd [ever] been out alone in the darkness. But I went and returned with the stone, which felt warm to my cold hands. I knew then it all had something to do with religion—something supernatural. That same night, after I came home, my older brother had to return the stone, but he refused to go because he was really scared. Many years later [CE 1890], one of my daughters took me to visit the old sweathouse area, and we found all the old stones had sunk into the ground (Ross 1968-2008).

The vision quest ritual was believed to help the young boy or girl to receive not only a guardian spirit (tutelary spirit = *sumés̆*), but to learn and benefit from the often long, solitary, and arduous period of training and conditioning, which was necessary to become a responsible and respected adult. For instance, boys were taught discipline when the sponsor—usually the *father* (*ʔes cutnélt* - "his child is on a vision quest") or father's brother—placed an article at the top of a mountain, after which the young boy would be sent to fetch the item in the dead of the night. This was to build bravery and endurance against the elements he must later confront during the vision quest and in life. It also encouraged the boy to learn how to align different topographical reference points later when he would be by himself.

A young girl never received a guardian spirit when confined during her menses (Smith 1936-8:1231; Elmendorf, pers. comm.). If prior to her menarche, a young girl experienced a vision or actual visitation by a future guardian spirit, she would be informed by her mother or grandmother that once she becomes a woman the guardian spirit would return.

It can only be posited that young girls more often received a sign or heard voices indicating the identity of their future tutelary spirit at an earlier age than did young boys. The apparent difficulty in drawing any conclusion is that nearly all contemporary accounts were from elderly women; and, until only a few years ago, women were often the only remaining cultural conservators in areas of medicine, language, and past domestic skills. In considering the many types of power and range of natural and cultural conditions under which one received his or her *suméš*, there appears to have been more opportunities of being approached by one's later tutelary spirit through dreaming, having a vision, or hearing voices that were prophetic. A testimony of the now-incomplete possession and knowledge of power was how in the recent past, even a person with no power could "see" a pending event if it was going to be one of considerable severity.

Growing up in an environment where power was a near-constant issue, one that explained success or failure in all human activities, it was known that young children were quite cogent of the supernatural and the many—but not all—ramifications that were of daily occurrence. For example, a common practice was for a mother to send her young daughter to fetch water from a spring with a bucket at twilight, preferably to a more distant spring or stream so that she had more of an opportunity to hear voices that would partially describe to the young girl what might happen in her later quest for power:

> She may not always see the animal, but she may, since all but a few animals *could speak in Indian* [*nqeʔlixʷcnm*]. Elders have always said that a guardian spirit would never appear to a person who didn't speak Indian. Nor would she [the potential recipient] understand all [that] the animal or unseen power told her, so her mother or grandmother would explain, as best they could (Ross 1968-2008).

A young boy, when bent over and looking into smooth, *clear water* (*hinxál*), could first learn of his guardian spirit. However, if the water suddenly became *muddy* (*hi ƛ'áʕʷč'*), he knew he was not ready to receive his tutelary spirit. In the past, a person did not have to possess a power to see future events in still water, or to have different forms of clairvoyance—a preternaturally clear or acute perception. One man's maternal or paternal grandfather was presumed to have had the power to see certain future events in an open fire, events which he felt were a *premonition* (*moyyxeʔ*) given him by his guardian spirit.

The interpretation of dreams and the individual significance of certain ideographic events of children were important, for there was consensus that some young boys and girls became first aware of later receiving a particular pending guardian spirit by dreaming of a certain animal, and the more vivid the dream, the more likely it would later come true. This applied to dreams that tended to be repetitive. The initial dream would frequently be incomplete and uncertain; but with each successive dream the animal would, in stages, reveal more details of its identity, associated taboos, privileges, and responsibilities required of the future recipient if the power was to be given.

The same phenomenon of sequential development of increasing detail while dreaming was common even after a person had received his or her power. A person's *suméš*, regardless of how it was acquired, remained with the person unless it was maliciously stolen by a more powerful person, or left a person who committed a serious moral transgression, or if the host purposely released his dependence upon his tutelary spirit when a person realized he was going to die. A man or woman, knowing they were dying, would, if possible, give up their *suméš* in a special ritual that involved constructing a small, secluded sweathouse, one away from the trails of men. The person would sing his power song and by chanting, thank his guardian spirit for its benevolent protection and assistance. But if a person attempted to keep his *suméš*, when he knew he should give it up—for whatever reason—then he could become the victim of debilitating arthritis, extreme difficulty in breathing, incessant nightmares, or some form of dementia—the universal explanation being that the person was selfish, and was trying to control what was only a temporary gift. After their contact with Euro-

676

Americans, it was believed that a person permanently lost power once they indulged in alcohol, and a drunk person's behavior and speech demonstrated that the man's *sumés̆* was working against him. Cox mentioned a policy regarding the prohibition of dispensing alcohol to indigenous people, first enacted by Thompson, "We never brought ardent sprits among them for the purposes of barter, and cannot say how far an abundance of it would seduce them to its intemperate use" (1832:235). With little effect, in July 1832, Congress passed a law that totally banned alcohol in Indian country.

Years ago, an elderly gentleman asked the author to make a sweathouse and attend him while he gave up his *sumés̆* in an area on Tschimakain Creek. Long after sunset, the elder entered the prepared structure alone and alternately sang his power song and *chanted* (*nkᵂnem*) until the stones had cooled as he released his *sumés̆*—the great blue heron (*Ardea herodias - skᵂer'š̆n* or *smóqᵂ'eʔ*). The man's singing in the clear night was not unlike an aria, one that 'spoke' of specific deeds that required a knowledge and strength that came only from his guardian spirit as he respectfully recited the many ways his *sumés̆* had helped him, and of how significant was the companionship of his guardian spirit. The sweathouse had been located in a secluded area on the opposite side of a shallow and wide *slow-moving stream* (*hec mowop*) only several meters from our temporary camp. The next morning, after tearing down the sweathouse and burying the stones, it was apparent that our footprints were still visible in the silt, showing where we had traversed the stream after he had sweated. Also visible were the imprints of where a heron had also walked across the stream during the night, stepping only on several of the old man's footprints; but none on the author's, which was unusual since herons invariably roost at night in a tree. Upon showing the prints of the heron to the man, he calmly explained, "Oh yes, now I know that my *sumés̆* has gone back, and it'll later come back to another person" (Ross 1968-2008).

Each individual circumstance of a person seeking and hopefully acquiring a guardian sprit varied, but generally, when a boy first experienced a voice change—usually from twelve to fourteen years of age—he would commence to prepare in earnest for his vision quest. This was always done under the tutelage of his sponsor, usually an uncle or close male agnate who would instruct the boy in the ritual and significance of the pending vigilance. This time of training was called *suxᵂtsuwntsút*. For several months to one year—prior to his vision quest—the young novice entered into a rigorous regime of intense physical exercise; never being permitted to sleep during the day, and learning how to hunt every day when away from the village or camp. As instructed, the time and distance spent from his village was increased each day.

In the evening, upon his return, the sponsor instructed the boy on how to *search for* (*λ'ʔem* or *λ'eʔi*) his *sumés̆*, and what he might expect to encounter during his one- to two-night vigil. Approximately one month before the boy left for his vision quest, he would commence periodic fasting, all the while maintaining a rigorous training of swimming, running, sweating, and spending long periods of solitude in the mountains. A neophyte's sponsor sometimes had the boy eat the immature, bitter white berries of dogwood to make him *strong* (*λic't*). When satisfied with the boy's training and condition, the sponsor would take his charge— usually in the winter—to a place for acquiring his *sumés̆*. He would instruct the boy to remain there—always in solitude—until his tutelary spirit appeared and recognized his spiritual needs necessary for his transformation to adulthood. It was common for a person, who many years later was to give up his *sumés̆*, to revisit the site *where he first claimed his tutelary spirit* (*snwčsuneštis*), *where his sumés̆ came to him* (*ʔe cčičš̆ łu sumés̆c*). The primary reason for returning to the site was to give up his guardian spirit where he had first acquired it, an area often characteristic of the tutelary' spirit's habitat.

A boy's vision quest usually took place after the winter dances, the coldest time of the winter. The actual site where one was to *seek one's sumés̆* (*qaqiʔti* or *qs wčsumés̆* - "he's seeking to acquire his personal guiding spirit") was invariably in an area that was topographically unusual, a place where one had a *sense of or heard something unusual* (*n'eʔ č'núm't*). It would be an environment that by itself created an *eerie feeling* (*čc'iqpiceʔ*), if not a sense of presence and anticipated power of a particular animal that was being sought as a guardian spirit. The location was, as mentioned, sometimes near a known habitat of the animal being sought.

For example, a high promontory near an eagle's aerie was chosen for eagle power; at the edge of a stream to acquire weasel, otter, beaver, or fish power; or any other environment associated with a particular creature. Such a site was *Sacred Mount* (*čłʔem'tu*), one that overlooks the Spokane River, and where numerous successful vision seekers left gifts in hopes of gaining the attention of a tutelary spirit.

Throughout the duration of the vision quest, the supplicant was warned never to sleep, not to eat; only take water. It was most important for him to concentrate on being 'owned' by a helping spirit, one which could appear in various forms. The power might first make its presence as a *song* (*qʷélm*) carried by a *gentle wind* (*q'ʷ oiʔ*) that created small visible whirlwinds in the water, dust, or fresh snow. Experiencing such a revelation, the boy would have visions of things he had never seen before—animals and even people of various sizes—moving sometimes in *slow motion* (*k'ʷak'ʷiet*), but who never took notice of the novice. One Spokan elder explained how during his grandfather's vision quest different small animals walked by him, and some turned their heads toward him and moved their mouths, but no sounds ever came out. His father later told him that there would be a time when they would speak to him.

Unlike the Euro-American notion of large animals being economically more important, powerful, or possessing greater significant anthropomorphic qualities necessary for domestication, the Amerindian in many instances considered smaller creatures as having certain unique skills for survival—wisdom, speed, guile, acute vision, or the ability to change form. The significance of a person's tutelary power was not necessarily represented by the size of the animal, for small creatures were respected such as the hummingbird, mouse, and chipmunk. These creatures were believed to have the power to temporarily transform a man into a small animal, thereby affording the human—now in animal form—the ability to outwit his enemy, or permit him to extricate himself from human sight, recognition, or a physical predicament that only a small creature could accomplish. Only men possessed deer, beaver, or bear power. Bear power could be used by a practitioner to *cure* (*puxʷntm*) a patient who had been afflicted by a different shaman—a sorcerer who possessed bear power.

A man or woman possessing coyote power had exceptional hearing; such a man was invaluable during a hunt. The most common and viable powers a sorcerer could have were those of rattlesnake, bear, spider, yellow jacket, and a type of large moth—all considered evil powers, but which were compatible with a benevolent tutelary. Ones with magpie or mole power were more successful in gambling.

Consequently, because of their diminutive size and often elusive characteristics, small creatures were considered important, and were, consequently, sought as tutelary spirits. As was once explained:

My father used to tell me and my brothers that it really didn't matter the size of a[n] animal a person's power came from, or even what type of animal. He told us how many years ago [ca. 1890], at a fair where some Indians were stick-gaming, when two of them started to have a fierce argument. Well, one man pulled a knife and stabbed the other man, then [he] went to a different part of the fair. The stabbed man did not die, and took his knife and found the other man, who he [then] stabbed several times in his chest, killing him. The first man thought he was going to die from loss of blood or faint into shock. Then he suddenly remembered his father, telling him [that] years earlier, no matter how small a man's guardian spirit was, it could help. So he called up his power—the salmon—to help, and he [the salmon] did when saying to him to breathe slowly and deeply, just the way the salmon does, and the blood was like sea water. He got well and had no scars (Ross 1968-2008).

When asked about a person having an animal's ability and characteristics, one observing and perceptive elder remarked, with considerable enjoyment, how:

You white people name your cars after animals, like the Pinto, Bronco, Mustang, and Cougar. Even some football teams, like the Colts, Bears, Seahawks, Rams, Ravens, Dolphins, and Eagles are named after animals. My grandson proudly served with the Screaming Eagles (82nd Air Borne Division); all the groups were named after animals, but we never forgot the little animals or birds we used to honor and pray [*t'áx̣ʷa* or *č'aʕʷ*] to (Coleman, pers. comm.).

There were numerous accounts of small animals—particularly all species of salmon—possessing power that was a definite advantage during warfare, and for curing serious wounds sustained through combat. The theme of salmon power assisting with knife wounds, appeared several times from different elders. For instance, the following brief account by an elderly man acknowledges the person's ability to spiritually acquire certain physical anthropomorphic features or characteristics which some animals possess:

A good *suméš* for fighting is trout [salmon] power because of how they must struggle and really fight to get upstream. A man having this type of power can be used for other things. Once, many years ago, my uncle was at an Indian fair [at Arlee] watching a stick-game when another man [a Flathead] started arguing with my uncle. After a while a terrible fight broke out, and the other man hit my uncle on the head with a wooden club— knocking him out. After a while my uncle came to, and he took the club which was left beside him, and he went and found the Flathead and hit him on the head. Finally, after a while, the Flathead man came to my father and stabbed him in the chest [with a knife]. My uncle really thought he was going to die because he was bleeding real bad. Now, my uncle had three helping animals, and so he called on each of them to help him. The first two animals couldn't help him, but the third power, trout, saved his life because the trout said to him: "Blood is like water, like the knife in your body is like the trout in water—swift water—and the water comes in and goes out." My uncle was now cured (Ross 1968-2008).

During the novice's vision quest the boy would *speak softly* (*k'ᵂkᵂiy'ecn*) to animals and birds near him, and in his solitude and stillness would undoubtedly gain their attention. Any one of these creatures—and often not his tutelary spirit—would be considered as a *companion* (*xᵂec'n' - sxcútéłxᵂ*). He could communicate with the creature, as it could understand Indian, and would be a *living thing which kept him company* (*ntekᵂls*) (STHC).

The type of tutelary spirit a person desired was best sought if one's vigil took place in the environment of that animal. The following was an explanation by an elderly Spokan to a question concerning how a boy's sponsor selected a particular environment or site to do his vision quest. The man explained that the story was about his mother's father's father when he was a young boy (1800), and his father's brother told him that they would both go on a long fishing trip near Priest Lake in late spring. Well, when they finally got there the man left the boy on a small boulder in mid-stream. Before leaving, the man tied around the boy's waist and chest several long connected strips of mink hide with the fur on. The man paddled away and left the boy on the rock. The boy stayed all night, just standing on the rock and shivering because the man had told him not to sit down or relax in any way. When the sun rose over the trees along the stream edge, a power came to him in the form of a fish, and spoke to him of his new power and gave the boy his power song, which he had only to sing when he wanted to catch any kind of fish.

A similar account of seeking power from aquatic creatures was told by a man whose grandfather had muskrat power, and who was never beaten in swimming events or when holding his breath in underwater contests:

When I was old enough to understand things, my father told me of how his father, when he was probably pretty young, was taken to the West End, just north of where the Spokane and Columbia Rivers come together. Late in the evening, my grandfather was told by his father that he'd come back the next day to get the boy, but first he had to take all his clothes off and jump in the water, staying down as long as he could. He was told to repeat this all through the night.

Early the next evening the boy's sponsor came back with the boy's clothes, but he couldn't find any trace of the boy; no foot prints, no pools of water, nothing to say the boy had been there. The man waited and waited until it was dark, and then he paddled the route home. The next day he came back, only earlier to the site, but there was still no sign of the boy. He did this one last day, returning with the sad news that the boy had drowned.

That night when all the boy's family and friends mourned his loss, there was a knock on the door jam, and in walked the boy, his waist and chest still covered by the muskrat skins. After everyone had thrown away their sadness, and the boy explained how he'd stayed underwater for three days and nights, living with a family of muskrats who'd taught him how to breathe under water and catch fish. He now had muskrat *suméš* power for fishing (Ross 1968-2008).

When a young man or older boy wanted to gain *fishing power* (*sqmeyeʔ ey slaq'ost*), he would spend four days and nights at a large lake or stream, a place where fish were always present. Usually the *day after* (*x̌alíp kʷákʷst*) his night vigil, or during his night's dream, a tutelary spirit would inform him that his *suméš* was going to appear, which it would, giving him a song in addition to delineating certain taboos and other behaviors. If a novice wanted deer or bear power for curing, he would spend four days in an area where the desired animal would most likely inhabit. A girl would do the same thing for deer power, only to be better able to hunt with a bow and arrow, "My grandmother was an excellent shot [with a rifle], and she killed many deer."

Despite the fact that all children were brought up with seemingly endless stories of how most men and women acquired their guardian spirits through a vision quest, there were, however, numerous accounts of how most children were frightened by the prospect of being sent out alone to seek their *suméš*, and that some were too frightened to maintain a successful vigil. One elderly man explained how when an animal appeared to the spirit-seeker, and spoke in a spirit language or Spokan, and then proceeded to open its stomach or pull back its face to reveal a humanoid or some animal, a child would often become frightened and run away. A further example was when a young girl was told to go in the late night and fetch water from the stream, and even though the girl was probably *scared to death* (*x̌'étíł'* - "fainted"), she did as she'd been told by her mother's brother [her sponsor]. Yet when the girl got to the stream with her bucket, the near-petrified girl was even more frightened, when out of the darkness she saw two huge yellow eyes staring right at her. Dropping the bucket, she ran all the way home and told her uncle what had happened. And he said to her, "That was your *suméš*, and now you'll never have it."

Often the novice would be sent out in the night to conduct a chore, and it was rarely if ever explained to the child that the chore was part of their receiving a guardian spirit. It must be kept in mind that children never experienced such demands before, because they had never been permitted to trespass outside, the night being a time when a nocturnal monster or theriomorphic creature could capture and take a child away. There is an account of a seven year old girl's apprehension and fright on being sent out in the night to conduct such a chore:

> Once, in the dead of winter, my father told me to take a stone he'd given to me, and put it out on a[n] old apple tree stump, way past the horse shed. I was awful scared, but after a while of walking very slow, all the time looking as best I could back to the house and a kerosene lamp on a table near the window. But before I got to the stump, I was so scared I dropped the stone, and ran home. When I opened the door my father asked if I'd gotten the stone to the stump. I said yes, but he knew I was lying—I never had [lied] before. He told me to go back again, pick up the stone, and put it on the stump. Well, the same thing happened again, and I went home and told my father I'd put the stone on the stump. I knew he was getting upset, and didn't believe me, so I went back a third time, but this time I did put the stone on the stump. My *suméš* came to me, but I can't to this day remember going home, but I remember how happy my father and mother were, and I never lied again (Ross 1968-2008).

There are several accounts of when young prepubescent boys had dreams that told them that they would receive their *power song* (*qʷelem'*). This was never a problem if the boy was sleeping alone, but when several boys of varying age slept in the same room or dwelling (which was often the case), another boy—one who had no power—could steal power from the recipient who was sleeping and experiencing the reception of his first power song. An account of such a happening was related by an elderly man:

> [...] one person I knew real well was maybe 11 years old, and was sleeping in a room with other kids and adults. During the night the boy's *suméš* came to him while he was sleeping, and the boy started to sing his new song, but before really understanding what was happening to him, an older boy stole his song and then he had the younger boy's *suméš* (Ross 1968-2008).

On occasion, during the vision quest, the animal would leave several sacred items: a medicine bundle, part of the animal's body, a *medicine song* (*qʷeʔm'*), and perhaps a feather, plant, unusual fossil, crystal (particularly *one that is clear* - *čx̌alssn*), or a small anthropomorphic or zoomorphic-like mud concretion. All of these items were symbolic of significant aspects of the recipient's new power. Any gifted sacred object would be retained by the boy to later place in his medicine bundle. Some medicine bundles of a curing shaman also contained four or five loose woodpecker feathers, which when sung over could rise collectively or in any combination, indicating the power was complete. The noted arrangement often revealed a person's particular malady when the shaman mentioned a certain person's name. If the feathers failed to stand up, the shaman knew the man had been sorcerized.

Prior to doing the vision quest—often many years before—most seekers had an inclination or even an intense desire to receive a specific type of *suméš*, which understandably may be fulfilled. Yet one or several sacred objects—nearly always symbolic of his *suméš* received during the quest—were not always understood by the recipient, and were shown to his sponsor, who in turn would interpret their significance. A sponsor would, similarly, explain to the boy the importance and true meaning of any song he heard during the quest, particularly if the tutelary spirit was relatively powerful. For example, the song and sacred paraphernalia of a younger *medicine man* (*sλ'e ?kʷilš* or *λ'eλ'e ?kʷlš* or *suxʷnmici* or *sxʷmryemist* or *tlkʷílš* or *λ'e ?kʷíλš* or *tlkʷílš*) might be interpreted by a practicing medicine man in the village, a person who over time would guide and further train the neophyte. A new shaman would add to his power song during the Mid-Winter Ceremony, or after a unique healing session if he successfully cured a person. The Mid-Winter Ceremony also served as if "The choreographic drama of the spirit dance is therapeutic psychodrama" (Jilek 1974:92).

Sometimes it took many years for a medicine man to fully develop his curing techniques. Even after feeling he was competent, he might, under varying circumstances, hear a song, usually one that came to him in a dream, which he might relate to an older and trusted medicine man who would explain the significance of the new song and any associated ritual necessary for curing. A critical role and responsibility of a medicine-prescribing medicine man in the curing of a patient, was to interpret what the curing practitioner or another person had dreamed about the patient, for a dream invariably revealed the cause of the patient's malady. This ability would be heightened after long meditation and accompanying ritual.

It was not unusual for a man or woman to have different types of *suméš*, and of course each from a different guardian spirit. These powers sometimes represented seemingly different powers, such as for hunting a certain animal, or being an accomplished gambler, exceptional dancer, or a renowned author of love songs. A *suméš* could even render him *invisible* (*ta-ys winxʷ*) to other humans, usually by assuming the character of his tutelary spirit. The last Spokan medicine man—known and accompanied many times by the author—was a powerful curing shaman who had five separate *suméš*; each for diagnosing and treating a specific illness, skills that were widely sought throughout the eastern Plateau and parts of the western Plains, where he travelled quite frequently.

As will be discussed later, during the vision quest or later, while renewing his power at the Mid-Winter Ceremony, a person was nearly always completely powerless when possessed by his *suméš*, a state that was publicly demonstrated when a man *would be thrown to the ground* (*c'aq'em'in'e ?m*) (STHC), made to assume extremely difficult body positions, speak in glossolalia, or assume the body attitudes or make the sounds characteristic of his tutelary animal. A person so possessed appeared to be in a trance or sometimes unconscious, and when revived might have no memory of his performance or his immediate surroundings. Yet he would recall certain occurrences while in a trance. No elder could recall if in the past, an attending shaman had the ability to translate what was said in glossolalia.

Guardian Spirit

The most important relationship a man or woman had between the supernatural world and their sociocultural and natural world was through his or her guardian or tutelary spirit (*suméš* or *čšt'ncútn* - "helper" or *snc ?uncu ?tis* - "to initiate your *suméš*" or *snwučsuméštis* - "going to be sick" or "shaman to see"). (Alternate spellings and pronunciations may be found in some of the literature and the appendices here.) The guardian spirit was an individual's religious power, believed to come to a human only from a supernatural force via an animal, plant, or inanimate object. Yet some said that a guardian spirit never came from an inanimate object, only from something that could breathe or was animated. And yet there were several known past instances when a person's *sumếš* was derived from an inanimate object, such as a quiver, a tipi or a tipi pole, a waterfall, a large fishing weir, etc. There was agreement that whether malevolent or benevolent, all forms of power enabled a person to perform specific tasks in different subsistence activities, gambling, curing, warfare, love, dancing, etc.

A person acquired a guardian or tutelary spirit most commonly during the vision quest, through dreaming or by inheritance, when the individual would be known as *x'eʔkʷilš* ("one who has searched"), a man who has found his helper (Elmendorf 1935-6, 1:21). All guardian spirits were different in the amount and type of power given to a neophyte, and the most powerful *sumếš* came to the person in a dream; most often during late December through to late January, a time when the most powerful *medicine men* (*λ'eλ'eʔkʷlš* - pl.) received their guardian spirit(s). All terrestrial animals are medicine animals.

A person's tutelary spirit often appeared as an animal, such as a bear, who would peel back his scalp to show a human face, or a wolverine who would stand erect and open his stomach, showing a different miniature animal, one of his many helpers. A person's tutelary spirit might appear in any animate or inanimate form, judging the novice's reaction before revealing its true form. A boy's guardian spirit often spoke to him in Spokan or in spirit language, both of which the boy readily understood even though he had never before heard spirit language being spoken. The boy was told the nature of his new power, certain rituals he must observe as well as moral prohibitions, which if violated would leave him without a guardian spirit, may even cause his illness or his death (Elmendorf 1978-89 pers. comm.).

Regardless of the form his guardian spirit assumed—in either animal or human form—the novitiate was always told, "this is your song, sing it for this purpose—use it in this manner—whenever you have need for it and how often you may need it" (STHC). He was further instructed how:

> His own sacrifices took shape in the form of a "give-away." His wealth was measured by the many precious gifts of horses, blankets, buckskin articles, etc., that he bestowed upon his friends and relatives. Personal possessions weren't to be hoarded, but to be shared. In this sharing, he knew he pleased his *sumếš* and these same articles could be replenished over and above what he had given away (STHC).

A novitiate might have a vision of a potential guardian spirit when alone during the day experiencing a life-threatening situation, when a guardian spirit might appear and provide assistance. A tutelary or guardian spirit may appear when one was having a death-like illness, and recovered through the presence and assistance of an animal, who often became the person's guardian spirit. There were a few knowledgeable elders who claimed a young male can only receive his tutelary spirit while in the sweathouse, on a vision quest, or by inheritance from a deceased kinsman. It was known, however, that one's *sumếš* could come in an unexpected way, "Even what looks like a human walking over a hill can finally come to you, and turn into a[n] animal, always talking to you in Indian, sometimes telling what power you'll get later. It was most common for one's tutelary spirit to appear and speak to a gifted man or woman when they were dreaming, but not always.

Though not common, it was possible for an elderly man or woman to leave his or her power to a grandchild, niece, or *nephew (sqʷsʔel't)*.

> I remember my great uncles and grandfather telling me when I was a boy to do this or that, and, if I was good, one of them would leave [his] power to me. I was foolish and I didn't always listen to them. An older woman would sometimes tell her daughter or granddaughter the same thing (Ross 1968-2008).

Prior to the start of the Mid-Winter Ceremony Medicine Dance, persons who hoped to participate did so when they were conscious of the compelling need to sing their *medicine song (snkʷnmếʔlsi)* (STHC), often considered a *medicine man's language (nλ'eʔkʷlšcín)*. Before singing his medicine song in public for the first time, one never indicated the intended name of his tutelary spirit, thereby not identifying his guardian spirit song until he sang his gifted song during the dance, and sometimes only after the recipient had been told by his guardian spirit that he could make such an announcement. It was always apparent when a young man in public received his tutelary spirit, as he fainted and would be revived by attending shamans. Before regaining consciousness, the man's new *sumés̆* would leave his body—sometimes departing from the lodge—and come back and speak to the man while he was unconscious, often telling him to be aware of certain near-future misfortunes that he should avoid (Elmendorf 1935-6, 1:35). The guardian spirit's identity was then no longer a secret, but known to all who were present. Therefore, one rarely—if ever—identified his specific tutelary spirit in public, even though the identity of his *sumés̆* was revealed when he sang the song at the ceremonial pole or cane during the Mid-Winter Ceremony.

It could happen if a young boy or girl were at the Mid-Winter Ceremony, a tutelary spirit would explain to the child what animal power s/he would later acquire—telling the neophyte, "You must put all your mind and faith in me" (Eli, pers. comm.). There was no set time when a boy received this tutelary spirit, which could occur, depending upon circumstances, commonly between the age of five and fourteen. Some recall accounts of girls just learning to talk and sometimes receiving their *sumés̆*. Elmendorf explained:

> [...] when girls were young, just starting to talk they usually got *sumés̆*—[and] in [the] evening [parents] would dress little girls up and tell them to go to a certain place & come back—they'd get it then—didn't have to stay all night—[they] saw a person who would tell her how she'd be when older—then when he [guardian spirit] turned to go away she'd see an animal running—few women were λ'e?k̆ʷíl̆š [a type of medicine men] but those who were had been awful good (1935-6, 2:8).

In certain circumstances when two or more children were together, one or two of the children might receive a song at the same time. But such multiple gifting was rare. An elder related his experience:

> When I was about 6 years old [born in 1883], one winter evening, my brother and me were caught listening to our parents speaking privately [in a one-room log house] about a Blue Jay curing ceremony [probably during the Mid-Winter Ceremony]. So, they sent us from the house to sleep in the sweathouse, probably 400 yards away. We were told that before we could come back in the morning—just before dawn, we were to each bring a sweathouse stone. My brother was 3 years older than me, and he got scared and ran to the house, but my dad sent him back to the sweathouse where we'd spent the night, not sleeping 'cause it was so damn cold. We each packed back a stone and were told to later put each stone at the foot of the power pole [in the ceremonial lodge], which we did, but nothing happened until that night when me and my brother each heard our songs. Mine was for spider, but you know I never hurt anyone (Ross 1968-2008).

A person's *sumés̆* invariably reflected certain characteristics and strengths of their guardian spirit, regardless if that tutelary spirit was animal, plant, or an element of nature. They were often examples of the Doctrine of Signatures—'like brings like'. For example, it was said that one man's power was from a whirlwind, and whenever he gambled he had the power to scoop up everything on the blanket. A person possessing *sumés̆* from magpie would be, in keeping with the bird's characteristics, always collecting bright or unusually shaped items, and later be quite capable of amassing wealth—usually at stick-gaming. An account was given of the power and ability of a person possessing the *sumés̆* of a house or *field mouse* (*sx̆ʷlx̆lsč'em'éy'e?*), a presumably insignificant creature:

> I'm now [1969] 84 years old, and my father's great grandfather told him this story. It would have been in the early 1800s. The area was the Chewelah Meadows, to the north. In the early evening, four to six young men—probably in their 40s, some in early their 50s—would erect a deer hide tipi and sit inside, and all the while they would sing very softly, never with drums or flutes.
>
> After many hours the door flap [that was] held with a section of broken leister spear would jiggle and finally move enough to whip the door about, and after some of this a small mouse would come in and speak to one of the men. After a while, a number of different small animals would also come in.
>
> Each animal, you understand, was a man's *sumés̆*, and one by one they'd each speak to a man they represented. One time, a field mouse came to my great great-grandfather and told him he'd been to visit the Flathead on the back of an eagle, and the people there told him they would win the next big stick-game when they came up to fish [at Kettle Falls]. The mouse said it wasn't true [that] the Flathead would win, but rather the Spokan would and that my great-great-grandfather should play and bet everything. He did and he won (Ross 1968-2008).

A man who is drowning might be saved by a salmon, a weasel, or some other type of aquatic animal that represented his power. Many types of animals were believed to dwell underwater, even land mammals and certain birds—any of which could become guardian spirits. Any animal that spoke to a young person could possibly become a guardian spirit, and the only living thing that could not be a guardian spirit was a louse. Presumably, a person's animal tutelary spirit could, either in the sweathouse or during the person's medicine dance, appear in human form, but was said to always retain certain animal characteristics (Benedict 1923:48). A person could have his guardian sprit stolen by a more powerful person, usually a sorcerer, when attending the Mid-Winter Medicine Dance; it was often impossible to recover.

A person would receive his guardian spirit most often during winter, usually before the age of twelve to fourteen. Most but not all adults had a guardian spirit, and if one had not received a tutelary spirit, it was not necessary to have *suméš* for a man to marry, nor did such a person have less status. It was the way things sometimes happened, regardless of a person's efforts and sacrifice. There was also agreement that inherited power was not as strong as power received through a vision quest.

A power could appear in different forms, but usually as animals that represented certain types of *suméš*. Also, an individual might have numerous guardian spirits, each representing a different animal or power object. Given the particular animal a person had as a tutelary or guardian spirit, it could be either a good or bad spirit. For example, all insects that bite or sting were *evil* (*t'éye?*), such as the yellow jacket and wasp. The western diamondback rattler, bear, wolverine, red ants, and certain types of moths and birds were respected but feared as potential malevolent tutelary or guardian spirits, and a person possessing such a guardian spirit would invariably be a sorcerer who was capable of using one or more of his evil spirits to effect illness or death upon a person. A few men were known to have an extremely powerful guardian spirit, one so powerful he worried about thinking angrily or hatefully about another person, for his *suméš* could harm or even kill whom he was thinking of (Elmendorf 1935-6, 4:2).

If a person did not have a guardian spirit, it was known that he might receive his guardian spirit directly from a deceased kinsperson, usually a year or more after the death of the deceased. If a guardian spirit from a deceased person appeared in the form of a person or some *theriomorphic* (*nqlix*ʷ*étk*ʷ*e?e?*) half-human and half-animal form, it was really a human. In either case, it was always considered to be evil, and if it were inherited from one generation to the next, the malevolent spirit always became more evil and powerful with each successive inheritance (Elmendorf pers. comm.). Fortunately, a person could reject such a spirit, even when the malevolent spirit continued to harass and threaten the person, often appearing disguised in different forms. By doing so, the spirit made apparent its true nature and intent, asking the person to do evil things. An individual was frequently forewarned that it might happen since it was known that the deceased person had been a mean person possessing an evil disposition, or was a dysfunctional person who had been socially marginal. Such an apparition was never taken to be a ghost, but simply as a lonely spirit. When inquiring about a sorcerer's nature or characteristics, it was common to hear that such a person often talked too much because of the evil, or that a sorcerer spoke from one side of his mouth, and that a smile was never really a smile, "only with his mouth, never his eyes."

Inherited spirits seem to have always come directly to a man from a father or uncle who has been killed in the past year, and would appear in human form while the young man was dreaming, but not if the dreamer already has a tutelary spirit, on which case he need not accept the intended inherited spirit, even though the spirit threatens to kill him. And as Smith explained:

> It is the inherited spirits that are the real bad ones. The more it is inherited (for example if he inherits one from his father who inherited it from an uncle), the farther it goes, the meaner it gets [...] If an inherited guardian spirit comes in the form of a person, it is bad. Sometimes it is a half Skelton. Sometimes this shows up before the relative who had it and sometimes after the person leaves. This is the worse kind; it is angry all the time, in misery all the time; it hates itself and everything else. This is the kind that is generally turned down. It is an animal which appears in this form (1936-8:1233).

684

Through time and loss of ritual and language, there is now incomplete knowledge of the various types of guardian spirits and the principal functions each animal spirit once served for its host. Basically, all anatomical features of any type of snake were considered an integral and viable part of a sorcerer's paraphernalia and ritual, and even after the sorcerer's death, the skin retained its deadly power, unless the skin was thrown into a fire. A person sorcerized by snake could best be cured by a shaman with snake power. The Western diamond-back rattler was the most feared. Any bird was the most popular tutelary spirit, most notably the bluebird and the humming-bird. The first for general good fortune and the latter for gambling power since the humming-bird could speak with his or her benefactor. The skin of a dead bird was saved by the son or daughter of the parent, and after being carefully wrapped with his or her power bundle, the bird would regain its shape, song, and power for the explicit benefit of the new owner. Smaller birds and fish were considered more powerful than larger species. Grasshoppers and butterflies were considered good guardian spirits, but all types of ants were bad guardian spirits. Most power songs came directly from tutelary spirits, and the recipient may receive several different power songs.

Given the personal relationship and dependence of a man upon his tutelary spirit, there was always the question of what happens to his tutelary spirit when a man dies. When Ray conducted his fieldwork with the Sanpoil and the Lower Spokan, he learned that there was agreement regarding the indigenous attitude toward one's spirit power after a man died, and that the intensity of one's relationship to his or her *suméš* could only be understood by acknowledging the spirit ghost concept:

> When a man died his tutelary did not return to its genus, disappear, or merely become non-existent. It was inconceivable that an identity so intimately associated with the deceased should not undergo a major transformation likewise. Consequently, the spirit "died" also, becoming thereby transformed in form to the ghost of the soul. The identifying character closely resembled in form to the ghost of the soul. The identifying character of the spirit were no longer retained, the new form being vaguely anthropomorphic (1937:594).

One origin of a soul ghost was if a person knew he was dying and failed to make an appropriate confession; he would—after dying—be fated to continually roam and suffer torment for his moral transgressions, or if one had not made retribution to those whom he had harmed. Conversely, a person who heard another's dying confession, but failed to fulfill the wishes of the *dying woman or man* (*šels-λ'lil*), would, upon his or her death—in retribution—become a soul ghost. Or a soul ghost may have been a living person who had been the subject of intense ridicule or slander. Consequently, soul ghosts were always a manifestation of malignant power and force. Soul ghosts—as other ghosts—were believed to never achieve peace as long as they wandered among the living; but once they leave, they never again appeared among the living.

Power Songs

The most enduring and perhaps important aspect of first receiving one's power was when a young and uninitiated supplicant, always in solitude, or during a dream, was initially engulfed by a particular guardian spirit when bestowing upon the seeker a unique *suméš* and a *power song* ($q^wélm$). Depending upon the season of the year, as noted earlier, this epiphany was on occasion first presaged for the novitiate by a gentle, warm wind that created small visible *whirlwinds* ($sx^wλék^w$ or $sx^wx^wl'e'k^w$ - "wind is blowing") in the water, in fresh snow, or moved the leaves and grass, but always making audible sounds. At first barely audible, the song might gradually increase in tempo as it approached or passed by the novitiate. Occasionally the song would make an echo, or was accompanied by unusually strange sounds—sometimes of different animals, one of which may eventually be identified as the seeker's particular animal guardian spirit. The unusual behavior of birds could register the presence of supernatural power by their erratic flight, songs, or even flying backwards.

Due to fasting, sleeplessness, and focused anticipation during the vision quest, the boy might see a vision as he *hallucinates* (*snw'ečm'tús*) of a guardian spirit who repeated the words of a song he may have previously heard as a child in a dream or previously told that he would later receive from his guardian spirit.

685

The person was told, "This is your song, sing it for this purpose—use it in this manner—whenever you have need for it and how often you may have need for it" (STHC). By singing a power song, the person may experience prophetic visions, even gain unusual strength and courage, or assume the physical identity and abilities of his guardian spirit.

It was universally agreed that fasting was the most expedient way to *attract and gain the attention of one's sumèš* (*čicntm*), for presumably one's tutelary spirit recognized the individual's sacrifice, and appeared as his charge. Fasting was believed to intensify one's unique relationship with one's *sumèš*.

Depending upon circumstances, a person seldom acquired all of his or her power song during the vision quest, but gradually, with repeated visits by his or her tutelary spirit during the Mid-Winter Dances, or sometimes in the sweat-house or when dreaming. The realization of receiving and knowing all of one's power song became apparent when the person felt he should sing his power song publicly for the first time during the Mid-Winter Ceremony—the major annual rite of intensification. During this public presentation of singing one's power song, the person could feel the active and powerful possession of their *sumèš* even though the singing was in a trance. The identity of the singer's guardian spirit was immediately recognized by all those attending the ceremony.

Hereafter, the power song was sung whenever a person needed council, strength, or the need to use his *sumèš* when confronted with a certain purpose or a daunting *challenge* (*č'scn'éyeʔn'tm*). After a usual and sometimes difficult but successful use of one's power, always through the assistance and active presence of one's *sumèš*, a person might add phrases to his gifted song; ones that may later increase his ability in gambling, hunting, curing, being song leader for the war dance, bravery in warfare, or whatever excellence he was now endowed with.

A power song or chant phrases were sung in what often sounded as a repetitious monotone, characterized by distinctly different mood, tenor, and tempo (STHC). Some have remarked how relaxing and even hypnotic a power song was upon those attending a ceremony, most notably a curing ritual.

Some power songs were so powerful that once they were sung, the song would never come back; even if the man could remember the song and tried to sing it, his words would have no sound. Or, if a shaman attempted to bring back a powerful curing song, it could make the shaman quite sick or even kill him. It was recognized that after a curing shaman's death, his *sumèš* songs often remained in the area. If a man became ill, the song could come to him and he might recover his health upon singing it. When the most powerful *sumèš* songs were sung, it was frequently forgotten, but it was recalled and sung only on special occasions. Presumably, it was always in the song's power if it would be sung again, and only by a deserving practitioner. A shaman would never sing his power song without reason, and then too only with the spiritual presence of his tutelary spirit.

Shamanism

As previously noted, men and women who were shamans occasionally possessed more than one form of *sumèš*, but guardian spirits are frequently noted as being quite different. No matter how many guardian spirits (*sumèš*) one may possess, s/he is, "inseparably conjoined, each possesses the other" (Lewis 1971:190). However, if a curing shaman had more than one *sumèš*, the usually all his or her powers were concerned with treating various maladies: forms of specialization. Not only did shamans exhibit an unusual appearance and strange behavior quite often, even in public, but were invariably eccentric of habit and authoritarian in demeanor. One cannot help but recall Wissler's (1938) work with different Indian groups, and the fact that he "seriously proposed that the Indian shaman 'may be a veritable idiot'" (Jilek 1982:131). Devereux (1980:14-15) was even more critical of Indian shamans: "my position is that the shaman is mentally deranged [...] In brief, there is no reason and no excuse for not considering the shaman to be a severe neurotic or even psychotic in a state of temporary remission." Earlier, Devereux facetiously asked, "how many Indian psychotics have turned into shamans" (1942:73). Yet among the Spokan, there was no memory or evidence that seizure was dangerous to the shaman or others present. Lewis felt that shamans "have found culturally accepted techniques for controlling private neurotic proclivities" (1971:191). Kroeber (1952) considered shamans as "less insane" than in judgments made by non-Indian, as did Linton (1956). Lewis (1971:180-181) quotes Devereux, who later concluded that "shamanism is 'culture dystonic', just as the shaman is 'ego-dystonic'" (1956a:23-48). Lewis quoted Socrates's judgment that, "Our greatest blessings come to us by way of madness" (1971:184).

This view of shamans being unstable was, in some ways, reinforced by shamans who often—but not always—lived socially and physically marginally—away from people or just on the edge of a camp or village. It was remembered from grandparents how "unusual" a shaman looked and often behaved, even scaring or frightening children. Briefly, some anthropologists feel that shamans were mentally *deranged* (*qʷoʔqʷawʔwʔ*), being manic-depressive psychotics, according to Devereux (2001:120). But generally, anthropologists recognize and acknowledge the need and value of shamans, as many people do of psychiatrists.

People with power, particularly sorcerers, never liked to be looked at directly; certainly not be stared at, which could be sufficient reason for revenge. Once, when discussing the differences between a shaman and a sorcerer, an elder once said:

> When out walking you could always tell if a shaman was behind you because the birds would be singing, a rabbit may run across your path, and if the sun was behind you, your back was always warm. But if the person was a real powerful sorcerer, you'd never hear the birds, even before they all scattered [flew] away, and if there was a sun behind you, your back would be cold. No more, but not long ago, if I took you to a big ceremony, even you'd know the ones with power; sometimes you couldn't say if it was good or bad, but you'd know who had *suméš*. A man with *suméš* could take anything into his two fisted hands, shake them in a special way, and before opening them, no one could see what he had in his hands; 'cause when he opened his hands, nothing was there. Shamans never played "games" like this except to entertain kids, 'cause he might lose his power. You never played with power (Ross 1968-2008).

Prior to the late 1930s or early 1940s, shamans were truly and exceptionally gifted individuals, capable of mediating between the spirit world and the natural world—believing that they had not only the ability, but the conviction of their power to cure. Eliade (1951), in a most comprehensive study of shamanism, commented upon the change of the early relationship a shaman has with his spirit, one that, "should [not] be understood in terms of individual psychopathology, but on the contrary as a culturally defined initiation ritual" (Lewis: 1971:189). With many anthropologists, Silverman also pointed out how, during a shaman's dramatic and convincing performance of power, the participant "becomes hysterical in his spirit possession, and how the members of the group anticipate that they will soon be visited by powerful spirits able to divine their vital problems. He goes on to describe the situation in more detail: "When he transports himself to the spirit world to divine or cure, his 'returning' pronouncements are received respectfully and obediently" (1967, 1:22).

Any shamanistic power performance was invariably enhanced and made more convincing—even unpredictable—of the group's anticipated reception of power by the predetermined visual and audible setting of the partially darkened room or dwelling, which was totally dominated by the performing shaman or curing practitioner. It is correct to say that no two performances were ever the same, never predictable; but the participants never looked away from the principal shaman. Often unusual sounds came from one or more of his tutelary spirits; sounds that may intermittently seem to originate from any source but the shaman: such as the fire, a water basket, a small pile of wood, from the patient, from anywhere since most shamans were gifted *ventriloquists* (*es-kʷuʔcin*). This ability, plus his seemingly facile manipulative skills of legerdemain and feared abilities of hypnotism, were reported to have absolute control over all who were present, most notably the patient. His visual powers were so powerful that he could 'see' who was coming from afar, or 'see' if a participant was foolish enough to bring a scrap of food in her purse or small bag. Some elders claimed how a

687

shaman could presumably change his appearance, most notably his very size, or even vary the gender of his voice (berdache?). If fear is a basis of respect, these shamans were greatly respected.

In the past, several elders who had been patients explained how absolutely convinced they were in the curing shaman's commitment and in his ability to cure the patient. This would be dramatized by seeing him shivering or in a trance, when being possessed by his guardian spirit prior to his administering a cure. Many years ago, one elder related this interesting episode:

> I was very sick, and I thought I'd die, but I got back my will to live when I realized the medicine man knew in his heart and mind that he could make me well. He'd convinced me I'd live and stay with my family. When my brother was in the hospital—where he died, he knew the physician didn't know him from the paper [chart] in his hand [physician's]. He'd look and find my brother's name; he never really got near him because he was an Indian; only asked a lot of questions about things my brother or any of us didn't understand, or was too embarrassed to tell he'd been fixed [sorcerized]. I had the feeling he was always talking down to my brother, and he ignored my family. But after a while he even uncovered my brother who was almost naked in front of my daughters. He had no sense of shame and I could see he'd no respect for older people (Ross 1968-2008).

An elderly curing shaman, with whom I traveled to distances off-reservation, visiting people he knew as a young adult, or doing different chores at his place, once related the following:

> During World War I, when I was young, I rode my horse to around Blue Creek looking for berries. I'd hobbled my horse and looked around, and in a small clearing was an older man who I knew was a Nez Perce doctor [shaman], but he talked Spokan real well. He was talking to himself or to an animal or bird I couldn't tell because nothing moved, not even the wind which was blowing just before I saw the man. Later, when I had my *suméš*, and when travelling alone in the woods, everything would go quiet until I talked to the animals and birds so they'd get normal (Ross 1968-2008).

Among the Spokan there were shamans who varied in the type of specific power they possessed. But the powers most actively sought were prophetic ones or—as with all hunting and gathering peoples—the ability for curing. Curing shamans typically enjoyed the status and satisfaction of curing others. On the other hand, a *curing shaman* (*sxʷmryém* or *sxʷmryemist* or *tlkʷílš* or *ƛ'eʔkʷíƛš*) was not only under intense psychological pressure and physical strain, but also ran the risk of being accused of sorcery. For this reason, a practitioner would always say if he could or could not help the patient. If he did commence treatment, but was unable to cure, the practitioner admitted that—in the case of sorcery—the sorcerer's power was greater than his. When a patient lingered in his recuperation, it was suspected that the shaman was actually a sorcerer.

Nor was it unusual for both female and male curing shamans to have more than one name if they possessed multiple types of power. Each name indicated a specific power which was apparent by the rituals, songs, and sometimes the dress of a shaman as s/he elicited assistance from a particular power. For example, a berdache might—when discussing the burning of tule beds—have water power, an ability, he might demonstrate, if necessary, when traveling in a desert-like dry *inland area* (*wutémtč*), as was once explained:

> [...] all the people got off their horses; gather around the shaman who would pull a sagebrush from the ground as he recited his prayer aloud, and water *erupted out of the ground* (*p't'ič*). After their needs were satisfied, the bush was replaced and the water would stop flowing (Ross 1968-2008).

When a shaman renewed multiple powers during the Mid-Winter Ceremonies, the sometimes lengthy process was initiated by appealing to the first power s/he had received, completing the propitiation with the power he has initially received. Whenever a person was discussing matters concerning a shaman, the *speaker* (*sxʷqʷlqʷeltm* or *saxʷʔuw'ew'lšm*) exercised discretion by not making reference to the shaman's power and associated tutelary. However, a shaman's power was generally made public first at the Mid-Winter ceremonies when the man held onto a sacred power pole and called for a *suméš* to attend him.

In addition to being able to speak in glossolalia, some shamans were capable of talking backwards and being understood by anyone having that *suméš*, particularly by his fellow Bluejays during the Mid-Winter Ceremony.

It was believed that Spokan shamans never sold or gave away their power name or their power songs. One could, however, have his power name stolen by a *jealous* (*sml'l'xweúse?i* or *č'łhém'ist*) or a more powerful shaman during the Mid-Winter Ceremony, usually when the unsuspecting participant was in a vulnerable trance when publicly renewing his tutelary relationship and power. If this occurred, then the situation was extremely dangerous since the loss of one's power name and corresponding power could result in prolonged *sickness* (*cq'ilt* - "he is sick") or even *sudden death* (*qe? č'łλ'llmiłlst*) of the victim. Sudden death was considered the result of the malicious machinations of a sorcerer when the *victim's eyes rolled back* (*čs?ol?olqncút*). To simply roll one's eyes back was termed *čʕʷol's*, but that did not necessarily indicate death. A curing shaman's methods were based on the techniques related to his particular power, but also on the force of his authority, as related by an elder: "One of the strongest shamans I ever saw, right here it was, at the house of old John Joseph's, at the late winter dances, could walk around in a dark room and blue-yellow flame would flash from both his hands. You really knew when his power was with him" (Ross 1968-2008).

Certain shamans, besides Bluejays, were known for their ability to predict the future, even declare long-term prophesies regarding humans or a specific ideographic natural occurrence. These men or women were called *kułanouél* or *kułtsínélsti*. In the past, an animal, most often a bird, could communicate in a dream or directly in the daytime with a person who had no *suméš*, a person of either gender or any age who was told what s/he should or should not do, usually to avoid a certain place or situation.

There was one other type of shaman, one who had mostly prophetic powers, but who was seldom a Bluejay. Such a person would be called an *ét'stúti* ("a man who was cut in half"), because he would have a thin but strong length of rawhide tied tightly around his exposed waist. When the cord was tightened by an assistant, the shaman could "see things" that were going to happen, as well as the location of lost or stolen items:

> A friend of my grandfather badly wanted a beautiful sorrel, a magnificent horse that had been stolen from him. My granddad went to a known *ét'stúti* who was able to tell him where it was and who'd stolen his horse. When these persons [*ét'stúti*] are cut in half, they become very weak, look awful because their *suméš* is gone in search of things—just up and left him (Ross 1968-2008).

Sorcery

A major area of behavior of any Amerindian medical system was the active and often malicious role of the *sorcerer* (*suxʷq'ewm*), who in the past was capable of causing death or various forms of maladies in his or her victims. By definition, belief, and practice, the Spokan had no witches, though it had been customary for the Middle Columbia Salishans (Miller 1998:166), the Northern Okanogan, Lakes, and Colville (Kennedy and Bouchard 1998:250). However, there was a Spokan word *wičwuče?t* that once described any strange and unexplainable fate or event, which was in some respects similar to witchcraft. Other Plateau ethnographers, when speaking of the Sanpoil, have maintained that, "Although sorcery could be practiced by anyone, and accusations of witchcraft were often made against shamans with care, of course, since it did not do to invite the enmity of a shaman" (Spencer, Jennings, *et al.* 1965:224). Though interpersonal conflict was the reason for being sorcerized, in some instances, however, "Sickness attributed to sorcery is hypothesized as representing a societal sanction of socially unacceptable behavior rather than interpersonal enmity" (Rubel and Hass 1996:115). Since the Spokan practiced a personalistic medical system "in which disease is explained as due to the active, purposeful intervention of an agent, who may be human (a witch or sorcerer), or supernatural (a deity or other powerful being). The sick person literally is a victim, the object of aggression or punishment directed specifically against him, for reasons that concern him alone" (Foster 1978:775).

The two major reasons why a man or woman became a sorcerer were either by inheritance or by the vision quest, as previously mentioned. A person was "born into sorcery" because of a painful and difficult delivery, or because the mother never wanted the child. One elderly woman claimed that a person could acquire such malevolent abilities from a living or even a deceased consanguineal parent or grandparent who was living or had been a sorcerer until death. Some felt that a child who was always too quiet, and with frequent fits of temper—really an unhappy child, or a child who had a congenital deformity and felt unaccepted by the group–could become a sorcerer.

A person may be trained in the use of poisons by a kinsman, but never about how to become a sorcerer; the methods and uses of sorcery were general knowledge, which always depended upon a person possessing one or more malevolent guardian spirits to actually practice sorcery. There were, as with all types of supernatural power, varying malicious consequences of being sorcerized, from discomfort to death, depending upon the wishes and abilities of the particular sorcerer.

A community was aware of those shamans who possessed malevolent guardian spirits, and was careful to avoid offending any such person; always taking care to avoid making a public or private accusation of sorcery, even if one suspected a spouse of malevolent acts using power. A person who had been publicly humiliated or offended, and had not the power to seek revenge by enlisting the assistance of a sorcerer, may leave his community. Even though the community knew or at least suspected who were sorcerers, they occasionally permitted a suspected sorcerer to treat a patient, particularly if the sorcerer had dreamed of the patient's condition. In such a case, "The healer functions in a dual role as sorcerer and must be capable of the kind of cognitive adjustment that will incorporate both roles" (Landy 1974, 1:103).

Sorcery (*wičwuče?t* or *čƛ?ax^wk^wisqelix^wtn* or *q^wu?q^wl* - "evil influence on people") was an effective means of social control, since a person was always careful to never humiliate or offend another person, particularly since a sorcerer could harm or kill a person in a group of people if he possessed projective powers. A sorcerer's projective power was so effective, "His mere look, if inimical to the victim, can kill [... and others] will hide or avert their heads in his presence to escape his glances" (Alvord 1857:15). Sorcery was effective for one assuming that he or she was too perfect, or a person who had publicly humiliated another, or who was too greedy or *spoke ill* (*su-siw* - "spoke ill of someone") of others. The reasons varied according to the sorcerer's interpretation. It was said that a *sorcerer's powers* (*k'áu*) were sought by others for a variety of reasons, usually to cause sickness or even kill, gain control of a person's spouse, or simply as a malicious act against someone who had knowingly or unknowingly humiliated the sorcerer:

A shaman may know of someone [in the village] who had maliciously embarrassed another man. The shaman would sometimes dream of what a sorcerer would do to the man who started the trouble [humiliation]. The shaman who had the dream must tell the man with bad words—warn him, of what may happen to him. I know [that] in the old days the dreamer [shaman] would be hurt if he didn't warn the man. Old people said if he didn't warn the man, then the dreamer would be harmed (Ross 1968-2008).

Just as *sumé* assumed different procedures, projective sorcery could have immediate effects:

A powerful sorcerer was known to be able to take a fresh leaf from the ground, and he'd put it in his mouth, and then roll it into a small compacted ball, which, if he wanted, he could snap at a person with his thumb and forefinger, like kids do with marbles or small rounded stones. When it hit his victim, the person would die, almost immediately. The victim always knew when he had been "hit" (Ross 1968-2008).

Any person *who presumed to live above others* (*?amotqn*) was often sorcerized. Not only was such a person more susceptible to sorcery, but a certain area of his or her body was considered to be a war zone—an area a sorcerer may attack to kill the person more easily, sometimes indiscriminately, for the slightest provocation. This may be used to make a woman barren.

The most dangerous and feared sorcerer was one who possessed *bad medicine* (*k^wlk^wleče? sqpusi'*) and used this *power* (*k^wlk^wleče? sqpusl' sumé*) indiscriminately—usually "succumbing to greed, personal gain" (STHC), with unrestrained personal impulses. A major clinical sign of sorcery was *physical depression* (*nλúx^w*), a condition that acknowledged for the patient and the family the power of thought which could be sufficient to kill the afflicted victim. There were different degrees of depression, such as *despair* (*piccx^wt*), and what psychologists called *hopelessness* (*picx^wt*).

690

The identity of a sorcerer was not always confirmed, though members of a group either knew or had strong suspicions of a sorcerer's identity. One may know a sorcerer was in the immediate vicinity if there was no discernable sounds from animals, bird or wind. Elders claimed that, "If you walked into a crowded longhouse, and you knew nothing about us, even you'd know who the powerful shaman was." Most powerful shamans were noted not by their clothing, but more through behavior and physical appearance. A few claimed how, "You'd just know, like feeling, smelling, hearing that something is different; like a tense coolness, like you're being watched."

It may seem confusing how at times a seemingly innocuous object in nature could be used as an instrument of evil when manipulated by a sorcerer, but at the same time serve as a prophylactic device against sorcery—like cheatgrass. Such situations were a testimony to the ever present and often precarious balance between the forces of good and evil, ones that were on occasion manipulated, even controlled temporarily by a sorcerer wanting to harm or kill his victim.

A sorcerer would always enlist the assistance of his *suméš* when he wanted to kill a person by attempting to *sorcerize* (*q'ew'* or *k'a'u*) in a manner that rendered the victim with little or no control. Some sorcerers possessed such a powerful *suméš* that even though the sorcerer might not actually dislike or want to intentionally harm or have illness befall a particular person, that person still became the victim of the sorcerer's *suméš*. It was said how a sorcerer may only think of hurting someone, and because his power was so great, his thoughts alone would harm the person. It was not always possible for a sorcerer to kill or harm a person who had a more powerful *suméš*. When a *medicine man's power leaves him* (*čɬwentm* or *čɬʔuwentm*), it might have been caused by sorcery, or by his own volition, or when he felt that he is too old and his power had commenced to work against him. If this happened, he was forewarned by his *suméš* to be released. Another problem that confronted all sorcerers was that they could lose their *suméš* if they failed when attempting to steal another's *suméš*, usually because the other person's power was greater or more devious than the sorcerer's *suméš*.

There will always be disagreement about the effectiveness of a sorcerer's defenses when he manifested and sent his power to harm or kill another person. Several elders claimed that once a sorcerer's power had temporarily left him, he was susceptible to sorcery by another sorcerer—one who knew when the former was without his power. Some elders believed that a *sorcerer* (*suxʷq'éwm* or *λ'eʔkʷilš*) always had some power of defense when targeting an individual. There was agreement that a sorcerer could not harm wild animals, only domesticated animals—particularly non-indigenous animals that were of economic worth to a person whom the sorcerer wanted to harm indirectly. For example, a horse would *become lame* (*tlxʷncut*), a *milk cow* (*čt esč'ɬp'eʔp'eʔmí*) would cease to produce milk, or chickens would lay only eggs with clots of blood inside. The author knew an elderly woman, a non-Spokan, who claimed to have once had cow *suméš*, and was able to ride her horse near a neighbor's unfenced herd and have the cows scatter throughout the bordering woods by just thinking of what she wanted them to do. This was done only to antagonize her neighbor, who would have to spend many hours getting his herd back to pasture. Years before, the neighbor's dog had killed some of her chickens.

Any curing shaman knew whether a patient of his or hers had been sorcerized by an individual who possessed a greater power, one that could possibly kill them during the *curing ceremony* (*ʔesníxúm*), or not long after. The identity of the sorcerer was revealed to a curing shaman since it was not unusual for him to 'see' the sorcerer sitting next to the patient "just as tho[ugh] he was alive; it is his soul; it does not make any noise as it comes" (Smith 1936-8:1301).

One elderly Spokan woman explained how she thought her particular illness was due to sorcery, and how she was treated and cured:

> I knew someone was trying to kill me because during that winter I kept losing my strength, had awful headaches, lost my appetite, and all my joints kept me from sleeping right. One late afternoon, without my asking, in walked [a curing shaman] who told me he'd dreamed of my condition, and wanted to help me get better.

First he hung new rosehip bundles in the corners of the room and put fresh crushed fir boughs [needles] in the coffee can with some water on the [wood] stove. After he unplugged and covered all the electric things, and when it was near-dark, he commenced working on me, all night as he kept singing and chanting several of his power songs, all the time he used two rattles made of deer dewclaws. During the ceremony, my dog started to growl and make awful painful-like noises so we knew someone evil was nearby. [...] said his power could see a[n] evil woman [whom] he named to all of us. He then took both his rattles and held them straight out in front of him, pointing towards where the barking dog was looking. Finally my dog stopped barking, and my son went outside and found a dead dog wedged against the backdoor. We all knew the evil had been sent as a dog by the woman [sorcerer].

The *x̣ʼeʔkʷil̓š* ("Indian doctor") said he now knew his power wasn't as strong as the evil woman's, but he'd still work to try and cure me, which he did. Before morning, my doctor said he'd cured me, but that he also had killed the woman, but that he'd also be the second person to die. Two months later he did die with what the Indian Health Service doctor said was a heart attack, but we all knew the real reason for him dying (Ross 1968-2008).

There were as many ways to protect oneself from sorcery as there were to sorcerize a person. Though personal prophylactic rituals and devices were not always adequate for personal protection, they were still used. A rather common means of protection was to wear a bag of nettles under one's shirt, or in a bag suspended from a shoulder so as to *hang in the person's axilla (č'tl̓ʕʼʷoax̣n)*. Some men preferred to *carry their power bag under their shirt (č'tl̓ʕʼʷoax̣iɬtm)*.

The author observed an incident of prophylactic ritual when visiting an elderly sick lady who suspected she was being sorcerized by a woman she had known since childhood, and who on occasion even sweated with her. When my hostess observed the sorcerer's imminent arrival in a car—followed by a cloud of dust— she asked to be carried from the living room to the kitchen, where she was propped up in a chair at her table. When the sorcerer came into her home, she was offered a glass of water, which the guest drank. But after the sorcerer left, the woman filled the glass with water and, without explanation, had all of her three young grandchildren drink a few sips from the 'contaminated' glass so that they would be immune to the sorcerer's malevolent power. When asked why she wanted to be propped up in the chair, she simply said that she wanted to give the impression that the sorcerer's power was not working, and would possibly improve my hostess's condition if the sorcerer doubted her ability.

Contagious magic was often the most powerful, involving either direct or indirect contact with the intended victim by the sorcerer or one of his familials. There were numerous methods of indirect contagious magic, but a common and much feared form involved a type of *evil medicine (qʼʷuʔqʼʷuʔt)* which required a sorcerer to place a special feather from *any bird (x̣ʷlx̣ʷeyʼut̓)* of the woodpecker family in the path or field of vision of an intended victim, but always in such a way that the intended victim became aware of its presence. It was said that in such a case, there was little the victim could do, whereas there were counter methods in the past. Less explicable was the application of the seeds from *common rush (Juncus communis - mlkʷtʼéstʼyeʔ)* when used by a sorcerer, sprinkled on an intended victim's stoop or on the intended victim's saddle horn, which would work only if he was in the saddle

A sorcerer could *place a curse (qʼew)* on anyone, including a medicine man, after his *sumés̓* was taken away. According to the will of the medicine man, the curse could serve simply as a warning, and was usually only an aggravating nuisance, or possibly cause the person's death. A powerful and feared form of contagious magic was when a sorcerer placed one or more hairs of his intended victim upon a recent burial site. If not properly treated in time, the intended victim would die through emaciation, simply wither away until dead. There were different explanations for such a death—one being that the life/spirit soul of the already deceased person had become lonely during the spell, knowing his host would die and simply wanted company before the actual death.

One example of the occurrence of sorcery and its effect upon nature, if misused, involved the so-called ironwood or ocean spray bush, which during early missionization some Christian Spokan Indians were led to believe was sacred, and was once a tree, but that it ceased to grow tall because Christ was crucified on this type of tree (STHC Anon., n.d.). One elderly Christian woman said she always wore a talisman of ironwood to protect her. Sorcerers commonly transplanted two of these bushes, always placing them in a secluded place, and tending them by methodically pruning each bush as needed; one plant represented a male and the other a female. Eventually, one would wither and die, either the male or female tree, signifying the eventual death of either a husband or his wife whom the sorcerer had been recruited to kill.

If a married woman attempted to sorcerize another woman whom she was jealous of, but nothing happened to the intended victim, then the married woman knew that the sorcerer had been sorcerized, or that the intended victim had a more powerful sorcerer who was attacking the married woman:

> This woman became very sick—just commenced to wither away until her family took her to a hospital to get better. She got a bit better, but never really OK. The woman once had power, but as she got older her power got weak—like her. She stopped going to ceremonies, for fear someone would hurt her like she tried to hurt the other lady (Ross 1968-2008).

It should not be surprising that during the history of Christianized England, every church yard had a well-tended yew and mountain ash (rowan tree) to protect the laity from evil, a practice that continues to exist in some areas today. An old English proverb explaining the belief of the powers of this tree was, "Rowan tree red thread. Put the witches to their spread." Yew trees in Great Britain were once so located as to produce bows in times of warfare.

A sorcerer's medicine bag often contained small *human bones* (*sqlix{^{w}}sc'am'*), presumably the first phalanges taken from young victims, most often infants and small children and the elderly who were more susceptible to a sorcerer's malevolent power. There was an array of evil things that sorcerers could store in their bags, such as spiders, yellow jackets, and cheatgrass—items that were capable of harming or killing a victim, but only after the sorcerer sang over them before use. Both the *non-poisonous spider* (*stey't*) and *poisonous spider* (*tupl'*) were commonly sought by a person attempting to become a sorcerer, one who might acquire spider *suméš*. Years ago, an account was given by an elderly Spokan woman who presumably had this power:

> My *suméš* is with the [poisonous] spider, and I can, if I want, kill anyone, and often no one can tell how or why the man or woman died. This power I'd gotten was sometimes helped by two other powers, both cow and bull *suméš*. You know some of my family who were near death [*či'łmnu'x*], and cured. If one of my family is sick, I will sacrifice something of great value to a curing shaman to get them back healthy. About 10 years ago I cured a young woman who had [undetermined] cancer inside her, and I did it all by sucking it away, little by little, until it was all gone (Ross 1968-2008).

However, the following situation of a curing shaman being afflicted with spider power from another woman occurred immediately after a Mid-Winter Ceremony:

> In December and January power is loose—everywhere, and I'm always very careful; everyone who believes this is careful, a time when we used to follow [observe] tabus and not hurt anyone. My colors are red and green because I saw these in my first power dream. All other colors were black and white. So, when I 'm curing, I always wear a red dress so my *suméš* will help me. I never cover my face with red paint [hematite] like they [shamans] did before.

> Once an old lady tried to kill me because she was awful jealous of me and my curing power; everyone told me this. One time she'd sent a black spider to jump on me when I was in a car with a friend I always sweated with. The huge black spider of the woman [sorcerer] came, it seemed from nowhere and landed on my right upper arm on my dress sleeve. I couldn't get the spider off until I started to sing my song, and then I could brush the spider away with no harm (Ross 1968-2008).

As mentioned, cheatgrass was used more often in various beneficial ways, but a sorcerer could surreptitiously leave a small bundle of this grass in a person's home, which later would tell the sorcerer what was being said. If not handled properly, dried cheatgrass can sting and cause a person considerable pain. And yet, as cited earlier, some carried cheatgrass to ward off malevolent spirits. Some sorcerers used dried, powdered cheatgrass to blow in a victim's face when in a crowd or ceremony. Using cheatgrass, a presumably innocuous plant, was an example of the sorcerer's power to take any benign plant or animal, and through ritual, instill within the object his or her malevolent power. For that matter, any organic item, plant, or animal that was a sorcerer's tutelary spirit could harm a person with illness or even kill the victim if the proper ritual was executed.

Once sorcerized, a person almost always realized that he had been forewarned by a sorcerer to change his behavior or attempt to make restitution to someone whom he had offended or spoken ill of, or had unknowingly humiliated. The common method for accomplishing this was to use a powerful projective *powder medicine* (*p'q'ᵂomín*), one that could be administered to a victim without the victim's knowledge. It was made by grinding with mortar and pestle the dried heart of a robin, which was placed in the sorcerer's mouth and administered to the victim by sneezing or atomizing a fine spray in the direction of the intended victim, similar in principle to the aforementioned powdered cheatgrass. As cited earlier, atomizing was also used for good purposes, being a method for purifying an area of malevolent forces.

A bird's heart was used by some sorcerers, more often of the *kingbird* (*Tyrannus tryannus - t'esŧ*), known for its ability to capture flies on the wing, and for its courage in attacking large predatory birds near its nest. The heart of a *calliope hummingbird* (*Stellula calliope - x̌ᵂn'ímx̌ᵂn'im*), a black-chinned hummingbird, a mourning dove, a turtle, a coyote, or a yellow-shafted woodpecker, was ground into a powder—but never mixed, since each type of powder brought different results. Adhering to the principles of contagious magic, any of these *projective powders* (*p'q'ᵂmín*) were effective when placed surreptitiously upon another's clothing, bedding, or food. Each type of powder was carefully kept by the sorcerer in a separate bag, always being extremely careful to never mix the elements unless required.

Several personal experiences involved taking older and more traditional Spokan who believed that they had sorcerer-caused maladies that required traveling to other reservations for treatment, since consensus was that on the Spokane Indian Reservation there were:

[... few] people who still know how to cure sickness and disease, but on some reservations, like the Umitilla, Nez Perce, and Yakima Reservations (Sahptian-speakers) there are some, and some of us still have old [traditional] sicknesses. Most of our health problems are ones we got—and still get—from the whites. Once, all our old sicknesses were cured by our doctors [curing shamans]. Our young people are [now] more and more like you whites (Ross 1968-2008).

During the early 1960s, the conflict of the government termination of Indian land rights and Indian status confronted both the Colville and Spokane Indian Reservations, creating intense and often bitter political and social factionalism. These conflicts tended to polarize the often more acculturated Indians from the more traditional enrolled tribal members, and it became apparent there was a revitalization of sorcery, typically by those opposed to termination against those advocating termination. Some felt that former *spiritual powers* (*nx̌ᵂlx̌ᵂíltn*) could be resurrected in their fight against the "more white-like faction members"—self-designated as the "Terminators." The following, by an elderly Spokan married to a Colville, explains the machinations of certain aspects of this religious revitalization, which illustrates their frustration by assuming they could jointly acquire the necessary *sumés* to achieve their purposes:

Both my wife and me looked for a special [power] we knew would help our people. After a while, we found [the] ones [plants] we're looking for, and picked a bag of them; but very carefully, and we kind of thinned them because they're now real hard to find. As we dug each plant, we did so slowly while singing our old songs. We needed only twenty or so, but before [too] long, we had a whole bag. Each plant we dug, I'd hold in my left hand, and I'd give each plant the name of a Terminator, and we knew something bad would happen to each of these people trying to sell our land [reservations]. Then I'd dig some more—many more, and I'd have my wife hold each [of the same] plant in her right hand, and I'd give each plant the name of [the] non-Terminators, before she put them in another bag, because we hoped their [non-Terminators] number would increase. After digging, we walked until we found a spot with a large gopher hole. I put all the plants named after [the] Terminators [in the hole]. When all the Terminator plants were carefully stuffed into the hole, I quickly filled the hole with dirt. The plants my wife carried in the other bag, I carefully placed on the ground, in the sun, so they'd become many [propagate from their seeds]; they'd be new non-Terminators (Ross 1968-2008).

With the loss of traditional Indian religion, and the adoption of Christianity, many of the elders suspected anyone professing to have individual power or *suméš* were, "People who had power that was evil; power that came directly from what is now called the Devil, and these people are like what our evil people [sorcerers] were once like." This was often the basis for certain types of religious factionalism, such as between some Catholic and Protestant Indians, or between Christians and non-Christians, but was even more intense with certain revitalized Indian religious groups—several being on other Indian reservations—who would participate in some funerals of traditional Indians who had opposed termination of reservation and loss of Indian status.

Ghosts

Until recently, ghosts and *ghosting* (*šk'ʷsčqélixʷ* - "being ghosted") were, at some point, inextricably related to certain illnesses and death, discussed to some extent in the life cycle chapter, particularly in the section on death. However, the behavioral aspects of *ghosts* (*st'qʷt'qʷnʔulexʷ* or *sk'ʷússč'eʔ* or *k'ʷsk'ʷsč'aʔsqélixʷ* or *sk'úsk'a*) were important elements within Spokan religion, and are here expanded upon with regard to other aspects of Spokan culture. All Amerindian peoples believed that ghosts fulfilled different functions: individual and group social control, explanations of unusual aberrant *nocturnal* (*skʷkʷʔéc*) noises and visions, lost game animals, and sometimes malodorous scents—reasons for certain self-induced illnesses and deaths; even an explanation of illnesses and deaths caused by sorcerers controlled by spirit ghosts. Ghosts of persons who had been dead but a short time liked to visit people. If repelled they gave up their attempts, and afterwards appeared only in lonely places and near graves" (Teit 1930:183). Ghosts of drowned people haunted the water for some time.

After a person died, his or her ghost may remain in the area until it was satisfied the survivors were fulfilling their obligations to the deceased. Teit (1930:183), when speaking of ghosts among the Coeur d'Alene, noted how, "if repelled, they gave up their attempts, and afterwards, appeared only in lonely places and near recent graves," and that ghosts "harmed people and cast illness on them." This belief was also held by the Spokan.

The existence, behaviors, and inhabitation sites of ghosts were once recognized by all Spokan, and universally verified by the individual experiences of people who heard and had seen ghosts. An illustrative account has come from a Spokan man who was married to a woman from Inchelium on the Colville Indian Reservation. The man thought it would be pleasant if his wife could spend part of the summer with her people, while he helped in the construction of the Hall Creek Bridge:

> I'd get up very early, before wolf-dawn, eat, and stay with my wife before leaving. One early morning I went to the narrow space under the stairs. It was real dark, and I was bent over to get something when a ghost grabbed me: one hand on each shoulder, and he'd pick me up and slam me hard against the wall, then he'd slam my forehead against the stair treads. Before I passed out, I must've cried out, because my wife and her family came and found me unconscious. Later, at work that day, I must've looked like a chicken. And all the men asked if I was sick. I wasn't, only in my mind was I worried about the ghost. And I never told them what happened. Later that day, after I went home, I stayed away from the house, afraid to go in. After a while I went in, but only because my wife and new baby was there. After that I could always hear the ghost walking around the house, but no one heard anything that time, only me. After a time [several months] we left and came back home again. Even my wife's family moved away, and someone else bought the place, but in that fall they moved the *small house* (*tstsmáɫax* or *k'ukʷím'éɫax* - "small house") to the top of the hill near the Inchelium ferry, it finally burned down in the winter (Ross 1964-1967).

Consensus was that a ghost rarely if ever associated with another ghost, and never had human needs for water, food, or pleasures, only human company. With the loss of aboriginal culture, due to missionization, and the general denunciation of traditional religion, there now exist conflicting beliefs regarding the behavior and severity of ghosting. In the past, ghosts could harm people by psychological means (shear fright) or even physically, such as by throwing stones. Some elders claimed a ghost could kill a person by suddenly frightening an unsuspecting person. More recently, some Spokan deny the existence of ghosts, believing that ghosts had nothing to do with a person's death due to improper burial rituals—not fulfilling his wishes for the distribution of his property, or bringing harm to a person who had humiliated or hurt him in life. Elmendorf described how a man who has bad thoughts toward another person must confess to the other person, for if not, the person having malevolent thoughts could die and become a ghost (1935-6, 1:4).

If a dead person—known to have been traveling at night—was later found with no apparent reason to explain his or her death, a shaman might later decide that a ghost had been responsible for this person's demise if the victim's face was contorted by fear. The most common indication of a ghost inhabiting a swamp area was when a person observed at night either a shimmering blue light or flickering flames (possibly burning swamp methane gases), not believed to be the ghost itself, but rather a sign made by an article of clothing or some possession that belonged to the deceased person.

Though some Spokan still believe there are ghosts, and have provided numerous accounts in private conversation, they deny their existence when other people are present. Consequently, most Spokan are uncertain about any earlier and now forgotten classifications of ghosts, but they seem to believe that ghosts appeared to have assumed varying amorphous forms, even though a person may say how in the past a ghost could occasionally be identified as a person who had died.

One Spokan elder, born in 1870, remembered his *parents* (*p'x̌ʷp'x̌ʷutc*) saying that there were at one time four, maybe five types of ghosts: a hooded ghost, one who had forgotten his name and never knew how he died, an evil ghost thought to be the spiritual apparition of a deceased sorcerer, a spirit ghost, and a soul ghost. Often it was difficult to make a distinction between the last two types, the only difference was that the latter form somehow maintained a close relationship with a living shaman, a distinction which is said to exist no longer. Confusion arose when some elders contended that breath-ghost was actually a soul ghost, or simply a soul—another uncertainty and confusion of concept created by earlier missionization. Some claimed there were two types of ghosts: those one can see and ones that are invisible during daylight. Several elders suggested a simple dichotomy of evil and benevolent ghosts.

Animals were never thought to become ghosts after death, but, as stated earlier, an owl had the ability *to ghost someone* (*k'ʷússč'eʔxtm*) when assuming a humanoid form with recognizable speech.

Receiving a spirit ghost was thought to be accidental, bestowed by a close *deceased relative* (*n'ƛ'lil*) who once possessed such a power, and who for several years gave indications of a future bequest by influencing the dreams of the potential recipient. A spirit ghost often passed from *father to son* (*selk'ʷmn*), even though the power was believed to be dangerous, particularly if a person refused to accept the spirit ghost power, and when doing so might cause him illness or even death.

If a person accepted a spirit ghost, he learned a new song given him by the ghost; henceforth, when he sang the song, the power of the spirit ghost served the man's wishes. After receiving the spirit ghost power, the recipient's behavior in time would replicate that of the deceased person. It was said that a ghost often emulated the behavior of the deceased. It is no longer certain to what extent a ghost was able to manipulate a person using contagious magic.

As can be best reconstructed, an unwilling recipient could enlist the help of a powerful curing shaman to destroy the spirit ghost. The shaman would negate the ghost's powers by holding the withdrawn power in his hands and submerging it in water, or by blowing the ghost' power from his hands into a fire, or passing his hands through the fire. Some elders recalled that a spirit ghost could be killed by humans using only a bow and arrow, and 'power'. Upon investigation the next day, the man may find his arrow embedded in a human scapula" (Smith 1936-8:1221) at the site of the encounter.

Elders agreed, however, that ghosts resided in known localities, usually swamp areas or a place where a person had been murdered, or where a lost person was believed to have been last seen. A human grave was a favorite place for a ghost to reside, particularly if the person had been murdered. Elders often stated how even a person unfamiliar with the local history would be able to examine the landscape and identify the places of ghosts, simply by the general topography and natural settings that would be conducive for a ghost-dwelling. Also, associated birds and animals often displayed aberrant behavior, such as a bird flying backwards, a deer with unusually short legs, or a wind being confined only to one small area—not blowing elsewhere. Recognition would be apparent if a person developed a sense of a thing, or a place, or a *ghostly (coil')* feeling that an unseen evil was present.

At one time the sites of ghost inhabitation were geonomically designated, and adults were careful to explain to children that such areas were to be avoided. As was mentioned earlier, there is a road near Wellpinit still called Ghost Road, and of course there were numerous accounts of ghost encounters explaining why was is so named. Apparently the inhabitation sites of ghosts were well established, and taught to the young through oral history. A Spokan man related an incident that happened to his grandfather's brother in the mid-1860s:

> [...] a man was crossing a small stream early one evening, when he heard footsteps behind him after crossing the water. The faster the man walked, the faster were the footsteps. Finally, the man ran away. The next evening he came prepared to the same stream crossing, and he could hear the ghost behind him—following him. The man turned quickly and shot an arrow at the figure of a ghost, hitting the ghost in the right shoulder. The ghost fell dead, but after a few minutes only the *shoulder blade* [scapula] (*snq'ʷɬtáqs* or *sxʷƛ'ečst*) was pinned to the ground with his arrow. The man picked up the shoulder bone with the arrow still in it, saying: "Why do you always follow and trouble people?" So the man buried the shoulder blade away from the stream, and never again was anyone bothered or scared by a ghost in the area. The man felt that maybe a person had once drowned in the stream and was never given a proper burial (Ross 1968-2008).

To rid an area of a ghost, it was once thought possible that a man—if brave enough—could kill a ghost by using only a traditional type of weapon, usually a bow and arrow, never a pistol or a rifle, because the loud noise would only cause the ghost to move quickly from danger. With few exceptions, non-Indian technology has not traditionally been associated with any sacred rituals involving supernatural power. Yet some elders believed that a ghost could steal a metal tool from a person, one that was the same type as what the ghost may have once used:

> In early June in 1920, a friend of mine was cutting wood near the main highway where the Ford fish hatchery is now, when he decided to stop work. So he hid [his] cross-cut saw under a bush. Then, after the 11 day Memorial Day Celebration, the young man and a group of his friends returned home by way of Little Falls, and decided to have a swim; they all swam deep to the base of the new dam, save for the fellow who was a sawyer. The others teased him, calling him a coward. Finally, the man did go swimming, saying he wasn't able to swim deep. Finally the young man got cramps and drowned—no one could save him, though they all tried. After some time his body came up, and his body was brought to his house, near where he had been cutting wood earlier. When anyone went near the wood lot, a ghost would chase them. I was chased several times myself, always when it was getting dark. This went on from threshing time 'til early November when someone happened to find the man's saw under the bushes. The saw was taken to the man's house, and never again was anyone bothered. I always thought that the ghost was really protecting [the] whereabouts of the saw, which maybe the ghost thought was now his (Anon., n.d.).

Ghosts were known to occasionally reside temporarily in the dwelling of the person being ghosted; leaving their body parts, usually a finger bone, tooth, or some unusual thing from nature. If a man or woman found such an item the next day, the person would go some distance from the camp or village and bury the item so the ghost could now rest and not bother the living. Another caution to prevent *being ghosted* (*skʼʷsčʼaʔsqélixʷ* - "a ghost's crying voice") was explained by an old man whose

> father always told us kids what to do if a person passed over in a violent way [murder] You gotta [sic] get together all the spilled blood on the ground, and any bloody water. You mop it up, and take all the rags and the

mop head to the burial place, and bury them before the people coming later throw any dirt on the man's casket. Now, if you don't do this, the dead man's spirit [ghost] will always wander around looking for his blood and make crying sounds (Ross 1968-2008).

Ghosts were reported to have appeared only during the night, and never when there was lightning. Smith (2007 pers. comm.) said how lightning could reveal the presence of a ghost; never leaving footprints in mud or snow, and seldom any tangible physical evidence of their presence. Ghosts and all aberrant anthropomorphic and theriomorphic manifestations were recognized or sensed by *domesticated* (*txʷoxʷ* - "to have become straightened") animals. Horses would whinny, paw the air with their hoofs, even bang against corral fences if penned. Dogs would bark or howl and bay incessantly until the form leaves the area. Also, a dog may appear comatose; never making a sound, but instead shivering until the intruding form left the area. Different elderly hunters described how, many years ago, hunters or trappers sometimes had to spend long periods in the woods, often with inclement weather or while tracking a wounded animal. When alone, a trapper knew a ghost or some theriomorphic *creature* (*ccim'e?t* - "small") was present by the noises created when animals and birds fled the area.

The presence of a ghost could also be indicated by sounds that were said to resemble a moving non-articulated *skeleton* (*sqlixʷsc'óm'* - "human bones") with its bones rattling. Sometimes a person out at night would feel a sudden and chilling wind, even in the summer, indicating the nearness of a ghost. Others claimed that the presence of a ghost was indicated when the night air smelled of ozone, as it does briefly after lightning, but on many occasions there was no lightning.

Though Teit (1930:183) was told by the Coeur d'Alene that ghosts had no heads, and therefore, unable to whistle, the Spokan said ghosts seemed to be able to *whistle* (*síkʷ* or *sesíkʷm'*) in a unique manner, even while simultaneously *humming* (*nkʷenmey'e*) a repetitious melody. This was always sufficient cause for parents to warn their children against ever whistling at night, particularly when they were away from the village or camp, since it was believed that a whistling could attract a ghost, who could grab and twist the child's face so severely that only a curing shaman was able to restore the child's face to a normal appearance. Involuntary face-twisting, and often uncontrollable facial spasms were once believed to be the consequence of whistling at night.

Elders claimed that ghosts could make crying or singing sounds that resembled human speech. A personal experience occurred while camping in a remote area with an elderly man in his early 90s. Later, just before midnight, we were awakened and startled by a loud, piercing shriek from what was undoubtedly a cougar. The elder, however, was convinced it was a ghost, from the eerie and frightening sound. There was consensus that a cougar's cry can be easily mistaken for the shrieking of a woman who is being terrorized or throttled, and yet some younger Indians claim this type of cry is more frightening than any sound a ghost could possibly make. People in the past claimed that the cougar scream was to entice an unsuspecting—presumably a non-Indian to come to the rescue of the endangered woman. It was also claimed how the cougar could imitate a puppy or even a coyote.

Some stated that the presence of a ghost was indicated by the cry of the great horned owl at night, which, people admitted, may be easily confused with ghost sounds. Numerous accounts were given of how the hooting of an owl at night reminded one of a woman crying. More often, the owl's cackling alarm-like cries were interspersed with Spokan words that warned of an impending danger that could harm, but not kill the night-traveler. If one heard a coyote during the day, a friend or family member might die the next morning.

Though not associated with ghosts, other nocturnal animals were capable of warning humans to proceed no further, to return from whence they came. Ghosts were frequently believed to be omens of disaster, and were often believed to be capable of returning to avenge some neglect or offense a person received while living. These psychic projections might appear in a person's dreams, which always required the assistance of a curing shaman to interpret and, if possible, to be treated for what was called ghost sickness. Having been forewarned, regardless of how, a person might be preoccupied with a fear of sorcery, and ultimately death.

Among the Kalispel, however, "an owl was never known to tell something wrong, nor to lead anyone astray, they were always good" (Smith 1936-8:1310). Yet the Chewelah-Spokan Group did believe—as cited earlier—that an owl could maliciously mislead or lie to a person (Elmendorf 1978-89, pers. comm.).

Ghosts were never given names, though some people were able to identify certain presumably spoken sounds as belonging to a past relative or a deceased friend. The Spokan had no memory of believing that ghosts were clever; rather, they were easily fooled if a person kept his or her wits and did not panic. If a man travelled alone at night, and heard a noise, he would never draw near to investigate; but rather shoot an arrow in the direction of the sound, which usually stopped the noise. A paramount fear was that a person would die if touched by such an *apparition* (*sčicn* - "visit"), particularly a *ghostly apparition* (*sk'ʷússč'e?*), dying of cardiac arrest brought on by sudden and extreme fright. In some cases, the day before a man died, a ghost might appear to him as a real person at night, but the dying man would know he was being visited by a ghost even though he spoke to him in Indian.

It was explained how in the past ghosts tended to travel along pathways at a quick shuffle or a loping run, making noises to warn the living of their presence, sometimes by making sounds of *creaking bones* (*wéhwéhw'eh*) or *cracking sticks* (*yíq'q'q'*), even though they were rarely seen during the day. There were past accounts of large boulders being maliciously rolled onto paths when a person was traveling, nor was it unusual for a solitary night traveler to be accosted by missiles of stone or *mud* (*sƛoč'óle?xʷ*). More serious damage resulted when a ghost chose to release logs into a river, which could float and damage fishing weirs; something that the shaggy humanoid creature *sc'wen'éy'ti* was also known to do at night. In a hunting camp, picketed horses were sometimes released by a ghost, or all a man's traps would be maliciously sprung by a ghost. Some contended, however, that these malicious acts were the work of a *nocturnal monster* (*sc'wen'éy't*); not necessarily ghosts. It was thought that such incidents indicated a general displeasure for the group rather than for any individual.

With the construction of lumber houses, children were warned to always close the curtains before dark to prevent ghosts from looking in to see if there were babies or young children. Some dwellings of traditional building materials were vacated after a person's death, and burned to prevent the occupancy of the deceased person's ghost; a practice which essentially stopped once homes were constructed of *lumber* (*pɬpɬ'ɬalqʷ* or *scpíč*). Unusual sounds at night were sometimes attributed to a ghost's presence. Even off the reservation the deserted home of a white farmer or rancher may have been considered as being haunted. An erroneous instance of this was related to the author:

> Coming back (ca. 1911) from root fields way west of Reardon we stopped at a[n] empty [abandoned] house for the night. We'd eaten our supper, unhitched the horses, and rolled out on the kitchen floor for the night. Late that night we could hear someone walking up the stairs, which we knew was a ghost, then the ghost stopped and started to walk down the stairs, so all of us grabbed the kids and bedding and ran out. We slept on a high knoll across the road away from the house. The next day we got our cooking gear, and one man said the house wasn't ghosted; rather the noise was from a wood rat's tail hitting the steps when coming down, which after a long vacancy was filled with *rodent droppings* (*mmneč*) (Ross 1968-2008).

The following incident occurred in the late 1960s, when the author, several university students, six Spokan elders, and a contingent of USAF Survival School instructors, camped for several days and nights at the once-traditional root fields below Harrington. Since the students could eat only the plants they had collected or the animals they had snared, one student—unknown to the rest of the group—unfortunately killed and later roasted a diamondback rattlesnake, some of which he ate. During the last night of the encampment, a powerful wind came up suddenly and blew over the two Indian tipis. This caused both tipis to fall across the cooking fire and burn. The wind scattered only the Indian blankets and gear. Eventually one of the instructors elected to leave after the storm, and to take one elderly Indian woman home to the reservation. But as soon as they tried to leave, the pararescue instructor was unable to control the direction of his vehicle, which veered about the root field until he turned off the engine. Finally, he made their way over to the dirt road, and they were able to leave, but only after the elderly Indian woman explained how and why they were being punished by rattlesnake power for having killed the snake and not asking to be forgiven.

With the partial and often a syncretic acceptance of missionization and notions of heaven, there grew belief in the wandering soul or breath-soul of a young and innocent child, that the captured soul would presumably provide guidance and afford the malevolent force a place in the hereafter (STHC). Upon the death of a child's close friend, the surviving child's parents would be noticeably attentive and warn him or her to be extremely careful, because their dead friend's soul—being lonely—might come as a ghost to take their soul. Some years after the first teachings of missionaries, it was said that some Spokan:

> [...] believe that those who are good go to a happy hunting ground where there is an unlimited supply of game, etc., whilst the bad go to a place where there is eternal snow, hunger, and thirst, and they are tantalised by the sight of game they cannot kill, and water they cannot drink (Wilson 1866:303).

There is no longer any agreement as to how a *deceased person's* (*st'q'ʷtq'ʷniúlaʔxʷ*) (ghost), one that had become a soul ghost, might be seen by members of his family. But some believed a person can be ghosted by a *deceased spouse* (*ʔumsčiyem*), particularly if the living widower or widow did not observe a proper period of mourning, one who married or had intimate relations too soon after a husband's or wife's burial. Thus, it was also possible for the deceased—as a ghost—to create fright in a widow who violated her time of mourning, by speaking to her *in his voice* (*ck'ʷusč'eʔcínm*), or have an animal do this, usually an owl. A ghost could "appear later to people who are rude, disrespectful at a person's burial ceremony" (Rogers 1944:560). A widow or widower might become ill and even die if ghosted by a *loved one* (*nʔumsčíym*). If a betrothed woman was rejected by her lover, and committed suicide, then the *suitor* (*sx̣mnčew's*) could be ghosted or condemned to death by the ghost of the rejected woman. A major concern for a survivor of a friend's death was that the ghost might have made an after-death decision to remain among the living, particularly with a close friend, and would then ghost him until he dies—to renew a more compatible relationship.

A treatment for a person thought to have been ghosted was identical to the medicament for treating a cold or nasal congestion (described earlier in the section on inhalation and respiratory phytotherapy). This was believed to not only clear the person's head, but also indicate to the ghost that he wanted to be left alone. For example, a personal experience was when an elderly and traditional Spokan-speaking man had been diagnosed with cardiac complications, and was placed in a large urban *hospital* (*snčc'eʔr'elstn*) for observation. During day visits, the man seemed fairly relaxed, but after several days he began imploring to be returned home, for he knew he was going to die of a ghost illness. He explained that an elderly non-Indian patient, in a bed on the other side of his circular curtain, had died the night before, and he knew that since none of the man's kinspeople or friends had ever visited the now deceased person, the man's confused and sorrowful ghost would come back and take the soul of the elderly Indian for company and solace in his wanderings. Fortunately, the man was discharged and able to return with the author to the reservation that afternoon.

As stated, one reason for a ghost to torment kinspeople was if the deceased had not received a proper mortuary ritual, as in the case of a sorcerer whose decomposed body was found before the spring bloom after being lost (possibly murdered) in late fall. One elder could recall how the peripatetic form of this once rather powerful sorcerer's *suméš* had appeared as a ghost for several months to various people. As stated, a most common explanation given for the presence of a ghost was not necessarily revenge, but rather loneliness, the need to have another's spirit to accompany the ghost in its wanderings. As one elder woman explained: "We were told never [to] play or go outside, as this was a time when ghosts looked for anyone to join them. The ghost had only to touch us and we would be taken."

Another explanation of a ghost's loneliness—always given in a lowered and serious voice—was of how when she and her brother were children, the speaker's grandmother:

[...] warned us to never cry or feel bad when we're in darkness, because a ghost will always feel sorry for us, and then take our tears or rub [on] our heads. Ghosts can feel sorry for people and want to comfort them, particularly children. She always said that after we'd been crying to wash our faces and drink some water so the ghosts can't take our tears. We'd then be unconscious and could hear only the ghost, or else lose our minds. She warned us that when we're big people, ghosts could still come and get our tears if we cried at night (Ross 1968-2008).

It was also feared that a person who saw and recognized a ghost might immediately develop a type of ghost illness, which would be diagnosed by an attending shaman because the patient would be suffering from excruciating headaches, crying inconsolably, or vigorously rubbing his head and face. Ghost illness was sometimes successfully treated if the patient sought help from a powerful curing shaman, one who could recognize this form of illness, since the patient was often unable to speak; even appearing sometimes to be comatose with a weak pulse, shallow breathing, and dilated pupils. Patients diagnosed with ghost illness often *wandered* (*sʔamʔamtɫkʼˀʷu* or *člaʔpmƛkʼˀʷuʔ* - "one who drifts") away from a village or camp, and when found were returned to their camp or village and immediately incubated by being wrapped in robes or blankets and placed between two low fires to increase the blanket's warmth to provide a sense of security, and hopefully induce sleep. After an hour or so, the shaman would commence to sing over the man, while *slowly* (*kʼˀʷukʼˀʷiet*) beating a drum and gradually increasing the tempo until the patient commenced to awaken. He would then be taken by several friends and the attending shaman into the sweathouse, where he was comforted by the shaman speaking in a low and reassuring voice until the man's tutelary spirit fully returned and restored the man's health. It was believed that if a ghosted man were left unattended, then he would die, particularly if he became subject to unpredictable *convulsions* (*qčmím*). Yet a ghost might take pity on a person who was experiencing an incurable and excruciating illness, and end his life.

A dying person who refused to admit all of his moral transgressions was believed to spend his time forever as a ghost in torment and experience excruciating pain, being condemned to continuously wander to all those places he had ever visited, away from his home area. Or, his endless journey was spent in areas of burials and, later, in established graveyards—always in solitude. For one year, the survivors of a known ghost would carefully avoid those places that the deceased had once favored, for fear that his ghost would appear and frighten them, but would not physically harm anyone. With a few exceptions, a deceased person normally appeared as a *ghostly apparition* (*skʼˀʷússčʼeʔ*) before a *solitary person* (*ča-naqes*), always avoiding crowds. Some have said how in the past a ghost could change form to temporarily appear as a *human being* (*ʔecʼxíl t sqéixʷ*), and even to be able to speak as a human.

Eventually the ghost might reach the undescribed land of the dead, never to reappear on earth or in people's dreams as a ghost. Though a widow or widower might be *ghosted by a deceased spouse* (*ʔumsčyém*) *during a visit* (*stʼqʼˀʷnʼiʔúleʔxʷ* - "visited by a deceased relative"), and any ensuing conversation would invariably be considered a prophetic warning to be heeded by the living spouse. Yet not all visits made to a surviving spouse were by a ghost; rather, they were often made by an owl, who would imitate the voice of the deceased. However, if one imitated a dead person's voice or attempted to predict the death of an individual, one could become ghosted, a process called *ckʼˀʷsčʼeʔcinm* (STHC). The surviving spouse of a deceased son or daughter was known as *sčʼʔelp*.

Ghosting (*skʼˀʷsčeʔsqélixʷ* - "being ghosted"), if not properly treated, was generally an accepted psychosomatic explanation of a *prolonged illness* (*nʼčeʼčirʼs*) and even death. The Spokan believed a person could be ghosted if the individual had ever mocked a dead person's voice, and this was true at any age, but it was common for an older person or a person in *deep mourning* (*nčʼtʼip* - "his heart is cut out"), and he was more susceptible to such an affliction. A deceased husband or wife could *ghost a spouse* (*ʔumsčiyém*) by creating illness that could lead to the spouse's death. Regardless of reason, a person was called *stqʼˀʷnʼiʔúlʼeʔxʷ* if ghosted by a close relative. Usually such a ghost enunciated reasons of regret, or some misdeed of a relative during the burial ceremony. The etiquette of a living person's relationship with ghosts was clearly prescribed, and taught to children from an early age. There was, however, no compunction about discussing owls when it was dark, even though it was believed that owls could understand the Spokan language and could communicate with ghosts. Yet some elders maintained that a person should never speak of owls after dark, for any mention could bring misfortune to the speaker.

Ghosting normally resulted in any one of several conditions: temporary or permanent muscular atrophy, paralysis, temporary hysteria, nervousness, chronic fatigue, various forms of clonic *seizures* (*x̣'l'x̣'él'il'*), *epileptic seizure* (*ʔec qecm'stem'*), dementia, or pseudo-hypertrophic muscular dystrophy. Often a person with a prolonged *fixed stare* (*čxc'x̣íc's* or *čx̣ax̣áʔpús* - "to stare") was thought to have been ghosted. Also, the permanent or transient loss of sight, hearing or even speech would be attributed to a person having been *maliciously ghosted* (*k'ʷusč'ʔem* - "it ghosted me" or *x̣c'tmłtúmš* - "he ghosted somebody") by an individual who had engaged a sorcerer possessing such a power of debilitation. A common explanation for a person becoming permanently *deaf* (*ntqtqén*) may also have been attributed to seeing a ghost. The knowledge and fear of ghosting served as an effective means of social control, in addition to providing a general explanation for various expressions of *mental illness* (*wíl*) and related maladies of the central nervous system.

Only a few elders claimed that ghosts no longer exist today since many people do not believe in them, never see or hear them, and there is too much controlled electricity in the air, and the traditional Indian culture is gone. One elderly gentleman contended that environmental pollution was also a factor. Yet there are some acculturated Spokan who believe that a person can protect himself by praying to *God* (*k'ʷl'ncaln* or *k'ʷl'ncútn* - "Supreme Being"), while other more traditional Spokan said that those who are bad during their lives will remain here on earth as ghosts, and all of their afterlives will be spent *roaming endlessly* (*xʷilwisi*) in pain as ghosts. One elderly lady said, "No matter who, if you don't believe it, it means you don't know the stories [oral history], which means you don't speak the language, which means it don't [sic] happen."

Without exception, every elder, when asked of his or her greatest fear during childhood, said that all sorts of monsters and other theriomorphic creatures were greatly feared; but as an individual grew older, ghosts dominated their fears because the spiritual world became increasingly more meaningful and relevant. One woman summarized her childhood fears:

> How as children we were always being warned about not opening any door at night if there was knocking, especially if there were only three knocks. Whenever it happened, she'd always ask out loud who was it. If a human answered she'd open the door and ask them in. If there was no human-like voice, she knew it was a ghost, and the next day we'd hear bad news about someone real sick or who'd died (Ross 1968-2008).

Monsters and Theriomorphic Beings

At one time, children were repeatedly told stories describing the many different supposed creatures, such as various types of zoomorphic and anthropomorphic manifestations that existed in the Spokan world that were neither animal nor human, but had *humanoid form* (*čx̣ił t sqelixʷ*). These life forms were effective in maintaining social control and providing explanations for unusual occurrences, such as non-human sounds, smells, or observed feats no human could have performed. Such beings were classified by often unusual anatomical characteristics, sizes, colors, behavior, and degree of zoomorphic and anthropomorphic transformation.

The Spokan had definite classifications of autochthonous inhabitants, called *sxʷq'ixʷm*, including dwarfs (*sncmasqélixʷ*), weird beings, and *ogres* (*n'ełnaqálixʷ*). They also recognized the existence of creatures such as giants and large monsters, most notably two forms of giant *man-eating monsters* (*n'ałisqélixʷtn*). No offerings were ever made to monsters in order to placate them. A *water-being* (*nqlixʷétkʷeʔ*), such as a merman or mermaid-like creature, or any underwater creature, was always feared by anyone seeing this creature, for it was believed that person was certain to die (Egesdal 2002-1, pers. comm.). It was recalled how descriptions of water-beings were often slight distortions of appearance that varied with each account;

702

perhaps a form of anamorphosis brought on by fright. For example, in several of the small lakes on the Spokane Indian Reservation, there lived a particularly feared theriomorphic creature, a water monster who possessed half-human, half-fish form, and was considered dangerous to humans swimming, rafting or canoeing, since this creature could easily *capsize* (*nȿol'l'l'étkʷ*) their boats, sometimes perhaps inadvertently drowning the occupants. This half-human and half-fish creature also inhabited the deep, still, and shadowed backwaters of streams, and were capable—even during the day—of gaining a victim who foolishly bent over close to the water to see his or her image.

Teit fortunately offers the only recorded description of early humanoids who were called *tree men* (*stémqestcínt*) who inhabited the areas of the Spokan and Coeur d'Alene:

They have a strong odor, dress in buffalo skins, and have the power of transforming themselves into trees and bushes. Once a number of people were dancing in the Spokan country near a small lake close to Cheney. Suddenly they smelled something, and one of them exclaimed, "That is *stc'qestínt!*" They looked around and saw four men standing a little apart from one another and wearing around their shoulders buffalo skins, the hair inside out. Immediately they disappeared and four bushes remained where they had stood. These four bushes could still be seen lately. Possibly the power of the people's glance killed them or prevented them from transforming themselves back into men. However, there are trees which have been in one spot a very long time, but they are *stc'mqestcín* just the same, although they seem merely trees to people looking at them [...] Often when things were seen and people approached them they disappeared, and only trees or bushes could be found (Ray1930:180-181).

Giants were believed to capture humans and hold a person for an unspecified time before releasing the individual, who, upon being released, would have no memory of the ordeal. Yet some say this could have been an explanation for a mental illness, prolonged coma, or paralysis in a person, due simply to shock from the experience. Elders, particularly women, would entertain and enculturate young people with seemingly endless stories of other *giants* (*sc'wené*), weird beings, and dwarfs. A few elders could recall accounts of terrestrial and other aquatic creatures that were *half-animal* and *half-human monsters* (*nqƛixʷét'k'ʷeʔ*) who always dwelled in larger bodies of water, and *only at night* (*čmi-n-skʷukʷuec*) would come onto shore, returning before wolf-dawn to their watery habitant. Their presence was proved by unusual swellings of water, unusual currents, or the surfacing of hydrophytes normally restricted to bottom depths. *Benjamin Lake* (*sčkʷlkʷlta čɬq'l'iʔs*) was known as a place where these creatures once dwelled; yet they never bothered women who annually harvested tules, cattails, and turtle eggs on the water's edge. It was once claimed that Benjamin Lake is connected with Turtle Lake by an *underground flowing stream* (*čɬmemélmn*), which permits the movement of turtles in early spring. There were several accounts of when Benjamin Lake was used to water horses, and of how one horse was dragged to the bottom and never surfaced. There is no recall of propitiatory words or gifts being given to appease aquatic monsters before harvesting turtles or aquatic plants.

Different land mammals were also believed to be dwelling underwater. As noted earlier, beavers were once thought by some to be partially human because they dwelled in lodges and cut down trees in a fashion that they presumably taught to early Indians. Once, when the author camped with an elderly Spokan man near a large pond, there was a series of loud and distinct slaps on the water in the middle of the night. In the morning, my host explained that the disturbance was a beaver flapping its tail to warn us, but of what he could not say. He remembered hearing, as a boy, that some beavers were once abnormally huge and too clever to ever be trapped by humans.

Certain land mammals, such as abnormally *huge toads* (*snakʷkʷan'eʔ*), and a *legendary large toad* (*sɬiʔɬay'eʔ*) were thought to inhabit aquatic environments, always waiting to take a solitary human child who foolishly ventured too close to the water. In the past, there was a rather ubiquitous and much feared lizard known as *člčlšéw's*, that would *growl deeply* (*ɬoml'š*); but their number greatly diminished with deforestation, and the once natural environment has been reduced and made inhabitable and further endangered by grazing cattle.

A particularly dangerous creature was a *giant toad* (*snaqʷuqʷeneʔ*) that was dangerous to the early inhabitants and to small animals; often characteristic of theriomorphic creatures. One knew of its whereabouts less by its stealth than by the horrible odor it could emit. In oral accounts children were once told stories regarding a large skunk feared for its obnoxious and sometimes poisonous spray, a creature called *snqʷalaʔxʷmin* (STHC).

The giant most commonly referred to was the Plateau's *Indian humanoid monster* (*sc'wen'éy'ti*), or called today as Big Foot by both non-Indians and Spokane Indians who do not speak Spokan, a creature that has commanded considerable attention and study by even some physical anthropologists (Grover Kranz 1971, pers. comm.). Many Spokan elders and some whites are adamant that the creature is human; at least part humanoid or an earlier form of humans. Not too many years ago, many Spokan elders could provide one or more personal accounts of an encounter with *sc'wen'éy'ti*, a shaggy creature that would roam about only at night. A universally agreed upon indication of this creature's presence was an overpowering malodorous scent that always accompanied *sc'wen'éy'ti* wherever it travelled. Some believed that the *odor* (*kʷiʔ*) resembled that of burning wet hair (Fusch 1992:6).

Domesticated animals, particularly horses and dogs, always displayed agitated behavior that indicated the presence of *sc'wen'éy'ti*. Yet no one ever attempted to kill or capture this creature since he was humanoid and could walk or run in an upright (orthograde) posture. Many Indians believed these creatures were former people, not animals; and there was consensus among adult Spokan that this creature was harmless—never killing people—only scaring them and their domesticated animals. The only known violence was against deer and bear-hunting dogs, of which there are several accounts. This creature was not known to be malicious.

An elderly Spokan woman, in the early 1920s, wrote an unpublished account of corral traps (included earlier in that section of this mongraph), and she also noted:

> In those days the big man creature was known to them as *Zwa-Nay-tee*. These big things had been seen by men and children at play. These must be fish loving things or man, creatures [...] Some times they wrecked our salmon traps and scattered fish all over the bank. They were big, powerful and fast, never was told of him hurting any one (Anon. n.d.)

Rev. Walker wrote: "They frequently come in the night & steal their [Indian] salmon from their nets, & eat them raw" (Drury 1976:122 fn). There were also numerous accounts of *se'wen'éy'ti* who presumably slept during the day, and quite soundly; thus, making possible the following encounter, as recorded many years ago:

> [...] three sisters and two or three other women drove stakes down into the ground around *sc'wen'éy'ti*. [It's known that when a *sc'wen'éy'ti* sleeps, he sleeps very soundly. They sleep during the day.] These 5 or 6 women laced their braided Indian ropes over and over him, tying him to the stakes they'd driven into the ground. When it appeared he was awaking, they all sat on him, hoping to keep him down. They said he appeared to pay no attention to them, [and] arose effortlessly, breaking his bonds, [while] the women fell off him as he got up and walked away! They had to destroy their clothing because of the stench from their contact with *se'wen'éyti* (STHC).

Another recorded episode described how a man had staked his horse near a stream, which flowed close to his home:

> One morning, they found the horse had been moved and staked quite ways further up the creek! [...] and had *sc'wen'éy'ti* stench on him for about a week! The horse didn't appear scared or anything out of the ordinary about him. They surmised that *sc'wen'éy'ti* probably hypnotizes horses and people (STHC).

This claim that *sc'wen'éy'ti* was capable of hypnotizing both humans and other animals provided an explanation for a young girl who many years ago was missing, and thought to have been abducted by *sc'wen'éy'ti*, but who was found some years later unharmed and asleep along a creek bed where she had last been seen. The woman, upon awakening, had no recollection of where she had been or any details during her

704

noted absence (STHC; Fusch 1992:9). However, some missing women were described as having lost all their senses when later found (STHC). Fusch, a popular writer of *sc'wen'éy'ti* also wrote how this creature "probably hypnotizes horses and people" (1992:5).

A letter of 1840, as recorded in the diaries of Elkanah Walker, described other types of theriomorphic creatures, and how the Spokan:

> [...] believe in the existence of a race of giants which inhabit a certain mountain, off to the west of us. This mountain is covered with perpetual snow. They inhabit its top [...] They hunt & do all their work in the night. They are men stealers. They come to the people's lodges in the night, when the people are asleep & take them & put them under their skins & take to their place of abode without their even awakening. When they awake in the morning, they are wholly lost, not knowing in what direction their home is [...] They say their track is about a foot & a half long [...] they frequently come in the night & steal their salmon from their nets, & eat them raw. If the people are awake, they always know when they are coming near, by the smell which is intolerable (Drury 1976:122-123).

A particularly fearsome creature was a *two-headed snake that had a head on each end* (*šmšmn'oʔsayaʔqn* or *šmšmnosaqs*), and like nearly all wild creatures (*stmsʕác* or *łu ʔuw'aq'ʷuʔt* - "wild"), this *two-headed snake* (*ʔasʔasálqn*) was known and feared, but not always seen by good people, more frequently by a *mean man* (*n'ałisqélixʷtn*) or a *bad man* (*nałisqéƛxʷ,*) the results of which were no longer remembered. Another aberrant form of snake was the *double-headed snake* (*šmšmnoʔsáy'aqn*), one with a head at both ends, said to have once been related to the Western blue-tailed skink, and existed during the time of Bank beaver and Tree Indians.

There is little agreement as to the different types of *anthropomorphic giants* (*sc'wen'éy'ti*) that the Spokan feared in the past, nor is there agreement about dwarfs, though they had until recently been part of Spokan stories, when some elders would occasionally see *little people* (*coʔtálixʷ* - "agents of confusion"), or some of the *lost people* (*smtéw'si*). When speaking of monsters and other theriomorphic creatures, Smith made a valid point, one that was also accepted by the Spokan, that the "Kalispel never pry into anything to see if they can learn any more about it; they let every thing go just as it looks" (1936-8:1225). On occasions, when inquiring about giants and theriomorphic beings, some elderly people would discuss and even describe them. However, other older and traditional Spokan often—after some reflection and considerable consternation—hesitantly explained why they would rather not talk of such creatures; though some did:

> It is better to never talk about something, something you don't want to happen, like ghosts and strange people or animals who are out at night; ones you can hear and sometimes smell. We were taught by older people and their elders before them that talking about things you don't believe, will happen. I think talking, or even thinking about them, will bring them around. My grandmother always told me how talking of something will make you then dream of that thing, which is now a part of you; [that] can be very dangerous. I know some whites even talk about *sc'wenéy'ti* and little people, but they're making fun of our beliefs. Even today I know some young [Indian] people [who] are disrespectful of the rock paintings, and that maybe a reason why so many young folk are confused and in different [forms of] trouble (Ross 1968-2008).

Children were told vivid and dramatic accounts of a type of supernatural creature called *słiʔiłá*—thought by some to be a transformed bull frog—which would appear before misbehaving children in human form either as male or female. As in all cultures, the Spokan undoubtedly turned to the supernatural when explaining to children how and why monsters and other theriomorphic and nocturnal creatures inhabited their area. Though little can be recounted, there was a large anthropomorphic creature known as *n'słnásqálxʷ*, who, unlike *sc'wen'éy'ti*, was a predator of certain smaller animals and people.

From an early age, all children were aware of the numerous monsters and theriomorphic creatures that inhabited their natural and supernatural worlds, and it was expected that adults had the answers to any child's inquiry, answers that not only elaborated upon the group's morals, but were an integral part of the *mythical charter* (*sqʷell'úm't* - "mythical account"), which served to explain and reiterate prescribed acceptable behavior. It served as a pragmatic charter of primitive faith and moral wisdom (Malinowski 1954:102). The primary reason for claiming and explaining the existence of potential malevolent life forms was to control the behavior of non-compliant children, but it once obviously concerned adults as well.

Stick and Bank Indians

Elders spoke of personal encounters with *stick Indians* (*eλčλčé*), who would dart quickly across a woodland path, but never came near human habitations. When camped at night, a deer hunter would occasionally hear but not necessarily see these inoffensive creatures. Elders acknowledged the acts and appearance of stick Indians. In many stories there is consensus that stick Indians were and are invariably present at night, and even if one cannot see them, one is readily aware of their presence by the malodorous scent they give off; similar to *sc'wen'éy'ti*. A further indication of their presence was often the sharp sounds of a stick being broken or beaten against a boulder, which probably gave rise to their designation.

These creatures travelled in small groups, for rarely was a lone stick Indian seen. One elder claimed how in the winter, when his father ran a trap-line near a frozen lake (?), he could distinctly hear loud noise emanating from the far end of the lake as great sections of ice were being broken and stacked by stick Indians. Similar to this was an account given by a Spokan woman of ice being piled up by stick Indians at Turtle Lake while two kinsmen were winter camping:

> They heard a loud crack of something big hitting the ice and breaking through to water, but they couldn't tell where it was coming from. The sound echoed off the cold air and hills and seemed to come from every direction at once. They listened to the rock and splash of ice hitting ice for a long while before it grew silent again (Lesley 1991:18).

Since stick Indians are rarely seen, only known to be present by their sounds and odor, nearly all contemporary accounts of stick Indians, mostly from oral history, unfortunately provide rather vague descriptions of their general appearance: suggesting they vary in height from less than a meter to several meters. Given a situation, a stick Indian is capable of changing its height and form when confronting a human, but usually at a distance, and no one could recall accounts of being touched by stick Indians. One elder said how as a young man he and a friend ran a trap-line near Chewelah, having as a base camp a sheet tin-roofed log cabin where they slept, stored equipment, and dressed pelts. One late fall night, after preparing their winter traps and equipment before returning when the snow would arrive, they were awakened by noises from one or more animals prancing on the tin roof. Arming themselves, they ran outside to investigate, and claim there were at least three stick Indians jumping about, who were clothed but revealed their identity of being humanoid but very "thin boned."

Stories are recalled of an earlier race so-called bank beavers, creatures thought to have once lived in trees or in south-facing stream banks, and which were much larger and in some ways more humanoid than present-day beavers. Neither the stick Indians nor the bank beavers were malicious, and presumably did not interfere in the affairs of the then-present Spokan Indians.

Omens and Dreams

Omens were rightfully believed to indicate dangerous and unpredictable future events, ones universally associated with all aspects of life, particularly those occurring in dreams and in physical manifestations. The lives of the Spokan were also influenced by a person's interpretation of culturally agreed upon *omens* (*čʼɫxáʕlstn*), usually discerned by a shaman who possessed the power to foretell a prophecy, and was called *λʼkʷλʼekʷʷílš*, or simply a *foretelling shaman* (*kuɫanavél*). Apart from dreaming, omens were presented to humans by both animals and birds and through the agencies of wind and other unique or aberrant sights and sounds of nature. Every aspect of a person's physical survival and spiritual existence was inextricably related to his awareness of the natural and spiritual surroundings, and even though an omen might prophetically signify a specific event, the recipient was not always certain of the significance or correct meaning of the omen, and would consult an *older person* (*pʼxʷpʼxʷút*) for interpretation, often an elderly shaman.

Despite the Spokan acknowledging a great number of omens, there were individual variations and interpretations of meanings; nuances that again may require a shaman's conclusion. However, an omen could be an explicit description of what would happen, or it might appear as a metaphor, or even a riddle; it may even be propitious. Furthermore, a revelation could occur at any time, such as in the sweathouse, when dreaming, or when resting after working one's trapline, but seldom when engaged in an activity requiring concentration. Explaining the significance and occurrence of omens, an elder once explained that when a person's hands are busy, nothing comes to his head.

Because many omens first appeared in dreams, children were instructed upon awakening to explain as best they could the details of any unusual dreams that they may have had to an elder. The listener, typically a grandmother, would explain the significance of the dream. If the revealed omen or dream was thought to be a forewarning, there would always be certain restrictions upon the child's activities for that day. Children were instructed to recognize and acknowledge omens, which—if ignored or violated—could affect an individual as well as the family or the community, depending upon the nature of the dream.

A child experiencing or witnessing an unusual occurrence of wind or sound would ask an adult for an explanation, such as a cool wind blowing upon the child on a warm day, called *xʕáʕ*, and was always considered ominous and sometimes a portent of evil. A *pending doom* (*čʼɫxaʕlstn*) was indicated if a cool, ill wind blew across a person's chest. Omens were often revealed to a solitary person during situations of contrast, such as light and dark, usually during darkness and during extremely hot and cold temperatures, and when the weather suggested impending change or uncertainty. For protection, and to mitigate one's apprehensions, a fearful person might sing his power song to his guardian spirit for guidance and protection.

Certain dreams were further understood to be prophetic, and often were a distinct image of a known person who was going to die, who was always warned by the dreamer. If the dreamer failed to do so, then s/he would die. The dream might not be an omen of death, but rather one that identified a range of situations that confronted someone, who similarly, if not told, would suffer the consequences of the omen or dream. It was imperative upon the dreamer to always warn the person, who, if possible, would avoid the *impending danger* (*moyyxei*) and later thank the dreamer for giving prior warning. The dreamer might receive a small keepsake in appreciation.

As was noted with the Flathead by Turney-High (1937:30), the Spokan had ministrants who could dream or see, not prophetically, currently occurring events. The ability and role of such a *seer* (*squmoíqa*) may have been that of a person who was, according to Turney-High (1937:30), often entertaining about even the most intimate behavioral details of a couple engaged in sexual intercourse.

There were two types of dreams: common and special dreams; the former were of no real significance, often being cognitive composites of secular past occurrences which came true only by chance. However, special dreams always came true, and were very significant, and dealt with supernatural subjects, which were directly communicated by the medicine man's tutelary spirit, or, on occasion by another person's animal helper. Such a dream might be communicated by a person whom the medicine man knew, but never came from a ghost, though a recently deceased individual—often a kinsperson—could 'appear' and speak directly to the dreamer. Invariably such dreams and messages were warnings of personal misfortune for one's family or even a friend or acquaintance.

Many nocturnal animals, particularly certain birds such as owls, if heard or seen at night, were considered to be omens of certain malevolent acts that would befall the hearer or observer. Despite its size, the most feared owl was the burrowing owl (*Achene cuniculana - sq'q'ax^w* or *nččw'e?*), for in mythical times this small ground-dwelling owl was actually a monster, a *cannibal* (*n'ełnasqélix^w*) known to eat children, but was destroyed when Coyote pushed the owl into a huge fire he was making to cook some captured children (Elmendorf 1935-6, 3:24). Any owl screeching—particularly the burrowing owl—for three consecutive nights meant one of the group would die before the fourth nightfall. Such a fate was also indicated when either a wolf, dog, or coyote howled and cried persistently for *three days* (*ča?ła*). One nocturnal animal, the brown bat (*t'en'w'éy'e?*), was not remembered as being an omen by some Indian groups. Even an "owl's hooting out of season is a bad omen - [or] if an owl lights near one & 'talks' [or] makes noises it is an indication that something terrible is going to happen" (Elmendorf 1935-6, 3:26).

Many Spokan omens predicted who would die or become seriously ill and when. For example, it was once believed that:

> When you see clouds forming "ribs" in the sky, you're going to hear about a death. If the clouds are red, especially at sun-set or sun-rise, it will be a "bloody" death or death by fire. If the "rib" clouds are huge, stretching across the skies, it will mean a famous or a well-known person's death. It [the news] will also come from whichever direction the clouds are formed (STHC).

Omens of illness or death assumed many forms, and did not necessarily involve any animal. For example, an *uncontrollable twitching* (*ʕʷoc ʔe ʕó ʕe ʕʷoc*) of a person's eye, ear, hand, or foot was considered to indicate a serious illness or some misfortune to a known person or to the dreamer. Spasms in one's left eye, foot, or hand were of serious consequences to the dreamer or one whom he had *dreamed* (*qey's*) of, indicating a permanent clonic-type seizure, or even the death of oneself, a close friend, or a kinsperson. (The meaning or significance of any spasms on the right side was not established ethnographically.) But if the threat was the result of the person being *haunted* (*sk'ʷússč'e*) by a ghost, then it could be cured.

Numerous omens and taboos determined how one interacted with most animals. When hunting, if a person sneezed, someone would immediately pick up a stick and break it, or else someone would die. If they failed to do this, the hunter might toss a sharpened stick into the air, and upon falling the sharpened end of the stick would point to the dwelling of pending death. Hearing unexplainable noises while in a wooded area by oneself was an omen of serious illness or death within one's family; and the person's identity might be later revealed in a dream. If the flames of an open fire were crying or even speaking to a solitary person that was taken as a pending omen of misfortune; an occurrence called *n'cll'úsmłt* (STHC). A woman stepping over a piece of food or a dead animal being dressed meant that the group would experience a famine (Elmendorf 1935-6, 1:68).

Children were told to avoid certain reptiles and amphibians—even the water snake (*Nerodia sipedon - sč'w'íl'e?*), which was believed to be the river spirit, as well as the frog, who was water snake's helper (Elmendorf 1935-6, 3:9). There once existed a type of frog called *č'łwáxls*, which was a bad omen for anyone who saw it turn over on its back (STHC). The rattlesnake—though feared—was held in reverence, and if one were killed, even accidentally, the person responsible quickly dug a hole and buried the snake, after which he would take a stick, wrap a thread or hair around it, and place it *upright* (*c'lc'il*) in the ground as a marker (Elmendorf 1935-6, 3:7).

An elderly man could receive an omen from his guardian spirit indicating it was time for him to give up his power. Failing to do so could cause his illness or death. Consequently, a person willingly gave up his guardian spirit if so cautioned, of which there were once numerous accounts.

Omens could be manifested as different types of physical or mental illness, often commencing with incipient or inconclusive premonitory symptoms, typically diagnosed only through a shaman's dreaming. As indicated, omens were often concerned with illness and death. For example, many years ago, just before a formal memorial ceremony, when the author was helping a person arrange a new headstone into place, an adult black bear wandered some 60 m away, suddenly stopped to watch us, and then looked away and continued his journey. The elder explained that this was an obvious omen for the relatives and friends of the deceased to be brave, have strength, and give up their sorrow.

During nocturnal traveling, a person was susceptible to suggestive omens, which, upon reflection, were usually interpreted for their true significance. For instance, seeing an unusually bright star near a full moon meant that a member of the village or camp would usually die within three days unless the person was forewarned. Unexplainable sounds—usually at night—also served as an ominous prediction of illness or death. Even the seasonal proximity of celestial bodies, or a shooting star, could be prophetic. The following incident was related by an elderly man who was explaining the significance of some celestial omens:

> Speaking of stars, many years ago [1930], Í was driving a sleigh that was pulled by two horses, and my partner said he could see a star falling. It seemed to last for maybe a minute, when suddenly it crashed to right where we were and broke the tongue of the sleigh in half. The star went right on into the frozen ground; never saw it again, even in the spring (Ross 1968-2008).

An omen may be good or bad, though the meaning was not always apparent when first heard or observed. An example was if a solitary person observed a large expanse of bear-grass moving in waves when there was no perceptible wind, that could mean a person was going to die, or the person was going to meet a friend whom he had not seen for some time. Another example was if a person accidentally stepped on a dry stick, the sound of it snapping would give an incomplete message that was made clear later by some other sign. One woman said that in the past her mother explained how one of her favorite bone awls—by speaking—would warn her of coming events, those she should avoid.

The way *lightning struck* (*scq'ém*) was always viewed with considerable apprehension. For example, a person would *become* sic*k* (*čcq'méƛtn*) if he used the wood from a lightning-struck tree in any manner, and the person may later have a stroke or a minor form of paralysis. The same physical symptoms would occur if a person ate the meat of an animal killed by lightning. Smith (1936-8:1306) mentioned how among the Kalispel, a person could tell that someone else was going to die if he saw a standing dead tree fall over when there was absolutely no perceptible wind. Or, when a solitary person saw a rotten tree falling when there was no apparent wind, he would expect to die, not immediately, but in the near future.

In the case of certain omens, there was no way to prevent an individual's illness or death, regardless of prophylactic rituals. Elders explained how in the past there existed a definite belief in *fait accompli*, and that when one thought it was time to die, for whatever reason, a person *resigned* (*hóy*) himself to his fate. Any disrespect to a dead animal was sure to cause a person illness; or, as explained earlier, if a man's wife was pregnant, the baby might be born with a congenital defect. Ominous consequences were unavoidable if a person ignored certain omens.

During a ritual gathering, a man who received an omen through a dream or directly from a non-tutelary animal—often a bird—will stand before the congregation and describe a future occurrence of illness, misfortune, or even death that will befall a named person. The recipient of the omen would then ask him if the prophecy was correct, and if so, an attending shaman will publicly attempt—through ritual—to prevent the occurrence of the pending danger or physical affliction (STHC). The dreamer may offer the intended victim a *medicinal root* (*mir'yemistn*), explaining that if he refused to eat it he would die.

Some omens were a *forecast* (*ʔac'xnúxʷ*) of good fortune, and as noted elsewhere, an individual tended to avoid contact with most reptiles, including the Western blue-tailed skink. However, some have said that if a person caught a blue-tailed skink in his hand, and the tail came off, then they would have good fortune when next gambling. Omens or signs of good fortune were more often detected by observing a certain bird, or hearing its call. To see either a *Western bluebird* (*Sialia mexicana* - *nqʷiqʷáyičn'* or *syoʕ'ʷy'aw'*) or a *mountain bluebird* (*Sialia corrucoides* - *nqʷiqʷay'ác'eʔ*) early in the morning meant a day's good fortune for the person. The same good omen was indicated upon seeing a mourning dove, a *Western meadowlark* (*Sturnella neglecta* - *w'aw'íckʷl'e* or *w'ew'íckʷl'eʔ*), or a *yellow warbler* (*Dendroica petechia* - *sxʷíwxʷu*).

However, if a certain bird demonstrated unusual behavior, it would be interpreted as a warning to the observer. A robin flying in or striking a family's dwelling while in flight meant one of the occupants would die. When in the woods, if a person found the feather of a certain bird, particularly the blackbird (*mláqlg*) or common raven (*sč'lúpeʔ*), he may interpret this as an ominous sign if the feather happened to fall near him, warning him to be exceptionally wary of danger. Finding a feather of a *brown or yellow-shafted flicker* (*Colaptes auratus* - *kʷlkʷléčeʔ* or *kʷλkʷλé*), or a red-headed woodpecker, served as an ominous sign. It often meant that the first person to find the feather was going to be sorcerized, it having been purposely placed there by the sorcerer. The tail or primary wing feather of either of these two birds was commonly used by a sorcerer, often attached to some personal item of the intended victim.

A person sensing that he was losing or had already lost certain long-established predation skills—such as trapping, hunting, or fishing—would *interpret* (*nmi-cin*) this as an omen of his impending illness or death, knowing that his own *sumés* had left or was leaving him. Prior to a scheduled hunt, a man dreaming of failure would often not participate, for it could be an omen that none in the group would have success if he participated. Upon making such an *announcement* (*łaq'ʷmstm* - "to announce"), a man was never criticized or mocked, but rather accorded respect for only a brave person would admit to a situation that would endanger his fellow warriors. The same was true if a person dreamed that his participation in warfare would cause a friend to die; in which case, he would not venture forth with the war party. Thus, all apparitions of death, sickness, or failure were obviously considered as bad omens, except when a man wanted to commit suicide against an enemy, often as a result of humiliation or loss of love.

Dreams of any adults were interpreted as containing significant omens, regardless of the subject, and were always related privately to the chief, who later in the fall would describe the person's dream publicly; but never reveal the informing medicine man's identity. Later, during the Medicine Dance, the medicine man who led the group was often the one who had the dream, thereby identifying himself as the recipient of the dream mentioned by the chief several months earlier. The main message of the dream was where they would first camp in the spring after leaving the winter village, even though it was known from long experience where they would go. But despite predictions and habits, nothing was certain, particularly when engaged in subsistence-getting activities, as best illustrated with the First Salmon Ceremony. Nothing was ever taken for granted, as failure to participate in a certain ritual or ignoring the prophecy of a dream, was tantamount to sacrilegious behavior, and warranted grievous consequences—not always immediately, but within a year. Thus, an appointed medicine man often assisted a chief in interpreting dreams and most omens brought to him by an individual, and it could happen that a chief had such powers.

Most dreams were believed to be influenced—even controlled—by one's guardian spirit, or on occasion by an offended and powerful sorcerer, and it was assumed that one's guardian spirit could come anytime to a person in his *dream* (*snspsú*). The source or reasons for omens naturally varied, but often an individual's guardian spirit was instrumental in such a warning, through a dream, an announcement while in the sweathouse that may appear in the true form of his *sumés*, or having another animal warn the person. Apparitions took many forms, but two common ones were seeing a person at a distance from a camp or village, and learning upon returning that the person had never left an omen foretelling the person's *approaching death* (*šels λ'lil*). Another was seeing a known deceased person in the woods, which surely indicated that the viewer would die. If a person happened to *sneeze* (*at'só?m* or *?at'š?o*), then he knew someone was speaking ill of him, but never knew who the speaker was.

The Spokan were deeply aware of literally hundreds of both good and bad omens. Furthermore, there were multiple variations of personal interpretations, and even though there are currently far fewer omens, those that remain are viable and continue to reinforce certain taboos, and occasionally afford explanations for misfortune. As with ritual, omens seem to have always been even more important for a person engaged, or planning to be engaged, in a particularly dangerous activity, such as bear hunting or warfare. This was true even of financial ventures, such as betting or gambling.

Most Spokan omens were based upon the Doctrine of Signatures: like brings like, in both form and function. For example, it was believed that a colt could attain greater speed and endurance as it grew older if it was given a secret name, or by attaching a time-tested power object, which would later make the horse even swifter. In accordance with the principles of the Doctrine of Signatures, the owner of the colt might take a primary spurious wing feather from a predator bird, usually an eagle, and tie the feather in the horse's mane, renewing the feather as needed. To insure speed in turning or negotiating tread areas, the body of a hummingbird was securely tied to the withers of a horse (G. Flett, pers. comm.).

The immediacy between ritual and actual occurrence of certain expectations was seldom lessened by time or distance, but was solely dependent upon a participant's spiritual and psychological commitment and belief in his *suméš*. Though there were not always discernable omens that served as explanations for a person's unique behavior or physical disability, elders once believed that any event could be revealed by a certain person's ability to recognize the fortuitous presence of what others failed to see or dreamed about. Once, when doing fieldwork on a different Salish-speaking reservation for several summers, the author spent time with an elderly gentleman who had joined thumbs on his right hand. One day he remarked:

> John, I notice how you sometimes look at my thumb, and I'd like to explain how it came to be. Many years ago [CE 1880s] when my mother was pregnant with me, she was collecting freshwater crabs in the river [San Poil] below where we lived, and one bit her bad on her right hand. So you see, that's why my double thumb looks just like a crab claw (Ross 1964-67).

The recognition and use of omens and prophecies were once prevalent in Spokan culture and it was used to explain or prevent illness, death, or misfortune. Most are almost unrecognizable today. An early recorded prophecy of Euro-Americans was recorded by Elmendorf:

> Alex Pierre - close to 100 - [an] elder in [the] Presbyterian church at Wellpinit - tells of [a] prophecy he heard when [as] a young child - already old then - a prophet had foretold the coming of the whites & how they would change the face of the country & introduce new animals (1935-6, 3:24a).

Mid-Winter Ceremony

The major sacred rite of Spokan intensification involving purification, spirit acquisition, and world renewal was the *Mid-Winter Ceremony* (*sλ'e?kʷlšscút*), celebrated in conjunction with the *Mid-Winter Medicine Dance* (*st'axʷa?*), Jump Dance, and Bluejay Ceremony. Most of the ceremony was conducted in a specially built *large long-house* (*siy'aʕ'iʕqs*), one that always had four large linear-spaced firepits, each large enough to accommodate a large cooking basket (STHC).

The Mid-Winter Ceremony was traditionally held during a four-to eight-day period in late December or early January, when it was believed that theriomorphic forces and malevolent spirits were the most powerful and prevalent within the natural environment. This brief yet violent period was a perceived manifestation of the rampant forces of nature, characterized with a change in atmosphere pressure—a heaviness like before a severe winter's ice storm, a time when animals sometimes exhibit erratic behavior, "The sky is black, but you know the clouds are swirling; animals make no noises and run with no direction, the only sound is the incessant winds, and even the birds sometimes fly backwards." This presumed potential near-apocalyptic conflict among the forces of nature, man, and the spiritual world, would gradually gain in intensity and assume devastating proportions if the Mid-Winter Ceremony was not conducted. The most predominant and omnipresent fear was being temporarily possessed by an omnipotent evil force, one that was in no way associated with sorcery, but by nature's "wildness" of nature and all its beings. One elderly woman explained her parents' brief description of how a malevolent power could:

> [...] come and take [possess] a person for four to five days. You could easily tell when someone had the evil power, you'd just sense or feel it; always at night. You knew all kinds of animals were near, but you couldn't see them, just sense they're about, sometimes making strange noises or no noises at all. You could protect yourself from evil by wearing under your arm or under your shirt a buckskin bag of fresh nettles. Then, after four or five days, everything would get sort of calm and settled, and you knew it was over, and maybe the sun would come— like a new world. People today don't talk about it because they don't know how it used to be, probably because the world is out of balance and our old ways and beliefs are gone. We no longer know how to renew our world, only destroy it (Ross 1968-2008).

During Mid-Winter rites of intensification and world renewal, any participant who had received his *suméš* and power song since the last Mid-Winter Dances would announce this occurrence (Olsen 1998:555). Critical to any recipient of *suméš* was the, "Self-expressive dramatization of effects through the personification of supernatural beings who are culturally at hand for ritual possessions [... and were] utilized for psychotherapeutic purposes" (Jilek 1982:92). Therefore, an important function of this annual rite of intensification was when "individualism and competition of contemporary life threaten[ed] tribal unity, the Winter Dance promote[d] group identification and group solidarity" (Randolph 1957:144). As previously cited, one could, however, have his or her *suméš* stolen.

During the ceremonies, any man or woman could become possessed by a new or alternate power, and would be thrown into a motionless trance while receiving instructions from their *suméš* or someone else's more powerful guardian spirit, which if followed would eventually prove beneficial. Consequently, the strict subjection and adherence to ritual was always believed to restore the balance of malevolent and benevolent power for the individual and the group, and of course their relationship with nature. Elmendorf's field notes recorded such an account:

> A woman from *stsqaístsi̓n* married *q'ʷłtłq'* ["a man who lead this dance"] and lived at *ntuʔúlm*—and she was thrown into a trance at a *st'áx̌ʷeʔ* a [winter dance] and [when she had gained consciousness,] they asked her what they should do—and after she had come to she told them to take off the clothes from [her] upper part of [her] body and grease her from [the] waist up and sprinkle down (duck or goose) over her and all over her hair—a horse hair rope [was placed] around her head with an end in [the] back for a woman to hold on to—(all of this procedure was ordered by the woman's *suméš*)—and another woman went in front—and the woman in the middle danced the *t'áx̌ʷa* [step] (*tcrápi*)—they went through every [camp] house that way—then they went through every house that way—then when she got back she could sing her song and tell her story—when she got back to her own home (where she had started) she stood in the middle and seemed to be normal—then they let go of the rope and she sang her song—[she] told the people the *suméš* (a bird of some kind) had told her she would be fortunate and get many horses if she followed directions and the people would be able to see for themselves if she succeeded—she did become quite successful—[she] acquired many horses—her name was *kʷlkʷlst'cáʔanim* (1935-6 1:24-25).

The Mid-Winter Ceremony was also a time for the ritual renewal of one's tutelary spirit, participating in prophylactic rituals, curing and, for some, receiving their Bluejay power when adults and older children were particularly careful, even fastidious, in their attendance and support and were careful to always be respectful to the other participants. A further reason for anxiety was a fearful concern all adults had for people with exceptional powers, who were thought to be capable of 'seeing' or discerning any type of disrespectful behavior or thoughts by others, which if revealed might warrant sanctioned retribution by the congregation.

There were different phases of the *Mid-Winter Dance* (*nix̌ʷmí*). The phase and ritual concerned with an individual's power renewal and ability to secure game was dependent upon the individual's *suméš*. The actual curing performance was known as *nix^wmI*. The *song dance* (*snk^wnk^wnám* - "power song") that called for good weather, personal wealth, and good hunting was called *staraqám*.

Probably the earliest and quite lengthy but succinct description of the Spokan Mid-Winter Ceremony was given by Curtis, who is the only source for certain elements revealed to him by elders when fortunately he:

[...] observed in Mid-Winter, after the people had begun to live in long-houses. One lodge of four fires [*siy'aʕ'iʕaqs*] was made for the medicine chant. It was occupied like any ordinary lodge, one of the families being that of a medicine-man whose title was *niuliwiuliumíhl*. He was the one who had charge of the ceremony, and the right to do this was given him by his guardian spirit. In Mid-Winter [January], in the middle of the night, this man would be heard singing his medicine-song. To any one who came inquiring why he was singing (although everyone knew what it meant), he said, as he sat by the fire, 'We are going to have this *átstiílakamísh*.' He named the day on which it was to begin. On the appointed night those who had *su'másh* [*suméš*], and any others who desired, assembled in the long-house. In the centre stood a slender fir pole beside a small platform of hewn logs. The leader advanced, stepped upon the platform, grasped the pole with his hands, and began to sing one of his medicine-songs, at the same time dancing up and down, while the people joined in his song and half marches, half danced, in single file around the pole. When the leader felt that one song had been repeated a sufficient number of times, he started another, and so continued to do until all of his personal songs had been used. Then any other person, man or woman, who had a guardian spirit, took his place on the platform, and his songs were repeated. If there was present anyone who, though he possessed medicine, had never revealed the fact, this was his opportunity, if the spirit so directed him, to declare himself; which he did by grasping the pole, singing the songs given by the spirit and relating what it had told him. All night, and usually for four nights, this continued. Excitement ran high. Occasionally a man would have some one gash his scalp until the blood streamed, believing that unless this were done he would die. Throughout the entire night, except when he stood singing his songs, the leader sat beside the pole.

About daylight the leader opened a roll of tule matting, inside of which appeared several feathers of a kind of wood-pecker. These all at once would arise and stand on end, without visible aid, and the medicine-man would call the name of some person present and say that a certain feather represented his soul, that he was going to be very sick and die on a certain day; but that he, the medicine-man, would tie the feather on the head of the person named, and if it was allowed to remain there all the day, and if the person would eat a certain food which the medicine-man named and on the following night brought back the feather, still tied to his hair, the evil spell would be then overcome and no harm would be done. Sometimes he would point out two feathers, and say that they represented two young persons, whom he then named, and they were to be married. Or he might say that the two feathers represented a man and his wife who were separated, and pronounce that if the woman tied both in her hair, the husband would come back to her. On the following night the people returned to the lodge, and as each one whom a feather had been given entered, he, or she, went to the medicine-man, who took the feather out of the hair and imposed on the person some trifling commission, such as; " [...] get a blanket of a certain kind in the early spring and wear it until the end of summer, and you will have good lucks." To others he would tell what was going to happen to them, or what had already happened. After all was over, he would say, "Now, next winter we will see how you are then. My *su'másh* [*suméš*] will be with you all the summer." As he took each feather, he laid it back on the tule matting, which at the end of the ceremony he rolled up. Each dancer tied some offering to the pole, and at the conclusion of the ceremony the pole and the offerings were carried to the hills and placed among the branches of a tree in a place known only to the one appointed to perform this duty [...] He first ordered certain young men to make a sweat-lodge and place the stones on the fire. Then he entered the sudatory and directed a man, choosing him at random, to bring in two of the red-hot stones in his bare hands. The man, it is said, did so, and the medicine-man would call upon others each to bring two stones, until all the heated stones had been carried in. Then these men went in to sweat, as well as any others who were going to hunt, until the lodge was filled.

At night the medicine-man took his place beside the fir pole in the long-house, and two assistants sat, one at each end of the lodge. Then at sunrise the people in the camp stood in a row in front of their lodges, while the medicine-man with a besom of leafy twigs went along brushing out each lodge and passing his bunch of twigs over the body of each person [...] To the last person in the row he gave the besom, telling him to run away with it. As the man started to run, the other people pursued, and if they caught him they were at liberty to strike him with

713

sticks and whips. This was believed to drive sickness out of the camp. That same day the hunters set out the village (Curtis 1907-30, 7:86-9).

Apart from the aforementioned account of the Mid-Winter and Bluejay Ceremony by Curtis, there is a brief but significant description by Elmendorf, who explains how the Mid-Winter Ceremony—actually a world renewal ceremony—was initiated by the Spokan:

> [...] when [a] leader's *suméš* comes to him in his sleep he starts singing and the leader sings too—*suméš* tells him what to do to hold a *st'áx̌ʷa*—[he] wakes up singing—tells people to fix [the] sweathouse—if the man does not sing when his *suméš* sings he will sicken and die—a medicine man could save him—he would come & touch the crown of the patient's head & find out what is the matter—he did not sing when his g[uardian]-sp[irit] did—[who] tells him what is the matter & then the m[edicine]-man starts singing the patient's song & the patient joins in & is saved– if he doesn't sing he's going to die [... the] one who has the most [powerful] *suméš*, he's going to be the [leader] of the *st'áx̌ʷa* [...] The *st'áx̌ʷa* [will start] in the morning—with sweat-bathing as described— after breakfast nobody can eat—they are in the ["lodge" - *sy'ay'qséłx̌ʷ*] all day—all the people in the evening go home & eat & come back—(they can go in and out [of the lodge] any time) anytime they want to go out they had to sing a song first—the *cíitús* [leader] is singing a song all the time inside and they join in when they came [back] in—after dinner they go back again and at midnight [they] go home & rest until morning (1935-6, 2:37).

Throughout the Mid-Winter Ceremony, all the Bluejays resided together in a number of secluded sweathouses during the day when not performing, or in several hastily built grouped shelters that had, at best, only a roof of fir boughs supported by a simple four-pole structure. Early every morning, before daylight, the Bluejays would gather and share the same sweathouse, observing the ritual of three spiritual sweats; during each session a Bluejay sang one or more of his power songs before leaving the sweathouse and rolling naked in the snow. It was said, "Bluejays would lie about all day, but sometimes, if you were lucky, you'd see one of them running away through the trees, almost naked, and sometimes cawing like a blue jay bird".

Prior to the reservation period, these ceremonies were traditionally staged in a large double-ended tule long-house, often built just prior to the ceremony. It was recorded how some of the Spokan would journey to *Three Mountain* (*čeʔɫx̌ʷc'ut*) for the Mid-Winter Ceremony, where they would erect a series of tipis and rebuild a long-house for the ceremony (STHC). However, by the early reservation period, with the occasion of lumber buildings, traditional structures were forsaken and each Spokan group would simultaneously conduct several Mid-Winter Ceremonies in either a large ceremonial lodge, or in the largest dwelling of a village. Eventually there were only four Spokan Mid-Winter Ceremonies structures that were used simultaneously at different locations. One structure remained until the early 1960s, when it was dismantled and unfortunately destroyed for a new logging road crew. There remains only one such structure just north of Turtle Lake, used until recently as a *hay barn* (*snamisqaʔx̌estn*).

During the Mid-Winter Ceremonies, participants were not permitted to leave the lodge or dwelling except for urinating or defecating. Even when a person had to urinate—except at daybreak, they first had to ask a Bluejay leader if he could go out. One elder said how, "Sometimes, every morning—a little before dawn—we were given permission to leave; the men would go one way and the women went the other direction to meet our need."

Another major concern was thirst, "because generally we'd dance a lot; jumping up and down, all the while going in a great clockwise circle, and get real thirsty." Approximately every hour a special man was sent out with a *bucket* (*ɫčep*) to get drinking water that he had to secure in a special way: He would first break the ice by plunging the bucket into the trough, keeping his arms straight, as he sang a short song of thanksgiving. Then he would pour two bucketfuls onto the frozen ground, and bring a third back to the lodge. The water man knew that if he conducted the brief water ritual incorrectly, the Bluejays would know, being able to see through the walls or any solid obstacle. Bluejays always knew everything. After drinking the water, one of the Bluejays might rhetorically ask the gathering "where does water come from?" No one would answer, knowing that the Bluejay would say, "Not just this spring or stream, but from hundreds of miles away."

714

The previously discussed tension during the Mid-Winter Ceremony might be alleviated by a humorous prank anecdote publicly narrated by a Bluejay:

Right here, on the hill, where old John Joseph's house used to be, we would have our winter dances and ceremonies. One time a man who was *showing off* (*q'ex*ʷ*m'scút*), was sent out in the night to fetch water from the spring; one right close to the house. The man with his bucket became lost and he wandered all over. All of this the head Blue Jay could see and told us what he could see to the assembled crowd. Finally the lost man stumbled in— almost frozen to death, and had to lay down for a long time to thaw out. After that, no one remembers him showing off (Ross 1968-2008).

During the Mid-Winter Ceremony, when a person was at the power pole singing his medicine song to renew his power and intensify his relationship with his guardian spirit, the leader would also be singing while the congregation danced as they sang or gave out their individual recognition of their *sumés̆*. Then, suddenly, the leader would order all of the fires to be put out, after which the medicine man would run outdoors to search for enemies and to learn of any illnesses or acts of sorcery. Possessing prophetic powers, he could foresee coming accidents or misfortune, or an unknown person whom he 'saw' some distance away coming to the ceremony, which he pronounced (STHC). After a while—upon reentering the lodge—he would order the fires to be relit, and would proceed to repeat to the participants what had been revealed to him while he was outside. For instance, he would often identify a member of the congregation who would soon be arriving, or the details of a coming illness, death, or pending misfortune to one or more of the village.

Given the time of the year, and the very nature of the world revitalization ceremony, the Mid-Winter Ceremony was extremely stressful; people had considerable apprehension, knowing that any human was now susceptible to violating certain moral prohibitions—or the recollection—of committing acts of indiscretion, or ignoring the details of established protocol that were an integral part of the Mid-Winter Ceremony.

Certainly the most stressful aspect of this ceremony was when a participant was at the power pole to renew his *sumés̆*, a time when a person—usually a sorcerer—could *steal* (*naq'*ʷ*is*) the other person's *sumés̆* for his or her own purposes. The stealing of another's *sumés̆* could also occur during a power duel, when a shaman attempted to steal another's power as they openly fought, never with physical contact, as each man's *sumés̆* violently struggled with the other person's *sumés̆*. It was explained how, in the dim light, each man was physically thrown repeatedly to the ground by an unknown force, until one combatant turned and walked away. Some power duels were less apparent, as we find in this account of an elderly person about how the participants were not always aware that one was stealing another's power:

[...] no [audible] noises, only if you were near one person you'd feel the air was sort of solid, even smelled different, like maybe after a lightning strike, or you'd see [the] man's face kind of contorted, his eyes were different, very large and sort of white, and his clothes looked solid. You'd never look to where he was staring, you'd be too afraid you'd get sort of caught up. I only seen this once, a long time ago, so I don't know how long it [the duel] lasts, but long ago old people told my father [it happens] very quick, so few ever see it. Later, after everyone is back home, you might see someone who seems much different, or you'd have heard about someone who has his *sumés̆* taken away by someone evil (Ross 1968-2008).

A person's *sumés̆* could also be stolen, or at least an attempt could be made to do so, by people whom the individual was close to and whom he presumably trusted:

[...] a person was sleeping and dreamed of his power song, and was told that another person can steal your *sumés̆* if he wants. I knew of an old woman who had very strong power and a powerful song. N-----, her daughter and her two older daughters all tried to steal the woman's song. Within three weeks after the ceremony, the daughter died while trying to do this. The reason everyone said she died was because the old woman's song didn't want to go, and so the song eventually killed the two granddaughters as well (Ross 1968-2008).

Just prior to completion of the Mid-Winter Ceremony, an important ceremony was conducted in preparation for a large collective deer hunt. The participants would sing and dance to entice large numbers of deer to return to the immediate area so they could be hunted more easily, and as a test of a shaman's ability to influence—never control—an aspect of nature. After the pre-hunt ceremony, there was a large dinner, and

715

afterwards the hunters left to set out *special little sticks* (*čnqʷul*) in a large perimeter—but with an opening that permitted the deer to enter, which was guarded by several of the more older hunters after the hunt. A once-famous woman, Spokan Mary, was known for her curing power when treating Indians as well as whites. An elder described how:

> During the time of the Mid-Winter Ceremony, Spokan Mary and my grandmother [a Lakes woman born in 1880] were always asked to cook meals for after the Winter ceremonies. In those days, huge cauldrons were used to cook and boil foods. Since no tools could be used to stir [the] cooking, the women had to stir with their bare arms and hands. They always wore *sleeveless garments* (*sxʷatáxn'*). Spokan Mary had power to stir the cauldrons and never got burned, but only when a shaman was there to help her—I suppose you'd say her *sumés* looked over her. My grandmother also has the power to do this, and she was never burned (Ross 1968-2008).

When perched precariously in the rafters of the ceremonial structure, Bluejays acted as sentinels, but also "observed intently the actions of those below to detect any breach of the formal rules of conduct" (Ray 1937:595) while in the *dancehouse* or *lodge* (*sntrqmín* or *snwenštn*).

Bluejay Ceremony

The Bluejay Ceremony was restricted to certain Salish-speaking groups: namely the Coeur d'Alene, Colville, Flathead, Kalispel, Spokan (Stewart 1946, 2:329), Southern Kutenai, Sanpoil and Nespelem, and Sinkaietk. Ray discussed the distribution and diffusion of the Bluejay complex in the Plateau, and claimed that it was not found among the Kutenai (1939:116), and suggested that the search for lost items involving owl power was used only by the Sanpoil and Kutenai (1939:118). However, several Spokan elders said the Spokan also had and used owl power. The Spokan were more similar to the Kalispel in the Bluejay ritual (Elmendorf 1935-6, 2:35, 2:37-38; Ray 1937:597, 1939:112; Smith 1936-8; and Himmleberg, n.d.). The Kalispel were presumably the last people to celebrate this annual ceremony, and who were noted for their dancing and physical endurance (STHC).

The *Bluejay Dance* (*sqʷasqʷiʔ* or *stλ'qm*) was an integral ceremony, always held in conjunction with the Mid-Winter Ceremony and Winter Dance. This annual ritual was concerned primarily with world renewal, propitiation to renew food resources, rituals of purification and curing, and bringing a warm Chinook wind in mid-winter (Turney-High 1933; Elmendorf 1935-6; Ray 1933, 1937, 1939, 1945; Smith 1936-8; Turney-High, 1933, 1937; Cline 1938, and Ross 1982).

Social relief to sedentary winter living, and reduced food supplies was provided by the Mid-Winter and Bluejay Ceremonies, which were actually psychodramas and reiterations of religious and supernatural forces, effectively dramatized by dancing, curing, and various prophetic performances, throughout late December and early January. Winter was a time of leisure and sometimes intense participation by all adults, who provided explanations and pronouncements of certain aspects of esoteric and sacred rituals to their grandchildren. These ceremonies also dramatically demonstrated their beliefs, needs, and the benefits of good character and generosity. Also, in conjunction with the Mid-Winter Ceremony, the group always wished to *bring a change in weather* (*xeʔnuxʷ*), and Bluejays—believed to be capable of blowing the cold weather away—would hold a *Chinook Dance* (*xwʔ nuxʷm*), presaging the arrival of warmer weather (STHC).

At the time of the Mid-Winter Ceremonies, those men with Bluejay power underwent a transformation which stripped them of certain human physical characteristics and behavior. Substituted were all of the traits of their tutelary spirit Bluejay, a mythological being who took possession of them throughout the entire ceremony. Since the usual guise and behavior of the mythological character was similar to that of the blue jay bird, it was believed that certain men—acting as blue jay birds—believed they could be physically and spiritually transformed into Bluejays by replicating the behavior, sounds, and the appearance of blue jays.

Bluejays renewed their unique *sumés* just prior to the Mid-Winter Ceremony when they blackened their faces, arms, and legs below their knees with charcoal. It was claimed they also rubbed charcoal into their hair, but never wore any blue jay feathers. All clothing was discarded, except for a breech cloth of willow bark from which they hung twigs of fir, which they wore throughout the ceremony. The only known painting of a Bluejay is one done by Paul Kane (1859:12) when he identified the subject as an "*El-ko-ka-shin*," a Salish designation for a shaman (Ray 1937:597). During this time, they were unable to speak Spokan, but could enunciate only in a glossolalia (a so-called spirit language); or, more often, they imitated the various calls of blue jays as they leapt with apparent ease to the ridge pole of the ceremonial winter lodge. Each group had a special ceremonial lodge for the Bluejay Ceremony, called a (*sntrqmín* or *snwenšt*).

The figure below is from a painting by Paul Kane (1859:12) titled "Chinewos & Ill-cauck-a-shin." The latter is apparently the name of this Spokan Bluejay dancer, identified elsewhere as "El-ko-ka-shin."

Figure 39. Bluejay dancer

Before entering the Mid-Winter lodge, everyone took lampblack or charcoal and made one or more spots approximately the size of a quarter on each cheek to show their respect prior to the entry of the Bluejays. On the first night of the ceremony, the head Bluejay—standing in the middle of the floor—would commence the ceremonies by tapping his dewclaw staff as he directed all the non-Bluejay participants to form a great circle as they entered in a clockwise direction. Women were never Bluejays.

More specifically, Ray (1945, 78:), citing the Spokan as perhaps best representing the Bluejay character, noted:

At the time of the winter dances all persons with Bluejay "power" undergo a transformation which strips them completely of human characteristics; substituted are all traits of the mythological being. Since the usual guise of the mythological character was similar to the human being today, complete identification is possible.

During the night's ceremony, some Bluejays would 'speak' the language of their familial, not always the call of a bluejay. For example, when communicating with humans, a Bluejay's guardian spirit would say that a *beaver can speak very slowly through his nose (sqléw')*, and that he wanted his human protégé to learn how to speak in such a manner. A definitive sound of a Bluejay was when he 'whistled' as the bluejays do when excited or agitated. Ray contends that the Colville, Spokane, and Flathead all used a negated speech, even speech inversion when a Bluejay always said the opposite of what was meant (Ray 1945:79). "The Flathead use it least although they are nearest the Plains where the practice is common" (Ray 1945:82). Bluejays could also speak backwards, lapsing into trances, perform excruciatingly painful demonstrations of power-possession; going sometimes naked out-of-doors during the Mid-Winter Ceremony and demonstrating other public manifestations of peculiar, unusual behavior that characterized Bluejays. Some have said how Bluejays were so possessed that they appeared "out of their minds," or *crazy (qʷaʕʷ* or *qʷúʔqʷawʼwuʔ* or *qʷoqʷáw* - "they are crazy"), and often required the smudging of a Bluejay with sweet grass smoke as well as being coaxed back to reality by the caller. It was also necessary to smoke a Bluejay's medicine bundle, thought to be largely responsible for his unorthodox behavior.

In addition to their various ways of speaking, Bluejays were further distinguished by their unusual appearance, behavior, and diet, to further dramatize the power transformation that they had undergone. The following peculiarities may be noted:

> Home contacts are completely severed; normal human associations adjured; and no food is eaten except pitch. The Bluejay's hair and ears are always full of pitch; likewise the spaces between his fingers and toes. At the dances he may be seen from time to time removing bits of this pitch and eating it. Usually he perches among the rafters at the dance lodge. He may dance with the others upon occasion but with unnatural and irregular steps. He is easily frightened; his defense is to clamber into the framework of the roof and hide. The dancers attract him to the floor again by making miniatures of various objects such as bows and arrows. These have an irresistible attraction for him; the dancers offer these objects as compensation for the services of the Bluejay in the recovery of lost objects. His clairvoyant powers toward this end are very great; it is especially easy for him to find objects which lie buried under the snow. Upon undertaking such a task he sights through a ring made of a twig. Then he leaves the dance house but returns after a moment's absence. The brief period suffices for even the most lengthy journey he is reputed to undertake. Upon his entry the recovered object is seen fastened to a small staff which he always carries (Ray 1945:78).

A frequent demonstration of a Bluejay's spiritual and physical transformation, during the ceremony, was his ability to leap considerable heights to a horizontal beam where he would squat, sometimes on one leg for long periods of time as he 'spoke' like a bluejay. During the Mid-winter Dance, a person "will come to the dance imitating those animals, as the bellowing of the buffalo, or the howling of the wolf" (Alvord 1857:16).

The following is an account of this ability, when four men attempted to *restrain (héc lic')* a fellow Bluejay just prior to his leaping to the beam. It also briefly described the method for restoring his humanoid behavior:

> [...] it must have been about 8 feet, 9 feet high [...] He'd just jump over their heads up to the highest [beam-like] pole [in a long-house], they couldn't reach him [...] They said, there were about four husky men who grabbed him, they brought him down, but still they couldn't hold him down [still ...] But they went after "that man" and "smoke[d] him." They "doctored" him and brought him back to normal (STHC).

Every Ceremony had one individual Bluejay designated as a leader, one who possessed the most power. Many years ago an elderly Chewelah-Spokan man paraphrased his father's description of a Bluejay Ceremony leader who was obviously quite:

> [...] different from all the other Bluejays. Even you'd be able to spot him 'cause he'd always stay on the ground and never leap about on the ridge pole in the rafters. I'll never forget this one Bluejay, I can't remember his name, but as I said, he'd stay on the ground and hop about, rolling his head all the time as he cawed at the

other Bluejays in the rafters. Physically, or by age, I can't recall if he was different from the others, except in his acting [behavior] he was totally different. Another thing, the special Bluejay was not from here, but out of the area. Prior to this ceremony, in a special lodge, they ran [*naked*] (*čłtmelx*ʷ), except for a brief loincloth of willow bark, and never wore footwear in the snow when looking for lost items (Ross 1968-2008).

During this intense period, and after the first communal *breakfast* (*sk*ʷ*ék*ʷ*st*), Bluejays maintained a strict fast throughout the entire ceremony, some even longer. During their fast, they drank only water, and some ate only pitch. If a small child later became hungry and cried, and was given a piece of food, anyone with *q*ʷ*ásq*ʷ*i?* power could see the transgression and would quickly run to the offender and snatch the food from the child's fingertips, taking it to the Bluejay leader. The leader would again warn everyone to refrain from eating; otherwise, the food would become stuck in the person's throat. Each morning, just before dawn, all of the Bluejays conducted a ritual sweat, one that always preceded each day's Mid-Winter Ceremony, and was led by the Bluejay with the strongest power. However, the first night prior to this special sweat was an important and dramatic ceremony, recorded only in Elmendorf's Spokan and Lakes field notes, which provided complete description, a part of which is related here:

[...] when they are going to hold a *st'áx*ʷ*a?*—they take a sweat bath before—[after the] heated rocks [...] On fire [are] red hot—four/5 people go in the sweathouse at a time—one man the leader asks for a red hot rock—picks out a person & tells him to bring 4 or 5 red hot rocks from the fire—he brings them & gives them to the leader who takes them in his hand and puts them in a depression in the center of the sweathouse—each of the other men in the sweathouse asks different people to do the same—*ci?itús* goes outside & tells anyone who wants to heat rocks & bring them in—about 3, 4, or 5 of them do so—any one can do this after the *ci?itús* tells them they can—he takes the rocks from them & puts them in the sweathouse—they close the sweathouse & the leader asks who of the five wants to make the steam—one volunteers to do this & he starts singing his *suméš* song—[he] takes & pours a basket of water on the rocks while singing—then all sing their g[uardian] sp[irit] songs at the same time—[it becomes] hot in there like fire—[when they] started cooling off after a while—someone outside who hears the men inside singing—& then his *suméš* comes to him (not necessarily [for the] first time) and he falls down in a faint & someone picks him up & after a little [while] he comes to & sings his g[uardian] sp[irit] song—and then he feels all right—the 5 in the sweathouse come out & pick him up & they rub a bone that sticks out of the front leg of a deer near the hoof—[they] wrap it up in buckskin and then it is called *tsósl*—the *ci?itús* shakes this over the head of the man *átstcítsnm t sumécs*—"his *suméš* has come to him" with a noise like *tsstsstss*—when they go back into the sweathouse they are still singing & then the *ci?itús* has a cane *ck'*ʷ*étcst* with the *tsósl* in the end & he shakes it *tqóqtes* etc.—when he touches the ground with the bottom of the cane is when he shakes it—then they stop singing—after they stop singing the leader tells them to get ready for breakfast—it is early in the morning when they went into the sweathouse—nobody in the village can't eat until [the] leader told them—then he tells everybody they can eat—after the breakfast then nobody can eat all day—if anyone had been going to eat the food would stick in their throat & the bluejay man would know it and run over to where the person was & as he went into their house he'd say *ká..?* & then he'd take the food right out through their throat & look at it and kind of laugh at it & then he'd take it to the *ci?itús* [... At the] beginning of the last night the leader tell[s] everybody they are going to eat now—four fires in a big long-house [are] built for the occasion, called *siáiqs*—& 4 holes big enough to hold [a] cooking basket—[the] rocks [were] heated on the fires—[they] let the fires die down and it's [now] dark except for the red hot rocks [He] tells 2 people to [take] each basket to put red hot rocks in them—they do this with their bare hands—[and] kept putting rocks in and stirring the soup around with their [bare] hands until it was boiling—after each one was cooked the 2 [men] on that place would remove the rocks with their bare hands & then all the 4 baskets were done they lit up the fires & the meal was ready [... Later] while it was dark in the *syáyqs* the people all went to growling & hollering like different animals according to their different *suméš*—their *suméš* would also let them know in a kind of dream where they would find game in a certain place or get wealth, etc.—when they see these things in a dream in the dark in the *syáyqs* they seize the vision and hold it in their hands and kind of wrap it up in a piece of fur or little animal in his skin in his hands then [he] came to—[he] rubbed the fur & kept the fur around his person—then he'd get the vision—[he] can only get this when they were *tt'áx*ʷ*aing*—the fur is good for the rest of his life & it's always good (Elmendorf 1935-6, 2:33-6).

There were different ways for a person to acquire *Bluejay power* (*hepɫ q*ʷ*asq*ʷ*i?* - "he has the Bluejay power"). It was said that a person knew when he had received such power. Most men received their Bluejay *suméš* while participating in the Mid-Winter Ceremony, hence the person—while standing and gripping the power pole, fainted, and when upon being revived made the repetitive call of a bluejay, "*ká..?.*" A young man might receive his Bluejay *suméš* in the Bluejay sweathouse, and upon emerging, his face would be covered with charcoal, and he "then acts as the 'eyes' of the *ci?tús*—finds who is eating against orders [...] Generally about 5 [years of age] would [he] have this power & get it at a *st'áx*ʷ*a* and act as policemen" (Elmendorf 1935-6, 2:38).

Some elders have said that a young boy learned to make the call of the Bluejay when he received the *suméš*, which could also render him unconscious; and upon being revived, he would find next to himself the required staff affixed with the deer dew claw rattles. For the next four or five nights and days, the novice would experience an intensity of power for curing and exercising his prophetic abilities, but after being smudged and revived at the end of the ceremony, those powers left him, to be renewed at the next Mid-Winter Ceremony (Ross 1982). Later, as a grown man he might become a Bluejay medicine man (*q*ʷ*ássq*ʷ*i?em*). As such he was accepted by other Bluejays as having extraordinary supernatural power that lasted approximately five days and four nights or the length of the ceremony.

These abilities were even more dramatically demonstrated when the Bluejay was placed under a blanket, or, as in the past, behind a tule mat that was hung from a rafter by hemp rope, and always in a lodge or room that was dimly lit by only a low open ember fire. Later, a *kerosene lantern* (*sčšréčst*) was used, but never electrical light, as this form of non-traditional power would negate the spiritual power of any man, even kill him. While behind a barrier, the performer often had his big toes tied together and his hands secured to his sides with rawhide, and some had their hands tied together behind their back.

After the Bluejay was tied, he was pushed behind the suspended blanket or tule mat. Immediately after his disappearance, he would toss the rawhide ties [from his hands] over the blanket, and then place [display] his tied toes over the blanket [possibly standing on his hands]. What awed everyone even after the ties were thrown over the screen, his toes were still tied in place. After being released and [his hands] retied, the Bluejay repeated this ritual three times, and after the performance, he would race off into the mountains, returning the same night (Ross 1968-2008).

A similar account of the Bluejay's power and ability to see things through solid barriers was given by an old woman, who was probably fourteen (circa 1880) when she attended her first Bluejay Ceremony:

Years ago I was at my first Bluejay Ceremony [...] we all entered the room before the Bluejays. Finally, they came in just before I'd put several white camas bulbs away I had been gnawing on. I carefully hid them in my cornhusk bag. When Bluejay came in he immediately came to me, staring very hard, and since Bluejays can't speak like humans, he violently banged his staff on the floor. Then he stormed out, leaving me very embarrassed because everyone was staring at me, even my poor family. A friend explained that Bluejay could see through anything, and he saw your camas. I can't remember leaving the lodge, but I did, and I tossed the camas bulbs away before returning. [The] Bluejay later came back in, smiling as though nothing bad had happened. After that, I never forgot how to behave right (Ross 1968-2008).

All Bluejays knew if there was any alcohol on the premises—realizing that the ingestion of any amount of alcohol would cause a person to lose his *suméš*, and everyone claimed that their *suméš* would never return if they drank alcohol. Despite their power and apparent success in locating lost items or people, they were not always successful; or, on occasion, a Bluejay would say he had not found a lost item, but speaking in reverse, he had located the object (Ray 1937:597). In later years, some Bluejays said this was due to the interference of electricity, or the presence of participants even casually subscribing to Christian beliefs and practices. The following account described such an incident:

The Bluejays would always look for people who were lost in the woods or even drown[ed]. B. B. was a[n] Indian gambler who had good *suméš*, but one time he told [the] tribal police about an Indian still near Gifford— long ago, just before WW I. The Indian moonshiners tied a car engine to B. B.'s neck and threw him alive into the

Columbia [River]. At the time there were huge braided cables strung across the Columbia, right where a bridge was being built. Well, after a few days word got out that maybe B. B. was murdered and his body tossed in the river. So the chief asked several Bluejays if they'd find the body, which they couldn't because they said too [much] mud was covering the body (Ross 1968-2008).

An elderly lady from *Inchelium* (*nceʔliy'm* or *snceʔliʔ*), who married a Chewelah-Spokan man, and later resided on the Spokane Indian Reservation with her enrolled husband, gave an interesting account similar to the one above:

> In the 1920s, a white man killed an Indian man in a *welukʷs* gambling game because the Indian had better gambling power and was not losing at all. The white man suddenly reached across the gambling blanket and hit the poor Indian, killing him. So several whites took the Indian to around the Daisey Ferry, and tied an old Model A engine block to him and then threw him into the river. Well later, two *qʷasqʷiʔ* searched all around the river, but nowhere was he to be found. They even walked on the narrow sloping ferry cables to get a better view, but no luck. Another Indian who always pretended to possess Bluejay power, came and said he could "see" where the body was. All they pulled up was a[n] old store manikin. Later, when these men were working on Grand Coulee Dam, two women with power killed the imposter (Ross 1968-2008).

There were, incidentally, stories of how during this bridge construction over the Columbia River (*nkʷtnetkʷ* or *ntxʷetkʷ* - "big river"), there was a favorite activity for Bluejays during the winter to demonstrate their abilities to one another by balancing precariously on cables without fear, "These cables were [a] game to the *qʷasqʷiʔ* as they'd scamper back and forth on the sagging cables, even when high winds would make the cables swing back and forth, but they were never known to fall." Another dramatic demonstration of Bluejay's power was his ability to travel great distances overland to collect a known object, and upon returning provided public proof of his power by displaying the retrieved object. Presumably they could easily travel as far away as the area of Missoula, Montana, in one night.

When a Bluejay was inside the ceremonial lodge, he could sing a man's power song of someone who was outside, and that man would know this and would come as if summoned. This was said to be possible because of one's *suméš*, not intuitive fears that *danger may befall them* (*ʔec móyxeʔey'*) if he did not comply.

Given the diversity among those groups practicing the Bluejay Ceremony, there were considerable differences regarding what illnesses a Bluejay could treat. Unfortunately, there is no recorded evidence or oral history that substantiates the claim that Bluejays were able to cure people except during the Mid-Winter. Perhaps the general and often misused term medicine man has caused some to assume that such an individual had a *suméš* for curing, and all medicine men were curing shamans, which was not true. Only during the Mid-Winter Dances did Bluejays have the power to cure (Ray 1945:82), and then more often when working with a curing shaman. As one Spokan elder explained:

> The Bluejay can't really cure all sickness, but would work closely with a medicine man, sometimes two or three of them [curing shamans] together when someone was really very sick. Then Bluejays will sometimes talk to a [curing] shaman who may or may not decide to offer help to the unsuspecting man. I think Bluejays can help cure other Bluejays, but only when they've got their power during the ceremony. The most important thing about Bluejays is that they've [prophetic] power, but they could cure some folks, those who'd swallowed anything that'd choke (*ntxʷumt*) them (Ross 1968-2008).

Elmendorf's Spokan field notes cite an incident that occurred (circa 1885) with a Bluejay who successfully extracted a needle that had been lodged in a young boy's throat while sucking:

> [...] there was a man at *stsq* - *a ƛ'eʔkʷíls* - whose *suméš* was bluejay [and] there was a boy [his son] who swallowed a needle & it stuck in his throat & they couldn't get it out. His mother told this med[icine] man about it—he got all excited about it, for the boy was just about dying—the father knew where the needle was already—he came up and said *káʔ* & then he bent down and inhaled through his mouth over the boy's neck and when he straightened up the needle was in his mouth & and the boy was saved—the skin was not broken (1935-6, 2:38).

Nearly all accounts of a Bluejay's power to cure deal primarily with the removal of foreign objects from a patient's body. Ray, when working with the Sanpoil and Nespelem, made a similar observation regarding the Bluejay's ability to extract a foreign object from a person's body, or food from a patient's stomach, by

721

manually extracting it via the patient's throat (1937:597). He first noted how the role of the curing shaman was assumed by the Bluejay, and later how the Bluejay may also be employed in a pseudo-shamanistic capacity. He is capable of removing from the stomach any foreign matter unintentionally swallowed (Ray 1945:79). This ability is an analogue of the (bird) bluejay's grasping power. Ray (1937, 1945) does not present any conclusions regarding the curing roles of the Bluejay. However, he does posit that these people were not true shamans capable of curing general illness, but only those maladies contracted by participants during the actual Bluejay Ceremony, which were probably caused by sorcerers using projective magic to manipulate or force something to a site for removal by sucking and passing of hands. There is no indication that Spokan Bluejays acted as sorcerers, as Turney-High claims the Flathead did, and usually for a fee:

> A person may upon occasion persuade a Bluejay shaman to set an illness upon an enemy by "throwing a bluejay feather into him." The shaman demands a fee because he fears his own *sumés*. If the feather is thrown into the vitals of a man, that person will surely die unless it is removed by another Bluejay shaman. In this case the shaman who cast the spell will surely die unless he can persuade the Bluejay to accept his client as a victim (1937:41).

Typically, a non-Bluejay curing shaman was presumably restricted to curing by sucking only on the patient's left side, regardless of where the object-intrusion or spirit-entry was located, except when removing an object from a person's throat. However, a Bluejay possessing any of the aforementioned tutelary spirits could work on either side of a patient, but only during the Mid-Winter Ceremonies. Before removing an intrusion, the Bluejay medicine man would slowly wash his hands in the presence of the patient and others, and, after sufficient acupressure and massage, would remove the debilitating object or malevolent spirit with his hands, sit upright, and then blow the neutralized malevolent force away.

During the Bluejay Ceremony, one or many near-naked Bluejays would run, cawing, from the ceremonial structure to the mountains. Later, upon returning, several more dramatic rituals were performed by three Bluejays who also possessed other tutelary spirits:

> One had fish power, another had rabbit power, and the third possessed lynx power. These Bluejays assumed their respective tutelary's forms before entering the darkened structure, and the first drama involved the rabbit and lynx, each appearing with a stone knife, fighting one another, sending blood in all directions and eventually reaching the door, only to continue their duel out in the snow. Lynx was always the victor, as he was considered an evasive and sly animal. People were never allowed outside during this combat; but the next day, they could see great amounts of blood upon the snow. After this, Fish would come in and go behind a screen. A delegated Bluejay then filled his stone elbow pipe with tobacco—a mixture of kinnikinnick and wild licorice root, light his pipe, take three puffs, and then slide the pipe under the screen. Fish would take one strong breath that burned all the tobacco in the bowl. This was done three times, and when his pipe was being refilled by another Bluejay, Fish told anyone where something that was missing could be found, be it lost or stolen. Fish then told anyone what they wanted to know, and after the third pipe bowl, he would recite the fighting episode of lynx and rabbit (STHC).

At the termination of the Bluejay Ceremony, there was an important ritual, namely, the smoking or smudging ceremony, using "sweet grass or throwing wetted ginseng root upon the body" (Ray 1945:79), which was done to transform the temporary speech and behavior of the Bluejays to human identity and function. Each Bluejay was first covered with black tree moss by using tamarack pitch over his entire body, with small balled sections of moss behind his ears and in his nostrils. Then, after the ceremony, all the moss and pitch was removed and carefully placed on a flat rock near the edge of an open fire so that the material could be burned—to prevent a sorcerer from getting even a small piece of unburned moss. All of the Bluejays would stand together and inhale the fumes, known to clear their vision and to complete their transformation to humans. It was important for all of this material to be carefully collected and burned:

> [...] if for some reason all the pitch and moss wasn't removed, the Bluejay would leave the ceremony and become crazy and run away, not knowing what he was doing. Once, when I was very young, I saw this happen when before the other Bluejays could remove all this stuff, the man ran out into the woods and spent the rest of the winter and most of the spring living with a bunch of wild horses. Once in a while someone would see him

riding bareback on one of the horses. The Bluejay was all skin and bones. When the older women were digging white camas, they saw him again, and finally the older people were able to catch him and remove all the tufts of moss and pitch (Ross 1968-2008).

There were actually several methods of reviving Bluejays from their transformed state; most commonly with the roots of rosy pussy-toes (*Antennaria rosea* ssp. *rosea* Greene - *sp'ic'pic'ulex*), which were pounded into powder and mixed with powdered *x̱ásax̱*, and then sprinkled on "hot coals at a winter dance. The smoke was used to drive away malevolent spirits in the dance house, and to 'revive' new dancers who had passed out or 'gone bluejay'" (Turner *et al.* 1980:75). Ray, in his cross-cultural study of the Bluejay Ceremony, provided an account of how the Bluejay dance ended and the dancer revived:

> During the erratic dancing to their regular singing of the Bluejays, a predetermined dancer grasps the "destitute" character around the waist, a struggle ensues, and finally the Bluejay "dies." He is held head downward, feet in the air, by his captor, while the dancers gather round. A smudge is prepared of sweet grass, sometimes mixed with a particular root [*x̱áxas*], and the character is held over it. This brings him to life in normal condition. The black paint is washed off and he once more takes his place among the dancers. He becomes the center of attention as he tells of his "wandering" while a Bluejay. Some of the characters are allowed to remain untransformed until the following evening. The dance is concluded on the fourth night (1939:122).

A problem that could occur was when a Bluejay attempted to assume human form, for occasionally the man lacked any ability to make the transition (Turney-High 1933:103-105), and would fight against the efforts of other Bluejays to assist him in this change:

> At the end of the dance period the Bluejays must be captured and returned to the human state, else they would remain in that character permanently. They resist capture until physically overcome by the dancers, who sometimes pursue them for great distances. Then the pitch is carefully removed from their bodies, the paint likewise. Retransformation is accomplished by smudging with sweet grass or throwing wet gingseng root upon the body (Ray 1945:78-79).

Here is an account of such a transition related to the author, one which occurred within the Chewelah-Spokan Group, as was explained by a 97-year-old man, whose mother's father's father had been a *Bluejay man* (*q"ássq"i?em'*):

> According to my great, grandmother, to revive the Bluejay, they had to be brought back to consciousness, which they'd do by giving *x̱ásx̱a* that was ground or pounded into small pieces and carefully placed in a tanned buckskin pouch, one that was closed with a tie. After a Bluejay had performed his dance and song it was always necessary to revive the Bluejay participant, 'cause a dancer can't do this by himself. Another Bluejay will take the pouch of *x̱ásx̱a* and pass it under the dancer's nose until he is OK. If this isn't done, the Bluejay will continue to dance and sing, and he'll never be able to stop, nor would he ever be normal again. That is to say, he'd always remain as a Bluejay. The Bluejay dances generally went on for at least one week, and during this time there were only certain times when a non-Bluejay could eat, and then only when the Bluejay said so. Even small children couldn't eat when they wanted, only when told by a Bluejay. Of course if someone tried to sneak a bit of food, the Bluejay would always be able to 'see' what was happening, even if the person was outside and away from the longhouse. My great, grandmother told me when she was a teenager—before her marriage—she was attending a Bluejay ceremony and she had forgotten she had some biscuit in her cornhusk bag. Well, the Bluejay could "see" this bit of food and sent her from the longhouse, much to her family's humiliation. And as you know, the Bluejays were known for their [prophetic] visions, and being able to find lost things. This was true for needles, things considered very valuable, certainly when steel needles were introduced. They could locate lost things any time of the year, not just during [the] ceremony. Bluejays were restricted in their ability to cure, or so I was told. I did hear stories of how they could remove needles from people's throats, also fish bones, most often *squaw fish* [*q'"e?č*] bones. Once, when I was young, I saw a Bluejay remove a steel needle from a child's throat, only he actually sucked it from where her Adam's apple is. There was no hole and no blood. At all the Bluejay ceremonies there was a special type of Bluejay [*ci?itús*] who was very different from all the others. This one Bluejay would always remain on the ground and never leap about on the ridge pole or rafters. This one Bluejay, I can't remember what he was called, but he would stay, as I said, on the ground and hop about, rolling his head all the while [he was] cawing at the other Bluejays in the rafters. Physically, or by age, I can't remember if he [was]

723

in any way different. Another thing I know, this special Bluejay was not a local, rather someone from out of the area—maybe [from] Canada because their government didn't stop some of the old ceremonies, like the Sun Dance. Also, the different Bluejay would smoke a tobacco [made] from "wild manure"—from a deer or coyote. This smoke he'd blow up towards the rafter dancers to give them strength to squat on only one leg for hours at a time; I've seen this (Ross 1968-2008).

Sometimes a Bluejay would be absent from the dance for several days at a time, and seen sleeping on the branches of a tree. Even though he might fall from his precarious perch to the frozen ground, he would never be injured, but simply 'fly' back to the limbs of a nearby tree; jumping from one tree to another with ease, and would finally settle down once more.

Fortunately, during the 1930s, Ray, Elmendorf, and Smith had the opportunity to interview several Bluejays and the sons and grandsons of former Bluejays, noting there was not always agreement on the form of ritual, particularly on the distinctions between a curing shaman and a curing Bluejay; a point that Ray (1937) makes with Turney-High's Flathead work (1937). Ray also did an earlier comparative study of the Sanpoil and Lower Spokan, which incidentally demonstrates how many cultural similarities existed between these two contiguous groups:

> Among the [Lower] Spokane, adjoining the Sanpoil on the east, a new element appears in the participation of the Bluejay character in the dance as a pseudo-shaman. Treatment was limited, however, to cases where the peculiar attributes of the bluejay indicated aptitude. Thus, just as among the Sanpoil the sentry retrieved food from a person's throat, among the Spokan he withdrew from a patient's stomach foreign matter which inadvertently had been swallowed (1937:597).

In the early 1900s, with the decline of this ceremony, some Spokan said how the most powerful Bluejays were Sinkaietk men, "who came down from Canada" (STHC). A few Spokan elders could recall how during the early 1900s, because of deculturation, the general effects of missionization, and off-reservation labor demands, there occurred a gradual but perceptive demise of Bluejay ceremonies. This was undoubtedly true for even the few who had Bluejay power, which nearly always was inherited through the so-called patrilineage. A noted exception was among the Chewelah-Spokan Group, when two women were thought to have Bluejay power, even though they never danced during the Bluejay Ceremonies, nor could they cure sickness; but were said to occasionally assist curing shamans who had female patients. One elderly Chewelah-Spokan Group man said the only female Bluejays were all from his area, but never gave any reason. Yet one person recalled—with no detail—a woman who had been a Bluejay, one she thought was a berdache (man-woman?).

Another elderly Spokan lady maintained that long after the loss of Bluejay power from the Spokan tribe (late 1920s)—and before she was crippled as an adult—she had Bluejay power, but never participated in any ceremonies. Her explanation for having such unique power was that the Spokan men were losing the power of becoming Bluejays. It seems reasonable to assume that the intractable and persistent encroachment of non-Indian beliefs and ways simply caused the men to be less convinced, and committed to traditional beliefs regarding physical transformation. Presumably, this may have resulted in women being forced to assume active roles in certain areas of religion and medicine.

Bluejay's flower (qʷásqʷiʔs scʼʔékʼʷ) was larkspur (šcʼʔekʼʷ or ntaqeneʔ), which was placed by a Bluejay upon the new grave of any Stellar bluejay (qʷásqwiʔ). Out of respect—even fear—bluejay meat was never eaten, and was reputed to have a bitter and unpleasant taste, termed hi táx̣ɫcʼeʔ (STHC). It is known that only a shaman with Bluejay suméš could properly bury a dead bluejay bird.

Proto-historical and Historical Syncretic and Prophetic Movements and Religions

Numerous syncretic or proto-historical revivalist religions, such as the Prophetic Dance (Dreamers and Dream Dance and Northwest Prophet Cult), Feather Cult, Seven Drum Religion, and more recently, the Indian and Bible Shaker Church (both continue to be different versions of the Native American Church) appeared, created prior to Euro-American contact when these prophetic movements occurred with the often devastating pandemics and several natural cataclysmic events. John Slocum, creator of the Shaker movement, "opposed the old Indian religion and especially the medicine men" (Eliade 1951:321), wanting to regenerate past cultural ways and values. Walker and Schuster identify other reasons for the development and spread of prophetic movements and the belief of world renewal:

> [...] the diversity of cults and prophetic figures apparent in the Plateau at the time of contact, the archaeological evidence from altered burial practices, increasing non-Indian trade goods in the region, the extinction or catastrophic reduction of various groups through epidemic disease, and oral tradition among contemporary Plateau religious leaders (1998:499).

However, the accumulative devastating effects of missionization and deculturation could not be altered by revitalization movements (Ray 1936:69, 73-75). These pan-Indian movements attempted to restore past cultural ways and beliefs, and as Cebula noted:

> [...] the Plateau world [had] changed, the ground shifted under some of the old beliefs and they became unstable. The waves of epidemic disease were especially corrosive to religion whose leaders were supposed to excel at healing. The Prophet Dance of the late proto-historical era was a last attempt to revive traditional beliefs in their pristine form. When smallpox returned to the plateau in 1800, it became clear that a simple revival of faith would not meet the new challenges. Indians began to look beyond their own belief system for the religious answers they needed [...] The Prophet Dance, the Columbian Religion, and Christianity all failed to improve the lives of the Plateau Indians. None was integrated with the plateau environment as their traditional faith had been. The new faiths fell short of the aboriginal standard, set in the precontact era (2003:132-33).

More specifically, Walker and Schuster contended that, "The Prophet Dance has been linked with proto-historical events in the Plateau such as epidemic disease, trade, the impact of the horse, the introduction of Christianity and other nonindigenous beliefs and practices, and the presence of various prophets seen by early explorers (1998:499):

> By employing more recent ethnographic, ethnohistorical, and archaeological research, it is possible to show (1) that population decimation most probably brought about cult activity on the Coast as well as in the Plateau, and (2) that the Nez Perces (and probably the rest of the Plateau groups) and the Northwest Coast groups were sharply affected by White influence before 1800 (Walker 1969:247).

In 1850, Father Joset wrote in his diary of the increased numbers of French-Canadians, Iroquois, and other former employees of the HBC who came and settled around the mission and Kettle Falls. He also described how he and other Jesuits attended to the needs of the sick and dying Indians during the 1853-54 smallpox epidemic, and, thus, were able to "garner a great harvest of souls" (Bischoff 1945:154), and the missionary presence probably stimulated renewed widespread interest in the Dreamer Religion and the Prophet dance (Spier 1935) within many Plateau groups. "Man dreamed he saw strange people and heard strange new songs. Everyone, young and old, gathered to hear him and then danced for joy every day every night. He predicted the arrival of whites and their marvelous possessions (Spier 1935:16-17).

Hunn explains how increasing Euro-American immigrants, particularly in the Willamette Valley, brought with them to the Plateau the various contagious diseases, noting how, "These epidemics were not simply biological disasters, but social and spiritual catastrophes as well. Prophets called their people home in a desperate effort to salvage their way of life and to resurrect their dead" (1990:375).

Though there is question as to when the Spokan knew of white people, most anthropologists—as mentioned earlier—believe Woodland Indians, most notably the Iroquois and northeastern trappers, had limited contact with eastern Plateau groups. However, a singular prophecy was made circa 1790 by a medicine man, Cornelius (Bighead), who proclaimed the eventual appearance of non-Indians. It should be noted that the Spokan were, by this time, familiar with Iroquois who had ventured west with trapper-trader groups.

However, the first estimated dates of eruptions and tephra ash fall affecting the interior were circa 1789 to 1799; however, a major and wide-spread cataclysmic event occurred in 1842, when approximately 14 to 20

725

cm of Mount St. Helen's ash fell upon the Lower Spokan (Majors 1980:18-19); a prediction given fifty years earlier. Between 1831 and 1847 there were a series of sporadic eruptions. Paul Kane painted the 1847 eruption, but the one accounted for in oral history was a major eruption between 1790 and 1800. Not long after this catastrophic event, Wilkes referred to the popular belief that "some forty or fifty years ago there was a great fall of ashes [...] They feared the world would fall to pieces & their hearts were very small. The quantity which fell was about six inches" (1845, 4:439; Drury 1940:130). Holmes (1955, 3:201-202) later recorded an early account by Pickering who provided the most complete statement of a Spokan prophecy regarding the coming of a different people when he interviewed Cornelius or Big Head (pronounced by non-Spokan speakers as "silimxnotylmilakabok"), a chief within the Spokan tribe, who actually was a Flathead, some 60 years after the eruption:

He gives an account of a singular prophecy that was made by one of their medicine-men, some fifty years ago [circa 1790], before they knew any thing of white people, or had heard of them. Cornelius, when about ten years of age, was sleeping in a lodge with a great many people, and was suddenly awakened by his mother, who called out to him that the world was falling to pieces. He then heard a great noise of thunder overhead, and all the people crying out in great terror. Something was falling very thick, which at first they took for snow, but on going out they found it to be dirt: it proved to be ashes, which fell to the depth of six inches, and increased their fears, by causing them to suppose that the end of the world was actually at hand. The medicine-man arose, told them to stop their fear and crying, for the world was not about to fall to pieces, 'Soon.' said he, 'there will come from the rising sun a different kind of men from any you have yet seen, who will with them bring a book, and will teach you every thing, and soon after that the world will fall to pieces [...] (Pickering 1888, 4:439).

Naturally, depending upon the location of the ash fall, there were varying accounts of the effects upon different groups in areas covered with ash. For example, Major Richard D. Gwydir (1845-1925) was told by *Whis-tel-po-sum* [Lot], a Spokan chief, how the earth quaked for two days, how the ash fell for several weeks, and, "The game abandoned the country, the waters of the lake receded, dry land appeared and desolation spread over the entire country. The Indians died by [the] thousands from starvation" (1907, 1:136-7). Teit also wrote of the dire effects of the eruption of ash upon the Nespelem and their environment: "the following winter, which happened to be rather long and severe, they ran out of supplies. A few of the old people died of starvation and others became so weak that they could not hunt" (1930:292). William Burke, Verne Ray's principal Sanpoil chief informant gave the following description of the effects of the eruption:

Everybody was so badly scared that the whole summer was spent in praying. The people even danced—something they never did except in winter. They didn't gather any food but what they had to live on. That winter meant people starved to death. Besides that the epidemic of smallpox (?) killed a lot of people. And the next spring some warriors from the south came and killed still more. What was worst, people even ate the flesh of their dead neighbors. Other people picked up prairie chicken [sharp-tailed grouse] droppings and made soup of them (Ray 1933, 5:108).

There are conflicting accounts (Gwydir 1917:243 fn; Cline 1938:173; Du Bois 1938) of when and under what conditions Kolaskin, a crippled orphan, became a self-acclaimed prophet of a revitalization movement, claiming the rights and powers of this position. Ray's work (1936) described how Kolaskin—at age twenty—after gambling and winning a blanket from a crippled man, refused to give it up when asked and as a result, became very ill and unable to walk because of paralyzed legs. His body swelled and his skin was covered in sores, which no curing shaman could cure, despite the many who practiced their skills and power on him. Eventually Kolaskin became unconscious, but upon awakening, proclaimed the intent and main tenets of his cult.

There is no evidence to show if the Spokan ever adopted the millennium Dream Dance, which was somewhat similar to the Plains Ghost Dance of 1870 and 1890, in that:

[...] a man "dies" and returns from the dead with a message to his fellows to lead a more upright life, at the same time announcing the impending return of the dead. These contacts with the supernatural follow the traditional power quest pattern. It is evident that this complex, which closely resembles the doctrine of the Ghost Dance movements of the 1870 and 1890, is of very considerable antiquity (Cline 1938:172).

Cline noted how *qʷélaskén* [Skolaskin] acknowledged that he sang a new song he had received while unconscious during the earthquake of 10-11 December 1872 (Howay *et al.* 1917, 3:227fn.), which was felt by the Colville, Spokan and Sinkaietk (Cline 1938:172). Initially, Skolaskin took advantage of this severe earthquake in the area of the Lower Spokan:

[...] he had been transported to heaven and had been commissioned to return to the earth with directions to build a great ark to save the remnant[s] of his race. The destructive agency was to be a flood of mud, which was to engulf the whites and restore the land to the natives, who would heed the warning, and such whites as might avail themselves of the opportunity and contribute tools and materials toward the undertaking (Kingston 1950:np).

As a result, a prophet movement was the *Dream Dance* (*ʔesotín'i*), a religious revitalization movement in the Plateau (1878-1885). However, having certain notions of Christianity, it never became an indigenous cult, but did have varying effect upon the Spokan. Du Bois summarizes the principal elements of the Dreamer religion and the Prophet dance as:

(1) dreamed revelation and songs, (2) necessity for publicizing one's dreams, (3) dances held in dwellings, (4) headbands, often bandanas, into which feathers were thrust, (5) feather wands, (6) peaked feather caps worn by some of the men dancers. All of these elements were probably pre-Ghost Dance. New features added about this time were: (7) stress on return of the dead, and (8) use of a square skin drum. The dream dance later became the Feather dance, in which the ritual was retained but not the supernatural inspiration through dreaming (1938:26).

Bischoff, drawing upon Joset's writing (1860), stated that the effects of the Dreamer religion were not particularly deleterious on Indians who had already converted to Catholicism:

It became almost the vogue to have visions and conversations with the angels. The credulous Indians were difficult people to convince of their delusion. Fortunately, they remained firm in their faith and attendance at church and approach to the sacraments (1945:154-155).

Curtis, when speaking of Kolaskin's syncretic cult, noted the leaders presumed prophet powers and influence; even control over many of the Sanpoil:

The belief in the efficacy of dreams and the power of prophecy was absolute, and still remains among the older Sanpoel [sic]. Some years ago the dreamer Skoláskîn predicted the end of the world, and commanded the people to build an ark in which to ride the flood that was to destroy the earth (1907-30, 7:78).

Gwydir, Indian Agent on the Colville Reservation from 1887 to 1890, described Kolaskin "as shrewd, cunning and the power he had over his people was almost absolute [...] " (1917:243). Later, Gwydir attended one of the early meetings when Kolaskin explained his prophecies and main objections to certain U.S. Government policies, particularly placing "Joseph's [Nez Perce chief] band on the land of the San Poil" (1917:246).

Ray had this to say about the involvement of the Spokan:

At this time some missionary work had been done among the Spokane by the Presbyterian branch of the Protestant church. The chief of the Lower Spokane *(snakált)*, a *óʔpaxan*, had become a convert by the missionary who periodically visited the people. The chief did not actively resist Kolaskin in his efforts to organize the new cult, but his passive opposition and the influence of the missionary undoubtedly were factors in the failure of Kolaskin among the Spokane (1936, 1:69).

Not unlike the Ghost Dance of the Plains, with resurrection of the dead, due to the often deadly effects of pandemics during the 1860s and 1870s, Ekland described how among certain indigenous religions of the Plateau, the prophet dance was an integral part of their ritual, one that acknowledged the rising of Christ from the dead:

The cult was characterized by a belief in the imminent destruction of the world and the resurrection of the dead; the earth was personified as Earth Woman. Prophets died, visited the land of the dead and returned with a message. By teaching a peculiar dance form, they prepared converts for the destruction of the earth. The prophet Cult allowed Christianity to be readily accepted and diffused among the Indians. The doctrines were analogous and the ritual did not conflict. Both told "of an apocalyptic end with the return to earth of its pristine happiness and the resurrection of the dead; the way prepared by a righteous life and a strict adherence to devotions (Ekland 1969, 2:123).

The Northwest Prophet cult was a revitalization movement and a messianic cult, much like the 1890 Ghost Dance. Spier provided an explanation for its development, which was predicated on belief in:

[...] the impending destruction and renewal of the world, when the dead would return, in conjunction with which there was a dance of the dead, and a conviction that intense preoccupation with the dance would hasten the happy day. From time to time men 'died' and returned to life with renewed assurances of the truth of the doctrine; at intervals cataclysms of nature occurred which were taken as portents of the end. Each of these events led to the performance of the dance with a renewed fervor, only to have it fall into abeyance again when their expectations remained unfulfilled (1935:5).

Much later, in the 1870s, the Smohalla cult flourished; "among the Salishian Cayuse, Spokane, Wasco and Wishram it had sympathetic followers. The wide-spread acceptance of such a religion would influence the effectiveness if any policies which would settle the Indians on farms" (Ekland 1969, 2:124).

Both the Indian Shaker Church and the Indian Bible Shaker Church were revivalist syncretic religious movements, whereas the latter group obviously used the *bible* (*swč̓miˀsepl'eˀtn*) in its teachings. Many of these religious movements were more established and active with Sahaptian groups; but among the Spokan—during the 1960s and 1970s—only the Native American Church was active for a relatively brief period when a few members became Peyotists (Walker and Schuster 1998:519). Because there was consensus that peyote was a debilitating drug, and not acceptable among the elders or the Spokane Tribal Council, or tribal members for that matter, this church is no longer on the Spokane Reservation.

Mythology

Prior to the effects of Euro-American diffusion, contact, and eventual Christian missionization, the Spokan mythical charter had been developed some ten to twelve thousand years ago, and was an elaborate oral tradition that provided explanations for the origin of all plants, animals, and eventually humans. Everything that was natural, supernatural, and cultural, as perceived within the Spokan *Weltanschauung* ("worldview"), was an integral part of their mythical charter. It also provided adequate explanations of their cosmos, pantheon, and folklore. More specifically, the mythical charter identified and explained the origins of land forms, stars, seasons, plants, and animals; it identified the spirits in their animistic religion, and it gave credence to even the principles of kinship and sociopolitical structure. Attitudes and practices of what were sacred or profane were clearly delineated in the moral order or religion, once based upon lengthy and complex interpretations that were inextricably related to mythology. The, "Myth era [was] called a time when they made hemp" (Elmendorf 1935-6, 3:7). The numerous accounts of mythical characters invariably served to teach and maintain the values of strength, endurance, justice, revenge, "and the defeat of animal characters who acted against group welfare" (Walker 1978:164). (See Appendix P.)

Father Gregory Mengarini, S.J. (1811-1886), spent time (1841-1850) with the Flathead, and was a serious student of their mythology and language, and mentions an invisible god called Amotkan, who in a creation *myth* (*sqʷell'úm't*) observed:

[...] from his mountaintop that man had greatly multiplied and had become evil and degenerate, attempting to persuade mankind to return to its senses. But growing angry when man failed to heed him, he caused all men to perish in a general flood in which the waters rose higher than the tallest mountain tops (1977:150).

An interesting and plausible interpretation of the aforementioned natural catastrophe caused by the glacial Lake Missoula flood may have been the basis for the interpretation of Amotkan's action upon the Flathead people (Scholz, pers. comm.).

There are many recorded *Indian legends* (*sqʷell'um't*) (STHC) that once were exceptionally detailed, resulting in a *long legend* (*č̓ɫkʷen'xʷcin'* or *n'qaspapl'qs* - "old story"). Unfortunately, it is now difficult to discern if a particular myth is from aboriginal Spokan or from another group, or a synthesis from one of the

728

contiguous tribes' mythical charter. There are several lengthy and rather idealized explanations of Spokan creation accounts (cf. Wynecoop 1985) that have been written or recited to historians by Indians who were Christians. Many of these Spokans presumably did not subscribe to the indigenous faith, even in syncretic form, and, thus, their renditions are sometimes inconclusive and even suspect. It is for this reason that a specific explanation for the origin of the Spokan world— recorded by Elmendorf—is so important, for while it is unfortunately rather brief, it is the only known mythological explanation not influenced by Christian missionization:

> Everything in [the] beginning was formless & one [was] moved by *snxpéw's* ("my double") = *sumíx*—the spirit—the creator in vapor forms & took forms of animals & were endowed with power to create—[they] planned out the way the world [was] to be—were *sxʷkʼɫpáʔxám* ("planners" of world)—they still have power but not as before—[they] reached this stage by eating food—but the animal spirits are still intermediate—fasting is for this reason necessary before attaining any spirit powers (1935-6, 2:55a).

Actually there are numerous accounts of Spokan origin, one being a recording by Lord who had an interest in the explanation of origin and an afterlife, and was informed that:

> The Flatheads (Salish and *Kalleespelm* [Kalispel]), it is said, believed the Sun to be the Supreme Being, and that after death the good, i.e., the brave and generous, went to the Sun, while the bad remained near the earth and troubled the living; others supposed that the worthless ceased to exist at death (1866, 2:239-240).

Another explanation of origin was how in the *very beginning* (*ɫwtn'šit*) there was only a *creator* (*kʼʷƛ'ancútn* certainly pre-Christian) and *an animal kingdom time* (*kʼʷakʼʷaʔqinm*) with a *chief of animals* (*axʷʔaxʷiná*). But in time there was an *end of animal kingdom and the beginning of people* (*č'et'lm'xʷil'š* or *ne' ɫuʔ st'llsqelixʷ* or *ƛwéʔʔntn - when the animal kingdom ends and the real people world began* or *šet'l'xʷil'š*). The *first Indians* (*šiʔtmasqélixʷ* - "first people") were *foolish and ignorant mythical people, smtéʔusi*, who initially spoke not an animal language, but the *mother tongue* (*nšiʔtcin*). They were considered to have been the *first ancestor* (*šiʔšʔít*) (STHC). In time, power was first given by birds to long-ago people, and:

> It is said that in the earliest times people did not die. After a time death was introduced into the world by a woman, and since then all people have died, and their flesh has rotted, leaving only bones. After a time even these decay and disappear. It seems that there was no belief that Coyote or others brought back the dead (Teit 1930:183).

In mythical times the climate was vastly different; characterized by little rain or snow, rather intense heat, considerable thunder and lightning, and incessant wind which was bothersome and even injurious to animals. *Coyote* (*Canus latrans - spílyeʔ* or *snč'lép*), a trickster, was important in origin myth, as initially the world was always dark, a time when the Little People and animals would have to carefully grope about to locate things. After Coyote created the earth and all its natural features, and the animals in one week, reflecting Christian influence upon an already established mythology, he then went to the heavens and created the moon and sun for the benefit of all living creatures:

> The world was dominated by severe hot and cold winds, but eventually Coyote made a snare to capture the wind, which he released only after the wind vowed to never hurt living things. To make certain this would happen, Coyote gave both the cold wind and the warm wind to the "wind people" who were two brothers; one would keep the cold wind in a bag and the other brother did likewise with the warm wind (STHC).

This illustrates the universal concept of complementary opposition, the basic premise that balance (homeostasis) was achieved through opposing duality. The warm wind brother was handsome, whereas the cold wind brother was *ugly* (*č'ssʕac'x*). Coyote explained to them how the cold wind would only be released when the weather was too warm, and conversely the warm wind would be released when the weather was too cold. Adelphic differences created conflict, leading to the ugly brother killing many living creatures, including humans, by indiscriminately releasing too much cold wind. Realizing his brother's harmful use of his powers, the warm wind brother killed him and restored a balance that was beneficial to living things. He first created the moon. Initially, Coyote was the moon, and was always bright, allowing him to see everything. He even divulged the nakedness of people, which *embarrassed* (*čkʷlkʷílneʔ*) them. The *great-great-grandfather* (*túpyeʔ* = one name for sweathouse) intervened and removed Coyote, but left the moon as it is now seen, changing monthly as the frog jumps back and forth (STHC).

The importance of Coyote continues as the major figure in the oral history of the Spokan; a figure who had a grandmother whom he called *ččiyeʔ*. Coyote possessed a guardian spirit, because even though he was married to Mrs. Mole or Gopher, *he bore his own children* (*ʔecpʼispʼsm*). Coyote had five sons, and while they were delivered successively, Coyote endured considerable pain, struggling while holding onto a small tree, all the while *beseeching his guardian spirit* (*pʼíspʼsm*) for assistance. The first son was called *nmyołtʼkʼʷótqn* ("he has brains" - "knows it all"). The second son was named *čʼłtattałʼáʔqʷ* ("he lies prone under a log," or "lay straight out on one's stomach under a log"). His third son was *pʼcʼalqʷewʼeʔsčšnʼ* ("he has feces on his hind legs"). The fourth son was known as *yerčnʼełpáwʔastqn* ("he has red berries [currants] on his head"). Coyote's fifth son was *scʼaʔcínʼšn* ("he has skinny ankles," or *cʼaʔ* - "skinny ankles").

Mole was Coyote's wife (*pulʼyehalʼ* - big toe (*stúmʼšnʼ* - "mother toe"), and until recently is still a common metaphorical expression, in which one's "big toe" represents a person, usually one's wife or good friend who is more stable and more reliable and capable of extracting the speaker from a difficult or untenable situation. A person without a big toe has poor balance and usually unsound judgement. Fox was Coyote's *stúmʼšnʼ*.

Different elders provided various reasons as to why their once important sacred relationship with animals disappeared:

Before there were so many *suyápi* [white people who] came to our country, all the wild animals would talk to us Indians, in Spokan. No matter where you went, animals and birds [would] call out and talk to us, and always those with your *suméš*. If a person was in bad trouble, or was hungry with no food, he'd go to the woods, and suddenly a[n] animal would come out to be used for food. Now, today, there are too many [...] *suyápi* everywhere, every place you go or look, you'd first hear them, then you'd see them, then smell them. White people have scared and driven all the animals away. Also, there're too many electrical things, and I've told you how this also keeps the animals away (Ross 1968-2008).

Chapter XIX: Natural Phenomena

Constellations

Unfortunately there is no recall of once existing classifications by the Spokan of the major stellar bodies—only of certain major celestial phenomena such as the *milky way* (*ʔesqʼxáx* or *qʼʷosqʼʷos*), which, some Spokan believed, were taught by missionaries to be the stairway to heaven, upon which the souls of the deceased would travel, sometimes slowly, given their earthly offences. Elmendorf, however, wrote how "long ago people believed the dead travelled across the Milky Way—doesn't know any name for it" (1935-6, 4:25). The Spokan also acknowledged the *northern lights* (*sčpʼaxʷásqʼt* or *spʼeʔxʷéwʼlš* or *spaʔaqʼéʔwxš* - "a lot of sudden light") (Smith 1936-8:1053), which indicated the coming of cold weather; even *extreme cold weather* (*hixʷmusm*). Both the *Little Dipper* (*sntkʼʷkʼʷłmʼúlmn*) and *Big Dipper* (*skʷłiłnkʼʷmulmn*) were acknowledged, and undoubtedly they are important in Spokan cosmology, but there are no recorded or remembered detailed explanations of their significance.

A number of the major *stars* (*skʷkʷusmʼ*) were named; few can be remembered, and Elmendorf stated that the Spokan "never paid much attention to the stars—had no names for them at all" (1935-6, 4:25)—apart from the *sun* (*spʼqʼnʼíʔ*), which was seen as the *morning star* (*ʔeskʼʷłaccncút* - "it is tied to something"). "It may show that the Spokan knew the evening star and the morning star were the same planet (Venus), as one being tied to the other" (Egesdal, pers. comm.). The *northern* or *polar star* (*smxiʔčnʼasqʼt* - "Grizzly Bear star"), as well as the *moon* (*spʼqʼniʔ* or *škʷkʷspʼqniʔ*), and the occasional occurrence of a *shooting star* (*kʷkʷúsmʼ* or *hwíthut*), were all named and they became the basis of a now all but forgotten mythology that once explained certain relationships between significant animals within their earthly environment. The Spokan recognized a constellation involving Orion's Belt, called *sqálixʷqn* ("skull" and "pumpkin"), which was a *cannibal* (*nʼełnasqélixʷ* - "eaters of people") who made a blanket of scalps, and "she sewed three spots in the blanket for her brothers" (Egesdal, pers. comm.). The Spokan recognized *Pleiades* (*qʼʷósqʼʷs*) as the Big Dipper, which it is not, but rather a cluster of stars sometimes called "Seven Sisters" (Egesdal, pers. comm.).

Some claimed that any occurrence of a *sunbeam* (*čłkʷllʼenʼéʔ* or *skʷkʷlʼilʼ*) was once important in their mythology, but details have been forgotten. Yet elders recalled how in the past all major constellations were recognized and presumably named after animals, and in some instances they represented various inter-species relationships, that served for their pedagogical value in stories to children. During fall and winter, any two stars close together were thought to be the two daughters of the louse, and once served as the corpus for a long recitation. The three nearest stars to the North Star were three human brothers who were always stalking the bear, but now only a cryptic explanation remains. The sun was the most important celestial body, being recognized as bringing life to all living things on the *earth* (*stʼúlixʷ*); thus, the annual Sun Dance Ceremony was an important annual renewal ritual.

Various patterns on the moon were thought to be a representation of a frog; being most apparent during a *full moon* (*čkʼʷaʔkʼʷʔásqʼtm*), and, until recently, several elders delighted in describing to their children the significance of the moon's various patterns. The *sky* (*sččʼmásqʼt*) and *heaven* (*čmlkʼʷmasqt*) (the latter being a post-Christian concept) were of no known significance—only, as taught by Christians, that the rain comes from God to help the sun give life to the earth and all plants and animals. Both lightning and thunder were considered extremely dangerous, the occurrence being explained by rather lengthy accounts that frequently involved animals, but often the indiscriminate behavior of humans were thought to cause one or both of these forces to be released, and in some instances they were believed to occur as the result of a single person's acts. Both lightning and *loud thunder claps* (*tʼrʼtreʔmʼ*) were feared, and they were in turn often taken to be ominous indications of immediate personal misfortune to an offender who was responsible for such dangerous displays of natural power.

Numerous elders felt that the world is coming to an apocalyptic end, recalling oral accounts handed down over many generations of when Mount. St. Helens erupted in 1847, covering the Spokan area in fine gray-white ash that people thought was flour being sent by God (Ross 1968-2008). Some women attempted to *bake* (*sč'ɬóʕ's*) the ash, but others were certain it was a warning to those who had given up their traditional ways of belief and living. Perhaps, more practically, a few men used the ash for tracking deer. These apocalyptic interpretations—once held by many elders—tended to be reinforced for those who watched television, who at times misinterpreted fictional shows as being occurring in reality. The most notable concern of elders was the spatial and temporal proximity of U.S. conflict abroad, seen most evenings on TV. The Spokan were quite aware of the phenomenon of an *earthquake* (*xʷrpúleʔxʷ* or *st'úlix* – "it's trembling the land" or *hec xʷrqmi y'e st'úlixʷ* or *st'úlixʷ hec xʷrpmi*), as they had experienced some severe ones recorded in memory and oral history.

Meteorology

Given both the immediate and projected long-term effects of weather upon the aquatic and terrestrial resources of hunting and gathering people, the Spokan were concerned primarily with the occurrence of rain fall and snow, which they believed could at least be influenced by ritual behavior. Consequently, the prediction of *weather* (*xeʔnúxʷ*) was of paramount concern to a people whose living conditions and dependence upon food within an environment was greatly influenced by changing climates. For example, during winter, a major concern of deer hunters was their reduced ability to track or trap game if there was only limited sporadic snow fall, or worse, an unusually mild winter with little snow. It was not recorded as to whether hunters ever prayed or made any sort of propitiation for *snow* (*smék'ʷt*). However, a *medicine man would sing a special song to bring snow on the ground* (*smek'ʷt*), or for rain to carry away late winter snows (Smith 1936-8:1273). Presumably it was common for a man with wolf power to propitiate his guardian spirit for snow; but only a few medicine men had this power. Those shamans who did sing for a weather change, did so only at night. Attempting to influence types of weather—*fog* (*shem'ip*), rain and *cold rain* (*yixʷmeys*), wind, or snow—was apparently seldom practiced in the late spring, the summer, or the fall. Elders claim that long ago one or two medicine men had the power to influence all types of weather, but they did not exercise their powers lightly, only when the group was confronted with a long and severe winter.

According to Schaeffer, the Flathead prediction of the severity of the winter was by measuring "The amount of marrow in the foreleg of a deer [...] ; if the marrow is thick, the winter will be hard" (1934-37, I-142:13).

During *extremely cold weather* (*hixʷmusm*), when people were more confined, elders would say to younger generations that it was a time to tell stories. There was a classification of varying degrees of cold weather: *hepɬ xxl'xl'eʔxʷ* was when, during a blizzard, one had the sensation of many small, biting teeth. *k'ʷusk'ʷusk'ʷus* was a condition when the cold was so severe that one's feet, when traveling over cold-crusted snow, made a *k'ʷič' k'ʷič'* sound (STHC). Until recently, elders who had spent time in the woods claimed that, once freezing weather sets in, a person can determine three distinct gradations of sub-zero temperature by the sound made when walking on snow. With sub-zero temperatures and an extreme chill factor, trees would crack and make popping sounds, a condition called *hec t't'qʷalqʷi* or *t't'qal'qmntm* ("severe winter when the trees popped and snapped") (STHC). A *chilly wind* (*c'aλtisúʔi*) came predominantly from the north or northeast.

Weather Control

It is presumptuous to say the Spokan felt they could control weather; rather there was behavior and ritual which they believed could sometimes influence weather. All major elements of weather, such as lightning, thunder, rain, and wind, were not natural or without reason. Rather, they were an extension or direct manifestation of a supernatural force, one that can communicate with shamans who possessed the power to have knowledge about and a limited influence upon such phenomena. Tormenting any animal, particularly a snake, would bring rain, thunder, and lightning. Thunder was a powerful force, and there were numerous explanations regarding its relationships to humans and nature, and it was thunder, not lightning, that struck people. The Spokan knew that thunder frightened animals, and of course occasionally even panicked a horse. Consequently, every effort was made to appease thunder—often by making a smoke fire, upon which sweet grass or dried boughs of either sub-alpine fir or white fir would be placed while a shaman prayed for the thunder to pass. According to Smith, the Kalispel, Upper Spokan, and Chewelah-Spokan Group would rejoice with the first claps of thunder in the spring, for it meant the coming of the *warm weather* (*snqʷecpm*) and that "the monotony and the *sickness* (*swéyt*) of the winter were gone" (1936-8:1325). It was said that a *flying squirrel* (*Glacomys sabrinus* - *sxʷupxʷup*) was recognized as a sure sign of spring.

The destructive effects of lightning were well understood, and yet the most feared was thunder, given that the noise was thought to knock down or uproot trees, and cause rock slides. On the Spokane Indian Reservation, there was a large and still discernible *landslide* (*ntmpenč*) into the Spokane River, circa 1874, one that some elders believed was due to a severe thunder *storm* (*sč'sasq't*). They felt that it was not caused by incessant rain, erosion, or an earth tremor, but thunder that shook the ground loose. We find the interesting ritual of a shaman pounding the roots of the herbaceous perennial bloodstone or, as previously cited, stoneseed roots to release drops of red juice to bring rain, all the while singing a rain chant. One account of this event, which occurred near Chelan, was reported by a settler woman:

> One day there was an earthquake and a big landslide somewhere near Chelan. The Indians said that there was a rumble, a smell of sulphur and that the earth opened up in cracks, taking some of the Indians, one of whom was left with a hand sticking out. The water of the Columbia was all muddy from the landslide, which for some time blocked the river (Coone 1917:20).

All apparent aspects of nature, including lightning, thunder, and rain, affected humans, just as any disrespect in voice or deed by a human would suffer nature's wrath. It was readily acknowledged that lightning could strike and kill a person or animal, or burn anything organic; but it was also believed that thunder could strike and kill a person or any animal. One way to protect oneself during the early reservation period from lightning strikes was to "always keep a large butcher knife in a post near your tent or house." The phenomena of lightning and thunder were always present, but they were dangerous only when one could hear it, for it was the sound that would kill. *Rolling thunder* (*st'rt're?m*) was said to be a most frightening experience since it was thought to be more ominous and unpredictable, and the same was true when there was an observed *simultaneous thunderclap and lightning strike* (*sq'em* or *si?xʷelm*). Some elders recall how in the past lightning in the north was caused by ice breaking up in late winter or early spring, and that burning a lightning-struck dead tree for firewood would only cause more lightning. Because of vegetation cover, a *dust storm* (*qʷu?łmncut*) was a *rare occurrence* (*y'aʕp'y'aʕ't*), and occurred only in late summer when stream sand was exposed.

As previously noted, prior to the arrival of commercially generated electricity, a person's tutelary power was temporarily inactive or greatly diminished when he was in the immediate vicinity of a lightning strike. With the advent of commercial electricity, guardian spirits went elsewhere; away from generators, power lines, and any type of electrical appliance. Some felt it was difficult, if not impossible, to acquire one's *sumés* if the seeker was near any source or outlet of electricity.

After the so-called Indian summer, a medicine man could, through appropriate ritual, influence the *weather to turn cold* (*c'er'tm*) so that deer would seek food at lower elevations. Through ritual, a shaman could rid an area of a *cold north wind* (*hi xʷmsm'aʔłq*) or sometimes *freezing temperatures* (*hixʷmusm*).

The power to bring needed rain was often given by a water-dwelling mammal, such as a muskrat, beaver, or otter. Smith explains how a Spokan woman had such a power, and when "The cold weather would not let the muskrat go out of his den and he was hungry and he was going to cause it to *rain* (*st'ípeys*) and thaw when she [the Spokan woman] sang" (1936-8:1319). Smith further explains how:

> Medicine men with muskrat for a guardian spirit are the ones who make rain; and all kinds of water animals, fish, otter, mink, could make rain. Upland guardian spirit animals, like wolves, would make snow. The guardian spirit would have to tell a person that he could control the weather before he could do it and not all guardian spirit animals would confer this power (1936-8:1323).

Of interest is that Walker's diary entry for 18 January 1843 addressed the matter of weather control by shamans, particularly for the occurrence of snow. Walker, when speaking with an elderly shaman, remarked, "that it rained. He made the reply that he could not get them to make medicine for snow. They all said their medicine was good for rain that they might have some roots & plenty of small fish" (Drury 1976:225).

This ritual for making rain was similar to what a medicine man did when he took an untanned pelt of any aquatic mammal, which was first submerged in water, and then removed and shaken so that the water was distributed over the ground. It should be noted that Spokan children were instructed never to harm or kill a frog for Spokan recognized that if a frog was molested in any way, it could cause rain. Some say such an act could bring adverse weather such as *sleet* (*sp'p'atn't*) or *hail* (*c'os*). Hail stones were called *c'sl'úe*.

The following is a brief story about a frog that attempted to *predict* (*hec q'ewn*) weather for the Chewelah-Spokan Group, a notion based on the belief that accidentally killing a frog would bring rain, even a *Pacific Treefrog* (*Hyla regilla* - *čłwax̣ ls* or *łameye'*):

> I well recall my grandfather and grandmother telling us kids [CE. 1860-70] a funny story one winter evening. The people of Chewelah sent a frog to Cusik to see what the weather was like, and if it was warmer because they thought they may go to pay the people around Coeur d'Alene a visit. Well, the frog went off to check the weather. When he got to the last mountain before *Cusick* [*tcm'k'ók'anú*], he stood up on his hind legs and held his head back. Of course this meant his eyes were on the "back of this head," so what he really saw was the weather in Chewelah. So to Chewelah came the frog, and all the Indians asked what the weather was like. Well, he said: "I stood on my hind legs and I could see they were having the same weather we're having." After a while, all the Indians began to laugh (Ross 1968-2008).

People were extremely cautious when conducting ceremonies or rituals to bring rain, for there was always the possibility that the conjurer might be struck by any accompanying lightning when beseeching the powers to recognize and comply with perceived human needs.

There were different rituals to stop rain. Again using the Chewelah-Spokan Group as an example, Smith (1936-8:1320) cites a procedure that required tying a hair around a louse, which was then hung outside a dwelling to stop the rain. Omens were sometimes predictors of weather change. For instance, if it had been raining during a child's birthing, but stopped during or right after the procedure, it was thought that there would be an annual recurrence of incessant rain, at least throughout the spring. The event of a birthing was believed to change the weather, either from good to bad, or vice versa. A good weather day was known as *xsasq't*, whereas a bad weather day was designated as *č'sasq't*.

Elders would direct children of four to six years of age to venture out, gather a basket of pine cones, and use them to make a circle around the dwelling firepit with the base ends toward the fire. The rain would stop once the cones had completely dried out (STHC). Another method to stop heavy rain was to hang up balled head lice on a tree or a door, a ritual known as *xeʔnuxʷ*. In the late 1880s, there was an elderly Spokan woman, known throughout this area as Spokane Rose, not only by the non-Indians through a much reproduced photograph of her carrying a huge load of winter wood, but also by the Spokan who

734

acknowledged her ability to bring or stop rain. An elderly woman whose grandmother knew Spokane Rose had this to say about her:

> Old Spokane Rose could always make it rain when she wanted. She would gather people in a large circle and tell them to dance clockwise to drumming while she'd joined with them. After a while the rain would start to fall. To stop the rain, she'd do the same dance with all the people, but then she'd suddenly stop and start to dance counter clockwise, and the rain would stop. But, if no money or little things were tossed to her, the rain would not stop (Ross 1968-2008).

There were accounts of how—through ritual—the Spokan could either stop or start rain. One such ritual was explained by a man who could stop rain when he wanted to go deer hunting:

> When it's raining hard, and I wanted to go hunting, I'd go to a huge red ant hill, right up behind that low hill, and sing my song as I took my "ant stick" [always of hardwood], and run it back and forth near the earth around the ant hill, and then through the hill. After a while the hill was flattened and ants [were] running everywhere— they'd never bite me. I'd be all the time singing my song: "Give your children the sunshine." Hearing my song, the red piss-ants would get on their backs and piss in the air, and the rain would stop (Ross 1968-2008).

Weather Indications

As with all cultures, there existed a wide variety of signs to predict or at least *guess* (*esč'ɬʕaqʔáwi*) the change of weather and the consequences. Though medicine men were the most proficient, observed behavior of domestic and wild animals—and even young children—were often indications of weather change. There was, however, consensus that different types of winds—directions and temperature—and lunar phases preceded major weather changes. It was agreed that a *rocking quarter moon with a south bulge* (*eč'stctešlš*) was a certain prediction that cold weather was coming, often accompanied by bad personal or group misfortune.

The abilities of all these supernatural forces—thunder, lightning, rain, high winds—suggest their unique characteristics, which were based on the Doctrine of Signatures, an example being the wind, a force called *snéʔut*, which caused the *wind to sing* (*swawlqʷ*) with every movement. Different people within a village or larger band had a shaman whose tutelary spirit would tell the individual what type of weather could be expected, or even how it would affect the productivity of a certain plant crop because the spirit communicated with a shaman possessing such a *suméš*. People without such a guardian spirit also were naturally able to make similar predictions of coming weather simply by analyzing conditions based on many years of observation.

Given the time of the year and the intensity of a meteorological occurrence, for example, thunder in early spring was a fortuitous indication of coming warmer weather, a time to prepare for leaving the winter village in quest of plant foods.

More than likely, the most dangerous type of inclement weather, for man or beast, was the *blizzard* (*quʔɬmncut*), because it caused severe wind chill, negative visibility, and general disorientation when one was in the woods. In such a condition, the rule of survival was for the person or group to go to ground by hastily constructing a temporary tree-well or snow bank excavation, which was, if possible, floored with *fir bough mats* (*t'agéλp*) for improved ground insulation.

Without the means of measuring barometric pressure per say, elders were often able to make reasonably accurate weather predictions based upon the severity of their aches and joint pains. Other natural signs included coyotes barking and calling back and forth, which indicated the weather was going to change; but one never knew if it would improve or worsen. The erratic behavior of some older dogs could be diagnostic of coming rain or snow, such as moaning and becoming *restless* (*meʔ*) (repeatedly get up and then lie down). Some elders said that the uneasy behavior of dogs could forecast other changes in weather, particularly of a coming spring *windstorm* (*sλ'ʕʷóɬmc'ʕʷot*) when there was little the Spokan could do except to empty and secure their drying racks and avoid being struck by flying objects.

735

The duration and severity of winter was also believed to be indicated by the appearance or behavior of other animals. A presumed omen for a long and possibly severe winter was if squirrels were seen hoarding large amounts of pine nuts, or if the migratory birds, ducks, and geese made an early departure. Recognizing these effects of weather upon animals, the Spokan believed that the observable behavior of smaller animals and birds, even insects, was an indication of future weather, most notably of coming snow and the severity of a winter as seen in greater amounts of food being stored by animals.

Medicine men, recognizing certain existing weather conditions, were capable of *forecasting weather* (*ac'xnúxʷ*). One elderly shaman had a reputation as a *weather forecaster* (*sxʷʔac'xnuxʷm*), and was presumably capable of predicting two to three days of weather. A more predictable forecast of cold weather occurred when there was a *circle around the moon* (*snq'l'ʔełxʷm*); this was interpreted as a sign of potentially stormy weather, accompanied with a *snow or sleet storm* (*sp'p'at'n't*) or *frozen rain* (*šetiš*). The apparent size and luminosity of the ring was meaningful, as when a close *circle around the moon* (*č'łqʷéccni* - [pulling a scarf close around the throat] or *snq'l'ełxʷm* - "circle around the moon) meant cold weather was coming, or when the *moon's halo was unusually large and bright* (*snq'l'ʔełxʷm'* - "ice or moon necklace") (STHC). It was believed that when there was a circle around the moon, the moon was sending a message, one that was predictive according to a viewer's interpretation.

The appearance of a *sun dog* (*ʔesʔesk'ʷléltn*) forecasted that the wind would swing about and come out of the north, bringing snow, rain, or a mild early spring *snow to rain or rain to snow* (*p'lč'seysm*) situation, or a simultaneous *mix of snow and rain* (*p'p'at'nt*) which would be often accompanied by wind. There are usually two sun dogs that appear opposite each other on a horizontal plane, appearing as a small cross section of a rainbow with one or even both ends of the main arc obscured by clouds or fog. There is no remembered or recorded significance or term for this phenomenon. People were always careful to never speak too loudly when there was a *sunset rainbow* (*snsuxʷm'eʔcn*), for voices could carry great distances due to the *quiet after sunset* (*snsem'm'c'*) (STHC), not unlike sound carrying over still water.

Forecasting weather was also done by signs known as *ʔac'xnuxʷ*, such as blue smoke, which meant the weather would remain hot whereas the weather would turn cold if a camp or cooking fire smoke was white, indicating the approach of a cold weather front. The appearance of a *spring rainbow* (*skʷmkʷmiw'ešn* - "the rainbow colors") indicated a series of warm but gentle rain cells, just as the *rainbow colors at sunrise or sunset* (*nsxʷm'eʔcn*) could predict weather.

Clouds were also important for forecasting weather and temperature changes. A *mackerel sky* (*sčt'kúʔusásq't*) of cirrocumulus clouds, suggesting rows of sand or articulated fish bones, indicated precipitation, or, in cold weather, that a snow storm was imminent. Any of the now-mostly-forgotten thirty-some cloud formations, depending on the season of the year, wind direction, and the time of day, was a means of forecasting weather, which for hunters and gatherers was often important. For example, *brown clouds were a definite sign of rain* (*čskʷiy'asq'tm*). These were most often altocumulus clouds observed in the summer. Another sign of impending rain was if the top of a shaman's head or his eyelids commenced to twitch (Smith 1936-1938:1307).

The presence of *continual rain* (*sšer'šr'w'l'š*) indicated the coming of spring and early summer, being beneficial to both plants and animals, which the Spokan were thankful for. Though not a prediction of weather, a late snowfall in early or even mid-spring was commonly called *crow's stockings* (*scʔaʔ snq'ʷuλ'šis*), since the snow would simply "fly away" before settling in (STHC).

Even children were knowledgeable of the *various harbingers of spring* (*st'aqt*), such as the first occurrence of robins, geese or squirrels *whistling, wind before the rain* (*snxʕáp*), and a *bad new moon* (*cč'sšcteššiš sp'q'n'iʔ*). On the other hand, a *bad season moon* (*čk'ʷaʔk'ʷʔasq't*) (which looked like a bowl facing upwards) was a sign of future adverse weather. The flying squirrel was another indication of spring, when at night one would hear *their sound* (*xʷupxʷup*) (STHC). A *good season moon* (*hec čššr'ew's*) appeared as a *half moon* (*ntx̣ʷew's sp'q'ni*) with the points facing to the viewer's left. All adults were quite capable of making *weather predictions* (*ʔac'x̣núx̣ʷ*) by simply noting the type of *sunset* (*čk'ʷƛ'ip* - "to slip off from" or *nsúx̣ʷmeʔcn*) or *sunrise* (*ck'ʷk'ʷƛ'ip*). A definite sign of warmer weather was when *snow sticks to one side of the tree* (*čsač'tal'q'ʷm'*), or a wet driving rain, or a snow storm in early spring—particularly if there were *large snow flakes* (*p'sƛ'ʔeys* - "big teeth").

A predictor of spring was a late snowfall, when the snow was not deep and would blow away. Another sign of an early summer was rolling thunder, or the first *sudden cloudburst* (*čspʔƛ'čsteneʔłt*). Many years ago when a small Spokan child heard a *summer's thunderclap* (*síʔx̣ʷilm*), this was an adequate reason for a grandmother to explain the noise as a consequence of a foolish act of Coyote. Smith (1936-8:1324) describes how even during summer, the Kalispel were always careful to cover the blood of a butchered deer with dirt, lest it should bring a summer snow storm.

Seasons

Both the equinoxes and the solstices, the longest and shortest days, were recognized as a type of *calendar* (*snsay'n'ʔásq'tn'*), which delineated the four seasons of a year:

- *winter* (*sʔistč - česmek'ʷeln* - "the first snow" - winter commences).
- *spring* (*sqepc*).
- *summer* (*sʔanłq*), summer months called *piʔitx̣ʷa*.
- *autumn* (*sč'lw'és* or *sč'ʔey*).

Each season was naturally recognized as having predictable climatic changes based on predominating wind directions and associated temperature changes, as well as differences in vegetation. For example, autumn arrived when the tamarack commenced to turn a *golden color* (*kʷr'i*), a time known as *čkʷr'r'ʔečt*. During the winter, *winds* generally from the *north* (*hix̣ʷmsúleʔx̣*) meant snow. But these same winds in spring and summer brought rain, certainly the so-called *April shower* (*qsšer'šr'w'l'ši* or *šeršrw'ls* - "tiresome"), which was a welcome occurrence and a sign of spring, a time when *frost leaves the trees* (*łʕaʔwalqʷ*) and the bark is easy to peel. Warm winds that *blew before rain* (*snx̣qap*) were also harbingers of spring and the start of root-digging. Such a wind would be similar to a *warm Chinook wind* (*heschátqi* or *chałqm*). A *spring quarter moon with a west bulge* (*cššr'ew's*) was also interpreted as a good indicator of incoming warm rain. The annual *early spring thaw following showers* (*titiʔm'ep*) was a joyous time for preparing the various technologies for gathering, hunting, and fishing. The thoughts of many an elder was, "My heart warms with the coming sun."

Given the influence of trade and goods, especially the introduction of aniline dyes and various types of trade items such as trade beads, it is not known when seasons became color-coded. Nonetheless, there are now accepted colors designating particular seasons in certain ceremonial clothing decorations. The colors in nature or culturally displayed ones have significance: white represents snow or winter, green for spring, orange for summer, and red for fall (STHC).

The predominant *weather* (*eʔnúx̣ʷ*), mainly in spring, summer, and fall for the Spokan area, was out of the south to the southwest, from whence most of the rain comes. The weather out of the west in the spring, summer, and early fall varies little from the southwest winds. The winds and accompanying weather and moisture in autumn can be quite variable, sometimes out of the east bringing cooler weather.

Lunar Months

The Spokan divided the year into lunar months, each of which commenced with a full moon and ended with the moon's waning. They also recognized the *winter* solstice (*skʷsus* - "hunting drives" or *hoy yaʔkʷáqs łu sʔanłq*) and *summer solstice* (*sʔanłq* or *hoy yaʔkʷáqs łu sʔistč*), which commenced on a full moon (Elmendorf 1935-6, 2:42); each lunation reflected a specific economic activity or condition of the environment:

- *January* (*čsmék'ʷlt* - "month of the frozen face"),
- *February* (*sčn'ir'm'n'* - "buttercup" - time of people starving in village),
- *March* (*sqépc* - "beginning of spring" - spring equinox - snow is melting),
- *April* (*sc'ʔek'ʷ* - "flowers bloom"),
- *May* (*sp'eƛ'm* - "bitterroot"),
- *June* (*sx̌ʷaʔlitx̌ʷeʔ* - "camas"),
- *July* (*sʔanɫq* - "berry harvesting" - time of summer solstice),
- *August* (*slamp* - "Indian summer days"),
- *September* (*sč'ʔey* - "beginning of autumn" - time of special hunting trips in mountains),
- *October* (*sč'lwes* - "dog salmon"),
- *November* (*čnʔuy'uy'eɫx̌ʷtn* - "setting up of winter houses"), and
- *December* (*časmek'ʷeln* - "the big snows" - the time spirits arrive).

Each Mid-Winter Ceremony acknowledged the end of *one year* (*nk'ʷspentč*) and the start of a *new year* (*sic spentč*). The *year* (*spentč*) commenced with a new moon, just as a lunar month began with a new moon, and ended with a waning moon. A year was delineated by phases of the moon. Some have contended that the year actually commenced with the start of summer.

The various cyclical stages of the moon were:

- *full moon* (*čk'ʷaʔk'ʷʔásq'tm* or *yrncút* or *sp'q'n'iʔ*),
- *moon* (*skʷkʷsp'qníʔ*),
- *three-quarter moon* (*qʔeɫc'sip sp'q'n'iʔ*),
- *half moon* (*qʔeɫc'síp* or *ntx̌ʷew's*), and
- *new moon* (*ntx̌ʷéw's* or *ctéšlš* or *čk'ʷak'ʷʔasq't* - "bite size" - *hec čšr'r'ew's* - "with a right bulge").

There was no recollection of any climatological significance for an *č'ɫqʷélstn* or *č'ɫč'loʔmncút* of the sun—only a mythological explanation that a *total eclipse* (*č'ɫloʔmncút*) was caused when the sun once killed some of Coyote's children, and in revenge Coyote cut the heart out the sun, bringing total darkness, but later restored it (STHC). Moon eclipses were explained to children as times when the moon covers his face.

Calendar Sticks

Undoubtedly, the main influence, even pressure, to devise a universal calendrical system to delineate days of the week and months of the year was introduced by Christian missionaries who wanted the Indians to acknowledge the Sabbath. Various methods of counting were used, including keeping track of days, months, and thus seasons, by using a calendar stick, though Wilson (1866:305) noted how men accounted for days of the month by counting strung beads. The only known and definitive description of the calendar stick is found in Smith's Kalispel material, which also applies to the Spokan, specifically the Chewelah-Spokan Group:

Just as soon as [a] man got up, he would notch his stick. But when the man was gone, the women would mark it. There was one stick to each house. The stick was generally about 4 feet or 5 feet long and about 5/8 inches or a little bigger in diameter. If it was not big enough, as they found out, to take the notches of the whole year, they fill out the year with a small stick and the next year, they get a little longer stick.

They make a notch in a line for each day down the end. Then they begin on another line. The stick would have 4 sides, and they would notch the corners [...] They start to notch in the summer and go clear to the summer again. They start as soon as the snow goes away and notch one stick until the snow comes in the fall. Then they get another stick for the winter time and notch it until it has as many notches as the one which they had in the summer. Then they knew that a year has passed. Then they begin over again.

738

Even if they have a short summer, they begin when the first snow falls and they begin the second stick for the winter and go until they have the same number of notches as in the summer, even if there is still snow on the ground (1936-8:1042-3).

Days of the Week

Prior to missionization, the Spokan never recognized a week (*nqéw's*) as a unit of time, nor had they any need to divide an arbitrary week into seven named days. During the process of Christianization, the missionaries imposed their concepts of weeks and days, presumably to regulate and schedule the lives of converts, and to help them in recognizing and attending church services on Sunday. The seven days of the week were known in Spokan as:

- *Sunday* (*sčʕacew's* - "the day the flag is tied up high") from a flag pole to announce the day of religious services;
- *Monday* (*čp'ƛ'ew'sm* - "the day the church flag is hauled down);"
- *Tuesday* (*aslʔasq't* - "the second day after the flag was lowered);"
- *Wednesday* (*čaʔⱡʔasq't* - "the third day after the flag was lowered);"
- *Thursday* (*mosq't* - "the fourth day after the flag was lowered);"
- *Friday* (*clčⱡtasq't* - "the fifth day after the flag was lowered);"
- *Saturday* (*čⱡʔeʔ* - "it is near to" the day before the flag is raised) (STHC).

The various phases of the day were delineated as well, which did not involve the raising and lowering of a church flag. They were:

- *predawn* (*ikʷékʷst*),
- *dawn* (*eⱡƛƛ'eʔéč* or *x̱x̱l'púleʔxʷ*),
- *morning* (*skʷékʷst*),
- *noon* (*ntx̱x̱qín*),
- *midday* (*n'iyaq'qín'* or *nt x̱ʷúx̱ʷqin* - "sun straight up"),
- *afternoon* (*n'iyaq'qín'*),
- *night* (*skʷkʷʔéc*), and
- *midnight* (*yéʔusmskukʷéc* or *tx̱ʷuʔskʷkʷée* - "moon overhead")

Measurements

Most aboriginal *measurement* (*súxʷmeʔtn*) of weight and distance was relative to one's perception. But smaller and more easily comparable measurements were indicated by using one's hands or arms. For example, if describing the length of a salmon, a man may indicate his *arm's length* (*sxʷépčst*), or if describing the length of an eel, he might indicate the length by extending both arms out parallel to the *earth* (*lexʷ*) to what was *understood* (*nk'ʷsxʷé*) as approximately 2 meters. The length of smaller objects was indicated by the display of so many knuckles, or the distance between the extended thumb and forefinger. Until recently, a man would indicate the length or diameter of an object by measuring from the tip of his extended fingers to a place indicated with his other hand on his forearm or upper arm. Eventually, the perception and designation of a mile was called *súxʷmeʔtn.*

Overland distance was described by the number of days required to reach a certain place, an explanation that invariably depended on what route was taken, for a person seldom travelled in a straight line, to avoid certain elevation gains and other natural obstacles. "They sometimes measure [*súxʷm'en*] distances by a day's journey. When an Indian travels alone, his day's journey will be 50 or 60 English miles, but only 15 or 20 when he moves with the camp" (DeSmet 1843:155). Alexander Ross claimed that Indians calculated distance by time: "a day's ride is estimated about seventy miles on horseback, thirty-five miles on foot" (1904 7:309).

Directions

All children from an early age were quite cognizant of the four major cardinal directions:

- *north* (*hixʷmsuleʔxʷ* - "cold land"),
- *south* (*ƛ'áq'leʔxʷ* - "hot earth"),
- *east* (*sčk'ʷƛ'ptín* - "sunrise"), and
- *west* (*nč'lxʷtin* or *sč'lxʷtín* - "sun going out of sight").

People seldom travelled at night, certainly not during a *moonless night* (*č'l'xʷepm'* or *sč'lxʷepm'* or *shemip*), nor when their vision was impaired by heavy fog. If they were caught in such conditions, they would stop, make a camp, and wait until the weather improved. If night travel were necessary, a person would use the North Star and other significant constellations for orientation. In dense wooded areas, they could identify the north by looking for the side of the trees with the most amount of moss. Knowing the approximate time of day from the sun's position was probably an unconscious process. The Spokan recognized a nadir and a zenith, *midday* (*ntxʷúxʷqin* - "sun straight up") and *midnight* (*txʷuʔskʷkʷec* - "moon overhead").

Adults were instructed as young children, when alone and traversing an unfamiliar, open, and treeless mountainous area, that they should always stop before every major turn and look back at the terrain from where they had come, which, otherwise, would be unfamiliar when returning. If a person was lost, s/he would follow one stream to another—all the while losing elevation—until they came upon one of the four major streams that emptied into either the Spokane or Columbia River. Elders claimed that it was unusual for a hunter to become lost. But if it did happen in a severe snow storm, then the person would construct, if possible, a tree-well or basic survival structure until the storm had passed.

Numbers

The defining cardinal numbers were:

- 1 - *nk'ʷuʔ*
- 2 - *ʔesél*
- 3 - *čeʔɬes*
- 4 - *mus*
- 5 - *cil*
- 6 - *t'aq'n*
- 7 - *sisp'l'*
- 8 - *hʔen'm*
- 9 - *x̣x̣n'ut*
- 10 - *upn*
- 11 - *upn ʔeɬ nk'ʷuʔ*
- 20 - *esl ʔupn*
- 21 - *esl ʔupn eɬ n'k'ʷuʔ*
- 30 - *čeʔ ɬl ʔupn*
- 40 - *msɬ ʔupn*
- 50 - *clt čɬ ʔupnʔ*
- 60 - *t'q'nt čɬ ʔupn*
- 70 - *ssp'l č'ɬ ʔupn*
- 80 - *heʔnm ɬ ʔupn*
- 90 - *x̣x̣n'tɬ ʔupn*
- 100 - *nk'ʷ oʔ qin*

740

- 200 - *esln k'ʷoʔ qin*
- 300 - *čeʔɬ nk'ʷoʔ qin*
- 1000 - *oʔ pn'tčst qn'*

Geonomic Designations

When explaining a distant or a more immediate feature or site area, every adult and some older children were cognizant of certain geonomically designated physical features that provide a descriptive explanation. A child's attention was maintained often by a speaker's dramatic and lengthy explanation of a unique or supernatural ideographic event that might have occurred or was responsible for a particular or unique land feature, whose geonomic designation summarized how the feature had been formed in mythical times. Consequently, every prominent earth form or feature was assigned a specific *geonomic designation* (*skʷkʷskʷstul'eʔxʷs*), one that invariably denoted a unique physical aspect. For example, an area would likely be named after a certain resource found there, or a traditional inhabitation site, or how a mythical creature modified the earth during a particular activity. Or, as Duff's toponomastic research has aptly explained:

> A place name is a reminder of history, indelibly stamped on the land. To enquire about it is to retell some [or all] of that history. To work with Indian place names is to learn something about the Indian versions of what happened in history (1969:3).

Physical topographical features were never given personal names of humans or so-called nicknames, but were assigned designations that explained the feature's physical uniqueness, or how the unique topographical feature originated within the Spokan mythical charter. Some land areas or sites were identified by a particular utilitarian or food resource. However, most of the significant topographical features within the Spokan territory were named to acknowledge the dramatic encounters between regional mythical animals during the genesis of the local environment, "a time before humans." The oral history of this genesis served to effectively explain the transformations of animals, plants, waterways, and the earth's surface.

For example, not far from where Latah Creek flows into the Spokane River, there still exists on a terrace of the main channel a rather prominent geological feature—a tall, almost cylindrical stratified rock column, approximately 7 m in height. Both the Spokan and the contiguous Coeur d'Alene have different accounts to explain the column's origin. In short, the Coeur d'Alene elders believed that this feature represented a once forgotten standing stack of tipi poles left by Coyote. However, the Spokan maintain that after an unusually cold and long winter, Coyote, upon awakening, was walking along the Spokane River when he happened to see what he thought was a female black bear, one that was still not fully awake after her long winter hibernation. Realizing he could fulfill his long pent-up sexual desires, and not realizing his mistake, he leapt upon what was a male bear, only to be thrown to the ground with great force by the enraged and larger creature. During the ensuing battle, amid great blood and pain, Coyote was defeated. Part of his humiliation was also the loss of twenty feet of his one hundred foot penis (which when traveling, he kept coiled in a great basket on his back). Hence, the Spokan elders always believed that the column in question is part of Coyote's penis, not simply an ordinary stack of tipi poles.

Important to a child's *learning* (*m'iʔpn'úy's* or *c'xʷm'ʔšétw'elxʷiʔ*) of oral history was the occasion when a visitor, having travelled from a distant area, would entertain the children and other occupants of his host's dwelling in the evening, with long accounts of the unusual places he had seen during his journey. The repeated descriptions of physical features encountered along the journey tended to reinforce the cognitive mapping and knowledge of areas that lay beyond the listeners' experience. Upon becoming adults, people would continue to *explain* (*c'xʷm'ʔšétw'eʔxʷiʔ*) their unique experiences with the natural and spiritual world to their children and people they would meet during their own travels.

Chapter XX: Conclusion

The three Spokan composite macro bands were a riverine-oriented Interior Salishan-speaking peoples of the southeastern Plateau, living along the banks, terraces, and upland areas of the Spokane River east to the territory of the Coeur d'Alene, west to the mouth and lower part of the Spokane River, north to the Kalispel, and south to the area of the Palouse.

The dialects of the Middle and Upper Spokan differed slightly from that of the Lower Spokan, and reflected some minor cultural adaptations, particularly in fishing technology. All Spokan group dialects were mutually intelligible, and the Spokan could converse easily with the Flathead, Coeur d'Alene, and Kalispel Indians. These linguistic abilities reinforced a commonly shared cultural core of socioeconomic relationships that were necessitated, and further strengthened, by intergroup marriage, trade, and the mutual exploitation of resources. Multilingualism and a concept of usufruct were responsible for later confusion by many non-Indians in delineating ethnic boundaries and the actual location of aboriginal groups. A Spokan person typically spoke at least two languages, namely, their native Spokan, as well as one of the contiguous dialects of other groups, since one or more grandparents were sometimes from a non-Spokan group.

Accurate protohistoric Spokan population figures are not really known, since the introduction of *disease* (*swéyt*) drastically reduced the aboriginal population long before the actual incursion of whites. The inaccuracy of these population figures is further exacerbated by the high degree of mobility, change of residence at different times of the year, language problems of the reviewers, and the typical Euro-American's difficulty with an *Indian name* (*snqlix*ʷ*sk*ʷʷ*est*), which often did not reflect progenitors or lineage.

Plateau intergroup relations were established generally through geographic proximity of ethnic groups, linguistic polyglotism, and occurrence of differential resources. Established intergroup relations facilitated mutual exploitation of resources through marriage, trade, and task-grouping for warfare when venturing onto the Plains for bison and other products, particularly after the arrival of the horse. However, most conflicts among the Interior Plateau groups were limited and sporadic. Such conflicts seem to have increased temporarily with the horse into eastern Washington in approximately 1730. Factionalism was introduced by Christian missionaries, and proved to have severe effects upon all Plateau groups. It wrought incalculable dysfunction to people who once subscribed to the belief of animism for explaining their intricate relationship to the natural and supernatural worlds. Religious factionalism was quickly overlaid with political factionalism, which in some instances remains today, as is the case with regional and religious factions (Ross 1967).

The primary unit of social control was the autonomous village, headed by a chief who retained his office through consensus, generosity, skill in decision-making, oratory abilities, adroitness in arbitration, and the possession of religious power. Children were enculturated to a large extent by resident grandparents and extended kin group, but primarily by the grandmother. This arrangement permitted the child's parents to pursue out-of-home economic tasks, such as subsistence-getting activities. All children and adults actively engaged in numerous forms of games, which taught and encouraged hand-eye coordination required for later adult food-getting endeavors. Puberty rites recognized the transition to adulthood and equipped them for the concomitant responsibilities and obligations.

Individual status was based upon respect and generosity toward elders. A woman's reputation would be based on her domestic skills, generosity, and accommodation of in-laws. Women were the principal force in meeting the family's physical and social needs, and for maintaining familial tranquility. She was "the rock around which all fish swam and ate at. My mother and grandmother were the second and third suns that came up every morning, even on a dark and rainy day." Men achieved status through oratory skills, courage, generosity, and various predation skills. Possession of individual forms of *sumé**š* by both men and women further enhanced their contributions to the group.

Each territorial band had two or three minor chiefs. During times of mutual resource exploitation, a leader would be an individual who possessed the power necessary for exploiting a particular resource. War leaders were self-designated; after experiencing a dream of a pending event, they organized and supervised horse-stealing parties. *Councils (sq'm'qmilš)* connived on important issues confronting the group, and deliberated in lengthy sessions to achieve consensus over a pending issue. Both male and female adults enjoyed the right to participate and present their opinions in the council.

All permanent and temporary dwellings were located according to task-orientation, proximity of floral and faunal resources, topographic features, water, and logistics of transporting and storage of food resources. Spokan structures reflected the duration of occupancy, available structural resources, and the population size of the particular group.

Of the various types of residence patterns after marriage, neolocal and patrilocal residence were the most common. Patripotestal authority was the norm, and based upon a type of bilateral descent with incipient composite band structure. The sweathouse, though *sacred (xaʔxeʔt)*, was used for both sacred rites and secular activities, which supported socialization, enculturation, spiritual and physical cleansing, curing, social control, and joking relationships between fictives.

The Spokan annual subsistence base was not always predictable, particularly with hunting; thus, it required the sharing of short-term or migratory resources, particularly fish from the Spokane River. The most reliable and plentiful sources of caloric intake were roots and fish; plants constituted nearly 40 to 45 percent of their food, and fish approximately the same, whereas land mammal hunting provided less than twelve percent of their food. These figures would vary from year to year. The Spokan possessed a specialized fishing technology, and had adequate means of storage. Food procurement was based upon a relatively strict division of labor, and enjoyed the customs and obligations of distribution and redistribution to all members of the group, regardless of their participation. The Spokan practiced wise stewardship of resources, including annual controlled burning of certain areas for the purposes of eliminating windfall and deadfall, reducing insects, preventing crown fires, improving communication, and encouraging grazing animals and the occurrence of certain plants, particularly huckleberries. The Spokan were cognizant of food chains and food webs, and always aware of the carrying capacity of particular ecozones.

All rites of passage, purification, and intensification were based upon prescribed behavioral and dietary prohibitions, which were closely regulated by a person's family, kin group, and communal population. Social control and enculturation were fulfilled by an elaborate mythical charter was based upon an animistic religion, as well as extensive prescribed mores, which, if violated, explained aberrant behaviors, sickness, and eventual death. Intergroup relations were developed and sustained through polyglotism, intergroup marriage, task-grouping, and well-defined trade networks. The only true specialization of role with esoteric knowledge was shamanism and sorcery. The animistic religion of the Spokan encouraged individual recognition and practice of certain powers through a tutelary spirit, one that was acquired in a variety of ways. "It is an anthropological commonplace that shamanism, not prostitution, is the first profession" (Moerman 1979, 1:59). Lewis, paraphrasing Nadel's view (1946), visualizes shamanism as an attempt to enrich the spiritual armory of a community beset by chronic environmental uncertainty, or rapid and inexplicable social change (1971:203-204).

The advent of white incursion was preceded by a tremendous decimation of population due to non-traditional diseases, which effectively commenced the process of deculturation. Sadly, this was exacerbated by aggressive government policies, warfare, confinement to a reservation system, partial loss of the *Spokan Indian language (č'n nmyeɫspoqinišcn)* through government and mission schooling, and the concerted effort to restrict the traditional subsistence orientation of the Spokan to agriculture, although they had always been a foraging people who had once enjoyed a successful physical and spiritual adaptation to their natural environment. Additional problems that restricted Spokan adaptation was the confinement to a sedentary life

743

on reservations, and eventually to the isolation of reservations and limitations of access to newly developing urban economies of Anglo settlements.

Numerous explorers, trapper-traders, missionaries, and certainly the military and the settlers have also commented upon the physical characteristics and examples of character of eastern Plateau peoples, and there was generally a consensus—with some exceptions—that during the time of early contact, aboriginal cultures were more stable, and certainly more adaptive, prior to Euro-American incursions and occupancy.

Afterword

I suspect that most ethnographers, while conducting fieldwork, must ultimately wonder about the significance of the ethnographic material they are gathering over a period of weeks, months, or even years—particularly material from a relatively small, distinct ethnic community of elders.

The eventual publication of that information becomes more critical when only a few of the indigenous people can speak their native language and can still recall the past ways of their parents, grandparents, and, in a few instances, a great-grandparent. Will the published material be of more value to the academic community—such as ethnographers and ethnohistorians—or to the general community, as represented by patrons of libraries and bookstores? How will the ethnography be of value and use to the now-younger Indian population, comprising non-speakers already acculturated by non-Indian films, books, music, and any unfortunate derogative racial or ethnic designations.

While performing my ethnographic research on the Spokane Indian Reservation, it was clear that with each "winter," fewer elders remained. In turn, fewer indigenous plants could be identified, and the details and significance of many rituals were being forgotten, as was the extensive language that described the people's spiritual and natural worlds. Most sad to any ethnographer is when an elderly man or woman says, "I'll answer your question so one day, maybe my granddaughter or grandson might, when not watching television, read what I have told you."

Despite decades of speaking with Spokan elders, I still had no real answer to my field inquiries of how this ethnography would be of benefit to the younger and future Spokan generations, let alone to my gracious mentors. I spent a morning with a delightful 94-year-old Spokan woman who had, during countless hours and over many years, shared with me her personal songs and her detailed descriptions of past experiences and group events. After she had spoken without interruption for perhaps three hours, she very quietly said, "I have for many years told you of my past and the ways of my people. And now that I have told you all that I can remember, I can tell you no more. So now I can die in happiness, because my children and their children will know some of what my elders believed was sacred and important."

Appendices

Of the following oral history accounts, some have appeared elsewhere in various publications and numerous unpublished manuscripts. Over the years, they have unfortunately been shortened and edited for grammatical corrections. In addition, many of the oral authors are anonymous or have simply been forgotten.

These accounts were collected over a long period by enrolled Spokan who had an interest in recording what was quickly fading from the memories of their elders. It was clear that these oral histories were being lost to time, with the decline in knowledge and use of the old Spokane language, and with the weakening of the storytelling tradition that used their language to keep alive their histories. Such storytelling, once a crucial element of their culture, has unfortunately been replaced by other types of private and public communication, primarily television.

Margaret Sherwood, Ignace Pascal, and Louie Camille were largely responsible for providing the following accounts, which at one time were considerably greater in length and detail. A major problem with any folk translation is the loss of linguistic nuances and general knowledge of the characters participating in the account. Little or no attempt has been made to improve the grammar, spelling, or clarity of these entries. Only errors that might inadvertently be interpreted as due to this ethnography's author are indicated with "[sic]".

Appendix A: Prehistoric Spokane—An Indian Legend

Recorded by United States Colville Agent Major R. D. Gwydir in 1907, later recorded in *History of the City Spokane and Spokane County*. Nelson W. Durham, 3 vols. 1912, (1:645). Chicago. Originally Published in *Washington Historical Quarterly*, v. 1, April 1907:136-137.

Whis-tel-po-sum [Lot], chief of one of the three Spokane tribes of Indians, one of the best and most truthful Indians that I have ever met with, gave me, amongst others, a traditional history of Spokane and the country surrounding it, which, as well as I can remember, was as follows:

Centuries ago, long before the paleface was known on this continent, where Spokane is now situated and for many days travel east of it, was and beautiful lake [Lake Missoula], with many islands resting on its surface. The country swarmed with game and the lake abounded with fish—veritably a hunter's paradise. Many well-populated villages [Flathead] lay along the shores of the lake.

One summer morning the entire population were startled by the rumbling and shaking of the earth. The waters of the lake began rising, and pitching, and tossed into mountainous waves, which threatened to engulf the entire country. To add to the horrors of the situation, the sun became obscured by an eclipse, and darkness added its horrors to the scene. The terror-stricken inhabitants fled to the hills for safety. The shaking of the earth continued for two days, when a rain of ashes began to fall, and so heavy was the fall of them that there was little difference between day and night. The fall of ashes continued for several weeks. The game abandoned the country, the waters of the lake receded and dry land filled its place, and desolation spread over the entire country. The Indians died by the thousands from starvation. The remnant who escaped starvation followed the course of the receding waters until they arrived at the Falls (now Spokane) (Gwydir 1907, 1:645).

Their first village was located in the neighborhood of where the Galland-Burke brewery now stands. The bay north of Bridge Avenue and between Post and Monroe Streets was their swimming or bathing pool.

The tradition further states that the devil, in the form of a coyote, gave them a great deal of trouble, but finally they snared him and all the Indians were in at the killing, after which they divided the carcass among the people of the different tribes. After this prosperity smiled upon them and continued to do so until the coming of the paleface race, whom they could not snare, and who proved the worse devil of the two, for he left them nothing—their present condition.

Appendix B: How the Spokane River was Formed

Anonymous, n.d.

Ages ago the land was devastated by a monstrous dragon of fetid, reeking breath and claws that uprooted in a single stroke the largest pine tree. The people everywhere stood in constant dread and awe of it. An Indian girl, who was gathering berries on a summer day, discovered the monster sleeping in the *sunshine* [*sk^wk^wlil*] on a hillside near the present mouth of the *Spokane River* [*čx^wiyy'ep*]. Slipping away, she ran to the village of her tribe and reported the scene that had burst upon her astonished vision. Instantly, the chief assembled his warriors, and gathering every cord and thong in the village; they stole upon the sleeping dragon and stealthily bound it to an old and huge adjacent tree and crag. This accomplished, the tribe fell upon the drowsy mammoth with all their implements of chase and war. Under this rude reveille the dragon bestirred himself, and by a single mighty lunge broke all his bonds, and vanished like the wind, tearing as he went a deep gorge and channel to Lake Coeur d'Alene. The imprisoned waters of the lake rolled down the dragon's course, and ever since the pleasant Spokane River has gone fretting to the sea.

Appendix C: Coyote Creates Spokane Falls

Account by Lawrence Aripa, Coeur d'Alene Elder, 1977

So Coyote was always by himself, and he was always wandering around. And this one day he was along the Spokane River, and he was jumping around and all of a sudden he saw a camp that had smoke coming out of it, this big camp. And there were people laughing and singing, and so he was across the river, and he looked over and saw a group of women who were cleaning fish, and preparing to smoke and dry it. And there were others washing clothes. And these were the ones that were singing, these were the ones having fun. And he looked at them and we was just going to leave and he looks and there is one girl that stands out.

Oooohh boy! She's beautiful. Gosh, I want that girl.

He thought, what could I do, how could I get her? So he starts thinking about it, and then they all go back to camp. So he thought, well the only thing to do is to go to her father. So he goes into the camp and the Indians look at him: "Hey look, there's Coyote! What's he doing?" So he asks about the girl and who her father is. And he found out that the father was the chief of the Coeur d'Alene people. So he goes up to the chief and said: I saw your daughter at the river today, and I want to marry her.

The chief looked down at him and says: What do you want?

He says: I want to marry your daughter.

And the chief started to laugh. He says: You can't do that, you're Coyote and she's human. You can't marry her.

Coyote says: But she's beautiful and I want her.

And the chief said: No! You can't! Anyway, when I do let my daughter go you'll have to bring me things and you'll have to be a great warrior. You'll have to prove yourself in battle and help others. You don't do that. No!

So Coyote leaves and then he thought, Kalispels are good friends of the Coeur d'Alene people. So he goes there, to the Kalispels, and tells the chief the same thing: I want to marry that girl and I want you to help me get her.

And the Kalispel chief started to laugh, and again he was chased out of camp, and he was ashamed. But he was still determined. So, he went to the Spokane Tribe and the same thing happened. They laughed at him and threw sticks and rocks at him, and chased him out of camp. Then he went to the Colvilles and the same thing happened. And so he finally came back to the Coeur d'Alenes and then he used his magic powers and he moved big rocks and dirt into the river. And he saw the salmon coming up the river, but they couldn't go over the dam that he had made. So he stopped the water from coming down and then the water finally filled up and came over anyway.

And then he went over to the chief and he said: I am going to leave that the way it is; no more salmon will be coming up until you change your mind and you let me know and I'll come and get the girl.

And the chief said: No way! It is impossible, you can't have my daughter, you can't marry a human.

But Coyote was determined. And the young man who was more or less courting her, the one that had been going out in battles and proving himself as a warrior, getting horses and deer skins and other things to use to give to the parents, for he intended to get the girl as his wife. Coyote left and the young man followed him. And they left the camp and neither one was ever heard of again. So nobody knows what happened.

But the falls remains, and to this day no more salmon are able to come to the Coeur d'Alene people because Coyote couldn't marry the young girl.

A brief version of this legend was recorded by Hale in 1846 (4:449):

On one occasion, it is related that the wolf was desirous of having a wife, and visited the tribe on the Spokane for that purpose, demanding a young woman in marriage. This request being granted, he promised that the salmon should be abundant, and for this purpose he raised the rapids, that they might be caught with facility. After he had been gratified in this instance, he made the same request of the others, among them, of the *Sketsui* (Coeur d'Alene) tribe, who were the only ones to refuse; he thereupon formed the great falls of the Spokane, which have ever since prevented the fish ascending to their territory.

Appendix D: How the Sun Disc Came to Spokane

Catherine Pascal, *Northwest Indian Times* I:1, 7 February 1969

There lived on the prairies of the Spokan before the time of man, two friends, Coyote and the fleet-footed Antelope. They were neighbors. Coyote had four sons, and the Antelope had twin sons. They had their lodges by a little spring, one across from the other.

Every morning before sunrise the Antelope twins would get up and have a light meal and take their daily exercise for swiftness and endurance. They had packed only a light snack to eat at midday. From morning until sunset they made a complete circle of their home, running in one direction until the sun was halfway across the sky and back toward their home the rest of the day. In the evening they would reach home where their father would have their meal ready for them. Immediately after, they would fall asleep from sheer weariness.

Now Coyote's four sons were supposed to be training for endurance and swiftness, but they didn't see any point in wasting so many beautiful days just running and running. So they would leave after breakfast and go swimming in the cool rippling waters, or pick wild berries and loll most of the day away in idle play. Instead of getting lithe and strong, they grew fat and clumsy.

After weeks of running, the Antelope twins decided they were ready to make the long trip east to Blackfoot country to steal the Sun Disc from the Blackfoot. When they announced the date of their departure, Coyote's four sons naturally said they were ready too. Early one morning the twins and the four Coyote boys together departed for the Blackfoot country.

They travelled for days crossing bodies of water and mountains and valleys until they reached the far plains of the Blackfoot. They rested for two nights, watching the Blackfoot braves playing and racing with the Sun Disc. They noted the course and made their plans for taking the disc. Early on the second morning, they took up their positions as planned. The oldest of the Coyotes concealed himself where the Sun Disc fell, the next brother behind him a little, and on down to the youngest of the brothers. The Antelope twins had the rear position, together as always.

At the first opportunity the first Coyote picked up the Sun Disc and started rolling it. He did fairly well for a while, but being fat and easily tired, he didn't go very far before the Blackfoot overtook him and killed him. The next Coyote took over the Disc, but like his brother, he didn't go too far. Finally, the youngest of the four Coyote brothers took the Sun Disc. He was a little faster and held out longer than his older brothers, but he too was slain. Now it was up to the Antelope twins to bring the Sun Disc home or to fail like their friends. As soon as the youngest of the Coyotes fell, the two Antelopes started rolling the Disc, one on each side. When it started to waver, they just gave it another little push. The Blackfoot were amazed at the speed of these two; they were as one with the Disc rolling at full speed. After hours of this losing race, all the Blackfoot runners commenced to fall out of the chase. Finally the swiftest and best runner could go no further and had to give up the chase.

The Antelope twins were far out on the plains before they dared to rest and continue their way home at a slower pace. After days of travel, they finally reached their home territory. From a high hill they could see the lodge of their father and Coyote with the smoke curling lazily through the poles. They felt very sorry for Coyote, for he would never see his four sons again, but at the same time they were relieved to be home.

Coyote and Antelope had finished their evening meal and had curled up by their respective lodge fires warming their backs, when all of a sudden out of the stillness they heard a loud voice say: "Antelope, your sons were slain by the Blackfoot." Coyote and Antelope were startled, and again the loud voice repeated the message. This time there was no doubt as to the meaning of the message. Coyote was overjoyed his sons had returned. He picked up a burning limb from his fire and entered his friend's lodge. "See, what did I tell you?

Your sons didn't have a chance. They were so lazy. They shouldn't have gone. They were probably just a hindrance to my sons." With his burning limb, Coyote singed Antelope's back.

Coyote had hardly finished when they heard the loud voice again. This time the voice said: "Coyote, your sons were slain by the Blackfoot." He recognized his son's voice. "Coyote, you worthless creature, burn my back, will you? I'll show you." Antelope took a burning limb from the fire and gave Coyote a dose of his own medicine.

By the time the Antelope twins reached home, their father had meat cooking over the fire for their homecoming meal. Meanwhile, Coyote was shedding puddles of tears and burning his hair off in his grief, all the while scheming and looking for an opportunity to get the Sun Disc for himself. "Ah, I know what I'll do."

Coyote went to Antelope's lodge and pleaded to see and feel the Sun Disc. "I want to see and feel it. I want to see the Sun Disc that was responsible for the loss of my sons. If I could just have a moment alone with it, it would be such a comfort." Antelope, feeling sorry for Coyote, bade his sons to let Coyote have the Sun Disc for a moment if it would ease his sorrow a little. The moment that Coyote had the Sun Disc in his hands, alone outside of the lodge, he immediately spat on the ground. The spittle carried on the sobbing, while Coyote rolled the disc across the prairie. Antelope wondered why Coyote's yelping got farther and farther away, so they decided to look outside their lodge. No Coyote! No Disc! Looking around, they could see Coyote and the Sun Disc getting farther and farther away. The two Antelope twins started after Coyote, but he had a good head start and was doing his best.

Coyote had decided that he would get rid of the Sun Disc. He headed for [Spokane] Falls. He could see that the Antelope twins would outrun him, so he headed toward the Falls. He reached the river's bank just a few feet ahead of the Antelope twins, and then rolled the Disc into the river.

As the Sun Disc hit the water and sank, the great Spirit announced in a loud voice that animal supremacy was at an end, and from that moment on a new being would be master of the universe.

If you should walk across the present Monroe Street Bridge, at the north end of the bridge just below the small park, you will see a *whirlpool* [*nyánqʷeʔ* or *nxʷletkʷ*]. When the water is low and the sun is out, you will always see a rainbow—from the reflections of the Sun Disc. Before the railroad bridge was constructed, one could have seen Coyote, and a few feet behind him, the Antelope, where they had all been turned to stone at the Great Spirit's voice.

Appendix E: Spokan Consanguineal Kin Terms

The next two pages show a chart depicting relationships among the kinship terms used in the Spokan language. (The chart is split between those pages due to its dimensions. Some of the terms near the center of the chart are shown on both sides of the book's gutter, to facilitate tracing from any central term to others on its respective page.)

Readers unfamiliar with standard kinship charts should note that: A triangle indicates the person is male, and a circle denotes a female. An equal sign (=) means the two connected male and female are married. A single horizontal line connecting two or more people indicates they are siblings. When a vertical line connects a male/female pair to a horizontal line, then that pair are the parents of the children connected by the horizontal line.

The top half of the chart, "Male Ego," shows the terms that would be used by a male, who is represented in the chart by the square near the center. Similarly, the bottom half of the chart, "Female Ego," shows the terms that would be used by a female, who is represented in the chart its square.

Male terms (left)

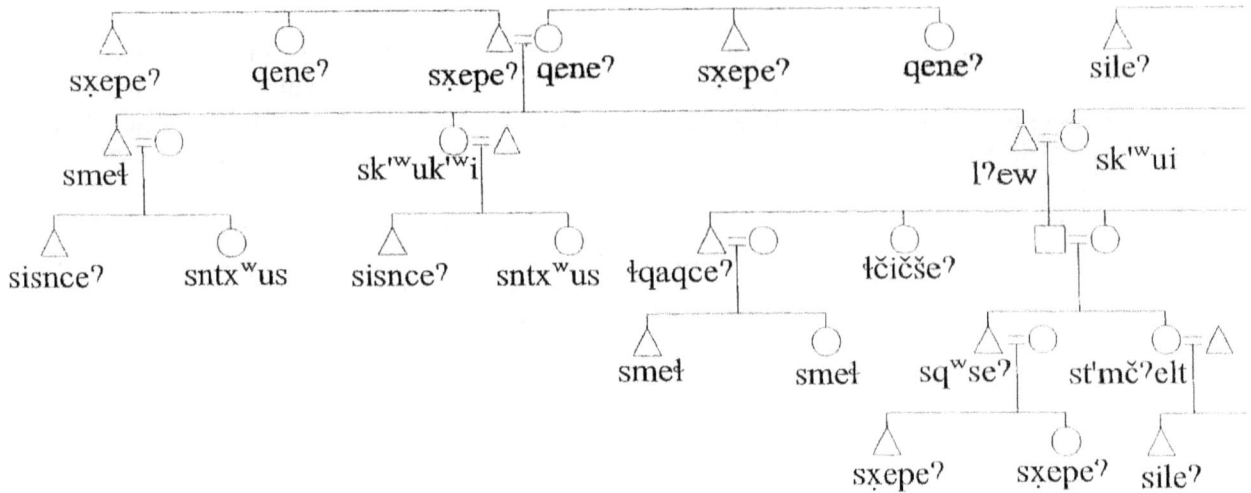

Female terms (left)

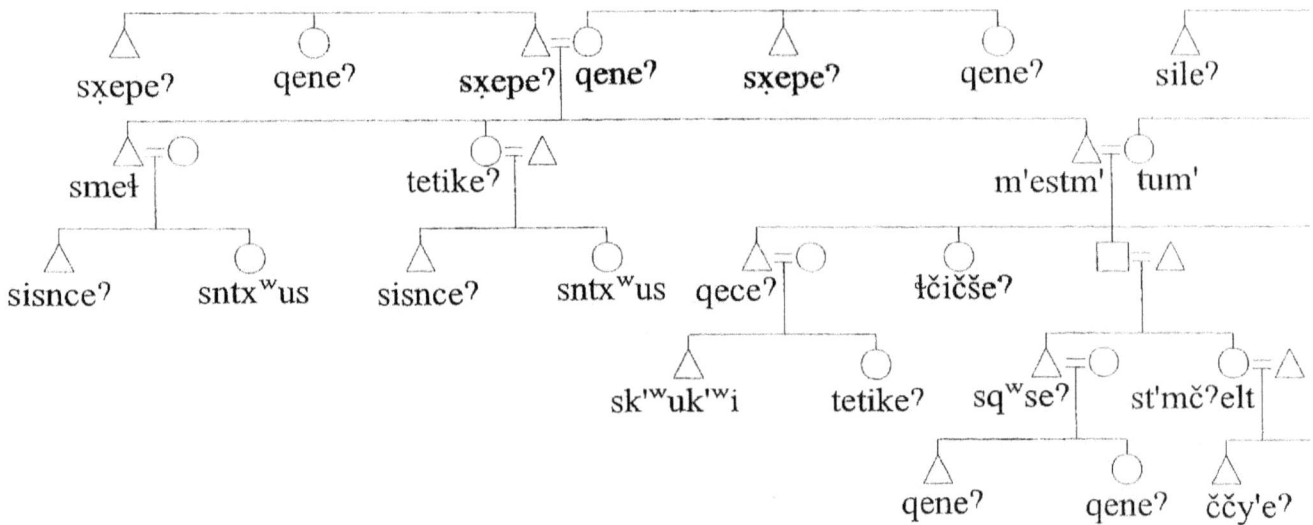

754

Male terms (right)

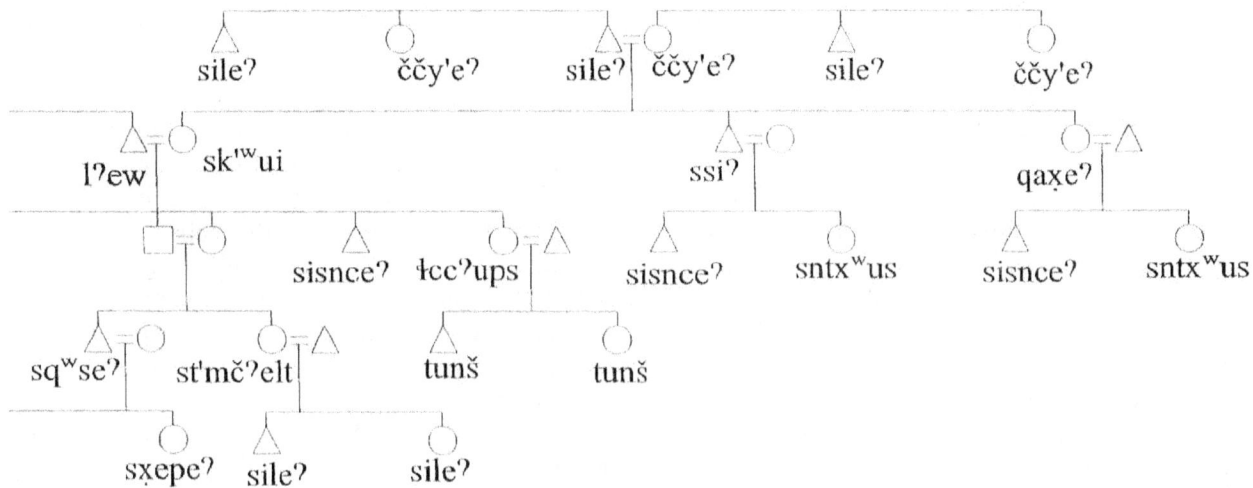

Female terms (right)

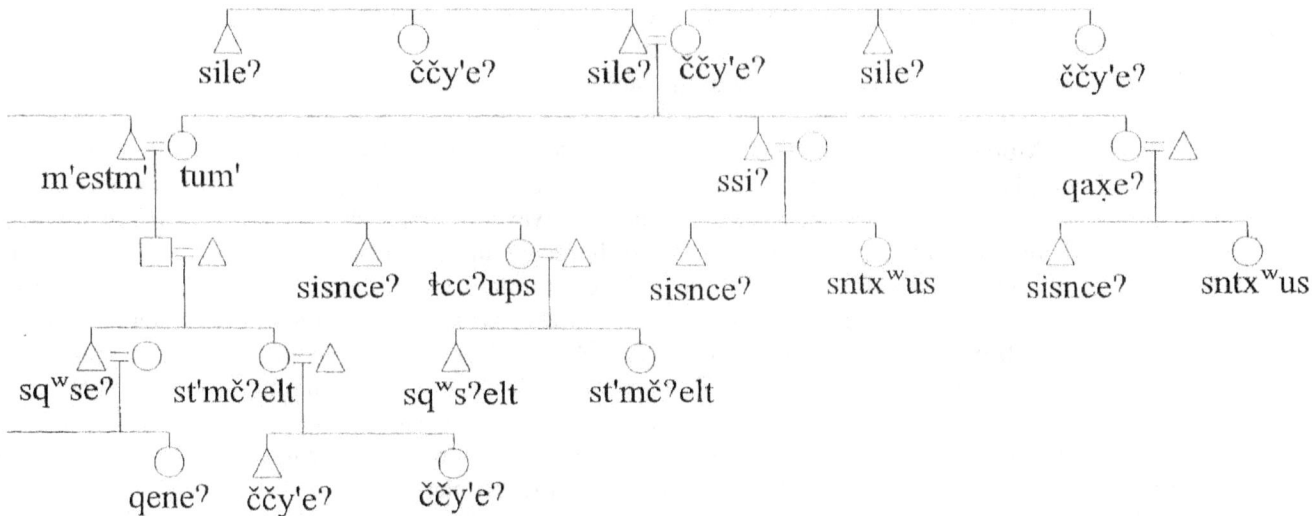

755

Appendix F: Story of a Small Boy's Adoption by Bears

Spokane Tribal History Collection, Anon., n.d.

[The bears] came upon him—one of the little cubs rolled him over—as they rolled him, the boy on the ground, the little cub yelled, I guess it was a little female, the little girl bear, she hollered to her mother, she said— "Mother, this thing lying here is a person! I wish he were our little brother [*sisnce?*]—it would be good if he was to be our little brother!" Then she was told: "No way! No way! You don't need him! Evil! He's nasty, don't you know! Bad! Leave him alone! Leave him there!" The little she-cub pleaded, begged, tried *to coax* (*čmnečstm*) her mother. All in vain. No! They finally walked away from there. This little boy jumped up quickly, moved to the side, he went around a little bend, he could see the direction they were going—he laid down—right in their pathway. Soon, they came upon him again—these same two little cubs—again, they rolled him over—they examined him closely—nudging him, this way, that way. She yelled again—to her mother: "He should become our relative—he should be our little brother!" With this, the Mother Bear came over, she examined him pretty closely also—"Well [...] if you must! But you must try hard, work hard. You must carry water. If you decide to carry water—remember how far away the water is located at—if you decide on packing water back, then I'll fix him up suitably for you both." They both said, "We will fetch the water!" So from a nearby tree, the mother pulled the bark off, she peeled it off. She peeled long strips of bark off, she then fixed it just like a water-bucket—she told her children: "Both of you, go! Both of you bring water back! Oh boy! The little cubs ran off toward the water—they ran—they dipped up pails of water, and headed back up the hill, again they reached their mother. The mother slapped, slashed her hand, she slapped the belly of the little boy, the mother bear did—the boy's belly popped open! It lay open! She told her cubs: "Come, look at him! See! How bad, evil, ugly he is on the insides, didn't I tell you?" Then she proceeded to wash him out—she washed and washed. The Mother Bear did—"He has a little *suméš*—it is tiny! His *suméš* is a tiny, little white weasel!" She washed this also—she put it back where she found it—she put the boy back together also—she brushed her paw over the boy's form, it instantly healed up—Oh, he came alive again! He went along, naturally, being family now—he ate what they dug up—of all their food, they fed him—he ate what they ate! All summer long like this, finally in the fall, I guess when it began to get cold—the Mother Bear told all of them: "Your attention, please! Let us all go to our house—that is where we will stay." They started walking—they walked, walked, climbed up steep hills—here, they seen a hole—what a large opening—this hole had! They went through this opening—hey, this is their house! Oh how huge it was! On the inside! Wow! The Mother Bear went to a corner, and laid down—but the two little bear cubs and the little boy—they played and played—as children do. Finally, they were told by their Mother Bear—"It's time to go back outdoors—let's go outdoors—the snow must've melted away by now!" They went out. Right outside their doorway, yet there was a little bit of snow—also in the dense underbrush—they began to climb up the mountain, reached the top—they went to the flat part of the mountain top—over toward the east, where the sun rises, already—it is (the ground) beginning to get green—the grass is a pretty green. They began to forage for food—shortly, they all were told by their Mother Bear, she said: "Come on, let's all go across to that other mountain—that one way over there." They all left, they went down, down the mountain—they came to a ledge—like on the mountainside—here, they all sat down, Mother Bear said to the boy—"Your father and mother, they are already camped over there at the lake—at the place where all the people are camped. There is where your father, your mother are, too. Go—it's time for you to go back to them. Go back to your father, your mother. Even though the boy protested, Mother Bear told him: "No—you are now to go back—go see them—your father, your mother!" He finally said: "Alright, I will go back." She answered: "Yes." She told him: "When you grow up, become a man and go hunting—do not kill your little sister. This brother of yours, he's the one you may kill—but your little sister here, you must never kill!" She said. "Also your little sister, this certain part of her flesh—[I can't recall what part of her flesh was named.] Mother Bear said: "Don't eat it! Whenever you go out hunting—don't ever eat it!—this part of her flesh!" When you finally retire and quit hunting—then you may eat it!" She finally finished preaching to the boy. He started down the hill, she instructed: "Go through here." He walked, down, down, he reached the bottom—got to the lake—oh, my! There are a lot of camps, lot of people—he walked forward—some of the people spied him—walking toward them—they kept watching him—more and more people—saw him—he got real near– to their camps—he began to stagger, reel around, then he fell! The people came forward towards him—there he lay—this young person! Someone picked him up—brought him to a house– there they laid him down—they brought out this certain grass—*sx̣sest'iy'e?*, this grass is called—they would use this on him—there was a fire there, they laid the grass on the fire—smudged his nose—smudged around his mouth, he finally came to, –alive again—He was revived! His dad was present—time went on—time passed—then more time passed—this was not at the same time—it must have been three years later or so—always he would go to this certain place to hunt—He was already a man! Already he must have been [...] He was already a man, a mature person! Finally, this one year, they were going to move again—he already had a wife—he was married—they were moving also— back to the lake—they went—arrived—to this camp site. He went out hunting. Seems like he'd just go out, in a short time, he'd be back, already he would have grizzly bear, a male grizzly bear! He killed one easily. Then this new woman he'd just gained, his wife, she'd start on the meat, cutting, jerking it. He told her, his woman: "This certain part of the meat—don't eat it! Don't eat from any part of it! Only when I retire from my hunting—then we can eat it!" So he went out to hunt again—he hunted—and he hunted –and every day he was killing a grizzly bear! This one time again, he went out to hunt, it was an early morning, he took off, of course there were a bunch of them, he was not alone. Meanwhile his wife joined the others in preparing the meat for jerking—they were cutting meat into strips—oh, my! She passed by the hanging-to-dry meat rack, here is a little piece, one little part, just barely hanging onto a larger piece, just hanging down—it was the forbidden piece—that she was not to eat—it's about ready to drop off! She barely brushed it, it broke off in her hand, she popped it into her mouth—she ate it! Finally, that evening, the men got home—the men returned from hunting—her man wasn't among them! She kept waiting—it got dark, night—still gone! He did not get home! All night, she waited, finally it's morning—still gone! The men said: "We'll go out looking for him– yesterday from the place we parted for our hunt—this man did have a little smoking tobacco—very little—from there, yesterday, our dispersing point—we will follow him, find his tracks and follow him." They all took off on foot—they went and went and found the dispersal point when hunting yesterday one fellow went one way, another went this way—looking—suddenly someone said: "Here are his tracks—this is the way he went." They began trailing his tracks, they went along—not very far—had they gone—they found one shoe on top of the snow—just one shoe—what of the other, it must be in the snow also laying – there, they found both—they discovered from that point grizzly bear tracks! Grizzly bear's claw-nails plainly showing not far from this, the shoes, the tracks, bear tracks were his pants—laying on top of the snow—further, a little bit, was his shirt, everything, every article of clothing was shed and found by the searchers, the only tracks showing was grizzly bear tracks! They all had to concede that this certain man had turned into a grizzly bear!

Appendix G: Boy Receiving His Tutelary Spirit
Unedited Field Notes of W. W. Elmendorf 1935-6, 2:1-5

[A] young boy, about 17 [years old] was sent up to Benjamin Lake from *stsqaistsc'łm*—[he] went up and took off [his] clothes & dived into the water—as he had been told—[he] dove down & saw [a] rock ledge [and he] swam down below there & began to smother [and] came up to [the] surface just in time and was almost across the lake—[he] had dived in early morning—put on [his] clothes & went back to the settlement [Wellpinit]—[and] his father asked him if he had dived—he told him what he had done & [the] father told him to go back & dive again once next morning—early in [the] morning [and] put on just [a] shirt & shoes & [he] went to [the] lake & got ready to dive again—then about 9 o'clock—his parents told him to holler at the water [...] (falsettos)—then he dived & passed 2 ledges of rock & reached the bottom & stood up on it—when he hit bottom he saw 2 water animals and then a voice from the side started talking to him—the 2 animals talked to him like this A *hu [...] ʔu* (falsetto)—black and white stripes [were] all over [their] bellies—called *uʔusíutł*—("the voice from the side")—he dove down there to get [his] *suméč* when the unseen voice from [the] side spoke both the 2 animals were *uʔusíutł*—the mother one spoke to him first it *uʔusíutł* said now look at me and you will see how I look—he looked & saw it—he was all covered with arrows—not a space left—he said "everytime [sic] I come to the surface people shoot at me but it never bothers me—that's how you'll be"—then the beaver [*sqléw'*] spoke again and showed him two containers—one [with] red liquid & [one with] yellow liquid—he was to drink them when he was hurt and the red (first) would come out of his mouth—then the yellow and it would go through him as waste—then *ltkú* [mink or otter]—pulled a knife out of this body and told the boy to make one just like it when he got home & always carry it with him—then he said look at me—I have these scars all over my body but it never hurt[s] me—all you have to do when you get wounded—the wounds got poisoned—is to drink the yellow liquid and to dive & the liquid would come out as waste and he'd be all right—then he said the boy could go back & make a knife like this and keep it with him always—but never hurt his fellow men—when the boy got ashore his clothes were gone so he had to go home naked—when [he] got home [he] found his mother crying—[he] asked [her] what [was] the matter— she said he had been given up for dead—[he] had been under water for 2 days—his father had found his clothes & brought them home—[the] boy wouldn't believe he had been gone [for] 2 days—[he] said he had just gone out that morning—soon his father came home & said he had been lost nearly 3 days—at first [the] boy wouldn't believe him but was finally convinced—[he] said they had told him he needn't come back again—[he] said there were 3 who had talked to him— *uʔusíutł, sqlán, & ltkʷú* [otter]— [the] next day the boy went out [and] got a piece of rock to make the knife out of—[but] his father asked him what he was making but he pretended it was nothing & and when he was finished he put it away—[he] worked every day until he had it as he wanted it—then it was time to trap the salmon—they [people] had the nets in & were starting to drive them—[the] boy would never go under where they were spearing salmon—every night they'd come back and tell how a boy of the *snxʷmén'a'i* ("the Upper Spokan," or *snxʷmen'eʔey'*) was acting awful mean there—stabbing people in the back when they didn't know he was there—they came back & the boy [*stsq*] heard them tell [all] about it—[the] next morning the boy who had dived went down where they were spearing—[he] saw a boy out on a big rock sticking out in the water and giving orders all around—the *stsq.* [Spokan] boy left for a minute & left his spear there & the others went down and cut the rope on his spearhead with his knife & and took the head with him—when the *stsq.* Boy came back he cried ["] who's got my spearhead"—no one knew—finally the *stsq.* Boy said "here, I've got your spearhead!"—[he] said give me back my spearhead—[the boy] refused & said he was going to keep it—the *stsq.* drew his knife & and so did the other—the *stsq.* Lifted up his arm & said "here, stab here"—he did & then they went to stabbing each other—each [was] right handed—until their left sides were all torn to pieces—at last the *stsq* boy got the other down & stabbed him some more & he didn't get up—then he said, here who'll come & get the *snx^w*.—the *snx^w*. Said to take him to the water & the *stsq*, was dragged down to the water & he swam there a while & made a noise like *ltk^wú* & *sqlán*—then he dived down & when he came up he walked ashore and said he was all right now—they took the *snx*. To the water too & he swam there & mimicked *tctclánx* a small brown or black animal & *nha'wátk^wa* a kind of bird—& then he walked ashore & said he was all right—then the stsq. Offered to fight again till one of them came to an end—but the *snx^w*. Wanted to be friends—but the other said for them to fight but *snx* said no, let's be friends—and the stsq. Said all right if you'll quit bothering the boys [and] sticking them in the back & killing them without cause—the *snx*. Promised to do that– [he] said he had just been trying out his power & he would never do anything out of his power & he would never do anything like that again unless in some big affair where they both had cause to fight for each other together—& the *stsq* said all right—so they became friends—this really happened—[a] generation before [the] narrator.

Appendix H: Boy's Vision Quest

Unedited Field notes of W. W. Elmendorf (1935-6, 1:50-53)

The sponsor would take the boy to the vision quest site and build for him [...] a ring of rocks and puts a robe in there for the boy to sit on—[and] he stays there awake & when he falls asleep he does so—if he doesn't hear anything he goes home in the morning & goes up again [the] next night—if he hears something (his parents ask him in the morning), he tells them & goes again [for] 3 nights—on [the] 3rd night the *suméš* tells him not to come any more—on those nights the [*suméš*] tells him how to go about *strqám* etc.—It comes just before dawn & he sees it—in [a] form of a man—when it turns after imparting information—it goes off in the form of some animal—it teaches a song [for the boy] to sing later when he needs it—every person has a different song—when he gets home he tells his folks that [this] is the last time & goes no more—he tells no one what his vision was—never does anything with his *suméš* until later—if he does forget about his experience—later when his spirit comes out of his mouth & they have to get a doctor to doctor him—then when he gets well he rises up and sings the song his *suméš* told him—med[icine] man examined him and finds out [his] *tcítsnm sumécs* his *suméš* has come to him—[the] med[icine] man sits him up when [he] cured of his own accord—the med[icine] man does not need to doctor him—he gets up & sings his song—when he is done singing he tells how he went up on the mountain & was led to house by bluejay & he saw 2 old men, one yellow & the other very old & the other young—[the] younger man speaks to him & tells him [and] after he is done speaking the old man will talk to him—the house on one side was all made of flowers—and leaves & the other part of feathers & fir boughs [and] the young man tells him that is the way he should decorate the place where he will hunt when he is older—then the old man speaks—tells him to look at him—you too will be old & yellow in [the] future—he can't get up—but he draws apart curtains & the boy sees deer & the old man sings a song that the boy will use when older & tells him things like *stłałáq'm*—then he is told to go back—bluejay opens the fir branches & the boy goes out [and] comes to his senses [while] on the mountain & goes home—this is what he tells them—the performance has no name—this might [be when the boy will] go & seek [his] *suméč* [at] any time of year but it comes [the] first time to him only in Mid-Winter [ceremony]— [but] *suméš* is always him, [and] if he is shot he goes *ntsah mést'cítm* deep exhalation and the blood gushes out & he is all right.

Appendix I: Boy's Lake Vision Quest

Unedited Field Notes of W. W. Elmendorf (1935-6, I:57-59)

A man told [his] son about 10 or 11 to go out on a *suméč* hunt - [and] the father told him "we are very poor so if anything talks to you we will have wealth—[he] told him not to be scared & to go & camp on [the] bank of a lake all night—his father brought him [the] first evening & he stayed there on a robe in the ring of rocks—nothing seemed to speak to him till toward dawn he had his vision—he went home at day break & his father asked him if he had seen anything—[the boy] told him yes & he had to go again [the] next evening. [His] father brought him again & he stayed there the second evening—[a] man came to him [the] 2nd night [and] told him he had 2 more nights to come yet & he would see the real old man who was to speak to him— when [he returned] home pa asked if he saw anything—[I] have to go 2 more nights." [His father] again brought him—toward midnite [the] same man came & gave him a chant he was to sing when [he was] older—[the man] told him [an] old man [was] yet to speak to him—[and] again he came back [the] next night—the same man came & talked to him & toward day break the bluejay took him to the house of the old man & he drew aside the curtain & there were all sorts of animals—[all] started chanting [a] tune—the tune he was to use at *st'áxʷa* [a] song he was to sing when his *suméč* came to him—[the] old man told him that [this] was the last time he should come there by the lake—when he went home in the morning—[he] told his father that he was not to go there anymore—his father said he must be telling a lie because he was scared— his father was going to take him over there again in the evening—[the] boy objected but [the] father said he was only scared [and] said he would take him back this time for the last time—[the] boy cried but [his] father got after him about it—his father brought him back & felt uneasy all the time & when the birds stared singing just before dawn he saw the same man "[I] told you not to come back here but now you're going to stay here"—[He] turned around and jumped into [the] lake & [the] boy followed him involuntarily in[to] [and he] saw [the] man was [an] enormous animal with horns—[he] sat on [the] back of it & dived down—[his] parents waited until noon [the] next day—[and] they realized what had happened [and] grieved—[they] started on [a] search—all afternoon & [the] next day—[the] mother stayed at [the] shore of [the] lake all night & thus for many days–[waiting while [the] father [was] hunting for him—then one morning she saw big horns coming out [of the water] & then [with] the boy on top of the animal—"don't worry about me, I'm alive but father will have to work hard to get me back"—[he must] hunt all winter & save all [the] fur & feathers & then next spring bring [the] fur & feathers & throw them on [the] lake & that way buy [the] boy back—[he] told [his] father–[he] hunted all winter & skinned all the birds & animals they got—[he] saved them—[his] mother took them all & went to [the] lake toward noon—waves on [the] lake [and] the beast appeared—[the] boy on it—[he] told her to throw them out on the lake—[she] did so—[and] the animal swam toward her & the boy seemed to grow fainter & fainter & when he got to the shore he fell off & died—[the] mother put all sorts of herbs together & smoked the boy with them—he revived & was a great *t'łáqʷíle* after that.

Appendix J: Account of Starvation

Unedited Field Notes of W. W. Elmendorf 1935-6, 2:15-20

[...] long ago in winter, people had their camp down on the Spokane river at *stsqaistsiɫm*—about 10 houses—people started getting short of food toward Spring when [the] snow [was] knee deep—[the] snow [was] too soft to go hunting—even snowshoes would sink about a foot—one man from *snáitctsti* had a *stsq* wife & lived down here—he was a good hunter but just [would] lay around—his wife's father was so hungry he couldn't do anything—and all the people were so hungry they just [would] lay around—too weak to go out—the Lakes man was about to die but he resolved to go hunting—[and] said he'd better die trying to get game for his wife and the people—[he] sat up with [some] difficulty & pulled on his moccasins with [the] fur inside—[and] his wife asked him what he was doing—[and] he said he'd rather go out & try to get something to eat than die there—[and] his wife said she'd go with him [and] he said no—but she said it would be better than for her to stay & die worrying about him—so he finally consented—[and] he got up and almost fell over [as] he was so weak—[and his] wife told her father they were going out & she was going with him because she wasn't going to stay there and die away from her husband—[they] put on their snowshoes and left—he'd walk a little ways and stand a little while then walk on—[and] every little while he'd stop to catch his breath—about [every] half mile [and he] had to start climbing a mountain—[he] hadn't gone a mile when night came on—[they] looked for a place to camp & found a tree with many branches & they stopped under it—[and] they made a fire & put [some] branches where they were going to sleep—[they] stayed all night—[and they] could hardly move around in [the] morning, but [the] woman felt a little better than the man, having had more to eat just before the food gave out—so she built the fire—[and] the man was terribly weak & could hardly stand—[but] they set off—first the woman told her husband to watch out for a big animal that would be lying across their path—[and] about noon [they] reached the big hill back of Wellpinit—[and they] sat up on the hill & rested & the husband said "right over this hill is where we are going to have our camp"— so they camped where he had indicated—[where] last Fall's lean-to [was] on the other side of a little creek— [and] there was a big animal across [from] from where they were going to camp—[which was] dead not long ago, blood [was] still coming from [its] nose—[and] looked like [an] elk—[and] they went over & he slit it open & got some ribs out of it—[and] not far from the fir-branch shelter—they went over there and were making soup out of some of the meat—they [then] heated rocks in the fire & and she a *yamxʷeʔ* from the shelter & filled it with water & cut the meat up small & boiled the soup with the hot rocks after wiping them out—after the rocks had been in the cooking-basket [for] some time they took them out & put in [some] new hot ones—[and] kept it boiling—[and] when [the meat was] cooked [they] took the rocks out and let it cool— [and the] man said [that] in their condition they must not eat any meat—[they] could [only] drink a little soup & he would fix the amount for both of them—so he fixed a little for them—[and] when they had done drinking it—he said they couldn't have any more until it began to make them feel stronger—after a while they drank a little larger amount—[and] in the evening they drank a little more & that made them feel better and he said after a while he'd go down & cut up the animal—[and] they took a small amount of soup again after awhile—and then he went down & butchered the animal & brought it back & stored it for the night—[and] slept awhile & got up before dawn & roasted and ate a good meal of meat—roasted (*stsq'wál*) all the meat on a willow frame four or 5 feet over the fire—[and] all day [they] did this—[and] in the evening she said she would go back with meat & feed her father if he was not dead—[she] felt normal in the morning so [she] packed & got ready to leave—[and she] took as much meat as she thought she could carry & started back—[it was] easier going back [and she] went back [the] same way they'd come—[she] got home and found her parents still alive but nearly starved—[they were] all thin & their eyes [were] stuck out—[she] started a fire and went through the same process of making soup—[and] while [the] rocks [were] heating she went & found

762

the neighbors [who were] still alive & told them she was making soup & shortly they'd have some—[she] gave [each] one [a] swallow [and] to her father when [it was] lukewarm—[and she] gave everyone a swallow, taking it around to all the neighbors—[it] took her an hour to make the whole round & then she started again, giving them a little more than before—[and she] said they could have no meat until [the] next day—[she] got up in the morning & heated the soup—[and] gave everyone a little piece of meat with a drink of soup—just enough to chew on—[and she] took 2 big *ɬitctsín* full of soup to feed everyone—[and she] gave each some meat & told her father she was going back to her husband—[and she] would come back in 2 days with more meat & they could come to where her husband was with her—[and] when she arrived at the camp where her husband was she saw some black-tailed deer lying there—[and] her husband had killed over 10, about 12 of them—[and they] ate some [of the] meat—[and] then went to get some of them [deer] to bring down to [the] camp—[and] they spent [the] rest of [the] evening skinning & butchering—& all [the] next day—[and] the next day [they] roasted all [of] the meat by [using the] *stsqyéɬts* a frame method—[and the wife] told [her] husband she was going back to the people—[and] he said to tell them to bring their camp up to where he was—[so] packed a load of meat & returned—[and] found smoke in her house & her mother squatting by a fire—[and] she told her everyone was all right—[and] she distributed the meat & told them if they wished they could come up to where her husband was—[and] that they had lots of meat there which her husband had killed—and said this was the last time she was going to bring meat down to them—[and] she went back & she & her husb[and] continued roasting the meat—and 2 days late her father arrived—[and the] next day another bunch came & it was not long until all the people were up there & all the men [were] hunting [and] lots of deer & the snowshoes did not sink very much, but the snow handicapped the deer.

[Immediately appended to the aforementioned true episode, Elmendorf paraphrases an interpretation made by Sam Boyd, his interpreter:] S. B. Thinks the women must have had *suméč* to foretell finding the animal—the man was smart but the woman was smarter yet—his *t'ópie* was alive when this happened—they fixed the place where the *snáítstcti* got the deer as a hunting camp—no name—near where a mine is today—when there is a lot of snow is the time when people starve.

Appendix K: Origin of the Bullhead

"How the Son of the Beaver Populated the Columbia River with the Large Bullhead and the Spokane River with the Small Bullhead"

Anonymous, n.d.

Once upon a time, before the time of chiefs, there lived on the banks of the Spokane River an old woman and her young grandson who was very handsome and always laughing to please the old lady. He was gifted with all the knowledge and forest lore of his grandmother and mother. His mother died when the boy was still young.

When the boy was about 16 years of age, his grandmother told him about other people whom he had never seen or met outside his village. He thought: "I have idled my time away, staying here always shut up in the woods with nothing but birds and animals for my friends. Now it is spring and I have decided to go forth to the north country where the sun sets and where snow has not yet vanished. In spring and summer the food will be easily attained. I will gather a great deal of food and return to my grandmother and the people of my village in the fall, just before nature puts on her white mantle of snow over our land, and the waters have not yet frozen so that man may walk as he would on land.

His grandmother carefully prepared for him things he would require on his long northward journey. When the sun was directly overhead, and the mist from the water had disappeared, the day for his departure had arrived but the boy felt fatigued. He began to doze and was awakened suddenly by a voice which seemed to come from the water and said: "Where are you going without a guide, and why did you not remain with your grandmother who is the first cousin of the Beaver, and who Too-mi-lax has always hated? If you continue on your way I shall surely overcome you and drown you." The youth replied: "Those words are idle, Too-mix-lax, and I shall have revenge for your hasty and foolish words." The head part grew a new tail and the tail grew a new head. The largest part of the Too-mi-lax shall go into the river which flows southward, and the little part shall remain in the stream and tributaries forever more. "I have spoken." And even today the large bullhead is caught in the Columbia River and the small bullhead in the Spokane River and its tributaries.

Appendix L: Observations of Beavers

The following quote is cited as a remarkable and even an unusually rare instance of cultural relativism by a European who not only appreciated the holistic adaptation and perception of an indigenous people, but more importantly reflects Cox's astute and insightful appreciation of nature and understanding of Amerindian intimate relations with Nature. Perhaps more critical and insightful is Cox's rather rare understanding of the seldom expressed intricate behavioral relationship of Indians with Nature.

Ross Cox (1832:127)

They [Flathead Group] have a curious tradition with respect to beavers. They firmly believe that these animals are a fallen race of Indians, who, in consequence of their wickedness, vexed the Good Spirit, and were condemned by him to their present shape; but that in due time they will be restored to their humanity. They allege that [t]he beavers have the powers of speech; and that they have heard them talk with each other, and seen them sitting in council on an offending member.

The lovers of natural history are already well acquainted with the surprising sagacity of these wonderful animals; with their dexterity in cutting down trees, their skill in constructing their houses, and their foresight in collecting and storing provisions sufficient to last them during the winter months: but few are aware, I should imagine, of a remarkable custom among them, which, more often than any other, confirms the Indians in believing them a fallen race. Towards the latter end of autumn a certain number, varying from twenty to thirty, assemble for the purpose of building their winter habitations. They immediately commence cutting down trees; and nothing can be more wonderful than the skill and patience which they manifest in this laborious undertaking; to see them anxiously looking up, watching the leaning of the trees when the trunk is nearly severed, and, when its creaking announces its approaching fall, to observe them scampering off in all directions to avoid being crushed.

When the tree is prostrated they quickly strip it of its branches; after which, with their dental chisels, they divide the trunk into several pieces of equal lengths, which they roll to the rivulet across which they intend to erect their house. Two or three old ones generally superintend the others; and it is no unusual sight to see them beating those who exhibit any symptoms of laziness. Should; however, any fellow be incorrigible, and persist in refusing to work, he is driven unanimously by the whole tribe to seek shelter and provisions elsewhere. These outlaws are obliged to pass a miserable winter, half-starved in a burrow on the banks of some stream, where they are easily trapped. The Indians call them "lazy beaver," and their fur is not half so valuable as that of the other animals.

Note: The above Flathead characterization of the beaver is nearly identical to the one by L. B. Palladino, S.J. (1894:7-8), Jesuit missionary at the Catholic Mission and School at St. Ignatious, Montana.

Appendix M: Origin of Chewelah-Spokan Group—Oral History
Allan H. Smith (1936-8:901-902)

A man and his wife and children left the Kalispel tribe and went there [Chewelah] and started the Chewelah tribe. He may have been angry or his guardian spirit might have told him to leave. He had a big family with a lot of children. This happened a long time ago. (Bob Sherwood, his wife, and his children and a couple more families are all that are left of the Chewelah.) (When the whites came, this tribe was as big as the Kalispel tribe.) After they went, the other Kalispel went after them and stayed with them. Tom [informant of AHS] knew a long time ago what was the name of the first man but he has now forgotten.

The Chewelah had two chiefs at once. One died and the other went to the Spokan reservation and died there when he got old. Only the Kalispel (no Spokan or others) went to form this tribe. The *sk'óyéł'pi* or *sk'ónit'kʷi* tribe "owned" [quotation marks added] the land before the Chewelah tribe. The *sk'óyéł'pi* lived at the falls which they called *sk'ónit'kʷi*. The first man (Kalispel) didn't have to fight to get the land to settle there. When these first Kalispel settlers got hungry they went to the *sk'óyéł'pi* and these people gave them salmon. Tom doesn't know the English name for these falls, nor does he know the English name for the *sk'óyéł'pi* people. When the whites came the Chewelahs were speaking pure Kalispel. The Kalispel language was not mixed up by the Chewelah with the *sk'óyéł'pi*, whose language is a whole lot different from that of the Kalispel—so different that the Kalispel had to learn to understand them. The Chewelah could understand the Kalispel and the *sk'óyéł'pi* because they spoke both languages. The Chewelah might have married some *sk'óyéł'pi* but Tom doesn't know. The Kalispel thought of the Chewelah long ago as being Kalispel.

NOTE: There are several versions of why some Kalispel left the larger group and went to the Chewelah Valley. One account claims the group in question had to leave as one of their younger men had stabbed and killed a Kalispel chief.

The Chewelah-Spokan Group occupied three different village sites: (1) *stca'wíla* - Chewelah, (2) *tcłewísctn* - Long Prairie, and (3) *sq'úmctn* - place toward Wellpinit (Elmendorf 1935-6, 1:79).

After the allotment of land for the Spokane Indian Reservation, the *sloʕʷtew'si* (the Valley people) were given a choice of settling on the Spokane Reservation or allotted land around Chewelah; most choose the newly established reservation, whereas some went north to Chewelah.

766

Appendix N: Account of Bluejay

Spokane Tribal History Collection, Anon., n.d.

[...] they would go there, clean the snow off, put their teepees up and get their wood. About 3-6 teepees lined up and they would put up their "longhouse." After they finish, they fix a sweathouse. Then they'll sweat for about four days, then they'll start their dance and go all night, until the day light! Then the night comes, they would start. Then finally, the other one has an animal song, gets pretty hot, one gets pretty sick and that's how one gets to be a *q^wasq^wiʔ* [Bluejay]. Then there are about 3 or 4 who get that way [...] And on his building they'd fixed is [sic] pretty high—there would be a pole up there—they'd jump clear up there, sit there with their legs hanging down—there they would sing, their faces all black with coal; from the fire (ashes) they would blacken their faces—no clothes on—just litt[l]e breech clothes—they don't eat for eight days—so they start— the first night—second night—there were 3 or 4 of them who got to be a *q^wasq^wiʔ* [...] (STHC).

Appendix O: Ghosts and Mental Illness

"What I Know About Ghosts and What Causes Mental Illness"

Anonymous Spokan Woman, 1978

When I was a child, my mother had always told us never to whistle at night, particularly bright *moonlight* (*sʔoq'eʔm*) because a ghost could grab your face and twist it. Then one would have to see an Indian doctor to make it go back again to normal.

She also told us to close the curtains as soon as the sun set. She always told us never to look outside at night, because you'll never know what could be looking back at you. Night time was a time when ghosts would be out. They would become overactive when someone passed on. This was a time when young children and babies were cautiously cared for, because of their innocence, the dead would try to take their spirits for guidance into the spirit world. They weren't safe until the dead were buried.

Many times my mother warned us to be very watchful of the dead; especially [if] it was a family member who was close to you. She believed that its spirit would try to take you with them because of the bond. She also said that if the body's eyes were partly open, that someone was going to follow that person in death.

We were always warned about answering the door at night, especially if there were just three knocks. When this happened, she would ask who is it or tell them to come in. If it was a human being they would usually answer, or they would come in. If not, then she told us that we were going to *hear* (*séwneʔ*) bad news, that someone we knew was going to die. The ghost was there to deliver a warning of what was about to happen.

My mother always told us that we were never to clean the house at night, because that was a time for the ghosts to be out, and if we didn't want to have a funeral in our family, we were to wait until morning.

She wouldn't let us play outside at night because that was the time when ghosts were out looking for someone to join them, and if we didn't want one touching us, then we were to stay inside. She also warned us never to cry—or even *pretend to cry* [*c'aqʷqʷey'eʔ*]—or feel bad while we were in the dark. Because a ghost could feel sorry for us and take our *tears* [*sč̓awʔpús*] or rub our heads. If this happened we could pass on or we could lose our minds.

My dad told me that one could also kill a ghost and the next morning one would find a bone or something unfamiliar to the room lying on the floor. Then you were to take the object and *bury* [*laq'x̌*] it in a cemetery so the ghost would no longer bother anyone. He always told the family that if someone passed on in a violent way, you were to take the blood that was on the ground or the bloody water that had been mopped up and put it in to the burial site before the dirt of the people has been thrown in the grave. This way it won't have to wander the earth in search of what was left behind. He also told us that there are more than one type of ghost. The hooded ghost—one in search of something—ones that sometimes don't know their dead, and the evil ones that cause harm, just to mention a few.

Ghosts can come to you in your dreams, usually to deliver a message. This happened to me the night after my oldest child was born. I dreamed I was visited by my four grandparents, three of them were dead and only one was still living. My dad's dad, -----, wouldn't let me touch him. He said he was there to visit me and see his granddaughter, for me not to worry because they weren't there to harm any of us. We had a very long visit. Grand pa ----- was the only one who was allowed to touch me because he was still alive at that time. Just before daybreak they all left me. They said it would be a very long time before I would see them again. That morning when I woke up I was very tired. It was as though I'd been up all night. When my mom came to see me I told her about my dream. She said they came to visit us because ----- was my first child and those two old men said she was special. Up to this day I've never dreamed about them.

768

As I've mentioned before, a ghost can cause mental illness if someone has been crying or feeling sorry for himself by wiping away any tears or rubbing one's head. The ghost is feeling sorry for this person and they see that they need comforting. If they don't seek help, then many times these sad people die or become mentally ill and then they take their own lives. Mom has always said to us children that after crying to wash our faces and drink water, and that way they [ghosts] can't take our tears.

Sometimes one's guardian spirit will cause a person to become mentally ill. Usually that person didn't know they had one [guardian spirit]. This is why the guardian spirit is causing it to happen [to cry] so that the person will seek help so they will find out what they are to do to remain healthy. Many times another medicine person has hooded you so that you can't dream and the guardian spirit will cause this to happen is if you have been using your powers to harm others or for self gain. The human being is a dumb creature and animals choose who they want to give their power to, be it gambling, fishing, hunting, gathering food, or for curing. If it [suméš] is misused then they will punish you in one way or another and if that doesn't work then they will take your mind from you. Many times that means they will leave you and since your spirit becomes one with their spirit, you will become whole.

Sometimes it is a medicine person who is the cause, or a person who knows about evil work and even someone who has a guardian spirit. The reasons are many, but here are a few examples.

Either it's a man or a woman who wants you so they can cause you to go crazy in hopes that you or your family will seek them out to cure you. If they do then they can make you or your family believe they cured you. Sometimes they caused this to happen because they were jealous of you or maybe of your children. Or maybe they caused this to happen because they wanted you for their mate even if you were already married. Many times when this happened the person would go crazy because they were doing something they didn't want to do. Their inner self was fighting for control of themselves. This is often the cause of mental illness when one's inner self [suméš] is fighting for control.

Appendix P: Creation, to an Indian

N. Wynecoop (1985:40-41)

In the beginning everything was one: spirit, heat, cold, sound, color, water and solid matter. Spirit, the greatest, formed into fantastic animal shapes which floated into the limpid whole. As time passed the great fleecy forms became active in developing other elements, such as separating light, heat and solid matter from the main body, and as the solid forms, like the earth, were put into place darkness followed. All things were made without labor, being done for pleasure and not to eat or wear. The creatures understood all things and enjoyed the wonderful creations they caused.

There was no hunger, thirst or cold. There were no selfish motives. They arranged the stars, moon or first sun, and eventually the present sun. They loved the earth.

Historically Significant Contributions by Selected Early Explorers and Naturalists

I would like to make brief recognition of what now may sound like arcane ethnocentric acclaims by some major observers and recorders, individuals who were nonetheless cognizant of Amerindian occupied ecological systems, and how human populations interacted with these systems that predated the recognition of cultural science by a century or more that acknowledged the now invaluable contributions of these aboriginal societies.

George Catlin (1796-1872), was one of the first and debatably the most famous painter of North American Indians who abandoned his law career to spend the rest of his life painting (watercolors and oils), sketching, and recording the cultures and customs of many Indian groups. He is noted for the detail and authenticity of environment, people, and material culture. Catlin died penniless.

Henry Thomas T. Cowley (1837-1917) "was guide, counsellor, teacher, and friend of the Spokanes" (Drury 1949:149) who, being quite acculturated for a minister, spoke their language and was committed to protecting the Spokan land from white encroachment.

Ross Cox (1793-1853), who was once described as a person "who bore the soubriquet 'Little Irishman'" (Franchère 1854:276 fn), faithfully recorded Plateau ethnographic conditions and practices. He was a prolific writer, which greatly influenced and continues to influence anthropological studies of the region.

Edward S. Curtis (1868-1952), a self-taught pioneer photographer, ethnographer, and linguist, who recorded 10,000 wax cylinders of Indian language and music and over 40,000 photographs. His *magnum opus*, an extensive documentary, was 20 volumes with 1,500 photographs of 80 Indian tribes. Although he was initially sponsored by JP Morgan in 1906 with a grant of $75,000, he died penniless.

Elliott Coues, MD, PhD, (1842-1899), a dedicated American army surgeon (1878, 1880, and 1903), botanist, ornithologist, naturalist, and prolific writer, was attached to the United States Geographic and Geological Survey of the Territories (U.S. Northern Boundary Commission). He was called by some the 'Father of Lewis and Clark.'

David Douglas (1799 -1834), the son of a stonemason, was an early mountaineer in North America and a brilliant and resourceful Scottish botanist who explored the Pacific Northwest and northeastern Plateau under the auspices of the Royal Hortricultural Society, exploring the Columbia River regions in 1830 and in 1832-33. He introduced over 250 new plant species to Britain and was a friend of William Hooker.

George Gibbs (1815-1873) was surveyor and ethnologist for the Northern Railroad Survey from the Mississippi to the Pacific, and later, in 1857, he served as a geologist and interpreter until 1862. Gibbs was known as the "most apt student of Indian languages and customs in the Northwest." He gathered and preserved geological and botanical specimens for the Smithsonian and studied Indian languages when conducting census surveys of Indians. Gibbs was later hired by I. I. Stevens to help negotiate Indian treaties, and to categorize each of the tribes geographically and linguistically.

Jacques Raphael ('Jocko') Finlay (1768-1828) was a Canadian-born Nor'wester Metis, whose wife was Chippewa. Noted as a good linguist, cartographer, and as a well-educated man, he worked as a clerk for the Hudson's Bay Company and helped build Spokane House in 1810.

Gabriel Franchère (1786-1863), a young explorer who came to the Northwest as a clerk for John Jacob Astor (1763-1848) in 1811, was an early observer and recorder of indigenous peoples along the Middle Columbia. He later worked for the American Fur Company. Franchère is, "Useful for correcting W. Irving's excesses, abuses, and misrepresentations regarding establishment of Astor's post at mouth of Columbia River."

Horatio Emmons Hale (1817-1896) was an accomplished linguist and artist who, as an undergraduate at Harvard, published "a vocabulary of a hitherto unrecorded Algonquin dialect" (Stanton 1975:65-6). He was later a member of the United States Exploring Expedition (1838-1842) (Morgan *et al.* 1978), and once in the Columbia River area he requested permission to remain there to conduct fieldwork and pursue his own way home, as he had done earlier with the Iroquois.

George Heron (1834-1874) was raised among Indians by Francis Heron, and later he was the chief trader for Hudson's Bay Company. Consequently, both he and his father were part Colville. George spoke French and all dialects of Northwest and Plateau Indians. In fact, he was acknowledged as one of the best Government Indian interpreters. In 1863, he married an Indian woman and they had five children.

Paul Kane (1810-1871) was a self-taught Irish-born artist who was the most brilliant of all 19th century painters, and a thorough ethnographer. His exceptional representations of Indian cultures and the landscapes they inhabited are accurate extensions of his ethnographic knowledge.

Alexander Kennedy (1781-1832) was a fur-trader and Chief Factor for the Hudson's Bay Company. His wife was Cree (Aggathas). Working closely with trapper-traders and Indians of the area, he later anticipated the dire effects of missionaries and settlers upon indigenous peoples and their culture. He made valuable descriptions of the types and numbers of fish in the Columbia River and the Little Spokane River, and the fishing predation technologies (Scholz, pers. comm.).

John Keast Lord (1819-1872), a British veterinarian surgeon and natural scientist, served as assistant naturalist to the British North American Land Boundary Commission (1858-62) while surveying and establishing the 49th parallel between British Columbia and the United States (originally established in 1846 and ratified on 17 June 1846) when British Columbia was formed into a colony after the gold discoveries on the Fraser River in 1858. Lord apparently spoke Chinook.

Sir Alexander Mackenzie (1763-1820), a Scottish explorer, made two major courageous and enterprising explorations across North America: one to the Arctic Ocean in 1789, and the other to the Pacific Ocean in 1793; the last trip—the first across North America—he accomplished by canoe. His skills and devotion were recognized and his exploits influenced Thomas Jefferson to initiate the Lewis and Clark Expedition to survey and claim previously unknown land. It was said, "He never harmed an Indian."

Doctor Charles Pickering (1805-1878), a physician, anthropologist, and chief naturalist of the Wilkes Expedition of 1838-42, published *The Races of Man and Their Geographical Distribution* in 1848. Spencer F. Baird, Assistant Secretary and noted ornithologist, herpetologist and ichthyologist at the Smithsonian Institution, once described Pickering as "a man who combined in himself the scientific accomplishments necessary to make a dozen eminent naturalists" (Dall, 1915:163). Pickering was "carried away from descriptive natural history and into the field of geographical distribution" (Stanton 1975:340) after reading Malthus's *An Essay on the Principles of Population* (1798), which influenced Charles Darwin regarding the isolation of species and uniqueness of populations.

Alexander Ross (1783-1856), a Scottish teacher, fur trader, author, came with the first group of settlers in Oregon. He had an Indian wife and was a clerk for John Jacob Astor's Pacific Fur Company; later with Northwest Company. He made word lists of Chinook jargon, and was one of the earliest Europeans to note the beneficial effects of indigenous selective burning upon the environment.

Brigadier General I. I. Stevens (1818-1862) was the first governor of the territory, and was instrumental in establishing reservations in the region; always emphasizing the importance of Indian fisheries and the rights to productive agricultural land to promote good citizenship. He always made great efforts when negotiating to achieve peace without the use of force, particularly when Superintendent of Indian Affairs; yet his defense of Indian tribes was not always popular.

David Thompson (1770-1857) was an accomplished Scottish astronomer, cartographer, and surveyor whose writings established the Spokan ethnographically as early as 1810. "David Thompson was one of the most remarkable men whose name is associated with the Columbia River" (Elliott 1919, 10:17). Geologist Joseph Burr Tyrrell, FRSC (1858-1957) described Thompson as the "greatest practical land geographer who ever lived" (1916:1), and who mapped 3.9 million square kilometers of North America. Thompson was the first to navigate the full length of the Columbia River.

Dr. William Fraser Tolmie (1812-1886) was a Scottish-Canadian surgeon and fur-trader who did comparative linguistics in British Columbia, and was Chief Factor for HBC and friend of John Work (Elliott 1912, 3:198-228). Tolmie was the first man to summit Mt. Rainer in 1823.

Captain Charles Wilkes (1798-1877), an American naval officer, was a strict disciplinarian, and despite his two court-martials, his major accomplishments were in the Antarctic—and those of his men were in western North America, most notably by Pickering and Hale.

William Parkhurst Winans (1836-1915) was an Indian Agent who demonstrated his concern for the welfare and protection of Indians in his area against white encroachment. He was a conscientious ethnographer, and made meticulous descriptions (1857-65, 1867, 68, 1876-78, and 1897-98) of once traditional ways of subsistence activities, food preparation and storage, including fishing, hunting, and trapping as well as the Indians' adaptation to farming.

Sir Charles W. Wilson (1826-1905), a captain and engineer with the British Royal Naval Engine, was secretary and member of the British North American Land Boundary Commission survey party; sent with others to map the U.S. and Canadian border (49th parallel). He spent the period from 1858 to 1862 gathering ethnographic and biological data for the British Boundary Commission, which concluded in 1846 as the agreed boundary (Gallatin1846:24; Merk 1950:5 fn) by both the ABC and BBC.

John Work (originally Wark) (1792?-1861) was born in Ireland and worked with the HBC from 1814 to1826. He was known as the "old gentleman." His wife "was of Spokane blood and a very intelligent woman" (Elliott 1914, 4:270 fn). His work was critical, fair, and objective in his prodigious recordings of Salish cultures.

Bibliography

Abrahamson, Lucinda
    1989   Spokane Tribe of Indians: Comprehensive Community Health Planning Project. Submitted to Spokane Tribe of Indians, Portland Area Indian Health Service.

Ackerknecht, Erwin H.
    1942   Primitive Medicine and Cultural Patterns, In *Bulletin of the History of Medicine*. November, 12:545-574.

Ackerman, Lillian A.
    1982   Sexual Equality in the Plateau Culture Area. Ph.D. Dissertation in Anthropology, Washington State University, Pullman. Microfilm: University Microfilms International, Ann Arbor, Michigan, 1982.
    1987   The Effects of Missionary Ideals on Family Structure and Women's Roles in Plateau Indian Culture. *Idaho Yesterdays* 31(1-2):64-73. Boise.
    1994   Nonunilinear descent groups in the Plateau Culture. *American Ethnologist* 21(2):286-309.

Adney, Edwin Tappan, and Howard I. Chapelle
    1964   *The Bark Canoes and Skin Boats of North America*. Washington: Smithsonian Institution.

Allen, Paula Gunn
    1986   The Sacred Hoop: Recovering the Feminine in American Indian Tradition. Boston: Beacon Press.

Alvord, Brevit Major Benjamin
    1857   Except from Report of Brevet Major Benjamin Alvord, Captain 4th Infantry. Concerning the Indians of the Territories of Oregon and Washington, East of the Cascades, etc. 1853. In *34th Congress. House Executive Document* 76, Report 3S (33-1) 721: Indian Affairs on the Pacific. Washington: U.S. Government Printing Office.

Ames, Kenneth M., Don E. Dumond, Jerry R. Galm, and Rick Minor
    1998   Prehistory of the Southern Plateau. In *Handbook of North American Indians. Plateau.* 12:103-119, Deward E. Walker, Jr., ed. Washington: Smithsonian Institution Press.

Anastasio, Angelo
    1955   Intergroup Relations in the Southern Plateau. Unpublished Ph.D. Dissertation, Department of Anthropology. University of Chicago.
    1972   The Southern Plateau: An Ecological Analysis of Intergroup Relations. Rev. ed. *Northwest Anthropological Research Notes* 6(2):109-229. Moscow: University of Idaho.
    1974   Ethnohistory of the Spokan Indians. In *Interior Salish and Eastern Washington Indians* IV. David A. Horr, ed. New York: Garland Publishing Inc.

Angelino, Henry, and Charles L. Shedd
    1955   A Note on Berdache. *American Anthropologist* 57:121-126.

Anonymous
    1881   Untitled MS in possession of the author.

Anonymous
    1887   Untitled. *The Morning Herald*, 7(139):3; 15 June, Spokane, Washington

Anonymous
1904   "Here's How the Stick-game is Played." Unpublished manuscript in possession of the author.

Anonymous
1904   Untitled document in possession of the author.

Anonymous
1911   *Spokesman-Review.* 23 July 1911, Pt 4:2.

Anonymous
1922   *Spokane Chronicle.* 13 May 1922, 36(202):4.

Anonymous
n.d.   Hand-written account (c. 1940) by a Spokane Indian of fishing at the confluence of the Spokane River and Latah Creek. In possession of the author.

Anonymous
1932   Salmon on move; Indians happy. *Spokane Chronicle* 5 August 1932, State history box 141.

Anonymous
1958   Untitled document in possession of the author.

Anonymous
1962   Untitled document in possession of the author.

Anonymous
1966   Foreword. In *Adventures of the First Settlers on the Columbia River by Alexander Ross* 1849. London: Steward & Murray, Reprinted New York: Readex Reprint.

Anonymous
1967   Spokane student paper of stories by elderly Spokan men and women. In possession of the author.

Anonymous
1967a   Spokane student paper on Spokan stick-gaming. In possession of the author.

Anonymous
1978   "What I know about ghosts, and what causes mental disorders." By a Spokan student. In possession of the author.

Anonymous
1974   *Cornhusk Bags of the Plateau Indians.* Pamphlet (pp. 1-17) by the Cheney Cowles Memorial Museum. Spokane, Washington.

Anonymous
1978   Certificate of Analysis for the Colville Confederated Tribes. Food, Chemical & Research Associates Laboratories, Inc. Seattle, Washington.

Armstrong, A. N.
1857   *Oregon: Comprising a Brief History and Full Description of the Territories of Oregon and Washington.* Chicago: Charles Scott & Co.

Arno, Stephen
1976   The Historical Role of Fire on the Bitterroot National Forest. *USDA Forest Service Research Paper,* INT-187. Ogden, Utah.

Avery, Mary W.
  1956   Guide to the W. P. Winans papers, 1815-1917. *Pacific Northwest Quarterly* 47:15-20.

Back, Francis
  1991   The Canadian Capote. *Journal of the Fur Trade Quarterly.* Fall 27(3):4-15.

Bagley, Clarence B.
  1924   The Acquisition and Pioneering of Old Oregon. 41, 17 plates. Seattle: Argus Press: Reprinted
               as The Acquisition and Pioneering of Old Oregon; In Beginning: Pioneer Reminiscences.
               Fairfield, Washington: Ye Galleon Press.
  1930   *Indian Myths of the Northwest.* Seattle: Lowman & Hanford Company

Bailey, Garry, and Jack Saltes
  1982   Fishery Assessment of the Upper Spokane River. *State of Washington Water Research Center,
               Report* No. 46, Washington State University, Pullman.

Ball, Howard T.
  1941   Disinterments at Grand Coulee. *Casket and Sunnyside.* 71(4):35-38.

Bamonte, Tony and Suzanne Schaeffer Bamonte
  1999   *Spokane and the Inland Northwest: Historical Sketches.* Marceline: Missouri: Walsworth
               Publishing Company. (Painting in Container 4, Folder 33 of Cage 37. Original in the Elkanah
               and Mary Walker Papers, Washington State University Libraries.)

Bancroft, Hubert Howe
  1875   *The Native Races of the Pacific States of North America.* New York: Appleton. Reprinted
               1883. Reprinted in 1883. San Francisco: A. L. Bancroft & Company, Publishers.

Barrett, Stephen W.
  1980   Indians and Fires. *Western Wildlands* 6(3):17-21.
  1980a   Indian Fires in the Pre-Settlement Forests of Western Montana. Proceedings of the Fire History
               Workshop, pp. 20-24, October, Tucson, Arizona. *General Technical Report* RM-81. Fort
               Collins, Colorado, U.S. Department of Agriculture Forest Service, Rocky Mountain Forest and
               Range Experiment Station.
  1981   Relationship of Indian-Caused Fires to the Ecology of Western Montana Forest. *U.S.
               Department of Agriculture Northern Region, Report* No. 4. University of Montana, Missoula,
               Montana.

Barrett, Stephen W., and Stephen F. Arno
  1999   Indian Fires in the Northern Rockies: Ethnohistory and Ecology, pp. 50-64. *Indians, Fire and
               the Land.* Robert Boyd, ed. Corvallis: Oregon State University Press.

Barry, J. Neilson
  1920   Pickering's Journey to Fort Colville in 1841. *Washington Historical Quarterly.* January,
               20(1):54-63.
  1927   The Indians in Washington, Their Distribution by Languages. *Oregon Historical Quarterly.*
               June, 28 (2):147-162.
  1929   Use of Soil Products by Indians. *Oregon Historical Quarterly.* March, 30(2):43-52.

Bayer, Jennifer, T. Craig Robinson, and James G. Smelye
  2001   *Upstream Migration of Pacific Lamprey in the John Day River.* Portland: Bonneville Power
               Administration.

Beach, L. P.
  1869   Field notes of the Colville Guide Meridian through Townships 25 to 36 North Latitude Inclusive. *Bureau of Land Management Survey Report.* vol. 78.

Becher, Edmund T.
  1965   *History, Government and Resources of the Spokane Area.* Spokane: Spokane Community College Print Shop.
  1974   *Spokane Corona: Eras and Empires.* Spokane: C. W. Hill Printers.

Bean, B. A.
  1895   Notes on William's Whitefish in Breeding Colors from the Little Spokane River, Washington and Remarks and Distribution of the Species. *Miscellaneous. Document* No. 200. U.S. Senate Report.

Beiningen, K. T.
  1976   Fish Runs. In *Investigative Reports of Columbia River Fisheries Project.* Pacific Northwest Regional Commission. Vancouver, Washington.

Benedict, Ruth Fulton
  1923   The Concept of the Guardian Spirit in North America, Memoirs, *American Anthropologist* n.s. 29, 4:1-97, Menasha, Wisconsin: George Banta Publishing Agent.
  1932   Configurations of Culture in North America. *American Anthropologist*, n.s. January-March, vol. 34, 1:1-27.

Berkhofer, Robert F., Jr.
  1965   *Salvation and the Savage: An Analysis of Protestant Missions and American Indian Responses.* Lexington: University of Kentucky Press.

Bernard, James
  1930   Sworn deposition. Colville Indians *et al. v.* United States. On file at Colville Indian Agency, Nespelem, Washington.

Bischoff, William H.
  1945   *The Jesuits in Old Oregon.* Caldwell: The Caxton Printers, Ltd.

Blackwood, Evelyn
  1984   Sexuality and Gender in Certain North American Indian Tribes: The Case of Cross-gender Females. *Signs* 10:27-42.

Blasser, Michael
  2000   Beaver Fever Giardia. *Wilderness Way* 6:27-8.

Boas, Franz
  1911   *Handbook of American Indian Languages,* vol. 1. Smithsonian Institution, Bureau of Ethnology, Bulletin 40. Washington: Government Printing office.

Boas, Franz, and James Teit
  1930   *Coeur d'Alene, Flathead and Okanogan Indians.* Fairfield, Washington: Ye Galleon Press.

Bohm, F. C., and Craig E. Holstine
  1983   The People's History of Stevens County Historical Society. Colville, Washington.

Bond, Roland
    1971   *The Original Northwester David Thompson and the Native Tribes of North America.* Nine Miles Falls, Washington: Spokane House Enterprises.

Boreson, Keo
    1987   Documentation of the Alberton Pictograph Site (24MO505) in Western Montana. Unpublished report prepared for Bonneville Power Administration, Archaeological Services, Eastern Washington University, Cheney.
    1998   Rock Art. In *Handbook of North American Indians. Plateau* 12:611-619, Deward E. Walker, Jr., ed. Washington: Smithsonian Institution.

Botkin, Daniel B.
    1995   *Discordant Harmonies: A New Ecology for the Twenty-First Century.* New York: Oxford University Press.

Bouchard, Randall T., and Dorothy Kennedy
    1975   *Utilization of Fish by the Mount Currie Lillooet Indian People of British Columbia.* British Columbia Indian Language Project. Victoria, Vancouver: University of British Columbia.
    1984   *Indian Land Use and Occupancy in the Franklin D. Roosevelt Lake Area of Washington State.* Prepared for The Colville Confederated Tribes and the United States Bureau of Reclamation. British Columbia Indian Language Project. Victoria, British Columbia.
    1984a   *Indian History and Knowledge of the Lower Similkameen River-Palmer Lake Area, Okanogan County, Washington.* Report to the U.S. Army Corps of Engineers, Seattle District, North Pacific Division. Manuscripts in British Columbia Indian Language Project, Victoria.
    1985   *Lakes Indians: Ethnography and History.* Report prepared for the British Columbia Heritage Conservation Branch. Victoria, British Columbia.

Bourke, J. B.
    1967   A Review of the Paleopathology of the Arthritic Diseases. *Diseases in Antiquity: A Survey of the Disease, Injuries, and Survey of Early Populations.* Don Brothell and A. T. Sandison, ed. pp. 352-70. Springfield: Charles C. Thomas.

Boyd, Robert Thomas
    1985   The Introduction of Infectious Diseases Among the Indians of the Pacific Northwest 1774-1874. Doctoral dissertation, Department of Anthropology. University of Washington, Seattle, University Microfilms International, Ann Arbor, Michigan.
    1998   Demographic History Until 1990. In *Handbook of North American Indians. Plateau* 12:467-98. Deward E. Walker, Jr., ed. Washington: Smithsonian Institution.
    1999   *Indians, Fire and the Land in the Pacific Northwest.* Robert Boyd, ed. Corvallis: Oregon State University Press.

Boyd, Robert Thomas, and Cecilia D. Gregory
    2007   "Disease and Demography in the Plateau". 2007 Journal of Northwest Anthropology. Spring, 41, 1:37-70.

Boyd, Robert Thomas, and Yvonne Hajda
    1987   Seasonal Population Movement along the Lower Columbia River: The Social and Ecological Context. *American Ethnology* 14(2):303-326.

Brown, Jennifer S. H., and Sylvia M. Van Kirk
 1966   Barnston, George, HBC fur-trader and naturalist; b.c. 1800 in Edinburgh, Scotland; 14 March
         1883 in Montreal, Que. http://www.biographi.ca/009004-119.01-e.php?&id_nbr=5360.
         Dictionary of Canadian Biography. Toronto: University of Toronto Press.

Brown, Peter J., Marcia C. Inhorn, and Daniel J. Smith
 1996   Disease, Ecology, and Human Behavior. pp. 183-218. In *Medical Anthropology: Contemporary
         Theory and Method. ed.,* Carolyn F. Sargent and Thomas M. Johnson. London: Praeger.

Brown, William Compton
 1911   *Early Okanogan history: gives an account of the first coming of the white men to this section
         and briefly narrates the events leading up to and attending the establishment of the first
         settlement in the State of Washington under the American flag, an event which occurred at the
         mouth of the Okanogan River, September 1st, 1811.* Okanogan: Press of the Okanogan
         Independent.

Bruchac, Marge
 1999   Reclaiming the Word "Squaw" in the Name of the Ancestors. pp. 1-5.
         http://www.nativeweb.org//pages/legal/squaw.html.

Brunton, Bill B.
 1994   The Stick-game. In *Handbook of North American Indians. Plateau.* 12:573-583. Deward E.
         Walker, Jr., ed. Washington: Smithsonian Institution.

Bryant, Floyd G., and Zell E. Parkhurst
 1950   Survey of the Columbia River and Its Tributaries - Part IV, Area III: Washington Streams from
         the Klickitat and Snake Rivers to Grand Coulee Dam, with Notes on the Columbia and Its
         Tributaries above Grand Coulee Dam. U.S. Fish and Wildlife Service, *Scientific Report,
         Fisheries*, No. 37.

Bullough, Bonnie, and Vern L. Bullough
 1972   *Poverty, Ethnic Identity and Health Care.* New York: Appleton, Century, Crofts.

Bulmer, Stanley H.
 2003-7 Personal communication.

Bureau of Indian Affairs
 1880   Reports Concerning Indians of Washington Territory, *Annual Report of the Commissioner of
         Indian Affairs.* Colville Agency, August 18, 1880.
 1885   Reports Concerning Indians of Washington Territory, *Annual Report of the Commissioner of
         Indian Affairs.* Colville Agency, Agent Benjamin P. Moore. August 12, 1885.
 1887   Reports Concerning Indians of Washington Territory, *Annual Report of the Commissioner of
         Indian Affairs.* Colville Agency, August 31, 1887.
 1897   U.S. Bureau of Indian Affairs, *Annual Report* (120,1:897), pp. 288-291.
 1903   Report of Agent for Colville Agency. Agent Albert M. Anderson. *Annual Report of the
         Commissioner of Indian Affairs to the Secretary of the Interior for the Year 1902.* 57th
         Congress. Washington: U.S. Government Printing Office.

Burnett, Peter H.
 1904   Recollections and Opinions of an Old Pioneer. *Quarterly of the Oregon Historical Society.*
         March 5(1):64-99, 5(2):150-198.

Burns, Robert Ignatius, S.J.
    1966   *The Jesuits and the Indian Wars of the Northwest*. New Haven: Yale University Press.

Bushnell, David I., Jr.
    1924   John Mix Stanley, Artist-Explorer. In Annual Report of the Board of Regents of the Smithsonian Institution, Offprint - from the Smithsonian Report for 1924, pp. 507-512, No. 2816. Offprint - from the Smithsonian Annual Report. Washington, DC, U.S. Government Printing Office.

Butler, B. Robert
    1961   Additional Notes and Comments on Atlatl Weights in the Northwest. *TEBIA: The Journal of the Idaho State College Museum* 4 (1):29-31.

Butler, B. Robert, and Douglas Osborne
    1959   Archaeological Evidence for the Use of Atatl Weights in the Northwest. *American Antiquity* 25 (1):215-24.

Cain, A. John
    1856   Report of Agent A. J. Cain, Acting Superintendent, Indian affairs, No. 97 in *Annual Report of the Commissioner of Indian Affairs* 1855:192-194, Washington.
    1860   Report of A. J. Cain, agent for the Cayuse, Walla-Walla, Palouse, Nez Perce and Spokane Indians. No. 189 in *Report of the Commissioner of Indian Affairs* 1859:413-417, Washington.

Callender, Charles, and Lee M. Kochems
    1983   The North American Berdache. *Current Anthropology* 5:443-445.

Cardozo, Christopher
    2005   *Edward S. Curtis: The Women*. New York: Bulfinch Press.

Carlson, Barry F.
    1972   A Grammar of Spokane: A Salish Language of Eastern Washington. *Working Papers in Linguistics* 4(4). Honolulu: University of Hawaii.

Carlson, Barry F., and Pauline Flett
    1989   *Spokane Dictionary*. University of Montana Occasional Papers in Linguistics, No. 6. Missoula.

Catlin, George
    1846   *Indian Gallery: View of the American West.* 29th Congress, 1st Session, HR 806.

Caywood, Louis R.
    1950   Exploratory Excavations at Fort Spokane Ms, pp. 21-36. National Park Service, Vancouver, Washington.
    1952   Archaeological Excavations at Fort Spokane, 1951. Ms, National Park Service, Vancouver, Washington.
    1954   Archaeological Excavations at Fort Spokane, 1951, 1952, and 1953. United States Department of the Interior, National Park Service. San Francisco, California.
    1956   Spokane House. *The Beaver.* Winter, 287: 44-7.
    1981   Exploratory Excavations at Fort Spokane, 1950. Ms. National Park Service. San Francisco. In *The Journal of Northwest Discovery.* January, 2(1):4-25.

Cebula, Larry
    2003   *Plateau Indians and the Quest for Spiritual Power, 1700-1850*. Lincoln: University of Nebraska Press.

Chalfant, Stuart A.
    1954   Testimony Before the Indian Claims Commission. October, 1954. Docket 181, microfiche.
            New York: Clearwater Publishing Company.
    1974   An Ethnohistorical Report on Aboriginal Land Use and Occupancy by the Spokan Indians. In
            Interior Salish and Eastern Washington Indians (4)1:25-142. [Spokan] David Agee Horr, ed.
            New York & London: Garland Publishing Inc.

Chance, David H.
    1967   Archaeological Survey of Coulee Dam National Recreational Area, Part 2: Spring Draw-Down
            of 1967. *Washington State University Report of Investigations* 42. Pullman, Washington.
    1973   Influences of the Hudson's Bay Company on the Native Cultures of the Colville District.
            Northwest Anthropological Research Notes 7 (1, Pt. 2); Memoir 2. Moscow: University of
            Idaho.
    1978   Archaeological Excavations of 1978 in Lake Roosevelt. *Quarterly Report to the U.S. Bureau of
            Reclamation.* Laboratory of Anthropology, University of Idaho, Moscow.

Chance, David H., Jennifer V. Chance, and John L. Fagan
    1977   Kettle Falls; Salvage Archaeology in Lake Roosevelt. *University of Idaho Anthropological
            Research Manuscript Series* No. 31. Laboratory of Anthropology, University of Idaho.
            Moscow, Idaho.

Chance, David H., and Lorelea Hudson
    1981   *A Cultural Resource Overview for the Colville and Idaho Panhandle National Forests and the
            Bureau of Land Management – Spokane and Coeur d'Alene Districts 1 and 2.* Sandpoint,
            Idaho: Cultural Resource Consultants, Inc.

Chase, E. B.
    1896   The Indian Life. *Spokesman-Review* pg. 15, 15 March.

Chittenden, Hiram Martin
    1902   *The American Fur Trade of the Far West. A History of the Pioneer Trading Posts and Early
            Fur Companies of the Missouri Valley and the Rocky Mountains and the Overland Commerce
            with Santa Fe.* New York: Francis P. Harper.

Chittenden, Hiram Martin, and Alfred Talbot Richardson, eds.
    1905   *Life, Letters, and Travels of Father Pierre Jean DeSmet, S.J.*, 4 vols. New York: Francis P.
            Harper.

Clark, Robert A.
    1994   The Spokane Mission: Nine Years of Love and Conflict. *Pacific Northwesterner* 38(1):1-16.

Clark, Robert C.
    1938   The Archives of the Hudson's Bay Company. *The Pacific Northwest Quarterly.* January, 29:3-
            15.

Clark, William P.
    1885   *The Indian Sign Language.* Philadelphia: L. R. Hammersly & Co. Reprinted in 1959, also by
            L. R. Hammersly & Co.

Clements, Forrest E.
    1932   Primitive Concepts of Disease. *University of California Publications in American Archaeology
            and Ethnology* 32(2):185-252.

Cline, Walter, *et al.*
  1938   The Sinkaietk or Southern Okanogan of Washington. Religion and World View. *General Series in Anthropology.* Leslie Spier, ed., 6:131-182, Contributions from the Laboratory of Anthropology 2. Menasha, Wisconsin: George Banta Publishing Agent.

Close, David A., Aaron D, Jackson, Brian P. Conner, and Hiram W. Li
  2004   Traditional Ecological Knowledge of Pacific Lamprey (*Lampetra tridenta*) in Northeastern Oregon and Southeastern Washington from Indigenous Peoples of the Confederated Tribes of the Umatilla Indian Reservation. *Journal of the Northwest Anthropology 38:141-161.*

Clune, Francis J., Jr.
  1976   Witchcraft, the Shaman, and Active Pharmacopoeia. In *Medical Anthropology.* Francis X. Grollig, S.J. and Harold B. Halet, eds., Pre-Congress Conference on Medical Anthropology. The Hague: Mouton Press.

Coan, Charles Florius
  1922   The Adoption of the Reservation Policy in Pacific Northwest, 1853-1855. *Oregon Historical Quarterly.* March, 23, (1):1-38. Portland: The Ivy Press.

Cohen, Felix S.
  1953   Indian Wardship: The Twilight of a Myth. *The American Indian,* Summer, vol. 6, 4:8-14.

Coleman, Michael C.
  1980   Not Race, But Grace; Presbyterian Missionaries and American Indians, 1837-1893. *The Journal of American History* 67(1):41-60.
  1985   *Presbyterian Missionary Attitudes towards American Indians,* 1837-1893. Jackson & London: University of Mississippi Press.

Coleman, Susan S.
  1968   Congenital Dysplasia of the Hip in the Navaho Infant. *Clinical Orthopedics and Related Research*, January-February 56:179-193.

Coleman, Walter H.
  2004   Personal communication.

Collier, Donald, Alfred E. Hudson, and Arlo Ford
  1942   Archaeology in the Upper Columbia Region. *University of Washington Publications in Anthropology* 9(1):1-178. Seattle: University of Washington Press.

Collier, John
  1938   *Annual Report of the Secretary of the Interior*, 1938. Washington: U.S. Government Printing Office.

Collins, Cary C.
  2000   The Broken Crucible of Assimilation: Forest Grove Indian and Origins of Off-Reservation Boarding-School Education in the West. *Oregon Historical Quarterly* Fall, 101(4):466-507.

Combs, John D.
  1962   Excavations at Fort Spokane, Summer of 1962: A *Preliminary Report. Report of Investigations* 20. Laboratory of Anthropology, Washington State University.
  1964   Excavation at Spokane House-Fort Spokane Historical Site, 1962-1963. *Report of Investigations* 29. Laboratory of Anthropology, Washington State University.

Conn, Richard G., and Mary Dodds Schlick
    1998   Basketry. In *Handbook of North American Indians. Plateau* 12:600-610. Deward E. Walker, Jr. ed., Washington: Smithsonian. Institution.

Connolly, Thomas, S.J.
    1990   Personal communication.

Cook, Francis H.
    1925   *The territory of Washington: as described by an impartial pen, in the hand of Francis H. Cook, who is perfectly familiar with the country of which he has attempted to draw a plain pen picture.* edited with and an introduction by J. Orin Oliphant. Cheney, Washington: State Normal School.

Cook, Katsi
    1984   Berry Plants in Women's Medicine. Reprinted from *Indian Studies* 1(2):33-35. Ithaca: Cornell University.

Coone, Ann Elizabeth
    1917   Reminiscences of a Pioneer Woman. *Washington Historical Quarterly.* January, 8(1):14 -21.

Cooper, James G.
    1860   *Reports of Explorations and Surveys to Ascertain the Most Probable and Economic Route for a Railroad From the Mississippi River to the Pacific Ocean, Made Under the Direction of the Secretary of War, in 1853-5, According to the Acts of Congress of March 3, 1853, May 31, 1854, and August 5, 1854.* Part 2, vol. 12, Book 2:135. Washington: Thomas H. Ford, Printer.

Coues, Dr. Elliott
    1878   Field notes on Birds Observed in Dakota and Montana Along the Forty-ninth Parallel During the Season of 1873 and 1874. Article XXV, pp. 545-661 In *Bulletin of the U.S. Geological and Geographic Survey*, vol. IV. Washington: U.S. Government Printing Office.
    1880   Sketch of North American Ornithology in 1879. *American Naturalist*, January, 14 (1):20-25.
    1893   *History of the Expedition Under the Command of Lewis and Clark: To the Sources of the Missouri River, Thence Across the Rocky Mountains and Down the Columbia River to the Pacific Ocean, Performed During the Year* 1804-5-6. New ed. 4 vols. New York: Francis P. Harper. (Reprinted in 3 vols. New York: Dover Publication,1965.)
    1897   New Light on the Early History of the Greater Northwest: The Manuscript Journals of Alexander Henry, Fur Trader of the Northwest Company, and of David Thompson, Official Geographer and Explorer of the Same Company, 1799-1814, Exploration and Columbia Rivers. 32 vols. New York: Francis P. Harper. (Reprinted in 3 vols. Minneapolis: Ross & Haines, 1965.)
    1903   *Key to North American Birds.* Revised edition, pp. 537-1152. Boston: Dana Estes and Company.
    1914   Journal of John Work, June 21, 6 October, 1825. Introduction and Commentaries by T. C. Elliott. *Washington Historical Quarterly.* July, (3):163-191; October, 5 (2):83-115; 5 (4):258-287.

Cowley, Henry Thomas
    1916   *Early Times in Spokane County.* Pamphlet, Special Collections. The Reminiscences of H. T. Cowley. From *Spokane Chronicle*, November-December. Holland Library, Cage 28. Washington State University, Pullman.

Cox, Ross

1831   *The Columbia River or Scenes and Adventures During a Residence of Six Years on the Western Side of the Rocky Mountains, among Various Tribes of Indians Hitherto Unknown; Together with a Journey Across the American Continent.* Two vols. in One. [3rd ed.] London: H. Colburn.

1832   *Adventures on the Columbia River, Including the Narrative of a Residence of Six Years on the Western Side of the Rocky Mountains, Among Various Tribes of Indians Hitherto Unknown: Together with a Journey Across the American Continent.* New York: J. & J. Harper. (Orig. publ. Henry Colburn and Richard Bentley, London, 1831.)

1957   *The Columbia River, or, Scenes and Adventures on the Western Side of the Rocky Mountains, Among Various Tribes of Indians Hitherto Unknown: Together with a Journey Across the American Continent.* Edgar I. Stewart and Jane R. Stewart, eds. Norman: The University of Oklahoma Press.

Craig, Joseph A., and Robert L. Hacker

1940   The History and Development of the Fisheries of the Columbia River. *Bulletin of the U.S. Fisheries* 49:133-216.

Cressman, Luther S.

1940   Atlatls and Associated Artifacts from Southcentral Oregon. Early Man in Oregon: Archaeological Studies in the *Northern Great Basin. University of Oregon Monographs, Studies in Anthropology* 3:16, 52.

Cressman, Luther S., In collaboration with D. C. Cole, W. A. Davis, W. Howell, A. D. Kreiger, T. M. Newman, and D. J. Scheans.

1960   Cultural Sequences at The Dalles, Oregon: A Contribution to Pacific Northwest Prehistory. *Transactions of the American Philosophical Society* 50(10):51-85. Philadelphia.

Csordas, Thomas J., and Arthur Kleinman

1996   The Therapeutic Process, pp. 3-20. In *Medical Anthropology: Contemporary Theory and Method.* Revised, ed. Carolyn F. Sargent and Thomas M. Johnson, eds. Westport, Connecticut: Praeger.

Culin, Stewart

1907   Games of the North American Indians. In *24th Annual Report of the Bureau of American Ethnology.* U.S. Government Printing Office, Washington D.C. (revised ed. 1975). New York City: Dover Publications Inc.

Curtis, Edward Sheriff

1907-30 *The North American Indian, Being a Series of Volumes Picturing and Describing the Indians of the United States, the Dominion of Canada and Alaska.* Frederick W. Hodge, ed. 20 vols. Norwood, Massachusetts: Plimpton Press. (Reprinted: 1970, New York: Johnson Reprint.)

Czorny, Dr Vasil P.

1969   Personal communication.

Dall, William Healey

1915   *Spencer Fullerton Baird: A biography including selections from his correspondence with Audubon, Agassiz, Dana, and others.* Philadelphia: J. P. Lippincott Company.

Dart, Dr. Anson
    1851   Report of Anson Dart, Superintendent of Indian Affairs in the Oregon Territory. No. 68 in *Report of the Commissioner of Indian Affairs,* 1851. pp. 472-73, Washington.

Daubenmire, Rexford
    1968   Steppe Vegetation of Washington. *Technical Bulletin* 62, Washington Agriculture Experiment Station, Washington State University, Pullman.

Daubenmire, Rexford, and Jean Daubenmire
    1968   *Forest Vegetation of Eastern Washington and Ida*ho. Cooperative Extension Service, Washington State University, Pullman

Davenport, T. Woodridge
    1907   Recollections of an Indian Agent. *Quarterly of the Oregon Historical Society.* March, 8:1-14.

Davies, Laurie
    2006   Personal communication.

Day, Gordon M.
    1953   The Indians as an Ecological Factor in the Northeastern Forest. *Ecology* 34(2):329-346.

de Lom d'Arce, Louise Armand, Baron de Lahontan
    1702   *Mémories de l'Amerique septentrionale ou La suite de voyage de M. le Lahontan.* Tome I. La Haye, les fréres. L'Honoré. Later translated and published in 1997 by International Marmot Network Publisher.

Dease, John Warren
    1827   Extracts from "Report of Colville District" 16 April 1827. *Hudson's Bay Company Archives* B.45/e/1, fo. 1-1d.

DeSmet, Pierre-Jean, S.J.
    1843   *Letters & Sketches: With a Narrative of a Year's Residence Among the Indian Tribes of the Rocky Mountains, 1841-1842.* Philadelphia: M. Fithian. Reprinted in *Early Western Travels,* vol. XXVII. Reuben Gold Thwaites, ed.
    1847   *Oregon Missions and Travels over the Rocky Mountains in 1845-46.* New York: Edward Dunigan.
    1905   *Life, Letters of Father Pierre-Jean DeSmet, S.J., 1801-1873: Missionary Labors and Adventures Among the Wild Tribes of North America, Edited from the Original Unpublished Manuscript Journals and Letter Books and from His Printed Works with Historical, Geographical, Ethnological and Other Notes; Also Letters. and Life of Father Pierre Jean DeSmet, S.J.* eds., Hiram M. Chittenden and Alfred T. Richardson, 4 vols. New York: Cleveland: Arthur H. Clark. (Reprinted in 1969, New York: Amo Press.1969.)
    1966   DeSmet's Letters and sketches. In *Early Western Travels: 1748-1846, A Series of Annotated Reprints of some of the best and rarest contemporary volumes of travel, descriptive of the Aborigines and Social and Economic Conditions in the Middle and Far West, during the Period of Early American Settlement,* 1966,7:349. Edited with Notes, Introduction, Index, etc., by Reuben Gold Twaites. New York: AMS Press, Inc

Deutsch, H. J.

1956   Indian and white in the Inland Empire: the Contest for the Land, 1880-1912. *Pacific Northwest Quarterly.* April, 47:44-51.

1976   *Foreword In Chief Spokan Garry 1811-1892: Christian Statesman, and Friend of the White Man.* by T. E. Jessett, pp. 5-6. Minneapolis: Denison & Company, Inc..

Devereux, George

1942   The Mental Hygiene of the American Indian. *Mental Hygiene* 26:71-91.

1956   *Therapeutic Education: Its Theoretical Bases and Practices.* New York: Harper & Brothers.

1956a   Normal and Abnormal: the Key Problem of Psychiatric Anthropology. Pp. 23-48. In *Some Uses of Anthropology: Theoretical and Applied.* J. Casagrande and T. Gladwin (eds.). Washington: American Anthropological Society. Washington.

1980   *Basic Problems of Ethnopsychiatry.* Chicago: University of Chicago Press.

2001   The Shaman in Mentally Deranged (1936). pp. 119-120. In *Shamans Through Time: 500 Years on the Path to Knowledge.* Jeremy Narby and Francis Huxley, eds. New York: Jeremy P. Tarcher/Putnam.

DeVoto, Bernard

1953   *The Journals of Lewis and Clark.* Boston: Houghton Mifflin Company.

Dinwoodie, David W.

2000   Review of Plateau. Handbook of the North American Indians. *Plateau* 12. Deward E. Walker, Jr., ed. In *American Anthropologist.* 102(4):918-19.

Diomedi, Alexander, S.J.

1878   *Sketches of Modern Indian Life.* St. Ignatius, Montana: St. Ignatius Press. (Reprinted: Woodstock Letters 22-23, Woodstock, Md., 1893-1894. Ye Galleon Press, Fairfield, Washington, 1978. ed., Edward J. Kowrach.)

Dixon, Cyril W.

1962   *Smallpox.* London: J. and A. Churchill.

Douglas, David

1904   Sketch of a Journey to Northwestern Parts of the Continent of North America During the Years 1824-'25-'26-'27, *Oregon Historical Quarterly.* March 1904 - December 1904. 5(3):230-271, (4):324-369; 6(1):76-95, (2):206:225. (Reprinted from *The Companion to the Botanical Magazine*, vol. 2, 1836, London.)

1914   *Journal Kept by David Douglas During His Travels in North America 1823-1847.* Published under the direction of the Royal Horticultural Society. London: William Wesley and Son.

1972   *The Oregon Journals of David Douglas: of his travels and adventures among the traders & Indians in the Columbia, Willamette and Snake River regions during the years 1825, 1826 & 1827.* Ashland, Oregon: The Oregon Book Society

Doughty, Ted

2006   Personal communication.

Douglas, Mary

1966   *Purity and Danger.* Baltimore: Penguin Books.

Downey, Tom, Darin Rilatos, Annette Sondenna, and Bob Zybach
1996   *Swakol: The Decline of the Siletz Lamprey Eel Population During the 20th Century.* Corvallis, Oregon: Oregon State University.

Dressler, William W.
1996   Culture, Stress, and Disease, pp. 252-271. In *Medical Anthropology: Contemporary Theory and Method.* Carolyn F. Sargent and Thomas M. Johnson, eds. Westport, Connecticut: Prager.

Drury, Reverend Clifford Merrill
1940   *Elkanah and Mary Walker, Pioneers among the Spokanes.* Caldwell, Idaho: The Caxton Printers.
1949   *A Tepee in His Front Yard. A Biography of H. T. Cowley, One of the Four Founders of the City of Spokane, Washington.* Portland: Binfords & Mort, Publishers.
1973   *Marcus and Narcissa Whitman and the Opening of Old Oregon,* 2 vols. Glendale: The Arthur H. Clark Co. Reprinted 1986, Pacific Northwest National Parks and Forests Association.
1976   *Nine Years With the Spokane Indians, The Diary, 1838-1848, of Elkanah Walker.* Northwest Historical Series XIII. Glendale, California: The Arthur H. Clark Company.
1976a   The Spokane Indian Mission at Tschimakain, 1838-1848. *Pacific Northwest Quarterly,* January, 67:1-9.

Dryden, Cecil P.
1949   *Up the Columbia for Furs.* Caldwell: The Caxton Printers, Ltd.

Du Bois, Cora
1938   The Feather Cult of the Middle Columbia. *General Series in Anthropology* 7. Menasha, Wisconsin: The George Banta Publishing Company.

Duff, Wilson
1969   *The Indian History of British Columbia,* vol. 1: The Impact of the White Man. 2d ed. Anthropology in British Columbia. Memoir 5. Victoria: British Columbia Provincial Museum.

Dunn, Frederick L.
1978   Epidemiological Factors: Health and Disease in Hunters and Gatherers. pp. 107-118. In *Health and The Human Condition: Perspectives on Medical Anthropology.* Michael H. Logan and Edward E. Hunt, Jr. North Scituate, Massachusetts: Duxbury Press.

Dunn, Jacob P., Jr.
1886   *Massacre of the Mountains: A History of the Indian Wars of the Far West, 1815-1875.* New York: Harper and Brothers. (Reprinted: Archer House, New York, 1958.)

Durham, Nelson Wayne
1912   Whis-tel-po-sum, In *History of the City of Spokane and Spokane Country, Washington, From its Earliest Settlement to its Present Time.* 1:645 (complied by Richard D. Gwydir). 3 vols. *Spokane,* Chicago, Philadelphia: S. J. Clarke Publishing Company. Also in *Work Progress Administration,* 1938. [citation in main text gives vol. and page and compilation]

Edwards, Reverend Jonathan
1900   *An Illustrated History of Spokane County, State of Washington.* San Francisco: W. H. Lever Publishers

Eells, Myron
> 1889   Hymns in the Chinook Jargon Language: The Worship and Traditions of the Aborigines of America Compiled by Rev M. Eells. *Portland, Oregon: D. Steel.*
> 1894   *Father Eells: or the Results of 55 Years of Missionary Labours in Washington and Oregon.* Boston: Congregational Sunday-School and Publishing Society.

Egerton, Robert B.
> 1964   Pokot Intersexuality: An East African Example of the Resolution of Sexual Incongruity. In *American Anthropologist* 66:1288-1299.

Egesdal, Steven M.
> 2002   Personal communication.

Ehrenberg, C. G.
> 1868   *Über die roten Erden als Speise der Guinea-Neger.* Berlin.

Ekland, Roy E.
> 1969   The 'Indian Problem': Pacific Northwest, 1879. *Oregon Historical Quarterly* 70(2):101-38.

Eli, Gibson
> 1974   Interview at KPBX by Rick Riley, Hank Swoboda, Elaine Melior, and Father Thomas Connolly, S.J. Tape in possession of the author.

Eliade, Mircea
> 1951   *Le Chamanisme et les Techniques Archaiques de l' Extase.* Paris: Libraire Payot.

Elliott, Thompson Coit
> 1909   The Peter Skene Ogden Journals of Snake Expedition 1825-1826. Editorial notes by T. C. Elliott. *The Quarterly of the Oregon Historical Society.* December, 10(4):331-365.
> 1911   David Thompson and the Columbia River. *The Quarterly of the Oregon Historical Society.* September, 12(3):195-205.
> 1912   Documents - Journals of William Fraser Tolmie. *Washington Historical Quarterly.* July, 3:198-228.
> 1913   Journal of Alexander Ross – Snake Country Expedition, 1824. second half. Dec. 15th, 1825, to June 12th 1826. Editorial Notes by T. C. Elliott. *The Quarterly of the Oregon Historical Society.* September, 14(3):280-314, December, 14(4):366-388.
> 1914   Journal of John Work, September, 7th to Dec. 14th, 1825. December, 15th, 1825, to *The Quarterly of Oregon Historical Society.* April, 5(2):83-115; July, 15(3):163-191; October, 5(4):258-287.
> 1914a   Journal of David Thompson's Journeys in the Spokane Country. *The Quarterly of the Oregon Historical Society.* April-December. Editorial Introduction by T. C. Elliott. March, 1914 - December, 1914, 5(1):39-63, June, 5(2):104-125).
> 1915   The Fur Trade in the Columbia River Basin Prior to 1811. *The Quarterly of the Oregon Historical Society.* January, 6(1):3-10; 6(1):26-49.
> 1917   The Fur Trade in the Columbia River Basin Prior to 1811, *Washington Historical Quarterly.* April 8(2):102-113, July 8(3):183-187, July 8(3):197 fn, October, 8(4):261-264.
> 1918   David Thompson's Journeys in the Spokane Country. *Washington Historical Quarterly.* January, 9(1):11-16; March, 9(1):36-63; April 9(2):103-106; July 9(3); 169-173; October 9(4):284-287.
> 1919   David Thompson's Journeys in the Spokane Country. *Washington Historical Quarterly.* January, 10(1):17-20.

1920   Francis Heron, Fur Trader. David Thompson' Journals. *Washington Historical Quarterly* January, 11(1):29-36.

1925   Journal of John Work, December 15, 1825, to June 12, 1826. *Washington Historical Quarterly.* October, 4(4):258-287.

1925a   David Thompson, Pathfinder and the Columbia River. *Oregon Historical Society.* September, 26(3):191-205.

1930   Spokane House. *Washington Historical Quarterly.* January, 2I(1):3-7.

1932   The Chinook Wind. *Oregon Historical Quarterly.* September, 33(3):243-249.

Ellis, M. M.
1937   Detection and Measurement of Stream Pollution. *U.S. Bureau of Fisheries.* Bulletin 22.

Elmendorf, William Wellcome
1935-6   Unpublished Lakes and Spokan field notes. Bancroft Library, University of California, Berkeley.

1961   System Change in Salish Kinship Terminologies. *Southwestern Journal of Anthropology* 17(4):365-82.

1965   Linguistic and Geographic Relations in the Northern Plateau. *Southwestern Journal of Anthropology* 21(1):63-77. Albuquerque.

1967   Soul Loss Illness in Western North America. pp. 104-114. In *Indian Tribes of Aboriginal America: Selected Papers of the XXIXth International Congress of Americanists.* Sol Tax, ed. New York: Cooper Square Publishers, Inc.

1978-89 Personal communication.

Elpel, Thomas J.
2005   The Atlatl and Dart: An Ancient Hunting Weapon. http://www.hollowtop.com/atlatlbob.htm.

Elrod, Martin J.
1906   An attempt on Mount St. Nicholas. Unpublished manuscript, University of Montana Archives, Missoula.

Erickson, Kevin
1990   Marine Shell Utilization in the Plateau Culture Area. *Northwest Anthropological Research Notes.* 24(1):91-144.

Ermatinger, Charles Oakes
1914   The Columbia River Under Hudson's Bay Company Rule. *Washington Historical Quarterly.* July, 5(3):192-206.

Erwin, Richard P.
1930   Indian Rock Painting in Idaho pp. 35-111. In *12th Biannual Report of the State Historical Society of Idaho for the Years 1929-1930.*

Ewers, John C.
    1948   *Gustavus Sohan's Portraits of Flathead and Pend d'Oreille Indians, 1854.* Smithsonian Miscellaneous Collections, (110):7:14. City of Washington. Published by the Smithsonian Institution, 26 November 1948.
    1955   The Horse in Blackfoot Indian Culture: With Comparative Material from Other Western Tribes. *Bureau of American Ethnology Bulletin* 159. (Reprinted: Smithsonian Institution Press, Washington, 1980.)

Fabrega, H.
    1978   Ethnomedicine and Ethnoscience. In *Medical Anthropology* 2:11-28.

Fahey, John
    1974   *The Flathead Indians.* Norman: University of Oklahoma Press.
    1987   Personal communication.
    1988   *The Spokane River: Its Miles and Its History.* Ms on file, Spokane Centennial Trail Committee, Spokane.

Ferris, Warren Angus
    1940   *Life in the Rocky Mountains: A Dairy of Wandering on the sources of the rivers Missouri, Columbia, and Colorado from February, 1830, to November, 1835.* Paul C, Phillips, ed. Denver: Old West Publishing Company. [His exploration and trading sojourn, 1830 to 1835 were first serialized in the *Western Literary Messenger* from 11 January 1843 until 8 May 1844.]

Flett, George
    1968-99 Personal communication.

Flett, Nancy
    n.d.   Oral History file 432-A, Eastern Washington State Historical Society. Spokane, Washington.

Flett, Pauline
    1968-79 Personal communication.

Foote, E. Barnard
    1888   An Indian Burying-Ground. In *The West Shore*, September, 14(9):471.

Forbes, Thomas R.
    1968   Medical Lore in the Bestiaries. In *Medical History.* July, 12(3):245-53. London: Wellcome Historical Medical Library.

Ford, Guy
    2000   Personal communication.

Forsberg, Michael
    2005   Hovering on the Edge of Existence. *National Wildlife Federation.* 43(6):22-30.

Foster, George M.
    1965   Peasant Society and the Image of Limited Good. *American Anthropologist* 67(2):293-315.
    1978   Disease Etiologies in Non-Western Systems. *American Anthropologist* 78(4):773-782.

Foster, George M., and Barbara G. Anderson
    1978   *Medical Anthropology.* New York: John Wiley & Sons, Inc.

Franchère, Gabriel

1854   *Narrative Voyage to the Northwest Coast of America in the Years 1811, 1812, 1813, and 1814. Early Western Travels: 1784-1846, Or the First Settlement on the Pacific.* Translated and edited by J. V. Huntington. New York: J. S. Redfield. (Reprinted in vol. 6 of *Early Western Travels*,1748-1846, by Reuben G. Twaites, Arthur H. Clark, ed. Cleveland, 1904-1907 AMS Press, New York, 1966.)

1967   Adventures at Astoria, 1810-1814. Hoyt C. Franchère ed., and Translated by Hoyt C. Franchère. Norman: University of Oklahoma Press.

1969   *Journal of a Voyage on the North West Coast of North America during the Years 1811, 1812, 1813 and 1814.* Transcribed and Translated by Wessie Tipping Lamb and edited by W. Kaye Lamb. Toronto: The Champlain Society.

Frank, Jerome D.

1975   Physiotherapy of Bodily Diseases: An Overview. *Psychotherapy and Psychosomatics* 26:192-207.

Frank, Jerome D., and Florence Powdermaker

1959   Group Psychotherapy. *In American Handbook of Psychiatry 2*, Silvano Arieti, ed. New York: Basic Books.

French, David

1961   Wasco-Wishram In *Perspectives in American Indian Culture Change.* pp. 337-430. Edward H. Spicer, ed. Chicago: The University of Chicago Press.

Frey, Rodney

2001   *Landscape Travelled by Coyote and Crane: The World of the Schitsu'umsh (Coeur d'Alene Indians).* A McLellan Book, Seattle: University of Washington Press.

Fuller, George W.

1931   *A History of the Pacific Northwest.* New York: Knopf.

Fulton, Leonard A.

1968   Spawning Areas and Abundance of Chinook Salmon (*Oncorhynchus tshawytscha*) In *Columbia River Basin-Past and Present. U.S. Fish Wildlife Service. Special. Scientific Report. Fish.* No. 571: 1-37.

1970   Spawning Areas and Abundance of Steelhead Trout and Coho, Sockeye, and Chum Salmon in the Columbia River Basin-Past and Present. *U.S. Fish Wildlife Service Special Scientific Report, Fish.* No. 116:1-26.

1994   A Design for Management of Cultural Resources in the Lake Roosevelt Basin of Northeastern Washington. Eastern Washington University Reports in Archaeology and History, 100-183. Archaeological and Historical Services.

Fulton, Robert, and Steven W. Anderson

1992   The Amerindian "Man-Woman": Gender, Liminality, and Cultural Continuity. *Current Anthropology.* December 33(5):603-610.

Fusch, Ed

1992   A Research Study on "*S'cwene'y'ti*," Large, Bipedal Hominids as Reported by Spokane Indians. Also titled, *sicwenEy'ti* and the Stick Indians of the Colvilles: The interaction of Large Bipedal Hominids with American Indians as Reported to Dr Ed Fusch, Anthropologist. pp. 1-27. An unpublished research paper. Department of Anthropology, Washington State University.

Gabriel, Louise
1954   Food and Medicines of the Okanakanes. (As compiled by Hester White.) 18th *Report of the Okanagan Historical Society*. pp. 24-29.

Gailbraith, Glenn
2007   Personal communication.

Gallatin, Albert
1846   *The Oregon Question*. New York: Bartlett & Welford.
1848   Hale's Indians of Northwest America, and Vocabularies of North America: With an Introduction. pp. xxiii-clxxxviii, 1-130 in *Transactions of the American Ethnological Society*. vol. 2. New York.

Galm, Jerry R.
1994   Prehistoric Trade and Exchange in the Interior Plateau of Northwestern North America. pp. 227-305. In *Prehistoric Exchange Systems in North America*. Timothy G. Baugh and Jonathon E. Ericson, eds. New York and London: Plenum Press.
2001-8   Personal communication.

Galm, Jerry R., and Fred Nials
1994   Modeling Prehistoric Land Use in the Lake Roosevelt Basin. In *A Design for Management of Cultural resources in the Lake Roosevelt Basin of Northeastern Washington*, Jerry R. Galm, ed., pp. 4:80. Eastern Washington University Reports in Archaeology and History 100-83, Archaeological Services. Cheney, Washington.

Galm Jerry R., and R. Lee Layman
1988   Archaeological Investigations at 45DO182. *Eastern Washington University Reports in Archaeology and History* Jerry Galm, ed. pp. 100-61. Archaeological and Historical Services. Cheney, Washington.
1988a   The Artifact Assemblage. In *Archaeological Investigations at River Mile 590: The Excavations at 45DO189*, Jerry R. Galm and R. Lee Lyman, eds. pp. 59-96. Eastern Washington Reports in Archaeology and History 100-61, Archaeological and Historical Services. Cheney, Washington.

Galm, Jerry R., *et al.*
1994   *A Design for Management of Cultural Resources in the Lake Roosevelt Basin of Northeastern Washington*. Eastern Washington University Reports in Archaeology and History 100-83 Archaeological and Historical Services.

Garbarino, Merwyn S., and Robert F. Sasso
1994   *Native American Heritage* 3rd ed. Prospect Heights, Illinois: Waveland Press.

Garth, Thomas R.
1964   Early Nineteenth Century Tribal Relations in the Columbia Plateau. In *Southwestern Journal of Anthropology* 20:43-57.
1965   The Plateau Whipping Complex and Its Relationship to Plateau-Southwest Contacts. *Ethnohistory* 12(2):141-70.

Garvin, John W., ed.
1927   *Master-works of Canadian Authors*. Toronto: The Radison Society of Canada.

Garry, Spokane
 1873   Spokan Garry Letters. Whitman College, Walla Walla, Washington.

Gaston, James Orin
 1927   The Story of Lt. William K. Abercrornbie. In *Early History of Spokane, Washington, Told by Contemporaries*, pp.162-166. Edited, with an introduction and notes by J. Orin Oliphant. State Normal School Cheney, Washington.

Gaston, Herbert
 1914   The Back Trail, #6 Interview with Mrs. J. L. Paine. *Spokane Chronicle*, November-December, 1916, 1914-1917, 6 items. The Story of Mrs. J. L. Paine. In Mr. Cowley's *Reminiscences of Pioneers of the Inland Empire*. Washington State University Libraries Manuscripts, Archives, and Special Collections. New Holland Library.

Geyer, Charles (Karl Andreas) Augustus
 1846   *Notes on the Vegetation and General Character of the Missouri and Oregon Territories, Made during a Botanical Journey from the State of Missouri, across the South-Pass of the Rocky Mountains to the Pacific, during the years of 1843 and 1844.* Hooker's London Journal of Botany 5 (continued from pg. 622 of vol. 4 1845:22-41). Retyped version, copied from the original by Harold Agustus St. John for Washington State College Library, Pullman, Washington.

Gibbs, George
 1854   *Report on the Indian Tribes of the Territory of Washington.* Secretary of War Reports of Explorations 1:400-449. Washington: U.S. Government Printing Office.
 1855   Report of Mr. George Gibbs to Captain McClellan, on the Indian Tribes of the Territory of Washington. [Dated] Olympia, Washington Territory, March 4, 1854. pp. 402-434. In *Report of Explorations for a Route for the Pacific Railroad, near the Forty-seventh and Forty-ninth Parallels of North Latitude, from St. Paul to Puget Sound by I. I. Stevens, Governor of Washington Territory.* In vol. 1, *Reports of Explorations and Surveys [...] from the Mississippi River to the Pacific Ocean,* 1:402-434. 33d Congress, 2nd Session, *Senate Executive Documents,* vol. 12, No. *78.* (Serial Set No. 758); and *House Executive Documents.* vol. 11, Part 1, No. 791. Washington: Beverly Tucker, Printer. Reprinted in 1978 as *Indian Tribes of Washington Territory.* Fairfield, Washington: Ye Galleon Press.
 1877   Tribes of Western Washington and Northeastern Oregon. pp. 157-361. In *Contributions to North American Ethnology* 1(2). John Wesley Powell, ed. Washington: U.S. Geographical and Geological Survey of the Rocky Mountain Region. (Reprinted: Storey Bookstore, Seattle, Washington, 1970.
 1877a   Vocabulary of the Spokan. Contributions to North American Ethnology vol. I, Department of the Interior, United States Geographical and Geological Survey of the Rocky Mountain Region. In *Department of the Interior, U.S. Geographical and Geological Survey of the Rocky Mountain Region.* J. W. Powell, Geologist in Charge. Appendix to Part II, Linguistics, pp. 252-265. Washington: U.S. Government Printing Office.
 1967   *Indian Tribes of Washington Territory.* Fairfield, Washington: Ye Galleon Press.

Gibby, Lon, and Donald Ball
 1997   Echoes of Yesterday - Moving 1388 Indian Graves. *Pacific Northwestern Quarterly* 41(4):52-56.

Gibson, Arrell Morgan
1980   *The American Indian: Prehistory to the Present.* Lexington, Massachusetts: D. C. Heath and Company.

Gidley, M.
1979   *With One Sky Above Us: Life on an Indian Reservation at the Turn of the Century.* New York: G. P. Putnam's Sons.

Gilbert, C. H., and B. W. Evermann
1895   A Report Upon Investigations in the Columbia River Basin, With Descriptions of Four New Species. *Bulletin of U.S. Fish Commission* 14:169-207.

Gilbert, Cathy A.
1984   The Historic Landscape of Fort Spokane: A Design Proposal. U.S. National Park Service.

Gile, Albion
1955   Notes on Columbia River Salmon. In *Oregon Historical Quarterly.* March, 56:140-53).

Glick, Leonard B.
1967   Medicine as an Ethnographic Category: The Gimi of the New Guinea Highlands. In *Ethnology* 6:31-56.

Glover, James N.
1927   The Reminiscences of James N. Glover. pp. 85-145. *The Early History of Spokane, Washington, Told by Contemporaries.* Orvin Oliphant, ed. Fairfield, Washington: Ye Galleon Press.
1985   *Reminiscences of James N. Glover.* Based on Interviews from the *Spokane Chronicle.* Fairfield, Washington: Ye Galleon Press.

Glover, Richard, ed.
1962   David Thompson's Narrative of His Explorations in Western America, 1784-1812. A new edition with added material [...]. Richard Glover, ed. Publications of the Champlain Society, 40:209-239; 375-398. Toronto: The Champlain Society. (Orig. pub: Joseph B. Tyrrell, ed. The Toronto Society, Toronto, 1916.)

Glover, Sheldon L.
1941   Clays and Shales of Washington. Bulletin No. 24. Olympia: Department of Conservation and Development. Olympic State Printing Plant.

Gottfred, Angela
1991   The Canadian Capot (Capote). *Journal of the Fur Trade Quarterly.* Fall 27 (3):4-17
1995   Art. II. *Femmes du Pays:* Women of the Fur Trade, 1774-1821. *The Northwest Journal* or *Transactions of the Northwest Brigade Club* 12:1-16. Calgary.

Gough, Stan
2005-8 Personal communication.

Gould, Harold A.
1965   Modern Medicine and Folk Cognition in Rural India. *Human Organization.* 24:201-208).

Graham, Thomas
1929   Steven County Fifty Years Ago. Unpublished manuscript in possession of the author.

Grant, Frank, ed.
1994   *A Forest and A Tribe in Transition: A History of the Spokane Indian Reservation Forest 1870-1994*. Frank Grant, ed. Missoula: Historical Research Associated, Inc.

Griswald, Gilbert
1970   Aboriginal Patterns of Trade Between the Columbia Basin and the Northern Plains. *Archaeology in Montana* 11(2-3):1-96. Missoula. (Original issued as the author's M.A. thesis in Anthropology, Montana State University, Missoula, 1953.)

Grover, C.
1855   *Final Report of Lieutenant C. Grover. By Isaac I. Stevens. Reports of His Examinations on a Trip from the Headwaters of the Missouri to the Dalles of the Columbia. Explorations and Surveys to Ascertain the most Practical Economic Route for a Railroad from the Mississippi River to the Pacific Ocean* 1:498-515. 33d Congress, 2d Session, Senate Executive Document 78 (Serial No. 758). Washington: Tucker, Printer.

Guerra, Francisco
1971   *The pre-Columbian mind: A study in the aberrant nature of sexual drives, drugs affecting behavior, and the attitude towards life and death, with a survey of psychotherapy, in pre-Columbian America*. London: Seminar Press.

Gunther, Erna
1950   The Indian Background of Washington History. *Pacific Northwest Quarterly*. July, 41(1):189-212.

Gwydir, R. D.
1907   Prehistoric Spokane–An Indian Legend. *Washington Historical Quarterly*. April, 1(3):136-37.
1917   A Record of the San Poil Indians. *Washington Historical Quarterly*. October, 8(4):243-250.

Haas, Theodore H.
1957   The Legal Aspects of Indian Affairs from 1887 to 1957. In American Indians and American Life. ed., George E. Simpson [and] J. Milton Yinger. *The Annuals of Political and Social Science of the American Academy*. May, 311:12-22. Philadelphia.

Hahn, Robert A., and Arthur Kleinman
1983   Belief as Pathogen, Belief as Medicine. *Medical Anthropological Quarterly*. August, 14, (4):3,16-19.

Haines, Guy
1879   Letter to John A. Simms, 3 March. File 12, Box 1, Cage 213, Holland Library Archives, Washington State University, Pullman.

Haines, D. Francis, Jr.
1938   Where Did the Plains Indians Get Their Horses? *American Anthropologist,* n.s. 40(1)112-117. Mensha, Wisconsin: Banta Publishing Agent.
1938a   The Northward Spread of Horses among the Plains Indians. *American Anthropologist,* n.s. 40(3):429-437. Mensha, Wisconsin: Banta Publishing Agent.
1940   The Western Limits of the Buffalo Range. *Washington Historical Quarterly*. October, 31:389-398.
1950   Problems of Indian Policy. *Pacific Northwest Quarterly*. July, 41 (3):203-212.
1955   *The Nez Perces: Tribesmen of the Columbia Plateau*. Norman: University of Oklahoma Press.

Hale, Horatio Emmons
  1846   *Ethnography and Philology. (With Map.). vol. 6 of United States Exploring Expedition During the Years 1838, 1839, 1840, 1841, 1842, Under the Command of Charles Wilkes, U.S.N.*, 5 vols. Philadelphia: Lea & Blanchard. (Reprinted 1968 by Gregg Press, Ridgewood, N. J.)

Hallowell, A. Irving
  1935   Discussion and Correspondence: Primitive Concepts of Disease. *American Anthropologist*, n.s. 37, No. (2) Part 1 (April - June), pp. 365-368.
  1977   The Social Function of Anxiety in a Primitive Society, pp. 132-138. In *Culture, Disease, and Healing: Studies in Medical Anthropology*, ed., David Landy. New York: Macmillan Publishing Co., Inc.

Hansen, C. E., Jr.
  1972   Castoreum, Butcher Knives as Historical Sources; Trade Goods in Ojo Indian Costumes. *Museum of the Fur Trade Quarterly*. Spring, 8:1-4.

Harman, Denham
  1992   Native American Medicine. *Energy Times*, 2(4):39-40.

Harvard, V.
  1895   Food Plants of the American Indians. *Bulletin of the Torrey Botanical Club* 22:98-123.

Harvey, George W.
  1874   Letter from G. A. Harvey, Farmer, to J. A. Simms, Special Indian Agent, 30 April 1874. *Records of the Bureau of Indian Affairs*, Washington Superintendency.

Hayden, Brian, and Rick Schulting
  1997   The Plateau Interaction Sphere and late Prehistoric Cultural Complexity. *American Antiquity*. January, 62(1):51-85.

Helman, Cecil G.
  2000   *Culture, Health, and Illness.* Oxford: Butterworth-Heinemann

Henry, Alexander
  1897   *New Light on the Early History of the Greater Northwest: The Manuscript Journals of Alexander, Fur Trader of the Northwest Company, and of David Thompson, Official Geographer and Explorer of the Same Company, 1799-1814, Exploration and Adventure among the Indians on the Red, Saskatchewan, Missouri, and Columbia Rivers, vol. 2. The Saskatchewan and Columbia Rivers.* Elliott Coues, ed. 3 vols. New York: Francis P. Harper.
  1901   Travels and Adventures in Canada and the Indian Territories Between the Years 1760 and 1776. Boston: Little Brown.

Hensold, Theodore
  2001   Personal communication.

Hewes, Gordon W.
  1973   Indian Fisheries Productivity in Precontact Times in the Pacific Salmon Area. *Northwest Anthropological Research Notes* 7(2):133-55. Moscow, Idaho.
  1998   Fishing. *Handbook of North American Indians*, Plateau 12:620-52. Deward E. Walker, Jr. ed., Washington: Smithsonian Institution.

Himes, George H.
   1913   Letters of Burr Osborn, Survivor of the Howison Exhibition to Oregon, 1846. *Quarterly of the Oregon Historical Society*. December, 14 (2):355-65.

Himmelberg, Claudia
   n.d.   Bluejay Dancers. Unpublished manuscript in possession of the author. Colville Historical Society Museum, Stevens County, Washington.
   1997   Letter from Dr Allan H. Smith to Claudia Himmelberg concerning Chewelah-Spokan Group.

Hitchcock, C. Leo, and Arthur Cronquist
   1981   *Flora of the Pacific Northwest: An Illustrated Manual*. Seattle: University of Washington Press.

Hocart, A. H.
   1952   *The Life-Giving Myth*. London: Methuen

Hodge, Frederick Webb, ed.
   1912   *Handbook of American Indians North of Mexico*. Smithsonian Institution, Bureau of American Ethnology, Bulletin 30. Two vols. Second Impression. Washington: U.S. Government Printing Office. Republished 1968. Grosse Pointe, Michigan: Scholarly Press.

Holbrook, Stewart H.
   1956   *The Columbia*. New York: Rinehart and Company, Inc.

Holden, Edward Singleton
   1898   *A Catalogue of Earthquakes on the Pacific Coast 1796-1897*. vol. 37, No. 5. Washington: Smithsonian Institution Miscellaneous Collections, 1087.

Holder, A. B.
   1889   The Bote: Description of a particular sexual perversion found among North American Indians. In *New York Medical Journal*, 50(23):623-5).

Holder, Preston
   1958   A survey of published primary and secondary research by early historians and observers, type recorded on six hundred 5X7 cards with attached 8X11 typed sheets. In possession of the author.

Holmes, Kenneth L.
   1955   Mount St. Helens' Recent Eruption. *Oregon Historical Quarterly*. September 55(3):197-211.

Hough, Walter
   1890   Fire as an Agent in Human Culture. *Bulletin of the United States National Museum*; 139. Washington, D.C. U.S. Printing Office, reprinted in 1926.

Howard, Helen
   1980   Spokan. *Dictionary of Indian Tribes of the Americas* 3:316-21. Newport Beach: American Indian Publishers, Inc.

Howay, F. W., William S. Lewis, and Jacob A. Meyers, eds.
   1917   Angus McDonald: A Few Items of the West. *Washington Historical Quarterly*. July 8(3):188-229.

Howison, Neil M.
  1913   Report of Lieutenant Neil M. Howison on Oregon, 1846. A reprint. *The Quarterly of the Oregon Historical Society.* March 1913-December 1913, 14:1-60.

Hudson, Lorelea, S. Boswell, C. D. Carley, W. Choquette, C. Miss, D. Chance, and M. A. Stamper
  1981   *A Cultural Resource Overview for the Colville and Idaho Panhandle National Forests and the Bureau of Land Management - Spokane and Coeur d'Alene Districts Northeastern Washington/Northern Idaho.* 2 vols. in 3. Sandpoint, Idaho: Cultural Resource Consultants.

Hulbert, Archer Butler, and Dorothy Printup Hulbert, eds.
  1936   *Marcus Whitman, Crusader. 3 Pts. Pt. 1: 1802 to 1839; Pt. 2: 1839 to 1843; Pt. 3: 1843-1847. Overland to the Pacific 6, 7, and 8.* Denver: The Stewart Commission of Colorado College and The Denver Public Library.

Hunn, Eugene S.
  1990   The Plateau Culture Area. In *Native North Americans: An Ethnological Approach.* Daniel Boxberger, ed. pp. 361-82. Dubuque: Kendall/Hunt Publishing Company.

Hunn, Eugene S., and David French
  1981   Lomatium: A Key Resource For Columbia Plateau Native Subsistence. Northwest Science 55(2):87-94.

Hunn, Eugene S., Nancy J. Turner, and David H. French
  1998   Ethnobiology and Subsistence. In *Handbook of North American Indians. Plateau* 12:525-545. Deward E. Walker, Jr., ed. Washington: Smithsonian Institution.

Hunt, Claire
  1916a   South Half or Diminished Colville Indian Reservation: General Description of the Climate, Soil, Products, and the Habits and Characteristics of Indian Inhabitants. Published by the author, Kettle Falls, Washington.
  1936   Manuscript on file with Dellwo, Rudolf, and Schroeder, P. S. Spokane, Washington.

Hunt, Garrett B.
  1966   Indian Wars of the Inland Empire. Reprinted by Spokane Community College Library, Spokane, Washington.

Hunt, H. F.
  1918   Slavery Among the Indians of Northwest America. *Washington Historical Quarterly.* October, 9(4):277-283.

Ingles, Lloyd G.
  1965   *Mammals of the Pacific States.* Stanford: Stanford University Press.

Irving, Washington
  1836   *The Adventures of Captain Bonneville, U.S. A. in the Rocky Mountains and the Far West.* New York: G. P. Putman. (Several reprints, incl: 1850, 1851, 1868; also edited by Edgeley W. Todd, University of Oklahoma Press, 1961; and, Twayne, New York, 1977.)
  1843   *The Rocky Mountains: or, Scenes, Incidents, and Adventures in the Far West; Digested from the Journal of Captain B. L. E. Bonneville, of the Army of the United States, and Illustrated from Various Other Sources.* In two vols., vol. 1. Philadelphia: Lea. & Blanchard.
  1851   *Adventures of Captain Bonneville.* New York: G. P. Putman.

Ispasescu, Dr. de Mihai
  1968   Unpublished manuscript in possession of the author.

Jilek, Wolfgang George
  1974   Salish Indian Mental Health and Culture Change. *Toronto: Holt, Rinehart and Winston.*
  1982   *Indian Healing: Shamanic Ceremonialism in the Pacific Northwest Today.* Blaine: Hancock
            House Publishers Ltd.

Johnson, Alice M.
  1972   *Dictionary of Canadian Biography* 10:1871-1880. Toronto: University of Toronto Press.

Johnson, Olga Weydemeyer
  1969   Flathead and Kootnay: The Rivers, the Tribes and the Region's Traders. *Northwest Historical
            Series* 9. Glendale, California: Arthur H. Clark.

Jorgensen, Joseph G.
  1969   Salish Language and Culture. Bloomington: Indiana University Press.

Joseph, Alice
  1942   Physician and Patient: Some Aspects of Inter-Personal Relations and Patients, with Special
            Regard to the Relationships Between White Physicians and Indian Patients. *Applied
            Anthropology* 1(4):1-6).

Josephy, Alvin M., Jr.
  1965   *The Nez Perce Indians and the Opening of the Northwest.* New Haven, Connecticut: Yale
            University Press.

Joset, Joseph
  1860   *Rocky Mountains: The History of the Colville Mission.* Translated from the French by Bernard
            Thomas. Manuscript, Joseph Jost Papers, Oregon Provincial Archives of the Society Jesus,
            Foley Library, Gonzaga University, Spokane.

Kane, Paul
  1859   *Wanderings of an Artist Among the Indians of North America, from Canada to Vancouver's
            Island and Oregon Through the Hudson's Bay Company's Territory and Back Again.*
            Edmonton, Canada: M. G. Hurtig Ltd. Reprinted 1968 by Charles E. Tuttle Co. Publishers,
            Rutland, Vermont.
  1925   *Master-Works of Canadian Authors.* 25 vols., ed., John W. Garvin, vol. 7. Introduction and
            Notes by Lawrence J. Burpee. Toronto: The Radisson Society of Canada Limited.
  1971   Paul Kane's frontier: including Wanderings of an artist among the Indians of North America by
            Paul Kane; edited with a biographical introduction and a catalogue raisonné by J. Russell
            Harper. Austin: Published for the Amon Carter Museum, Fort Worth, and the National Gallery
            of Canada by the University of Texas, c. 1971.

Kappler, Charles J., ed.
  1904-41   *Indian Affairs: Laws and Treaties.* 5 vols. (vol. 2, 1904) 446, 449, 453, 662, 670-1, 682, 694-5,
            699, 720. Washington: U.S. Government Printing Office.
  1913   Indian Affairs: Laws and Treaties. vol. III (Laws), 116, 170, 754, 1:925. 62nd Congress, 2nd
            Session, Senate Executive Document No. 719. Washington: U.S. Government Printing Office.

Keane, Robert E., Stephen F. Arno, and James K. Brown
    1990   Simulating Cumulative Fire Effects in Ponderosa Pine/Douglas-Fir Forests. *Ecology* 71(1):189-203.

Keeler, Robert W.
    1973   An Upland Hunting Camp on the North Fork of the Clearwater River, North-Central Idaho. *Occasional Papers of the Idaho State University Museum* 30. Pocatello.

Keenan, J.
    1997   Coeur d'Alene War of 1958. In *Encyclopedia of American Indian Wars: 1492-1890.* Santa Barbara: ABC-CLIO, Inc.

Kendeigh, S. C.
    1964   *Animal Ecology.* Englewood Cliffs: Prentice Hall.

Kennedy, Alexander
    1823   Spokan House Report 1822-23. Manuscript B. 208/e/1, in Hudson's Bay Company Archives, Provincial Archives of Manitoba, Winnipeg.

Kennedy, Dorothy
    1984   The Quest for a Cure: A Case Study in the Use of Health Care Alternatives. *Culture* 4(2):21-31.

Kennedy, Dorothy, and Randy Bouchard
    1998   Northern Okanagan, Lakes, and Colville. *Handbook of North American Indians*, *Plateau* 12:238-252. Deward E. Walker, Jr., ed. Washington: Smithsonian Institution.

Keyser, James D.
    1992   *Indian Rock Art of the Columbia Plateau.* Seattle: University of Washington Press.

Kingston, C. S.
    1923   Introduction of Cattle in the Northwest. *Washington Historical Quarterly.* July, 14(3):163-175.
    1932   Buffalo in the Pacific Northwest. *Washington Historical Quarterly.* July, 23(3):163-172.
    1950   Mr. Cowley's Reminiscences. MS #89024 on file with Dellwo, Rudolf, and Schroeder, P. S. Spokane, Washington.

Kip, Lawrence
    1859   *Army Life of the Pacific; A Journal of the Expedition Against the Northern Indians, The Tribes of the Coeur d'Alenes, Spokans, and Palouzes, in the Summer of 1858.* New York: Redfield.

Kirk, Donald
    1975   *Wild Edible Plants of the Western States.* Healdsburg, California: Naturegraph Publishers, Inc.

Kleinman, Leonard A.
    1978   International Health Care Planning from an Ethnomedical Perspective. In *Medical Anthropology.* Spring, Part 4, 2:71-96.

Knudson, Ruthann
    1978   The Columbia Plateau: Foods and Trade. *Journal of Forestry* 78(9):542-45.
    1982   Ancient Peoples of the Columbia Plateau. *Landmarks* Spring, pp. 31-32.

Koch, D. L.
    1976   Estimate of the size of the salmon and steelhead trout populations of the upper Columbia River, 1872-1939. The Confederate Tribes on the Colville Reservation *v*. the United States of America. Indian Claims Commission. Docket No. 181-C.

Kohnen, Patricia
    2007   *At the End of the Trail: Clackamas County, Oregon.*
            http://www.usgennet.org/usa/or/county/clackamas/

Kozlowski, T. T., and C. E. Ahlgren, eds.
    1974   *Fire and Ecosystems.* New York: Academic Press.

Kranz, Grover
    1971   Personal communication.

Krieger, Herbert W.
    1928   Prehistoric Inhabitants of the Columbia River Valley. *Smithsonian Institution, Explorations and Field-Work*, 1927, pp. 133-40. [Smithsonian Publication 2957]. Washington

Kroeber, Albert. L.
    1939   Cultural and Natural Areas of Native America. *University of California Publications in American Archaeology and Ethnology* 38:1-242, Berkeley and Los Angeles: University of California Press.
    1952   *The Nature of Culture.* Chicago: University of Chicago Press.

La Farge, Oliver
    1940   *As Long as the Grass Shall Grow.* New York: Alliance Book Company.

Lahren, Sylvester L.
    1998   Kalispel. *Handbook of North American Indians. Plateau.* 12:283-96. Deward E. Walker, Jr., ed. Washington: Smithsonian Institution.
    1998a   Reservations and Treaties. *Handbook of North American Indians. Plateau* 12:484-98. Deward E. Walker, Jr., ed. Washington: Smithsonian Institution.

Landeen, Dan, and Allen Pickham
    1999   *Salmon and His People: Fish & Fishing in Nez Perce Culture*. Lewiston, Idaho: Confluence Press.

Landy, David
    1974   Role Adaptation: Traditional Curers under the Impact of Western Medicine. In *American Ethnologist*. February, 1:103-127.
    1977   Role Adaptation: Traditional Curers under the Impact of Western Medicine, pp. 468-480. In *Culture, Disease and Healing*. David Landy, ed., New York: John Wiley and sons.
    1978   Role Adaptation: Traditional Curers Under the Impact of Western Medicine, pp. 217-241. In *Health and the Human Condition: Perspectives on Medical Anthropology.* North Scituate: Duxbury Press.

Lantz, Trevor C., Kristina Swerhun, and Nancy J. Turner
    2004   Devil's Club (*Oplopanaax horridum*): An Ethnobotanical Review. *The Journal of the American Botanical Council* (62):33-48.

Larrabee, Edward M., and Susan Kardas
1966   *Archaeology Survey of Grand Coulee Dam National Recreational Area: Part 1: Lincoln County Above Normal Pool,* Washington State University, Laboratory of Anthropology, Report of Investigations 38. Pullman, Washington.

Laufer, Berthold
1930   Geophagy. In *Field Museum of Natural History.* Publication 280, Anthropology Series 18(2):99-198. Chicago.

Laurie, Nancy O.
1953   Winnebago Berdache. In *American Anthropologist* 55:708-12.

Lavender, David
1963   Westward Vision. New York: Rinehart and Company, Inc.
1964   *The First in the Wilderness.* Garden City: Doubleday & Company, Inc.

Lavender, David, ed.,
1972   *The Oregon Journals of David Douglas: of his travels and the adventures among the traders & Indians in the Columbia, Willamette and Snake River regions during the years 1825, 1826, and 1827.* 2 vols. Ashland: The Oregon Book Society.

Leechman, Douglas
1932   *Aboriginal Paints and Dyes in Canada. Proceedings and Transactions of the Royal Society of Canada.* 3rd set, vol. 26, Sect. 2:37-42. Ottawa, Canada.

Lerman, Norman
1952   Okanogan (Salish) Ethnology. Field notes and Unpublished Manuscript. Original from Melville Jacobs Collection, Suzzallo Library of Washington Archives, Box 78, files 1 and 2. University of Washington Library, Seattle; microfilmed in the British Columbia Indian Language Project files, Victoria)
1954   An Okanagan Winter Dance. In *Anthropology in British Columbia* 4:35-6. Victoria.

Lesley, Craig
1991   *Talking Leaves.* New York: Bantam Doubleday Dell Publishing Group, Inc.

Lévi-Strauss, Claude
1963   Structural Anthropology. Trans. C. Jacobson. New York: Macmillan and St. Martin's Press.

Lewis, Albert Buell
1906   Tribes of the Columbia Valley and the Coast of Washington and Oregon. In *Memoirs, American Anthropological Association* 1(2):147-209. Lancaster, Pennsylvania. (Reprinted: Kraus Reprint, New York, 1964; [and] Millwood, New York, 1983.)

Lewis, Henry T.
1977   Maskura: The Ecology of Indian Fires in Northern Alberta. *Western Canadian Journal of Anthropology,* 7(1):15-52.
1982   A Time for Burning. *Occasional Publications.* Number 17, Boreal Institute for Northern Studies, The University of Alberta, Edmonton, Alberta.

Lewis, Ioan M.
1971   *Ecstatic Religion: An Anthropological Study of Spirit Possession and Shamanism.* New York: Penguin Books.

Lewis, Meriwether, and William Clark

1814   *History of the Expedition Under the Command of Captains Lewis and Clark, to the Sources of the Missouri; Thence Across the Rocky Mountains and Down the River Columbia to the Pacific Ocean; Performed during the Years 1804-5-6.* [1st Nicholas Biddle edition.] Paul Allen, ed. Philadelphia: Bradford and Inskeep.

Lewis, William Stanley

1917   David Thompson's Journeys in the Spokane Country. *Washington Historical Quarterly.* October, 8(4):261-264.

1920   Francis Heron, Fur Trader: Other Herons. *Washington Historical Quarterly.* January, 11(1):29-34.

1925   Information Concerning the Establishment of Fort Colville. *Washington Historical Quarterly.* April, 9(2):102-7.

1925a   "Old Hudson's Bay Post was His First Home." H. C. Burnett Recalls Log Ruins of Settlement at Mouth of Little Spokane River. In *Sidelights On The Early History of Spokane, Washington. Spokesman-Review*, 3rd Printing, pp. 22-26. 8 November.

1925b   Old Indian Campsite His First Home Here: Ben Norman Settled at Fishing Grounds at the Mouth of Little Spokane River. Ousting Fish Traps. In *Reminiscences of Pioneers of the Inland Empire*, Foreword and Edited by J. Orin Oliphant. Old Hudson Bay Post Was His First Home of *The Inland Empire. Spokane-Review*, 8 November 1925, 2nd Printing, vol. 178, Part 4, pp. 1-2.

1925c   Preparing Private Cache. In *Reminiscences of Pioneers of the Inland Empire. Sidelights On The Early History of Spokane, Washington.* Foreword and Notes by J. Orin Oliphant. Cheney: State Normal School. 2nd Printing, pp. 144-149. (First published in the *Spokesman-Review* on 1 November 1924).

1925d   Belated Honor Merited. In *Reminiscences of Pioneers of the Inland Empire. Spokesman-Review.* 15 November 1925:100.

1926   Parting the Indian From His Land. In *Reminiscences of Pioneers of the Inland Empire. Spokesman-Review*, Foreword and edited by William S. Lewis, 11 October 1925:12-13.

1927   The Story of Chief Louis Wildshoe. Sidelights On the Early History of Spokane, Washington. In *Spokane Daily Chronicle.* 21 August 1919. Foreword and Edited by J. Orin Oliphant. pp. 9-11.

1955   Came in by Ox Team. *Spokesman-Review*, 14 June 1955:31-38.

n.d.   Spokane House, The History of an Old Trading Post. Typed manuscript in Spokane Public Library Archives.

Lewis, William Stanley, and Jacob A. Meyers

1925   Life at Old Fort Colville. *Washington Historical Quarterly*, June, 16(3):198-205.

Lieban, Richard W.

1960   Sorcery Illness and Social Control in a Philippine Municipality. In *Southwestern Journal of Anthropology* 16:127-43.

Liljeblad, Sven

1972   The Idaho Indians in Transition, 1805-1960. *A Special Publication of the Idaho State University Museum.* Pocatello, Idaho.

Linklater, Andron

2002   *Measuring America.* London: HarperCollins Publications.

Linton, Ralph
1956   *Culture and Mental Illnesses.* George Devereux, ed. Springfield: Charles Thomas Publishers.

Lockwood, Jeffery A.
2004   *Locust: The Devastating Rise and Mysterious Disappearing of the Insect that Shaped the American Frontier.* New York: Basic Books.

Lord, John Keast
1866   *The Naturalist in Vancouver Island and British Columbia.* 2 vols. London: Richard Bentley.
1867   *At Home in the Wilderness by 'The Wanderer': What to Do and How to Get There.* 2nd edition. London: Robert Hardwicke.

Lugenbeel, Pinkney
1859   Capt. Pinkney to E. R. Geary, Harney Depot, Colville Valley, 15 July 1859. Washington Superintendent of Indian Affairs, microfilm series roll No. 20, Washington.

Lupibereza, Todor
1951   *Glina.* Belgrade, Yugoslavia

Luttrell, Charles T.
1994   Development of Agricultural Settlements in the Upper Columbian Region. In *A Design for the Management of Cultural Resources in the Lake Roosevelt Basin of Northeastern Washington.* (7):7.1-30. Jerry R. Galm, ed., Eastern Washington University Reports on Archaeology and History 100-83. Archaeological and Historical Services

Lyght, Charles E., editor
1966   *The Merck Manual of Diagnosis and Therapy.* 11th edition. West Point, Pennsylvania: Merck Sharp & Dohme Research Laboratories.

Lyman, R. Lee
1980   Freshwater Bivalve Molluscs. In Southern Plateau Prehistory: A Discussion and Description of Three Genera. *Northwest Science* 56 (2):121-136.
1984   A Model of Large Freshwater Clam Exploitation in the Prehistoric Southern Columbia Plateau Culture Area. *Northwest Anthropological Research Notes* 18:97-107.

Lyons, Kevin J.
2000-7   Personal communication.

McBeth, Kate
1908   *The Nez Perce since Lewis and Clark.* New York: Revell.

McCarty, Ella
1965-8   Personal communication.

McDonald, M.
1894   The Salmon Fisheries of the Columbia River Basin. *Report of the Commissioner of Fish and Fisheries on Investigations in the Columbia River Basin in Regards to the Salmon Fisheries* 53rd Congress, 2nd Session. Miscellaneous Document No. 200.

McLaughlin, Castle
2003   *Arts of Diplomacy Lewis & Clark's Indian Collection.* Seattle: University of Washington Press.

McWhorter, Lucullus Virgil
    1904-14 McWhorter Native American Collection. Ten typed MS pages entitled "A Study of the Spokane Indians in order to be profitable should cover the following phases: Ethnology, folk lore and language." Cage 55, folder 349, File 1-H, Section 2, pp. 1-10. Manuscripts, Archives, and Special Collections, Holland Library Archives, Washington State University, Pullman.

MacDonald, Donald
    1927 Testimony of Donald McDonald, 22 December 1927, Spokane City, Washington. Manuscript in Record Group 75, No.2295, Record of the Bureau of Indian Affairs, National Archives, Washington.

Makepeace, Anne
    2000 *Coming to Light: Edward S. Curtis and the North American Indian.* 86 min. Documentary video recording, DVD 3194, also VHS Video/c 4380. Washington, National Geographic.

Mackenzie, Sir Alexander
    1801 *The Journals of Alexander Mackenzie's Voyages from Montreal, on the River St. Laurence, Through the Continent of North America, To the Frozen and Pacific Oceans In the Years, 1789 and 1733, With a Preliminary Account of the Rise, Progress, and Present State of the Fur Trade of that Country.* London: Printed for T. Cadwel, W. Davies and W. Creech by Noble. Reprinted by The Narrative Press in 2001.

Madsen, William
    1964 Value Conflicts and Folk Psychotherapy in South Texas. In *Magic, Faith, and Healing.* Ari Kiev, ed. pp. 420-40. Glencoe: The Free Press.

Majors, Harry M.
    1980 The Great Tephra Eruption in circa 1802. *Northwest Discovery: The Journal of Northwest History and Natural History.* June, 1(1):9-31.

Malinowski, Bronislaw
    1954 *Magic, Society, and Religion.* New York: Doubleday and Company, Inc.

Malouf, Carling
    1974 Economy and Land Use by the Indians of Western Montana. pp. 117-78. In *Interior Salish and Eastern Washington Indians II. American Indian Ethnohistory: Indians of the Northwest.* New York: Garland Publishing.

Mandelbaum, May
    1938 The Sinkaietk or Southern Okanogan of Washington, The Individual Life Cycle. pp. 101-129. Leslie Spier, ed. *General Series in Anthropology* 6. Contributions from the Laboratory of Anthropology, 2. Menasha, Wisconsin: George Banta Publishing Company Agent.

Manring, Benjamin F.
    1912 *The Conquest of the Coeur d'Alene, Spokanes, and Palouses: The Expeditions of Colonels E. J. Steptoe and George Wright against the "Northern Indians" in 1858.* Spokane, Washington: Inland Printing. (Reprinted: Ye Galleon Press, Fairfield, Washington, 1975.)

Mason, Otis Tufton, and Meriden S. Hill
    1901 *Pointed Bark Canoes of the Kutenai and Amu.* Report of U.S. National Museum for 1899. pp. 525-37. Washington: Smithsonian Institution.

Maximilian, Alexander Philipp von, Prince zu Weid-Neuweid and Karl Bodmer
    1834   *Travels in the Interior of North America, in the Years 1832, 1833, and 1834,* Part III. Cobienz: J. Howscher. Reprinted In *Early Western Travels* (1748-1846), 1906. vol. 22-25. Reuben Gold Twaites ed., Cleveland: The A. H. Clark Company.

May, Robert
    n.d.   Interview with Antoine Andrew, Reel Lo3.1.003.T01. Translated by Ann McCrea 17 August 2006.
    1969-80 Personal communication.

Meany, Edward S
    1922   Origin of Washington Geographic Names. *Washington Historical Quarterly.* July, 13, 3:212-24.
    1923   *Origin of Washington Geographic Names.* Seattle: University of Washington Press.
    1925   Documents - Diary of Wilkes in the Northwest. *Washington Historical Quarterly.* May, 16(1):49-55; July, 16(2):137-145; October 1841, 16(4):290-301.

Mehl-Madrona, Lewis
    2010   Comparisons of Health Education, Group Medical Care, and Collaborative Health Care for Controlling Diabetes. *The Permanente Journal.* Summer, Vol. 14, 2:4-10.

Meinig, D. W.
    1968   *The Great Columbia Plain: a historical geography* 1805-1910. Seattle: University of Washington Press.

Mengarini, Gregory, S.J.
    1977   *Recollections of the Flathead Mission: Containing Brief Observations both Ancient and Contemporary Concerning this Particular Nation.* Translated and Edited with a Biographical Introduction by Gloria Ricci Lothrop. Glendale, California: The Arthur H. Clark Company.

Merk, Frederick, ed.
    1931   *Fur Trade and Empire: George Simpson's Journal; Remarks Connected with the Fur Trade in the Course of a Voyage from York Factory to Fort George and Back to York Factory, 1824-1825; Together with Accompanying Documents.* Frederick Merk, ed. Cambridge: Harvard University Press.
    1950   *Albert Gallatin and the Oregon Problem: A Study on Anglo-American Diplomacy.* Cambridge: Harvard University Press.

Merriam, Alan P.
    1951   Flathead Indian Instruments and Their Music. *The Musical Quarterly.* July 37(3):368-375.
    1967   Ethnomusicology of the Flathead Indians *Viking Fund Publication in Anthropology* 44. New York: Wenner-Gren Foundation for Anthropological Research.

Meyer, Karen
    2004   Personal communication.

Meyers, Jacob. A.
    1919   Jacques Raphael Finlay. *Washington Historical Quarterly.* July, 10(3):163-167.

Miller, Christopher
    2003   *Prophetic Worlds: Indians and Whites on the Columbia Plateau.* Seattle: University of Washington Press.

Miller, Jay, ed.

1990   *Mourning Dove: A Salishan Autobiography.* Lincoln: University of Nebraska Press.

1998   Middle Columbia River Salishans. *Handbook of North American Indians. Plateau* 12:253-270. Deward E. Walker, Jr., ed. Washington: Smithsonian Institution.

Mitchell, Howard I., ed.

1963   *The Journals of William Fraser Tolmie, Physician and Fur Trader.* Vancouver, Canada: Mitchell Press Limited.

Modigliani, Eljo

1892   *Fra i Batacchi indipendenti.* Rome.

Moerman, Daniel E.

1979   Anthropology of Symbolic Healing [and Comments and Replys]. In *Current Anthropology* 20(1):59-80.

1983   General Medical Effectiveness and Human Biology: Placebo Effects in the Treatment of Ulcer Disease. In *Medical Anthropology Quarterly.* August, 14(4):3+13-16.

2009   *Native American Medicinal Plants: An Ethnobotanical Dictionary.* Portland: Timber Press Inc.

Mooney, James

1896   The Ghost-dance Religion and the Sioux Outbreak of 1890. pp. 641-1136 in Pt 2 of *14th Annual Report of American Ethnology for 1892-'93.* Washington. (Reprinted: Dover Publications, New York, 1973 with an Introduction by Raymond J. DeMallie, Lincoln: University of Nebraska Press.

1928   *The Aboriginal Population of America North of Mexico.* J. R. Swanton, ed. Smithsonian Miscellaneous Collections, vol. 80, 7 (Publication 2955), Washington: U.S. Government Printing Office.

Moore, W. R.

1974   From Fire Control to Fire Management. *Western Wildlands* 1(3):11-5.

Morgan, W. J., D. B. Tyler, J. L. Leonhart, and M. F. Loughlin, eds.

1978   *Autobiography of Rear Admiral Charles Wilkes, U.S. Navy 1798-1877.* Washington: Naval Division, Department of the Navy.

Moser, Charles, and Peggy J. Klemplatz

2002   Transvestic Fetishism: Psychopathology or Iatrogenic Artifact? *New Jersey Psychologist,* 52(2):16-17.

Mullan, John

1854   Report of an Exploration from the Bitterroot Valley to Fort Hall and back. In I. I. Stevens (compiler) Report of Exploration of a Route for the Pacific Railroad. Governor Stevens' Report to the Secretary of War. Senate Executive Document, No. 78, 33rd Congress. 2nd Session, vol. 1. U.S. War Department. Washington: U.S. Government Printing Office.

1861   United States Military Road Expedition from Fort Walla Walla to Fort Benton, W. T., by Lieutenant John Mullan, 2nd Artillery. Appendix 17, Pp. 549-569 in Report of the Secretary of War for 1861. *37th Congress. 2nd Session. Senate Executive Document* 2(1). (Serial No.1118). Washington: U.S. Government Printing Office.

1862   *Army Corps of Topographical Engineers Report on the Construction of a Military Road from Fort Walla Walla to Fort Benton.* Washington: GPO.

1863   U.S. Army Corps of Engineers Report on the Construction of a Military Road from Fort Walla Walla to Fort Benton. *37th Congress.3d Session. Senate Executive Document 43,* ("The Mullan Report"). Washington: U.S. Government Printing Office.

Murray, Stephen O.

1994   On Subordinating Native American Cosmologies to the Empire of Gender. *Current Anthropology* 35:59-61.

Nadel, Siegfried Frederick

1946   A Study of Shamanism in the Nubu Hills. *Journal of the Royal Anthropological Institute of Great Britain and Ireland,* 75:25-37.

Nelson, C. M.

1973   Prehistoric Cultural Change in the Intermontane Plateau of Western North America. In *The Explanation of Culture Change: Models in Prehistory.* C. Renfrew, ed. pp. 371-390. London: Gerald Duckworth & Company.

Nesmith, J. W.

1858   Report of J. W. Nesmith, No. 79 in *Report of the Commissioner of Indian Affairs for 1858,* pp. 214-222. Washington: U.S. Government Printing Office.

Newcomb, William W., Jr.

1974   *North American Indians: An Anthropological Perspective.* Pacific Palisades: Goodyear Publishing Company.

Neuman, Alex

2007   Aboriginal Use of Lamprey on the Columbia River. (Unpublished MA thesis. Departments of Biology and Anthropology. Eastern Washington University, Cheney.)

Nicandri, David L.

1986   *Northwest Chiefs: Gustav Sohon's Views of the 1855 Stevens Treaty Councils.* Washington State Historical Society. Manuscript in Eastern Washington, John F. Kennedy Memorial Library Archives. Cheney, Washington.

Nisbet, Jack

2005   *Mapmaker's Eye: David Thompson on the Columbia River.* Pullman: Washington State University Press.

2007   *Visible Bones: Journeys Across Time in the Columbia River Country.* Seattle: Sasquatch Books.

Norman, Ben
    1911   Personal communication, 26 Nov 1911 to W. S. Lewis. Lewis manuscript coll. Eastern Washington State Historical Society, MS-25:1/13.

O'Hara, Edwin V.
    1909   DeSmet in Oregon Country. *The Quarterly of the Oregon Historical Society.* September, 10(3):239-262.

Oliphant, James Orin
    1925   Old Fort Colville. *Washington Historical Quarterly.* April, 16(2):83-101.
    1927   *Sidelights On The Early History of Spokane, Washington, Told by Contemporaries.* Edited with an Introduction and Notes by J. Orin. pp. 123-126, and 162-166.
    1927a   The Eastward Movement of Cattle from The Oregon Country. *Mississippi Valley Historical Review* 13:30-49. Reprinted, *Agricultural History* 1946, 20 (1):19-43).
    1932   Winter Losses of Cattle in the Oregon Country, 1847-1890. *Washington Historical Quarterly.* January, 23(1):3-17.
    1934   Botanical Labors of the Reverend Henry H. Spaulding. *Washington Historical Quarterly.* April, 25 (2):93-102.
    1948   History of Livestock in the Pacific Northwest. *Oregon Historical Quarterly.* March, 49 (1):3-29.
    1950   Encroachments of Cattle on Indian Reservations of the Pacific Northwest, 1870-1890. *Agricultural History.* January, 24(1):42-58.

Olsen, Loran
    1998   Music and Dance. *Handbook of North American Indians. Plateau.* 12:546-72. Deward E. Walker, Jr., ed. Washington: Smithsonian Institution Press.

O'Neill, Phillip Michael
    1962   The Spokane Indian Tribe. (Unpublished Master's thesis. Department of History, Gonzaga University. Spokane, Washington.)

Osborne, Douglas D.
    1953   Archaeological Occurrence of Pronghorn Antelope, Bison, and Horse in the Columbia Plateau. *Scientific Monthly* 77(5):260-9.

Osterman, Deane
    1995   The Ethno-ichthyology of the Spokan Indian People. (Unpublished Master's thesis, Departments of Anthropology and Biology. Eastern Washington University, Cheney, Washington.)

Owen, John
    1858   Copy of Letter of John Owen, No. 95 in *Report of the Commissioner of Indian Affairs for 1858*, pp. 266-69. Washington: U.S. Government Printing Office.

Pacioni, Giovanni
    1999   *Simon & Schuster's Guide to Mushrooms.* New York: Simon & Schuster, Inc.

Paige, George A.
    1865   Report of George A. Paige, Fort Colville special agency, No. 10 in *Report of the Commission of Indian Affairs,* Dated 1865, 98-101. Washington: U.S. Government Printing Office.
    1866   Report of George A. Paige, Indian Agent to Superintendent W. H. Waterman of Bureau of Indian Affairs. Dated 19 September 1866, 73. (Manuscript in Letters Received, M234, Reel 909 (3), Folder W521-W697 *Records of the Bureau of Indian Affairs,* 1824-81 [microfilm] *Record Group* 75, National Archives and Records Service, Washington, D.C.)
    1868   Annual Report of George A. Paige, Special Agent, Fort Colville Reservation. No. 10 in *Report on Indian Affairs for the Year 1867*, pp. 52-57. Washington: U.S. Printing Office.

Palladino, Father Lawrence B.
    1894   *Indian and White in the Northwest: or, A History of Catholicity in Montana.* With an Introduction by Right Reverend John B. Brondel, D. D. Baltimore: John Murphy and Company.

Palmer, Gary B.
    2001   Indian Pioneers: The Settlement of N'lukhwalqw (*Upper Latah Creek*, Idaho). by the Schitsu'umsh (*Coeur d'Alene Indians*). *Oregon Historical Quarterly* 102(1):22-47.

Pambrun, Andrew Dominique
    1979   *The Story of His Life as He Tells It.* Eastern Washington University, Hargraves Library MS, in print as *Andrew Dominique Pambrum, Sixty Years on the Frontier in the Pacific Northwest.* Edward J. Kowrach, ed. Fairfield, Washington: Ye Galleon Press.

Pankonin, Lynn
    2008   Personal communication

Parker, Reverend Samuel D.
    1838   *Journal of an Exploring Tour Beyond the Rocky Mountains in the Years 1836-37.* Lancaster: Wickersham Publishing Company.
    1840   *Journal of An Exploring Tour Beyond the Rocky Mountains, Under the Direction of the A. B. C. F. M., in the Years 1835, '36, and '37: Containing a Description of the Geography, Geology, Climate, Productions of the Country, and the Numbers, Manners, and Customs of the Natives, with a Map of Oregon Territory.* Revised 2d ed. Ithaca: Mack, Andrus, & Woodruff, c. 1838. Reprinted in 1844 also Ross and Haines, Minneapolis, 1967; University of Idaho Press, Moscow, 1990.)
    1844   *Journal of an Exploring Tour Beyond the Rocky Mountains in the Years 1835-37.* Lancaster: Wickersam Publishing Company. (Fifth Edition Published in 1846 by J. C. Derby and Company in Auburn.)

Parson, Talcott
    1958   *The Social System.* New York: Free Press.

Paterek, Josephine
    1994   *Encyclopedia of American Indian Costume.* Santa Barbara: ABC-CLIO, Inc.

Peets, Orville H.
    1960   Experiments in the Use of Atlatl Weights in Northwestern Arizona. *American Antiquity* 26(1):108-110.

Peltier, Jerome
  1975   *Manners and Customs of the Coeur d'Alene Indians.* Spokane: Peltier Publications.
  1990   The Fur Trade Was Equitable in the Far West. *The Pacific Northwesterner* 34(1):1-12.
  1996   *Northwest History.* Fairfield, Washington: Ye Galleon Press.

Perkins, William R.
  1993   Atlatl Weights: Function and Classification. *Bulletin of Primitive Technology* No. 5. Spring
          issue, n.p.
  1996   Personal communication
  2005   Atlatl and Mechanics: A Brief Discussion. (Unpublished MS in possession of author.)

Petzer, Peter C.
  1994   *Grand Coulee: Harnessing A Dream.* Pullman: Washington State University Press.

Pfeiffer, Michael A.
  1981   Clay Tobacco Pipes from Spokane House and Fort Colville. *Northwest. Anthropological
          Research Notes* 15(2):221-235).

Pickering, Charles
  1888   *The Races of Man and Their Geographical Distribution.* London: George Bell & Sons.

Point, Nicolas, S.J.
  1967   *Wilderness Kingdom: Indian Life in the Rocky Mountains: 1840-1847. The Journal and
          Paintings of Nicolas Point, S.J.* Translated and Introduced by Joseph P. Donnelly, S.J.
          Reprinted in 1967 with an appreciation by John C. Ewers. New York, Chicago, San Francisco:
          Holt, Rinehart and Winston.

Post, Richard H.
  1938   The Subsistence Quest. pp. 9-34. In *General Series in Anthropology*, No. 6. *Contributions
          from the Laboratory of Anthropology*, 2. The Sinkaietk or Southern Okanogan of Washington.
          By Walter Cline, Rachel S. Commons, May Mandelbaum, Richard H. Post, and L.V.W.
          Walters. Leslie Spier, ed. Menasha, Wisconsin: George Banta Publishing Company Agent.

Post, Richard H., and Rachel S. Commons
  1938   Material Culture. pp. 35-70. In *General Series in Anthropology* No. 6. *Contributions from the
          Laboratory of Anthropology*, 2. The Sinkaietk or Southern Okanogan of Washington. By
          Walter Cline, Rachael S. Commons, May Mandelbaum, Richard H. Post, and L.V.W. Walters.
          Leslie Spier, ed. Menasha, Wisconsin: George Banta Publishing Company Agent.

Powell, John Wesley
  1891   *Seventh Annual Report of the Bureau of Ethnology to the Smithsonian Institution, 1885-'86.*
          Washington: U.S. Government Printing Office.

Press, Irwin
  1978   Urban Folk Medicine: A Functional Overview. In *American Anthropologist* 80:71-84.

Prucha, Francis Paul, S.J.
  1969   Andrew Jackson's Indian Policy: A Reassessment. *Journal of American History.* December, 56
          (3):527-538.
  1988   Two Roads to Conversion Protestant and Catholic Missionaries in the Pacific Northwest.
          Pacific Northwest Quarterly. October, 79(4):130-137.

Pyne, Stephen J.
  1983   Indian Fires: The fire practices of North American Indians transformed large areas from forest
            to grassland. *Natural History* 2:6-11.

Quinn, Robert R.
  1984   Climate of the Northern Columbia Plateau. In *Northern Columbia Plateau Landscapes*:
            Narrative and Field Guide. pp. 31-36. Michael M. Folsom, ed. Cheney: Eastern Washington
            University Press.

Quintasket, Charles
  1964-99   Personal communication.

Quintasket, Christine (Mourning Dove or *hemIshemis*)
  1990   *Mourning Dove: A Salishan Autobiography.* Jay Miller, ed. Lincoln: University of Nebraska
            Press.

Randolph, June
  1957   Witness of Indian Religion: Present-Day Concepts of the Guardian Spirit. *Pacific Northwest
            Quarterly.* October, 48 (4):139-45.

Raufer, Maria Ilma
  1965   *Black Robes and Indians on the Last Frontier.* Milwaukee: The Bruce Publishing Company.

Ray, Verne F.
  1928   Spokan War Shirt, Unpublished field notes and photograph. Accession Record, 2346, State
            Museum, University of Washington, Burke Museum. Deaccessed to Spokane Tribe of Indians,
            FR Document 03-27525 Filed 31.10.03.
  1932   Pottery on the Middle Columbia. *American Anthropologist*, n.s., 34(1):127-133.
  1933   *The Sanpoil and Nespelem: Salishan Peoples of Northeastern Washington* 5. University of
            Washington Publications in Anthropology.
  1936   Native Villages and Groupings of the Columbia Basin. *Pacific Northwest Quarterly.* April,
            27(2):99-152.
  1936a   The Kolaskin Prophet Cult. *American Anthropologist* n.s., 38(1):67-75.
  1937   The Bluejay Character in the Plateau Spirit Dance. *American Anthropologist* n.s. October-
            December, 39(4):593-601. Mensha, Wisconsin: George Banta Publishing Agent.
  1939   Cultural Relations in the Plateau of Northwestern America. *Publications of the Frederick Web
            Hodge Anniversary Publication Fund,* vol. 3. Los Angeles: Southwest Museum.
  1942   Cultural Element Distributions: XXII. Plateau. *Anthropological Records* 8(2):98-262. Oxford:
            Clarendon Press.
  1945   The Contrary Behavior Pattern in American Ceremonialism. *Southwestern Journal of
            Anthropology* 1:73-113.
  1954   Testimony before the Indians Claims Commission, Docket No. 181, The Confederated Tribes
            of the Colville Reservation *et al. v.* The United States of America, and Docket No. 331,
            Spokane Tribe of Indians *v.* United States of America. (Microfiche). New York: Clearwater
            Publishing.
  1960   Testimony before the Indian Claims Commission, Dockets 161 and 222, in the matter of the
            Confederated Tribes of the Colville Indian Reservation, as the Representative of the Palus
            Band. (Microfiche.) New York: Clearwater Publishing.

1977   Ethnic Impact of the Events Incident to the Federal Power Development on the Colville and
            Spokane Indian Reservations. (Reports prepared for the Confederated Tribes of the Colville and
            the Spokane Tribe of Indians, Nespelem, Washington

Ray, Verne F., and others (G. P. Murdock, B. Blyth, O. C. Stewart, J. Harris, E. H. Hoebel, and D. B.
Shimkin)
1938   Tribal Distribution in Eastern Oregon and Adjacent Regions. *American Anthropologist*, n.s,.
            40:384-415. Mensha: Banta Publishing Agent.

Reagan, Albert B.
1917   Archaeological Notes on Western Washington and Adjacent British Columbia. *Proceedings of
            the California Academy of Sciences. Fourth Series* 7(1):1-31.

Reddick, SuAnn M.
2000   The Evolution of Chemawa Indian School: From Red River to Salem, 1825-1885. *Oregon
            Historical Quarterly.* 101(4):442-465.

Reddick, SuAnn M., Cary C. Collins
2000   Forest Grove and Chemawa Indian School: The First Off-Reservation Boarding School in the
            West. *Oregon Historical Society.* Fall, 101(4):444-465.

Reddy, Marlita A., ed.
1993   *Statistical Record of Native North Americans.* Washington: Gale Research Inc.

Redfield, Robert
1953   *The Primitive World and its Transformation.* Ithaca: Cornell University Press.

Reimers, Henry L.
1973   *Indian Country: Inland Northwest Native People.* Minneapolis: T. S. Denison & Co., Inc.
1993   The County Commissioner's Son. *Pacific Northwesterner.* 38(1):1-13.

Rice, David G.
1970   Basin-Plateau Cultural Relations in Light of Finds from Marmes Rockshelter in The Lower
            Snake River Region of the Southern Columbia Plateau. Paper Presented at the Cultural
            Relations between the Plateau and Great Basin Symposium. Later published in *Northwest
            Anthropological Research Notes* 5(1):82-98. ed., Earl H. Swanson.

Rice, Harvey S.
1984   Native American Dwellings and Attendant Structures of the Southern Plateau. Unpublished
            Ph.D. dissertation, Department of Anthropology, Washington State University.
2005   Native American Dwellings of the Southern Plateau. pp. 45-63. In *Spokane and the Inland
            Empire: An Interior Pacific Northwest Anthology,* David Stratton, ed. Pullman: Washington
            State University Press.

Rice, Harvey S, and John A. Ross
1980   *Cultural Resource Survey of the Southern and Eastern Boundaries of the Spokane Indian
            Reservation.* Project Report Number 101. Washington Archaeological Research Center,
            Washington State University, Pullman.

Richards, J. E. and F.W.H. Beamish
1981   Initiation of feeding and salinity tolerance in the Pacific lamprey *Lampetra tridentata. Marine
            Biology* 63:73-7.

Richardson, Ron
    2006   Mary Richardson Walker (1811-1897). *The Outline Encyclopedia of Washington State History.* pp. 1-9. http://www.historylink.org/?DisplayPage=output.cfm&file_id=7204.

Rigsby, Bruce
    1996   Some Aspects of Plateau Linguistic Prehistory: Sahaptain/Interior Salishan Relations. pp. 141-146. In *Chin Hills to Chiloquin: Papers Honoring the Versatile Career of Theodore Stern.* University of Oregon Anthropological Papers No. 52.

Roe, Frank Gilbert
    1955   *The Indian and the Horse.* Norman: University of Oklahoma Press (Reprinted in 1968 and1974).

Roehrig, R. B.
    1881   Comparative Vocabulary of the Selish Languages, 50 pp. In *First Annual Report of the Bureau of Ethnology to the Secretary of the Smithsonian Institution 1879-'80.* Powell, J. W., ed. Washington: U.S. Government Printing Office.

Rogers, Spencer L.
    1944   Disease Concepts in North America; Brief Communications. *American Anthropologist* n.s. 46(4):559-564.

Römer, Bela J.
    1976   The Use of Argillaceous Earth as a Medicament. In *Medical Anthropology.* Pre-Congress Conference on Medical Anthropology. pp. 269-278. Francis X. Grollig, S.J. and Harold B. Haley. eds., The Hague: Mouton Publishers.

Roscoe, Will
    1987   Bibliography of Berdache and Alternate Gender Roles Among North American Indians. *Journal of Homosexuality* 14(3/4):81-171.
    1988   Wewha and Klah: The American Indian Berdache as Artist and Priest. *The American Indian Quarterly.* 12:127-50.

Ross, Alexander
    1849   *Adventures of the First Settlers on the Oregon or Columbia River: Being a Narrative of the Expedition Fitted Out by John Jacob Astor, to Establish the "Pacific Fur Company"; with an Account of Some Indian Tribes of the Coast of the Pacific.* By Alexander Ross, One of the Adventures. London: Smith, Elder and Co. (Reprinted: vol. 7 (1810-1814) of Early Western Travels. 1748-1846. Reuben G. Twaites, ed., Cleveland: Arthur C. Clark, 1904.
    1855   *The Fur Hunters of the Far West; A Narrative of Adventures in The Oregon. and Rocky Mountains.* 2 vols. London: Smith, Elder and Co.
    1877   *Contributions to North America Ethnology.* Vol. III, pp. 306-309.
    1904   *Adventures of the First Settlers on the Oregon or Columbia River, 1810-1813.* Vol. 7. Cleveland: Arthur H. Clark. Reprinted in 1926 by Reuben Gold Thwaites, ed.

Ross, John Alan
    1964   Flathead ethnographic field notes. (Manuscripts in author's possession.)
    1964-67 Colville ethnographic field notes. (Manuscripts in author's possession.)
    1965   The Puberty Ceremony of the Chimbu Girl in the Eastern Highlands of New Guinea. *Anthropos*, 60:423-432.

1968-2008 Spokan, Kalispel, and Coeur d'Alene ethnographic field notes from sixty-seven informants. (Manuscripts in author's possession.)

1967 Factionalism on the Colville Reservation. (Unpublished M.A. thesis. Department of Anthropology. Washington State University, Pullman.)

1968 Political Conflict on the Colville Reservation. *Northwest Anthropological Research Notes* 2(1):29-91.

1979 An Ethnographic Report of Aboriginal Use and Occupancy of the Spokane River and its Tributaries by the Upper Spokan Indians. Historical Landmark Survey: *A Report and Site Inventory of Spokane's Historic Resources. Spokane City Planning Commission.* Pullman: National Heritage, Inc.

1980 Aboriginal and Historical Use and Occupancy of the Spokane River and Chamokane Creek Contiguous with the Spokane Indian Reservation. Harvey S. Rice, ed. *Cultural Resource Survey of the Southern and Eastern Boundaries of the Spokane Indian Reservatio*n. Project Report No. 101, Washington Archaeological Research Center.

1980a Prophetic Medical Procedures in the Plateau: Some Forms and Functions Among the Aboriginal Salish. 65th Northwest Scientific Associations Annual Conference. Moscow, Idaho.

1980b The Role of Syncretic Medicine in Accommodating Non-traditional Therapy by Indigenous Medico-Religious Systems. 22nd Annual Western Science Associations. 24-25 April. Albuquerque, New Mexico.

1980c Interpersonal Relations of Physicians, Shamans, and Indian Patients. Sixty-First Annual Pacific Division, American Association for the Advancement of Science, Section K. 22-27 June, Davis, University of California.

1981 Shakerism and Emerging Patterns in Reservation Communal Health Care. 22nd Annual Western Association of Sociology and Anthropology. Paper read by Julie A. Ross. University of Manitoba. 4-6 March, Winnipeg, Canada.

1981a Controlled Burning: A Case of Aboriginal Resource and Forest Management in the Columbia Plateau. In 54th Annual Meeting of the Northwest Scientific Association Abstract, 26-28 March. Corvallis: Oregon State University.

1981b Geophagy Amongst Plateau Salish-Speakers: Aboriginal Use of Argillaceous Earth as Medicaments. 34th Northwest Anthropological Conference, 26-28 March. Portland State University, Portland, Oregon.

1981c The Structure and Function of the Group Medical inquest in Traditional and Syncretic Medical Systems. 23rd Annual Western Social Science Association Conference. 23-25 April, San Diego, California.

1981d Traditional Medical Beliefs and Practices: The Value of Accommodating Alternative Medical Systems. Washington State Public Health Association/Washington Association of Social Workers. 4-6 October. Spokane, Washington.

1982 The Significance of the Bluejay Ceremony in Columbia Plateau Syncretic Medicine (L' importance de la séré monie de l'oiseau "Bluejay" dans la pratique de la medecine syncrétique du Plateau Columbique. 35th Northwest Anthropological Conference, 7-9 April. Simon Fraser University, Burnaby, British Columbia.

1982a The Function of Traditional Medicine Amongst the Spokan Indians. 44th International Congress of Americanists. Symposium on American Indian Medicine. 5-10 September. University of Manchester. Manchester, England.

1983 Plateau Indian Health: Fallacies of Conflict and Acceptance of Syncretic Medicine. With Kaven di Pignatelli. 24th Annual Conference of Western Association of Sociology and Anthropology. Brandon University. 11-13 February, Brandon, Manitoba, Canada.

1983a   An Anthropological View of the Change in Attitudes toward Mental Illness and Physical Handicaps. *The History and Social Science Teacher*, March, 18(3), pp. 135-140.

1983b   The Role of Plateau Syncretix Indian Religion in the Treatment of Traditional and Non-traditional Illnesses. 25th Conference of the Western Social Science Association. Albuquerque Hilton, 27-30 April. Albuquerque, New Mexico.

1983c   The Persistence of Prophetic Beliefs and Practices Amongst Columbia Plateau Salish. IXth International Congress of Anthropological and Ethnological Sciences, Phase II. University of British Columbia. 20-25 August. Vancouver, British Columbia, Canada.

1984   The Occurrence and Significance of the Berdache Among the Southern Plateau Salish. With Kaven di Pignatelli. 37th Northwest Anthropological Conference, 21-23 March. Spokane, Washington.

1984a   An Archaeological, Ethnographic, and Historical Survey of the Spokane Indian Reservation. Unpublished manuscript in possession of the Spokane Indian Tribe.

1984b   An Ethnographic Report on Aboriginal Use and Occupancy of the Spokane River and Tributaries by the Upper Spokan Indians. Pullman: National Heritage, Inc.

1984c   The Persistence of Syncretic Medicine Amongst the Spokan Indians. First Annual Canadian Association of Medical Anthropology. Read by Julie A. Ross. University of Montreal. 11-13 May. Montreal, Quebec, Canada.

1988   Games of the Plateau Indians. *The Journal of Physical Education, Recreation, and Dance* 59(9):29-33.

1989   Indian Shamans of the Spokan Indians: Past and Present. *Medical Bulletin* 62(3):52-57. Spokane Medical Association.

1989a   Contributions in Cultural Resource Management No. 27. An Ethnographic and Ethnohistorical Survey of the Proposed Spokane Centennial Trail, pp. 65-93. In *A Cultural Resource Survey of the Spokane River Centennial Trail: Phase I - Spokane to the Washington/Idaho Border*. Randall Schalk and Marilyn Wyss ed. Submitted to the Washington State Parks and Recreation Commission by The Center for Northwest Anthropology, Washington State University, Pullman.

1991   Ethnographic and Ethnohistorical Investigations Along the Spokane River. Part 1: An Ethnographic and Ethnohistorical Survey of the Proposed Spokane River Centennial Trail, and Part 2: Use of the Spokane River by the Middle and Upper Spokan. John A. Draper and William Andrefsky, Jr., eds. *Archaeology of the Middle Spokan River Valley: Investigations Along the Spokane Centennial Trail.* Project Report No. 17, Center for Northwest Anthropology, Washington State University. Pullman, Washington.

1991a   Traditional Health and Healing in a Contemporary Context: Issues and Concerns in Health Service.44th Annual Northwest Anthropological Conference. 28-30 March 1991. Missoula, Montana.

1993   An Ethnoarchaeological Cultural Resource Survey of the Spokane Indian Reservation (1991-1993), 17 vols. U.S. Bureau of Indian Affairs and the U.S. Department of Forestry. Spokane Tribal Archives, Wellpinit, Washington.

1993a   Aboriginal Spokan Utilization and Stewardship of Forested Areas and Specific Floral/Faunal Resource Sites. National Social Science Conference. 10-13 November, San Antonio, Texas.

1994   The Spokan. *Native Americans in the 20th Century: An Encyclopedia.* pp. 611-612. Mary B. Davis, ed. (Garland Reference Library of Social Science 452.) New York and London: Garland Publishing Company.

1994a   A Forest and a Tribe in Transition: *A History of the Spokane Indian Reservation Forest. 1870-1994*. Frank Grant, ed., and Principal Investigator. Missoula: Historical Research Associates, Inc.

1995   An Ethnographic and Historical Analysis of the Spokan People. John Alan Ross, John Fahey, and Deane Osterman, eds. U.S. Bureau of Reclamation and the Spokane Indian Tribal Council, Wellpinit, Washington.

1995a   Medicines and Modes of Curing. In *Ready Reference: American Indians* pp. 472-75. James L. Magill, ed. Pasadena: Salem Press, Inc

1995b   Spokan. In *American Indian Tribes* 2:497-499. R. Kent Rasmussen, ed. Pasadena: Salem Press, Inc.

1995c   Spokan. In *Magill's Ready Reference: American Indians* 3:746. ed., Harvey Markowitz. Pasadena: Salem Press, Inc.

1995d   Traditional Social Control. In *Magill's Ready Reference: American Indians* 3:731-2. Chris Moose, ed. Pasadena: Salem Press, Inc.

1995e   Tattooing. In *Magill's Ready Reference: American Indian*s. 3:769. James L. Magill, ed. Pasadena: Salem Press Inc.

1995f   Hides and Hidework. In *Magill's Ready Reference: American Indians.* pp. 3:323. James Magill, ed. Pasadena: Salem Press Inc.

1995g   Plateau. In *Magill's Ready Reference: American Indians.* 3:600-603. James Magill, ed. Pasadena: Salem Press Inc.

1995h   Resources. In *Magill's Ready Reference: American Indians.* 3:671-672. James Magill, ed. Pasadena: Salem Press Inc.

1995i   Traditional Social Control. In *Magill's Ready Reference: American Indians* 3:731-732. Pasadena: Salem Press Inc.

1996   The Significance and Relationship of Traditional Spokan Indian Religious Beliefs Explaining Congenital Birth Defects *Pacific Northwest Forum* – Special Issue, "Indians of the Columbia Plateau." 9(1-2):14-29.

1998   Spokan. *Handbook of North American Indians. Plateau* 12:271-282. Deward E. Walker, Jr., ed. Washington: Smithsonian Institution Press.

1999   Proto-historical and Historical Spokan Prescribed Burning and Stewardship of Resource Areas pp. 277-291. In *Indians, Fire and The Land in the Pacific Northwest.* Robert Boyd, ed. Corvallis: Oregon State University Press.

1999c   Spokane Garry. In *American Indian Biographies.* Harvey Makowitz, ed., pp. 118. Pasadena: Salem Press, Inc.

2000   Plateau. In *American Indian Tribes* 2:50-56. ed., R. Kent Rasmussen. Pasadena: Salem Press, Inc.

2008   Spokan Burial Rituals and Associated Mortuary Beliefs. In *Journal of Northwest Anthropology,* 42(1):17-70.

Ross, Julie Ann

1963-64   Unpublished Flathead field notes in possession of author.

Ross, Samuel

1870   [Letter of September 1, 1870.] pp. 480-494 in *41st Congress. 3d Session. House Executive Document* 1. (Serial No. 1449). Washington.

Rousseau, Jean Jacques
  1913   Discourse on Inequality. In *The Social Contract and Discourses*. Translated by G.D.A. Cole.
            pp. 207-238. London: J. M. Dent

Roy, Prodipto
  1961   Assimilation of the Spokane Indians. Washington Agriculture Experiment Stations, Institute of
            Agricultural Sciences, Washington State University, Bulletin 628 pp. 1-55.

Royce, Charles C.
  1899   Indian Land Cessions in the United States. In *Eighteenth Annual Report of the Bureau of
            American Ethnology*, Part 2, Washington.

Rubel, Arthur J., and Michael R. Hass
  1996   Ethnomedicine pp. 114-130. In *Medical Anthropology: Contemporary Theory and Method*.
            eds., Carolyn F. Sargent and Thomas M. Johnson. Westport, Connecticut: Prager.

Ruby, Robert H., and John A. Brown
  1981   *Indians of the Pacific Northwest.* Norman: University of Oklahoma Press.
  1982   *The Spokane Indians, Children of the Sun.* Norman: University of Oklahoma Press.
  1986   *A Guide to the Indian Tribes of the Pacific Northwest.* Norman: University of Oklahoma Press.
  1993   *Indian Slavery in the Pacific Northwest.* Spokane: The Arthur H. Clark Company.

Sahlins, Marshall
  1965   On the Sociology of Primitive Exchange. The Relevance of Models for Social Anthropology.
            Association of Social Anthropologists Monographs 1. New York: Praeger.

Santora, Dolores, and Penny Starkey
  1982   Research Studies in American Indian Suicide. *Journal of Psychological Nursing in Mental
            Health Service* 20(8):25-29.

Sapir, Edward
  1916   Terms of Relationship and the Levirate. *American Anthropologist,* n.s July-September (3):327-
            337.
  1965   The Kutenai Berdache: Courier, Guide, Prophetess, and Warrior. *Ethnohistory* 12(3):193-236.

Sargent, Carolyn F., and Thomas M. Johnson
  1996   The Professionalization of Indigenous Healers pp. 374-395. In *Medical Anthropology;
            Comparative Theory and Method.* Westport, Connecticut: Prager Press.

Schaeffer, Claude Everett
  1934-37   Unpublished Flathead and Kutenai Field Notes. The Glenbow Foundation, Calgary, Alberta.
  1937   The First Jesuit Mission to the Flathead, 1840-1850: A Study in Conflicts. *Pacific Northwest
            Quarterly.* July, 28(3):227-250.
  1940   The Subsistence Quest of the Kutenai: A Study of the Interaction of Culture and Environment.
            (Unpublished Doctoral Dissertation in Anthropology, University of Pennsylvania,
            Philadelphia.)
  1952   Molded Pottery Among the Kutenai Indians. *Occasional Anthropology and Sociology Papers*,
            No. 6. Department of Anthropology, University of Montana, Missoula.
  1965   The Kutenai Female Berdache: Courier, Guide, Prophetess and Warrior. *Ethnohistory*
            12(3):193-236.

Schafer, Joseph, ed.

1909   Documents Relative to Harry J. Warre and Alfred Vavasour's Military Reconnaissance in Oregon, 1845-6. *The Quarterly of the Oregon Historical Society.* March-December, 10 (1):1-109.

Schalk, Randall F.

1977   The Structure of an Anadromous Fish Resource. In *Theory Building in Archaeology: Aquatic Resources, Spatial Analysis, and Systemic Modeling.* Lewis R. Binford, ed. pp. 207-249. New York: Academic Press.

1981   Land Use and Organizational Complexity Among Foragers of Northwestern North America. In *Senn Ethnology Studie*s. S. Koyama and D. H. Thomas, ed. 9:53-75. National Museum of Ethnology. Senri, Osaka, Japan.

1986   Estimating Salmon and Steelhead Usage in the Columbia Basin Before 1850: The Anthropological Perspective. *The Northwest Environmental Journal*, 2(2):1-29.

Schalk, Randall F., and Gregory C. Cleveland

1983   A Sequence of Adaptations in the Columbia-Fraser Plateau. Cultural Resource Investigations for the Lyons Ferry Fish Hatchery Project, near Lyons Ferry, Washington. Randall F. Schalk, ed. pp. 11-56. *Laboratory of Archaeology and History Project Reports* No. 8. Washington State University, Pullman.

Scholz, Allan T., *et al.*

1985   *Compilation of Information on Salmon and Hydropower Related Losses in the Upper Columbia River Basin, Above Grand Coulee Dam. Fisheries.* Technical Report No. 2. Upper Columbia United Tribes Fisheries Center. Cheney: Eastern Washington University.

Scholz, Allan T. and Holly J. McLellan

2009   *Filed Guide to the Fishes of Eastern Washington.* Cheney: Eagle Printing.

Schoolcraft, Henry Rowe

1857   *History of the Indian Tribes of the United States: Their Present Condition and Prospects, and a Sketch of Their Ancient Status.* 6 vols. Published by Order of Congress Under the Direction of the Department of the Interior – Indian Bureau. Philadelphia: J. B. Lippincott, Grambo & Company.

Schroedl, Gerald F.

1973   The Archaeological Occurrence of Bison in the Southern Plateau. *Washington State University. Laboratory of Anthropology, Reports of Investigations* 51. Pullman. (Originally presented as the Author's Thesis in Anthropology, Washington State University, Pullman, 1972, under title: The Association of Bison Remains in the Columbia Plateau of Washington.)

Scott, Harvey Whitefield

1924   *History of Oregon Country.* Complied by Leslie M. Scott, ed., vol. 2. Cambridge: Riverside Press.

Scott, Leslie M.

1928   Indian Diseases as Aids to Pacific Northwest Settlements. *Oregon Historical Quarterly.* June, 29(2)144-161.

1941   Indian Woman as Food Providers and Tribal Counselors. *Oregon Historical Quarterly.* September, 42(3):208-19.

Scott, O. A.
  1968   *Pioneer Days on the Shadowy St. Joe*. Coeur d'Alene, Idaho.

Shetler, Sidney G.
  1982   *A Biography of S. G. Shelter (1871-1942), Bishop, Evangelist, Pastor, and Preacher*. Scottdale,
           Pennsylvania: Herald Press.

Sherwood, Alex
  1967   Personal communication.

Shinn, Dean
  1980   Historical Perspectives on Range Burning in the Inland Pacific Northwest *Journal of Range
           Management* 33(6):415-23.

Sigerist, Henry E.
  1944   *Civilization and Disease*. Ithaca: Cornell University Press.
  1970   The Special Position of the Sick. In *Henry E. Sigerist on the Sociology of Medicine* pp. 388-
           394. Milton I. Roemer, ed. New York: MD Publications. Reprinted in 1977, The Special
           Position of the Sick. pp. 43:388-394. In *Culture, Disease, and Healing: Studies in Medical
           Anthropology*. David Landy, ed. New York: Macmillan Publishing Co., Inc.

Silverman, Julian
  1967   Shamans and Acute Schizophrenia. *American Anthropologist*. February, 69(1):21-31.

Simms, John A.
  1875   Letter of John A. Simms, September 1, 1875 In *Annual Reports of Agents in Washington
           Territory*. Colville Indian Agency, September 1. Records of the Colville Agency, Cage 213,
           Series 2, Box 2, Folder 16. (Reports on the Colville and Reports of Employees in Service at
           Colville Agency, 1872-79.
  1876   *Annual Report, Commissioner of Indian Affairs*. Packet 11B. Washington State University
           Archives. Petitioner's Exhibit 65, Pt. 2:55-149. Kalispel Tribe *v.* United States, Docket No. 94.
  1880   Letter from John A. Simms, August 18, 1880 In *Annual Report of the Commissioner of Indian
           Affairs*, 153, Washington: Washington State University Archives.
  1882   Section of Population, Sources of Subsistence, Religious, Vital, and Criminal Statistics. *Annual
           Report 0f the Commissioner of Indian Affairs to the Secretary of the Interior for the Year* 1882.
           Washington: U.S. Government Printing Office.

Simpson, Sir George E.
  1847   *Narrative of a Journey Round the World, During the Years 1841 and 1842*. 2 vols. London:
           Henry Colburn, Publisher.
  1968   *Fur Trade and Empire. George Simpson's Journal*. Entitled Remarks Connected with the Fur
           Trade in the Course of a Voyage from the York Factory to Fort George and Back to York
           Factory 1824-25. With Related Documents. Revised Edition. Edited with a New Introduction
           by Frederick Merk. Cambridge, Massachusetts: Belknap Press.

Sleeper-Smith, Susan
  2000   Women, Kin, and Catholicism: New perspectives on the fur trade. *Ethnohistory*. Spring,
           47(2):423-452.

Smith, Allan H.

1936-8   Kalispel field notes Ms., Kalispel Tribal Archives, Lewis and Clark College, Clarkston, Idaho.

1941   The Dynamics of Cultural Diffusion in the Plateau Area: With Particular Reference to Slavery and Trade (Unpublished Ph.D. dissertation, Department of Anthropology, Yale University.)

1950   Kalispel ethnography. Manuscript, Exhibit 65, and (pp. 151-300, incl.). Kalispel Ethnography. Washington, Commission). Docket 94.

1951   Lower Pend d' Oreille or Kalispel Tribe of Indians *v.* The United States of America. Docket 94, (pp. 1-104). Deposition of Allan H, Smith taken at Spokane, Washington, Box 1077. National Archives of the United States, Indian Claims Commission, Washington. Lower Pend d' Oreille or Kalispel Tribe *v.* The United States of America. Deposition of Allan H, Smith taken at Spokane, Washington, Box 1077. National Archives of the United States, Indian Claims Commission, Washington.

1953   *The Indians of Washington.* Research Studies of the State College of Washington, June, (21) 85-113.

1961   An Ethnological Analysis of David Thompson's 1809-1811 Journeys in the Lower Pend Oreille Valley, Northeast Washington. *Ethnohistory* Fall, 8(4):309-357.

1965   Linguistic and Geographic Relations in the Northern Plateau Area. *Southwestern Journal of Anthropology* 21(1):63-78.

1983   The Native Peoples. pp. 135-334. In *Cultural Resources of the Rocky Reach of the Columbia River*, vol. 1. Randall Schalk and Robert Mierendorf, eds. *Washington State University for Northwest Anthropology, Project Papers Report* 1. Pullman, Washington.

1991   Kalispel Ethnography and Ethnohistory. The Calispel Valley Archaeological Project, Project Report No. 16. Center for Northwest Anthropology. Paul Sanders, William Andrefsky and Stephen Samuels, ed. Department of Anthropology. Washington State University, Pullman, Washington.

1989-96   Personal communication

2000   *Kalispel Ethnography and Ethnohistory, in The Calispel Valley Archaeological Project*, pp. 8-1.154. Paul Sanders, William Anfrefsky, and Stephen Samuels, eds. Center for Northwest Anthropology, Department of Anthropology, Washington State University, Pullman.

Smith, Courtland

1979   *Salmon Fishers of the Columbia.* Corvallis: Oregon State University Press.

Smith, Harlan I.

1900   Archaeology of the Thompson River Region, *British Columbia. American Museum of Natural History, Anthropology Papers* 2(6):401-454. New York: The Jesup North Pacific Expedition 6.

Smith, Kenneth M.

1946   Spirit-Possession in Native America. *Southwestern Journal of Anthropology.* 2:323-339).

Smith, Robin T.

2007   Personal communication.

Smith, William C.

1977   *Archaeological Explorations in the Columbia Plateau: A Report on the Mesa Project 1973-1975.* Central Washington Archaeological Survey. Central Washington University. Ellensburg, Washington.

Snowden, Clinton A.

1909   *History of Washington: The Rise and Progress of an American State.* Cornelius H. Hanford, Miles C. Moore, eds. William D. Tyler, and Stephen J. Chadwick. vol. 4. New York: The Century Publishing Company.

Spencer, Robert F., Jesse D. Jennings, *et al.*

1965   *The Native Americans: History and Ethnology of the North American Indians.* New York: Harper & Row Publishers.

Sperlin, Otis Bedney

1913   Exploration of The Upper Columbia *Washington Historical Quarterly.* January 4(1):3-11.

1917   Fur Trade Forts in Washington, *Washington Historical Quarterly.* April, 8(2):102-113

1930   Two Kootenay Women Masquerading as Men? Or Were They One? *Washington Historical Quarterly.* January, 21(1):120-130.

Spier, Leslie

1930   Klamath Ethnography. In *University of California Publications in American Archaeology and Ethnology* 30:224-325. Berkeley.

1935   The Prophet Dance of the Northwest and Its Derivatives: The Source of the Prophet Dance. *General Series in Anthropology* No. 1. Menasha, Wisconsin: George Banta Publishing Company.

1936   Tribal Distribution in Washington. *General Series in Anthropology* No. 3. Menasha, Wisconsin: George Banta Publishing Company.

1938   The Sinkaietk or Southern Okanogan of Washington. By Walter Cline, Rachel S. Commons, May Mandlebaum, Richard H. Post, and L.V.W. Waters. *General Series in Anthropology* 6. Contributions from the Laboratory of Anthropology 2. Menasha, Wisconsin: George Banta.

Spier, Leslie and Edward Sapir

1930   Wishram Ethnography. *University Publications in Anthropology.* May, 3(3):151-300.

Spinden, Herbert Joseph

1908   The Nez Perce Indians. *Memoirs of the American Anthropologist Association* 2(3):167-274. Lancaster, Pennsylvania.

Spokane Chronicle

1922   Indian Tragedy 800 Years Old. *Spokane Chronicle*, 36(202):4; 15 May. Spokane.

Spokane Tribal History Collection (STHC)

n.d.   Field notes and electronic recordings of the Spokane Tribal History Collection. Eastern Washington University Archival Collection, JFK Library, SPC 986-0248. Cheney, Washington.

Spokesman-Review

1911   Brought Back to Rest With Indian Fathers Near Spokane. *Spokesman-Review*, 9(33) Part 4:2; 23 July. Spokane, Washington.

Sprague, Roderick
1959   A Comparative Cultural Analysis of an Indian Burial Site in Southern Washington. Master's Thesis, Washington State University. Pullman.
1967   Aboriginal Burial Practices on the Plateau Region of North America. Doctoral dissertation, University of Arizona. Tucson. University Microfilms International, Ann Arbor, Michigan.
1985   Glass Trade Beads: A Progress Report. *Historical Archaeology* 19(2):87-105.
1991   Description of Glass Beads, 10-CW-4. In *Archaeological Investigations at the Clearwater Fish Hatchery Site (45-CW-4)*, by Robert Lee Sappington, pp. 86-87. University of Idaho Anthropological Report Series, No. 91. Moscow.
1998-2006 Person communication.

Sprague, Roderick, and Walter H. Birkby
1970   Miscellaneous Columbia Plateau Burial. *Tebiwa* 13(2):1-32.

Sprague, Roderick, and Jay Miller
1979   Burial Relocation Survey, Chief Joseph Reservoir, 1977-78. *University of Idaho Anthropological Research Manuscript Series*, No. 51. Moscow.

St. John, Harold
1963   *Flora of Southeastern Washington and of Adjacent Idaho*. 3rd ed. Escondido, California: Outdoor Pictures.

Stanley, John Mix
1862   Portraits of North American Indians, with Sketches of Scenery, etc., Painted by J. M. Stanley. *Smithsonian Institution Miscellaneous Collections 2(3), Washington. Reports of Explorations and Surveys to Ascertain the Most Practicable and Economical Route for a Railroad from the Mississippi River to the Pacific Ocean*. vol. 12, part 1. Washington: B. Tucker, printer, 1855 - 1860.

Stanley, George F. G., ed.
1970   *Mapping the Frontier: Charles Wilson's Diary of the Survey of the 49th Parallel, 1856-1862, While Secretary of the British Boundary Commission*. Seattle: University of Washington Press.

Stanton, William
1975   *The Great United States Exploring Expedition of 1838-1842*. Berkeley: University of California Press.

Stapp, Darby C.
1984   Late Prehistoric Burials with Copper Artifacts in the Pacific Northwest. (Master's thesis. Department of Anthropology. University of Idaho, Moscow, Idaho.)

Stern, Theodore
1993   Chiefs & Chief Traders: Indian Relations at Fort Nez Percés, 1818-1855. [vol. 2]. Corvallis: Oregon State University Press.
1998   Columbia River Trade Network. In *Handbook of North American Indians. Plateau*. 12:641-652. Deward E. Walker, Jr., ed. Washington: Smithsonian Institution.

Stevens, Hazard
1856   *The Life of Isaac Ingalls Stevens*. (Steven's report to the Indian Department, 22 October 1856.)
1900   *The Life of Isaac Ingalls Stevens by His Son Hazard Stevens*. Epston: Houghton, Mifflin and Company.

Stevens, Isaac Ingalls

1855   *Narrative and Final Report of Explorations for a Route for the Pacific Railroad, near the Forty-Seventh and Forty-Ninth Parallel of North Latitude from St. Paul to Puget Sound.* 33d Congress. Made Under the Direction of the Secretary of War, in 1853-5, According to the Acts of Congress of March 3, 1853, May 31, 1854, and August 5, 1854. 2nd Session, House Executive Document 56, vols. 1 and 12, Washington, D.C.: Thomas H. Ford, Printer

1860   *Reports of Explorations and Surveys to Ascertain the Most Probable and Economic Route for a Railroad From the Mississippi River to the Pacific Ocean, Made Under the Direction of the Secretary of War, in 1853-5.* According to Acts of Congress of March 2, 1853, May 31, 1854, and August 5, 1854. 36th Congress, 1st Session, House Executive Document 56, Serial 1055, vol. 12, Book 1 and 2. Washington, D.C.: Thomas H. Ford, Printer.

1861   *Explorations And Surveys For A Railroad From The Mississippi River To The Pacific Ocean, Under the Direction of the Secretary of Wa, in 1834-5 Near The Forty-Seventh And Forty-Ninth Parallels Of North Latitude.* vol. 12. Washington: Thomas H. Ford

Stevens, Rebecca A.

2000   Freshwater Mussel shell Middens and the Nutritional Value of *Margaritifera falcata* on the Upper Wenatchee River. (Unpublished M.A. thesis. Department of Anthropology and Geography. Eastern Washington State University, Cheney.)

2007   Personal communication.

Stewart, Egar I., and Jane R. Stewart, eds.

1957   *The Columbia River; or, Scenes and Adventures on the Western Side of the Rocky Mountains, Among Various Tribes of Indians Hitherto Unknown: Together with a Journey Across the American Continent.* Edgar I. Stewart and Jane R. Stewart, eds. Norman: The University of Oklahoma Press.

Stewart, Kenneth M.

1946   Spirit Possession in Native America. *Southwestern Journal of Anthropology* 2:323-339.

Stewart, Omar C.

1951   Burning and Natural Vegetation in the United States. *Geographical Review* 41(2):317-20.

1954   Forest fires with a purpose. *Southwestern Lore* 20(4):59-64.

1956   Fire as the First Great Force Employed by Man. In *Man's Role in Changing the Face of the Earth*, pp. 115-133. W. L. Thomas, ed. Chicago: University of Chicago Press.

1963   Barriers to understanding the influence of use of fire by aborigines on vegetation. Proceedings of Tall Timbers Fire Ecology Conference. 2:117-126.

Stewart, Sir William Drummond

1846   *Altowan, or, Incidents of Life and Adventures in the Rocky Mountains, By an Amateur Traveller.* 2 vols., ed. James Wilson Webb. New York: Harper & Brothers

Stimson, W.

1985   *A View of the Falls: An Illustrated History of Spokane.* Northridge, California: Windsor Publications, Inc.

Stone, Livingston
 1883   Scarcity of salmon in the Little Spokane and other streams on the Pacific Coast. 3:476-477.
          Bulletin United States Fish Commission
 1885   Explorations on the Columbia River from the head of Clark's Fork to the Pacific Ocean, made
          in the summer of 1883. pp. 237-258. Washington: U.S. Government Printing Office.

Strong, William Duncan
 1945   The Occurrence and Wider Implications of a "Ghost Cult" on the Columbia River Suggested by
          Carvings in Wood, Bone and Stone. *American Anthropologist*, n.s. 47(2):244-261.

Suckley, George, MD
 1855   Report of Dr. George Suckley, Assistant Surgeon, U.S.A., of His Trip in Canoe from Fort
          Owen, down the Bitter Root, Clark's Fork, and Columbia Rivers to Vancouver. pp. 291-300. In
          I. I. Stevens, 1855 *Reports of Explorations and Surveys, to As the Most Practical and
          Economical Route for a Railroad From the Mississippi River to the Pacific Ocean.* vol. I, Part
          2. 33rd Congress, 2nd Session, Senate Executive Document No. 78 and House Executive
          Document No. 91. Washington.

Suttles, Wayne
 1951   The Early Diffusion of the Potato among the Coast Salish. *Southwestern Journal of
          Anthropology* 7:272-85.
 1972   On the Cultural Track of the Sasquatch. Northwest Anthropological Research Notes. 6(1):65-
          90.

Swanton, John R.
 1952   *The Indian Tribes of Washington, Oregon, and Idaho.* Bureau of American Ethnology, Bulletin
          145. Washington: U.S. Government Printing Office.

Swindell, Earl H., Jr.
 1942   *Report on Source, Nature and Extent of the Fishing, Hunting and Miscellaneous Related Rights
          of Certain Indian Tribes in Washington and Idaho Together with Affidavits Showing Location
          of a Number of Usual and Accustomed Fishing Grounds and Station.* U.S. Department of
          Interior, Office of Indian Affairs, Division of Forestry and Grazing. Washington, D.C.

Sykes, Cherip
 2007   *Glycyrrhiza lepidota* (Nutt.) Pursh: Wild licorice, American licorice. pp. 1-5.
          www4.geometry.net/detail/basic_b/blackfoot-indians-native-amer.

Szasz, Ferenc Morson
 2000   *Scots in the North American West as Cultural Brokers, 1790-1917.* Norman: University of
          Oklahoma Press.

Taylor, M. Scott
 2007   Buffalo Hunt: International Trade and the Virtual Extinction of the North American Bison.
          Working Paper no. W12969. University of Calgary - Economics, National Bureau of Economic
          Research.

Teit, James Alexander

1904   Field notes on Thompson and Neighboring Salish languages. Manuscript No. 30 (S1b.7) [Freeman No. 2492] in the American Philosophical Society Library, Philadelphia.

1908   Vocabulary in Okanagan and Related Dialects. Manuscript No.30 (S1d.2) (Freeman No. 2552) in the American Philosophical Society Library, Philadelphia.

1909   The Shuswap. Franz Boas, ed. In *Memoirs of the American Museum of Natural History* 4(7); *Publication of the Jesup North Pacific Expedition* 2(7). New York. (Reprinted by AMS Press, New York, 1975.)

1928   The Middle Columbia Salish. Franz Boas, ed. *University of Washington Publications in Anthropology* 2(4). Seattle.

1930   The Salishan Tribes of the Western Plateau. Franz Boas, ed. pp. 23-396 in 45th *Annual Report of the Bureau of American Ethnology for 1927-1928*. Washington, D.C.

1963   The Indian Claims Commission 301. The Yakima Tribe v. The United States. Def., The Confederated Tribes of the Colville Reservation *et al*. Pet, Ex. 441:103, 104. Doc. No. 161:301-361.

Thayer, James Steel

1980   The Berdache of the Northern Plains: A Socioreligious Perspective. *Journal of Anthropological Research*, 37(3):287-93.

Thompson, David

1916   *Narrative of Explorations in Western America, 1784-1812*. ed., Joseph Burr Tyrrell Publications of the Champlain Society. 12. Toronto. The Champlain Society. Reprinted: Richard Glover, ed. 1962. (Greenwood Press, New York, 1968.)

1950   David Thompson's Journals Relating to Montana and Adjacent Regions, 1808-1812. Transcribed from a Photostatic Copy of the Original Manuscripts and edited with an Introduction by M. Catherine White. *Montana State University Studies* 1. Missoula.

1962   David Thompson's Narrative of His Explorations in Western America, 1784-1812. A new ed. with added material [...]. *Richard Glover, ed. Publications of the Champlain Society* 40. Toronto: The Champlain Society. (Original publication: Joseph B. Tyrrell, ed. The Champlain Society, Toronto, 1916.)

Thoms, Alston

1983   Population Decimation and the Antiquity of Plateau Culture. Unpublished manuscript in possession of the author.

1989   The Northern Roots of Hunter-Gatherer Intensification: Camas and the Pacific Northwest. Ph.D. dissertation, Department of Anthropology, Washington State University, Pullman. Photocopy: University Microfilms International, Ann Arbor, Michigan, 1991.

1991   Landscape Evolution and Economic Resource Structure of the Middle 10-11 December 1872 Spokane River Valley. In *Archaeology of the middle Spokane River Valley: Investigations Along the Spokane Centennial Trail, Project Report* Number 17. John A Draper and William Andrefsky, Jr., eds. Center for Northwest Anthropology, Department of Anthropology, Washington State University

2005   The Fire Stones Carry: Ethnographic and Archaeological Expectations for Hot-Rock Cookery in Western North America. pp. 1-30. Learning From Once Hot-Rocks. Jeffery Leach, ed. In *International Series of British Anthropological Reports*. Oxford: Archaeopress.

Thwaites, Reuben Gold, ed.

1904   *Early Western Travels: 1748-1846. A Series of Annotated Reprints of some of the best and rarest contemporary volumes of travel descriptive of the Aborigines and Social and Economic Conditions in the Middle and Far West, during the period of Early American Settlement. 38 vols. Franchère's Voyage to Northwest, 1811-1814*, vol. 6. Cleveland: The Arthur H. Clark Company.

1966   *Early Western Travels: 1748-1846. A series of Annotated Reprints of some of the best and rarest contemporary volumes of travel, descriptive of the Aborigines and Social and Economic Conditions in the Middle and Far West, during the period of Early American Settlement.* vol. 7. *Ross's Adventures of the First Settlers on the Oregon or Columbia River, 1810-1813.* Edited and Notes, Introduction, Index, etc., by Reuben Gold Twaites. New York: AMS Press, Inc.

Tolmie, William Fraser

1963   *The Journals of William Fraser Tolmie, Physician and Fur Trader.* Vancouver, Canada: Mitchell Press.

Townsend, John Kirk

1839   Narrative of a Journey Across the Rocky Mountains to the Columbia River. Philadelphia: H, Henry Perkins & Marvin. Reprinted in 1905, *Early Western*, vol. 8. Reubens Gold Twaites, ed. Cleveland: Arthur H. Clark.

Trimble, W. J.

1914   American and British Treatment of Indians in the Pacific Northwest. *Washington Historical Quarterly.* January-October, 5(1):32-54.

Turner, Nancy J.

1975   The Ethnobotany of the Okanogan Indians of British Columbia and Washington State. *Occasional Papers of the British Columbia Provincal Museum* 21. The British Columbia Language Study Project. Victoria.

1977   Economic Importance of Black Tree Lichens (*Bryoria fremontii*) to the Indians of Western North America. *Economic Botany* No. 31:461-470.

1978   Food Plants of British Columbia Indians: Part 2, Interior Peoples. *British Columbia Provincial Museum Handbook* 36. Victoria.

1979   Plants In British Columbia Indian Technology. *British Columbia Provincial Museum. Handbook.* 38. Victoria.

1982   Traditional Use of Devil's-Club (*Oplopanax horridus*; araliaceae) by Native Peoples in Western North America. *Journal of Ethnobiology.* May, 2(1):17-38.

1984   Counter-irritant and other medicinal uses of plants in Ranuncularceae by Native Peoples of British Columbia and neighboring areas. *Journal of Ethnopharmacology* 11:181-201.

1995   *Food Plants of Coastal First People.* Royal British Columbia Museum Handbook.

2003-10 Personal communication.

Turner, Nancy J., and M. A. M. Bell

1973   The Ethnobotany of the Southern Kwakiutl Indians of British Columbia. *Economic Botany* 27(3):257-319).

Turner, Nancy, J. R. Bouchard, and D. Kennedy

1980   Ethnobotany of the Okanogan-Colville Indians of British Columbia and Washington. *Occasional Papers of the British Columbia Provincial Museum*, No. 21. Victoria: British Columbia Provincial Museum.

Turner, Nancy J., L. C. Thompson, and M. Terry Thompson, and A. Z. York
  1990   *Thompson Ethnobotany: Knowledge and Usage of Plants by the Thompson Indians of British Columbia*. Royal British Columbia Museum Memoir No. 3.

Turner, Nancy J., and Adam F. Szczawinski
  1991   *Common Poisonous Plants and Mushrooms of North America*. Portland: Timber Press, Inc.

Turner, Victor
  1964   An Adembu Doctor in Practice. In *Magic, Faith, and Healing*. Ari Kiev, ed. New York: Free Press.
  1967   *Forest of Symbols: Aspects of Ndembu Ritual*. Ithaca: Cornell University Press.

Turney-High, Harry Holbert
  1933   The Bluejay Dance. *American Anthropologist* 35(1):103-107.
  1933a   Flathead Cooking of Camas and Bitterroot. *The Scientific Monthly* 2 (4)36:262-263.
  1937   The Flathead Indians of Montana, *American Anthropological Association, Memoir* No. 48. Menasha, Wisconsin. (Reprinted: Kraus Reprint, New York, 1969.).
  1941   Ethnography of the Kutenai. *Memoirs of the American Anthropological Association*. No. 56. Menasha, Wisconsin. (Reprinted: Kraus Reprint, New York, 1974.)

Tyrrell, Joseph Burr, ed.
  1916   *David Thompson's Narrative of the Explorations in Western America (1784-1812)*. Toronto: Champlain Society

Van Gennep, Arnold
  1969   *Rites of Passage: A Classic Study of Cultural Celebrations*. Chicago: University of Chicago Press.

Van Kirk, Sylvia
  1980   *Many Tender Ties: Woman in Fur-Trade Society in Western Canada, 1670-1870*. Winnipeg: Watson & Dwyer.

Viall, John
  1871   *Pioneering Days*. London: Smith, Elder and Company

Vitt, Dale H., Janet E. Marsh, and Robin B. Bovey
  1988   *Mosses, Lichens & Ferns of Northwest North America*. Edmonton, Alberta: Lone Pine Publishing.

Walcott, Randy
  1986   The Bluejay Ceremony: A Study of Change in an Intensification Ritual and Its Analysis as a Metaphor. Paper presented at the 41st Annual Northwest Anthropological Association Conference, 10-13 March. Sheraton Inn, Tacoma.

Walker, Deward E., Jr.

1963-64　Nez Perce field notes. Unpublished MS.

1966　A Nez Perce Ethnographic Observation of Archaeological Significance. *American Antiquity* 31(3):436-437.

1967　Mutual Cross-Utilization of Economic Resources in the Plateau: An Example from Aboriginal Nez Perce Fishing Practices. *Washington State University, Laboratory of Anthropology, Report of Investigations No. 41.* Pullman.

1968　*Conflict and Schism in Nez Perce Acculturation: A Study of Religion and Politics.* Pullman: Washington State University Press. (Reprinted, with a Foreword by Robert A. Hackenberg: University of Idaho Press, Moscow, 1985.).

1969　New Light on the Prophet Dance Controversy. *Ethnohistory* 16(3):245-253.

1973　*Indians of Idaho,* vol. 1: Aboriginal Cultures. University of Idaho. Department of Sociology/Anthropology. Anthropological Monographs 1. Moscow, Idaho.

1977　Anthropological Guide for the Coulee Dam National Recreation. Area. University of Idaho *Anthropological Research Manuscript Series No. 33,* Moscow.

1978　*Indians of Idaho.* Moscow, Idaho: University of Idaho Press.

1989　Plateau: Nez Perce. In *Witchcraft and Sorcery of the American Native Prophet,* Deward E. Walker, Jr., ed. Moscow: University of Idaho Press.

Walker, Deward E., Jr., and Sylvester H. Lahren, Jr.

1977　Anthropological Guide for the Coulee Dam National Recreation Area. University of Idaho. *Anthropological Research Manuscript Series 3.* Moscow, Idaho

Walker, Deward E., Jr., and Roderick Sprague

1998　History Until 1846. *Handbook of North American Indians. Plateau.* 12:138-148, Deward E. Walker, Jr., ed. Washington: Smithsonian Institution Press.

Walker, Deward E., Jr. and Helen H. Schuster

1998　Religious Movements. *Handbook of North American Indians.* 12 *Plateau.* 12:499-514, Deward E. Walker, Jr., ed. Washington: Smithsonian Institution Press.

Wallace, Anthony F. C.

1999　*Jefferson and The Indians: The Tragic Fate of the First Americans* Cambridge, Massachusetts: The Belknap Press of Harvard University Press.

Wallmo, O. C.

1981　Mule and black-tailed deer distribution and habitats. In *Mule and black-tailed deer of North America.* pp. 1-15. O. C. Wallmo, ed., Lincoln: University of Nebraska Press.

Walters, L.V.W.

1938　Social Structure. The Sinkaietk or Southern Okanagan of Washington. pp. 73-99. *General Series in Anthropology,* No. 6. Leslie Spier, ed. Menasha, Wisconsin: George Banta Publishing Company Agent.

Ward, Jean M. and Elaine A. Maveety

1995　Nancy Perkins Wynecoop, 1875-1939 and The Song of the Generous Supply and Able-One, My Grandmother. pp. 16-26. In *Pacific Northwest Women, 1815-1925: Lives, Memories, and Writings.* Corvallis: Oregon State University Press.

Warren, Henry J.

1848　*Sketches in North America and the Oregon Territory.* London: Dickinson.

Weaver, Harold
    1957   Effects of Prescribed Burning in Second Growth Ponderosa Pine. *Journal of Forestry* 55(11)719-722.
    1967   *Reports on Prescribed Burning on the Colville Indian Reservation, Washington, during 1943 and 1944.* U.S. Dept. of the Interior. Washington, D.C.

Webb, James Watson
    1846   *Annual Report of the Board of Regents of the Smithsonian Institution.* 2 vols. New York: Harper & Brothers.

Whitman, Marcus, MD
    1843   Letters to Elkanah Walker. Beinecke Rare Book Room and Manuscript Library. New Haven: Yale University.

Wiggins, Marianne
    2007   The Shadow Catcher. Reviewed by Richard R. Woodward. *The New York Times Book Review,* July vol. 62, no. 26, pg. 11.

Wihr, William Saxe
    1995   "You Toad-Sucking Fool": An Inquiry into the Possible Use of Butotenine by Northern Northwest Coast Shamans. *Northwest Anthropological Research Notes* 29(1):51-59.

Wilkes, Charles, U.S.N.
    1845   *Lieutenant Wilkes' Narrative of the United States Exploring Expedition During the Years 1838, 1839, 1840, 1841, 1842.* 5 vols. and Atlas. Philadelphia: Lea and Blanchard.

Wilkinson, M. C.
    1877   Official Report of M. C. Wilkinson, 1st Lieut., 3rd Inf., Aide-de-Camp, made in accordance with the following order: S.O. 167, Headquarters. Dept. of the Columbia. Manuscript in *Records of the War Department, U.S. Army Commands*, Department of the Columbia, No. 2473, 1877, National Archives, Washington.

Williams, Christina M. M.
    1922   A Daughter of Angus MacDonald, In *Washington Historical Quarterly* 13, 2:107-117.

Williams, Gerald W.
    2005   *References on the use of the American Indian use of fire in ecosystems.* USDA Forest Service. Washington.

Wilson, Charles William
    1861   Watercolor of Spokan Plains. PdP0321 in *British Columbia Archives.*
    1866   Report on the Indian Tribes Inhabiting the Country in the Vicinity of the 49th Parallel of North Latitude. *Transactions of the Ethnological Society of London*, New Series, 1865, 4:275-332. London.

Winans, William Parkhurst
    1870   Census Roster of the Spokane Indians. William Parkhurst Winans Papers 16.1 ms.(44-F/Box 6). Washington State University Library Archives, Pullman.
    1871   *Annual Report to the Commissioner of Indian Affairs.* William Parkhurst Winans Papers, 292-5, Washington State University Library Archives, Pullman. Box 4, No. 34.
    1873   *Annual Report to the Commissioner of Indian Affairs.* William Parkhurst Winans Papers, 1815-1891,7. Easter Washington State University, Cheney, Washington.

Winkelman, Michael
  1986   Trance states: A Theoretical model and cross-cultural analysis. *Ethos.* 14:174-2034.
  1989   A Cross-cultural Study of Shamanistic Healers. *Journal of Psychoactive Drugs* 21(1):17-24, January-March.

Winthrop, Theodore
  1863   *The Canoe and The Saddle, Adventures Among the Northwestern Rivers and Forests, and Isthmiana.* Boston: Ticknor & Fields.

Wishart, David J.
  1979   *The Fur Trade of the American West 1807-1840: A Geographic Synthesis.* Lincoln: University of Nebraska Press.

Wissler, Clark
  1914   The Influence of the Horse in the Development of Plains Culture. *American Anthropologist,* n.s. Jan. - Mar., 16(1):1-25.
  1938   *The America Indian.* New York: American Museum of Natural History and Oxford University Press.

Wolman, C.
  1970   The Cradleboard of the Western Indians: A Baby-tending Device of Cultural Importance. *Clinical Pediatrics* 9(5):306-308.

Wood, W. Raymond
  1957   Perforated Elk Teeth: A Functional and Historical Analysis. *American Antiquity* 22(4):381-386).

Work, John
  1820   John Work's Journal of a Trip From Fort Colville to Fort Vancouver and Return in 1828. Introduced and Annotated by T. C. Elliott. *Washington Historical Quarterly,* 1914, 5 (4):258-87.
  1823-24 Journal, 18 July to 28 October 1823, York Factory to Spokane House. Typescript A/B/40/W89.1A. British Columbia Archives and Record Service, Victoria.
  1829   Extracts from "Answers to Queries on Natural History," Fort Colville, 1 April 1829. Manuscript B.45/e/2, fos. 1, 2d-3, 3d-4, 9d. Appendix A. Hudson's Bay Company Archives, Provincial Archives of Winnipeg, Manitoba.
  1830   [Some information relative to the Colville District, Fort Colville Report, April 1830.] (Manuscript B.45/e/3/1-14), Hudson's Bay Company Archives, Provincial Archives of Manitoba, Winnipeg.)
  1971   *The Snake Country Expedition of 1830-1831: John Work's Field Journal.* ed., Francis D. Haines, Jr. Norman: University of Oklahoma Press.

Wynecoop, Arnold
  2002-10 Personal communication.

Wynecoop, David C.
  1969   *Children of the Sun: A History of the Spokane Indians.* Spokane: Comet and Cole.

Wynecoop, Nancy Perkins
  1938   Nancy Winecoop [sic]. WPA Interviews and Autobiographical Narrative. Told by the Pioneers' Reminiscences of Pioneer Life in Washington. 1:114-119. Olympia: State of Washington.

1985   *The Stream: An Indian Story.* Edited and sections added by authors, daughter N. Wynecoop Clark. Self-published manuscript in possession of the author's daughter.

1996   Reminiscences of Nancy Wynecoop. *The Pacific Northwest Forum Second Series* 9(1-2:62-67). First published in *Told by the Pioneers: Tales of Frontier Life as Told by Those Who Remember the Days of the Territory and Early Statehood of Washington,* 3 vols. F. I. Trotter, F. H. Loutzenhiser, and J. R. Loutzenhiser, eds. Olympia: Works Progress Administration, 1937-38:114-119.

Wynecoop, Tina
2000-2010 Personal communication.

Wynne-Davies, R.
1972   The epidemiology of congenital dislocation of the hip. *Developmental Medicine and Child Neurology* 14 (4):515-517.

Yantis, B. F.
1857   Letter from B. F. Yantis to J. W. Nesmith, Superintendent of Indian Affairs, Oregon Territory, 20 July 1857.

Young, Allan
1976   Some Implications of Medical Beliefs and Practices for Social Anthropology. *American Anthropologist* 78(1):5-24.

Zimmerman, William, Jr.
1957   The Role of the Bureau of Indian Affairs Since 1933. In American Indians and American Life. eds. George E Simpson and J. Milton Yinger. Reprinted in The Annals of The Academy of Political and Social Science. American Indians and American Life. ed., Thorsten Sellin, and Marvin E. Wolfgang, Assistant Editor. May, 311:31-40. Edited with an introduction by Richard N. Ellis. Lincoln: University of Nebraska Press [1972].

Index

A

abalone   33, 494, 497, 500
Abrahamson, Lucinda   560, 589, 774
abscesses   618
abstinence   53, 94, 362
Ackerknecht, Erwin H.   561, 774
Ackerman, Lillian A.   59, 82, 155, 160, 774
acne   614, 618
acupressure   571-2, 584-5, 592-3, 722
Adney, Edwin Tappan   453, 774
adultery   87, 89-90, 114, 152, 161-2, 172
adulthood   132, 134-5, 157, 677, 742
afterlife   170, 187, 231, 326, 666, 729
agnomens   118-19, 131, 513, 741
agriculture   13, 61-2, 65-9, 73, 251, 275, 334,
      348, 365-6, 457, 464, 485, 512, 608, 652
AHS *see* Archaeological and Historical Services
Alberta   10, 802, 818, 828
alcohol   47, 53, 57, 628, 677, 720
Allen, Paula Gunn   164, 774
alliances   46, 69, 149
Alvord, Brevit Major Benjamin   151, 160, 339,
      690, 718, 774
Ames, Kenneth M.   15, 201-2, 205, 225, 774
ammunition   55, 58, 322-3, 659
Anastasio, Angelo   13, 15, 17, 20-1, 33, 36-7, 49-
      50, 81-2, 140, 154, 318, 360, 460, 482, 774
anchors   225-6, 366, 440, 451
Angelino, Henry   165-6, 774
anger   3, 112, 119, 287-8
animal bones   356, 420, 510, 633
   breaking large   225
   burned   630
   discarded   356
   small   284
animal carcasses   257, 293, 303, 321, 324, 375,
      431, 457, 747
animal claws   474, 548
animal contamination   274, 354
animal fat   342, 430, 507, 616, 618, 648
animal feces   566, 652
animal foods   95, 276, 433

animal fur   482, 484
   small   485
animal grease   343, 621, 660
animal hairs   210
animal hides   263, 284, 483, 585
   frozen   457
   tanned   508
   untanned   508
animal husbandry   68, 357, 551
animal intestines   240, 564
animal kingdom   238, 330, 729
animal livers   258, 262, 266, 387, 429
animal organs   96, 420
animal predation   298, 360
animal predators   293, 311
animal species   234, 329
animal spirit   280, 284, 570, 682
animal traps   239, 247, 295, 353
animals   95-8, 122-4, 126-31, 256-60, 287-94,
      296-300, 302-26, 466-70, 482-6, 531-6, 661-
      8, 678-85, 707-12, 728-31, 760-5
   aquatic   302, 367, 684
   brains   316, 324, 622
   dead   95-6, 262, 709
   domesticated   97, 131, 171, 249, 270, 652, 691,
      704
   dressed   206, 321
   farm   49, 526
   ground-dwelling   252, 325, 335, 354, 357
   head   284, 289, 293, 302
   large   124, 224, 256, 258, 260, 263-4, 283, 289,
      294, 311-12, 317, 321, 435, 531
   leg bones   473
   marauding   243, 437, 441
   nocturnal   321, 576, 698, 708
   non-indigenous   551, 691
   pack   463
   pelts   53, 60, 290, 292, 321, 323-5, 482, 485-6,
      539-40
   scavenging   190, 339, 430
   small   41, 111-12, 123, 147, 261, 282, 285, 287-
      91, 293, 307, 323-5, 337, 355, 375, 678-9
   species   163, 240, 242-3, 246, 260, 306, 328-9,
      339-40, 343, 350, 361-2, 370-1, 504-5, 564,
      622-3
   water-dwelling   486, 734, 758
   wounded   465, 467, 698

836

mid-winter 134, 208, 271, 299, 304, 329, 492, 538-9, 547, 550, 681, 683, 688-9, 711-16, 720-2

mortuary 183-4

name-changing 129

name-giving 494

water 663

chairs 121, 194, 250, 692

Chalfant, Stuart A. 13, 15, 17-18, 22, 24, 29-30, 48, 69-70, 74, 82, 781

Chance, David H. 55, 318, 400, 452, 781

chants 298-9, 395, 517-18, 552, 761

charcoal 43-4, 192, 436, 492-3, 496, 499, 515, 530, 610, 716-17, 720

ground deer bone 99

charms 111, 113, 143, 234, 386, 489, 498

Chase, E. B. 410, 781

cheatgrass 414, 691, 693-4

Cheney 18, 24, 32, 703, 778, 783, 792, 803, 808-9, 812, 819, 822, 824, 831

chests 185, 197, 259, 444, 457-8, 466-7, 517, 551, 590, 593, 601, 606, 627, 678-9

Chewelah Indians 20, 25-6, 81, 140, 191, 218, 236, 317, 599, 706, 734, 766

Chewelah-Spokan Group 20, 25, 38, 118, 140, 148, 167, 188-9, 218, 295, 317-21, 382-3, 723-4, 733-4, 766

chewing 115, 280, 325, 613, 622, 624-5, 628, 631, 633, 635, 651, 655

chickens 324, 469, 538, 604, 691, 695

chief Spokane Garry 21, 63-4, 74, 76, 86, 234, 776, 786, 793, 817

chiefs 38-9, 41-2, 46, 73-4, 82-91, 141-2, 149-50, 153, 177-80, 185-6, 277, 404-5, 710, 726-7, 747-9

sub- 41, 84, 86, 88-9, 177

childbirth 93-6, 98-109, 115, 129, 134, 137-8, 155, 181, 196, 568, 626-7, 632, 658, 734

abortions (feticide) 99, 106, 114-15

infanticide 114, 116-17, 433

placenta 104-5

umbilical cords 40, 95-7, 104-5, 111

childhood 105, 109, 127, 131-2, 365, 692, 702

children 76-7, 79-81, 94-8, 101-18, 120-32, 145-60, 163, 194-5, 511-13, 523-4, 527-36, 634-8, 648-9, 697-702, 704-8

adopted 117, 163

betrothal 147

brother's 123

camp's 432

first 98, 100, 127, 155, 158, 768

husband's 152

illegitimate 117

infants 45, 103, 109-12, 115-17, 147, 463, 627, 633, 693

misbehaving 87, 89, 111, 118, 122, 125-6, 498, 705

newborn 102-4, 106, 108, 110, 116-17, 129-30, 639

orphan 74, 116-17, 121

twins 98, 103-4, 117, 751

unborn 94, 97-100, 129

young 117, 120, 122-3, 129, 131, 147, 170, 174, 186, 214, 219, 242, 345, 658, 675-6

Chinese 69-70, 496

Chinook language 26-7, 30, 35, 45, 60, 62, 112-13, 329, 635, 654, 772

chipmunks 41, 176, 221, 271, 307, 425, 678

Chittenden, Hiram Martin 47, 267, 402-3, 781, 785

chocolate tips 608, 623, 653

chokecherries 99, 228, 344-5, 347-8, 424, 446, 486, 600-1, 615, 625, 640

choreography 488, 539, 544-5

chores 53, 122, 135-7, 154, 219, 532, 555, 680, 688

Christianity 51, 59-61, 63-7, 74, 78, 551, 664, 693, 695, 725, 727

missionization 171, 558, 666, 728-9

churches 51-2, 62, 66, 543, 640, 693, 727-8

Clark, Robert A. 438, 781

Clark, Robert C. 58, 781

Clark, William P. 9, 21, 28, 47, 52, 58, 71, 222, 315, 318, 339, 369, 781, 803-4, 831-2

clay 5, 33, 41, 110, 203, 209, 236, 421, 424-5, 499, 507-8, 530-1, 594, 606, 631-4

ground 492, 621, 636

white 44, 139, 236, 263, 460, 488, 617, 626-7, 631, 633

cleansing 95, 104, 137, 139-40, 157, 189-90, 195, 246-7, 299, 564-5, 625-6, 630, 658-9, 661-2, 671-2

ritual 140, 175, 564, 671

Clements, Forrest E. 560, 781

838

premasticated 108
stone-boiled 419
defects, congenital 10, 94-5, 97-8, 709
dens 314, 317, 324
deodorants 246, 661-2
designs 190, 215, 219, 287, 427, 432, 453, 461-2, 472-3, 479, 481-2, 485-8, 492, 496-7, 791-2
  geometric 219, 252, 483-4
DeSmet, Pierre-Jean, S.J. 12, 21, 32, 37, 47, 58, 63, 302-3, 318, 325-7, 354-5, 402, 454-5, 468-9, 785
Deutsch, H. J. 65, 74, 786
Devereux, George 551, 686-7, 786, 804
DeVoto, Bernard 268, 786
diabetes 3, 656
diarrhea 109, 248, 350, 369, 625, 628-30, 632-4, 649
  treating 236, 625, 629, 632-3, 664
digging sticks 101, 124, 164, 172, 187, 190, 264, 297, 325, 333-6, 342, 395, 422, 527, 565
Dinwoodie, David W. 15, 786
Diomedi, Alexander, S.J. 82, 303, 395, 455, 786
diuretics 601, 631-2, 634, 643
Dixon, Cyril W. 93, 786
Doctrine of Signatures 40, 92-3, 95-6, 100, 108, 126, 143, 283, 460, 467, 526, 528, 534, 561-2, 711
dogs 39, 188, 207, 218, 259, 294, 300-2, 304, 310, 313-14, 320-4, 359, 404, 440-1, 464-9
  training 465-7, 681
dolls 198, 257, 512, 530
doorways 95, 206, 208, 219, 435, 441, 669, 756
Doughty, Ted 486, 786
Douglas, David 12, 181, 185, 369, 381, 384, 391, 408, 486, 640, 651, 771, 786, 802
Douglas, Mary 165, 185
Douglas firs 242-3, 246, 270, 356, 390, 412, 609, 626
dream dances 545, 724, 727
dream medicines 564-5
dreamer religion 725, 727
dreaming 85, 120, 129, 193, 314, 316, 545, 564-5, 575-6, 580-2, 673-6, 682, 684, 690, 707-10
  shaman's 571-2, 709
dreams 127, 129-30, 175, 193-4, 298-9, 564-5, 570-2, 575-6, 581-3, 590, 674-6, 680-2, 689-90, 707-10, 768-9

bad 107, 126, 576, 600
  patient's 571, 576
Dressler, William W. 577, 787
driftwood 75, 201, 203, 228, 395, 412, 427, 450, 452
drowning 113, 173, 183, 386, 684, 703
drummers 180, 543, 545, 555-6, 578
drumming 180, 511, 546, 555-6, 577-8, 580, 735
drums 32, 44, 180, 415, 539, 541-6, 552-3, 555-6, 580, 683, 701
Drury, Reverend Clifford Merrill 61-8, 76, 125, 172, 207-10, 244, 301-2, 438, 457, 465, 469-70, 571, 625, 650, 654
Dryden, Cecil P. 55, 188, 201, 787
Du Bois, Cora 19, 654, 726-7, 787
Duff, Wilson 741, 787
Dunn, Frederick L. 357, 787
Dunn, Jacob P., Jr. 70, 787
Durham, Nelson Wayne 19, 21, 28, 51, 54-8, 62, 64, 76, 112, 170, 205-6, 315, 318, 354-5, 388-9
dyes 234, 243, 246-7, 252, 349, 472, 485, 498-9, 802
  mineral 493, 499
  plant 252, 494, 498-9, 509
dysentery 634, 654

E

eagles 81, 240, 295-6, 327, 553, 672, 678, 683, 711
  feathers 33, 112, 190, 483, 487, 489, 539-40, 545, 556, 592, 675
ears 12, 43, 87, 143, 174, 182-3, 186, 218, 314, 464, 466, 493-4, 497, 499-501, 636
  aches 636
earthquakes 90, 356, 727, 732-3, 797
eclipses 604, 747
eddies 122, 382, 385, 390, 395
Edwards, Reverend Jonathan 20, 77, 360, 787
Eells, Myron 30, 37, 61-3, 209, 359-60, 400, 470, 788
eels 33, 346, 361, 371-3, 406, 428-9, 739
Egerton, Robert B. 166, 788
Egesdal, Steven M. 6, 9, 12, 14, 93-5, 115-17, 125, 150-2, 176, 311-12, 351, 412-13, 532, 552, 731

eggs 33, 98, 276, 327-8, 330-2, 364, 369-70, 429, 448, 646, 650, 691
  turtle 331-2, 703
Ehrenberg, C. G. 632, 788
Ekland, Roy E. 727-8, 788
elderberries 390, 394, 396, 455, 553, 585, 634, 636
  blue 347, 564, 617, 623, 653
elders 79-80, 104-7, 123-31, 136-8, 158-63, 168-70, 265-72, 412-14, 531-7, 603-8, 636-42, 655-8, 695-8, 705-7, 730-5
  accounts 207, 221, 223, 295, 297, 307, 343, 351, 374, 415, 496, 524, 642, 648-9, 732-3
  sorcerized 657
  Spokan 12, 96, 112, 173, 177, 217, 234, 245, 263, 268, 270, 282, 336, 394, 462
  traditional 79, 350, 588, 666
  widows 138
  women 98-102, 105, 113-14, 123-4, 139-40, 151-2, 244-6, 249, 254, 262-3, 334, 342-3, 371-2, 532-3, 640
Eli, Gibson 546, 569, 587, 683, 788
Eliade, Mircea 687, 725, 788
elk 216, 258, 260, 267, 271-2, 280-2, 284-5, 291, 300-1, 308, 319-21, 426, 473, 490, 497-8
  meat 426-7
  skins 216, 220, 230, 260-1, 471, 473, 489
Elliott, Thompson Coit 20-2, 52-8, 241, 261, 354-5, 370-1, 384-5, 399-400, 402, 437, 453-4, 465, 772-3, 783, 788
Ellis, M. M. 68, 365, 401, 789
Elmendorf, William Wellcome 20, 28-33, 40-3, 83-6, 88-91, 116-18, 128-30, 145-56, 158-9, 190-5, 205-9, 361-4, 452-4, 474-5, 480-6
Elmendorf's fieldwork 12, 25, 28, 187, 205, 212, 469, 586, 719, 721
elopement 145
Elpel, Thomas J. 286, 789
Elrod, Martin J. 267, 789
emetic 239, 255, 506, 631, 671
enclosures 279, 297, 304, 315, 320, 379, 381, 407
enculturation 77, 120-2, 157, 535, 538, 666, 668, 743
enemies 22, 37, 39-44, 71, 81, 117, 171, 177, 181, 282, 285, 309, 489-91, 540-1, 548-50
  camp 40-2

common 37, 49
Erickson, Kevin 494-5, 789
Ermatinger, Charles Oakes 113, 789
Erwin, Richard P. 499, 774, 789
escaping 43, 45, 103, 384, 403
ethnic groups 18, 20-1, 36, 50, 52, 148, 359-60, 407, 742
ethnobotany 10-11, 76, 275, 827
ethnographers 9, 14, 20, 24, 34, 48, 129, 167, 213, 269, 375, 490, 745, 771-2
ethnographies 9, 82, 164, 490, 530, 745, 778, 796, 828
etiologies 560, 603, 610, 619, 652
eulogies 176-8
Euro-Americans 19-20, 47, 51-2, 56-9, 66-70, 82, 90-1, 168-9, 461-2, 655, 694, 704-5, 711, 727, 742
  early 13, 20, 67, 267, 346
evil 53, 149, 171, 179, 184, 540, 542, 563, 573, 585, 591, 684, 691-3, 695-6, 756
  powers 678, 712
  spirits 111, 177, 184, 399, 516, 540-1, 574, 584, 586, 595, 684
Ewers, John C. 37, 459, 790, 811
excrement 5, 252, 306
eyes 1, 39, 92, 103, 113, 121, 134, 138, 174-5, 259, 265-6, 419-20, 537, 638-41, 684
  baby's 639
  cataracts 607, 638-9
  child's 639, 648
  lids 174, 640-1, 736
  soreness 638-41, 643
  wash 639-41, 643

F

Fabrega, H. 558, 790
faces 40, 43-4, 88, 186, 192, 492, 543, 588, 659, 701, 716, 767, 769
  painting 471, 491-2, 499
Fahey, John 140, 326, 357, 360, 459, 781, 790, 817
familials 87, 93, 172, 584, 692, 718
families 73-7, 81-4, 90-2, 114-17, 126-30, 137-44, 146-7, 154-63, 172-80, 192-8, 205-7, 210-12, 405, 431-9, 564-7
  grieving 178, 180, 194-5, 541

843

845

851

lynx   95, 290-1, 312, 324, 482, 722
Lyons, Kevin J.   10, 207, 248, 334, 373, 804

M

Mackenzie, Sir Alexander   52, 57, 318, 805
Madsen, William   578, 805
magic   113, 667-8, 805, 828
  contagious   143, 668, 692, 694
  projective   121, 142, 668
  sympathetic   99, 612, 667-8
Majors, Harry M.   726, 805
Makepeace, Anne   70, 805
Malinowski, Bronislaw   665, 667, 706, 805
Malouf, Carling   75, 340, 805
mammals
  land   113, 131, 231, 263, 289, 302, 307, 322,
      333, 380, 512, 703-4
  small   40, 293-4, 663
  water   455, 734
Mandelbaum, May   112-13, 169, 182, 189, 805
Manring, Benjamin F.   70, 85, 488, 805
marmots   33, 221, 287, 290, 323, 325, 477
marriage   30, 34, 36, 45-6, 49, 55, 59-60, 92, 114-
      15, 134-5, 140-2, 144-57, 159-63, 193-6,
      742-3
  bigamy   153
  ceremonies   144, 147-8
  couples   51, 95, 141-2, 144-8, 154-5, 159-60,
      707
  divorce   118, 144, 146, 148, 159-60
  intergroup   366, 742-3
  intermarriage   20, 29-30, 39, 46, 50, 54, 84,
      140, 149, 383, 421, 453
  levirate   146, 151-3, 160, 195, 612, 818
  monogamous   148-9
  polyandry   87, 148-9, 151-2
  polygamy   82, 144, 148-50
  polygyny   17, 59, 148-50
  prescribed   134, 142, 144, 146-8
  remarriage   160
  sororal polygyny   150-1
  sororate   146, 151-3, 160
  spouses   130, 150-1, 154, 159-61, 171, 193-4,
      690, 702
martingales   254, 461-2
Mason, Otis Tufton   453, 805

massage   100, 104, 262, 592-3, 604, 610-11, 722
mats   168, 189-90, 201-3, 205-8, 216-17, 239,
      247-51, 402-3, 411, 429-30, 432, 434, 436-7,
      441, 582-3
  cattail   135, 203-4, 207-8, 211, 217, 219-20,
      231, 248, 250, 256, 399, 442, 473, 524
  grass   217, 250, 453
  tule   31, 58, 102, 127, 135, 185, 204-8, 211-13,
      248-51, 337-9, 343-5, 428-9, 432, 713, 720
mauls   225, 229-30, 265, 412-14, 430-1, 452, 454
Maximilian, Alexander Philipp von   25, 806
May, Robert   143, 339, 374, 639, 806
McBeth, Kate   274, 804
McCarty, Ella   2, 9, 213, 448, 804
McDonald, M.   318, 369, 405, 410, 622, 804
McLaughlin, Castle   331, 473, 553, 804
McWhorter, Lucullus Virgil   170, 254, 805
meadowlark   87, 329, 668
Meany, Edward   21, 48, 53, 406, 461, 806
meat   33, 95-6, 144, 157-8, 256-60, 283, 290-2,
      316-25, 327-8, 330-3, 374-5, 419-20, 424-8,
      430-3, 762-3
  broth   108, 345, 351, 430
  butchering   256-8, 321, 367, 419, 763
  cooking   424-5, 447-8, 752
  dishes   347, 349, 351
  distribution of   257, 541
  dried   3-4, 39, 150, 207, 229, 421, 426-7, 430-2,
      436, 445-6, 637
  drying   321, 429
  exposed   427, 601
  jerky   316, 418, 430
  roasting   54, 420, 425
  squirrel   324, 476
  stored   419, 430, 438, 443
  supplies   55, 355
  white   95, 137, 324, 397
medicine   106-7, 113, 241-3, 246-7, 255, 558,
      561-2, 564-5, 567-72, 599-600, 608-11, 616-
      19, 629-35, 641-5, 734-6
  application   224, 238, 241, 254, 264, 484, 492-
      3, 495, 558, 561-2, 612-14, 617-20, 639, 644-
      5, 652-3
  bags   41, 186, 233, 569-70, 594, 693
  bundles   217, 240, 486, 509, 562, 569-70, 581,
      602, 674, 680-1

missionaries   4, 30, 47, 51, 57, 60-3, 65-7, 69, 89-90, 148, 170, 191, 420, 469, 727
missionization   12-13, 61, 77-8, 90, 93, 165, 177, 538, 551, 665-6, 696, 700, 724-5, 739
Mississippi River   393, 477, 783, 793, 795, 823-5
Mitchell, Howard I.   60, 807
mittens   473, 484
moccasins   39, 59, 109, 111, 129, 143, 188, 194, 246, 251, 259, 298-300, 471-2, 480-1, 619
  strings   481
Modigliani, Eljo   632, 807
Moerman, Daniel E.   116, 559, 561-2, 609, 635, 643, 743, 807
moles   133, 324-5, 730
moon   61, 533, 709, 729-31, 736-40, 770
  new   738
Mooney, James   19, 21, 47, 74, 807
moose   33, 258, 317, 319, 455, 489, 817
mortars and pestles   225, 227-9, 237, 266, 342, 344, 347-8, 350, 429, 431-2, 597, 612, 618, 625, 694
Moser, Charles   168, 807
moss   110, 140, 209, 237, 244-6, 275-6, 354-6, 417, 419, 436, 458, 476, 478, 662, 722-3
  ground   246, 481, 658
mothers   92-9, 101-12, 116-18, 120-2, 129-30, 134-7, 139, 144-7, 150, 156-9, 246-9, 314-15, 329-30, 501-2, 756
  girl's   115, 135, 142, 341, 530
  in-law   97, 143, 147, 155-6, 238, 636
  little   123, 146
  new   104-5, 108, 150, 155
  nursing   108, 212, 627
  unwed   117
  uterine   108, 150
  young   108, 155, 628
moths   176, 268, 473, 584, 684
Mount Spokane   22, 637
mountain ash berries   319, 351, 494
mountain goat   264, 319, 321
  hair   474, 480, 485
mountain lion   322
mountains   2, 32, 56-7, 81, 110, 186, 275-6, 310, 318, 326, 399, 674-5, 705, 756, 760
mouths   18-19, 24-7, 29-31, 317-19, 360-2, 388-9, 407-10, 427-8, 520-2, 586-8, 590-2, 612-14, 637-8, 641-2, 757-8

soreness   613-14
mud   246, 326, 339, 412, 424, 455, 595-6, 606, 698-9, 721, 727
mule deer   258, 308, 310, 319
mule-ears   615, 617, 645
mules   144, 464, 470, 649, 829
Mullan, John   52, 70, 245, 267, 302, 383, 485, 808
mullein   101, 104, 110, 135, 137, 140, 220, 245, 331, 339, 419, 422-3, 458, 481, 651
murder   38, 64, 81, 89-91, 465, 629, 698
Murray, Stephen O.   166, 808
mushrooms   255, 809, 828
music   147, 282, 511, 539, 545, 552-4, 745, 771, 806, 809
  instruments   239, 256, 353, 380, 552-3
muskrats   248-9, 284, 290, 302, 323, 355, 465, 476, 482, 519, 734
mussels   11, 356, 373-5, 427, 494, 500
  freshwater   239, 374-5, 380, 529
  shells   495
mythology   13, 665-7, 728-9, 731
  charter   535, 665, 706, 728-9, 741, 743

N

Nadel, Siegfried Frederick   743, 808
NAGPRA (Native American Graves Protection and Repatriation Act)   198
names   18-19, 21-2, 29, 40, 49, 112-13, 116-17, 121-2, 127-30, 142-4, 188, 400-1, 591-2, 694-6, 730-1
  diminutive   333, 421
  English   127, 766
  first   128, 670
  given personal   280, 530, 741
  Indian   127, 401, 742
  new   128-30
  temporary change   130
naming   54, 92, 127-31, 144, 196, 263, 361, 449
  ceremony   128-9, 174
nasal septum   113, 491, 493
Native American Graves Protection and Repatriation Act (NAGPRA)   198
nausea   93, 626, 629, 631, 633
necklaces   33, 142, 315, 325, 495, 497-8, 546

857

predators 214, 292-3, 307, 330-1, 706
pregnancy 93, 95-7, 99, 107, 114-15, 122, 129,
    135, 137, 141, 633
  difficult birth 94, 97-8, 103, 106-7, 627, 690
  fetus 93, 95-8, 107, 115, 264, 618, 627, 632
  lactating 105, 108, 375
  morning sickness 93, 99, 626
  third trimester 94-5, 98-100, 155
  wife's 96-7, 129, 155
  woman's 93-101, 104, 107, 109, 116, 127, 255,
    618, 633
  woman's husband 95, 97
  woman's mother 155
Press, Irwin 578, 811
priests 64, 197-8, 543, 567, 814
prisoners 45-6, 153
prongs 334, 389, 393-4
property 36, 58, 62, 77, 80-1, 90, 150, 178-9,
    185-8, 239, 246, 301, 437, 511, 561
prophecies 166, 581-2, 584, 707, 709-11, 724-7,
    818
  powers 329, 689, 715
prostitution 60, 114, 151, 169, 743
protection 30, 36, 41, 43, 138, 190, 194, 210-11,
    213-14, 477-80, 482, 489-90, 540, 639, 707
Protestants 61-2, 65, 67, 74, 76
  missionaries 12, 62-3, 65, 105, 148
protocols 80, 87, 171, 184, 223, 257, 319, 418-
    19, 502, 504, 506, 546, 715
protohistoric period 201-2, 223, 487
Prucha, Francis Paul, S.J. 61-2, 319, 811
puberty 92, 105, 124, 128, 131-2, 135, 138, 140,
    147, 196, 468, 493, 501, 532, 582
  ceremony 132, 134, 814
puff-ball 255
pulp 343, 431-2, 615
punishment 51, 71, 83, 87-91, 125-7, 161, 326,
    527, 579, 584, 624, 689
punk wood 2, 262-3, 366, 414
purification 105, 175, 182, 184, 187, 189, 402,
    504-5, 569, 584, 594, 596, 631, 673, 711
pylons 361, 377-8, 380, 382
Pyne, Stephen J. 267, 812

Q

quills 283, 324, 494

Quinn, Robert R. 15, 812
Quintasket, Charles 9, 184-5, 192, 603, 812
Quintasket, Christine 257, 812

R

rabbitbrush 239, 602, 642-3, 658
rabbits 95, 290-2, 295, 324, 425, 476, 482-3, 687,
    722
  jack 123, 324
  skins 33, 104, 473, 476
racks 316, 370, 399, 427-9, 432, 443, 478, 649
  fish-drying 383, 403, 427
  meat-drying 426-7
rafts 91, 226, 399, 414, 433, 450-1, 454
raiding 37-8, 469
rain 61, 203, 211, 306, 403, 434-5, 440, 478,
    731-7, 747
Randolph, June 133, 593, 712, 812
rape 90, 161-3
rashes 597, 616-18, 657
  diaper 111
raspberries 350, 369, 629, 632
rattles 103, 539, 549, 552, 557, 592, 603, 647,
    692
  shaman's 332, 554
rattlesnakes 94, 103, 332, 462, 614, 640, 647-8,
    678, 708
  skins 279, 483
ravens 48, 96, 329, 538, 648, 678
rawhide 228-9, 237, 260-1, 263-4, 285, 334-5,
    344, 420-1, 430-2, 444-6, 461-2, 464, 482-3,
    486-8, 490
  lengths of 445, 456
  wet 224, 229-30, 237, 282, 462, 502, 557, 612
Ray, Verne F. 12, 15-18, 24-6, 29-30, 46-7, 81-3,
    163-4, 169, 200-4, 489-90, 559-61, 637-40,
    665-7, 716-18, 720-7
Reagan, Albert B. 339, 813
red osier dogwood 216, 250-1, 282, 334, 350,
    426
red willow 104, 139, 239, 253, 350, 376, 420,
    427, 432, 499, 505, 555, 614, 624, 671
  berries 350, 588
Reddick, SuAnn M. 76-7, 813
Reddy, Marlita A. 77, 813
Redfield, Robert 573, 791, 800, 813

859

863

865

whistles 6, 308-9, 532-3, 539, 552, 554-5, 567, 698, 768

whistling 326, 532-3, 698

White Physicians and Indian Patients 799

white pine 237, 241-2, 263-4, 343, 453, 599-600, 616

white pine roots 447

white trappers 357, 471

whitefish 31, 361, 370, 396, 398, 400

Whitman, Marcus 57, 61-2, 64, 389, 625, 798, 830

widowers 117, 124, 160, 172-3, 190, 192-5, 197, 259, 353, 656, 700-1

  elderly 173

widows 44, 117, 121, 130, 151-3, 173, 175, 187, 190, 192-6, 198, 277, 352, 541-2, 700-1

  brother's 152-3

  elderly 124, 175, 542

Wiggins, Marianne 70, 830

Wihr, William Saxe 647, 656, 830

wild animals 91, 97, 99, 730, 735

wild carrot 33, 339, 342, 423, 438, 613, 629, 631

wild licorice 256, 661, 825

wild licorice root 104, 107, 505, 570, 598, 615, 622, 636-7, 641, 669, 673, 722

wild strawberry 348, 350, 613, 634-5

wild tobacco 504, 615

Wilkes, Charles, U.S.N. 47, 53, 58, 66, 82, 135, 186, 192, 277-8, 355, 367, 371, 405, 524-5, 830

Wilkinson, M. C. 20, 49, 502, 830

Williams, Christina M. M. 191, 830

Williams, Gerald W. 268, 830

willow 111, 125, 127, 135, 207, 239, 242, 285, 314, 326, 350, 377-8, 380-1, 388, 555

willow bark 204, 231, 239, 377, 380, 396, 436, 453-4, 469, 482, 522, 602, 624, 637, 651

Willow hoops 392, 446-7

willow mats 211, 381, 595

willow sticks 421, 672

willow withes 203, 208, 378, 380-1, 391, 469, 671

Wilson, Charles William 12, 14, 38, 45, 49, 82, 103, 106, 262, 280, 325, 385-6, 452-3, 461-3, 528, 830

Winans, William Parkhurst 49, 64, 68, 71, 76, 407, 776, 830

wind 30, 99, 127, 136-7, 159, 210-11, 218, 253, 303, 399, 534-6, 707, 729, 732-3, 735-7

  cold 729

winds, warm 685, 729, 737

Winkelman, Michael 570, 831

winner 513-14, 520, 523-4, 528, 531, 538

winning 73, 513, 516-19, 526, 528, 726

winter 201-2, 204-7, 249-51, 274-6, 309-17, 321-6, 336-9, 347-51, 355-7, 429-34, 462-5, 467-8, 477-83, 731-3, 736-7

  late 240, 242, 245, 274, 301, 336, 342, 353, 356, 361, 375, 399, 406-7, 433, 438

  severe 37, 58, 270, 325, 355, 465, 732, 736

winter camps 25, 214, 336

winter ceremonies 208, 332, 716

winter consumption 275, 277, 336, 346, 349-51, 402, 405, 445

Winter Dance 542, 546-7, 712, 723

winter dances 674, 677, 715, 718

winter deer camp 425

winter deer hunt 299

winter dwellings 201-2, 205, 211, 219, 374, 433, 440, 445

winter fishing 399

winter food 245, 274, 339, 344, 347, 349, 367, 370, 374, 428, 433, 435-6, 440-1

  important 374

  protecting 441

  stored 633

  supplemental 245

winter food storage containers 447

winter food storage house 441

winter food storage pits 438

winter game 295, 312, 523-4

winter hunting 302, 433, 467, 480, 484

winter hunts 265, 320-1, 436

winter lodges 201, 215, 274

winter provisions 240, 249, 270, 338

winter riverine villages 269

winter storage 245, 251, 267, 269, 276, 321, 333-4, 337-8, 344-5, 348, 350, 368, 431-2, 440-1, 444

winter storage areas 228, 335

winter survival food 356

winter time 213, 738

winter tutelary spirit dances 17

winter village dwelling 447

871

Wynecoop, David C. 21, 483, 831
Wynecoop, Nancy Perkins 217, 229, 237, 239,
    257, 353, 410, 412-13, 502, 729, 770, 831
Wynecoop, Tina 99, 108, 110-11, 341, 636, 832
Wynne-Davies, R. 112, 832

Y

Yakima Indians 38, 488
  reservation 657

Yantis, B. F. 49, 832
yarrow 261, 292, 619, 624, 628-9, 641-3
  roots 108, 116, 580, 601, 613, 616, 619, 629,
    634
Young, Allan 560, 832

Z

Zimmerman, William, Jr. 75, 832

www.ingramcontent.com/pod-product-compliance
Lightning Source LLC
Chambersburg PA
CBHW052127020426
42334CB00023B/2633